TEST CRICKET LISTS

The Complete Book of Test Cricket from 1877

Compiled by Graham Dawson — Statistics by Charlie Wat

The Five Mile Press

The Five Mile Press Pty Ltd
22 Summit Road
Noble Park Victoria 3174 Australia

First edition published 1989
Second edition published 1992
This edition published 1996

Editor: Emma Short
Formatting: Emma Short, Charlie Wat
Production: Emma Borghesi
Cover design: Peter Bourne

Printed in Australia by the Australian Print Group

National Library of Australia Cataloguing-in-Publication Data

Test cricket lists.

3rd ed.
ISBN 1 87597 152 1

1. Cricket - Records. 2. Cricket - Statistics. 3. Test matches (Cricket).
I. Dawson, Graham. II. Wat, Charlie.
796.35865

FRONT COVER PHOTOGRAPHS:
Top: Shane Warne, Australia v England 1994-95
(Darrin Braybrook/Sport.The Library.)
Bottom: Greg Blewett, Australia v Pakistan, 1995
(Darren England/Sport.The Library.)

INTRODUCTION

Since the second edition of *Test Cricket Lists* was published in 1992, Test cricket matches continue to be played at an ever-increasing rate — in fact there were 136 matches contested between October 1992 and August 1996.

The past four years have produced many highlights. Brian Lara broke Sir Garfield Sobers' world record Test score with his 375 against England at the Recreation Ground in St Johns, Antigua, in April 1994. And in a couple of the most thrilling encounters in the game's history, the West Indies defeated Australia by one run at the Adelaide Oval in January 1993; while Pakistan, with an unbroken tenth wicket partnership of 57 runs, downed Australia by one wicket at Karachi in October 1994. Complete scorecards and descriptions of these matches, as well as many more magnificent contests, appear in the expanded 'Famous Test Matches' section of this edition.

Once again, statistician Charlie Wat has been magnificent. His attention to detail and presentation of the statistics are matched only by his great knowledge, understanding and love of the game — all of which have proved to be a constant source of strength.

In compiling this volume, I am again indebted to the works of some far more knowledgable students of the game than me. In particular, I acknowledge my debt to the *Wisden Book of Test Cricket*, compiled and edited by Bill Frindall; the *Wisden Cricketers' Almanack*, edited by Matthew Engel; and *The Complete Who's Who of Test Cricketers* by Christopher Martin-Jenkins.

In order to meet publication deadlines, figures and statistics are current up to and including the third Test between England and Pakistan at The Oval in August 1996.

Graham Dawson

Graham Dawson
September 1996

CONTENTS

FAMOUS TEST MATCHES 11

TEST CRICKET LISTS 65

TEST MATCH RESULTS AND RECORDS 109

PART 1

FAMOUS TEST MATCHES

A Guide to the Symbols

Throughout this book we have used asterisks (*) alongside individual scores to indicate that the player was not out.

In the score cards, we have used an asterisk after a player's name to indicate the captain of the team, and a dagger (†) to indicate the wicketkeeper.

All other symbols are explained where they occur.

Spelling

Players' names have been spelt as they appear in the cricketing records of their own country.

AUSTRALIA v ENGLAND 1876-77

The Melbourne Cricket Ground, Melbourne
15, 16, 17, 19 March 1877
Australia won by 45 runs

Australia 245 (C. Bannerman 165 retired hurt) and 104; England 196 (H. Jupp 63, W.E. Midwinter 5 for 78) and 108 (T. Kendall 7 for 55)

This is regarded as the first official Test match. England was represented by professional players who had been touring Australia during the 1876-77 season, but it would have been a stronger team had it included the leading amateur cricketers of the day.

Australia won the toss and batted first. Charles Bannerman dominated the innings and, after receiving the first ball in Test cricket, went on to score the first Test century. He eventually retired hurt after making 165 in an Australian total of 245. Surrey opener Harry Jupp top-scored in England's first innings with a patient knock of 63.

Shaw and Ulyett combined to bowl Australia out for 104, but the target of 154 proved too much for the England batsmen. The Victorian Kendall captured seven wickets for 55 runs as England was dismissed for 208; Australia won by 45 runs. A collection at the ground for the injured Bannerman raised £165. See page 14 for the complete scoreboard.

AUSTRALIA v ENGLAND 1878-79

The Melbourne Cricket Ground, Melbourne
2, 3, 4 January 1879
Australia won by 10 wickets

England 113 (C.A. Absalom 52, F.R. Spofforth 6 for 48) and 160 (F.R. Spofforth 7 for 62), Australia 256 (A. C. Bannerman 73, T. Emmett 7 for 68) and 0 for 19

This was the only Test match played on this tour by the England team led by Lord Harris. Unlike Lillywhite's combination in the first Test, it was composed chiefly of amateurs and was not as strong a team. The Australians, however, formed a more formidable outfit than their earlier counterparts.

Murdoch and Bannerman strengthened the batting, while the bowling of Spofforth ('the Demon') proved too much for the England batsmen. He claimed the first hat-trick in Test cricket, his victims being Royle, Mackinnon and Emmett, and bowled Australia to a convincing victory. He finished the match with the fine figures of 13 for 110.

ENGLAND v AUSTRALIA 1880

The Oval, London
6, 7, 8 September 1880
England won by 5 wickets

England 420 (W.G. Grace 152, A.P. Lucas 55, Lord Harris 52) and 5 for 57; Australia 149 (F. Morley 5 for 56) and 327 (W.L. Murdoch 153 not out)

This was the first Test match to be played on English soil, and the Australian team was weakened by the absence of its greatest bowler of the time, Spofforth.

The England team, led by Lord Harris, included for the first time three brothers, E.M., W.G. and G.F. Grace. E.M. Grace opened the England innings with W.G. Grace, whose 152 was the first Test century scored by an Englishman. The third and youngest brother, G.F. Grace, made the first 'pair' of ducks in Test cricket, but his outfield catch to dismiss the Australian Bonnor was also long remembered. The batsmen were on their way back for the third run when he held the catch. He died less than a month later after catching a severe cold in a club game. The cold developed into congestion of the lungs, and he was dead within three days.

ENGLAND v AUSTRALIA 1882

The Ashes Match
The Oval, London
28, 29 August 1882
Australia won by 7 runs

Australia 63 (R.G. Barlow 5 for 19) and 122 (H.H. Massie 55); England 101 (F.R. Spofforth 7 for 46) and 77 (F.R. Spofforth 7 for 44)

This most remarkable and exciting match will be remembered for as long as cricket history exists. The Ashes match was Australia's first Test victory in England. The win was set up by Spofforth's magnificent bowling, and his figures of 14 for 90 enhanced his reputation as the finest bowler in the world.

Australia was bundled out for 63 after winning the toss. England's reply was not much better, and the team was dismissed for 101. Australia's second innings was an improvement on the first, and Massie led the way with 55 in an opening stand of 66 with Bannerman, but the rest struggled. By mid-afternoon on the second day, Australia had been dismissed for 122, with a lead of just 84 runs. England looked comfortable in

AUSTRALIA v ENGLAND 1876-77 (First Test)

Melbourne Cricket Ground, 15, 16, 17, 19 March. — Australia won by 45 runs

AUSTRALIA

Batsman	1st innings	Runs		2nd innings	Runs
C.Bannerman	retired hurt	165		b Ulyett	4
N.D.F.Thomson	b Hill	1		c Emmett b Shaw	7
T.P.Horan	c Hill b Shaw	12		c Selby b Hill	20
D.W.Gregory*	run out	1	(9)	b Shaw	3
B.B.Cooper	b Southerton	15		b Shaw	3
W.E.Midwinter	c Ulyett b Southerton	5		c Southerton b Ulyett	17
E.J.Gregory	c Greenwood b Lillywhite	0		c Emmett b Ulyett	11
J.M.Blackham†	b Southerton	17		lbw b Shaw	6
T.W.Garrett	not out	18	(4)	c Emmett b Shaw	0
T.K.Kendall	c Southerton b Shaw	3		not out	17
J.Hodges	b Shaw	0		b Lillywhite	8
Extras	(B 4, LB 2, W 2)	8		(B 5, LB 3)	8
Total		245			104

ENGLAND

Batsman	1st innings	Runs		2nd innings	Runs
H.Jupp	lbw b Garrett	63	(3)	lbw b Midwinter	4
J.Selby†	c Cooper b Hodges	7	(5)	c Horan b Hodges	38
H.R.J.Charlwood	c Blackham b Midwinter	36	(4)	b Kendall	13
G.Ulyett	lbw b Thompson	10	(6)	b Kendall	24
A.Greenwood	c E.J.Gregory b Midwinter	1	(2)	c Midwinter b Kendall	5
T.Armitage	c Blackham b Midwinter	9	(8)	c Blackham b Kendall	3
A.Shaw	b Midwinter	10		st Blackham b Kendall	2
T.Emmett	b Midwinter	8	(9)	b Kendall	9
A.Hill	not out	35	(1)	c Thompson b Kendall	0
J.Lillywhite*	c and b Kendall	10		b Hodges	4
J.Southerton	c Cooper b Garrett	6		not out	1
Extras	(LB 1)	1		(B 4, LB 1)	5
Total		196			108

ENGLAND	O	M	R	W		O	M	R	W
Shaw	55.3	34	51	3	Shaw	34	16	38	5
Hill	23	10	42	1	Ulyett	19	7	39	3
Ulyett	25	12	36	0	Hill	14	6	18	1
Southerton	37	17	61	3	Lillywhite	1	0	1	1
Armitage	3	0	15	0					
Lillywhite	14	5	19	1					
Emmett	12	7	13	0					

AUSTRALIA	O	M	R	W		O	M	R	W
Hodges	9	0	27	1	Kendall	33.1	12	55	7
Garrett	18.1	10	22	2	Midwinter	19	7	23	1
Kendall	38	16	54	1	D.W.Gregory	5	1	9	0
Midwinter	54	23	78	5	Garrett	2	0	9	0
Thompson	17	10	14	1	Hodges	7	5	7	2

FALL OF WICKETS

Wkt	A 1st	E 1st	A 2nd	E 2nd
1st	2	23	7	0
2nd	40	79	27	7
3rd	41	98	31	20
4th	118	109	31	22
5th	142	121	35	62
6th	143	135	58	68
7th	197	145	71	92
8th	243	145	75	93
9th	245	168	75	100
10th	245	196	104	108

Umpires: C.A.Reid and R.B.Terry

the second innings when W.G. Grace and Ulyett took the score to 51 after the early loss of Hornby and Barlow, but inspired bowling by 'the Demon' (Spofforth) and Boyle, supported by magnificent fielding, carried Australia to a thrilling victory. See page 16 for the complete scoreboard.

The day after the match, *The Sporting Times* carried an 'In Memoriam' announcement as follows:

'IN AFFECTIONATE REMEMBRANCE
OF
ENGLISH CRICKET
which died at the Oval
on
29th August 1882.
Deeply lamented by a large
circle of sorrowing friends and
acquaintances.
R.I.P.
N.B. — The body will be cremated and
the ashes taken to Australia.'

ENGLAND v AUSTRALIA 1884

The Oval, London
11, 12, 13 August 1884
Drawn

Australia 551 (W.L. Murdoch 211, P.S. McDonnell 103, H.J.H. Scott 102); England 346 (W.W. Read 117, W.H. Scotton 90) and 2 for 85

Murdoch won the toss for Australia and the team piled on the runs — 2 for 363 on the first day before being dismissed for 551 (the first score of over 500 in a Test innings). Murdoch's 211 was the first double-century in Test cricket and his partnership with Scott realised a then-record 207 for the third wicket.

During Australia's record-breaking innings every member of the England team had a bowl. The most successful was actually the wicketkeeper, the Hon. A. Lyttelton, who took the last four wickets with lobs.

England was in trouble in the first innings at 8 for 181, but was saved by the partnership of the opener Scotton, and Read, who added 151 for the ninth wicket. (Scotton batted for 340 minutes and was at the wicket for 332 of England's total of 346 runs.)

AUSTRALIA v ENGLAND 1884-85

Sydney Cricket Ground, Sydney
20, 21, 23, 24 February 1885
Australia won by 6 runs

Australia 181 (T.W. Garrett 51 not out, W. Flowers 5 for 46) and 165 (W. Bates 5 for 24); England 133 (T.P. Horan 6 for 40) and 207 (W. Fellows 56, J.M. Reid 56, F.R. Spofforth 6 for 90)

Australia crawled to 0 for 40 at lunch before a violent storm hit the ground. When play finally resumed on the damp pitch Australia collapsed, finishing the day at 8 for 97. When Spofforth went at 101 Australia was in real trouble. But fortunately Garret, 51, and Evans, 33, added 80 runs for the last wicket in a match-winning partnership. Barnes — the leading wicket-taker on the tour — refused to bowl after a disagreement with his captain, Shrewsbury.

The England innings finished quickly as Horan and Spofforth bundled out the visitors for 133, Flowers top-scoring with 24. Australia then built on its first-innings lead of 48 before Bates struck. England's target was now 214. At 5 for 61 and then 6 for 92 the game appeared lost. It was Flowers and Reid who combined for a 102-run partnership that turned the game the visitors' way, before Australia's great bowlers, Spofforth and Trumble, wrapped up the England tail. 'The Demon' Spofforth captured ten wickets in a match for the third time.

AUSTRALIA v ENGLAND 1886-87

Sydney Cricket Ground, Sydney
28, 29, 31 January 1887
England won by 13 runs

England 45 (C.T.B. Turner 6 for 15, J.J. Ferris 4 for 27) and 184 (J.J. Ferris 5 for 76); Australia 119 and 97 (W. Barnes 6 for 28)

After being sent into bat, England was bundled out for its lowest score against Australia (45). Turner and Ferris, both on debut, bowled unchanged in England's innings. Australia gained a first-innings lead of 74 after being dismissed for 119. Moses and Jones top-scored with 31 each. England's lead was only 29 with just three wickets in hand. On the final day, England's Briggs compiled the top score for the game, 33, to set Australia 111 runs for victory. Moses, 24, and Jones, 18, again batted well, but it was Barnes and Lohmann who triumphed and bowled England to a great win.

ENGLAND v AUSTRALIA 1882 (Only Test)

Kennington Oval, London, 28, 29 August. Australia won by 7 runs

AUSTRALIA

Batsman	1st innings	Runs		2nd innings	Runs
A.C.Bannerman	c Grace b Peate	9		c Studd b Barnes	13
H.H.Massie	b Ulyett	1		b Steel	55
W.L.Murdoch*	b Peate	13	(4)	run out	29
G.J.Bonnor	b Barlow	1	(3)	b Ulyett	2
T.P.Horan	b Barlow	3		c Grace b Peate	2
G.Giffen	b Peate	2		c Grace b Peate	0
J.M.Blackham†	c Grace b Barlow	17		c Lyttelton b Peate	7
T.W.Garrett	c Read b Peate	10	(10)	not out	2
H.F.Boyle	b Barlow	2	(11)	b Steel	0
S.P.Jones	c Barnes b Barlow	0	(8)	run out	6
F.R.Spofforth	not out	4	(9)	b Peate	0
Extras	(B 1)	1		(B 6)	6
Total		63			122

ENGLAND

Batsman	1st innings	Runs		2nd innings	Runs
R.G.Barlow	c Bannerman b Spofforth	11	(3)	b Spofforth	0
W.G.Grace	b Spofforth	4	(1)	c Bannerman b Boyle	32
G.Ulyett	st Blackham b Spofforth	26	(4)	c Blackham b Spofforth	11
A.P.Lucas	c Blackham b Boyle	9	(5)	b Spofforth	5
Hon.A.Lyttelton†	c Blackham b Spofforth	2	(6)	b Spofforth	12
C.T.Studd	b Spofforth	0	(10)	not out	0
J.M.Read	not out	19	(8)	b Spofforth	0
W.Barnes	b Boyle	5	(9)	c Murdoch b Boyle	2
A.G.Steel	b Garrett	14	(7)	c and b Spofforth	0
A.N.Hornby*	b Spofforth	2	(2)	b Spofforth	9
E.Peate	c Boyle b Spofforth	0		b Boyle	2
Extras	(B 6, LB 2, NB 1)	9		(B 3, LB 1)	4
Total		101			77

ENGLAND	O	M	R	W		O	M	R	W
Peate	38	24	31	4	Peate	21	9	40	4
Ulyett	9	5	11	1	Ulyett	6	2	10	1
Barlow	31	22	19	5	Barlow	13	5	27	0
Steel	2	1	1	0	Steel	7	0	15	2
					Barnes	12	5	15	1
					Studd	4	1	9	0

AUSTRALIA	O	M	R	W		O	M	R	W
Spofforth	36.3	18	46	7	Spofforth	28	15	44	7
Garrett	16	7	22	1	Garrett	7	2	10	0
Boyle	19	7	24	2	Boyle	20	11	19	3

FALL OF WICKETS

	A	E	A	E
Wkt	1st	1st	2nd	2nd
1st	6	13	66	15
2nd	21	18	70	15
3rd	22	57	70	51
4th	26	59	79	53
5th	30	60	79	66
6th	30	63	99	70
7th	48	70	114	70
8th	53	96	117	75
9th	59	101	122	75
10th	63	101	122	77

Umpires: L.Greenwood and R.Thoms

ENGLAND V AUSTRALIA 1890

The Oval, London
11, 12 August 1890
England won by 2 wickets

Australia 92 (F. Martin 6 for 50) and 102 (F. Martin 6 for 52); England 100 and 8 for 95 (J.J. Ferris 5 for 49)

Played on a slow wicket soaked by heavy rain, this was a match dominated by the ball. In his only Test against Australia, the Kent bowler Martin spearheaded England's victory with match figures of 12 for 102.

In a nerve-tingling finish with England needing one run to tie and two to win, Sharpe joined MacGregor at the wicket. The Australian bowler Ferris continually beat Sharpe, but wasn't able to claim the wicket Australia desperately needed. At last, Sharpe put bat to ball; he and his partner MacGregor ran for a suicidal single, but Barrett's return was too high for Ferris to reach. England won the match on the overthrow.

AUSTRALIA v ENGLAND 1894-95

Sydney Cricket Ground, Sydney
14, 15, 17, 18, 19, 20 December 1895
England won by 10 runs

Australia 586 (S.E. Gregory 201, G. Giffen 161, F.A. Iredale 81, J. Blackham 74, T. Richardson 5 for 181) and 166 (J. Darling 53, R. Peel 6 for 67); England 325 (A. Ward 75, J. Briggs 57) and 437 (A. Ward 117, J.T. Brown 53)

This high-scoring match was one of many highlights and records: the aggregate of 1514 runs was a new mark, Australia's score of 586 remained an Australian record for 30 years, the ninth-wicket partnership of 154 by Gregory and Blackham still remains Australia's best, and, for the first time, a team won after following-on. Giffen produced an outstanding all-round performance for Australia: 161 and 41 with the bat, and 8 for 238 from 118 overs with the ball. But luck went against the Australians. First, Blackham sustained a severe thumb injury and couldn't keep wicket in England's second innings. Then, after five days' play, with Australia needing just 64 runs with eight wickets in hand to win, the heavens opened and the rain tumbled down. The next day followed with blazing sunshine, and Australia was caught on a classic 'sticky' wicket. Briggs and Peel took full advantage of the conditions to bowl England to a memorable victory. The details of this absorbing Test are set out on page 19.

ENGLAND v AUSTRALIA 1896

Old Trafford, Manchester
16, 17, 18 July 1896
Australia won by 3 wickets

Australia 412 (F.A. Iredale 108, G. Giffen 80, G. H. S. Trott 53, T. Richardson 7 for 168) and 7 for 125. (T. Richardson 6 for 76); England 231 (A.A. Lilley 65 not out, K. S. Ranjitsinhji 62) and 305 (K.S. Ranjitsinhji 154 not out)

In this classic match, the two outstanding performers were on the defeated England team. Richardson returned match figures of 13 for 239 from 110 overs, and Ranjitsinhji, playing in his first Test, scored 62 and a masterly 154 not out. Australia's victory was set up by the top-order batsmen. Iredale, 108, Giffen, 80, and Trott, 53, led the way to the Australian first-innings total of 412. In England's first innings, Lilley and the 'Prince' (Ranjitsinhji) both compiled half-centuries, but it was not enough to avoid the follow-on. In their second innings, Ranjitsinhji played one of the great Test innings. He scored 154 not out in his three hours and ten minutes at the crease, but the team was all out for 305. What should have been a formality for Australia almost turned into a nightmare. Richardson bowled superbly. He had Australia on the brink at 7 for 100 before Trumble and Kelly were able to scramble for the last 25 runs needed to record Australia's first Test win in England for eight years.

ENGLAND v AUSTRALIA 1902

Old Trafford, Manchester
24, 25, 26 July 1902
Australia won by 3 runs

Australia 299 (V.T. Trumper 104, C. Hill 65, R.A. Duff 54, J. Darling 51, W.H. Lockwood 6 for 48); and 86 (W.H. Lockwood 5 for 28); England 262 (Hon. F.S. Jackson 128, L.C. Braund 65) and 120 (H. Trumble 6 for 53)

Australia went into this vital Test one up with two matches to play, and England had made four changes to the team that had lost the previous Test at Sheffield. Significantly, Jessop and Hirst were left out of the team, and F.W. Tate, a bowler with no batting ability, was included for his first Test. Trumper played a magnificent innings for Australia and posted his century before lunch. With Hill, 65, Duff, 54, and Darling, 51, making useful contributions, Australia posted 299, a somewhat disappointing total after the opening stand of 135. England's reply was dominated by

Jackson, 128, and Braund, 65, who scored 193 out of 262. With a lead of 37, Australia collapsed in its second innings and was dismissed for a paltry 86. Only Darling, 37, and Gregory, 24, reached double figures. Tate dropped Darling early in his innings; if the catch had been taken, Australia would have struggled to reach 50.

With light rain falling, England needed 124 to square the series. After a steady start, the wickets began to tumble — 15 runs were needed with two wickets to fall when Rhodes joined Lilley. But shortly afterwards Lilley fell to a magnificent outfield catch by Hill.

With eight runs required, Tate was the last man, and the rain was coming down in torrents. After a delay of 45 minutes, play resumed. Rhodes calmly played three balls from Trumble, then Tate faced Saunders. The first ball was snicked for four; Tate survived the next two and was then clean-bowled by the fourth ball of the over.

Australia had snatched victory by three runs. Both Lockwood and Trumble bowled superbly: Lockwood claimed eleven wickets and Trumble claimed ten.

ENGLAND v AUSTRALIA 1902

The Oval, London
11, 12, 13 August 1902
England won by 1 wicket

Australia 324 (H. Trumble 64 not out, M.A. Noble 52, G.H. Hirst 5 for 77) and 121 (W.H. Lockwood 5 for 45); England 183 (H. Trumble 8 for 65) and 9 wickets for 263 (G.L. Jessop 104, G.H. Hirst 58 not out)

This classic contest is always referred to as 'Jessop's match' for it was Jessop (known as 'the Croucher') who eventually won the game for England.

Darling called correctly, and Australia took advantage of the good weather and pitch to compile 324. Trumble's 64 not out proved his all-round ability.

England made a modest reply, scoring 183 with Trumble claiming 8 for 65.

Australia's second innings started disastrously with Trumper being run out for 2. After this early setback, the Australian batsmen struggled and only Hill, 34, and Armstrong, 21, were able to score more than 20. Australia was all out for 121, for a lead of 262.

England collapsed and was at one point only 5 for 48. The match looked to be over. Then 'the Croucher' joined Jackson, and the pair turned the game around for the home team. In 75 minutes, Jessop smashed 104 runs with 17 boundaries and a five. But 15 runs were still required when the last man, Rhodes, joined Hirst.

Legend has it that Hirst said to Rhodes, "We'll get them in singles." However, although these men of Yorkshire did manage to score the runs needed to record a famous victory, they did not do it in singles.

AUSTRALIA v ENGLAND 1903-04

Sydney Cricket Ground, Sydney
11, 12, 14, 15, 16, 17 December 1903
England won by 5 wickets

Australia 285 (M.A. Noble 133) and 485 (V.T. Trumper 185 not out, R.A. Duff 84, C. Hill 51, W. Rhodes 5 for 94); England 577 (R.E. Foster 287, L.C. Braund 102, J.T. Tyldesley 53) and 5 for 194 (T.W. Hayward 91, G.H. Hirst 60 not out)

Under the leadership of Pelham Warner, this touring party was the first to come to Australia under the MCC's banner. Previous tours to Australia had been privately sponsored, and team selection had been undertaken by individuals.

Noble was Australia's new captain, and he started well by winning the toss and making the top score, 133, in a respectable total of 285. England struggled at first, but Foster and Braund turned the tide. After two days' play, the visitors trailed by 42 runs with six wickets in hand. On the third day, Foster's innings blossomed. He struck 38 boundaries in a new Test record score of 287. England's total of 577 was a new innings high for Test cricket.

Foster shared century partnerships with Braund, 192, Relf, 115, and Rhodes, 130. The Foster-Rhodes last-wicket partnership still stands as an English record.

A superb, unbeaten century from Trumper, with valuable contributions from Duff and Hill, carried Australia's second innings to 485. Rhodes was once more the pick of England's bowlers. He finished with 5 for 94 from a marathon bowling spell of 40 overs.

England's target was 194 runs. The team was in trouble at 4 for 82, then Hirst was missed by Laver after just one run had been added. After the let-off, the Yorkshireman assisted Hayward to wipe off the deficit. Hirst and Hayward saw England home by five wickets with Hayward, 91, being dismissed near the end of the match.

AUSTRALIA v ENGLAND 1894-95 (First Test)

Sydney Cricket Ground, 14, 15, 17, 18, 19, 20 December. England won by 10 runs

AUSTRALIA

J.J.Lyons	b Richardson	1		b Richardson	25
G.H.S.Trott	b Richardson	12		c Gay b Peel	8
G.Giffen	c Ford b Brockwell	161		lbw b Briggs	41
J.Darling	b Richardson	0		c Brockwell b Peel	53
F.A.Iredale	c Stoddart b Ford	81	(6)	c and b Briggs	5
S.E.Gregory	c Peel b Stoddart	201	(5)	c Gay b Peel	16
J.C.Reedman	c Ford b Peel	17		st Gay b Peel	4
C.E.McLeod	b Richardson	15		not out	2
C.T.B.Turner	c Gay b Peel	1		c Briggs b Peel	2
J.M.Blackham*†	b Richardson	74	(11)	c and b Peel	2
E.Jones	not out	11	(10)	c MacLaren b Briggs	1
Extras	(B 8, LB 3, W 1)	12		(B 2, LB 1, NB 4)	7
Total		586			166

ENGLAND

A.C.MacLaren	c Reedman b Turner	4	b Giffen	20
A.Ward	c Iredale b Turner	75	b Giffen	117
A.E.Stoddart*	c Jones b Giffen	12	c Giffen b Turner	36
J.T.Brown	run out	22	c Jones b Giffen	53
W.Brockwell	c Blackham b Jones	49	b Jones	37
R.Peel	c Gregory b Giffen	4	b Giffen	17
F.G.J.Ford	st Blackham b Giffen	30	c and b McLeod	48
J.Briggs	b Giffen	57	b McLeod	42
W.H.Lockwood	c Giffen b Trott	18	b Trott	29
L.H.Gay†	c Gregory b Reedman	33	b Trott	4
T.Richardson	not out	0	not out	12
Extras	(B 17, LB 3, W 1)	21	(B 14, LB 8)	22
Total		325		437

ENGLAND	O	M	R	W		O	M	R	W
Richardson	55.3	13	181	5	Richardson	11	3	27	1
Peel	53	14	140	2	Peel	30	9	67	6
Briggs	25	4	96	0	Lockwood	16	3	40	0
Brockwell	22	7	78	1	Briggs	11	2	25	3
Ford	11	2	47	1					
Stoddart	3	0	31	1					
Lockwood	3	2	1	0					

AUSTRALIA	O	M	R	W		O	M	R	W
Jones	19	7	44	1	Jones	19	0	57	1
Turner	44	16	89	2	Turner	35	14	78	1
Giffen	43	17	75	4	Giffen	75	25	164	4
Trott	15	4	59	1	Trott	12.4	2	22	2
McLeod	14	2	25	0	McLeod	30	7	67	2
Reedman	3.3	1	12	1	Reedman	6	1	12	0
Lyons	2	2	0	0	Lyons	2	0	12	0
					Iredale	2	1	3	0

FALL OF WICKETS

	A	E	E	A
Wkt	1st	1st	2nd	2nd
1st	10	14	44	26
2nd	21	43	115	45
3rd	21	78	217	130
4th	192	149	245	135
5th	331	155	290	147
6th	379	211	296	158
7th	400	211	385	159
8th	409	252	398	161
9th	563	325	420	162
10th	586	325	437	166

Umpires: C.Bannerman and J.Phillips

Note: McLeod and Reedman deputised for Blackham for part of the second innings.

SOUTH AFRICA v ENGLAND 1905-06

Old Wanderers, Johannesburg
2, 3, 4 January 1906
South Africa won by 1 wicket

England 184 and 190 (P.F. Warner 51); South Africa 91 (W Lees 5 for 34) and 9 wickets for 287 (A. W. Nourse 93 not out, G. C. White 81)

In this low-scoring match, England gained a first-innings lead of 93. Faulkner bowled superbly to capture 4 for 26 and restrict England's second innings to 190. Crawford batted well in both innings, scoring 44 and 43.
When Nourse joined White, the home team was struggling at 6 for 105 and England appeared likely to win. Nourse played with remarkable maturity as he and White carried the score to 226. After White's departure, Vogler and Schwarz fell at 230 and 239 respectively. The last man in was South Africa's captain Sherwell; when he arrived at the crease, 45 runs were still required for victory. Amid great excitement Nourse and Sherwell hit the runs needed to win. It was South Africa's first Test victory.

AUSTRALIA v ENGLAND 1907-08

Sydney Cricket Ground, Sydney
13, 14, 16, 17, 18, 19 December 1907
Australia won by 2 wickets

England 273 (G. Gunn 119, A. Cotter 6 for 101) and 300 (G. Gunn 74, J. Hardstaff Sr 63); Australia 300 (C. Hill 87, A. Fielder 6 for 82) and 8 for 275 (H. Carter 61)

With A.O. Jones indisposed, Fane took over the captaincy of England. He called correctly, and took first use of a good pitch. George Gunn was called up to take Jones's place in the team and, on debut, made 119 and 74 to top-score in both of England's innings.
Australia gained a lead of 27 runs after compiling a first-innings total of 300. Hill top-scored with 87, while Fielder was best with the ball, claiming 6 for 82. England matched Australia's 300, so the home team needed to score 274 to win the first match of the series.
Trumper, Hill and Macartney fell cheaply, and the innings continued to stutter. With just three wickets remaining, 89 runs were still needed; however, keeper Carter, 61 (the top score), Cotter, 34 not out, and Hazlitt, 33 not out, steered Australia to an exciting win. The ninth-wicket partnership between Cotter and Hazlitt realised 56 in just 39 minutes.

AUSTRALIA v ENGLAND 1907-08

Melbourne Cricket Ground, Melbourne
1, 2, 3, 4, 6, 7 January 1908
England won by 1 wicket

Australia 266 (M.A. Noble 61, J.N. Crawford 5 for 79) and 397 (W.W. Armstrong 77, M.A. Noble 64, V.T. Trumper 63, C.G. Macartney 54, H. Carter 53, S.F. Barnes 5 for 72); England 382 (K.L. Hutchings 126, J.B. Hobbs 83, A. Cotter 5 for 142) and 9 wickets for 282 (F.L. Fane 50)

The first Test in Sydney was close, but this one was even closer.
Australia's 266 was a modest effort after an 84-run opening stand by Trumper and Macartney. The skipper, Noble, top-scored with 61.
This match saw the Test debut of J.B. Hobbs. He made 83 and paved the way for Hutchings to smash 126 with 25 fours and a six. England finished with 382 for a lead of 116.
Five batsmen scored half-centuries as Australia compiled a second-innings total of 397, despite the untiring effort of S.F. Barnes who captured 5 for 72 from 27.4 overs.
England needed to score 282 to win the match and level the series. After the fifth day, it was 4 for 159 and anyone's game. When Rhodes was run out, it was 8 for 209 with 73 runs still required. Barnes and Humphries added 34, but 39 were still needed when the last pair was at the crease. Finally, with one run needed, the batsmen went for a suicidal single. But Hazlitt's throw was wild and England scored a thrilling victory.

AUSTRALIA v SOUTH AFRICA 1912

Old Trafford, Manchester
27, 28 May 1912
Australia won by an innings and 88 runs

Australia 448 (W. Bardsley 121, C. Kelleway 114, S.J. Pegler 6 for 105); South Africa 265 (G.A. Faulkner 122 not out, W.J. Whitty 5 for 55) and 95 (C. Kelleway 5 for 33)

This was the first match in the triangular tournament of 1912. The Australians started confidently as Kelleway and Bardsley scored freely, compiling a 202-run partnership for the third wicket. Low-order batsmen Matthews and Whitty hit lustily in a last-wicket stand of 63.
Faulkner played a lone hand for South Africa. Dropped at 36, he carried his bat for 122. Whitty had broken the back of the batting with a fiery spell before Matthews ended the innings with the first of his two hat-tricks for the day. Beaumont

was bowled, and both Pegler and Ward were trapped lbw.
Forced to follow-on, South Africa's second innings was a dismal effort. At 5 for 70 Matthews bowled Taylor and then caught and bowled both Schwarz and Ward, capturing his second hat-trick. Ward bagged a 'king pair', being the third victim of both hat-tricks.

SOUTH AFRICA v ENGLAND 1922-23

Newlands, Cape Town
1, 2, 3, 4 January 1923
England won by one wicket

South Africa 113 and 242 (R.H. Catterall 76, H.W. Taylor 68, G.G. Macaulay 5 for 64); England 183 (J.M. Blanckenberg 5 for 61) and 9 for 173 (A.E. Hall 7 for 63)

England gained the ascendancy on the first day, dismissing South Africa for 113 and being 4 for 128 in reply.
Fender was the best of England's bowlers and finished with 4 for 29. Carr, 42 and Russell, 39, batted well for the visitors.
However, though the first day went well for the visitors, the second day saw a complete turnaround in fortunes. South African bowlers Blanckenberg and Hall demolished the middle- and lower-order England batsmen and the English lead was restricted to just 70 runs.
After Hearne went out at two for his second 'duck' in the match, Catterall and Taylor dominated the batting and, at the close of the day's play, they had taken the South African's second-innings score to 134.
Macaulay and Kennedy bowled England back into the match on the third day. South Africa's lead was 172. Inspired by Hall's fine bowling, the home team struck back and England finished the day at 6 for 86.
The England captain, Mann, and Jupp added 68 for the seventh wicket to give the visitors a glimmer of hope. When the last man, Macaulay, joined Kennedy, five runs were still needed for victory. Kennedy hit a four before a single by Macaulay finished the match.
As well as the exciting finish, this match was a memorable game for a number of reasons: Macaulay took the wicket of Hearne with his very first ball in Test cricket, and he also made the winning run; Hall, the other debutante in the match, took 11 for 112 and almost bowled South Africa to victory.

AUSTRALIA v ENGLAND 1924 -1925

Adelaide Oval, Adelaide
16, 17, 19, 20, 21, 22, 23 January 1925
Australia won by 11 runs

Australia 489 (J. Ryder 201 not out, T.J.E. Andrews 72, A.J. Richardson 69) and 250 (J. Ryder 88); England 365 (J.B. Hobbs 119, E.H. Hendren 92) and 363 (W.W. Whysall 75, H. Sutcliffe 59, A.P.F. Chapman 58)

England went into the game, the third of the series, two matches down. Gilligan called incorrectly for the third time, so Australia again had the advantage of batting first.
Luck was against the visitors, for their two top bowlers were injured: the spearhead Tate broke down with Australia 3 for 22, and then Gilligan's strained thigh sent him away from the field as well. At this point, Australia was struggling at 6 for 119, but the last four wickets added 370 to carry the home team out of danger. Ryder's 201 not out was scored in six and a half hours.
England's batting order was shuffled with the innings starting late on the second day. Hobbs, at no. 5 played beautifully for 119; Hendren was also in fine form and scored 92. The deficit was 124.
In its second innings, Australia was caught on a sticky wicket. After Ryder, 88, Ponsford, 43, and Taylor, 34, had laid the foundations for another big total, the England bowlers Kilner and Woolley captured the last seven wickets to keep the series alive. Hobbs and Sutcliffe were superb on the difficult wicket, and then Whysall and Chapman gave the visitors a glimmer of hope. On the seventh morning, 27 runs were needed with two wickets in hand. Gilligan holed out to V.Y. Richardson off Gregory and when Mailey had Freeman caught by Oldfield, Australia was home by eleven runs.

ENGLAND v AUSTRALIA 1926

The Oval, London
14, 16, 17, 18 August 1926
England won by 289 runs

England 280 (H. Sutcliffe 76, A.A. Mailey 6 for l38) , and 436 (H. Sutcliffe 161, J.B. Hobbs 100); Australia 302 (J.M. Gregory 73, H.L. Collins 61) and 125

It was decided this match should be played to a result because the previous matches in the series had been drawn.
England appointed Percy Chapman as captain, recalled Rhodes at the age of 48 years and 10 months and selected the 21-year-old fast bowler Larwood for his second Test match.

Hobbs and Sutcliffe opened with a 53-run partnership for England, but the rest struggled against Mailey's spin and the result was a modest 280.

Australia fared little better before Collins and Gregory added 107 for the seventh wicket. Oldfield and Grimmett then posted 67 for the ninth to establish a meagre 22-run lead.

Hobbs and Sutcliffe produced the batting of the match on a rain-affected pitch, scoring 172 for the first wicket. The openers both made centuries and laid the foundations for an English victory. The visitors needed to score 415 to retain the Ashes on a difficult pitch.

With pace and hostility, Larwood made the early break before the 'Old Master' took over. Rhodes justified the selectors' gamble by capturing 4 for 44 in Australia's second innings and 6 for 79 for the match. England regained the Ashes that were lost in Australia in 1920-21.

ENGLAND v AUSTRALIA 1928-29

Exhibition Ground, Brisbane
30 November 1928, 1, 3, 4, 5 December 1928
England won by 675 runs

England 521 (E.H. Hendren 169, H. Larwood 70, A.P.F. Chapman 50) and 8 for 342 dec. (C.P. Mead 72, D.R. Jardine 65 not out, C.V. Grimmett 6 for 131); Australia 122 (H. Larwood 6 for 32) and 66

This was Brisbane's first Test match and one of only two to be played at the Exhibition Ground. The 675-run winning margin is the largest Test match victory, by runs, ever recorded.

Under Chapman, who had regained the Ashes at the Oval in 1926, England had one of its strongest teams. But many of the Australian stalwarts, including Collins, Bardsley, Macartney, Andrews, Taylor and Mailey, had retired after the last tour of England.

Hendren, playing perhaps his finest innings against Australia, scored a masterly 169 as England reached 521. Towards the end of the innings, Gregory injured his knee attempting to take a return catch and was told by the doctor that he would never play again.

It was in this match that Bradman made his debut, although he failed, scoring only 18 and 1. He was subsequently left out of the team for the second Test.

Larwood crashed through Australia's batting. He captured 6 for 32, and, with Tate claiming 3 for 50, the home team was bundled out for 122.

With Kelleway indisposed with food poisoning and Gregory out of the match, Chapman decided to bat again. He eventually made the first declaration in a Test in Australia at 8 for 342.

Australia's target: just 742 runs! On a difficult pitch, the effort put up by the home team was abysmal: all out for 66 in just 25.3 overs. Woodfull carried his bat in making 30.

Larwood had an outstanding match: he scored 70 and 37 and took 6 for 32 and 2 for 30. And, to round it off, he took four catches in Australia's second innings.

AUSTRALIA v ENGLAND 1928-29

Adelaide Oval, Adelaide
1, 2, 4, 5, 6, 7, 8 February 1929
England won by 12 runs

England 334 (W.R. Hammond 119 not out, J.B. Hobbs 74, H. Sutcliffe 64, C.V. Grimmett 5 for 102) and 383 (W.R. Hammond 177, D.R. Jardine 98); Australia 369 (A. Jackson 164, J. Ryder 63, J.C White 5 for 130) and 336 (J. Ryder 87, D.G. Bradman 58, A.F. Kippax 51, J.C. White 8 for 126)

The tension in this match is indicated by the scores: 334, 369, 383, and 336. England came home in a thriller by twelve runs. Hammond, whose three previous innings had been 251, 200 and 32 run out, was once again England's premier batsman. After Hobbs and Sutcliffe had provided their customary century opening partnership, Hammond held the innings together, scoring 72 of the last 88 runs to finish with 119 not out.

This was Jackson's first Test. He opened the innings with Woodfull, but soon his three partners, Woodfull, Hendry, and Kippax, were back in the pavilion for just 19. Jackson reached his century with a slashing square cut off Larwood, and was eventually dismissed for 164.

Although Hobbs and Sutcliffe fell cheaply this time, Hammond and Jardine ground out a 262-run partnership for the third wicket. England finished with 383 — Australia required 349 to win. The home team was in with a real chance until Hobbs, one of the finest fieldsmen, ran Bradman out for 58. It was then 8 for 320 before 'Farmer' White snared the last two wickets to win the match for England.

WEST INDIES v ENGLAND 1929-30

Sabina Park, Kingston, Jamaica
3, 4, 5, 7, 8, 9, 10, 11, 12 April 1930
Drawn

England 849 (A. Sandham 325, L.E.G. Ames 149, G. Gunn 85, E.H. Hendren 61, R.E.S. Wyatt 58, J. O'Connor 51, O.C. Scott 5 for 266) and 9 for 272 dec. (E.H. Hendren 55, A. Sandham 50); West Indies 286 (R.K. Nunes 66) and 5 for 408 (G.A. Headley 223, R.K. Nunes 92)

This was the final Test of the first series played between these teams in the Caribbean. England had won at Port-of-Spain by 167 runs, and then the West Indies won at Georgetown by 289. With the series level, it was decided to play the Test in Kingston to a finish.

Sandham, who batted for more than ten hours, posted the first triple-century in Test cricket. His innings was the backbone of the massive England total of 849. (This is still the second-highest innings total in Test history.) The West Indies trailed by 563, but the England captain, the Hon. F.S.G. Calthorpe, did not enforce the follow-on. Sandham scored 50 in the second innings to give himself a match aggregate of 375.

The West Indies was set 836 to win and posted a highly respectable 5 for 408 before rain and a waiting ship ended the match. The 20-year-old George Headley made his debut in the series, scoring 703 runs with four centuries and an average of 87.

ENGLAND v AUSTRALIA 1930

Lord's Cricket Ground, London
27, 28, 30 June, 1 July 1930
Australia won by 7 wickets

England 425 (K.S. Duleepsinhji 173, M.W. Tate 54) and 375 (A.P.F. Chapman 121, G.O.B. Allen 57, C.V. Grimmett 6 for 167); Australia 6 wickets for 729 dec. (D.G. Bradman 254, W.M. Woodfull 155, A.F. Kippax 83, W.H. Ponsford 81) and 3 for 72

This was the match in which Bradman played the innings he considered to be (technically) the best in his life.

Australia had gone to Lord's one down, but determined to square the series. Duleepsinhji emulated his famous uncle Ranjitsinhji by contributing a century, 173, in his first Test against Australia to England's total of 425.

Woodfull and Ponsford gave Australia a flying start and posted 162 for the first wicket. With Bradman's arrival, the scoring rate increased. At stumps, 'the Don' was 155 not out, with Australia 2 for 404 — 829 runs had been scored in two days' play. On the third day, Bradman and Kippax continued on to post a 192-run partnership. Woodfull declared at tea with a new record score for Australia of 729 (since broken). Bradman's chanceless 254 had taken just five and a half hours to compile.

Grimmett struck early in England's second innings, dismissing Hobbs and Woolley. And when he removed Hammond just after play resumed on the final day, Australia knew victory was a distinct possibility. Chapman scored a fine century, but it wasn't enough to save the match. Australia's target was 72, and they had plenty of time to polish off the runs. The Bradman era had dawned!

AUSTRALIA v WEST INDIES 1930-31

Sydney Cricket Ground, Sydney
27, 28 February, 2, 3, 4 March 1931
West Indies won by 30 runs

West Indies 6 for 350 dec. (F.R. Martin 123 not out, G. Headley 105, G.C. Grant 62) and 5 for 124 dec.; Australia 224 (A.G. Fairfax 54) and 220 (A.G. Fairfax 60 not out)

This match was the first Test win for the West Indies against Australia. It was a fine achievement, for they had been soundly beaten in the first four matches of the series.

Grant won the toss, and the West Indies went in to bat. Centuries by the opener, Martin, and Headley, plus 62 by the skipper took the visitors to 6 for 350 on the second day.

Overnight rain followed by hot morning sunshine produced a classic sticky wicket. The West Indies collapsed from an overnight 2 for 298 to 6 for 350 when Grant declared. Considering the state of the pitch, Australia did well to score 224. And, when the West Indies batted again, wicket conditions had deteriorated further.

Grant on 27 not out decided to declare with a lead of just 250. The gamble came off, for Australia was bowled out for 220 to give the West Indies a memorable win. Bradman went for a duck in Australia's second innings.

AUSTRALIA v ENGLAND 1932-33

Sydney Cricket Ground, Sydney
2, 3, 5, 6, 7 December 1932
England won by 10 wickets

Australia 360 (S.J. McCabe 187 not out, H. Larwood 5 for 96) and 164 (H. Larwood 5 for 28); England 524 (H. Sutcliffe 194, W.R. Hammond 112, Nawab of Pataudi, Sr. 102) and 0 for 1

This was the first Test of the infamous 'Bodyline Series', but unfortunately illness prevented 'the Don' from taking part in the game.

McCabe played one of the truly great Test innings. He hit 25 boundaries in his four-hour stay at the crease and scored 51 of a 55-run last-wicket partnership in just 33 minutes. In a sign of what was to come throughout the series, Larwood and Voce did the damage for England with five and four wickets respectively.
The Nawab of Pataudi, Sr., playing for England, became the third Indian prince after 'Ranji' and 'Duleep' to score a century in his first Test against Australia. Sutcliffe and Hammond were the other century-makers as England gained a lead of 164. Then Larwood, bowling with great pace, ripped the heart out of the Australian batting. Only Fingleton, 40, and McCabe, 32, offered any resistance, and England wrapped up the match.

AUSTRALIA v ENGLAND 1932-33

Melbourne Cricket Ground, Melbourne
30, 31 December 1932, 2, 3 January 1933
Australia won by 111 runs
Australia 228 (J.H.W. Fingleton 83) and 191 (D.G. Bradman 103 not out); England 169 (H. Sutcliffe 52, W.J. O'Reilly 5 for 63) and 139 (W.J. O'Reilly 5 for 66)

The great Don Bradman returned to the Australian line-up after missing the first Test in Sydney. Woodfull elected to bat first and was quickly back in the pavilion. When O'Brien went shortly afterwards 'the Don' strode out to join Fingleton. On his first ball he attempted to hook Bowes but only succeeded in edging it onto his stumps.
Fingleton was the mainstay of Australia's innings, top-scoring with a patient 83, and England could not match the home side's modest total of 228. Wall and O'Reilly were the chief destroyers for Australia.
The third day crowd of 70 000 was a record and the patrons did not go home disappointed as their hero Bradman scored a superb 103 not out in a total of 191.
England's target was 251 runs. When the fourth day began this had been reduced to 208 with all wickets in hand. Once again it was O'Reilly, this time with the assistance of Ironmonger, who proved to be damaging on the responsive pitch. O'Reilly's match-winning ten-wicket haul was the first of three he was to claim in Test cricket.

AUSTRALIA v ENGLAND 1932-33

Adelaide Oval, Adelaide
13, 14, 16, 17, 18, 19 January 1933
England won by 338 runs
England 341 (M. Leyland 83, R.E.S. Wyatt 78, E. Paynter 77, T.W. Wall 5 for 72) and 412 (W.R. Hammond 85, L.E.G. Ames 69) D.R. Jardine 56); Australia 222 (W.H. Ponsford 85) and 193 (W.M. Woodfull 73 not out, D.G. Bradman 66)

This must have been one of the most unpleasant Test matches ever played. The 'Bodyline' controversy had reached its ugliest; in fact, ill-feeling was so great that Jardine had to persuade local officials to close the ground to spectators while the England team had its final practice session the day before the match.
Jardine elected to bat first, but his team was soon in desperate trouble with the score at 4 for 30. Leyland, 83, and Wyatt, 78, added 156 for the fifth wicket before Verity helped Paynter carry the total beyond 300.
The crowd became hostile early in Australia's innings when Woodfull was struck a painful blow above the heart by a Larwood thunderbolt. Later in the innings, Oldfield went down after misjudging a Larwood delivery. This incident stirred the crowd to fever pitch, and they began to count the England team 'out'—'one, two, three, four, five, six, seven, eight, nine, ten, out!'. Australia was dismissed for 222 with Ponsford, 85, top-scoring.
England produced an even team performance in its second innings. With six batsmen reaching 40, the total climbed to 412. Australia's target was 532, which proved far too difficult a task. Only Bradman, 66, and Woodfull, who carried his bat for 73, offered any resistance.
It was during this match that the Australian captain, Woodfull, made his famous utterance to the MCC tour management, Sir Pelham Warner and Lionel Palairet: 'There are two teams out there and one of them is trying to play cricket.'

AUSTRALIA v ENGLAND 1932-33

Woolloongabba, Brisbane
10, 11, 13, 14, 15, 16 February 1933
England won by 6 wickets
Australia 340 (V.Y. Richardson 83, D.G. Bradman 79, W.M. Woodfull 67) and 175; England 356 (H. Sutcliffe 86, E. Paynter 83) and 4 for 162 (M. Leyland 86)

England regained the Ashes with their third win of the 'Bodyline' series on the day that Archie Jackson died. Woodfull took Richardson in with him first and they posted Australia's best opening partnership of the series. Bradman built on the solid foundation and, along with Woodfull, carried the total to 200. However, the middle and lower order failed to capitalise on the home team's promising start.

In reply, England really struggled after a painstaking opening partnership between Jardine and Sutcliffe had realised 114. Paynter was the English hero. Suffering from acute tonsillitis he left a nursing home sick-bed to play a match-winning innings of 83. He added 92 with Verity for the ninth wicket, to gain a 16-run lead for the visitors.

Australia's top order failed in the second innings. A mix-up between debutants Darling and Bromley saw Darling run out, and the innings quickly folded. Leyland played one of his finest knocks to take England within sight of victory before the first-innings hero Paynter won the match by hitting McCabe for six.

ENGLAND v AUSTRALIA 1934

Lord's Cricket Ground, London
22, 23, 25 June 1934
England won by an innings and 38 runs
England 440 (L.E.G. Ames 120, M. Leyland 109, C.F. Walters 82); Australia 284 (W.A. Brown 105, H. Verity 7 for 61) and 118 (H. Verity 8 for 43)

This Test became known as 'Verity's Match'. Batting first, England compiled 440, with Leyland and the wicketkeeper, Ames, both scoring centuries. Walters, who was relieved of the captaincy after the first Test, returned to form with 82. By the close of play on the second day (Saturday) Australia had reached 2 for 192, but rain over the weekend drenched the pitch. The England left-arm spinner Verity was able to exploit the conditions perfectly when play resumed.

Australia lost its last 8 wickets for 81, with Verity claiming 6 for 37. Forced to follow-on, the visitors were demolished by this Yorkshireman. Australia was all-out for 118 — Verity taking 8 for 43. On the final day, he took 14 wickets for 80 runs and so equalled Rhodes' earlier record of 15 wickets in Anglo-Australian Tests.

This was England's first win against Australia at Lord's since 1896, and they have not won against Australia at the home of cricket since.

ENGLAND v AUSTRALIA 1934

The Oval, London
18, 20, 21, 22 August 1934
Australia won by 562 runs
Australia 701 (W.H. Ponsford 266, D.G. Bradman 244) and 327 (D.G. Bradman 77, S.J. McCabe 70, W.E. Bowes 5 for 55, E.W. Clark 5 for 98); England 321 (M. Leyland 110, C.F. Walters 64) and 145 (C.V. Grimmet 5 for 64)

This was the final Test of the summer and with the series tied at one apiece, there was no restriction on the number of days' play to get a result. England recalled Woolley at the age of 47 to make the last Test appearance by a pre-1914 Test player, but this move backfired. Woolley scored 4 and 0 and while deputising for the injured Ames in Australia's second innings, conceded a record number of byes (37) for a Test innings.

After Brown had fallen cheaply, Ponsford and Bradman combined to create one of the greatest partnerships in the game's history. Australia's champion batsmen added 451 for the second wicket in five and a quarter hours. Bradman's classic knock included one six and 32 fours; while Ponsford hit a five and 27 boundaries in his highest ever Test innings.

After an opening stand of 104 between the English batsmen Walters and Sutcliffe, only Leyland provided resistance against the Australians. In a superb knock he added 110 of 185 runs to the score. Despite leading by 380, Woodfull did not enforce the follow-on. England, left to make 708 for victory, were bundled out for just 145 with Grimmet doing most of the damage. For the second time in four years, Australia regained the Ashes on the captain's birthday.

WEST INDIES v ENGLAND 1934-35

Kensington Oval, Bridgetown, Barbados 8, 9, 10 January 1935
England won by 4 wickets
West Indies 102 and 6 for 51 dec. (C.I.J. Smith 5 for 16); England 7 for 81 dec. and 6 for 75 (E.A. Martindale 5 for 22)

This was a low-scoring match played on a rain-affected pitch where the respective captains, Grant and Wyatt, became involved in an absorbing tactical battle. England sent the West Indies in to bat and they were all out for a miserable 102. The visitors hardly did any better, reaching 5 for 81 at the end of the first day's play. More rain delayed the start of the second day until after tea. Hammond and Holmes went out in the first over, so Wyatt immediately declared, 21 runs behind.

Grant changed the batting order to protect his best batsmen, but by stumps the West Indies were 3 for 33. More rain fell overnight and delayed the

resumption until mid-afternoon. Before tea, three wickets fell for 18 runs. Grant declared at 6 for 51, leaving England 73 to win.
Wyatt reversed his batting order but the move backfired — six wickets fell for 48 before Hammond and Wyatt managed to score the runs needed for victory.

SOUTH AFRICA v AUSTRALIA 1935-36

Old Wanderers, Johannesburg
24, 26, 27, 28 December 1935
Drawn

South Africa 157 and 491 (A.D. Nourse 231); Australia 250 (J.H.W. Fingleton 62, W.A. Brown 51) and 2 for 274 (S.J. McCabe189 not out)

Australia gained a 93-run lead on the first innings. In the second, Dudley Nourse hammered the Australian spinners, Grimmett, O'Reilly and Fleetwood-Smith, to score 231 in under five hours and give South Africa a lead of 398. But then McCabe played an innings to be compared with his 187 not out at Sydney in the 'Bodyline' series. He joined Fingleton after Brown fell cheaply, and reached 50 in 40 minutes before a light appeal was granted. The next morning, he raced to his century in 90 minutes, and scored 100 in the pre-lunch session (59-159) — with twenty boundaries. Australia's 250 was posted in 199 minutes, but when the score reached 2 for 274 there was an appeal against the light — from the fielding captain. Herbie Wade felt his fieldsmen were in danger of being hit by McCabe's aggressive strokes. Shortly after the players left the ground, the pitch was under water.

ENGLAND v AUSTRALIA 1938

The Oval, London
20, 22, 23, 24 August 1938
England won by an innings and 579 runs

England 7 wickets for 903 dec. (L. Hutton 364, M. Leyland 187, J. Hardstaff Jnr 169 not out, W.R. Hammond 59, A. Wood 53); Australia 201 (W.A. Brown 69, W.E. Bowes 5 for 49) and 123

This will always be remembered as 'Hutton's match'. On a belter of a pitch, he and Leyland added 318 on the first day after Edrich had become O'Reilly's 100th wicket against England. The second-wicket partnership was broken with the run-out of Leyland, but not before 382 had been added to the score.
By stumps on the second day, England had reached 5 for 634 with Hutton 300 not out. Australia's fielding was outstanding as the team attempted to defend Bradman's record Test score for Anglo-Australian tests. Hutton eventually was dismissed for 364, the highest Test innings at the time. He played the then longest innings in first-class cricket, batting for more than 13 hours.
Hammond finally declared at 7 for 903, which is still the highest total in Test cricket. With both Bradman (who injured an ankle bowling) and Fingleton unable to bat, Australia's reply was a moderate 201. Brown, who opened, was last man out for 69. The second innings was even worse — all out for 123 — and England had inflicted the heaviest defeat in Test history. The margin was an innings and 579 runs.

SOUTH AFRICA v ENGLAND 1938-39

Kingsmead, Durban
3, 4, 6, 7, 8 9, 10, 11 ,13, 14 March 1939
Drawn

South Africa 530 (P.G.V. Van der Bijl 125, A.D. Nourse 103, A. Melville 78, R.E. Grieveson 75, E.L. Dalton 57, R.T.D. Perks 5 for 100) and 481 (A. Melville 103, P.G.V. Van der Bijl 97, B. Mitchell 89, K.G. Viljoen 74); England 316 (L.E.G Ames 84, E. Paynter 62) and 5 for 654 (W.J. Edrich 219, W.R. Hammond 140, P.A. Gibb 120, E. Paynter 75, L. Hutton 55)

This was the famous 'timeless' Test. There was play on nine out of ten possible days, and the game only ended because the ship that was to take the England team home could wait no longer. After the tenth day, England was just 40 runs away from achieving an amazing victory.
Details of the close-of-play scores on each day were as follows:

Day 1: South Africa 2 for 229
Day 2: South Africa 6 for 423
Day 3: South Africa all out 530
England 1 for 35 (rain stopped play)
Day 4: England 7 for 268 (bad light stopped play)
Day 5: England all out 316
South Africa 3 for 193
Day 6: South Africa all out 481
England 0 for 0 (bad light stopped play)
Day 7: England 1 for 253 (bad light)
Day 8: Rain
Day 9: England 3 for 496 (bad light)
Day 10: England 5 for 654 (interruptions because of rain)

NEW ZEALAND v AUSTRALIA 1945-46

Basin Reserve, Wellington
29, 30 March 1946
Australia won by an innings and 103 runs
New Zealand 42 (W.J. O'Reilly 5 for 14) and 54; Australia 8 for 199 dec. (W.A. Brown 67, S.G. Barnes 54, J. Cowie 6 for 40)

This was the first Test to be played between the countries and the first for Lindwall, Miller and Tallon — who were to become three of Australia's finest Test players. New Zealand batted first on a rain-affected pitch. The Kiwis lost their last eight wickets for just five runs as O'Reilly, playing in his final Test, captured five wickets in an innings for the eleventh time.

The match ended on the second afternoon after eight and a half hours of play. New Zealand's aggregate of 96 was their lowest score in all Tests, and the match aggregate of 295 was the third lowest of any completed Test. Australia and New Zealand would not meet again in a Test until 1973-74.

ENGLAND v AUSTRALIA 1948

Headingley, Leeds
22, 23, 24, 26, 27 July 1948
Australia won by 7 wickets
England 496 (C. Washbrook 143, W.J. Edrich 111, L. Hutton 81, A.V. Bedser 79) and 8 for 365 dec. (D.C.S. Compton 66, C. Washbrook 65, L. Hutton 57, W.J. Edrich 54); Australia 458 (R.N. Harvey 112, S.J.E. Loxton 93, R.R. Lindwall 77, K.R. Miller 58) and 3 for 404 (A.R. Morris 182, D.G. Bradman 173 not out)

This was a memorable match with many highlights. England batted better than at any other stage in the series, and was content to have scored 496. But it should have been more, for at one stage on the second day they were 2 for 423. Australia started poorly and lost Morris, Hassett and Bradman cheaply (3 for 68). Then Harvey, in his first Test against England, joined Miller, and they proceeded to hit themselves out of trouble. After Miller departed, Loxton took over and he smashed 5 sixes and 8 fours in an innings of 93. The 19-year-old Harvey reached his century; then Lindwall added 77 and Australia trailed by only 38 runs. England again batted soundly in the second innings and, by the end of the fourth day, was 8 for 362 (a lead of 400). Yardley batted on for five minutes the following morning, so he could use the heavy roller in the hope that it would further break up the pitch.

Australia only needed to draw the match to retain the Ashes, but when Bradman joined Morris they went for victory. They got there with less than fifteen minutes remaining. Bradman fed the strike to Harvey to allow him to hit the winning runs.

It was the Don's last innings at Leeds. In four Tests at the ground, he scored 963 runs at an average of 192.6.

SOUTH AFRICA v ENGLAND 1948-49

Kingsmead, Durban
16, 17, 18, 20 December 1948
England won by 2 wickets
South Africa 161 and 219 (W.W. Wade 63); England 253 (L. Hutton 83, D.C.S. Compton 72, N.B.F Mann 6 for 59) and 8 for 128 (C.N. McCarthy 6 for 43)

This match was played on the same pitch as the 'timeless' Test ten years before. (See page 26). However, this time the pitch played at varying heights and with the ball swinging late in the humid atmosphere, conditions were not easy for batting. Bedser and Gladwin utilised the conditions beautifully and with the support of some magnificent fielding, the South Africans were dismissed for a disappointing 161.

England's batsmen, apart from Hutton and Compton, struggled against the South African spinners Mann and A.M.B. Rowan. The pitch started turning appreciably on the second day and they were able to take advantage of the conditions. Two and a quarter hours were left for play when South Africa's second innings ended — England's target for victory was 128 runs.

England's final innings was played in drizzling rain and poor light but both teams were determined to play on. McCarthy, in his first Test, claimed 6 for 33 in a devastating spell that gave South Africa a winning chance.

Compton and Jenkins added 45 for the seventh wicket to stem the tide for England.

Bedser and Gladwin were at the crease with Tuckett to bowl the last over.

Eight runs were required from the eight-ball over. With three balls left, any one of four results (a win, loss, draw or tie) was possible. Bedser levelled the scores with a single from the sixth delivery, then Gladwin missed the seventh, and after a mid-pitch conference, the batsmen decided to run whatever happened on the final ball. Gladwin swung at the last ball, missed, but then ran the leg bye that gave England the most narrow and exciting of victories.

SOUTH AFRICA v ENGLAND 1948-49

St George's Park, Port Elizabeth
5, 7, 8, 9 March 1949
England won by 3 wickets

South Africa 379 (W.W. Wade 125, B. Mitchell 99, A.D. Nourse 73) and 3 for 189 dec. (B. Mitchell 56); England 395 (F.G. Mann 136 not out, A.M.B. Rowan 5 for 167) and 7 for 174

South Africa recovered from yet another bad start but as had been the case throughout the series, there was never any urgency about their batting. Mitchell's 99 was scored in over six and a half hours of an innings that lasted more than nine hours.

England was in trouble with the top five batsmen out and only 168 runs on the board. The captain, F.G. Mann, played his finest innings to save the side. With the support of the tail he carried England to a 16-run lead.

When Nourse declared South Africa's second innings, he left England needing 172 in 95 minutes to win. Hutton hit the first ball of the innings for four and Washbrook smacked his first ball for six — their opening stand of 58 in 27 minutes set the visitors on the road to victory. Compton and Washbrook carried the total to 104 in 53 minutes. Six wickets fell for 49 and the run chase was on in earnest! In the final over of the match, Crapp made ten runs from three successive balls bowled by Mann to get England home with just one minute of the match remaining. England won the series 2-0, both matches coming down to the wire in the final over.

SOUTH AFRICA v AUSTRALIA 1949-50

Kingsmead, Durban
20, 21, 23, 24 January 1950
Australia won by 5 wickets

South Africa 311 (E.A.B. Rowan 143, A.D. Nourse 66) and 99 (I. W. Johnson 5 for 34); Australia 75 (H.J. Tayfield 7 for 23) and 5 for 101. (R.N. Harvey 151 not out, S.J.E. Loxton 54)

This was a truly remarkable victory by Australia after South Africa gained a first-innings lead of 236 runs. Rowan's patient knock of 143 was the backbone of the Springboks' innings which carried on well into the second day. It is contended that Hassett, the Australian captain, in conjunction with his bowlers, Miller and Johnston, did not attempt to take South African wickets on the second day. The South Africa innings eventually finished on 311. By stumps, Australia was dismissed for a paltry 75, with ten wickets falling for 44. Tayfield, the off-spinner, claimed 7 for 23. Nourse, South Africa's skipper, had the weekend to decide whether he should enforce the follow-on. With rain threatening, he decided to bat again. South Africa's collapse was worse than Australia's, with the last eight wickets falling for just 14 runs. South Africa was dismissed for 99 — and Australia needed 336 to win.

On a wearing, turning pitch, Harvey proceeded to play possibly his finest Test innings. He finished on 151 not out and was involved in match-winning partnerships with Loxton (135 for the fifth wicket), and McCool (106 unbroken for the sixth).

Australia got home by five wickets to be 2-0 up in the series.

ENGLAND v WEST INDIES 1950

Lord's Cricket Ground, London
24, 26, 27, 28, 29 June 1950
West Indies won by 326 runs

West Indies 326 (A.F. Rae 106, E.D. Weekes 63, F.M.M. Worrell 52, R.O. Jenkins 5 for 116) and 6 for 425 dec. (C.L. Walcott 168 not out, G.E. Gomez 70, E.D. Weekes 63); England 151 (S. Ramadhin 5 for 66) and 274 (C. Washbrook 114, S. Ramadhin 6 for 86)

In this match, the West Indies scored its first Test win in England, and at the 'home' of cricket. No pace attack here! It was the 'spin twins', Ramadhin and Valentine, who bowled their team to victory. Rae scored a century in the visitors' first innings total of 326. England replied with only 151; the opening stand realised 62, and the last wicket added 29 — with not much in between.

Walcott, who was dropped at 9, went on to remain 168 not out. With Gomez, he added 211 for the sixth wicket. England's task was to score 601 to win, or to bat for two days to save the game.

It was all over early on the final morning. Washbrook offered the most resistance, and scored 114 in a determined five and a half hours at the crease.

The 'spin twins' bowling figures were as follows:

England's first innings:

Valentine	45-28-48-4
Ramadhin	43-27-66-5

England's second innings:

Valentine	71-47-79-3
Ramadhin	72-43-86-6

AUSTRALIA v ENGLAND 1950-51

Woolloongabba, Brisbane
1, 2, 4, 5 December 1950
Australia won by 70 runs

Australia 228 (R.N. Harvey 74) and 7 for 32 dec.; England 7 for 62 dec. (W.A. Johnston 5 for 35) and 122 (L. Hutton 62 not out)

Hassett won the toss for Australia and decided to take advantage of the near-perfect batting conditions.

England did remarkably well to bowl out the home team on the first day for 228. Only Harvey, 74, and Lindwall, with a patient 41, took advantage of the conditions. Bedser and Bailey were the pick of the English bowlers.

A typical Brisbane thunderstorm washed out play on Saturday and rain delayed the start until half an hour before lunch on Monday. What followed was one of the most amazing day's play in Test Cricket history — twenty wickets fell for just 102 runs!

Brown declared England's innings while still 160 runs behind in the hope that his bowlers would also be able to take advantage of the conditions. They were — and Australia was soon 3 for 0. Hassett declared the innings at 7 for 32 for an overall lead of 192 runs. Bedser and Bailey were the only two bowlers used in the innings, both finishing with seven wickets for the match.

With a target of 193, England's innings started disastrously with Lindwall bowling Simpson first ball. Brown shuffled his order with his finest batsmen, Hutton and Compton, coming in at eight and nine respectively. Hassett's bold declaration was vindicated as England crashed to 6 for 30 at stumps.

On the fourth day, Hutton played one of the great Test innings. He made 62 not out while 92 runs were added on the treacherous pitch. Unorthodox spinner Iverson claimed four wickets in his first Test to seal the Australian victory.

AUSTRALIA v ENGLAND 1950-51

Melbourne Cricket Ground, Melbourne
22, 23, 26, 27 December 1950
Australia won by 28 runs

Australia 194 (A.L. Hassett 52) and 181; England 197 (F.R. Brown 62) and 150

Hassett won the toss as he had done in the first match of the series. However, this time Brown may not have have been sorry to lose — the square had been completely covered for several days to protect it from heavy rain and this had made the pitch green and fast.

Morris fell cheaply as Australia's top order struggled for runs. The home team owed much to the captain Hassett and Loxton who added 84 for the fifth wicket. This was the best partnership of the match and contributed greatly to Australia's success. The last four wickets of the innings fell for just two runs.

On the second day, with conditions more favourable for batting, England struggled against the Australian pace attack of Lindwall, Miller, Johnston and the 'mystery' spin of Iverson. At 6 for 61 the visitors were in desperate trouble. The fightback was again led by the captain who received admirable support from Evans and Bailey. England gained a three-run lead. A two-day break followed for Sunday and Christmas Day and when play resumed on Boxing Day cracks had appeared in the pitch — the result of scorching sunshine on the two rest days.

Australia batted poorly again, debutant K.A. Archer top-scoring with 46. England was left with more than three days to score the 179 required for victory. However, more poor batting and sustained hostile bowling by the Australian attack saw them fall short of the target. Compton's absence from the match because of injury may have proved crucial to the result.

AUSTRALIA v WEST INDIES 1951-52

Melbourne Cricket Ground, Melbourne
31 December 1951, 1, 2, 3 January 1952
Australia won by 1 wicket

West Indies 272 (F.M.M. Worrell 108, K.R. Miller 5 for 60) and 203 (J.B. Stollmeyer 54, G.E. Gomez 52); Australia 216 (R.N. Harvey 83, J. Trim 5 for 34) and 9 for 260 (A.L. Hassett 102, A.L. Valentine 5 for 88)

The injured Worrell scored a superb century in the first innings to carry the West Indies to 272, but Miller captured 5 for 60 to spearhead Australia's attack. The visitors, however, gained a first-innings lead of 56 after a disappointing reply from Australia. Only Harvey, 83, mastered the attack of which Trim, with 5 for 34, was the star.

Despite half-centuries by Stollmeyer and Gomez, the West Indies could only manage 203 in the second innings for a lead of 259. The captain, Hassett, scored a superb 102, but, despite his efforts, Australia looked beaten when the ninth wicket fell at 222. With 38 runs needed, Johnston joined Ring at the crease. As they crept closer to

the target, confusion became evident in the West Indies's team: Ring and Johnson took 13 off a Valentine over, and seven off the next by Ramadhin. Then Ramadhin limped off and nearly everyone was trying to set the field.
Johnston deflected Worrell to fine leg for the single that won an unlikely victory. Later, Johnston was reported to have said: "I was never worried. I knew we couldn't make the runs."

INDIA v ENGLAND 1951-52

Chepauk (Chidambaram Stadium), Madras
6, 8, 9, 10 February 1952
India won by an innings and 8 runs

England 266 (J.D.B. Robertson 77, R.T. Spooner 66, M.H. Mankad 8 for 55) and 183 (J.D.B. Robertson 56); India 9 for 457 dec. (P.R. Umrigar 130 not out, Pankaj Roy 111, D.G. Phadkar 61)

This was India's first Test victory after almost 20 years and 24 previous matches. Carr, deputising for the ill Howard, won the toss and made first use of the excellent batting conditions.
Robertson, Spooner and Graveney gave England a sound start until Mankad produced his match-winning spell — his figures of 38.5-15-55-8 are the best by an Indian bowler in all Tests against England — and wicketkeeper Sen assisted with four stumpings.
The death of King George VI was announced during the first day's play and arrangements were changed to make the following day the rest day.
India batted far more positively than in the previous matches of the series. Umrigar, who had originally been left out of the team, led the way with an unbeaten 130 — his maiden Test century. (Umrigar gained his reprieve when Adhikari sustained a wrist injury just before the game.)
Pankaj Roy scored the second century of his series and this got the home team's innings away to a flying start.
Trailing by 191 runs and with the pitch deteriorating, England struggled in the second innings. Robertson top-scored again but the consistent Watkins was the only other batsman to offer any real resistence to the Indian spinners, Mankad and Ghulam Ahmed.
Both bowlers collected four wickets, giving Mankad a total of twelve for the match. The Indian players and officials were jubilant at the victory after such a long wait for success.

ENGLAND v AUSTRALIA 1953

Lord's Cricket Ground, London
25, 26, 27, 29, 30 June 1953
Match drawn

Australia 346 (A.L. Hassett 104, A.K. Davidson 76, R.N. Harvey 59, A.V. Bedser 5 for 105) and 368 (K.R. Miller 109, A.R. Morris 89, R.R. Lindwall 50); England 372 (L. Hutton 145, T.W. Graveney 78, D.C.S. Compton 57, R.R. Lindwall 5 for 56) and 7 for 282 (W. Watson 109, T.E. Bailey 71)

England recalled its Chairman of Selectors, F.R. Brown, at the age of 42 to play his first Test for two years. After the Australians won the toss, Hassett went in first with Morris. They posted an opening stand of 65 before Morris was brilliantly stumped by Evans off Bedser.
Harvey joined the captain Hassett and they proceeded to add 125 for the second wicket. But the Englishman Wardle then picked up three wickets in ten deliveries to rip the heart out of the Australian middle order. Davidson held the tail together with an aggressive 76 scored out of 117 runs made while he was at the crease.
Hutton and Graveney launched England's innings with an impressive range of stroke play that had been missing from Test cricket for some years. Hutton, playing one of his finest knocks in a five and a quarter hour stay at the crease, passed 2000 runs in Tests against Australia.
Like the Australian innings, the England middle and lower order collapsed, the last eight wickets falling for just 93 runs.
Trailing by 26 runs, Australia's second innings followed a similar pattern to the first, although this time it was Morris and Miller who added 165 for the second wicket. Lindwall's half-century in 45 minutes gave the tail some sting and Australia a lead of 342.
England had an hour to bat on the fourth day and in that time lost Hutton, Kenyon and Graveney for 20 runs. Watson was dropped in the last over of the day.
When Compton fell early on the final morning an Australian victory looked assured. Bailey joined Watson at 12.42 pm and this pair stayed together until 5.50 pm, 40 minutes before stumps.
Their partnership was worth 163 runs and it saved the English team from defeat, with the Australian spinners failing to capitalise on the favourable conditions.

ENGLAND v AUSTRALIA 1953

The Oval, London
15, 17, 18, 19 August 1953
England won by 8 wickets
Australia 275 (R.R. Lindwall 62, A.L. Hassett 53) and162 (G.A.R. Lock 5 for 45); England 306 (L. Hutton 82, T.E. Bailey 64) and 2 for 132 (W.J. Edrich 55 not out)

In this match, England regained the Ashes which had been in Australia's possession for 19 years. The first four Tests in this damp summer had been drawn. The final match began with Hassett giving Australia a solid start after calling correctly for the fifth time in the series. A shower of rain during the luncheon break freshened up the wicket, and the England bowler Trueman (playing his only Test of the summer) took full advantage of the lively strip. Australia slumped from 2 for 107 to 5 for 118. Only aggressive late-order batting by Lindwall gave Australia's innings respectability.

Hutton, 82, played a fine captain's knock for England. Bailey and Bedser added 44 for the last wicket, and England gained a first-innings lead of 31.

After Hassett's dismissal, Morris and Hole (promoted to No.3) carried Australia's second-innings score to 59. Then followed a sensational fifteen minutes in which the Ashes were lost: Hole was given lbw to Laker then Lock's first ball to Harvey bowled him. Miller was caught at short leg off Laker for a duck, and Morris was trapped in front from the first ball of Lock's next over. Four wickets had fallen for just two runs.

Archer scored 49 with some strong hitting before Australia was all out for 162.

England, needing just 132 to regain the Ashes, acquired the runs with little difficulty. Compton made the winning hit off Morris; this was the signal for thousands of delighted fans to stream on to the ground to acknowledge their heroes.

WEST INDIES v ENGLAND 1953-54

Bourda, Georgetown, British Guiana
24, 25, 26, 27 February, 1, 2, March 1954
England won by 9 wickets
England 435 (L. Hutton 169, D.C.S. Compton 64, S. Ramadhin 6 for 113) and 1 for 75; West Indies 251 (E.deC. Weekes 94, C.A. McWatt 54) and 256 (J.K. Holt 64)

There was controversy before the match when the Englishman Hutton objected to the appointed umpires standing in the Test. Inter-island jealousies meant that two other Georgetown umpires had to be used. Hutton won the toss but the advantage seemed lost with the early dismissal of Watson and May. Hutton then proceeded to play one of his best Test innings. His knock of 169 was the foundation of the sizeable England total and the innings lasted until early on the third day. Then in the thirty-five minutes play before lunch Statham, bowling with great hostility, removed Worrell, Stollmeyer and Walcott. Rain washed out play for the remainder of the day.

The batting collapse continued the next morning until seven wickets were down for 139. Of these runs, Weekes had made a memorable 94. McWatt and Holt set about restoring the West Indies' innings. Holt, batting with a runner because of a pulled leg muscle, went in at number nine rather than opening as usual. Ninety-nine had been added by this pair before McWatt was run out by May. Sections of the crowd disagreed with Umpire Menzies' decision and started hurling bottles and wooden packing-cases on to the field. It was an ugly scene with several players lucky to escape injury. The British Guiana Cricket Association officials suggested to Hutton that he take his players from the field, but Hutton wanted to remain on the ground to press home his team's advantage.

England enforced the follow-on and although several of the West Indian batsmen got a reasonable start, no-one played the big innings that was required to save the game.

In England's final innings, Watson completed the visitors' victory by hitting a six.

ENGLAND v PAKISTAN 1954

The Oval, London
12, 13, 14, 16, 17 August 1954
Pakistan won by 24 runs
Pakistan 133 and 164 (J.H. Wardle 7 for 56); England 130 (D.C.S. Compton 53, Fazal Mahmood 6 for 53) and 143 (P.B.H. May 53, Fazal Mahmood 6 for 46)

England rested Bailey and Bedser from the game and included Loader and Tyson to boost their Test match experience. This pair had been selected for the MCC tour to Australia later in the year, but Bailey's omission left England with a long 'tail'.

Rain prevented play starting until 2.30 pm and Pakistan, after winning the toss, soon found themselves in trouble. The debutants, Loader and Tyson, had the visitors reeling at 7 for 51. Kardar

led the fightback with a patient 36 before 56 was added for the last two wickets.
Further rain washed out play on the second day. When play resumed, conditions were difficult for batting with the ball rising awkwardly from a good length. Fazal Mahmood and Mahmood Hussain exploited the conditions superbly with Fazal bowling 30 overs unchanged throughout the innings.
With the pitch drying out in Pakistan's second innings, the English spinners came into their own. It was Wardle who looked likely to spin the home side to victory as the visitors slumped to 8 for 82. But once again the tail wagged — Wazir Mohammad and Zulfiqar Ahmed posting 58 for the ninth wicket.
England needed 168 for victory and looked likely to score the runs on the fourth afternoon. Simpson and May added 51 in forty minutes for the second wicket; but the aggressive approach and the absence of Bailey's steadiness from the middle order saw the wickets tumble. When the final day began, England required 43 for victory with four wickets in hand. Fazal captured six wickets for the second time in the match to bowl Pakistan to a memorable win. It was their first victory over England and the first time a visiting country had won a Test match on their first tour of England.

AUSTRALIA v ENGLAND 1954-55

Sydney Cricket Ground, Sydney
17, 18, 20, 21, 22 December 1954
England won by 38 runs
England 154 and 296 (P.B.H. May 104, M.C. Cowdrey 54); Australia 228 and 184 (R.N. Harvey 92 not out, F.H. Tyson 6 for 85)

Morris, captaining Australia in the absence of the injured Johnson, invited England to bat first. The decision was vindicated with the visitors bowled out for a modest total of 154. The Australian pace quartet of Lindwall, Archer, Davidson and Johnston shared the wickets with two, three, two and three respectively. Wardle, coming in at number nine, top-scored with an invaluable 35.
Australia's reply was disappointing. They gained a lead of only 74 runs despite the fact that six batsmen 'got a start' — Archer led the way with a hard-hitting 49. England's speedsters did the damage. Bailey and Tyson captured four wickets each while Statham picked up the other two.
England then looked to be in real trouble with Hutton, Bailey and Graveney out and only 55 runs on the board. However, May and Cowdrey gave the visitors some hope with a partnership of 116. May went on to compile his first century against Australia in just under five hours. Again the England tail wagged, and this time Appleyard and Statham put on 46 for the last wicket. Tyson had been knocked out when he turned his back on a Lindwall bouncer and was struck on the back of the head.
Australia required 223 for victory and Tyson bowled with great pace and hostility despite his painful blow. He was superbly supported by Statham who operated into a strong wind. Only Harvey offered any resistance to the pace of the English pair. He played one of his finest innings to remain 92 not out and almost single-handedly pulled off an Australian victory. However, Tyson's six wickets gave him ten for the match, spearheading England to victory.

AUSTRALIA v ENGLAND 1954-55

Melbourne Cricket Ground, Melbourne
31 December 1954, 1, 3, 4, 5, January 1955
England won by 128 runs
England 191 (M.C. Cowdrey 102) and 279 (P.B.H. May 91, W.A. Johnston 5 for 25); Australia 231 (J.B. Statham 5 for 60) and 111 (F.H. Tyson 7 for 27)

More than 300 000 people attended this New Year Test. It has been remembered as the 'watering of the wicket' match. The respected Melbourne *Age* cricket writer Percy Beames saw the MCG curator watering the pitch on the Sunday rest day! Fortunately, this watering helped England more than Australia.
Cowdrey rescued England with one of his great innings. After the magnificent bowling of Miller had England reeling at 4 for 41, Cowdrey's century carried the visitors to 191. Australia's reply was not much better, but the tail wagged sufficiently to give the home team a 40-run lead. The pitch was at its best the Monday following the Sunday watering. Johnston bowled superbly for Australia, but England's 279 (including 91 runs from May) set Australia a target of 240.
With Morris and Favell out, Australia was 2 for 75 at the end of the fourth day, needing only a further 165 to win. When Harvey fell to a brilliant leg-side catch by Evans off Tyson, England's danger-man was gone. Australia crashed, losing eight wickets for 36 in only 80 minutes on the final morning. A 'typhoon' had wrecked Australia: Tyson returned 7 for 27 as England went 2-1 up in the series.

ENGLAND v AUSTRALIA 1956

Old Trafford, Manchester
26, 27, 28, 30, 31 July 1956
England won by an innings and 170 runs
England 459 (Rev. D.S. Sheppard 113, P.E. Richardson 104, M.C. Cowdrey 80); Australia 84 (J.C. Laker 9 for 37) and 205 (C.C. McDonald 89, J.C. Laker 10 for 53)

This was 'Laker's Match' on a dust bowl of an Old Trafford pitch. Groundsman Bert Stack as good as admitted he was instructed to prepare the wicket to suit the England spinners, Laker and Lock. (See final scoreboard on page 34.)
There were no problems for Richardson and Cowdrey. They compiled 174 for the first wicket and, with Sheppard scoring a century, England posted a daunting 459. McDonald and Burke started Australia's innings steadily, scoring 48 for the first wicket. But after McDonald's dismissal, the rest capitulated, and Australia was all out for 84. After tea on the second day, Laker had taken seven wickets for eight runs from 22 balls. Laker's first nine overs had yielded 0 for 21; his next 7.4 returned 9 for 16.
Australia followed-on, 375 runs behind. McDonald was soon to retire hurt and out came Harvey who was dismissed on his first ball, a full toss from Laker to Cowdrey (the great left-hander made a pair on the same day!). Rain permitted only 49 minutes play on the third day (Saturday) when Burke was dismissed. On Monday, there was more rain, and only 19 overs of play were possible, but McDonald and Craig survived on the soft, rain-affected pitch. On the final day, they continued until lunch to give the visitors some hope of survival.
Sunshine ended Australia's hopes. Laker utilised the sticky wicket to spin a web over the batsmen. Craig went just after lunch after almost four and a half hours of defiant defence. Mackay, Miller and Archer followed in quick succession. When McDonald went for 89 after more than five and a half resolute hours at the crease, it was all but over. Maddocks was trapped in front to give Laker 'all ten'. All hell erupted, the result and retention of the Ashes forgotten in the thrill of Laker's historic achievement. His figures were 16.4-4-39-9 and 51.2-23-53-10.

PAKISTAN v AUSTRALIA 1956-57

National Stadium, Karachi
11, 12, 13, 15, 17 October 1956
Pakistan won by 9 wickets
Australia 80 (Fazal Mahmood 6 for 34) and 187 (R. Benaud 56, Fazal Mahmood 7 for 80); Pakistan 199 (A.H. Kardar 69, Wazir Mohammad 67) and 1 for 69

This Test match, the first between Pakistan and Australia, was played on a matting wicket. Fazal Mahmood, the 'Bedser of Pakistan', and Khan Mohammad bowled unchanged to rout Australia. The visitors were bundled out for just 80. The match featured some of the slowest scoring in the game's history — only 95 in five and a half hours on the first day and 112 on the fourth.
There was little joy for the Australians. Ray Lindwall, however, captured his 200th Test wicket (the second Australian, after Grimmett, to do so). Australia dismissed the leading Pakistan batsman, Hanif Mohammad, cheaply in both innings.
Fazal ripped through Australia's second innings to set up the historic victory. The great bowler finished with 13 for 114 from 75 overs.

SOUTH AFRICA v ENGLAND 1956-57

Old Wanderers, Johannesburg
15, 16, 18, 19, 20 February 1957
South Africa won by 17 runs
South Africa 340 (R.A. McLean 93, T.L. Goddard 67, J.H.B. Waite 61) and 142; England 251 (P.B.H. May 61) and 214 (D.J. Insole 68, M.C. Cowdrey 55, H.J. Tayfield 9 for 113

South Africa won the toss for the first time in the series and decided to adopt a more positive approach to its batting. Goddard and Waite set up the innings with a 112-run partnership for the second wicket. McLean, who top-scored with a hard-hitting 93, was dropped at slip on 3. South Africa's total of 340 was their highest score of the series in a rubber dominated by the bowlers of both sides.
England were making reasonable progress at 2 for 131, with May and Insole having added 71 for the third wicket, when Insole was run out in unusual circumstances. Tayfield unsuccessfully appealed for lbw. The ball flew to Goddard at slip, but Insole thought the ball had gone through the slips and started for a run — Goddard ran in and easily removed the bails. Compton, with the support of the tailenders, struggled to take England's total to 251.
South Africa's 89-run lead proved decisive, although a lion-hearted effort by the England attack restricted the Springboks' second innings to 142. Goddard completed a fine double, top-scoring with 49.

ENGLAND v AUSTRALIA 1956 (Fourth Test)

Old Trafford, Manchester, 26, 27, 28, 30, 31 July. England won by an innings and 170 runs

ENGLAND

P.E.Richardson	c Maddocks b Benaud	104
M.C.Cowdrey	c Maddocks b Lindwall	80
Rev.D.S.Sheppard	b Archer	113
P.B.H.May*	c Archer b Benaud	43
T.E.Bailey	b Johnson	20
C.Washbrook	lbw b Johnson	6
A.S.M.Oakman	c Archer b Johnson	10
T.G.Evans†	st Maddocks b Johnson	47
J.C.Laker	run out	3
G.A.R.Lock	not out	25
J.B.Statham	c Maddocks b Lindwall	0
Extras	(B 2, LB 5, W 1)	8
Total		459

AUSTRALIA

C.C.McDonald	c Lock b Laker	32		c Oakman b Laker	89
J.W.Burke	c Cowdrey b Lock	22		c Lock b Laker	33
R.N.Harvey	b Laker	0		c Cowdrey b Laker	0
I.D.Craig	lbw b Laker	8		lbw b Laker	38
K.R.Miller	c Oakman b Laker	6	(6)	b Laker	0
K.D.Mackay	c Oakman b Laker	0	(5)	c Oakman b Laker	0
R.G.Archer	st Evans b Laker	6		c Oakman b Laker	0
R.Benaud	c Statham b Laker	0		b Laker	18
R.R.Lindwall	not out	6		c Lock b Laker	8
L.V.Maddocks†	b Laker	4	(11)	lbw b Laker	2
I.W.Johnson*	b Laker	0	(10)	not out	1
Extras		-		(B 12, LB 4)	16
Total		84			205

AUSTRALIA	O	M	R	W		O	M	R	W
Lindwall	21.3	6	63	2					
Miller	21	6	41	0					
Archer	22	6	73	1					
Johnson	47	10	151	4					
Benaud	47	17	123	2					
ENGLAND	O	M	R	W		O	M	R	W
Statham	6	3	6	0	Statham	16	10	15	0
Bailey	4	3	4	0	Bailey	20	8	31	0
Laker	16.4	4	37	9	Laker	51.2	23	53	10
Lock	14	3	37	1	Lock	55	30	69	0
					Oakman	8	3	21	0

FALL OF WICKETS	E	A	A
1st	174	48	28
2nd	195	48	55
3rd	288	62	114
4th	321	62	124
5th	327	62	130
6th	339	73	130
7th	401	73	181
8th	417	78	198
9th	458	84	203
10th	459	84	205

Umpires: D.E.Davies and F.S.Lee

The visitors needed 232 for victory. They lost Bailey late on the fourth afternoon and started the final day requiring 213 to win. Tayfield bowled unchanged for four hours and fifty minutes sending down 35 eight-ball overs. He was to bowl South Africa to its first home win against England for 26 years and its first win at home on a turf pitch. Tayfield was the first South African bowler to take nine wickets in an innings and 13 in a match. Loader, the last wicket to fall, was caught by Tayfield's brother Arthur who was substituting for Funston.

WEST INDIES v PAKISTAN 1957-58

Kensington Oval, Bridgetown, Barbados
17, 18, 20, 21, 22, 23 January 1958
Match drawn

West Indies 9 for 579 declared (E.deC. Weekes 197, C.C. Hunte 142, O.G. Smith 78, G.St.A. Sobers 52) and 0 for 28; Pakistan 106 and 8 for 657 declared (Hanif Mohammad 337, Imtiaz Ahmed 91, Saeed Ahmed 65)

This was the first Test to be played between the two countries and it was a match of many records. Nasim-Ul-Ghani, aged 16 years and 248 days, became the youngest Test player ever. On the first day of the game, Hunte scored a brilliant century on debut to set up a sizeable West Indies total. Weekes then proceeded to blast the Pakistani attack all over the ground.

Pakistan followed on 473 runs behind after a miserable display with the bat realised only 106. Hanif then proceeded to play the longest innings in Test history — he batted for 16 hours and 53 minutes, hitting 24 boundaries in a great knock of 337. He shared in century partnerships with Imtiaz Ahmed (152), Alimuddin (112), Saeed Ahmed (154) and his brother Wazir (121).

Hanif was finally dismissed after tea on the final (sixth) day, having started his innings mid-afternoon on the third day. Although the match resulted in a draw, Pakistan's 8 for 657 will be remembered as the highest total after following-on in all Tests.

WEST INDIES v PAKISTAN 1957-58

Sabina Park, Kingston, Jamaica
26, 27, 28 February, 1, 3, 4, March
West Indies won by an innings and 174 runs

Pakistan 328 (Imtiaz Ahmed 122, W. Mathias 77, Saeed Ahmed 52, E.St.E. Atkinson 5 for 42) and 288 (Wazir Mohammad 106, A.H. Kardar 57); West Indies 3 for 790 dec. (G.St.A. Sobers 365 not out, C.C. Hunte 260, C.L. Walcott 88 not out)

This crushing win by the West Indies was dominated by Sobers' great innings. The 21-year-old left-hander broke the Test record individual score of 364, set by Hutton for England against Australia at the Oval in 1938.

Sobers batted for just over ten hours, which was three hours less than Hutton. He received grand support from Hunte — their partnership was worth 446 and was only broken by the run-out of Hunte for 260. They became only the fourth pair to bat through a whole day's play and it was also Sobers' first century in Test cricket.

Pakistan was limited to two fit bowlers after the first five balls with Nasim-Ul-Ghani (fractured thumb) and Mahmood Hussain (pulled thigh muscle) unable to bowl. The captain Kardar went into the match with a broken finger on his left hand yet he bowled 37 overs of left-arm spinners.

Because of these injuries, Pakistan batted two men short in the second innings and despite a determined rearguard action by Wazir Mohammad and Karder, the match finished early on the final day with victory going to the West Indies.

INDIA v AUSTRALIA 1959-60

Green Park (Modi Stadium), Kanpur
19, 20, 21, 23, 24 December 1959
India won by 119 runs

India 152 (A.K. Davidson 5 for 31) and 291 (N.J. Contractor 74, R.B. Kenny 51, A.K. Davidson 7 for 93); Australia 219 (C.C. McDonald 53, R.N. Harvey 51, J.M. Patel 9 for 69) and 105 (J.M. Patel 5 for 55)

The pitch at Green Park had recently been relaid, and Davidson and Benaud took full advantage of the conditions to bundle India out for 152. McDonald and Harvey both scored half-centuries as Australia replied with 219. Jasu Patel, a 35-year-old off-spinner, played the fifth of his seven Tests and proceeded to wreck the Australian batsmen with 9 for 69.

India batted with more application in the second innings and, despite a magnificent effort by Davidson (7 for 93 from 57 overs), reached 291. Contractor and Kenny compiled half-centuries. The task of scoring 225 proved too great for Australia, and the team was bowled out for a disappointing 105. Patel again exploited the conditions superbly to finish with 5 for 55, giving him 14 wickets for the match.

AUSTRALIA v WEST INDIES 1960-61

Woolloongabba, Brisbane
9, 10, 12, 13, 14 December 1960
Match tied

West Indies 453 (G.S. Sobers 132, F.M.M. Worrell 65, J.S. Solomon 65, F.C.M. Alexander 60, W.W. Hall 50, A.K. Davidson 5 for 135) and 284 (F.M.M. Worrell 65, R.B. Kanhai 54, A.K Davidson 6 for 87); Australia 505 (N.C. O'Neill 181, R.B. Simpson 92, C.C. McDonald 57) and 232 (A.K. Davidson 80, R. Benaud 52, W.W. Hall 5 for 63)

This Test will live forever in cricket history. It was the first tie in almost 500 matches, and was truly one of the great games highlighted by many outstanding individual efforts.

Sobers, 132 with 21 fours, played one of the greatest innings ever, according to the Australian captain, Benaud. The grace of Worrell (who scored 65 in each innings), the 181 runs scored by O'Neill, the fast bowling of Hall, and the magnificent all-round performance of Davidson (who scored 44 and 80 and captured 5 for 135 and 6 for 87) also contributed to the memorable impact of this match

So to the final day: Hall and Valentine added 25 valuable runs to the West Indies's tally, leaving Australia 233 to win in just over five hours. Midway through the afternoon session, all looked lost as Simpson, Harvey, McDonald, O'Neill, Favell and Mackay were back in the pavilion with only 92 on the board. But Davidson and Benaud staged a tremendous fightback, adding 134 for the seventh wicket before Solomon threw Davidson out.

Grout joined his captain with seven runs needed to win. He took a single and faced the last over which was to be bowled by Hall (at this time they were still bowling eight-ball overs). The first ball took Grout on the thigh for one leg-bye so now five were needed. The next delivery was a bouncer; Benaud swung, got a faint edge, and was caught behind by Alexander.

Meckiff was the new batsman. He played his first ball defensively, then Grout called him for a bye from the next. Four were now needed to win from four balls, with two wickets in hand. Grout skied the next ball towards square leg; Kanhai was waiting to take the catch, but Hall charged towards the ball, causing his team-mates to scatter. The big fast bowler, however, muffed the chance, and the batsmen ran a single.

Three balls to go, three runs to win. Meckiff swung the next ball towards the mid-wicket boundary, and the game looked over as the batsmen turned to complete the third run. But Conrad Hunte returned fast and flat to Alexander beside the bails, with Grout just short of his crease.

The scores were tied as the last man, Kline, joined Meckiff with two balls left. He pushed the first ball to square leg, and Meckiff called for the single. Joe Solomon gathered, and from 20 metres and with one stump at which to aim, ran Meckiff out — a thrilling finish to a magnificent game of cricket and the first tie in Test match history. See the final scoreboard on page 37.

AUSTRALIA v WEST INDIES 1960-61

Adelaide Oval, Adelaide
27, 28, 30, 31 January, 1 February 1961
Drawn

West Indies 393 (R.B. Kanhai 117, F.M.M. Worrell 71, F.C.M. Alexander 63 not out, R. Benaud 5 for 96) and 6 for 432 dec. (R.B. Kanhai 115, F.C.M. Alexander 87 not out, C.C. Hunte 79, F.M.M. Worrell 53); Australia 366 (R.B. Simpson 85, R.Benaud 77, C.C. McDonald 71, L.R. Gibbs 5 for 97) and 9 for 273 (N.C. O'Neill 65, K.D. Mackay 62 not out)

This match produced an even longer period of suspense than did the tied Test in Brisbane. Kanhal produced his best batting of the series, ripping a century off Australia's attack in each innings. The West Indian wicketkeeper Alexander added great depth to his team's batting, scoring 63 not out and 87 not out from the lower order. Worrell was again among the run-scorers with 71 and 53. Australia sorely missed the injured Davidson on a belter of an Adelaide pitch.

The highlight of Australia's first innings was the hat-trick taken by Gibbs. The victims were Mackay, Grout and Misson. It was the first hat-trick in Australia-West Indies Tests, and the first to be taken in Australia for 57 years.

Worrell's declaration left Australia 460 to score in about six and a half hours. When McDonald, Favell and Simpson fell before stumps on the fourth day, things were serious.

O'Neill, 65, Burge, 49, and Grout, 42, batted well. But the match seemed over just after tea when Australia was 9 for 207 with 110 minutes still to play. The last man, Kline (who had been dismissed repeatedly in the nets), walked out to join Mackay. The pair remained calm in the crisis as Worrell continually changed his bowlers. The new ball was seen off and the spinners kept out. Mackay faced the last over from Hall and was so determined to save the game that he took several deliveries on the body. His courage was rewarded! The last pair saved the day for Australia.

AUSTRALIA v WEST INDIES 1960-61 (First Test)

Woolloongabba, Brisbane, 9, 10, 12, 13, 14 December. Match tied

WEST INDIES

C.C.Hunte	c Benaud b Davidson	24	c Simpson b Mackay	39
C.W.Smith	c Grout b Davidson	7	c O'Neill b Davidson	6
R.B.Kanhai	c Grout b Davidson	15	c Grout b Davidson	54
G.S.Sobers	c Kline b Meckiff	132	b Davidson	14
F.M.M.Worrell*	c Grout b Davidson	65	c Grout b Davidson	65
J.S.Solomon	hit wkt b Simpson	65	lbw b Simpson	47
P.D.Lashley	c Grout b Kline	19	b Davidson	0
F.C.M.Alexander†	c Davidson b Kline	60	b Benaud	5
S.Ramadhin	c Harvey b Davidson	12	c Harvey b Simpson	6
W.W.Hall	st Grout b Kline	50	b Davidson	18
A.L.Valentine	not out	0	not out	7
Extras	(LB 3, W 1)	4	(B 14, LB 7, W 2)	23
Total		453		284

AUSTRALIA

C.C.McDonald	c Hunte b Sobers	57	b Worrell	16
R.B.Simpson	b Ramadhin	92	c sub (L.R.Gibbs) b Hall	0
R.N.Harvey	b Valentine	15	c Sobers b Hall	5
N.C.O'Neill	c Valentine b Hall	181	c Alexander b Hall	26
L.E.Favell	run out	45	c Solomon b Hall	7
K.D.Mackay	b Sobers	35	b Ramadhin	28
A.K.Davidson	c Alexander b Hall	44	run out	80
R.Benaud*	lbw b Hall	10	c Alexander b Hall	52
A.T.W.Grout†	lbw b Hall	4	run out	2
I.Meckiff	run out	4	run out	2
L.F.Kline	not out	3	not out	0
Extras	(B 2, LB 8, NB 4, W 1)	15	(B 2, LB 9, NB 3)	14
Total		505		232

AUSTRALIA	O	M	R	W		O	M	R	W
Davidson	30	2	135	5	Davidson	24.6	4	87	6
Meckiff	18	0	129	1	Meckiff	4	1	19	0
Mackay	3	0	15	0	Benaud	31	6	69	1
Benaud	24	3	93	0	Mackay	21	7	52	1
Simpson	8	0	25	1	Kline	4	0	14	0
Kline	17.6	6	52	3	Simpson	7	2	18	2
					O'Neill	1	0	2	0

WEST INDIES	O	M	R	W		O	M	R	W
Hall	29.3	1	140	4	Hall	17.7	3	63	5
Worrell	30	0	93	0	Worrell	16	3	41	1
Sobers	32	0	115	2	Sobers	8	0	30	0
Valentine	24	6	82	1	Valentine	10	4	27	0
Ramadhin	15	1	60	1	Ramadhin	17	3	57	1

FALL OF WICKETS

	W	A	W	A
Wkt	1st	1st	2nd	2nd
1st	23	84	13	1
2nd	42	138	88	7
3rd	65	194	114	49
4th	239	278	127	49
5th	243	381	210	57
6th	283	469	210	92
7th	347	484	241	226
8th	366	489	250	228
9th	452	496	253	232
10th	453	505	284	232

Umpires: C.J.Egar and C.Hoy

AUSTRALIA v WEST INDIES 1960-61

Melbourne Cricket Ground, Melbourne
10, 11, 13, 14, 15 February 1961
Australia won by 2 wickets

West Indies 292 (G.St.A. Sobers 64) and 321 (F.C.M. Alexander 73, C.C. Hunte 52, A.K. Davidson 5 for 84); Australia 356 (C.C. McDonald 91, R.B. Simpson 75, P.J.P. Burge 68, G.StA. Sobers 5 for 120) and 8 for 258 (R.B. Simpson 92, P.J.P. Burge 53)

This was the deciding match of one of the most exciting series ever played. Both teams agreed to play a sixth day, if required, to obtain a result. Benaud surprised most people when he invited the West Indian visitors to bat. However, it was not the spearhead Davidson who did the damage but Misson and the spinners who claimed most of the wickets. Six of the West Indies batsmen reached 20 but no-one was able to play the commanding innings required to lay the foundation for a sizeable total.

Before a world-record MCG crowd of 90 800 on the second day, Simpson and McDonald posted the highest opening partnership of the series (146) to place the home team in a sound position. The middle order, apart from Burge, failed to capitalise on the excellent start and at the end of the innings Australia's lead was just 64 runs.

Once again, most of the West Indies' batsmen made a reasonable start but only Alexander and Hunte reached 50. Simpson dismissed the dangerous Sobers — caught at the wicket for the second time in the match — while tragically for the visitors, Solomon was run out again after being well set.

Simpson started the chase for victory at breakneck speed. Eighteen runs came from the first over and 24 from the first ten balls he received. The innings ebbed and flowed until Grout, with Australia 7 for 254, late-cut Valentine. The off-bail fell to the ground and wicketkeeper Alexander pointed to the bail, while the batsmen ran two. Umpire Egar conferred with square leg umpire Hoy and they decided that Grout was not out. Ironically, Grout was then dismissed without further addition to the score.

Mackay and Martin ran a bye to win a thrilling Test and thousands from the final-day crowd of 41 186 swarmed on to the ground to celebrate the climax of a memorable series. The teams were given a ticker-tape parade through the streets of Melbourne two days later.

ENGLAND v AUSTRALIA 1961

Old Trafford, Manchester
27, 28, 29, 31 July, 1 August 1961
Australia won by 54 runs

Australia 190 (W.M. Lawry 74, J.B. Statham 5 for 53) and 432 (W.M. Lawry 102, A.K. Davidson 77 not out, N.C. O'Neilll 67, R.B. Simpson 51); England 367 (P.B.H. May 95, K.F. Barrington 78, G. Pullar 63) and 201 (E.R. Dexter 76, R.Benaud 6 for 70)

It was one Test apiece when the English and Australian teams arrived in Manchester for the fourth match of the series. The pitch was the complete opposite to the 'dust bowl' of 1956. Once again, Australia's innings was held together by Lawry, who scored 74 in a disappointing total of just 190. Statham exploited the conditions and bowled superbly, returning 5 wickets for 53 from 21 overs.

England reached 6 for 358 before Simpson crashed through the English lower order, capturing 4 for 2 off just 26 balls. Simpson was bowling because Benaud was still struggling with the shoulder injury which caused him to miss the second Test at Lord's.

The Ashes were at stake, and Australia's batsmen put their heads down. Lawry scored his second century of the series, and with O'Neill, 67, and Simpson, 51, gave Australia a lead of 154 runs with four wickets in hand at the start of the final day's play.

Mackay, Benaud and Grout fell for the addition of three runs when the No.11 batsman, McKenzie, joined Davidson. The pair produced one of the finest last-wicket partnerships seen, so that when Flavell bowled the 19-year-old McKenzie, 98 runs had been added. The home team was left with 256 to score at 67 per hour. After a steady start by Pullar and Subba Row that realised 40, 'Lord Ted' Dexter accepted the challenge. He hammered the Australian attack to score 76 in 84 minutes, before Benaud switched to bowl around the wicket. The change worked! Dexter was caught behind, with England 2 for 150. Then two balls later, May was bowled around his legs and the tide had turned in Australia's favour.

From 1 for 150, England crashed to 9 for 193, with Australia's captain producing a match-winning spell at the crease. Benaud's return — injured shoulder and all — was 6 for 70 from 32 overs. When Davidson captured the last wicket, Australia had won by 54 runs and, more importantly, they had retained the Ashes.

ENGLAND v WEST INDIES 1963

Lord's Cricket Ground, London
20, 21, 22, 24, 25 June 1963
Drawn

West Indies 301 (R.B. Kanhai 73, J. S. Solomon 56, F.S. Trueman 6 for 100) and 229 (B.F. Butcher 133, F.S. Trueman 5 for 52); England 297 (K.F. Barrington 80, E.R. Doxtor 70, F.J. Titmus 52 not out, C.C.Griffith 5 for 91) and 9 for 228 (D.B.Close 70, K.F. Barrington 60)

This Test did much for cricket in England. Fortunes fluctuated over five days before the game ended in a thrilling draw.

The West Indies opened proceedings with 301. 'Fiery Fred' (F.S. Trueman) took 6 for 100 before Shackleton, with three wickets from four balls, finished off the innings. Dexter savaged the attack for 70 and, with Barrington's 80, England's deficit was only four runs. The West Indies started the second innings poorly: 2 for 15 became 5 for 104 before Butcher rescued the side with a superb 133. There was another late-order collapse when five wickets fell for 15 runs on the fourth morning, leaving England 234 runs to win and almost two days' play to make them.

England slumped to 3 for 31, and lost Cowdrey with a broken arm. At the close of play on the fourth day, England needed 118 with 6 wickets in hand. The pre-lunch session on the final day was washed out, and England had 200 minutes to score the 118 required. At tea, the score had advanced to 5 for 171, with 63 needed in 85 minutes. Close continued to score freely and seemed likely to take England to victory. When the 200 was posted, 34 runs were needed in 45 minutes, with five wickets still in hand. Then the drama started — Hall had Titmus and Trueman out in one over, and then Griffiths dismissed Close. Now fifteen runs were needed in twenty minutes, with two wickets in hand, including the injured Cowdrey. Allen and Shackleton reduced the margin to six runs from three balls. Shackleton was run out! Cowdrey came out with his broken left arm in plaster (fortunately for England, he went to the non-striker's end). Allen blocked the last two balls for the game to end in a nail-biting draw.

AUSTRALIA v SOUTH AFRICA 1963-64

Adelaide Oval, Adelaide
24, 25, 27, 28, 29 January 1964
South Africa won by 10 wickets

Australia 345 (P.J.P. Burge 91, R.B. Simpson 78, B.K. Shepherd 70, B.C. Booth 58, T.L. Goddard 5 for 60) and 331 (B.K. Shepherd 78, N.C. O'Neill 66); South Africa 595 (E.J. Barlow 201, R.G. Pollock 175, N.J.N. Hawke 6 for 139) and 0 for 82

This match is best-remembered for producing South Africa's highest partnership in Test matches. Barlow and Pollock blasted the Australian attack to score 341 in only 283 minutes. Pollock raced to his century in just over two hours, and his 175 was compiled in 283 minutes with 18 fours and 3 sixes. Barlow was not quite as aggressive, his 201 coming in six and a half hours with 27 fours. South Africa's 595 was its record total against Australia, and lasted until the first match of the next series. Barlow dismissed Shepherd, Benaud and McKenzie on the final morning to finish with 3 for 6 from 5 overs, then proceeded to score 47 not out. He and Goddard scored the 82 needed for victory.

ENGLAND v AUSTRALIA 1964

Headingley, Leeds
2, 3, 4, 6 July 1964
Australia won by 7 wickets

England 268 (J.M. Parks 68, E.R. Dexter 66, N.J.N. Hawke 5 for 75) and 229 (K.F. Barrington 89); Australia 389 (P.J.P Burge 160, W.M. Lawry 78) and 3 for 111 (I.R. Redpath 58 not out)

Australia did well to bowl England out on the first day. Hawke and McKenzie were in fine form as they restricted the home team to 268 — Dexter and Parks played many handsome strokes but neither were able to get through the sixties.

Burge joined Lawry with Australia in a comfortable position at 2 for 124. Lawry was run out five runs later and the middle order collapsed, leaving the visitors 7 for 178 and struggling against the English spinners, Titmus and Gifford. Burge was 38 not out when Dexter decided to take the new ball with Australia 7 for 187.

Forty-two runs came from the first seven overs bowled by Trueman and Flavell. Burge and Hawke added 105 for the eighth wicket, in better than even time. Burge reached his century just before stumps.

The following morning, Grout assisted Burge in compiling an 89-run partnership for the ninth wicket. The last three wickets had realised 211 runs and Burge had played one of the great innings in Anglo-Australian Tests, batting for five and a quarter hours and hitting 24 boundaries.

Apart from Barrington, England's batsmen struggled against the Australian attack which was supported by superb fielding. Australia was never troubled to make the 109 required for victory.
The win in this match was the only result in the series and enabled Australia to retain the Ashes. It will always be remembered as 'Burge's Match'.

INDIA v AUSTRALIA 1964-65

Brabourne Stadium, Bombay
10, 11, 12, 14, 15 October 1964
India won by 2 wickets

Australia 320 (P.J.P. Burge 80, B.N. Jarman 78, T.R. Veivers 67) and 274 (R.M. Cowper 81, B.C. Booth 74, W.M. Lawry 68); India 341 (Nawab of Pataudi Jnr 86, M.L. Jaisimha 66, V.L. Manjrekar 59) and 8 for 256 (D.N. Sardesai 56, Nawab of Pataudi Jnr 53)

This was a Test that could have gone either way. Australia was unfortunate to lose its No.3 batsman, O'Neill, who went down with 'Delhi belly' and couldn't bat in either innings.
The game appeared likely to finish in a draw until Australia lost 6 for 28 in its second innings, crashing from 3 for 246 to all out for 274. Steady batting carried India to 8 for 224 shortly after tea on the final day. The experienced Borde with the wicketkeeper, Indrajitsinhji, managed to score the 32 runs needed for victory in what was a great game, and India's second Test win over Australia.

ENGLAND v AUSTRALIA 1972

Lord's Cricket Ground, London
22, 23, 24, 26 June 1972
Australia won by 8 wickets

England 272 (A.W. Greig 54, R.A.L. Massie 8 for 84) and 116 (R.A.L. Massie 8 for 53); Australia 308 (G.S. Chappell 131, I.M.Chappell 56, R.W. Marsh 50, J.A. Snow 5 for 57) and 2 for 81 (K.R. Stackpole 57 not out)

This was 'Massie's Match'. In his Test debut, the 25-year-old West Australian returned figures of 32.5-7-84-8 and 27.2-9-53-8 — a total of 16 wickets for 137. Only Laker with 19 and Barnes with 17 have taken more wickets in a Test. He was supported in the attack by the fast and fiery Lillee, who captured just four wickets for 140.
Because of Massie's outstanding bowling, Greg Chappell's innings tends to be overlooked. He, however, played one of his greatest innings, scoring 131 after Australia had lost 2 for 7.
Massie bowled unchanged from the nursery end in England's second innings to cut a swathe through the line-up (as he had done in the first innings). Australia continued its great record at the 'home' of cricket and won by eight wickets.

SOUTH AFRICA v AUSTRALIA 1966-67

Old Wanderers, Johannesburg
23, 24, 26, 27, 28 December 1966
South Africa won by 233 runs

South Africa 199 (J.D. Lindsay 69, G.D. McKenzie 5 for 46) and 620 (J. D. Lindsay 182, R.G. Pollock 90, P.L. Van der Merwe 76, H.R. Lance 70, A. Bacher 63, E.J. Barlow 50); Australia 325 (W.M. Lawry 98, R.B. Simpson 65) and 261 (T.R. Veivers 55, T.L. Goddard 6 for 53)

This was Australia's first defeat in a Test match on South African soil. Although the ground had been saturated by days of rain, Van der Merwe put South Africa in first after winning the toss. It certainly looked like he had made a grave mistake when the score stood at 5 for 41. Lindsay and Lance added some respectability with a stand of 110, but 199 looked anything but a winning total. Simpson and Lawry posted 118 before the captain was dismissed for 65. Australia passed South Africa's total with the loss of just one wicket but then Australia collapsed losing 9 for 121, resulting in a lead of 126.
Lindsay made a match-winning century in his maiden Test and R.G. Pollock also produced a classic innings of 90. The Australians put down some vital chances, the most crucial when Lindsay was 10 and Van der Merwe 2 — this pair shared a record seventh-wicket partnership of 221. South Africa's score proved to be way beyond the visitors, with Goddard returning career-best figures of 6 for 53 to bowl his team to a historic victory.

INDIA v WEST INDIES 1966-67

Eden Gardens, Calcutta
31 December 1966, 1, 3, 4, 5 January 1967
West Indies won by an innings and 45 runs

West Indies 390 (R.B. Kanhai 90, G.St.A. Sobers 70, S.M. Nurse 56); India 167 (L.R. Gibbs 5 for 51) and 178

This match will be remembered not for the cricket but for the riot that caused the second day's play to be abandoned. The authorities had sold more tickets than there were seats so the disappointed Indian spectators invaded the ground, clashed with police and set fire to several of the stands. The players, naturally concerned for their own

safety, were reluctant to continue the match. It came close to being abandoned until assurances were received from important government officials that there would be no further trouble.
The game was played on an under-prepared pitch so the toss virtually decided the outcome. After both openers were run out, cautious batting placed the visitors in a match-winning position. With the ball spinning viciously and coming off the pitch at an uneven height, Sobers and Gibbs triumphed, leading the West Indies to a comprehensive victory.

WEST INDIES v ENGLAND 1967-68

Queen's Park Oval, Port-of-Spain, Trinidad
14, 15, 16, 18, 19 March 1968
England won by 7 wickets

West Indies 7 for 526 dec. (R.B. Kanhai 153, S.M. Nurse 136, S. Camacho 87) and 2 for 92 dec.; England 414 (M.C. Cowdrey 148, A.P.E. Knott 69 not out, G. Boycott 62, B.F. Butcher 5 for 34) and 3 for 215 (G. Boycott 80 not out, M.C. Cowdrey 71)

This was the fourth match of the series and the only one in which a result was obtained. England had had the better of the first three matches but this time the West Indies dominated proceedings until the final day.
An aggressive start by Camacho laid the foundation for Nurse and Kanhai to plunder the bowling. This pair added 273 for the third wicket to leave the home side in a seemingly impregnable position.
Cowdrey played a superb captain's knock to lead the fightback until the part-time spinner Butcher ran through the lower middle order to record career-best figures of 5 for 34. With a lead of 112 and the success of the leg spinners, Rodriguez and Butcher, Sobers gambled and declared for the West Indies at 2 for 92 — leaving England to reach 215 in two and three quarter hours.
Again it was Cowdrey and Boycott who led the way for the visiting team. They paced the innings perfectly after Edrich, 29, had laid the foundation for an improbable victory. Boycott was there when the match was won with three minutes and eight balls remaining. The West Indian captain Sobers was severely criticised in the Caribbean for the generosity of his declaration.

ENGLAND v AUSTRALIA 1968

Kennington Oval, London
22, 23, 24, 26, 27, August 1968
England won by 226 runs

England 494 (J.H. Edrich 164, B.L. D'Olivera 158, T.W. Graveney 63) and 181; Australia 324 (W.M. Lawry 135, I.R. Redpath 67) and 125 (R.J. Inverarity 56, D.L. Underwood 7 for 50)

England was to win this memorable match with just five minutes of the match remaining.
Rain sent the players from the field one minute before lunch on the last day with Australia in real trouble at 5 for 86. Then a freak storm flooded the ground during the interval and looked likely to prevent the English victory. However, the ground staff mopped up — assisted by volunteers from the crowd — to enable play to resume at 4.45 pm with just 75 minutes of the match remaining. Rain had played havoc with earlier matches in the rubber and again looked likely to deprive England of a win. No-one will ever forget the sight of hundreds of people mopping up pools of water on the Oval!
Inverarity and Jarman continued to defend stoutly on the deadened pitch. Cowdrey tried his front-line bowlers — Snow, Brown, Illingworth and Underwood — then introduced D'Oliveira who bowled Jarman with the last ball of his second over. Cowdrey immediately recalled Underwood to the attack and the left-armer found the pitch more to his liking as it dried out in the afternoon sun. He removed Mallett and McKenzie in his first over, Gleeson survived until twelve minutes to six, and Inverarity — who had batted for over four hours since the start of the innings — was the last man out at five to six. England thoroughly deserved the victory to square the series.
Of the four centuries scored in the series, three were made in this match — Edrich and D'Oliveira for England, and Lawry for Australia.

WEST INDIES v AUSTRALIA 1973

Queen's Park Oval, Port-of-Spain, Trinidad
23, 24, 25, 27, 28 March 1973
Australia won by 44 runs

Australia 332 (KD. Walters 112, I.R. Redpath 66, G.S. Chappell 56) and 281 (I.M. Chappell 97, L.R. Gibbs 5 for 102); West Indies 280 (R.B. Kanhai 56, A.I. Kallicharran 53) and 289 (A.I. Kallicharran 91, R.C. Fredericks 76)

Australia pulled off a fighting victory on a turning pitch in Trinidad. Walters played one of his great Test innings. He scored 100 between lunch and tea on the first day (Later, in December 1974 in Perth, he was to score 100 between tea and stumps against England.)

The West Indies replied with 280 to trail by 52 runs in the first innings. They were disadvantaged by the fact that their No.3 batsman, Rowe, tore the ligaments in his right ankle on the first day and was therefore unable to bat in either innings of the match.
Ian Chappell's gutsy 97 was the foundation of Australia's second effort with the bat. He was seventh out at 231, and then some strange bowling by Gibbs allowed the last three wickets to add 50 (including 33 for the last wicket between Walker and Hammond).
The home team's target was 334. At lunch on the final day, an improbable victory seemed likely when Kallicharran and Foster were together with the score at 4 for 268. The tireless Walker snared 'Kalli' on the first ball after lunch and then O'Keeffe removed Foster. The rout continued with O'Keefe picking up one of his best returns in the Test arena taking 4 for 57 from 24.1 overs.

ENGLAND v AUSTRALIA 1975

Headingley, Leeds
14, 15, 16, 18, 19 (no play) August 1975
Drawn

England 288 (D.S. Steele 73, J. H. Edrich 62, A.W. Greig 51, G.J. Gilmour 6 for 85) and 291 (D.S. Steele 92); Australia 135 (P.H. Edmonds 5 for 28) and3 for 220 (R.B. McCosker 95 not out, I.M. Chappell 62)

This game at Headingley was the third Test of a four-match series. Australia, holding the Ashes, was leading 1-0.
England collapsed from 5 for 268 to be all out for 288. Gilmour was the wrecker, capturing a career-best 6 for 85 from 31 overs. Australia was bundled out for 135 in reply. Edmonds, on debut, was the destroyer with 5 for 28 from 20 overs.
Steele with 92 (after 73 in the first innings) and Greig, 49 (after his 51 in the first 'dig'), carried the home team to 291. The lead was 444 runs as Australia chased an improbable victory. By the end of the fourth day, they were in with a chance at 3 for 220.
When the ground staff arrived the next morning, they discovered to their horror that the pitch had been vandalised. Not only had the wicket been dug up but oil had also been poured onto it. Play was impossible and so the game was abandoned. Ironically, it started raining at about midday so little play would have been possible on the final day anyway.

WEST INDIES v INDIA 1975-76

Queens Park Oval, Port-of-Spain, Trinidad
7, 8, 10, 11, 12 April 1976
India won by 6 wickets

West Indies 359 (I.V.A. Richards 177, C.H. Lloyd 68, B.S. Chandrasekhar 6 for 120) and 6 for 271 dec.(A.I. Kallicharran 103 not out); India 228 (M.A. Holding 6 for 65) and 4 for 406 (G.R. Viswanath 112, S.M. Gavaskar 102, M. Amarnath 85)

In this match, India scored over 400 in the fourth innings to win. The only previous occasion had been at Headingley in 1948 (see page 27). Richards, with 177, mastered the Indian spinners, and made nearly half of the West Indies first-innings total of 359. The youthful Holding ripped through the visitors, who were bowled out for 228, leaving a deficit of 131. The home team built on that first-innings lead and, after Kallicharran reached his century, Lloyd declared. India needed to score 403 in a day and a half. (Australia's target at Leeds had been 404.)
Gavaskar, at his best, smashed 86 with twelve fours before stumps were drawn at 1 for 134. India needed 269 runs in six hours. After Gavaskar's early departure, Viswanath took over and, with Amarnath as the sheet anchor, they progressed steadily towards an improbable victory. The West Indian spinners bowled poorly and without the skill of their opposite numbers. Even though 'Vishy' and Amarnath were run out, Patel took over and India was home with seven overs to spare.

WEST INDIES v INDIA 1975-76

Sabina Park, Kingston, Jamaica
21, 22, 24, 25 April 1976
West Indies won by 10 wickets

India 6 for 306 dec. (A.D. Gaekwad 81 retired hurt, S.M. Gavaskar 66) and 97 (M. Amarnath 60), West Indies 391 (R.C. Fredericks 82, D.L. Murray 71, I.V.A. Richards 64, M.A. Holding 55, B.S. Chandrasekhar 5 for 135) and 0 for 13

This match was the one that followed India's great victory at Port-of-Spain. The pitch at Sabina Park had been relaid, and played with an unpredictable and uneven bounce.
Lloyd sent the Indians in on winning the toss. Before bad light stopped play on the first day, they had scored 1 for 175. On the second morning however, everything went wrong for India. Viswanath, on being caught off the glove, suffered a fractured finger. Gaekwad, who had batted through the first day, was struck above the left

ear and retired hurt on 81. Patel top-edged Holding, and was also forced off the field. Bedi declared just before tea at 6 for 306.

India struck back strongly, with Julien the sixth batsman out at 217. With the bowlers tiring, Murray and Holding added 107 for the seventh wicket.

With a first innings lead of 85, the West Indies struck early with Holding trapping Gavaskar. At 5 for 97, India's second innings closed as five batsmen were absent hurt. In addition to Viswanath, Gaekwad and Patel, Bedi and Chandrasekhar sustained finger injuries while fielding. At first it was thought that Bedi had declared again, but after the West Indies won the match, India's captain issued a statement that the second innings should be recorded as completed.

AUSTRALIA v ENGLAND 1976-77

The Centenary Test
Melbourne Cricket Ground, Melbourne
12, 13, 14, 16, 17 March 1977
Australia won by 45 runs

Australia 138 and 9 for 419 dec. (R.W. Marsh 110 not out, I.C. Davis 68, K.D. Walters 66, D.W. Hookes 56); England 95 (D.K. Lillee 6 for 26) and 417 (D.W. Randall 174, D.L. Amiss 64, D.K. Lillee 5 for 139)

The Centenary of Test cricket was celebrated with a special match at Melbourne 100 years after that first match in March 1877. Australia, sent in on a lively pitch, was bundled out for just 138. The huge Sunday crowd roared as Lillee and Walker crashed through England's batting. England was all out for 95 as a result of the onslaught — Lillee took 6 for 26 and Walker took 4 for 54.

The MCC officials were concerned; the match seemed certain to be over by the fourth day of play. However, the Queen and Duke of Edinburgh were not due to attend until the afternoon of the fifth day.

The pitch was now favouring the batsmen. Although the home side was in trouble at 3 for 53 in the second innings, they were able to turn that situation around. Rodney Marsh reached his first Test century against England, and the 21-year-old Hookes, on debut, hit Greig for five successive fours. The gutsy McCosker (who had his jaw fractured in the first innings) batted at No.10 and scored 25 in an invaluable partnership of 54 with Marsh. Chappell declared Australia's innings with his team leading by 462.

Randall and Amiss gave England a glimmer of hope with a third-wicket stand of 166. O'Keeffe had both Randall and Greig caught at short leg by Cosier, then Lillee trapped Knott in front.

The result was an Australian victory by 45 runs — the same margin by which they had won the first match 100 years earlier. See page 44 for the final scoreboard.

NEW ZEALAND v ENGLAND 1977-78

Basin Reserve, Wellington
10, 11, 12, 14, 15 February l978
New Zealand won by 72 runs

New Zealand 228 (J.G. Wright 55, C.M. Old 6 for 54) and 123 (R.G.D. Willis 5 for 32); England 215 (G. Boycott 77) and 64 (R.J. Hadlee 6 for 26)

This was the forty-eighth match in 48 years between the two countries. Wright, playing his first Test, laid the foundation for New Zealand's innings. His 55 was scored in almost six hours and, with Congdon, 44, the home team reached a modest 228. Old bowled into the howling gale and finished with 6 for 54 from 30 overs. If Wright was laborious, then Boycott was, too. His 77 took almost seven and a half hours to compile. England lost its last six wickets for 32 runs to trail by 13 runs on the first innings. New Zealand's second-innings collapse was just as dramatic. The home team went from 1 for 82 to be all out for 123, with the last nine wickets falling for 41 runs. Willis was the destroyer, taking 5 for 32. England's target was 137, but by the end of the fourth day the innings was in tatters: eight wickets had fallen for 53 runs. Rain delayed the inevitable on the final morning for 40 minutes. It then took the Kiwis 49 minutes to claim the last two wickets, both falling to Richard Hadlee, who finished with 6 for 26. England was all out for 64.

New Zealand defeated England for the first time amid chaotic scenes at the Basin Reserve.

NEW ZEALAND v WEST INDIES 1979-80

Carisbrook, Dunedin
8, 9, 10, 12, 13 February 1980
New Zealand won by 1 wicket

West Indies 140 (D.L. Haynes 55, R.J. Hadlee 5 for 34) and 212 (D.L. Haynes 105, R.J. Hadlee 6 for 68); New Zealand 249 (B.A. Edgar 65, R.J. Hadlee 51) and 9 for 104

After Lloyd called correctly, Hadlee tore the heart out of the visitors' innings. They were 3 for 4 after Hadlee had bowled 13 deliveries. Haynes with

AUSTRALIA v ENGLAND 1976-77 (Centenary Test)

Melbourne Cricket Ground, 12, 13, 14, 16, 17 March. Australia won by 45 runs

AUSTRALIA

I.C.Davis	lbw b Lever	5		c Knott b Greig	68
R.B.McCosker	b Willis	4	(10)	c Greig b Old	25
G.J.Cosier	c Fletcher b Lever	10	(4)	c Knott b Lever	4
G.S.Chappell*	b Underwood	40	(3)	b Old	2
D.W.Hookes	c Greig b Old	17	(6)	c Fletcher b Underwood	56
K.D.Walters	c Greig b Willis	4	(5)	c Knott b Greig	66
R.W.Marsh†	c Knott b Old	28		not out	110
G.J.Gilmour	c Greig b Old	4		b Lever	16
K.J.O'Keeffe	c Brearley b Underwood	0	(2)	c Willis b Old	14
D.K.Lillee	not out	10	(9)	c Amiss b Old	25
M.H.N.Walker	b Underwood	2		not out	8
Extras	(B 4, LB 2, NB 8)	14		(LB 10, NB 15)	25
Total		138		(9 wkts dec.)	419

ENGLAND

R.A.Woolmer	c Chappell b Lillee	9		lbw b Walker	12
J.M.Brearley	c Hookes b Lillee	12		lbw b Lillee	43
D.L.Underwood	c Chappell b Walker	7	(10)	b Lillee	7
D.W.Randall	c Marsh b Lillee	4	(3)	c Cosier b O'Keeffe	174
D.L.Amiss	c O'Keeffe b Walker	4	(4)	b Chappell	64
K.W.R.Fletcher	c Marsh b Walker	4	(5)	c Marsh b Lillee	1
A.W.Greig*	b Walker	18	(6)	c Cosier b O'Keeffe	41
A.P.E.Knott†	lbw b Lillee	15	(7)	lbw b Lillee	42
C.M.Old	c Marsh b Lillee	3	(8)	c Chappell b Lillee	2
J.K.Lever	c Marsh b Lillee	11	(9)	lbw b O'Keeffe	4
R.G.D.Willis	not out	1		not out	5
Extras	(B 2, LB 2, NB 2, W 1)	7		(B 8, LB 4, NB 7, W 3)	22
Total		95			417

ENGLAND	O	M	R	W		O	M	R	W
Lever	12	1	36	2	Lever	21	1	95	2
Willis	8	0	33	2	Willis	22	0	91	0
Old	12	4	39	3	Old	27.6	2	104	4
Underwood	11.6	2	16	3	Greig	14	3	66	2
					Underwood	12	2	38	1

AUSTRALIA	O	M	R	W		O	M	R	W
Lillee	13.3	2	26	6	Lillee	34.4	7	139	5
Walker	15	3	54	4	Walker	22	4	83	1
O'Keeffe	1	0	4	0	Gilmour	4	0	29	0
Gilmour	5	3	4	0	Chappell	16	7	29	1
					O'Keeffe	33	6	108	3
					Walters	3	2	7	0

FALL OF WICKETS

	A	E	A	E
Wkt	1st	1st	2nd	2nd
1st	11	19	33	28
2nd	13	30	40	113
3rd	23	34	53	279
4th	45	40	132	290
5th	51	40	187	346
6th	102	61	244	369
7th	114	65	277	380
8th	117	78	353	385
9th	136	86	407	410
10th	138	95	-	417

Umpires: T.F.Brooks and M.G.O'Connell

55 played a lone hand, as the West Indies were bowled out for 140.
Against hostile fast bowling, Edgar and Howarth played with great courage and determination for New Zealand, with Edgar taking almost five hours to score 65. After a middle-order collapse, Hadlee and Cairns added 64 in 34 minutes for the eighth wicket. Cairns hit Parry for 3 sixes in one over, and Hadlee's 51 runs included nine fours.
New Zealand's lead was a valuable 109 runs. Again it was Haynes who held the visitors innings together. He scored 105 out of 212, and added 88 for the fifth wicket with King and 63 for the sixth with Murray to save the side.
New Zealand needed 104 to win. By lunch on the final day they had reached 2 for 33. Under intense pressure from the pace battery (Holding, Croft and Garner), they crashed to be 7 for 54 and appeared to be beaten.
Again Hadlee and Cairns came to the rescue. They added 19 for the eighth wicket before Cairns and Troup put on 27 for the ninth. At tea it was 8 for 95. With one run added, Holding hit Cairns' off-stump without dislodging the bail. Cairns went when the score reached 100. Boock, the No.11 batsman, joined Troup. He survived the last five balls of Holding's over. Garner continued the attack. The first ball produced a bye. On the second ball, Boock survived an appeal for lbw. He defended the next two before pushing the fifth ball behind point for two runs. With scores level, the batsmen scampered a leg bye to produce a thrilling New Zealand victory.
Hadlee's 11 wickets included a Test record of 7 lbw decisions (of the total 12 lbw decisions made in the match).

AUSTRALIA v INDIA 1980-81

Melbourne Cricket Ground, Melbourne
7, 8, 9, 10, 11 February 1981
India won by 59 runs

India 237 (G.R. Viswanath 114) and 324 (C.P.S. Chauhan 85, S.M. Gavaskar 70); Australia 419 (A.R. Border 124, K.D. Walters 78, G.S. Chappell 76) and 83 (Kapil Dev 5 for 28)

This was a sensational match — not only because of Australia's amazing second-innings collapse on the final day, but because India had come near to forfeiting the match on the previous day when the captain, Gavaskar, disagreed with an lbw decision and wanted to call off the game.
Chappell sent India in on an MCG pitch that had been criticised all summer. The decision was vindicated when India slumped to 6 for 115. They were kept in the match by Viswanath, who went in at 2 for 22, and was ninth man out making 114.
In reply, Australia struggled early before Chappell and Border added 108 for the fourth wicket. Border reached his century on the third morning, and then Walters and Marsh held the lower order together.
Australia had a significant lead of 182, although resolute batting by Gavaskar and Chauhan had reduced this to 74 at the end of the third day. Then, 35 minutes before lunch, the 'Gavaskar incident' occurred. Gavaskar was given out, but he indicated that he had hit the ball on to his pad. As he walked past his partner, Chauhan, he urged him to leave the field with him. Fortunately, the Indian team manager, Wing Commander Durrani, intervened and ordered Chauhan to continue his innings.
When Chauhan was dismissed shortly after, Lillee became Australia's leading Test wicket-taker.
Vengsarkar, Viswanath and Patil helped rebuild India's innings, but a late-order collapse left Australia needing only 143 to win.
India's attack was seriously depleted. Kapil Dev had pulled a thigh muscle and didn't bowl on the fourth evening. Yadav suffered a fractured toe batting in the first innings when he was struck by a Pascoe yorker, and Doshi had a fractured instep and was greatly distressed. Nevertheless Australia was reeling at 3 for 24 at the end of the day, with Dyson, Wood, and Chappell all back in the pavilion. The injured Kapil Dev joined the fray on the final morning and, despite the disability, bowled unchanged to capture five of the last seven wickets to fall. India managed an unlikely victory by 59 runs.

ENGLAND v AUSTRALIA 1981

Headingley, Leeds
16, 17, 18, 20, 21 July 1981
England won by 18 runs

Australia 9 for 401 dec. (J. Dyson 102, K.J. Hughes 89, G.N. Yallop 58, I.T. Botham 6 for 95) and 111 (R.G.D. Willis 8 for 43); England 174 (I.T. Botham 50) and 356 (I.T. Botham 149 not out, G.R. Dilley 56, T.M. Alderman 6 for 135)

For this third Test of the series, Brearley replaced Botham as England's captain. Hughes won the toss for the third time in succession for Australia, and batted first. Dyson's solid century and the skipper's 89 steered Australia to the relative safety of 401 before declaring.

Australia's pace bowlers, Lillee, Alderman and Lawson, bundled England out for 174. The deposed Botham, who had taken six wickets in Australia's innings, top-scored with 50.

England followed on, 227 runs behind, but the second innings proceeded along similar lines to the first. Taylor became Alderman's fourth victim for the innings, and England's score was 7 for 135.

Botham proceeded to play one of the great Test hands and, with admirable support from the tail, at least avoided the innings defeat and gave his team a glimmer of hope. With Dilley, 56, he added 117 for the eighth wicket in 80 minutes; with Old, 29, it was 67 for the ninth; and with Willis, 2, it was 37 for the last. Botham finished with 149 not out and posted his century from 87 balls. (Jessop had smashed 104 in 75 minutes at The Oval in 1902 — see page 18.)

Australia had almost the entire final day to score 130 to win. With the score at 1 for 56, Willis changed ends to bowl with the wind. He proceeded to take eight of the last nine wickets to fall and, in a career-best performance, returned 8 for 43 from 15.1 overs as England snatched a dramatic 18-run victory.

This was only the second time that a team following-on had won a Test match. The previous occasion was in Sydney in December 1894 (see page 17 and 19).

Early in England's second innings, odds of 500 to 1 for an England victory were posted in the betting tents at Headingley.

AUSTRALIA v ENGLAND 1982-83

Melbourne Cricket Ground, Melbourne
26, 27, 28, 29, 30 December 1982
England won by 3 runs

England 284 (C.J. Tavare 89, A.J. Lamb 83) and 294 (G. Fowler 65); Australia 287 (K.J. Hughes 66, D.W. Hookes 53, R.W. Marsh 53) and 288 (D.W. Hookes 68, A.R. Border 62 not out, N.G. Cowans 6 for 77)

This was one of the great Test matches. In terms of runs, the only closer Tests were a tie between Australia and the West Indies in Brisbane, 1960-61 (page 36); a tie between India and Australia in Madras, 1986-87 (page 51); and the West Indies' one run win over Australia in Adelaide, 1992-93 (page 59).

Chappell sent England in on a slightly damp pitch. The visitors were soon struggling at 3 for 56 before Tavare and Lamb added 161 for the fourth wicket in sparkling fashion. England's tail failed to wag, and the innings ended at 284.

On the second day, Australia was bowled out for 287. After Cowans dismissed Dyson and Chappell with successive deliveries, Hughes grafted a patient 66 to hold the Australian innings together. Both Hookes and Marsh, with a mixture of aggression and good fortune, scored half-centuries.

The pattern continued on the third day with England being dismissed for 294. This time, it was the lower order that held the innings together. Botham scored his 46 at a run a ball before Pringle and Taylor realised 61 in an eighth wicket partnership.

Australia's target was 292. An occasional ball was keeping low on the relaid pitch, but the outfield was unusually fast (the result of a prolonged drought that had restricted the watering of the ground).

Fortunes fluctuated throughout Australia's innings. Early on, England was on top. Chappell fell cheaply, again to Cowans, and when Dyson was brilliantly caught by Tavare at slip it was 3 for 71. Australia regained the initiative when Hughes and Hookes posted a century partnership for the fourth wicket.

Then an inspired spell from Cowans tipped the scales England's way. He captured 4 for 19 in seven overs to have the home team in desperate trouble at 9 for 218. Thomson joined Border with 74 runs still required. By stumps, the last pair had taken the score to 255 — they were halfway there.

On the final morning 18 000 spectators turned up for the climax to what had been the most enthralling Test since the tie at the Gabba 22 years earlier.

Willis kept the field back for Border to enable him to take singles. The pugnacious left-hander had been out of touch, and the lack of pressure helped play him back to form.

The new ball had been taken early on the final morning with the score at 259, but still the last pair defied the England team. Botham started the eighteenth over of the day with four runs needed for an improbable victory. Thomson fended at the first ball, edging it to Tavare at second slip. The straightforward catch bounced out, but within reach of Miller at first slip. He completed the catch, and England won the titanic struggle by three runs. With that final wicket, Botham became only the second English Test player (Rhodes being the other) to score 1000 runs and take 100 wickets against Australia.

PAKISTAN v INDIA 1982-83

Niaz Stadium, Hyderabad
14, 15, 16, 18, 19 January 1983
Pakistan won by an innings and 119 runs

Pakistan 3 for 581 dec. (Javed Miandad 280 not out, Mudassar Nazar 231); India 189 (B.S. Sandhu 71, M. Amarnath 61, Imran Khan 6 for 35), 273 (M. Amarnath 64, S.M. Gavaskar 60, D.B. Vengsarkar 50 not out)

The feature of this match was the third-wicket partnership between Mudassar Nazar and Javed Miandad. Their stand realised 451 runs which equalled the then world Test record for any wicket (Legendary Australian batsmen Ponsford and Bradman had added 451 for the second wicket at the Oval in 1934.) Mudassar and Miandad both made their highest Test score.

Pakistan outclassed India for the third successive match to record its most emphatic series victory over its subcontinental neighbour.

In this game, Viswanath played his eighty-fifth consecutive Test to equal the then record of G.S. Sobers. In the series, Pakistan's captain, Imran Khan, was outstanding. He captured 40 wickets.

ENGLAND v NEW ZEALAND 1983

Headingley, Leeds
28, 29, 30 July, 1 August 1983
New Zealand won by 5 wickets

England 225 (C.J. Tavare 69, A.J. Lamb 58, B.L Cairns 7 for 74) and 252 (D.I. Gower 112 not out, E.J.Chatfield 5 for 95); New Zealand 377 (J.G. Wright 93, B.A. Edgar 84, R.J. Hadlee 75) and 5 for 103 (R.G.D. Willis 5 for 35)

After a long run of seventeen defeats and eleven draws, this was New Zealand's first Test victory in England.

Howarth sent the home team in on a seamer's pitch. It was a successful opening day for the visitors, and England was bowled out for 225. Just before tea, only two wickets had fallen when Martin Crowe took a brilliant diving catch at square leg to remove Lamb. Cairns, with 7 for 74, became the first New Zealand bowler to capture seven wickets in a Test innings against England.

Edgar was forced to retire hurt early on the second day, but his opening partner, Wright, became New Zealand's sheet anchor. On his way to scoring 93 in almost five hours, he was involved in two tragic run-outs — both Howarth and Jeff Crowe were victims of his indecision. Later, Edgar returned and with the hard-hitting Hadlee, carried New Zealand's first-innings total to 377.

England's second effort was only a slight improvement on the first. But Gower, in scoring his first century at home in four years, held the innings together.

New Zealand required 101 to win, but, with Willis in full flight, Kiwi hearts were fluttering as Coney walked to the crease with the score at 4 for 61. Jeff Crowe went at 83, then Hadlee joined Coney, and they proceeded to wipe off the deficit with more than a day to spare.

NEW ZEALAND v ENGLAND 1983-84

Lancaster Park, Christchurch
3, 4, 5 February 1984
New Zealand won by an innings and 132 runs

New Zealand 307 (R.J. Hadlee 99); England 82 and 93 (R.J. Hadlee 5 for 28)

This match, played on a suspect pitch at Lancaster Park, was completed in just under twelve hours' playing time. New Zealand recorded its largest ever victory in a Test match.

The England touring party had been hit by injuries, but that was no excuse for the wayward bowling on the first day. Hadlee took full advantage of the erratic attack to blast 99 from 81 balls in less than two hours.

When Fowler was bowled in the last over of the opening day England was in trouble. On the second day, the team was in deeper trouble when play resumed after tea. Hadlee and Chatfield exploited the conditions perfectly as the visitors tumbled to 7 for 53.

The follow-on was not avoided as Chatfield and Cairns cleaned up the tail. Starting the second innings 225 runs behind, England was soon in desperate trouble at 6 for 33. (The lowest score for England against New Zealand was 64 at Wellington in 1977-78.)

Randall and Taylor added 39 before Taylor was run out. Fittingly, Hadlee captured the last three wickets to finish with match figures of 8 for 44 from 35 overs — and with his 99 he was undoubtedly the 'Man of the Match'.

PAKISTAN v ENGLAND 1983-84

National Stadium, Karachi
2, 3, 4, 6 March 1984
Pakistan won by 3 wickets

England 182 (D.I. Gower 58, Abdul Qadir 5 for 74) and 159 (D.I. Gower 57); Pakistan 277 (Saleem Malik 74, Mohsin Khan 54, N.G.B. Cook 6 for 65) and 7 for 66 (M.G.B. Cook 5 for 18)

This was Pakistan's first victory over England in thirteen home Tests. England arrived on the subcontinent after the tour of New Zealand and, with no time to acclimatise to the different conditions, went straight into the first match of the series.
Gower called correctly, and England reached 1 for 90 in the afternoon session before the Pakistani bowlers Sarfraz and Qadir took over. Only Gower's patient 58 prevented a complete rout.
Pakistan's innings followed a similar pattern. Cook ripped through the middle order to have the home team struggling at 6 for 138. Qadir, who was dropped on 1, showed his all-round capabilities to add 75 with Saleem Malik for the seventh wicket. Saleem finished with 74, and, when the last pair, Tauseef and Azeem, added 37 runs, Pakistan's lead had stretched to 95.
England's second innings followed a similar pattern to the first with only Gower providing stout resistance.
Pakistan, with a target of just 65, was quickly in trouble. Cook was on for the fourth over of the innings: 3 for 26 soon became 6 for 40 before the 20-year-old wicketkeeper, Anil Dalpat, steadied the innings. Cook finished the match with 11 wickets for 83, while Abdul Qadir claimed 8 for 133.

ENGLAND v WEST INDIES 1984

Lord's Cricket Ground, London
28, 29, 30 June, 2, 3 July 1984
West Indies won by 9 wickets
England 286 (G. Fowler 106, B.C. Broad 55, M.D. Marshall 6 for 85) and 9 for 300 dec. (A.J. Lamb 110, I.T. Botham 81); West Indies 245 (I.V.A. Richards 72, I.T. Botham 8 for 103) and 1 for 344 (C.G. Greenidge 214 not out, H.A. Gomes 92 not out)

England controlled the match for four of the five days, only to be convincingly defeated at the end.
Fowler and Broad, on debut, scored a rare century opening stand against the West Indies pace battery. Fowler applied himself for over six hours to post his second Test century. The last six England wickets fell for only 43 as Marshall cleaned up the tail to finish with 6 for 70.
Botham knocked over the top order to have the West Indies in trouble at 3 for 35. Richards and Lloyd dug in until Botham trapped Richards in front for 72.
Umpire Barry Meyer later admitted that he had considered recalling Richards, fearing he may have made a mistake. Botham was magnificent, and finished with 8 for 103 as England gained a first innings lead of 41 runs.
This advantage was quickly lost as the home team slumped to 3 for 36. Lamb, with support from Gatting and Botham, turned the innings around. The irrepressible Botham hammered 81, while Lamb finished with 110.
When Gower declared early on the final morning the West Indies required 342 to win in five and a half hours.
Greenidge proceeded to play a superb innings. He made the England attack look pedestrian as he plundered 29 boundaries in compiling a brilliant double-century. Greenidge and Gomes added an unbroken 287 for the second wicket to bring the West Indies home with almost twelve overs to spare.
For the first time, a 'Man of the Match' award was shared — Botham joined Greenidge for the honour.
Finally, of the 30 dismissals in the match, twelve were lbw, thereby equalling the record set at Dunedin in 1979-80.

AUSTRALIA v WEST INDIES 1984-85

Sydney Cricket Ground, Sydney
30, 31 December 1984, 1, 2 January 1985
Australia won by an innings and 55 runs
Australia 9 for 471 dec. (K.C. Wessels 173, A.R. Border 69); West Indies 163 (R.G. Holland 6 for 54) and 253 (C.H. Lloyd 72, I.V.A. Richards 58)

This was the 110th and final Test for the West Indian captain, Lloyd. It was his seventy-fourth match as skipper.
The Sydney pitch had favoured the spinners all season, so it came as a surprise when the visitors left out their only slow bowler, Harper, to include Holding, who was returning after injury.
Two days of rain had left the pitch and outfield damp, but Border decided to bat first. Wood and Wessels were both missed early in their innings. These missed chances were to cost the West Indies dearly.
Wessels was the sheet anchor of Australia's innings. He occupied the crease for more than eight hours in compiling his fourth Test century. The home team batted on for an hour on the third day, and before stumps the West Indies was following on.
Australia's leg spinner, Holland, was the destroyer. He returned career-best figures of 6 for 54.

Lord Harris at the crease as captain of the England team which toured Australia in 1878-79.

W.G. Grace played for England from 1880 to 1899 and is regarded as the father of the modern game.

The visitors performed only slightly better in the second innings. Although Richards and Lloyd both threatened to play the big innings required by the West Indies, Australia held all the aces.
Lloyd top-scored with 72 and he received a standing ovation from the crowd of 25 000 as he returned to the pavilion. It was the first time in 27 matches that the West Indies had been defeated (since Melbourne in 1981-82), and it was their first loss by a whole innings since 1968-69 (also in Melbourne).

NEW ZEALAND v PAKISTAN 1984-85

Carisbrook, Dunedin
9, 10, 11, 13, 14 February 1985
New Zealand won by 2 wickets
Pakistan 274 (Qasim Omar 96, Javed Miandad 79, R.J. Hadlee 6 for 51) and 223 (Qasim Omar 89); New Zealand 220 (M.D. Crowe 57, Wasim Akram 5 for 56) and 8 for 278 (J.V. Coney 111 not out, M.D. Crowe 84, Wasim Akram 5 for 72)

On a seamer's pitch, both teams went into the match without a spinner! Howarth won the toss and, not surprisingly, decided to bowl first.
Coming together at 2 for 100, Qasim Omar and Javed Miandad added 141 in a brilliant batting display. Along the way, Javed Miandad, at 27, became the youngest player to reach 5000 Test runs. A dramatic collapse — five wickets falling for ten runs in the last 30 minutes of play on the first day — tipped the scales in favour of New Zealand. Hadlee, as was normally the case, did the damage. The final return for the Kiwi champion was 6 for 51.
New Zealand struggled against the Pakistan pace quartet particularly the 18-year-old Wasim Akram, (who was playing in only his second Test).
Qasim Omar was again the dominant Pakistan batsman. He followed his first innings 96 with 89. Rashid and Akram added 42 for the last wicket to lift the overall lead to 277.
New Zealand was soon in desperate trouble at 4 for 23. Akram had three wickets when Coney joined Martin Crowe at the crease. They survived for the remainder of the afternoon, and in the process carried the score to 114. The pair continued to bat patiently on the final morning until Crowe was out for 84 just before lunch. His stand with Coney had realised 157.
Pakistan then regained the upper hand, taking the seventh wicket at 216. Cairns, who was not wearing a helmet, was struck on the head by Akram and retired hurt. Chatfield joined Coney after Bracewell was dismissed at 228. The last pair was required to make 50, as Cairns was severely concussed and was to spend three days in hospital. By tea the score had advanced to 235. Coney, on 97, was dropped by the keeper from the first ball of the final session. The excitement was intense as the final pair carried New Zealand to a thrilling victory.
With the field set deep for Coney, he faced 48 balls in the partnership, while Chatfield, in compiling his highest Test score, received 84 deliveries.

ENGLAND v AUSTRALIA 1985

Lord's Cricket Ground, London
27, 28, 29 June, 1, 2 July 1985
Australia won by 4 wickets
England 290 (D.I. Gower 86, C.J. McDermott 6 for 70) and 261 (I.T. Botham 85, M.W. Gatting 75 not out, R.G. Holland 5 for 68); Australia 425 (A.R. Border 196, G.M. Ritchie 94, I.T. Botham 5 for 109) and 6 for 127

Australia kept its great record at the 'home' of cricket intact, in a game that was dominated by its captain, Border. He scored 196 and 41 not out, which comprised 43 per cent of his team's total runs.
Border sent England in to bat. Inspired fast bowling by McDermott soon had the home side in trouble, and only another brilliant knock by Gower saved his team from total collapse.
Australia was struggling at 4 for 101 when Ritchie joined Border. They added 216 for the fifth wicket before Botham returned to restrict the visitors' lead to 135. He picked up five wickets in a Test innings for the twenty-fifth time.
Gower used two nightwatchmen on the third evening. But when they went early on Monday morning, together with Lamb and the skipper himself, England was on the ropes at 6 for 98. Enter Botham who, with Gatting , put on 131 for the seventh wicket. Australia's leg spinner Holland decided to bowl around the wicket. He finally lured Botham into going for a big hit — 'Beefy' holed out to Border at deep point.
Australia, needing 127 to win, slumped to 3 for 46 by the close of play on the fourth day. It was soon 5 for 65 on the final morning before Border and Phillips carried the score to 116 and relative safety Australia won by four wickets. It was Australia's fifth victory at Lord's since Verity's match in 1934 (see page 25).

SRI LANKA v INDIA 1985-86

P. Saravanamutta Stadium, Colombo
6, 7, 8, 10, 11 September 1985
Sri Lanka won by 149 runs

Sri Lanka 385 (S.A.R. Silva 111, R.L. Dias 95, R.S. Madugalle 54, L.R.D. Mendis 51, Chetan Sharma 5 for 118) and 3 for 206 dec. (P.A. de Silva 75, R.L. Dias 60 not out); India 244 (K. Srikkanth 64, M. Amarnath 60, S.M. Gavaskar 52) and 198 (Kapil Dev 78, R.J. Ratnayake 5 for 49)

This was Sri Lanka's first Test win in only their fourteenth Test match.

After slow batting on the opening day, Silva's century and Dias's polished 95 provided the nucleus for the home team's total of 385. This score was achieved even though the last six wickets fell for 17 runs.

India never recovered from a catastrophic start to its first innings. Half-centuries to Srikkanth, Gavaskar and Amarnath helped after it was 3 for 3, but the team still trailed by 141 runs.

Quick scoring by Aravinda de Silva and Dias enabled Sri Lanka to declare 347 ahead. Only a hard-hitting 78 by the skipper Kapil Dev saved India from complete humiliation. Ratnayake was the chief wrecker. He followed 4 for 76 with 5 for 49. Silva's century and nine dismissals were an unprecedented feat by a wicketkeeper in a Test match.

AUSTRALIA v NEW ZEALAND 1985-86

Woolloongabba, Brisbane
8, 9, 10, 11, 12 November 1985
New Zealand won by an innings and 41 runs

Australia 179 (K.C. Wessels 70, R.J. Hadlee 9 for 52) and 333 (A.R. Border 152 not out, G.R.J. Matthews 115, R.J. Hadlee 6 for 71); New Zealand 7 for 553 dec. (M.D. Crowe 188, J.F. Reid 108, R.J. Hadlee 54)

In this match, New Zealand scored its most overwhelming Test victory yet away from home. The New Zealand victory was engineered by the champion Kiwi fast bowler, Richard Hadlee, who cut through Australia's batting line-up like a warm knife slicing butter.

Hadlee captured the first eight wickets before taking a very well-judged outfield catch — off the bowling of Brown — to dismiss Lawson. Brown later returned the favour, catching Holland for a duck.

Australia was all out for 179. Hadlee finished with 9 for 52. Only Laker (twice at Manchester in 1956) and Lohmann (in Johannesburg in 1895-96) had recorded better figures in Test cricket.

Centuries to Reid and Martin Crowe placed the visitors in an impregnable position. Coney declared on the fourth morning with a lead of 374 runs.

In just over two hours, Hadlee, Chatfield and Snedden had reduced Australia to 5 for 67, but then Border and Matthews added a solid 197 for the sixth wicket to offer Australia just a glimmer of hope. But the tail failed to offer Border enough assistance to make New Zealand bat again.

Hadlee captured 6 for 71 to finish with match figures of 52.3-13-123-15, the best by a New Zealand bowler.

WEST INDIES v ENGLAND 1985-86

Recreation Ground, St John's, Antigua
11, 12, 13, 15, 16 April 1986
West Indies won by 240 runs

West Indies 474 (D.L Haynes 131, M.D. Marshall 76, M.A. Holding 73, R.A. Harper 60) and 2 for 246 dec. (I.V.A. Richards 110 not out, D.L. Haynes 70); England 310 (D.I. Gower 90, W.N. Slack 52, G.A. Gooch 51) and 170 (G.A. Gooch 51)

This was the final Test of a five-match series, and was historic on two counts.

Firstly, the West Indies emulated Australia's achievement in winning all five home Tests on more than one occasion — they had previously defeated India 5-0 in the 1961-62 series. Secondly, and more significantly, Richards, in scoring 110 not out in the West Indies second innings, recorded the fastest Test century ever produced in terms of balls faced — he faced 56 to reach three figures, and 58 in all. The previous best had been J.M. Gregory's 67 against South Africa at Johannesburg in 1921-22.

Richards' innings was played without blemish while England was trying to make run-scoring as difficult as possible. For the most part, there were six men on the boundary and sometimes as many as nine. His innings occupied 83 minutes, and he scored 110 of the 146 runs made in that time. The details were as follows:

..36126141	(24 off 10)
.211.412.1	(36 off 20)
112.2111..	(45 off 30)
.1.1624441	(68 off 40)
12..664612	(96 off 50)
..21.461	(110 off 58)

INDIA v AUSTRALIA 1986-87

Chepauk (Chidambaram Stadium), Madras
18, 19, 20, 21, 22 September 1986
Match tied

Australia 7 for 574 dec. (D.M. Jones 210, D.C. Boon 122, A.R. Border 106) and 5 for 170 dec.; India 397 (Kapil Dev 119, R.J. Shastri 62, K.R. Srikkanth 53, M. Azharuddin 50, G.R.J. Matthews 5 for 103) and 347 (S.M. Gavaskar 90, M. Amarnath 51, G.R.J. Matthews 5 for 146, R.J. Bright 5 for 94)

This match resulted in the second tie in Test history. (Australia was also involved in the first tie — against the West Indies — in 1960-61. See page 35.) At the finish, it was Australia who managed to avoid defeat, even though they had dominated proceedings for the first four days' play. Australia declared both its innings, and lost only twelve wickets in the match.

Australia's first innings continued until early on the third day. Jones' double-century was the cornerstone of the visitors' highest Test score in India, and Boon and Border were the other centurions. However, the Indian skipper, Kapil Dev, made sure that Australia batted again by blasting a century off 109 balls with 21 fours.

The off-spinner Matthews picked up five wickets in an innings for the first time. From the 49 overs remaining on the fourth day, Australia scored 170. This allowed Border to declare on the final morning, setting India 348 to win from a minimum of 87 overs.

After a steady start, Gavaskar and Amarnath picked up the batting tempo and, when they went to tea at 2 for 190, India had a realistic chance of winning the match. The target for the final session was 158 runs from 30 overs. At the start of the final 20 overs, 118 runs were needed with seven wickets in hand.

Gavaskar, 90, went out at 251; when Kapil Dev was out two runs later, Australia again had a chance. Shastri, Pandit and Chetan Sharma turned the game India's way until only 18 runs were needed from 30 balls. The situation changed again when Sharma and More were dismissed in an over by Bright. Yadav, who had hit Matthews for six, was ninth out at 344, bowled by Bright.

With just eight balls remaining, Maninder Singh joined Shastri and defended two balls from Bright, giving Shastri the strike for the last over from Matthews. The first ball was blocked. He went for a big hit off the second ball, and mistimed the stroke, but after a misfield he was able to take two runs.

The third ball was pushed to mid-wicket for a single, and the scores were tied. Maninder defended the fourth, but from the fifth delivery he was trapped lbw. The match ended in a thrilling tie before 30 000 excited fans. Matthews picked up his second five-wicket haul, and the left-armer Bright gained the other five. All ten wickets in India's second innings had fallen to spin. See page 52 for the final scoreboard.

PAKISTAN v WEST INDIES 1986-87

Iqbal Stadium, Faisalabad
24, 26, 27, 28, 29 October 1986
Pakistan won by 186 runs

Pakistan 159 (Imran Khan 61) and 328 (Wasim Akram 66, Saleem Yousuf 61); West Indies 248 (R.B. Richardson 54, Wasim Akram 6 for 91) and 53 (Abdul Qadir 6 for 16)

This was an amazing match in which fortunes fluctuated continually until the fourth afternoon when the wily Qadir destroyed the West Indies. The second-innings total of 53 was the visitors' lowest score in a Test match.

Imran decided to bat first, but it wasn't long before the innings was in tatters at 5 for 37. He rescued the sinking ship with a hard-hitting 61, and had support from Saleem Malik, until a lifting delivery broke Malik's arm just above the wrist.

With Richards ill and forced to bat down the order, the West Indies failed to establish its first innings. Wasim Akram ran through the tail to restrict the visitor's lead to 89 runs.

Resolute batting by Moshin, Qasim Omar and the wicketkeeper, Saleem Yousuf (who had been sent in as nightwatchman), gave Pakistan some hope. The lead was 135 when Akram joined Imran. Akram proceeded to punish the West Indies attack to post his first Test half-century. The Pakistan fightback was epitomised by Saleem Malik, who came out to bat with his arm in plaster, and helped Akram add 32 for the last wicket.

The West Indies required 240 to win in four sessions; after one, their innings was destroyed by Imran and Qadir. Qadir picked up the final wicket next morning to finish with 6 for 16. Pakistan had won easily after an absorbing battle.

INDIA v PAKISTAN 1986-87

Karnataka State Cricket Association Stadium (Chinnaswamy Stadium), Bangalore
13, 14, 15, 17 March 1987
Pakistan won by 16 runs

INDIA v AUSTRALIA 1986-87 (First Test)

Chidambaram Stadium, Chepauk, Madras, 18, 19, 20, 21, 22 September. A tie

AUSTRALIA

D.C.Boon	c Kapil Dev b Sharma	122	(2)	lbw b Maninder Singh	49
G.R.Marsh	c Kapil Dev b Yadav	22	(1)	b Shastri	11
D.M.Jones	b Yadav	210		c Azharuddin b Maninder Singh	24
R.J.Bright	c Shastri b Yadav	30			
A.R.Border*	c Gavaskar b Shastri	106	(4)	b Maninder Singh	27
G.M.Ritchie	run out	13	(5)	c Pandit b Shastri	28
G.R.J.Matthews	c Pandit b Yadav	44	(6)	not out	27
S.R.Waugh	not out	12	(7)	not out	2
T.J.Zoehrer†					
C.J.McDermott					
B.A.Reid					
Extras	(B 1, LB 7, NB 6, W 1)	15		(LB 1, NB 1)	2
Total	(7 wkts dec.)	574		(5 wkts dec.)	170

INDIA

S.M.Gavaskar	c and b Matthews	8		c Jones b Bright	90
K.Srikkanth	c Ritchie b Matthews	53		c Waugh b Matthews	39
M.Amarnath	run out	1		c Boon b Matthews	51
M.Azharuddin	c and b Bright	50		c Ritchie b Bright	42
R.J.Shastri	c Zoehrer b Matthews	62	(7)	not out	48
C.S.Pandit	c Waugh b Matthews	35	(5)	b Matthews	39
Kapil Dev*	c Border b Matthews	119	(6)	c Bright b Matthews	1
K.S.More†	c Zoehrer b Waugh	4	(9)	lbw b Bright	0
C.Sharma	c Zoehrer b Reid	30	(8)	c McDermott b Bright	23
N.S.Yadav	c Border b Bright	19		b Bright	8
Maninder Singh	not out	0		lbw b Matthews	0
Extras	(B 1, LB 9, NB 6)	16		(B 1, LB 3, NB 2)	6
Total		397			347

INDIA	O	M	R	W		O	M	R	W
Kapil Dev	18	5	52	0	Sharma	6	0	19	0
Sharma	16	1	70	1	Kapil Dev	1	0	5	0
Maninder Singh	39	8	135	0	Shastri	14	2	50	2
Yadav	49.5	9	142	4	Maninder Singh	19	2	60	3
Shastri	47	8	161	1	Yadav	9	0	35	0
Srikkanth	1	0	6	0					

AUSTRALIA	O	M	R	W		O	M	R	W
McDermott	14	2	59	0	McDermott	5	0	27	0
Reid	18	4	93	1	Reid	10	2	48	0
Matthews	28.2	3	103	5	Matthews	39.5	7	146	5
Bright	23	3	88	2	Bright	25	3	94	5
Waugh	11	2	44	1	Border	3	0	12	0
					Waugh	4	1	16	0

FALL OF WICKETS

	A	I	A	I
Wkt	1st	1st	2nd	2nd
1st	48	62	31	55
2nd	206	65	81	158
3rd	282	65	94	204
4th	460	142	125	251
5th	481	206	165	253
6th	544	220	-	291
7th	573	245	-	331
8th	-	330	-	334
9th	-	334	-	344
10th	-	397	-	347

Umpires: D.N.Dotiwalla and V.Vikramraju

Pakistan 116 (Maninder Singh 7 for 27) and 249; India 145 (D.B. Vengsarkar 50, Iqbal Qasim 5 for 48, Tauseef Ahmed 5 for 54) and 204 (S.M. Gavaskar 96)

This was the fifth and final match in a series in which the first four games had been drawn. The Test was played on a pitch that encouraged the spinners, although both teams thought the conditions would be helpful to the seamers.

Imran batted first after winning the toss. It wasn't long before the visitors were in deep trouble. Maninder Singh produced career-best figures of 7 for 27 as he spun Pakistan out for their lowest score against India of 116.

Vengsarkar played resolutely in scoring 50, placing the home team in a position to establish a sizeable first-innings lead. But Tauseef and Iqbal captured the last six wickets for 19 runs. India's lead was deteriorating rapidly.

Imran shuffled his batting order in the second innings and sent Miandad in first with Rameez. It was a titanic struggle with first one team, then the other, gaining the ascendancy until Yousuf and Tauseef added 51 for the ninth wicket. Pakistan's lead was 220.

Gavaskar played a great innings on a pitch that enabled the off-spinner to bowl bouncers. Unfortunately, India's master batsman didn't get enough support, with only Vengsarkar, Azharuddin and Binny reaching double figures. The Test victory gave Pakistan its first series win in India, and only its third victory in any Test series outside Pakistan.

PAKISTAN v ENGLAND 1987-88

Iqbal Stadium, Faisalabad
7, 8, 9, 11, 12 December 1987
Drawn

England 292 (B.C. Broad 116, M.W. Gatting 79, Iqbal Qasim 5 for 83) and 6 for 137 dec. (G.A. Gooch 65); Pakistan 191 (Saleem Malik 60) and 1 for 51

This was one of the most acrimonious Test matches in history. The loss of a whole day's play and 30 minutes from another may have cost England the chance to level the series.

Gatting won the toss, and, on a pitch that had been prepared for the spinners, batted first. Broad was at the crease for seven hours for 116. Gatting's innings was exactly the opposite. Sparked by anger at the standard of umpiring, he smashed 79 off 81 deliveries.

With three balls remaining to complete the second day, Pakistan was struggling at 5 for 106 in reply to England's 292. Gatting moved Capel from deep square leg to save the single. As Hemmings came in to bowl, Gatting signalled to Capel that he had come in close enough. Then umpire Shakoor Rana, at square leg, stopped play to inform batsman Saleem Malik of Capel's position. The umpire claimed that Gatting had unfairly moved the fieldsman behind the batsman's back. Gatting objected, suggesting that Shakoor Rana had overstepped his bounds.

The umpire refused to play on until he received an apology from the England skipper. By the time Gatting's enforced apology had restored an uneasy truce, six hours' playing time had been lost. A further three and a half were then lost to rain and bad light on the fourth day.

The Pakistan officials refused to make up for the lost third day, and so the game petered out to a tame draw. The home team thereby retained their one match lead in the series.

AUSTRALIA v NEW ZEALAND 1987-88

Melbourne Cricket Ground, Melbourne
26, 27, 28, 29, 30 December 1987
Drawn

New Zealand 317 (J.G. Wright 99, M.D. Crowe 82, C.J. McDermott 5 for 97) and 286 (M.D. Crowe 79, A.I.C. Dodemaide 6 for 58); Australia 357 (P.R. Sleep 90, S.R.Waugh 55, A.I.C. Dodemaide 50, R.J. Hadlee 5 for 109) and 9 for 230 (D.C. Boon 54, R.J. Hadlee 5 for 67)

This final Test of the three-match series was a classic contest that developed into a nail-biting finish. New Zealand was put in to bat and had reached 1 for 119 when Jones deflected McDermott; Australia's wicketkeeper, Dyer, rolled over, then held the ball aloft claiming the catch. The umpires conferred, and the decision was given against the batsman. The television replays, however, showed the ball leaving the 'keeper's gloves and rolling on the ground. With that controversy behind them, the visitors went on to score 317.

Wright became the third New Zealand batsman to be dismissed for 99 in a Test innings.

Australia's middle and lower order staged a grand recovery to give the home team a 40-run first-innings lead. Sleep, 90, Waugh, 55, and the Victorian Dodemaide, 50 on debut, led the fightback after Australia had slumped to 5 for 121. Martin Crowe again played beautifully in New Zealand's second innings and struck twelve majestic boundaries in an innings of 79.

The all-rounder Dodemaide followed his first innings half-century with 6 for 58 from 28.3 overs in the second — and in doing so made a fine start to his Test career.
With the New Zealand second innings ending on the third ball of the final day, Australia required 247 for victory from a minimum of 92 overs. At 4 for 176, the target was only 71 from 28 overs when Hadlee was recalled to the attack. He bowled superbly until the end of the match, and almost single-handedly pulled off an improbable victory for the visitors.
McDermott and Whitney, the last pair, had to survive for 4.5 overs to save the match and give Australia the Trans-Tasman Trophy for the first time. Hadlee had taken ten wickets in a Test match for a record eighth time, and had joined Botham on 373 wickets.

INDIA v WEST INDIES 1987-88

Chepauk (Chidambaram Stadium), Madras
11, 12, 14, 15 January 1988
India won by 255 runs

India 382 (Kapil Dev 109, Arun Lal 69) and 8 for 217 dec. (W.V. Raman 83); West Indies 184 (I.V.A. Richards 68, N.D. Hirwani 8 for 61) and 160 (A.L. Logie 67, N.D. Hirwani 8 for 75)

In this match India recorded the most convincing of its six victories over the West Indies. The player mainly responsible was a new cap, the 19-year-old leg spinner Hirwani. He captured eight wickets in each innings, which equalled the performance of Australia's Massie at Lord's in 1972. Coincidentally, Hirwani returned match figures of 16 for 136 — Massie's were an almost identical 16 for 137.
Shastri was captaining India for the first time. He won the toss and batted first on what was an under-prepared pitch. The home team was struggling at 5 for 156 but then the former captain, Kapil Dev, joined another new cap, Ajay Sharma, at the crease. This pair added 113 runs for the sixth wicket, and Kapil Dev's contribution was a match-winning 109 runs from 119 balls. Given the difficult batting conditions, 382 was a most respectable score.
The West Indies struggled from the start of its innings, and certainly missed the experienced opener Greenidge. Richardson batted for two hours at the crease to make 36, and Richards produced some amazing strokes in compiling 68. The follow-on was avoided on the third morning as Hirwani, on debut, finished with 8 for 61 from 18.3 overs.
With time on its side, India steadily increased its lead. Raman, yet another new cap, showed considerable maturity in making 83. Walsh was again the pick of the West Indies bowlers toiling manfully to finish with 4 for 55.
The West Indies required 416 to win, or more realistically, to bat for one and a half days to save the game. Their batsmen played as if it were a limited overs match, and the Test was over on the fourth day.
This time, Hirwani finished with 8 for 75 from 15.2 overs, and India's wicketkeeper, More, excelled in the difficult conditions. He stumped six batsmen in the match, five of them in the second innings, and in doing so made two Test records.

WEST INDIES v PAKISTAN 1987-88

Queens's Park Oval, Port-of-Spain, Trinidad
14, 15, 16, 17, 19 April 1988
Drawn

West Indies 174 and 391 (I.V.A. Richards 123, P.J.L. Dujon 106 not out, Imran Khan 5 for 115); Pakistan 194 (Saleem Malik 66) and 9 for 341 (Javed Miandad 102)

Pakistan had won the first Test of the three-match series by nine wickets, so this second game was vitally important. The West Indies' captain, Richards, and the team's No.1 fast bowler, Marshall, returned after missing the first match through illness and injury.
It was Richards who top-scored with 49 in a disappointing first-innings total of 174. Richardson was next best with 42, and the home team was out by tea on the first day. Worse was to follow for Pakistan as they slumped to 5 for 50, then 7 for 68 early on the second morning.
Saleem Malik and Saleem Yousuf saved the side with a 94-run partnership for the eighth wicket. The tail wagged sufficiently for Pakistan to gain a 20-run lead on the first innings, and Marshall celebrated his return by claiming 4 for 55.
Early on the third day, the West Indies was struggling at 4 for 81 until Richards took over. He added 94 with Hooper for the fifth wicket, and 97 with Dujon for the sixth, and scored his twenty-second Test century off 134 balls. Dujon went on to complete his fifth Test century, and along the way added 90 runs for the last two wickets with Benjamin and Walsh.
Pakistan's target was 372. When Javed Miandad was seventh out after scoring a flawless 102, only

84 runs were needed for victory. Marshall tipped the scales in favour of the home team when he dismissed Wasim Akram, but then Saleem Yousuf and Ijaz Faqih defended stoutly. In the last over, Yousuf was trapped in front by Richards. Abdul Qadir survived the final five balls with the fieldsmen clustered around the bat. Pakistan retained their lead in the series.

WEST INDIES v PAKISTAN 1987-88

Kensington Oval, Bridgetown, Barbados
22, 23, 24, 26, 27 April 1988
West Indies won by 2 wickets
Pakistan 309 (Ramiz Raja 54, Shoaib Mohammad 54) and 262 (Shoaib Mohammad 64, M.D. Marshall 5 for 65); West Indies 306 (I.V.A. Richards 67, C.L. Hooper 54) and 8 for 268 (R.B. Richardson 64)

The West Indies went into this last match of the series one down and needing to win. They had not lost a home series since 1972-73 when Ian Chappell's Australian team was successful, and furthermore they had not lost a match at Bridgetown since 1935.

Richards won the toss and sent the visitors in to bat. Pakistan's innings was a mixed bag. Shoaib Mohammad and Ramiz Raja both scored half-centuries, and Aamer Malik played well for 32 runs. But with the score at 7 for only 218 the team was in trouble.

Then Saleem Yousuf and Wasim Akram added 67 for the eighth wicket, with the 50-run partnership coming in only five overs. Yousuf then deflected a ball from Marshall on to his face. His nose was broken in two places, and Aamer Malik had to keep wicket in both innings for Pakistan.

The West Indies reply followed a similar pattern to Pakistan's innings. Haynes grafted for almost five hours to score 48, while Richards attacked the bowling and reached 67 from 80 balls.

The home team's tail wagged; Marshall and Benjamin put on 58 for the ninth wicket and the last pair, Benjamin and Walsh, added 23 to bring the West Indies to within three runs of Pakistan's total.

By the end of the third day the West Indies had struck back and Pakistan was 6 for 177. Shoaib scored his second half-century of the match, while Mudassar, 41, and Javed Miandad, 34, both made useful contributions.

On the fourth morning Imran bravely held the tail together. The Pakistan skipper scored 43 not out as the visitors gained a lead of 265. Marshall finished with 5 for 65 to complete a nine-wicket haul for the match Throughout the final innings, fortunes fluctuated as first one team, and then the other, gained the ascendancy.

When Richards and Ambrose fell early on the final day, to be followed shortly afterwards by Marshall, the West Indies still required 59 runs to win with two wickets in hand.

Careful batting by Dujon, and some lusty hitting by Benjamin, saw the West Indies through to victory just after lunch. Benjamin, batting at No.10 had a fine double, scoring 31 run out and 40 not out in successive innings.

The victory levelled the series for the West Indies. But Pakistan had done well! It was the first time since 1973-74 that a visiting team had squared a rubber in the Caribbean.

PAKISTAN v AUSTRALIA 1988-89

National Stadium, Karachi
15, 16, 17, 19, 20 September 1988
Pakistan won by an innings and 188 runs
Pakistan 9 for 469 dec. (Javed Miandad 211, Shoaib Mohammad 94); Australia 165 (P.L. Taylor 54 not out, Iqbal Qasim 5 for 35) and 116

This match will be remembered more for what happened off the field than on it.

When Waugh was given out lbw to the left-arm spinner Iqbal Qasim, to leave Australia 5 for 54, all hell broke loose. Manager Egar, a former Test umpire, and coach Simpson went to the Pakistan Board officials' room to lodge their protest in no uncertain terms. Then, during the tea interval, they called the Australian journalists to a press conference at which they criticised the pitch and umpire Mahboob Shah's decisions.

After the match, the Australian captain, Border, described the pitch at Karachi as the worst pitch he had seen anywhere. He also hinted that the tourists might return home and not complete the tour.

Back to the cricket! Javed Miandad scored his fifth Test double-century while steering his team to a formidable total of 469 runs. Reid, Dodemaide and May toiled manfully for Australia but with poor support from the field. Several chances were missed. Australia's batsmen had no answer to Pakistan's spinners, Iqbal Qasim, Abdul Qadir and Tauseef Ahmed. Only Peter Taylor, batting at No.7, reached 50. The match was over early on the final day with the home team scoring a resounding victory.

ENGLAND v AUSTRALIA 1989

Old Trafford, Manchester
27, 28, 29, 31 July, 1 August 1989
Australia won by 9 wickets

England 260 (R.A. Smith 143, G.F. Lawson 6 for 72) and 264 (R.C. Russell 128 not out, J.E. Emburey 64, T.M. Alderman 5 for 66); Australia 447 (S.R. Waugh 92, M.A. Taylor 85, A.R. Border 80, D.M. Jones 69) and 1 for 81

This was the fourth Test of a six-match series. Australia had won the first two Tests and the third was drawn. Gower decided to bat first after winning the toss. This time Lawson made the early breakthrough and England was soon in trouble at 3 for 57. Smith played superbly to score his maiden Test century, but only Gower and Foster offered any support. Foster contributed 39 in an eighth-wicket partnership of 74.

Taylor and Marsh put on 135 for the first wicket as Australia set about building a sizeable first-innings advantage. When the innings ended early on the morning of the fourth day, the visitors' lead had reached 187.

Just after lunch, the match was all but over. England had crashed, losing 6 for 59, with Lawson and Alderman claiming three wickets apiece. Rain delayed the inevitable — after all, the match was being played in Manchester!

On the final day, Russell and Emburey batted through the first session. Emburey finally went for 64 after adding 142 with the gritty wicketkeeper Russell for the seventh wicket. Russell became the fourth England player to score his maiden first-class century in a Test match. Alderman, who was surprisingly 'wicketless' in the first innings, picked up five in the second, while Lawson claimed three to finish with nine for the match.

The target of 78 presented no problems for Australia and, when Boon hit Cook to the boundary, there was great rejoicing in the visitors' camp. The Ashes had been regained in England for the first time since 1934.

ENGLAND v INDIA 1990

Lord's Cricket Ground, London
26, 27, 28, 30, 31 July 1990
England won by 247 runs

England 4 for 653 dec. (G.A. Gooch 333, A.J. Lamb 139, R.A. Smith 100 not out) and 4 for 272 dec. (G.A. Gooch 123, M.A. Atherton 72): India 451 (M. Azharuddin 121, R.J. Shastri 100, Kapil Dev 77 not out, D.B. Vengsarkar 52, A.R.C. Fraser 5 for 104) and 224

This high-scoring Test was a match of many records. The aggregate number of runs, 1603, was two more than the previous record for Lord's (established in 1930 when England played Australia).

Azharuddin sent England in to bat. Late on the second day, Gooch was able to declare at 4 for 653. The skipper was dropped behind by More on 36, and then went on to record the highest Test score at Lord's. Gooch's 333 included 3 sixes and 43 fours; it was the third-highest Test score made by an English cricketer and the sixth-highest overall. Lamb and Smith also compiled centuries, while the partnership of 308 by Gooch and Lamb was the best for any wicket for England against India.

The visitors replied in a positive manner: Azharuddin scored his century off just 88 balls; Shastri, in a new role as opener, also reached three figures. It was 9 for 430 when the last man, Hirwani, joined Kapil Dev, and India needed 24 runs to avoid the follow-on. Hirwani survived one ball from Fraser; then Hemmings bowled to Kapil Dev. The champion all-rounder blocked the first two balls before launching an unbelievable assault on the hapless off-spinner. Four successive deliveries were smashed down the pitch for six. Fraser dismissed Hirwani with the next ball.

Gooch continued on from his first-innings massacre of the Indian attack. His 123 came off only 113 balls, and included 4 sixes and 13 fours. His match aggregate of 456 was 76 more than the previous record held by Greg Chappell. India was left with seven hours to bat to save the match, or score 472 to win. On a wearing pitch, the task was always going to prove too difficult, and it was Gooch who ended the game by throwing out Sharma. England won handsomely by 247 runs.

NEW ZEALAND v SRI LANKA 1990-91

Basin Reserve, Wellington
31 January, 1, 2, 3, 4, February 1991
Drawn

New Zealand 174 and 4 for 671 (M.D. Crowe 299, A.H. Jones 186, J.G. Wright 88); Sri Lanka 497 (P.A. de Silva 267, A.P. Gurusinha 70, A. Ranatunga 55, D.K. Morrison 5 for 153)

This match will be remembered forever as the Test in which a new world Test record partnership for any wicket was established. Sri Lanka dominated the first half of the match and had played itself into a winning position before New Zealand produced a superb fightback to save the game. Ratnayake and Labrooy, with four wickets apiece, combined on the opening day to bowl the home team out for 174. Aravinda de Silva then hammered the New Zealand bowlers to all parts of the ground as he posted his country's highest Test score. His 267 contained 40 fours, and was scored from 378 balls. Sri Lanka declared on the third day with a lead of 323. New Zealand had the task of batting for 15 hours to save the game. Wright and Franklin posted 134 for the opening stand, but then both batsmen were out within 14 runs. This set the stage for the highest partnership in test history. The New Zealand captain, Martin Crowe, joined Jones and in just over nine hours together they added 467, surpassing the previous best of 451. (Ponsford and Bradman scored 451 for the second wicket against England in 1934, and Mudassar Nazar and Javed Miandad made their partnership of 451 against India in 1982-83.) Jones was out for 186, and Crowe was dismissed in the final over of the match for 299.

WEST INDIES v SOUTH AFRICA 1991-92

Kensington Oval, Bridgetown, Barbados
18, 19, 20, 22, 23 April 1992
West Indies won by 52 runs

West Indies 262 (K.L.T. Arthurton 59, D.L. Haynes 58) and 283 (J.C. Adams 79 not out, B.C. Lara 64); South Africa 345 (A.C. Hudson 163, K.C. Wessels 59) and 148 (K.C. Wessels 74, P.N. Kirsten 52, C.E.L. Ambrose 6 for 34, C.A. Walsh 4 for 31)

It was an historic occasion when Wessels led his team-mates out at the Kensington Oval in Barbados. It was South Africa's first Test for 22 years and its first ever clash against the West Indies. The West Indies Board selected Bridgetown as the venue for the only Test match; the home team had not lost there since 1935 when England won by four wickets.

Wessels followed the accepted procedure for Kensington Oval and sent the West Indies in to bat. Haynes and Simmons added 99 before lunch, but then both openers fell in the space of nine balls from Snell. Richardson and Athurton put on 82 for the fourth wicket before the middle and lower order collapsed. The last six wickets fell for only 22 runs.

South Africa gained a first-innings lead of 83. Opener Hudson scored 163 on debut to become the first South African cricketer to score a century in his first Test match. It was his country's 173rd Test. Only Wessels, 59, and Kuiper, 34, offered any worthwhile contributions apart from the century-maker. Adams was the most successful bowler with 4 for 43. By stumps on the third day, South Africa had a firm grip on the match. The West Indies' lead was only 101 with just three wickets in hand. Donald and Snell had ripped the heart out of the home team's batting, taking three wickets apiece. After the rest day, however, the tail wagged and 99 runs were added on the fourth day, including 62 for the last wicket by Adams and Patterson. Adams, on debut, completed a fine double. He held the middle and lower order together with 79 not out.

South Africa's target was 201. By the end of the fourth day's play, they were just 79 runs away from victory with eight wickets in hand. Wessels had played magnificently and was 74 at the close (he and Kirsten had added 95 for the third wicket after the openers Hudson and Rushmere had gone cheaply). On the final day, the visitors were routed by sustained hostile fast bowling from Ambrose and Walsh. Both bowlers claimed four wickets apiece as South Africa lost 8 for 26. Only Wessels and Kirsten reached double figures. 'Extras' was third top score on 11, Pringle was next best with 4. The West Indies won a memorable match by 52 runs.

ENGLAND v PAKISTAN 1992

Lord's Cricket Ground, London
18, 19, 20, 21 June 1992
Pakistan won by 2 wickets

England 255 (A.J. Stewart 74, G.A. Gooch 69, Waqar Younis 5 for 91) and 175 (A.J. Stewart 69 not out); Pakistan 293 (Aamer Sohail 73, Asif Mujtaba 59, Saleem Malik 55) and 8 for 141

This was the most tense and exciting end to a Test Match at Lord's since England drew with the West Indies in 1963 (see page 39). England has not defeated Pakistan at Lord's since 1978, and since then has only won four Tests at the 'home' of cricket against seven defeats.

Gooch decided to bat first on a pitch that was noticeably cracked from the outset. The skipper, with Stewart, gave the home team the best possible start, putting on 123 for the first wicket. From the moment Wasim Akram bowled Gooch for 69, England's innings lost momentum and only Lamb, 30, and Russell, 22 not out, played with authority. Stewart had been the sheet anchor, taking four hours to score 74, and Waqar Younis was at his destructive best. He ripped the heart out of England's middle order to finish with 5 for 91.

The fact that Pakistan failed to sew up the match in the first innings was a result of fast and hostile bowling by Malcolm on the third afternoon. He claimed 4 for 70 as the visitors crashed from 3 for 228, to be all out for 293 with a lead of just 38. Before Malcolm's blitz, Aamir Sohail, 73, Asif Mujtaba, 59, and Saleem Malik, 55, had laid the foundation for a sizeable Pakistani total.

England, however, failed to capitalise on the fightback, and its second innings never gained any momentum. Alec Stewart played a lone hand and he became the first Englishman to carry his bat in a Test match at Lord's. Pace bowler Wasim Akram was the chief destroyer, this time taking 4 for 66. The leg spinner Mushtaq Ahmed picked up a further three wickets, giving him a total of five for the match.

Against the apparent ease of Pakistan's task (138 to win), England fought back magnificently to grab the balance of power. With De Freitas and Botham injured and unable to bowl, the burden was left to Lewis and the new cap Salisbury. The leg spinner, operating around the wicket to the left-handers, almost achieved the impossible.

In the end, it was the bowlers Wasim and Waqar who guided Pakistan to victory. They came together with their side in desperate trouble at 8 for 95 with 43 runs still required. In the space of an hour, they won the match, Wasim driving Salisbury to the cover boundary after the extra half hour of play had been claimed by the umpires.

SRI LANKA v AUSTRALIA 1992-93

Sinhalese Sports Club, Colombo, Sri Lanka
17, 18, 19, 21, 22 August 1992
Australia won by 16 runs

Australia 256 (I.A. Healy 66 not out) and 471 (D.C. Boon 68, G.R.J. Matthews 64, D.M. Jones 57, M.E. Waugh 56); Sri Lanka 8 for 547 dec. (A.P. Gurusinha 137, R.S. Kaluwitharana 132 not out, A. Ranatunga 127, R.S. Mahanama 78) and 164

Because of the civil unrest in Sri Lanka, this was the first time a Test match had been played there in six years.

Australia was sent in to bat on a pitch that was expected to assist the seam bowlers. It did, to the extent that the Australians lost seven wickets in the afternoon session after Taylor and Boon had added 76 for the second wicket. The unlikely destroyer was the opening batsman Hathurusingha, bowling gentle medium pace. He finished with 4 for 66. The innings was rescued by the wicketkeeper Healy, who, together with Warne and Whitney, added 94 runs for the last two wickets. Still, 256 was a disappointing total.

The home team then batted for the best part of two days to gain a lead of 291 runs. Gurusinha was the sheet anchor of the innings. He was at the crease for nearly nine hours in compiling 137 runs. With Ranatunga, he added 230 for the fourth wicket; this was only ten runs short of their own all-time partnership record for Sri Lanka.

The coup-de-grace was delivered by the pint-sized Sri Lankan wicketkeeper, Kaluwitharana. On debut, he smashed the bowling to score 132 not out from only 158 balls with 26 boundaries. With Kaluwitharana in full flight, the declaration made by Ranatunga with just over one hour's play remaining on the third day was surprising.

Moody was dismissed early on the fourth morning, but from then on the Australians fought hard in a desperate attempt to save the match. Nearly all the recognised batsmen started well, but not one managed to go on and make the big score that was needed.

Over 360 runs were added on the fourth day, for the loss of seven wickets. Once again, the Australian tail wagged, with Matthews holding the innings together while the bowlers McDermott, 40, Warne, 35, and Whitney, 10 not out, all made useful contributions.

Sri Lanka needed 181 runs to win from a minimum of 58 overs. When Mahanama and Hathurusingha opened with a stand of 76 it appeared almost certain that the home team would record its first Test victory over Australia.

Mahanama, 39, was first out in the second last over before tea. In the next over, Hathurusingha, 36, was run out by Moody, who threw the stumps down at the wicketkeeper's end. Then came the turning point. Border, after running more than 25 metres, caught de Silva for 37, and it was 3 for 127. When Ranatunga, Atapattu and Kaluwitharana went cheaply, it was 6 for 137. With 15 overs remaining, Sri Lanka needed 36 runs to win; Australia needed four wickets.

Matthews trapped Ramanayake, and then Warne proceeded to clean up the tail. The leg-spinner captured 3 for 0 from his last eleven balls. Australia had scored an amazing victory by 16 runs after trailing by 291 on the first innings. Only once before had Australia won a Test after trailing by more than 200 on the first innings. That was against South Africa at Durban in 1949-50 (see page 28).

AUSTRALIA v WEST INDIES 1992-93

Adelaide Oval, Adelaide
23, 24, 25, 26 January 1993
West Indies won by 1 run

West Indies 252 (B.C. Lara 52, M.G. Hughes 5 for 64) and 146 (R.B. Richardson 72, T.B.A. May 5 for 9); Australia 213 (C.E.L. Ambrose 6 for 74) and 184 (J.L. Langer 54)

This was one of the greatest Test matches ever played and the closest of all Tests decided on a run basis. (See scoreboard on page 59).

Haynes, 45, and Simmons, 46, got the West Indies off to a flying start with an opening stand of 84 but the visitors failed to capitalise on this foundation. On a pitch that offered more assistance to the bowlers than normal, only Lara and Murray — apart from the openers — played an innings of consequence. The lion-hearted Hughes was rewarded for his persistence with another five-wicket haul for the Australians.

Australia had a taste of what was in store for them when Taylor fell on the first evening and the debutant Langer had his helmet split by some fierce bowling from the West Indies. Australia's woes continued on the rain-shortened second day when Boon was forced to retire hurt after being struck on the arm.

Ambrose was at the peak of his form and bowled the visitors to a 39-run first innings lead.

The third day of this fluctuating match saw 17 wickets fall for 259 runs. A hostile spell of fast-bowling from McDermott reduced the visitors to 4 for 65 before Richardson and Hooper added 59 for the fifth wicket. However, careless batting then saw the West Indies lose their last six wickets for only 22 runs. May, playing his first Test for almost four years, captured 5 for 5 from 32 deliveries.

Australia had two days in which to score 186 and thus regain the Frank Worrell Trophy. The openers went cheaply but Langer and M. Waugh carefully carried the score beyond fifty. Waugh went out for 26 with the total on 54. Shortly after lunch Ambrose removed S. Waugh, Border and Hughes with Walsh chipping in to dismiss Healy — Australia had lost 4 for 10 and the team was now reeling at 7 for 74.

Langer's determined resistance continued and 28 more runs were added before Warne fell to Bishop. May — on his 31st birthday and with a fractured finger — valiantly continued the struggle. It was Bishop who finally removed the doughty Langer — his great effort of four and a quarter hours at the crease had yielded the home team's only half-century of the match.

McDermott, at No. 11, supported May bravely. They carried Australia to within two runs of victory before a lifting delivery from Walsh brushed McDermott's glove and Umpire Hair upheld the West Indies appeal. So it was the visitors who were celebrating on Australia Day, winning a thrilling match by the narrowest possible margin.

SRI LANKA v ENGLAND 1992-93

Sinhalese Sports Club, Colombo
13, 14, 15, 17, 18 March 1993
Sri Lanka won by 5 wickets

England 380 (R.A. Smith 128, G.A. Hick 68, A.J. Stewart 63) and 228 (J.E. Emburey 59); Sri Lanka 469 (H.P. Tillakeratne 93 not out, P.A. De Silva 80, R.S. Mahanama 64, A. Ranatunga 64, V.C. Hathurusingha 59) and 5 for 142

This was Sri Lanka's fourth Test win and their first against England. Smith, in a new role as opening batsman, was the sheet anchor of England's innings. He put on 112 runs for the third wicket with Hick and 122 runs for the fourth wicket with Stewart. Although the tail failed to wag, the last five wickets fell for 22, the last 7 for 64, and the score of 380 appeared to have taken the visitors to relative safety.

The Sri Lankan top order showed its class and unlike the England innings, the bowlers chimed in with valuable runs. Tillakeratne and Muralidaran added 83 for the ninth wicket and the home team finished with a lead of 89.

England's second innings was disappointing. The top order self-destructed against the off-spin of Warnaweera and at 5 for 96 humiliation was on the cards. Lewis and Emburey gave the innings some respectability; however, and Sri Lanka was left to score 140 for victory.

Emburey and Tufnell gave England a glimmer of hope as the home team slumped to 4 for 61. However, Sri Lankan Captain Ranatunga and Tillakeratne played with admirable maturity and patience and took their side within four runs of victory. The skipper was dismissed but then Jayasuriya smashed his first ball for six to pull off the historic victory for Sri Lanka.

AUSTRALIA v WEST INDIES 1992-93 (Fourth Test)

Adelaide Oval, 23, 24, 25, 26, 27 January. West Indies won by 1 run

WEST INDIES

D.L.Haynes	st Healy b May	45	c Healy b McDermott	11
P.V.Simmons	c Hughes b S.R.Waugh	46	b McDermott	10
R.B.Richardson*	lbw b Hughes	2	c Healy b Warne	72
B.C.Lara	c Healy b McDermott	52	c S.R.Waugh b Hughes	7
K.L.T.Arthurton	c S.R.Waugh b May	0	c Healy b McDermott	0
C.L.Hooper	c Healy b Hughes	2	c Hughes b May	25
J.R.Murray†	not out	49	c M.E.Waugh b May	0
I.R.Bishop	c M.E.Waugh b Hughes	13	c M.E.Waugh b May	6
C.E.L.Ambrose	c Healy b Hughes	0	st Healy b May	1
K.C.G.Benjamin	b M.E.Waugh	15	c Warne b May	0
C.A.Walsh	lbw b Hughes	5	not out	0
Extras	(LB 11, NB 12)	23	(LB 2, NB 12)	14
Total		252		146

AUSTRALIA

M.A.Taylor	c Hooper b Bishop	1	(2) c Murray b Benjamin	7
D.C.Boon	not out	39	(1) lbw b Ambrose	0
J.L.Langer	c Murray b Benjamin	20	c Murray b Bishop	54
M.E.Waugh	c Simmons b Ambrose	0	c Hooper b Walsh	26
S.R.Waugh	c Murray b Ambrose	42	c Arthurton b Ambrose	4
A.R.Border*	c Hooper b Ambrose	19	c Haynes b Ambrose	1
I.A.Healy†	c Hooper b Ambrose	0	b Walsh	0
M.G.Hughes	c Murray b Hooper	43	lbw b Ambrose	1
S.K.Warne	lbw b Hooper	0	lbw b Bishop	9
T.B.A.May	c Murray b Ambrose	6	not out	42
C.J.McDermott	b Ambrose	14	c Murray b Walsh	18
Extras	(B 7, LB 3, NB 19)	29	(B 1, LB 8, NB 13)	22
Total		213		184

AUSTRALIA	O	M	R	W		O	M	R	W
McDermott	16	1	85	1	McDermott	11	0	66	3
Hughes	21.3	3	64	5	Hughes	13	1	43	1
S.R.Waugh	13	4	37	1	S.R.Waugh	5	1	8	0
May	14	1	41	2	May	6.5	3	9	5
Warne	2	0	11	0	Warne	6	2	18	1
M.E.Waugh	1	0	3	1					

WEST INDIES	O	M	R	W		O	M	R	W
Ambrose	28.2	6	74	6	Ambrose	26	5	46	4
Bishop	18	3	48	1	Bishop	17	3	41	2
Benjamin	6	0	22	1	Benjamin	12	2	32	1
Walsh	10	3	34	0	Walsh	19	4	44	3
Hooper	13	4	25	2	Hooper	5	1	12	0

FALL OF WICKETS

	W	A	W	A
Wkt	1st	1st	2nd	2nd
1st	84	1	14	5
2nd	99	16	49	16
3rd	129	46	63	54
4th	130	108	65	64
5th	134	108	124	72
6th	189	112	137	73
7th	206	181	145	74
8th	206	181	146	102
9th	247	197	146	144
10th	252	213	146	184

Umpires: D.B.Hair and L.J.King

AUSTRALIA v SOUTH AFRICA 1993-94

Sydney Cricket Ground, Sydney
2, 3, 4, 5, 6 January 1994
South Africa won by 5 runs

South Africa 169 (G. Kirsten 67, S.K. Warne 7 for 56) and 239 (J.N. Rhodes 76 not out, S.K. Warne 5 for 72); Australia 292 (M.J. Slater 92, D.R. Martyn 59) and 111 (P.S. De Villiers 6 for 43)

South Africa scored a thrilling victory after Australia had held control for most of the match. The visitors were bowled out on a suspect pitch for a disappointing 169. Hudson fell cheaply before G. Kirsten and Cronje added 90 for the second wicket. Warne ripped through the middle and lower order — in one spell he claimed 5 for 5 in 22 balls — while his figures of 7 for 56 are the best for Australia against South Africa at home. Apart from Kirsten and Cronje, only De Villiers reached double figures.

Michael Slater, playing with unusual caution, guided Australia to a 123-run lead. The other major contributions came from Martyn and the captain Border. The Australian supporters may have been concerned that the lead wasn't greater as the team had to bat last in the match and the Australians had a poor record when chasing a target. South Africa's opening bowlers, Donald and De Villiers, stuck to their task and claimed four wickets apiece.

When the fifth wicket of the South African second innings had fallen for 110, the match looked lost for the Springboks. However, Rhodes played superbly and with the assistance of Richardson and Donald, South Africa gained a lead of 116. Rhodes and Richardson put on 72 for the sixth wicket while 36 was added for the last by Rhodes and Donald.

The brilliant Warne once again mesmerised the South African batsmen as he claimed his first ten-wicket haul in Test cricket. Australia needed 117 to win its first Test against South Africa for 27 years. Shortly before stumps on the penultimate day, the home team was cruising at 1 for 51. Then De Villiers removed Taylor, Boon and nightwatchman May to set the stage for an exciting finish to what had been a truly absorbing match.

With free admission, an estimated crowd of 12 000 turned up on the final morning. When Donald bowled Border in the very first over of the day the game had swung South Africa's way. Then Donald struck again, removing M. Waugh with a fast yorker, and when the acting captain Cronje threw down the stumps to run out Warne, the Australian team was on the ropes at 8 for 75.

McDermott made some telling blows and while he and Martyn were together the Australians still had some hope. After 35 had been added for the ninth wicket, Martyn holed out to cover and was caught. McGrath was dismissed in the next over and South Africa had pulled off a stunning victory. The Australian score of 111 was the same as that recorded in 'Botham's match' at Headingley in 1981.

WEST INDIES v ENGLAND 1993-94

Queen's Park Oval, Port-of-Spain, Trinidad
25, 26, 27, 29, 30 March 1994
West Indies won by 147 runs

West Indies 254 (R.B. Richardson 63) and 269 (S. Chanderpaul 50, A.R. Caddick 6 for 65); England 328 (G.P. Thorpe 86, C.E.L. Ambrose 5 for 60) and 46 (C.E.L. Ambrose 6 for 24)

The West Indies pulled off an amazing victory after England had held the upper hand for the first three days of the match.

Richardson elected to bat on a somewhat suspect pitch. He was the sheet anchor of the team's struggle for runs on the opening day, taking more than four hours to score 63. From the relative safety of 1 for 158, the middle order capitulated against the accuracy of Fraser and Lewis with the last nine wickets falling for 94 runs.

England gained a first innings lead of 76 after some resolute batting by Thorpe, Atherton and Hick and some spirited hitting by Salisbury at the end. Ambrose collected yet another five-wicket haul in an innings and was largely responsible for restricting England's lead.

When Richardson, Lara and Haynes had been dismissed with the deficit still 25, the visitors were in the box seat. Arthurton and Adams added 80 carefully compiled runs for the fourth wicket. But both fell shortly before stumps to once again leave the advantage with England. Chanderpaul, who was dropped twice, with the support of the 'keeper Murray and the bowlers, put on 126 valuable runs on the fourth day to give the West Indies a handy lead of 193.

Because of rain interruptions, 15 overs remained to complete the day's play. Atherton fell lbw to the first ball of the innings, Ramprakash ran himself out off the fifth and Smith was bowled by the second ball of Ambrose's second over. Worse was to follow; Hick went at 21, and Stewart, the

only batsman to reach double figures, was bowled at 26. Walsh at last got into the act and had Salisbury caught at slip. Ambrose then removed Thorpe and Russell to leave England in tatters at 8 for 40.
Walsh claimed the last two wickets early the next morning but not before six runs had been scored. England's lowest Test innings of 45 was narrowly avoided — but at least the team of 1887 won that match in Sydney! Ambrose and Walsh had bowled through the innings, Ambrose taking his third ten-wicket haul in Test cricket.

PAKISTAN v AUSTRALIA 1994-95

National Stadium, Karachi
28, 29, 30 September, 1, 2 October 1994
Pakistan won by 1 wicket

Australia 337 (M.G. Bevan 82, S.R. Waugh 73, I.A. Healy 57) and 232 (D.C. Boon 114 not out, M.E. Waugh 61, Wasim Akram 5 for 63); Pakistan 256 (Saeed Anwar 85) and 9 for 315 (Saeed Anwar 77, Inzamamul Haq 58 not out, S.K. Warne 5 for 89)

This was the seventh Test to be decided by a margin of one wicket. It was the first Test Australia had played since the retirement of former captain Allan Border, who had appeared in 153 successive matches. Mark Taylor, the new captain, did win the toss but unfortunately he became the first player to mark his first Test as captain by 'bagging a pair'.
Australia took the honours on the opening day compiling 7 for 325. Bevan, on debut, scored a stylish 82. He added 121 in better than even time with S. Waugh, whose 73 included 13 boundaries. Keeper Healy contributed yet another useful half-century.
The last three wickets fell for just twelve runs on the second morning. Pakistan started brightly with Saeed Anwar and Aamir Sohail posting 90 for the first wicket in even time. A middle-order collapse left the home side struggling at 7 for 209 at stumps on the second day. A breezy 39 from Wasim Akram carried the Pakistan total to 256.
Despite Taylor going cheaply again, the visitors built on the 81-run lead, with Boon and M. Waugh pushing the score to 2 for 171 shortly before the close of the day's play. Pakistan then struck back with Waqar Younis removing M. Waugh for 61 and Wasim Akram dismissing both Bevan and S. Waugh first ball. The determined Tasmanian Boon posted his nineteenth Test century, which was his first against Pakistan, but the Australian tail failed to wag.
The home team's target was 314 with almost two full days' play remaining. Saeed Anwar again batted positively giving his side a good start for the second time in the match. However, when Saleem Malik fell for 43 runs just before stumps the game was evenly balanced with the home team at 3 for 155.
The spinner Warne ripped out the Pakistan middle order on the final morning to set up what looked a certain Australian victory. When the last man in for the home side, Mushtaq Ahmed, joined Inzamamul Haq, 56 runs were still needed. Some brave batting brought the scores closer until just three were required.
Warne bowled to Inzamamul Haq who went down the pitch to a ball pitched outside the leg stump. It missed the bat, flicked the pad and sped away for four leg byes. Pakistan had won a thrilling match to retain its unbeaten record in Karachi. (See final scoreboard on page 62.)

ZIMBABWE v PAKISTAN 1994-95

Harare Sports Club, Harare
31 January, 1, 2, 4 February 1995
Zimbabwe won by an innings and 64 runs

Zimbabwe 4 for 544 dec. (G.W. Flower 201 not out, A. Flower 156, G.J. Whittall 113); Pakistan 322 (Inzamamul Haq 71, Ijaz Ahmed 65, Aamir Sohail 61, H.H. Streak 6 for 90) and 158 (Inzamamul Haq 65)

This was Zimbabwe's first Test victory in only its eleventh Test match.
The match started in dramatic fashion. Referee Hendriks missed the toss, which was won by Pakistan captain Saleem Malik, and then ruled that a replay should take place. This time Zimbabwe won. (Match referees had only been present at the toss since 1994 when Saleem Malik had claimed the call somewhat dubiously against New Zealand in Auckland.)
The home team started poorly losing 3 for 42 before the Flower brothers came together in a record-breaking partnership. They added 269 for the fourth wicket, beating the Chappell brothers' 264 for the third at Wellington in 1973-74. The skipper went for 156 before Whittall and G. Flower combined for an unbroken fifth-wicket stand of 233.
The bowler Streak returned Zimbabwe's best Test figures of 6 for 90 from 39 hostile overs. Only half-centuries from Inzamamul Haq, Ijaz Ahmed and Aamir Sohail gave Pakistan any hope of avoiding the follow-on. In the second innings it was only Inzamamul Haq and Rashid Latif who offered any

PAKISTAN v AUSTRALIA 1994-95 (First Test)

National Stadium, Karachi, 28, 29, 30 September, 1, 2 October. Pakistan won by 1 wicket

AUSTRALIA

M.J.Slater	lbw b Wasim Akram	36	lbw b Mushtaq Ahmed	23
M.A.Taylor*	c and b Wasim Akram	0	c Rashid Latif b Waqar Younis	0
D.C.Boon	b Mushtaq Ahmed	19	not out	114
M.E.Waugh	c Zahid Fazal b Mushtaq Ahmed	20	b Waqar Younis	61
M.G.Bevan	c Aamer Sohail b Mushtaq Ahmed	82	b Wasim Akram	0
S.R.Waugh	b Waqar Younis	73	lbw b Wasim Akram	0
I.A.Healy†	c Rashid Latif b Waqar Younis	57	c Rashid Latif b Wasim Akram	9
S.K.Warne	c Rashid Latif b Aamer Sohail	22	lbw b Waqar Younis	0
J.Angel	b Wasim Akram	5	c Rashid Latif b Wasim Akram	8
T.B.A.May	not out	1	b Wasim Akram	1
G.D.McGrath	b Waqar Younis	0	b Waqar Younis	1
Extras	(B 2, LB 12, NB 8)	22	(B 6, LB 4, NB 5)	15
Total		337		232

PAKISTAN

Saeed Anwar	c M.E.Waugh b May	85	(1)	c and b Angel	77
Aamer Sohail	c Bevan b Warne	36	(2)	run out	34
Zahid Fazal	c Boon b May	27	(3)	c Boon b Warne	3
Saleem Malik*	lbw b Angel	26	(4)	c Taylor b Angel	43
Basit Ali	c Bevan b McGrath	0	(6)	lbw b Warne	12
Inzamamul Haq	c Taylor b Warne	9	(8)	not out	58
Rashid Latif†	c Taylor b Warne	2	(9)	lbw b S.R.Waugh	35
Wasim Akram	c Healy b Angel	39	(7)	c and b Warne	4
Akram Raza	b McGrath	13	(5)	lbw b Warne	2
Waqar Younis	c Healy b Angel	6	(10)	c Healy b Warne	7
Mushtaq Ahmed	not out	2	(11)	not out	20
Extras	(LB 7, NB 4)	11		(B 4, LB 13, NB 3)	20
Total		256		(9 wkts)	315

PAKISTAN	O	M	R	W		O	M	R	W
Wasim Akram	25	4	75	3	Wasim Akram	22	3	64	5
Waqar Younis	19.2	2	75	3	Waqar Younis	18	2	69	4
Mushtaq Ahmed	24	2	97	3	Mushtaq Ahmed	21	3	51	1
Akram Raza	14	1	50	0	Akram Raza	10	1	19	0
Aamer Sohail	5	0	19	1	Aamer Sohail	7	0	19	0
Saleem Malik	1	0	7	0					

AUSTRALIA	O	M	R	W		O	M	R	W
McGrath	25	6	70	2	McGrath	6	2	18	0
Angel	13.1	0	54	3	Angel	28	8	92	2
May	20	5	55	2	S.R.Waugh	15	3	28	1
Warne	27	10	61	3	Warne	36.1	12	89	5
S.R.Waugh	2	0	9	0	May	18	4	67	0
					M.E.Waugh	3	1	4	0

FALLOF WICKETS

	A	P	A	P
Wkt	1st	1st	2nd	2nd
1st	12	90	1	45
2nd	41	153	49	64
3rd	75	154	171	148
4th	95	157	174	157
5th	216	175	174	174
6th	281	181	213	179
7th	325	200	218	184
8th	335	234	227	236
9th	335	253	229	258
10th	337	256	232	-

Umpires: H.D.Bird and Khizer Hayat

resistance. Brain, Streak and Whittall captured three wickets apiece to bowl Zimbabwe to this historic victory.

PAKISTAN v SRI LANKA 1995-96

Iqbal Stadium, Faisalabad
15, 16, 17, 18, 19 September 1995
Sri Lanka won by 42 runs

Sri Lanka 223 (H.P. Tillakeratne 115) and 361 (P.A. de Silva 105, U.C. Hathurusinghe 83, Aqib Javed 5 for 84); Pakistan 333 (Ramiz Raja 75, Saeed Anwar 54, Inzamamul Haq 50, M. Muralitharan 5 for 68) and 209 (Saeed Anwar 50, Moin Khan 50)

This was the second Test of a three-match series. Pakistan had won the first match by an innings and 40 runs.

The Sri Lankans were strengthened by the inclusion of experienced batsman de Silva, who had joined the team after a successful season with Kent in the English County Championships.

Sri Lanka was sent in on a firm, grassy pitch and when the score was 4 for 34, the decision by Ramiz Raja looked vindicated. However, an 83-run partnership by Hathurusinghe and Tillakeratne restored Sri Lankan hopes.

Consistent batting by Pakistan saw the home team establish a lead of 110. Controversial off-spinner Muriltharan picked up another five-wicket haul for the visitors to become Sri Lanka's leading Test wicket-taker.

A shoulder injury prevented Wasim Akram bowling in the Sri Lankan second innings. Vital partnerships of 176 for the third wicket by Hathurusinghe and de Silva and 67 for the eighth by Dharmasena and Vaas carried the Sri Lankans to a modest lead of 251 runs.

Pakistan's second innings was most disappointing with only Saeed Anwar and Moin Khan scoring half-centuries. Vaas and Dharmasena, this time with the ball, spearheaded Sri Lanka to a historic victory. It was Sri Lanka's first Test win in Pakistan.They continued the good form and won the deciding Test at Sialkot by 144 runs to win their second series overseas.

PART 2
TEST CRICKET LISTS

40 NOTABLE DEBUTS

1 G. Gunn (England), on holidays in Australia for health reasons in 1907-08, was called into the injury-hit England side for the Sydney Test. Playing his very first innings on Australian soil — and his first Test match innings — Gunn hit a brilliant 119 in two and a half hours and followed up with 74 in the second innings.

2 H.L. Collins (Australia) began his Test career with consecutive scores of 70 and 104 (Sydney), 64 (Melbourne) and 162 (Adelaide) against England in 1920-21.

3 A.L. Valentine (West Indies), making his debut in the match against England at Manchester in 1950, took the first eight wickets to fall.

4 L.G. Rowe (West Indies) made history by scoring 214 and 100* in his first Test match, which was against New Zealand at Kingston in 1971-72. Rowe is the only batsman to make 100 in each innings on his Test debut, and only one of three players — R.E. Foster (England) and D.S.B.P. Kuruppu (Sri Lanka) being the others — to make a double-century on debut.

5 R.E. Foster (England) made his debut against Australia at Sydney in 1903-04, and after an uncertain start, helped himself to a glorious 287, with 38 boundaries in 420 minutes. Foster added 192 for the fifth wicket with G.H. Hirst, 115 for the ninth with R.E. Relf, and 130 for the tenth with W. Rhodes, the latter being scored in an amazing 66 minutes.

6 D.S.B.P. Kuruppu (Sri Lanka), achieved a rare feat by being on the field throughout his maiden Test. He took 776 minutes to reach his double- century — the slowest 200 in first class cricket — and batted for 777 minutes for his 201* against New Zealand at Colombo in 1986-87.

7 R.A.L. Massie (Australia), confounded the opposition batsmen with an astonishing display of swing-bowling in overcast conditions during the match against England at Lord's in 1972. He took 8 for 53 and 8 for 84 for an Australian record Test match 'bag' of 16 wickets.

8 N.D. Hirwani (India), exacting great turn on an under-prepared pitch, exploited the weakness of the West Indies batsmen to take 8 for 61 and 8 for 75 at Madras in 1987-88, thereby establishing an Indian record for wickets in a Test.

9 H.B. Taber (Australia), playing against South Africa at Johannesburg in 1966-67, caught seven and stumped one, a 'bag' never equalled by a wicketkeeper in his first Test. *Note:* A.T.W. Grout of Australia caught 6 in an innings in his first Test against South Africa in 1957-58.

10 J.E. Barrett became the first Australian player to carry his bat through a completed innings in a Test against England. Barrett scored 67* in Australia's second innings at Lord's in 1890 — his first Test match.

11 F. Martin (England) took twelve wickets in his first Test appearance against Australia at The Oval in 1890. His figures were 6 for 50 and 6 for 52.

12 A.E. Trott (Australia), playing his first Test against England at the Adelaide Oval in January 1895, scored 110 runs (38* and 72*) without being dismissed, and bowled unchanged throughout the second innings, to take eight wickets for 43 runs.

13 E.G. Arnold (England) took the wicket of the great Victor Trumper with his first delivery in a Test match at Sydney in December 1903.

14 A. Warren (England), in his only Test match took five wickets for 57 in the first innings against Australia at Leeds in 1905.

15 G.M. Parker, a South African cricketer playing Bradford League cricket during the South African tour of England in 1924, was called up to play for his country in the first Test at Birmingham, although he was not a member of the touring party. He took six wickets for 152 in England's only innings.

16 W.R. Hammond (England) scored 51 runs and took five wickets in his first Test, against South Africa at Johannesburg in 1927-28.

17 M.J.C. Allom (England), playing in his first Test against New Zealand in Christchurch in 1930, took four wickets in just five balls, including a hat-trick.

18 H.D. Smith (New Zealand) bowled E. Paynter (England) with his first ball in Test cricket at Christchurch in 1932-33. It was his only wicket in his only Test.

19 C.S. Marriott (England) took eleven wickets in his first and only Test, against the West Indies at The Oval in 1933.

20 J.C. Laker (England), playing against West Indies at Bridgetown during the 1947-48 season, took seven wickets for 103 runs in his very first Test innings.

21 H.H.H. Johnson (West Indies) played in his first Test at the age of 37 when he appeared against England at Kingston during 1947-48. He took 5 for 41 in the first innings, and 5 for 55 in the second.

22 A.T.W. Grout (Australia) kept wickets against South Africa in his first Test which was at Johannesburg in 1957-58, and set a then world Test record of six catches in an innings.

23 C.A. Milton (England) played his first Test against New Zealand at Leeds in 1958. He scored 104* in England's only innings, and became the first England player to be on the ground throughout an entire Test match (although there was no play on the first two days).

24 J.D.F. Larter (England) took nine wickets in his first Test against Pakistan at The Oval in1962.

25 P.J. Petherick (New Zealand) took a hat-trick in his first Test, played against Pakistan at Lahore in October 1976. In the same match, Javed Miandad scored 163 and 25* in his first Test.

26 Yajurvindra Singh (India) equalled two Test records in his first Test. Playing against England at Bangalore in the fourth Test of the 1976-77 season, he took five catches in the first innings and a total of seven for the match — both records for non-wicketkeepers.

27 R.A. Duff (Australia) played against England at Melbourne in his first Test in 1901-02. He top-scored in the first innings with 32 and again in the second with 104. He also shared in the first hundred partnership for the tenth wicket with W.W. Armstrong (who was also playing in his first Test).

28 C.V. Grimmett (Australia) took eleven wickets in his first Test. Playing against England in Sydney during the 1924-25 season, he captured 5 for 45 in the first innings and 6 for 37 in the second.

29 B.R.Taylor (New Zealand) is the only Test cricketer to have made 100 and to have taken five wickets in an innings on debut. He scored 105 and took 5 for 86 in the match against India at Calcutta in 1964-65.

30 A.V. Bedser (England) took eleven wickets in each of his first two Test matches. In his first, against India at Lord's in June 1946, he took 7 for 49 and 4 for 96. In his second, the following month at Manchester, he captured 4 for 41 and 7 for 52.

31 J.K. Lever (England), playing against India at Delhi in 1976-77, scored 53 and took 7 for 46 and 3 for 24. It was his first Test match.

32 M. Azharuddin (India) began his Test career with 110 at Calcutta, 48 and 105 at Madras, and 122 and 54* at Kanpur — all against England in 1984-85.

33 A.I.C. Dodemaide (Australia) was brought in as a late replacement for the injured B.A. Reid, and scored 50 in his first innings and took 6 for 58 in the second against New Zealand at Melbourne in 1987-88.

34 When A.C. Hudson scored 163 and 0 against the West Indies at Bridgetown in 1991-92, he became the first South African to score a century on Test debut and the first player to score a 'ton' and a 'duck' in his first Test.

35 D.L. Houghton (Zimbabwe) emulated the feat of C. Bannerman (in the match between Australia and England at Melbourne in 1876-77) by scoring a century in his country's inaugural Test in 1992-93.

36 D.W. Fleming (Australia) captured 4 for 75 and 3 for 86, including a hat trick, against Pakistan at Rawalpindi in 1994-95.

37 G.S. Blewett (Australia) followed his 102* and 12 against England at Adelaide during the 1994-95 season with 20 and 115 at Perth.

38 C.I. Dunusinghe (Sri Lanka) scored 11 and 91 against New Zealand at Napier in 1994-95 — as well as taking seven catches behind the stumps.

39 D.G. Cork (England) captured 7 for 43 in the match against the West Indies at Lord's in 1995.

40 S. Ganguly (India), playing against England in 1996, became the third player to score a century in his first two Test innings. He scored 131 in a match at Lord's, and then 136 and 48 at Nottingham.

7 INGLORIOUS DEBUTS

1 M. Leyland was dismissed for a 'duck' during England's only innings in the third Test against the West Indies at The Oval in 1928 — his first appearance for his country.

2 D.G. Bradman scored only 18 and 1 in his debut in the first Test against England at Brisbane in the 1928-29 season. He was subsequently dropped from the team for the second Test, but was reinstated for the third, in which he scored 79 and 112.

3 L. Hutton (England) scored a 'duck' and 1 in his debut Test match against New Zealand at Lord's in 1937. In his second match, at Manchester, he made 100 and 14.

4 I.M. Chappell (Australia) made a modest 11 runs and bowled 26 overs without a wicket in his debut Test against Pakistan at Melbourne in 1964-65.

5 New Zealand batsman J.M. Parker fractured a bone in his hand while fielding against Pakistan at Wellington in 1973, and was unable to bat in his debut match.

6 G.A. Gooch (England) recorded a pair of 'ducks' in his first Test, which was against Australia at Birmingham in 1975.

7 In 1991-92, S.K. Warne (Australia) took 1 for 150 against India at Sydney on his Test debut.

A NOTABLE UMPIRING DEBUT

Umpire W.E. Alley, standing in his first Test match (England v India at Birmingham in 1974), was given little time to settle in, being required to make a decision about the first ball of the match. His verdict? S.M. Gavaskar, out, caught behind by Knott, bowled Arnold.

20 RAPID RISES

1 Joseph Emile Patrick McMaster (England) deserves his spot in the record books. His Test appearance for England against South Africa at Cape Town in 1888-89 was his only match in first-class cricket. As he scored a 'duck', McMaster must be the only cricketer of Test match status who has never scored a run in his entire first-class career.

2 L. Hone, of Ireland, kept wicket for England against Australia at Melbourne in 1878-79. Hone never appeared in English county cricket.

3 B.A.F. Grieve (England) appeared in only three first-class matches, of which two (against South Africa in 1888-89 at Port Elizabeth and Cape Town) were Test matches.

4 Edric Leadbeater (England) was flown to India as a replacement for A.E.G. Rhodes during the 1951-52 season. He played in his first Test before being capped for his county.

5 G.M. Parker (South Africa) came into the South African Test side from the Bradford League to play against England at Birmingham in 1924. It was only his second first-class match. His entire first-class career comprised three games, two of which were Tests.

6 D.W. Carr (England) played his first first-class game for Kent at The Oval on 27 May 1909, aged 37. He was chosen for the Gentlemen v Players on 8 July, made his debut in county cricket on 29 July, and appeared for England against Australia on 9 August. It was his sixth first-class game, and he had risen to Test honours within ten weeks of his first-class debut.

7 A.L. Valentine and S. Ramadhin (West Indies) were selected to tour England in 1950 after each had played in only two first-class games.

8 S.F. Barnes (England) was selected to tour Australia in 1901-02 after only six first-class games and 13 first-class wickets.

9 I.A.R. Peebles (England) played against South Africa at Johannesburg in 1927-28, before he had made his debut in county cricket.

10 A.G. Chipperfield (Australia) was selected to tour England in 1934 after playing only three first-class games.

11 T.R. McKibbin (Australia) played against England in 1894-95 in only his sixth first-class match. A.G. Fairfax, E.L. A'Beckett, D.G. Bradman, W.J. O'Reilly, J.R. Thomson and I.C. Davis (all Australia) also made their Test debuts within ten matches of their first-class debut.

12 G.J. Bonnor (Australia) was selected to tour England in 1880 without ever having played a first-class game.

13 G.E. Vivian (New Zealand) was selected to tour India, Pakistan and England in 1965 without having appeared in a first-class match. He made his first-class debut in the Test against India at Calcutta in 1964-65.

14 C.C. Griffith (West Indies) was chosen for his first Test against England at Port-of-Spain in 1959-60, after only one first-class match.

15 M.D. Marshall (West Indies) was selected for the tour of India 1978-79 after only one first-class appearance, and played in his first Test in 1978-79 after only three matches.

16 J.E.F. Beck (South Africa, 1954-55) and J.C. Alabaster (India 1955-56) were chosen for New Zealand tours during the 1950s without having made first-class appearances. They made their Test debuts after five matches and one match respectively.

17 Wasim Akram (Pakistan) was selected to tour New Zealand in 1984-85 after only two first-class games. He made his Test debut at Auckland in his fourth match.

18 A. Ranatunga (Sri Lanka) made his first-class debut against the touring English team in February 1982 and made his Test debut in his next game a week later.

19 G.F. Labrooy (Sri Lanka) was chosen to tour India in 1986-87 without any first-class experience, and made his Test debut in only his second game.

20 Saleem Elahi (Pakistan) made his first-class debut on the tour of Australia in 1995-96 and his Test debut in his third first-class match. He had made his Limited Over International debut two months earlier (scoring a century).

GREAT CRICKETING FAMILIES

1 Gregory (Australia). The family produced four Test cricketers, two of whom (Dave and Syd) captained Australia. Father of the clan was Edward William who played in Sydney in the 1820s. Four of his children played cricket for NSW — Dave (Australia's first captain), Ned, Charlie and Arthur. Ned's sons were Syd and Charles (the latter scored the first triple century in a first-class game in Australia). Jack, who arrived on the scene in the 1920s, was the grandson of Edward William, and so he became a cricket star about a century after his grandfather.

2 Mohammad (Pakistan). At least one Mohammad brother represented Pakistan in 100 of that country's first 101 Tests in 27 years of Test cricket between 1952-80. A fifth brother, Raees, was once Pakistan's twelfth man against India (1954-55). Three brothers — Hanif, Mushtaq and Sadiq — all played together in one Test against New Zealand in 1969, and all batted and bowled during the match. Between them, Hanif, Mushtaq, Sadiq and Wazir aggregated almost 11 000 Test runs with 29 centuries. They have also held 115 catches and taken 80 wickets.

3 Amarnath (India). Father 'Lala' and son Surinder are the only father-son combination to record centuries on debut. The second son, Mohinder, narrowly missed becoming one of the few to score a century in each innings when he made 90 and 100 against Australia in Perth in 1977-78.

4 Bannerman (Australia). Elder brother Charles faced the first ball bowled in Test cricket, scored the first run, the first 50 and the first 100. He was also the first Australian to make a century in England, New Zealand and Canada. Younger brother Alec scored the first run in a Test on English soil.

5 Chappell (Australia). The grandsons of Victor Richardson, Ian, Greg and Trevor represent only the fourth set of three brothers to appear in Test cricket. Ian and Greg captained Australia more than 50 times, and are the only brothers to have scored centuries in each innings of a Test, and were the first brothers to score a century in the same Test. They are the only brothers who have each scored over 5000 Test runs.

111 TEST CRICKETERS WHO BATTED RIGHT-HANDED AND BOWLED LEFT-ARM

Australia

M.J. Bennett
R.J. Bright
H.L. Collins
A.R. Dell
L.O. Fleetwood-Smith
J.B. Gannon
T.G. Hogan
R.J. Inverarity
B.P. Julian
C.G. Macartney
I. Meckiff
D.J. Sincock
E.R.H. Toshack
M.R. Whitney
W.J. Whitty

England

J.C. Balderstone
R.G. Barlow
C. Blythe
J.B. Bolus
J. Briggs
H.R. Bromley-Davenport
D.B. Carr
D.C.S. Compton
C. Cook
G. Cook
N.G.B. Cook
P.H. Edmonds
P.R. Foster
M.J. Hilton
G.H. Hirst
J.L. Hopwood
J. Iddon
R.K. Illingworth
I.J. Jones
J.K. Lever
G.A.R. Lock
B.W. Luckhurst
G.A.E. Paine
C.W.L. Parker
W. Rhodes
F.E. Rumsey
D.S. Steele
P.C.R. Tufnell
D.L. Underwood
H. Verity
W. Voce
A. Waddington
P.M. Walker
J.C. White
H.I. Young
J.A. Young

South Africa

P.R. Adams
W.H. Ashley
C.P. Carter
G.A. Chevalier
M.K. Elgie
A.E. Hall
G.A. Kempis
M.J. Macaulay
A.H. McKinnon
Q. McMillan
J.B. Plimsoll
N.A. Quinn
A. Rose-Innes
G.A. Rowe
P.L. van der Merwe

West Indies

M.R. Bynoe
G.M. Carew
B.D. Julien
R.R. Jumadeen
C.B. Lambert
S. Shivnarine
A.L. Valentine
F.M.M. Worrell

New Zealand

S.L. Boock
T.B. Burtt
M.E. Chapple
R.O. Collinge
F.E. Fisher
N. Gallichan
E.J. Gray
A.F. Lissette
J.F.M. Morrison
D.R. O'Sullivan
M.W. Priest
G.B. Troup
B.W. Yuile

India

B.S. Bedi
R.J.D. Jamshedji
Maninder Singh
M.H. Mankad
Mushtaq Ali
R.G. Patel
A.K. Sharma
R.J. Shastri
K.K. Tarapore
S.L. Venkatapathy Raju

Pakistan

Inzamam-ul-Haq
Kabir Khan
Liaqat Ali
Mufasir-ul-Haq
Nadeem Ghauri
Nadeem Khan
Pervez Sajjad
Saleem Jaffer
Shujauddin

Sri Lanka

S.D. Anurasiri
S. Jeganathan
A.K. Kuruppuarachchi
A.N. Ranasinghe
K.J. Silva
R.G.C.E. Wijesuriya
P.K. Wijetunge

Zimbabwe

M.H. Dekker
G.W. Flower
M.P. Jarvis
B.C. Strang

114 TEST CRICKETERS WHO BATTED LEFT-HANDED AND BOWLED RIGHT-ARM

Australia

J. Angel
D.D. Blackie
I.W. Callen
R.M. Cowper
L.S. Darling
R.A. Gaunt
J.M. Gregory
R.N. Harvey
T.V. Hohns
W.P. Howell
J.L. Langer
T.J. Laughlin
E.L. McCormick
K.D. Mackay
T.R. McKibbin
R.W. McLeod
A.L. Mann
R.W. Marsh
R.L.A. Massie
G.R.J. Matthews
L.C. Mayne
J.D.A. O'Connor
W.J. O'Reilly
G.F. Rorke
B.K. Shepherd
P.L. Taylor
T.R. Veivers
K.C. Wessels

England

R.W. Barber
J. Birkenshaw
B.C. Broad
D.B. Close
G.R. Dilley
J.H. Edrich
R.M. Ellison
J.A. Flavell
G. Fowler
D.I. Gower
K. Higgs
J.T. Ikin
H. Morris
M.S. Nichols
C.M. Old
P.H. Parfitt
R.T.D. Perks

J.S.E. Price
G. Pullar
P.E. Richardson
T.F. Smailes
J.B. Statham
R. Subba Row
R. Tattersall
G.P. Thorpe
C.L. Townsend
D.W. White

South Africa

D.J. Cullinan
G. Kirsten
J.F.W. Nicolson
A.W. Nourse
R.G. Pollock
K.C. Wessels

West Indies

C.E.L. Ambrose
M.C. Carew
S. Chanderpaul
J.D.C. Goddard
H.A. Gomes
A.B. Howard
A.I. Kallicharran
B.C. Lara
P.D. Lashley
C.H. Lloyd
C.A. McWatt
G.C. Shillingford

New Zealand

V.R. Brown
D.C. Cleverley
G.F. Cresswell
B.A. Edgar
S.P. Fleming
R.J. Hadlee
C.Z. Harris
E.G. McLeod
L.S.M. Miller
B.D. Morrison
G.W.F. Overton
J.F. Reid
I.M. Sinclair
M.C. Snedden
B.R. Taylor
R.G. Twose
J.T.C. Vaughan
G.E. Vivian
J.G. Wright

India

S. Amarnath
N.J. Contractor
V.G. Kambli
A.G. Milka Singh
S.V. Nayak
A.M. Pai

Pakistan

Sadiq Mohammad
Wasim Raja

Sri Lanka

F.S. Ahangama
E.A.R. de Silva
A.P. Gurusinha
R.S. Kalpage
M.A.W.R. Madurasinghe
A. Ranatunga
S. Ranatunga
J.R. Ratnayeke
C.P. Senanayake
H.P. Tillakeratne
K.P.J. Warnaweera

Zimbabwe

A. Flower
S.G. Peall
A.H. Shah

16 TEST CRICKETERS WHO HAVE BEEN KNIGHTED

Australia

Sir Donald George Bradman

England

Sir George Oswald Browning Allen
Sir Michael Colin Cowdrey
Sir John Berry Hobbs
Sir Leonard Hutton
Sir Francis Stanley Jackson
Sir Henry Dudley Gresham Leveson Gower
Sir Charles Aubrey Smith
Sir Pelham Francis Warner

West Indies

Sir Learie Nicholas Constantine
Sir Garfield St Auburn Sobers
Sir Frank Mortimor Maglinne Worrell
Sir Clyde Leopold Walcott
Sir Everton de Courcy Weekes

New Zealand

Sir Richard John Hadlee
Sir Jack Newman

CRICKETERS' ROLL OF HONOUR: TEST CRICKETERS KILLED IN THE BOER WAR, WORLD WAR I AND WORLD WAR II

Boer War

J.J. Ferris (Australia/England)

World War I

A. Cotter (Australia)
C. Blythe (England)
K.L. Hutchings (England)
R.M.H. Hands (South Africa)
E.B. Lundie (South Africa)
R.O. Schwarz (South Africa)
G.C. White (South Africa)

World War II

R.G. Gregory (Australia)
K. Farnes (England)
G.B. Legge (England)
G.G. Macaulay (England)
M.J.L. Turnbull (England)
H. Verity (England)
A.W. Briscoe (South Africa)
A.B.C. Langton (South Africa)
D.A.R. Moloney (New Zealand)

TEST CAREERS THAT ENDED IN TRAGEDY

1 K.J. Wadsworth (New Zealand). One of his country's finest wicketkeepers, Ken Wadsworth died of cancer at the peak of his career, aged 29, on 19 August 1979.

2 O.G. Smith (West Indies). 'Collie' Smith, a versatile all-rounder, died of injuries received in a car accident in England in 1959. He was 26 years old.

3 G.B. Street (England). A good county wicketkeeper and useful tail-end batsmen. He played one Test for England against South Africa in 1922-23, but was tragically killed at the age of 24 years in a motorcycle accident just before the 1924 season.

4 F. Morley (England). A left-arm fast bowler, Morley was a member of the Hon. Ivo Bligh's team that sailed to Australia for the 1882-83 season. Morley was apparently hurt in a collision at sea, but carried on throughout the tour with an injured hip. Upon his return to England, his health deteriorated and he died the following year, aged 33.

5 H.B. Cameron (South Africa). 'Jock' Cameron was a wicketkeeper and gifted batsman who captained his country in nine Tests. He contracted enteric fever on the way home from the 1935 tour of England and died at the age of 30, ten weeks after playing in his final Test.

6 N.B.F. Mann (South Africa). 'Tufty' Mann was a versatile middle-order batsman and left-arm spinner who died aged 31, after an abdominal operation.

TEST CRICKETERS WHO WERE RHODES SCHOLARS

C.B. Van Ryneveld	South Africa
J.P. Duminy	South Africa
P.A. M.Hands	South Africa
R.H. M.Hands	South Africa
H.G. Owen-Smith	South Africa
D.B. Pithey	South Africa
J.A. Dunning	New Zealand

TEST CRICKET CAPTAINS WHO WERE BORN ABROAD

Australia

P.S. McDonnell	England
T.P. Horan	Ireland

England

Lord Harris	West Indies
P.F. Warner	West Indies
F.L. Fane	Ireland
D.R. Jardine	India
G.O.B. Allen	Australia
F.R. Brown	Peru
M.C. Cowdrey	India
E.R. Dexter	Italy
A.R. Lewis	Wales
M.H. Denness	Scotland
A.W. Greig	South Africa
A.J. Lamb	South Africa

South Africa

E.A. Halliwell	England

Pakistan

A.H. Kardar	India
Fazal Mahmood	India
Asif Iqbal	India
Majid J. Khan	India

Zimbabwe

A. Flower	South Africa

TEN CRICKETERS WHO RETIRED HURT

1 J.J. Kelly (Australia). A useful batsman and outstanding wicketkeeper, Kelly played 36 Tests for Australia around the turn of the Century. He retired from first-class cricket after his last tour of England because of the effects of a damaged finger and a blow over the heart from a ball received in a Test at Manchester.

2 C. Milburn (England). One of the most punishing batsmen seen on the Test arena for many years, Colin Milburn was involved in a car accident in 1969 which cost him his left eye. He attempted a county come-back in 1973, but to all intents and purposes his career was finished by the crash.

3 R.K. Oxenham (Australia). An excellent all-rounder, Oxenham represented his country in seven Tests during the late 1920s and 1930s. He was seriously injured in a car accident in 1937 and never fully recovered. He died in 1939.

4 N.J. Contractor (India). An opening bat and occasional medium-pace bowler, Contractor captained India on twelve occasions. During a match against Barbados, on the 1961-62 tour of the West Indies, he was hit on the head by a ball from C.C. Griffith. His skull was fractured and he remained gravely ill for some days. Fortunately he recovered but never again played international cricket.

5 G.F. Rorke (Australia). A big man, Gordon Rorke played four Tests for Australia and was a very effective fast bowler in Sheffield Shield cricket. His Test career was unfortunately cut short in 1959-60 when he contracted hepatitis while on tour in India.

6 G.B. Stevens (Australia). An opening batsman, Gavin Stevens played four Tests for Australia in 1959-60. He dehydrated badly from the same strain of hepatitis that G.F. Rorke picked up. He lost 13 kilograms and was sent home early from the sub-continent. He never played first-class cricket again.

7 R.C. Motz (New Zealand). One of New Zealand's most successful Test bowlers, Motz took 100 Test wickets but was forced to retire from first-class cricket when it was discovered he had been bowling for some time with a displaced vertebra.

8 I.J. Jones (England). A Welshman, Jones represented England on 15 occasions taking 44 wickets as a fast bowler. In May 1968, yet to reach his peak, he tore the ligaments in his elbow. From then on, he was a spent force in top cricket.

9 W. Bates (England). In a short but brilliant career, Billy Bates represented England 15 times, scoring 656 runs and taking 50 wickets in the late 1880s. His career came to an abrupt end in Melbourne in 1887 when he was struck in the eye at net practice. He suffered permanent damage to his sight, and was forced to retire.

10 J. Briggs (England). A regular member of the England team during the late 1880s, Briggs scored over 800 runs and took 118 wickets. During a Test against Australia in 1899, he was struck over the heart by a ball while fielding, and suffered what was believed to be an epileptic fit. He retired from the game and, although he attempted a first-class come-back the following year, his Test career was over.

39 TEST CRICKETERS WHO WERE TEST UMPIRES

Australia

C. Bannerman
G. Coulthard
T.W. Garrett *
P.G. McShane #
H.H. Massie **

A.J. Richardson
J.P.F. Travers

* T.W. Garrett, who was playing in the game, replaced umpire Hodges after tea on the last day in the match between Australia and England at Melbourne in 1884-85.

P.G. McShane played and umpired in the same series between Australia and England in Australia in 1884-85.

** H.H. Massie substituted for E.H. Elliott in the match between Australia and England at Sydney in 1884-85.

England

R.G. Barlow
J. Birkenshaw
L.C. Braund
H.R. Butt
J.F. Crapp
A. Dolphin
H. Elliott
A.E. Fagg
W. Gunn*
J.H. Hampshire
J. Hardstaff Snr
F. Hearne
A. Hill
J.W. Hitch
J. Lillywhite
A.S.M. Oakman**
N. Oldfield
K.E. Palmer
W.F.F. Price
M. Sherwin
E.J. Smith
G.J. Thompson
P. Willey
H. Young

* W. Gunn replaced the injured umpire Swift during the match between England and Australia at Sydney in 1886-87. (He had been playing in the Test.)

** A.S.M. Oakman deputised for H.D. Bird (who had an injured back) after tea on the third day of the first Test between England and Australia at Birmingham in 1975.

West Indies

E.E. Achong
G.E. Gomez

South Africa

W.W. Wade

New Zealand

J.A. Cowie
E.W.T. Tindill

India

S. Venkataraghavan

Pakistan

Javed Akhtar
Mohammad Aslam

PLAYERS WHO HAVE OPENED THE BATTING AND BOWLING IN THE SAME MATCH*

* First innings only apply in this record

Australia

G. Giffen	v England, Sydney 1882-83
G.E. Palmer	v England, Sydney 1884-85
W. Bruce	v England, Melbourne 1884-85
C.T.B. Turner	v England, Lord's 1890
C.T.B. Turner	v England, The Oval 1890
G.H.S. Trott	v England, Sydney 1894-95
G.H.S. Trott	v England, Melbourne 1894-95
W.W. Armstrong	v South Africa, Johannesburg 1902-03
V.T. Trumper	v South Africa, Johannesburg, 1902-03
M.A. Noble	v England, Sydney 1907-08
F.J. Laver	v England, Lord's 1909
C. Kelleway	v England, Melbourne 1911-12
J.M. Gregory	v South Africa, Durban 1921-22

England

A. Shaw	v Australia, Melbourne 1876-77
G. Ulyett	v Australia, Melbourne 1878-79
C.T. Studd	v Australia, Melbourne 1882-83
R.G. Barlow	v Australia, Sydney 1882-83
G. Ulyett	v Australia, Sydney 1884-85
G.A. Lohmann	v South Africa, Port Elizabeth 1895-96
G.A. Lohmann	v South Africa, Johannesburg 1895-96
G.L. Jessop	v Australia, Melbourne 1901-02
J.B. Hobbs	v South Africa, Johannesburg 1909-10
J.B. Hobbs	v South Africa, Durban 1909-10
J.B. Hobbs	v South Africa, Cape Town 1909-10
M.W. Tate	v Australia, Adelaide 1924-25
W.R. Hammond	v South Africa, Cape Town 1930-31
W.R. Hammond	v South Africa, Durban 1930-31
R.E.S. Wyatt	v West Indies, Port-of-Spain 1934-35

R.E.S. Wyatt	v West Indies, Georgetown 1934-35
R.E.S. Wyatt	v South Africa, Lord's 1935
W.J. Edrich	v South Africa, Johannesburg 1938-39
T.E. Bailey	v West Indies, Kingston 1953-54
T.E. Bailey	v Australia, Sydney 1954-55
T.E. Bailey	v South Africa, Port Elizabeth 1956-57

South Africa

A. Rose-Innes	v England, Cape Town 1888-89
J.H. Sinclair	v England, Johannesburg 1895-96
G.A. Faulkner	v England, The Oval 1907
D.J. Meintjes	v England, Johannesburg 1922-23
T.L. Goddard	v England, Nottingham 1955
T.L. Goddard	v England, The Oval 1955
T.L. Goddard	v Australia, Cape Town 1957-58

West Indies

F.M.M. Worrell	v England, Nottingham 1957
F.M.M. Worrell	v England, Leeds 1957
F.M.M. Worrell	v England, The Oval 1957

India

Pankaj Roy	v West Indies, Delhi 1958-59
M.L. Jaisimha	v England, Delhi 1961-62
M.L. Jaisimha	v England, Madras 1961-62
M.L. Jaisimha	v England, Delhi 1963-64
M.L. Jaisimha	v England, Kanpur 1963-64
M.L. Jaisimha	v Australia, Madras 1964-65
M.L. Jaisimha	v Australia, Bombay 1964-65
M.L. Jaisimha	v Australia, Calcutta 1964-65
M.L. Jaisimha	v New Zealand, Calcutta 1964-65
M.L. Jaisimha	v New Zealand, Bombay 1964-65
M.L. Jaisimha	v New Zealand, Madras 1964-65
M.L. Jaisimha	v New Zealand, Delhi 1964-65
M.L. Jaisimha	v West Indies, Bombay 1966-67
B.K. Kunderan	v England, Birmingham 1967
S. Abid Ali	v New Zealand, Wellington 1967-68
S. Abid Ali	v New Zealand, Bombay 1969-70
S. Abid Ali	v New Zealand, Nagpur 1969-70
S. Abid Ali	v New Zealand, Hyderabad 1969-70
S. Abid Ali	v West Indies, Kingston 1970-71
S. Abid Ali	v West Indies, Port-of-Spain 1970-71
S.M. Gavaskar	v England, Madras 1972-73
E.D. Solkar	v England, Manchester 1974
M. Amarnath	v England, Madras 1976-77
S.M. Gavaskar	v England, Bombay 1976-77
S.M. Gavaskar	v Australia, Melbourne 1977-78
S.M. Gavaskar	v Pakistan, Lahore 1978-79
M. Prabhakar	v New Zealand, Napier 1989-90
M. Prabhakar	v New Zealand, Auckland 1989-90
M. Prabhakar	v Sri Lanka, Chandigarh 1990-91
M. Prabhakar	v South Africa, Cape Town 1992-93
M. Prabhakar	v England, Calcutta, 1992-93
M. Prabhakar	v England, Madras, 1992-93
M. Prabhakar	v England, Bombay, 1992-93
M. Prabhakar	v Zimbabwe, Delhi, 1992-93
M. Prabhakar	v Sri Lanka, Colombo, 1993-94
M. Prabhakar	v Sri Lanka, Colombo, 1993-94
M. Prabhakar	v Sri Lanka, Lucknow, 1993-94
M. Prabhakar	v Sri Lanka, Bangalore, 1993-94
M. Prabhakar	v Sri Lanka, Motera, 1993-94
M. Prabhakar	v West Indies, Bombay, 1994-95
M. Prabhakar	v West Indies, Nagpur, 1994-95
M. Prabhakar	v West Indies, Mohali, 1994-95
M. Prabhakar	v New Zealand, Bangalore, 1994-95
M. Prabhakar	v New Zealand, Cuttack, 1994-95

Pakistan

Mudassar Nazar	v New Zealand, Lahore 1984-85
Mudassar Nazar	v New Zealand, Hyderabad 1984-85
Mudassar Nazar	v New Zealand, Karachi 1984-85
Mudassar Nazar	v New Zealand, Wellington 1984-85
Mudassar Nazar	v England, Lahore 1987-88
Mudassar Nazar	v England, Faisalabad 1987-88
Mudassar Nazar	v Australia, Karachi 1988-89
Mudassar Nazar	v Australia, Faisalabad 1988-89
Mudassar Nazar	v Australia, Lahore 1988-89

Sri Lanka

B. Warnapura	v England, Colombo 1981-82
J.R. Ratnayeke	v India, Nagpur 1986-87
J.R. Ratnayeke	v India, Calcutta 1986-87

SOME NOTABLE 'FIRSTS' AND 'LASTS'

1 L. Hone was the first player to represent England in a Test without playing for a county. (England v Australia in 1878-79.)

2 D.C.H. Townsend was the last player to represent England in a Test match without having played for a first-class county. (England v West Indies at Port-of-Spain, Georgetown and Kingston, 1934-35.)

3 Rt. Rev. D.S. Sheppard (later Bishop of Liverpool) was the first ordained minister to play Test cricket. Although he played his first Test in 1950, he played his first Test as an ordained minister in 1956.

4 A. Sandham (England) was the first batsman to score 300 in a Test innings. He scored 325 in the match against the West Indies at Kingston in 1929-30.

5 W. Bardsley (Australia) was the first batsman to score a century in each innings of a Test match. He scored 136 and 130 in the match against England at The Oval in 1909.

6 A.K. Davidson (Australia) was the first player to complete the match double of 100 runs and ten wickets in a Test. Playing against the West Indies at Brisbane in 1960-61, he scored 44 and 80 runs, and his bowling figures were 30-2-135-5 and 24.6-4-87-6.

7 S. Morris (Australia) was the first black man to play in a Test match against England at Melbourne in 1884-85. Morris was born in Hobart of West Indian parents. When the eleven players from the first Test at Adelaide demanded 50 per cent of the gate money for the second Test, and were refused by officials, Morris got his chance when a new team was formed as a result. He scored 4 and 10* and took 2 for 73 in his only Test.

8 Gloucestershire-born W.E. Midwinter is the first cricketer to have played for and against Australia in Test matches. Midwinter played eight times for Australia against England — 1876-77 (2), 1882-83 (1), 1884 (3), 1886-87 (2). He played four times for England against Australia in 1881-82.

9 K.C. Wessels is the last player to play for and against Australia in Test cricket. He represented Australia in 24 Tests between 1982-83 and 1985-86; and represented South Africa in 16 Tests between 1991-92 and 1994.

10 In the second Test at Melbourne in 1882-83, W. Bates achieved the first hat-trick for England when he dismissed P.S. McDonnell, G. Giffen and G.J. Bonnor in Australia's first innings. He became the first player to score a fifty and take ten or more wickets in the same Test. He scored 55 runs and his bowling figures were 26.2-14-28-7 and 33-14-74-7. This was the first Test to be won by an innings.

11 The first double century in Test cricket was scored by the Australian captain W.L. Murdoch (211) in the match against England at The Oval in 1884.

12 P.S. McDonnell (Australia) was the first batsman to score two centuries in successive Test innings. He scored 103 against England at The Oval in 1884, and 124 at Adelaide, also against England, in 1884-85.

13 A. Shrewsbury (England) became the first batsman to score 1000 runs in Test cricket. He scored his 1000th run in a match against Australia played at Lord's in 1893.

14 J. Briggs (England) became the first player to take 100 Test wickets, during the fourth Test against Australia played at Sydney in 1894-95. In the same match, C.T.B. Turner became the first Australian bowler to capture 100 Test wickets.

15 G.A. Lohmann (England) was the first bowler to take nine wickets in a Test innings. This occurred during a match against South Africa played at Johannesburg in 1895-96. His figures were 14.2-6-28-9.

16 J. Darling (Australia) was the first left-hander to score a century in a Test match with 101 against England at Sydney in 1897-98. During the season, Darling became the first batsman to score three centuries in the same series, and to aggregate 500 runs in the same series.

A FEW MORE FIRSTS

1 *First time a country won a Test series after losing the first two matches:* In the 1936-37 series played in Australia, Australia won the last three matches in the five-match series to defeat England 3-2.

2 *First drawn match in Australia since 1881-82:* The third Test between Australia and England at Melbourne in 1946-47.

3 *First time an extra day was added to a Test:* This occurred during the match between New Zealand and England at Christchurch in 1946-47. The third day had been washed out, but rain prevented play on the extra day as well.

4 *First time Test cricket was played on Christmas Day:* This occurred during the third Test between Australia and the West Indies at Adelaide in 1951-52.

5 *First ball bowled in Test cricket:* A. Shaw (England), from the eastern end of the MCG. (Australia v England, Melbourne, 1876-77.)

6 *First run in Test cricket:* C. Bannerman (Australia) scored the first run off the second ball of A. Shaw's first over. (Australia v England, Melbourne, 1876-77.)

7 *First wicket taken in Test cricket:* A. Hill (England) clean-bowled N.D.F. Thomson (Australia) in the fourth over bowled in the very first Test cricket match. (Australia v England 1876-77.)

8 *First 5-wickets-in-an-innings haul:* W.E. Midwinter (Australia), 5 for 78. (Australia v England, Melbourne, 1876-77.)

9 *First 10-wickets-in-a-match haul:* F.R. Spofforth (Australia), 6 for 48 and 7 for 62. (Australia v England, Melbourne, 1878-79.)

10 *First catch taken in Test cricket:* A. Hill (England) caught T.P. Horan (Australia) at third man. (Australia v England, Melbourne, 1876-77.)

11 *First stumping completed in Test cricket:* J.M. Blackham stumped England's A. Shaw for 2 in the second innings of the first Test match. (Australia v England, Melbourne, 1876-77.)

12 *First boundary hit:* T.P. Horan (Australia) hit the first boundary with a snick through slips. (Australia v England, Melbourne, 1876-77.)

13 *First 100 partnership:* W.G. Grace (152) and A.P. Lucas (55) put on 120 for England's second wicket against Australia. (England v Australia, The Oval 1880.)

14 *First century:* C. Bannerman (Australia), 165, retired hurt. (Australia v England, Melbourne, 1876-77.)

15 *First to score 50 in each innings:* G. Ulyett (England), 52 and 63*. (England v Australia, Melbourne, 1876-77.)

Note: Ulyett also became the first cricketer to score a century and 50 in the same Test. This occurred in the match against Australia played in Melbourne in 1881-82.

16 *First hat-trick in Test cricket:* F.R. Spofforth (Australia) dismissed the England batsmen V.P.F.A. Royle (bowled), F.A. McKinnon (bowled), and T. Emmett (caught by T.P. Horan) for a hat-trick. (Australia v England, Melbourne, 1878-79.)

17 *First declaration in test cricket:* A.E. Stoddart (England) declared at 8 for 234 during a match that was eventually drawn. (England v Australia, Lord's, 1893.)

18 *First six (without overthrows) in a Test:* J. Darling (Australia) hit the first six in Test cricket. To be a six in those early days, the ball had to be hit out of the ground, and not merely over the boundary. (Australia v England, Melbourne, 1897-98.)

19 *First bowler to be 'no-balled' for throwing:* B. Jones (Australia) was given the first no-ball by Umpire J. Phillips. (Australia v England, Melbourne, 1897-98.)

20 *First century before lunch:* K.S. Ranjitsinhitji (England) finished not-out on 154 in his first Test. 'Ranji' was also the first Indian to play Test cricket. (England v Australia, Manchester, 1896.)

21 *First batsman to carry his bat through a completed innings:* A.B. Tancred (South Africa) carried his bat with 26* from a team total of 47. (South Africa v England, Cape Town, 1888-89.)

22 *First Sunday Test match play:* India v England, Bombay, 1933-34 (first Test).

23 *First Test match streaker:* Michael Angelow streaked on the fourth day of the second Test between England and Australia at Lord's in August 1975. He did it to win a bet, but lost the proceeds to the magistrate's court the next day.

24 *First US President to watch a Test match:* Dwight D. Eisenhower. (Pakistan v Australia, Karachi, 1959-60.)

25 *First batsman to wear a protective helmet in a Test:* D.L. Amiss. (England v West Indies, The Oval, 1976.)

ATTENDANCE RECORDS

Single day: On 11 February 1961, 90 800 spectators watched the second day of the fifth Test between Australia and the West Indies at the MCG.

Match: The third Test at Melbourne between Australia and England in 1936-37 attracted 350 534 spectators, the record for any cricket match. The Test was played on 1, 2, 4, 5, 6, 7 January 1937.

Series: The five matches in the 1936-37 series between Australia and England attracted 943 000 spectators, the biggest attendance for any Test rubber.

GAMES ABANDONED WITHOUT A BALL BEING BOWLED

1 England v Australia, Manchester 1890. Rain washed out play on each day.

2 England v Australia, Manchester 1938. Rain washed out play on each day.

3 Australia v England, Melbourne, 1970-71. This game, originally scheduled as the third Test of the series, was abandoned after solid rain on the first three days. A replacement Test, becoming an historic seventh Test of the series, was arranged to replace the washed-out game.

4 West Indies v England, Georgetown, 1980-81. Two days before this match was due to start, England bowler Robin Jackman (who had been flown to Georgetown to replace the injured Bob Willis) had his visitor's permit revoked by the Guyanese government and was ordered to leave the country. This was because he had spent several English winters in South Africa (as, incidentally, had several other members of the England team). The Tour Manager Alan Smith issued a statement saying that England would not play this second Test of the series 'as it is no longer possible for the Test team to be chosen without restrictions being imposed.' The game was then abandoned.

5 New Zealand v Pakistan, Dunedin, 1988-89. Heavy sweeping rain caused the match to be called off on the third day.

6 West Indies v England, Georgetown, 1989-90. Torrential rain, falling nightly for five days, left the ground under water, and a contentiously early decision to abandon the match was made on the rest day.

7 Sri Lanka v Pakistan, Sinhalese Sports Club Ground, Colombo, 1994-95. This match was cancelled due to a post-election curfew in Sri Lanka.

FAVOURITE GROUNDS

1 W.R. Hammond (England) scored 808 runs at Sydney: 251 (1928-29); 112; 101 and 75* (1932-33); 231* (1936-37); 1 and 37 (1946-47). Average: 161.60.

2 L. Hutton (England) scored 1521 runs at The Oval: 12 (1937); 73 and 165* (1939); 25 (1946); 83 and 36 (1947); 30 and 64 (1948); 206 (1949); 20* and 2 (1950); 28 and 27 (1951); 86 (1952); 82 and 17 (1953); and 14 and 5 (1954). Average: 89.47.

3 D.C.S. Compton (England) scored 955 runs at Nottingham: 102 (1938); 65 and 163 (1947); 19 and 184 (1948); 112 and 5 (1951); 0 (1953); 278 (1954); 27 (1955). Average: 95.50.

4 D.G. Bradman (Australia) scored 963 runs at Leeds: 334 (1930); 304 (1934); 103 and 16 (1938); 33 and 173* (1948). Average 192.60.

5 D.G. Bradman (Australia) scored 1671 runs at Melbourne: 79 and 112; 123 and 37* (1928-29); 152 (1930-31); 2 and 167 (1931-32); 0

and 103* (1932-33); 13 and 270; 169 (1936-37); 79 and 49 (1946-47); 132 and 127*; 57 retired hurt (1947-48). Average 129.30.

6 S.M. Gavaskar (India) scored 793 runs at Port-of-Spain: 64 and 67*; 124 and 220 (1970-71); 156; 26 and 10 (1975-76); 1 and 32 (1982-83). Average 113.28.

7 H. Sutcliffe (England) scored 724 runs at Melbourne: 176 and 127; 143 (1924-25); 58 and 135 (1928-29); 52 and 53 (1932-33). Average: 103.50.

8 E.D. Weekes (West Indies) scored 1074 runs at Port-of-Spain: 30 and 20 (1947-48); 207; 161 and 55*(1952-53); 206 and 1 (1953-54); 139 and 87* (1954-55); 78 and 24; 51 and 9 (1957-58). Average 97.63.

9 G.S. Sobers (West Indies) scored 1354 runs at Kingston: 14* and 26 (1953-54); 35* and 64 (1954-55); 365* (1957-58); 147 and 19 (1959-60); 153; 104 and 50 (1961-62); 30 and 27 (1964-65); 0 and 113* (1967-68); 44 and 93 (1967-68); 44 and 93 (1970-71); 13* (1971-72); 57 (1973-74). Average 104.15.

10 W.M. Lawry (Australia) scored 1023 runs at Melbourne: 52 and 57 (1962-63); 157 and 20 (1963-64); 41 and 19 (1964-65); 88 and 78; 108 (1965-66); 100 (1967-68); 205 (1968-69); 56 and 42 (1970-71). Average 78.69.

11 J.B. Hobbs (England) scored 1178 runs at Melbourne: 83 and 28; 57 and 0 (1907-08); 6 and 126*; 178 (1911-12); 122 and 20; 27 and 13 (1920-21); 154 and 22; 66 (1924-25); 20 and 49; 142 and 65 (1928-29). Average 69.29.

12 G.S. Chappell (Australia) scored 1006 runs at Brisbane (Woolloongabba): 58 and 71 (1974-75); 123 and 109* (1975-76); 74 and 124 (1979-80); 35 (1980-81); 201 (1981-82); 53 and 8 (1982-83); 150* (1983-84). Average 111.78.

13 Zaheer Abbas (Pakistan) scored 1093 runs at Lahore: 18 and 33 (1974-75); 15 and 15 (1976-77); 235* and 34* (1978-79); 134 (1981-82); 52 (v Australia 1982-83); 215; 13 (v India 1982-83); 82* and 5 (1983-84); 168* (v India 1984-85); 43 and 31 (v New Zealand 1984-85). Average 99.36.

14 Javed Miandad (Pakistan) scored 1068 runs at Faisalabad: 154* and 6* (1978-79); 106* (1979-80); 50 and 22 (1980-81); 18 and 36 (1981-82); 6 (v Australia 1982-83); 126; 16 (v India 1982-83); 203* (1985-86); 1 and 30 (1986-87); 19 (1987-88); 43 and 107 (1988-89); 13 (1989-90); 25 and 55 (v New Zealand 1990-91); 7 and 9 (v West Indies 1990-91); 14 and 2 (1991-92). Average 56.21.

15 A.R. Border (Australia) scored 1415 runs at Adelaide: 11 and 1 (1978-79); 54 and 24 (1979-80); 57 and 7 (1980-81); 78 and 126 (1981-82); 26 (1982-83); 117* and 66 (1983-84); 21 and 18 (1984-85); 49 (1985-86); 70 and 100* (1986-87); 205 (1987-88); 64 and 6* (1988-89); 13 and 8 (1989-90); 12 and 83* (1990-91); 0 and 91* (1991-92); 19 and 1 (1992-93); 84 and 4 (1993-94). Average 58.95.

16 M.D. Crowe (New Zealand) scored 1123 runs at Wellington: 9 (1981-82); 13 and 100 (1983-84); 37 and 33 (1984-85); 19 (1985-86); 3 and 119 (1986-87); 143 (1987-88); 174 and 0 (1988-89); 30 and 299 (1989-90); 30 and 13* (1991-92); 98 and 3 (1992-93). Average 70.18.

17 D.C. Boon (Australia) scored 1127 runs at Sydney: 49 (1984-85); 0 and 81 (v New Zealand 1985-86); 131 and 25 (v India 1985-86); 12 and 184* v England (1987-88); 149 and 10 (1988-89); 97 and 29 (1990-91); 129* and 7 (1991-92); 76 and 63* (1992-93); 50 and 38 (1993-94); 3 and 17 (1994-95); 16 and 6 (1995-96). Average 62.61.

BATTING CURIOSITIES

1 A.C. Bannerman scored off only five of 208 balls bowled to him by W. Attewell. Attewell bowled 46 overs (6-ball), 24 of which were maidens, for figures of 1 for 43. Bannerman batted for 421 minutes for his 91 (Australia v England, Sydney, 1891-92).

2 C.F. Root (England) played in three Test matches during his career — failing to get a hit in any of them (all against Australia in 1926).

3 C.S. Nayudu (India) played only four scoring strokes in a stay of 145 minutes during the match against England at Calcutta in 1933-34. He hit a six, two fours and a single.

4 W.J. Edrich (England) played two innings before lunch on the third day of the Test against South Africa at Nottingham in 1947. Edrich had been not out at the start of play, and came in at No.3 when England followed-on.

5 A.R. Morris (Australia) batted at one end and D.G. Bradman and I.W. Johnson at the other for 100 minutes during the match against England at The Oval in 1948. The first single was eventually scored and the batsmen changed ends.

6 Three batsmen in the Australian team playing against England at Nottingham in 1953 scored a combined total of 237 out of 244 runs from the bat in Australia's first innings of 249. A.R. Morris hit 67, A.L. Hassett hit 115, and K.R. Miller hit 55. Morris and Hassett shared a stand of 122 for the second wicket, and Hassett and Miller shared one of 109 for the fourth. The next highest score was 4.

7 Each batsman to go to the crease in the India v New Zealand Test at Delhi in 1955-56 reached double figures. The highest score of the fifteen players who batted was 230*. (B. Sutcliffe, New Zealand) and the lowest 10* (J.W. Guy, also playing for New Zealand).

8 There have been eight instances of all eleven batsmen reaching double figures in an innings of a Test match. On each occasion, a team score of over 350 has been recorded; most recently by India in the match against New Zealand at Kanpur in 1976-77.

9 Only once has an innings been completed without a single batsman reaching double figures. This occurred when South Africa was all out for 30 against England at Birmingham in 1924. The highest score was 7 (H.W. Taylor, South Africa) and there were 11 extras.

10 In 1932, the Nawab of Pataudi Snr scored a century in his first Test against Australia. Thirty-two years later, his son, the Nawab of Pataudi Jnr, achieved the same distinction against Australia, playing at Madras in 1964-65.

11 W.J. Edrich (England), who batted on 83 occasions for his country at an average of 40.00, had an incredible run of failures during 1938 and 1939. In consecutive innings he scored 5,0,10,12,28,12,4,10,0,6 and 1. In his next innings he notched up 219.

12 In the second Test between South Africa and New Zealand in 1953-54, two New Zealand batsmen retired hurt before scoring. Both had been hit by balls from N.A.T. Adcock — B. Sutcliffe on the head, and L.S.M. Miller on the chest. Both returned later — Sutcliffe scoring 80*, including seven sixes.

13 In the first Test of the 1957-58 series between the West Indies and Pakistan at Bridgetown, Pakistan scored 106 in its first innings and 8 dec. for 657 in its second — a difference of 551 between the two innings.

14 R.E. Foster's score of 287 at Sydney in the first Test of the 1903-04 series is the highest score by any player in his first Test. He was the first player to share in three century partnerships in the same innings.

15 In the first Test of the Triangular Tournament at Manchester in 1912, T.A. Ward (South Africa) bagged a 'king pair'. He was the third victim of T.J. Matthews' two hat-tricks and was dismissed twice on the one day (May 28).

16 In the fourth Test between Australia and England at Melbourne in 1920-21, J.W.H. Makepeace (England) became the oldest player to score a maiden Test century. He was aged 38 years and 173 days.

17 At Lord's in 1926, W. Bardsley, aged 42 years and 201 days, carried his bat in scoring 193.* His record (the oldest player to score a century for Australia against England) still stands.

18 G.A. Headley (West Indies) is the only batsman to have scored four Test centuries before turning 21 (176, 114, 112 and 223).

19 With scores of 53* and 71*, G.C. Grant (West Indies) was the first batsman to score a not-out fifty in each innings of a Test in the match against Australia at Adelaide in 1930-31.

20 A.G. Ganteaume (West Indies) scored 112 in his only Test innings at Port-of-Spain against England in 1947-48.

21 At Durban in 1964-65, K.F. Barrington (England) became the first batsman to score a Test century in all seven Test-playing countries. (Since Barrington's retirement, Sri Lanka was granted Test match status in 1981 and Zimbabwe in 1992.)

22 Playing against the West Indies at Bridgetown in 1964-65, Australia's W.M. Lawry, 210, and R.B. Simpson, 201, became the first opening pair to score double-centuries in the same Test innings.

23 I.M. Chappell (Australia), 165, scored the 1000th Test century in the match against West Indies played at Melbourne in 1968-69. This was the 643rd Test match.

24 G.M. Turner (New Zealand) became the youngest player to carry his bat through a completed Test innings. Turner was 22 years and 63 days when he scored 43* in the match against England played at Lord's in 1969.

25 In South Africa's last official Test series against Australia before its 22-year isolation, B.A. Richards became the only batsman to score 500 runs in his first series for South Africa (508 runs, average 72.57).

26 The record aggregate for a batsman playing in his first series is 774 (average 154.80), scored by S.M. Gavaskar (India) against the West Indies in 1970-71.

27 The highest aggregate by a batsman in his debut calendar year is 1219 (average 64.15), by M.A. Taylor (Australia) in 1989.

28 The first time brothers scored centuries in the same innings of a Test was at The Oval in 1972. I.M. Chappell scored 118 and his brother, G.S. Chappell, 113 for Australia in this match against England.

29 The first time brothers scored centuries in each innings of the same Test was at Wellington in 1973-74. I.M. Chappell (145 and 121) and G.S. Chappell (247* and 133) scored four centuries between them for Australia in this match against New Zealand.

30 R.E. Redmond (New Zealand) scored 107 and 56 in his only Test match, at Auckland against Pakistan in 1972-73.

31 M.E. Waugh and S.R. Waugh (Australia) provided the first instance in Test cricket of twins playing in the same Test, playing against the West Indies at Port-of-Spain in 1990-91.

32 G.S. Chappell (Australia) became the first player to score centuries in each innings of his first Test as captain with 123 and 109* against the West Indies at Brisbane, 1975-76.

33 When S. Amarnath (India) scored 124 against New Zealand at Auckland in 1975-76, he became the first player to emulate his father by scoring a century in his first Test. 'Lala' Amarnath scored 118 against England in 1933-34.

34 The record number of runs scored in Tests in a calendar year was achieved by I.V.A. Richards (West Indies) with 1710 runs in 1976 (average 90.00).

35 In the second Test at Kanpur in 1976-77, India scored 524 against New Zealand. This is the highest total in Test cricket in which no batsman has scored a century.

36 At Leeds in 1977, G. Boycott (England) became the first batsman to score his 100th first-class century in a Test match, when he scored 191 against Australia.

37 C. Hill (Australia) became the only batsman to be dismissed for three consecutive 90s. This occurred in the series against England in 1901-02. He scored 99 in the second innings of the second Test, and 98 and 97 in the third Test. He also became the first player to score 500 runs in a series without making a century. His scores were 46 and 0, 15 and 99, 98 and 97, 21 and 30, and 28 and 87. In his career Hill made the following nervous nineties scores: 96, 99, 98, 87, 91*, 98.
The only other batsmen to score 500 runs in a series without making a century are: C.C. Hunte (West Indies) against Australia in 1964-65 — his scores were 41 and 81, 89 and 53, 31 and 38, 75 and 31, 1 and 60*; M.A. Atherton (England) against Australia in 1993 — his scores were 19 and 25, 80 and 99, 11 and 9,

55 and 63, 72 and 28, 50 and 42; G.P. Thorpe (England) against the West Indies 1995 — his scores were 20 and 61, 52 and 42, 30 and 0, 94 and 0, 19 and 76, 74 and 38.

38 In the West Indies first innings of the fourth Test against England at Leeds in 1957, F.C.M. Alexander, who went in at the fall of the seventh wicket, was not called upon to face a single ball. F.S. Trueman took a wicket with the last ball of the over, and in the next P.J. Loader took a hat-trick to dismiss the last three batsmen and end the innings. Four wickets fell in consecutive balls.

39 M.C. Cowdrey (England) became the first cricketer to play 100 Tests, when he played against Australia at Birmingham in 1968. He duly celebrated this feat by scoring 104.

MOST RUNS OFF ONE BALL

1 8: E.H. Hendren (169) England v Australia, Brisbane 1928-29 (four boundary overthrows).

2 8: J.G. Wright (44) New Zealand v Australia, Melbourne 1980-81 (four boundary overthrows).

3 7: A. Sandham (325) England v West Indies, Kingston 1929-30 (four boundary overthrows).

4 7: A.P.E. Knott (116) England v West Indies, Leeds 1976 (one, plus two overthrows, plus four boundary overthrows).

5 7: Majid Khan (74) Pakistan v Australia, Melbourne 1981-82 (ran four plus three overthows).

FAMOUS BATSMEN WHO SCORED A 'DUCK' IN THEIR FIRST TEST INNINGS

It's been said of some cricketers, 'he batted so badly he was lucky to make a "duck."' One occasion which seems to have overawed otherwise reliable batsmen is their first Test innings. Below is a list of some who failed in their first big test. Their second appearance is shown in brackets.

Hon.I.F.W. Bligh‡	England	v Australia	Melbourne	1882-83	(3)
S.E.Gregory	Australia	v England	Lord's	1890	(9)
J.Darling	Australia	v England	Sydney	1894-95	(53)
V.T.Trumper	Australia	v England	Nottingham	1899	(11)
G.E.Tyldesley	England	v Australia	Nottingham	1921	(7)
R.E.S.Wyatt	England	v South Africa	Johannesburg	1927-28	(2)†
M.Leyland	England	v West Indies	The Oval	1928	(137)†
L.Hutton	England	v New Zealand	Lord's	1937	(1)
G.E.Gomez	West Indies	v England	Manchester	1939	(11)
D.B.Close	England	v New Zealand	Manchester	1949	(0)†
J.G.Leggatt	New Zealand	v West Indies	Auckland	1951-52	(6*)
K.F.Barrington	England	v South Africa	Nottingham	1955	(34)†
M.J.K.Smith	England	v New Zealand	Birmingham	1958	(7)
C.Milburn	England	v West Indies	Manchester	1966	(94)
A.P.E.Knott	England	v Pakistan	Nottingham	1967	(28)†
K.W.R.Fletcher	England	v Australia	Leeds	1968	(23*)
G.M.Turner	New Zealand	v West Indies	Auckland	1968-69	(40)
G.R.Viswanath	India	v Australia	Kanpur	1969-70	(137)
A.R.Lewis	England	v India	Delhi	1972-73	(70*)
G.A.Gooch	England	v Australia	Birmingham	1975	(0)
J.M.Brearley	England	v West Indies	Nottingham	1976	(17)
Saeed Anwar	Pakistan	v West Indies	Faisalabad	1990-91	(0)

‡ captained England on first Test appearance
† not in the same match

FAMOUS BATSMEN WHO BAGGED A TEST MATCH 'PAIR'

	Career Runs	Career Average	HS	100s
Australia				
A.C. Bannerman	1108	23.08	94	-
R. Benaud	2201	24.45	122	3
A.R. Border	11174	50.56	205	27
J. Darling	1657	28.56	178	3
R. Edwards	1171	40.37	170*	2
J.H.W. Fingleton	1189	42.46	136	5
S.E. Gregory	2282	24.53	201	4
R.N. Harvey	6149	48.41	205	21
I.A. Healy	2803	27.21	113*	2
D.W. Hookes	1306	34.36	143*	1
K.J. Hughes	4415	37.41	213	9
D.M. Jones	3631	46.55	216	11
P.S. McDonnell	950	28.78	147	3
R.W. Marsh	3633	26.51	132	3
M.A. Noble	1997	30.25	133	1
V.Y. Richardson	706	23.53	138	1
K.R. Stackpole	2807	37.42	207	7
M.A. Taylor	5502	45.85	219	14
V.T. Trumper (three 'ducks' in a row)	3163	39.04	214*	8
M.E. Waugh (twice)	3627	44.23	140	10
G.M. Wood	3374	31.83	172	9
England				
D.L. Amiss (twice)	3612	46.30	262*	11
T.E. Bailey	2290	29.74	134*	1
I.T. Botham	5200	33.54	208	14
G.A. Gooch	7571	43.76	333	17
A.P.E. Knott	4389	32.75	135	5
B.W. Luckhurst	1298	36.05	131	4
G. Pullar	1974	43.86	175	4
M.J.K. Smith	2278	31.61	121	3
R.A. Woolmer	1059	33.09	149	3
South Africa				
W.R. Endean	1630	33.95	162*	3
D.J. McGlew	2440	42.06	255*	7
Pakistan				
Aamer Sohail	1960	35.63	205	2
Imtiaz Ahmed	2079	29.28	209	3
Javed Burki	1341	30.47	140	3
Majid J. Khan	3930	38.91	167	8
Mudassar Nazar	4114	38.09	231	10
Saeed Anwar	1038	41.52	169	2
Wazir Mohammad	801	27.62	189	2

	Career Runs	Career Average	HS	100s
West Indies				
F.C.M. Alexander	961	30.03	108	1
K.L.T. Arthurton	1382	30.71	157*	2
P.J.L. Dujon	3322	31.94	139	5
C.G. Greenidge	7558	44.72	226	19
A.I. Kallicharran (twice)	4399	44.43	187	12
A.L. Logie	2470	35.79	130	2
D.L. Murray	1993	22.90	91	-
C.A. Roach (twice)	952	30.70	209	2
O.G. Smith	1331	31.69	168	4
J.S. Solomon	1326	34.00	100*	1
E.D. Weekes	4455	58.61	207	15
F.M.M. Worrell	3860	49.48	261	9
New Zealand				
J.V. Coney	2668	37.57	174*	3
T.W. Jarvis	625	29.76	182	1
I.D.S. Smith	1815	25.56	173	2
J.G. Wright	4964	37.61	185	12
India				
M. Amarnath (twice in run of 0 + 0, 1 + 0, 0 + 0)	4378	42.50	138	11
F.M. Engineer	2611	31.08	121	2
V.S. Hazare	2192	47.65	164*	7
M.L. Jaisimha	2056	30.68	129	3
Pankaj Roy	2442	32.56	173	5
G.S. Ramchand	1180	24.58	109	2
D.N. Sardesai	2001	39.23	212	5
D.B. Vengsarkar	6868	42.13	166	17
Yashpal Sharma	1606	33.45	140	2
Sri Lanka				
A. Ranatunga	2023	34.87	135*	3

BATSMEN WHO SCORED THEIR ONE AND ONLY TEST CENTURY IN THEIR DEBUT MATCH

C. Bannerman	Australia	165*	v England	1876-77
P.F. Warner	England	132*	v South Africa	1898-99
R.E. Foster	England	287	v Australia	1903-04
R.J. Hartigan	Australia	116	v England	1907-08
A. Jackson	Australia	164	v England	1928-29
J.E. Mills	New Zealand	117	v England	1929-30
Nawab of Pataudi Snr	England	102	v Australia	1932-33
N.B. Amarnath	India	118	v England	1933-34
S.C. Griffith	England	140	v West Indies	1947-48
A.G. Ganteaume	West Indies	112	v England	1947-48
R.H. Shodhan	India	110	v Pakistan	1952-53
B.H. Pairaudeau	West Indies	115	v India	1952-53
A.G. Kripal Singh	India	100*	v New Zealand	1955-56
C.A. Milton	England	104*	v New Zealand	1958
A.A. Baig	India	112	v England	1959
Hanumant Singh	India	105	v England	1963-64
Khalid Ibadulla	Pakistan	166	v Australia	1964-65
J.H. Hampshire	England	107	v West Indies	1969
R.E. Redmond	New Zealand	107	v Pakistan	1973
F.C. Hayes	England	106*	v West Indies	1973
L. Baichan	West Indies	105*	v Pakistan	1974-75
S. Amarnath	India	124	v New Zealand	1986-87
D.M. Wellham	Australia	103	v England	1981
D.S.B.P. Kuruppu	Sri Lanka	201*	v New Zealand	1986-87
R.S. Kaluwitharana	Sri Lanka	132*	v Australia	1992-93
P.K. Amre	India	103	v South Africa	1992-93

SOME SIXES TO WIN TEST MATCHES

1 In the fifth Test played between Australia and England at Sydney in 1932-33, W.R. Hammond (England) won the match by hitting a six.

2 In the first Test between the West Indies and England played at Bridgetown in 1934-35, W.R. Hammond (England) won the match by hitting a six.

3 In the fifth Test between South Africa and Australia played at Port Elizabeth in 1966-67, H.R. Lance (South Africa) won the match by hitting a six.

4 In the fourth Test between Australia and England played at Brisbane in 1932-33, E. Paynter won the match, and the Ashes, for England by hitting a six.

5 In the only Test played between Sri Lanka and England at Colombo in 1992-93, S.T. Jayasuriya (Sri Lanka) won the match by hitting the first ball he faced for six.

PARTNERSHIP FEATS

1 H. Sutcliffe (England) playing against Australia at Sydney in 1932-33, shared in century stands for the first three wickets.

2 J.B. Hobbs and H. Sutcliffe (England) shared four century opening stands against Australia in 1924-25. Three of these were recorded in the first three innings in which they partnered each other.

3 L. Hutton and C. Washbrook (England) shared three consecutive opening stands of over 100 against Australia in 1946-47.

4 R.S. Modi and V.S. Hazare (India) shared three consecutive century stands for the third wicket against the West Indies in 1948-49.

5 C.G. Greenidge partnered D.L. Haynes in sixteen century opening stands for the West Indies.

6 J.B. Hobbs (England) shared in 24 century opening stands (15 with H. Sutcliffe, 8 with W. Rhodes and one with C.B. Fry). S.M. Gavaskar (India) and C.G. Greenidge (West Indies) in 22; H. Sutcliffe (England) 21; G. Boycott (England) 20.

7 G. Boycott, B.W. Luckhurst and J.H. Edrich (England) figured in four successive opening stands of more than 100 against Australia in 1970-71. In eight successive innings, these pairs registered six century opening stands.

8 I.M. Chappell (Australia) and S.M. Gavaskar (India) figured in 18 century partnerships for the second wicket.

9 Batsmen who have featured in the most century partnerships are: A.R. Border (Australia) 62; S.M. Gavaskar (India) 58; Javed Miandad (Pakistan) 50; G. Boycott (England) 47; C.G. Greenidge (West Indies) 46; G.S.Chappell (Australia) and I.V.A. Richards (West Indies) 44; G.S. Sobers (West Indies) 43; D.C. Boon (Australia) and M.C. Cowdrey (England) 42; G.A. Gooch (England), L. Hutton (England) and C.H. Lloyd (West Indies) 41.

CENTURIES BY TAIL-ENDERS

* (lower than No. 8 in order)

1 W.W. Read (England). Read batted at No. 10 in the match against Australia at The Oval in 1884, and in the second innings came in with England facing defeat at 8 for 181. It was said that Read was in a towering rage at his captain's decision to place him so low in the order, and he made his point with a brilliant 117 in two hours, during which time he added 151 with W.H. Scotton (90 in five and three quarter hours).

2 R.A. Duff (Australia). Duff batted at No. 6 in the first innings of the second Test against England at Melbourne in 1901-02, but was held back to No. 10 in the second innings. Duff scored 104 and shared in a tenth wicket partnership of 120 with fellow debutant W.W. Armstrong.

3 R.J. Hartigan (Australia). Hartigan, batting at No. 9 in his Test debut against England at Adelaide in 1907-08, came in when Australia, in its second innings, led by only 102 runs with seven wickets down. He joined C. Hill (who was suffering a bout of influenza) but the two defied the English bowling and the 42°C heat to put on 243 for the eighth wicket, of which Hartigan's share was 116. Their record stand enabled Australia to win the match.

4 J.M. Gregory (Australia). After taking 7 for 69 earlier in the match against England at Melbourne in 1920-21, Gregory, batting at No. 9, joined C.E. Pellew with Australia 7 for 282 in its second innings. Together they put on 173. Gregory's share was exactly 100.

5 G.O.B. Allen (England). Batting at No. 9, Allen joined wicketkeeper L.E.G. Ames with England 7 for 190 in their first innings against New Zealand at Lord's in 1931. The two added 246 runs, with Allen making 122.

6 R.R. Lindwall (Australia). Batting at No. 9 in Australia's second innings against England at Melbourne in 1946-47, Lindwall joined wicketkeeper D. Tallon with Australia at 7 for 341. These two then shared a blistering partnership, adding 154 runs in 88 minutes of brilliant hitting, Lindwall making a perfect century (one six and 13 fours) in 109 minutes.

7 J.T. Murray (England). Batting at No. 9 in England's only innings against the West Indies at The Oval in 1966, Murray joined T.W. Graveney with England at 7 for 166 in reply to the West Indies' total of 268. This pair then added 217 for the eighth wicket to take England to the lead. Then a tenth wicket stand of 128 by K. Higgs and J.A. Snow helped gain an innings victory.

8 Asif Iqbal (Pakistan). Batting at No. 9 in Pakistan's second innings against England at the Oval in 1967, Asif was joined by compatriot Intikhab Alam with Pakistan 8 for 65 and still 139 runs in arrears. They added 190 — a new

Test record for the ninth wicket, which still stands.

9 I.D.S. Smith (New Zealand). Batting at No. 9 in New Zealand's first innings against India at Auckland in 1989-90, Smith joined R.J. Hadlee with the score at 7 for 131. He then added 101 with Hadlee for the eighth wicket and 136 for the ninth wicket with M.C. Snedden. His innings of 173 included 24 off a single over (2, 4, 4, 2, 6, 6) from A.S. Wassan.

SOME VALUABLE EFFORTS BY 'NIGHTWATCHMEN'

1 H. Carter (Australia) went in late on the third day against England at Adelaide in 1911-12, with Australia at 1 for 86 in its second innings. He scored 71 and shared in a 124-run stand for the fourth wicket with C. Hill.

2 H. Larwood (England) playing against Australia at Sydney in 1932-33 went in to bat late on the second evening when England were 2 for 153. The Australian bowlers did not see his back until the score had reached 310, of which Larwood's share in 135 minutes was a grand 98. His innings was ended by a catch to Bert Ironmonger, who was not noted as a safe catcher (he held only 3 in 14 Test matches).

3 A.V. Bedser (England) came in late on the first day in the match against Australia at Leeds with England at 2 for 268. The following morning, Bedser defied the Australian attack of R.R. Lindwall, K.R. Miller, W.A. Johnston, E.R.H. Toshack and I.W. Johnson to make his highest Test score, 79, and to help add 155 for the third wicket with W.J. Edrich.

4 Nasim-ul-Ghani (Pakistan) played against England at Lord's in 1962. Normally batting at No. 8, he was promoted two places and sent in as a nightwatchman when Pakistan was 4 for 77 in its second innings. Nasim stayed to score 101 and shared in a Pakistan record fifth wicket partnership of 197 with Javed Burki — a record which still stands. Nasim's century was his first in first-class cricket and the first by a Pakistan batsman in England.

5 A.P.E. Knott (England), playing against Australia at Brisbane 1970-71, was sent in as nightwatchman with England at 1 for 92 late on the second day. He stayed long enough to score 73.

6 A.L. Mann (Australia), playing against India at Perth in 1977-78, came in with the score at 1 for 13 late on the fourth day, having batted at No. 8 in the first innings. The following day he scored 105 out of a total of 8 for 342, sharing a partnership of 139 for the third wicket with P.M. Toohey. Mann's other seven Test innings in a four Test career netted a mere 84 runs.

7 D.R. Parry (West Indies), playing against Australia at Georgetown in 1977-78, was sent in with the West Indies at 2 for 95 in its second innings. He went on to score 51 — his only Test fifty.

8 Wasim Bari (Pakistan) was sent in as nightwatchman in the match against India at Lahore in 1978-79. The score was 1 for 19. He achieved a Test career-high score of 85, sharing in a second wicket partnership stand of 115 with Majid J. Khan, and was dismissed when the score was 3 for 161.

9 R.R. Jumadeen (West Indies) came in late on the third day in the match against India at Kanpur in 1978-79. The score was 2 for 134, but Jumadeen stayed long enough to score his only Test fifty (56) and shared a third-wicket stand of 129 with S.F.A.F. Bacchus.

10 S.M.H. Kirmani (India), when playing against Australia at Bombay in 1979-80, came in late on the first day when India was 3 for 231. Scoring 0* overnight, Kirmani (in the side as a wicketkeeper) batted for the remainder of the innings until India declared at 8 for 458. He scored 101* in five hours, adding 127 with K.D. Ghavri for the eighth wicket.

11 Iqbal Qasim (Pakistan), playing against Sri Lanka at Karachi in 1981-82, came in late on the third day with Pakistan 1 for 16 in the second innings. He scored his highest Test score of 56 before he was dismissed at 3 for 107.

12 E.E. Hemmings (England) came in late on the fourth day of the match against Australia at

Sydney in 1982-83. England was 1 for 3 in the second innings, but Hemmings batted for 226 minutes to record his highest Test score of 95.

13 W.W. Davis (West Indies) played against England at Manchester in 1984. He came in late on the first day when the score was 5 for 267 and scored 77, sharing in a sixth wicket stand of 170 with C.G. Greenidge.

14 C. Sharma (India) came in late on the second day against Australia at Adelaide in 1985-86. With India at 1 for 97, he scored 54 runs as the nightwatchman.

15 Saleem Yousuf (Pakistan), playing against the West Indies at Faisalabad in 1986-87, came in late on the second day with Pakistan at 2 for 19 in the second innings. He scored 61, adding 94 for the third wicket with Qasim Omar.

16 B.N. French (England), playing against Pakistan at Manchester in 1987, came in late on the first day with the score 3 for 133. He scored 59, adding 113 for the fourth wicket with R.T. Robinson.

17 R.C. Russell (England) v Sri Lanka at Lord's 1988, making his Test debut, was sent in late on the first day as 'nightwatchman' with the score at 1 for 40. He scored 94 and shared in a second wicket stand of 131 with G.A.Gooch.

18 R.C. Russell (England) was sent in late on the fourth day in the match against the West Indies at Bridgetown in 1989-90. The score was 3 for 10 in England's second innings. He was eventually sixth out for 55 but helped push the score to 166.

19 P.L. Taylor (Australia), was sent in as nightwatchman on the third day against New Zealand at Wellington in 1989-90, with Australia at 2 for 54. He top-scored with 87, adding 103 for the fourth wicket with A.R. Border.

20 I.A. Healy (Australia), playing against England in the match against Sydney in 1990-91, came in as nightwatchman late on the fourth day with Australia at 1 for 21 in the second innings. He went on to top-score in the innings with 69.

HIGHEST SCORES BY A NO. 11

1 68*: R.O. Collinge (New Zealand), New Zealand v Pakistan, Auckland 1972-73. He added 151 for the tenth wicket with B.F. Hastings (110) — a record for Test cricket.

2 62*: A.E.E. Vogler (South Africa), South Africa v England, Cape Town, 1905-06.

3 60*: Wasim Bari (Pakistan), Pakistan v West Indies, Bridgetown, 1976-77.

4 59*: J.A. Snow (England), England v West Indies, The Oval, 1966.

5 52: R.M. Hogg (Australia), Australia v West Indies, Georgetown, 1984-85.

6 50*: W.W. Hall (West Indies), West Indies v India, Port-of-Spain, 1961-62.

7 50: F.R. Spofforth (Australia), Australia v England, Melbourne, 1884-85.

8 50: Ghulam Ahmed (India), India v Pakistan, Delhi, 1952-53.

SLOW SCORING MEMORABILIA

1 Fourteen consecutive (four-ball) maiden overs were bowled to A.C. Bannerman and W.L. Murdoch (Australia) during their second wicket partnership against England at Melbourne in 1882-83.

2 A.C. Bannerman (Australia) scored 19 runs in 200 minutes during the match against England at Sydney in 1886-87. Bannerman made 15* in two hours in the first innings and 4 in 80 minutes in the second.

3 Australia's total of 175 in 325 minutes against England at Manchester in 1921 included 58 maiden overs.

4 B. Mitchell, on debut for South Africa against England at Birmingham in 1929, made a combined total of 149 in 575 minutes — 88 in 420 minutes and 61* in 155 minutes.

5 England scored only 37 runs before lunch against Australia at Adelaide in 1932-33.

6 I.D. Craig (Australia) scored 38 in four and a half hours, spread over four days, in the match against England at Manchester in 1956.

7 P.G. van der Bijl (South Africa) scored 125 against England at Durban in 1938-39, but did not hit his first boundary until he had been at the wicket for three hours. The first four of the South African innings came after 130 minutes.

8 England took 972 minutes and 1723 balls to score 442 runs against Australia at Leeds in 1953 — 167 in 386 minutes (658 balls) and 275 in 586 minutes (1065 balls).

9 England scored only 27 (39 overs) before lunch on the third day against the West Indies at Bridgetown in 1953-54. The new ball (at that time taken after 65 overs) arrived with the score at 77.

10 Hanif Mohammad scored 59 runs in 337 minutes in the match against England at Lord's in 1954 — 20 in 197 minutes and 39 in 140 minutes.

11 New Zealand had scored only 24 at lunch (after 90 minutes) on the first day of the match against England at Dunedin in 1954-55. The total for the day was 125 in 292 minutes.

12 New Zealand scored only 69 off 90 six-ball overs (56 maidens) against Pakistan at Dacca in 1955-56.

13 New Zealand scored 6 for 32 and 3 for 37 in two pre-lunch sessions against England at Birmingham in 1958.

14 England scored only 19 runs before lunch (90 minutes) in the match against Australia at Brisbane in 1958-59, taking an overnight score of 2 for 92 to 4 for 111. T.E. Bailey scored 8 of the 19 runs in the session.

15 Pakistan scored 24 before lunch against Australia at Karachi in 1959-60. The innings of 8 (dec.) for 194 lasted eight hours.

16 M.L. Jaisimha (India), v Australia at Calcutta in 1959-60, batted through a whole day's play, taking his overnight score of 0* to 59*.

17 T.E. Bailey (England), in the first Test against Australia in Brisbane in 1958-59, scored 68 runs in 458 minutes — less than nine runs an hour. He took 357 minutes to reach fifty and scored off only 40 of the 425 balls bowled to him.

COURAGEOUS PERFORMANCES

1 During the second Test of the 1970-71 series between Australia and England at Perth, the England batsman B.W. Luckhurst damaged his thumb early in his innings but carried on to score 131 runs. In the fifth Test, played a little over a month later at Melbourne, Luckhurst's left little finger was fractured early in his innings and on this occasion he scored 109 runs.

2 During the first Test at Dunedin of the 1967-68 series between New Zealand and India, R.B. Desai (India) had his jaw fractured by a rising ball from R.C. Motz, but went on to score 32* in a tenth-wicket partnership of 57 with B.S. Bedi.

3 A.R. Border (Australia), despite batting in considerable pain from a broken finger during the 1981 series against England, scored in succession 123*, 106* and 84, batting in all for 15 hours and two minutes before losing his wicket.

4 E. Paynter (England) was hospitalised with acute tonsillitis during the fourth Test against Australia in 1932-33, but he insisted on taking his place at the crease where he stayed for four hours, scoring 83 runs. In the second innings, Paynter struck a six which won the match, and regained the Ashes, for England.

5 A.D. Nourse (South Africa) batted for 550 minutes to score 208 in the first Test against England at Nottingham in 1951 — with a broken thumb.

6 W.M. Lawry (Australia) had ten stitches inserted in a head wound caused by a fast rising ball from P.M. Pollock in the third Test against South Africa at Durban in 1966-67. He returned to the crease and top-scored with 44 out of the first innings total of 147.

7 R.B. McCosker (Australia) suffered a fractured jaw while batting in the first innings of the Centenary Test between Australia and England at Melbourne in March 1977. He returned to the crease, however, his face swathed in bandages to help Australia to a second innings total of 9 (dec.) for 419.

8 S.M. Patil (India), playing in the first Test against Australia at Sydney in 1980-81, was knocked unconscious by a 'bouncer' from L.S. Pascoe. Three weeks later in the second Test at Adelaide, Patil proceeded to score 174 runs in 301 minutes.

SHORTEST TEAM TEST MATCH INNINGS

1 50 minutes: South Africa was all out for 30 in 12.3 overs (six-ball) in the first innings against England at Birmingham in 1924.

2 80 minutes: England was all out for 45 in 35.3 overs (four-ball) in the first innings against Australia at Sydney in 1886-87.

3 90 minutes: Australia was all out for 30 in 23 overs (six-ball) in the first innings against England at Birmingham in 1902.

4 225 minutes: India was all out twice in one day for 58 in 21.4 overs (six-ball) and 82 in 37.3 overs, when playing against England at Manchester in 1952.

UNUSUAL DISMISSALS

1 S.J. Snooke (South Africa) was stumped for 53 by N.C. Tufnell (England) at Durban in 1909-10. Tufnell was keeping wicket as a substitute for H. Strudwick (injured).

2 A. Ducat (England) had scored three runs against Australia at Leeds in 1921 when the shoulder of his bat was broken by an express delivery from E.A. McDonald. The broken piece knocked off a bail and the ball was caught by J.M. Gregory. The umpire's decision was 'out caught.'

3 W.H. Brann (South Africa) was given 'not out' for a catch at the wicket during the Test against South Africa in Cape Town in 1922-23. The bowler, G.G. Macauley, appealed for lbw and the appeal was granted.

4 Mushtaq Ali (India) playing in the match against England at Manchester in 1936, was run out when a ball hit by his partner, V.M. Merchant, hit the back of Mushtaq Ali's bat and deflected to mid off; there A.E. Fagg fielded and threw down the non-striker's wicket with Mushtaq Ali out of his ground.

5 D.G. Bradman (Australia) was batting against India at Brisbane in 1947-48 when he played back so far to N.B. 'Lala' Amarnath that the downward swing of his bat broke the wicket from behind. Bradman was out 'hit wicket' to Amarnath for 185.

6 W.A. Brown (Australia) was run out by the bowler, M.H. Mankad, when batting for Australia against India at Sydney in 1947-48. Brown had been backing up too far and Mankad removed the bails as he ran in to bowl. Mankad did not deliver a warning as he had been involved in a similar incident with Brown only four weeks before in a match between an Australian XI and the touring Indian team.

7 L. Hutton (England) was dismissed for 'obstructing the field' when playing against South Africa at The Oval in 1951. A delivery hit Hutton's bat handle or hand and lobbed into the air where wicketkeeper W.R. Endean prepared to take the catch. Hutton, however, hit the ball away as it fell (with the intention of preventing it hitting his wicket) and upon appeal was given out.

8 Ironically, W.R. Endean (South Africa) was given out 'handled the ball' against England at Cape Town in 1956-57; a ball from J.C. Laker rose sharply and Endean palmed it away with his hand in hockey-goalkeeper style.

9 Pervez Sajjad (Pakistan) was stumped by B.E. Congdon (New Zealand) at Lahore in 1964-65. Congdon was substituting as wicketkeeper for A.E. Dick, who had been injured.

10 I.R. Redpath (Australia) was run out by bowler C.C. Griffith (West Indies), when backing-up too far, at Adelaide in 1968-69. (Interestingly,

I.M. Chappell was caught out of his ground in the same way by bowler D.A.J. Holford only minutes later, but in this instance the bowler refrained from removing the bails.)

11 D.W. Randall (England) was run out by bowler E.J. Chatfield (New Zealand) in the Test at Christchurch in 1977-78.

12 Sikander Bakht (Pakistan) was similarly dismissed by bowler A.G. Hurst (Australia) at Perth in 1978-79.

13 A.M.J. Hilditch (Australia) when batting against Pakistan at Perth in 1978-79, took pity on the perspiring fast bowler Sarfraz Nawaz. He bent down and collected the ball by his feet at the bowler's end, and handed it to Sarfraz. Instead of thanking Hilditch, the bowler appealed for 'handled the ball' and the umpire had no option but to uphold the appeal.

14 R.M. Hogg (Australia), when batting against Pakistan at Melbourne in 1978-79, ran a single then, between deliveries, walked up the pitch to prod down some loose turf. The ball, however, was still in the possession of a fielder, Javed Miandad, who put down the stumps with Hogg yards down the wicket to run the batsman out for 9.

15 West Indies batsman J.S. Solomon was judged out 'hit wicket' when his cap fell off, dislodging the bails during the second Test of the 1960-61 series against Australia at Melbourne.

16 J.W. Zulch (South Africa), playing against Australia in the second Test at Johannesburg in 1921-22, was given out 'hit wicket' when a splinter of wood from his bat, dislodged by a ball from E.A. McDonald, removed the bails.

17 B.L. d'Oliveira (England) batted with J.M. Parks in the first innings of the second Test against the West Indies at Lord's in 1966. Parks, facing W.W. Hall, drove a ball back down the pitch which rebounded off d'Oliveira's boot onto the stumps while he was out of his crease. Thinking he was run out, d'Oliveira 'walked', whereupon Hall picked up the ball and removed a stump with the hand holding the ball, thus correctly completing the dismissal. Had the batsman stood his ground he would not have been out as no fielder had touched the ball when the wicket was first broken.

18 S.P. Jones (Australia), playing against England in the 1882 Ashes Test at The Oval, was run out by W.G. Grace when, after completing a run, he left his crease to pat the pitch down. This was said to so infuriate F.R. Spofforth that he bowled like a man possessed; taking 7 for 44 in England's second innings, Spofforth was instrumental in gaining Australia's first-ever win in a Test on English soil.

19 D.M. Jones (Australia), against the West Indies at Georgetown in 1990-91, was bowled by a no-ball from C.A. Walsh. Because of his helmet and the noise from the crowd, he did not hear the umpire's call and started to walk off the field. C.L. Hooper grabbed the ball and snatched up a stump with the hand holding the ball. The umpire then, incorrectly, gave the batsman out. The laws of cricket had been changed in 1980 so that the umpire can call back a batsman leaving the ground under a misapprehension that he had been dismissed.

Note: In 1973-74 at Port-of-Spain, A.W. Greig (England) ran out I.A. Kallicharran. B.D. Julien played the last ball of the second day's play down the pitch, Greig picked up the ball and, seeing Kallicharran out of his ground, threw down the non-striker's wicket and appealed. Umpire D. Sang Hue ruled Kallicharran 'run out'. That evening, lengthy off-field discussions between the captains, officials and umpires led to the appeal being withdrawn in the interests of cricket.

A FEW SURPRISE SELECTIONS

1 E.J.K. Burn (Australia) was selected in the 1890 Australian team to tour England as the second wicketkeeper. Only when the team was assembled in Adelaide did it become known that he had never kept wicket in his life!

2 S.F. Barnes (England) was selected to tour Australia in 1901-02, mainly at the instigation of A.C. McLaren. Barnes, then a professional with Burnley in the Lancashire League, had taken only nine wickets in first-class cricket — but then proceeded to take 19 wickets in his first two Tests on the way to becoming one of

the greatest bowlers the world has ever seen.

3 A.L. Valentine (West Indies) was taken to England in 1950 after only two first-class matches in which he took two wickets for 190 runs.

4 S. Ramadhin (West Indies) was pulled out of Trinidad club cricket to tour England in 1950. While on tour, he and A.L. Valentine mystified the best batsmen in England, and both were on their way to becoming Test 'greats'. Ramadhin, like Valentine, had played only two games of first-class cricket — both on matting.

5 G.S. Sobers (West Indies) was called into the West Indies Test side to play against England at Kingston in 1953-54. Previously, Sobers (who replaced the injured A.L. Valentine) had played only two first-class matches.

6 J.E.F. Beck (New Zealand) had played only club cricket and never appeared in a first-class match when chosen to tour South Africa in 1953-54. He was run out for 99 at Cape Town in his second Test match.

7 J.R. Watkins (Australia) was chosen to play against Pakistan in Sydney in 1972-73 after A.A. Mallett had announced his unavailability for the forthcoming tour of the West Indies. Although Watkin's first-class record for New South Wales was not particularly distinguished, he made a fine 36 in the second innings, and shared in a stand of 83 with R.A.L. Massie after Australia had collapsed to 8 for 101; and, with the ball, delivered probably the six most inaccurate overs ever bowled at Sydney.

8 The English selectors pulled off three of the most amazing selections in history for the 1956 series against Australia.
For the third Test at Leeds, they included 41-year-old C. Washbrook, who had not played Test cricket for five years. Coming in to bat at 3 for 17, Washbrook made 98 and shared in a stand of 177 with P.B.H. May.
For the next Test at Manchester, the Rev. David Sheppard was included. Because of clerical duties, he had played only four innings that year for Sussex — but promptly made 113 to help England win the Test.
For The Oval Test, the selectors brought in Denis Compton — 18 years after he had played his first Test and not long after he had undergone an operation for the removal of a knee-cap. Compton completed the 'hat-trick' for the selectors with scores of 94 and 35*.

9 Australian selectors had a 'double' selection bonanza in 1907-08 when they brought J.D.A. O'Connor and R.J. Hartigan into the side for the Adelaide Test against England. Hartigan scored 48 and 116 (sharing in a record stand of 243 with C. Hill after Australia had been 7 for 180) and O'Connor bowled Australia to victory with 5 for 40 in the vital fourth innings of the match.

10 W. Rhodes (England) was brought back into the England team for the vital fifth Test of the 1926 series against Australia. He was aged 48! With England needing a win to regain the Ashes, Rhodes bowled them to victory with 2 for 35 and 4 for 44.

11 M.R. Whitney (Australia) was in England to play League cricket, and to appear occasionally for Gloucestershire, when he was brought into the Australian Test team in 1981 (after injuries to G.F. Lawson and R.M. Hogg had left the team short). Previously, Whitney had made only four appearances for NSW.

12 P.L. Taylor (Australia) was selected for the fifth Test against England at Sydney 1986-87 after only six first-class matches, and only one of them during the season. There was speculation in the media whether the selectors had chosen the wrong Taylor, for M.A. Taylor, an opening batsmen for NSW, had experienced a successful debut in first-class cricket the previous season. P.L. Taylor, bowling off-spin, took a career-best 6 for 78 and 2 for 76, as well as scoring a crucial 42 runs in Australia's second innings; Australia won its first Test against England since June 1985.

UNUSUAL INCIDENTS

1 In the series between Australia and England played in Australia in 1936-37, Middlesex captain R.W.V. Robins played under the leadership of his county vice-captain, G.O.B.

Allen. A similar situation occurred in the 1980 series between England and the West Indies when Somerset captain B.C. Rose played under the leadership of Somerset vice-captain I.T. Botham. And in 1995, Lancashire captain M. Watkinson played under the leadership of his county colleague M.A. Atkinson against both the West Indies and South Africa.

2 The West Indies, playing against England at St John's in 1980-81, opened the Test by scoring 45 from the first seven overs — made up of eleven fours and a single.

3 The start of the Test between Pakistan and the West Indies at Multan in 1980-81 was delayed due to the late arrival of one of the umpires.

4 When given out lbw in the match against Australia at Melbourne in 1980-81, the Indian captain S.M. Gavaskar indicated that the ball had hit his pad, and was so angry at the decision that he ordered his batting partner, C.P.S. Chauhan, to accompany him from the field and forfeit the match. Both players were only metres inside the boundary when the Indian manager Wing-Commander Durani intervened and ordered Chauhan back to the crease. The following day, Kapil Dev and D.R. Doshi bowled India to victory as Australia was dismissed for 83 (chasing a target of 143).

5 In the match between the West Indies and Pakistan at Multan in 1980-81, bowler S.T. Clarke (West Indies) was bombarded by a shower of oranges, as well as a brick, thrown from the crowd, as he fielded on the fine-leg fence. Enraged, Clarke picked up the brick and threw it back into the crowd, injuring a young student. Play was immediately held up, and only West Indies vice-captain A.I. Kallicharran's calming plea restored order in the angry crowd. Clarke was later suspended for three matches by the West Indies Cricket Board of Control.

6 During the Test between India and Australia at Bangalore in 1979-80, the Australian pace-bowler R.M. Hogg, became upset with the feather-bed pitch and with his own spate of no-balls (seven in five overs) so he kicked down the stumps at the bowler's end. His captain, K.J. Hughes tendered an immediate apology to the umpire, an action which Hogg duplicated at the end of play.

7 In the New Zealand v West Indies Test at Christchurch 1979-80, the West Indies fast-bowler C.E.H. Croft took bad sportsmanship to the brink. After being no-balled and showing his displeasure several times, Croft ran in very close to umpire F.R. Goodall — so close that the batsman could not see him — and shouldered Goodall heavily. Croft was later suspended, but the West Indians were so upset about Goodall's umpiring that they refused to take the field after tea on the third day unless he was replaced. They were finally persuaded to resume, twelve minutes late.

8 In the seventh Test between Australia and England at Sydney in 1970-71, England nearly became the first team to forfeit a Test. England paceman J.A. Snow felled Australian tail-ender T.J. Jenner with a 'bouncer', and became involved in a war of words with the umpire, L.P. Rowan, when warned for 'intimidatory' bowling. R. Illingworth, England's captain, joined in, and the crowd began to boo and hiss. Cans came flying onto the field and, when Snow was sent to field right on the fine-leg boundary, a drunken spectator leaned over the fence and grabbed his arm. Illingworth immediately motioned his team from the ground, and it was only the umpire's advice that if they did not return they would forfeit the match that persuaded Illingworth to resume.

9 In the Test between Australia and England at Perth in 1979-80, Australian batsman D.K. Lillee, not out overnight, continued his innings the next morning using an aluminium bat, (which he had used once previously). After two balls had been played (rather noisily), England captain J.M. Brearley complained to the umpires that the aluminium bat was damaging the ball! The umpires asked Lillee to change his bat, but Lillee, quite within his rights, refused and argued heatedly with Brearley. Finally, the umpires ordered him off for a replacement, but after stalking from the ground, Lillee re-appeared — still carrying his aluminium bat. More argument ensued. Eventually Lillee threw the bat away in disgust, accepted a willow replacement, and play was allowed to resume.

10 G.J. Bonnor (Australia), in making 87 against England at Sydney in 1882-83, was dropped eight (yes, eight!) times. A.G. Steel dropped four of the chances, when Bonnor was 2, 17, 24 and 80. When England batted, Steel himself was dropped four times — but went on to make 135*.

CAPTAINCY CURIOSITIES

1 H.M. Taberer captained South Africa in his one and only Test match appearance when he led his country in the match against England at Johannesburg in the first Test of 1902-03. For the second Test, less than a week later, J.H. Anderson led South Africa in his only Test appearance.

2 N. Betancourt captained the West Indies in his only Test match, which was against England in 1929-30.

3 In the fourth Test between the West Indies and England at Kingston in 1934-35, both captains were forced off the field through injury. England's R.E.S. Wyatt suffered a broken jaw and the West Indies's C.G. Grant retired with an ankle injury.

4 C.A. Smith (England) captained his country at his only appearance in a Test match, which was against South Africa in 1888-89. Smith, later knighted, was afterwards famous as an Hollywood film actor.

5 P.W. Sherwell (South Africa) captained his country in his very first Test appearance, in the match against England at Johannesburg in 1905-06.

6 During his period as captain of England (twelve matches from June 1980 to July 1981), I.T. Botham scored 276 runs at an average of 13.80 and took 35 wickets at 32.00 average. Compare these figures to his overall career statistics of 33.54 runs per innings and 28.40 for each wicket.

ODDMENTS

1 In the second Test match between Australia and England in 1877, played at the Melbourne Cricket Ground, Australian batsman T.J.D. Kelly hit eight consecutive fours in the second innings and C. Bannerman scored 30 in 15 minutes. Despite these spirited efforts, Australia lost by four wickets.

2 In the first Test of the 1881-82 season between Australia and England played at Melbourne, W.E. Midwinter made his debut for England having played for Australia in the first two Tests between the two countries. (In the same match T.P. Horan and G. Giffen scored Australia's first-ever century partnership — 107 for the fifth wicket.)

3 W.L. Murdoch of Australia scored the first double-century in Test cricket when he knocked up 211 against England at The Oval during the third Test in 1884. In the same match, all eleven English players were called upon to bowl while Australia scored 551 runs. The match was drawn.

4 The only other instance of all eleven players bowling in an innings occurred at Faisalabad in 1979-80 during the second Test between Pakistan and Australia. The entire Australian team, including the wicketkeeper R.W. Marsh, had a spell at the bowling crease during Pakistan's only innings, and the match was drawn. Australia made 617 and Pakistan 2 for 382.

5 In the fifth Test between Australia and England at Melbourne during the 1884-85 season, umpire J. Hodges refused to take the field after tea on the third day because of complaints made by some English players about his decisions. The Australian player T.W. Garrett deputised for Hodges during the last session and the English manager, J. Lillywhite, took over on the last day. There is nothing in the records to indicate how Garrett performed in this unusual role.

6 The appearance of a mouse on the field held up play for several minutes during the Test between England and Pakistan at Birmingham in 1962.

7 Four players with the same surname played in the Test between South Africa and England at Cape Town in 1891-92: A., G.E., and J.T. Hearne for England; F. Hearne for South Africa.

8 In his debut Test match, G.G. Macaulay (playing for England in the match against South Africa at Cape Town in 1922-23) took a wicket with his first ball, and later he made the winning hit when England won the match — by just one wicket.

9 In the Test between Pakistan and England at Lahore in 1977-78, England off-spinner G.A. Cope dismissed Abdul Qadir lbw and then bowled Sarfraz Nawaz with the first ball. Iqbal Qasim then snicked the next delivery to J.M. Brearley, the English captain, at slip and the umpire confirmed the catch and Copes' hat-trick. However, Brearley indicated that the 'catch' had been taken on the bounce and Qasim was allowed to bat on. It would be difficult to get much closer to a Test hat-trick than Cope did on that day.

10 M.H. Mankad (India), in 72 innings, and W. Rhodes (England), in 98 innings, are the only two batsmen in the history of Test cricket to bat in every position in the team — from No. 1 to No. 11 — in their respective Test match careers.

11 The only occasion when one country has simultaneously played official Test matches in two different countries was in 1929-30 when England played New Zealand at Christchurch on 10, 11, and 13 January, and played the West Indies at Bridgetown on 11, 13, 14, 15, and 16 January.

12 In 1880, an Australian team advertised for opponents. This unique event occurred during the the Australians' visit to England: apparently it was not certain until the late spring of that year that the Australians would be touring, and consequently the county programmes had already been drawn up. The Australians therefore found the large part of their tour consisted of fixtures with local clubs in the North and Midlands, usually against odds. It was during this period that the team took out newspaper advertisements for opponents.
Finally, at the end of August, and mainly through the efforts of one man, C.W. Alcock, a match against a representative English team was organised. This became the first Test match on English soil.

13 The most expensive miss occurred when B.A. Barnett, while keeping wicket for Australia, missed stumping L. Hutton off L.O. Fleetwood-Smith in the match against England at The Oval in 1938. Hutton was on 40, and went on to make 364.

14 In the first Test against India at Madras in 1979-80, Australia's first seven batsmen in the batting order each opened their score with a boundary. The batsmen were: A.M.J. Hilditch, G.M. Wood, A.R. Border, K.J. Hughes, G.N. Yallop, D.F. Whatmore and K.J. Wright.

EIGHT BOWLERS NO-BALLED FOR THROWING IN TEST MATCHES

The following bowlers have been no-balled for throwing:

1 E. Jones (Australia) once by umpire J. Phillips in the second Test against England at Melbourne in 1897-98.

2 G.A.R. Lock (England) in the first Test against the West Indies at Kingston in 1953-54.

3 G.M. Griffin (South Africa) eleven times by umpire F.S. Lee in the second Test against England at Lord's in 1960. In England's only innings, Griffin claimed the only Test hat-trick for South Africa when he took the wickets of M.J.K. Smith, P.M. Walker and F.S. Trueman.

4 Haseeb Ahsan (Pakistan) in the first Test against India at Bombay in 1960-61.

5 I. Meckiff (Australia) four times by umpire C.J. Egar in his only over in the first Test against South Africa at Brisbane in 1963-64.

6 S. Abid Ali (India) once by umpire F.R. Goodall in the second Test against New Zealand at Christchurch in 1967-68. He deliberately threw the ball in protest at the action of G.A. Bartlett who had not been 'called' for throwing.

7 D.I. Gower (England) deliberately threw the only ball he 'bowled' in the second Test against New Zealand at Nottingham in 1986. The scores were level and New Zealand had eight wickets in hand.

The 'Prince' of batsmen, Ranjitsinhji, playing at Manchester in 1896. He scored 154 not out for England in this match against Australia.

Australian cricket stars of the 19th century: George Giffen, Harry Boyle, Billy Murdoch and Hugh Trumble.

8 M. Muralidaran (Sri Lanka) by umpire D.B. Hair in the second Test against Australia at Melbourne in 1995-96. This is the only instance of a player being 'called' by the umpire at the bowler's end.

HAT-TRICKS TO END A TEST

1 In the second Test between Australia and England at Melbourne in 1901-02. H. Trumble completed Australia's win by taking a hat-trick. He dismissed A.O. Jones, J.R. Gunn and S.F. Barnes. Australia won by 229 runs.

2 In the second Test between South Africa and Australia at Cape Town in 1957-58, L.F. Kline completed Australia's win when he did the hat-trick. He dismissed E.R.H. Fuller, H.J. Tayfield and N.A.T. Adcock. Australia won by an innings and 141 runs.

Note: In the third Test between England and Pakistan at Leeds in 1971, P. Lever completed England's win by taking three wickets in four balls. He dismissed Wasim Bari, Asif Masood and Pervez Sajjad. England won by 25 runs.

BOWLING CURIOSITIES

1 J. Briggs (England), playing against South Africa at Cape Town in 1888-89, took all of his wickets unaided. He bowled 14 and trapped one lbw. His figures were 7 for 17 and 8 for 11.

2 W.W. Armstrong (Australia), playing against England at Nottingham in 1905, bowled off-breaks wide outside leg stump in an attempt to slow the scoring. From 204 consecutive balls, the England batsmen scored off only 25. Of the remaining 179 balls, only 19 were played by the batsmen, the other 160 being allowed to go through to the wicketkeeper.

3 T.J. Matthews (Australia) took a hat-trick in each innings of the match between Australia and South Africa at Manchester in 1912. This is the only instance of its kind in all Test cricket history. These six wickets were the only ones taken by Matthews in the match, and constituted over a third of his Test career 'bag'.

4 W.W. Armstrong (Australia) became the first man in Test history to bowl two consecutive overs — against England at Manchester in 1921. England closed its innings on the second day but, as the first day had been washed out, it was discovered that Australia was left with insufficient batting time under the laws of cricket (as they then stood). After some confusion, the England innings resumed and Armstrong, who had bowled the last over before the break, bowled the first one after it.

5 G.O.B. Allen (England) opened the bowling in the match against Australia at Manchester in 1934 with a 13-ball over — three wides and four no-balls.

6 England's score of 7 (dec.) for 469 against South Africa at Durban in 1938-39 did not include a single maiden over (eight-ball overs).

7 N.B.F. Mann (South Africa), making his debut against England at Nottingham in 1947, bowled eight consecutive maiden overs before conceding his first run in Test cricket.

8 A.M. Moir (New Zealand) equalled the achievement of W.W. Armstrong by sending down two consecutive overs. Moir bowled the last over before tea in the Test against England at Wellington in 1950-51, and then the first over after tea.

9 H.J. Tayfield (South Africa), playing against New Zealand at Johannesburg in 1953-54, bowled 14 eight-ball overs, seven of which were maidens, for figures of 6 for 13. Only nine scoring shots were made from 112 balls.

10 H.J.Tayfield (South Africa), while playing against England at Durban in 1956-57, bowled 16 consecutive (eight-ball) maiden overs — he delivered 137 successive balls all told from which no runs were scored.

11 K.R. Miller (Australia) bowled unchanged before lunch on the first day against England at Melbourne in 1954-55, for figures of 9-8-5-3. All five runs scored off Miller came in his fourth over.

12 S. Ramadhin (West Indies), playing against England at Lord's in 1950, bowled ten consecutive maidens in the first innings and eleven in the second.

13 In the Test between England and Australia at The Oval in 1882, English bowlers E. Peate and R.G. Barlow delivered 14 consecutive maidens during Australia's first innings of 63. Peate's return for the innings was 24 maidens in 38 overs, while Barlow's 31 overs included 22 maidens.

14 In the third Test between the West Indies and England played at Bridgetown in the 1973-74 season, a total of 79 no-balls were bowled. With 20 runs scored off them, the bowlers had given away almost a century.

15 In the six-match Test series between Australia and England played in Australia in 1970-71, not one lbw appeal was upheld against an Australian batsman.

16 In the second innings of the Test between the West Indies and India in 1961-62 at Bridgetown, L.R. Gibbs (West Indies) achieved figures of 53.3 overs 37 maidens, 38 runs and eight wickets. These included figures of 15.3-14-6-8 in the final session of the match.

17 In the Test between India and England played at Madras in 1963-64, R.G. Nadkarni bowled 21 consecutive maiden overs in the first innings but didn't take a wicket. His first innings figures were 32-27-5-0. In the second innings, he took 2 for 6 off six overs (with four maidens).

18 H. Verity (England) bowled a Chinaman when he dismissed E.E. Achong (West Indies) in the second Test at Manchester in 1933.

19 Because of an umpiring error, J.T. Sparling (New Zealand) bowled an eleven-ball over (excluding no-balls and wides) in the first Test against England, played at Auckland during the 1962-63 season.

20 At Lord's in 1972, R.A.L. Massie (Australia) returned match figures of 16 for 137: 32.5-7-84-8 and 27.2-9-53-8. At Madras in 1987-88, N.D. Hirwani equalled this feat by taking 16 for 136: 18.3-3-61-8 and 15.2-3-75-8. This is the record for any bowler in his first Test. A.E. Trott and A.L. Valentine are the only other bowlers to have taken eight wickets in an innings in their first Test.

MOST CONSECUTIVE MAIDENS

Six-ball overs

1 21: R.G Nadkarni, India v England, Madras, 1963-64. (He bowled 131 consecutive balls from which no runs were scored.)

2 15: M.C. Carew, West Indies v England, Port-of-Spain, 1967-68. (He bowled 90 consecutive balls from which no runs were scored.)

3 13: J.H. Wardle, England v South Africa, Nottingham, 1955.

4 11: J.A. Young, England v Australia, Nottingham, 1948.

5 11: S. Ramadhin, West Indies v England, Lord's 1950 (second innings).

6 10: S. Ramadhin, West Indies v England, Lord's 1950 (first innings).

Eight-ball overs

1 16: H.J. Tayfield, South Africa v England, Durban, 1956-57. (He bowled 137 consecutive balls from which no runs were scored.)

2 9: H.J. Tayfield, South Africa v Australia, Melbourne, 1952-53.

LONG BOWLING SPELLS

1 The Australian bowlers G.E. Palmer (53-36-68-7) and E. Evans (57-32-64-3) bowled unchanged for the entire English innings of 133, scored in 190 minutes during the match between England and Australia played at Sydney in 1881-82.

2 T. Richardson, playing for England in the match against Australia at Manchester in 1896, bowled unchanged for three hours during the second innings to try and stave off an England defeat. Richardson, a pace-bowler, delivered 42.3 overs, with 16 maidens, and took 6 for 76.

3 A.M.B. Brown (South Africa) bowled unchanged for 46 six-ball overs against England at Leeds in 1947, for figures of 46-12-89-1.

4 Ghulam Ahmed, playing for India against Pakistan at Dacca in 1954-55, bowled 40 overs unchanged on the first day, his figures being 40-8-84-4.

5 T.L. Goddard (South Africa) bowled 46 overs unchanged on the last day of the match against England at Leeds in 1955. His spell resulted in figures of 46-27-45-4.

6 H.J. Tayfield (South Africa) had an unchanged spell of 53.4-29-60-5 during England's second innings in the match played at The Oval in 1955.

7 T.R. Veivers (Australia) bowled 55 consecutive overs in the Test against England at Manchester during the 1964 season. Veivers bowled 75 of the last 80 overs sent down from the city end.

GOOD BOWLING SPELLS

1 7 wickets for 1 run in 26 balls: Sarfraz Nawaz, Pakistan v Australia, Melbourne, 1978-79.

2 7 wickets for 1 run in 32 balls: C.E.L. Ambrose, West Indies v Australia, Perth 1992-93.

3 7 wickets for 8 runs in 22 balls: J.C. Laker, England v Australia, Manchester, 1956.

4 6 wickets for 6 runs in 45 balls: S. Haigh, England v South Africa, Cape Town, 1898-99.

5 7 wickets for 17 runs in 46 balls: M.A. Noble, Australia v England, Melbourne, 1901-02.

6 8 wickets for 7 runs in 49 balls: G.A. Lohmann, England v South Africa, Johannesburg, 1895-96.

7 6 wickets for 7 runs in 29 balls: S.J. Pegler, South Africa v England, Lord's, 1912.

8 5 wickets for 1 run in 17 balls: G.R. Hazlitt, Australia v England, The Oval, 1912.

9 5 wickets for 7 runs in 31 balls: E.P. Nupen, South Africa v England, Durban, 1927-28.

10 6 wickets for 11 runs in 24 balls: E.P. Nupen, South Africa v England, Johannesburg, 1930-31.

11 6 wickets for 8 runs in 36 balls: H. Ironmonger, Australia v South Africa, Melbourne, 1931-32.

12 6 wickets for 9 runs in 56 balls: C.V. Grimmett, Australia v South Africa, Adelaide, 1931-32.

13 5 wickets for 1 run in 28 balls: I.T. Botham, England v Australia, Birmingham, 1981.

14 5 wickets for 2 runs in 19 balls: E.R.H. Toshack, Australia v India, Brisbane, 1947-48.

MOST WIDES BY ONE BOWLER

1 9: Kabir Khan, Pakistan v South Africa, Johannesburg, 1994-95. (He also bowled five wides in the first innings).

2 8: B.J.T. Bosanquet, England v Australia, Leeds, 1905.

3 8: M.B. Owens, New Zealand v Sri Lanka, Moratuwa, 1992-93.

4 8: A.D. Mullally, England v India, Lord's, 1996.

5 6: M.A. Noble, Australia v England, Leeds, 1905.

6 6: J.R. Watkins, Australia v Pakistan, Sydney, 1972-73.

INEXPENSIVE ANALYSES

1 25-19-18-0: Fazal Mahmood, Pakistan v India, Dacca, 1954-55.

2 28-17-21-2: A.H. Kardar, Pakistan v New Zealand, Dacca, 1955-56.

3 30-19-20-2: Khan Mohammad, Pakistan v New Zealand, Dacca, 1955-56.

4 32-27-5-0: R.G. Nadkarni, India v England, Madras, 1963-64.

5 32-23-24-4: J.H. Wardle, England v South Africa, Nottingham, 1955.

6 36-23-27-3: J.C. Laker, England v New Zealand, Leeds, 1958.

7 45-28-48-4: A.L. Valentine, West Indies v England, Lord's, 1950.

8 45-26-42-6: K.D. Mackay, Australia v Pakistan, Dacca, 1959-60.

9 46-24-43-1: W. Attewell, England v Australia, Sydney, 1891-92.

10 46.1-20-42-1: G.E. Gomez, West Indies v India, Port-of-Spain, 1952-53.

11 46.3-24-42-6: Zulfiqar Ahmed, Pakistan v New Zealand, Karachi, 1955-56.

12 47-29-42-5: H. Ironmonger, Australia v South Africa, Brisbane, 1931-32.

13 47-28-39-3: C.V. Grimmett, Australia v England, Nottingham, 1934.

14 53-30-50-4: S. Ramadhin, West Indies v England, Bridgetown, 1953-54.

15 53.3-37-38-8: L.R. Gibbs, West Indies v India, Bridgetown, 1961-62.

16 54-38-43-4: B.W. Yuile, New Zealand v Pakistan, Auckland, 1964-65.

17 57-30-64-1: J.C. White, England v Australia, Melbourne, 1928-29.

18 61-34-71-1: M.H. Mankad, India v Pakistan, Peshawar, 1954-55.

19 61-32-51-3: W. Attewell, England v Australia, Melbourn,e 1891-92.

20 62-37-69-4: T.L. Goddard, South Africa v England, Leeds, 1955.

21 62-35-61-1: D.S. Atkinson, West Indies v Pakistan, Bridgetown, 1957-58.

22 69-34-79-2: D.R. Doshi, India v New Zealand, Auckland, 1980-81.

23 71-47-79-3: A.L. Valentine, West Indies v England, Lord's, 1950.

24 72-43-86-6: S. Ramadhin, West Indies v England, Lord's, 1950.

25 76-47-58-4: M.H. Mankad, India v England, Delhi 1951-52.

26 81-36-105-5: G. Geary, England v Australia, Melbourne, 1928-29.

All of the above instances were six-ball overs.

EXPENSIVE ANALYSES

1 87-11-298-1: L.O. Fleetwood-Smith, Australia v England, The Oval, 1938.

2 80.2-13-266-5: O.C. Smith, West Indies v England, Kingston, 1929-30.

3 54-5-259-0: Khan Mohammad, Pakistan v West Indies, Kingston, 1957-58.

4 85.2-20-247-2: Fazal Mahmood, Pakistan v West Indies, Kingston, 1957-58.

5 70-10-229-1: S.L. Boock, New Zealand v Pakistan, Auckland, 1988-89.

6 82-17-228-5: M.H. Mankad, India v West Indies, Kingston, 1952-53.

7 64.2-8-226-6: B.S. Bedi, India v England, Lord's, 1974.

8 54-3-224-2: M. Muralidaran, Sri lanka v Australia, Perth, 1995-96.

9 38.4-3-220-7; Kapil Dev, India v Pakistan, Faisalabad, 1982-83.

10 54-7-217-3: I.T. Botham, England v Pakistan, The Oval, 1987.

11 71-8-204-6: I.A.R. Peebles, England v Australia, The Oval, 1930.

12 75-16-202-3: M.H. Mankad, India v West Indies, Bombay, 1948-49.

13 84-19-202-6: Haseeb Ahsan, Pakistan v India, Madras, 1960-61.

WICKETKEEPING CURIOSITIES

1 In the first-ever Test between England and South Africa, played at Port Elizabeth in March

1889, both wicketkeepers were at one stage off the field. South Africa's W.H. Milton deputised for regular keeper F.W. Smith in England's second innings while M.P. Bowden filled in for H. Wood when the England keeper was unavailable. Ironically, deputy Milton was caught behind by deputy Bowden.

2 In the first Test between England and New Zealand at Lord's in 1986, four different players shared the wicketkeeping duties for England in the New Zealand first innings. The selected 'keeper, B.N. French, was injured while batting. C.W.J. Athey kept wickets for the first two overs before handing over the gloves to R.W. Taylor (substitute). After a further 74 overs, R.J. Parks (substitute) took over the gloves until the end of the 140th over of the innings. B.N. French then returned and kept wicket for the remainder of the innings — namely, one ball!

WICKETKEEPERS WHO HAVE OPENED THE BOWLING IN A TEST MATCH

C.L. Walcott (West Indies) opened the bowling in England's second innings against Manchester in 1950, replacing the injured H.H.H. Johnson. R.J. Christiani deputised behind the stumps, while Walcott bowled four overs without success.

BOUNDARY CURIOSITIES

1 E.H. Hendren (England), playing against Australia at Brisbane in 1928-29, scored an eight (including four overthrows) from the bowling of P.M. Hornibrook.

2 G.S. Sobers (West Indies) hit ten fours in an innings of 43 in the Test against Australia at Bridgetown in 1954-55. His other scoring shots consisted of three singles.

3 J.H. Edrich (England) scored 238 in boundaries (five sixes and 52 fours) in an innings of 310* against New Zealand at Lord's in 1965. Edrich is the only batsman to accumulate more than 200 runs through boundaries in a Test innings.

4 K.H. Weekes (West Indies), playing against England at The Oval in 1939, scored four successive fours from the bowling of R.T.D. Perks.

5 D.T. Lindsay (South Africa) scored five consecutive fours from the bowling of J.W. Gleeson in the match against Australia at Port Elizabeth in 1969-79.

6 R.E. Redmond (New Zealand) scored five consecutive fours from the bowling of Majid J. Khan in the match against Pakistan at Auckland in 1972-73.

7 D.W. Hookes (Australia) scored five successive fours from the bowling of A.W. Greig against England at Melbourne in 1976-77.

8 S.M. Patil (India) scored six successive fours from the bowling of R.G.D. Willis in the match against England at Manchester in 1982.

9 B.Sutcliffe (New Zealand) hit four sixes (three in four balls) from one eight-ball over bowled by H.J.Tayfield in the match against South Africa at Johannesburg in 1953-54 .

10 F.S. Trueman (England) hit three sixes from one six-ball over bowled by S. Ramadhin in against the West Indies at Lord's in 1957.

11 W.R. Hammond (England) hit three successive sixes from the bowling of J. Newman in the match against New Zealand at Auckland in 1932-33.

12 W. Voce (England) hit three sixes from four balls bowled by A.E. Hall in the match against South Africa in Johannesburg in 1930-31.

13 R.C. Motz (New Zealand) hit three sixes from five balls bowled by D.A. Allen in the match against England played at Dunedin in the 1965-66 season.

14 A.M.E. Roberts (West Indies) hit three sixes and a four from five balls bowled by I.T. Botham in the match against England at Port-of-Spain in 1980-81.

15 S.T. Clarke (West Indies) hit three sixes from three successive balls bowled by Mohammad Nazir in the match against Pakistan at Faisalabad in 1980-81.

16 I.V.A. Richards (West Indies), in making 145 against England at Lord's in 1980, hit 106 runs in boundaries — 25 fours and one six.

17 B.L. Cairns (New Zealand) hit three sixes in one over off the bowling of D.R. Parry in the match against the West Indies at Dunedin in 1979-80.

18 Intikhab Alam (Pakistan) hit eleven fours in his score of 48 against Australia at Melbourne in 1972-73.

19 Kapil Dev (India) scored 70 runs from boundaries in an innings of 89 during the match against England at Lord's in 1982. He hit 13 fours and three sixes.

20 Kapil Dev (India) hit four successive sixes off the last four balls of an over from E.E. Hemmings — this was to avoid the follow-on in the match played against England at Lord's in 1990.

ALPHABETICAL TEAMS

After studying the information in this book, one cannot help wondering what great teams could be assembled if different cricketers from different countries and times were available for selection. And so, just for fun — and as an exercise in team selection — we have compiled 'Alphabetical Teams', based on the players' family names. In doing so, we have produced some very interesting combinations!
We soon found that selecting a Test Team was much more difficult than first expected. How can one compare the career performances of John Briggs and Bishen Bedi, or the batting deeds of J.T. Tyldesley and Sachin Tendulkar? There were some hard decisions to make, but in all cases we strived to select the best-balanced team to play in all types of conditions.
Which of these teams would you back? Do you agree with our selections? Should Alexander or Ames be the wicketkeeper for the 'A' team, and why did we leave Bardsley, Butcher, Blyth and Briggs out of the 'B' team? Which players would you choose? Let's have a look at the line-ups:

The 'A's: One of the strongest teams. The bowling has hostility and variety. The batting has depth, with all players through to Ames, the wicketkeeper at No. 7, having scored Test centuries.

The 'B's: A difficult team to beat. The batting has a perfect mix of stroke-players and defenders. The attack has variety and penetration, with Barlow and Border a bonus.

The 'C's: Another of the strong teams, with the batting going to No. 8. Once again, the attack has a hostile new-ball battery, with plenty of variety to back it up.

The 'D's: Another powerful batting line-up that goes down to No. 9; however, despite the inclusion of A.A. Donald, this combination may struggle to bowl some of the better teams out.

The 'E's: This side would struggle against some of the more powerful opposition, although the batting looks stronger than the bowling, and there are no problems with wicketkeeping or fielding.

The 'F's: Not in the silk department, but a more than useful outfit, just the same. Runs would be scored quickly, while the bowlers would be hard to keep out.

The 'G's: One of the favourites. An outstanding all-round team with a superbly balanced attack, top-quality batting and excellent wicketkeeping and fielding.

The 'H's: This outfit is almost unbeatable. Hanif will keep and bat at No. 7, and that thought would be enough to break any bowler's heart. The all-pace attack would be capable of breaking through the strongest batting line-up.

The 'I's: This is not likely to be one of the stronger teams, despite the useful inclusion of Inzamam-Ul-Haq of Pakistan. The spin attack could pose some problems while Imran would be required to carry the pace department.

The 'J's: Batting is the strength of this outfit with the Jacksons leading the way. The attack has variety, but Jones is the only bowler with real pace.

The 'K's: Other teams look classier than this one. It does, however, bat right down the order, with Knott at No. 9 and Knight at No. 10 being century-makers. Kapil Dev would have to carry the attack.

The 'L's: This is a team to contend with, with its solid batsmen, dashing stroke-players such as

Brian Lara, and a lethal attack. There would not be many batsmen lining up to open the innings against the likes of bowlers such as Larwood, Lillee and Lindwall.

The 'M's: Another one of the favourites. The batting is all class and should score heavily. The bowling doesn't have the same quality as the batting, but it is still strong enough to bowl out the opposition.

The 'Mc's/Mac's: The Australian influence is to the fore in this team. The batting is sound and has flair while the pace attack is aggressive.

The 'N's: A team not likely to trouble the toughest teams; however, any side that is led by 'Monty' Noble should not be taken lightly.

The 'O's: This team would be down the table, but 'Tiger' O'Reilly would make sure the opposition earned each and every run.

The 'P's and 'Q's: One of the surprise packets. Not too may 'Q's have played Test cricket, but Qasim Omar deserves his place at No. 3 in this powerful line-up.

The 'R's: The strength of this team is the batting. Runs would be scored quickly and with elegance. Reid (who does his share of bowling) would be required to keep wickets here. Rhodes and Richardson were two of the finest bowlers ever to play for England.

The 'S's: Another of the strong teams, comprising a superb batting line-up and a pace quartet of the highest standard that could capture wickets under any conditions.

The 'T's: The batting may be a little thin, but the bowling is the opposite. Some of these champions would have to wait patiently to get a turn at the crease. Close-to-the-wicket catching would be another strength.

The 'U's and 'V's: A team that would struggle, but it should not be discounted entirely. What about the array of left-armers: Underwood, Valentine, and Verity would be hard to get away.

The 'W's: Another of the strong combinations. Walcott could bat anywhere from No. 1 to No. 7, but in this team he would have to be satisfied with the latter and with taking the gloves. Wasim Akram, Waqar Younis and Shane Warne provide the variety in a more than useful attack.

The 'X,Y,Z's: Not a particularly competitive team, but there weren't many players to select from.

The 'Left-Overs': Several quality 'left-over' sides could have been selected, but this one is a more than useful line-up.

And now for the teams — note that since the previous edition the selectors have made the following changes:

1 *to the 'D's:* A.A. Donald (South Africa) for G.R. Dilley (England)

2 *to the 'F's:* A. Flower (Zimbabwe) for G.M. Fullerton (South Africa)

3 *to the 'I's:* Inzamamul Haq (Pakistan) for D.J. Insole (England)

4 *to the 'K's:* G. Kirsten (South Africa), V.G. Kambli (India) and A.R. Kumble (India) for B.K. Kunderan (India), A.G. Kripal Singh (India) and L.F. Kline (Australia)

5 *to the 'L's:* B.C. Lara (West Indies) for A.J. Lamb (England)

6 *to the 'Mc,Mac's:* B.M. MacMillan (South Africa) for K.D. Mackay (Australia)

7 *to the 'W's:* S.R. Waugh (Australia), S.K. Warne (Australia) and Waqar Younis (Pakistan) for C. Washbrook (England), M.H.N. Walker (Australia) and J.H. Wardle (England)

THE TEAMS

A

1	D.L. Amiss	England
2	R. Abel	England
3	M. Amarnath	India
4	M. Azharuddin	India
5	Asif Iqbal	Pakistan
6	W.W. Armstrong	Australia (C)
7	L.E.G. Ames	England (WK)
8	Abdul Qadir	Pakistan
9	C.E.L. Ambrose	West Indies

10	N.A.T. Adcock	South Africa
11	T.M. Alderman	Australia

B

1	G. Boycott	England
2	E.J. Barlow	South Africa
3	D.G. Bradman	Australia (C)
4	K.F. Barrington	England
5	A.R. Border	Australia
6	I.T. Botham	England
7	R. Benaud	Australia
8	A.V. Bedser	England
9	J.McC. Blackham	Australia (WK)
10	B.S. Bedi	India
11	S.F. Barnes	England

C

1	M.C. Cowdrey	England
2	H.L. Collins	Australia
3	I.M. Chappell	Australia (C)
4	G.S. Chappell	Australia
5	D.C.S. Compton	England
6	M.D. Crowe	New Zealand
7	H.B. Cameron	South Africa (WK)
8	L.N. Constantine	West Indies
9	C.E.H. Croft	West Indies
10	A. Cotter	Australia
11	B.S. Chandrasekhar	India

D

1	R.A. Duff	Australia
2	C.S. Dempster	New Zealand
3	E.R. Dexter	England
4	J. Darling	Australia (C)
5	M.P. Donnelly	New Zealand
6	K.S. Duleepsinhji	England
7	P.J.L. Dujon	West Indies (WK)
8	B.L. D'Oliveira	England
9	A.K. Davidson	Australia
10	A.A. Donald	South Africa
11	D.R. Doshi	India

E

1	B.A. Edgar	New Zealand
2	F.M. Engineer	India
3	J.H. Edrich	England (C)
4	W.J. Edrich	England
5	W.R. Endean	South Africa
6	R. Edwards	Australia
7	T.G. Evans	England (WK)
8	J.E. Emburey	England
9	P.H. Edmonds	England
10	R.M. Ellison	England
11	Ehtesham-ud-din	Pakistan

F

1	R.C. Fredericks	West Indies
2	J.H.W. Fingleton	Australia
3	C.B. Fry	England (C)
4	R.E. Foster	England
5	K.W.R. Fletcher	England
6	A.G. Fairfax	Australia
7	G.A. Faulkner	South Africa
8	A. Flower	South Africa (WK)
9	Fazal Mahmood	Pakistan
10	J.J. Ferris	England/Australia
11	A.P. Freeman	England

G

1	S.M. Gavaskar	India
2	C.G. Greenidge	West Indies
3	W.G. Grace	England (C)
4	D.I. Gower	England
5	T.L. Goddard	South Africa
6	J.M. Gregory	Australia
7	G. Giffen	Australia
8	A.W.T. Grout	Australia (WK)
9	J. Garner	West Indies
10	L.R. Gibbs	West Indies
11	C.V. Grimmett	Australia

H

1	J.B. Hobbs	England
2	L. Hutton	England (C)
3	R.N. Harvey	Australia
4	W.R. Hammond	England
5	G.A. Headley	West Indies
6	C. Hill	Australia
7	Hanif Mohammed	Pakistan (WK)
8	R.J. Hadlee	New Zealand
9	M.A. Holding	West Indies
10	T.H. Hirst	England
11	W.W. Hall	West Indies

I

1	F.A. Iredale	Australia
2	Imtiaz Ahmed	Pakistan (WK)
3	B.L. Irvine	South Africa
4	Ijaz Ahmed	Pakistan
5	Inzamamul Haq	Pakistan
6	Imran Khan	Pakistan
7	R. Illingworth	England (C)
8	Intikhab Alam	Pakistan
9	Iqbal Qasim	Pakistan
10	J.B. Iverson	Australia
11	H. Ironmonger	Australia

J

1	A. Jackson	Australia
2	T.W. Jarvis	New Zealand
3	D.R. Jardine	England (C)
4	Javed Miandad	Pakistan
5	D.M. Jones	Australia
6	Hon. F.S. Jackson	England
7	G.L. Jessop	England
8	I.W. Johnson	Australia
9	B.N. Jarman	Australia (WK)
10	E. Jones	Australia
11	W.A. Johnston	Australia

K

1	G. Kirsten	South Africa
2	D.S.B.P. Kuruppu	Sri Lanka
3	R.R. Kanhai	West Indies
4	A.I. Kallicharran	West Indies
5	A.F. Kippax	Australia
6	V.G. Kambli	India
7	Kapil Dev	India (C)
8	C. Kelleway	Australia
9	A.P.E. Knott	England (WK)
10	B.R. Knight	England
11	A.R. Kumble	India

L

1	W.M. Lawry	Australia
2	B.W. Luckhurst	England
3	B.C. Lara	West Indies
4	M. Leyland	England
5	C.H. Lloyd	West Indies (C)
6	D.T. Lindsay	South Africa (WK)
7	R.R. Lindwall	Australia
8	H. Larwood	England
9	D.K. Lillee	Australia
10	G.A. Lohmann	England
11	J.C. Laker	England

Mc & Mac

1	C.C. McDonald	Australia
2	D.J. McGlew	South Africa
3	C.G. Macartney	Australia
4	S.J. McCabe	Australia
5	A.C. MacLaren	England (C)
6	K.D. Mackay	Australia
7	C.L. McCool	Australia
8	J.A. Maclean	Australia (WK)
9	C.J. McDermott	Australia
10	G.D. McKenzie	Australia
11	E.A. McDonald	Australia

M

1	A.R. Morris	Australia
2	W.L. Murdoch	Australia
3	B. Mitchell	South Africa
4	P.B.H. May	England (C)
5	C.P. Mead	England
6	Mushtaq Mohammad	Pakistan
7	K.R. Miller	Australia
8	M.H. Mankad	India
9	R.W. Marsh	Australia (WK)
10	M.D. Marshall	West Indies
11	A.A. Mailey	Australia

N

1	Nazar Mohammad	Pakistan
2	A.W. Nourse	South Africa
3	A.D. Nourse	South Africa
4	S.M. Nurse	West Indies
5	M.A. Noble	Australia (C)
6	R.G. Nadkarni	India
7	Nasim Ul-Ghani	Pakistan
8	M.S. Nichols	England
9	R.K. Nunes	West Indies (WK)
10	E.P. Nupen	South Africa
11	J.M. Noreiga	West Indies

O

1	L.P.J. O'Brien	Australia
2	H.G. Owen-Smith	South Africa (C)
3	N.C. O'Neill	Australia
4	N. Oldfield	England
5	S. O'Linn	South Africa
6	J. O'Connor	England
7	C.M. Old	England
8	K.J. O'Keeffe	Australia
9	W.A.S. Oldfield	Australia (WK)
10	J.D.A. O'Connor	Australia
11	W.J. O'Reilly	Australia

P&Q

1	W.H. Ponsford	Australia
2	G. Pullar	England
3	Qasim Omar	Pakistan
4	R.G. Pollock	South Africa
5	Pataudi, Nawab of Jnr.	India (C)
6	E. Paynter	England
7	J.M. Parks	England (WK)
8	M.J. Procter	South Africa
9	P.M. Pollock	South Africa
10	R. Peel	England
11	E.A.S. Prasanna	India

R

1	B.A. Richards	South Africa
2	I.R. Redpath	Australia
3	R.B. Richardson	West Indies
4	I.V.A. Richards	West Indies (C)
5	K.S. Ranjitsinhji	England
6	C.A.G. Russell	England
7	J.R. Reid	NewZealand (WK)
8	W. Rhodes	England
9	A.M.E. Roberts	West Indies
10	T. Richardson	England
11	S. Ramadhin	West Indies

S

1	H. Sutcliffe	England
2	R.B. Simpson	Australia
3	B. Sutcliffe	New Zealand
4	A. Shrewsbury	England (C)
5	G.S. Sobers	West Indies
6	Salim Malik	Pakistan
7	P.W. Sherwell	South Africa (WK)
8	J.A. Snow	England
9	Sarfraz Nawaz	Pakistan
10	J.B. Statham	England
11	F.R. Spofforth	South Africa (C)

T

1	G.M. Turner	New Zealand
2	M.A. Taylor	Australia
3	V.T. Trumper	Australia
4	H.W. Taylor	South Africa (C)
5	S.R. Tendulkar	India
6	M.W. Tate	England
7	D. Tallon	Australia (WK)
8	H. Trumble	Australia
9	H.J. Tayfield	South Africa
10	F.S. Trueman	England
11	C.T.B. Turner	Australia

U & V

1	P.G.V. Van Der Bijl	South Africa
2	H.G. Vivian	New Zealand
3	D.B. Vengsarkar	India
4	G.R. Vishwanath	India
5	K.G. Vilijoen	South Africa (WK)
6	P.R. Umrigar	India (C)
7	G. Ulyett	England
8	W. Voce	England
9	H. Verity	England
10	D.L. Underwood	England
11	A.L. Valentine	West Indies

W

1	W.M. Woodfull	Australia
2	F.M.M. Worrell	West Indies (C)
3	E.D. Weekes	West Indies
4	F.E. Woolley	England
5	S.R. Waugh	Australia
6	K.D. Walters	Australia
7	C.L. Walcott	West Indies (WK)
8	Wasim Akram	Pakistan
9	S.K. Warne	Australia
10	Waqar Younis	Pakistan
11	R.G.D. Willis	England

X,Y & Z

1	J.W. Zulch	South Africa
2	Yashpal Sharma	India
3	Zaheer Abbas	Pakistan
4	G.N. Yallop	Australia
5	Younis Ahmed	Pakistan
6	N.W.D. Yardley	England (C)
7	T.J. Zoehrer	Australia (WK)
8	B. Yardley	Australia
9	N.S. Yadav	India
10	Zulfiqar Ahmed	Pakistan
11	H.I. Young	England

THE LEFT OVERS

1	G.A. Gooch	England
2	C.C. Hunte	West Indies
3	W. Bardsley	Australia
4	V.S. Hazare	India
5	E.H. Hendren	England
6	A.L. Hassett	Australia (C)
7	A.W. Greig	England
8	Wasim Bari	Pakistan (WK)
9	J.R. Thomson	Australia
10	F.H. Tyson	England
11	G.A.R. Lock	England

A TEAM OF PLAYERS WHO APPEARED IN ONLY ONE TEST

* Figures represent each player's Test match figures

		BATTING		BOWLING	
		1st	**2nd**	**1st**	**2nd**
1	A.G. Ganteaume (WI)	112	-	-	-
2	R.E. Redmond (NZ)	107	56	-	-
3	V.H. Stollmeyer (WI)	96	-	-	-
4	N. Oldfield (E)	80	19	-	-
5	Patiala, Yuvaraj (I) Captain	24	60	-	-
6	Azmat Rana (P)	49	-	-	-
7	G.B. Street (E)	4	7*	1 stumping	
8	M.F. Malone (A)	46	-	5-63	1-14
9	L.J. Johnson (A)	25*	-	3-66	3-8
10	G.A. Chevalier (SA)	0	0*	3-68	2-32
11	C.S. Marriott (E)	0	-	5-37	6-59

A TEAM OF PLAYERS WHO APPEARED IN ONLY TWO TESTS

* Figures represent each player's career figures

	RUNS	H.S.	BATTING AVE.	WKTS	BOWLING AVE.
1 S.K. Coen (SA)	101	41*	50.50	-	-
2 R.J. Hartigan (A)	170	116	42.50	-	-
3 K.H. Weekes (WI)	173	137	57.66	-	-
4 R.G. Gregory (A) Captain	153	80	51.00	-	-
5 C. Ramaswami (I)	10	60	56.66	-	-
6 R.E. Grieveson (SA)	114	75	57.00	-	-
7 I.L. Mendonca (WI) WK	81	78	40.50	8 catches, 2 stumpings	
8 H.I. Young (E)	43	43	21.50	12	21.83
9 H.J. Butler (E)	15	15*	15.00	12	17.91
10 T.K. Kendall (A)	39	17*	13.00	14	15.35
11 F. Martin (E)	14	13	7.00	14	10.07

SOME TEST CRICKETERS WHO PLAYED OTHER SPORTS AT INTERNATIONAL LEVEL

B.C. Booth (Australia) Hockey
(1956 Olympics)
B. Dooland (Australia) Baseball
V.Y. Richardson (Australia) Baseball
C.B. Fry (England)
Athletics
(Fry held the world long jump record for 21 years)
D.C. Cleverley (New Zealand) Boxing
J.W.H.T. Douglas (England) Boxing
(Douglas won the gold medal in the middleweight boxing division in the 1908 London Olympics, and also represented England in amateur soccer)
R.C. Grant (West Indies) Boxing
(Heavyweight Champion)
M.L.C. Foster (West Indies) Table tennis
(Jamaican Champion)
E.M. Grace (England) Triple jump
(world record 1866)
P.A. Horne (New Zealand) Badminton
(Commonwealth Games)
E.L. Dalton (South Africa) Golf
(South African Amateur Champion 1950)
Farooq Hamid (Pakistan) Athletics
(Olympic level)
P.W. Sherwell (South Africa) Tennis
(Champion 1904)
K. Thomson (New Zealand) Hockey
E.G. McLeod (New Zealand) Hockey
Nawab of Pataudi, Snr (India) Hockey
J.N Rhodes (South Africa) Hockey
M.J. Gopalan (India) Hockey
W.R. Endean (South Africa) Hockey
D.L. Houghton (Zimbabwe) Hockey
C. Ramaswami (India) Hockey

SOME OF CRICKET'S DOUBLE INTERNATIONALS

E = England A = Australia
SA = South Africa NZ = New Zealand
W = Wales WI = West Indies
Sc = Scotland An = Antigua

	Cricket	Rugby	Soccer
A.N. Hornby	E	E	-
S.M.J. Woods	A/E	E	-
G. McGregor	E	Sc	-
A.E. Stoddard	E	E	-
C.B. Fry	E	-	E
(Missed at rugby due to injury)			
F. Mitchell	E/SA	E	-
L.B. Fishlock	E	-	E
J.H. Sinclair	SA	SA/E	E
R.O. Schwarz	SA	E	-
L.H. Gay	E	-	E
R.H. Spooner	E	E	-
R.E. Foster	E	-	E
(Only man to captain England at cricket and soccer)			
A. Ducat	E	-	E
H.T.W. Hardinge	E	-	E
J.W.H. Makepeace	E	-	E
K.W. Hough	NZ	-	NZ/A
A.E. Knight	E	-	E
M.J. Turnbull	E	W	-
(Also played hockey for Wales)			
J.Arnold	E	-	E
W. Gunn	E	-	E
G.C. White	SA	-	SA
J. Sharp	E	-	E
R.S. Grant	WI	-	E
J.M.M. Commaille	SA	-	SA
M.K. Elgie	SA	Sc	-
S. O'Linn	SA	-	SA
C.A. Smith	E	-	E
Hon. A. Lyttelton	E	-	E
G.F. Vernon	E	E	-
H.G. Owen-Smith	SA	E	-
D.C.S. Compton	E	-	E
J.H. Anderson	SA	SA	-
G.R.P. Dickinson	NZ	NZ	-
M.P. Donnelly	NZ	E	-
T.A. Harris	SA	SA	-
R.H.M. Hands	SA	E	-
P.S.T. Jones	SA	SA	-
W. Watson	E	-	E
W.H. Milton	SA	E	-
C.A. Milton	E	-	E
O.E. Nothling	A	A	-
M.L. Page	NZ	NZ	-
A.W. Powell	SA	SA	-
A. Richards	SA	SA	-
M.J.K. Smith	E	E	-
E.W.T. Tindill*	NZ	NZ	-
C.B. Van Ryneveld	SA	E	-
F.C.M. Alexander	WI	-	E
(Amateur International)			
I.V.A. Richards	WI	-	An
R.B. Richardson	WI	-	An

TEST CRICKETERS WHO WON F.A. CUP WINNERS' MEDALS

E.G. Wynyard — with Old Carthusians 1880-81
J. Sharp — with Everton 1905-06
H. Makepeace — with Everton 1905-06
A. Ducat — with Aston Villa 1919-20
D.C.S. Compton — with Arsenal 1949-50
Other Test cricketers who were well-known soccer players in England include:
I.T. Botham (Scunthorpe United)
D.B. Close (Leeds United, Bradford City, Arsenal)
J. Dewes (Middleborough, Plymouth Argyle, Walsall)
S. O'Linn (Charlton Athletic)
C.J. Poole (Gillingham, Mansfield Town)
D.R. Smith (Bristol City, Millwall)
F. Sugg (Sheffield Wednesday, Derby County, Burnley)
K. Taylor (Huddersfield Town, Bradford P.A.)
F.J. Titmus (Watford)
A.J. Watkins (Plymouth Argyle, Cardiff City)
E.G. Wynyard (Old Carthusians)
D.L. Bairstow (Bradford City)
R.W.V. Robins (Nottingham Forest)
M. Sherwin (Notts County)
M.J. Stewart (Charlton Athletic)
L.E.G. Ames (Clapton Orient, Gillingham)
J.C. Balderstone (Huddersfield Town, Carlisle United, Doncaster Rovers)
H.E. Dollery (Reading)
W.J. Edrich (Tottenham Hotspurs)
J.A. Flavell (Walsall)
W. Gunn (Notts County)
W.R. Hammond (Bristol Rovers)
J. Hardstaff Snr. (Nottingham Forest)
E.H. Hendren (Manchester City, Brentford)
H. Howell (Wolverhampton Wanderers, Accrington Stanley)
W.W. Keeton (Sunderland, Nottingham Forest)
J.W. Sharpe (Notts County)
A. Sidebottom (Manchester United, Huddersfield Town, Halifax)
W. Storer (Derby County)
A. Waddington (Halifax Town)
F. Barratt (Aston Villa, Sheffield Wednesday)

* also a Test umpire and international rugby referee

PART 3
TEST MATCH RESULTS & RECORDS

Summary of Tests

SUMMARY OF ALL TEST MATCHES 1876-77 TO 1996

	Opponent	Tests	won by A	E	SA	WI	NZ	I	P	SL	Z	Tied	Draw
Australia	v England	285	111	90	-	-	-	-	-	-	-	-	81
	v South Africa	59	31	-	13	-	-	-	-	-	-	-	15
	v West Indies	81	32	-	-	27	-	-	-	-	-	1	21
	v New Zealand	32	13	-	-	-	7	-	-	-	-	-	12
	v India	50	24	-	-	-	-	8	-	-	-	1	17
	v Pakistan	40	14	-	-	-	-	-	11	-	-	-	15
	v Sri Lanka	10	7	-	-	-	-	-	-	0	-	-	3
	v Zimbabwe	0	-	-	-	-	-	-	-	-	-	-	0
England	v South Africa	110	-	47	20	-	-	-	-	-	-	-	43
	v West Indies	115	-	27	-	48	-	-	-	-	-	-	40
	v New Zealand	75	-	34	-	-	4	-	-	-	-	-	37
	v India	84	-	32	-	-	-	14	-	-	-	-	38
	v Pakistan	55	-	14	-	-	-	-	9	-	-	-	32
	v Sri Lanka	5	-	3	-	-	-	-	-	1	-	-	1
	v Zimbabwe	0	-	-	-	-	-	-	-	-	-	-	0
South Africa	v New Zealand	21	-	-	12	-	3	-	-	-	-	-	6
	v West Indies	1	-	-	0	1	-	-	-	-	-	-	0
	v India	4	-	-	1	-	-	0	-	-	-	-	3
	v Sri Lanka	3	-	-	1	-	-	-	-	0	-	-	2
	v Pakistan	1	-	-	1	-	-	-	0	-	-	-	0
	v Zimbabwe	1	-	-	1	-	-	-	-	-	0	-	0
West Indies	v New Zealand	28	-	-	-	10	4	-	-	-	-	-	14
	v India	65	-	-	-	27	-	7	-	-	-	-	31
	v Pakistan	31	-	-	-	12	-	-	7	-	-	-	12
	v Sri Lanka	1	-	-	-	0	-	-	-	0	-	-	1
	v Zimbabwe	0	-	-	-	-	-	-	-	-	-	-	0
New Zealand	v India	35	-	-	-	-	6	13	-	-	-	-	16
	v Pakistan	37	-	-	-	-	4	-	17	-	-	-	16
	v Sri Lanka	13	-	-	-	-	4	-	-	2	-	-	7
	v Zimbabwe	4	-	-	-	-	1	-	-	-	0	-	3
India	v Pakistan	44	-	-	-	-	-	4	7	-	-	-	33
	v Sri Lanka	14	-	-	-	-	-	7	-	1	-	-	6
	v Zimbabwe	2	-	-	-	-	-	1	-	-	0	-	1
Pakistan	v Sri Lanka	17	-	-	-	-	-	-	9	3	-	-	5
	v Zimbabwe	6	-	-	-	-	-	-	4	-	1	-	1
Sri Lanka	v Zimbabwe	3	-	-	-	-	-	-	-	-	-	-	3
		1332	232	247	49	125	33	54	64	7	1	2	518

	Tests	**Won**	**Lost**	**Drawn**	**Tied**	**Toss Won**
Australia	557	232	156	167	2	276
England	729	247	207	275	-	359
South Africa	200	49	82	69	-	96
West Indies	322	125	77	119	1	169
New Zealand	245	33	101	111	-	125
India	298	54	98	145	1	150
Pakistan	231	64	53	114	-	115
Sri Lanka	66	7	31	28	-	34
Zimbabwe	16	1	7	8	-	8
	1332	812	812	1036	4	1332

The Grounds

TEST MATCH GROUNDS

The Test played at Centurion Park, Pretoria has lifted the number of Test match grounds to 76. Colombo has now used four grounds, Johannesburg and Mumbai three apiece, whilst Brisbane, Bulawayo, Durban, Karachi, Lahore, Lucknow, Chennai and Peshawar have each played Test matches on two different grounds. For these eleven cities the exact ground is denoted by a superscript numeral (e.g. Brisbane[1]) except for Colombo, where the ground is shown in brackets. This key to this numeral is given in the tables below. The tables show the full title, date of the first day's play and number of Tests staged for each ground.

Test Match Centres	Grounds	First Test Match Day	No.of Tests
AUSTRALIA			(290)
Adelaide	Adelaide Oval	12 Dec 1884	54
Brisbane	[1]Exhibition Ground (1928-29 to 1930-31)	30 Nov 1928	2
	[2]Woolloongabba	27 Nov 1931	38
Hobart	Bellerive Oval	16 Dec 1989	3
Melbourne	Melbourne Cricket Ground	15 Mar 1877	88
Perth	Western Australia Cricket Association (W.A.C.A.) Ground	11 Dec 1970	23
Sydney	Sydney Cricket Ground (No.1)	17 Feb 1882	82
ENGLAND			(368)
Birmingham	Edgbaston	29 May 1902	32
Leeds	Headingley	29 Jun 1899	57
Lord's, London	Lord's Cricket Ground	21 Jul 1884	94
Manchester	Old Trafford	†10 Jul 1884	62
Nottingham	Trent Bridge	1 Jun 1899	44
The Oval, London	Kennington Oval	6 Sep 1880	78
Sheffield	Bramall Lane	3 Jul 1902	1
SOUTH AFRICA			(114)
Cape Town	Newlands	25 Mar 1889	28
Durban	[1]Lord's (1909-10 to 1921-22)	21 Jan 1910	4
	[2]Kingsmead	18 Jan 1923	23
Johannesburg	[1]Old Wanderers (1895-96 to 1938-39)	2 Mar 1896	22
	[2]Ellis Park (1948-49 to 1953-54)	27 Dec 1948	6
	[3]Wanderers Stadium	24 Dec 1956	16
Port Elizabeth	St George's Park	12 Mar 1889	14
Pretoria	Centurion Park	16 Nov 1995	1
WEST INDIES			(140)
Bridgetown, Barbados	Kensington Oval	11 Jan 1930	32
Georgetown, Guyana	Bourda	21 Feb 1930	23
Kingston, Jamaica	Sabina Park	3 Apr 1930	31
Port-of-Spain, Trinidad	Queen's Park Oval	1 Feb 1930	44
St John's, Antigua	Recreation Ground	27 Mar 1981	10
NEW ZEALAND			(118)
Auckland	Eden Park	#14 Feb 1930	38
Christchurch	Lancaster Park	10 Jan 1930	34
Dunedin	Carisbrook	11 Mar 1955	9
Hamilton	Trust Bank Park	22 Feb 1991	4
Napier	McLean Park	16 Feb 1979	3
Wellington	Basin Reserve	24 Jan 1930	30

INDIA			(159)
Ahmedabad	Gujarat Stadium, Motora	12 Nov 1983	3
Bangalore	M.Chinnaswamy Stadium (Karnataka State Cricket Association Stadium)	22 Nov 1974	11
Calcutta	Eden Gardens	5 Jan 1934	27
Chandigarh	Sector 16 Stadium	23 Nov 1990	1
Chennai	[1]M.A.Chidambaram Stadium (Chepauk)	10 Feb 1934	22
(formerly Madras)	[2]Nehru (Corporation) Stadium (1955-56 to 1964-65)	6 Jan 1956	9
Cuttack	Barabati Stadium	4 Jan 1987	2
Delhi	Feroz Shah Kotla (Willingdon Pavillion)	10 Nov 1948	23
Hyderabad (Deccan)	Lal Bahadur Shastri Stadium (Fateh Maidan)	19 Nov 1955	3
Jaipur	Sawai Mansingh Stadium (Chogan Stadium)	21 Feb 1987	1
Jullundur	Burlton Park (B.S.Bedi Stadium)	24 Sep 1983	1
Kanpur	Green Park (Modi Stadium)	12 Jan 1952	16
Lucknow	[1]University Ground (1952-53 only)	23 Oct 1952	1
	[2]K.D.Singh Babu Stadium (Central Sports Stadium)	19 Jan 1994	1
Mohali	Punjab Cricket Association Stadium	10 Dec 1994	1
Mumbai	[1]Gymkhana (1933-34 Only)	15 Dec 1933	1
(formerly	[2]Brabourne Stadium (1948-49 to 1972-73)	9 Dec 1948	17
Bombay)	[3]Wankhede Stadium	23 Jan 1975	15
Nagpur	Vidarbha Cricket Association Ground	3 Oct 1969	4
PAKISTAN			(103)
Bahawalpur	Bahawal Stadium (Dring Stadium)	15 Jan 1955	1
Dacca	Dacca Stadium	1 Jan 1955	7
Faisalabad	Iqbal Stadium (Lyallpur Stadium)	16 Oct 1978	17
Gujranwala	Municipal Stadium	20 Dec 1991	1
Hyderabad (Sind)	Niaz Stadium	16 Mar 1973	5
Karachi	[1]National Stadium	26 Feb 1955	31
	[2]Defence Stadium	1 Dec 1993	1
Lahore	[1]Bagh-e-Jinnah (Lawrence Gardens) (1954-55 to 1958-59)	29 Jan 1955	3
	[2]Gaddafi Stadium (Lahore Stadium)	21 Nov 1959	27
Multan	Ibn-e-Qasim Bagh Stadium (Old Fort)	30 Dec 1980	1
Peshawar	[1]Services Club Ground (Peshawar Club Ground) (1954-55 only)	13 Feb 1955	1
	[2]Arbab Niaz Stadium	8 Sep 1995	1
Rawalpindi	[1]Army Sports Stadium (Pindi Club Ground) (1964-65 only)	27 Mar 1965	1
	[2]Pindi Cricket Stadium	9 Dec 1993	2
Sialkot	Jinnah (Park) Stadium	27 Oct 1985	4
SRI LANKA			(27)
Colombo	P.Saravanamuttu Stadium (PSS)	17 Feb 1982	6
	Sinhalese Sports Club Ground (SSC)	16 Mar 1984	7
	Colombo Cricket Club Ground (CCC)	24 Mar 1984	3
	Premadasa (Khettamara)International Stadium (PIS)	28 Aug 1992	1
Kandy	Asgiriya Stadium	22 Apr 1983	6
Moratuwa	Tyrone Fernando Stadium	8 Sep 1992	4
ZIMBABWE			(10)
Bulawayo	[1]Bulawayo Athletic Club Ground (1992-93 only)	1 Nov 1992	1
	[2]Queens Sports Oval	§18 Oct 1994	2
Harare	Harare (Salisbury) Sports Club Ground	18 Oct 1992	7

† Rain prevented play until 11 Jul 1884. # Rain prevented play until 17 Feb 1930. § Rain prevented play until 20 Oct 1994.
The 1890 and 1938 Tests at Manchester, the 1970-71 Third Test at Melbourne, the 1988-89 Test at Dunedin and the 1989-90 Test at Georgetown, all abandoned without a ball being bowled, plus the cancelled 1980-81 Second Test at Georgetown and 1994-95 Second Test at Kandy are excluded from these figures.

RECORD TOTALS FOR EACH TEST MATCH GROUND

AUSTRALIA

Centre		Highest Total			Lowest Total	
Adelaide	674	Australia v India	1947-48	82	Australia v West Indies	1951-52
Brisbane[1]	558	Australia v West Indies	1930-31	66	Australia v England	1928-29
Brisbane[2]	645	Australia v England	1946-47	58	Australia v England	1936-37
				58	India v Australia	1947-48
Hobart	544-6d	Australia v New Zealand	1993-94	161	New Zealand v Australia	1993-94
Melbourne	604	Australia v England	1936-37	36	South Africa v Australia	1931-32
Perth	617-5d	Australia v Sri Lanka	1995-96	62	Pakistan v Australia	1981-82
Sydney	659-8d	Australia v England	1946-47	42	Australia v England	1887-88

ENGLAND

Centre		Highest Total			Lowest Total	
Birmingham	633-5d	England v India	1979	30	South Africa v England	1924
Leeds	601-7d	Australia v England	1989	67	New Zealand v England	1958
Lord's	729-6d	Australia v England	1930	42	India v England	1974
Manchester	656-8d	Australia v England	1964	58	India v England	1952
Nottingham	658-8d	England v Australia	1938	88	South Africa v England	1960
The Oval	903-7d	England v Australia	1938	44	Australia v England	1896
Sheffield	289	Australia v England	1902	145	England v Australia	1902

SOUTH AFRICA

Centre		Highest Total			Lowest Total	
Cape Town	559-9d	England v South Africa	1938-39	35	South Africa v England	1898-99
Durban[1]	450	England v South Africa	1913-14	111	South Africa v England	1913-14
Durban[2]	654-5	England v South Africa	1938-39	75	Australia v South Africa	1949-50
Johannesburg[1]	482	England v South Africa	1895-96	85	South Africa v Australia	1902-03
Johannesburg[2]	608	England v South Africa	1948-49	79	New Zealand v South Africa	1953-54
Johannesburg[3]	620	South Africa v Australia	1966-67	72	South Africa v England	1956-57
Port Elizabeth	549-7d	Australia v South Africa	1949-50	30	South Africa v England	1895-96
Pretoria	381-9d	England v South Africa	1995-96		no instance	

WEST INDIES

Centre		Highest Total			Lowest Total	
Bridgetown	668	Australia v West Indies	1954-55	94	New Zealand v West Indies	1984-85
Georgetown	569	West Indies v Australia	1990-91	109	West Indies v Australia	1972-73
Kingston	849	England v West Indies	1929-30	97†	India v West Indies	1975-76
Port-of-Spain	681-8d	West Indies v England	1953-54	46	England v West Indies	1993-94
St John's	593-5d	West Indies v England	1993-94	154	England v West Indies	1989-90
	593	England v West Indies	1993-94			

NEW ZEALAND

Centre		Highest Total			Lowest Total	
Auckland	616-5d	Pakistan v New Zealand	1988-89	26	New Zealand v England	1954-55
Christchurch	560-8d	England v New Zealand	1932-33	65	New Zealand v England	1970-71
Dunedin	507-6d	Pakistan v New Zealand	1972-73	74	New Zealand v West Indies	1955-56
Hamilton	374-6d	New Zealand v Sri Lanka	1990-91	93	New Zealand v Pakistan	1992-93
Napier	402	New Zealand v Pakistan	1978-79	129	New Zealand v Sri Lanka	1994-95
Wellington	671-4	New Zealand v Sri Lanka	1990-91	42	New Zealand v Australia	1945-46

INDIA

Centre		Highest Total			Lowest Total	
Ahmedabad	395	Pakistan v India	1986-87	103	India v West Indies	1983-84
Bangalore	541-6d	India v Sri Lanka	1993-94	116	Pakistan v India	1986-87
Calcutta	614-5d	West Indies v India	1958-59	90	India v West Indies	1983-84
Chandigarh	288	India v Sri Lanka	1990-91	82	Sri Lanka v India	1990-91

Centre		Highest Total			Lowest Total	
Chennai[1]	652-7d	England v India	1984-85	83	India v England	1976-77
Chennai[2]	539-9d	India v Pakistan	1960-61	138	India v Australia	1959-60
Cuttack	400	India v Sri Lanka	1986-87	142	Sri Lanka v India	1986-87
Delhi	644-8d	West Indies v India	1958-59	75	India v West Indies	1987-88
Hyderabad	498-4d	India v New Zealand	1955-56	89	India v New Zealand	1969-70
Jaipur	465-8d	India v Pakistan	1986-87	341	Pakistan v India	1986-87
Jullundur	374	India v Pakistan	1983-84	337	Pakistan v India	1983-84
Kanpur	676-7	India v Sri Lanka	1986-87	105	Australia v India	1959-60
Lucknow[1]	331	Pakistan v India	1952-53	106	India v Pakistan	1952-53
Lucknow[2]	511	India v Sri Lanka	1993-94	174	Sri Lanka v India	1993-94
Mohali	443	West Indies v India	1994-95	114	India v West Indies	1994-95
Mumbai[1]	438	England v India	1933-34	219	India v England	1933-34
Mumbai[2]	629-6d	West Indies v India	1948-49	88	India v New Zealand	1964-65
Mumbai[3]	604-6d	West Indies v India	1974-75	102	England v India	1981-82
Nagpur	546-9d	India v Sri Lanka	1994-95	109	India v New Zealand	1969-70

PAKISTAN

Centre		Highest Total			Lowest Total	
Bahawalpur	312-9d	Pakistan v India	1954-55	235	India v Pakistan	1954-55
Dacca	439	England v Pakistan	1961-62	70	New Zealand v Pakistan	1955-56
Faisalabad	674-6	Pakistan v India	1984-85	53	West Indies v Pakistan	1986-87
Gujranwala	109-2	Pakistan v Sri Lanka	1991-92		no instance	
Hyderabad	581-3d	Pakistan v India	1982-83	189	India v Pakistan	1982-83
				189	New Zealand v Pakistan	1984-85
Karachi[1]	565-9d	Pakistan v New Zealand	1976-77	80	Australia v Pakistan	1956-57
Karachi[2]	423	Pakistan v Zimbabwe	1993-94	134	Zimbabwe v Pakistan	1993-94
Lahore[1]	561	Pakistan v New Zealand	1955-56	104	Pakistan v West Indies	1958-59
Lahore[2]	699-5	Pakistan v India	1989-90	77	Pakistan v West Indies	1986-87
Multan	249	West Indies v Pakistan	1980-81	166	Pakistan v West Indies	1980-81
Peshawar[1]	245	India v Pakistan	1954-55	182	Pakistan v India	1954-55
Peshawar[2]	459-9d	Pakistan v Sri Lanka	1995-96	186	Sri Lanka v Pakistan	1995-96
Rawalpindi[1]	318	Pakistan v New Zealand	1964-65	79	New Zealand v Pakistan	1964-65
Rawalpindi[2]	537	Pakistan v Australia	1994-95	187	Zimbabwe v Pakistan	1993-94
Sialkot	423-5d	Pakistan v Sri Lanka	1991-92	157	Sri Lanka v Pakistan	1985-86

SRI LANKA

Centre		Highest Total			Lowest Total	
Colombo (PSS)	446	India v Sri Lanka	1993-94	175	Sri Lanka v England	1981-82
Colombo (SSC)	547-8d	Sri Lanka v Australia	1992-93	102	New Zealand v Sri Lanka	1992-93
Colombo (CCC)	459	New Zealand v Sri Lanka	1983-84	132	Pakistan v Sri Lanka	1985-86
Colombo (PIS)	296-6d	Australia v Sri Lanka	1992-93	247	Australia v Sri Lanka	1992-93
Kandy	514-4d	Australia v Sri Lanka	1982-83	71	Sri Lanka v Pakistan	1994-95
Moratuwa	337	Australia v Sri Lanka	1992-93	190	Sri Lanka v West Indies	1993-94

ZIMBABWE

Centre		Highest Total			Lowest Total	
Bulawayo[1]	325-3d	New Zealand v Zimbabwe	1992-93	219	Zimbabwe v New Zealand	1992-93
Bulawayo[2]	462-9d	Zimbabwe v Sri Lanka	1994-95	146	Zimbabwe v Pakistan	1994-95
Harare	544-4d	Zimbabwe v Pakistan	1994-95	137	Zimbabwe v New Zealand	1992-93

†Five men were absent hurt. The second lowest total at Kingston is 103 by England in 1934-35.

HIGHEST INDIVIDUAL SCORE FOR EACH TEST MATCH GROUND

Ground	Score	Player	Match	Season
AUSTRALIA				
Adelaide	299*	D.G.Bradman	Australia v South Africa	1931-32
Brisbane[1]	223	D.G.Bradman	Australia v West Indies	1930-31
Brisbane[2]	226	D.G.Bradman	Australia v South Africa	1931-32
Hobart	168	M.J.Slater	Australia v New Zealand	1993-94
Melbourne	307	R.M.Cowper	Australia v England	1965-66
Perth	219	M.J.Slater	Australia v Sri Lanka	1995-96
Sydney	287	R.E.Foster	England v Australia	1903-04
ENGLAND				
Birmingham	285*	P.B.H.May	England v West Indies	1957
Leeds	334	D.G.Bradman	Australia v England	1930
Lord's	333	G.A.Gooch	England v India	1990
Manchester	311	R.B.Simpson	Australia v England	1964
Nottingham	278	D.C.S.Compton	England v Pakistan	1954
The Oval	364	L.Hutton	England v Australia	1938
Sheffield	119	C.Hill	Australia v England	1902
SOUTH AFRICA				
Cape Town	209	R.G.Pollock	South Africa v Australia	1966-67
Durban[1]	119	J.W.H.T.Douglas	England v South Africa	1913-14
Durban[2]	274	R.G.Pollock	South Africa v Australia	1969-70
Johannesburg[1]	231	A.D.Nourse	South Africa v Australia	1935-36
Johannesburg[2]	195	C.Washbrook	England v South Africa	1948-49
Johannesburg[3]	185*	M.A.Atherton	England v South Africa	1995-96
Port Elizabeth	167	A.L.Hassett	Australia v South Africa	1949-50
Pretoria	141	G.A.Hick	England v South Africa	1995-96
WEST INDIES				
Bridgetown	337	Hanif Mohammad	Pakistan v West Indies	1957-58
Georgetown	259	G.M.Turner	New Zealand v West Indies	1971-72
Kingston	365*	G.S.Sobers	West Indies v Pakistan	1957-58
Port-of-Spain	220	S.M.Gavaskar	India v West Indies	1970-71
St John's	375	B.C.Lara	West indies v England	1993-94
NEW ZEALAND				
Auckland	336*	W.R.Hammond	England v New Zealand	1932-33
Christchurch	258	S.M.Nurse	West Indies v New Zealand	1968-69
Dunedin	201	Mushtaq Mohammad	Pakistan v New Zealand	1972-73
Hamilton	133	M.J.Greatbatch	New Zealand v Pakistan	1992-93
Napier	119*	Majid Khan	Pakistan v New Zealand	1978-79
Wellington	299	M.D.Crowe	New Zealand v Sri Lanka	1990-91
INDIA				
Ahmedabad	152	M.Azharuddin	India v Sri Lanka	1993-94
Bangalore	172	S.M.Gavaskar	India v England	1981-82
Calcutta	256	R.B.Kanhai	West Indies v India	1958-59
Chandigarh	88	R.J.Shastri	India v Sri Lanka	1990-91
Chennai[1]	236*	S.M.Gavaskar	India v West Indies	1983-84
Chennai[2]	231	M.H.Mankad	India v New Zealand	1955-56
Cuttack	166	D.B.Vengsarkar	India v Sri Lanka	1986-87
Delhi	230*	B.Sutcliffe	New Zealand v India	1955-56
Hyderabad	223	P.R.Umrigar	India v New Zealand	1955-56
Jaipur	125	R.J.Shastri	India v Pakistan	1986-87
Jullundur	201	A.D.Gaekwad	India v Pakistan	1983-84
Kanpur	250	S.F.A.F.Bacchus	West Indies v India	1978-79
Lucknow[1]	124*	Nazar Mohammad	Pakistan v India	1952-53
Lucknow[2]	142	S.R.Tendulkar	India v Sri Lanka	1993-94

Mohali	174*	J.C.Adams	West Indies v India	1994-95
Mumbai[1]	136	B.H.Valentine	England v India	1933-34
Mumbai[2]	223	M.H.Mankad	India v New Zealand	1955-56
Mumbai[3]	242*	C.H.Lloyd	West Indies v India	1974-75
Nagpur	179	S.R.Tendulkar	India v West Indies	1994-95
PAKISTAN				
Bahawalpur	142	Hanif Mohammad	Pakistan v India	1954-55
Dacca	165	G.Pullar	England v Pakistan	1961-62
Faisalabad	235	G.S.Chappell	Australia v Pakistan	1979-80
Gujranwala	51*	Rameez Raja	Pakistan v Sri Lanka	1991-92
Hyderabad	280*	Javed Miandad	Pakistan v India	1982-83
Karachi[1]	211	Javed Miandad	Pakistan v Australia	1988-89
Karachi[2]	81	Shoaib Mohammad	Pakistan v Zimbabwe	1993-94
Lahore[1]	217	R.B.Kanhai	Pakistan v India	1978-79
Lahore[2]	235*	Zaheer Abbas	Pakistan v India	1978-79
Multan	120*	I.V.A.Richards	West Indies v Pakistan	1980-81
Peshawar[1]	108	P.R.Umrigar	India v Pakistan	1954-55
Peshawar[2]	95	Inzamamul Haq	Pakistan v Sri Lanka	1995-96
Rawalpindi[1]	76	B.R.Taylor	New Zealand v Pakistan	1964-65
Rawalpindi[2]	237	Saleem Malik	Pakistan v Australia	1994-95
Sialkot	117*	Moin Khan	Pakistan v Sri Lanka	1995-96
SRI LANKA				
Colombo (PSS)	151	R.S.Mahanama	Sri Lanka v India	1993-94
Colombo (SSC)	137	A.P.Gurusinha	Sri Lanka v Australia	1992-93
Colombo (CCC)	201*	D.S.B.P.Kuruppu	Sri Lanka v New Zealand	1986-87
Colombo (PIS)	100*	D.M.Jones	Australia v Sri Lanka	1992-93
Kandy	143*	D.W.Hookes	Australia v Sri Lanka	1982-83
Moratuwa	153	R.S.Mahanama	Sri Lanka v New Zealand	1992-93
ZIMBABWE				
Bulawayo[1]	119	R.T.Latham	New Zealand v Zimbabwe	1992-93
Bulawayo[2]	266	D.L.Houghton	Zimbabwe v Sri Lanka	1994-95
Harare	201*	G.W.Flower	Zimbabwe v Pakistan	1994-95

HIGHEST WICKET PARTNERSHIPS FOR EACH TEST GROUND

	Runs	Wkt			
AUSTRALIA					
Adelaide	341	3rd	E.J.Barlow, R.G.Pollock	South Africa v Australia	1963-64
Brisbane[1]	229	2nd	W.H.Ponsford D.G.Bradman	Australia v West Indies	1930-31
Brisbane[2]	276	3rd	D.G.Bradman, A.L.Hassett	Australia v England	1946-47
Hobart	260*	6th	D.M.Jones, S.R.Waugh	Australia v Sri Lanka	1989-90
Melbourne	346	6th	J.H.W.Fingleton, D.G.Bradman	Australia v England	1936-37
Perth	259	2nd	W.B.Phillips, G.N.Yallop	Australia v Pakistan	1983-84
Sydney	405	5th	S.G.Barnes, D.G.Bradman	Australia v England	1946-47
ENGLAND					
Birmingham	411	4th	P.B.H.May, M.C.Cowdrey	England v West Indies	1957
Leeds	388	4th	W.H.Ponsford, D.G.Bradman	Australia v England	1934
Lord's	370	3rd	W.J.Edrich, D.C.S.Compton	England v South Africa	1947
Manchester	246	3rd	E.R.Dexter, K.F.Barrington	England v Australia	1964
Nottingham	329	1st	G.R.Marsh, M.A.Taylor	Australia v England	1989
The Oval	451	2nd	W.H.Ponsford, D.G.Bradman	Australia v England	1934
Sheffield	107	4th	C.Hill, S.E.Gregory	Australia v England	1902

SOUTH AFRICA

Cape Town	260	1st	B.Mitchell, I.J.Siedle	South Africa v England	1930-31
Durban[1]	143	4th	G.C.White, A.W.Nourse	South Africa v England	1909-10
Durban[2]	280	2nd	P.A.Gibb, W.J.Edrich	England v South Africa	1938-39
Johannesburg[1]	230	2nd	H.Sutcliffe, G.E.Tyldesley	England v South Africa	1927-28
Johannesburg[2]	359	1st	L.Hutton, C.Washbrook	England v South Africa	1948-49
Johannesburg[3]	221	7th	D.T.Lindsay, P.L.van der Merwe	South Africa v Australia	1966-67
Port Elizabeth	187	3rd	A.R.Morris, R.N.Harvey	Australia v South Africa	1949-50
Pretoria	142	4th	M.A.Atherton, G.A.Hick	England v South Africa	1995-96

WEST INDIES

Bridgetown	399	4th	G.S.Sobers.F.M.M.Worrell	West Indies v England	1959-60
Georgetown	387	1st	G.M.Turner, T.W.Jarvis	New Zealand v West Indies	1971-72
Kingston	446	2nd	C.C.Hunte, G.S.Sobers	West Indies v Pakistan	1957-58
Port-of-Spain	338	3rd	E.D.Weekes, F.M.M.Worrell	West Indies v England	1953-54
St John's	308	3rd	R.B.Richardson, I.V.A.Richards	West Indies v Australia	1983-84

NEW ZEALAND

Auckland	266	4th	M.H.Denness, K.W.R.Fletcher	England v New Zealand	1974-75
Christchurch	242	5th	W.R.Hammond, L.E.G.Ames	England v New Zealand	1932-33
Dunedin	350	4th	Mushtaq Mohammad, Asif Iqbal	Pakistan v New Zealand	1972-73
Hamilton	161	1st	T.J.Franklin, J.G.Wright	New Zealand v Sri Lanka	1990-91
Napier	195	2nd	J.G.Wright, G.P.Howarth	New Zealand v Pakistan	1978-79
Wellington	467	3rd	M.D.Crowe, A.H.Jones	New Zealand v Sri Lanka	1990-91

INDIA

Ahmedabad	154	7th	Imran Khan, Ijaz Faqih	Pakistan v India	1986-87
Bangalore	207	4th	C.G.Greenidge, C.H.Lloyd	West Indies v India	1974-75
Calcutta	344*	2nd	S.M.Gavaskar, D.B.Vengsarkar	India v West Indies	1978-79
Chandigarh	76	2nd	R.J.Shastri, S.V.Manjrekar	India v Sri Lanka	1990-91
Chennai[1]	316	3rd	G.R.Viswanath, Yashpal Sharma	India v England	1981-82
Chennai[2]	413	1st	M.H.Mankad, P.Roy	India v New Zealand	1955-56
Cuttack	111	6th	D.B.Vengsarkar, Kapil Dev	India v Sri Lanka	1986-87
Delhi	267	4th	C.L.Walcott, G.E.Gomez	West Indies v India	1948-49
Hyderabad	238	3rd	P.R.Umrigar, V.L.Manjrekar	India v New Zealand	1955-56
Jaipur	130	5th	M.Azharuddin, R.J.Shastri	India v Pakistan	1986-87
Jullundur	121	6th	A.D.Gaekwad, R.M.H.Binny	India v Pakistan	1983-84
Kanpur	272	6th	M.Azharuddin, Kapil Dev	India v Sri Lanka	1986-87
Lucknow[1]	63	8th	Nazar Mohammad, Zulfiqar Ahmed	Pakistan v India	1952-53
Lucknow[2]	142	4th	S.R.Tendulkar, M.Azharuddin	India v Sri Lanka	1993-94
Mohali	145*	4th	J.C.Adams, K.L.T.Arthurton	West Indies v India	1994-95
Mumbai[1]	186	3rd	N.B.Amarnath, C.K.Nayudu	India v England	1933-34
Mumbai[2]	254	5th	K.W.R.Fletcher, A.W.Greig	England v India	1972-73
Mumbai[3]	298*	6th	D.B.Vengsarkar, R.J.Shastri	India v Australia	1986-87
Nagpur	202	5th	S.R.Tendulkar, M.Azharuddin	India v West Indies	1994-95

PAKISTAN

Bahawalpur	127	1st	Hanif Mohammad, Alimuddin	Pakistan v India	1954-55
Dacca	198	1st	G.Pullar, R.W.Barber	England v Pakistan	1961-62
Faisalabad	397	3rd	Qasim Omar, Javed Miandad	Pakistan v Sri Lanka	1985-86
Gujranwala	59	2nd	Rameez Raja, Zahid Fazal	Pakistan v Sri Lanka	1991-92
Hyderabad	451	3rd	Mudassar Nazar, Javed Miandad	Pakistan v India	1982-83
Karachi[1]	252	4th	Javed Miandad, Mushtaq Mohammad	Pakistan v New Zealand	1976-77
Karachi[2]	95	1st	Aamer Sohail, Shoaib Mohammad	Pakistan v Zimbabwe	1993-94
Lahore[1]	308	7th	Waqar Hassan, Imtiaz Ahmed	Pakistan v New Zealand	1955-56
Lahore[2]	281	5th	Javed Miandad, Asif Iqbal	Pakistan v New Zealand	1976-77
Multan	100	3rd	Majid Khan, Javed Miandad	Pakistan v West Indies	1980-81
Peshawar[1]	91	3rd	P.R.Umrigar, V.L.Manjrekar	India v Pakistan	1954-55

Peshawar[2]	132	3rd	Rameez Raja, Inzamamul Haq	Pakistan v Sri Lanka	1995-96
Rawalpindi[1]	114	2nd	Mohammad Ilyas, Saeed Ahmed	Pakistan v New Zealand	1964-65
Rawalpindi[2]	176	1st	M.A.Taylor, M.J.Slater	Australia v Pakistan	1994-95
Sialkot	128	3rd	S.V.Manjrekar, M.Azharuddin	India v Pakistan	1985-86
SRI LANKA					
Colombo (PSS)	240*	4th	A.P.Gurusinha, A.Ranatunga	Sri Lanka v Pakistan	1985-86
Colombo (SSC)	230	4th	A.P.Gurusinha, A.Ranatunga	Sri Lanka v Australia	1992-93
Colombo (CCC)	246*	6th	J.J.Crowe, R.J.Hadlee	New Zealand v Sri Lanka	1986-87
Colombo (PIS)	131	6th	D.M.Jones, G.R.J.Matthews	Australia v Sri Lanka	1992-93
Kandy	216	4th	R.L.Dias, L.R.D.Mendis	Sri Lanka v India	1985-86
Moratuwa	151	5th	K.R.Rutherford, C.Z.Harris	New Zealand v Sri Lanka	1992-93
ZIMBABWE					
Bulawayo[1]	127	2nd	R.T.Latham, A.H.Jones	New Zealand v Zimbabwe	1992-93
Bulawayo[2]	121	4th	D.L.Houghton, A.Flower	Zimbabwe v Sri Lanka	1994-95
Harare	269	3rd	G.W.Flower, A.Flower	Zimbabwe v Pakistan	1994-95

BEST INNINGS BOWLING ANALYSIS FOR EACH TEST GROUND

AUSTRALIA

Adelaide	8-43	A.E.Trott	Australia v England	1894-95
Brisbane[1]	6-32	H.Larwood	England v Australia	1928-29
Brisbane[2]	9-52	R.J.Hadlee	New Zealand v Australia	1985-86
Hobart	6-31	S.K.Warne	Australia v New Zealand	1993-94
Melbourne	9-86	Sarfraz Nawaz	Pakistan v Australia	1978-79
Perth	8-87	M.G.Hughes	Australia v West Indies	1988-89
Sydney	8-35	G.A.Lohmann	England v Australia	1886-87

ENGLAND

Birmingham	7-17	W.Rhodes	England v Australia	1902
Leeds	8-43	R.G.D.Willis	England v Australia	1981
Lord's	8-34	I.T.Botham	England v Pakistan	1978
Manchester	10-53	J.C.Laker	England v Australia	1956
Nottingham	8-107	B.J.T.Bosanquet	England v Australia	1905
The Oval	9-57	D.E.Malcolm	England v South Africa	1994
Sheffield	6-49	S.F.Barnes	England v Australia	1902

SOUTH AFRICA

Cape Town	8-11	J.Briggs	England v South Africa	1888-89
Durban[1]	7-56	S.F.Barnes	England v South Africa	1913-14
Durban[2]	8-69	H.J Tayfield	South Africa v England	1956-57
Johannesburg[1]	9-28	G.A.Lohmann	England v South Africa	1895-96
Johannesburg[2]	6-13	H.J.Tayfield	South Africa v New Zealand	1953-54
Johannesburg[3]	9-113	H.J.Tayfield	South Africa v England	1956-57
Port Elizabeth	8-7	G.A.Lohmann	England v South Africa	1895-96
Pretoria	3-50	B.M.McMillan	South Africa v England	1995-96

WEST INDIES

Bridgetown	8-38	L.R.Gibbs	West Indies v India	1961-62
Georgetown	7-44	I.W.Johnson	Australia v West Indies	1954-55
Kingston	7-34	T.E.Bailey	England v West Indies	1953-54
Port-of-Spain	9-95	J.M.Noreiga	West Indies v India	1970-71
St John's	6-54	C.A.Walsh	West Indies v Australia	1994-95

NEW ZEALAND				
Auckland	8-76	E.A.S.Prasanna	India v New Zealand	1975-76
Christchurch	7-75	F.S.Trueman	England v New Zealand	1962-63
Dunedin	7-52	Intikhab Alam	Pakistan v New Zealand	1972-73
Hamilton	5-22	Waqar Younis	Pakistan v New Zealand	1992-93
Napier	5-43	W.P.U.J.C.Vaas	Sri Lanka v New Zealand	1994-95
Wellington	7-23	R.J.Hadlee	New Zealand v India	1975-76
INDIA				
Ahmedabad	9-83	Kapil Dev	India v West Indies	1983-84
Bangalore	7-27	Maninder Singh	India v Pakistan	1986-87
Calcutta	7-49	Ghulam Ahmed	India v Australia	1956-57
Chandigarh	6-12	S.L.Venkatapathy Raju	India v Sri Lanka	1990-91
Chennai[1]	8-55	M.H.Mankad	India v England	1951-52
Chennai[2]	7-43	R.R.Lindwall	Australia v India	1956-57
Cuttack	6-59	N.D.Hirwani	India v New Zealand	1995-96
Delhi	8-52	M.H.Mankad	India v Pakistan	1952-53
Hyderabad	7-128	S.P.Gupte	India v New Zealand	1955-56
Jaipur	4-88	G.Sharma	India v Pakistan	1986-87
Jullundur	4-50	Wasim Raja	Pakistan v India	1983-84
Kanpur	9-69	J.M.Patel	India v Australia	1959-60
Lucknow[1]	7-42	Fazal Mahmood	Pakistan v India	1952-53
Lucknow[2]	7-59	A.R.Kumble	India v Sri Lanka	1993-94
Mohali	5-55	K.C.G.Benjamin	West Indies v India	1994-95
Mumbai[1]	5-55	M.S.Nichols	England v India	1933-34
Mumbai[2]	7-157	B.S.Chandrasekhar	India v West Indies	1966-67
Mumbai[3]	7-48	I.T.Botham	England v India	1979-80
Nagpur	7-51	Maninder Singh	India v Sri Lanka	1986-87
PAKISTAN				
Bahawalpur	6-74	P.R.Umrigar	India v Pakistan	1954-55
Dacca	6-21	Khan Mohammad	Pakistan v New Zealand	1955-56
Faisalabad	7-52	C.Pringle	New Zealand v Pakistan	1990-91
Gujranwala	1-27	G.P.Wickramasinghe	Sri Lanka v Pakistan	1991-92
Hyderabad	7-87	S.L.Boock	New Zealand v Pakistan	1984-85
Karachi[1]	8-60	Imran Khan	Pakistan v India	1982-83
Karachi[2]	7-91	Waqar Younis	Pakistan v Zimbabwe	1993-94
Lahore[1]	5-87	W.W.Hall	West Indies v Pakistan	1958-59
Lahore[2]	9-56	Abdul Qadir	Pakistan v England	1987-88
Multan	5-62	Imran Khan	Pakistan v West Indies	1980-81
Peshawar[1]	5-63	S.P.Gupte	India v Pakistan	1954-55
Peshawar[2]	5-55	Wasim Akram	Pakistan v Sri Lanka	1995-96
Rawalpindi[1]	4-5	Pervez Sajjad	Pakistan v New Zealand	1964-65
Rawalpindi[2]	5-56	H.H.Streak	Zimbabwe v Pakistan	1993-94
Sialkot	8-83	J.R.Ratnayeke	Sri Lanka v Pakistan	1985-86
SRI LANKA				
Colombo (PSS)	6-33	J.E.Emburey	England v Sri Lanka	1981-82
Colombo (SSC)	6-85	R.J.Ratnayake	Sri Lanka v India	1985-86
Colombo (CCC)	5-29	R.I.Hadlee	New Zealand v Sri Lanka	1983-84
Colombo (PIS)	4-53	C.J.McDermott	Australia v Sri Lanka	1992-93
Kandy	6-34	Waqar Younis	Pakistan v Sri Lanka	1994-95
Moratuwa	5-69	A.A.Donald	South Africa v Sri Lanka	1993-94
ZIMBABWE				
Bulawayo[1]	6-113	D.N.Patel	New Zealand v Zimbabwe	1992-93
Bulawayo[2]	5-43	Wasim Akram	Pakistan v Zimbabwe	1994-95
Harare	8-71	A.A.Donald	South Africa v Zimbabwe	1995-96

BEST MATCH BOWLING ANALYSIS FOR EACH TEST GROUND

AUSTRALIA

Ground	Analysis	Bowler	Match	Season
Adelaide	14-199	C.V.Grimmett	Australia v South Africa	1931-32
Brisbane[1]	9-144	C.V.Grimmett	Australia v West Indies	1930-31
Brisbane[2]	15-123	R.J.Hadlee	New Zealand v Australia	1985-86
Hobart	9-67	S.K.Warne	Australia v New Zealand	1993-94
Melbourne	15-124	W.Rhodes	England v Australia	1903-04
Perth	13-217	M.G.Hughes	Australia v West Indies	1988-89
Sydney	12-87	C.T.B.Turner	Australia v England	1887-88

ENGLAND

Ground	Analysis	Bowler	Match	Season
Birmingham	12-119	F.S.Trueman	England v West Indies	1963
Leeds	15-99	C.Blythe	England v South Africa	1907
Lord's	16-137	R.A.L.Massie	Australia v England	1972
Manchester	19-90	J.C.Laker	England v Australia	1956
Nottingham	14-99	A.V.Bedser	England v Australia	1953
The Oval	14-90	F.R.Spofforth	Australia v England	1882
Sheffield	11-103	M.A.Noble	Australia v England	1902

SOUTH AFRICA

Ground	Analysis	Bowler	Match	Season
Cape Town	15-28	J.Briggs	England v South Africa	1888-89
Durban[1]	14-144	S.F.Barnes	England v South Africa	1913-14
Durban[2]	13-173	C.V.Grimmett	Australia v South Africa	1935-36
Johannesburg[1]	17-159	S.F.Barnes	England v South Africa	1913-14
Johannesburg[2]	8-61	H.J.Tayfield	South Africa v New Zealand	1953-54
Johannesburg[3]	13-192	H.J.Tayfield	South Africa v England	1956-57
Port Elizabeth	15-45	G.A.Lohmann	England v South Africa	1895-96
Pretoria	3-50	B.M.McMillan	South Africa v England	1995-96

WEST INDIES

Ground	Analysis	Bowler	Match	Season
Bridgetown	11-120	M.D.Marshall	West Indies v New Zealand	1984-85
Georgetown	11-121	Imran Khan	Pakistan v West Indies	1987-88
Kingston	10-96	H.H.H.Johnson	West Indies v England	1947-48
Port-of-Spain	13-156	A.W.Greig	England v West Indies	1973-74
St John's	9-146	C.A.Walsh	West Indies v Australia	1994-95

NEW ZEALAND

Ground	Analysis	Bowler	Match	Season
Auckland	11-123	D.K.Lillee	Australia v New Zealand	1976-77
Christchurch	12-97	D.L.Underwood	England v New Zealand	1970-71
Dunedin	11-102	R.J.Hadlee	New Zealand v West Indies	1979-80
Hamilton	9-81	Waqar Younis	Pakistan v New Zealand	1992-93
Napier	10-90	W.P.J.U.C.Vaas	Sri Lanka v New Zealand	1994-95
Wellington	13-55	C.A.Walsh	West Indies v New Zealand	1994-95

INDIA

Ground	Analysis	Bowler	Match	Season
Ahmedabad	11-125	S.L.Venkatapathy Raju	India v Sri Lanka	1993-94
Bangalore	10-126	Maninder Singh	India v Pakistan	1986-87
Calcutta	11-105	R.Benaud	Australia v India	1956-57
Chandigarh	8-37	S.L.Venkatapathy Raju	India v Sri Lanka	1990-91
Chennai[1]	16-136	N.D.Hirwani	India v West Indies	1987-88
Chennai[2]	11-122	R.G.Nadkarni	India v Australia	1964-65
Cuttack	6-83	Maninder Singh	India v Sri Lanka	1986-87
Delhi	13-131	M.H.Mankad	India v Pakistan	1952-53
Hyderabad	8-109	E.A.S.Prasanna	India v New Zealand	1969-70
Jaipur	4-88	G.Sharma	India v Pakistan	1986-87
Jullundur	4-50	Wasim Raja	Pakistan v India	1983-84

Ground	Figures	Player	Match	Season
Kanpur	14-124	J.M.Patel	India v Australia	1959-60
Lucknow[1]	12-94	Fazal Mahmood	Pakistan v India	1952-53
Lucknow[2]	11-128	A.R.Kumble	India v Sri Lanka	1993-94
Mohali	8-171	K.C.G.Benjamin	West Indies v India	1994-95
Mumbai[1]	8-108	M.S.Nichols	England v India	1933-34
Mumbai[2]	11-235	B.S.Chandrasekhar	India v West Indies	1966-67
Mumbai[3]	13-106	I.T.Botham	England v India	1979-80
Nagpur	10-107	Maninder Singh	India v Sri Lanka	1986-87

PAKISTAN

Ground	Figures	Player	Match	Season
Bahawalpur	7-124	Khan Mohammad	Pakistan v India	1954-55
Dacca	12-100	Fazal Mahmood	Pakistan v West Indies	1958-59
Faisalabad	12-130	Waqar Younis	Pakistan v New Zealand	1990-91
Gujranwala	1-27	G.P.Wickramasinghe	Sri Lanka v Pakistan	1991-92
Hyderabad	8-80	Imran Khan	Pakistan v India	1982-83
Karachi[1]	13-114	Fazal Mahmood	Pakistan v Australia	1956-57
Karachi[2]	13-135	Waqar Younis	Pakistan v Zimbabwe	1993-94
Lahore[1]	7-167	S.P.Gupte	India v Pakistan	1954-55
Lahore[2]	14-116	Imran Khan	Pakistan v Sri Lanka	1981-82
Multan	5-89	Imran Khan	Pakistan v West Indies	1980-81
Peshawar[1]	6-115	S.P.Gupte	India v Pakistan	1954-55
Peshawar[2]	7-79	Wasim Akram	Pakistan v Sri Lanka	1995-96
Rawalpindi[1]	8-47	Pervez Sajjad	Pakistan v New Zealand	1964-65
Rawalpindi[2]	9-138	Waqar Younis	Pakistan v Zimbabwe	1993-94
Sialkot	9-95	Imran Khan	Pakistan v Sri Lanka	1985-86

SRI LANKA

Ground	Figures	Player	Match	Season
Colombo (PSS)	9-125	R.J.Ratnayake	Sri Lanka v India	1985-86
Colombo (SSC)	9-106	B.N.Schultz	South Africa v Sri Lanka	1993-94
Colombo (CCC)	10-102	R.J.Hadlee	New Zealand v Sri Lanka	1983-84
Colombo (PIS)	6-85	C.J.McDermott	Australia v Sri Lanka	1992-93
Kandy	11-119	Waqar Younis	Pakistan v Sri Lanka	1994-95
Moratuwa	8-157	C.P.H.Ramanayake	Sri Lanka v Australia	1992-93

ZIMBABWE

Ground	Figures	Player	Match	Season
Bulawayo[1]	7-173	D.N.Patel	New Zealand v Zimbabwe	1992-93
Bulawayo[2]	8-83	Wasim Akram	Pakistan v Zimbabwe	1994-95
Harare	11-113	A.A.Donald	South Africa v Zimbabwe	1995-96

Series by Series Records

• denotes batted first (Where a captain's name appears only once he was captain throughout the entire series).

AUSTRALIA V ENGLAND	Australia		England		Captains	
Venue and Result	1st	2nd	1st	2nd	Australia	England
1876-77 in AUSTRALIA						
Melbourne-Australia 45 runs	•245	104	196	108	D.W.Gregory	J.Lillywhite
Melbourne-England 4 wkts	•122	259	261	6-122		
1878-79 in AUSTRALIA						
Melbourne-Australia 10 wkts	256	0-19	•113	160	D.W.Gregory	Lord Harris
1880 in ENGLAND						
The Oval-England 5 wkts	149	327	•420	5-57	W.L.Murdoch	Lord Harris
1881-82 in AUSTRALIA						
Melbourne-Drawn	320	3-127	•294	308	W.L.Murdoch	A.Shaw
Sydney-Australia 5 wkts	197	5-169	•133	232		
Sydney-Australia 6 wkts	260	4-66	•188	134		
Melbourne-Drawn	300	-	•309	2-234		
1882 in ENGLAND						
The Oval-Australia 7 runs	•63	122	101	77	W.L.Murdoch	A.N.Hornby
1882-83 in AUSTRALIA						
Melbourne-Australia 9 wkts	•291	1-58	177	169	W.L.Murdoch	Hon.I.F.W.Bligh
Melbourne-England inns & 27 runs	114	153	•294	-		
Sydney-England 69 runs	218	83	•247	123		
Sydney-Australia 4 wkts	262	6-199	•263	197		
1884 in ENGLAND						
Manchester-Drawn	182	-	•95	9-180	W.L.Murdoch	A.N.Hornby
Lord's-England inns & 5 runs	•229	145	379	-		Lord Harris
The Oval-Drawn	•551	-	346	2-85		Lord Harris
1884-85 in AUSTRALIA						
Adelaide-England 8 wkts	•243	191	369	2-67	W.L.Murdoch	A.Shrewsbury
Melbourne-England 10 wkts	279	126	•401	0-7	T.P.Horan	
Sydney-Australia 6 runs	•181	165	133	207	H.H.Massie	
Sydney-Australia 8 wkts	309	2-40	•269	77	J.M.Blackham	
Melbourne-England inns & 98 runs	•163	125	386	-	T.P.Horan	
1886 in ENGLAND						
Manchester-England 4 wkts	•205	123	223	6-107	H.J.H.Scott	A.G.Steel
Lord's-England inns & 106 runs	121	126	•353	-		
The Oval-England inns & 217 runs	68	149	•434	-		
1886-87 in AUSTRALIA						
Sydney-England 13 runs	119	97	•45	184	P.S.McDonnell	A.Shrewsbury
Sydney-England 71 runs	84	150	•151	154		
1887-88 in AUSTRALIA						
Sydney-England 126 runs	42	82	•113	137	P.S.McDonnell	W.W.Read

AUSTRALIA v ENGLAND (cont.)	Australia		England		Captains	
Venue and Result	1st	2nd	1st	2nd	Australia	England
1888 in ENGLAND						
Lord's-Australia 61 runs	•116	60	53	62	P.S.McDonnell	A.G.Steel
The Oval-England inns & 137 runs	•80	100	317	-		W.G.Grace
Manchester-England inns & 21 runs	81	70	•172	-		W.G.Grace
1890 in ENGLAND						
Lord's-England 7 wkts	•132	176	173	3-137	W.L.Murdoch	W.G.Grace
The Oval-England 2 wkts	•92	102	100	8-95		
Manchester-Abandoned	-	-	-	-		
1891-92 in AUSTRALIA						
Melbourne-Australia 54 runs	•240	236	264	158	J.M.Blackham	W.G.Grace
Sydney-Australia 72 runs	•145	391	307	157		
Adelaide-England inns & 230 runs	100	169	•499			
1893 in ENGLAND						
Lord's-Drawn	269	-	•334	8d-234	J.M.Blackham	A.E.Stoddart
The Oval-England inns & 43 runs	91	349	•483	-		W.G.Grace
Manchester-Drawn	•240	236	243	4-118		W.G.Grace
1894-95 in AUSTRALIA						
Sydney-England 10 runs	•586	166	325	437	J.M.Blackham	A.E.Stoddart
Melbourne-England 94 runs	123	333	•75	475	G.Giffen	
Adelaide-Australia 382 runs	•238	411	124	143	G.Giffen	
Sydney-Australia inns & 147 runs	•284	-	65	72	G.Giffen	
Melbourne-England 6 wkts	•414	267	385	4-298	G.Giffen	
1896 in ENGLAND						
Lord's-England 6 wkts	•53	347	292	4-111	G.H.S.Trott	W.G.Grace
Manchester-Australia 3 wkts	•412	7-125	231	305		
The Oval-England 66 runs	119	44	•145	84		
1897-98 in AUSTRALIA						
Sydney-England 9 wkts	237	408	•551	1-96	G.H.S.Trott	A.C.MacLaren
Melbourne-Australia inns & 55 runs	•520	-	315	150		A.C.MacLaren
Adelaide-Australia inns & 13 runs	•573	-	278	282		A.E.Stoddart
Melbourne-Australia 8 wkts	•323	2-115	174	263		A.E.Stoddart
Sydney-Australia 6 wkts	239	4-276	•335	178		A.C.MacLaren
1899 in ENGLAND						
Nottingham-Drawn	•252	8d-230	193	7-155	J.Darling	W.G.Grace
Lord's-Australia 10 wkts	421	0-28	•206	240		A.C.MacLaren
Leeds-Drawn	•172	224	220	0-19		A.C.MacLaren
Manchester-Drawn	196	7d-346	•372	3-94		A.C.MacLaren
The Oval-Drawn	352	5-254	•576	-		A.C.MacLaren
1901-02 in AUSTRALIA						
Sydney-England inns & 124 runs	168	172	•464	-	J.Darling	A.C.MacLaren
Melbourne-Australia 229 runs	•112	353	61	175	J.Darling	
Adelaide-Australia 4 wkts	321	6-315	•388	247	J.Darling	
Sydney-Australia 7 wkts	299	3-121	•317	99	H.Trumble	
Melbourne-Australia 32 runs	•144	255	189	178	H.Trumble	

AUSTRALIA v ENGLAND (cont.)	Australia		England		Captains	
Venue and Result	1st	2nd	1st	2nd	Australia	England
1902 in ENGLAND						
Birmingham-Drawn	36	2-46	•9d-376	-	J.Darling	A.C.MacLaren
Lord's-Drawn	-	-	•2-102	-		
Sheffield-Australia 143 runs	•194	289	145	195		
Manchester-Australia 3 runs	•299	86	262	120		
The Oval-England 1 wkt	•324	121	183	9-263		
1903-04 in AUSTRALIA						
Sydney-England 5 wkts	•285	485	577	5-194	M.A.Noble	P.F.Warner
Melbourne-England 185 runs	122	111	•315	103		
Adelaide-Australia 216 runs	•388	351	245	278		
Sydney-England 157 runs	131	171	•249	210		
Melbourne-Australia 218 runs	•247	133	61	101		
1905 in ENGLAND						
Nottingham-England 213 runs	221	188	•196	5d-426	J.Darling	Hon.F.S.Jackson
Lord's-Drawn	181	-	•282	5-151		
Leeds-Drawn	195	7-224	•301	5d-295		
Manchester-England inns & 80 runs	197	169	•446	-		
The Oval-Drawn	363	4-124	•430	6d-261		
1907-08 in AUSTRALIA						
Sydney-Australia 2 wkts	300	8-275	•273	300	M.A.Noble	F.L.Fane
Melbourne-England 1 wkt	•266	397	382	9-282		F.L.Fane
Adelaide-Australia 245 runs	•285	506	363	183		F.L.Fane
Melbourne-Australia 308 runs	•214	385	105	186		A.O.Jones
Sydney-Australia 49 runs	•137	422	281	229		A.O.Jones
1909 in ENGLAND						
Birmingham-England 10 wkts	•74	151	121	0-105	M.A.Noble	A.C.MacLaren
Lord's-Australia 9 wkts	350	1-41	•269	121		
Leeds-Australia 126 runs	•188	207	182	87		
Manchester-Drawn	•147	9d-279	119	3-108		
The Oval-Drawn	•325	5d-339	352	3-104		
1911-12 in AUSTRALIA						
Sydney-Australia 146 runs	•447	308	318	291	C.Hill	J.W.H.T.Douglas
Melbourne-England 8 wkts	•184	299	265	2-219		
Adelaide-England 7 wkts	•133	476	501	3-112		
Melbourne-England inns & 225 runs	•191	173	589	-		
Sydney-England 70 runs	176	292	·324	214		
1912 in ENGLAND						
Lord's-Drawn	7-282	-	•7d-310	-	S.E.Gregory	C.B.Fry
Manchester-Drawn	0-14	-	•203	-		
The Oval-England 244 runs	111	65	•245	175		
1920-21 in AUSTRALIA						
Sydney-Australia 377 runs	•267	581	190	281	W.W.Armstrong	J.W.H.T.Douglas
Melbourne-Australia inns & 91 runs	•499	-	251	157		
Adelaide-Australia 119 runs	•354	582	447	370		
Melbourne-Australia 8 wkts	389	2-211	•284	315		
Sydney-Australia 9 wkts	392	1-93	•204	280		

AUSTRALIA v ENGLAND (cont.)	Australia		England		Captains	
Venue and Result	1st	2nd	1st	2nd	Australia	England
1921 in ENGLAND						
Nottingham-Australia 10 wkts	232	0-30	•112	147	W.W.Armstrong	J.W.H.T.Douglas
Lord's-Australia 8 wkts	342	2-131	•187	283		J.W.H.T Douglas
Leeds-Australia 219 runs	•407	7d-273	259	202		Hon.L.H.Tennyson
Manchester-Drawn	175	-	•4d-362	1-44		Hon.L.H.Tennyson
The Oval-Drawn	389	-	•8d-403	2-244		Hon.L.H.Tennyson
1924-25 in AUSTRALIA						
Sydney-Australia 193 runs	•450	452	298	411	H.L.Collins	A.E.R.Gilligan
Melbourne-Australia 81 runs	•600	250	479	290		
Adelaide-Australia 11 runs	•489	250	365	363		
Melbourne-England inns & 29 runs	269	250	•548	-		
Sydney-Australia 307 runs	•295	325	167	146		
1926 in ENGLAND						
Nottingham-Drawn	-	-	•0-32	-	H.L.Collins	A.W.Carr
Lord's-Drawn	•383	5-194	3d-475	-	H.L.Collins	A.W.Carr
Leeds-Drawn	•494	-	294	3-254	W.Bardsley	A.W.Carr
Manchester-Drawn	•335	-	5-305	-	W.Bardsley	A.W.Carr
The Oval-England 289 runs	302	125	•280	436	H.L.Collins	A.P.F.Chapman
1928-29 in AUSTRALIA						
Brisbane[1]-England 675 runs	122	66	•521	8d-342	J.Ryder	A.P.F.Chapman
Sydney-England 8 wkts	•253	397	636	2-16		A.P.F.Chapman
Melbourne-England 3 wkts	•397	351	417	7-332		A.P.F.Chapman
Adelaide-England 12 runs	369	336	•334	383		A.P.F.Chapman
Melbourne-Australia 5 wkts	491	5-287	•519	257		J.C.White
1930 in ENGLAND						
Nottingham-England 93 runs	144	335	•270	302	W.M.Woodfull	A.P.F.Chapman
Lord's-Australia 7 wkts	6d-729	3-72	•425	375		A.P.F.Chapman
Leeds-Drawn	•566	-	391	3-95		A.P.F.Chapman
Manchester-Drawn	•345	-	8-251	-		A.P.F.Chapman
The Oval-Australia inns & 39 runs	695	-	•405	251		R.E.S.Wyatt
1932-33 in AUSTRALIA						
Sydney-England 10 wkts	•360	164	524	0-1	W.M.Woodfull	D.R.Jardine
Melbourne-Australia 111 runs	•228	191	169	139		
Adelaide-England 338 runs	222	193	•341	412		
Brisbane[2]-England 6 wkts	•340	175	356	4-162		
Sydney-England 8 wkts	•435	182	454	2-168		
1934 in ENGLAND						
Nottingham-Australia 238 runs	•374	8d-273	268	141	W.M.Woodfull	C.F.Walters
Lord's-England inns & 38 runs	284	118	•440	-		R.E.S.Wyatt
Manchester-Drawn	491	1-66	•9d-627	0d-123		R.E.S.Wyatt
Leeds-Drawn	584	-	•200	6-229		R.E.S.Wyatt
The Oval-Australia 562 runs	•701	327	321	145		R.E.S.Wyatt
1936-37 in AUSTRALIA						
Brisbane[2]-England 322 runs	234	58	•358	256	D.G.Bradman	G.O.B.Allen
Sydney-England inns & 22 runs	80	324	•6d-426	-		
Melbourne-Australia 365 runs	•9d-200	564	9d-76	323		
Adelaide-Australia 148 runs	•288	433	330	243		
Melbourne-Australia inns & 200 runs	•604	-	239	165		

AUSTRALIA v ENGLAND (cont.)	Australia		England		Captains	
Venue and Result	1st	2nd	1st	2nd	Australia	England
1938 in ENGLAND						
Nottingham-Drawn	411	6-427	•8d-658	-	D.G.Bradman	W.R.Hammond
Lord's-Drawn	422	6-204	•494	8d-242		
Manchester-Abandoned	-	-	-	-		
Leeds-Australia 5 wkts	242	5-107	•223	123		
The Oval-England inns & 579 runs	201	123	•7d-903	-		
1946-47 in AUSTRALIA						
Brisbane[2]-Australia inns & 332 runs	•645	-	141	172	D.G.Bradman	W.R.Hammond
Sydney-Australia inns & 33 runs	8d-659	-	•255	371		W.R.Hammond
Melbourne-Drawn	•365	536	351	7-310		W.R.Hammond
Adelaide-Drawn	487	1-215	•460	8d-340		W.R.Hammond
Sydney-Australia 5 wkts	253	5-214	•280	186		N.W.D.Yardley
1948 in ENGLAND						
Nottingham-Australia 8 wkts	509	2-98	•165	441	D.G.Bradman	N.W.D.Yardley
Lord's-Australia 409 runs	•350	7d-460	215	186		
Manchester-Drawn	221	1-92	•363	3d-174		
Leeds-Australia 7 wkts	458	3-404	•496	8d-365		
The Oval-Australia inns & 149 runs	389	-	•52	188		
1950-51 in AUSTRALIA						
Brisbane[2]-Australia 70 runs	•228	7d-32	7d-68	122	A.L.Hassett	F.R.Brown
Melbourne-Australia 28 runs	•194	181	197	150		
Sydney-Australia inns &13 runs	426	-	•290	123		
Adelaide-Australia 274 runs	•371	8d-403	272	228		
Melbourne-England 8 wkts	•217	197	320	2-95		
1953 in ENGLAND						
Nottingham-Drawn	•249	123	144	1-120	A.L.Hassett	L.Hutton
Lord's-Drawn	•346	368	372	7-282		
Manchester-Drawn	•318	8-35	276	-		
Leeds-Drawn	266	4-147	•167	275		
The Oval-England 8 wkts	•275	162	306	2-132		
1954-55 in AUSTRALIA						
Brisbane[2]-Australia inns & 154 runs	•8d-601	-	190	257	I.W.Johnson	L.Hutton
Sydney-England 38 runs	228	184	•154	296	A.R.Morris	
Melbourne-England 128 runs	231	111	•191	279	I.W.Johnson	
Adelaide-England 5 wkts	•323	111	341	5-97	I.W.Johnson	
Sydney-Drawn	221	6-118	•7d-371	-	I.W.Johnson	
1956 In ENGLAND						
Nottingham-Drawn	148	3-120	•8d-217	3d-188	I.W.Johnson	P.B.H.May
Lord's-Australia 185 runs	•285	257	171	186		
Leeds-England inns & 42 runs	143	140	•325	-		
Manchester-England inns & 170 runs	84	205	•459	-		
The Oval-Drawn	202	5-27	•247	3d-182		
1958-59 In AUSTRALIA						
Brisbane[2]-Australia 8 wkts	186	2-147	•134	198	R.Benaud	P.B.H.May
Melbourne-Australia 8 wkts	308	2-42	•259	87		
Sydney-Drawn	357	2-54	•219	7d-287		
Adelaide-Australia 10 wkts	•476	0-36	240	270		
Melbourne-Australia 9 wkts	351	1-69	•205	214		

AUSTRALIA v ENGLAND (cont.)	Australia		England		Captains	
Venue and Result	1st	2nd	1st	2nd	Australia	England
1961 In ENGLAND						
Birmingham-Drawn	9d-516	-	•195	4-401	R.Benaud	M.C.Cowdrey
Lord's-Australia 5 wkts	340	5-71	•206	202	R.N.Harvey	M.C.Cowdrey
Leeds-England 8 wkts	•237	120	299	2-62	R.Benaud	P.B.H.May
Manchester-Australia 54 runs	•190	432	367	201	R.Benaud	P.B.H.May
The Oval-Drawn	494	-	•256	8-370	R.Benaud	P.B.H.May
1962-63 in AUSTRALIA						
Brisbane²-Drawn	•404	4d-362	389	6-278	R.Benaud	E.R.Dexter
Melbourne-England 7 wkts	•316	248	331	3-237		
Sydney-Australia 8 wkts	319	2-67	•279	104		
Adelaide-Drawn	•393	293	331	4-223		
Sydney-Drawn	349	4-152	•321	8d-268		
1964 in ENGLAND						
Nottingham-Drawn	168	2-40	•8d-216	9d-193	R.B.Simpson	E.R.Dexter
Lord's-Drawn	•176	4-168	246	-		
Leeds-Australia 7 wkts	389	3-111	•268	229		
Manchester-Drawn	•8d-656	0-4	611	-		
The Oval-Drawn	379	-	•182	4-381		
1965-66 in AUSTRALIA						
Brisbane²-Drawn	•6d-443	-	280	3-186	B.C.Booth	M.J K.Smith
Melbourne-Drawn	•358	426	558	0-5	R.B.Simpson	
Sydney-England inns & 93 runs	221	174	•488	-	B.C.Booth	
Adelaide-Australia inns & 9 runs	516	-	•241	266	R.B.Simpson	
Melbourne-Drawn	8d-543	-	•9d-485	3-69	R.B Simpson	
1968 in ENGLAND						
Manchester-Australia 159 runs	•357	220	165	253	W.M.Lawry	M.C.Cowdrey
Lord's-Drawn	78	4-127	•7d-351	-	W.M.Lawry	M.C.Cowdrey
Birmingham-Drawn	222	1-68	•409	3d-142	W.M.Lawry	M.C.Cowdrey
Leeds-Drawn	•315	312	302	4-230	B.N.Jarman	T.W.Graveney
The Oval-England 226 runs	324	125	•494	181	W.M.Lawry	M.C.Cowdrey
1970-71 in AUSTRALIA						
Brisbane²-Drawn	•433	214	464	1-39	W.M.Lawry	R.Illingworth
Perth-Drawn	440	3-100	•397	6d-287	W.M.Lawry	
Melbourne-Abandoned	-	-	-	-	W.M.Lawry	
Sydney-England 299 runs	236	116	•332	5d-319	W.M.Lawry	
Melbourne-Drawn	•9d-493	4d-169	392	0-161	W.M.Lawry	
Adelaide-Drawn	235	3-328	•470	4d-233	W.M.Lawry	
Sydney-England 62 runs	264	160	•184	302	I.M.Chappell	
1972 in ENGLAND						
Manchester-England 89 runs	142	252	•249	234	I.M.Chappell	R.Illingworth
Lord's-Australia 8 wkts	308	2-81	•272	116		
Nottingham-Drawn	•315	4d-324	189	4-290		
Leeds-England 9 wkts	•146	136	263	1-21		
The Oval-Australia 5 wkts	399	5-242	•284	356		

AUSTRALIA v ENGLAND (cont.)	Australia		England		Captains	
Venue and Result	1st	2nd	1st	2nd	Australia	England
1974-75 in AUSTRALIA						
Brisbane²-Australia 166 runs	•309	5d-288	265	166	I.M.Chappell	M.H.Denness
Perth-Australia 9 wkts	481	1-23	•208	293		M.H.Denness
Melbourne-Drawn	241	8-238	•242	244		M.H.Denness
Sydney-Australia 171 runs	•405	4d-289	295	228		J.H.Edrich
Adelaide-Australia 163 runs	304	5d-272	172	241		M.H.Denness
Melbourne-England inns & 4 runs	•152	373	529	-		M.H.Denness
1975 in ENGLAND						
Birmingham-Australia inns & 85 runs	•359	-	101	173	I.M.Chappell	M.H.Denness
Lord's-Drawn	268	3-329	•315	7d-436		A.W.Greig
Leeds-Drawn	135	3-220	•288	291		A.W.Greig
The Oval-Drawn	•9d-532	2-40	191	538		A.W.Greig
1976-77 in AUSTRALIA (CENTENARY TEST)						
Melbourne-Australia 45 runs	•138	9d-419	95	417	G.S.Chappell	A.W.Greig
1977 in ENGLAND						
Lord's-Drawn	296	6-114	•216	305	G.S.Chappell	J.M.Brearley
Manchester-England 9 wkts	•297	218	437	1-82		
Nottingham-England 7 wkts	•243	309	364	3-189		
Leeds-England inns & 85 runs	103	248	•436	-		
The Oval-Drawn	385	-	•214	2-57		
1978-79 in AUSTRALIA						
Brisbane²-England 7 wkts	•116	339	286	3-170	G.N.Yallop	J.M.Brearley
Perth-England 166 runs	190	161	•309	208		
Melbourne-Australia 103 runs	•258	167	143	179		
Sydney-England 93 runs	294	111	•152	346		
Adelaide-England 205 runs	164	160	•169	360		
Sydney-England 9 wkts	198	143	308	1-35		
1979-80 in AUSTRALIA						
Perth-Australia 138 runs	•244	337	228	215	G.S.Chappell	J.M.Brearley
Sydney-Australia 6 wkts	145	4-219	•123	237		
Melbourne-Australia 8 wkts	477	2-103	•306	273		
1980 in ENGLAND (CENTENARY TEST)						
Lord's-Drawn	•5d-385	4d-189	205	3-244	G.S.Chappell	I.T.Botham
1981 in ENGLAND						
Nottingham-Australia 4 wkts	179	6-132	•185	125	K.J.Hughes	I.T.Botham
Lord's-Drawn	345	4-90	•311	8-265		I.T.Botham
Leeds-England 18 runs	•9-401	111	174	356		J.M.Brearley
Birmingham-England 29 runs	258	121	•189	219		J.M.Brearley
Manchester-England 103 runs	130	402	•231	404		J.M.Brearley
The Oval-Drawn	•352	9d-344	314	7-261		J.M.Brearley
1982-83 in AUSTRALIA						
Perth-Drawn	9d-424	2-73	•411	358	K.J.Hughes	R.G.D.Willis
Brisbane²-Australia 7 wkts	341	3-190	•219	309		
Adelaide-Australia 8 wkts	•438	2-83	216	304		
Melbourne-England 3 runs	287	288	•284	294		
Sydney-Drawn	•314	382	237	7-314		

AUSTRALIA v ENGLAND (cont.)	Australia		England		Captains	
Venue and Result	1st	2nd	1st	2nd	Australia	England
1985 in ENGLAND						
Leeds-England 5 wkts	•331	324	533	5-123	A.R.Border	D.I.Gower
Lord's-Australia 4 wkts	425	6-127	•290	261		
Nottingham-Drawn	539	-	•456	2-196		
Manchester-Drawn	•257	5-340	9d-482	-		
Birmingham-England inns & 118 runs	•335	142	5d-595	-		
The Oval-England inns & 94 runs	241	129	•464	-		
1986-87 in AUSTRALIA						
Brisbane[2]-England 7 wkts	248	282	•456	3-77	A.R.Border	M.W.Gatting
Perth-Drawn	401	4-197	•8d-592	8d-199		
Adelaide-Drawn	•5d-514	3d-201	455	2-39		
Melbourne-England inns & 14 runs	•141	194	349	-		
Sydney-Australia 55 runs	•343	251	275	264		
1987-88 in AUSTRALIA (BICENTENNIAL TEST)						
Sydney-Drawn	214	2-328	•425	-	A.R.Border	M.W.Gatting
1989 in ENGLAND						
Leeds-Australia 210 runs	•7d-601	3d-230	430	191	A.R.Border	D.I.Gower
Lord's-Australia 6 wkts	528	4-119	•286	359		
Birmingham-Drawn	•424	2-158	242	-		
Manchester-Australia 9 wkts	447	1-81	•260	264		
Nottingham-Australia inns & 180 runs	•6d-602	-	255	167		
The Oval-Drawn	•468	4d-219	285	5-143		
1990-91 in AUSTRALIA						
Brisbane[2]-Australia 10 wkts	152	0-157	•194	114	A.R.Border	A.J.Lamb
Melbourne-Australia 8 wkts	306	2-197	•352	150		G.A.Gooch
Sydney-Drawn	•518	205	8d-469	4-113		G.A.Gooch
Adelaide-Drawn	•386	6d-314	229	5-335		G.A.Gooch
Perth-Australia 9 wkts	307	1-120	•244	182		G.A.Gooch
1993 in ENGLAND						
Manchester-Australia 179 runs	•289	5d-432	210	332	A.R.Border	G.A.Gooch
Lord's-Australia inns & 62 runs	•4d-632	-	205	365		G.A.Gooch
Nottingham-Drawn	373	6-202	•321	422		G.A.Gooch
Leeds-Australia inns & 148 runs	•4d-653	-	200	305		G.A.Gooch
Birmingham-Australia 8 wkts	408	2-120	•276	251		M.A.Atherton
The Oval-England 161 runs	303	229	•380	313		M.A.Atherton
1994-95 in AUSTRALIA						
Brisbane[2]-Australia 184 runs	•426	8d-248	167	323	M.A.Taylor	M.A.Atherton
Melbourne-Australia 295 runs	•279	7d-320	212	92		
Sydney-Drawn	116	7-344	•309	2d-255		
Adelaide-England 106 runs	419	156	•353	328		
Perth-Australia 329 runs	•402	8d-345	295	123		

Test Match Results Summary

AUSTRALIA v ENGLAND — IN AUSTRALIA

		Result			Melbourne			Sydney			Adelaide			Brisbane[1]			Brisbane[2]			Perth		
	Tests	A	E	D	A	E	D	A	E	D	A	E	D	A	E	D	A	E	D	A	E	D
1876-77	2	1	1	-	1	1	-	-	-	-	-	-	-	-	-	-	-	-	-	-	-	-
1878-79	1	1	-	-	1	-	-	-	-	-	-	-	-	-	-	-	-	-	-	-	-	-
1881-82	4	2	-	2	-	-	2	2	-	-	-	-	-	-	-	-	-	-	-	-	-	-
1882-83	4	2	2	-	1	1	-	1	1	-	-	-	-	-	-	-	-	-	-	-	-	-
1884-85	5	2	3	-	-	2	-	2	-	-	-	1	-	-	-	-	-	-	-	-	-	-
1886-87	2	-	2	-	-	-	-	-	2	-	-	-	-	-	-	-	-	-	-	-	-	-
1887-88	1	-	1	-	-	-	-	-	1	-	-	-	-	-	-	-	-	-	-	-	-	-
1891-92	3	2	1	-	1	-	-	1	-	-	-	1	-	-	-	-	-	-	-	-	-	-
1894-95	5	2	3	-	-	2	-	1	1	-	1	-	-	-	-	-	-	-	-	-	-	-
1897-98	5	4	1	-	2	-	-	1	1	-	1	-	-	-	-	-	-	-	-	-	-	-
1901-02	5	4	1	-	2	-	-	1	1	-	1	-	-	-	-	-	-	-	-	-	-	-
1903-04	5	2	3	-	1	1	-	-	2	-	1	-	-	-	-	-	-	-	-	-	-	-
1907-08	5	4	1	-	1	1	-	2	-	-	1	-	-	-	-	-	-	-	-	-	-	-
1911-12	5	1	4	-	-	2	-	1	1	-	-	1	-	-	-	-	-	-	-	-	-	-
1920-21	5	5	-	-	2	-	-	2	-	-	1	-	-	-	-	-	-	-	-	-	-	-
1924-25	5	4	1	-	1	1	-	2	-	-	1	-	-	-	-	-	-	-	-	-	-	-
1928-29	5	1	4	-	1	1	-	-	1	-	-	1	-	-	1	-	-	-	-	-	-	-
1932-33	5	1	4	-	1	-	-	-	2	-	-	1	-	-	-	-	-	1	-	-	-	-
1936-37	5	3	2	-	2	-	-	-	1	-	1	-	-	-	-	-	-	1	-	-	-	-
1946-47	5	3	-	2	-	-	1	2	-	-	-	-	1	-	-	-	1	-	-	-	-	-
1950-51	5	4	1	-	1	1	-	1	-	-	1	-	-	-	-	-	1	-	-	-	-	-
1954-55	5	1	3	1	-	1	-	-	1	1	-	1	-	-	-	-	1	-	-	-	-	-
1958-59	5	4	-	1	2	-	-	-	-	1	1	-	-	-	-	-	1	-	-	-	-	-
1962-63	5	1	1	3	-	1	-	1	-	1	-	-	1	-	-	-	-	-	1	-	-	-
1965-66	5	1	1	3	-	-	2	-	1	-	1	-	-	-	-	-	-	-	1	-	-	-
1970-71	6	-	2	4	-	-	1	-	2	-	-	-	1	-	-	-	-	-	1	-	-	1
1974-75	6	4	1	1	-	1	1	1	-	-	1	-	-	-	-	-	1	-	-	1	-	-
1976-77	1	1	-	-	1	-	-	-	-	-	-	-	-	-	-	-	-	-	-	-	-	-
1978-79	6	1	5	-	1	-	-	-	2	-	-	1	-	-	-	-	-	1	-	-	1	-
1979-80	3	3	-	-	1	-	-	1	-	-	-	-	-	-	-	-	-	-	-	1	-	-
1982-83	5	2	1	2	-	1	-	-	-	1	1	-	-	-	-	-	1	-	-	-	-	1
1986-87	5	1	2	2	-	1	-	1	-	-	-	-	1	-	-	-	-	1	-	-	-	1
1987-88	1	-	-	1	-	-	-	-	-	1	-	-	-	-	-	-	-	-	-	-	-	-
1990-91	5	3	-	2	1	-	-	-	-	1	-	-	1	-	-	-	1	-	-	1	-	-
1994-95	5	3	1	-	1	-	-	-	-	1	-	1	-	-	-	-	1	-	-	1	-	-
	150	73	52	25	25	18	7	23	20	7	13	8	5	-	1	-	8	4	3	4	1	3

AUSTRALIA v ENGLAND-IN ENGLAND

		Result			The Oval			Manch.			Lord's			Notting.			Leeds			Birming.			Sheffield		
	Tests	A	E	D	A	E	D	A	E	D	A	E	D	A	E	D	A	E	D	A	E	D	A	E	D
1880	1	-	1	-	-	1	-	-	-	-	-	-	-	-	-	-	-	-	-	-	-	-	-	-	-
1882	1	1	-	-	1	-	-	-	-	-	-	-	-	-	-	-	-	-	-	-	-	-	-	-	-
1884	3	-	1	2	-	-	1	-	-	1	-	1	-	-	-	-	-	-	-	-	-	-	-	-	-
1886	3	-	3	-	-	1	-	-	1	-	-	1	-	-	-	-	-	-	-	-	-	-	-	-	-
1888	3	1	2	-	-	1	-	-	1	-	1	-	-	-	-	-	-	-	-	-	-	-	-	-	-
1890	2	-	2	-	-	1	-	-	-	-	-	1	-	-	-	-	-	-	-	-	-	-	-	-	-
1893	3	-	1	2	-	1	-	-	-	1	-	-	1	-	-	-	-	-	-	-	-	-	-	-	-
1896	3	1	2	-	-	1	-	1	-	-	-	1	-	-	-	-	-	-	-	-	-	-	-	-	-
1899	5	1	-	4	-	-	1	-	-	1	1	-	-	-	-	1	-	-	1	-	-	-	-	-	-
1902	5	2	1	2	-	1	-	1	-	-	-	-	1	-	-	-	-	-	-	-	-	1	1	-	-
1905	5	-	2	3	-	-	1	-	1	-	-	-	1	-	1	-	-	-	1	-	-	-	-	-	-
1909	5	2	1	2	-	-	1	-	-	1	1	-	-	-	-	-	1	-	-	-	1	-	-	-	-
1912	3	-	1	2	-	1	-	-	-	1	-	-	1	-	-	-	-	-	-	-	-	-	-	-	-
1921	5	3	-	2	-	-	1	-	-	1	1	-	-	1	-	-	1	-	-	-	-	-	-	-	-
1926	5	-	1	4	-	1	-	-	-	1	-	-	1	-	-	1	-	-	1	-	-	-	-	-	-
1930	5	2	1	2	1	-	-	-	-	1	1	-	-	-	1	-	-	-	1	-	-	-	-	-	-
1934	5	2	1	2	1	-	-	-	-	1	-	1	-	1	-	-	-	-	1	-	-	-	-	-	-
1938	4	1	1	2	-	1	-	-	-	-	-	-	1	-	-	1	1	-	-	-	-	-	-	-	-
1948	5	4	-	1	1	-	-	-	-	1	1	-	-	1	-	-	1	-	-	-	-	-	-	-	-
1953	5	-	1	4	-	1	-	-	-	1	-	-	1	-	-	1	-	-	1	-	-	-	-	-	-
1956	5	1	2	2	-	-	1	-	1	-	1	-	-	-	-	1	-	1	-	-	-	-	-	-	-
1961	5	2	1	2	-	-	1	1	-	-	1	-	-	-	-	-	-	1	-	-	-	1	-	-	-
1964	5	1	-	4	-	-	1	-	-	1	-	-	1	-	-	1	1	-	-	-	-	-	-	-	-
1968	5	1	1	3	-	1	-	1	-	-	-	-	1	-	-	-	-	-	1	-	-	1	-	-	-
1972	5	2	2	1	1	-	-	-	1	-	1	-	-	-	-	1	-	1	-	-	-	-	-	-	-
1975	4	1	-	3	-	-	1	-	-	-	-	-	1	-	-	-	-	-	1	1	-	-	-	-	-
1977	5	-	3	2	-	-	1	-	1	-	-	-	1	-	1	-	-	1	-	-	-	-	-	-	-
1980	1	-	-	1	-	-	-	-	-	-	-	-	1	-	-	-	-	-	-	-	-	-	-	-	-
1981	6	1	3	2	-	-	1	-	1	-	-	-	1	1	-	-	-	1	-	-	1	-	-	-	-
1985	6	1	3	2	-	1	-	-	-	1	1	-	-	-	-	1	-	1	-	-	1	-	-	-	-
1989	6	4	-	2	-	-	1	1	-	-	1	-	-	1	-	-	1	-	-	-	-	1	-	-	-
1993	6	4	1	1	-	1	-	1	-	-	1	-	-	-	-	1	1	-	-	1	-	-	-	-	-
	135	38	38	59	5	14	12	6	7	13	12	5	13	5	3	9	7	6	8	2	3	4	1	-	-
Totals	285	111	90	84																					

Key to ground abbreviations: Manch. - Manchester; Notting. - Nottingham; Birming. - Birmingham.
The matches abandoned without a ball being bowled at Manchester in 1890 and 1938 and at Melbourne in 1970-71 are excluded from these tables.

HIGHEST INNINGS TOTALS

Australia in England	6d-729	Lord's	1930
Australia in Australia	8d-659	Sydney	1946-47
England in England	7d-903	The Oval	1938
England in Australia	636	Sydney	1928-29

LOWEST INNINGS TOTALS

Australia in England	36	Birmingham	1902
Australia in Australia	42	Sydney	1887-88
England in England	52	The Oval	1948
England in Australia	45	Sydney	1886-87

HIGHEST MATCH AGGREGATE	1753 for 40 wickets	Adelaide	1920-21
LOWEST MATCH AGGREGATE	291 for 40 wickets	Lord's	1888

HIGHEST INDIVIDUAL INNINGS

Australia in England	334	D.G.Bradman	Leeds	1930
Australia in Australia	307	R.M.Cowper	Melbourne	1965-66
England in England	364	L.Hutton	The Oval	1938
England in Australia	287	R.E.Foster	Sydney	1903-04

HIGHEST AGGREGATE OF RUNS IN A SERIES

Australia in England	974 (av 139.14)	D.G.Bradman	1930
Australia in Australia	810 (av 90.00)	D.G.Bradman	1936-37
England in England	732 (av 81.33)	D.I.Gower	1985
England in Australia	905 (av 113.12)	W.R.Hammond	1928-29

RECORD WICKET PARTNERSHIPS-AUSTRALIA

1st	329	G.R.Marsh (138), M.A.Taylor(219)	Nottingham	1989
2nd	451	W.H.Ponsford (266), D.G.Bradman (244)	The Oval	1934
3rd	276	D.G.Bradman (187), A.L.Hassett (128)	Brisbane2	1946-47
4th	388	W H.Ponsford (181), D.G.Bradman (304)	Leeds	1934
5th	405	S.G.Barnes (234), D.G.Bradman (234)	Sydney	1946-47
6th	346	J.H.W Fingleton (136), D.G Bradman (270)	Melbourne	1936-37
7th	165	C.Hill (188), H.Trumble (46)	Melbourne	1897-98
8th	243	R.J.Hartigan (113), C.Hill (160)	Adelaide	1907-08
9th	154	S.E.Gregory (201), J.M.Blackham (74)	Sydney	1894-95
10th	127	J.M.Taylor (108), A.A.Mailey (46*)	Sydney	1924-25

RECORD WICKET PARTNERSHIPS-ENGLAND

1st	323	J.B.Hobbs (178), W.Rhodes (179)	Melbourne	1911-12
2nd	382	L.Hutton (364), M.Leyland (187)	The Oval	1938
3rd	262	W.R.Hammond (177), D.R.Jardine (98)	Adelaide	1928-29
4th	222	W.R.Hammond (240), E.Paynter (99)	Lord's	1938
5th	206	E.Paynter (216*), D.C.S.Compton (102)	Nottingham	1938
6th	215	L.Hutton (364), J.Hardstaff, jr (169 *)	The Oval	1938
	215	G.Boycott (107), A.P.E.Knott (135)	Nottingham	1977
7th	143	F.E.Woolley (133 *), J.Vine (36)	Sydney	1911-12
8th	124	E.H.Hendren (169), H.Larwood (70)	Brisbane[1]	1928-29
9th	151	W.H.Scotton (90), W.W.Read (117)	The Oval	1884
10th	130	R.E.Foster (287), W.Rhodes (40 *)	Sydney	1903-04

BEST INNINGS BOWLING ANALYSIS

Australia in England	8-31	F.J.Laver	Manchester	1909
Australia in Australia	9-121	A.A.Mailey	Melbourne	1920-21
England in England	10-53	J.C.Laker	Manchester	1956
England in Australia	8-35	G.A.Lohmann	Sydney	1886-87

BEST MATCH BOWLING ANALYSIS

Australia in England	16-137	R.A.L.Massie	Lord's	1972
Australia in Australia	13-77	M.A.Noble	Melbourne	1901-02
England in England	19-90	J.C.Laker	Manchester	1956
England in Australia	15-124	W.Rhodes	Melbourne	1903-04

HIGHEST AGGREGATE OF WICKETS IN A SERIES

Australia in England	42 (av 21.26)	T.M.Alderman	1981
Australia in Australia	41 (av 12.85)	R.M.Hogg	1978-79
England in England	46 (av 9.60)	J.C.Laker	1956
England in Australia	38 (av 23.18)	M.W.Tate	1924-25

AUSTRALIA V SOUTH AFRICA	Australia		South Africa		Captains	
Venue and Result	1st	2nd	1st	2nd	Australia	South Africa
1902-03 in SOUTH AFRICA						
Johannesburg[1]-Drawn	296	7d-372	•454	4-101	J.Darling	H.M.Taberer
Johannesburg[1]-Australia 159 runs	•175	309	240	85		J.H.Anderson
Cape Town-Australia 10 wkts	•252	0-59	85	225		E.A.Halliwell
1910-11 in AUSTRALIA						
Sydney-Australia inns &114 runs	•528	-	174	240	C.Hill	P.W.Sherwell
Melbourne-Australia 89 runs	•348	327	506	80		
Adelaide-South Africa 38 runs	465	339	•482	360		
Melbourne-Australia 530 runs	•328	578	205	171		
Sydney-Australia 7 wkts	•364	3-198	160	401		
1912 in ENGLAND						
Manchester-Australia inns & 88 runs	•448	-	265	95	S.E.Gregory	F.Mitchell
Lord's-Australia 10 wkts	390	0-48	•263	173		F.Mitchell
Nottingham-Drawn	219	-	•329	-		L.J.Tancred
1921-22 in SOUTH AFRICA						
Durban[1]-Drawn	•299	7d-324	232	7-184	H.L.Collins	H.W.Taylor
Johannesburg[1]-Drawn	•450	0-7	243	8d-472		
Cape Town-Australia 10 wkts	396	0-1	•180	216		
1931-32 in AUSTRALIA						
Brisbane[2]-Australia inns & 163 runs	•450	-	170	117	W.M.Woodfull	H.B.Cameron
Sydney-Australia inns & 155 runs	469	-	•153	161		
Melbourne-Australia 169 runs	•198	554	358	225		
Adelaide-Australia 10 wkts	513	0-73	•308	274		
Melbourne-Australia inns & 72 runs	153	-	•36	45		
1935-36 in SOUTH AFRICA						
Durban[2]-Australia 9 wkts	429	1-102	•248	282	V.Y.Richardson	H.F.Wade
Johannesburg[1]-Drawn	250	2-274	•157	491		
Cape Town-Australia inns & 78 runs	•8d-362	-	102	182		
Johannesburg[1]-Australia inns & 184 runs	439	-	•157	98		
Durban[2]-Australia inns & 6 runs	455	-	•222	227		
1949-50 in SOUTH AFRICA						
Johannesburg[2]-Australia inns & 85 runs	•413	-	137	191	A.L.Hassett	A.D.Nourse
Cape Town-Australia 8 wkts	•7d-526	2-87	278	333		
Durban[2]-Australia 5 wkts	75	5-336	•311	99		
Johannesburg[2]-Drawn	•8d-465	2-259	352	-		
Port Elizabeth-Australia inns & 259 runs	•7d-549	-	158	132		
1952-53 in AUSTRALIA						
Brisbane[2]-Australia 96 runs	•280	277	221	240	A.L.Hassett	J.E.Cheetham
Melbourne-South Africa 82 runs	243	290	•227	388		
Sydney-Australia inns & 38 runs	443	-	•173	232		
Adelaide-Drawn	•530	3d-233	387	6-177		
Melbourne-South Africa 6 wkts	•520	209	435	4-297		

AUSTRALIA v SOUTH AFRICA (cont)	Australia		South Africa		Captains	
Venue and Result	1st	2nd	1st	2nd	Australia	South Africa
1957-58 in SOUTH AFRICA						
Johannesburg[3]-Drawn	368	3-162	•9d-470	201	I.D.Craig	D.J.McGlew
Cape Town-Australia inns & 141 runs	•449	-	209	99		C.B.van Ryneveld
Durban[2]-Drawn	•163	7-292	384	-		C.B.van Ryneveld
Johannesburg[3]-Australia 10 wkts	•401	0-1	203	198		C.B.van Ryneveld
Port Elizabeth-Australia 8 wkts	291	2-68	•214	144		C.B.van Ryneveld
1963-64 in AUSTRALIA						
Brisbane[2]-Drawn	•435	1d-144	346	1-13	R.Benaud	T.L.Goddard
Melbourne-Australia 8 wkts	447	2-136	•274	306	R.B.Simpson	
Sydney-Drawn	•260	9d-450	302	5-326	R.B.Simpson	
Adelaide-South Africa 10 wkts	•345	331	595	0-82	R.B.Simpson	
Sydney-Drawn	•311	270	411	0-76	R.B.Simpson	
1966-67 in SOUTH AFRICA						
Johannesburg[3]-South Africa 233 runs	325	261	•199	620	R.B.Simpson	P.L.van der Merwe
Cape Town-Australia 6 wkts	•542	4-180	353	367		
Durban[2]-South Africa 8 wkts	147	334	•300	2-185		
Johannesburg[3]-Drawn	•143	8-148	9d-332	-		
Port Elizabeth-South Africa 7 wkts	•173	278	276	3-179		
1969-70 in SOUTH AFRICA						
Cape Town-South Africa 170 runs	164	280	•382	232	W.M.Lawry	A.Bacher
Durban[2]-South Africa inns &129 runs	157	336	•9d-622	-		
Johannesburg[3]-South Africa 307 runs	202	178	•279	408		
Port Elizabeth-South Africa 323 runs	212	246	•311	8d-470		
1993-94 in AUSTRALIA						
Melbourne-Drawn	•7d-342	-	3-258	-	A.R.Border	K.C.Wessels
Sydney-South Africa 5 runs	292	111	•169	239		K.C.Wessels
Adelaide-Australia 191 runs	•7d-469	6d-124	273	129		W.J.Cronje
1993-94 in SOUTH AFRICA						
Johannesburg[3]-South Africa 197 runs	248	256	•251	9d-450	A.R.Border	K.C.Wessels
Cape Town-Australia 9 wkts	435	1-92	•361	164		
Durban[2]-Drawn	•269	4-297	422	-		

Test Match Results Summary

AUSTRALIA v SOUTH AFRICA-IN AUSTRALIA

		Result			Sydney			Melbourne			Adelaide			Brisbane[2]		
	Tests	A	SA	D	A	SA	D	A	SA	D	A	SA	D	A	SA	D
1910-11	5	4	1	-	2	-	-	2	-	-	-	1	-	-	-	-
1931-32	5	5	-	-	1	-	-	2	-	-	1	-	-	1	-	-
1952-53	5	2	2	1	1	-	-	-	2	-	-	-	1	1	-	-
1963-64	5	1	1	3	-	-	2	1	-	-	-	1	-	-	-	1
1993-94	3	1	1	1	-	1	-	-	-	1	1	-	-	-	-	-
	23	13	5	5	4	1	2	5	2	1	2	2	1	2	-	1

AUSTRALIA v SOUTH AFRICA-IN SOUTH AFRICA

		Result			Jo'burg[1]			Cape Town			Durban[1]			Durban[2]			Jo'burg[2]			P.Elizabeth			Jo'burg[3]		
	Tests	A	S	D	A	S	D	A	S	D	A	S	D	A	S	D	A	S	D	A	S	D	A	S	D
1902-03	3	2	-	1	1	-	1	1	-	-	-	-	-	-	-	-	-	-	-	-	-	-	-	-	-
1921-22	3	1	-	2	-	-	1	1	-	-	-	-	1	-	-	-	-	-	-	-	-	-	-	-	-
1935-36	5	4	-	1	1	-	1	1	-	-	-	-	-	2	-	-	-	-	-	-	-	-	-	-	-
1949-50	5	4	-	1	-	-	-	1	-	-	-	-	-	1	-	-	1	-	1	1	-	-	-	-	-
1957-58	5	3	-	2	-	-	-	1	-	-	-	-	-	-	-	1	-	-	-	1	-	-	1	-	1
1966-67	5	1	3	1	-	-	-	1	-	-	-	-	-	-	1	-	-	-	-	-	1	-	-	1	1
1969-70	4	-	4	-	-	-	-	-	1	-	-	-	-	-	1	-	-	-	-	-	1	-	-	1	-
1993-94	3	1	1	1	-	-	-	1	-	-	-	-	-	-	-	1	-	-	-	-	-	-	-	1	-
	33	16	8	9	2	-	3	7	1	-	-	-	1	3	2	2	1	-	1	2	2	-	1	3	2

AUSTRALIA v SOUTH AFRICA-IN ENGLAND

		Result			Manchester			Lord's			Nottingham		
	Tests	A	SA	D	A	SA	D	A	SA	D	A	SA	D
1912	3	2	-	1	1	-	-	1	-	-	-	-	1
Totals	59	31	13	15									

HIGHEST INNINGS TOTALS

Australia in Australia	578	Melbourne	1910-11
Australia in South Africa	7d-549	Port Elizabeth	1949-50
South Africa in Australia	595	Adelaide	1963-64
South Africa in South Africa	9d-622	Durban[2]	1969-70

LOWEST INNINGS TOTALS

Australia in Australia	111	Sydney	1993-94
Australia in South Africa	75	Durban[2]	1949-50
South Africa in Australia	36	Melbourne	1931-32
South Africa in South Africa	85	Johannesburg[1]	1902-03
	85	Cape Town	1902-03

HIGHEST MATCH AGGREGATE	1646 for 40 wickets	Adelaide	1910-11
LOWEST MATCH AGGREGATE	234 for 29 wickets	Melbourne	1931-32

HIGHEST INDIVIDUAL INNINGS

Australia in Australia	299*	D.G.Bradman	Adelaide	1931-32
Australia in South Africa	203	H.L.Collins	Johannesburg[1]	1921-22
South Africa in Australia	204	G.A.Faulkner	Melbourne	1910-11
South Africa in South Africa	274	R.G.Pollock	Durban[2]	1969-70

HIGHEST AGGREGATE OF RUNS IN A SERIES

Australia in Australia	834 (av 92.66)	R.N.Harvey	1952-53
Australia in South Africa	660 (av 132.00)	R.N.Harvey	1949-50
South Africa in Australia	732 (av 73.20)	G.A.Faulkner	1910-11
South Africa in South Africa	606 (av 86.57)	D.T.Lindsay	1966-67

RECORD WICKET PARTNERSHIPS-AUSTRALIA

1st	233	J.H.W.Fingleton (112), W.A.Brown (121)	Cape Town	1935-36
2nd	275	C.C.McDonald (154), A.L.Hassett (163)	Adelaide	1952-53
3rd	242	C.Kelleway (102), W.Bardsley (164)	Lord's	1912
4th	169	M.A.Taylor (170), M.E.Waugh (84)	Melbourne	1993-94
5th	208	A.R.Border (84), S.R.Waugh (164)	Adelaide	1993-94
6th	107	C.Kelleway (59), V.S.Ransford (75)	Melbourne	1910-11
7th	160	R.Benaud (90), G.D.McKenzie (76)	Sydney	1963-64
8th	83	A.G.Chipperfield (109), C.V.Grimmett (15)	Durban[2]	1935-36
9th	78	D.G.Bradman (299*), W.J.O'Reilly (23)	Adelaide	1931-32
	78	K.D.Mackay (83*), I.Meckiff (26)	Johannesburg[3]	1957-58
10th	82	V.S.Ransford (95), W.J.Whitty (39*)	Melbourne	1910-11

RECORD WICKET PARTNERSHIPS-SOUTH AFRICA

1st	176	D.J.McGlew (108), T.L.Goddard (90)	Johannesburg[3]	1957-58
2nd	173	L.J.Tancred (97), C.B.Llewellyn (90)	Johannesburg[1]	1902-03
3rd	341	E.J.Barlow (201), R.G.Pollock (175)	Adelaide	1963-64
4th	206	C.N.Frank (152), A.W.Nourse (111)	Johannesburg[1]	1921-22
5th	129	J.H.B.Waite (59), W.R.Endean (77)	Johannesburg[3]	1957-58
6th	200	R.G.Pollock (274), H.R.Lance (61)	Durban[2]	1969-70
7th	221	D.T.Lindsay (182), P.L.van der Merwe (76)	Johannesburg[3]	1966-67
8th	124	A.W.Nourse (72), E.A.Halliwell (57)	Johannesburg[1]	1902-03
9th	85	R.G.Pollock (209), P.M.Pollock (41)	Cape Town	1966-67
10th	53	L.A.Stricker (48), S.J.Pegler (24*)	Adelaide	1910-11

BEST INNINGS BOWLING ANALYSIS

Australia in Australia	7-56	S.K.Warne	Sydney	1993-94
Australia in South Africa	7-34	J.V.Saunders	Johannesburg[1]	1902-03
South Africa in Australia	7-81	H.J.Tayfield	Melbourne	1952-53
South Africa in South Africa	7-23	H.J.Tayfield	Durban[2]	1949-50

BEST MATCH BOWLING ANALYSIS

Australia in Australia	14-199	C.V.Grimmett	Adelaide	1931-32
Australia in South Africa	13-173	C.V.Grimmett	Durban[2]	1935-36
South Africa in Australia	13-165	H.J.Tayfield	Melbourne	1952-53
South Africa in South Africa	10-116	C.B.Llewellyn	Johannesburg[1]	1902-03

HIGHEST AGGREGATE OF WICKETS IN A SERIES

Australia in Australia	37 (av 17.08)	W.J.Whitty	1910-11
Australia in South Africa	44 (av 14.59)	C.V.Grimmett	1935-36
South Africa in Australia	30 (av 28.10)	H.J.Tayfield	1952-53
South Africa in South Africa	26 (av 16.23)	T.L.Goddard	1966-67
	26 (av 13.57)	M.J.Procter	1969-70

AUSTRALIA V WEST INDIES	Australia		West Indies		Captains	
Venue and Result	1st	2nd	1st	2nd	Australia	West Indies
1930-31 in AUSTRALIA						
Adelaide-Australia 10 wkts	376	0-172	•296	249	W.M.Woodfull	G.C.Grant
Sydney-Australia inns & 172 runs	•369	-	107	90		
Brisbane[1]-Australia inns & 217 runs	•558	-	193	148		
Melbourne-Australia inns & 122 runs	8d-328	-	•99	107		
Sydney-West Indies 30 runs	224	220	•6d-350	5d-124		
1951-52 in AUSTRALIA						
Brisbane[2]-Australia 3 wkts	226	7-236	•216	245	A.L.Hassett	J.D.C.Goddard
Sydney-Australia 7 wkts	517	3-137	•362	290	A.L.Hassett	J.D.C.Goddard
Adelaide-West Indies 6 wkts	•82	255	105	4-233	A.R.Morris	J.D.C.Goddard
Melbourne-Australia 1 wkt	216	9-260	•272	203	A.L.Hassett	J.D.C.Goddard
Sydney-Australia 202 runs	•116	377	78	213	A.L.Hassett	J.B.Stollmeyer
1954-55 in WEST INDIES						
Kingston-Australia 9 wkts	•9d-515	1-20	259	275	I.W.Johnson	D.S.Atkinson
Port-of-Spain-Drawn	9d-600	-	•382	4-273		J.B.Stollmeyer
Georgetown-Australia 8 wkts	257	2-133	•182	207		J.B.Stollmeyer
Bridgetown-Drawn	•668	249	510	6-234		D.S.Atkinson
Kingston-Australia inns & 82 runs	8d-758	-	•357	319		D.S.Atkinson
1960-61 in AUSTRALIA						
Brisbane[2]-Tied	505	232	•453	284	R.Benaud	F.M.M.Worrell
Melbourne-Australia 7 wkts	•348	3-70	181	233		
Sydney-West Indies 222 runs	202	241	•339	326		
Adelaide-Drawn	366	9-273	•393	6d-432		
Melbourne-Australia 2 wkts	356	8-258	•292	321		
1964-65 in WEST INDIES						
Kingston-West Indies 179 runs	217	216	•239	373	R.B.Simpson	G.S.Sobers
Port-of-Spain-Drawn	516	-	•429	386		
Georgetown-West Indies 212 runs	179	144	•355	180		
Bridgetown-Drawn	•6d-650	4d-175	573	5-242		
Port-of-Spain-Australia 10 wkts	294	0-63	•224	131		
1968-69 in AUSTRALIA						
Brisbane [2]-West Indies 125 runs	284	240	•296	353	W.M.Lawry	G.S.Sobers
Melbourne-Australia inns & 30 runs	510	-	•200	280		
Sydney-Australia 10 wkts	547	0-42	•264	324		
Adelaide-Drawn	533	9-339	•276	616		
Sydney-Australia 382 runs	•619	8d-394	279	352		
1972-73 in WEST INDIES						
Kingston-Drawn	•7d-428	2d-260	428	3-67	I.M.Chappell	R.B.Kanhai
Bridgetown-Drawn	•324	2d-300	391	0-36		
Port-of-Spain-Australia 44 runs	•332	281	280	289		
Georgetown-Australia 10 wkts	341	0-135	•366	109		
Port-of-Spain-Drawn	•8d-419	7d-218	319	5-135		

AUSTRALIA V WEST INDIES	Australia		West Indies		Captains	
Venue and Result	1st	2nd	1st	2nd	Australia	West Indies
1975-76 in AUSTRALIA						
Brisbane²-Australia 8 wkts	366	2-219	·214	370	G.S.Chappell	C.H.Lloyd
Perth-West Indies inns & 87 runs	•329	169	585	-		
Melbourne-Australia 8 wkts	485	2-55	•224	312		
Sydney-Australia 7 wkts	405	3-82	•355	128		
Adelaide-Australia 190 runs	•418	7d-345	274	299		
Melbourne-Australia 165 runs	•351	3d-300	160	326		
1977-78 in WEST INDIES						
Port-of-Spain-West Indies inns & 106 runs	·90	209	405	-	R.B.Simpson	C.H.Lloyd
Bridgetown-West Indies 9 wkts	•250	178	288	1-141		C.H.Lloyd
Georgetown-Australia 3 wkts	286	7-362	•205	439		A.I.Kallicharran
Port-of-Spain-West Indies 198 runs	290	94	•292	290		A.I.Kallicharran
Kingston-Drawn	•343	3d-305	280	9-258		A.I.Kallicharran
1979-80 in AUSTRALIA						
Brisbane²-Drawn	•268	6d-448	441	3-40	G.S.Chappell	D L.Murray
Melbourne-West Indies 10 wkts	•156	259	397	0-22		C.H.Lloyd
Adelaide-West Indies 408 runs	203	165	•328	448		C.H.Lloyd
1981-82 in AUSTRALIA						
Melbourne-Australia 58 runs	•198	222	201	161	G.S.Chappell	C H.Lloyd
Sydney-Drawn	267	4-200	•384	255		
Adelaide-West Indies 5 wkts	•238	386	389	5-239		
1983-84 in WEST INDIES						
Georgetown-Drawn	•279	9d-273	230	0-250	K.J.Hughes	C.H.Lloyd
Port-of-Spain-Drawn	•255	9d-299	8d-468	-		I.V.A.Richards
Bridgetown-West Indies 10 wkts	•429	97	509	0-21		C.H.Lloyd
St John's-West Indies inns & 36 runs	•262	200	498	-		C.H.Lloyd
Kingston-West Indies 10 wkts	•199	160	305	0-55		C.H.Lloyd
1984-85 in AUSTRALIA						
Perth-West Indies inns & 112 runs	76	228	•416	-	K.J.Hughes	C.H.Lloyd
Brisbane²-West Indies 8 wkts	•175	271	424	2-26	K.J.Hughes	
Adelaide-West Indies 191 runs	284	173	•356	7d-292	A.R.Border	
Melbourne-Drawn	298	8-198	•479	5d-186	A.R.Border	
Sydney-Australia inns & 55 runs	•9d-471	-	163	253	A.R.Border	
1988-89 in AUSTRALIA						
Brisbane²-West Indies 8 wkts	•167	289	394	2-63	A.R.Border	I.V.A.Richards
Perth-West Indies 169 runs	8d-395	234	•449	9d-349		
Melbourne-West Indies 285 runs	242	114	•280	9d-361		
Sydney-Australia 7 wkts	401	3-82	•224	256		
Adelaide-Drawn	•515	4d-224	369	4-233		

AUSTRALIA v WEST INDIES (cont.) Venue and Result	Australia 1st	Australia 2nd	West Indies 1st	West Indies 2nd	Captains Australia	Captains West Indies
1990-91 in WEST INDIES						
Kingston-Drawn	371	-	•264	3-334	A.R.Border	I.V.A.Richards
Georgetown-West Indies 10 wkts	•348	248	569	0-31		
Port-of-Spain-Drawn	•294	3-123	227	-		
Bridgetown-West Indies 343 runs	134	208	•149	9d-536		
St John's-Australia 157 runs	•403	265	214	297		
1992-93 in AUSTRALIA						
Brisbane²-Drawn	•293	308	371	8-133	A.R.Border	R.B.Richardson
Melbourne-Australia 139 runs	•395	196	233	219		
Sydney-Drawn	•9d-503	0-117	616	-		
Adelaide-West Indies 1 run	213	184	•252	146		
Perth-West Indies inns & 25 runs	•119	178	322	-		
1994-95 in WEST INDIES						
Bridgetown-Australia 10 wkts	346	0-39	•195	189	M.A.Taylor	R.B.Richardson
St John's-Drawn	•216	7d-300	260	2-80		
Port-of-Spain-West Indies 9 wkts	•128	105	136	1-98		
Kingston-Australia inns & 53 runs	531	-	•265	213		

Test Match Results Summary

AUSTRALIA v WEST INDIES-IN AUSTRALIA

	Tests	Result A	W	D	T	Adelaide A	W	D	T	Sydney A	W	D	T	Brisbane¹ A	W	D	T	Melbourne A	W	D	T	Brisbane² A	W	D	T	Perth A	W	D	T
1930-31	5	4	1	-	-	1	-	-	-	1	1	-	-	1	-	-	-	1	-	-	-	-	-	-	-	-	-	-	-
1951-52	5	4	1	-	-	-	1	-	-	2	-	-	-	-	-	-	-	1	-	-	-	1	-	-	-	-	-	-	-
1960-61	5	2	1	1	1	-	-	1	-	-	1	-	-	-	-	-	-	2	-	-	-	-	-	-	1	-	-	-	-
1968-69	5	3	1	1	-	-	-	1	-	2	-	-	-	-	-	-	-	1	-	-	-	-	1	-	-	-	-	-	-
1975-76	6	5	1	-	-	1	-	-	-	1	-	-	-	-	-	-	-	2	-	-	-	1	-	-	-	-	1	-	-
1979-80	3	-	2	1	-	-	1	-	-	-	-	-	-	-	-	-	-	-	1	-	-	-	-	1	-	-	-	-	-
1981-82	3	1	1	1	-	-	1	-	-	-	-	1	-	-	-	-	-	1	-	-	-	-	-	-	-	-	-	-	-
1984-85	5	1	3	1	-	-	1	-	-	1	-	-	-	-	-	-	-	-	-	1	-	-	1	-	-	-	1	-	-
1988-89	5	1	3	1	-	-	-	1	-	1	-	-	-	-	-	-	-	-	1	-	-	-	1	-	-	-	1	-	-
1992-93	5	1	2	2	-	-	1	-	-	-	-	1	-	-	-	-	-	1	-	-	-	-	-	1	-	-	1	-	-
	47	22	16	8	1	2	5	3	-	8	2	2	-	1	-	-	-	9	2	1	-	2	3	2	1	-	4	-	-

AUSTRALIA v WEST INDIES-IN WEST INDIES

	Tests	Result A	W	D	T	Kingston A	W	D	T	Port-of-Spain A	W	D	T	Georgetown A	W	D	T	Bridgetown A	W	D	T	St John's A	W	D	T
1954-55	5	3	-	2	-	2	-	-	-	-	-	1	-	1	-	-	-	-	-	1	-	-	-	-	-
1964-65	5	1	2	2	-	-	1	-	-	1	-	1	-	-	1	-	-	-	-	1	-	-	-	-	-
1972-73	5	2	-	3	-	-	-	1	-	1	-	1	-	1	-	-	-	-	-	1	-	-	-	-	-
1977-78	5	1	3	1	-	-	-	1	-	-	2	-	-	1	-	-	-	-	1	-	-	-	-	-	-
1983-84	5	-	3	2	-	-	1	-	-	-	-	1	-	-	-	1	-	-	1	-	-	-	1	-	-
1990-91	5	1	2	2	-	-	-	1	-	-	-	1	-	-	1	-	-	-	1	-	-	1	-	-	-
1994-95	4	2	1	1	-	1	-	-	-	-	1	-	-	-	-	-	-	1	-	-	-	-	-	1	-
	34	10	11	13	-	3	2	3	-	2	3	5	-	3	2	1	-	1	3	3	-	1	1	1	-
Totals	81	32	27	21	1																				

HIGHEST INNINGS TOTALS

Australia in Australia	619	Sydney	1968-69
Australia in West Indies	8d-758	Kingston	1954-55
West Indies in Australia	616	Adelaide	1968-69
West Indies in West Indies	573	Bridgetown	1964-65

LOWEST INNINGS TOTALS

Australia in Australia	76	Perth	1984-85
Australia in West Indies	90	Port-of-Spain	1977-78
West Indies in Australia	78	Sydney	1951-52
West Indies in West Indies	109	Georgetown	1972-73

HIGHEST MATCH AGGREGATE	1764 for 39 wickets	Adelaide	1968-69
LOWEST MATCH AGGREGATE	467 for 31 wickets	Port-of-Spain	1994-95

HIGHEST INDIVIDUAL INNINGS

Australia in Australia	242	K.D.Walters	Sydney	1968-69
Australia in West Indies	210	W.M.Lawry	Bridgetown	1964-65
West Indies in Australia	277	B.C.Lara	Sydney	1992-93
West Indies in West Indies	226	C.G.Greenidge	Bridgetown	1990-91

HIGHEST AGGREGATE OF RUNS IN A SERIES

Australia in Australia	702 (av 117.00)	G.S.Chappell	1975-76
Australia in West Indies	650 (av 108.33)	R.N.Harvey	1954-55
West Indies in Australia	537 (av 59.66)	D.L.Haynes	1988-89
West Indies in West Indies	827 (av 82.70)	C.L.Walcott	1954-55

RECORD WICKET PARTNERSHIPS-AUSTRALIA

1st	382	W.M.Lawry (210), R.B.Simpson (201)	Bridgetown	1964-65
2nd	298	W.M.Lawry (205), I.M.Chappell (165)	Melbourne	1968-69
3rd	295	C.C.McDonald (127), R.N.Harvey (204)	Kingston	1954-55
4th	336	W.M.Lawry (151), K.D.Walters (242)	Sydney	1968-69
5th	220	K.R.Miller (109), R.G.Archer (128)	Kingston	1954-55
6th	206	K.R.Miller (137), R.G.Archer (98)	Bridgetown	1954-55
7th	134	R.Benaud (52), A.K.Davidson (80)	Brisbane[2]	1960-61
8th	137	R.Benaud (128), I.W.Johnson (27*)	Kingston	1954-55
9th	114	D.M.Jones (216), M.G.Hughes (72*)	Adelaide	1988-89
10th	97	T.G.Hogan (42*), R.M.Hogg (52)	Georgetown	1983-84

RECORD WICKET PARTNERSHIPS-WEST INDIES

1st	250*	C.G.Greenidge (120*), D.L.Haynes (103*)	Georgetown	1983-84
2nd	297	D.L.Haynes (111), R.B.Richardson (182)	Georgetown	1990-91
3rd	308	R.B.Richardson (154), I.V.A.Richards (178)	Antigua	1983-84
4th	198	L.G.Rowe (107), A.I.Kallicharran (101)	Brisbane[2]	1975-76
5th	210	R.B.Kanhai (84), M.L.C.Foster (125)	Kingston	1972-73
6th	165	R.B.Kanhai (105), D.L.Murray (90)	Bridgetown	1972-73
7th	347	D.S.Atkinson (219), C.C.Depeiza (122)	Bridgetown	1954-55
8th	87	P.J.L.Dujon (70), C.E.L.Ambrose (53)	Port-of-Spain	1990-91
9th	122	D.A.J.Holford (80), J.L.Hendriks (37*)	Adelaide	1968-69
10th	56	J.Garner (60), C.E.H.Croft (2*)	Brisbane[2]	1979-80

BEST INNINGS BOWLING ANALYSIS

Australia in Australia	8-71	G.D.McKenzie	Melbourne	1968-69
Australia in West Indies	7-44	I.W.Johnson	Georgetown	1954-55
West Indies in Australia	7-25	C.E.L.Ambrose	Perth	1992-93
West Indies in West Indies	6-29	L R.Gibbs	Georgetown	1964-65

BEST MATCH BOWLING ANALYSIS

Australia in Australia	13-217	M.G.Hughes	Perth	1988-89
Australia in West Indies	10-115	N.J.N.Hawke	Georgetown	1964-65
West Indies in Australia	11-107	M.A.Holding	Melbourne	1981-82
West Indies in West Indies	9-80	L.R.Gibbs	Georgetown	1964-65

HIGHEST AGGREGATE OF WICKETS IN A SERIES

Australia in Australia	33 (av 17 96)	C.V.Grimmett	1930-31
	33 (av 18 54)	A.K.Davidson	1960-61
Australia in West Indies	26 (av 20.73)	M.H.N.Walker	1972-73
West Indies in Australia	33 (av 16.42)	C.E.L.Ambrose	1992-93
West Indies in West Indies	31 (av 16.87)	J.Garner	1983-84

AUSTRALIA V NEW ZEALAND	Australia		New Zealand		Captains	
Venue and Result	1st	2nd	1st	2nd	Australia	New Zealand
1945-46 in NEW ZEALAND						
Wellington-Australia inns & 103 runs	8d-199	-	•42	54	W.A.Brown	W.A.Hadlee
1973-74 in AUSTRALIA						
Melbourne-Australia inns & 25 runs	•8d-462	-	237	200	I.M.Chappell	B.E.Congdon
Sydney-Drawn	162	2-30	•312	9d-305		
Adelaide-Australia inns & 57 runs	•477	-	218	202		
1973-74 in NEW ZEALAND						
Wellington-Drawn	•6d-511	8-460	484	-	I.M.Chappell	B.E.Congdon
Christchurch-New Zealand 5 wkts	•223	259	255	5-230		
Auckland-Australia 297 runs	•221	346	112	158		
1976-77 in NEW ZEALAND						
Christchurch-Drawn	•552	4d-154	357	8-293	G.S.Chappell	G.M.Turner
Auckland-Australia 10 wkts	377	0-28	•229	175		
1980-81 in AUSTRALIA						
Brisbane[2]-Australia 10 wkts	305	0-63	•225	142	G.S.Chappell	G.P.Howarth
Perth-Australia 8 wkts	265	2-55	•196	121		M.G.Burgess
Melbourne-Drawn	•321	188	317	6-128		G.P.Howarth
1981-82 in NEW ZEALAND						
Wellington-Drawn	1-85	-	•7d-266	-	G.S.Chappell	G.P.Howarth
Auckland-New Zealand 5 wkts	•210	280	387	5-109		
Christchurch-Australia 8 wkts	•353	2-69	149	272		
1985-86 in AUSTRALIA						
Brisbane[2]-New Zealand inns & 41 runs	•179	333	7d-553	-	A.R.Border	J.V.Coney
Sydney-Australia 4 wkts	227	6-260	•293	193		
Perth-New Zealand 6 wkts	•203	259	299	4-164		
1985-86 in NEW ZEALAND						
Wellington-Drawn	•435	-	6-379	-	A.R.Border	J.V.Coney
Auckland-Drawn	•364	7d-219	339	1-16		
Christchurch-New Zealand 8 wkts	•314	103	258	2-160		
1987-88 in AUSTRALIA						
Brisbane[2]-Australia 9 wkts	305	1-97	•186	212	A.R.Border	J.J.Crowe
Adelaide-Drawn	496	-	•9d-485	7-182		
Melbourne-Drawn	357	9-230	•317	286		
1989-90 in AUSTRALIA						
Perth-Drawn	•9d-521	-	231	7-322	A.R.Border	J.G.Wright
1989-90 in NEW ZEALAND						
Wellington-New Zealand 9 wkts	•110	269	202	1-181	A.R.Border	J.G.Wright
1992-93 in NEW ZEALAND						
Canterbury-Australia inns & 60 runs	•485	-	182	243	A.R.Border	M.D.Crowe
Wellington-Drawn	298	-	•329	7-210		
Auckland-New Zealand 5 wkts	•139	285	224	5-201		

AUSTRALIA v NEW ZEALAND (cont.)	Australia		New Zealand		Captains	
Venue and Result	1st	2nd	1st	2nd	Australia	New Zealand
1993-94 in AUSTRALIA						
Perth-Drawn	·398	1d-323	9d-419	4-166	A.R.Border	M.D.Crowe
Hobart-Australia inns & 222 runs	·6d-544	-	161	161		K.R.Rutherford
Brisbane²-Australia inns & 96 runs	6d-607	-	·233	278		K.R.Rutherford

Test Match Results Summary

AUSTRALIA v NEW ZEALAND-IN AUSTRALIA

		Result			Melbourne			Sydney			Adelaide			Brisbane²			Perth			Hobart		
	Tests	A	NZ	D	A	NZ	D	A	NZ	D	A	NZ	D	A	NZ	D	A	NZ	D	A	NZ	D
1973-74	3	2	-	1	1	-	-	-	-	1	1	-	-	-	-	-	-	-	-	-	-	-
1980-81	3	2	-	1	-	-	1	-	-	-	-	-	-	1	-	-	1	-	-	-	-	-
1985-86	3	1	2	-	-	-	-	1	-	-	-	-	-	-	1	-	-	1	-	-	-	-
1987-88	3	1	-	2	-	-	1	-	-	-	-	-	1	1	-	-	-	-	-	-	-	-
1989-90	1	-	-	1	-	-	-	-	-	-	-	-	-	-	-	-	-	-	1	-	-	-
1993-94	3	2	-	1	-	-	-	-	-	-	-	-	-	1	-	-	-	-	1	1	-	-
	16	8	2	6	1	-	2	1	-	1	1	-	1	3	1	-	1	1	2	1	-	-

AUSTRALIA v NEW ZEALAND-IN NEW ZEALAND

		Result			Wellington			Christchurch			Auckland		
	Tests	A	NZ	D	A	NZ	D	A	NZ	D	A	NZ	D
1945-46	1	1	-	-	1	-	-	-	-	-	-	-	-
1973-74	3	1	1	1	-	-	1	-	1	-	1	-	-
1976-77	2	1	-	1	-	-	-	-	-	1	1	-	-
1981-82	3	1	1	1	-	-	1	1	-	-	-	1	-
1985-86	3	-	1	2	-	-	1	-	-	1	-	1	-
1989-90	1	-	1	-	-	1	-	-	-	-	-	-	-
1992-93	3	1	1	1	-	-	1	1	-	-	-	1	-
	16	5	5	6	1	1	4	2	1	2	2	3	-
Totals	32	13	7	12									

HIGHEST INNINGS TOTALS			
Australia in Australia	6d-607	Brisbane²	1993-94
Australia in New Zealand	552	Christchurch	1976-77
New Zealand in Australia	7d-553	Brisbane²	1985-86
New Zealand in New Zealand	484	Wellington	1973-74
LOWEST INNINGS TOTALS			
Australia in Australia	162	Sydney	1973-74
Australia in New Zealand	103	Auckland	1985-86
New Zealand in Australia	121	Perth	1980-81
New Zealand in New Zealand	42	Wellington	1945-46
HIGHEST MATCH AGGREGATE	1455 for 24 wickets	Wellington	1973-74
LOWEST MATCH AGGREGATE	295 for 28 wickets	Wellington	1945-46

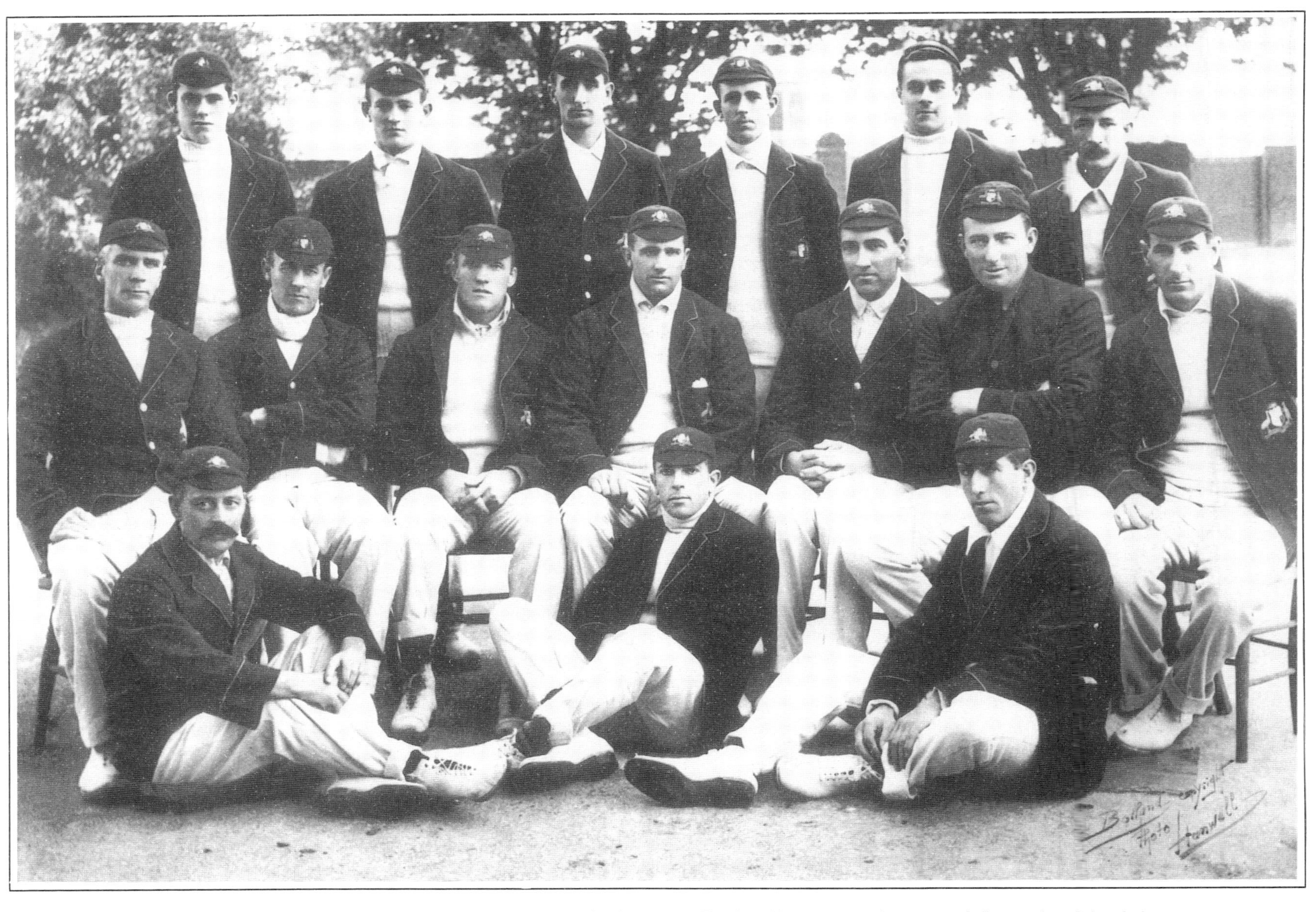

The Australian team, captained by Monty Noble, which toured England in 1909 and successfully retained the Ashes.

'The Big Ship' and captain of the Australian team, Warwick Armstrong, scoring a fine 158 against England in Sydney during the 1920-21 series.

HIGHEST INDIVIDUAL INNINGS

Australia in Australia	205	A.R.Border	Adelaide	1987-88
Australia in New Zealand	250	K.D.Walters	Christchurch	1976-77
New Zealand in Australia	188	M.D.Crowe	Sydney	1985-86
New Zealand in New Zealand	161	B.A.Edgar	Auckland	1981-82

HIGHEST AGGREGATE OF RUNS IN A SERIES

Australia in Australia	305 (av 76.25)	M.J.Slater	1993-94
Australia in New Zealand	449 (av 89.80)	G.S.Chappell	1973-74
New Zealand in Australia	396 (av 66.00)	M.D.Crowe	1987-88
New Zealand in New Zealand	403 (av 100.75)	G.M.Turner	1973-74

RECORD WICKET PARTNERSHIPS-AUSTRALIA

1st	198	M.J.Slater (99), M.A.Taylor (142*)	Perth	1993-94
2nd	235	M.J.Slater (168), D.C.Boon (106)	Hobart	1993-94
3rd	264	I.M.Chappell (145), G.S.Chappell (247*)	Wellington	1973-74
4th	150	M.E.Waugh (111), A.R.Border (60)	Hobart	1993-94
5th	213	G.M.Ritchie (92), G.R.J.Matthews (130)	Wellington	1985-86
6th	197	A.R.Border (152*), G.R.J.Matthews (115)	Brisbane[2]	1985-86
7th	217	K.D.Walters (250), G.J.Gilmour (101)	Christchurch	1976-77
8th	93	G.J.Gilmour (64), K.J.O'Keeffe (32)	Auckland	1976-77
9th	69	I.A.Healy (113*), C.J.McDermott (35)	Perth	1993-94
10th	60	K.D.Walters (107), J.D.Higgs (6*)	Melbourne	1980-81

RECORD WICKET PARTNERSHIPS-NEW ZEALAND

1st	112	M.J.Greatbatch (61), J.G.Wright (72)	Wellington	1992-93
2nd	128	J.G.Wright (45), A.H.Jones (150)	Adelaide	1987-88
	128*	J.G.Wright (117*), A.H.Jones (33*)	Wellington	1989-90
3rd	224	J.F.Reid (108), M.D.Crowe (188)	Brisbane[2]	1985-86
4th	229	B.E.Congdon (132), B.F.Hastings (101)	Wellington	1973-74
5th	88	J.V.Coney (71), M.G.Burgess (43)	Perth	1980-81
6th	109	K.R.Rutherford (65), J.V.Coney (101*)	Wellington	1985-86
7th	132*	J.V.Coney (101*), R.J.Hadlee (81*)	Wellington	1985-86
8th	88*	M.J.Greatbatch (146*), M.C.Snedden (33*)	Perth	1989-90
9th	73	H.J.Howarth (60), D.R.Hadlee (37)	Christchurch	1976-77
10th	124	J.G.Bracewell (83*), S.L.Boock (37)	Sydney	1985-86

BEST INNINGS BOWLING ANALYSIS

Australia in Australia	6-31	S.K.Warne	Hobart	1993-94
Australia in New Zealand	6-72	D.K.Lillee	Auckland	1976-77
New Zealand in Australia	9-52	R.J.Hadlee	Melbourne	1985-86
New Zealand in New Zealand	7-89	D.K.Morrison	Wellington	1992-93

BEST MATCH BOWLING ANALYSIS

Australia in Australia	10-174	R.G.Holland	Sydney	1985-86
Australia in New Zealand	11-123	D.K.Lillee	Auckland	1976-77
New Zealand in Australia	15-123	R.J.Hadlee	Brisbane[2]	1985-86
New Zealand in New Zealand	10-146	J.G.Bracewell	Auckland	1985-86

HIGHEST AGGREGATE OF WICKETS IN A SERIES

Australia in Australia	18 (av 16.94)	S.K.Warne	1993-94
Australia in New Zealand	17 (av 15.05)	S.K.Warne	1992-93
New Zealand in Australia	33 (av 12.15)	R.J.Hadlee	1985-86
New Zealand in New Zealand	17 (av 25.64)	R.O.Collinge	1973-74
	17 (av) 16.94)	D.K.Morrison	1992-93

AUSTRALIA V INDIA	Australia		India		Captains	
Venue and Result	1st	2nd	1st	2nd	Australia	India
1947-48 in AUSTRALIA						
Brisbane[2]-Australia inns & 226 runs	•8d-382	-	58	98	D.G.Bradman	N.B.Amarnath
Sydney-Drawn	107	-	•188	7-61		
Melbourne-Australia 233 runs	•394	4d-255	9d-291	125		
Adelaide-Australia inns & 16 runs	•674	-	381	277		
Melbourne-Australia inns & 177 runs	•8d-575	-	331	67		
1956-57 in INDIA						
Chennai[2]-Australia inns & 5 runs	319	-	•161	153	I.W.Johnson	P.R.Umrigar
Mumbai[2]-Drawn	7d-523	-	•251	5-250	R.R.Lindwall	
Calcutta-Australia 94 runs	•177	9d-189	136	136	I.W.Johnson	
1959-60 in INDIA						
Delhi-Australia inns & 127 runs	468	-	•135	206	R.Benaud	G.S.Ramchand
Kanpur-India 119 runs	219	105	•152	291		
Mumbai[2]-Drawn	8d-387	1-34	•289	5d-226		
Chennai[2]-Australia inns & 55 runs	•342	-	149	138		
Calcutta-Drawn	331	2-121	•194	339		
1964-65 in INDIA						
Chennai[2]-Australia 139 runs	•211	397	276	193	R.B.Simpson	Nawab of Pataudi, jr
Mumbai[2]-India 2 wkts	•320	274	341	8-256		
Calcutta-Drawn	•174	1-143	235	-		
1967-68 in AUSTRALIA						
Adelaide-Australia 146 runs	•335	369	307	251	R.B.Simpson	C.G Borde
Melbourne-Australia inns & 4 runs	529	-	•173	352	R.B.Simpson	Nawab of Pataudi, jr
Brisbane[2]-Australia 39 runs	•379	294	279	355	W M.Lawry	Nawab of Pataudi, jr
Sydney-Australia 144 runs	•317	292	268	197	W.M.Lawry	Nawab of Pataudi, jr
1969-70 in INDIA						
Mumbai[2]-Australia 8 wkts	345	2-67	•271	137	W.M.Lawry	Nawab of Pataudi, jr
Kanpur-Drawn	348	0-95	•320	7d-312		
Delhi-India 7 wkts	•296	107	223	3-181		
Calcutta-Australia 10 wkts	335	0-42	•212	161		
Chennai[1]-Australia 77 runs	•258	153	163	171		
1977-78 in AUSTRALIA						
Brisbane[2]-Australia 16 runs	•166	327	153	324	R.B.Simpson	B.S.Bedi
Perth-Australia 2 wkts	394	8-342	•402	9d-330		
Melbourne-India 222 runs	213	164	•256	343		
Sydney-India inns & 2 runs	•131	263	8d-396	-		
Adelaide-Australia 47 runs	•505	256	269	445		
1979-80 in INDIA						
Chennai[1]-Drawn	•390	7-212	425	-	K.J.Hughes	S.M.Gavaskar
Bangalore-Drawn	•333	3-77	5d-457	-		
Kanpur-India 153 runs	304	125	•271	311		
Delhi-Drawn	298	413	•7d-510	-		
Calcutta-Drawn	•442	6d-151	347	4-200		
Mumbai[3]-India inns & 100 runs	160	198	•8d-458	-		

AUSTRALIA v INDIA (cont.)	Australia		India		Captains	
Venue and Result	1st	2nd	1st	2nd	Australia	India
1980-81 In AUSTRALIA						
Sydney-Australia inns & 4 runs	406	-	•201	201	G.S.Chappell	S.M.Gavaskar
Adelaide-Drawn	•528	7d-221	419	8-135		
Melbourne-India 59 runs	419	83	•237	324		
1985-86 In AUSTRALIA						
Adelaide-Drawn	•381	0-17	520	-	A.R.Border	Kapil Dev
Melbourne-Drawn	•262	308	445	2-59		
Sydney-Drawn	396	6-119	•4d-600	-		
1986-87 in INDIA						
Chennai[1]-Tied	•7d-574	5d-170	397	347	A.R.Border	Kapil Dev
Delhi-Drawn	•3d-207	-	3-107	-		
Mumbai[3]-Drawn	•345	2-216	5d-517	-		
1991-92 in AUSTRALIA						
Brisbane[2]-Australia 10 wkts	340	0-58	•239	156	A.R.Border	M.Azharuddin
Melbourne-Australia 8 wkts	349	2-128	•263	213		
Sydney-Drawn	•313	8-173	483	-		
Adelaide-Australia 38 runs	•145	451	225	333		
Perth-Australia 300 runs	•346	6d-367	272	141		

Test Match Results Summary

AUSTRALIA v INDIA-IN AUSTRALIA

		Result				Brisbane[2]				Sydney				Melbourne				Adelaide				Perth			
	Tests	A	I	D	T	A	I	D	T	A	I	D	T	A	I	D	T	A	I	D	T	A	I	D	T
1947-48	5	4	-	1	-	1	-	-	-	-	-	1	-	2	-	-	-	1	-	-	-	-	-	-	-
1967-68	4	4	-	-	-	1	-	-	-	1	-	-	-	1	-	-	-	1	-	-	-	-	-	-	-
1977-78	5	3	2	-	-	1	-	-	-	-	1	-	-	-	1	-	-	1	-	-	-	1	-	-	-
1980-81	3	1	1	1	-	-	-	-	-	1	-	-	-	-	1	-	-	-	-	1	-	-	-	-	-
1985-86	3	-	-	3	-	-	-	-	-	-	-	1	-	-	-	1	-	-	-	1	-	-	-	-	-
1991-92	5	4	-	1	-	1	-	-	-	-	-	1	-	1	-	-	-	1	-	-	-	1	-	-	-
	25	16	3	6	-	4	-	-	-	2	1	3	-	4	2	1	-	4	-	2	-	2	-	-	-

AUSTRALIA v INDIA-IN INDIA

		Result				Chennai[2]				Mumbai[2]				Calcutta				Delhi				Kanpur				Bang.				Chennai[1]				Mumbai[3]			
	Tests	A	I	D	T	A	I	D	T	A	I	D	T	A	I	D	T	A	I	D	T	A	I	D	T	A	I	D	T	A	I	D	T	A	I	D	T
1956-57	3	2	-	1	-	1	-	-	-	-	-	1	-	1	-	-	-	-	-	-	-	-	-	-	-	-	-	-	-	-	-	-	-	-	-	-	-
1959-60	5	2	1	2	-	1	-	-	-	-	-	1	-	-	-	1	-	1	-	-	-	-	1	-	-	-	-	-	-	-	-	-	-	-	-	-	-
1964-65	3	1	1	1	-	1	-	-	-	-	1	-	-	-	-	1	-	-	-	-	-	-	-	-	-	-	-	-	-	-	-	-	-	-	-	-	-
1969-70	5	3	1	1	-	-	-	-	-	1	-	-	-	1	-	-	-	-	1	-	-	-	-	1	-	-	-	-	-	1	-	-	-	-	-	-	-
1979-80	6	-	2	4	-	-	-	-	-	-	-	-	-	-	-	1	-	-	-	1	-	-	1	-	-	-	-	1	-	-	-	1	-	-	1	-	-
1986-87	3	-	-	2	1	-	-	-	-	-	-	-	-	-	-	-	-	-	-	1	-	-	-	-	-	-	-	-	-	-	-	-	1	-	-	1	-
	25	8	5	11	1	3	-	-	-	1	1	2	-	2	-	3	-	1	1	2	-	-	2	1	-	-	-	1	-	1	-	1	1	-	1	1	-
Totals	50	24	8	17	1																																

HIGHEST INNINGS TOTALS

Australia in Australia	674	Adelaide	1947-48
Australia in India	7d-574	Chennai[1]	1986-87
India in Australia	4d-600	Sydney	1985-86
India in India	5d-517	Mumbai[3]	1986-87

LOWEST INNINGS TOTALS

Australia in Australia	83	Melbourne	1980-81
Australia in India	105	Kanpur	1959-60
India in Australia	58	Brisbane[2]	1947-48
India in India	135	Delhi	1959-60

HIGHEST MATCH AGGREGATE	1488 for 32 wickets	Chennai[1]	1986-87
LOWEST MATCH AGGREGATE	538 for 28 wickets	Brisbane[2]	1947-48

HIGHEST INDIVIDUAL INNINGS

Australia in Australia	213	K.J.Hughes	Adelaide	1980-81
Australia in India	210	D.M.Jones	Chennai[1]	1986-87
India in Australia	206	R.J.Shastri	Sydney	1991-92
India in India	164*	D.B.Vengsarkar	Mumbai[3]	1986-87

HIGHEST AGGREGATE OR RUNS IN A SERIES

Australia in Australia	715 (av 178.75)	D.G.Bradman	1947-48
Australia in India	594 (av 59.40)	K.J.Hughes	1979-80
India in Australia	473 (av 52.55)	G.R.Viswanath	1977-78
India in India	518 (av 74.00)	G.R.Viswanath	1979-80

RECORD WICKET PARTNERSHIPS-AUSTRALIA

1st	217	D.C.Boon (172), G.R.Marsh (116)	Sydney	1985-86
2nd	236	S.G.Barnes (112), D.G.Bradman (201)	Adelaide	1947-48
3rd	222	A.R.Border (162), K.J.Hughes (100)	Chennai[1]	1979-80
4th	178	D.M.Jones (210), A.R.Border (106)	Chennai[1]	1986-87
5th	223*	A.R.Morris (100*), D.G.Bradman (127*)	Melbourne	1947-48
6th	151	T.R.Veivers (67), B.N.Jarman (78)	Mumbai[2]	1964-65
7th	66	G.R.J.Matthews (100), R.J.Bright (28)	Melbourne	1985-86
8th	73	T.R.Veivers (74), G.D.McKenzie (27)	Chennai[2]	1964-65
9th	87	I.W.Johnson (73), W.P.A.Crawford (34)	Chennai[2]	1956-57
10th	77	A.R.Border (163), D.R.Gilbert (10*)	Melbourne	1985-86

RECORD WICKET PARTNERSHIPS-INDIA

1st	192	S.M.Gavaskar (123), C.P.S.Chauhan (73)	Mumbai[3]	1979-80
2nd	224	S.M.Gavaskar (172), M.Amarnath (138)	Sydney	1985-86
3rd	159	S.M.Gavaskar (115), G.R.Viswanath (131)	Delhi	1979-80
4th	159	D.B.Vengsarkar (112), G.R.Viswanath (161*)	Bangalore	1979-80
5th	196	R.J.Shastri (206), S.R.Tendulkar (148*)	Sydney	1991-92
6th	298*	D.B.Vengsarkar (164*), R.J.Shastri (121*)	Mumbai[3]	1986-87
7th	132	V.S.Hazare (145), H.R.Adhikari (51)	Adelaide	1947-48
8th	127	S.M.H.Kirmani (101*), K.D.Ghavri (86)	Mumbai[3]	1979-80
9th	81	S.R.Tendulkar (114), K.S.More (67*)	Perth	1991-92
10th	94	S.M.Gavaskar (166*), N.S.Yadav (41)	Adelaide	1985-86

BEST INNINGS BOWLING ANALYSIS

Australia in Australia	7-27	M.R.Whitney	Perth	1991-92
Australia in India	7-43	R.R.Lindwall	Chennai[2]	1956-57
India in Australia	6-52	B.S.Chandrasekhar	Melbourne	1977-78
India in India	9-69	J.M.Patel	Kanpur	1959-60

BEST MATCH BOWLING ANALYSIS

Australia in Australia	12-126	B.A.Reid	Melbourne	1991-92
Australia in India	12-124	A.K.Davidson	Kanpur	1959-60
India in Australia	12-104	B.S.Chandrasekhar	Melbourne	1977-78
India in India	14-124	J.M.Patel	Kanpur	1959-60

HIGHEST AGGREGATE OF WICKETS IN A SERIES

Australia in Australia	31 (av 21.61)	C.J.McDermott	1991-92
Australia in India	[illegible] (av 14.[illegible])	A.K.Davidson	1959-60
	29 (av 19.58)	R.Benaud	1959-60
India in Australia	31 (av 23.87)	B.S.Bedi	1977-78
India in India	28 (av 22.32)	Kapil Dev	1979-80

AUSTRALIA V PAKISTAN	Australia		Pakistan		Captains	
Venue and Result	1st	2nd	1st	2nd	Australia	Pakistan
1956-57 In PAKISTAN						
Karachi[1]-Pakistan 9 wkts	•80	187	199	1-69	I.W.Johnson	A.H.Kardar
1959-60 In PAKISTAN						
Dacca-Australia 8 wkts	225	2-112	•200	134	R.Benaud	Fazal Mahmood
Lahore[2]-Australia 7 wkts	9d-391	3-123	•146	366		Imtiaz Ahmed
Karachi[1]-Drawn	257	2-83	•287	8d-194		Fazal Mahmood
1964-65 in PAKISTAN						
Karachi[1]-Drawn	352	2-227	•414	8d-279	R.B.Simpson	Hanif Mohammad
1964-65 in AUSTRALIA						
Melbourne-Drawn	448	2-88	•287	326	R.B.Simpson	Hanif Mohammad
1972-73 in AUSTRALIA						
Adelaide-Australia inns & 114 runs	585	-	•257	214	I.M.Chappell	Intikhab Alam
Melbourne-Australia 92 runs	•5d-441	425	8d-574	200		
Sydney-Australia 52 runs	•334	184	360	106		
1976-77 in AUSTRALIA						
Adelaide-Drawn	454	6-261	•272	466	G.S.Chappell	Mushtaq Mohammad
Melbourne-Australia 348 runs	•8d-517	8d-315	333	151		
Sydney-Pakistan 8 wkts	•211	180	360	232		
1978-79 in AUSTRALIA						
Melbourne-Pakistan 71 runs	168	310	•196	9d-353	G.N.Yallop	Mushtaq Mohammad
Perth-Australia 7 wkts	327	3-236	•277	285	K.J.Hughes	
1979-80 in PAKISTAN						
Karachi[1]-Pakistan 7 wkts	•225	140	292	3-76	G.S.Chappell	Javed Miandad
Faisalabad-Drawn	•617	-	2-382	-		
Lahore[2]-Drawn	•7d-407	8-391	9d-420	-		
1981-82 in AUSTRALIA						
Perth-Australia 286 runs	•180	8d-424	62	256	G.S.Chappell	Javed Miandad
Brisbane[2]-Australia 10 wkts	9d-512	0-3	•291	223		
Melbourne-Pakistan inns & 82 runs	293	125	•8d-500	-		
1982-83 in PAKISTAN						
Karachi[1]-Pakistan 9 wkts	•284	179	9d-419	1-47	K.J.Hughes	Javed Miandad
Faisalabad-Pakistan inns & 3 runs	168	330	•6d-501	-		
Lahore[2]-Pakistan 9 wkts	•316	214	7d-467	1-64		
1983-84 in AUSTRALIA						
Perth-Australia inns & 9 runs	•9d-436	-	129	298	K.J.Hughes	Zaheer Abbas
Brisbane[2]-Drawn	7d-506	-	•156	3-82		Zaheer Abbas
Adelaide-Drawn	•465	7-310	624	-		Zaheer Abbas
Melbourne-Drawn	555	-	•470	7-238		Imran Khan
Sydney-Australia 10 wkts	6d-454	0-35	•278	210		Imran Khan
1988-89 in PAKISTAN						
Karachi[1]-Pakistan inns & 188 runs	185	116	•9d-469	-	A.R.Border	Javed Miandad
Faisalabad-Drawn	321	3-67	•316	9d-378		
Lahore[2]-Drawn	•340	3d-161	233	8-153		

AUSTRALIA V PAKISTAN (cont.) Venue and Result	Australia 1st	Australia 2nd	Pakistan 1st	Pakistan 2nd	Captains Australia	Captains Pakistan
1989-90 in AUSTRALIA						
Melbourne-Australia 92 runs	•223	8d-312	107	336	A.R.Border	Imran Khan
Adelaide-Drawn	341	6-233	•257	9d-387		
Sydney-Drawn	2-176	-	•199	-		
1994-95 in PAKISTAN						
Karachi[1]-Pakistan 1 wkt	•337	232	256	9-315	M.A.Taylor	Saleem Malik
Rawalpindi[2]-Drawn	•9d-521	1-14	260	537		
Lahore[2]-Drawn	455	-	•373	404		
1995-96 in AUSTRALIA						
Brisbane[2]-Australia inns & 126 runs	•463	-	97	240	M.A.Taylor	Wasim Akram
Hobart-Australia 155 runs	•267	306	198	220		
Sydney-Pakistan 74 runs	257	172	•299	204		

Test Match Results Summary

AUSTRALIA v PAKISTAN-IN AUSTRALIA

		Result			Melbourne			Adelaide			Sydney			Perth			Brisbane[2]			Hobart		
	Tests	A	P	D	A	P	D	A	P	D	A	P	D	A	P	D	A	P	D	A	P	D
1964-65	1	-	-	1	-	-	1	-	-	-	-	-	-	-	-	-	-	-	-	-	-	-
1972-73	3	3	-	-	1	-	-	1	-	-	1	-	-	-	-	-	-	-	-	-	-	-
1976-77	3	1	1	1	1	-	-	-	-	1	-	1	-	-	-	-	-	-	-	-	-	-
1978-79	2	1	1	-	-	1	-	-	-	-	-	-	-	1	-	-	-	-	-	-	-	-
1981-82	3	2	1	-	-	1	-	-	-	-	-	-	-	1	-	-	1	-	-	-	-	-
1983-84	5	2	-	3	-	-	1	-	-	1	1	-	-	1	-	-	-	-	1	-	-	-
1989-90	3	1	-	2	1	-	-	-	-	1	-	-	1	-	-	-	-	-	-	-	-	-
1995-96	3	2	1	-	-	-	-	-	-	-	-	1	-	-	-	-	1	-	-	1	-	-
	23	12	4	7	3	2	2	1	-	3	2	2	1	3	-	-	2	-	1	1	-	-

AUSTRALIA v PAKISTAN-IN PAKISTAN

		Result			Karachi[1]			Dacca			Lahore[2]			Faisalabad			Rawalpindi[2]		
	Tests	A	P	D	A	P	D	A	P	D	A	P	D	A	P	D	A	P	D
1956-57	1	-	1	-	-	1	-	-	-	-	-	-	-	-	-	-	-	-	-
1959-60	3	2	-	1	-	-	1	1	-	-	1	-	-	-	-	-	-	-	-
1964-65	1	-	-	1	-	-	1	-	-	-	-	-	-	-	-	-	-	-	-
1979-80	3	-	1	2	-	1	-	-	-	-	-	-	1	-	-	1	-	-	-
1982-83	3	-	3	-	-	1	-	-	-	-	-	1	-	-	1	-	-	-	-
1988-89	3	-	1	2	-	1	-	-	-	-	-	-	1	-	-	1	-	-	-
1994-95	3	-	1	2	-	1	-	-	-	-	-	-	1	-	-	-	-	-	1
	17	2	7	8	-	5	2	1	-	-	1	1	3	-	1	2	-	-	1
Totals	40	14	11	15															

HIGHEST INNINGS TOTALS

Australia in Australia	585	Adelaide	1972-73
Australia in Pakistan	617	Faisalabad	1979-80
Pakistan in Australia	624	Adelaide	1983-84
Pakistan in Pakistan	537	Rawalpindi[2]	1994-95

LOWEST INNINGS TOTALS

Australia in Australia	125	Melbourne	1981-82
Australia in Pakistan	80	Karachi[1]	1956-57
Pakistan in Australia	62	Perth	1981-82
Pakistan in Pakistan	134	Dacca	1959-60

HIGHEST MATCH AGGREGATE	1640 for 33 wickets	Melbourne	1972-73
LOWEST MATCH AGGREGATE	535 for 31 wickets	Karachi[1]	1956-57

HIGHEST INDIVIDUAL INNINGS

Australia in Australia	268	G.N.Yallop	Melbourne	1983-84
Australia in Pakistan	235	G.S.Chappell	Faisalabad	1979-80
Pakistan in Australia	158	Majid Khan	Melbourne	1972-73
Pakistan in Pakistan	237	Saleem Malik	Rawalpindi[2]	1994-95

HIGHEST AGGREGATE ON RUNS IN A SERIES

Australia in Australia	554 (av 92.33)	G.N.Yallop	1983-84
Australia in Pakistan	395 (av 131.66)	A.R.Border	1979-80
Pakistan in Australia	390 (av 43.33)	Mohsin Khan	1983-84
Pakistan in Pakistan	557 (av 92.83)	Saleem Malik	1994-95

RECORD WICKET PARTNERSHIPS-AUSTRALIA

1st	176	M.A.Taylor (69), M.J.Slater (110)	Rawalpindi[2]	1994-95
2nd	259	W.B.Phillips (159), G.N.Yallop (141)	Perth	1983-84
3rd	203	G.N.Yallop (268), K.J.Hughes (94)	Melbourne	1983-84
4th	217	G.S.Chappell (235), G.N.Yallop (172)	Faisalabad	1979-80
5th	171	G.S.Chappell (121), G.J.Cosier (168)	Melbourne	1976-77
5th	171	A.R.Border (118), G.S.Chappell (150*)	Brisbane[2]	1983-84
6th	139	R.M.Cowper (83), T.R.Veivers (88)	Melbourne	1964-65
7th	185	G.N.Yallop (268), G.R.J.Matthews (75)	Melbourne	1983-84
8th	117	G.J.Cosier (168), K.J.O'Keeffe (28*)	Melbourne	1976-77
9th	83	J.R.Watkins (36), R.A.L.Massie (42)	Sydney	1972-73
10th	52	D.K.Lillee (14), M.H.N.Walker (34*)	Sydney	1976-77
10th	52	G.F.Lawson (57*), T.M.Alderman (7)	Lahore[2]	1982-83

RECORD WICKET PARTNERSHIPS-PAKISTAN

1st	249	Khalid Ibadulla (166), Abdul Kadir (95)	Karachi[1]	1964-65
2nd	233	Mohsin Khan (149), Qasim Omar (113)	Adelaide	1983-84
3rd	223*	Taslim Arif (210*), Javed Miandad (106*)	Faisalabad	1979-80
4th	155	Mansoor Akhtar (111), Zaheer Abbas (126)	Faisalabad	1982-83
5th	186	Javed Miandad (131), Saleem Malik (77)	Adelaide	1983-84
6th	196	Saleem Malik (143), Aamer Sohail (105)	Lahore[2]	1994-95
7th	104	Intikhab Alam (64), Wasim Bari (72)	Adelaide	1972-73
8th	111	Majid Khan (110*), Imran Khan (56)	Lahore[2]	1979-80
9th	56	Intikhab Alam (61), Afaq Hussain (13*)	Melbourne	1964-65
10th	87	Asif Iqbal (152*), Iqbal Qasim (4)	Adelaide	1976-77

BEST INNINGS BOWLING ANALYSIS

Australia in Australia	8-59	A.A.Mallett	Adelaide	1972-73
Australia in Pakistan	7-75	L.F.Kline	Lahore[2]	1959-60
Pakistan in Australia	9-86	Sarfraz Nawaz	Melbourne	1978-79
Pakistan in Pakistan	7-49	Iqbal Qasim	Karachi[1]	1979-80

BEST MATCH BOWLING ANALYSIS

Australia in Australia	11-77	S.K.Warne	Brisbane[2]	1995-96
Australia in Pakistan	10-111	R.J.Bright	Karachi[1]	1979-80
Pakistan in Australia	12-165	Imran Khan	Sydney	1976-77
Pakistan in Pakistan	13-114	Fazal Mahmood	Karachi[1]	1956-57

HIGHEST AGGREGATE OF WICKETS IN A SERIES

Australia in Australia	24 (av 24.16)	G.F.Lawson	1983-84
Australia in Pakistan	18 (av 21.05)	R.Benaud	1959-60
	18 (av 28.00)	S.K.Warne	1994-95
Pakistan in Australia	19 (av 38.52)	Azeem Hafeez	1983-84
Pakistan in Pakistan	22 (av 25.54)	Abdul Qadir	1982-83

AUSTRALIA V SRI LANKA	Australia		Sri Lanka		Captains	
Venue and Result	1st	2nd	1st	2nd	Australia	Sri Lanka
1982-83 in SRI LANKA						
Kandy-Australia inns & 38 runs	•4d-514	-	271	205	G.S.Chappell	L.R.D.Mendis
1987-88 in AUSTRALIA						
Perth-Australia inns & 108 runs	•455	-	194	153	A.R.Border	R.S.Madugalle
1989-90 in AUSTRALIA						
Brisbane[2]-Drawn	•367	6-375	418	-	A.R.Border	A.Ranatunga
Hobart-Australia 173 runs	•224	5d-513	216	348		
1992-93 in SRI LANKA						
Colombo (SSC)-Australia 16 runs	•256	471	8d-547	164	A.R.Border	A.Ranatunga
Colombo (PIS)-Drawn	•247	6d-296	258	2-136		
Moratuwa-Drawn	•337	8-271	9d-274	-		
1995-96 in AUSTRALIA						
Perth-Australia inns & 36 runs	5d-617	-	•251	330	M.A.Taylor	A.Ranatunga
Melbourne-Australia 10 wkts	•6d-500	0-41	233	307		A.Ranatunga
Adelaide-Australia 148 runs	•9d-502	6d-215	317	252		P.A.de Silva

Test Match Results Summary

AUSTRALIA v SRI LANKA-IN AUSTRALIA

		Result			Perth			Brisbane[2]			Hobart			Melbourne			Adelaide		
	Tests	A	SL	D	A	SL	D	A	SL	D	A	SL	D	A	SL	D	A	SL	D
1987-88	1	1	-	-	1	-	-	-	-	-	-	-	-	-	-	-	-	-	-
1989-90	2	1	-	1	-	-	-	-	-	1	1	-	-	-	-	-	-	-	-
1995-96	3	3	-	-	1	-	-	-	-	-	-	-	-	1	-	-	1	-	-
	6	5	-	1	2	-	-	-	-	1	1	-	-	1	-	-	1	-	-

AUSTRALIA v SRI LANKA-IN SRI LANKA

		Result			Kandy			Colombo (SSC)			Colombo (PIS)			Moratuwa		
	Tests	A	SL	D	A	SL	D	A	SL	D	A	SL	D	A	SL	D
1982-83	1	1	-	-	1	-	-	-	-	-	-	-	-	-	-	-
1992-93	3	1	-	2	-	-	-	1	-	-	-	-	1	-	-	1
	4	2	-	2	1	-	-	1	-	-	-	-	1	-	-	1
Totals	10	7	-	3												

HIGHEST INNINGS TOTALS

Australia in Australia	5d-617	Perth	1995-96
Australia in Sri Lanka	4d-514	Kandy	1982-83
Sri Lanka in Australia	418	Brisbane²	1989-90
Sri Lanka in Sri Lanka	8d-547	Colombo (SSC)	1992-93

LOWEST INNINGS TOTALS

Australia in Australia	224	Hobart	1989-90
Australia in Sri Lanka	247	Colombo (PIS)	1992-93
Sri Lanka in Australia	153	Perth	1987-88
Sri Lanka in Sri Lanka	164	Colombo (SSC)	1992-93

HIGHEST MATCH AGGREGATE	1438 for 39 wickets	Colombo (SSC)	1992-93
LOWEST MATCH AGGREGATE	802 for 30 wickets	Perth	1987-88

HIGHEST INDIVIDUAL INNINGS

Australia in Australia	219	M.J.Slater	Perth	1995-96
Australia in Sri Lanka	143*	D.W.Hookes	Kandy	1982-83
Sri Lanka in Australia	167	P.A.de Silva	Brisbane²	1989-90
Sri Lanka in Sri Lanka	137	A.P.Gurusinha	Colombo (SSC)	1992-93

HIGHEST AGGREGATE ON RUNS IN A SERIES

Australia in Australia	362 (av 362.00)	S.R.Waugh	1995-96
Australia in Sri Lanka	329 (av 54.83)	G.R.J.Matthews	1992-93
Sri Lanka in Australia	314 (av 104.66)	P.A.de Silva	1989-90
Sri Lanka in Sri Lanka	250 (av 50.00)	R.S.Mahanama	1992-93

RECORD WICKET PARTNERSHIPS-AUSTRALIA

1st	228	M.J.Slater (219), M.A.Taylor (96)	Perth	1995-96
2nd	170	K.C.Wessels (141), G.N.Yallop (98)	Kandy	1982-83
3rd	158	T.M.Moody (106), A.R.Border (56)	Brisbane²	1989-90
3rd	158	M.J.Slater (219), M.E.Waugh (111)	Perth	1995-96
4th	163	M.A.Taylor (108), A.R.Border (85)	Hobart	1989-90
5th	155*	D.W.Hookes (143*), A.R.Border (47*)	Kandy	1982-83
6th	260*	D.M.Jones (118*), S.R.Waugh (134*)	Hobart	1989-90
7th	129	G.R.J.Matthews (96), I.A.Healy (49)	Moratuwa	1992-93
8th	56	G.R.J.Matthews (64), C.J.McDermott (40)	Colombo (SSC)	1992-93
9th	45	I.A.Healy (66*), S.K.Warne (24)	Colombo (SSC)	1992-93
10th	49	I.A.Healy (66*), M.R.Whitney (13)	Colombo (SSC)	1992-93

RECORD WICKET PARTNERSHIPS-SRI LANKA

1st	110	R.S.Mahanama (69), U.C.Hathurusingha (49)	Colombo (PIS)	1992-93
2nd	92	R.S.Mahanama (78), A.P.Gurusinha (137)	Colombo (SSC)	1992-93
3rd	125	S.T.Jayasuriya (125), S.Ranatunga (65)	Adelaide	1995-96
4th	230	A.P.Gurusinha (137), A.Ranatunga (127)	Colombo (SSC)	1992-93
5th	116	H.P.Tillakaratne (82), A.Ranatunga (48)	Moratuwa	1992-93
6th	96	A.P.Gurusinha (137), R.S.Kaluwitharana (132*)	Colombo (SSC)	1992-93
7th	144	P.A.de Silva (167), J.R.Ratnayeke (56)	Brisbane²	1989-90
8th	33	A.Ranatunga (55), C.P.H.Ramanayake (9)	Perth	1987-88
9th	46	H.D.P.K.Dharmasena (30), G.P.Wickramasinghe (28)	Perth	1995-96
10th	27	P.A.de Silva (167), C.P.H.Ramanayake (10*)	Brisbane²	1989-90

BEST INNINGS BOWLING ANALYSIS

Australia in Australia	5-39	P.R.Reiffel	Adelaide	1995-96
Australia in Sri Lanka	5-66	T.G.Hogan	Kandy	1982-83
Sri Lanka in Australia	6-66	R.J.Ratnayake	Hobart	1989-90
Sri Lanka in Sri Lanka	5-82	C.P.H.Ramanayake	Moratuwa	1992-93

BEST MATCH BOWLING ANALYSIS

Australia in Australia	8-156	M.G.Hughes	Hobart	1989-90
Australia in Sri Lanka	7-100	B.Yardley	Kandy	1982-83
Sri Lanka in Australia	8-189	R.J.Ratnayake	Hobart	1989-90
Sri Lanka in Sri Lanka	8-157	C.P.H.Ramanayake	Moratuwa	1992-93

HIGHEST AGGREGATE OF WICKETS IN A SERIES

Australia in Australia	21 (av 20.85)	G.D.McGrath	1995-96
Australia in Sri Lanka	14 (av 24.42)	C.J.McDermott	1992-93
Sri Lanka in Australia	9 (av 41.22)	W.P.U.J.C.Vaas	1995-96
Sri Lanka in Sri Lanka	17 (av 25.52)	C.P.H.Ramanayake	1992-93

ENGLAND V SOUTH AFRICA	England		South Africa		Captains	
Venue and Result	1st	2nd	1st	2nd	England	South Africa
1888-89 in SOUTH AFRICA						
Port Elizabeth-England 8 wkts	148	2-67	•84	129	C.A.Smith	O.R.Dunell
Cape Town-England inns & 202 runs	•292	-	47	43	M.P.Bowden	W.H.Milton
1891-92 in SOUTH AFRICA						
Cape Town-England inns & 189 runs	369	-	•97	83	W.W.Read	W.H.Milton
1895-96 in SOUTH AFRICA						
Port Elizabeth-England 288 runs	•185	226	93	30	Sir T.C.O'Brien	E.A.Halliwell
Johannesburg[1]-England inns & 197 runs	•482	-	151	134	Lord Hawke	E.A.Halliwell
Cape Town-England inns & 33 runs	265	-	•115	117	Lord Hawke	A.R.Richards
1898-99 in SOUTH AFRICA						
Johannesburg[1]-England 32 runs	•145	237	251	99	Lord Hawke	M.Bisset
Cape Town-England 210 runs	•92	330	177	35		
1905-06 in SOUTH AFRICA						
Johannesburg[1]-South Africa 1 wkt	•184	190	91	9-287	P.F.Warner	P.W.Sherwell
Johannesburg[1]-South Africa 9 wkts	•148	160	277	1-33		
Johannesburg[1]-South Africa 243 runs	295	196	•385	5d-349		
Cape Town-England 4 wkts	198	6-160	•218	138		
Cape Town-South Africa inns & 16 runs	•187	130	333	-		
1907 in ENGLAND						
Lord's-Drawn	•428	-	140	3-185	R.E.Foster	P.W.Sherwell
Leeds-England 53 runs	•76	162	110	75		
The Oval-Drawn	•295	138	178	5-159		
1909-10 in SOUTH AFRICA						
Johannesburg[1]-South Africa 19 runs	310	224	•208	345	H.D.G.Leveson Gower	S.J.Snooke
Durban[1]-South Africa 95 runs	199	252	•199	347	H.D.G.Leveson Gower	
Johannesburg[1]-England 3 wkts	322	7-221	•305	237	H.D.G.Leveson Gower	
Cape Town-South Africa 4 wkts	•203	178	207	6-175	F.L.Fane	
Cape Town-England 9 wkts	•417	1-16	103	327	F.L.Fane	
1912 in ENGLAND						
Lord's-England inns & 62 runs	337	-	•58	217	C.B.Fry	F.Mitchell
Leeds-England 174 runs	•242	238	147	159		L.J.Tancred
The Oval-England 10 wkts	176	0-14	•95	93		L.J.Tancred
1913-14 in SOUTH AFRICA						
Durban[1]-England inns & 157 runs	450	-	•182	111	J.W.H.T.Douglas	H.W.Taylor
Johannesburg[1]-England inns & 12 runs	403	-	•160	231		
Johannesburg[1]-England 91 runs	•238	308	151	304		
Durban[1]-Drawn	163	5-154	•170	9d-305		
Port Elizabeth-England 10 wkts	411	0-11	•193	228		
1922-23 in SOUTH AFRICA						
Johannesburg[1]-South Africa 168 runs	182	218	•148	420	F.T.Mann	H.W.Taylor
Cape Town-England 1 wkt	183	9-173	•113	242		
Durban[2]-Drawn	•428	1-11	368	-		
Johannesburg[1]-Drawn	•244	6d-376	295	4-247		
Durban[2]-England 109 runs	•281	241	179	234		

ENGLAND v SOUTH AFRICA (cont.)	England		South Africa		Captains	
Venue and Result	1st	2nd	1st	2nd	England	South Africa
1924 in ENGLAND						
Birmingham-England inns & 18 runs	•438	-	30	390	A.E.R.Gilligan	H.W.Taylor
Lord's-England inns & 18 runs	2d-531	-	•273	240	A.E.R.Gilligan	
Leeds-England 9 wkts	•396	1-60	132	323	A.E.R.Gilligan	
Manchester-Drawn	-	-	•4-116	-	J.W.H.T.Douglas	
The Oval-Drawn	8-421	-	•342	-	A.E.R.Gilligan	
1927-28 in SOUTH AFRICA						
Johannesburg[1]-England 10 wkts	313	0-57	•196	170	R.T.Stanyforth	H.G.Deane
Cape Town-England 87 runs	•133	428	250	224	R.T.Stanyforth	
Durban[2]-Drawn	430	2-132	•246	8d-464	R.T.Stanyforth	
Johannesburg[1]-South Africa 4 wkts	•265	215	328	6-156	R.T.Stanyforth	
Durban[2]-South Africa 8 wkts	•282	118	7d-332	2-69	G.T.S.Stevens	
1929 in ENGLAND						
Birmingham-Drawn	•245	4d-308	250	1-171	J C.White	H.G.Deane
Lord's-Drawn	•302	8d-312	322	5-90	J C.White	
Leeds-England 5 wkts	328	5-186	•236	275	J C.White	
Manchester-England inns & 32 runs	•7d-427	-	130	265	A.W.Carr	
The Oval-Drawn	•258	1-264	8d-492	-	A.W.Carr	
1930-31 in SOUTH AFRICA						
Johannesburg[1]-South Africa 28 runs	193	211	•126	306	A.P.F.Chapman	E.P.Nupen
Cape Town-Drawn	350	252	•8d-513	-		H.G.Deane
Durban[2]-Drawn	1d-223	-	•177	8-145		H.G.Deane
Johannesburg[1]-Drawn	•442	9d-169	295	7-280		H.B.Cameron
Durban[2]-Drawn	230	4-72	•252	7d-219		H.B.Cameron
1935 in ENGLAND						
Nottingham-Drawn	•7d-384	-	220	1-17	R.E.S.Wyatt	H.F.Wade
Lord's-South Africa 157 runs	198	151	•228	7d-278		
Leeds-Drawn	•216	7d-294	171	5-194		
Manchester-Drawn	•357	6d-231	318	2-169		
The Oval-Drawn	6d-534	-	•476	6-287		
1938-39 in SOUTH AFRICA						
Johannesburg[1]-Drawn	•422	4d-291	390	1-108	W.R.Hammond	A.Melville
Cape Town-Drawn	•9d-559	-	286	2-201		
Durban[2]-England inns & 13 runs	•4d-469	-	103	353		
Johannesburg[1]-Drawn	•215	4-203	8d-349	-		
Durban[2]-Drawn	316	6-654	•530	481		
1947 in ENGLAND						
Nottingham-Drawn	208	551	•533	1-166	N.W.D.Yardley	A.Melville
Lord's-England 10 wkts	•8d-554	0-26	327	252		
Manchester-England 7 wkts	478	3-130	•339	267		
Leeds-England 10 wkts	7d-317	0-47	•175	184		
The Oval-Drawn	•427	6d-325	302	7-423		
1948-49 in SOUTH AFRICA						
Durban[2]-England 2 wkts	253	8-128	•161	219	F.G.Mann	A.D.Nourse
Johannesburg[2]-Drawn	•608	-	315	2-270		
Cape Town-Drawn	•308	3d-276	356	4-142		
Johannesburg[2]-Drawn	•379	7d-253	9d-257	4-194		
Port Elizabeth-England 3 wkts	395	7-174	•379	3d-187		

ENGLAND V SOUTH AFRICA	England		South Africa		Captains	
Venue and Result	1st	2nd	1st	2nd	England	South Africa
1951 in ENGLAND						
Nottingham-South Africa 71 runs	9d-419	114	•9d-483	121	F.R.Brown	A.D.Nourse
Lord s-England 10 wkts	•311	0-16	115	211		
Manchester-England 9 wkts	211	1-142	•158	191		
Leeds-Drawn	505	-	•538	0-87		
The Oval-England 4 wkts	194	6-164	•202	154		
1955 in ENGLAND						
Nottingham-England inns & 5 runs	•334	-	181	148	P.B.H.May	J.E.Cheetham
Lord's-England 71 runs	•133	353	304	111		J.E.Cheetham
Manchester-South Africa 3 wkts	•284	381	8d-521	7-145		D.J.McGlew
Leeds-South Africa 224 runs	191	256	•171	500		D.J.McGlew
1956-57 in SOUTH AFRICA						
Johannesburg[3]-England 131 runs	•268	150	215	72	P.B.H.May	C.B.van Ryneveld
Cape Town-England 312 runs	•369	6d-220	205	72		D.J.McGlew
Durban[2]-Drawn	•218	254	283	6-142		C.B.van Ryneveld
Johannesburg[3]-South Africa 17 runs	251	214	•340	142		C.B.van Ryneveld
Port Elizabeth-South Africa 58 runs	110	130	•164	134		C.B.van Ryneveld
1960 in ENGLAND						
Birmingham-England 100 runs	•292	203	186	209	M.C.Cowdrey	D.J.McGlew
Lord's-England inns & 73 runs	•8d-362	-	152	137		
Nottingham-England 8 wkts	•287	2-49	88	247		
Manchester-Drawn	•260	7d-153	229	0-46		
The Oval-Drawn	•155	9d-479	419	4-97		
1964-65 in SOUTH AFRICA						
Durban[2]-England inns & 104 runs	•5d-485		155	226	M J K.Smith	T L.Goddard
Johannesburg[3]-Drawn	•531	-	317	6-336		
Cape Town-Drawn	442	0 15	•7d-501	346		
Johannesburg[3]-Drawn	384	6-153	•6d-390	3d-307		
Port Elizabeth-Drawn	435	1-29	•502	4d-178		
1965 in ENGLAND						
Lord's-Drawn	338	7-145	•280	248	M.J.K.Smith	P L.van der Merwe
Nottingham-South Africa 94 runs	240	224	•269	289		
The Oval-Drawn	202	4-308	•208	392		
1994 in ENGLAND						
Lord's-South Africa 356 runs	180	99	•357	8d-278	M.A.Atherton	K.C.Wessels
Leeds-Drawn	•9d-477	5d-267	447	3-116		
The Oval-England 8 wickets	304	2-205	•332	175		
1995-96 in SOUTH AFRICA						
Pretoria-Drawn	•9d-381	-	-	-	M.A.Atherton	W.J.Cronje
Johannesburg[3]-Drawn	200	5-351	•332	9d-346		
Durban[2]-Drawn	5-152		•225			
Port Elizabeth-Drawn	263	3-189	•428	9d-162		
Cape Town-South Africa 10 wkts	•153	157	244	0-70		

Test Match Results Summary

ENGLAND v SOUTH AFRICA-IN ENGLAND

		Result			Lord's			Leeds			The Oval			Birmingham			Manchester			Nottingham		
	Tests	E	SA	D	E	SA	D	E	SA	D	E	SA	D	E	SA	D	E	SA	D	E	SA	D
1907	3	1	-	2	-	-	1	1	-	-	-	-	1	-	-	-	-	-	-	-	-	-
1912	3	3	-	-	1	-	-	1	-	-	1	-	-	-	-	-	-	-	-	-	-	-
1924	5	3	-	2	1	-	-	1	-	-	-	-	1	1	-	-	-	-	1	-	-	-
1929	5	2	-	3	-	-	1	1	-	-	-	-	1	-	-	-	1	-	-	-	-	-
1935	5	-	1	4	-	1	-	-	-	1	-	-	1	-	-	-	-	-	1	-	-	1
1947	5	3	-	2	1	-	-	1	-	-	-	-	1	-	-	-	1	-	-	-	-	1
1951	5	3	1	1	1	-	-	-	-	1	1	-	-	-	-	-	1	-	-	-	1	-
1955	5	3	2	-	1	-	-	-	1	-	1	-	-	-	-	-	-	1	-	1	-	-
1960	5	3	-	2	1	-	-	-	-	-	-	-	1	1	-	-	-	-	1	1	-	-
1965	3	-	1	2	-	-	1	-	-	-	-	-	1	-	-	-	-	-	-	-	1	-
1994	3	1	1	1	-	1	-	-	-	1	1	-	-	-	-	-	-	-	-	-	-	-
	47	22	6	19	6	2	3	5	1	3	4	-	7	2	-	1	3	1	3	2	2	2

ENGLAND v SOUTH AFRICA-IN SOUTH AFRICA

		Result			P.Elizabeth			Cape Town			Johannesburg			Durban			Pretoria		
	Tests	E	SA	D	E	SA	D	E	SA	D	E	SA	D	E	SA	D	E	SA	D
1888-89	2	2	-	-	1	-	-	1	-	-	-	-	-	-	-	-	-	-	-
1891-92	1	1	-	-	-	-	-	1	-	-	-	-	-	-	-	-	-	-	-
1895-96	3	3	-	-	1	-	-	1	-	-	1	-	-	-	-	-	-	-	-
1898-99	2	2	-	-	-	-	-	1	-	-	1	-	-	-	-	-	-	-	-
1905-06	5	1	4	-	-	-	-	1	1	-	-	3	-	-	-	-	-	-	-
1909-10	5	2	3	-	-	-	-	1	1	-	1	1	-	-	1	-	-	-	-
1913-14	5	4	-	1	1	-	-	-	-	-	2	-	-	1	-	1	-	-	-
1922-23	5	2	1	2	-	-	-	1	-	-	-	1	1	1	-	1	-	-	-
1927-28	5	2	2	1	-	-	-	1	-	-	1	1	-	-	1	1	-	-	-
1930-31	5	-	1	4	-	-	-	-	-	1	-	1	1	-	-	2	-	-	-
1938-39	5	1	-	4	-	-	-	-	-	1	-	-	2	1	-	1	-	-	-
1948-49	5	2	-	3	1	-	-	-	-	1	-	-	2	1	-	-	-	-	-
1956-57	5	2	2	1	-	1	-	1	-	-	1	1	-	-	-	1	-	-	-
1964-65	5	1	-	4	-	-	1	-	-	1	-	-	2	1	-	-	-	-	-
1995-96	5	-	1	4	-	-	1	-	1	-	-	-	1	-	-	1	-	-	1
	63	25	14	24	4	1	2	9	3	4	7	8	9	5	2	8	-	-	1
Totals	110	47	20	43															

HIGHEST INNINGS TOTALS

England in England	8d-554	Lord's	1947
England in South Africa	5-654	Durban[2]	1938-39
South Africa in England	538	Leeds	1951
South Africa in South Africa	530	Durban[2]	1938-39

LOWEST INNINGS TOTALS

England in England	76	Leeds	1907
England in South Africa	92	Cape Town	1898-99
South Africa in England	30	Birmingham	1924
South Africa in South Africa	30	Port Elizabeth	1895-96

HIGHEST MATCH AGGREGATE	1981 for 35 wickets	Durban[2]	1938-39
LOWEST MATCH AGGREGATE	378 for 30 wickets	The Oval	1912

HIGHEST INDIVIDUAL INNINGS

England in England	211	J.B.Hobbs	Lord's	1924
England in South Africa	243	E.Paynter	Durban[2]	1938-39
South Africa in England	236	E.A.B.Rowan	Leeds	1951
South Africa in South Africa	176	H.W.Taylor	Johannesburg[1]	1922-23

HIGHEST AGGREGATE OF RUNS IN A SERIES

England in England	753 (av 94.12)	D.C.S.Compton	1947
England in South Africa	653 (av 81.62)	E.Paynter	1938-39
South Africa in England	621 (av 69.00)	A.D.Nourse	1947
South Africa in South Africa	582 (av 64.66)	H.W.Taylor	1922-23

RECORD WICKET PARTNERSHIPS-ENGLAND

1st	359	L.Hutton (158), C.Washbrook (195)	Johannesburg[2]	1948-49
2nd	280	P.A.Gibb (120), W.J.Edrich (219)	Durban[2]	1938-39
3rd	370	W.J.Edrich (189), D.C.S.Compton (208)	Lord's	1947
4th	197	W.R.Hammond (181), L.E.G.Ames (115)	Cape Town	1938-39
5th	237	D.C.S.Compton (163), N.W.D.Yardley (99)	Nottingham	1947
6th	206*	K.F.Barrington (148*), J.M.Parks (108*)	Durban[2]	1964-65
7th	115	J.W.H.T.Douglas (119), M.C.Bird (61)	Durban[1]	1913-14
8th	154	C.W.Wright (71), H.R Bromley-Davenport (84)	Johannesburg[1]	1895-96
9th	71	H.Wood (134), J.T.Hearne (40)	Cape Town	1891-92
10th	92	C.A.G.Russell (111), A.E.R.Gilligan (39*)	Durban[2]	1922-23

RECORD WICKET PARTNERSHIPS-SOUTH AFRICA

1st	260	B.Mitchell (123), I.J.Siedle (141)	Cape Town	1930-31
2nd	198	E.A.B.Rowan (236).C.B.van Ryneveld (83)	Leeds	1951
3rd	319	A.Melville (189), A.D.Nourse (149)	Nottingham	1947
4th	214	H.W.Taylor (121), H.G.Deane (93)	The Oval	1929
5th	157	A.J.Pithey (95), J.H.B.Waite (64)	Johannesburg[3]	1964-65
6th	171	J.H.B.Waite (113), P.L.Winslow (108)	Manchester	1955
7th	123	H.G.Deane (73), E.P.Nupen (69)	Durban[2]	1927-28
8th	109*	B.Mitchell (189*), L.Tuckett (40*)	The Oval	1947
9th	137	E.L.Dalton (117), A.B.C.Langton (73*)	The Oval	1935
10th	103	H.G.Owen-Smith (129), A.J.Bell (26*)	Leeds	1929

BEST INNINGS BOWLING ANALYSIS

England in England	9-57	D.E.Malcolm	The Oval	1994
England in South Africa	9-28	G.A.Lohmann	Johannesburg[1]	1895-96
South Africa in England	7-65	S.J.Pegler	Lord's	1912
South Africa in South Africa	9-113	H.J.Tayfield	Johannesburg[3]	1956-57

BEST MATCH BOWLING ANALYSIS

England in England	15-99	C.Blythe	Leeds	1907
England in South Africa	17-159	S.F.Barnes	Johannesburg[1]	1913-14
South Africa in England	10-87	P.M.Pollock	Nottingham	1965
South Africa in South Africa	13-192	H.J.Tayfield	Johannesburg[3]	1956-57

HIGHEST AGGREGATE OF WICKETS IN A SERIES

England in England	34 (av 8.29)	S F Barnes	1912
England in South Africa	49 (av 10.93)	S.F.Barnes	1913-14
South Africa in England	26 (av 21.84)	H.J.Tayfield	1955
	26 (av 22.57)	N.A T.Adcock	1960
South Africa in South Africa	37 (av 17.18)	H.J.Tayfield	1956-57

ENGLAND v WEST INDIES	England		West Indies		Captains	
Venue and Result	1st	2nd	1st	2nd	England	West Indies
1928 in ENGLAND						
Lord's-England inns & 58 runs	•401	-	177	166	A.P.F.Chapman	R.K.Nunes
Manchester-England inns & 30 runs	351	-	•206	115		
The Oval-England inns & 71 runs	438	-	•238	129		
1929-30 in WEST INDIES						
Bridgetown-Drawn	467	3-167	•369	384	Hon F.S.G.Calthorpe	E.L.G.Hoad
Port-of-Spain-England 167 runs	•208	8d-425	254	212		N.Betancourt
Georgetown-West Indies 289 runs	145	327	•471	290		M.P.Fernandes
Kingston-Drawn	•849	9d-272	286	5-408		R.K.Nunes
1933 in ENGLAND						
Lord's-England inns & 27 runs	•296	-	97	172	D.R.Jardine	G.C.Grant
Manchester-Drawn	374	-	•375	225	D.R.Jardine	
The Oval-England inns & 17 runs	•312	-	100	195	R.E.S.Wyatt	
1934-35 in WEST INDIES						
Bridgetown-England 4 wkts	7d-81	6-75	•102	6d-51	R.E.S.Wyatt	G.C.Grant
Port-of-Spain-West Indies 217 runs	258	107	•302	6d-280		
Georgetown-Drawn	•226	6d-160	184	5-104		
Kingston-West Indies inns & 161 runs	271	103	•7d-535	-		
1939 in ENGLAND						
Lord's-England 8 wkts	5d-404	2-100	•277	225	W.R.Hammond	R.S.Grant
Manchester-Drawn	•7d-164	6d-128	133	4-43		
The Oval-Drawn	•352	3d-366	498	-		
1947-48 in WEST INDIES						
Bridgetown-Drawn	253	4-86	•296	9d-351	K.Cranston	G.A.Headley
Port-of-Spain-Drawn	•362	275	497	3-72	G.O.B.Allen	G.E.Gomez
Georgetown-West Indies 7 wkts	111	263	•8d-297	3-78	G.O.B.Allen	J.D.C.Goddard
Kingston-West Indies 10 wkts	•227	336	490	0-76	G.O.B.Allen	J.D.C.Goddard
1950 in ENGLAND						
Manchester-England 202 runs	•312	288	215	183	N.W.D.Yardley	J.D.C.Goddard
Lord's-West Indies 326 runs	151	274	•326	6d-425	N.W.D Yardley	
Nottingham-West Indies 10 wkts	•223	436	558	0-103	N.W.D.Yardley	
The Oval-West Indies inns & 56 runs	344	103	•503	-	F.R.Brown	
1953-54 in WEST INDIES						
Kingston-West Indies 140 runs	170	316	•417	6d-209	L.Hutton	J.B.Stollmeyer
Bridgetown-West Indies 181 runs	181	313	•383	2d-292		
Georgetown-England 9 wkts	•435	1-75	251	256		
Port-of-Spain-Drawn	537	3-98	•8d-681	4d-212		
Kingston-England 9 wkts	414	1-72	•139	346		
1957 in ENGLAND						
Birmingham-Drawn	•186	4d-583	474	7-72	P.B.H.May	J.D.C.Goddard
Lord s-England inns & 36 runs	424	-	•127	261		
Nottingham-Drawn	•6d-619	1-64	372	367		
Leeds-England inns & 5 runs	279	-	•142	132		
The Oval-England inns & 237 runs	•412	-	89	86		

ENGLAND v WEST INDIES (cont.)	England		West Indies		Captains	
Venue and Result	1st	2nd	1st	2nd	England	West Indies
1959-60 in WEST INDIES						
Bridgetown-Drawn	•482	0-71	8d-563	-	P.B.H.May	F.C.M.Alexander
Port-of-Spain-England 256 runs	•382	9d-230	112	244	P.B.H.May	
Kingston-Drawn	•277	305	353	6-175	P.B.H.May	
Georgetown-Drawn	•295	8-334	8d-402		M.C.Cowdrey	
Port-of-Spain-Drawn	•393	7d-350	8d-338	5-209	M.C.Cowdrey	
1963 in ENGLAND						
Manchester-West Indies 10 wkts	205	296	•6d-501	0-1	E.R.Dexter	F.M.M.Worrell
Lord's-Drawn	297	9-228	•301	229		
Birmingham-England 217 runs	•216	9d-278	186	91		
Leeds-West Indies 221 runs	174	231	•397	229		
The Oval-West Indies 8 wkts	•275	223	246	2-255		
1966 in ENGLAND						
Manchester-West Indies inns & 40 runs	167	277	•484	-	M.J.K.Smith	G.S.Sobers
Lord's-Drawn	355	4-197	•269	5d-369	M.C.Cowdrey	
Nottingham-West Indies 139 runs	325	253	•235	5d-482	M.C.Cowdrey	
Leeds-West Indies inns & 55 runs	240	205	•9d-500	-	M.C.Cowdrey	
The Oval-England inns & 34 runs	527	-	•268	225	D.B.Close	
1967-68 in WEST INDIES						
Port-of-Spain-Drawn	•568	-	363	8-243	M.C.Cowdrey	G.S.Sobers
Kingston-Drawn	•376	8-68	143	9d-391		
Bridgetown-Drawn	449	-	•349	6-284		
Port-of-Spain-England 7 wkts	404	3-215	•7d-526	2d-92		
Georgetown-Drawn	371	9-206	•414	264		
1969 in ENGLAND						
Manchester-England 10 wkts	•413	0-12	147	275	R.Illingworth	G.S.Sobers
Lord's-Drawn	344	7-295	•380	9d-295		
Leeds-England 30 runs	•223	240	161	272		
1973 in ENGLAND						
The Oval-West Indies 158 runs	257	255	•415	255	R.Illingworth	R.B.Kanhai
Birmingham-Drawn	305	2-182	•327	302		
Lord's-West Indies inns & 226 runs	233	193	•8d-652	-		
1973-74 in WEST INDIES						
Port-of-Spain-West Indies 7 wkts	•131	392	392	3-132	M.H.Denness	R.B.Kanhai
Kingston-Drawn	•353	9-432	9d-583	-		
Bridgetown-Drawn	•395	7-277	8d-596	-		
Georgetown-Drawn	•448	-	4-198	-		
Port-of-Spain-England 26 runs	•267	263	305	199		
1976 in ENGLAND						
Nottingham-Drawn	332	2-156	•494	5d-176	A.W.Greig	C.H.Lloyd
Lord's-Drawn	•250	254	182	6-241		
Manchester-West Indies 425 runs	71	126	•211	5d-411		
Leeds-West Indies 55 runs	387	204	•450	196		
The Oval-West Indies 231 runs	435	203	•8d-687	0d-182		

ENGLAND v WEST INDIES (cont.)	England		West Indies		Captains	
Venue and Result	1st	2nd	1st	2nd	England	West Indies
1980 in ENGLAND						
Nottingham-West Indies 2 wkts	•263	252	308	8-209	I.T.Botham	C.H.Lloyd
Lord's-Drawn	•269	2-133	518	-		C.H.Lloyd
Manchester-Drawn	•150	7-391	260	-		C.H.Lloyd
The Oval-Drawn	•370	9d-209	265	-		C.H.Lloyd
Leeds-Drawn	•143	6d-227	245	-		I.V.A.Richards
1980-81 in WEST INDIES						
Port-of-Spain-West Indies inns & 79 runs	178	169	•9-426		I.T.Botham	C.H.Lloyd
Georgetown-match cancelled	-	-	-	-		
Bridgetown-West Indies 298 runs	122	224	•265	7d-379		
St John's-Drawn	•271	3-234	9d-468			
Kingston-Drawn	•285	6d-302	442	-		
1984 in ENGLAND						
Birmingham-West Indies inns & 180 runs	•191	235	606	-	D.I.Gower	C.H.Lloyd
Lord's-West Indies 9 wkts	•286	9d-300	245	1-344		
Manchester-West Indies 8 wkts	•270	159	302	2-131		
Leeds-West Indies inns & 64 runs	280	156	•500	-		
The Oval-West Indies 172 runs	190	346	162	202		
1985-86 in WEST INDIES						
Kingston-West Indies 10 wkts	•159	152	307	0-5	D.I.Gower	I.V.A.Richards
Port-of-Spain-West Indies 7 wkts	•176	315	399	3-95		
Bridgetown-West Indies inns & 30 runs	189	199	•418	-		
Port-of-Spain-West Indies 10 wkts	•200	150	312	0-39		
St John's-West Indies 240 runs	310	170	•474	2d-246		
1988 in ENGLAND						
Nottingham-Drawn	•245	3-301	9d-448	-	M.W.Gatting	I.V.A.Richards
Lord's-West Indies 134 runs	165	307	•209	397	J.E.Emburey	
Manchester-West Indies inns & 156 runs	•135	93	7d-384	-	J.E.Emburey	
Leeds-West Indies 10 wkts	•201	138	275	0-67	C.S.Cowdrey	
The Oval-West Indies 8 wkts	•205	202	183	2-226	G.A.Gooch	
1989-90 in WEST INDIES						
Kingston-England 9 wkts	364	1-21	•164	240	G.A.Gooch	I.V.A.Richards
Georgetown-match abandoned	-	-	-	-	G.A.Gooch	I.V.A.Richards
Port-of-Spain-Drawn	288	5-120	•199	239	G.A.Gooch	D.L.Haynes
Bridgetown-West Indies 164 runs	358	191	•446	8d-267	A.J.Lamb	I.V.A.Richards
St John's-West Indies inns & 32 runs	•260	154	446	-	A.J.Lamb	I.V.A.Richards
1991 in ENGLAND						
Leeds-England 115 runs	•198	252	173	162	G.A.Gooch	I.V.A.Richards
Lord's-Drawn	354	-	•419	2-12		
Nottingham-West Indies 9 wkts	•300	211	397	1-115		
Birmingham-West Indies 7 wkts	•188	255	292	3-157		
The Oval-England 5 wkts	•419	5-146	176	385		

ENGLAND v WEST INDIES (cont.)	England		West Indies		Captains	
Venue and Result	1st	2nd	1st	2nd	England	West Indies
1993-94 in WEST INDIES						
Kingston- West Indies 8 wkts	•234	267	407	2-95	M.A.Atherton	R.B.Richardson
Georgetown-West Indies inns & 44 runs	•322	190	556	-		R.B.Richardson
Port-of-Spain-West Indies 147 runs	328	46	•252	269		R.B.Richardson
Bridgetown-England 208 runs	•355	7d-394	304	237		R.B.Richardson
St John's-Drawn	493	-	•5d•593	0-43		C.A.Walsh
1995 in ENGLAND						
Leeds-West Indies 9 wkts	•199	208	282	1-129	M.A.Atherton	R.B.Richardson
Lord's-England 72 runs	•283	336	324	223		
Birmingham-West Indies inns & 64 runs	•147	89	300	-		
Manchester-England 6 wkts	437	4-94	•216	314		
Nottingham-Drawn	•440	9d-269	417	2-42		
The Oval-Drawn	•454	4-223	8d-692	-		

Test Match Results Summary

ENGLAND v WEST INDIES-IN ENGLAND

		Result			Lord's			Manchester			The Oval			Nottingham			Birmingham			Leeds		
	Tests	E	WI	D	E	WI	D	E	WI	D	E	WI	D	E	WI	D	E	WI	D	E	WI	D
1928	3	3	-	-	1	-	-	1	-	-	1	-	-	-	-	-	-	-	-	-	-	-
1933	3	2	-	1	1	-	-	-	-	1	1	-	-	-	-	-	-	-	-	-	-	-
1939	3	1	-	2	1	-	-	-	-	1	-	-	1	-	-	-	-	-	-	-	-	-
1950	4	1	3	-	-	1	-	1	-	-	-	1	-	-	1	-	-	-	-	-	-	-
1957	5	3	-	2	1	-	-	-	-	-	1	-	-	-	-	1	-	-	1	1	-	-
1963	5	1	3	1	-	-	1	-	1	-	-	1	-	-	-	-	1	-	-	-	1	-
1966	5	1	3	1	-	-	1	-	1	-	-	1	-	-	-	-	1	-	-	-	1	-
1969	3	2	-	1	-	-	1	1	-	-	-	-	-	-	-	-	-	-	-	1	-	-
1973	3	-	2	1	-	1	-	-	-	-	-	1	-	-	-	-	-	-	1	-	-	-
1976	5	-	3	2	-	-	1	-	1	-	-	1	-	-	-	1	-	-	-	-	1	-
1980	5	-	1	4	-	-	1	-	-	1	-	-	1	-	1	-	-	-	-	-	1	-
1984	5	-	5	-	-	1	-	-	1	-	-	1	-	-	-	-	-	1	-	-	1	-
1988	5	-	4	1	-	1	-	-	1	-	-	1	-	-	-	-	-	1	-	-	-	1
1991	5	2	2	-	-	-	1	1	-	-	1	-	-	-	-	1	-	-	-	-	-	1
1995	6	2	2	2	1	-	-	1	-	-	-	-	1	-	-	1	-	1	-	-	1	-
	65	18	28	19	5	4	6	5	5	3	5	6	3	-	3	5	1	2	2	2	6	2

ENGLAND v WEST INDIES-IN WEST INDIES

		Result			Bridgetown			Port-of-Spain			Georgetown			Kingston			St John's		
	Tests	E	WI	D	E	WI	D	E	WI	D	E	WI	D	E	WI	D	E	WI	D
1929-30	4	1	1	2	-	-	1	1	-	-	-	1	-	-	-	1	-	-	-
1934-35	4	1	2	1	1	-	-	-	1	-	-	-	1	-	1	-	-	-	-
1947-48	4	-	2	2	-	-	1	-	-	1	-	1	-	-	1	-	-	-	-
1953-54	5	2	2	1	-	1	-	-	-	1	1	-	-	1	1	-	-	-	-
1959-60	5	1	-	4	-	-	1	1	-	1	-	-	1	-	-	1	-	-	-
1967-68	5	1	-	4	-	-	1	1	-	1	-	-	1	-	-	1	-	-	-
1973-74	5	1	1	3	-	-	1	1	1	-	-	-	1	-	-	1	-	-	-
1980-81	4	-	2	2	-	1	-	-	1	-	-	-	-	-	-	1	-	-	1
1985-86	5	-	5	-	-	1	-	-	2	-	-	-	-	-	1	-	-	1	-
1989-90	4	1	2	1	-	1	-	-	-	1	-	-	-	1	-	-	-	1	-
1993-94	5	1	3	1	1	-	-	-	1	-	-	1	-	-	1	-	-	-	1
	50	9	20	21	2	4	5	4	6	5	1	3	4	2	5	5	-	2	2
Totals	115	27	48	40															

HIGHEST INNINGS TOTALS

England in England	6d-619	Nottingham	1957
England in West Indies	849	Kingston	1929-30
West Indies in England	8d-692	The Oval	1995
West Indies in West Indies	8d-681	Port-of-Spain	1953-54

LOWEST INNINGS TOTALS

England in England	71	Manchester	1976
England in West Indies	46	Port-of-Spain	1993-94
West Indies in England	86	The Oval	1957
West Indies in West Indies	102	Bridgetown	1934-35

HIGHEST MATCH AGGREGATE	1815 for 34 wickets	Kingston	1929-30
LOWEST MATCH AGGREGATE	309 for 29 wickets	Bridgetown	1934-35

HIGHEST INDIVIDUAL INNINGS

England in England	285*	P.B.H.May	Birmingham	1957
England in West Indies	325	A.Sandham	Kingston	1929-30
West Indies in England	291	I.V.A.Richards	The Oval	1976
West Indies in West Indies	375	B.C.Lara	St John's	1993-94

HIGHEST AGGREGATE OF RUNS IN A SERIES

England in England	489 (av 97.80)	P.B.H.May	1957
England in West Indies	693 (av 115.50)	E.H.Hendren	1929-30
West Indies in England	829 (av 118.42)	I.V.A.Richards	1976
West Indies in West Indies	798 (av 99.75)	B.C.Lara	1993-94

RECORD WICKET PARTNERSHIPS-ENGLAND

1st	212	C.Washbrook (102), R.T.Simpson (94)	Nottingham	1950
2nd	266	P.E.Richardson (126), T.W.Graveney (258)	Nottingham	1957
3rd	303	M.A.Atherton (135), R.A.Smith (175)	St John's	1993-94
4th	411	P.B.H.May (285*), M.C.Cowdrey (154)	Birmingham	1957
5th	150	A.J.Stewart (143), G.P.Thorpe (84)	Brigetown	1993-94
6th	196	G.A.Hick (96), R.C.Russell (91)	The Oval	1995
7th	197	M.J.K.Smith (96), J.M.Parks (101*)	Port-of-Spain	1959-60
8th	217	T.W.Graveney (165), J.T.Murray (112)	The Oval	1966
9th	109	G.A.R.Lock (89), P.I.Pocock (13)	Georgetown	1967-68
10th	128	K.Higgs (63), J.A.Snow (59*)	The Oval	1966

RECORD WICKET PARTNERSHIPS-WEST INDIES

1st	298	C.G.Greenidge (149), D.L.Haynes (167)	St John's	1989-90
2nd	287*	C.G.Greenidge (214*), H.A.Gomes (92*)	Lord's	1984
3rd	338	E.D.Weekes (206), F.M.M.Worrell (167)	Port-of-Spain	1953-54
4th	399	G.S.Sobers (226), F.M.M.Worrell (197*)	Bridgetown	1959-60
5th	265	S.M.Nurse (137), G.S.Sobers (174)	Leeds	1966
6th	274*	G.S.Sobers (163*), D.A.J.Holford (105*)	Lord's	1966
7th	155*†	G.S.Sobers (150*), B.D.Julien (121)	Lord's	1973
8th	99	C.A.McWatt (54), J.K.Holt (48*)	Georgetown	1953-54
9th	150	E.A.E.Baptiste (87*), M.A.Holding (69)	Birmingham	1984
10th	67*	M.A.Holding (58*), C.E.H.Croft (17*)	St John's	1980-81

† 231 runs were added for this wicket, G.S.Sobers retired ill and was replaced by K.D.Boyce after 155 had been scored.

BEST INNINGS BOWLING ANALYSIS

England in England	8-103	I.T.Botham	Lord's	1984
England in West Indies	8-75	A.R.C.Fraser	Bridgetown	1993-94
West Indies in England	8-92	M.A.Holding	The Oval	1976
West Indies in West Indies	8-45	C.E.L.Ambrose	Bridgetown	1989-90

BEST MATCH BOWLING ANALYSIS

England in England	12-119	F.S.Trueman	Birmingham	1963
England in West Indies	13-156	A.W.Greig	Port-of-Spain	1973-74
West Indies in England	14-149	M.A.Holding	The Oval	1976
West Indies in West Indies	11-84	C.E.L.Ambrose	Bridgetown	1993-94

HIGHEST AGGREGATE OF WICKETS IN A SERIES

England in England	34 (av 17.47)	F.S.Trueman	1963
England in West Indies	27 (av 18.66)	J.A.Snow	1967-68
West Indies in England	35 (av 12.65)	M.D.Marshall	1950
West Indies in West Indies	27 (av 16.14)	J.Garner	1985-86
	27 (av 17.65)	M.D.Marshall	1985-86

ENGLAND v NEW ZEALAND	England		New Zealand		Captains	
Venue and Result	1st	2nd	1st	2nd	England	New Zealand
1929-30 in NEW ZEALAND						
Christchurch-England 8 wkts	181	2-66	•112	131	A.H.H.Gilligan	T.C.Lowry
Wellington-Drawn	320	4-107	•440	4d-164		
Auckland-Drawn	•4d-330	-	1-96	-		
Auckland-Drawn	•540	3-22	387	-		
1931 in ENGLAND						
Lord's-Drawn	454	5-146	•224	9d-469	D.R.Jardine	T.C.Lowry
The Oval-England inns & 26 runs	•4d-416	-	193	197		
Manchester-Drawn	•3-224	-	-	-		
1932-33 in NEW ZEALAND						
Christchurch-Drawn	•8d-560	-	223	0-35	D.R.Jardine	M.L.Page
Auckland-Drawn	7d-548	-	•158	0-16	R.E.S.Wyatt	
1937 in ENGLAND						
Lord's-Drawn	•424	4d-226	295	8-175	R.W.V.Robins	M.L.Page
Manchester-England 130 runs	•9d-358	187	281	134		
The Oval-Drawn	7d-254	1-31	•249	187		
1946-47 in NEW ZEALAND						
Christchurch-Drawn	7d-265	-	•9d-345	-	W.R.Hammond	W.A.Hadlee
1949 in ENGLAND						
Leeds-Drawn	•372	4d-267	341	2-195	F.G.Mann	W.A.Hadlee
Lord's-Drawn	•9d-313	5-306	484	-	F.G.Mann	
Manchester-Drawn	9d-440	-	•293	7-348	F.R.Brown	
The Oval-Drawn	482	-	•345	9d-308	F.R.Brown	
1950-51 in NEW ZEALAND						
Christchurch-Drawn	550	-	•8d-417	3-46	F.R.Brown	W.A.Hadlee
Wellington-England 6 wkts	227	4-91	•125	189		
1954-55 in NEW ZEALAND						
Dunedin-England 8 wkts	8d-209	2-49	•125	132	L.Hutton	G.O.Rabone
Auckland-England inns & 20 runs	246	-	•200	26		
1958 in ENGLAND						
Birmingham-England 205 runs	•221	6d-215	94	137	P.B.H.May	J.R.Reid
Lord's-England inns & 148 runs	•269	-	47	74		
Leeds-England inns & 71 runs	2d-267	-	•67	129		
Manchester-England inns & 13 runs	9d-365	-	•267	85		
The Oval-Drawn	9d-219	-	•161	3-91		
1958-59 in NEW ZEALAND						
Christchurch-England inns & 99 runs	•374	-	142	133	P.B.H.May	J.R.Reid
Auckland-Drawn	7-311	-	•181	-		
1962-63 in NEW ZEALAND						
Auckland-England inns & 215 runs	•7d-562	-	258	89	E.R.Dexter	J.R.Reid
Wellington-England inns & 47 runs	8d-428	-	•194	187		
Christchurch-England 7 wkts	253	3-173	•266	159		

ENGLAND v NEW ZEALAND (cont.)	England		New Zealand		Captains	
Venue and Result	1st	2nd	1st	2nd	England	New Zealand
1965 in ENGLAND						
Birmingham-England 9 wkts	•435	1-96	116	413	M.J.K.Smith	J.R.Reid
Lord's-England 7 wkts	307	3-218	•175	347		
Leeds-England inns & 187 runs	•4d-546	-	193	166		
1965-66 in NEW ZEALAND						
Christchurch-Drawn	•342	5d-201	347	8-48	M.J.K.Smith	M.E.Chapple
Dunedin-Drawn	8d-254	-	•192	9-147		B.W.Sinclair
Auckland-Drawn	222	4-159	•296	129		B.W.Sinclair
1969 in ENGLAND						
Lord's-England 230 runs	•190	340	169	131	R.Illingworth	G.T.Dowling
Nottingham-Drawn	8d-451	-	•294	1-66		
The Oval-England 8 wkts	242	2-138	•150	229		
1970-71 in NEW ZEALAND						
Christchurch-England 8 wkts	231	2-89	•65	254	R.Illingworth	G.T.Dowling
Auckland-Drawn	•321	237	7d-313	0-40		
1973 in ENGLAND						
Nottingham-England 38 runs	•250	8d-325	97	440	R.Illingworth	B.E.Congdon
Lord's-Drawn	•253	9-463	9d-551	-		
Leeds-England inns &1 run	419	-	•276	142		
1974-75 in NEW ZEALAND						
Auckland-England inns & 83 runs	•6d-593	-	326	184	M.H.Denness	B.E.Congdon
Christchurch-Drawn	2-272	-	•342	-		
1977-78 in NEW ZEALAND						
Wellington-New Zealand 72 runs	215	64	•228	123	G.Boycott	M.G.Burgess
Christchurch-England 174 runs	•418	4d-96	235	105		
Auckland-Drawn	429	-	•315	8-382		
1978 in ENGLAND						
The Oval-England 7 wkts	279	3-138	•234	182	J.M.Brearley	M.G.Burgess
Nottingham-England inns &119 runs	•429	-	120	190		
Lord's-England 7 wkts	289	3-118	•339	67		
1983 in ENGLAND						
The Oval-England 189 runs	•209	6d-446	196	270	R.G.D.Willis	G.P.Howarth
Leeds-New Zealand 5 wkts	•225	252	377	5-103		
Lord's-England 127 runs	•326	211	191	219		
Nottingham-England 165 runs	•420	297	207	345		
1983-84 in NEW ZEALAND						
Wellington-Drawn	463	0-69	•219	537	R.G.D.Willis	G.P.Howarth
Christchurch-New Zealand inns & 132 runs	82	93	•307	-		
Auckland-Drawn	439	-	•9d-496	0-16		
1986 in ENGLAND						
Lord's-Drawn	•317	6d-295	342	2-41	M.W.Gatting	J.V.Coney
Nottingham-New Zealand 8 wkts	•256	230	413	2-77		
The Oval-Drawn	5d-388	-	•287	0-7		

ENGLAND v NEW ZEALAND (cont.)	England		New Zealand		Captains	
Venue and Result	1st	2nd	1st	2nd	England	New Zealand
1987-88 in NEW ZEALAND						
Christchurch-Drawn	•319	152	168	4-130	M.W.Gatting	J.J.Crowe
Auckland-Drawn	323	-	•301	7-350		J.J.Crowe
Wellington-Drawn	2-183	-	•6d-512	-		J.G.Wright
1990 in ENGLAND						
Nottingham-Drawn	9d-345	-	•208	2-36	G.A.Gooch	J.G.Wright
Lord's-Drawn	•334	4d-272	9d-462	-		
Birmingham-England 114 runs	•435	158	249	230		
1991-92 in NEW ZEALAND						
Christchurch-England inns & 4 runs	•9d-580	-	312	264	G.A.Gooch	M.D.Crowe
Auckland-England 168 runs	•203	321	142	214		
Wellington-Drawn	•305	7d-359	9d-432	3-43		
1994 in ENGLAND						
Nottingham-England inns & 90 runs	9d-567	-	•251	226	M.A.Atherton	K.R.Rutherford
Lord's-Drawn	281	8-254	•476	5d-211		
Birmingham-Drawn	•382	-	151	7-308		

Test Match Results Summary

ENGLAND v NEW ZEALAND-IN ENGLAND

		Result			Lord's			The Oval			Manchester			Leeds			Birmingham			Nottingham		
	Tests	E	NZ	D	E	NZ	D	E	NZ	D	E	NZ	D	E	NZ	D	E	NZ	D	E	NZ	D
1931	3	1	-	2	-	-	1	1	-	-	-	-	1	-	-	-	-	-	-	-	-	-
1937	3	1	-	2	-	-	-	-	-	1	1	-	-	-	-	-	-	-	-	-	-	-
1949	4	-	-	4	-	-	1	-	-	1	-	-	1	-	-	1	-	-	-	-	-	-
1958	5	4	-	1	1	-	-	-	-	1	1	-	-	1	-	-	1	-	-	-	-	-
1965	3	3	-	-	1	-	-	-	-	-	-	-	-	1	-	-	1	-	-	-	-	-
1969	3	2	-	1	1	-	-	1	-	-	-	-	-	-	-	-	-	-	-	-	-	1
1973	3	2	-	1	-	-	1	-	-	-	-	-	-	1	-	-	-	-	-	1	-	-
1978	3	3	-	-	1	-	-	1	-	-	-	-	-	-	-	-	-	-	-	1	-	-
1983	4	3	1	-	1	-	-	1	-	-	-	-	-	-	1	-	-	-	-	1	-	-
1986	3	-	1	2	-	-	1	-	-	1	-	-	-	-	-	-	-	-	-	-	-	1
1990	3	1	-	2	-	-	1	-	-	-	-	-	-	-	-	-	1	-	-	-	-	1
1994	3	1	-	2	-	-	1	-	-	-	-	-	1	-	-	-	-	-	-	1	-	-
	40	21	2	17	5	-	7	4	-	4	2	-	3	3	1	1	3	-	-	4	1	2

ENGLAND v NEW ZEALAND-IN NEW ZEALAND

		Result			Christchurch			Wellington			Auckland			Dunedin		
	Tests	E	NZ	D	E	NZ	D	E	NZ	D	E	NZ	D	E	NZ	D
1929-30	4	1	-	3	1	-	-	-	-	1	-	-	2	-	-	-
1932-33	2	-	-	2	-	-	1	-	-	-	-	-	1	-	-	-
1946-47	1	-	-	1	-	-	1	-	-	-	-	-	-	-	-	-
1950-51	2	1	-	1	-	-	1	1	-	-	-	-	-	-	-	-
1954-55	2	2	-	-	-	-	-	-	-	-	1	-	-	1	-	-
1958-59	2	1	-	1	1	-	-	-	-	-	-	-	1	-	-	-
1962-63	3	3	-	-	1	-	-	1	-	-	1	-	-	-	-	-
1965-66	3	-	-	3	-	-	1	-	-	-	-	-	1	-	-	1
1970-71	2	1	-	1	1	-	-	-	-	-	-	-	1	-	-	-
1974-75	2	1	-	1	-	-	1	-	-	-	1	-	-	-	-	-
1977-78	3	1	1	1	1	-	-	-	1	-	-	-	1	-	-	-
1983-84	3	-	1	2	-	1	-	-	-	1	-	-	1	-	-	-
1987-88	3	-	-	3	-	-	1	-	-	1	-	-	1	-	-	-
1991-92	3	2	-	1	1	-	-	-	-	1	1	-	-	-	-	-
	35	13	2	20	6	1	6	2	1	4	4	-	9	1	-	1
Totals	75	34	4	37												

HIGHEST INNINGS TOTALS

England In England	8d-567	Nottingham	1994
England in New Zealand	6d-593	Auckland	1974-75
New Zealand in England	9d-551	Lord's	1973
New Zealand in New Zealand	537	Wellington	1983-84

LOWEST INNINGS TOTALS

England in England	158	Birmingham	1990
England in New Zealand	64	Wellington	1977-78
New Zealand in England	47	Lord's	1958
New Zealand in New Zealand	26	Auckland	1954-55

HIGHEST MATCH AGGREGATE	1293 for 34 wickets	Lord's	1931
LOWEST MATCH AGGREGATE	390 for 30 wickets	Lord's	1958

HIGHEST INDIVIDUAL INNINGS

England in England	310*	J.H.Edrich	Leeds	1965
England in New Zealand	336*	W.R.Hammond	Auckland	1932-33
New Zealand in England	206	M.P.Donnelly	Lord's	1949
New Zealand in New Zealand	174*	J.V.Coney	Wellington	1983-84

HIGHEST AGGREGATE OF RUNS IN A SERIES

England in England	469 (av 78.16)	L.Hutton	1949
England in New Zealand	563 (av 563.00)	W.R.Hammond	1932-33
New Zealand in England	462 (av 77.00)	M.P.Donnelly	1949
New Zealand in New Zealand	341 (av 85.25)	C.S.Dempster	1929-30

RECORD WICKET PARTNERSHIPS-ENGLAND

1st	223	G.Fowler (105), C.J.Tavare (109)	The Oval	1983
2nd	369	J.H.Edrich (310*), K.F.Barrington (163)	Leeds	1965
3rd	245	J.Hardstaff, jr (114), W.R.Hammond (140)	Lord's	1937
4th	266	M H.Denness (188), K.W.R.Fletcher (216)	Auckland	1974-75
5th	242	W.R.Hammond (227), L.E.G.Ames (103)	Christchurch	1932-33
6th	240	P.H.Parfitt (131*), 8.R.Knight (125)	Auckland	1962-63
7th	149	A.P.E.Knott (104), P.Lever (64)	Auckland	1970-71
8th	246	L.E.G.Ames (137), G.O.B.Allen (122)	Lord's	1931
9th	163*	M.C.Cowdrey (128*), A.C.Smith (69*)	Wellington	1962-63
10th	59	A.P.E.Knott (49), N.Gifford (25*)	Nottingham	1973

RECORD WICKET PARTNERSHIPS-NEW ZEALAND

1st	276	C.S.Dempster (136), J.E.Mills (117)	Wellington	1929-30
2nd	241	J.G.Wright (116), A.H.Jones (143)	Wellington	1991-92
3rd	210	B.A.Edgar (83), M.D.Crowe (106)	Lord's	1986
4th	155	M.D.Crowe (143), M.J.Greatbatch (68)	Wellington	1987-88
5th	180	M.D.Crowe (142), S.A.Thomson (69)	Lord's	1994
6th	141	M.D.Crowe (115), A.C.Parore (71)	Manchester	1994
7th	117	D.N.Patel (99), C.L.Cairns (61)	Christchurch	1991-92
8th	104	D.A.R.Moloney (64), A.W.Roberts (66*)	Lord's	1937
9th	118	J.V.Coney (174*), B.L.Cairns (64)	Wellington	1983-84
10th	57	F.L.H.Mooney (46), J.Cowie (26*)	Leeds	1949

BEST INNINGS BOWLING ANALYSIS

England in England	7-32	D.L.Underwood	Lord's	1969
England in New Zealand	7-47	P.C.R.Tufnell	Christchurch	1991-92
New Zealand in England	7-74	B.L.Cairns	Leeds	1983
New Zealand in New Zealand	7-143	B.L.Cairns	Wellington	1983-84

BEST MATCH BOWLING ANALYSIS

England in England	12-101	D.L.Underwood	The Oval	1969
England in New Zealand	12-97	D.L.Underwood	Christchurch	1970-71
New Zealand in England	11-169	D.J.Nash	Lord's	1994
New Zealand in New Zealand	10-100	R.J.Hadlee	Wellington	1977-78

HIGHEST AGGREGATE OF WICKETS IN A SERIES

England in England	34 (av 7.47)	G.A.R.Lock	1958
England in New Zealand	17 (av 9.34)	K.Higgs	1965-66
	17 (av 12.05)	D.L.Underwood	1970-71
	17 (av 18.29)	I.T.Botham	1977-78
New Zealand in England	21 (av 26.61)	R.J.Hadlee	1983
New Zealand in New Zealand	15 (av 19.53)	R.O.Collinge	1977-78
	15 (av 24.73)	R.J.Hadlee	1977-78

ENGLAND v INDIA Venue and Result	England 1st	England 2nd	India 1st	India 2nd	Captains England	Captains India
1932 in ENGLAND						
Lord's-England 158 runs	•259	8d-275	189	187	D.R.Jardine	C.K.Nayudu
1933-34 in INDIA						
Mumbai[1]-England 9 wkts	438	1-40	•219	258	D.R.Jardine	C.K.Nayudu
Calcutta-Drawn	•403	2-7	247	237		
Chennai[1]-England 202 runs	•335	7d-261	145	249		
1936 in ENGLAND						
Lord's-England 9 wkts	134	1-108	•147	93	G.O.B.Allen	Maharaj Vizianagram
Manchester-Drawn	8d-571	-	•203	5-390		
The Oval-England 9 wkts	•8d-471	1-64	222	312		
1946 in ENGLAND						
Lord's-England 10 wkts	428	0-48	•200	275	W.R.Hammond	Nawab of Pataudi, sr
Manchester-Drawn	•294	5d-153	170	9-152		
The Oval-Drawn	3-95	-	•331	-		
1951-52 in INDIA						
Delhi-Drawn	•203	6-368	6d-418	-	N.D.Howard	V.S.Hazare
Mumbai[2]-Drawn	456	2-55	•9d-485	208	N.D.Howard	
Calcutta-Drawn	•342	5d-252	344	0-103	N.D.Howard	
Kanpur-England 8 wkts	203	2-76	•121	157	N.D.Howard	
Chennai[1]-India inns & 8 runs	•266	183	9d-457	-	D.B.Carr	
1952 in ENGLAND						
Leeds-England 7 wkts	334	3-128	•293	165	L.Hutton	V.S.Hazare
Lord's-England 8 wkts	537	2-79	•235	378		
Manchester-England inns & 207 runs	•9d-347	-	58	82		
The Oval-Drawn	•6d-326	-	98	-		
1959 in ENGLAND						
Nottingham-England inns & 59 runs	•422	-	206	157	P.B.H.May	D.K.Gaekwad
Lord's-England 8 wkts	226	2-108	•168	165	P.B.H.May	P.Roy
Leeds-England inns & 173 runs	8d-483	-	•161	149	P.B.H.May	D.K.Gaekwad
Manchester-England 171 runs	•490	8d-265	208	376	M C Cowdrey	D.K.Gaekwad
The Oval-England inns & 27 runs	361	-	•140	194	M C Cowdrey	D.K.Gaekwad
1961-62 in INDIA						
Mumbai[2]-Drawn	•8d-500	5d-184	390	5-180	E.R.Dexter	N.J.Contractor
Kanpur-Drawn	244	5-497	•8d-467	-		
Delhi-Drawn	3-256	-	•466	-		
Calcutta-India 187 runs	212	233	•380	252		
Chennai[2]-India 128 runs	281	209	•428	190		
1963-64 in INDIA						
Chennai[2]-Drawn	317	5-241	•7d-457	9d-152	M.J.K.Smith	Nawab of Pataudi, jr
Mumbai[2]-Drawn	233	3-206	•300	8d-249		
Calcutta-Drawn	267	2-145	•241	7d-300		
Delhi-Drawn	451	-	•344	4 463		
Kanpur-Drawn	•8d-559	-	266	3-347		

ENGLAND v INDIA (cont.) Venue and Result	England 1st	England 2nd	India 1st	India 2nd	Captains England	Captains India
1967 in ENGLAND						
Leeds-England 6 wkts	•4d-550	4-126	164	510	D.B.Close	Nawab of Pataudi, jr
Lord's-England inns & 124 runs	386	-	•152	110		
Birmingham-England 132 runs	•298	203	92	277		
1971 in ENGLAND						
Lord's-Drawn	•304	191	313	8-145	R.Illingworth	A.L.Wadekar
Manchester-Drawn	•386	3d-245	212	3-65		
The Oval-India 4 wkts	•355	101	284	6-174		
1972-73 In INDIA						
Delhi-England 6 wkts	200	4-208	•173	233	A.R.Lewis	A.L.Wadekar
Calcutta-India 28 runs	174	163	•210	155		
Chennai[1]-India 4 wkts	•242	159	316	6-86		
Kanpur-Drawn	397	-	•357	6-186		
Mumbai[2]-Drawn	480	2-67	•448	5d-244		
1974 in ENGLAND						
Manchester-England 113 runs	•9d-328	3d-213	246	182	M.H.Denness	A.L.Wadekar
Lord's-England inns & 285 runs	•629	-	302	42		
Birmingham-England inns & 78 runs	2d-459	-	•165	216		
1976-77 in INDIA						
Delhi-England inns & 25 runs	•381	-	122	234	A.W.Greig	B.S.Bedi
Calcutta-England 10 wkts	321	0-16	•155	181		
Chennai[1]-England 200 runs	•262	9d-185	164	83		
Bangalore-India 140 runs	195	177	•253	9d-259		
Mumbai[3]-Drawn	317	7-152	•338	192		
1979 in ENGLAND						
Birmingham-England inns & 83 runs	•5d-633	-	297	253	J.M.Brearley	S.Venkataraghavan
Lord's-Drawn	9d-419	-	•96	4-318		
Leeds-Drawn	•270	-	6-223	-		
The Oval-Drawn	•305	8d-334	202	8-429		
1979-80 in INDIA						
Mumbai[3]-England 10 wkts	296	0-98	•242	149	J.M.Brearley	G.R.Viswanath
1981-82 in India						
Mumbai[3]-India 138 runs	166	102	•179	227	K.W.R.Fletcher	S.M.Gavaskar
Bangalore-Drawn	•400	3-174	428	-		
Delhi-Drawn	•9d-476	0-68	487	-		
Calcutta-Drawn	•248	5d-265	208	3-170		
Chennai[1]-Drawn	328	-	•4d-481	3-160		
Kanpur-Drawn	•9d-378	-	7-377	-		
1982 in ENGLAND						
Lord's-England 7 wkts	•433	3-67	128	369	R.G.D.Willis	S.M.Gavaskar
Manchester-Drawn	•425	-	8-379	-		
The Oval-Drawn	•594	3d-191	410	3-111		

ENGLAND v INDIA (cont.)	England		India		Captains	
Venue and Result	1st	2nd	1st	2nd	England	India
1984-85 in India						
Mumbai[3]-India 8 wkts	•195	317	8d-465	2-51	D.I.Gower	S.M.Gavaskar
Delhi-England 8 wkts	418	2-127	•307	235		
Calcutta-Drawn	276	-	•7d-437	1-29		
Chennai[1]-England 9 wkts	7d-652	[illegible]	•272	412		
Kanpur-Drawn	417	0-91	•8d-553	1d-97		
1986 in ENGLAND						
Lord's-India 5 wkts	•294	180	341	5-136	D.I.Gower	Kapil Dev
Manchester-India 279 runs	102	128	•272	237	M.W.Gatting	
The Oval-Drawn	•390	235	390	5-174	M.W.Gatting	
1990 in ENGLAND						
Lord's-England 247 runs	•4d-653	4d-272	454	224	G.A.Gooch	M.Azharuddin
Manchester-Drawn	•519	4d-320	432	6-343		
The Oval-Drawn	340	4d-477	•9d-606	-		
1992-93 in India						
Calcutta-India 8 wkts	163	286	•371	2-82	G.A.Gooch	M.Azharuddin
Chennai[1]-India inns & 22 runs	286	252	•6d-560	-	A.J.Stewart	
Mumbai[3]-India inns & 15 runs	•347	227	591		G.A.Gooch	
1996 in ENGLAND						
Birmingham-England 8 wkts	313	2-121	•214	219	M.A.Atherton	M.Azharuddin
Lord's-Drawn	•344	9d-278	429	-		
Nottingham-Drawn	564	-	•521	211		

Test Match Results Summary

ENGLAND v INDIA-IN ENGLAND

		Result			Lord's			Manchester			The Oval			Leeds			Nottingham			Birmingham		
	Tests	E	I	D	E	I	D	E	I	D	E	I	D	E	I	D	E	I	D	E	I	D
1932	1	1	-	-	1	-	-	-	-	-	-	-	-	-	-	-	-	-	-	-	-	-
1936	3	2	-	1	1	-	-	-	-	1	1	-	-	-	-	-	-	-	-	-	-	-
1946	3	1	-	2	1	-	-	-	-	1	-	-	1	-	-	-	-	-	-	-	-	-
1952	4	3	-	1	1	-	-	1	-	-	-	-	1	1	-	-	-	-	-	-	-	-
1959	5	5	-	-	1	-	-	1	-	-	1	-	-	1	-	-	-	-	-	-	-	-
1967	3	3	-	-	1	-	-	-	-	-	-	-	-	-	-	-	1	-	-	1	-	-
1971	3	-	1	2	-	-	1	-	-	1	-	1	-	-	-	-	-	-	-	-	-	-
1974	3	3	-	-	1	-	-	1	-	-	-	-	-	-	-	-	-	-	-	1	-	-
1979	4	1	-	3	-	-	1	-	-	-	-	-	1	-	-	1	-	-	-	1	-	-
1982	3	1	-	2	1	-	-	-	-	1	-	-	1	-	-	-	-	-	-	-	-	-
1986	3	-	2	1	-	1	-	-	-	-	-	-	-	-	1	-	-	-	-	-	-	1
1990	3	1	-	2	1	-	-	-	-	1	-	-	1	-	-	-	-	-	-	-	-	-
1996	3	1	-	-	1	-	-	-	-	-	-	-	-	-	-	-	-	-	1	-	-	1
	41	22	3	16	10	1	2	3	-	5	2	1	5	3	1	1	1	-	1	3	-	2

ENGLAND v INDIA-IN INDIA

		Result			Mumbai			Calcutta			Chennai			Delhi			Kanpur			Bangalore		
	Tests	E	I	D	E	I	D	E	I	D	E	I	D	E	I	D	E	I	D	E	I	D
1933-34	3	2	-	1	1	-	-	-	-	1	1	-	-	-	-	-	-	-	-	-	-	-
1951-52	5	1	1	3	-	-	1	-	-	1	-	1	-	-	-	1	1	-	-	-	-	-
1961-62	5	-	2	3	-	-	1	-	1	-	-	1	-	-	-	1	-	-	1	-	-	-
1963-64	5	-	-	5	-	-	1	-	-	1	-	-	1	-	-	1	-	-	1	-	-	-
1972-73	5	1	2	2	-	-	1	-	1	-	-	1	-	1	-	-	-	-	1	-	-	-
1976-77	5	3	1	1	-	-	1	1	-	-	1	-	-	1	-	-	-	-	-	-	-	1
1979-80	1	1	-	-	1	-	-	-	-	-	-	-	-	-	-	-	-	-	-	-	-	-
1981-82	6	-	1	5	-	1	-	-	-	1	-	-	1	-	-	1	-	-	1	-	-	1
1984-85	5	2	1	2	-	1	-	-	-	1	1	-	-	1	-	-	-	-	1	-	-	-
1992-93	3	-	3	-	-	1	-	-	1	-	-	1	-	-	-	-	-	-	-	-	-	-
	43	10	11	22	2	3	5	1	3	5	3	4	2	3	-	4	1	-	5	-	1	1
Totals	84	32	14	38																		

HIGHEST INNINGS TOTALS

England in England	4d-653	Lord's	1990
England in India	7d-652	Chennai[1]	1984-85
India in England	9d-606	The Oval	1990
India in India	591	Mumbai[3]	1992-93

LOWEST INNINGS TOTALS

England in England	101	The Oval	1971
England in India	102	Mumbai[3]	1981-82
India in England	42	Lord's	1974
India in India	83	Chennai[1]	1976-77

HIGHEST MATCH AGGREGATE	1614 for 30 wickets	Manchester	1990
LOWEST MATCH AGGREGATE	482 for 31 wickets	Lord's	1936

HIGHEST INDIVIDUAL INNINGS

England in England	333	G.A.Gooch	Lord's	1990
England in India	207	M.W.Gatting	Chennai[1]	1984-85
India In England	221	S.M.Gavaskar	The Oval	1979
India in India	224	V.G.Kambli	Mumbai[3]	1992-93

HIGHEST AGGREGATE OF RUNS IN A SERIES

England in England	752 (av 125.33)	G.A.Gooch	1990
England in India	594 (av 99.00)	K.F.Barrington	1961-62
India in England	542 (av 77.42)	S.M.Gavaskar	1979
India in India	586 (av 83.71)	V.L.Manjrekar	1961-62

RECORD WICKET PARTNERSHIPS-ENGLAND

1st	225	G.A.Gooch(116), M.A.Atherton(131)	Manchester	1990
2nd	241	G.Fowler (201), M.W.Gatting (207)	Chennai[1]	1984-85
3rd	308	G.A.Gooch(333), A.J.Lamb(139)	Lord's	1990
4th	266	W.R.Hammond (217), T.S.Worthington (128)	Oval	1936
5th	254	K.W.R.Fletcher (113), A.W.Greig (148)	Mumbai[2]	1972-73
6th	171	I.T.Botham (114), R.W.Taylor (43)	Mumbai[3]	1979-80
7th	125	D.W.Randall (126), P.H.Edmonds (64)	Lord's	1982
8th	168	R.Illingworth (107), P.Lever (88*)	Manchester	1971
9th	83	K.W.R.Fletcher (97*), N.Gifford (19)	Chennai[1]	1972-73
10th	70	P.J.W.Allott (41*), R.G.D.Willis (28)	Lord's	1982

RECORD WICKET PARTNERSHIPS-INDIA

1st	213	S.M.Gavaskar (221), C.P.S.Chauhan (80)	The Oval	1979
2nd	192	F.M.Engineer (121), A.L.Wadekar (87)	Mumbai[2]	1972-73
3rd	316†	G.R.Viswanath (222), Yashpal Sharma (140)	Chennai[1]	1981-82
4th	222	V.S.Hazare (89), V.L.Manjrekar (133)	Leeds	1952
5th	214	M.Azharuddin (110), R.J.Shastri (111)	Calcutta	1984-85
6th	130	S.M.H.Kirmani (43), Kapil Dev (97)	The Oval	1982
7th	235	R.J.Shastri (142), S.M.H.Kirmani (102)	Mumbai[3]	1984-85
8th	128	R.J.Shastri (93), S.M.H.Kirmani (67)	Delhi	1981-82
9th	104	R.J.Shastri (93), S.Madan Lal (44)	Delhi	1981-82
10th	51	R.G.Nadkarni (43'), B.S.Chandrasekhar (16)	Calcutta	1963-64
	51	S.M.H.Kirmani (75), C.Sharma (17*)	Chennai[1]	1984-85

† 415 runs were added for this wicket. D.B.Vengsarkar retired hurt after he had added 99 with Viswanath.

BEST INNINGS BOWLING ANALYSIS

England in England	8-31	F.S.Trueman	Manchester	1952
England in India	7-46	J.K.Lever	Delhi	1976-77
India in England	6-35	L.Amar Singh	Lord's	1936
India in India	8-55	M.H.Mankad	Chennai[1]	1951-52

BEST MATCH BOWLING ANALYSIS

England in England	11-93	A.V.Bedser	Manchester	1946
England in India	13-106	I.T.Botham	Mumbai[3]	1979-80
India in England	10-188	C.Sharma	Birmingham	1986
India in India	12-108	M.H.Mankad	Chennai[1]	1951-52

HIGHEST AGGREGATE OF WICKETS IN A SERIES

England in England	29 (av 13.31)	F.S.Trueman	1952
England in India	29 (av 17.55)	D.L.Underwood	1976-77
India in England	17 (av 34.64)	S.P.Gupte	1959
India in India	35 (av 18.91)	B.S.Chandrasekhar	1972-73

ENGLAND v PAKISTAN	England		Pakistan		Captains	
Venue and Result	1st	2nd	1st	2nd	England	Pakistan
1954 in ENGLAND						
Lord's-Drawn	9d-117	-	•87	3-121	L.Hutton	A.H.Kardar
Nottingham-England inns &129 runs	6d-558	-	•157	272	D.S.Sheppard	
Manchester-Drawn	•8d-359	-	90	4-25	D.S.Sheppard	
The Oval-Pakistan 24 runs	130	143	•133	164	L.Hutton	
1961-62 in PAKISTAN						
Lahore[2]-England 5 wkts	380	5-209	•9d-387	200	E.R.Dexter	Imtiaz Ahmed
Dacca-Drawn	439	0-38	•7d-393	216		
Karachi[1]-Drawn	507	-	•253	8-404		
1962 in ENGLAND						
Birmingham-England inns & 24 runs	•5d-544	-	246	274	E.R.Dexter	Javed Burki
Lord's-England 9 wkts	370	1-86	•100	355	E.R.Dexter	
Leeds-England inns & 117 runs	•428	-	131	180	M.C.Cowdrey	
Nottingham-Drawn	•5d-428	-	219	6-216	E.R.Dexter	
The Oval-England 10 wkts	•5d-480	0-27	183	323	E.R.Dexter	
1967 in ENGLAND						
Lord's-Drawn	•369	9d-241	354	3-88	D.B.Close	Hanif Mohammad
Nottingham-England 10 wkts	8d-252	0-3	•140	114		
The Oval-England 8 wkts	440	2-34	•216	255		
1968-69 In PAKISTAN						
Lahore[2]-Drawn	•306	9d-225	209	5-203	M.C.Cowdrey	Saeed Ahmed
Dacca-Drawn	274	0-33	•246	6d-195		
Karachi[1]-Drawn	•7-502	-	-	-		
1971 in ENGLAND						
Birmingham-Drawn	353	5-229	•7d-608	-	R.Illingworth	Intikhab Alam
Lord's-Drawn	•2d-241	0-117	148	-		
Leeds-England 25 runs	•316	264	350	205		
1972-73 in PAKISTAN						
Lahore[2]-Drawn	•355	7d-306	422	3-124	A.R.Lewis	Majid Khan
Hyderabad-Drawn	•487	6-218	9d-569	-		
Karachi[1]-Drawn	386	1-30	•6d-445	199		
1974 in ENGLAND						
Leeds-Drawn	183	6-238	•285	179	M.H.Denness	Intikhab Alam
Lord's-Drawn	270	0-27	•9d-130	226		
The Oval-Drawn	545	-	•7d-600	4-94		
1977-78 in PAKISTAN						
Lahore[2]-Drawn	288	-	•9d-407	3-106	J.M.Brearley	Wasim Bari
Hyderabad-Drawn	191	1-186	•275	4d-259	J.M.Brearley	
Karachi[1]-Drawn	•266	5-222	281	-	G.Boycott	

ENGLAND v PAKISTAN (cont.)	England		Pakistan		Captains	
Venue and Result	1st	2nd	1st	2nd	England	Pakistan
1978 in ENGLAND						
Birmingham-England inns & 57 runs	8d-452	-	•164	231	J.M.Brearley	Wasim Bari
Lord's-England inns &120 runs	•364	-	105	139		
Leeds-Drawn	7-119	-	•201	-		
1982 in ENGLAND						
Birmingham-England 113 runs	•272	291	251	199	R.G.D.Willis	Imran Khan
Lord's-Pakistan 10 wkts	227	276	•8d-428	0-77	D.I.Gower	
Leeds-England 3 wkts	256	7-219	•275	199	R.G.D.Willis	
1983-84 in PAKISTAN						
Karachi[1]-Pakistan 3 wkts	•182	159	277	7-66	R.G.D.Willis	Zaheer Abbas
Faisalabad-Drawn	8d-546	-	•8d-449	4-137	D.I.Gower	
Lahore[2]-Drawn	•241	9d-344	343	6-217	D.I.Gower	
1987 in ENGLAND						
Manchester-Drawn	•447	-	5-140	-	M.W.Gatting	Imran Khan
Lord's-Drawn	•368	-	-	-		
Leeds-Pakistan inns & 18 runs	•136	199	353	-		
Birmingham-Drawn	521	7-109	•439	205		
The Oval-Drawn	232	4-315	•708	-		
1987-88 in PAKISTAN						
Lahore[2]-Pakistan inns & 87 runs	•175	130	392	-	M.W.Gatting	Javed Miandad
Faisalabad-Drawn	•292	6d-137	191	1-51		
Karachi[1]-Drawn	•294	9-258	353	-		
1992 in ENGLAND						
Birmingham-Drawn	7-459	-	•4d-448	-	G.A.Gooch	Javed Miandad
Lord's-Pakistan 2 wkts	•255	175	293	8-141		
Manchester-Drawn	390	-	•505	5d-239		
Leeds-England 6 wkts	320	4-99	•197	221		
The Oval-Pakistan 10 wkts	•207	174	380	0-5		
1996 in ENGLAND						
Lord's-Pakistan 164 runs	285	243	•340	5d-352	M.A.Atherton	Wasim Akram
Leeds-Drawn	501	-	•448	7d-242		
The Oval-Pakistan 9 wickets	•326	242	8d-521	1-48		

Test Match Results Summary

ENGLAND v PAKISTAN-IN ENGLAND

		Result			Lords			Nottingham			Manchester			The Oval			Birmingham			Leeds		
	Tests	E	P	D	E	P	D	E	P	D	E	P	D	E	P	D	E	P	D	E	P	D
1954	4	1	1	2	-	-	1	1	-	-	-	-	1	-	1	-	-	-	-	-	-	-
1962	5	4	-	1	1	-	-	-	-	1	-	-	-	1	-	-	1	-	-	1	-	-
1967	3	2	-	1	-	-	1	1	-	-	-	-	-	1	-	-	-	-	-	-	-	-
1971	3	1	-	2	-	-	1	-	-	-	-	-	-	-	-	-	-	-	1	1	-	-
1974	3	-	-	3	-	-	1	-	-	-	-	-	-	-	-	1	-	-	-	-	-	1
1978	3	2	-	1	1	-	-	-	-	-	-	-	-	-	-	-	1	-	-	-	-	1
1982	3	2	1	-	-	1	-	-	-	-	-	-	-	-	-	-	1	-	-	1	-	-
1987	5	-	1	4	-	-	1	-	-	-	-	-	1	-	-	1	-	-	1	-	1	-
1992	5	1	2	2	-	1	-	-	-	-	-	-	1	-	1	-	-	-	1	1	-	-
1996	3	-	2	1	-	1	-	-	-	-	-	-	-	-	1	2	-	-	-	-	-	1
	37	13	7	17	2	3	5	2	-	1	-	-	3	2	3	2	3	-	3	4	1	3

ENGLAND v PAKISTAN-IN PAKISTAN

		Result			Lahore[2]			Dacca			Karachi[1]			Hyderabad			Faisalabad		
	Tests	E	P	D	E	P	D	E	P	D	E	P	D	E	P	D	E	P	D
1961-62	3	1	-	2	1	-	-	-	-	1	-	-	1	-	-	-	-	-	-
1968-69	3	-	-	3	-	-	1	-	-	-	-	-	1	-	-	1	-	-	-
1972-73	3	-	-	3	-	-	1	-	-	-	-	-	1	-	-	1	-	-	-
1977-78	3	-	-	3	-	-	1	-	-	1	-	-	1	-	-	-	-	-	-
1983-84	3	-	1	2	-	-	1	-	-	-	-	1	-	-	-	-	-	-	1
1987-88	3	-	1	2	-	1	-	-	-	-	-	-	1	-	-	-	-	-	1
	18	1	2	15	1	1	4	-	-	2	-	1	5	-	-	2	-	-	2
Totals	55	14	9	32															

HIGHEST INNINGS TOTALS

England in England	6d-558	Nottingham	1954
England in Pakistan	8d-546	Faisalabad	1983-84
Pakistan in England	708	The Oval	1987
Pakistan in Pakistan	9d-569	Hyderabad	1972-73

LOWEST INNINGS TOTALS

England in England	130	The Oval	1954
England in Pakistan	130	Lahore[2]	1987-88
Pakistan in England	87	Lord's	1954
Pakistan in Pakistan	191	Faisalabad	1987-88

HIGHEST MATCH AGGREGATE	1274 for 25 wickets	Hyderabad	1972-73
LOWEST MATCH AGGREGATE	509 for 28 wickets	Nottingham	1967

HIGHEST INDIVIDUAL INNINGS

England in England	278	D.C.S.Compton	Nottingham	1954
England in Pakistan	205	E.R.Dexter	Karachi[1]	1961-62
Pakistan in England	274	Zaheer Abbas	Birmingham	1971
Pakistan in Pakistan	157	Mushtaq Mohammad	Hyderabad	1972-73

HIGHEST AGGREGATE OF RUNS IN A SERIES

England in England	453 (av 90.60)	D.C.S.Compton	1954
England in Pakistan	449 (av 112.25)	D.I.Gower	1983-84
Pakistan in England	488 (av 81.33)	Saleem Malik	1992
Pakistan in Pakistan	407 (av 67.83)	Hanif Mohammad	1961-62

RECORD WICKET PARTNERSHIPS-ENGLAND

1st	198	G.Pullar (165), R.W.Barber (86)	Dacca	1961-62
2nd	248	M.C.Cowdrey (182), E.R.Dexter (172)	The Oval	1962
3rd	227	A.J.Stewart (190), R.A.Smith (127)	Birmingham	1992
4th	188	E.R.Dexter (205), P.H.Parfitt (111)	Karachi[1]	1961-62
5th	192	D.C.S.Compton (278), T.E.Bailey (36*)	Nottingham	1954
6th	153*	P.H.Parfitt (101*), D.A.Allen (79*)	Birmingham	1962
7th	167	D.I.Gower (152), V.J.Marks (83)	Faisalabad	1983-84
8th	99	P.H.Parfitt (119), D.A.Allen (62)	Leeds	1962
9th	76	T.W.Graveney (153), F.S.Trueman (29)	Lord's	1962
10th	79	R.W.Taylor (54), R.G.D.Willis (28*)	Birmingham	1982

RECORD WICKET PARTNERSHIPS-PAKISTAN

1st	173	Mohsin Khan (104), Shoaib Mohammad (80)	Lahore[2]	1983-84
2nd	291	Zaheer Abbas (274), Mushtaq Mohammad (100)	Birmingham	1971
3rd	180	Mudassar Nazar (114), Haroon Rashid (122)	Lahore[2]	1977-78
4th	332	Javed Miandad (153*), Saleem Malik (165)	Birmingham	1992
5th	197	Javed Burki (101), Nasim-ul-Ghani (101)	Lord's	1962
6th	145	Mushtaq Mohammad (157), Intikhab Alam (138)	Hyderabad	1972-73
7th	122	Asif Mujtaba (51), Moin Khan (105)	Leeds	1996
8th	130	Hanif Mohammad (187*), Asif Iqbal (76)	Lord's	1967
9th	190	Asif Iqbal (146), Intikhab Alam (51)	The Oval	1967
10th	62	Sarfraz Nawaz (53), Asif Masood (4*)	Leeds	1974

BEST INNINGS BOWLING ANALYSIS

England in England	8-34	I.T.Botham	Lord's	1978
England in Pakistan	7-66	P.H.Edmonds	Karachi[1]	1977-78
Pakistan in England	7-40	Imran Khan	Leeds	1987
Pakistan in Pakistan	9-56	Abdul Qadir	Lahore[2]	1987-88

BEST MATCH BOWLING ANALYSIS

England in England	13-71	D.L.Underwood	Lord's	1974
England in Pakistan	11-83	N.G.B.Cook	Karachi[1]	1983-84
Pakistan in England	12-99	Fazal Mahmood	The Oval	1954
Pakistan in Pakistan	13-101	Abdul Qadir	Lahore[2]	1987-88

HIGHEST AGGREGATE OF WICKETS IN A SERIES

England in England	22 (av 19.95)	F.S.Trueman	1962
England in Pakistan	14 (av 31.71)	N.G.B.Cook	1983-84
Pakistan in England	22 (av 25.31)	Waqar Younis	1992
Pakistan in Pakistan	30 (av 14.56)	Abdul Qadir	1987-88

ENGLAND v SRI LANKA Venue and Result	England 1st	 2nd	Sri Lanka 1st	 2nd	Captains England	 Sri Lanka
1981-82 in SRI LANKA						
Colombo (PSS)-England 7 wkts	223	3-171	•218	175	K.W.R.Fletcher	B.Warnapura
1984 in ENGLAND						
Lord's-Drawn	370	-	•7d-491	7d-294	D.I.Gower	L.R.D.Mendis
1988 in ENGLAND						
Lord's-England 7 wkts	429	3-100	•194	331	G.A.Gooch	R.S.Madugalle
1991 in ENGLAND						
Lord's-England 137 runs	•282	3d-364	224	285	G.A.Gooch	P.A.de Silva
1992-93 in SRI LANKA						
Colombo (SSC)-Sri Lanka 5 wickets	•380	228	469	5-142	A.J.Stewart	A.Ranatunga

Test Match Results Summary

ENGLAND v SRI LANKA-IN ENGLAND

		Result			Lord's		
	Tests	E	SL	D	E	SL	D
1984	1	-	-	1	-	-	1
1988	1	1	-	-	1	-	-
1991	1	1	-	-	1	-	-
	3	2	-	1	2	-	1

ENGLAND v SRI LANKA-IN SRI LANKA

		Result			Colombo (PSS)			Colombo (SSC)		
	Tests	E	SL	D	E	SL	D	E	SL	D
1981-82	1	1	-	-	1	-	-	-	-	-
1992-93	1	-	1	-	-	-	-	-	1	-
	2	1	1	-	1	-	-	-	1	-
Totals	5	3	1	1						

HIGHEST INNINGS TOTALS

England in England	429	Lord's	1988
England in Sri Lanka	380	Colombo (SSC)	1992-93
Sri Lanka in England	7d-491	Lord's	1984
Sri Lanka in Sri Lanka	469	Colombo (SSC)	1992-93

LOWEST INNINGS TOTALS

England in England	282	Lord's	1991
England in Sri Lanka	223	Colombo (PSS)	1981-82
Sri Lanka in England	194	Lord's	1988
Sri Lanka in Sri Lanka	195	Colombo (PSS)	1981-82

HIGHEST MATCH AGGREGATE	1219 for 37 wickets	Colombo (SSC)	1992-93
LOWEST MATCH AGGREGATE	787 for 33 wickets	Colombo (PSS)	1981-82

HIGHEST INDIVIDUAL INNINGS

England in England	174	G.A.Gooch	Lord's	1991
England in Sri Lanka	128	R.A.Smith	Colombo (SSC)	1992-93
Sri Lanka in England	190	S.Wettimuny	Lord's	1984
Sri Lanka in Sri Lanka	93*	H.P.Tillakaratne	Colombo (SSC)	1992-93

HIGHEST AGGREGATE OF RUNS IN A SERIES

England in England	212 (av 90.60)	G.A.Gooch	1991
England in Sri Lanka	163 (av 81.50)	R.A.Smith	1992-93
Sri Lanka in England	205 (av 44.55)	L.R.D.Mendis	1984
Sri Lanka in Sri Lanka	129 (av —.—)	H.P.Tillakaratne	1992-93

RECORD WICKET PARTNERSHIPS-ENGLAND

1st	78	G.A.Gooch (174), H.Morris (23)	Lord's	1991
2nd	139	G.A.Gooch (174), A.J.Stewart (43)	Lord's	1991
3rd	112	R.A.Smith (128), G.A.Hick (68)	Colombo (SSC)	1992-93
4th	122	R.A.Smith (128), A.J.Stewart (63)	Colombo (SSC)	1992-93
5th	40	A.J.Stewart (113*), I.T.Botham (22)	Lord's	1991
6th	87	A.J.Lamb (107), R.M.Ellison (41)	Lord's	1984
7th	63	A.J.Stewart (113*), R.C.Russell (17)	Lord's	1991
8th	20	J.E.Emburey (59), P.W.Jarvis (3)	Colombo (SSC)	1992-93
9th	37	P.J.Newport (26), N.A.Foster (14*)	Lord's	1988
10th	40	J.E.Emburey (59), D.E.Malcolm (8*)	Colombo (SSC)	1992-93

RECORD WICKET PARTNERSHIPS-SRI LANKA

1st	99	R.S.Mahanama (64), U.C.Hathurusingha (59)	Colombo (SSC)	1992-93
2nd	83	B.Warnaweera (38), R.L.Dias (77)	Colombo (PSS)	1981-82
3rd	101	S.Wettimuny (190), R.L.Dias (32)	Lord's	1984
4th	148	S.Wettimuny (190), A.Ranatunga (84)	Lord's	1984
5th	150	S.Wettimuny (190), L.R.D.Mendis(111)	Lord's	1984
6th	138	S.A.R.Silva (102*), L.R.D.Mendis (94)	Lord's	1984
7th	74	U.C.Hathurusingha (66), R.J.Ratnayake (52)	Lord's	1991
8th	28	R.J.Ratnayake (17), C.P.H.Ramanayake (34*)	Lord's	1991
9th	83	H.P.Tillakaratne (93*), M.Muralidharan (19)	Colombo (SSC)	1992-93
10th	64	J.R.Ratnayeke (59*), G.F.Labrooy (42)	Lord's	1988

BEST INNINGS BOWLING ANALYSIS

England in England	7-70	P.A.J.DeFreitas	Lord's	1991
England in Sri Lanka	6-33	J.E.Emburey	Colombo (PSS)	1981-82
Sri Lanka in England	5-69	R.J.Ratnayake	Lord's	1991
Sri Lanka in Sri Lanka	4-70	A.L.F.de Mel	Colombo (PSS)	1981-82

BEST MATCH BOWLING ANALYSIS

England in England	8-115	P.A.J.DeFreitas	Lord's	1991
England in Sri Lanka	8-95	D.L.Underwood	Colombo (PSS)	1981-82
Sri Lanka in England	5-160	R.J.Ratnayake	Lord's	1991
Sri Lanka in Sri Lanka	8-188	K.P.J.Warnaweera	Colombo (SSC)	1992-93

HIGHEST AGGREGATE OF WICKETS IN A SERIES

England in England	8 (av 14.37)	P.A.J.DeFreitas	1991
England in Sri Lanka	8 (av 11.87)	D.L.Underwood	1981-82
Sri Lanka in England	5 (av 32.00)	R.J.Ratnayake	1991
	5 (av 36.00)	S.D.Anurasiri	1991
Sri Lanka in Sri Lanka	8 (av 23.50)	K.P.J.Warnaweera	1992-93

SOUTH AFRICA v NEW ZEALAND Venue and Result	South Africa 1st	 2nd	New Zealand 1st	 2nd	Captains South Africa	 New Zealand
1931-32 In NEW ZEALAND						
Christchurch-South Africa inns & 12 runs	451	-	•293	146	H.B.Cameron	M.L.Page
Wellington-South Africa 8 wkts	410	2-150	•364	193		
1952-53 In NEW ZEALAND						
Wellington-South Africa inns & 180 runs	•8d-524	-	172	172	J.E.Cheetham	W.M.Wallace
Auckland-Drawn	•377	5d-200	245	2-31		
1953-54 In SOUTH AFRICA						
Durban[2]-South Africa inns & 58 runs	•9d-437	-	230	149	J.E.Cheetham	G.O.Rabone
Johannesburg[2]-South Africa 132 runs	•271	148	187	100		G.O.Rabone
Cape Town-Drawn	326	3-159	•505	-		G.O.Rabone
Johannesburg[2]-South Africa 9 wkts	•243	1-25	79	188		B.Sutcliffe
Port Elizabeth-South Africa 5 wkts	237	5-215	•226	222		B.Sutcliffe
1961-62 In SOUTH AFRICA						
Durban[2]-South Africa 30 runs	•292	149	245	166	D.J.McGlew	J.R.Reid
Johannesburg[3]-Drawn	•322	6d-178	223	4-165		
Cape Town-New Zealand 72 runs	190	335	•385	9d-212		
Johannesburg[3]-South Africa inns & 51 runs	464	-	•164	249		
Port Elizabeth-New Zealand 40 runs	190	273	•275	228		
1963-64 in NEW ZEALAND						
Wellington-Drawn	•302	2d-218	253	6-138	T.L.Goddard	J.R.Reid
Dunedin-Drawn	223	3-42	•149	138		
Auckland-Drawn	•371	5d-200	263	8-191		
1994-95 In SOUTH AFRICA						
Johannesburg[3]-New Zealand 137 runs	279	189	•411	194	W.J.Cronje	K.R.Rutherford
Cape Town-South Africa 8 wkts	226	2-153	•185	192		
Durban[2]-South Africa 7 wkts	440	3-89	•288	239		
1994-95 in NEW ZEALAND						
Auckland-South Africa 93 runs	•294	6d-308	328	181	W.J.Cronje	K.R.Rutherford

Test Match Results Summary

SOUTH AFRICA v NEW ZEALAND-IN SOUTH AFRICA

	Tests	Result			Durban[2]			Johannesburg			Cape Town			P.Elizabeth		
		SA	NZ	D	SA	NZ	D	SA	NZ	D	SA	NZ	D	SA	NZ	D
1953-54	5	4	-	1	1	-	-	2	-	-	-	-	1	1	-	-
1961-62	5	2	2	1	1	-	-	1	-	1	-	1	-	-	1	-
1994-95	3	2	1	-	1	-	-	-	1	-	1	-	-	-	-	-
	13	8	3	2	2	-	-	3	-	1	-	1	1	1	1	-

SOUTH AFRICA v NEW ZEALAND-IN NEW ZEALAND

		Result			Christchurch			Wellington			Auckland			Dunedin		
	Tests	SA	NZ	D	SA	NZ	D	SA	NZ	D	SA	NZ	D	SA	NZ	D
1931-32	2	2	-	-	1	-	-	1	-	-	-	-	-	-	-	-
1952-53	2	1	-	1	-	-	-	1	-	-	-	-	1	-	-	-
1963-64	3	-	-	3	-	-	-	-	-	1	-	-	1	-	-	1
1994-95	1	1	-	-	-	-	-	-	-	-	1	-	-	-	-	-
	8	4	-	4	1	-	-	2	-	1	-	-	2	-	-	1
Totals	21	12	3	6												

HIGHEST INNINGS TOTALS

South Africa in South Africa	464	Johannesburg[3]	1961-62
South Africa in New Zealand	8d-524	Wellington	1952-53
New Zealand in South Africa	505	Cape Town	1953-54
New Zealand in New Zealand	364	Wellington	1931-32

LOWEST INNINGS TOTALS

South Africa in South Africa	148	Johannesburg[2]	1953-54
South Africa in New Zealand	223	Dunedin	1963-64
New Zealand in South Africa	79	Johannesburg[2]	1953-54
New Zealand in New Zealand	138	Dunedin	1963-64

HIGHEST MATCH AGGREGATE	1122 for 39 wickets	Cape Town	1961-62
LOWEST MATCH AGGREGATE	535 for 31 wickets	Johannesburg[2]	1953-54

HIGHEST INDIVIDUAL INNINGS

South Africa in South Africa	127*	D.J.McGlew	Durban[2]	1961-62
South Africa in New Zealand	255*	D.J.McGlew	Wellington	1952-53
New Zealand in South Africa	142	J.R.Reid	Johannesburg[3]	1961-62
New Zealand in New Zealand	138	B.W.Sinclair	Auckland	1963-64

HIGHEST AGGREGATE OF RUNS IN A SERIES

South Africa in South Africa	426 (av 60.85)	D.J.McGlew	1961-62
South Africa in New Zealand	323 (av 161.50)	D.J.McGlew	1952-53
New Zealand in South Africa	546 (av 60.66)	J.R.Reid	1961-62
New Zealand in New Zealand	264 (av 44.00)	B.W.Sinclair	1963-64

RECORD WICKET PARTNERSHIPS-SOUTH AFRICA

1st	196	J.A.J.Christy (103), B.Mitchell (113)	Christchurch	1931-32
2nd	97	G.Kirsten (66*), J.B.Commins (45)	Durban[2]	1994-95
3rd	112	D.J.McGlew (120), R.A.McLean (78)	Johannesburg[3]	1961-62
4th	135	K.J.Funston (39), R.A McLean (101)	Durban[2]	1953-54
5th	130	W.R.Endean (116), J.E.Cheetham (54)	Auckland	1952-53
6th	83	K.C.Bland (83), D.T.Lindsay (37)	Auckland	1963-64
7th	246	D.J.McGlew (255*), A.R.A.Murray (109)	Wellington	1952-53
8th	95	J.E.Cheetham (89), H.J.Tayfield (34)	Cape Town	1953-54
9th	60	P.M.Pollock (54), N.A.T.Adcock (24)	Port Elizabeth	1961-62
10th	47	D.J.McGlew (28*), H.D.Bromfield (21)	Port Elizabeth	1961-62

RECORD WICKET PARTNERSHIPS-NEW ZEALAND

1st	126	G.O.Rabone (56), M.E.Chapple (76)	Cape Town	1953-54
2nd	72	D.J.Murray (25), S.P.Fleming (48)	Johannesburg[3]	1994-95
3rd	94	M.B.Poore (44), B.Sutcliffe (66)	Cape Town	1953-54
4th	171	B.W.Sinclair (138), S.N.McGregor (62)	Auckland	1963-64
5th	174	J.R.Reid (135), J.E.F.Beck (99)	Cape Town	1953-54
6th	100	H.G.Vivian (100), F.T Badcock (53)	Wellington	1931-32
7th	84	J.R.Reid (142), G.A.Bartlett (33)	Johannesburg[3]	1961-62
8th	74	S.A.Thomson (84), D.J.Nash (18)	Johannesburg[3]	1994-95
9th	69	C.F.W.Allcott (26), I.B.Cromb (51*)	Wellington	1931-32
10th	57	S.B.Doull (31*), R.P.de Groen (21)	Johannesburg[3]	1994-95

BEST INNINGS BOWLING ANALYSIS

South Africa in South Africa	8-53	G.B.Lawrence	Johannesburg[3]	1961-62
South Africa in New Zealand	6-47	P.M.Pollock	Wellington	1963-64
New Zealand in South Africa	6-68	G.O.Rabone	Cape Town	1953-54
New Zealand in New Zealand	6-60	J.R.Reid	Dunedin	1963-64

BEST MATCH BOWLING ANALYSIS

South Africa in South Africa	11-196	S.F.Burke	Cape Town	1961-62
South Africa in New Zealand	9-127	Q.McMillan	Christchurch	1931-32
New Zealand in South Africa	8-134	M.N.Hart	Johannesburg[3]	1994-95
New Zealand in New Zealand	7-142	R.W.Blair	Auckland	1963-64

HIGHEST AGGREGATE OF WICKETS IN A SERIES

South Africa in South Africa	28 (av 18.28)	G.B.Lawrence	1961-62
South Africa in New Zealand	16 (av 20.18)	Q.McMillan	1931-32
New Zealand in South Africa	22 (av 20.63)	A.R.MacGibbon	1953-54
	22 (av 28.04)	J.C.Alabaster	1961-62
New Zealand in New Zealand	12 (av 23.16)	J.R.Reid	1963-64
	12 (av 27.16)	R.W.Blair	1963-64

SOUTH AFRICA v WEST INDIES	South Africa		West Indies		Captains	
Venue and Result	1st	2nd	1st	2nd	South Africa	West Indies
1991-92 In WEST INDIES						
Bridgetown-West Indies 52 runs	345	148	•262	283	K.C.Wessels	R.B.Richardson

Test Match Results Summary

SOUTH AFRICA v WEST INDIES-IN WEST INDIES

		Result			Bridgetown		
	Tests	SA	W	D	SA	W	D
1991-92	1	-	1	-	-	1	-

HIGHEST INNINGS TOTALS

South Africa in West Indies	345	Bridgetown	1991-92
West Indies in West Indies	283	Bridgetown	1991-92

LOWEST INNINGS TOTALS

South Africa in West Indies	148	Bridgetown	1991-92
West Indies in West Indies	262	Bridgetown	1991-92

HIGHEST MATCH AGGREGATE

1038 for 40 wickets	Bridgetown	1991-92

HIGHEST INDIVIDUAL INNINGS

South Africa in West Indies	163	A.C.Hudson	Bridgetown	1991-92
West Indies in West Indies	79*	J.C.Adams	Bridgetown	1991-92

HIGHEST AGGREGATE OF RUNS IN A SERIES

South Africa in West Indies	163 (av 81.50)	A.C.Hudson	1991-92
West Indies in West Indies	90 (av 90.00)	J.C.Adams	1991-92

HIGHEST WICKET PARTNERSHIP-SOUTH AFRICA

1st	14	M.W.Rushmere (3), A.C.Hudson (163)	Bridgetown	1991-92
2nd	125	A.C.Hudson (163), K.C.Wessels (59)	Bridgetown	1991-92
3rd	96	K.C.Wessels (74), P.N.Kirsten (52)	Bridgetown	1991-92
4th	19	A.C.Hudson (163), W.J.Cronje (5)	Bridgetown	1991-92
5th	92	A.C.Hudson (163), A.P.kuiper (34)	Bridgetown	1991-92
6th	14	A.C.Hudson (163), D.J.Richardson (8)	Bridgetown	1991-92
7th	19	A.C.Hudson (163), R.P.Snell (16)	Bridgetown	1991-92
8th	5	D.J.Richardson (2), M.W.Pringle (4)	Bridgetown	1991-92
9th	20	M.W.Pringle (15), A.A.Donald (0)	Bridgetown	1991-92
10th	9	M.W.Pringle (15), T.Bosch (5*)	Bridgetown	1991-92

HIGHEST WICKET PARTNERSHIP-WEST INDIES

1st	99	D.L.Haynes (58), P.V.Simmons (35)	Bridgetown	1991-92
2nd	56	D.L.Haynes (23), B.C.Lara (64)	Bridgetown	1991-92
3rd	31	B.C.Lara (17), R.B.Richardson (44)	Bridgetown	1991-92
4th	82	R.B.Richardson (44), K.L.T.Arthurton (59)	Bridgetown	1991-92
5th	21	K.L.T.Arthurton (59), J.C.Adams (11)	Bridgetown	1991-92
6th	25	J.C.Adams (79*), D.Williams (5)	Bridgetown	1991-92
7th	10	J.C.Adams (79*), C.E.L.Ambrose (6)	Bridgetown	1991-92
8th	22	J.C.Adams (79*), K.C.G.Benajmin (7)	Bridgetown	1991-92
9th	27	J.C.Adams (79*), C.A.Walsh (13)	Bridgetown	1991-92
10th	62	J.C.Adams (79*), B.P.Patterson (11)	Bridgetown	1991-92

BEST INNINGS BOWLING ANALYSIS

South Africa in West Indies	4-74	R.P.Snell	Bridgetown	1991-92
West Indies in West Indies	6-34	C.E.L.Ambrose	Bridgetown	1991-92

BEST MATCH BOWLING ANALYSIS

South Africa in West Indies	8-157	R.P.Snell	Bridgetown	1991-92
West Indies in West Indies	8-81	C.E.L.Ambrose	Bridgetown	1991-92

HIGHEST AGGREGATE OF WICKETS IN A SERIES

South Africa in West Indies	8 (av 19.62)	R.P.Snell	1991-92
West Indies in West Indies	8 (av 10.12)	C.E.L.Ambrose	1991-92

SOUTH AFRICA v INDIA	South Africa		India		Captains	
Venue and Result	1st	2nd	1st	2nd	South Africa	West Indies
1992-93 In SOUTH AFRICA						
Durban²-Drawn	•254	3-176	277	-	K.C.Wessels	M.Azharuddin
Johannesburg³-Drawn	•292	252	227	4-141		
Port Elizabeth-South Africa 9 wkts	275	1-155	•212	215		
Cape Town-Drawn	•9d-360	6d-130	276	1-29		

Test Match Results Summary

SOUTH AFRICA v INDIA-IN SOUTH AFRICA

		Result			Durban²			Johannesburg³			P.Elizabeth			Cape Town		
	Tests	SA	I	D	SA	I	D	SA	I	D	SA	I	D	SA	I	D
1992-93	4	1	-	3	-	-	1	-	-	1	1	-	-	-	-	1

HIGHEST INNINGS TOTALS

South Africa in South Africa	9d-360	Cape Town	1992-93
India in South Africa	277	Durban²	1992-93

LOWEST INNINGS TOTALS

South Africa in South Africa	254	Durban²	1992-93
India in South Africa	212	Port Elizabeth	1992-93

HIGHEST MATCH AGGREGATE	912 for 37 wickets	Johannesburg³	1992-93
LOWEST MATCH AGGREGATE	767 for 23 wickets	Durban²	1992-93

HIGHEST INDIVIDUAL INNINGS

South Africa in South Africa	135	W.J.Cronje	Port Elizabeth	1992-93
India in South Africa	129	Kapil Dev	Port Elizabeth	1992-93

HIGHEST AGGREGATE OF RUNS IN A SERIES

South Africa in South Africa	295 (av 52.20)	K.C.Wessels	1992-93
India in South Africa	202 (av 40.40)	Kapil Dev	1992-93
	202 (av 33.66)	S.R.Tendulkar	1992-93

HIGHEST WICKET PARTNERSHIP-SOUTH AFRICA

1st	98	K.C.Wessels (95*), A.C.Hudson (33)	Port Elizabeth	1992-93
2nd	117	A.C.Hudson (52), W.J.Cronje (135)	Port Elizabeth	1992-93
3rd	60	K.C.Wessels (118), P.N.Kirsten (13)	Durban²	1992-93
4th	82	K.C.Wessels (118), J.N.Rhodes (41)	Durban²	1992-93
5th	99	D.J.Cullinan (46), J.N.Rhodes (86)	Cape Town	1992-93
6th	85	J.N.Rhodes (91), B.M.McMillan (98)	Johannesburg³	1992-93
7th	37	B.M.McMillan (52), D.J.Richardson (21)	Cape Town	1992-93
8th	65	B.M.McMillan (98), C.R.Matthews (31)	Johannesburg³	1992-93
9th	31*	B.M.McMillan (98), M.W.Pringle (3+)	Johannesburg³	1992-93
10th	15*	C.R.Matthews (28*), A.A.Donald (1*)	Cape Town	1992-93

HIGHEST WICKET PARTNERSHIP-INDIA

1st	68	R.J.Shastri (23), A.D.Jadeja (43)	Johannesburg[3]	1992-93
2nd	85	M.Prabhakar (62), S.V.Manjrekar (46)	Cape Town	1992-93
3rd	17	S.V.Manjrekar (7), S.R.Tendulkar (111)	Johannesburg[3]	1992-93
4th	39	S.V.Manjrekar (23), M.Azharuddin (60)	Port Elizabeth	1992-93
5th	87	M.Azharuddin (36), P.K.Amre (103)	Durban[2]	1992-93
6th	47	S.R.Tendulkar (73), S.L.Venkatapathy Raju (18)	Cape Town	1992-93
7th	128	S.R.Tendulkar (111), Kapil Dev (25)	Johannesburg[3]	1992-93
8th	101	P.K.Amre (103), K.S.More (55)	Durban[2]	1992-93
9th	77	Kapil Dev (129), A.R.Kumble (17)	Port Elizabeth	1992-93
10th	18	Kapil Dev (129), S.L.Venkatapathy Raju (2*)	Port Elizabeth	1992-93

BEST INNINGS BOWLING ANALYSIS

South Africa in South Africa	7-84	A.A.Donald	Port Elizabeth	1992-93
India in South Africa	6-53	A.R.Kumble	Johannesburg[3]	1992-93

BEST MATCH BOWLING ANALYSIS

South Africa in South Africa	12-139	A.A.Donald	Port Elizabeth	1992-93
India in South Africa	8-113	A.R.Kumble	Johannesburg[3]	1992-93

HIGHEST AGGREGATE OF WICKETS IN A SERIES

South Africa in South Africa	20 (av 19.70)	A.A.Donald	1992-93
India in South Africa	18 (av 25.94)	A.R.Kumble	1992-93

SOUTH AFRICA v SRI LANKA	South Africa		Sri Lanka		Captains	
Venue and Result	1st	2nd	1st	2nd	South Africa	Sri Lanka
1993-94 in SRI LANKA						
Moratuwa-Drawn	267	7-251	•331	6d-300	K.C.Wessels	A.Ranatunga
Colombo(SSC)-Sth.Africa inns & 208 runs	495	-	•168	119		
Colombo(PSS)-Drawn	•316	4-159	9d-296	-		

Test Match Results Summary

SOUTH AFRICA v SRI LANKA-IN SRI LANKA

		Result			Moratuwa			Colombo(SSC)			Colombo(PSS)		
	Tests	SA	SL	D	SA	SL	D	SA	SL	D	SA	SL	D
1993-94	3	1	-	2	-	-	1	1	-	-	-	-	1

HIGHEST INNINGS TOTALS

South Africa in Sri Lanka	495	Colombo (SSC)	1993-94
Sri Lanka in Sri Lanka	331	Moratuwa	1993-94

LOWEST INNINGS TOTALS

South Africa in Sri Lanka	267	Moratuwa	1993-94
Sri Lanka in Sri Lanka	119	Colombo (SSC)	1993-94

HIGHEST MATCH AGGREGATE	1149 for 33 wickets	Moratuwa	1993-94
LOWEST MATCH AGGREGATE	771 for 23 wickets	Colombo (PSS)	1993-94

HIGHEST INDIVIDUAL INNINGS

South Africa in Sri Lanka	122	W.J.Cronje	Colombo (SSC)	1993-94
Sri Lanka in Sri Lanka	131	A.Ranatunga	Moratuwa	1993-94

HIGHEST AGGREGATE OF RUNS IN A SERIES

South Africa in Sri Lanka	237 (av 59.25)	W.J.Cronje	1993-94
	237 (av 47.40)	D.J.Cullinan	1993-94
Sri Lanka in Sri Lanka	250 (av 40.40)	A.Ranatunga	1993-94

HIGHEST WICKET PARTNERSHIP-SOUTH AFRICA

1st	137	K.C.Wessels (92), A.C.Hudson (58)	Colombo (SSC)	1993-94
2nd	48	A.C.Hudson (90), W.J.Cronje (17)	Moratuwa	1993-94
3rd	105	W.J.Cronje (122), D.J.Cullinan (52)	Colombo (SSC)	1993-94
4th	94	W.J.Cronje (73*), J.N.Rhodes (19)	Colombo (PSS)	1993-94
5th	35	D.J.Cullinan (46), J.N.Rhodes (101*)	Moratuwa	1993-94
6th	122	D.J.Cullinan (102), D.J.Richardson (63)	Colombo (PSS)	1993-94
7th	68	W.J.Cronje (122), P.L.Symcox (50)	Colombo (SSC)	1993-94
8th	79	P.L.Symcox (50), R.P.Snell (48)	Colombo (SSC)	1993-94
9th	7	R.P.Snell (48), A.A.Donald (4*)	Colombo (SSC)	1993-94
10th	8	A.A.Donald (4*), B.N.Schultz (6)	Colombo (SSC)	1993-94

HIGHEST WICKET PARTNERSHIP-SRI LANKA

1st	26	R.S.Mahanama (17), U.C.Hathurusingha (9)	Moratuwa	1993-94
2nd	72	R.S.Mahanama (53), A.P.Gurusinha (26)	Moratuwa	1993-94
3rd	45	U.C.Hathurusingha (34), P.A.de Silva (34)	Colombo (SSC)	1993-94
4th	101	P.A.de Silva (82), A.Ranatunga (50)	Colombo (PSS)	1993-94
5th	121	P.A.de Silva (68), A.Ranatunga (131)	Moratuwa	1993-94
6th	103	A.Ranatunga (131), H.P.Tillakaratne (33*)	Moratuwa	1993-94
7th	26	S.T.Jayasuriya (44), K.Dharmasena (5)	Colombo (SSC)	1993-94
8th	21	S.T.Jayasuriya (65), D.K.Liyanage (0)	Colombo (PSS)	1993-94
9th	28	H.P.Tillakaratne (92), G.P.Wickramasinghe (11)	Moratuwa	1993-94
10th	18	H.P.Tillakaratne (92), M.Muralidharan (2*)	Moratuwa	1993-94
	18	P.B.Dassanayake (10), M.Muralidharan (14*)	Colombo (SSC)	1993-94

BEST INNINGS BOWLING ANALYSIS

South Africa in Sri Lanka	5-48	B.N.Schultz	Colombo (SSC)	1993-94
Sri Lanka in Sri Lanka	5-101	M.Muralidharan	Colombo (SSC)	1993-94

BEST MATCH BOWLING ANALYSIS

South Africa in Sri Lanka	9-106	B.N.Schultz	Colombo (SSC)	1993-94
Sri Lanka in Sri Lanka	6-152	M.Muralidharan	Moratuwa	1993-94

HIGHEST AGGREGATE OF WICKETS IN A SERIES

South Africa in Sri Lanka	20 (av 16.30)	B.N.Schultz	1993-94
Sri Lanka in Sri Lanka	16 (av 22.25)	M.Muralidharan	1993-94

SOUTH AFRICA v PAKISTAN	South Africa		Pakistan		Captains	
Venue and Result	1st	2nd	1st	2nd	South Africa	Pakistan
1994-95 In SOUTH AFRICA						
Johannesburg[3]-South Africa 324 runs	•460	7d-259	230	165	W.J.Cronje	Saleem Malik

Test Match Results Summary

SOUTH AFRICA v PAKISTAN-IN SOUTH AFRICA

		Result			Johannesburg[3]		
	Tests	SA	P	D	SA	P	D
1994-95	1	1	-	-	1	-	-

HIGHEST INNINGS TOTALS

South Africa in South Africa	460	Johannesburg[3]	1994-95
Pakistan in South Africa	230	Johannesburg[3]	1994-95

LOWEST INNINGS TOTALS

South Africa in South Africa	460	Johannesburg[3]	1994-95
Pakistan in South Africa	165	Johannesburg[3]	1994-95

HIGHEST MATCH AGGREGATE 1114 for 37 wickets Johannesburg[3] 1994-95

Sunil Gavaskar made his highest Test score of 236 not out against the West Indies in Madras, during the 1983-84 season. He holds the world record for Test cricket centuries (34) and scored 10 122 career runs — the second highest total ever.

The great New Zealand bowler Sir Richard Hadlee claims one of his ten wickets in the third Test against Australia in Melbourne, December 1987.

HIGHEST INDIVIDUAL INNINGS

South Africa in South Africa	113	B.M.McMillan	Johannesburg[3]	1994-95
Pakistan in South Africa	99	Saleem Malik	Johannesburg[3]	1994-95

HIGHEST AGGREGATE OF RUNS IN A SERIES

South Africa in South Africa	146 (av 73.00)	B.M.McMillan	1994-95
Pakistan in South Africa	114 (av 57.00)	Inzamamul Haq	1994-95

HIGHEST WICKET PARTNERSHIP-SOUTH AFRICA

1st	69	G.Kirsten (42), P.J.R.Steyn (17)	Johannesburg[3]	1994-95
2nd	54	G.Kirsten (62), J.B.Commins (13)	Johannesburg[3]	1994-95
3rd	59	W.J.Cronje (48), D.J.Cullinan (69*)	Johannesburg[3]	1994-95
4th	79	G.Kirsten (62), W.J.Cronje (41)	Johannesburg[3]	1994-95
5th	30	G.Kirsten (62), J.N.Rhodes (72)	Johannesburg[3]	1994-95
6th	157	J.N.Rhodes (72), B.M.McMillan (113)	Johannesburg[3]	1994-95
7th	4	D.J.Cullinan (69*), D.J.Richardson (0)	Johannesburg[3]	1994-95
8th	12	B.M.McMillan (113), C.E.Eksteen (13)	Johannesburg[3]	1994-95
9th	22	C.E.Eksteen (13), P.S.de Villiers (66*)	Johannesburg[3]	1994-95
10th	71	P.S.de Villiers (66*), A.A.Donald (15)	Johannesburg[3]	1994-95

HIGHEST WICKET PARTNERSHIP-PAKISTAN

1st	20	Aamer Sohail (23), Saeed Anwar (2)	Johannesburg[3]	1994-95
2nd	0	Aamer Sohail (23), Asif Mujtaba (0)	Johannesburg[3]	1994-95
	0	Saeed Anwar (2), Asif Mujtaba (26)	Johannesburg[3]	1994-95
3rd	24	Aamer Sohail (23), Saleem Malik (99)	Johannesburg[3]	1994-95
4th	93	Asif Mujtaba (26), Inzamamul Haq (95)	Johannesburg[3]	1994-95
5th	28	Saleem Malik (99), Inzamamul Haq (19)	Johannesburg[3]	1994-95
6th	24	Saleem Malik (99), Moin Khan (9)	Johannesburg[3]	1994-95
7th	35	Saleem Malik (99), Wasim Akram (41)	Johannesburg[3]	1994-95
8th	40	Inzamamul Haq (95), Kabir Khan (10)	Johannesburg[3]	1994-95
9th	23	Wasim Akram (41), Aaqib Javed (0*)	Johannesburg[3]	1994-95
10th	1	Aaqib Javed (0), Aamer Nazir (1*)	Johannesburg[3]	1994-95

BEST INNINGS BOWLING ANALYSIS

South Africa in South Africa	6-81	P.S.de Villiers	Johannesburg[3]	1994-95
Pakistan in South Africa	3-102	Aaqib Javed	Johannesburg[3]	1994-95

BEST MATCH BOWLING ANALYSIS

South Africa in South Africa	10-108	P.S.de Villiers	Johannesburg[3]	1994-95
Pakistan in South Africa	5-184	Aaqib Javed	Johannesburg[3]	1994-95

HIGHEST AGGREGATE OF WICKETS IN A SERIES

South Africa in South Africa	10 (av 10.80)	P.S.de Villiers	1994-95
Pakistan in South Africa	5 (av 36.80)	Aaqib Javed	1994-95

SOUTH AFRICA v ZIMBABWE	South Africa		Zimbabwe		Captains	
Venue and Result	1st	2nd	1st	2nd	South Africa	Zimbabwe
1995-96 in ZIMBABWE						
Harare-South Africa 7 wkts	346	3-108	•170	283	W.J.Cronje	A.Flower

Test Match Results Summary

SOUTH AFRICA v ZIMBABWE-IN ZIMBABWE

		Result			Harare		
	Tests	SA	Z	D	SA	Z	D
1995-96	1	1	-	-	1	-	-

HIGHEST INNINGS TOTALS

South Africa in Zimbabwe	346	Harare	1995-96
Zimbabwe in Zimbabwe	283	Harare	1995-96

LOWEST INNINGS TOTALS

South Africa in Zimbabwe	346	Harare	1995-96
Zimbabwe in Zimbabwe	170	Harare	1995-96

HIGHEST MATCH AGGREGATE

907 for 33 wickets	Harare	1995-96

HIGHEST INDIVIDUAL INNINGS

South Africa in Zimbabwe	135	A.C.Hudson	Harare	1995-96
Zimbabwe in Zimbabwe	63	A.Flower	Harare	1995-96

HIGHEST AGGREGATE ON RUNS IN A SERIES

South Africa in Zimbabwe	139 (av 69.50)	A.C.Hudson	1995-96
Zimbabwe in Zimbabwe	70 (av 35.00)	A.Flower	1995-96

RECORD WICKET PARTNERSHIPS-SOUTH AFRICA

1st	6	G.Kirsten (13), A.C.Hudson (4)	Harare	1995-96
2nd	30	G.Kirsten (13), W.J.Cronje (56*)	Harare	1995-96
3rd	35	A.C.Hudson (135), D.J.Cullinan (11)	Harare	1995-96
4th	60*	W.J.Cronje (56*), B.M.McMillan (25*)	Harare	1995-96
5th	60	A.C.Hudson (135), J.N.Rhodes (15)	Harare	1995-96
6th	101	A.C.Hudson (135), B.M.McMillan (98*)	Harare	1995-96
7th	15	B.M.McMillan (98*), D.J.Richardson (13)	Harare	1995-96
8th	4	B.M.McMillan (98*), P.L.Symcox (4)	Harare	1995-96
9th	79	B.M.McMillan (98*), A.A.Donald (33)	Harare	1995-96
10th	2	B.M.McMillan (98*), B.N.Schultz (0)	Harare	1995-96

RECORD WICKET PARTNERSHIPS-ZIMBABWE

1st	13	M.H.Dekker (24), G.W.Flower (5)	Harare	1995-96
2nd	51	M.H.Dekker (24), A.D.R.Campbell (28)	Harare	1995-96
3rd	10	G.W.Flower (24), D.L.Houghton (5)	Harare	1995-96
4th	31	D.L.Houghton (21), A.Flower (63)	Harare	1995-96
5th	97	A.Flower (63), G.J.Whittall (38)	Harare	1995-96
6th	13	G.J.Whittall (29), C.B.Wishart (24)	Harare	1995-96
7th	25	C.B.Wishart (13), P.A.Strang (37)	Harare	1995-96
8th	43	C.B.Wishart (24), H.H.Streak (53)	Harare	1995-96
9th	48	P.A.Strang (37), B.C.Strang (25*)	Harare	1995-96
10th	42	H.H.Streak (53), A.C.I.Lock (8*)	Harare	1995-96

BEST INNINGS BOWLING ANALYSIS

South Africa in Zimbabwe	8-71	A.A.Donald	Harare	1995-96
Zimbabwe in Zimbabwe	5-101	B.C.Strang	Harare	1995-96

BEST MATCH BOWLING ANALYSIS

South Africa in Zimbabwe	11-113	A.A.Donald	Harare	1995-96
Zimbabwe in Zimbabwe	5-105	A.C.I.Lock	Harare	1995-96

HIGHEST AGGREGATE OF WICKETS IN A SERIES

South Africa in Zimbabwe	11 (av 10.27)	A.A.Donald	1995-96
Zimbabwe in Zimbabwe	5 (av 21.00)	A.C.I.Lock	1995-96
	5 (av 23.80)	B.C.Strang	1995-96

WEST INDIES v NEW ZEALAND

Venue and Result	West Indies 1st	West Indies 2nd	New Zealand 1st	New Zealand 2nd	Captains West Indies	Captains New Zealand
1951-52 in NEW ZEALAND						
Christchurch-West Indies 5 wkts	287	5-142	•236	189	J.D.C.Goddard	B.Sutcliffe
Auckland-Drawn	•6d-546	-	160	1-17		
1955-56 in NEW ZEALAND						
Dunedin-West Indies inns & 71 runs	353	-	•74	208	D.S.Atkinson	H.B.Cave
Christchurch-West Indies inns & 64 runs	•386	-	158	164		J.R.Reid
Wellington-West Indies 9 wkts	•404	1-13	208	208		J.R.Reid
Auckland-New Zealand 190 runs	145	77	•255	9d-157		J.R.Reid
1968-69 in NEW ZEALAND						
Auckland-West Indies 5 wkts	276	5-348	•323	8d-297	G.S.Sobers	G.T.Dowling
Wellington-New Zealand 6 wkts	•297	148	282	4-166		
Christchurch-Drawn	•417	-	217	6-367		
1971-72 in WEST INDIES						
Kingston-Drawn	•4d-508	3d-218	386	6-236	G.S.Sobers	G.T.Dowling
Port-of-Spain-Drawn	341	5-121	•348	3d-288		G.T.Dowling
Bridgetown-Drawn	•133	8-564	422	-		B.E.Congdon
Georgetown-Drawn	•7d-365	0-86	3d-543	-		B.E.Congdon
Port-of-Spain-Drawn	•368	194	162	7-253		B.E.Congdon
1979-80 in NEW ZEALAND						
Dunedin-New Zealand 1 wkt	•140	212	249	9-104	C.H.Lloyd	G.P.Howarth
Christchurch-Drawn	•228	5d-447	460	-		
Auckland-Drawn	•220	9d-264	305	4-73		
1984-85 in WEST INDIES						
Port-of-Spain-Drawn	•307	8d-261	262	6-187	I.V.A.Richards	G.P.Howarth
Georgetown-Drawn	•6d-511	6d-268	440	-		
Bridgetown-West Indies 10 wkts	336	0-10	•94	248		
Kingston-West Indies 10 wkts	•363	0-59	138	283		
1986-87 in NEW ZEALAND						
Wellington-Drawn	345	2-50	•228	5d-386	I.V.A.Richards	J.V.Coney
Auckland-West Indies 10 wkts	•9d-419	0-16	157	273		
Christchurch-New Zealand 5 wkts	•100	264	9d-332	5-33		
1994-95 in NEW ZEALAND						
Christchurch-Drawn	312	-	•8d-341	2-61	C.A.Walsh	K.R.Rutherford
Wellington-West Indies inns & 322 runs	•5d-660	-	216	122		
1995-96 in WEST INDIES						
Bridgetown-West Indies 10 wkts	472	0-29	•195	305	C.A.Walsh	L.K.Germon
St John's-Drawn	•7d-548	184	437	5-130		

Test Match Results Summary

WEST INDIES v NEW ZEALAND-IN WEST INDIES

		Result			Kingston			Port-of-Spain			Bridgetown			Georgetown			St John's		
	Tests	WI	NZ	D	WI	NZ	D	WI	NZ	D	WI	NZ	D	WI	NZ	D	WI	NZ	D
1971-72	5	-	-	5	-	-	1	-	-	2	-	-	1	-	-	1	-	-	-
1984-85	4	2	-	2	1	-	-	-	-	1	1	-	-	-	-	1	-	-	-
1995-96	2	1	-	1	-	-	-	-	-	-	1	-	-	-	-	-	-	-	1
	11	3	-	8	1	-	1	-	-	3	2	-	1	-	-	2	-	-	1

WEST INDIES v NEW ZEALAND-IN NEW ZEALAND

		Result			Christchurch			Auckland			Dunedin			Wellington		
	Tests	WI	NZ	D	WI	NZ	D	WI	NZ	D	WI	NZ	D	WI	NZ	D
1951-52	2	1	-	1	1	-	-	-	-	1	-	-	-	-	-	-
1955-56	4	3	1	-	1	-	-	-	1	-	1	-	-	1	-	-
1968-69	3	1	1	1	-	-	1	1	-	-	-	-	-	-	1	-
1979-80	3	-	1	2	-	-	1	-	-	1	-	1	-	-	-	-
1986-87	3	1	1	1	-	1	-	1	-	-	-	-	-	-	-	1
1994-95	2	1	-	1	-	-	1	-	-	-	-	-	-	1	-	-
	17	7	4	6	2	1	3	2	1	2	1	1	-	2	1	1
Totals	28	10	4	14												

HIGHEST INNINGS TOTALS

West Indies in West Indies	8-564	Bridgetown	1971-72
West Indies in New Zealand	5d-660	Wellington	1994-95
New Zealand in West Indies	3d-543	Georgetown	1971-72
New Zealand in New Zealand	460	Christchurch	1979-80

LOWEST INNINGS TOTALS

West Indies in West Indies	133	Bridgetown	1971-72
West Indies in New Zealand	77	Auckland	1955-56
New Zealand in West Indies	94	Bridgetown	1984-85
New Zealand in New Zealand	74	Dunedin	1955-56

HIGHEST MATCH AGGREGATE	1348 for 23 wickets	Kingston	1971-72
LOWEST MATCH AGGREGATE	634 for 39 wickets	Auckland	1955-56

HIGHEST INDIVIDUAL INNINGS

West Indies in West Indies	214	L.G.Rowe	Kingston	1971-72
West Indies in New Zealand	258	S.M.Nurse	Christchurch	1968-69
New Zealand in West Indies	259	G.M.Turner	Georgetown	1971-72
New Zealand in New Zealand	147	G.P.Howarth	Christchurch	1979-80

HIGHEST AGGREGATE OF RUNS IN A SERIES

West Indies in West Indies	487 (av 54.11)	R.C.Fredericks	1971-72
New Zealand in New Zealand	558 (av 111.60)	S.M.Nurse	1968-69
New Zealand in West Indies	672 (av 98.00)	G.M.Turner	1971-72
New Zealand in New Zealand	328 (av 65.60)	M.D.Crowe	1986-87

RECORD WICKET PARTNERSHIPS-WEST INDIES

1st	225	C.G.Greenidge (97), D.L.Haynes (122)	Christchurch	1979-80
2nd	269	R.C.Fredericks (163), L.G.Rowe (214)	Kingston	1971-72
3rd	221	B.C.Lara (147), J.C.Adams (151)	Wellington	1994-95
4th	162	E.D.Weekes (123), O.G.Smith (64)	Dunedin	1955-56
	162	C.G.Greenidge (91), A.I.Kallicharran (75)	Christchurch	1979-80
5th	189	F.M.M.Worrell (100), C.L.Walcott (115)	Auckland	1951-52
6th	254	C.A.Davis (183), G.S.Sobers (142)	Bridgetown	1971-72
7th	143	D.S Atkinson (85), J.D.C.Goddard (83*)	Christchurch	1955-56
8th	83	I.V.A.Richards (105), M.D.Marshall (63)	Bridgetown	1984-85
9th	70	M.D.Marshall (63), J.Garner (37*)	Bridgetown	1984-85
10th	31	T.M.Findlay (44*), G.C.Shillingford (15)	Bridgetown	1971-72

RECORD WICKET PARTNERSHIPS-NEW ZEALAND

1st	387	G.M.Turner (259), T.W.Jarvis (182)	Georgetown	1971-72
2nd	210	G.P.Howarth (84), J.J.Crowe (112)	Kingston	1984-85
3rd	241	J.G.Wright (138), M.D.Crowe (119)	Wellington	1986-87
4th	175	B.E.Congdon (126), B.F.Hastings (105)	Bridgetown	1971-72
5th	144	N.J.Astle (125), J.T.C.Vaughan (24)	Bridgetown	1995-96
6th	220	G.M.Turner (223*), K.J.Wadsworth (78)	Kingston	1971-72
7th	143	M.D.Crowe (188), I.D.S.Smith (53)	Georgetown	1984-85
8th	136	B.E.Congdon (166*), R.S.Cunis (51)	Port-of-Spain	1971-72
9th	62*	V.Pollard (51*), R.S.Cunis (20*)	Auckland	1968-69
10th	45	D.K.Morrison (26*), R.J.Kennedy (22)	Bridgetown	1995-96

BEST INNINGS BOWLING ANALYSIS

West Indies in West Indies	7-80	M.D.Marshall	Bridgetown	1984-85
West Indies in New Zealand	7-37	C.A.Walsh	Wellington	1994-95
New Zealand in West Indies	7-74	B.R.Taylor	Bridgetown	1971-72
New Zealand in New Zealand	6-50	R.J.Hadlee	Christchurch	1986-87

BEST MATCH BOWLING ANALYSIS

West Indies in West Indies	11-120	M.D.Marshall	Bridgetown	1984-85
West Indies in New Zealand	13-55	C.A.Walsh	Wellington	1994-95
New Zealand in West Indies	10-124	E.J.Chatfield	Port-of-Spain	1984-85
New Zealand in New Zealand	11-102	R.J Hadlee	Dunedin	1979-80

HIGHEST AGGREGATE OF WICKETS IN A SERIES

West Indies in West Indies	27 (av 18.00)	M.D.Marshall	1984-85
West Indies In New Zealand	20 (av 15.80)	S.Ramadhin	1955-56
New Zealand in West Indies	27 (av 17.70)	B.R.Taylor	1971-72
New Zealand In New Zealand	19 (av 19.00)	R.J Hadlee	1979-80

WEST INDIES v INDIA

Venue and Result	West Indies 1st	West Indies 2nd	India 1st	India 2nd	Captains West Indies	Captains India
1948-49 in INDIA						
Delhi-Drawn	•631	-	454	6-220	J.D.C.Goddard	N.B.Amarnath
Mumbai²-Drawn	•6d-629	-	273	3-333		
Calcutta-Drawn	•366	9d-336	272	3-325		
Chennai¹-West Indies inns & 193 runs	•582	-	245	144		
Mumbai²-Drawn	•286	267	193	8-355		
1952-53 in WEST INDIES						
Port-of-Spain-Drawn	438	0-142	•417	294	J.B.Stollmeyer	V.S.Hazare
Bridgetown-West Indies 142 runs	•296	228	253	129		
Port-of-Spain-Drawn	315	2-192	•279	7d-362		
Georgetown-Drawn	364	-	•262	5-190		
Kingston-Drawn	576	4-92	•312	444		
1958-59 in INDIA						
Mumbai²-Drawn	•227	4d-323	152	5-289	F.C.M.Alexander	P.R.Umrigar
Kanpur-West Indies 203 runs	•222	7d-443	222	240		Ghulam Ahmed
Calcutta-West Indies inns & 336 runs	•5d-614	-	124	154		Ghulam Ahmed
Chennai²-West Indies 295 runs	•500	5d-168	222	151		M.H.Mankad
Delhi-Drawn	8d-644	-	•415	275		H.R.Adhikari
1961-62 in WEST INDIES						
Port-of-Spain-West Indies 10 wkts	289	0-15	•203	98	F.M.M.Worrell	N.J.Contractor
Kingston-West Indies inns & 18 runs	8d-631	-	•395	218		N.J.Contractor
Bridgetown-West Indies inns & 30 runs	475	-	•258	187		Nawab of Pataudi, jr
Port-of-Spain-West Indies 7 wkts	•9d-444	3-176	197	422		Nawab of Pataudi, jr
Kingston-West Indies 123 runs	•253	283	178	235		Nawab of Pataudi, jr
1966-67 in INDIA						
Mumbai²-West Indies 6 wkts	421	4-192	•296	316	G.S.Sobers	Nawab of Pataudi, jr
Calcutta-West Indies inns & 45 runs	•390	-	167	178		
Chennai¹-Drawn	406	7-270	•404	323		
1970-71 in WEST INDIES						
Kingston-Drawn	217	5-385	•387	-	G.S.Sobers	A.L.Wadekar
Port-of-Spain-India 7 wkts	•214	261	352	3-125		
Georgetown-Drawn	•363	3d-307	376	0-123		
Bridgetown-Drawn	•5d-501	6d-180	347	5-221		
Port-of-Spain-Drawn	526	8-165	•360	427		
1974-75 in INDIA						
Bangalore-West Indies 267 runs	•289	6d-356	260	118	C.H.Lloyd	Nawab of Pataudi, jr
Delhi-West Indies inns & 17 runs	493	-	•220	256		S.Venkataraghavan
Calcutta-India 85 runs	240	224	•233	316		Nawab of Pataudi, jr
Chennai¹-India 100 runs	192	154	•190	256		Nawab of Pataudi, jr
Mumbai³-West Indies 201 runs	•6d-604	3d-205	406	202		Nawab of Pataudi, jr
1975-76 in WEST INDIES						
Bridgetown-West Indies inns & 97 runs	9d-488	-	•177	214	C.H.Lloyd	B.S.Bedi
Port-of-Spain-Drawn	•241	8-215	5d-402	-		
Port-of-Spain-India 6 wkts	•359	6d-271	228	4-406		
Kingston-West Indies 10 wkts	391	0-13	•6d-306	97		

WEST INDIES v INDIA (cont.)

Venue and Result	West Indies 1st	West Indies 2nd	India 1st	India 2nd	Captains West Indies	Captains India
1978-79 in INDIA						
Mumbai[3]-Drawn	493	-	•424	2-224	A.I.Kallicharran	S.M.Gavaskar
Bangalore-Drawn	•437	8-200	371	-		
Calcutta-Drawn	327	9-197	•300	1d-361		
Chennai[1]-India 3 wkts	•228	151	255	7-125		
Delhi-Drawn	172	3-179	•8d-566	-		
Kanpur-Drawn	8-452	-	•7d-644	-		
1982-83 in WEST INDIES						
Kingston-West Indies 4 wkts	254	6-173	•251	174	C.H.Lloyd	Kapil Dev
Port-of-Spain-Drawn	394	-	•175	7-469		
Georgetown-Drawn	•470	-	3-284	-		
Bridgetown-West Indies 10 wkts	486	0-1	•209	277		
St John's-Drawn	550	-	•457	5d-247		
1983-84 in INDIA						
Kanpur-West Indies inns & 83 runs	•454	-	207	164	C.H.Lloyd	Kapil Dev
Delhi-Drawn	384	2-120	•464	233		
Ahmedabad-West Indies 138 runs	•281	201	241	103		
Mumbai[3]-Drawn	393	4-104	•463	5d-173		
Calcutta-West Indies inns & 46 runs	377	-	•241	90		
Chennai[1]-Drawn	•313	1-64	8d-451	-		
1987-88 in INDIA						
Delhi-West Indies 5 wkts	127	5-276	•75	327	I.V.A.Richards	D.B.Vengsarkar
Mumbai[3]-Drawn	337	1-4	•281	173		D.B.Vengsarkar
Calcutta-Drawn	•5d-530	2-157	565	-		D.B.Vengsarkar
Chennai[1]-India 255 runs	184	160	•382	8d-217		R.J.Shastri
1988-89 in WEST INDIES						
Georgetown-Drawn	•437	-	1-86	-	I.V.A.Richards	D.B.Vengsarkar
Bridgetown-West Indies 8 wkts	377	2-196	•321	251		
Port-of-Spain-West Indies 217 runs	•314	266	150	213		
Kingston-West Indies 7 wkts	384	3-60	•289	152		
1994-95 in INDIA						
Mumbai[3]-India 96 runs	243	266	•272	333	C.A.Walsh	M.Azharuddin
Nagpur-Drawn	428	5-132	•9d-546	7d-208		
Mohali-West Indies 243 runs	•443	3d-301	387	114		

Test Match Results Summary

WEST INDIES v INDIA-IN WEST INDIES

	Tests	Result			Port-of-Spain			Bridgetown			Georgetown			Kingston			St John's		
		WI	I	D	WI	I	D	WI	I	D	WI	I	D	WI	I	D	WI	I	D
1952-53	5	1	-	4	-	-	2	1	-	-	-	-	1	-	-	1	-	-	-
1961-62	5	5	-	-	2	-	-	1	-	-	-	-	-	2	-	-	-	-	-
1970-71	5	-	1	4	-	1	1	-	-	1	-	-	1	-	-	1	-	-	-
1975-76	4	2	1	1	-	1	1	1	-	-	-	-	-	1	-	-	-	-	-
1982-83	5	2	-	3	-	-	1	1	-	-	-	-	1	1	-	-	-	-	1
1988-89	4	3	-	1	1	-	-	1	-	-	-	-	1	1	-	-	-	-	-
	28	13	2	13	3	2	5	5	-	1	-	-	4	5	-	2	-	-	1

WEST INDIES v INDIA-IN INDIA

	Tests	Result			Delhi			Mumbai			Calcutta			Chennai		
		WI	I	D	WI	I	D	WI	I	D	WI	I	D	WI	I	D
1948-49	5	1	-	4	-	-	1	-	-	2	-	-	1	1	-	-
1958-59	5	3	-	2	-	-	1	-	-	1	1	-	-	1	-	-
1966-67	3	2	-	1	-	-	-	1	-	-	1	-	-	-	-	1
1974-75	5	3	2	-	1	-	-	1	-	-	-	1	-	-	1	-
1978-79	6	-	1	5	-	-	1	-	-	1	-	-	1	-	1	-
1983-84	6	3	-	3	-	-	1	-	-	1	1	-	-	-	-	1
1987-88	4	1	1	2	1	-	-	-	-	1	-	-	1	-	1	-
1994-95	3	1	1	1	-	-	-	-	1	-	-	-	-	-	-	-
	34	13	4	17	2	-	4	2	-	6	3	1	3	2	3	2
Totals	62	26	6	30												

	Kanpur			Bang.			Ahmed.			Nagpur			Mohali		
	WI	I	D	WI	I	D	WI	I	D	WI	I	D	WI	I	D
1948-49	-	-	-	-	-	-	-	-	-	-	-	-	-	-	-
1958-59	1	-	-	-	-	-	-	-	-	-	-	-	-	-	-
1966-67	-	-	-	-	-	-	-	-	-	-	-	-	-	-	-
1974-75	-	-	-	1	-	-	-	-	-	-	-	-	-	-	-
1978-79	-	-	1	-	-	1	-	-	-	-	-	-	-	-	-
1983-84	1	-	-	-	-	-	1	-	-	-	-	-	-	-	-
1987-88	-	-	-	-	-	-	-	-	-	-	-	-	-	-	-
1994-95	-	-	-	-	-	-	-	-	-	-	-	1	1	-	-
	2	-	1	1	-	1	1	-	-	-	-	1	1	-	-

Key to ground abbreviation: Bang. - Bangalore; Ahmed. - Ahmedabad.

HIGHEST INNINGS TOTALS

West Indies in West Indies	8d-631	Kingston	1961-62
West Indies in India	8d-644	Delhi	1958-59
India in West Indies	7-469	Port-of-Spain	1982-83
India in India	7d-644	Kanpur	1978-79

LOWEST INNINGS TOTALS

West Indies in West Indies	214	Port-of-Spain	1970-71
West Indies in India	127	Delhi	1987-88
India in West Indies	97	Kingston	1975-76
India in India	75	Delhi	1987-88

HIGHEST MATCH AGGREGATE	1478 for 38 wickets	Port-of-Spain	1970-71
LOWEST MATCH AGGREGATE	605 for 30 wickets	Port-of-Spain	1961-62

HIGHEST INDIVIDUAL INNINGS

West Indies in West Indies	237	F.M.M.Worrell	Kingston	1952-53
West Indies in India	256	R.B.Kanhai	Calcutta	1958-59
India in West Indies	220	S.M.Gavaskar	Port-of-Spain	1970-71
India in India	236*	S.M.Gavaskar	Chennai[1]	1983-84

HIGHEST AGGREGATE OF RUNS IN A SERIES

West Indies in West Indies	716 (av 102.28)	E.D.Weekes	1952-53
West Indies in India	779 (av 111.28)	E.D.Weekes	1948-49
India in West Indies	774 (av 154.80)	S.M.Gavaskar	1970-71
India in India	732 (av 91.50)	S.M.Gavaskar	1978-79

RECORD WICKET PARTNERSHIPS-WEST INDIES

Wicket	Runs	Partners	Venue	Season
1st	296	C.G.Greenidge (154*), D.L.Haynes (136)	St John's	1982-83
2nd	255	E.D A.S.McMorris (125), R.B.Kanhai (158)	Kingston	1961-62
3rd	220	I V.A Richards (142), A.I.Kallicharran (93)	Bridgetown	1975-76
4th	267	C.L.Walcott (152) ,G.E.Gomez (101)	Delhi	1948-49
5th	219	E.D.Weekes (207) ,B.H.Pairaudeau (115)	Port-of-Spain	1952-53
6th	250	C.H.Lloyd (242), D.L.Murray (91)	Mumbai[3]	1974-75
7th	130	C.G.Greenidge (194), M.D.Marshall (92)	Kanpur	1983-84
8th	124	I.V.A Richards (192), K.D.Boyce (68)	Delhi	1974-75
9th	161	C.H.Lloyd (161*), A.M.E.Roberts (68)	Calcutta	1983-84
10th	98*	F.M.M.Worrell (73*), W.W.Hall (50*)	Port-of-Spain	1961-62

RECORD WICKET PARTNERSHIPS-INDIA

Wicket	Runs	Partners	Venue	Season
1st	153	S.M.Gavaskar (73), C.P.S.Chauhan (84)	Mumbai[3]	1978-79
2nd	344*	S.M.Gavaskar (182), D.B.Vengsarkar (157)	Calcutta	1978-79
3rd	177	N.S.Sidhu (107), S.R.Tendulkar (179)	Nagpur	1994-95
4th	172	G.R.Viswanath (179), A.D.Gaekwad (102)	Kanpur	1978-79
5th	204	S.M.Gavaskar (156), B.P.Patel (115)	Port-of-Spain	1975-76
6th	170	S.M.Gavaskar (236*), R.J.Shastri (72)	Chennai[1]	1983-84
7th	186	D.N.Sardesai (150), E.D.Solkar (65)	Bridgetown	1970-71
8th	107	Yashpal Sharma (63), B.S.Sandhu (68)	Kingston	1982-83
9th	143*	S.M.Gavaskar (236*), S.M.H.Kirmani (63*)	Chennai[1]	1983-84
10th	62	D.N.Sardesai (150), B.S.Bedi (20*)	Bridgetown	1970-71

BEST INNINGS BOWLING ANALYSIS

West Indies in West Indies	9-95	J.M.Noreiga	Port-of-Spain	1970-71
West Indies in India	7-64	A.M.E.Roberts	Chennai[1]	1974-75
India in West Indies	7-162	S.P.Gupte	Port-of-Spain	1952-53
India in India	9-83	Kapil Dev	Ahmedabad	1983-84

BEST MATCH BOWLING ANALYSIS

West Indies in West Indies	11-89	M.D.Marshall	Port-of-Spain	1988-89
West Indies in India	12-121	A.M.E.Roberts	Chennai[1]	1974-75
India in West Indies	8-118	Kapil Dev	Kingston	1982-83
India in India	16-136	N.D.Hirwani	Chennai[1]	1987-88

HIGHEST AGGREGATE OF WICKETS IN A SERIES

West Indies in West Indies	28 (av 29.57)	A.L.Valentine	1952-53
West Indies in India	33 (av 18.81)	M.D.Marshall	1983-84
India in West Indies	27 (av 29.22)	S.P.Gupte	1952-53
India in India	29 (av 18.51)	Kapil Dev	1983-84

WEST INDIES v PAKISTAN Venue and Result	West Indies 1st	 2nd	Pakistan 1st	 2nd	Captains West Indies	 Pakistan
1957-58 In WEST INDIES						
Bridgetown-Drawn	•9d-579	0-28	106	8d-657	F.C.M.Alexander	A.H.Kardar
Port-of-Spain-West Indies 120 runs	•325	312	282	235		
Kingston-West Indies inns & 174 runs	3d-790	-	•328	288		
Georgetown-West Indies 8 wkts	410	2-317	•408	318		
Port-of-Spain-Pakistan inns & 1 run	•268	227	496	-		
1958-59 In PAKISTAN						
Karachi[1]-Pakistan 10 wkts	•146	245	304	0-88	F.C.M.Alexander	Fazal Mahmood
Dacca-Pakistan 41 runs	76	172	•145	144		
Lahore[1]-West Indies & 156 runs	•469	-	209	104		
1974-75 in PAKISTAN						
Lahore[2]-Drawn	214	4-258	•199	7d-373	C.H.Lloyd	Intikhab Alam
Karachi[1]-Drawn	493	0-1	•8d-406	256		
1976-77 in WEST INDIES						
Bridgetown-Drawn	421	9-251	•435	291	C.H.Lloyd	Mushtaq Mohammad
Port-of-Spain-West Indies 6 wkts	316	4-206	•180	340		
Georgetown-Drawn	448	1-154	•194	540		
Port-of-Spain-Pakistan 266 runs	154	222	•341	9d-301		
Kingston-West Indies 140 runs	•280	359	198	301		
1980-81 in PAKISTAN						
Lahore[2]-Drawn	297	-	•369	7-156	C.H.Lloyd	Javed Miandad
Faisalabad-West Indies 156 runs	•235	242	176	145		
Karachi[1]-Drawn	169	-	•128	9-204		
Multan-Drawn	•249	5-116	166	-		
1986-87 in PAKISTAN						
Faisalabad-Pakistan 186 runs	248	53	•159	328	I.V.A.Richards	Imran Khan
Lahore[2]-West Indies inns & 10 runs	218	-	•131	77		
Karachi[1]-Drawn	•240	211	239	7-125		
1987-88 in WEST INDIES						
Georgetown-Pakistan 9 wkts	•292	172	435	1-32	C.G.Greenidge	Imran Khan
Port-of-Spain-Drawn	•174	391	194	9-341	I.V.A.Richards	
Bridgetown-West Indies 2 wkts	306	8-268	•309	262	I.V.A.Richards	
1990-91 in PAKISTAN						
Karachi[1]-Pakistan 8 wkts	•216	181	345	2-98	D.L.Haynes	Imran Khan
Faisalabad-West Indies 7 wkts	195	3-130	•170	154		
Lahore[2]-Drawn	•294	173	122	6-242		
1992-93 in WEST INDIES						
Port-of-Spain-West Indies 204 runs	•127	382	140	165	R.B.Richardson	Wasim Akram
Bridgetown-West Indies 10 wkts	•455	0-29	221	262		
St John's-Drawn	•438	4-153	326			

Test Match Results Summary

WEST INDIES v PAKISTAN-IN WEST INDIES

		Result			Bridgetown			Port-of-Spain			Kingston			Georgetown			St John's		
	Tests	WI	P	D	WI	P	D	WI	P	D	WI	P	D	WI	P	D	WI	P	D
1957-58	5	3	1	1	-	-	1	1	1	-	1	-	-	1	-	-	-	-	-
1976-77	5	2	1	2	-	-	1	1	1	-	1	-	-	-	-	1	-	-	-
1987-88	3	1	1	1	1	-	-	-	-	1	-	-	-		1		-	-	-
1992-93	3	2	-	1	1	-	-	1	-	-	-	-	-	-	-	-	-	-	1
	16	8	3	5	2	-	2	3	2	1	2	-	-	1	1	1	-	-	1

WEST INDIES v PAKISTAN-IN PAKISTAN

		Result			Karachi[1]			Dacca			Lahore			Faisalabad			Multan		
	Tests	WI	P	D	WI	P	D	WI	P	D	WI	P	D	WI	P	D	WI	P	D
1958-59	3	1	2	-	-	1	-	-	1	-	1	-	-	-	-	-	-	-	-
1974-75	2	-	-	2	-	-	1	-	-	-	-	-	1	-	-	-	-	-	-
1980-81	4	1	-	3	-	-	1	-	-	-	-	-	1	1	-	-	-	-	1
1986-87	3	1	1	1	-	-	1	-	-	-	1	-	-	-	1	-	-	-	-
1990-91	3	1	1	1	-	1	-	-	-	-	-	-	1	1	-	-	-	-	-
	15	4	4	7	-	2	3	-	1	-	2	-	3	2	1	-	-	-	1
Totals	31	12	7	12															

HIGHEST INNINGS TOTALS

West Indies in West Indies	3d-790	Kingston	1957-58
West Indies in Pakistan	493	Karachi[1]	1974-75
Pakistan in West Indies	8d-657	Bridgetown	1957-58
Pakistan in Pakistan	8d-406	Karachi[1]	1974-75

LOWEST INNINGS TOTALS

West Indies in West Indies	127	Port-of-Spain	1992-93
West Indies in Pakistan	53	Faisalabad	1986-84
Pakistan in West Indies	106	Bridgetown	1957-58
Pakistan in Pakistan	77	Lahore[2]	1986-84

HIGHEST MATCH AGGREGATE	1453 for 32 wickets	Georgetown	1957-58
LOWEST MATCH AGGREGATE	426 for 30 wickets	Lahore[2]	1986-84

HIGHEST INDIVIDUAL INNINGS

West Indies in West Indies	365	G.S.Sobers	Kingston	1957-58
West Indies in Pakistan	217	R.B.Kanhai	Lahore[1]	1958-59
Pakistan in West Indies	337	Hanif Mohammad	Bridgetown	1957-58
Pakistan in Pakistan	123	Mushtaq Mohammad	Lahore[2]	1974-75
	123	Imran Khan	Lahore[2]	1980-81

HIGHEST AGGREGATE OF RUNS IN A SERIES

West Indies in West Indies	824 (av 137.33)	G.S.Sobers	1957-58
West Indies in Pakistan	364 (av 72.80)	I.V.A.Richards	1980-81
Pakistan in West Indies	628 (av 69.77)	Hanif Mohammad	1957-58
Pakistan in Pakistan	285 (av 57.00)	Saleem Malik	1990-91

RECORD WICKET PARTNERSHIPS-WEST INDIES

1st	182	R.C.Fredericks (83), C.G.Greenidge (82)	Kingston	1976-77
2nd	446	C.C.Hunte (260), G.S.Sobers (365*)	Kingston	1957-58
3rd	169	D.L.Haynes (143*), B.C.Lara (96)	Port-of-Spain	1992-93
4th	188*	G.S Sobers (365*), C.L.Walcott (88*)	Kingston	1957-58
5th	185	E.D.Weekes (197), O.G Smith (78)	Bridgetown	1957-58
6th	151	C.H.Lloyd (157), D.L.Murray (52)	Bridgetown	1976-77
7th	70	C.H.Lloyd (157), J.Garner (43)	Bridgetown	1976-77
8th	60	C.L.Hooper (178*) A.C.Cummins (14)	St John's	1992-93
9th	61*	P.J.L.Dujon (29*), W.K.M.Benjamin (40*)	Bridgetown	1987-88
10th	106	C.L.Hooper (178*), C.A.Walsh (30)	St John's	1992-93

RECORD WICKET PARTNERSHIPS-PAKISTAN

1st	159†	Majid Khan (167), Zaheer Abbas (80)	Georgetown	1976-77
2nd	178	Hanif Mohammad (103), Saeed Ahmed (78)	Karachi[1]	1958-59
3rd	169	Saeed Ahmed (97), Wazir Mohammad (189)	Port-of-Spain	1957-58
4th	174	Shoaib Mohammad (86), Saleem Malik (102)	Karachi[1]	1990-91
5th	88	Basit Ali (56), Inzamamul Haq (123)	St John's	1992-93
6th	166	Wazir Mohammad (106), A.H.Kardar (57)	Kingston	1957-58
7th	128	Wasim Raja (107*), Wasim Bari (58)	Karachi[1]	1974-75
8th	94	Saleem Malik (66), Saleem Yousuf (39)	Port-of-Spain	1987-88
9th	96	Inzamamul Haq (123), Nadeem Khan (25)	St John's	1992-93
10th	133	Wasim Raja (71), Wasim Bari (60*)	Bridgetown	1976-77

† 219 runs were added for this wicket, Sadiq Mohammad retired hurt and was replaced by Zaheer Abbas after 60 had been scored.

BEST INNINGS BOWLING ANALYSIS

West Indies in West Indies	8-29	C.E.H.Croft	Port-of-Spain	1976-77
West Indies in Pakistan	5-33	M.D.Marshall	Lahore[2]	1986-87
Pakistan in West Indies	7-80	Imran Khan	Georgetown	1987-88
Pakistan in Pakistan	6-16	Abdul Qadir	Faisalabad	1986-87

BEST MATCH BOWLING ANALYSIS

West Indies in West Indies	9-95	C.E.H.Croft	Port-of-Spain	1976-77
West Indies in Pakistan	9-187	A.M.E.Roberts	Lahore[2]	1974-75
Pakistan in West Indies	11-121	Imran Khan	Georgetown	1987-88
Pakistan in Pakistan	12-100	Fazal Mahmood	Dacca	1959-60

HIGHEST AGGREGATE OF WICKETS IN A SERIES

West Indies in West Indies	33 (av 20.48)	C E.H.Croft	1976-77
West Indies in Pakistan	17 (av 17.76)	C.E.H.Croft	1980-81
Pakistan in West Indies	25 (av 31.60)	Imran Khan	1976-77
Pakistan in Pakistan	21 (av 15.85)	Fazal Mahmood	1958-59
	21 (av 14.19)	Wasim Akram	1990-91

WEST INDIES v SRI LANKA	West Indies		Sri Lanka		Captains	
Venue and Result	1st	2nd	1st	2nd	West Indies	Sri Lanka
1993-94 in SRI LANKA						
Moratuwa-Drawn	·190	2-43	204	-	R.B.Richardson	A.Ranatunga

Test Match Results Summary

WEST INDIES v SRI LANKA-IN SRI LANKA

	Tests	Result WI	SL	D	Moratuwa WI	SL	D
1993-94	1	-	-	1	-	-	1

HIGHEST INNINGS TOTALS

West Indies in Sri Lanka	204	Moratuwa	1993-94
Sri Lanka in Sri Lanka	190	Moratuwa	1993-94

LOWEST INNINGS TOTALS

West Indies in Sri Lanka	204	Moratuwa	1993-94
Sri Lanka in Sri Lanka	190	Moratuwa	1993-94

HIGHEST MATCH AGGREGATE

437 for 22 wickets — Moratuwa — 1993-94

HIGHEST INDIVIDUAL INNINGS

West Indies in Sri Lanka	62	C.L.Hooper	Moratuwa	1993-94
Sri Lanka in Sri Lanka	53	P.A.de Silva	Moratuwa	1993-94

HIGHEST AGGREGATE OF RUNS IN A SERIES

West Indies in Sri Lanka	62 (av 62.00)	C.L.Hooper	1993-94
Sri Lanka in Sri Lanka	68 (av 68.00)	P.A.de Silva	1993-94

HIGHEST WICKET PARTNERSHIP-WEST INDIES

1st	42	D.L.Haynes (20), P.V.Simmons (17)	Moratuwa	1993-94
2nd	0	P.V.Simmons (17), R.B.Richardson (51)	Moratuwa	1993-94
3rd	36	R.B.Richardson (51), B.C.Lara (18)	Moratuwa	1993-94
4th	6	R.B.Richardson (51), K.L.T.Arthurton (0)	Moratuwa	1993-94
5th	84	R.B.Richardson (51), C.L.Hooper (62)	Moratuwa	1993-94
6th	10	C.L.Hooper (62), R.A.Harper (3)	Moratuwa	1993-94
7th	13	C.L.Hooper (62), J.R.Murray (7)	Moratuwa	1993-94
8th	0	C.L.Hooper (62), W.K.M.Benjamin (2)	Moratuwa	1993-94
9th	13	W.K.M.Benjamin (2), C.E.L.Ambrose (7*)	Moratuwa	1993-94
10th	0	C.E.L.Ambrose (7*), C.A.Walsh (0)	Moratuwa	1993-94

HIGHEST WICKET PARTNERSHIP-SRI LANKA

1st	18	R.S.Mahanama (11), D.P.Samaraweera (16)	Moratuwa	1993-94
2nd	2	H.P.Tillakaratne (0), D.P.Samaraweera (16)	Moratuwa	1993-94
3rd	37	D.P.Samaraweera (16), P.A.de Silva (53)	Moratuwa	1993-94
4th	49	P.A.de Silva (53), A.Ranatunga (31)	Moratuwa	1993-94
5th	0	A.Ranatunga (31), S.T.Jayasuriya (0)	Moratuwa	1993-94
6th	24	A.Ranatunga (31), R.S.Kalpage (39)	Moratuwa	1993-94
7th	51	R.S.Kalpage (39), P.B.Dasanayake (18)	Moratuwa	1993-94
8th	1	R.S.Kalpage (39), G.P.Wickramasinghe (0)	Moratuwa	1993-94
9th	6	R.S.Kalpage (39), S.D.Anurasiri (1)	Moratuwa	1993-94
10th	2	R.S.Kalpage (39), M.Muralidharan (1*)	Moratuwa	1993-94

BEST INNINGS BOWLING ANALYSIS

West Indies in Sri Lanka	4-46	W.K.M.Benjamin	Moratuwa	1993-94
Sri Lanka in Sri Lanka	4-47	M.Muralidharan	Moratuwa	1993-94

BEST MATCH BOWLING ANALYSIS

West Indies in Sri Lanka	5-51	W.K.M.Benjamin	Moratuwa	1993-94
Sri Lanka in Sri Lanka	4-47	M.Muralidharan	Moratuwa	1993-94

HIGHEST AGGREGATE OF WICKETS IN A SERIES

West Indies in Sri Lanka	5 (av 10.20)	W.K.M.Benjamin	1993-94
Sri Lanka in Sri Lanka	4 (av 11.75)	M.Muralidharan	1993-94

NEW ZEALAND v INDIA	New Zealand		India		Captains	
Venue and Result	1st	2nd	1st	2nd	New Zealand	India
1955-56 in INDIA						
Hyderabad-Drawn	326	2-212	•4d-498	-	H.B.Cave	Ghulam Ahmed
Mumbai²-India inns & 27 runs	258	136	•8d-421	-		P.R.Umrigar
Delhi-Drawn	•2d-450	1-112	7d-531	-		P.R.Umrigar
Calcutta-Drawn	336	6-75	•132	7d-438		P.R.Umrigar
Chennai²-India inns & 109 runs	209	219	•3d-537	-		P.R.Umrigar
1964-65 in INDIA						
Chennai²-Drawn	315	0-62	•397	2d-199	J.R.Reid	Nawab of Pataudi, jr
Calcutta-Drawn	•9d-462	9d-191	380	3-92		
Mumbai²-Drawn	•297	8-80	88	5d-463		
Delhi-India 7 wkts	•262	272	8d-465	3-73		
1967-68 in NEW ZEALAND						
Dunedin-India 5 wkts	•350	208	359	5-200	B.W.Sinclair	Nawab of Pataudi, jr
Christchurch-New Zealand 6 wkts	•502	4-88	288	301	G.T.Dowling	
Wellington-India 8 wkts	•186	199	327	2-59	G.T.Dowling	
Auckland-India 272 runs	140	101	•252	5d-261	G.T.Dowling	
1969-70 in INDIA						
Mumbai²-India 60 runs	229	127	•156	260	G.T.Dowling	Nawab of Pataudi, jr
Nagpur-New Zealand 167 runs	•319	214	257	109		
Hyderabad-Drawn	•181	8d-175	89	7-67		
1975-76 in NEW ZEALAND						
Auckland-India 8 wkts	•266	215	414	2-71	G.M.Turner	S.M.Gavaskar
Christchurch-Drawn	403	-	•270	6-255		B.S.Bedi
Wellington-New Zealand inns & 33 runs	334	-	•220	81		B.S.Bedi
1976-77 in INDIA						
Mumbai³-India 162 runs	298	141	•399	4d-202	G.M.Turner	B.S.Bedi
Kanpur-Drawn	350	7-193	•9d-524	2d-208		
Chennai¹-India 216 runs	140	143	•298	5d-201		
1980-81 in NEW ZEALAND						
Wellington-New Zealand 62 runs	•375	100	223	190	G.P.Howarth	S.M.Gavaskar
Christchurch-Drawn	5-286	-	•255	-		
Auckland-Drawn	366	5-95	•238	284		
1988-89 in INDIA						
Bangalore-India 172 runs	189	164	•9d-384	1d-141	J.G.Wright	D.B.Vengsarkar
Mumbai³-New Zealand 136 runs	•236	279	234	145		
Hyderabad-India 10 wkts	•254	124	358	0-22		
1989-90 in NEW ZEALAND						
Christchurch-New Zealand 10 wkts	•459	0-2	164	296	J.G.Wright	M.Azharuddin
Napier-Drawn	1-178	-	•358	-		
Auckland-Drawn	•391	5d-483	482	0-149		
1993-94 in NEW ZEALAND						
Hamilton-Drawn	•187	7d-368	246	3-177	K.R.Rutherford	M.Azharuddin
1995-96 in INDIA						
Bangalore-India 8 wkts	228	2-151	•145	233	L.K.Germon	M.Azharuddin
Chennai²-Drawn	-	-	•2-144	-		
Cuttack-Drawn	8-175	-	•8d-296	-		

Test Match Results Summary

NEW ZEALAND v INDIA-IN NEW ZEALAND

		Result			Dunedin			Christchurch			Wellington			Auckland			Napier			Hamilton		
	Tests	NZ	I	D	NZ	I	D	NZ	I	D	NZ	I	D	NZ	I	D	NZ	I	D	NZ	I	D
1967-68	4	1	3	-	-	1	-	1	-	-	-	1	-	-	1	-	-	-	-	-	-	-
1975-76	3	1	1	1	-	-	-	-	-	1	1	-	-	-	1	-	-	-	-	-	-	-
1980-81	3	1	-	2	-	-	-	-	-	1	1	-	-	-	-	1	-	-	-	-	-	-
1989-90	3	1	-	2	-	-	-	1	-	-	-	-	-	-	-	1	-	-	1	-	-	-
1993-94	1	-	-	1	-	-	-	-	-	-	-	-	-	-	-	-	-	-	-	-	-	1
	14	4	4	6	-	1	-	2	-	2	2	1	-	-	2	2	-	-	1	-	-	1

NEW ZEALAND v INDIA-IN INDIA

		Result			Hyder.			Mumbai			Delhi			Calcutta			Chennai			Nagpur			Kanpur			Bang.			Cuttack		
	Tests	NZ	I	D	NZ	I	D	NZ	I	D	NZ	I	D	NZ	I	D	NZ	I	D	NZ	I	D	NZ	I	D	NZ	I	D	NZ	I	D
1955-56	5	-	2	3	-	-	1	-	1	-	-	-	1	-	-	1	-	1	-	-	-	-	-	-	-	-	-	-	-	-	-
1964-65	4	-	1	3	-	-	-	-	-	1	-	1	-	-	-	1	-	-	1	-	-	-	-	-	-	-	-	-	-	-	-
1969-70	3	1	1	1	-	-	1	-	1	-	-	-	-	-	-	-	-	-	-	1	-	-	-	-	-	-	-	-	-	-	-
1976-77	3	-	2	1	-	-	-	-	1	-	-	-	-	-	-	-	-	1	-	-	-	-	-	-	1	-	-	-	-	-	-
1988-89	3	1	2	-	-	1	-	1	-	-	-	-	-	-	-	-	-	-	-	-	-	-	-	-	-	-	1	-	-	-	-
1995-96	3	-	1	2	-	-	-	-	-	-	-	-	-	-	-	-	-	-	1	-	-	-	-	-	-	1	-	-	-	-	1
	21	2	9	10	-	1	2	1	3	1	-	1	1	-	-	2	-	2	2	1	-	-	-	-	1	1	1	-	-	-	1
Totals	35	6	13	16																											

Key to ground abbreviation: Hyder. - Hyderabad; Bang. - Bangalore.

HIGHEST INNINGS TOTALS

New Zealand in New Zealand	502	Christchurch	1967-68
New Zealand in India	9d-462	Calcutta	1964-65
India in New Zealand	482	Auckland	1989-90
India in India	3d-537	Chennai[2]	1955-56

LOWEST INNINGS TOTALS

New Zealand in New Zealand	100	Wellington	1980-81
New Zealand in India	124	Hyderabad	1988-89
India in New Zealand	81	Wellington	1975-76
India in India	88	Mumbai[2]	1964-65

HIGHEST MATCH AGGREGATE	1505 for 25 wickets	Auckland	1989-90
LOWEST MATCH AGGREGATE	635 for 29 wickets	Wellington	1975-76

HIGHEST INDIVIDUAL INNINGS

New Zealand in New Zealand	239	G.T.Dowling	Christchurch	1967-68
New Zealand in India	230*	B.Sutcliffe	Delhi	1955-56
India in New Zealand	192	M.Azharuddin	Auckland	1989-90
India in India	231	M.H.Mankad	Chennai[2]	1955-56

HIGHEST AGGREGATE OF RUNS IN A SERIES

New Zealand in New Zealand	471 (av 58.87)	G.T.Dowling	1967-68
New Zealand in India	611 (av 87.28)	B.Sutcliffe	1955-56
India in New Zealand	330 (av 47.14)	A.L.Wadekar	1967-68
India in India	526 (av 105.20)	M.H.Mankad	1955-56

RECORD WICKET PARTNERSHIPS-NEW ZEALAND

1st	149	T.J.Franklin (50), J.G.Wright (113*)	Napier	1989-90
2nd	155	G.T.Dowling (143), B.E.Congdon (58)	Dunedin	1967-68
3rd	222*	B.Sutcliffe (230*), J.R Reid (119*)	Delhi	1955-56
4th	125	J.G.Wright (185), M.J.Greatbatch (46)	Christchurch	1989-90
5th	119	G.T.Dowling (239), K Thomson (69)	Christchurch	1967-68
6th	87	J.W.Guy (102), A.R MacGibbon (59)	Hyderabad	1955-56
7th	163	B.Sutcliffe (151*), B.R Taylor (105)	Calcutta	1964-65
8th	103	R.J.Hadlee (87), I.D.S.Smith (173)	Auckland	1989-90
9th	136	I.D.S.Smith (173), M.C.Snedden (22)	Auckland	1989-90
10th	61	J.T.Ward (35*), R.O.Collinge (34)	Chennai[2]	1964-65

RECORD WICKET PARTNERSHIPS-INDIA

1st	413	M.H.Mankad (231), P.Roy (173)	Chennai[2]	1955-56
2nd	204	S.M Gavaskar (116), S Amarnath (124)	Auckland	1975-76
3rd	238	P.R Umrigar (223), V.L.Manjrekar (118)	Hyderabad	1955-56
4th	171	P R Umrigar (223), A.G Kripal Singh (100*)	Hyderabad	1955-56
5th	127	V.L.Manjrekar (177), G.S Ramchand (72)	Delhi	1955-56
6th	193*	D.N Sardesai (200), Hanumant Singh (75*)	Mumbai[3]	1964-65
7th	128	S.R.Tendulkar (88), K.S.More (73)	Napier	1989-90
8th	143	R.G.Nadkarni (75), F.M.Engineer (90)	Chennai[2]	1964-65
9th	105	S.M.H.Kirmani (88), B.S.Bedi (36)	Mumbai[3]	1976-77
	105	S.M.H.Kirmani (78), N.S.Yadav (43)	Auckland	1980-81
10th	57	R.B.Desai (32*), B.S.Bedi (22)	Dunedin	1967-68

BEST INNINGS BOWLING ANALYSIS

New Zealand in New Zealand	7-23	R.J.Hadlee	Wellington	1975-76
New Zealand in India	6-49	R.J.Hadlee	Mumbai[3]	1964-65
India in New Zealand	8-76	E.A.S.Prasanna	Auckland	1975-76
India in India	8-72	S.Venkataraghavan	Delhi	1964-65

BEST MATCH BOWLING ANALYSIS

New Zealand in New Zealand	11-58	R.J.Hadlee	Wellington	1975-76
New Zealand in India	10-88	R.J.Hadlee	Mumbai[3]	1969-70
India in New Zealand	11-140	E.A.S.Prasanna	Auckland	1975-76
India in India	12-152	S.Venkataraghavan	Delhi	1964-65

HIGHEST AGGREGATE OF WICKETS IN A SERIES

New Zealand in New Zealand	16 (av 27.87)	D.K.Morrison	1989-90
New Zealand in India	18 (av 14.00)	R.J.Hadlee	1988-89
India in New Zealand	24 (av 18.79)	E.A.S.Prasanna	1967-68
India in India	34 (av 19.17)	S.P.Gupte	1955-55

NEW ZEALAND v PAKISTAN Venue and Result	New Zealand 1st	New Zealand 2nd	Pakistan 1st	Pakistan 2nd	Captains New Zealand	Captains Pakistan
1955-56 in PAKISTAN						
Karachi[1]-Pakistan inns & 1 run	•164	124	289	-	H.B.Cave	A.H.Kardar
Lahore[1]-Pakistan 4 wkts	•348	328	561	6-117		
Dacca-Drawn	•70	6-69	6d-195	-		
1964-65 in NEW ZEALAND						
Wellington-Drawn	•266	7d-179	187	7-140	J.R.Reid	Hanif Mohammad
Auckland-Drawn	214	7-166	•226	207		
Christchurch-Drawn	202	5-223	•206	8d-309		

NEW ZEALAND v PAKISTAN (cont.) Venue and Result	New Zealand 1st	New Zealand 2nd	Pakistan 1st	Pakistan 2nd	Captains New Zealand	Captains Pakistan
1964-65 in PAKISTAN						
Rawalpindi[1]-Pakistan inns & 64 runs	•175	79	318	-	J.R.Reid	Hanif Mohammad
Lahore[2]-Drawn	6d-482	-	•7d-385	8d-194		
Karachi[1]-Pakistan 8 wkts	•285	223	8d-307	2-202		
1969-70 in PAKISTAN						
Karachi[1]-Drawn	274	5-112	•220	8d-283	G.T.Dowling	Intikhab Alam
Lahore[2]-New Zealand 5 wkts	241	5-82	•114	208		
Dacca-Drawn	•273	200	7d-290	4-51		
1972-73 in NEW ZEALAND						
Wellington-Drawn	325	3-78	•357	6d-290	B.E.Congdon	Intikhab Alam
Dunedin-Pakistan inns & 166 runs	156	185	•6d-507	-		
Auckland-Drawn	402	3-92	•402	271		
1976-77 in PAKISTAN						
Lahore[2]-Pakistan 6 wkts	157	360	•417	4-105	G.M.Turner	Mushtaq Mohammad
Hyderabad-Pakistan 10 wkts	219	254	•8d-473	0-4	G.M.Turner	
Karachi[1]-Drawn	468	7-262	•9d-565	5d-290	J.M.Parker	
1978-79 in NEW ZEALAND						
Christchurch-Pakistan 128 runs	290	176	•271	6d-323	M.G.Burgess	Mushtaq Mohammad
Napier-Drawn	402	-	•360	3d-234		
Auckland-Drawn	•254	8d-281	359	0-8		
1984-85 in PAKISTAN						
Lahore[2]-Pakistan 6 wkts	•157	241	221	4-181	J.V.Coney	Zaheer Abbas
Hyderabad-Pakistan 7 wkts	•267	189	230	3-230		
Karachi[1]-Drawn	426	-	•328	5-308		
1984-85 in NEW ZEALAND						
Wellington-Drawn	•492	4-103	322	-	G.P.Howarth	Javed Miandad
Christchurch-New Zealand inns & 99 runs	9d-451	-	•169	183		
Dunedin-New Zealand 2 wkts	220	8-278	•274	223		
1988-89 in NEW ZEALAND						
Dunedin-Abandoned	-	-	-	-	J.G.Wright	Imran Khan
Wellington-Drawn	•447	8-186	7d-438	-		
Auckland-Drawn	403	3-99	•5d-616	-		
1990-91 in PAKISTAN						
Karachi[1]-Pakistan inns & 43 runs	•196	194	6d-433	-	M.D.Crowe	Javed Miandad
Lahore[2]-Pakistan 9 wkts	•160	287	9d-373	1-77		
Faisalabad-Pakistan 65 runs	217	177	•102	357		
1992-93 in NEW ZEALAND						
Auckland-Pakistan 33 runs	264	93	•216	174	K.R.Rutherford	Javed Miandad
1993-94 in NEW ZEALAND						
Auckland-Pakistan 5 wkts	•242	110	215	5-141	K.R.Rutherford	Saleem Malik
Wellington-Pakistan inns & 12 runs	•175	361	5d-548	-		
Christchurch-New Zealand 5 wkts	200	5-324	•344	179		
1995-96 in NEW ZEALAND						
Christchurch-Pakistan 161 runs	286	195	•208	434	L.K.Germon	Wasim Akram

Test Match Results Summary

NEW ZEALAND v PAKISTAN-IN NEW ZEALAND

		Result			Wellington			Auckland			Christchurch			Dunedin			Napier			Hamilton		
	Tests	NZ	P	D	NZ	P	D	NZ	P	D	NZ	P	D	NZ	P	D	NZ	P	D	NZ	P	D
1964-65	3	-	-	3	-	-	1	-	-	1	-	-	1	-	-	-	-	-	-	-	-	-
1972-73	3	-	1	2	-	-	1	-	-	1	-	-	-	-	1	-	-	-	-	-	-	-
1978-79	3	-	1	2	-	-	-	-	-	1	-	1	-	-	-	-	-	-	1	-	-	-
1984-85	3	2	-	1	-	-	1	1	-	-	-	-	-	1	-	-	-	-	-	-	-	-
1988-89	2	-	-	2	-	-	1	-	-	1	-	-	-	-	-	-	-	-	-	-	-	-
1992-93	1	-	1	-	-	-	-	-	-	-	-	-	-	-	-	-	-	-	-	-	1	-
1993-94	3	1	2	-	-	-	1	-	-	1	1	-	-	-	-	-	-	-	-	-	-	-
1995-96	1	-	1	-	-	-	-	-	-	-	-	1	-	-	-	-	-	-	-	-	-	-
	19	3	6	10	-	-	5	1	-	5	1	2	1	1	1	-	-	-	1	-	1	-

NEW ZEALAND v PAKISTAN-IN PAKISTAN

		Result			Karachi[1]			Lahore			Dacca			Rawalpindi[1]			Hyderabad			Faisalabad		
	Tests	NZ	P	D	NZ	P	D	NZ	P	D	NZ	P	D	NZ	P	D	NZ	P	D	NZ	P	D
1955-56	3	-	2	1	-	1	-	-	1	-	-	-	1	-	-	-	-	-	-	-	-	-
1964-65	3	-	2	1	-	1	-	-	-	1	-	-	-	-	1	-	-	-	-	-	-	-
1969-70	3	1	-	2	-	-	1	1	-	-	-	-	1	-	-	-	-	-	-	-	-	-
1976-77	3	-	2	1	-	-	1	-	1	-	-	-	-	-	-	-	-	1	-	-	-	-
1984-85	3	-	2	1	-	-	1	-	1	-	-	-	-	-	-	-	-	1	-	-	-	-
1990-91	3	-	3	-	-	1	-	-	1	-	-	-	-	-	-	-	-	-	-	-	1	-
	18	1	11	6	-	3	3	1	4	1	-	-	2	-	1	-	-	2	-	-	1	-
Totals	37	4	17	16																		

HIGHEST INNINGS TOTALS

New Zealand in New Zealand	492	Wellington	1984-85
New Zealand in Pakistan	6d-482	Lahore[2]	1964-65
Pakistan in New Zealand	5d-616	Auckland	1988-89
Pakistan in Pakistan	9d-565	Karachi[1]	1976-77

LOWEST INNINGS TOTALS

New Zealand in New Zealand	93	Hamilton	1992-93
New Zealand in Pakistan	70	Dacca	1955-56
Pakistan in New Zealand	169	Auckland	1984-85
Pakistan in Pakistan	102	Faisalabad	1990-91

HIGHEST MATCH AGGREGATE	1585 for 31 wickets	Karachi[1]	1976-77
LOWEST MATCH AGGREGATE	572 for 30 wickets	Rawalpindi[1]	1964-65

HIGHEST INDIVIDUAL INNINGS

New Zealand in New Zealand	174	M.D.Crowe	Wellington	1988-89
New Zealand in Pakistan	152	W.K.Lees	Karachi[1]	1976-77
Pakistan in New Zealand	201	Javed Miandad	Auckland	1988-89
Pakistan in Pakistan	209	Imtiaz Ahmed	Lahore[1]	1955-56

HIGHEST AGGREGATE OF RUNS IN A SERIES

New Zealand in New Zealand	333 (av 83.25)	J.F.Reid	1984-85
New Zealand in Pakistan	296 (av 59.20)	J.R.Reid	1964-65
Pakistan in New Zealand	389 (av 194.50)	Javed Miandad	1988-89
Pakistan in Pakistan	507 (av 169.00)	Shoaib Mohammad	1990-91

RECORD WICKET PARTNERSHIPS-NEW ZEALAND

1st	159	R.E.Redmond (107), G.M.Turner (58)	Auckland	1972-73
2nd	195	J.G.Wright (88), G.P.Howarth (114)	Napier	1978-79
3rd	178	B.W.Sinclair (130), J.R.Reid (88)	Lahore[2]	1964-65
4th	128	B.F.Hastings (72), M.G.Burgess (79)	Wellington	1972-73
5th	183	M.G.Burgess (111), R.W.Anderson (92)	Lahore[2]	1976-77
6th	145	J.F.Reid (148), R.J.Hadlee (87)	Wellington	1984-85
7th	186	W.K.Lees (152), R.J.Hadlee (87)	Karachi[1]	1976-77
8th	100	B.W.Yuile (47*), D.R.Hadlee (56)	Karachi[1]	1969-70
9th	96	M.G.Burgess (119*), R.S.Cunis (23)	Dacca	1969-70
10th	151	B.F.Hastings (110), R.O.Collinge (68*)	Auckland	1972-73

RECORD WICKET PARTNERSHIPS-PAKISTAN

1st	172	Rameez Raja (78), Shoaib Mohammad (203*)	Karachi[1]	1990-91
2nd	139	Ijaz Ahmed (103), Inzamamul Haq (82)	Christchurch	1995-96
3rd	248	Shoaib Mohammad (112), Javed Miandad (271)	Auckland	1988-89
4th	350	Mushtaq Mohammad (201), Asif Iqbal (175)	Dunedin	1972-73
5th	281	Javed Miandad (163), Asif Iqbal (166)	Lahore[2]	1976-77
6th	217	Hanif Mohammad (203*), Majid Khan (80)	Lahore[2]	1964-65
7th	308	Waqar Hassan (189), Imtiaz Ahmed (209)	Lahore[1]	1955-56
8th	89	Anil Dalpat (52), Iqbal Qasim (45*)	Karachi[1]	1984-85
9th	52	Intikhab Alam (45), Arif Butt (20)	Auckland	1964-65
10th	65	Salahuddin (34*), Mohammad Farooq (47)	Rawalpindi[1]	1964-65

BEST INNINGS BOWLING ANALYSIS

New Zealand in New Zealand	6-51	R.J.Hadlee	Dunedin	1984-85
New Zealand in Pakistan	7-52	C.Pringle	Faisalabad	1990-91
Pakistan in New Zealand	7-52	Intikhab Alam	Dunedin	1972-73
Pakistan in Pakistan	7-52	Waqar Younis	Faisalabad	1990-91

BEST MATCH BOWLING ANALYSIS

New Zealand in New Zealand	9-70	F.J.Cameron	Auckland	1964-65
New Zealand in Pakistan	11-152	C.Pringle	Faisalabad	1990-91
Pakistan in New Zealand	11-130	Intikhab Alam	Dunedin	1972-73
Pakistan in Pakistan	12-130	Waqar Younis	Faisalabad	1990-91

HIGHEST AGGREGATE OF WICKETS IN A SERIES

New Zealand in New Zealand	18 (av 23.00)	R.J.Hadlee	1978-79
New Zealand in Pakistan	16 (av 20.18)	H.J.Howarth	1969-70
Pakistan in New Zealand	25 (av 17.24)	Wasim Akram	1993-94
Pakistan in Pakistan	29 (av 10.86)	Waqar Younis	1990-91

NEW ZEALAND v SRI LANKA	New Zealand		Sri Lanka		Captains	
Venue and Result	1st	2nd	1st	2nd	New Zealand	Sri Lanka
1982-83 in NEW ZEALAND						
Christchurch-New Zealand inns & 25 runs	•344	-	144	175	G.P.Howarth	D.S.de Silva
Wellington-New Zealand 6 wkts	201	4-134	•240	93		
1983-84 in SRI LANKA						
Kandy-New Zealand 165 runs	•276	8d-201	215	97	G.P.Howarth	L.R.D.Mendis
Colombo (SSC)-Drawn	198	4-123	•174	9d-289		
Colombo (CCC)-New Zealand inns & 61 runs		459	-	•256	142	
1986-87 in SRI LANKA						
Colombo (CCC)-Drawn	5-406	-	•9d-397	-	J.J.Crowe	L.R.D.Mendis
1990-91 in NEW ZEALAND						
Wellington-Drawn	•174	4-671	497	-	M.D.Crowe	A.Ranatunga
Hamilton-Drawn	•296	6d-374	253	6-344	M.D.Crowe	
Auckland-Drawn	317	5-261	•380	319	I.D.S.Smith	
1992-93 in SRI LANKA						
Moratuwa-Drawn	•288	5-195	6d-327	-	M.D.Crowe	A.Ranatunga
Colombo (SSC)-Sri Lanka 9 wkts	102	361	•394	1-70		
1994-95 in NEW ZEALAND						
Napier-Sri Lanka 241 runs	109	185	•183	352	K.R.Rutherford	A.Ranatunga
Dunedin-Drawn	307	0-0	•233	411		

Test Match Results Summary

NEW ZEALAND v SRI LANKA-IN NEW ZEALAND

		Result			Christchurch			Wellington			Hamilton			Auckland			Napier			Dunedin		
	Tests	NZ	SL	D	NZ	SL	D	NZ	SL	D	NZ	SL	D	NZ	SL	D	NZ	SL	D	NZ	SL	D
1982-83	2	2	-	-	1	-	-	1	-	-	-	-	-	-	-	-	-	-	-	-	-	-
1990-91	3	-	-	3	-	-	-	-	-	1	-	-	1	-	-	1	-	-	-	-	-	-
1994-95	2	-	1	1	-	-	-	-	-	-	-	-	-	-	-	-	-	1	-	-	-	1
	5	2	1	4	1	-	-	1	-	1	-	-	1	-	-	1	-	1	-	-	-	1

NEW ZEALAND v SRI LANKA-IN SRI LANKA

		Result			Kandy			Colombo (SSC)			Colombo (CCC)			Moratuwa		
	Tests	NZ	SL	D	NZ	SL	D	NZ	SL	D	NZ	SL	D	NZ	SL	D
1983-84	3	2	-	1	1	-	-	-	-	1	1	-	-	-	-	-
1986-87	1	-	-	1	-	-	-	-	-	-	-	-	1	-	-	-
1992-93	2	-	1	1	-	-	-	-	1	-	-	-	-	-	-	1
	6	2	1	3	1	-	-	-	1	1	1	-	1	-	-	1
Totals	11	4	2	7												

HIGHEST INNINGS TOTALS

New Zealand in New Zealand	4-671	Wellington	1990-91
New Zealand In Sri Lanka	459	Colombo (CCC)	1983-84
Sri Lanka in New Zealand	497	Wellington	1990-91
Sri Lanka in Sri Lanka	9d-397	Colombo (CCC)	1986-87

LOWEST INNINGS TOTALS

New Zealand in New Zealand	109	Napier	1994-95
New Zealand in Sri Lanka	102	Colombo (SSC)	1992-93
Sri Lanka in New Zealand	93	Wellington	1987-88
Sri Lanka in Sri Lanka	97	Kandy	1983-84

HIGHEST MATCH AGGREGATE	1342 for 23 wickets	Wellington	1990-91
LOWEST MATCH AGGREGATE	663 for 30 wickets	Christchurch	1982-83

HIGHEST INDIVIDUAL INNINGS

New Zealand in New Zealand	299	M.D.Crowe	Wellington	1990-91
New Zealand in Sri Lanka	180	J.F.Reid	Colombo (CCC)	1983-84
Sri Lanka in New Zealand	267	P.A.de Silva	Wellington	1990-91
Sri Lanka in Sri Lanka	201*	D.S.B.P.Kuruppu	Colombo (CCC)	1986-87

HIGHEST AGGREGATE ON RUNS IN A SERIES

New Zealand in New Zealand	513 (av 102.60)	A.H.Jones	1990-91
New Zealand in Sri Lanka	243 (av 48.60)	J.F.Reid	1983-84
Sri Lanka in New Zealand	493 (av 98.60)	P.A.de Silva	1990-91
Sri Lanka in Sri Lanka	291 (av 97.00)	R.S.Mahanama	1992-93

RECORD WICKET PARTNERSHIPS-NEW ZEALAND

1st	161	T.J.Franklin (69), J.G.Wright (101)	Hamilton	1990-91
2nd	76	J.G.Wright (84), A.H.Jones (27)	Auckland	1990-91
3rd	467	A.H.Jones (188), M.D.Crowe (299)	Wellington	1990-91
4th	82	J.F.Reid (180), S.L.Boock (35)	Colombo (CCC)	1983-84
5th	151	K.R.Rutherford (105), C.Z.Harris (56)	Moratuwa	1992-93
6th	246*	J.J.Crowe (120*), R.J.Hadlee (151*)	Colombo (CCC)	1986-87
7th	47	D.N.Patel (52), M.L.Su'a (20*)	Dunedin	1994-95
8th	79	J.V.Coney (84), W.K.Lees (89)	Christchurch	1982-83
9th	42	W.K.Lees (89), M.C.Snedden (22)	Christchurch	1982-83
10th	52	W.K.Lees (89), E.J.Chatfield (10*)	Christchurch	1982-83

RECORD WICKET PARTNERSHIPS-SRI LANKA

1st	102	R.S.Mahanama (109), U.C.Hathurusingha (27)	Colombo (SSC)	1992-93
2nd	137	R.S.Mahanama (153), A.P.Gurusinha (43)	Moratuwa	1992-93
3rd	159*†	S.Wettimuny (65), R.L.Dias (108)	Colombo (SSC)	1983-84
4th	192	A.P.Gurusinha (127), H.P.Tillakaratne (108)	Dunedin	1994-95
5th	130	R.S.Madugalle (79), D.S.de Silva (61)	Wellington	1982-83
6th	109§	R.S.Madugalle (89*), A.Ranatunga (37)	Colombo (CCC)	1983-84
	109	D.S.B.P.Kuruppu (201*), R.S.Madugalle (60)	Colombo (CCC)	1986-87
7th	89	C.I.Dunusinghe (91), W.P.J.U.C.Vaas (36)	Napier	1994-95
8th	69	H.P.Tillakaratne (93), M.Muralidharan (24)	Colombo (SSC)	1992-93
9th	31	G.F.Labrooy (70*), R.J.Ratnayake (18)	Auckland	1990-91
	31	S.T.Jayasuriya (12*), R.J.Ratnayake (20)	Auckland	1990-91
10th	60	V.B.John (27*), A.M.J.G.Amerasinghe (34)	Kandy	1983-84

†163 runs were added for this wicket, S.Wettimuny retired hurt and was replaced by L.R.D.Mendis after 159 had been scored.

§ 119 runs were added for this wicket, R.S.Madugalle retired hurt and was replaced by D.S.de Silva after 109 had been scored.

BEST INNINGS BOWLING ANALYSIS

New Zealand in New Zealand	5-75	C.L.Cairns	Auckland	1990-91
New Zealand in Sri Lanka	5-28	S.L.Boock	Kandy	1983-84
Sri Lanka in New Zealand	6-87	W.P.J.U.C.Vaas	Dunedin	1994-95
Sri Lanka in Sri Lanka	5-42	J.R.Ratnayeke	Colombo (SSC)	1983-84

BEST MATCH BOWLING ANALYSIS

New Zealand in New Zealand	9-211	C.L.Cairns	Auckland	1990-91
New Zealand in Sri Lanka	10-102	R.J.Hadlee	Colombo (CCC)	1983-84
Sri Lanka in New Zealand	10-90	W.P.J.U.C.Vaas	Napier	1994-95
Sri Lanka in Sri Lanka	8-159	V.B.John	Kandy	1983-84

HIGHEST AGGREGATE OF WICKETS IN A SERIES

New Zealand in New Zealand	13 (av 36.61)	D.K.Morrison	1990-91
New Zealand in Sri Lanka	23 (av 10.00)	R.J.Hadlee	1983-84
Sri Lanka in New Zealand	16 (av 11.06)	W.P.J.U.C.Vaas	1994-95
Sri Lanka in Sri Lanka	16 (av 23.31)	V.B.John	1983-84

NEW ZEALAND v ZIMBABWE	New Zealand		Zimbabwe		Captains	
Venue and Result	1st	2nd	1st	2nd	New Zealand	Zimbabwe
1992-93 in ZIMBABWE						
Bulawayo[1]-Drawn	•3d-325	5d-222	219	1-197	M.D.Crowe	D.L.Houghton
Harare-New Zealand won by 177 runs	•335	5d-262	9d-283	137		
1995-96 in NEW ZEALAND						
Hamilton-Drawn	•8d230	5d222	196	6-208	L.K.Germon	A.Flower
Auckland-Drawn	•251	5d-441	9d-326	4-246		

Test Match Results Summary

NEW ZEALAND v ZIMBABWE-IN ZIMBABWE

		Result			Harare			Bulawayo[1]		
	Tests	NZ	Z	D	NZ	Z	D	NZ	Z	D
1992-93	2	1	-	1	1	-	-	-	-	1

NEW ZEALAND v ZIMBABWE-IN ZIMBABWE

		Result			Auckland			Hamilton		
	Tests	NZ	Z	D	NZ	Z	D	NZ	Z	D
1995-96	2	-	-	2	-	-	1	-	-	1

HIGHEST INNINGS TOTALS

New Zealand in New Zealand	5d-441	Auckland	1995-96
New Zealand in Zimbabwe	335	Harare	1992-93
Zimbabwe in New Zealand	9-326	Auckland	1995-96
Zimbabwe in Zimbabwe	9d-283	Harare	1992-93

LOWEST INNINGS TOTALS

New Zealand in New Zealand	251	Auckland	1995-96
New Zealand in Zimbabwe	335	Harare	1992-93
Zimbabwe in New Zealand	196	Hamilton	1995-96
Zimbabwe in Zimbabwe	137	Harare	1992-93

HIGHEST MATCH AGGREGATE	1417 for 34 wickets	Harare	1992-93
LOWEST MATCH AGGREGATE	852 for 29 wickets	Hamilton	1995-96

HIGHEST INDIVIDUAL INNINGS

New Zealand in New Zealand	120	C.L.Cairns	Auckland	1995-96
New Zealand in Zimbabwe	140	M.D.Crowe	Harare	1992-93
Zimbabwe in New Zealand	104+	D.L.Houghton	Auckland	1995-96
Zimbabwe in Zimbabwe	101*	K.J.Arnott	Bulawayo[1]	1992-93

HIGHEST AGGREGATE ON RUNS IN A SERIES

New Zealand in New Zealand	191 (av 47.75)	C.L.Cairns	1995-96
New Zealand in Zimbabwe	249 (av 62.25)	M.D.Crowe	1992-93
Zimbabwe in New Zealand	166 (av 83.00)	D.L.Houghton	1995-96
Zimbabwe in Zimbabwe	209 (av 69.66)	K.J.Arnott	1992-93

RECORD WICKET PARTNERSHIPS-NEW ZEALAND

1st	214	C.M.Spearman (112), R.G.Twose (94)	Auckland	1995-96
2nd	127	R.T.Latham (119), A.H.Jones (67*)	Bulawayo[1]	1992-93
3rd	71	A.H.Jones (67*), M.D.Crowe (42)	Bulawayo[1]	1992-93
4th	168	M.D.Crowe (140), K.R.Rutherford (74)	Harare	1992-93
5th	166	A.C.Parore (76*), C.L.Cairns (120)	Auckland	1995-96
6th	82*	A.C.Parore (84*), L.K.Germon (22*)	Hamilton	1995-96
7th	52	L.K.Germon (24), D.N.Patel (31)	Hamilton	1995-96
8th	10*	D.N.Patel (31), G.R.Loveridge (4*)	Hamilton	1995-96
9th	4*	R.J.Kennedy (2*), G.I.Allott (0*)	Hamilton	1995-96
10th	5	M.J.Haslam (3), D.J.Nash (11*)	Harare	1992-93
	5	D.N.Patel (7*), G.I.Allott (0)	Auckland	1995-96

RECORD WICKET PARTNERSHIPS-ZIMBABWE

1st	120	G.W.Flower (71), S.V.Carlisle (58)	Auckland	1995-96
2nd	107	K.J.Arnott (68), A.D.R.Campbell (52)	Harare	1992-93
3rd	26	G.W.Flower (59), D.L.Houghton (31)	Hamilton	1995-96
4th	88	D.L.Houghton (104+), A.Flower (35)	Auckland	1995-96
5th	58	D.L.Houghton (104+), A.D.R.Campbell (17)	Auckland	1995-96
6th	70	D.L.Houghton (36), A.Flower (81)	Bulawayo[1]	1992-93
7th	91	G.J.Whittall (54), P.A.Strang (49)	Hamilton	1995-96
8th	79	P.A.Strang (44), E.A.Brandes (39)	Auckland	1995-96
9th	46	G.J.Crocker (33), M.G.Burmester (17*)	Harare	1992-93
10th	8*	M.G.Burmester (30*), A.J.Traicos (1*)	Harare	1992-93

BEST INNINGS BOWLING ANALYSIS

New Zealand in New Zealand	4-56	C.L.Cairns	Hamilton	1995-96
New Zealand in Zimbabwe	6-50	D.N.Patel	Harare	1992-93
Zimbabwe in New Zealand	4-52	H.H.Streak	Hamilton	1995-96
Zimbabwe in Zimbabwe	3-39	M.P.Jarvis	Bulawayo[1]	1992-93

BEST MATCH BOWLING ANALYSIS

New Zealand in New Zealand	6-99	C.L.Cairns	Hamilton	1995-96
New Zealand in Zimbabwe	8-131	D.N.Patel	Harare	1992-93
Zimbabwe in New Zealand	7-160	H.H.Streak	Auckland	1995-96
Zimbabwe in Zimbabwe	4-101	D.H.Brain	Harare	1992-93

HIGHEST AGGREGATE OF WICKETS IN A SERIES

New Zealand in New Zealand	8 (av 27.62)	D.N.Patel	1995-96
	8 (av 30.00)	C.L.Cairns	1995-96
New Zealand in Zimbabwe	15 (av 20.26)	D.N.Patel	1992-93
Zimbabwe in New Zealand	12 (av 22.33)	H.H.Streak	1995-96
Zimbabwe in Zimbabwe	6 (av 48.33)	A.J.Traicos	1992-93

INDIA v PAKISTAN Venue and Result	India 1st	 2nd	Pakistan 1st	 2nd	Captains India	 Pakistan
1952-53 In INDIA						
Delhi-India inns & 70 runs	•372	-	150	152	N.B.Amarnath	A.H.Kardar
Lucknow[1]-Pakistan inns & 43 runs	•106	182	331	-		
Mumbai[2]-India 10 wkts	4d-387	0-45	•186	242		
Chennai[1]-Drawn	6-175	-	•344	-		
Calcutta-Drawn	397	0-28	•257	7d-236		
1954-55 In PAKISTAN						
Dacca-Drawn	148	2-147	•257	158	M.H.Mankad	A.H.Kardar
Bahawalpur-Drawn	•235	5-209	9d-312	-		
Lahore[1]-Drawn	251	2-74	•328	5d-136		
Peshawar[1]-Drawn	245	1-23	•188	182		
Karachi[1]-Drawn	145	2-69	•162	5d-241		
1960-61 In INDIA						
Mumbai[2]-Drawn	9d-449	-	•350	4-166	N.J.Contractor	Fazal Mahmood
Kanpur-Drawn	404	-	•335	3-140		
Calcutta-Drawn	180	4-127	•301	3d-146		
Chennai[2]-Drawn	9d-539	-	•8d-448	0-59		
Delhi-Drawn	•463	0-16	286	250		
1978-79 In PAKISTAN						
Faisalabad-Drawn	9d-462	0-43	•8d-503	4d-264	B.S.Bedi	Mushtaq Mohammad
Lahore[2]-Pakistan 8 wkts	•199	465	6d-539	2-182		
Karachi[1]-Pakistan 8 wkts	•344	300	9d-481	2-164		
1979-80 IN INDIA						
Bangalore-Drawn	416	-	•9d-431	2-108	S.M.Gavaskar	Asif Iqbal
Delhi-Drawn	126	6-364	•273	242	S.M.Gavaskar	
Mumbai[3]-India 131 runs	•334	160	173	190	S.M.Gavaskar	
Kanpur-Drawn	•162	2-193	249	-	S.M.Gavaskar	
Chennai[1]-India 10 wkts	430	0-78	•272	233	S.M.Gavaskar	
Calcutta-Drawn	•331	205	4d-272	6-179	G.R.Viswanath	
1982-83 In PAKISTAN						
Lahore[2]-Drawn	379	-	•485	1-135	S.M.Gavaskar	Imran Khan
Karachi[1]-Pakistan inns & 86 runs	•169	197	452	-		
Faisalabad-Pakistan 10 wkts	•372	286	652	0-10		
Hyderabad-Pakistan inns & 119 runs	189	273	•3d-581	-		
Lahore[2]-Drawn	3-235	-	•323	-		
Karachi[1]-Drawn	•8d-393	2-224	6d-420	-		
1983-84 IN INDIA						
Bangalore-Drawn	•275	0-176	288	-	Kapil Dev	Zaheer Abbas
Jullundur-Drawn	374	-	•337	0-16		
Nagpur-Drawn	•245	8d-262	322	1-42		
1984-85 In PAKISTAN						
Lahore[2]-Drawn	156	6-371	•9d-428	-	S.M.Gavaskar	Zaheer Abbas
Faisalabad-Drawn	•500	-	6-674	-		

INDIA v PAKISTAN (cont.) Venue and Result	India 1st	India 2nd	Pakistan 1st	Pakistan 2nd	Captains India	Captains Pakistan
1986-87 IN INDIA						
Chennai[1]-Drawn	9d-527	-	•9d-487	3-182	Kapil Dev	Imran Khan
Calcutta-Drawn	•403	3d-181	229	5-179		
Jaipur-Drawn	•8d-465	2-114	341	-		
Ahmedabad-Drawn	323	-	•395	2-135		
Bangalore-Pakistan 16 runs	145	204	•116	249		
1989-90 In PAKISTAN						
Karachi[1]-Drawn	262	3-303	•409	5d-305	K.Srikkanth	Imran Khan
Faisalabad-Drawn	•288	7-398	9d-423	-		
Lahore[2]-Drawn	•509	-	5-699	-		
Sialkot-Drawn	•324	7-234	250	-		

Test Match Results Summary

INDIA v PAKISTAN-IN INDIA

	T	Result I P D	Delhi I P D	Luck. I P D	Bomb. I P D	Chennai I P D	Calc. I P D	Kanpur I P D	Bang. I P D	Jull. I P D	Nagpur I P D	Jaipur I P D	Ahmed. I P D
1952-53	5	2 1 2	1 - -	- 1 -	1 - -	- - 1	- - 1	- - -	- - -	- - -	- - -	- - -	- - -
1960-61	5	- - 5	- - 1	- - -	- - 1	- - 1	- - 1	- - 1	- - -	- - -	- - -	- - -	- - -
1979-80	6	2 - 4	- - 1	- - -	1 - -	1 - -	- - 1	- - 1	- - 1	- - -	- - -	- - -	- - -
1983-84	3	- - 3	- - -	- - -	- - -	- - -	- - -	- - -	- - 1	- - 1	- - 1	- - -	- - -
1986-87	5	- 1 4	- - -	- - -	- - -	- - 1	- - 1	- - -	- 1 -	- - -	- - -	- - 1	- - 1
	24	4 2 18	1 - 2	- 1 -	2 - 1	1 - 3	- - 4	- - 2	- 1 2	- - 1	- - 1	- - 1	- - 1

INDIA v PAKISTAN-IN PAKISTAN

	Tests	Result I	Result P	Result D	Dacca I P D	Bah. I P D	Lahore I P D	Pesh. I P D	Karachi[1] I P D	Fais. I P D	Hyd. I P D	Sialkot I P D
1954-55	5	-	-	5	- - 1	- - 1	- - 1	- - 1	- - 1	- - -	- - -	- - -
1978-79	3	-	2	1	- - -	- - -	- 1 -	- - -	- 1 -	- - 1	- - -	- - -
1982-83	6	-	3	3	- - -	- - -	- - 2	- - -	- 1 1	- 1 -	- 1 -	- - -
1984-85	2	-	-	2	- - -	- - -	- - 1	- - -	- - -	- - 1	- - -	- - -
1989-90	4	-	-	4	- - -	- - -	- - 1	- - -	- - 1	- - 1	- - -	- - 1
	20	-	5	15	- - 1	- - 1	- 1 5	- - 1	- 2 3	- 1 3	- 1 -	- - 1
Totals	44	4	7	33								

Key to ground abbreviations: Luck. - Lucknow[1]; Bomb. - Mumbai; Calc. - Calcutta; Bang. - Bangalore; Jull. - Jullundur; Ahmed. - Ahmedabad; Bah. - Bahawalpur; Pesh. - Peshawar[1]; *Fais. - Faisalabad; Hyd. - Hyderabad.*

HIGHEST INNINGS TOTALS

India in India	9d-539	Chennai[2]	1960-61
India in Pakistan	509	Lahore[2]	1989-90
Pakistan in India	9d-487	Chennai[2]	1960-61
Pakistan in Pakistan	5-699	Lahore[2]	1989-90

LOWEST INNINGS TOTALS

India in India	106	Lucknow[1]	1952-53
India in Pakistan	145	Karachi[1]	1954-55

Pakistan in India	116	Delhi	1986-87
Pakistan in Pakistan	158	Dacca	1954-55

HIGHEST MATCH AGGREGATE	1331 for 28 wickets	Lahore[2]	1978-79
LOWEST MATCH AGGREGATE	619 for 30 wickets	Lucknow[1]	1952-53

HIGHEST INDIVIDUAL INNINGS

India in India	201	A.D.Gaekwad	Jullundur	1983-84
India in Pakistan	218	S.V.Manjrekar	Lahore[2]	1989-90
Pakistan in India	160	Hanif Mohammad	Mumbai[2]	1960-61
Pakistan in Pakistan	280*	Javed Miandad	Hyderabad	1982-83

HIGHEST AGGREGATE OF RUNS IN A SERIES

India in India	529 (av 52.90)	S.M.Gavaskar	1979-80
India in Pakistan	584 (av 73.00)	M.Amarnath	1982-83
Pakistan in India	460 (av 51.11)	Saeed Ahmed	1960-61
Pakistan in Pakistan	761 (av 126.83)	Mudassar Nazar	1982-83

RECORD WICKET PARTNERSHIPS-INDIA

1st	200	S.M.Gavaskar (91), K.Srikkanth (123)	Chennai[1]	1986-87
2nd	135	N.S.Sidhu (85), S.V.Manjrekar (113)	Karachi[1]	1989-90
3rd	190	M.Amarnath (120), Yashpal Sharma (63*)	Lahore[2]	1982-83
4th	186	S.V.Manjrekar (218), R.J.Shastri (61)	Lahore[2]	1989-90
5th	200	S.M.Patil (127), R.J.Shastri (139)	Faisalabad	1984-85
6th	143	M.Azharuddin (141), Kapil Dev (66)	Calcutta	1986-87
7th	155	R.M.H.Binny (83*), S.Madan Lal (74)	Bangalore	1983-84
8th	122	S.M.H.Kirmani (66), S.Madan Lal (54)	Faisalabad	1982-83
9th	149	P.G.Joshi (52*), R.B.Desai (85)	Mumbai[2]	1960-61
10th	109	H.R.Adhikari (81*), Ghulam Ahmed (50)	Delhi	1952-53

RECORD WICKET PARTNERSHIPS-PAKISTAN

1st	162	Hanif Mohammad (62), Imtiaz Ahmed (135)	Chennai[2]	1960-61
2nd	250	Mudassar Nazar (199), Qasim Omar (210)	Faisalabad	1984-85
3rd	451	Mudassar Nazar (230), Javed Miandad (280*)	Hyderabad	1982-83
4th	287	Javed Miandad (126), Zaheer Abbas (168)	Faisalabad	1982-83
5th	213	Zaheer Abbas (186), Mudassar Nazar (119)	Karachi[1]	1982-83
6th	207	Saleem Malik (107), Imran Khan (117)	Faisalabad	1982-83
7th	154	Imran Khan (72), Ijaz Faqih (105)	Ahmedabad	1986-87
8th	112	Imran Khan (135*), Wasim Akram (62)	Chennai[1]	1986-87
9th	60	Wasim Bari (49*), Iqbal Qasim (20)	Bangalore	1979-80
10th	104	Zulfiqar Ahmed (63*), Amir Elahi (47)	Chennai[1]	1952-53

BEST INNINGS BOWLING ANALYSIS

India in India	8-52	M.H.Mankad	Delhi	1952-53
India in Pakistan	8-85	Kapil Dev	Lahore[2]	1982-83
Pakistan In India	8-69	Sikander Bakht	Delhi	1979-80
Pakistan in Pakistan	8-60	Imran Khan	Karachi[1]	1982-83

BEST MATCH BOWLING ANALYSIS

India in India	13-131	M.H.Mankad	Delhi	1952-53
India in Pakistan	8-85	Kapil Dev	Lahore[2]	1982-83
Pakistan in India	12-94	Fazal Mahmood	Lucknow[1]	1952-53
Pakistan in Pakistan	11-79	Imran Khan	Karachi[1]	1982-83

HIGHEST AGGREGATE OF WICKETS IN A SERIES

India in India	32 (av 17.68)	Kapil Dev	1979-80
India in Pakistan	21 (av 22.61)	Kapil Dev	1982-83
Pakistan in India	24 (av 26.70)	Sikander Bakht	1979-80
Pakistan in Pakistan	22 (av 15.86)	Imran Khan	1982-83

INDIA v SRI LANKA	India		Sri Lanka		Captains	
Venue and Result	1st	2nd	1st	2nd	India	Sri Lanka
1982-83 in INDIA						
Chennai[1]-Drawn	6d-566	7-135	•346	394	S.M.Gavaskar	B.Warnaweera
1985-86 in SRI LANKA						
Colombo (SSC)-Drawn	•218	251	347	4-61	Kapil Dev	L.R.D.Mendis
Colombo (PSS)-Sri Lanka 149 runs	244	198	•385	3d-206		
Kandy-Drawn	•249	5d-325	198	7-307		
1986-87 in INDIA						
Kanpur-Drawn	7-676	-	•420	-	Kapil Dev	L.R.D.Mendis
Nagpur-India inns & 106 runs	6d-451	-	•204	141		
Cuttack-India inns & 67 runs	•400	-	191	142		
1990-91 in INDIA						
Chandigarh-India inns & 8 runs	•288	-	82	198	M.Azharuddin	A.Ranatunga
1993-94 in SRI LANKA						
Kandy-Drawn	-	-	•3-24	-	M.Azharuddin	A.Ranatunga
Colombo (SSC)-India 235 runs	•366	4d-359	254	236		
Colombo (PSS)-Drawn	446	-	351	6-352		
1993-94 in INDIA						
Lucknow[2]-India inns & 119 runs	•511	-	218	174	M.Azharuddin	A.Ranatunga
Bangalore-India inns & 95 runs	•6d-541	-	231	215		
Ahmedabad-India inns & 17 runs	358	-	119	222		

Test Match Results Summary

INDIA v SRI LANKA-IN INDIA

	Tests	Result			Chennai			Kanpur			Nagpur			Cuttack			Chand.			Lucknow			Bang.			Ahmed.		
		I	SL	D	I	SL	D	I	SL	D	I	SL	D	I	SL	D	I	SL	D	I	SL	D	I	SL	D	I	SL	D
1982-83	1	-	-	1	-	-	1	-	-	-	-	-	-	-	-	-	-	-	-	-	-	-	-	-	-	-	-	-
1986-87	3	2	-	1	-	-	-	1	-	-	-	-	1	1	-	-	-	-	-	-	-	-	-	-	-	-	-	-
1990-91	1	1	-	-	-	-	-	-	-	-	-	-	-	-	-	-	-	-	1	-	-	-	-	-	-	-	-	-
1993-94	3	3	-	-	-	-	-	-	-	-	-	-	-	-	-	-	-	-	-	1	-	-	1	-	-	1	-	-
	8	6	-	2	-	-	1	1	-	-	-	-	1	1	-	-	-	-	1	1	-	-	1	-	-	1	-	-

INDIA v SRI LANKA-IN SRI LANKA

	Tests	Result			Colombo (SSC)			Colombo (PSS)			Kandy		
		I	SL	D	I	SL	D	I	SL	D	I	SL	D
1985-86	3	-	1	2	-	-	1	-	1	-	-	-	1
1993-94	3	1	-	2	1	-	-	-	-	1	-	-	1
	6	1	1	4	1	-	1	-	1	1	-	-	2
Totals	14	7	1	6									

Key to ground abbreviations: Chand. - Chandigarh; Bang. - Bangalore; Ahmed. - Ahmedabad.

HIGHEST INNINGS TOTALS

India in India	7-676	Kanpur	1986-87
India in Sri Lanka	446	Colombo (PSS)	1993-94
Sri Lanka in India	420	Kanpur	1986-87
Sri Lanka in Sri Lanka	385	Colombo (PSS)	1985-86

LOWEST INNINGS TOTALS

India in India	288	Chandigarh	1990-91
India in Sri Lanka	198	Colombo (PSS)	1985-86
Sri Lanka in India	82	Chandigarh	1990-91
Sri Lanka in Sri Lanka	198	Kandy	1985-86

HIGHEST MATCH AGGREGATE	1441 for 33 wickets	Chennai[1]	1982-83
LOWEST MATCH AGGREGATE	568 for 30 wickets	Chandigarh	1990-91

HIGHEST INDIVIDUAL INNINGS

India in India	199	M.Azharuddin	Kanpur	1986-87
India in Sri Lanka	125	V.G.Kambli	Colombo (SSC)	1993-94
Sri Lanka in India	105 (twice)	L.R.D.Mendis	Chennai[1]	1982-83
Sri Lanka in Sri Lanka	151	R.S.Mahanama	Colombo (PSS)	1993-94

HIGHEST AGGREGATE ON RUNS IN A SERIES

India in India	376 (av 125.33)	D.B.Vengsarkar	1986-87
India in Sri Lanka	249 (av 83.00)	V.G.Kambli	1993-94
Sri Lanka in India	282 (av 47.00)	R.S.Mahanama	1993-94
Sri Lanka in Sri Lanka	310 (av 62.00)	L.R.D.Mendis	1985-86

RECORD WICKET PARTNERSHIPS-INDIA

1st	171	M.Prabhakar (94), N.S.Sidhu (104)	Colombo (SSC)	1993-94
2nd	173	S.M.Gavaskar (155), D.B.Vengsarkar (90)	Chennai[1]	1982-83
3rd	173	M.Amarnath (131), D.B.Vengsarkar (153)	Nagpur	1986-87
4th	163	S.M.Gavaskar (176), M.Azharuddin (199)	Kanpur	1986-87
5th	87	M.Azharuddin (108), S.V.Manjrekar (39)	Bangalore	1993-94
6th	272	M.Azharuddin (199), Kapil Dev (163)	Kanpur	1986-87
7th	78*	S.M.Patil (114*), S.Madan Lal (37*)	Chennai[1]	1982-83
8th	70	Kapil Dev (78), L.Sivaramakrishnan (21)	Colombo (PSS)	1985-86
9th	67	M.Azharuddin (152), R.K.Chauhan (9)	Ahmedabad	1993-94
10th	29	Kapil Dev (78), C.Sharma (0*)	Colombo (PSS)	1985-86

RECORD WICKET PARTNERSHIPS-SRI LANKA

1st	159	S.Wettimuny (79), J.R.Ratnayeke (93)	Kanpur	1986-87
2nd	95	S.A.R.Silva (111), R.S.Madugalle (54)	Colombo (PSS)	1985-86
3rd	153	R.L.Dias (60), L.R.D.Mendis (105)	Chennai[1]	1982-83
4th	216	R.L.Dias (106), L.R.D.Mendis (124)	Kandy	1985-86
5th	144	R.S.Madugalle (103), A.Ranatunga (111)	Colombo (SSC)	1985-86
6th	89	L.R.D.Mendis (105), A.N.Ranasinghe (77)	Chennai[1]	1982-83
7th	77	R.S.Madugalle (46), D.S.de Silva (49)	Chennai[1]	1982-83
8th	40*	P.A.de Silva (29*), A.L.F.de Mel (9*)	Kandy	1985-86
9th	60	H.P.Tillakaratne (55), M.A.W.R.Madurasinghe (11)	Chennai[1]	1982-83
10th	44	R.J.Ratnayake (32*), E.A.R.de Silva (16)	Nagpur	1986-87

BEST INNINGS BOWLING ANALYSIS

India in India	7-51	Maninder Singh	Nagpur	1986-87
India in Sri Lanka	5-87	A.R.Kumble	Colombo (SSC)	1993-94
Sri Lanka in India	5-68	A.L.F.de Mel	Chennai[1]	1982-83
Sri Lanka in Sri Lanka	6-85	R.J.Ratnayake	Colombo (SSC)	1985-86

BEST MATCH BOWLING ANALYSIS

India in India	11-128	A.R.Kumble	Lucknow[2]	1993-94
India in Sri Lanka	8-172	A.R.Kumble	Colombo (SSC)	1993-94
Sri Lanka in India	7-201	A.L.F.de Mel	Chennai[1]	1982-83
Sri Lanka in Sri Lanka	9-125	R.J.Ratnayake	Colombo (PSS)	1985-86

HIGHEST AGGREGATE OF WICKETS IN A SERIES

India in India	18 (av 15.50)	Maninder Singh	1986-87
India in Sri Lanka	14 (av 27.35)	C.Sharma	1985-86
Sri Lanka in India	12 (av 35.00)	M.Muralidharan	1993-94
Sri Lanka in Sri Lanka	20 (av 22.95)	R.J.Ratnayake	1985-86

INDIA v ZIMBABWE Venue and Result	India 1st	India 2nd	Zimbabwe 1st	Zimbabwe 2nd	Captains India	Captains Zimbabwe
1992-93 in ZIMBABWE						
Harare-Drawn	307	-	•456	4-146	M.Azharuddin	D.L.Houghton
1992-93 in India						
Delhi-India inns & 13 runs	•7d-536	-	322	201	M.Azharuddin	D.L.Houghton

Test Match Results Summary

INDIA v ZIMBABWE-IN ZIMBABWE

	Tests	Result I	Result Z	Result D	Harare I	Harare Z	Harare D
1992-93	1	-	-	1	-	-	1

INDIA v ZIMBABWE-IN INDIA

	Tests	Result I	Result Z	Result D	Delhi I	Delhi Z	Delhi D
1992-93	1	1	-	-	1	-	-
Totals	2	1	-	1			

HIGHEST INNINGS TOTALS

India in Zimbabwe	307	Harare	1992-93
India in India	7d-536	Delhi	1992-93
Zimbabwe in Zimbabwe	456	Harare	1992-93
Zimbabwe in India	322	Delhi	1992-93

LOWEST INNINGS TOTALS

India in Zimbabwe	307	Harare	1992-93
India in India	no instance	Delhi	1992-93
Zimbabwe in Zimbabwe	456	Harare	1992-93
Zimbabwe in India	201	Delhi	1992-93

HIGHEST MATCH AGGREGATE	1059 for 27 wickets	Delhi	1992-93
LOWEST MATCH AGGREGATE	909 for 24 wickets	Harare	1992-93

HIGHEST INDIVIDUAL INNINGS

India in Zimbabwe	104	S.V.Manjrekar	Harare	1992-93
India in India	227	V.G.Kambli	Delhi	1992-93
Zimbabwe in Zimbabwe	121	D.L.Houghton	Harare	1992-93
Zimbabwe in India	115	A.Flower	Delhi	1992-93

HIGHEST AGGREGATE ON RUNS IN A SERIES

India in Zimbabwe	104 (av 104.00)	S.V.Manjrekar	1992-93
India in India	227 (av 227.00)	V.G.Kambli	1992-93
Zimbabwe in Zimbabwe	162 (av 162.00)	D.L.Houghton	1992-93
Zimbabwe in India	177 (av 177.00)	A.Flower	1992-93

HIGHEST WICKET PARTNERSHIP-INDIA

1st	29	R.J.Shastri (11), W.V.Raman (43)	Harare	1992-93
2nd	107	N.S.Sidhu (61), V.G.Kambli (227)	Delhi	1992-93
3rd	137	V.G.Kambli (227), S.R.Tendulkar (62)	Delhi	1992-93
4th	107	V.G.Kambli (227), M.Azharuddin (42)	Delhi	1992-93
5th	64	V.G.Kambli (227), P.K.Amre (52*)	Delhi	1992-93
6th	96	S.V.Manjrekar (104), Kapil Dev (60)	Harare	1992-93
7th	43	P.K.Amre (52*), V.Yadav (14)	Delhi	1992-93
8th	68	S.V.Manjrekar (104), K.S.More (41)	Harare	1992-93
9th	7	K.S.More (41), A.R.Kumble (0)	Harare	1992-93
10th	13	K.S.More (41), J.Srinath (6*)	Harare	1992-93

HIGHEST WICKET PARTNERSHIP-ZIMBABWE

1st	100	K.J.Arnott (40), G.W.Flower (82)	Harare	1992-93
2nd	75	G.W.Flower (82), A.D.R.Campbell (45)	Harare	1992-93
3rd	77	K.J.Arnott(32), A.J.Pycroft (46)	Harare	1992-93
4th	192	G.W.Flower (96), A.Flower (115)	Delhi	1992-93
5th	51	A.J.Pycroft (39), D.L.Houghton (121)	Harare	1992-93
6th	165	D.L.Houghton (121), A.Flower (59)	Harare	1992-93
7th	28	D.L.Houghton (121), G.J.Crocker (23*)	Harare	1992-93
8th	1	A.H.Shah (25), D.H.Brain (0)	Delhi	1992-93
8th	1	A.Flower (62*), D.H.Brain (0)	Delhi	1992-93
9th	31	A.H.Shah(25), U.Ranchod (7)	Delhi	1992-93
10th	13	A.Flower (62*), A.J.Traicos (1)	Delhi	1992-93

BEST INNINGS BOWLING ANALYSIS

India in Zimbabwe	3-66	M.Prabhakar	Harare	1992-93
India in India	5-70	A.R.Kumble	Delhi	1992-93
Zimbabwe in Zimbabwe	5-86	A.J.Traicos	Harare	1992-93
Zimbabwe in India	3-186	A.J.Traicos	Delhi	1992-93

BEST MATCH BOWLING ANALYSIS

India in Zimbabwe	4-88	M.Prabhakar	Harare	1992-93
India in India	8-160	A.R.Kumble	Delhi	1992-93
Zimbabwe in Zimbabwe	5-86	A.J.Traicos	Harare	1992-93
Zimbabwe in India	3-186	A.J.Traicos	Delhi	1992-93

HIGHEST AGGREGATE OF WICKETS IN A SERIES

India in Zimbabwe	4 (av 22.00)	M.Prabhakar	1992-93
India in India	4 (av 22.00)	A.R.Kumble	1992-93
Zimbabwe in Zimbabwe	5 (av 17.20)	A.J.Traicos	1992-93
Zimbabwe in India	3 (av 62.00)	A.J.Traicos	1992-93

PAKISTAN v SRI LANKA	Pakistan		Sri Lanka		Captains	
Venue and Result	1st	2nd	1st	2nd	Pakistan	Sri Lanka
1981-82 in PAKISTAN						
Karachi[1]-Pakistan 204 runs	•396	4d-301	344	149	Javed Miandad	B Warnapura
Faisalabad-Drawn	270	7-186	•454	8d-154		L R D. Mendis
Lahore[2]-Pakistan inns & 102 runs	7d-500	-	•240	158		B. Warnapura
1985-86 in PAKISTAN						
Faisalabad-Drawn	3-555	-	•479	-	Javed Miandad	L. R. D. Mendis
Sialkot-Pakistan 8 wkts	259	2-100	•157	200		
Karachi[1]-Pakistan 10 wkts	295	0-98	•162	230		
1985-86 in SRI LANKA						
Kandy-Pakistan inns & 20 runs	230	-	•109	101	Imran Khan	L. R. D. Mendis
Colombo (CCC)-Sri Lanka 149 runs	•132	172	273	2-32		
Colombo (PSS)-Drawn	318	-	•281	3-323		
1991-92 in PAKISTAN						
Sialkot-Drawn	5d-423	-	•270	5-137	Imran Khan	P.A.de Silva
Gujranwala-Drawn	•2-109	-	-	-		
Faisalabad-Pakistan 3 wkts	221	7-188	•240	165		
1994-95 in SRI LANKA						
Colombo (PSS)-Pakistan 301 runs	•390	4d-318	226	181	Saleem Malik	A.Ranatunga
Colombo (SSC)-Match cancelled						
Kandy-Pakistan inns & 52 runs	9d-357	-	71	234		
1995-96 in PAKISTAN						
Peshawar[2]-Pakistan inns & 40 runs	•9d-459	-	186	233	Rameez Raja	A.Ranatunga
Faisalabad-Sri Lanka 42 runs	333	209	•223	361		
Sialkot-Sri Lanka 144 runs	214	212	•232	9d-338		

Test Match Results Summary

PAKISTAN v SRI LANKA-IN PAKISTAN

		Results			Karachi[1]			Faisalabad			Lahore[2]			Sialkot			Gujranwala			Peshawar[2]		
	Tests	P	SL	D	P	SL	D	P	SL	D	P	SL	D	P	SL	D	P	SL	D	P	SL	D
1981-82	3	2	-	1	1	-	-	-	-	1	1	-	-	-	-	-	-	-	-	-	-	-
1985-86	3	2	-	1	1	-	-	-	-	1	-	-	-	1	-	-	-	-	-	-	-	-
1991-92	3	1	-	2	-	-	1	1	-	-	-	-	-	-	-	1	-	-	1	-	-	-
1995-96	3	1	2	-	-	-	-	-	1	-	-	-	-	-	1	-	-	-	-	1	-	-
	12	6	2	4	2	-	1	1	1	2	1	-	-	1	1	1	-	-	1	1	-	-

PAKISTAN v SRI LANKA-IN SRI LANKA

		Result			Kandy			Colombo (CCC)			Colombo (PSS)			Colombo (SSC)		
	Tests	P	SL	D	P	SL	D	P	SL	D	P	SL	D	P	SL	D
1985-86	3	1	1	1	1	-	-	-	1	-	-	-	1	-	-	-
1994-95	2	2	-	-	1	-	-	-	-	-	1	-	-	-	-	-
	5	3	1	1	2	-	-	-	1	-	1	-	1	-	-	-
Totals	17	9	3	5												

HIGHEST INNINGS TOTALS

Pakistan in Pakistan	3-555	Faisalabad	1985-86
Pakistan in Sri Lanka	390	Colombo (PSS)	1994-95
Sri Lanka in Pakistan	479	Faisalabad	1985-86
Sri Lanka in Sri Lanka	3-323	Colombo (PSS)	1985-86

LOWEST INNINGS TOTALS

Pakistan in Pakistan	209	Faisalabad	1995-96
Pakistan in Sri Lanka	132	Colombo (CCC)	1985-86
Sri Lanka in Pakistan	149	Karachi[1]	1981-82
Sri Lanka in Sri Lanka	71	Kandy	1994-95

HIGHEST MATCH AGGREGATE	1190 for 34 wickets	Karachi[1]	1981-82
LOWEST MATCH AGGREGATE	440 for 30 wickets	Kandy	1985-86

HIGHEST INDIVIDUAL INNINGS

Pakistan in Pakistan	206	Qasim Omar	Faisalabad	1985-86
Pakistan in Sri Lanka	136	Saeed Anwar	Colombo (PSS)	1994-95
Sri Lanka in Pakistan	157	S.Wettimuny	Faisalabad	1981-82
Sri Lanka in Sri Lanka	135*	A.Ranatunga	Colombo (PSS)	1985-86

HIGHEST AGGREGATE OF RUNS IN A SERIES

Pakistan in Pakistan	306 (av 153.00)	Javed Miandad	1985-86
Pakistan in Sri Lanka	261 (av 87.00)	Saeed Anwar	1994-95
Sri Lanka in Pakistan	316 (av 52.66)	S.Wettimuny	1985-86
Sri Lanka in Sri Lanka	316 (av 79.00)	A.Ranatunga	1985-86

RECORD WICKET PARTNERSHIPS-PAKISTAN

Wkt	Runs	Partners	Venue	Season
1st	128	Rameez Raja (98), Shoaib Mohammad (43)	Sialkot	1991-92
	128	Saeed Anwar (136), Aamer Sohail (65)	Colombo (PSS)	1994-95
2nd	151	Mohsin Khan (129), Majid Khan (63)	Lahore[2]	1981-82
3rd	397	Qasim Omar (206), Javed Miandad (203*)	Faisalabad	1985-86
4th	162	Saleem Malik (100*), Javed Miandad (92)	Karachi[1]	1981-82
5th	132	Saleem Malik (101), Imran Khan (93*)	Sialkot	1991-92
6th	100	Zaheer Abbas (134), Imran Khan (39)	Lahore[2]	1981-82
7th	104	Haroon Rashid (153), Tahir Naqqash (57)	Karachi[1]	1981-82
8th	33	Inzamamul Haq (100*), Wasim Akram (12)	Kandy	1994-95
9th	127	Haroon Rashid (153), Rashid Khan (59)	Karachi[1]	1981-82
10th	65	Moin Khan (117*), Aamer Nazir (11)	Sialkot	1995-96

RECORD WICKET PARTNERSHIPS-SRI LANKA

Wkt	Runs	Partners	Venue	Season
1st	81	R.S.Mahanama (58), U.C.Hathurusingha (49)	Faisalabad	1991-92
2nd	217	S.Wettimuny (157), R.L.Dias (98)	Faisalabad	1981-82
3rd	176	U.C.Hathurusingha (83), P.A.de Silva (105)	Faisalabad	1995-96
4th	240*	A.P.Gurusinha (116*), A.Ranatunga (135*)	Colombo (PSS)	1985-86
5th	125	A.Ranatunga (76), H.P.Tillakaratne (48)	Peshawar[2]	1995-96
6th	121	A.Ranatunga (79), P.A.de Silva (122)	Faisalabad	1985-86
7th	66	P.A.de Silva (122), J.R.Ratnayeke (34)	Faisalabad	1985-86
8th	65	H.D.P.K.Dharmasena (49), W.P.J.U.C.Vaas (40)	Faisalabad	1995-96
9th	52	P.A.de Silva (122), R.J.Ratnayake (56)	Faisalabad	1985-86
10th	36	R.J.Ratnayake (356), R.G.C.E.Wijesuriya (7*)	Faisalabad	1985-86

BEST INNINGS BOWLING ANALYSIS

Pakistan in Pakistan	8-58	Imran Khan	Lahore[2]	1981-82
Pakistan in Sri Lanka	6-34	Waqar Younis	Kandy	1994-95
Sri Lanka in Pakistan	8-83	J.R.Ratnayeke	Faisalabad	1985-86
Sri Lanka in Sri Lanka	6-99	H.D.P.K.Dharmasena	Colombo (PSS)	1994-95

BEST MATCH BOWLING ANALYSIS

Pakistan in Pakistan	14-116	Imran Khan	Lahore[2]	1981-82
Pakistan in Sri Lanka	11-119	Waqar Younis	Kandy	1994-95
Sri Lanka in Pakistan	9-162	D.S.de Silva	Faisalabad	1981-82
Sri Lanka in Sri Lanka	8-183	H.D.P.K.Dharmasena	Colombo (PSS)	1994-95

HIGHEST AGGREGATE OF WICKETS IN SERIES

Pakistan in Pakistan	17 (av 15.94)	Imran Khan	1985-86
Pakistan in Sri Lanka	15 (av 18.00)	Imran Khan	1985-86
Sri Lanka in Pakistan	17 (av 28.94)	D.S.de Silva	1981-82
Sri Lanka in Sri Lanka	12 (av 21.50)	H.D.P.K.Dharmasena	1994-95

PAKISTAN v ZIMBABWE	Pakistan		Zimbabwe		Captains	
Venue and Result	1st	2nd	1st	2nd	Pakistan	Zimbabwe
1993-94 in PAKISTAN						
Karachi²-Pakistan 131 runs	•8d-423	3d-131	289	134	Waqar Younis	A.Flower
Rawalpindi²-Pakistan 52 runs	•245	248	254	187	Wasim Akram	
Lahore²-Drawn	•147	1-174	230	-	Wasim Akram	
1994-95 in ZIMBABWE						
Harare-Zimbabwe inns & 64 runs	322	158	•4d-544	-	Saleem Malik	A.Flower
Bulawayo²-Pakistan 8 wkts	260	2-61	•174	146		
Harare-Pakistan 99 runs	•231	250	243	139		

Test Match Results Summary

PAKISTAN v ZIMBABWE-IN PAKISTAN

		Result			Karachi¹			Rawalpindi²			Lahore²		
	Tests	P	Z	D	P	Z	D	P	Z	D	P	Z	D
1993-94	3	2	-	1	1	-	-	1	-	-	-	-	1

PAKISTAN v ZIMBABWE-IN ZIMBABWE

		Result			Harare			Bulawayo²		
	Tests	P	Z	D	P	Z	D	P	Z	D
1994-95	3	2	1	-	1	1	-	1	-	-
Totals	6	4	1	1						

HIGHEST INNINGS TOTALS			
Pakistan in Pakistan	8d-423	Karachi²	1993-94
Pakistan in Zimbabwe	322	Harare	1994-95
Zimbabwe in Pakistan	289	Karachi²	1993-94
Zimbabwe in Zimbabwe	4d-544	Harare	1994-95

LOWEST INNINGS TOTALS			
Pakistan in Pakistan	147	Lahore²	1993-94
Pakistan in Zimbabwe	158	Harare	1994-95
Zimbabwe in Pakistan	134	Karachi²	1993-94
Zimbabwe in Zimbabwe	139	Harare	1994-95

HIGHEST MATCH AGGREGATE	1024 for 24 wickets	Harare	1994-95
LOWEST MATCH AGGREGATE	551 for 21 wickets	Lahore²	1993-94

HIGHEST INDIVIDUAL INNINGS				
Pakistan in Pakistan	81	Shoaib Mohammad	Karachi²	1993-94
Pakistan in Zimbabwe	101	Inzamamul Haq	Harare	1994-95
Zimbabwe in Pakistan	75	A.D.R.Campbell	Rawalpindi²	1993-94
Zimbabwe in Zimbabwe	201*	G.W.Flower	Harare	1994-95

HIGHEST AGGREGATE OF RUNS IN A SERIES			
Pakistan in Pakistan	184 (av 61.33)	Asif Mujtaba	1993-94
Pakistan in Zimbabwe	367 (av 73.40)	Inzamamul Haq	1994-95
Zimbabwe in Pakistan	205 (av 41.00)	A.D.R.Campbell	1993-94
Zimbabwe in Zimbabwe	250 (av 50.00)	A.Flower	1994-95

RECORD WICKET PARTNERSHIPS-PAKISTAN

Wkt	Runs	Batsmen	Venue	Season
1st	95	Aamer Sohail (63), Shoaib Mohammad (81)	Karachi[2]	1993-94
2nd	118*	Shoaib Mohammad (53*), Asif Mujtaba (65*)	Lahore[2]	1993-94
3rd	83	Shoaib Mohammad (81), Javed Miandad (70)	Karachi[2]	1993-94
4th	116	Inzamamul Haq (83), Ijaz Ahmed (55)	Harare	1994-95
5th	76	Ijaz Ahmed (41), Inzamamul Haq (101)	Harare	1994-95
6th	96	Ijaz Ahmed (65), Inzamamul Haq (71)	Harare	1994-95
7th	120	Inzamamul Haq (71), Wasim Akram (27)	Harare	1994-95
8th	46	Rashid Latif (68*), Iqbal Qasim (18)	Harare	1994-95
9th	60*	Rashid Latif (68*), Tauseef Ahmed (21*)	Karachi[2]	1993-94
10th	27	Waqar Younis (17), Ashfaq Ahmed (1*)	Harare	1994-95

RECORD WICKET PARTNERSHIPS-ZIMBABWE

Wkt	Runs	Batsmen	Venue	Season
1st	20	G.W.Flower (30), M.H.Dekker (2)	Harare	1994-95
2nd	135	M.H.Dekker (68*), A.D.R.Campbell (75)	Rawalpindi[2]	1993-94
3rd	269	G.W.Flower (30), D.L.Houghton (50)	Harare	1994-95
4th	233*	D.L.Houghton (50), A.Flower (62*)	Harare	1994-95
5th	77	A.Flower (63), G.J.Whittall (33)	Karachi[2]	1993-94
6th	72	M.H.Dekker (68), H.H.Streak (29)	Rawalpindi[2]	1993-94
7th	48	G.K.Bruk-Jackson (31), S.G.Peall (0)	Bulawayo[2]	1994-95
8th	46	A.Flower (62*), D.H.Brain (28)	Lahore[2]	1993-94
9th	40	H.H.Streak (19*), E.A.Brandes (17)	Harare	1994-95
10th	19	M.H.Dekker (68*), S.G.Peall (10)	Rawalpindi[2]	1993-94

BEST INNINGS BOWLING ANALYSIS

Pakistan in Pakistan	7-91	Waqar Younis	Karachi[2]	1993-94
Pakistan in Zimbabwe	5-43	Wasim Akram	Bulawayo[2]	1994-95
Zimbabwe in Pakistan	5-42	D.H.Brain	Lahore[2]	1993-94
Zimbabwe in Zimbabwe	6-90	H.H.Streak	Harare	1994-95

BEST MATCH BOWLING ANALYSIS

Pakistan in Pakistan	13-135	Waqar Younis	Karachi[2]	1993-94
Pakistan in Zimbabwe	8-83	Wasim Akram	Bulawayo[2]	1994-95
Zimbabwe in Pakistan	8-114	H.H.Streak	Rawalpindi[2]	1993-94
Zimbabwe in Zimbabwe	9-105	H.H.Streak	Harare	1994-95

HIGHEST AGGREGATE OF WICKETS IN SERIES

Pakistan in Pakistan	27 (av 13.81)	Waqar Younis	1993-94
Pakistan in Zimbabwe	13 (av 24.07)	Wasim Akram	1994-95
Zimbabwe in Pakistan	13 (av 30.30)	E.A.Brandes	1993-94
Zimbabwe in Zimbabwe	22 (av 13.54)	H.H.Streak	1994-95

SRI LANKA v ZIMBABWE

Venue and Result	Sri Lanka 1st	Sri Lanka 2nd	Zimbabwe 1st	Zimbabwe 2nd	Captains Sri Lanka	Captains Zimbabwe
1994-95 in ZIMBABWE						
Harare-Drawn	•383	-	8-319	-	A.Ranatunga	A.Flower
Bulawayo²-Drawn	218	4-193	•9d-462	-		
Harare-Drawn	•402	3-89	375	-		

Test Match Results Summary

SRI LANKA v ZIMBABWE-IN ZIMBABWE

	Tests	Result SL	Result Z	Result D	Harare SL	Harare Z	Harare D	Bulawayo² SL	Bulawayo² Z	Bulawayo² D
1994-95	3	-	-	3	-	-	2	-	-	1

HIGHEST INNINGS TOTALS

Sri Lanka in Zimbabwe	402	Harare	1994-95
Zimbabwe in Zimbabwe	9-462	Bulawayo²	1994-95

LOWEST INNINGS TOTALS

Sri Lanka in Zimbabwe	218	Bulawayo²	1994-95
Zimbabwe in Zimbabwe	8-319	Harare	1994-95

HIGHEST MATCH AGGREGATE	873 for 23 wickets	Bulawayo²	1994-95
LOWEST MATCH AGGREGATE	702 for 18 wickets	Harare	1994-95

HIGHEST INDIVIDUAL INNINGS

Sri Lanka in Zimbabwe	128	A.P.Gurusinha	Harare	1994-95
Zimbabwe in Zimbabwe	266	D.L.Houghton	Bulawayo²	1994-95

HIGHEST AGGREGATE OF RUNS IN A SERIES

Sri Lanka in Zimbabwe	273 (av 68.25)	S.Ranatunga	1994-95
Zimbabwe in Zimbabwe	466 (av 155.33)	D.L.Houghton	1994-95

RECORD WICKET PARTNERSHIPS-SRI LANKA

1st	64	R.S.Mahanama (24), A.P.Gurusinha (54)	Harare	1994-95
2nd	217	A.P.Gurusinha (128), S.Ranatunga (118)	Harare	1994-95
3rd	50	S.Ranatunga (100*), H.P.D.K.Dharmasena (18)	Bulawayo²	1994-95
4th	84	S.Ranatunga (100*), P.A.de Silva (27)	Bulawayo²	1994-95
5th	75	H.P.Tillakaratne (116), A.Ranatunga (39)	Harare	1994-95
6th	13	H.P.Tillakaratne (116), S.T.Jayasuriya (10)	Harare	1994-95
7th	51	A.P.Gurusinha (63), H.P.D.K.Dharmasena (54)	Harare	1994-95
8th	37	H.P.Tillakaratne (116), H.P.D.K.Dharmasena (21)	Bulawayo²	1994-95
9th	22	H.P.D.K.Dharmasena (54), G.P.Wickramasinghe (7)	Bulawayo²	1994-95
10th	25	H.P.D.K.Dharmasena (54), M.Muralidharan (15*)	Bulawayo²	1994-95

RECORD WICKET PARTNERSHIPS-ZIMBABWE

1st	113	G.W.Flower (41), M.H.Dekker (40)	Harare	1994-95
2nd	15	M.H.Dekker (14), A.D.R.Campbell (99)	Harare	1994-95
3rd	194	A.D.R.Campbell (99), D.L.Houghton (142)	Harare	1994-95
4th	121	D.L.Houghton (266), A.Flower (50)	Bulawayo[2]	1994-95
5th	62	D.L.Houghton (142), G.J.Whittall (61*)	Harare	1994-95
6th	100	D.L.Houghton (266), W.R.James (33)	Bulawayo[2]	1994-95
7th	58	G.J.Whittall (61*), H.H.Streak (20)	Harare	1994-95
8th	84	D.L.Houghton (266), J.A.Rennie (19*)	Bulawayo[2]	1994-95
9th	43	J.A.Rennie (19*), S.G.Peall (30)	Bulawayo[2]	1994-95
10th	3	G.J.Whittall (61*), M.P.Jarvis (2)	Harare	1994-95

BEST INNINGS BOWLING ANALYSIS

Sri Lanka in Zimbabwe	7-116	K.R.Pushpakumara	Harare	1994-95
Zimbabwe in Zimbabwe	5-129	H.H.Streak	Harare	1994-95

BEST MATCH BOWLING ANALYSIS

Sri Lanka in Zimbabwe	7-116	K.R.Pushpakumara	Harare	1994-95
Zimbabwe in Zimbabwe	4-70	G.J.Whittall	Harare	1994-95

HIGHEST AGGREGATE OF WICKETS IN SERIES

Sri Lanka in Zimbabwe	10 (av 23.50)	W.P.U.J.C.Vaas	1994-95
Zimbabwe in Zimbabwe	13 (av 23.38)	H.H.Streak	1994-95

The Teams

HIGHEST INNINGS TOTALS

903-7d	England	v	Australia	The Oval	1938
849	England	v	West Indies	Kingston	1929-30
790-3d	West Indies	v	Pakistan	Kingston	1957-58
758-8d	Australia	v	West Indies	Kingston	1954-55
729-6d	Australia	v	England	Lord's	1930
708	Pakistan	v	England	The Oval	1987
701	Australia	v	England	The Oval	1934
699-5	Pakistan	v	India	Lahore[2]	1989-90
695	Australia	v	England	The Oval	1930
692-8d	West Indies	v	England	The Oval	1995
687-8d	West Indies	v	England	The Oval	1976
681-8d	West Indies	v	England	Port-of-Spain	1953-54
676-7	India	v	Sri Lanka	Kanpur	1986-87
674-6	Pakistan	v	India	Faisalabad	1984-85
674	Australia	v	India	Adelaide	1947-48
671-4	New Zealand	v	Sri Lanka	Wellington	1990-91
668	Australia	v	West Indies	Bridgetown	1954-55
660-5d	West Indies	v	New Zealand	Wellington	1994-95
659-8d	Australia	v	England	Sydney	1946-47
658-8d	England	v	Australia	Nottingham	1938
657-8d	Pakistan	v	West Indies	Bridgetown	1957-58
656-8d	Australia	v	England	Manchester	1964
654-5	England	v	South Africa	Durban[2]	1938-39
653-4d	England	v	India	Lord's	1990
653-4d	Australia	v	England	Leeds	1993
652-7d	England	v	India	Chennai[1]	1984-85
652-8d	West Indies	v	England	Lord's	1973
652	Pakistan	v	India	Faisalabad	1982-83
650-6d	Australia	v	West Indies	Bridgetown	1964-65
645	Australia	v	England	Brisbane[2]	1946-47
644-7d	India	v	West Indies	Kanpur	1978-79
644-8d	West Indies	v	India	Delhi	1958-59
636	England	v	Australia	Sydney	1928-29
633-5d	England	v	India	Birmingham	1979
632-4d	Australia	v	England	Lord's	1993
631-8d	West Indies	v	India	Kingston	1961-62
631	West Indies	v	India	Delhi	1948-49
629-6d	West Indies	v	India	Mumbai[2]	1948-49
629	England	v	India	Lord's	1974
627-9d	England	v	Australia	Manchester	1934
624	Pakistan	v	Australia	Adelaide	1983-84
622-9d	South Africa	v	Australia	Durban[2]	1969-70
620	South Africa	v	Australia	Johannesburg[3]	1966-67
619-6d	England	v	West Indies	Nottingham	1957
619	Australia	v	West Indies	Sydney	1968-69
617-5d	Australia	v	Sri Lanka	Perth	1995-96
617	Australia	v	Pakistan	Faisalabad	1979-80
616-5d	Pakistan	v	New Zealand	Auckland	1988-89
616	West Indies	v	Australia	Adelaide	1968-69
614-5d	West Indies	v	India	Calcutta	1958-59
611	England	v	Australia	Manchester	1964
608-7d	Pakistan	v	England	Birmingham	1971
608	England	v	South Africa	Johannesburg[2]	1948-49

606	West Indies	v	England	Birmingham	1984
606-9d	India	v	England	The Oval	1990
606	West Indies	v	Australia	Sydney	1992-93
604-6d	West Indies	v	India	Mumbai[3]	1974-75
604	Australia	v	England	Melbourne	1936-37
602-6d	Australia	v	England	Nottingham	1989
601-7d	Australia	v	England	Leeds	1989
601-8d	Australia	v	England	Brisbane[2]	1954-55
600-4d	India	v	Australia	Sydney	[illegible]
600-7d	Pakistan	v	England	The Oval	1974
600-9d	Australia	v	West Indies	Port-of-Spain	1954-55
600	Australia	v	England	Melbourne	1924-25

The highest total for the other countries are:

547-8d	Sri Lanka	v	Australia	Colombo (SSC)	1992-93
544-5d	Zimbabwe	v	Pakistan	Harare	1994-95

BOTH TEAMS SCORING 600

Australia (8d-656)	v	England (611)	Manchester	1964

RECORD SECOND INNINGS TOTALS *First innings in brackets (§ After following on.)*

671-4	(174)	New Zealand	v	Sri Lanka	Wellington	1990-91
657-8d §	(106)	Pakistan	v	West Indies	Bridgetown	1957-58
654-5	(316)	England	v	South Africa	Durban[2]	1938-39
620	(199)	South Africa	v	Australia	Johannesburg[3]	1966-67
616	(276)	West Indies	v	Australia	Adelaide	1968-69
583-4d	(186)	England	v	West Indies	Birmingham	1957
582	(354)	Australia	v	England	Adelaide	1920-21
581	(267)	Australia	v	England	Sydney	1920-21
578	(328)	Australia	v	South Africa	Melbourne	1910-11
564-8	(133)	West Indies	v	New Zealand	Bridgetown	1971-72
564	(200-9d)	Australia	v	England	Melbourne	1936-37
554	(198)	Australia	v	South Africa	Melbourne	1931-32
551 §	(208)	England	v	South Africa	Nottingham	1947

RECORD FOURTH INNINGS TOTALS

TO WIN

						Runs set in 4th innings
406-4	India	v	West Indies	Port-of-Spain	1975-76	403
404-3	Australia	v	England	Leeds	1948	404
362-7	Australia	v	West Indies	Georgetown	1977-78	359
348-5	West Indies	v	New Zealand	Auckland	1968-69	345
344-1	West Indies	v	England	Lord's	1984	342
342-8	Australia	v	India	Perth	1977-78	339
336-5	Australia	v	South Africa	Durban[2]	1949-50	336
332-7	England	v	Australia	Melbourne	1928-29	332
324-5	New Zealand	v	Pakistan	Christchurch	1993-94	323
317-2	West Indies	v	Pakistan	Georgetown	1957-58	317
315-6	Australia	v	England	Adelaide	1901-02	315
315-9	Pakistan	v	Australia	Karachi[1]	1994-95	314

TO TIE

347	India	v	Australia	Chennai[1]	1986-87

TO LOSE

						Losing Margin
445	India	v	Australia	Adelaide	1977-78	47
440	New Zealand	v	England	Nottingham	1973	38
417	England	v	Australia	Melbourne	1976-77	45

411	England	v	Australia	Sydney	1924-25	193
402	Australia	v	England	Manchester	1981	103
376	India	v	England	Manchester	1959	171
370	England	v	Australia	Adelaide	1920-21	119
363	England	v	Australia	Adelaide	1924-25	11
355	India	v	Australia	Brisbane[2]	1967-68	39
352	West Indies	v	Australia	Sydney	1968-69	382
348	Sri Lanka	v	Australia	Hobart	1989-90	173
345	New Zealand	v	England	Nottingham	1983	165
339	Australia	v	South Africa	Adelaide	1910-11	38
336	Australia	v	England	Adelaide	1928-29	12
336	Pakistan	v	Australia	Melbourne	1989-90	92
335	Australia	v	England	Nottingham	1930	93
335	South Africa	v	New Zealand	Cape Town	1961-62	72
333	Australia	v	England	Melbourne	1894-95	94
333	India	v	Australia	Adelaide	1991-92	38
332	England	v	Australia	Manchester	1993	179
327	England	v	West Indies	Georgetown	1929-30	289
326	West Indies	v	Australia	Melbourne	1975-76	165
324	India	v	Australia	Brisbane[2]	1977-78	16
323	England	v	Australia	Melbourne	1936-37	365
323	England	v	Australia	Brisbane[2]	1994-95	184
316	England	v	West Indies	Kingston	1953-54	140
313	England	v	West Indies	Bridgetown	1953-54	181
310	Australia	v	Pakistan	Melbourne	1978-79	71
307	England	v	West Indies	Lord's	1988	134
304	South Africa	v	England	Johannesburg[1]	1913-14	91
301	Pakistan	v	West Indies	Kingston	1976-77	140

TO DRAW						Runs set in 4th innings
654-5	England	v	South Africa	Durban[2]	1938-39	696
429-8	India	v	England	The Oval	1979	438
423-7	South Africa	v	England	The Oval	1947	451
408-5	West Indies	v	England	Kingston	1929-30	836
364-6	India	v	Pakistan	Delhi	1979-80	390
355-8	India	v	West Indies	Mumbai[2]	1948-49	361
351-5	England	v	South Africa	Johannesburg[3]	1995-96	479
344-6	Sri Lanka	v	New Zealand	Hamilton	1990-91	418
344-7	Australia	v	England	Sydney	1994-95	449
343-6	India	v	England	Manchester	1990	408
341-9	Pakistan	v	West Indies	Port-of-Spain	1987-88	372
339-9	Australia	v	West Indies	Adelaide	1968-69	360
335-5	England	v	Australia	Adelaide	1990-91	472
329-3	Australia	v	England	Lord's	1975	484
328-3	Australia	v	England	Adelaide	1970-71	469
326-5	South Africa	v	Australia	Sydney	1963-64	409
325-3	India	v	West Indies	Calcutta	1948-49	431
314-7	England	v	Australia	Sydney	1982-83	460
310-7	England	v	Australia	Melbourne	1946-47	551
308-4	England	v	South Africa	The Oval	1965	399
307-7	Sri Lanka	v	India	Kandy	1985-86	377
303-3	India	v	Pakistan	Karachi[1]	1989-90	453

RECORD MATCH AGGREGATES - BOTH SIDES

Runs	Wkts						Days Played
1981	35	South Africa	v	England	Durban[2]	1938-39	§10
1815	34	West Indies	v	England	Kingston	1929-30	†9
1764	39	Australia	v	West Indies	Adelaide	1968-69	5
1753	40	Australia	v	England	Adelaide	1920-21	6
1723	31	England	v	Australia	Leeds	1948	5
1661	36	West Indies	v	Australia	Bridgetown	1954-55	6
1646	40	Australia	v	South Africa	Adelaide	1910-11	6
1644	38	Australia	v	West Indies	Sydney	1968-69	6
1640	24	West Indies	v	Australia	Bridgetown	1964-65	6
1640	33	Australia	v	Pakistan	Melbourne	1972-73	5
1619	20	Australia	v	England	Melbourne	1924-25	7
1614	30	England	v	India	Manchester	1990	5
1611	40	Australia	v	England	Sydney	1924-25	7
1603	28	England	v	India	Lord's	1990	5
1601	29	England	v	Australia	Lord's	1930	4
1585	31	Pakistan	v	New Zealand	Karachi[1]	1976-77	5
1562	37	Australia	v	England	Melbourne	1946-47	6
1554	35	Australia	v	England	Melbourne	1928-29	8
1541	35	Australia	v	England	Sydney	1903-04	6
1528	24	West Indies	v	England	Port-of-Spain	1953-54	6
1514	40	Australia	v	England	Sydney	1894-95	6
1507	28	England	v	West Indies	The Oval	1976	5
1505	25	New Zealand	v	India	Auckland	1989-90	5
1502	29	Australia	v	England	Adelaide	1946-47	6

§ No play on one day. † No play on two days.

RECORD MATCH AGGREGATES - ONE SIDE

Runs	Wkts					
1121	19	England	v	West Indies	Kingston	1929-30
1028	20	Australia	v	England	The Oval	1934
1013	18	Australia	v	West Indies	Sydney	1968-69
1011	20	South Africa	v	England	Durban[2]	1938-39

LOWEST COMPLETED INNINGS TOTALS

26	New Zealand	v	England	Auckland	1954-55
30	South Africa	v	England	Port Elizabeth	1895-96
30	South Africa	v	England	Birmingham	1924
35	South Africa	v	England	Cape Town	1898-99
36	Australia	v	England	Birmingham	1902
36	South Africa	v	Australia	Melbourne	1931-32
42	Australia	v	England	Sydney	1887-88
42	New Zealand	v	Australia	Wellington	1945-46
42 §	India	v	England	Lord's	1974
43	South Africa	v	England	Cape Town	1888-89
44	Australia	v	England	The Oval	1896
45	England	v	Australia	Sydney	1886-87
45	South Africa	v	Australia	Melbourne	1931-32
46	England	v	West Indies	Port-of-Spain	1993-94
47	South Africa	v	England	Cape Town	1888-89
47	New Zealand	v	England	Lord's	1958
52	England	v	Australia	The Oval	1948
53	England	v	Australia	Lord's	1888
53	Australia	v	England	Lord's	1896
53	West Indies	v	Pakistan	Faisalabad	1986-87

54	New Zealand	v	Australia	Wellington	1945-46
58	South Africa	v	England	Lord's	1912
58 §	Australia	v	England	Brisbane[2]	1936-37
58	India	v	Australia	Brisbane[2]	1947-48
58	India	v	England	Manchester	1952
60	Australia	v	England	Lord's	1888
61	Australia	v	England	Melbourne	1901-02
61	England	v	Australia	Melbourne	1903-04
62	England	v	Australia	Lord's	1888
62	Pakistan	v	Australia	Perth	1981-82
63	Australia	v	England	The Oval	1882
64	England	v	New Zealand	Wellington	1977-78
65	England	v	Australia	Sydney	1894-95
65	Australia	v	England	The Oval	1912
65	New Zealand	v	England	Christchurch	1970-71

§ One batsman absent hurt/ill.

The lowest completed innings total for the other countries are:

71	Sri Lanka	v	Pakistan	Kandy	1994-95
134	Zimbabwe	v	Pakistan	Karachi[2]	1993-94

The following innings were closed at a low total:

32-7d	Australia	v	England	Brisbane[2]	1950-51
35-8	Australia	v	England	Manchester	1953
48-8	New Zealand	v	England	Christchurch	1965-66
51-6d	West Indies	v	England	Bridgetown	1934-35

DISMISSED FOR UNDER 100 IN BOTH INNINGS

42	82	Australia	v	England	Sydney	1887-88
53	62	England	v	Australia	Lord's	1888
81	70	Australia	v	England	Manchester	1888
47	43	South Africa	v	England	Cape Town	1888-89
97	83	South Africa	v	England	Cape Town	1891-92
65	72	England	v	Australia	Sydney	1894-95
93	30	South Africa	v	England	Port Elizabeth	1895-96
95	93	South Africa	v	England	The Oval	1912
36	45	South Africa	v	Australia	Melbourne	1931-32
42	54	New Zealand	v	Australia	Wellington	1945-46
58	98	India	v	Australia	Brisbane[2]	1947-48
58	82	India	v	England	Manchester	1952
89	86	West Indies	v	England	The Oval	1957
47	74	New Zealand	v	England	Lord's	1958
82	93	England	v	New Zealand	Christchurch	1983-84

RESULTS BY NARROW MARGINS - TIE

Australia (505 + 232)	v	West Indies (453 + 284)	Brisbane[2]	1960-61
India (397 + 347)	v	Australia (7d-574 + 5d-170)	Chennai[1]	1986-87

RESULTS BY NARROW MARGINS - WON BY ONE WICKET

				10th Wicket Partnership	
England (183 + 9-263)	v	Australia (324 + 121)	The Oval	15*	1902
South Africa (91 + 9-287)	v	England (184 + 190)	Johannesburg[1]	48*	1905-06
England (382 + 9-282)	v	Australia (266 + 397)	Melbourne	39*	1907-08
England (183 + 9-173)	v	South Africa (113 + 242)	Cape Town	5*	1922-23
Australia (216 + 9-260)	v	West Indies (272 + 203	Melbourne	38*	1951-52
New Zealand (249 + 9-104)	v	West Indies (140 + 212)	Dunedin	4*	1979-80
Pakistan (256 + 9-315)	v	Australia (337 + 232)	Karachi[1]	57*	1994-95

** (unbroken)*

RESULTS BY NARROW MARGINS - WON BY TWO WICKETS

England (100 + 8-95)	v	Australia (92 + 102)	The Oval	1890
Australia (300 + 8-275)	v	England (273 + 100)	Sydney	1907-08
§ England (253 + 8-128)	v	South Africa (161 + 219)	Durban[2]	1948-49
Australia (356 + 8-258)	v	West Indies (292 + 321)	Melbourne	1960-61
India (341 + 8-256)	v	Australia (320 + 274)	Mumbai[2]	1964-65
Australia (394 + 8-342)	v	India (402 + 9d-330)	Perth	1977-78
West Indies (308+ 8-209)	v	England (263 + 252)	Nottingham	1980
New Zealand (220 + 8-278)	v	Pakistan (274 + 223)	Dunedin	1984-85
West Indies (306 + 8-268)	v	Pakistan (309 + 262)	Bridgetown	1987-88
Pakistan (293 + 8-141)	v	England (255 + 175)	Lord's	1992

§ England won by a leg bye off the last possible ball

RESULTS BY NARROW MARGINS - LESS THAN TWENTY RUNS

1	West Indies (252 + 146)	v	Australia (213 + 184)	Adelaide	1992-93
3	Australia (299 + 86)	v	England (262 + 120)	Manchester	1902
3	England (284 + 294)	v	Australia (287 + 288)	Melbourne	1982-83
5	South Africa (169 + 239)	v	Australia (292 + 111)	Sydney	1993-94
6	Australia (182 + 165)	v	England (133 + 207)	Sydney	1884-85
7	Australia (63 + 122)	v	England (101 + 77)	The Oval	1882
10	England (325 + 437)	v	Australia (586 + 166)	Sydney	1894-95
11	Australia (489 + 250)	v	England (365 + 363)	Adelaide	1924-25
12	England (334 + 383)	v	Australia (369 + 336)	Adelaide	1928-29
13	England (115 + 184)	v	Australia (119 + 97)	Sydney	1886-87
16	Australia (166 + 327)	v	India (153 + 324)	Brisbane[2]	1977-78
16	Pakistan (116 + 249)	v	India (145 + 204)	Bangalore	1986-87
16	Australia (256 + 471)	v	Sri Lanka (8d-547 + 164)	Colombo (SSC)	1992-93
17	South Africa (340 + 142)	v	England (251 + 214)	Johannesburg[3]	1956-57
18	England (174 + 356)	v	Australia (9d-401 + 111)	Leeds	1981
19	South Africa (208 + 345)	v	England (310 + 224)	Johannesburg[1]	1909-10

At Port-of-Spain in 1934-35, West Indies took England's last second innings wicket with the fifth ball of the last possible over to win by 217 runs.

DRAWS

	Target	Total	Opponents		
India	361	355-8	West Indies	Mumbai[2]	1948-49
England	234	228-9	West Indies	Lord's	1963
Australia	360	339-9	West Indies	Adelaide	1968-69
Australia	246	238-8	England	Melbourne	1974-75
India	438	429-8	England	The Oval	1979
Australia	247	230-9	New Zealand	Melbourne	1987-88
Pakistan	372	341-9	West Indies	Port-of-Spain	1987-88

LOWEST MATCH AGGREGATES *(Completed match)*

Runs	Wkts						Days Played
234	29	Australia	v	South Africa	Melbourne	1931-32	§3
291	40	England	v	Australia	Lord's	1888	2
295	28	New Zealand	v	Australia	Wellington	1945-46	2
309	29	West Indies	v	England	Bridgetown	1934-35	3
323	30	England	v	Australia	Manchester	1888	2
363	40	England	v	Australia	The Oval	1882	2
374	40	Australia	v	England	Sydney	1887-88	†5
378	30	England	v	South Africa	The Oval	1912	2
382	30	South Africa	v	England	Cape Town	1888-89	2
389	38	England	v	Australia	The Oval	1890	2
390	30	England	v	New Zealand	Lord's	1958	3
392	40	England	v	Australia	The Oval	1896	3

§ No play on one day. † No play on two days.

GREATEST TEST VICTORIES BY AN INNINGS

Inns and 579 runs	England	v	Australia	The Oval	1938
Inns and 336 runs	West Indies	v	India	Calcutta	1958-59
Inns and 332 runs	Australia	v	England	Brisbane[2]	1946-47
Inns and 322 runs	West Indies	v	New Zealand	Wellington	1994-95
Inns and 285 runs	England	v	India	Lord's	1974
Inns and 259 runs	Australia	v	South Africa	Port Elizabeth	1949-50
Inns and 237 runs	England	v	West Indies	The Oval	1957
Inns and 230 runs	England	v	Australia	Adelaide	1891-92
Inns and 226 runs	Australia	v	India	Brisbane[2]	1947-48
Inns and 226 runs	West Indies	v	England	Lord's	1973
Inns and 225 runs	England	v	Australia	Melbourne	1911-12
Inns and 222 runs	Australia	v	New Zealand	Hobart	1993-94
Inns and 217 runs	England	v	Australia	The Oval	1886
Inns and 217 runs	Australia	v	West Indies	Brisbane[1]	1930-31
Inns and 215 runs	England	v	New Zealand	Auckland	1962-63
Inns and 208 runs	South Africa	v	Sri Lanka	Colombo (SSC)	1993-94
Inns and 207 runs	England	v	India	Manchester	1952
Inns and 202 runs	England	v	South Africa	Cape Town	1888-89
Inns and 200 runs	Australia	v	England	Melbourne	1936-37

GREATEST TEST VICTORIES BY A RUN MARGIN

675 runs	England	v	Australia	Brisbane[1]	1928-29
562 runs	Australia	v	England	The Oval	1934
530 runs	Australia	v	South Africa	Melbourne	1910-11
425 runs	West Indies	v	England	Manchester	1976
409 runs	Australia	v	England	Lord's	1948
408 runs	West Indies	v	Australia	Adelaide	1979-80
382 runs	Australia	v	England	Adelaide	1894-95
382 runs	Australia	v	West Indies	Sydney	1968-69
377 runs	Australia	v	England	Sydney	1920-21
365 runs	Australia	v	England	Melbourne	1936-37
356 runs	South Africa	v	England	Lord's	1994
348 runs	Australia	v	Pakistan	Melbourne	1976-77
343 runs	West Indies	v	Australia	Bridgetown	1990-91
338 runs	England	v	Australia	Adelaide	1932-33
329 runs	Australia	v	England	Perth	1994-95
326 runs	West Indies	v	England	Lord's	1950
324 runs	South Africa	v	Pakistan	Johannesburg[3]	1994-95
323 runs	South Africa	v	Australia	Port Elizabeth	1969-70
322 runs	England	v	Australia	Brisbane[2]	1936-37
312 runs	England	v	South Africa	Cape Town	1956-57
308 runs	Australia	v	England	Melbourne	1907-08
307 runs	Australia	v	England	Sydney	1924-25
307 runs	South Africa	v	Australia	Johannesburg[3]	1969-70
301 runs	Pakistan	v	Sri Lanka	Colombo (PSS)	1994-95
300 runs	Australia	v	India	Perth	1991-92

VICTORY LOSING FEWEST WICKETS

TWO WICKETS

England (2d-531)	v	South Africa (273 + 240)	Lord's	1924
England (2d-267)	v	New Zealand (67 + 129)	Leeds	1958
England (2d-459)	v	India (165 + 216)	Birmingham	1974

VICTORY AFTER FOLLOWING-ON

England (325 + 437)	beat	Australia (586 +166) by 10 runs	Sydney	1894-95
England (174 + 356)	beat	Australia (9d-401 + 111) by 12 runs	Leeds	1981

LONGEST MATCHES

10 days	South Africa	v	England	Durban[2]	1938-39
9 days	West Indies	v	England	Kingston	1929-30
8 days	Australia	v	England	Melbourne	1928-29

MATCHES COMPLETED IN TWO DAYS

England	(101 + 77)	v	Australia	(63 + 122)	The Oval	1882
England	(53 + 62)	v	Australia	(116 + 60)	Lord's	1888
England	(317)	v	Australia	(80 + 100)	The Oval	1888
England	(172)	v	Australia	(81 + 70)	Manchester	1888
South Africa	(84 + 129)	v	England	(148 + 2-67)	Port Elizabeth	1888-89
South Africa	(47 + 43)	v	England	(292)	Cape Town	1888-89
England	(100 + 8-95)	v	Australia	(92 + 102)	The Oval	1890
South Africa	(93 + 30)	v	England	(185 + 226)	Port Elizabeth	1895-96
South Africa	(115 + 117)	v	England	(265)	Cape Town	1895-96
England	(176 + 0-14)	v	South Africa	(95 + 93)	The Oval	1912
Australia	(448)	v	South Africa	(265 + 95)	Manchester	1912
England	(112 + 147)	v	Australia	(232 + 0-30)	Nottingham	1921
Australia	(8d-328)	v	West Indies	(99 + 107)	Melbourne	1930-31
South Africa	(157 + 98)	v	Australia	(439)	Johannesburg[1]	1935-36
New Zealand	(42 + 54)	v	Australia	(8d-199)	Wellington	1945-46

COMPLETE SIDE DISMISSED TWICE IN A DAY

					Day	
India	(58 + 82)	v	England	Manchester	3rd	1952

BATSMEN'S PARADISE (Over 60 runs per wicket)

Runs per Wkt	Runs-Wkts					
109.30	(1093-10)	India	v	New Zealand	Delhi	1955-56
99.40	(994-10)	West Indies	v	New Zealand	Georgetown	1971-72
86.87	(695-8)	New Zealand	v	England	Wellington	1987-88
83.25	(999-12)	Pakistan	v	Australia	Faisalabad	1979-80
82.27	(905-11)	England	v	Pakistan	Birmingham	1992
81.93	(1229-15)	West Indies	v	England	St John's	1993-94
80.53	(1208-15)	Pakistan	v	India	Lahore[2]	1989-90
79.53	(1034-13)	Pakistan	v	Sri Lanka	Faisalabad	1985-86
78.25	(1252-16)	India	v	West Indies	Calcutta	1987-88
73.37	(1174-16)	Pakistan	v	India	Faisalabad	1984-85
73.06	(1096-15)	India	v	West Indies	Kanpur	1978-79
70.61	(1271-18)	England	v	Australia	Manchester	1964
68.33	(1640-24)	West Indies	v	Australia	Bridgetown	1964-65
66.95	(1406-21)	West Indies	v	Pakistan	Kingston	1957-58
65.35	(1307-20)	England	v	Australia	Manchester	1934
65.00	(1235-19)	India	v	West Indies	Mumbai[2]	1948-49
64.75	(1036-16)	India	v	New Zealand	Hyderabad	1955-56
64.52	(1226-19)	Australia	v	West Indies	Sydney	1992-93
64.47	(1096-17)	India	v	Sri Lanka	Kanpur	1986-87
63.66	(1528-24)	West Indies	v	England	Port-of-Spain	1953-54
63.41	(1078-17)	India	v	Australia	Mumbai[3]	1986-87
62.33	(1496-24)	England	v	Australia	Nottingham	1938
62.22	(1369-22)	England	v	West Indies	The Oval	1995
62.11	(1118-18)	New Zealand	v	Pakistan	Auckland	1988-89
62.00	(1116-18)	West Indies	v	England	Bridgetown	1959-60
61.86	(1423-23)	England	v	India	The Oval	1990
61.52	(1042-17)	India	v	Pakistan	Chennai[2]	1960-61
60.94	(1158-12)	India	v	England	Kanpur	1984-85
60.62	(1455-24)	New Zealand	v	Australia	Wellington	1973-74

60.57	(1272-21)	Pakistan	v	India	Faisalabad	1978-79
60.45	(1209-20)	Australia	v	England	Adelaide	1986-87
60.20	(1505-25)	New Zealand	v	India	Auckland	1989-90

HIGHEST SCORES FOR EACH BATTING POSITION

No							
1	364	L.Hutton	England	v	Australia	The Oval	1938
2	325	A.Sandham	England	v	West Indies	Kingston	1929-30
3	375	B.C.Lara	West Indies	v	England	St John's	1993-94
4	307	R.M.Cowper	Australia	v	England	Melbourne	1965-66
5	304	D.G.Bradman	Australia	v	England	Leeds	1934
6	250	K.D.Walters	Australia	v	New Zealand	Christchurch	1976-77
7	270	D.G.Bradman	Australia	v	England	Melbourne	1936-37
8	209	Imtiaz Ahmed	Pakistan	v	New Zealand	Lahore[1]	1955-56
9	173	I.D.S.Smith	New Zealand	v	India	Auckland	1989-90
10	117	W.W.Read	England	v	Australia	The Oval	1884
11	68*	R.O.Collinge	New Zealand	v	Pakistan	Auckland	1972-73

HIGHEST SCORE AT THE FALL OF EACH WICKET

1st	413	India (3d-537)	v	New Zealand	Chennai[2]	1955-56
2nd	533	West Indies (3d-790)	v	Pakistan	Kingston	1957-58
3rd	615	New Zealand (4-671)	v	Sri Lanka	Wellington	1990-91
4th	671	New Zealand (4-671)	v	Sri Lanka	Wellington	1990-91
5th	720	England (849)	v	West Indies	Kingston	1929-30
6th	770	England (7d-903)	v	Australia	The Oval	1938
7th	876	England (7d-903)	v	Australia	The Oval	1938
8th	813	England (849)	v	West Indies	Kingston	1929-30
9th	821	England (849)	v	West Indies	Kingston	1929-30
10th	849	England (849)	v	West Indies	Kingston	1929-30

LOWEST SCORE AT THE FALL OF EACH WICKET

1st	0	Numerous instances				
2nd	0	Numerous instances				
3rd	0	{Australia(7d-32)	v	England	Brisbane[2]	1950-51
		{India (165)	v	England	Leeds	1952
4th	0	India (165)	v	England	Leeds	1952
5th	6	India (98)	v	England	The Oval	1952
6th	7	Australia (70)	v	England	Manchester	1888
7th	14	Australia (44)	v	England	The Oval	1896
8th	19	Australia (44)	v	England	The Oval	1896
9th	25	Australia (44)	v	England	The Oval	1896
10th	26	New Zealand (26)	v	England	Auckland	1954-55

MOST CENTURIES IN AN INNINGS

5	Australia (8d-758)	v	West Indies	Kingston	1954-55
4	England (8d-658)	v	Australia	Nottingham	1938
4	West Indies (631)	v	India	Delhi	1948-49
4	Pakistan (652)	v	India	Faisalabad	1982-83
4	West Indies (550)	v	India	St John's	1982-83

The most fifties in a Test innings is seven by England (9d-627) v Australia at Manchester in 1934.

MOST CENTURIES IN A MATCH (BOTH TEAMS)

7	England (4)	v	Australia (3)	Nottingham	1938
7	West Indies (2)	v	Australia (5)	Kingston	1954-55

The most fifties in a Test match is 17 by Australia (10) and West Indies (7) at Adelaide in 1968-69.

Australian captain Mark Taylor made his highest Test innings score of 219 at Trent Bridge in 1989. This formed part of a record opening partnership of 329 in matches against England. Taylor's partner was former Australian vice-captain Geoff Marsh.

Sashin Tendulkar (India) on his way to scoring 148 not out in the third Test against Australia in Sydney, January 1992. At 18 years and 256 days, Tendulkar became the youngest player ever to score a Test century in Australia.

MOST CENTURIES IN A SERIES (ONE TEAM)

				Venue		Tests
12	Australia	v	West Indies	West Indies	1954-55	5
12	Pakistan	v	India	Pakistan	1982-83	6
11	England	v	South Africa	South Africa	1938-39	5
11	West Indies	v	India	India	1948-49	5
11	Australia	v	South Africa	South Africa	1949-50	5
11	India	v	West Indies	India	1978-79	6

MOST CENTURIES IN A SERIES (BOTH TEAMS)

				Venue		Tests
21	West Indies (9)	v	Australia (12)	West Indies	1954-55	5
17	Australia (9)	v	England (8)	Australia	1928-29	5
17	South Africa (6)	v	England (11)	South Africa	1938-39	5
17	Pakistan (12)	v	India (5)	Pakistan	1982-83	6
16	India (5)	v	West Indies (11)	India	1948-49	5
16	Australia (10)	v	West Indies (6)	Australia	1968-69	5
16	Australia (10)	v	West Indies (6)	Australia	1975-76	6
15	Australia (10)	v	England (5)	Australia	1946-47	5
15	England (9)	v	India (6)	England	1990	3

TEAM UNCHANGED THROUGHOUT A SERIES

			Venue		Tests
England	v	Australia	Australia	1884-85	5
South Africa	v	England	South Africa	1905-06	5
West Indies	v	Australia	West Indies	1990-91	5
England	v	Australia	Australia	1881-82	4
Australia	v	England	England	1884	3
Australia	v	England	England	1893	3
Pakistan	v	New Zealand	Pakistan	1964-65	3
India	v	England	England	1971	3
Australia	v	New Zealand	New Zealand	1981-82	3
India	v	England	India	1992-93	3
India	v	Sri Lanka	India	1993-94	3
South Africa	v	Australia	South Africa	1993-94	3
Australia	v	West Indies	West Indies	1994-95	4
Australia	v	Pakistan	Australia	1995-96	3

MOST PLAYERS ENGAGED BY ONE SIDE IN A SERIES

				Venue	
30 in 5 Tests	England	v	Australia	England	1921
29 in 6 Tests	England	v	Australia	England	1989
28 in 5 Tests	Australia	v	England	Australia	1884-85
27 in 4 Tests	West Indies	v	England	West Indies	1929-30
26 in 5 Tests	India	v	Pakistan	India	1952-53
25 in 4 Tests	England	v	West Indies	England	1950
25 in 5 Tests	England	v	Australia	England	1909
25 in 5 Tests	England	v	South Africa	England	1935
25 in 5 Tests	England	v	South Africa	England	1955

South Africa used 20 players in the 3-match rubber of 1895-96 against England in South Africa.

WINNING EVERY TEST IN A SERIES (Minimum: 4 matches)

			Venue		Tests
Australia	v	England	Australia	1920-21	5
Australia	v	South Africa	Australia	1931-32	5
England	v	India	England	1959	5
West Indies	v	India	West Indies	1961-62	5
Australia	v	India	Australia	1967-68	4
South Africa	v	Australia	South Africa	1969-70	4
West Indies	v	England	England	1984	5
West Indies	v	England	West Indies	1985-86	5

The following countries won 6-match series in Australia by 5 Tests to one: Australia (v West Indies 1975-76) England (v Australia 1978-79).

MOST CONSECUTIVE WINS

11	West Indies	Bridgetown	1983-84	to	Adelaide	1984-85
8	Australia	Sydney	1920-21	to	Leeds	1921
7	England	Melbourne	1884-85	to	Sydney	1887-88
7	England	Lord's	1928	to	Adelaide	1928-29
7	West Indies	Bridgetown	1984-85	to	St John's	1985-86
7	West Indies	Lord's	1988	to	Melbourne	1988-89
6	England	The Oval	1888	to	The Oval	1890
6	England	Leeds	1957	to	Manchester	1958
6	West Indies	Port-of-Spain	1961-62	to	Manchester	1963

MOST CONSECUTIVE MATCHES WITHOUT DEFEAT

27	West Indies	Sydney	1981-82	to	Melbourne	1984-85
26	England	Lord's	1968	to	Manchester	1971
25	Australia	Wellington	1945-46	to	Adelaide	1950-51
18	England	Christchurch	1958-59	to	Birmingham	1961
17	Australia	Chennai[2]	1956-57	to	Delhi	1959-60
17	India	Kandy	1985-86	to	Ahmedabad	1986-87
16	Australia	Sydney	1920-21	to	Adelaide	1924-25
16	Pakistan	Karachi[1]	1986-87	to	Port-of-Spain	1987-88
15	England	Melbourne	1911-12	to	Port Elizabeth	1913-14
15	Pakistan	Wellington	1972-73	to	Adelaide	1976-77
15	India	Lord's	1979	to	Calcutta	1979-80
15	West Indies	Christchurch	1979-80	to	Kingston	1980-81
14	Australia	Sydney	1988-89	to	Sydney	1989-90
13	India	Port-of-Spain	1952-53	to	Chennai[2]	1955-56
13	Australia	The Oval	1972	to	Wellington	1973-74
12	England	The Oval	1938	to	The Oval	1946
12	Pakistan	Manchester	1954	to	Bridgetown	1957-58
12	England	The Oval	1966	to	Georgetown	1967-68
12	Pakistan	Karachi[1]	1982-83	to	Nagpur	1983-84

MOST CONSECUTIVE DEFEATS

8 †	South Africa	Port Elizabeth	1888-89	to	Cape Town	1898-99
8	England	Sydney	1920-21	to	Leeds	1921
7	Australia	Melbourne	1884-85	to	Sydney	1887-88
7	England	Lord's	1950	to	Adelaide	1950-51
7	India	Leeds	1967	to	Sydney	1967-68
7	England	Kingston	1985-86	to	Leeds	1986
7	England	The Oval	1992	to	Lord's	1993
6	South Africa	Melbourne	1910-11	to	Lord's	1912
6	New Zealand	Johannesburg[2]	1953-54	to	Lahore[1]	1955-56
6	India	Nottingham	1959	to	Delhi	1959-60
6	Australia	Bridgetown	1983-84	to	Adelaide	1984-85

† *South Africa's first 8 Tests*

MOST CONSECUTIVE MATCHES WITHOUT VICTORY

44 †	New Zealand	Christchurch	1929-30	to	Wellington	1955-56
31	India	Bangalore	1981-82	to	Faisalabad	1984-85
28	South Africa	Leeds	1935	to	Port Elizabeth	1949-50
24	India	Lord's	1932	to	Kanpur	1951-52
23	New Zealand	Auckland	1962-63	to	Dunedin	1967-68
22	Pakistan	Lahore[1]	1958-59	to	Christchurch	1964-65
21	Sri Lanka	Colombo (PSS)	1985-86	to	Moratuwa	1992-93
20	West Indies	Wellington	1968-69	to	Port-of-Spain	1972-73
18	New Zealand	Dacca	1969-70	to	Wellington	1973-74
18	England	Sydney	1986-87	to	The Oval	1988

16	South Africa	Melbourne	1910-11	to	Cape Town	1921-22
16	Pakistan	Lord's	1967	to	Wellington	1972-73
14	India	Chennai[2]	1956-57	to	Delhi	1959-60
14	Australia	Perth	1985-86	to	Melbourne	1986-87
14	India	Georgetown	1988-89	to	The Oval	1990
14	New Zealand	Durban[2]	1994-95	to	St John's	1995-96
13	India	Chennai[1]	1952-53	to	Hyderabad	1955-56
13	England	Wellington	1983-84	to	Mumbai[3]	1984-85
13	Sri Lanka	Colombo (PSS)	1981-82	to	Colombo (SSC)	1985-86
13	New Zealand	Nottingham	1990	to	Bulawayo[1]	1992-93
13	Sri Lanka	Kandy	1993-94	to	Harare	1994-95
12	South Africa	Cape Town	1922-23	to	Durban[2]	1927-28
12	England	Leeds	1963	to	The Oval	1964
12	England	Nottingham	1980	to	Lord's	1981

† *New Zealand's first 44 Tests.*

MOST CONSECUTIVE DRAWS

10	West Indies	Georgetown	1970-71	to	Bridgetown	1972-73
9	India	Port-of-Spain	1952-53	to	Hyderabad	1955-56
9	India	Calcutta	1959-60	to	Delhi	1961-62

DRAWING EVERY TEST IN A FIVE-MATCH SERIES

Pakistan	v	India	1954-55
Indiav	Pakistan	1960-61	
Indiav	England	1963-64	
West Indies	v	New Zealand	1971-72

ELEVEN BATSMEN REACHING DOUBLE FIGURES IN AN INNINGS

				Venue	Lowest Score
1894-95	England (475)	v	Australia	Melbourne	11
1905-06	South Africa (385)	v	England	Johannesburg[2]	10
1928-29	England (636)	v	Australia	Sydney	11
1931-32	South Africa (358)	v	Australia	Melbourne	10*
1947-48	Australia (8d-575)	v	India	Melbourne	11
1952-53	India (397)	v	Pakistan	Calcutta	11
1967-68	India (359)	v	New Zealand	Dunedin	12
1976-77	India (9d-524)	v	New Zealand	Kanpur	10*
1992-93	Australia (471)	v	Sri Lanka	Colombo (SSC)	10*

NO BATSMAN REACHING DOUBLE FIGURES IN A COMPLETED INNINGS

South Africa (30 - highest score 7)	v	England	Birmingham	1924

ONLY FOUR BOWLERS IN AN INNINGS OF OVER 400 RUNS

Australia	v	England (8d-403)	The Oval	1921
South Africa	v	England (8-421)	The Oval	1924
New Zealand	v	England (482)	The Oval	1949
England	v	Australia (426)	Sydney	1950-51
India	v	England (9d-419)	Lord's	1979
India	v	Australia (528)	Adelaide	1980-81
Australia	v	England (404)	Manchester	1981
England	v	India (428)	Bangalore	1981-82
Sri Lanka	v	Pakistan (7d-500)	Lahore[2]	1981-82
Pakistan	v	Australia (6d-454)	Sydney	1983-84
Australia	v	West Indies (8d-468)	Port-of-Spain	1983-84
Australia	v	West Indies (498)	St John's	1983-84
Australia	v	West Indies (416)	Perth	1984-85
Australia	v	England (456)	Nottingham	1985

Pakistan	v	England (447)	Manchester	1987
New Zealand	v	India (482)	Auckland	1989-90
England	v	West Indies (446)	Bridgetown	1989-90
England	v	West Indies (446)	St John's	1989-90
England	v	Australia (408)	Birmingham	1993
Pakistan	v	Australia (455)	Lahore[2]	1994-95

ELEVEN BOWLERS IN AN INNINGS

England	v	Australia (551)	The Oval	1884
Australia	v	Pakistan (2-382)	Faisalabad	1979-80

TWENTY BOWLERS IN A MATCH

South Africa (7d-501 + 346)	v	England (442 + 0-15)	Cape Town	1964-65

MOST RUNS IN ONE DAY - BY ONE TEAM

						Day
503-2	England (0-28 to 2d-531)	v	South Africa	Lord's	1924	2nd
494-6	Australia (6-496)	v	South Africa	Sydney	1910-11	1st
475-2	Australia (2-475)	v	England	The Oval	1934	1st
471-8	England (8d-471)	v	India	The Oval	1936	1st
458-3	Australia (3-458)	v	England	Leeds	1930	1st
455-1	Australia (3-93 to 4-494)	v	England	Leeds	1934	2nd
451-10	South Africa (451)	v	New Zealand	Christchurch	1931-32	2nd
450-10	Australia (450)	v	South Africa	Johannesburg[1]	1921-22	1st

MOST RUNS IN ONE DAY - BY BOTH TEAMS

						Day
588-6	England (2-173 to 8d-571)	v	India (0-190)	Manchester	1936	2nd
522-2	England (0-28 to 2d-531)	v	South Africa (0-19)	Lord's	1924	2nd
508-8	England (4-313- to 6d-534)	v	South Africa (6-287)	The Oval	1935	3rd
496-4	England (2-121 to 6d-558)	v	Pakistan (0-59)	Nottingham	1952	2nd
492-8	South Africa (6-297 to 476)	v	England (4-313)	The Oval	1935	2nd
491-7	New Zealand (9-312 to 341 + 2-195)	v	England (4d-267)	Leeds	1949	3rd
473-4	South Africa (5-283 to 8d-492)	v	England (1-264)	The Oval	1929	3rd
471-9	Australia (3-162 to 389)	v	England (2-244)	The Oval	1921	3rd
469-7	West Indies (6-395 to 498)	v	England (3d-366)	The Oval	1939	3rd
464-11	Australia (448)	v	South Africa (1-16)	Manchester	1912	1st
458-12	Australia (3-239 to 8d-394)	v	West Indies (7-303)	Sydney	1968-69	5th

FEWEST RUNS IN A FULL DAY'S PLAY

						Day
95-12	Australia (80 all out)	v	Pakistan (2-15)	Karachi[1]	1956-57	1st
104-5	Pakistan (5-104)	v	Australia	Karachi[1]	1959-60	4th
106-8	England (2-92 to 198 all out)	v	Australia	Brisbane[2]	1958-59	4th
112-5	Australia (6-138 to 187 all out)	v	Pakistan (1-63)	Karachi[1]	1956-57	4th
115-18	Australia (7-116 to 165 all out + 5-66)	v	Pakistan	Karachi[1]	1988-89	4th
117-5	India (5-117)	v	Australia	Chennai[2]	1956-57	1st
117-4	New Zealand (0-6 to 1-123)	v	Sri Lanka	Colombo (SSC)	1983-84	5th
122-8	England (9-110 to 110)	v	South Africa (7-122)	Port Elizabeth	1956-57	3rd
122-6	Australia (6-156 to 186)	v	England (2-92)	Brisbane[1]	1958-59	3rd
122-15	Australia (6-282 to 306 + 1-9)	v	England (87)	Melbourne	1958-59	4th
122-14	Australia (4-243 to 258)	v	England (8-107)	Melbourne	1978-79	2nd
123-9	England (2-123 to 191)	v	Pakistan (1-55)	Hyderabad	1977-78	3rd
124-7	Pakistan (4-74 to 134)	v	Australia (1-64)	Dacca	1959-60	4th
124-6	India (6-226 to 291)	v	Australia (2-59)	Kanpur	1959-60	4th
127-8	India (3-162 to 245)	v	Pakistan (1-44)	Peshawar[1]	1954-55	3rd
127-8	West Indies (2-291 to 353)	v	England (0-65)	Kingston	1959-60	4th
128-7	England (2-53 to 9-181)	v	West Indies	Bridgetown	1953-54	3rd
129-6	Pakistan (6-129)	v	India	Peshawar[1]	1954-55	1st
129-11	India (1-46 to 149 + 2-26)	v	Australia	Chennai[2]	1959-60	3rd

130-14	South Africa (7-200 to 243)	v	New Zealand (78 + 1-8)	Johannesburg[2]	1953-54	2nd
130-6	India (5-115 to 148)	v	Pakistan (1 07)	Dacca	1954-55	3rd
130-8	West Indies (7-349 to 386)	v	New Zealand (5-93)	Christchurch	1955-56	2nd
130-4	Pakistan (4-130)	v	India	Ahmedabad	1986-87	1st
134-9	England (1-333 to 439)	v	Pakistan (0-28)	Dacca	1961-62	4th
136-14	South Africa (5-138 to 164)	v	England (9-110)	Port Elizabeth	1956-57	2nd
136-6	New Zealand (0-9 to 6-145)	v	India	Bangalore	1988-89	3rd
138-6	Australia (6-138)	v	Pakistan	Karachi[1]	1956-57	3rd
[illegible]	South Africa (5-130)	v	England	Port Elizabeth	1956-57	1st
140-5	New Zealand (1-8 to 6-148)	v	South Africa	Johannesburg[2]	1953-54	3rd

MOST WICKETS IN ONE DAY

						Day
27-157	England (3-18 to 53 + 62)	v	Australia (60)	Lord's	1888	2nd
25-221	Australia (112 + 5-48)	v	England (61)	Melbourne	1901-02	1st
24-255	England (1-69 to 145 + 5-60)	v	Australia (61)	The Oval	1896	2nd
22-197	Australia (92 + 2-5)	v	England (100)	The Oval	1890	1st
22-207	Australia (82 + 2-0)	v	West Indies (105)	Adelaide	1951-52	1st
22-195	England (7-292 to 9d-347)	v	India (58 + 82)	Manchester	1952	3rd
21-278	England (185 + 1-0)	v	South Africa (93)	Port Elizabeth	1895-96	1st

MOST WICKETS BEFORE LUNCH

						Day
18	Australia (2-32 to 81 + 70)	v	England	Manchester	1888	2nd

NO WICKETS IN A FULL DAY'S PLAY

				Day	
England (0-283)	v	Australia	Melbourne	3rd	1924-25
West Indies (6-187 to 6-494)	v	Australia	Bridgetown	4th	1954-55
India (0-234)	v	New Zealand	Chennai[2]	1st	1955-56
West Indies (1-147 to 1-504)	v	Pakistan	Kingston	3rd	1957-58
West Indies (3-279 to 3-486)	v	England §	Bridgetown	5th	1959-60
West Indies (2-81 to 2-291)	v	England	Kingston	3rd	1959-60
Australia (0-263)	v	West Indies	Bridgetown	1st	1964-65
West Indies (7-310 to 7d-365)	v	New Zealand (0-163)	Georgetown	3rd	1971-72
India (1-70 to 1d-361)	v	West Indies 0-15)	Calcutta	4th	1978-79
India (2-178 to 395-2)	v	England	Chennai[2]	2nd	1981-82
Sri Lanka (3-83 to 3-323)	v	Pakistan	Colombo (PSS)	5th	1985-86
Australia (0-301)	v	England	Nottingham	1st	1989

§ G.S.Sobers (226) and F.M.M.Worrell (197) added 399 for the fourth wicket in the longest partnership in Test cricket (579 minutes) and remain the only pair of batsmen to bat throughout two consecutive days of Test cricket, although the final hour of the fourth day was lost to rain and a rest day intervened.*

The following pairs of batsmen have batted throughout one full day's play in the above matches: J.B.Hobbs and H.Sutcliffe (1924-25), D.S.Atkinson and C.C.Depeiza (1954-55), M.H.Mankad and Pankaj Roy (1955-56), C.C.Hunte and G.S.Sobers (1957-58) W.M.Lawry and R.B.Simpson (1964-65), G.R.Viswanath and Yashpal Sharma (1981-82), A.P.Gurusinha and A.Ranatunga (1985-86), and G.R.Marsh and M.A.Taylor (1989).

E XTRAS TOP SCORING IN A COMPLETED INNINGS

	Total	HS	Extras	Opponents		
South Africa	58	13	17	England	Lord's	1912
South Africa	30	7	11	England	Birmingham	1924
New Zealand	97	19	20	England	Nottingham	1973
England	126	24	25	West Indies	Manchester	1976
England	227	33	46	Pakistan	Lord's	1982
Australia	200	29	36	West Indies	St John's	1983-84
England	315	47	59	West Indies	Port-of-Spain	1985-86
New Zealand	160	33	38	Pakistan	Lahore[2]	1990-91
Australia	248	47	53	West Indies	Georgetown	1990-91
New Zealand	93	22	19	Pakistan	Hamilton	1992-93
(Zimbabwe	8-319	58	65	Sri Lanka	Harare	1994-95)

50 OR MORE EXTRAS IN AN INNINGS

71 (B 21, LB 8, NB 38, W 4)	Pakistan (435)	v	West Indies	Georgetown	1987-88
68 (B 29, LB 11, NB 28)	Pakistan (291)	v	West Indies	Bridgetown	1976-77
65 (B 10, LB 18, NB 36, W 1)	Zimbabwe (8-319)	v	Sri Lanka	Harare	1994-95
64 (B 12, LB 25, NB 27)	India (565)	v	West Indies	Calcutta	1987-88
64 (B 4, LB 18, NB 36, W 6)	South Africa (460)	v	Pakistan	Johannesburg[3]	1994-95
64 (B 18, LB 11, NB 34, W 1)	England (437)	v	West Indies	Manchester	1995
61 (B 17, LB 17, NB 25, W 2)	Pakistan (9-341)	v	West Indies	Port-of-Spain	1987-88
61 (B 6, LB 23, NB 29, W 3)	Australia (6d-602)	v	England	Nottingham	1989
60 (B 4, LB 27, NB 18, W 11)	England (5d-633)	v	India	Birmingham	1979
59 (B 20, LB 11, NB 27, W 1)	England (315)	v	West Indies	Port-of-Spain	1985-86
58 (LB 18, NB 40)	Australia (515)	v	West Indies	Adelaide	1988-89
58 (LB 23, NB 34, W 1)	Australia (471)	v	Sri Lanka	Colombo (SSC)	1992-93
57 (B 31, LB 16, NB 10)	New Zealand (387)	v	England	Auckland	1929-30
57 (B 7, LB 21, NB 19, W 10)	England (370)	v	West Indies	The Oval	1980
57 (B 16, LB 14, NB 26, W 1)	India (463)	v	West Indies	Mumbai[3]	1983-84
55 (B 6, LB 11, NB 32, W 6)	Australia (345)	v	England	Lord's	1981
55 (B 2, LB 16, NB 22, W 15)	India (288)	v	Pakistan	Faisalabad	1989-90
55 (B 16, LB 22, NB 12, W 5)	England (4-477)	v	India	The Oval	1990
55 (B 11, LB25,, NB 9, W 10)	India (429)	v	England	Lord's	1996
54 (B 7, LB 13, NB 34)	India (8d-566)	v	West Indies	Delhi	1978-79
54 (B 8, LB 10, NB 35, W 1)	England (419)	v	West Indies	The Oval	1991
53 (B 20, LB 8, NB 21, W 4)	India (487)	v	England	Delhi	1981-82
53 (B 6, LB 17, NB 28, W 2)	West Indies (606)	v	England	Birmingham	1984
53 (B 17, LB 6, NB 28, W 2)	Australia (248)	v	West Indies	Georgetown	1990-91
53 (B 8, LB 8, NB 35, W 2)	England (390)	v	Pakistan	Manchester	1992
52 (B 12, LB 7, NB 33)	New Zealand (468)	v	Pakistan	Karachi[1]	1976-77
52 (B 19, LB 13, NB 10, W 10)	England (252)	v	West Indies	Nottingham	1980
52 (B 8, LB 8, NB 35, W 1)	England (309)	v	Australia	Brsbane[2]	1982-83
52 (B 1, LB 24, NB 16, W 11)	England (521)	v	Pakistan	Birmingham	1987
52 (B 4, LB 23, NB 21, W 4)	Australia (371)	v	West Indies	Kingston	1990-91
52 (B 9, LB 20, NB 23)	England (593)	v	West Indies	Port-of-Spain	1993-94
51 (B 10, LB 20, NB 21)	India (7-469)	v	West Indies	Port-of-Spain	1982-83
51 (B 5, LB 6, NB 40)	England (310)	v	West Indies	St John's	1985-86
51 (B 14, LB 9, NB 25, W 3)	England (358)	v	West Indies	Bridgetown	1989-90
50 (B 37, LB 8, NB 4, W 1)	Australia (327)	v	England	The Oval	1934
50 (B 22, LB 19, NB 8, W 1)	England (7d-903)	v	Australia	The Oval	1938
50 (B 11, LB 8, NB 29, W 2)	India (6d-566)	v	Sri Lanka	Chennai[1]	1982-83
50 (B 13, LB 9, NB 28)	India (8d-393)	v	Pakistan	Karachi[1]	1982-83
50 (B 13, LB 11, NB 26)	England (464)	v	Australia	The Oval	1985
50 (B 8, LB 6, NB 36)	England (7d-394)	v	West Indies	Bridgetown	1993-94
50 (B 18, LB 18, NB 14)	England (564)	v	India	Nottingham	1996

25 OR MORE BYES IN AN INNINGS

37	Australia (327)	v	England	The Oval	1934
33	India (390)	v	England	Mumbai[2]	1961-62
33	West Indies (9d-391)	v	England	Kingston	1967-68
31	New Zealand (387)	v	England	Auckland	1929-30
29	Pakistan (291)	v	West Indies	Bridgetown	1976-77
28	India (372)	v	Pakistan	Delhi	1952-53

25 OR MORE LEG BYES IN AN INNINGS

30	West Indies (5d-411)	v	England	Manchester	1976
28	New Zealand (307)	v	Sri Lanka	Dunedin	1994-95
27	England (5d-633)	v	India	Birmingham	1979
27	England (336)	v	West Indies	Lord's	1995
26	England (8d-452)	v	Pakistan	Birmingham	1978

25	West Indies (509)	v	Australia	Bridgetown	1983-84
25	India (565)	v	West Indies	Calcutta	1987-88
25	India (429)	v	England	Lord's	1996

35 OR MORE NO BALLS IN AN INNINGS *(from which no runs were scored by batsmen)*

40	England (310)	v	West Indies	St John's	1985-86
40	Australia (515)	v	West Indies	Adelaide	1988-89
38	Pakistan (435)	v	West Indies	Georgetown	1987-88
37	Australia (234) (2nd innings)	v	West Indies	Perth	1988-89
36	England (7d-394)	v	West Indies	Bridgetown	1993-94
36	Zimbabwe (8-319)	v	Sri Lanka	Harare	1994-95
36	South Africa (460)	v	Pakistan	Johannesburg[3]	1994-95
35	West Indies (8d-596)	v	England	Bridgetown	1973-74
35	England (309)	v	Australia	Brisbane[2]	1982-83
35	Australia (8d-395) (1st innings)	v	West Indies	Perth	1988-89
35	New Zealand (4-671)	v	Sri Lanka	Wellington	1990-91
35	England (419)	v	West Indies	The Oval	1991
35	England (390)	v	Pakistan	Manchester	1992

10 OR MORE WIDES IN AN INNINGS

15	India (288)	v	Pakistan	Faisalabad	1989-90
15	England (260)	v	West Indies	St John's	1989-90
15	South Africa (7d-259)	v	Pakistan	Johannesburg[3]	1994-95
13	England (227)	v	Pakistan	Lord's	1982
12	India (6d-306)	v	West Indies	Kingston	1975-76
11	England (288)	v	Australia	Leeds	1975
11	England (5d-633)	v	India	Birmingham	1979
11	England (521)	v	Pakistan	Birmingham	1987
10	England (252)	v	West Indies	Nottingham	1980
10	England (370)	v	West Indies	The Oval	1980
10	India (371)	v	England	Calcutta	1992-93
10	India (366)	v	Sri Lanka	Colombo (SSC)	1993-94
10	India (429)	v	England	Lord's	1996

100 EXTRAS IN A MATCH

173 (B 37, LB 31, NB 103, W 2) West Indies	v	Pakistan	Bridgetown	1976-77
149 (B 25, LB 34, NB 90) Australia	v	West Indies	Perth	1988-89
140 (B 20, LB 48, NB 71, W 1) Australia	v	West Indies	Adelaide	1988-89
136 (B 28, LB 29, NB 75, W 4) West Indies	v	Australia	Georgetown	1990-91
129 (B 18, LB 35, NB 54, W 22) South Africa	v	Pakistan	Johannesburg[3]	1994-95
127 (B 22, LB 38, NB 62, W 5) West Indies	v	England	Bridgetown	1989-90
124 (B 21, LB 36, NB 63, W 4) West Indies	v	England	St John's	1985-86
122 (B 19, LB 33, NB 58, W 12) England	v	West Indies	Leeds	1976
122 (B 31, LB 39, NB 37, W 15) England	v	India	The Oval	1990
120 (B 4, LB 43, NB 68, W 5) Sri Lanka	v	Australia	Colombo (SSC)	1992-93
119 (B 25, LB 27, NB 66, W 1) West Indies	v	South Africa	Bridgetown	1991-92
117 (B 41, LB 43, NB 33) India	v	West Indies	Mumbai[3]	1994-95
117 (B 40, LB 36, NB 41) Pakistan	v	Sri Lanka	Sialkot	1995-96
114 (B 53, LB 30, NB 25, W 6) West Indies	v	Australia	Bridgetown	1964-65
114 (B 5, LB 36, NB 72, W 1) New Zealand	v	Sri Lanka	Auckland	1990-91
114 (B 25, LB 62, NB 26, W 1) England	v	Sri Lanka	Lord's	1991
113 (B 26, LB 32, NB 54, W1) Pakistan	v	West Indies	Lahore[2]	1990-91
112 (B 7, LB 39, NB 54, W 12) England	v	West Indies	The Oval	1980
112 (B 11, LB32, NB39, W30) Pakistan	v	India	Faisalabad	1989-90
112 (B 9, LB 22, NB81) West Indies	v	England	Bridgetown	1993-94
111 (B 10, LB 23, NB 68, W 10) Australia	v	West Indies	Brisbane[2]	1988-89
110 (B 27, LB 41, NB 27, W 15) England	v	West Indies	Nottingham	1980
110 (B 23, LB 36, NB 50, W 1) Pakistan	v	West Indies	Karachi[1]	1990-91

109 (B 16, LB 33, NB 59, W 1)	New Zealand	v	India	Christchurch	1967-68
109 (B 25, LB 49, NB 16, W 19)	England	v	Pakistan	Lord's	1982
108 (B 23, LB 25, NB 59, W 1)	India	v	Australia	Delhi	1979-80
108 (B 19, LB 24, NB 61, W 4)	Ebgland	v	West Indies	The Oval	1991
107 (B 36, LB 42, NB 29)	Australia	v	England	Melbourne	1970-71
107 (B 51, LB 38, NB 17, W 1)	West Indies	v	Australia	Port-of-Spain	1972-73
107 (B 10, LB 18, NB 79)	West Indies	v	England	Bridgetown	1973-74
106 (B 26, LB 39, NB 38, W 3)	Australia	v	England	Perth	1986-87
105 (B 26, LB 36, NB 42, W 1)	West Indies	v	England	Kingston	1973-74
105 (B 27, LB 39, NB 36, W 3)	Pakistan	v	India	Karachi[1]	1978-79
105 (B 47, LB 42, NB 12, W 4)	Pakistan	v	West Indies	Karachi[1]	1986-87
105 (B 27, LB 37, NB 39, W 2)	West Indies	v	Pakistan	Port-of-Spain	1987-88
105 (B 16, LB 34, NB 52, W 3)	South Africa	v	England	Johannesburg[3]	1995-96
104 (B 28, LB 32, NB 35, W 9)	England	v	West Indies	The Oval	1976
104 (B 30, LB 36, NB 38)	West Indies	v	New Zealand	Port-of-Spain	1984-85
104 (B 26, LB 25, NB 47, W 6)	Pakistan	v	New Zealand	Lahore[2]	1990-91
104 (B 25, LB 41, NB 28, W 10)	England	v	India	Lord's	1996
103 (B 20, LB 43, NB 32, W 8)	West Indies	v	New Zealand	Georgetown	1984-85
103 (B 22, LB 33, NB 42, W 6)	India	v	West Indies	Mohali	1994-95
103 (B 23, LB 23, NB 50, W 7)	England	v	West Indies	Manchester	1995
101 (B 12, LB 43, NB 32, W 14)	England	v	India	Birmingham	1979
101 (B 18, LB 39, NB 44)	India	v	West Indies	Calcutta	1987-88
100 (B 65, LB 22, NB 12, W 1)	West Indies	v	England	Kingston	1967-68
100 (B 15, LB 30, NB 42, W 13)	England	v	Australia	Leeds	1981
100 (B 27, LB 19, NB 50, W 4)	West Indies	v	Pakistan	Georgetown	1987-88
100 (B 19, LB 35, NB 40, W 6)	West Indies	v	Australia	Kingston	1990-91
100 (B 25, LB 31, NB 36, W 8)	England	v	India	Nottingham	1996

COMPLETED INNINGS WITHOUT EXTRAS

Total	Wicket-keeper					
328	N.S.Tamhane	India	v	Pakistan	Lahore[1]	1954-55
252	W.Farrimond	England	v	South Africa	Durban[2]	1930-31
247	J.M.Parks	England	v	South Africa	Nottingham	1960
236	G.MacGregor	England	v	Australia	Melbourne	1891-92
200	R.W.Marsh	Australia	v	Pakistan	Melbourne	1972-73
174	J.J.Kelly	Australia	v	England	Melbourne	1897-98
128	R.W.Marsh	Australia	v	West Indies	Sydney	1975-76
126	J.Hunter	England	v	Australia	Melbourne	1884-85
111	A.F.A.Lilley	England	v	Australia	Melbourne	1903-04
96	R.W.Taylor	England	v	India	Lord's	1979
94	T.G.Evans	England	v	New Zealand	Birmingham	1958
92	G.MacGregor	England	v	Australia	The Oval	1890
84	T.G.Evans	England	v	Australia	Manchester	1956
77	S.C.Guillen	New Zealand	v	West Indies	Auckland	1955-56
74	T.G.Evans	England	v	New Zealand	Lord's	1958
62	J.M.Blackham	Australia	v	England	Lord's	1888
42	A.P.E.Knott	England	v	India	Lord's	1974
30	H.R.Butt	England	v	South Africa	Port Elizabeth	1895-96
26	T.G.Evans	England	v	New Zealand	Auckland	1954-55

UNUSUAL DISMISSALS

Handled the ball

W.R.Endean (3)	South Africa	v	England	Cape Town	1956-57
A.M.J.Hilditch (29)	Australia	v	Pakistan	Perth	1978-79
Mohsin Khan (58)	Pakistan	v	Australia	Karachi[1]	1982-83
D.L.Haynes (55)	West Indies	v	India	Mumbai[3]	1983-84
G.A.Gooch (133)	England	v	Australia	Manchester	1993

Obstructed the field

L.Hutton (27)	England	v	South Africa	The Oval	1951

Run out by the bowler *(while backing up before the ball had been bowled)*

W.A.Brown (18) by M.H.Mankad	Australia	v	India	Sydney	1947-48
I.R.Redpath (9) by C.C.Griffith	Australia	v	West Indies	Adelaide	1968-69
D.W Randall (13) by E.J.Chatfield	England	v	New Zealand	Christchurch	1977-78
Sikander Bakht (0) by A.G.Hurst	Pakistan	v	Australia	Perth	1978-79

Stumped by a substitute

S.J.Snooke by N.C.Tufnell (sub for H.Strudwick)	South Africa	v	England	Durban[1]	1909-10
Pervez Sajjad by B.E.Congdon (sub for A.E.Dick)	Pakistan	v	New Zealand	Lahore[1]	1964-65

TEN BATSMEN CAUGHT IN AN INNINGS

Australia	v	England	Melbourne	1903-04
South Africa	v	Australia	Melbourne	1931-32
England	v	South Africa	Durban[2]	1948-49
New Zealand	v	England	Leeds	1949
England	v	Pakistan	The Oval	1954
England	v	Australia	Melbourne	1958-59
West Indies	v	Australia	Sydney	1960-61
New Zealand	v	India	Wellington	1967-68
New Zealand	v	West Indies	Auckland	1968-69
New Zealand	v	India	Mumbai[2]	1969-70
India	v	West Indies	Port-of-Spain	1970-71
India	v	England	Lord's	1971
Australia	v	England	Nottingham	1972
England	v	India	Chennai[1]	1972-73
England	v	West Indies	Lord's	1973
Australia	v	New Zealand	Auckland	1973-74
New Zealand	v	Pakistan	Auckland	1978-79
§ England	v	Australia	Brisbane[2]	1982-83
England	v	Australia	Melbourne	1982-83
India	v	West Indies	Bridgetown	1982-83
West Indies	v	India	Bridgetown	1982-83
Sri Lanka	v	Australia	Kandy	1982-83
England	v	New Zealand	Christchurch	1987-88
England	v	West Indies	The Oval	1988
India	v	New Zealand	Hyderabad	1988-89
Pakistan	v	India	Karachi[1]	1989-90
West Indies	v	Australia	Bridgetown	1990-91
Australia	v	India	Perth	1991-92
India	v	Australia	Perth	1991-92
India	v	South Africa	Port Elizabeth	1992-93
West Indies	v	England	Bridgetown	1993-94
Sri Lanka	v	Zimbabwe	Harare	1994-95
Pakistan	v	Zimbabwe	Harare	1994-95
New Zealand	v	Sri Lanka	Napier	1994-95
West Indies	v	Australia	Bridgetown	1994-95
West Indies	v	Australia	Port-of-Spain	1994-95

§ Australia held nine catches in England's second innings. This is the only occasion where a side has held 19 catches in a Test.

MOST BATSMEN CAUGHT IN A MATCH

33	Australia	v	India	Perth	1991-92

(of the 36 batsmen dismissed not one was bowled - a unique feat for a completed Test match)

32	England	v	Pakistan	Leeds	1971
32	New Zealand	v	Pakistan	Auckland	1993-94
32	Zimbabwe	v	Pakistan	Harare	1994-95
31	West Indies	v	England	Bridgetown	1993-94
30	India	v	West Indies	Mumbai[3]	1994-95

MOST BATSMEN CAUGHT AND BOWLED IN AN INNINGS

4	Australia	v	England	Lord's	1890
4	Australia	v	New Zealand	Sydney	1985-86

MOST BATSMEN CAUGHT AND BOWLED IN A MATCH

6	Australia	v	England	Lord's	1890

MOST BATSMEN BOWLED IN AN INNINGS

9	South Africa	v	England	Cape Town	1888-89

MOST BATSMEN BOWLED IN A MATCH

23	South Africa	v	England	Port Elizabeth	1895-96

MOST BATSMEN LBW IN AN INNINGS

6	England	v	South Africa	Leeds	1955
6	England	v	West Indies	Kingston	1959-60
6	England	v	Pakistan	Karachi[1]	1977-78
6	West Indies	v	England	Kingston	1985-86
6	Pakistan	v	Australia	Melbourne	1989-90
6	India	v	Sri Lanka	Chandigarh	1990-91
6	Pakistan	v	Sri Lanka	Faisalabad	1991-92
6	New Zealand	v	Pakistan	Hamilton	1992-93
6	South Africa	v	Australia	Durban[2]	1993-94
6	West Indies	v	India	Mohali	1994-95

MOST BATSMEN LBW IN A MATCH

17	West Indies (8)	v	Pakistan (9)	Port-of-Spain	1992-93
14	Pakistan (8)	v	Sri Lanka (6)	Faisalabad	1991-92
13	New Zealand (8)	v	England (5)	Auckland	1991-92
12	New Zealand (5)	v	West Indies (7)	Dunedin	1979-80
12	England (9)	v	West Indies (3)	Lord's	1984
12	Pakistan (5)	v	West Indies (7)	Faisalabad	1986-87
12	New Zealand (8)	v	Pakistan (4)	Hamilton	1992-93
12	Pakistan (8)	v	Zimbabwe (4)	Rawalpindi[2]	1993-94

MOST BATSMEN RUN OUT IN AN INNINGS

4	India	v	Pakistan	Peshawar[1]	1954-55
4	Australia	v	West Indies	Adelaide	1968-69

MOST BATSMEN RUN OUT IN A MATCH

7	Australia (3)	v	Pakistan (4)	Melbourne	1972-73
6	Australia (2)	v	England (4)	Adelaide	1901-02
6	Australia (4)	v	South Africa (2)	Melbourne	1910-11
6	Australia (5)	v	England (1)	Sydney	1920-21
6	England (2)	v	South Africa (4)	Leeds	1924
6	West Indies (3)	v	India (3)	Georgetown	1970-71

6	England (3)	v	New Zealand (3)	The Oval	1983
6	England (4)	v	Pakistan (2)	Birmingham	1987

MOST BATSMEN STUMPED IN AN INNINGS

5	West Indies	v	India (K.S.More)	Chennai[1]	1987-88
4	England	v	Australia (W.A.S.Oldfield)	Melbourne	1924-25
4	England	v	India (P.Sen)	Chennai[1]	1951-52

MOST BATSMEN STUMPED IN A MATCH

6	Australia	v	England	Sydney	1894-95
6	India	v	England	Chennai[1]	1951-52
6	West Indies	v	India (all by K.S.More)	Chennai[1]	1987-88

Batting

6000 RUNS IN TESTS

Player (Country)	M	I	Runs	Opponent A	E	SA	WI	NZ	I	P	SL	Z
A.R.Border (A)	156	265	**11174**	-	3548	298	2052	1500	1567	1666	543	-
S.M.Gavaskar (I)	125	214	**10122**	1550	2483	-	2749	651	-	2089	600	-
G.A.Gooch (E)	118	215	**8900**	2632	-	139	2197	1148	1725	683	376	-
Javed Miandad (P)	124	189	**8832**	1797	1329	-	834	1919	2228	-	582	143
I.V.A.Richards (W)	121	182	**8540**	2266	2869	-	-	387	1927	1091	-	-
D.I.Gower (E)	117	204	**8231**	3269	-	-	1149	1051	1391	1185	186	-
G.Boycott (E)	108	193	**8114**	2945	-	373	2205	916	1084	591	-	-
G.S.Sobers (W)	93	160	**8032**	1510	3214	-	-	404	1920	984	-	-
M.C.Cowdrey (E)	114	188	**7624**	2433	-	1021	1751	1133	653	633	-	-
C.G.Greenidge (W)	108	185	**7558**	1819	2318	-	-	882	1678	861	-	-
C.H.Lloyd (W)	110	175	**7515**	2211	2120	-	-	234	2344	606	-	-
D.L.Haynes (W)	116	202	**7487**	2233	2392	81	-	843	990	928	20	-
D.C.Boon (A)	107	190	**7422**	-	2237	433	1437	1187	1204	431	493	-
W.R.Hammond (E)	85	140	**7249**	2852	-	2188	639	1015	555	-	-	-
G.S.Chappell (A)	87	151	**7110**	-	2619	-	1400	1076	368	1581	66	-
D.G.Bradman (A)	52	80	**6996**	-	5028	806	447	-	715	-	-	-
L.Hutton (E)	79	138	**6971**	2428	-	1564	1661	777	522	19	-	-
D.B.Vengsarkar (I)	116	185	**6868**	1304	1589	-	1596	440	-	1284	655	-
K.F.Barrington (E)	82	131	**6806**	2111	-	989	1042	594	1355	715	-	-
R.B.Kanhai (W)	79	137	**6227**	1694	2267	-	-	-	1693	573	-	-
R.N.Harvey (A)	79	137	**6149**	-	2416	1625	1054	-	775	279	-	-
G.R.Viswanath (I)	91	155	**6080**	1538	1880	-	1455	585	-	611	11	-

2000 RUNS IN TESTS

AUSTRALIA	Tests	I	NO	Runs	HS	Avge	100	50
A.R.Border	156	265	44	11174	205	50.56	27	63
D.C.Boon	107	190	20	7422	200	43.65	21	32
G.S.Chappell	87	151	19	7110	247*	53.86	24	31
D.G.Bradman	52	80	10	6996	334	99.94	29	13
R.N.Harvey	79	137	10	6149	205	48.41	21	24
M.A.Taylor	72	129	9	5502	219	45.85	14	33
K.D.Walters	74	125	14	5357	250	48.26	15	33
I.M.Chappell	75	136	10	5345	196	42.42	14	26
W.M.Lawry	67	123	12	5234	210	47.15	13	27
S.R.Waugh	81	125	26	5002	200	50.52	11	28
R.B.Simpson	62	111	7	4869	311	46.81	10	27
I.R.Redpath	66	120	11	4737	171	43.45	8	31
K.J.Hughes	70	124	6	4415	213	37.41	9	22
R.W.Marsh	96	150	13	3633	132	26.51	3	16
D.M.Jones	52	89	11	3631	216	46.55	11	14
M.E.Waugh	54	86	4	3627	140	44.23	10	22
A.R.Morris	46	79	3	3533	206	46.48	12	12
C.Hill	49	89	2	3412	191	39.21	7	19
G.M.Wood	59	112	6	3374	172	31.83	9	12
V.T.Trumper	48	89	8	3163	214*	39.04	8	13
C.C.McDonald	47	83	4	3107	170	39.32	5	17
A.L.Hassett	43	69	3	3073	198*	46.56	10	11
K.R.Miller	55	87	7	2958	147	36.97	7	13
W.W.Armstrong	50	84	10	2863	159*	38.68	6	8
G.R.Marsh	50	93	7	2854	138	33.18	4	15

K.R.Stackpole	43	80	5	2807	207	37.42	7	14
I.A.Healy	79	117	14	2803	113*	27.21	2	17
N.C.O'Neill	42	69	8	2779	181	45.55	6	15
G.N.Yallop	39	70	3	2756	268	41.13	8	9
S.J.McCabe	39	62	5	2748	232	48.21	6	13
M.J.Slater	33	57	3	2611	219	48.35	7	10
W.Bardsley	41	66	5	2469	193*	40.47	6	14
W.M.Woodfull	35	54	4	2300	161	46.00	7	13
P.J.P.Burge	42	68	8	2290	181	38.16	4	12
S.E.Gregory	58	100	7	2282	201	24.53	4	8
R.Benaud	63	97	7	2201	122	24.45	3	9
C.G.Macartney	35	55	4	2131	170	41.78	7	9
W.H.Ponsford	29	48	4	2122	266	48.22	7	6
R.M.Cowper	27	46	2	2061	307	46.84	5	10

ENGLAND	Tests	I	NO	Runs	HS	Avge	100	50
G.A.Gooch	118	215	6	8900	333	42.58	20	46
D.I.Gower	117	204	18	8231	215	44.25	18	39
G.Boycott	108	193	23	8114	246*	47.72	22	42
M.C.Cowdrey	114	188	15	7624	182	44.06	22	38
W.R.Hammond	85	140	16	7249	336*	58.45	22	24
L.Hutton	79	138	15	6971	364	56.67	19	33
K.F.Barrington	82	131	15	6806	256	58.67	20	35
D.C.S.Compton	78	131	15	5807	278	50.06	17	28
J.B.Hobbs	61	102	7	5410	211	56.94	15	28
I.T.Botham	102	161	6	5200	208	33.54	14	22
J.H.Edrich	77	127	9	5138	310*	43.54	12	24
T.W.Graveney	79	123	13	4882	258	44.38	11	20
A.J.Lamb	79	139	10	4656	142	36.09	14	18
M.A.Atherton	62	114	3	4627	185*	41.68	10	29
H.Sutcliffe	54	84	9	4555	194	60.73	16	23
P.B.H.May	66	106	9	4537	285*	46.77	13	22
E.R.Dexter	62	102	8	4502	205	47.89	9	27
M.W.Gatting	79	138	14	4409	207	35.55	10	21
A.P.E.Knott	95	149	15	4389	135	32.75	5	30
R.A.Smith	62	112	15	4240	175	43.71	9	28
A.J.Stewart	58	103	6	3935	190	40.56	8	20
D.L.Amiss	50	88	10	3612	262*	46.30	11	11
A.W.Greig	58	93	4	3599	148	40.43	8	20
E.H.Hendren	51	83	9	3525	205*	47.63	7	21
F.E.Woolley	64	98	7	3283	154	36.07	5	23
K.W.R.Fletcher	59	96	14	3272	216	39.90	7	19
M.Leyland	41	65	5	2764	187	46.06	9	10
G.A.Hick	46	80	6	2672	178	36.10	4	15
C.Washbrook	37	66	6	2569	195	42.81	6	12
B.L.D'Oliveira	44	70	8	2484	158	40.06	5	15
D.W.Randall	47	79	5	2470	174	33.37	7	12
W.J.Edrich	39	63	2	2440	219	40.00	6	13
T.G.Evans	91	133	14	2439	104	20.49	2	8
L.E.G.Ames	47	72	12	2434	149	40.56	8	7
W.Rhodes	58	98	21	2325	179	30.19	2	11
T.E.Bailey	61	91	14	2290	134*	29.74	1	10
M.J.K.Smith	50	78	6	2278	121	31.63	3	11
G.P.Thorpe	32	59	5	2174	123	40.25	2	18
P.E.Richardson	34	56	1	2061	126	37.47	5	9

SOUTH AFRICA	Tests	I	NO	Runs	HS	Avge	100	50
B.Mitchell	42	80	9	3471	189*	48.88	8	21
A.D.Nourse	34	62	7	2960	231	53.81	9	14
H.W.Taylor	42	76	4	2936	176	40.77	7	17
E.J.Barlow	30	57	2	2516	201	45.74	6	15
T.L.Goddard	41	78	5	2516	112	34.46	1	18
D.J.McGlew	34	64	6	2440	255*	42.06	7	10
J.H.B.Waite	50	86	7	2405	134	30.44	4	16
R.G.Pollock	23	41	4	2256	274	60.97	7	11
A.W.Nourse	45	83	8	2234	111	29.78	1	15
R.A.McLean	40	73	3	2120	142	30.28	5	10

WEST INDIES	Tests	I	NO	Runs	HS	Avge	100	50
I.V.A.Richards	121	182	12	8540	291	50.23	24	45
G.S.Sobers	93	160	21	8032	365*	57.78	26	30
C.G.Greenidge	108	185	16	7558	226	44.72	19	34
C.H.Lloyd	110	175	14	7515	242*	46.67	19	39
D.L.Haynes	116	202	25	7487	184	42.29	18	39
R.B.Kanhai	79	137	6	6227	256	47.53	15	28
R.B.Richardson	86	146	12	5949	194	44.39	16	27
E.D.Weekes	48	81	5	4455	207	58.61	15	19
A.I.Kallicharran	66	109	10	4399	187	44.43	12	21
R.C.Fredericks	59	109	7	4334	169	42.49	8	26
F.M.M.Worrell	51	87	9	3860	261	49.48	9	22
C.L.Walcott	44	74	7	3798	220	56.68	15	14
P.J.L.Dujon	81	115	11	3322	139	31.94	5	16
C.C.Hunte	44	78	6	3245	260	45.06	8	13
B.C.Lara	33	55	2	3197	375	60.32	7	17
H.A.Gomes	60	91	11	3171	143	39.63	9	13
B.F.Butcher	44	78	6	3104	209*	43.11	7	16
C.L.Hooper	52	87	7	2548	178*	31.85	5	12
S.M.Nurse	29	54	1	2523	258	47.60	6	10
A.L.Logie	52	78	9	2470	130	35.79	2	16
G.A.Headley	22	40	4	2190	270*	60.83	10	5
J.B.Stollmeyer	32	56	5	2159	160	42.33	4	12
L.G.Rowe	30	49	2	2047	302	43.55	7	7

NEW ZEALAND	Tests	I	NO	Runs	HS	Avge	100	50
M.D.Crowe	77	131	11	5444	299	45.36	17	18
J.G.Wright	82	148	7	5334	185	37.82	12	23
B.E.Congdon	61	114	7	3448	176	32.22	7	19
J..R.Reid	58	108	5	3428	142	33.28	6	22
R.J.Hadlee	86	134	19	3124	151*	27.16	2	15
G.M.Turner	41	73	6	2991	259	44.64	7	14
A.H.Jones	39	74	8	2922	186	44.27	7	11
B.Sutcliffe	42	76	8	2727	230*	40.10	5	15
M.G.Burgess	50	92	6	2684	119*	31.20	5	14
J.V.Coney	52	85	14	2668	174*	37.57	3	16
G.P.Howarth	47	83	5	2531	147	32.44	6	11
K.R.Rutherford	56	99	8	2463	107*	27.06	3	15
G.T.Dowling	39	77	3	2306	239	31.16	3	11

INDIA	Tests	I	NO	Runs	HS	Avge	100	50
S.M.Gavaskar	125	214	16	10122	236*	51.12	34	45
D.B.Vengsarkar	116	185	22	6868	166	42.13	17	35
G.R.Viswanath	91	155	10	6080	222	41.93	14	35
Kapil Dev	131	184	15	5248	163	31.05	8	27

M.Amarnath	69	113	10	4378	138	42.50	11	24
M.Azharuddin	71	101	4	4362	199	41.96	14	15
R.J.Shastri	80	121	14	3830	206	35.79	11	12
P.R.Umrigar	59	94	8	3631	223	42.22	12	14
V.L.Manjrekar	55	92	10	3208	189*	39.12	7	15
C.G.Borde	55	97	11	3061	177*	35.59	5	18
S.R.Tendulkar	41	60	7	2911	179	54.92	10	14
Nawab of Pataudi, jr	46	83	3	2793	203*	34.91	6	16
S.M.H.Kirmani	88	124	22	2759	102	27.04	2	12
F.M.Engineer	46	87	3	2611	121	31.08	2	16
Pankaj Roy	43	79	4	2442	173	32.56	5	9
V.S.Hazare	30	52	6	2192	164*	47.65	7	9
A.L.Wadekar	37	71	3	2113	143	31.07	1	14
M.H.Mankad	44	72	5	2109	231	31.47	5	6
N.S.Sidhu	36	54	2	2087	107	40.13	6	10
C.P.S.Chauhan	40	68	2	2084	97	31.57	-	16
K.Srikkanth	43	72	3	2062	123	29.88	2	12
M.L.Jaisimha	39	71	4	2056	129	30.68	3	12
S.V.Manjrekar	35	59	6	2004	218	37.81	4	9
D.N.Sardesai	30	55	4	2001	212	39.23	5	9

PAKISTAN	Tests	I	NO	Runs	HS	Avge	100	50
Javed Miandad	124	189	21	8832	280*	52.57	23	43
Saleem Malik	90	134	21	5101	237	45.14	14	25
Zaheer Abbas	78	124	11	5062	274	44.79	12	20
Mudassar Nazar	76	116	8	4114	231	38.09	10	17
Majid Khan	63	106	5	3931	167	38.92	8	19
Hanif Mohammad	55	97	8	3915	337	43.98	12	15
Imran Khan	88	126	25	3807	136	37.69	6	18
Mushtaq Mohammad	57	100	7	3643	201	39.17	10	19
Asif Iqbal	58	99	7	3575	175	38.85	11	12
Saeed Ahmed	41	78	4	2991	172	40.41	5	16
Wasim Raja	57	92	14	2821	125	36.16	4	18
Rameez Raja	55	91	5	2747	122	31.94	2	21
Mohsin Khan	48	79	6	2709	200	37.10	7	9
Shoaib Mohammad	45	68	7	2705	203*	44.34	7	13
Sadiq Mohammad	41	74	2	2579	166	35.81	5	10
Inzamamul Haq	33	57	7	2367	148	47.34	5	16
Imtiaz Ahmed	41	72	1	2079	209	29.28	3	11
Aamer Sohail	32	59	2	2037	205	35.73	2	13

SRI LANKA	Tests	I	NO	Runs	HS	Avge	100	50
A.Ranatunga	61	104	6	3471	135*	35.41	4	23
P.A.de Silva	53	93	4	3176	267	35.68	8	13
A.P.Gurusinha	39	68	7	2312	143	37.90	7	6
H.P.Tillakaratne	36	61	8	2166	119	40.86	4	12

500 runs for Zimbabwe:

ZIMBABWE	Tests	I	NO	Runs	HS	Avge	100	50
D.L.Houghton	16	25	2	1113	266	48.39	4	2
A.Flower	16	26	5	1049	156	49.95	2	8
A.D.R.Campbell	16	27	1	815	99	31.34	0	7
G.W.Flower	16	27	1	794	201*	30.53	1	4

1000 RUNS AT A TEST GROUND

Player	Country	Ground	M	I	NO	Runs	HS	Avge	100's	50's	0's
Gooch,GA	Eng	Lord's	21	39	1	2015	333	53.02	6	5	2
Bradman,DG	Aust	Melbourne	11	17	4	1671	270	128.53	9	3	1
Hutton,L	Eng	The Oval	12	19	2	1521	364	89.47	4	5	0
Border,AR	Aust	Adelaide	16	29	5	1415	205	58.95	4	9	1
Javed Miandad	Pak	Karachi[1]	17	25	1	1393	211	58.04	3	8	0
Sobers,GS	WI	Kingston	11	18	5	1354	365*	104.15	5	4	0
Border,AR	Aust	Melbourne	20	36	3	1272	163	38.54	4	5	3
Chappell,GS	Aust	Melbourne	17	31	4	1257	121	46.55	4	9	4
Gower,DI	Eng	Lord's	17	30	2	1241	108	44.32	2	8	1
Kanhai,RB	WI	Port-of-Spain	16	31	3	1212	153	43.28	4	4	1
Haynes,DL	WI	Bridgetown	13	25	5	1210	145	60.50	4	6	1
Boycott,G	Eng	Lord's	16	29	3	1189	128*	45.73	3	6	1
Hobbs,JB	Eng	Melbourne	10	18	1	1178	178	69.29	5	4	1
Border,AR	Aust	Sydney	17	29	8	1177	89	56.04	0	11	0
Chappell,GS	Aust	Sydney	12	22	4	1150	204	63.88	4	3	2
Crowe,MD	NZ	Wellington	10	17	1	1123	299	70.18	5	1	1
Javed Miandad	Pak	Lahore[2]	17	23	3	1122	163	56.10	3	3	0
Gavaskar,SM	India	Mumbai[3]	11	20	0	1122	205	56.10	5	3	0
Gooch,GA	Eng	The Oval	12	22	1	1097	196	52.23	1	9	3
Zaheer Abbas	Pak	Lahore[2]	10	15	4	1093	235*	99.36	4	2	0
Boon,DC	Aust	Sydney	11	21	3	1127	184*	62.61	4	4	1
Weekes,ED	WI	Port-of-Spain	7	13	2	1074	207	97.63	4	4	0
Javed Miandad	Pak	Faisalabad	15	23	4	1068	203*	56.21	5	2	0
Wright,JG	NZ	Auckland	15	29	2	1060	130	39.25	3	5	1
Lloyd,CH	WI	Port-of-Spain	16	28	2	1035	143	39.80	2	1	0
Lawry,WM	Aust	Melbourne	8	13	0	1023	205	78.69	4	5	0
Gavaskar,SM	India	Chennai[1]	12	21	4	1018	236*	59.88	3	3	1
Richards,IVA	WI	Port-of-Spain	14	21	0	1015	177	48.33	3	4	1
Chappell,GS	Aust	Brisbane[2]	7	11	2	1006	201	111.77	5	4	0
Wright,JG	NZ	Wellington	13	23	2	1005	138	47.85	3	4	1

BATSMEN WITH 1000 RUNS IN THE CALENDAR YEAR

Player (Country)	Year	Tests	I	NO	Runs	HS	Avge	100	50
I.V.A.Richards (W)	1976	11	19	0	1710	291	90.00	7	5
S.M Gavaskar (I)	1979	18	27	1	1555	221	59.80	5	8
G.R.Viswanath (I)	1979	17	26	3	1388	179	60.34	5	6
R.B.Simpson (A)	1964	14	26	3	1381	311	60.04	3	7
D.L.Amiss (E)	1974	13	22	2	1379	262*	68.95	5	3
S.M.Gavaskar (I)	1983	18	32	4	1310	236*	46.78	5	5
G.A.Gooch (E)	1990	9	17	1	1264	333	79.00	4	5
D.C.Boon (A)	1993	16	25	5	1241	164*	62.05	4	7
B.C.Lara (W)	1995	12	20	2	1222	179	67.88	4	6
M.A.Taylor (A)	1989	11	20	1	1219	219	64.15	4	5 #
G.S.Sobers (W)	1958	7	12	3	1193	365*	132.55	5	3
D.B.Vengsarkar (I)	1979	18	27	4	1174	146*	51.04	5	6
K.J.Hughes (A)	1979	15	28	4	1163	130*	48.45	2	8
D.C.S.Compton (E)	1947	9	15	1	1159	208	82.78	6	3
C.G.Greenidge (W)	1984	14	22	4	1149	223	63.83	4	3
M.A.Atherton (E)	1995	13	24	1	1129	185*	49.08	2	7
M.A.Taylor (A)	1993	15	23	2	1106	170	52.66	4	4
A.R.Border (A)	1985	11	20	3	1099	196	64.64	4	2
D.M.Jones (A)	1989	11	18	3	1099	216	73.26	4	4
I.T.Botham (E)	1982	14	22	0	1095	208	49.77	3	6
K.W.R.Fletcher (E)	1973	13	22	4	1090	178	60.55	2	9
M.Amarnath (I)	1983	14	24	1	1077	120	46.82	4	7
A.R.Border (A)	1979	14	27	3	1073	162	44.70	3	6
C.Hill (A)	1902	12	21	2	1061	142	55.78	2	7
D.I.Gower (E)	1982	14	25	2	1061	114	46.13	1	8
D.I.Gower (E)	1986	14	25	1	1059	136	44.12	2	6
W.M.Lawry (A)	1964	14	27	2	1056	157	42.24	2	6
S.M.Gavaskar (I)	1978	9	15	2	1044	205	80.30	4	4
G.A.Gooch (E)	1991	9	17	1	1040	174	65.00	3	5
K.F.Barrington (E)	1963	12	22	2	1039	132*	51.95	3	5
E.R.Dexter (E)	1962	11	15	1	1038	205	74.14	2	6
K.F.Barrington (E)	1961	10	17	4	1032	172	79.38	4	5
Mohsin Khan (P)	1982	10	17	3	1029	200	73.50	4	4
D.G.Bradman (A)	1948	8	13	4	1025	201	113.88	5	2
S.M.Gavaskar (I)	1976	11	20	1	1024	156	53.89	4	4
A.R.Border (A)	1986	11	19	3	1000	140	62.50	5	3

 # Taylor achieved the feat in his debut calendar year.

HIGHEST INDIVIDUAL INNINGS

375	B.C.Lara	West Indies	v	England	St John's	1993-94
365*	G.S.Sobers	West Indies	v	Pakistan	Kingston	1957-58
364	L.Hutton	England	v	Australia	The Oval	1938
337	Hanif Mohammad	Pakistan	v	West Indies	Bridgetown	1957-58
336*	W.R.Hammond	England	v	New Zealand	Auckland	1932-33
334	D.G.Bradman	Australia	v	England	Leeds	1930
333	G.A.Gooch	England	v	India	Lord's	1990
325	A.Sandham	England	v	West Indies	Kingston	1929-30
311	R.B.Simpson	Australia	v	England	Manchester	1964
310*	J.H.Edrich	England	v	New Zealand	Leeds	1965
307	R.M.Cowper	Australia	v	England	Melbourne	1965-66
304	D.G.Bradman	Australia	v	England	Leeds	1934
302	L.G.Rowe	West Indies	v	England	Bridgetown	1973-74
299*	D.G.Bradman	Australia	v	South Africa	Adelaide	1931-32
299	M.D.Crowe	New Zealand	v	Sri Lanka	Wellington	1990-91
291	I.V.A.Richards	West Indies	v	England	The Oval	1976
287	R.E.Foster	England	v	Australia	Sydney	1903-04
285*	P.B.H.May	England	v	West Indies	Birmingham	1957
280*	Javed Miandad	Pakistan	v	India	Hyderabad	1982-83
278	D.C.S.Compton	England	v	Pakistan	Nottingham	1954
277	B.C.Lara	West Indies	v	Australia	Sydney	1992-93
274	R.G.Pollock	South Africa	v	Australia	Durban[2]	1969-70
274	Zaheer Abbas	Pakistan	v	England	Birmingham	1971
271	Javed Miandad	Pakistan	v	New Zealand	Auckland	1988-89
270*	G.A.Headley	West Indies	v	England	Kingston	1934-35
270	D.G.Bradman	Australia	v	England	Melbourne	1936-37
268	G.N.Yallop	Australia	v	Pakistan	Melbourne	1983-84
267	P.A.de Silva	Sri Lanka	v	New Zealand	Wellington	1990-91
266	W.H.Ponsford	Australia	v	England	The Oval	1934
266	D.L.Houghton	Zimbabwe	v	Sri Lanka	Bulawayo[2]	1994-95
262*	D.L.Amiss	England	v	West Indies	Kingston	1973-74
261	F.M.M.Worrell	West Indies	v	England	Nottingham	1950
260	C.C.Hunte	West Indies	v	Pakistan	Kingston	1957-58
260	Javed Miandad	Pakistan	v	England	The Oval	1987
259	G.M.Turner	New Zealand	v	West Indies	Georgetown	1971-72
258	T.W.Graveney	England	v	West Indies	Nottingham	1957
258	S.M.Nurse	West Indies	v	New Zealand	Christchurch	1968-69
256	R.B.Kanhai	West Indies	v	India	Calcutta	1958-59
256	K.F.Barrington	England	v	Australia	Manchester	1964
255*	D.J.McGlew	South Africa	v	New Zealand	Wellington	1952-53
254	D.G.Bradman	Australia	v	England	Lord's	1930
251	W.R.Hammond	England	v	Australia	Sydney	1928-29
250	K.D.Walters	Australia	v	New Zealand	Christchurch	1976-77
250	S.F.A.F.Bacchus	West Indies	v	India	Kanpur	1978-79
247*	G.S.Chappell	Australia	v	New Zealand	Wellington	1973-74
246*	G.Boycott	England	v	India	Leeds	1967
244	D.G.Bradman	Australia	v	England	The Oval	1934
243	E.Paynter	England	v	South Africa	Durban[2]	1938-39
242*	C.H.Lloyd	West Indies	v	India	Mumbai[3]	1974-75
242	K.D.Walters	Australia	v	West Indies	Sydney	1968-69
240	W.R.Hammond	England	v	Australia	Lord's	1938
240	Zaheer Abbas	Pakistan	v	England	The Oval	1974
239	G.T.Dowling	New Zealand	v	India	Christchurch	1967-68
237	F.M.M.Worrell	West Indies	v	India	Kingston	1952-53

237	Saleem Malik	Pakistan	v	Australia	Rawalpindi[2]	1994-95
236*	S.M.Gavaskar	India	v	West Indies	Chennai[1]	1983-84
236	E.A.B.Rowan	South Africa	v	England	Leeds	1951
235*	Zaheer Abbas	Pakistan	v	India	Lahore[2]	1978-79
235	G.S.Chappell	Australia	v	Pakistan	Faisalabad	1979-80
234	D.G.Bradman	Australia	v	England	Sydney	1946-47
234	S.G.Barnes	Australia	v	England	Sydney	1946-47
232	D.G.Bradman	Australia	v	England	The Oval	1930
232	S.J.McCabe	Australia	v	England	Nottingham	1938
232	I.V.A.Richards	West Indies	v	England	Nottingham	1976
231*	W.R.Hammond	England	v	Australia	Sydney	1936-37
231	A.D.Nourse	South Africa	v	Australia	Johannesburg[1]	1935-36
231	M.H.Mankad	India	v	New Zealand	Chennai[2]	1955-56
231	Mudassar Nazar	Pakistan	v	India	Hyderabad	1982-83
230*	B.Sutcliffe	New Zealand	v	India	Delhi	1955-56
227	W.R.Hammond	England	v	New Zealand	Christchurch	1932-33
227	V.G.Kambli	India	v	Zimbabwe	Delhi	1992-93
226	D.G.Bradman	Australia	v	South Africa	Brisbane[2]	1931-32
226	G.S.Sobers	West Indies	v	England	Bridgetown	1959-60
226	C.G.Greenidge	West Indies	v	Australia	Bridgetown	1990-91
225	R.B.Simpson	Australia	v	England	Adelaide	1965-66
224	V.G.Kambli	India	v	England	Mumbai[3]	1992-93
223*	G.M.Turner	New Zealand	v	West Indies	Kingston	1971-72
223	G.A.Headley	West Indies	v	England	Kingston	1929-30
223	D.G.Bradman	Australia	v	West Indies	Brisbane[1]	1930-31
223	P.R.Umrigar	India	v	New Zealand	Hyderabad	1955-56
223	M.H.Mankad	India	v	New Zealand	Mumbai[2]	1955-56
223	C.G.Greenidge	West Indies	v	England	Manchester	1984
222	G.R.Viswanath	India	v	England	Chennai[1]	1981-82
221	S.M.Gavaskar	India	v	England	The Oval	1979
220	C.L.Walcott	West Indies	v	England	Bridgetown	1953-54
220	S.M.Gavaskar	India	v	West Indies	Port-of-Spain	1970-71
219	W.J.Edrich	England	v	South Africa	Durban[2]	1938-39
219	D.S.Atkinson	West Indies	v	Australia	Bridgetown	1954-55
219	M.A.Taylor	Australia	v	England	Nottingham	1989
219	M.J.Slater	Australia	v	Sri Lanka	Perth	1995-96
218	S.V.Manjrekar	India	v	Pakistan	Lahore[2]	1989-90
217	W.R.Hammond	England	v	India	The Oval	1936
217	R.B.Kanhai	West Indies	v	Pakistan	Lahore[1]	1958-59
216*	E.Paynter	England	v	Australia	Nottingham	1938
216	K.W.R.Fletcher	England	v	New Zealand	Auckland	1974-75
216	D.M.Jones	Australia	v	West Indies	Adelaide	1988-89
215	Zaheer Abbas	Pakistan	v	India	Lahore[2]	1982-83
215	D.I.Gower	England	v	West Indies	Birmingham	1985
214*	V.T.Trumper	Australia	v	South Africa	Adelaide	1910-11
214*	D.Lloyd	England	v	India	Birmingham	1974
214*	C.G.Greenidge	West Indies	v	England	Lord's	1984
214	L.G.Rowe	West Indies	v	New Zealand	Kingston	1971-72
213	K.J.Hughes	Australia	v	India	Adelaide	1980-81
213	C.G.Greenidge	West Indies	v	New Zealand	Auckland	1986-87
212	D.G.Bradman	Australia	v	England	Adelaide	1936-37
212	D.N.Sardesai	India	v	West Indies	Kingston	1970-71
211	W.L.Murdoch	Australia	v	England	The Oval	1884
211	J.B.Hobbs	England	v	South Africa	Lord's	1924
211	Javed Miandad	Pakistan	v	Australia	Karachi[1]	1988-89

210*	Taslim Arif	Pakistan	v	Australia	Faisalabad	1979-80
210	W.M.Lawry	Australia	v	West Indies	Bridgetown	1964-65
210	Qasim Omar	Pakistan	v	India	Faisalabad	1984-85
210	D.M.Jones	Australia	v	India	Chennai[1]	1986-87
210	G.A.Gooch	England	v	New Zealand	Nottingham	1994
209*	B.F.Butcher	West Indies	v	England	Nottingham	1966
209	C.A.Roach	West Indies	v	England	Georgetown	1929-30
209	Imtiaz Ahmed	Pakistan	v	New Zealand	Lahore[1]	1955-56
209	R.G.Pollock	South Africa	v	Australia	Cape Town	1966-67
208*	J.C.Adams	West Indies	v	New Zealand	St John's	1995-96
208	D.C.S.Compton	England	v	South Africa	Lord's	1947
208	A.D.Nourse	South Africa	v	England	Nottingham	1951
208	I.T.Botham	England	v	India	The Oval	1982
208	I.V.A.Richards	West Indies	v	Australia	Melbourne	1984-85
208	S.L.Campbell	West Indies	v	New Zealand	Bridgetown	1995-96
207	E.D.Weekes	West Indies	v	India	Port-of-Spain	1952-53
207	K.R.Stackpole	Australia	v	England	Brisbane[2]	1970-71
207	M.W.Gatting	England	v	India	Chennai[1]	1984-85
206*	W.A.Brown	Australia	v	England	Lord's	1938
206	M.P.Donnelly	New Zealand	v	England	Lord's	1949
206	L.Hutton	England	v	New Zealand	The Oval	1949
206	A.R.Morris	Australia	v	England	Adelaide	1950-51
206	E.D.Weekes	West Indies	v	England	Port-of-Spain	1953-54
206	Javed Miandad	Pakistan	v	New Zealand	Karachi[1]	1976-77
206	Qasim Omar	Pakistan	v	Sri Lanka	Faisalabad	1985-86
206	R.J.Shastri	India	v	Australia	Sydney	1991-92
205*	E.H.Hendren	England	v	West Indies	Port-of-Spain	1929-30
205*	J.Hardstaff, jr	England	v	India	Lord's	1946
205	R.N.Harvey	Australia	v	South Africa	Melbourne	1952-53
205	L.Hutton	England	v	West Indies	Kingston	1953-54
205	E.R.Dexter	England	v	Pakistan	Karachi[1]	1961-62
205	W.M.Lawry	Australia	v	West Indies	Melbourne	1968-69
205	S.M.Gavaskar	India	v	West Indies	Mumbai[3]	1978-79
205	A.R.Border	Australia	v	New Zealand	Adelaide	1987-88
205	Aamer Sohail	Pakistan	v	England	Manchester	1992
204	G.A.Faulkner	South Africa	v	Australia	Melbourne	1910-11
204	R.N.Harvey	Australia	v	West Indies	Kingston	1954-55
204	G.S.Chappell	Australia	v	India	Sydney	1980-81
203*	Nawab of Pataudi, jr	India	v	England	Delhi	1963-64
203*	Hanif Mohammad	Pakistan	v	New Zealand	Lahore[2]	1964-65
203*	Javed Miandad	Pakistan	v	Sri Lanka	Faisalabad	1985-86
203*	Shoaib Mohammad	Pakistan	v	India	Lahore[2]	1989-90
203*	Shoaib Mohammad	Pakistan	v	New Zealand	Karachi[1]	1990-91
203	H.L.Collins	Australia	v	South Africa	Johannesburg[1]	1921-22
203	D.L.Amiss	England	v	West Indies	The Oval	1976
202*	L.Hutton	England	v	West Indies	The Oval	1950
201*	J.Ryder	Australia	v	England	Adelaide	1924-25
201*	D.S.B.P.Kuruppu	Sri Lanka	v	New Zealand	Colombo (CCC)	1986-87
201*	G.W.Flower	Zimbabwe	v	Pakistan	Harare	1994-95
201	S.E.Gregory	Australia	v	England	Sydney	1894-95
201	D.G.Bradman	Australia	v	India	Adelaide	1947-48
201	E.J.Barlow	South Africa	v	Australia	Adelaide	1963-64
201	R.B.Simpson	Australia	v	West Indies	Bridgetown	1964-65
201	S.M.Nurse	West Indies	v	Australia	Bridgetown	1964-65
201	Mushtaq Mohammad	Pakistan	v	New Zealand	Dunedin	1972-73

201	G.S.Chappell	Australia	v	Pakistan	Brisbane[2]	1981-82
201	A.D.Gaekwad	India	v	Pakistan	Jullundur	1983-84
201	G.Fowler	England	v	India	Chennai[1]	1984-85
200*	D.N.Sardesai	India	v	New Zealand	Mumbai[2]	1964-65
200*	D.I.Gower	England	v	India	Birmingham	1979
200*	A.R.Border	Australia	v	England	Leeds	1993
200	W.R.Hammond	England	v	Australia	Melbourne	1928-29
200	Mohsin Khan	Pakistan	v	England	Lord's	1982
200	D.C.Boon	Australia	v	New Zealand	Perth	1989-90
200	S.R.Waugh	Australia	v	West Indies	Kingston	1994-95

HIGHEST BATTING AVERAGES *(Qualification: 15 innings)*

Player	Country	Tests	I	NO	Runs	HS	Avge	100	50
D.G.Bradman	Australia	52	80	10	6996	334	**99.94**	29	13
J.C.Adams	West Indies	24	37	9	1851	208*	**66.10**	5	8
C.S.Dempster	New Zealand	10	15	4	723	136	**65.72**	2	5
S.G.Barnes	Australia	13	19	2	1072	234	**63.05**	3	5
R.G.Pollock	South Africa	23	41	4	2256	274	**60.97**	7	11
G.A.Headley	West Indies	22	40	4	2190	270*	**60.83**	10	5
H.Sutcliffe	England	54	84	9	4555	194	**60.73**	16	23
B.C.Lara	West Indies	33	55	2	3197	375	**60.32**	7	17
E.Paynter	England	20	31	5	1540	243	**59.23**	4	7
K.F.Barrington	England	82	131	15	6806	256	**58.67**	20	35
E.D.Weekes	West Indies	48	81	5	4455	207	**58.61**	15	19
K.S.Duleepsinhji	England	12	19	2	995	173	**58.52**	3	5
W.R.Hammond	England	85	140	16	7249	336*	**58.46**	22	24
G.S.Sobers	West Indies	93	160	21	8032	365*	**57.78**	26	30
J.B.Hobbs	England	61	102	7	5410	211	**56.94**	15	28
C.A.G.Russell	England	10	18	2	990	140	**56.87**	5	2
C.L.Walcott	West Indies	44	74	7	3798	220	**56.68**	15	14
L.Hutton	England	79	138	15	6971	364	**56.67**	19	33
S.Chanderpaul	West Indies	11	16	4	667	82	**55.58**	0	8
G.E.Tyldesley	England	14	20	2	990	122	**55.00**	3	6
S.R.Tendulkar	India	41	60	7	2911	179	**54.92**	10	14
C.A.Davis	West Indies	15	29	5	1301	183	**54.20**	4	4
V.G.Kambli	India	17	21	1	1084	227	**54.20**	4	3
G.S.Chappell	Australia	87	151	19	7110	247*	**53.86**	24	31
A.D.Nourse	South Africa	34	62	7	2960	231	**53.81**	9	14
Javed Miandad	Pakistan	124	189	21	8832	280*	**52.57**	23	43
A.Melville	South Africa	11	19	2	894	189*	**52.58**	4	3
C.F.Walters	England	11	18	3	784	102	**52.26**	1	7
S.L.Campbell	West Indies	11	18	1	885	208	**52.05**	1	6
J.Ryder	Australia	20	32	5	1394	201*	**51.62**	3	9
S.M.Gavaskar	India	125	214	12	10122	236*	**51.12**	34	45
A.R.Border	Australia	156	265	44	11174	205	**50.56**	27	63
S.R.Waugh	Australia	81	125	26	5002	200	**50.52**	11	28
I.V.A.Richards	West Indies	121	182	12	8540	291	**50.23**	24	45
D.C.S.Compton	England	78	131	15	5807	278	**50.06**	17	28

500 RUNS IN A TEST SERIES *(§ first Test series. # last Test series. † only Test Series)*

AUSTRALIA	Opp	Season	Tests	I	NO	Runs	HS	Avge	100	50
D.G.Bradman	ENG	1930	5	7	0	974	334	139.14	4	-
M.A.Taylor	ENG	1989	6	11	1	839	219	83.90	2	5
R.N.Harvey	SA	1952-53	5	9	0	834	205	92.66	4	3
D.G.Bradman	ENG	1936-37	5	9	0	810	270	90.00	3	1
D.G.Bradman	SA	1931-32	5	5	1	806	299*	201.50	4	-
D.G.Bradman	ENG	1934	5	8	0	758	304	94.75	2	1
D.G.Bradman	IND	1947-48	5	6	2	715	201	178.75	4	1
G.S.Chappell	WI	1975-76	6	11	5	702	182*	117.00	3	3
K.D.Walters	WI	1968-69	4	6	0	699	242	116.50	4	2
A.R.Morris	ENG	1948	5	9	1	696	196	87.00	3	3
D.G.Bradman	ENG	1946-47	5	8	1	680	234	97.14	2	3
W.M.Lawry	WI	1968-69	5	8	0	667	205	83.38	3	2
V.T.Trumper	SA	1910-11	5	9	2	661	214*	94.42	2	2
R.N.Harvey	SA	1949-50	5	8	3	660	178	132.00	4	1
R.N.Harvey	WI	1954-55	5	7	1	650	204	108.33	3	1
K.R.Stackpole	ENG	1970-71	6	12	0	627	207	52.25	2	2
M.J.Slater	ENG	1994-95	5	10	0	623	176	62.30	3	1
G.S.Chappell	ENG	1974-75	6	11	0	608	144	55.27	2	5
A.R.Border	ENG	1985	6	11	2	597	196	66.33	2	1
K.J.Hughes	IND	1979-80	6	12	2	594	100	59.40	1	5
W.M.Lawry	ENG	1965-66	5	7	0	592	166	84.57	3	2
I.R.Redpath	WI	1975-76	6	11	0	575	103	52.27	3	2
V.T.Trumper	ENG	1903-04	5	10	1	574	185*	63.77	2	3
W.Bardsley	SA	1910-11	5	9	0	573	132	63.66	1	5
W.H.Ponsford #	ENG	1934	4	7	1	569	266	94.83	2	1
D.M.Jones	ENG	1989	6	9	1	566	157	70.75	2	3
H.L.Collins §	ENG	1920-21	5	9	0	557	162	61.88	2	3
D.C.Boon	IND	1991-92	5	9	2	556	135	79.42	3	1
D.C.Boon	ENG	1993	6	10	2	555	164*	69.37	3	1
G.N.Yallop	PAK	1983-84	5	6	0	554	268	92.33	2	1
M.E.Waugh	ENG	1993	6	10	1	550	137	61.11	1	5
I.M.Chappell	WI	1968-69	5	8	0	548	165	68.50	2	3
I.M.Chappell	WI	1972-73	5	9	2	542	109	77.42	2	3
J.M.Taylor	ENG	1924-25	5	10	0	541	108	54.10	1	4
R.B.Simpson	IND	1977-78	5	10	0	539	176	53.90	2	2
J.Darling	ENG	1897-98	5	8	0	537	178	67.12	3	-
A.R.Border	ENG	1981	6	12	3	533	123*	59.22	2	3
B.C.Booth	SA	1963-64	4	7	1	531	169	88.50	2	3
D.C.Boon	ENG	1990-91	5	9	2	530	121	75.71	1	3
N.C.O'Neill	WI	1960-61	5	10	0	522	181	52.20	1	3
C.Hill	ENG	1901-02	5	10	0	521	99	52.10	-	4
A.R.Border	IND	1979-80	6	12	0	521	162	49.63	1	3
A.R.Border	WI	1983-84	5	10	3	521	100*	74.42	1	4
C.C.McDonald	ENG	1958-59	5	9	1	519	170	64.87	2	1
W.A.Brown	ENG	1938	4	8	1	512	206*	73.14	2	1
D.M.Jones	ENG	1986-87	5	10	1	511	184*	56.77	1	3
D.G.Bradman #	ENG	1948	5	9	2	508	173*	72.57	2	1
S.R.Waugh	ENG	1989	6	8	4	506	177*	126.50	2	1
K.C.Wessels	WI	1984-85	5	9	0	505	173	56.11	1	4
A.R.Morris §	ENG	1946-47	5	8	1	503	155	71.85	3	1

ENGLAND	Opp	Season	Tests	I	NO	Runs	HS	Avge	100	50
W.R.Hammond	AUST	1928-29	5	9	1	905	251	113.12	4	-
D.C.S.Compton	SA	1947	5	8	0	753	208	94.12	4	2
G.A.Gooch	IND	1990	3	6	0	752	333	125.33	3	2

H.Sutcliffe	AUST	1924-25	5	9	0	734	176	81.56	4	2
D.I.Gower	AUST	1985	6	9	0	732	215	81.33	3	1
E.H.Hendren	WI	1929-30	4	8	2	693	205*	115.50	2	5
L.Hutton	WI	1953-54	5	8	1	677	205	96.71	2	3
G.A.Gooch	AUST	1993	6	12	0	673	133	56.08	2	4
D.L.Amiss	WI	1973-74	5	9	1	663	262*	82.87	3	-
J.B.Hobbs	AUST	1911-12	5	9	1	662	187	82.75	3	1
G.Boycott	AUST	1970-71	5	10	3	657	142*	93.85	2	5
E.Paynter #	SA	1938-39	5	8	0	653	243	81.62	3	2
J.H.Edrich	AUST	1970-71	6	11	2	648	130	72.00	2	4
W.R.Hammond	SA	1938-39	5	8	1	609	181	87.00	3	2
K.F.Barrington	IND	1961-62	5	9	3	594	172	99.00	3	1
A.Sandham #	WI	1929-30	4	8	0	592	325	74.00	2	2
K.F.Barrington	AUST	1962-63	5	10	2	582	132	72.75	2	3
P.B.H.May	SA	1955	5	9	1	582	117	72.75	2	3
L.Hutton	SA	1948-49	5	9	0	577	158	64.11	2	2
M.W.Gatting	IND	1984-85	5	9	3	575	207	95.83	2	1
J.B.Hobbs	AUST	1924-25	5	9	0	573	154	63.66	3	2
W.R.Hammond	NZ	1932-33	2	2	1	563	336*	64.49	2	-
D.C.S.Compton	AUST	1948	5	10	1	562	184	62.44	2	2
J.H.Edrich	AUST	1968	5	9	0	554	164	61.55	1	4
R.A.Smith	AUST	1989	5	10	1	553	143	61.44	2	3
M.A.Atherton	AUST	1993	6	12	0	553	99	46.08	0	6
W.J.Edrich	SA	1947	4	6	1	552	191	110.40	2	2
C.Washbrook	SA	1948-49	5	9	0	542	195	60.22	1	2
J.B.Hobbs	SA	1909-10	5	9	1	539	187	67.37	1	4
M.C.Cowdrey	WI	1967-68	5	8	0	534	148	66.75	2	4
L.Hutton	AUST	1950-51	5	10	4	533	156*	88.83	1	4
K.F.Barrington	AUST	1964	5	8	1	531	256	75.85	1	2
M.W.Gatting	AUST	1985	6	9	3	527	160	87.83	2	3
E.R.Dexter	WI	1959-60	5	9	1	526	136*	65.75	2	2
G.E.Tyldesley	SA	1927-28	5	9	1	520	122	65.00	2	3
W.R.Hammond	SA	1930-31	5	9	1	517	136*	64.62	1	4
H.Sutcliffe	AUST	1929	5	9	1	513	114	64.12	4	-
M.A.Atherton	WI	1993-94	5	9	0	510	144	56.66	2	2
K.F.Barrington	SA	1964-65	5	7	2	508	148*	101.60	2	2
G.P.Thorpe	WI	1995	6	12	0	506	94	42.16	0	5
J.B.Hobbs	AUST	1920-21	5	10	0	505	123	50.50	2	1

SOUTH AFRICA	Opp	Season	Tests	I	NO	Runs	HS	Avge	100	50
G.A.Faulkner	AUST	1910-11	5	10	0	732	204	73.20	2	5
A.D.Nourse	ENG	1947	5	9	0	621	149	69.00	2	5
D.T.Lindsay	AUST	1966-67	5	7	0	606	182	86.57	3	1
E.J.Barlow	AUST	1963-64	5	10	2	603	201	75.37	3	1
B.Mitchell	ENG	1947	5	10	1	597	189*	66.33	2	3
H.W.Taylor	ENG	1922-23	5	9	0	582	176	64.66	3	2
K.C.Bland	ENG	1964-65	5	10	2	572	144*	71.50	1	4
A.Melville	ENG	1947	5	10	1	569	189	63.22	3	1
E.J.Barlow	ENG	1964-65	5	10	0	558	138	55.80	1	4
G.A.Faulkner	ENG	1909-10	5	10	1	545	123	60.55	1	3
R.G.Pollock	AUST	1966-67	5	9	2	537	209	76.71	2	2
A.D.Nourse	ENG	1948-49	5	10	3	536	129*	76.57	2	2
A.D.Nourse	AUST	1935-36	5	10	1	518	231	57.55	1	2
R.G.Pollock #	AUST	1969-70	4	7	0	517	274	73.85	1	3
E.A.B.Rowan #	ENG	1951	5	10	1	515	236	57.22	1	3
B.A.Richards †	AUST	1969-70	4	7	0	508	140	72.57	2	2
H.W.Taylor	ENG	1913-14	5	10	0	508	109	35.10	1	3

WEST INDIES	Opp	Season	Tests	I	NO	Runs	HS	Avge	100	50
I.V.A.Richards	ENG	1976	4	7	0	829	291	118.42	3	2
C.L.Walcott	AUST	1954-55	5	10	0	827	155	82.70	5	2
G.S.Sobers	PAK	1957-58	5	8	2	824	365*	137.33	3	3
B.C.Lara	ENG	1993-94	5	8	0	798	375	99.75	2	2
E.D.Weekes	IND	1948-49	5	7	0	779	194	111.28	4	2
B.C.Lara	ENG	1995	6	10	1	765	179	85.00	3	3
G.S.Sobers	ENG	1966	5	8	1	722	174	103.14	3	2
E.D.Weekes	IND	1952-53	5	8	1	716	207	102.28	3	2
G.S.Sobers	ENG	1959-60	5	8	1	709	226	101.28	3	1
G.A.Headley §	ENG	1929-30	4	8	0	703	223	87.87	4	-
C.L.Walcott	ENG	1953-54	5	10	2	698	220	87.25	3	3
C.H.Lloyd	IND	1974-75	5	9	1	636	242*	79.50	2	1
C.C.Hunte §	PAK	1957-58	5	9	1	622	260	79.75	3	-
R.B.Richardson	IND	1988-89	4	7	0	619	194	88.42	2	3
L.G.Rowe	ENG	1973-74	5	7	0	616	302	88.00	3	-
G.S.Sobers	IND	1970-71	5	10	2	597	178*	74.62	3	1
C.G.Greenidge	ENG	1976	5	10	1	592	134	65.66	3	2
C.G.Greenidge	ENG	1984	5	8	1	572	223	81.71	2	-
S.M.Nurse #	NZ	1968-69	3	5	0	558	258	111.60	2	1
G.S.Sobers	IND	1958-59	5	8	2	557	198	92.83	3	-
I.V.A.Richards	IND	1975-76	4	7	0	556	177	92.66	3	1
C.C.Hunte	AUST	1964-65	5	10	1	550	89	61.11	-	6
G.S.Sobers	ENG	1967-68	5	9	3	545	152	90.83	2	2
F.M.M.Worrell	ENG	1950	4	6	0	539	261	89.33	2	1
A.I.Kallicharran	IND	1978-79	6	10	1	538	187	59.77	1	3
R.B.Kanhai	IND	1958-59	5	8	0	538	256	67.25	1	2
C.G.Greenidge	PAK	1976-77	5	10	0	536	100	53.60	1	4
R.B.Kanhai	ENG	1967-68	5	10	1	535	153	59.44	2	1
C.A.Davis	IND	1970-71	4	8	4	529	125*	132.25	2	3
J.C.Adams	IND	1994-95	3	6	3	520	174*	173.33	2	2
R.C.Fredericks	ENG	1976	5	10	1	517	138	57.44	2	3
R.B.Kanhai	AUST	1960-61	5	10	0	503	117	50.30	2	2
S.M.Nurse	ENG	1966	5	8	0	501	137	62.65	1	4

NEW ZEALAND	Opp	Season	Tests	I	NO	Runs	HS	Avge	100	50
G.M.Turner	WI	1971-72	5	8	1	672	259	96.00	2	2
B.Sutcliffe	IND	1955-56	5	9	2	611	230*	87.28	2	1
J.R.Reid	SA	1961-62	5	10	1	546	142	60.66	1	4
B.E.Congdon	WI	1971-72	5	8	2	531	166*	88.50	2	3
A.H.Jones	SL	1990-91	3	6	1	513	186	102.60	3	1

INDIA	Opp	Season	Tests	I	NO	Runs	HS	Avge	100	50
S.M.Gavaskar §	WI	1970-71	4	8	3	774	220	154.80	4	3
S.M.Gavaskar	WI	1978-79	6	9	1	732	205*	91.50	4	1
D.N.Sardesai	WI	1970-71	5	8	0	642	212	80.25	3	1
M.Amarnath	WI	1982-83	5	9	0	598	117	66.44	2	4
V.L.Manjrekar	ENG	1961-62	5	8	1	586	189*	83.71	1	4
M.Amarnath	PAK	1982-83	6	10	2	584	120	73.00	3	3
S.V.Manjrekar	PAK	1989-90	4	7	1	569	218	94.83	2	3
G.R.Viswanath	WI	1974-75	5	10	1	568	139	63.11	1	3
R.S.Modi	WI	1948-49	5	10	0	560	112	56.00	1	5
P.R.Umrigar	WI	1952-53	5	10	1	560	130	62.22	2	4
V.S.Hazare	WI	1948-49	5	10	2	543	134*	67.87	2	3
S.M.Gavaskar	ENG	1979	4	7	0	542	221	77.42	1	4
S.M.Gavaskar	PAK	1979-80	6	11	1	529	166	52.90	1	2

Indian bowler Kapil Dev raises his arms to acknowledge the applause of the crowd during the fifth Test between Australia and India at the WACA ground in Perth, February 1992. Dev had just dismissed Australian opener Mark Taylor, who became the 400th Test wicket of Dev's career.

Former Australian captain Allan Border faces New Zealand in Hobart, November 1993.
Border's career total of 11 174 runs remains the highest in Test cricket.

	Opp	Season	Tests	I	NO	Runs	HS	Avge	100	50
M.H.Mankad	NZ	1955-56	4	5	0	526	231	105.20	2	-
B.K.Kunderan	ENG	1963-64	5	10	0	525	192	52.50	2	1
G.R.Viswanath	A	1979-80	6	8	1	518	161*	74.00	2	2
S.M.Gavaskar	WI	1983-84	6	11	1	505	236*	50.50	2	1
S.M.Gavaskar	ENG	1981-82	6	9	1	500	172	62.50	1	3

PAKISTAN	Opp	Season	Tests	I	NO	Runs	HS	Avge	100	50
Mudassar Nazar	IND	1982-83	6	8	2	761	231	126.83	4	1
Zaheer Abbas	IND	1982-83	6	6	1	650	215	130.00	3	-
Hanif Mohammad	WI	1957-58	5	9	0	628	337	39.10	1	3
Javed Miandad	IND	1982-83	6	6	1	594	280*	118.88	2	1
Zaheer Abbas	IND	1978-79	3	5	2	583	235	174.33	2	1
Saleem Malik	AUS	1994-95	3	6	0	557	237	92.83	2	1
Majid.J.Khan	WI	1976-77	5	10	0	530	167	53.00	1	3
Wasim Raja	WI	1976-77	5	10	1	517	117*	57.44	1	5
Saeed Ahmed §	WI	1957-58	5	9	0	508	150	56.44	1	4
Shoaib Mohammad	NZ	1990-91	3	5	2	507	203*	169.00	3	-
Javed Miandad §	NZ	1976-77	3	5	1	504	206	126.00	2	1

Most runs in a Test series for the other countries:

SRI LANKA	Opp	Season	Tests	I	NO	Runs	HS	Avge	100	50
P.A.de Silva	NZ	1990-91	3	5	0	493	267	98.60	2	1

ZIMBABWE	Opp	Season	Tests	I	NO	Runs	HS	Avge	100	50
D.L.Houghton	SL	1994-95	3	3	0	466	266	155.33	2	1

MOST RUNS IN A MATCH

456	G.A.Gooch (333 + 123)	England	v	India	Lord's	1990
380	G.S.Chappell (247* + 133)	Australia	v	New Zealand	Wellington	1973-74
375	A.Sandham (325 + 50)	England	v	West Indies	Kingston	1929-30
375	B.C.Lara (375)	West Indies	v	England	Bridgetown	1993-94
365	G.S.Sobers (365*)	West Indies	v	Pakistan	Kingston	1957-58
364	L.Hutton (364)	England	v	Australia	The Oval	1938
354	Hanif Mohammad (17 + 337)	Pakistan	v	West Indies	Bridgetown	1957-58

The most for the other countries are as follows:

344	S.M.Gavaskar (124 + 220)	India	v	West Indies	Port-of-Spain	1970-71
329	M.D.Crowe (30 + 299)	New Zealand	v	Sri Lanka	Wellington	1990-91
309	B.Mitchell (120 + 189*)	South Africa	v	England	The Oval	1947
267	P.A.de Silva (267)	Sri Lanka	v	New Zealand	Wellington	1990-91
266	D.L.Houghton (266)	Zimbabwe	v	Sri Lanka	Bulawayo[2]	1994-95

CARRYING BAT THROUGH A COMPLETED INNINGS

(§ on Test debut. # one or more batsmen absent or retired hurt)

AUSTRALIA	Score	Total	Opponents		
J.E.Barrett	67*	176 §	England	Lord's	1890
W.W.Armstrong	159*	309	South Africa	Johannesburg[1]	1902-03
W.Bardsley	193*	383	England	Lord's	1926
W.M.Woodfull	30*	66#	England	Brisbane[1]	1928-29
W.M.Woodfull	73*	193#	England	Adelaide	1932-33
W.A.Brown	206*	422	England	Lord's	1938
W.M.Lawry	49*	107	India	Delhi	1969-70
W.M.Lawry	60*	116#	England	Sydney	1970-71
I.R.Redpath	159*	346	New Zealand	Auckland	1973-74
D.C.Boon	58*	103	New Zealand	Auckland	1985-86

ENGLAND	Score	Total	Opponents		
R.Abel	132*	307	Australia	Sydney	1891-92
P.F.Warner	132*	237 §	South Africa	Johannesburg[1]	1898-99
L.Hutton	202*	344	West Indies	The Oval	1950
L.Hutton	156*	272	Australia	Adelaide	1950-51
G.Boycott	99*	215	Australia	Perth	1979-80
G.A.Gooch	154*	252	West Indies	Leeds	1991
A.J.Stewart	69*	175	Pakistan	Lord's	1992

SOUTH AFRICA	Score	Total	Opponents		
A.B.Tancred	26*	47	England	Cape Town	1888-89
J.W.Zulch	43*	103	England	Cape Town	1909-10
T.L.Goddard	56*	99	Australia	Cape Town	1957-58
D.J.McGlew	127*	292	New Zealand	Durban[2]	1961-62

WEST INDIES	Score	Total	Opponents		
F.M.M.Worrell	191*	372	England	Nottingham	1957
C.C.Hunte	60*	131	Australia	Port-of-Spain	1964-65
D.L.Haynes	88*	211	Pakistan	Karachi[1]	1986-87
D.L.Haynes	75*	176	England	The Oval	1991
D.L.Haynes	143*	382	Pakistan	Port-of-Spain	1992-93

NEW ZEALAND	Score	Total	Opponents		
G.M.Turner	43*	131	England	Lord's	1969
G.M.Turner	223*	386	West Indies	Kingston	1971-72

INDIA	Score	Total	Opponents		
S.M.Gavaskar	127*	286	Pakistan	Faisalabad	1982-83

PAKISTAN	Score	Total	Opponents		
Nazar Mohammad	124*	331	India	Lucknow[1]	1952-53
Mudassar Nazar	152*	323	India	Lahore[2]	1982-83

SRI LANKA	Score	Total	Opponents		
S.Wettimuny	63*	144	New Zealand	Christchurch	1982-83

ZIMBABWE	Score	Total	Opponents		
M.H.Dekker	68*	187	Pakistan	Rawalpindi[2]	1993-94

MOST CENTURIES

Player	Country	100	Inns	A	E	SA	WI	NZ	I	P	SL	Z
S.M.Gavaskar	India	**34**	214	8	4	-	13	2	-	5	2	-
D.G.Bradman	Australia	**29**	80	-	19	4	2	-	4	-	-	-
A.R.Border	Australia	**27**	265	-	8	-	3	5	4	6	1	-
G.S.Sobers	West Indies	**26**	160	4	10	-	-	1	8	3	-	-
G.S.Chappell	Australia	**24**	151	-	9	-	5	3	1	6	-	-
I.V.A.Richards	West Indies	**24**	161	5	8	-	-	1	8	2	-	-
Javed Miandad	Pakistan	**23**	189	6	2	-	2	7	5	-	1	-
G.Boycott	England	**22**	193	7	-	1	5	2	4	3	-	-
M.C.Cowdrey	England	**22**	188	5	-	3	6	2	3	3	-	-
W.R.Hammond	England	**22**	140	9	-	6	1	4	2	-	-	-
D.C.Boon	Australia	**21**	190	-	7	-	3	3	6	1	1	-
R.N.Harvey	Australia	**21**	137	-	6	8	3	-	4	-	-	-
K.F.Barrington	England	**20**	131	5	-	2	3	3	3	4	-	-
G.A.Gooch	England	**20**	215	4	-	-	5	4	5	1	1	-
C.G.Greenidge	West Indies	**19**	185	4	7	-	-	2	5	1	-	-

L.Hutton	England	**19**	138	5	-	4	5	3	2	-	-	-
C.H.Lloyd	West Indies	**19**	175	6	5	-	-	-	7	1	-	-
D.I.Gower	England	**18**	204	9	-	-	1	4	2	2	-	-
D.L.Haynes	West Indies	**18**	202	5	5	-	-	3	2	3	-	-
D.C.S.Compton	England	**17**	131	5	-	7	2	2	-	1	-	-
M.D.Crowe	New Zealand	**17**	131	3	5	-	3	-	1	2	2	1
D.B.Vengsarkar	India	**17**	185	2	5	-	6	-	-	2	2	-
R.B.Richardson	West Indies	**16**	146	9	4	-	-	1	2	-	-	-
H.Sutcliffe	England	**16**	84	8	-	6	-	2	-	-	-	-
J.B.Hobbs	England	**15**	102	12	-	2	1	-	-	-	-	-
R.B.Kanhai	West Indies	**15**	137	5	5	-	-	-	4	1	-	-
C.L.Walcott	West Indies	**15**	74	5	4	-	-	1	4	1	-	-
K.D.Walters	Australia	**15**	125	-	4	-	6	3	1	1	-	-
E.D.Weekes	West Indies	**15**	81	1	3	-	-	3	7	1	-	-
M.Azharuddin	India	**14**	96	1	6	-	-	1	-	3	3	-
I.T.Botham	England	**14**	161	4	-	-	-	3	5	2	-	-
I.M.Chappell	Australia	**14**	136	-	4	-	5	2	2	1	-	-
A.J.Lamb	England	**14**	139	1	-	-	6	3	3	-	1	-
Saleem Malik	Pakistan	**14**	134	2	4	-	1	2	3	-	2	-
M.A.Taylor	Australia	**14**	129	-	5	1	1	1	1	3	2	-
G.R.Viswanath	India	**14**	155	4	4	-	4	1	-	1	-	-
W.M.Lawry	Australia	**13**	123	-	7	1	4	-	1	-	-	-
P.B.H.May	England	**13**	106	3	-	3	3	3	1	-	-	-
J.H.Edrich	England	**12**	127	7	-	-	1	3	1	-	-	-
Hanif Mohammad	Pakistan	**12**	97	2	3	-	2	3	2	-	-	-
A.I.Kallicharran	West Indies	**12**	109	4	2	-	-	2	3	1	-	-
A.R.Morris	Australia	**12**	79	-	8	2	1	-	1	-	-	-
P.R.Umrigar	India	**12**	94	-	3	-	3	1	-	5	-	-
J.G.Wright	New Zealand	**12**	148	2	4	-	1	-	3	1	1	-
Zaheer Abbas	Pakistan	**12**	124	2	2	-	-	1	6	-	1	-
M.Amarnath	India	**11**	113	2	-	-	3	-	-	4	2	-
D.L.Amiss	England	**11**	88	-	-	-	4	2	2	3	-	-
Asif Iqbal	Pakistan	**11**	99	3	3	-	1	3	1	-	-	-
T.W.Graveney	England	**11**	123	1	-	-	5	-	2	3	-	-
D.M.Jones	Australia	**11**	89	-	3	-	1	-	2	2	3	-
R.J.Shastri	India	**11**	121	2	4	-	2	-	-	3	-	-
S.R.Waugh	Australia	**11**	125	-	3	1	2	1	-	1	3	-
M.A.Atherton	England	**10**	114	1	-	1	3	3	2	-	-	-
M.W.Gatting	England	**10**	138	4	-	-	-	1	3	2	-	-
A.L.Hassett	Australia	**10**	69	-	4	3	2	-	1	-	-	-
G.A.Headley	West Indies	**10**	40	2	8	-	-	-	-	-	-	-
Mudassar Nazar	Pakistan	**10**	116	-	3	-	-	1	6	-	-	-
Mushtaq Mohammad	Pakistan	**10**	100	1	3	-	2	3	1	-	-	-
R.B.Simpson	Australia	**10**	111	-	2	1	1	-	4	2	-	-
S.R.Tendulkar	India	**10**	60	2	4	1	1	-	-	-	2	-
M.E.Waugh	Australia	**10**	86	-	3	1	3	1	-	1	1	-

The leading century-maker for South Africa is A.D.Nourse (9 in 62 innings); for Sri Lanka P.A.de Silva (8 in 93 innings)and for Zimbabwe D.L.Houghton (4 in 25 innings).

MOST CENTURIES IN A SERIES

FIVE

C.L Walcott	West Indies	v Australia	1954-55

FOUR

D.G Bradman	Australia	v England	1930
	Australia	v South Africa	1931-32
	Australia	v India	1947-48
D.C.S.Compton	England	v South Africa	1947

S.M.Gavaskar	India	v	West Indies	1970-71
	India	v	West Indies	1978-79
W.R.Hammond	England	v	Australia	1928-29
R.N.Harvey	Australia	v	South Africa	1949-50
	Australia	v	South Africa	1952-53
G.A.Headley	West Indies	v	England	1929-30
Mudassar Nazar	Pakistan	v	India	1982-83
H.Sutcliffe	England	v	Australia	1924-25
	England	v	South Africa	1929
K.D.Walters	Australia	v	West Indies	1968-69
E.D.Weekes	West Indies	v	India	1948-49

MOST DOUBLE CENTURIES IN A SERIES

THREE				
D.G.Bradman	Australia	v	England	1930
TWO				
D.G.Bradman	Australia	v	South Africa	1931-32
	Australia	v	England	1934
	Australia	v	England	1936-37
C.G.Greenidge	West Indies	v	England	1984
W.R.Hammond	England	v	Australia	1928-29
	England	v	New Zealand	1932-33
M.H.Mankad	India	v	New Zealand	1955-56
I.V.A.Richards	West Indies	v	England	1976
G.M.Turner	New Zealand	v	West Indies	1971-72

CENTURIES IN MOST CONSECUTIVE INNINGS

			Opponents		
FIVE					
E.D.Weekes	West Indies	141	England	Kingston	1947-48
		128	India	Delhi	1948-49
		194	India	Mumbai[2]	1948-49
		162 }	India	Calcutta	1948-49
		101 }			

Weekes was run out for 90 in his next innings (Chennai[1] 1948-49).

			Opponents		
FOUR					
J.H.W.Fingleton	Australia	112	South Africa	Cape Town	1935-36
		108	South Africa	Johannesburg[1]	1935-36
		118	South Africa	Durban[2]	1935-36
		100	England	Brisbane[2]	1936-37
A.Melville	South Africa	103	England	Durban[2]	1938-39
		189 }	England	Nottingham	1947
		104* }			
		117	England	Lord's	1947

			Opponents		
THREE					
W.Bardsley	Australia	136 }	England	The Oval	1909
		130 }			
		132	South Africa	Sydney	1910-11
G.Boycott	England	119*	Australia	Adelaide	1970-71
		121*	Pakistan	Lord's	1971
		112	Pakistan	Leeds	1971
D G Bradman	Australia	132 }	India	Melbourne	1947-48
		127* }			
		201	India	Adelaide	1947-48
D.C.S.Compton	England	163	South Africa	Nottingham	1947
		208	South Africa	Lord's	1947
		115	South Africa	Manchester	1947
S.M.Gavaskar	India	117*	West Indies	Bridgetown	1970-71

		124 } 220 }	West Indies	Port-of-Spain	1970-71
S.M.Gavaskar		111 } 137 }	Pakistan	Karachi[1]	1978-79
		205	West Indies	Mumbai[3]	1978-79
G.A.Gooch	England	333 } 123 }	India	Lord's	1990
		116	India	Manchester	1990
C.G.Greenidge	West Indies	134 } 101 }	England	Manchester	1976
		115	England	Leeds	1976
V.S.Hazare	India	122	West Indies	Mumbai[2]	1948-49
		164*	England	Delhi	1951-52
		155	England	Mumbai[2]	1951-52
G.A.Headley	West Indies	270*	England	Kingston	1934-35
		106 } 107 }	England	Lord's	1939
A.H.Jones	New Zealand	186	Sri Lanka	Wellington	1990-91
		122 } 100* }	Sri Lanka	Hamilton	1990-91
V.G.Kambli	India	224	England	Mumbai[3]	1992-93
		227	Zimbabwe	Delhi	1992-93
		125	Sri Lanka	Colombo (SSC)	1993-94
C.G.Macartney	Australia	133*	England	Lord's	1926
		151	England	Leeds	1926
		109	England	Manchester	1926
A.R.Morris	Australia	155	England	Melbourne	1946-47
		122 } 124* }	England	Adelaide	1946-47
Mudassar Nazar	Pakistan	231	India	Hyderabad	1982-83
		152*	India	Lahore[2]	1982-83
		152	India	Karachi[1]	1982-83
G.S.Sobers	West Indies	365*	Pakistan	Kingston	1957-58
		125 } 109* }	Pakistan	Georgetown	1957-58
H.Sutcliffe	England	115	Australia	Sydney	1924-25
		176 } 127 }	Australia	Melbourne	1924-25
P.R.Umrigar	India	117	Pakistan	Chennai[2]	1960-61
		112	Pakistan	Delhi	1960-61
		147*	England	Kanpur	1961-62
E.D.Weekes	West Indies	123	New Zealand	Dunedin	1955-56
		103	New Zealand	Christchurch	1955-56
		156	New Zealand	Wellington	1955-56
Zaheer Abbas	Pakistan	215	India	Lahore[2]	1982-83
		186	India	Karachi[1]	1982-83
		168	India	Faisalabad	1982-83

CENTURY IN EACH INNINGS OF A MATCH

AUSTRALIA

			Opponents		
W.Bardsley	136	130	England	The Oval	1909
A.R.Morris	122	124*	England	Adelaide	1946-47
D.G.Bradman	132	127*	India	Melbourne	1947-48
J.Moroney	118	101*	South Africa	Johannesburg[2]	1949-50
R.B.Simpson	153	115	Pakistan	Karachi[1]	1964-65
K.D.Walters	242	103	West Indies	Sydney	1968-69

I.M.Chappell	145	121	New Zealand	Wellington	1973-74
G.S.Chappell	247*	133	New Zealand	Wellington	1973-74
G.S.Chappell	123	109*	West Indies	Brisbane[2]	1975-76
A.R.Border	150*	153	Pakistan	Lahore[2]	1979-80
A.R.Border	140	114*	New Zealand	Christchurch	1985-86
D.M.Jones	116	121*	Pakistan	Adelaide	1989-90

ENGLAND			Opponents		
C.A.G.Russell	140	111	South Africa	Durban[2]	1922-23
H.Sutcliffe	176	127	Australia	Melbourne	1924-25
W.R.Hammond	119*	177	Australia	Adelaide	1928-29
H.Sutcliffe	104	109*	South Africa	The Oval	1929
E.Paynter	117	100	South Africa	Johannesburg[1]	1938-39
D.C.S.Compton	147	103*	Australia	Adelaide	1946-47
G.A.Gooch	333	123	India	Lord's	1990
A.J.Stewart	118	143	West Indies	Bridgetown	1993-94

SOUTH AFRICA			Opponents		
A.Melville	189	104*	England	Nottingham	1947
B.Mitchell	120	189*	England	The Oval	1947

WEST INDIES			Opponents		
G.A.Headley	114	112	England	Georgetown	1929-30
G.A.Headley	106	107	England	Lord's	1939
E.D.Weekes	162	101	India	Calcutta	1948-49
C.L.Walcott	126	110	Australia	Port-of-Spain	1954-55
C.L.Walcott	155	110	Australia	Kingston	1954-55
G.S.Sobers	125	109*	Pakistan	Georgetown	1957-58
R.B.Kanhai	117	115	Australia	Adelaide	1960-61
L.G.Rowe	214	100*	New Zealand	Kingston	1971-72
C.G.Greenidge	134	101	England	Manchester	1976

NEW ZEALAND			Opponents		
G.M.Turner	101	110*	Australia	Christchurch	1973-74
G.P.Howarth	122	102	England	Auckland	1977-78
A.H.Jones	122	100*	Sri Lanka	Hamilton	1990-91

INDIA			Opponents		
V.S.Hazare	116	145	Australia	Adelaide	1947-48
S.M.Gavaskar	124	220	West Indies	Port-of-Spain	1970-71
S.M.Gavaskar	111	137	Pakistan	Karachi[1]	1978-79
S.M.Gavaskar	107	182*	West Indies	Calcutta	1978-79

PAKISTAN			Opponents		
Hanif Mohammad	111	104	England	Dacca	1961-62
Javed Miandad	104	103*	New Zealand	Hyderabad	1984-85

SRI LANKA			Opponents		
L.R.D.Mendis	105	105	India	Chennai[1]	1982-83
A.P.Gurusinha	119	102	New Zealand	Hamilton	1990-91

CENTURY AND A NINETY IN A MATCH *(§ In first Test. † in last Test)*

AUSTRALIA			Opponents		
R.M.Cowper	92	108	India	Adelaide	1967-68
P.M.Toohey	122	97	West Indies	Kingston	1977-78
A.R.Border	98*	100*	West Indies	Port-of-Spain	1983-84

ENGLAND			Opponents		
P.A.Gibb §	93	106	South Africa	Johannesburg[1]	1938-39
M.C.Cowdrey	114	97	West Indies	Kingston	1959-60
K.F.Barrington	101	94	Australia	Sydney	1962-63
A.P.E.Knott	101	96	New Zealand	Auckland	1970-71
G.Boycott	99	112	West Indies	Port-of-Spain	1973-74

SOUTH AFRICA			Opponents		
P.G.V.van der Bijl §	125	97	England	Durban[2]	1938-39

WEST INDIES			Opponents		
G.S.Sobers	152	92*	England	Georgetown	1967-68
S.M.Nurse	95	168	New Zealand	Auckland	1968-69
C.G.Greenidge §	93	107	India	Bangalore	1974-75

INDIA			Opponents		
C.G.Borde	109	96	West Indies	Delhi	1958-59
M.Amarnath	90	100	Australia	Perth	1977-78

PAKISTAN			Opponents		
Hanif Mohammad	104	93	Australia	Melbourne	1964-65
Zaheer Abbas	176	96	India	Faisalabad	1978-79
Mohsin Khan	94	101*	India	Lahore[2]	1982-83
Saeed Anwar	94	136	Sri Lanka	Colombo (PSS)	1993-94

SRI LANKA			Opponents		
L.R.D.Mendis	111	94	England	Lord's	1984
P.A.de Silva	96	123	New Zealand	Auckland	1990-91

NINETY IN EACH INNINGS OF A MATCH

AUSTRALIA			Opponents		
C.Hill	98	97	England	Adelaide	1901-02

ENGLAND			Opponents		
F.E.Woolley	95	93	Australia	Lord's	1921

WEST INDIES			Opponents		
C.G.Greenidge	91	96	Pakistan	Georgetown	1976-77
C.G.Greenidge	91	97	New Zealand	Christchurch	1979-80

FIRST THREE BATSMEN SCORING CENTURIES

England (2d-531)	v	South Africa	Lord's	1924
	(J.B.Hobbs 211; H.Sutcliffe 122; F.E.Woolley 134*)			
Australia (9d-600)	v	West Indies	Port-of-Spain	1954-55
	(C.C.McDonald 110; A.R.Morris 111; R.N.Harvey 133)			
Australia (6d-650)	v	West Indies	Bridgetown	1964-65
	(W.M.Lawry 210; R.B.Simpson 201; R.M.Cowper 102)			
India (4d-600)	v	Australia	Sydney	1985-86
	(S.M.Gavaskar 172; K.Srikkanth 116; M.Amarnath 138)			
Australia (4d-632)	v	England	Lord's	1993
	(M.A.Taylor 111; M.J.Slater 152; D.C.Boon 164*)			

CENTURIES IN MOST CONSECUTIVE MATCHES

SIX

D.G.Bradman	Australia	270, 212, 169, 144*, 102*, 103	1936-37 to 1938

Because of injury Bradman was unable to bat in his next Test but scored 187 and 234 in his following two matches in 1946-47.

CENTURY ON DEBUT

IN BOTH INNINGS

L.G.Rowe	214 / 100*	West Indies	v	New Zealand	Kingston	1971-72

IN FIRST INNINGS

C.Bannerman	165*	Australia	v	England	Melbourne	1876-77
W.G.Grace	152	England	v	Australia	The Oval	1880
H.Graham	107	Australia	v	England	Lord's	1893
R.E.Foster	287	England	v	Australia	Sydney	1903-04
G.Gunn	119	England	v	Australia	Sydney	1907-08
W.H.Ponsford †‡	110	Australia	v	England	Sydney	1924-25
A.Jackson	164	Australia	v	England	Adelaide	1928-29
J.E.Mills	117	New Zealand	v	England	Wellington	1929-30
Nawab of Pataudi, sr	102	England	v	Australia	Sydney	1932-33
B.H.Valentine	136	England	v	India	Mumbai[1]	1933-34
S.C.Griffith	140	England	v	West Indies	Port-of-Spain	1947-48
A.G.Ganteaume #	112	West Indies	v	England	Port-of-Spain	1947-48
P.B.H.May	138	England	v	South Africa	Leeds	1951
R.H.Shodhan	110	India	v	Pakistan	Calcutta	1952-53
B.H.Pairaudeau	115	West Indies	v	India	Port-of-Spain	1952-53
A.G.Kripal Singh	100*	India	v	New Zealand	Hyderabad	1955-56
C.C.Hunte	142	West Indies	v	Pakistan	Bridgetown	1957-58
C.A.Milton	104*	England	v	New Zealand	Leeds	1958
Hanumant Singh	105	India	v	England	Delhi	1963-64
Khalid Ibadulla	166	Pakistan	v	Australia	Karachi[1]	1964-65
B.R.Taylor	105	New Zealand	v	India	Calcutta	1964-65
K.D.Walters ‡	155	Australia	v	England	Brisbane[2]	1965-66
J.H.Hampshire	107	England	v	West Indies	Lord's	1969
G.S.Chappell †	108	Australia	v	England	Perth	1970-71
A.I.Kallicharran ‡	100*	West Indies	v	New Zealand	Georgetown	1971-72
R.E.Redmond #	107	New Zealand	v	Pakistan	Auckland	1972-73
G.J.Cosier	109	Australia	v	West Indies	Melbourne	1975-76
S.Amarnath ¥	124	India	v	New Zealand	Auckland	1975-76
Javed Miandad	163	Pakistan	v	New Zealand	Lahore[2]	1976-77
K.C.Wessels	162	Australia	v	England	Brisbane[2]	1982-83
W.B.Phillips	159	Australia	v	Pakistan	Perth	1983-84
M.Azharuddin §	110	India	v	England	Calcutta	1984-85
D.S.B.P.Kuruppu	201*	Sri Lanka	v	New Zealand	Colombo (CCC)	1986-87
M.E.Waugh	138	Australia	v	England	Adelaide	1990-91
A.C.Hudson	163	South Africa	v	West Indies	Bridgetown	1991-92
R.S.Kaluwitharana	132*	Sri Lanka	v	Australia	Colombo (SSC)	1992-93
D.L.Houghton	121	Zimbabwe	v	India	Harare	1992-93
P.K.Amre	103	India	v	South Africa	Durban[2]	1992-93
G.S.Blewett ‡	102*	Australia	v	England	Adelaide	1994-95
S.Ganguly ‡	131	India	v	England	Lord's	1996

IN SECOND INNINGS

K.S.Ranjitsinhji	154*	England	v	Australia	Manchester	1896
P.F.Warner	132*	England	v	South Africa	Johannesburg[1]	1898-99
R.A.Duff †	104	Australia	v	England	Melbourne	1901-02
R.J.Hartigan	116	Australia	v	England	Adelaide	1907-08
H.L.Collins	104	Australia	v	England	Sydney	1920-21
G.A.Headley	176	West Indies	v	England	Bridgetown	1929-30
N.B.Amarnath ¥	118	India	v	England	Mumbai[1]	1933-34
P.A.Gibb §	106	England	v	South Africa	Johannesburg[1]	1938-39
J.W.Burke	101*	Australia	v	England	Adelaide	1950-51

O.G.Smith	104	West Indies	v	Australia	Kingston	1954-55
A.A.Baig	112	India	v	England	Manchester	1959
G.R.Viswanath	137	India	v	Australia	Kanpur	1969-70
F.C.Hayes	106*	England	v	West Indies	The Oval	1973
C.G.Greenidge §	107	West Indies	v	India	Bangalore	1974-75
L.Baichan	105*	West Indies	v	Pakistan	Lahore[2]	1974-75
A.B.Williams	100	West Indies	v	Australia	Georgetown	1977-78
D.M.Wellham	103	Australia	v	England	The Oval	1981
Saleem Malik	100*	Pakistan	v	Sri Lanka	Karachi[1]	1981-82
M.J.Greatbatch	107*	New Zealand	v	England	Auckland	1987-88
G.P.Thorpe	114*	England	v	Australia	Nottingham	1993

 # Only Test. § Gibb and Greenidge both scored 93 in the first innings. † Duff, Ponsford and Chappell also scored a century in their last Test (Chappell also scored a century in each innings of his first Test as captain). ‡ Ponsford, Walters, Kallicharran, Blewett and Ganguly also scored a century in their second Test. § Azharuddin scored a century in each of his first three Tests. ¥ N.B. and S.Amarnath provide the only instance of a father and son scoring a century on debut.

MOST RUNS IN FIRST TEST MATCH

314	L.G.Rowe	(214 + 100*)	West Indies	v	New Zealand	Kingston	1971-72
306	R.E.Foster	(287 + 19)	England	v	Australia	Sydney	1903-04

B.M.Laird (92 and 75) scored 167 runs for Australia v West Indies at Brisbane[2] in 1979-80 the highest aggregate without a century by a player in his first Test.

MAIDEN FIRST-CLASS CENTURY IN A TEST MATCH

C.Bannerman §†	165*	Australia	v	England	Melbourne	1876-77
W.L.Murdoch	153*	Australia	v	England	The Oval	1880
P.S.McDonnell	147	Australia	v	England	Sydney	1881-82
H.Wood †	134*	England	v	South Africa	Cape Town	1891-92
H.Graham §	107	Australia	v	England	Lord's	1893
A.J.L.Hill	124	England	v	South Africa	Cape Town	1895-96
J.H.Sinclair	106	South Africa	v	England	Cape Town	1898-99
P.W.Sherwell	115	South Africa	v	England	Lord's	1907
H.G.Owen-Smith	129	South Africa	v	England	Leeds	1929
C.A.Roach	122	West Indies	v	England	Bridgetown	1929-30
S.C.Griffith §	140	England	v	West Indies	Port-of-Spain	1947-48
V.L.Manjrekar	133	India	v	England	Leeds	1952
C.C.Depeiza †	122	West Indies	v	Australia	Bridgetown	1954-55
P.L.Winslow	108	South Africa	v	England	Manchester	1955
S.N.McGregor	111	New Zealand	v	Pakistan	Lahore[1]	1955-56
F.C.M.Alexander †	108	West Indies	v	Australia	Sydney	1960-61
Nasim-ul-Ghani	101	Pakistan	v	England	Lord's	1962
B.R.Taylor §	105	New Zealand	v	India	Calcutta	1964-65
B.D.Julien	121	West Indies	v	England	Lord's	1973
W.K.Lees	152	New Zealand	v	Pakistan	Karachi[1]	1976-77
Kapil Dev	126*	India	v	West Indies	Delhi	1978-79
S.Wettimuny	157	Sri Lanka	v	Pakistan	Faisalabad	1981-82
S.A.R.Silva	102*	Sri Lanka	v	England	Lord's	1984
D.S.B.P.Kuruppu §	201*	Sri Lanka	v	New Zealand	Colombo (CCC)	1986-87
R.C.Russell	128*	England	v	Australia	Manchester	1989
I.A.Healy	102*	Australia	v	England	Manchester	1993

§ On Test debut. † Only century in first-class cricket. H.Graham (105 v England at Sydney in 1894-95), C.A.Roach (209 v England at Georgetown in 1929-30), B.R.Taylor (124 v West Indies at Auckland in 1968-69) and I.A.Healy (113 v New Zealand at Perth in 1993-94) also scored their second first-class century in a Test match.*

YOUNGEST PLAYERS TO SCORE A CENTURY

Years	Days	Player	Score	Team		Opponent	Venue	Season
17	82	Mushtaq Mohammad	101	Pakistan	v	India	Delhi	1960-61
17	112	S.R.Tendulkar	119*	India	v	England	Manchester	1990
18	251	Mushtaq Mohammad	100*	Pakistan	v	England	Nottingham	1962
18	256	S.R.Tendulkar	148*	India	v	Australia	Sydney	1991-92
18	285	S.R.Tendulkar	114	India	v	Australia	Perth	1991-92
18	328	Saleem Malik	100*	Pakistan	v	Sri Lanka	Karachi[1]	1981-82
19	26	Mohammad Ilyas	126	Pakistan	v	New Zealand	Karachi[1]	1964-65
19	119	Javed Miandad	163	Pakistan	v	New Zealand	Lahore[2]	1976-77
19	121	H.G.Vivian	100	New Zealand	v	South Africa	Wellington	1931-32
19	121	R.N.Harvey	153	Australia	v	India	Melbourne	1947-48
19	140	Javed Miandad	206	Pakistan	v	New Zealand	Karachi[1]	1976-77
19	152	A.Jackson	164	Australia	v	England	Adelaide	1928-29
19	192	A.P.Gurusinha	116*	Sri Lanka	v	Pakistan	Colombo (PSS)	1985-86
19	218	S.R.Tendulkar	111	India	v	South Africa	Johannesburg[3]	1992-93
19	264	Saleem Malik	107	Pakistan	v	India	Faisalabad	1982-83
19	290	R.N.Harvey	112	Australia	v	England	Leeds	1948
19	294	S.R.Tendulkar	165	India	v	England	Chennai[1]	1992-93
19	318	R.G.Pollock	122	South Africa	v	Australia	Sydney	1963-64
19	332	R.G.Pollock	175	South Africa	v	Australia	Adelaide	1963-64
19	357	K.D.Walters	155	Australia	v	England	Brisbane[2]	1965-66
20	1	P.A.de Silva	122	Sri Lanka	v	Pakistan	Faisalabad	1985-86
20	3	Ijaz Ahmed	122	Pakistan	v	Australia	Faisalabad	1988-89
20	14	K.D.Walters	115	Australia	v	England	Melbourne	1965-66
20	19	D.C.S.Compton	203	England	v	Australia	Nottingham	1938
20	21	Kapil Dev	126*	India	v	West Indies	Delhi	1978-79
20	23	P.A.de Silva	105	Sri Lanka	v	Pakistan	Karachi[1]	1985-86
20	58	Hanif Mohammad	142	Pakistan	v	India	Bahawalpur	1954-55
20	96	S.R.Tendulkar	104*	India	v	Sri Lanka	Colombo (SSC)	1993-94
20	129	D.G.Bradman	112	Australia	v	England	Melbourne	1928-29
20	131	A.A.Baig	112	India	v	England	Manchester	1959
20	148	H.G.Owen-Smith	129	South Africa	v	England	Leeds	1929
20	154	Saeed Ahmed	150	Pakistan	v	West Indies	Georgetown	1957-58
20	197	D.G.Bradman	123	Australia	v	England	Melbourne	1928-29
20	230	G.A.Headley	176	West Indies	v	England	Bridgetown	1929-30
20	240	J.W.Burke	101*	Australia	v	England	Adelaide	1950-51
20	249	R.J.Shastri	128	India	v	Pakistan	Karachi[1]	1982-83
20	253	V.L.Manjrekar	133	India	v	England	Leeds	1952
20	268	G.A.Headley	114	West Indies	v	England	Georgetown	1929-30
20	271	G.A.Headley	112	West Indies	v	England	Georgetown	1929-30
20	271	S.R.Tendulkar	142	India	v	Sri Lanka	Lucknow[2]	1993-94
20	281	G.R.Viswanath	137	India	v	Australia	Kanpur	1969-70
20	314	G.A.Headley	223	West Indies	v	England	Kingston	1929-30
20	317	C.Hill	188	Australia	v	England	Melbourne	1897-98
20	324	J.W.Hearne	114	England	v	Australia	Melbourne	1911-12
20	330	O.G.Smith	104	West Indies	v	Australia	Kingston	1954-55
20	332	Saleem Malik	116	Pakistan	v	England	Faislabad	1984-85
20	337	R.J.Shastri	102	India	v	West Indies	St John's	1982-83
20	351	R.G.Pollock	137	South Africa	v	England	Port Elizabeth	1964-65

YOUNGEST PLAYERS TO SCORE A DOUBLE CENTURY

Years	Days	Player	Score	Team		Opponent	Venue	Season
19	141	Javed Miandad	206	Pakistan	v	New Zealand	Karachi[1]	1976-77
20	315	G.A.Headley	223	West Indies	v	England	Kingston	1929-30

YOUNGEST PLAYERS TO SCORE A TRIPLE CENTURY

Years	Days							
21	216	G.S.Sobers	365*	West Indies	v	Pakistan	Kingston	1957-58
21	318	D.G.Bradman	334	Australia	v	England	Leeds	1930

OLDEST PLAYERS TO SCORE A CENTURY

Years	Days							
46	82	J.B.Hobbs	142	England	v	Australia	Melbourne	1928-29
45	241	J.B.Hobbs	159	England	v	West Indies	The Oval	1928
45	151	E.H.Hendren	132	England	v	Australia	Manchester	1934
43	294	A.W.Nourse	111	South Africa	v	Australia	Johannesburg[1]	1921-22
43	244	J.B.Hobbs	100	England	v	Australia	The Oval	1926
43	194	J.B.Hobbs	119	England	v	Australia	Lord's	1926
43	201	W.Bardsley	193*	Australia	v	England	Lord's	1926
42	61	F.E.Woolley	154	England	v	South Africa	Manchester	1929
42	35	J.B.Hobbs	119	England	v	Australia	Adelaide	1924-25
42	18	J.B.Hobbs	154	England	v	Australia	Melbourne	1924-25
42	6	J.B.Hobbs	115	England	v	Australia	Sydney	1924-25
42	6	E.A.B.Rowan	236	South Africa	v	England	Leeds	1951
41	360	R.B.Simpson	100	Australia	v	India	Adelaide	1977-78
41	318	R.B.Simpson	176	Australia	v	India	Perth	1977-78
41	266	W.W.Armstrong	123*	Australia	v	England	Melbourne	1920-21
41	264	T.W.Graveney	105	England	v	Pakistan	Karachi[1]	1968-69
41	242	H.W.Taylor	117	South Africa	v	England	Cape Town	1930-31
41	241	W.W.Armstrong	121	Australia	v	England	Adelaide	1920-21
41	213	W.W.Armstrong	158	Australia	v	England	Sydney	1920-21
41	197	J.B.Hobbs	211	England	v	South Africa	Lord's	1924
41	109	B.Sutcliffe	151*	New Zealand	v	India	Calcutta	1964-65
41	64	G.Boycott	105	England	v	India	Delhi	1981-82
41	21	E.H.Hendren	123	England	v	West Indies	Georgetown	1929-30
40	364	E.H.Hendren	205*	England	v	West Indies	Port-of-Spain	1929-30
40	315	G.A.Gooch	210	England	v	New Zealand	Nottingham	1994
40	312	G.Boycott	137	England	v	Australia	The Oval	1981
40	218	T.W.Graveney	118	England	v	West Indies	Port-of-Spain	1967-68
40	208	A.D.Nourse	208	South Africa	v	England	Nottingham	1951
40	184	E.A.B.Rowan	143	South Africa	v	Australia	Durban[2]	1949-50
40	162	G.Boycott	104*	England	v	West Indies	St John's	1980-81
40	105	H.W.Taylor	121	South Africa	v	England	The Oval	1929
40	85	C.H.Lloyd	114	West Indies	v	Australia	Brisbane[2]	1984-85
40	29	C.G.Macartney	109	Australia	v	England	Manchester	1926
40	22	V.J.Merchant	154	India	v	England	Delhi	1951-52
40	13	C.G.Macartney	151	Australia	v	England	Leeds	1926
40	8	T.W.Graveney	151	England	v	India	Lord's	1967
40	2	C.G.Macartney	133*	Australia	v	England	Lord's	1926

OLDEST PLAYERS TO SCORE A DOUBLE CENTURY

Years	Days							
42	7	E.A.B.Rowan	236	South Africa	v	England	Leeds	1951
41	197	J.B.Hobbs	211	England	v	South Africa	Lord's	1924
41	0	E.H.Hendren	205*	England	v	West Indies	Port-of-Spain	1929-30
40	316	G.A.Gooch	210	England	v	New Zealand	Nottingham	1994
40	208	A.D.Nourse	208	South Africa	v	England	Nottingham	1951
39	355	C.G.Greenidge	226	West Indies	v	Australia	Bridgetown	1990-91
39	349	A.Sandham	325	England	v	West Indies	Kingston	1929-30
39	149	D.G.Bradman	201	Australia	v	India	Adelaide	1947-48
38	270	M.H.Mankad	231	India	v	New Zealand	Chennai[2]	1955-56
38	112	D.G.Bradman	234	Australia	v	England	Sydney	1946-47

OLDEST PLAYERS TO SCORE A MAIDEN CENTURY

Years	Days							
43	294	A.W.Nourse	111	South Africa	v	Australia	Johannesburg[1]	1921-22
39	256	E.H.Bowley	109	England	v	New Zealand	Auckland	1929-30
39	191	A.Sandham	152	England	v	West Indies	Bridgetown	1929-30
39	173	J.W.H.Makepeace	117	England	v	Australia	Melbourne	1920-21
39	163	E.A.B.Rowan	156*	South Africa	v	England	Johannesburg[2]	1948-49
39	84	P.N.Kirsten	104	South Africa	v	England	Leeds	1994
38	324	G.E.Tyldesley	122	England	v	South Africa	Johannesburg[1]	1927-28
38	98	H.Wood	134*	England	v	South Africa	Cape Town	1891-92

DISTRIBUTION OF TEST MATCH CENTURIES

Conceded By	Scored For A	E	SA	WI	NZ	I	P	SL	Z	Total Conceded
Australia	0	201	38	78	19	35	36	7	-	414
England	232	0	62	107	38	64	38	3	-	544
South Africa	58	90	0	0	7	3	0	1	-	159
West Indies	76	95	1	0	20	58	18	0	-	268
New Zealand	30	79	14	31	0	22	38	10	2	226
India	51	76	2	78	21	0	41	9	2	280
Pakistan	42	47	1	24	21	31	0	9	3	178
Sri Lanka	15	4	3	0	10	17	11	0	2	62
Zimbabwe	-	-	1	-	4	2	1	4	0	12
Total Scored	504	592	122	318	140	232	183	43	9	2143

CENTURIES IN TEST CRICKET

§ Denotes century on first appearance against that country. Where known I have shown the batting time, balls faced and boundary details of the complete innings. The following abbreviations are used: m - minutes; h - minutes where time has been converted from hours e.g. $4^3/_4$ hours converts to 285h; a - about; n - nearly; > more than; †just over; < less than; ‡ just under; ¥ indicates that the ball was hit over the boundary but the match was played in Australia at a time when such hits were awarded only five runs, the ball having to be hit clear out of the ground for a six. Such sixes are indicated thus: !. The majority of this information was supplied by Dr Colin Clowes. ® indicates retired hurt.

AUSTRALIA (504)			Time	Balls	6/4	Opponents		
Archer,RG		128	213m		2/19	West Indies	Kingston	1954-55
Armstrong,WW	(6)	159*			-/16	South Africa	Johannesburg[1]	1902-03
		133*	289m		2!/14	England	Melbourne	1907-08
		132	208m		-/13	South Africa	Melbourne	1910-11
		158	205m	209	-/17	England	Sydney	1920-21
		121	206m		-/11	England	Adelaide	1920-21
		123*	214m		-/9	England	Melbourne	1920-21
Badcock,CL		118	205m		-/15	England	Melbourne	1936-37
Bannerman,C		165* §	285h		-/18	England	Melbourne	1876-77
		(The first century in Test cricket)						
Bardsley,W	(6)	136 }	228m	230	1/12	England	The Oval	1909
		130 }	200m	250	-/10			
		132 §	150m		-/16	South Africa	Sydney	1910-11
		121	150m	157	2/11	South Africa	Manchester	1912
		164	216m	283	1/16	South Africa	Lord's	1912
		193*	398m		-/14	England	Lord's	1926
Barnes,SG	(3)	234	642m	661	-/17	England	Sydney	1946-47
		112	227m		1/6	India	Adelaide	1947-48

		141	227m	286	2/14	England	Lord's	1948
Benaud,J		142	211m	207	2/18	Pakistan	Melbourne	1972-73
Benaud,R	(3)	121	96m		2/18	West Indies	Kingston	1954-55
		122	220m		-/20	South Africa	Johannesburg[3]	1957-58
		100	186m		1/9	South Africa	Johannesburg[3]	1957-58
Blewett,GS	(2)	102* §	261m	180	-/12	England	Adelaide	1994-95
		115	202m	158	-/19	England	Perth	1994-95
Bonnor,GJ		128	115m		3¥/14	England	Sydney	1884-85
Boon,DC	(21)	123 §	336m	255	-/14	India	Adelaide	1985-86
		131	345m	311	-/16	India	Sydney	1985-86
		122	332m	258	-/21	India	Chennai[1]	1986-87
		103	305m	274	-/14	England	Adelaide	1986-87
		143	342m	255	-/15	New Zealand	Brisbane[2]	1987-88
		184*	492m	431	-/14	England	Sydney	1987-88
		149	479m	425	-/10	West Indies	Sydney	1988-89
		200	451m	326	-/28	New Zealand	Perth	1989-90
		121	368m	276	-/9	England	Adelaide	1990-91
		109*	388m	253	-/9	West Indies	Kingston	1990-91
		129*	444m	361	-/13	India	Sydney	1991-92
		135	465m	352	-/16	India	Adelaide	1991-92
		107	377m	304	-/14	India	Perth	1991-92
		111	325m	259	-/13	West Indies	Brisbane[2]	1992-93
		164*	471m	378	-/15	England	Lord's	1993
		101	257m	177	-/17	England	Nottingham	1993
		107	310m	225	-/17	England	Leeds	1993
		106	317m	242	-/9	New Zealand	Hobart	1993-94
		114	336m	220	-/10	Pakistan	Karachi[1]	1994-95
		131	378m	277	-/14	England	Melbourne	1994-95
		110	408m	312	-/11	Sri Lanka	Melbourne	1995-96
Booth,BC	(5)	112	217m		-/14	England	Brisbane[2]	1962-63
		103	348m		-/19	England	Melbourne	1962-63
		169 §	330m		-/19	South Africa	Brisbane[2]	1963-64
		102*	306m	235	-/5	South Africa	Sydney	1963-64
		117	315m		-/13	West Indies	Port-of-Spain	1964-65
Border,AR	(27)	105 §	373m	275	-/7	Pakistan	Melbourne	1978-79
		162 §	416m		1/24	India	Chennai[1]	1979-80
		115	384m	296	-/13	England	Perth	1979-80
		150* }	397m		2/16	Pakistan	Lahore[2]	1979-80
		153 }	214m		5/16			
		124	303m	265	-/12	India	Melbourne	1980-81
		123*	415m	356	-/17	England	Manchester	1981
		106*	290m	230	-/13	England	The Oval	1981
		126	336m	278	-/9	West Indies	Adelaide	1981-82
		118	347m	254	-/10	Pakistan	Brisbane[2]	1983-84
		117*	310m	208	-/11	Pakistan	Adelaide	1983-84
		100*	279m	269	-/12	West Indies	Port-of-Spain	1983-84
		196	450m	317	-/22	England	Lord's	1985
		146*	346m	333	-/13	England	Manchester	1985
		152*	458m	301	2/20	New Zealand	Brisbane[2]	1985-86
		163	410m	358	-/16	India	Melbourne	1985-86
		140 }	386m	338	1/15	New Zealand	Christchurch	1985-86
		114* }	280m	201	-/10			
		106	252m	172	1/14	India	Chennai[1]	1986-87
		125	372m	282	-/17	England	Perth	1986-87
		100*	303m	253	-/11	England	Adelaide	1986-87
		205	599m	485	-/20	New Zealand	Adelaide	1987-88
		113*	354m	237	-/13	Pakistan	Faisalabad	1988-89

		106	217m	164	-/16	Sri Lanka	Moratuwa	1992-93
		110	350m	274	1/5	West Indies	Melbourne	1992-93
		200*	565m	399	-/26	England	Leeds	1993
		105	275m	193	-/15	New Zealand	Brisbane[2]	1993-94
Bradman,DG	(29)	112	247m	281	-/7	England	Melbourne	1928-29
		123	217m	247	-/8	England	Melbourne	1928-29
		131	258m	287	-/10	England	Nottingham	1930
		254	339m	376	-/25	England	Lord's	1930
		334	378m	446	-/46	England	Leeds	1930
		232	408m	410	-/16	England	The Oval	1930
		223	297m		-/24	West Indies	Brisbane[1]	1930-31
		152	154m		-/13	West Indies	Melbourne	1930-31
		226 §	277m		-/22	South Africa	Brisbane[2]	1931-32
		112	155m		-/10	South Africa	Sydney	1931-32
		167	183m		-/18	South Africa	Melbourne	1931-32
		299*	396m		-/23	South Africa	Adelaide	1931-32
		103*	185m	146	-/7	England	Melbourne	1932-33
		304	430m	466	2/44	England	Leeds	1934
		244	316m	277	1/32	England	The Oval	1934
		270	458m	375	-/22	England	Melbourne	1936-37
		212	441m	393	-/14	England	Adelaide	1936-37
		169	223m		-/15	England	Melbourne	1936-37
		144*	363m	377	-/5	England	Nottingham	1938
		102*	147m	132	-/15	England	Lord's	1938
		103	176m	181	-/9	England	Leeds	1938
		187	318m	313	-/19	England	Brisbane[2]	1946-47
		234	393m	396	-/24	England	Sydney	1946-47
		185 §	288m		-/20	India	Brisbane[2]	1947-48
		132	197m		-/8	India	Melbourne	1947-48
		127*	178m		-/12			
		201	272m		1/21	India	Adelaide	1947-48
		138	288m	315	-/10	England	Nottingham	1948
		173*	255m	294	-/29	England	Leeds	1948
Brown,WA	(4)	105	199m	199	-/14	England	Lord's	1934
		121	207m	225	1/5	South Africa	Cape Town	1935-36
		133	320m	377	-/13	England	Nottingham	1938
		206*	370m	386	-/22	England	Lord's	1938
Burge,PJP	(4)	181	411m		-/22	England	The Oval	1961
		103	331m	293	-/9	England	Sydney	1962-63
		160	314m	307	-/24	England	Leeds	1964
		120	255m		-/12	England	Melbourne	1965-66
Burke,JW	(3)	101* §	245m		-/9	England	Adelaide	1950-51
		161	504m		-/15	India	Mumbai[2]	1956-57
		189	578m		-/15	South Africa	Cape Town	1957-58
Chappell,GS	(24)	108 §	272m		-/10	England	Perth	1970-71
		131	372m		-/14	England	Lord's	1972
		113	272m		-/17	England	The Oval	1972
		116*	230m		-/12	Pakistan	Melbourne	1972-73
		106	255m		-/10	West Indies	Bridgetown	1972-73
		247*	410m	356	1/30	New Zealand	Wellington	1973-74
		133	186m	175	-/8			
		144	252m	209	-/16	England	Sydney	1974-75
		102	249m	177	-/11	England	Melbourne	1974-75
		123	231m	232	2/15	West Indies	Brisbane[2]	1975-76
		109*	161m	172	1/14			
		182*	366m	274	-/22	West Indies	Sydney	1975-76
		121	246m		-/9	Pakistan	Melbourne	1976-77

		112	282m	230	1/15	England	Manchester	1977
		124	376m	299	-/12	West Indies	Brisbane[2]	1979-80
		114	288m	213	-/14	England	Melbourne	1979-80
		235	441m		-/24	Pakistan	Faisalabad	1979-80
		204 §	408m	296	-/27	India	Sydney	1980-81
		201	417m	296	-/22	Pakistan	Brisbane[2]	1981-82
		176	257m	218	2/23	New Zealand	Christchurch	1981-82
		117	259m	174	2/11	England	Perth	1982-83
		115	209m	201	-/19	England	Adelaide	1982-83
		150*	334m	250	-/17	Pakistan	Brisbane[2]	1983-84
		182	526m	400	-/17	Pakistan	Sydney	1983-84
Chappell,IM	(14)	151	252m		-/21	India	Melbourne	1967-68
		117 §	247m		-/17	West Indies	Brisbane[2]	1968-69
		165	319m		-/16	West Indies	Melbourne	1968-69
		138	276m		-/21	India	Delhi	1969-70
		111	243m		-/12	England	Melbourne	1970-71
		104	326m		-/9	England	Adelaide	1970-71
		118	330m		-/20	England	The Oval	1972
		196	295m	243	4/21	Pakistan	Adelaide	1972-73
		106*	247m		-/15	West Indies	Bridgetown	1972-73
		109	302m		-/10	West Indies	Georgetown	1972-73
		145 }	283m	268	1/17	New Zealand	Wellington	1973-74
		121 }	199m	218	1/13			
		192	442m	367	-/17	England	The Oval	1975
		156	377m	261	-/19	West Indies	Perth	1975-76
Chipperfield,AG		109 §	171m	193	-/8	South Africa	Durban[2]	1935-36
Collins,HL	(4)	104 §	219m	278	-/11	England	Sydney	1920-21
		162	258m		-/20	England	Adelaide	1920-21
		203	277m		-/26	South Africa	Johannesburg[1]	1921-22
		114	236m		-/9	England	Sydney	1924-25
Cosier,GJ	(2)	109 §	254m	186	-/13	West Indies	Melbourne	1975-76
		168	228m		-/20	Pakistan	Melbourne	1976-77
Cowper,RM	(5)	143	339m		-/18	West Indies	Port-of-Spain	1964-65
		102	183m		-/13	West Indies	Bridgetown	1964-65
		307	727m	589	-/20	England	Melbourne	1965-66
		108	212m		-/13	India	Adelaide	1967-68
		165	321m	346	-/13	India	Sydney	1967-68
Darling,J	(3)	101	195m		-/19	England	Sydney	1897-98
		178	285m		1!/26	England	Adelaide	1897-98
		160	175m		-/30	England	Sydney	1897-98
Davis,IC		105 §	229m		1/14	Pakistan	Adelaide	1976-77
Duff,RA	(2)	104 §	206m		-/11	England	Melbourne	1901-02
		146	197m		-/20	England	The Oval	1905
Dyson,J	(2)	102	292m	233	-/14	England	Leeds	1981
		127* §	377m	321	-/11	West Indies	Sydney	1981-82
Edwards,R	(2)	170*	344m		-/13	England	Nottingham	1972
		115	322m	252	-/6	England	Perth	1974-75
Favell,LE		101				India	Chennai[2]	1959-60
Fingleton,JHW	(5)	112	191m	212	-/7	South Africa	Cape Town	1935-36
		108	132m	169	-/7	South Africa	Johannesburg[1]	1935-36
		118	224m	212	-/9	South Africa	Durban[2]	1935-36
		100	301m		-/6	England	Brisbane[2]	1936-37
		136	386m		-/6	England	Melbourne	1936-37
Giffen,G		161	254m		1¥/22	England	Sydney	1894-95
Gilmour,GJ		101	187m	146	1/20	New Zealand	Christchurch	1976-77
Graham,H	(2)	107 §	140m		-/12	England	Lord's	1893
		105	135m		-/14	England	Sydney	1894-95

Player	No.	Score	Time	Balls	6s/4s	Opponent	Venue	Season
Gregory,JM	(2)	100	137m		-/12	England	Melbourne	1920-21
		119	85m		2/19	South Africa	Johannesburg[1]	1921-22
		(Including the fastest Test century in 70 minutes)						
Gregory,SE	(4)	201	243m		-/28	England	Sydney	1894-95
		103	160m		-/17	England	Lord's	1896
		117	195m		-/15	England	The Oval	1899
		112	122m		-/15	England	Adelaide	1903-04
Hartigan,RJ		116 §	319m		-/18	England	Adelaide	1907-08
Harvey,RN	(21)	153	249m		-/11	India	Melbourne	1947-48
		112 §	188m	186	-/17	England	Leeds	1948
		178	237m	253	-/16	South Africa	Cape Town	1949-50
		151*	325m	361	-/14	South Africa	Durban[2]	1949-50
		100	133m	132	-/13	South Africa	Johannesburg[2]	1949-50
		116	130m	128	-/14	South Africa	Port Elizabeth	1949-50
		109	155m		-/16	South Africa	Brisbane[2]	1952-53
		190	361m		-/21	South Africa	Sydney	1952-53
		116	125m		-/14	South Africa	Adelaide	1952-53
		205	295m		-/19	South Africa	Melbourne	1952-53
		122	240m	248	-/11	England	Manchester	1953
		162	380m		-/17	England	Brisbane[2]	1954-55
		133	306m		-/20	West Indies	Kingston	1954-55
		133	242m		-/18	West Indies	Port-of-Spain	1954-55
		204	426m		1/24	West Indies	Kingston	1954-55
		140	244m		-/18	India	Mumbai[2]	1956-57
		167	370m	325	-/16	England	Melbourne	1958-59
		114	240h		-/14	India	Delhi	1959-60
		102	287m		-/9	India	Mumbai[2]	1959-60
		114	212m		-/18	England	Birmingham	1961
		154	326m		-/18	England	Adelaide	1962-63
Hassett,AL	(10)	128	394m	395	-/10	England	Brisbane[2]	1946-47
		198*	342m		-/16	India	Adelaide	1947-48
		137	352m	385	1/20	England	Nottingham	1948
		112 §	261m	283	-/7	South Africa	Johannesburg[1]	1949-50
		167	314m	314	1/14	South Africa	Port Elizabeth	1949-50
		132	381m		-/10	West Indies	Sydney	1951-52
		102	323m		-/10	West Indies	Melbourne	1951-52
		163	359m		-/15	South Africa	Adelaide	1952-53
		115	394m	315	-/9	England	Nottingham	1953
		104	296m	251	-/11	England	Lord's	1953
Healy,IA	(2)	102*	164m	133	-/12	England	Manchester	1993
		113*	262m	181	-/11	New Zealand	Perth	1993-94
Hendry,HSTL		112	233m	305	-/7	England	Sydney	1928-29
Hilditch,AMJ	(2)	113 §	339m	273	-/7	West Indies	Melbourne	1984-85
		119	245m	182	2/17	England	Leeds	1985
Hill,C	(7)	188	294m		-/21	England	Melbourne	1897-98
		135	240m		-/17	England	Lord's	1899
		119	145m		-/19	England	Sheffield	1902
		142 §	135m		1/16	South Africa	Johannesburg[1]	1902-03
		160	254m		-/12	England	Adelaide	1907-08
		191	202m		-/18	South Africa	Sydney	1910-11
		100	<100m		-/13	South Africa	Melbourne	1910-11
Hookes,DW		143* §	201m	152	2/17	Sri Lanka	Kandy	1982-83
Horan,TP		124	250m		-/7	England	Melbourne	1881-82
Hughes,KJ	(9)	129	481m	411	2/8	England	Brisbane[2]	1978-79
		100	278m		1/10	India	Chennai[1]	1979-80
		130* §	376m	244	1/17	West Indies	Brisbane[2]	1979-80
		117	205m	213	3/14	England	Lord's	1980

		213	383m	301	-/21	India	Adelaide	1980-81
		106	271m	198	-/17	Pakistan	Perth	1981-82
		100*	266m	200	-/11	West Indies	Melbourne	1981-82
		137	379m	316	3/12	England	Sydney	1982-83
		106	269m	245	1/11	Pakistan	Adelaide	1983-84
Iredale,FA	(2)	140	245m		-/17	England	Adelaide	1894-95
		108	220m		-/16	England	Manchester	1896
Jackson,AA		164 §	318m	331	-/15	England	Adelaide	1928-29
Jones,DM	(11)	210 §	502m	330	2/27	India	Chennai[1]	1986-87
		184*	540m	421	1/12	England	Sydney	1986-87
		102 §	251m	174	-/13	Sri Lanka	Perth	1987-88
		216	538m	347	-/16	West Indies	Adelaide	1988-89
		157	391m	295	-/17	England	Birmingham	1989
		122	214m	180	-/17	England	The Oval	1989
		118*	252m	178	-/6	Sri Lanka	Hobart	1989-90
		116 }	331m	239	-/7	Pakistan	Adelaide	1989-90
		121* }	260m	205	1/11			
		150*	395m	265	1/14	India	Perth	1991-92
		100*	281m	213	2/7	Sri Lanka	Colombo (PIS)	1992-93
Kelleway,C	(3)	114	201m	244	-/5	South Africa	Manchester	1912
		102	196m	279	-/7	South Africa	Lord's	1912
		147	422m		-/13	England	Adelaide	1920-21
Kippax,AF	(2)	100	217m	255	-/9	England	Melbourne	1928-29
		146 §	229m		-/18	West Indies	Adelaide	1930-31
Lawry,WM	(13)	130	369m		-/18	England	Lord's	1961
		102	270m		-/13	England	Manchester	1961
		157	329m		-/19	South Africa	Melbourne	1963-64
		106	281m	311	3/5	England	Manchester	1964
		210	544m		3/25	West Indies	Bridgetown	1964-65
		166	419m		1/23	England	Brisbane[2]	1965-66
		119	255m		1/9	England	Adelaide	1965-66
		108	369m		-/7	England	Melbourne	1965-66
		100	179m	186	-/8	India	Melbourne	1967-68
		135	447m		-/22	England	The Oval	1968
		105	286m		-/12	West Indies	Brisbane[2]	1968-69
		205	461m		1/12	West Indies	Melbourne	1968-69
		151	500m	367	-/12	West Indies	Sydney	1968-69
Lindwall,RR	(2)	100	113m	90	1/13	England	Melbourne	1946-47
		118	159m		2/15	West Indies	Bridgetown	1954-55
Loxton,SJE		101 §	144m	193	-/14	South Africa	Johannesburg[2]	1949-50
Lyons,JJ		134	165h		-/16	England	Sydney	1891-92
Macartney,CG	(7)	137	193m		-/16	South Africa	Sydney	1910-11
		170	244m	227	-/20	England	Sydney	1920-21
		115	186m	176	-/13	England	Leeds	1921
		116	114m		1/17	South Africa	Durban[1]	1921-22
		133*	205m		-/13	England	Lord's	1926
		151	170m		-/21	England	Leeds	1926
		109	178m		-/14	England	Manchester	1926
McCabe,SJ	(6)	187*	242m	233	-/25	England	Sydney	1932-33
		137	214m	205	-/22	England	Manchester	1934
		149	268m	266	-/6	South Africa	Durban[2]	1935-36
		189*	197m	232	-/29	South Africa	Johannesburg[1]	1935-36
		112	163m		-/16	England	Melbourne	1936-37
		232	235m	276	1/34	England	Nottingham	1938
McCool,CL		104*	183m	194	-/8	England	Melbourne	1946-47
McCosker,RB	(4)	127	372m	294	-/21	England	The Oval	1975
		109*	249m	267	-/7	West Indies	Melbourne	1975-76

		105	222m		-/10	Pakistan	Melbourne	1976-77
		107	371m	307	1/10	England	Nottingham	1977
McDonald,CC	(5)	154	316m		1/16	South Africa	Adelaide	1952-53
		110	257m		-/12	West Indies	Port-of-Spain	1954-55
		127	323m		-/11	West Indies	Kingston	1954-55
		170	487m	315	-/12	England	Adelaide	1958-59
		133	339m	249	-/7	England	Melbourne	1958-59
McDonnell,PS	(3)	147	250m		1¥/16	England	Sydney	1881-82
		103	136m	168	-/14	England	The Oval	1884
		124	195m		-/9	England	Adelaide	1884-85
McLeod,CE		112	244m		-/4	England	Melbourne	1897-98
Mann,AL		105	184m		-/11	India	Perth	1977-78
Marsh,GR	(4)	118	346m	287	-/14	New Zealand	Auckland	1985-86
		101	370m	300	-/11	India	Mumbai[3]	1986-87
		110 §	392m	311	-/12	England	Brisbane[2]	1986-87
		138	432m	382	-/15	England	Nottingham	1989
Marsh,RW	(3)	118 §	164m		4/10	Pakistan	Adelaide	1972-73
		132	305m	266	-/9	New Zealand	Adelaide	1973-74
		110*	297m	173	-/10	England	Melbourne	1976-77
Matthews,GRJ	(4)	115 §	229m	205	1/10	New Zealand	Brisbane[2]	1985-86
		100*	195m	152	2/9	India	Melbourne	1985-86
		130	306m	235	-/12	New Zealand	Wellington	1985-86
		128	242m	175	-/17	England	Sydney	1990-91
Miller,KR	(7)	141*	270m	198	1/9	England	Adelaide	1946-47
		145*	354m		1/6	England	Sydney	1950-51
		129	246m		-/15	West Indies	Sydney	1951-52
		109	292m	269	1/14	England	Lord's	1953
		147	346m		-/15	West Indies	Kingston	1954-55
		137	237m		-/22	West Indies	Bridgetown	1954-55
		109	328m		1/15	West Indies	Kingston	1954-55
Moody,TM	(2)	106 §	218m	179	-/12	Sri Lanka	Brisbane[2]	1989-90
		101 §	186m	149	-/9	India	Perth	1991-92
Moroney,J	(2)	118	321m	334	-/13	South Africa	Johannesburg[2]	1949-50
		101*	225m	197	-/17			
Morris,AR	(12)	155	364m	317	-/8	England	Melbourne	1946-47
		122	268m	255	2/12	England	Adelaide	1946-47
		124*	198m	171	-/12			
		100*	196m		-/7	India	Melbourne	1947-48
		105	209m	214	1/14	England	Lord's	1948
		182	291m	294	-/33	England	Leeds	1948
		196	406m	493	-/16	England	The Oval	1948
		111	267m	242	1/9	South Africa	Johannesburg[2]	1949-50
		157	301m	226	1/14	South Africa	Port Elizabeth	1949-50
		206	462m		-/23	England	Adelaide	1950-51
		153	419m		2/18	England	Brisbane[2]	1954-55
		111	322m		-/18	West Indies	Port-of-Spain	1954-55
Murdoch,WL	(2)	153*	330m		-/18	England	The Oval	1880
		211	484m	525	-/24	England	The Oval	1884
Noble,MA		133	287m		-/17	England	Sydney	1903-04
O'Neill,NC	(6)	134			-/17	Pakistan	Lahore[2]	1959-60
		163	360h		-/14	India	Mumbai[2]	1959-60
		113			-/15	India	Calcutta	1959-60
		181 §	401m		-/22	West Indies	Brisbane[2]	1960-61
		117	200m		-/14	England	The Oval	1961
		100	171m		-/13	England	Adelaide	1962-63
Pellew,CE	(2)	116	203m		-/8	England	Melbourne	1920-21
		104	123m		-/14	England	Adelaide	1920-21

Phillips,WB	(2)	159 §	307m	240	-/20	Pakistan	Perth	1983-84
		120	227m	197	4/14	West Indies	Bridgetown	1983-84
Ponsford,WH	(7)	110 §	228m		-/8	England	Sydney	1924-25
		128	222m		-/6	England	Melbourne	1924-25
		110	159m	206	-/11	England	The Oval	1930
		183	348m		-/11	West Indies	Sydney	1930-31
		109	165m		-/12	West Indies	Brisbane[1]	1930-31
		181	387m	425	-/19	England	Leeds	1934
		266	460m	418	-/27	England	The Oval	1934
Ransford,VS		143*	252m	260	-/21	England	Lord's	1909
Redpath,IR	(8)	132	267m	277	-/11	West Indies	Sydney	1968-69
		171	484m		-/14	England	Perth	1970-71
		135	277m		-/14	Pakistan	Melbourne	1972-73
		159*	348m	310	-/20	New Zealand	Auckland	1973-74
		105	344m	239	-/9	England	Sydney	1974-75
		102	320m	258	-/10	West Indies	Melbourne	1975-76
		103	220m	175	2/6	West Indies	Adelaide	1975-76
		101	325m	230	-/11	West Indies	Melbourne	1975-76
Richardson,AJ		100	186m		-/10	England	Leeds	1926
Richardson,VY		138	198m		-/13	England	Melbourne	1924-25
Rigg,KE		127 §	240m		-/12	South Africa	Sydney	1931-32
Ritchie,GM	(3)	106*	293m	216	3/9	Pakistan	Faisalabad	1982-83
		146	361m	308	-/16	England	Nottingham	1985
		128 §	389m	321	-/11	India	Adelaide	1985-86
Ryder,J	(3)	142	181m		-/12	South Africa	Cape Town	1921-22
		201*	385m		1/12	England	Adelaide	1924-25
		112	224m	219	1/6	England	Melbourne	1928-29
Scott,HJH		102	203m	216	-/15	England	The Oval	1884
Serjeant,CS		124	268m		1/18	West Indies	Georgetown	1977-78
Sheahan,AP	(2)	114	257m		-/20	India	Kanpur	1969-70
		127	275m	207	-/12	Pakistan	Melbourne	1972-73
Simpson, RB	(10)	311	762m	740	1/23	England	Manchester	1964
		153 § }	408m	361	-/12	Pakistan	Karachi[1]	1964-65
		115 § }	200m	192	-/15			
		201	414m		-/22	West Indies	Bridgetown	1964-65
		225	545m		1/18	England	Adelaide	1965-66
		153	386m		-/12	South Africa	Cape Town	1966-67
		103	232m		-/12	India	Adelaide	1967-68
		109	220m	170	-/8	India	Melbourne	1967-68
		176	391m	343	-/17	India	Perth	1977-78
		100	264m		-/6	India	Adelaide	1977-78
Slater,MJ	(7)	152	293m	263	-/18	England	Lord's	1993
		168	328m	235	-/17	New Zealand	Hobart	1993-94
		110	250m	155	-/14	Pakistan	Rawalpindi[2]	1994-95
		176	324m	244	-/25	England	Brisbane[2]	1994-95
		103	283m	236	-/10	England	Sydney	1994-95
		124	296m	231	-/13	England	Perth	1994-95
		219	460m	321	5/15	Sri Lanka	Perth	1995-96
Stackpole,KR	(7)	134	196m		2/18	South Africa	Cape Town	1966-67
		103 §	290m		-/14	India	Mumbai[2]	1969-70
		207	454m		1/25	England	Brisbane[2]	1970-71
		136	410m		-/16	England	Adelaide	1970-71
		114	335m		-/10	England	Nottingham	1972
		142	265m		-/22	West Indies	Kingston	1972-73
		122 §	222m	191	-/13	New Zealand	Melbourne	1973-74
Taylor,JM		108	164m		-/8	England	Sydney	1924-25
Taylor,MA	(14)	136 §	394m	315	-/16	England	Leeds	1989

		219	551m	461	-/23	England	Nottingham	1989
		164 §	425m	334	2/17	Sri Lanka	Brisbane[2]	1989-90
		108	291m	291	-/12	Sri Lanka	Hobart	1989-90
		101 §	322m	240	-/11	Pakistan	Melbourne	1989-90
		101*	258m	227	-/8	Pakistan	Sydney	1989-90
		144	361m	277	-/12	West Indies	St John's	1990-91
		100	395m	303	-/9	India	Adelaide	1991-92
		124	325m	234	2/12	England	Manchester	1993
		111	323m	245	1/10	England	Lord's	1993
		142*	360m	255	-/8	New Zealand	Perth	1993-94
		170 §	495m	349	-/12	South Africa	Melbourne	1993-94
		113	364m	248	-/9	England	Sydney	1994-95
		123	356m	243	-/13	Pakistan	Hobart	1995-96
Toohey,PM		122	313m	293	-/10	West Indies	Kingston	1977-78
Trott,G HS		143	210m		-/24	England	Lord's	1896
Trumper,VT	(8)	135*	195m		-/20	England	Lord's	1899
		104	115m		-/14	England	Manchester	1902
		185*	230m		-/25?	England	Sydney	1903-04
		113	189m		-/12	England	Adelaide	1903-04
		166	241m		-/18	England	Sydney	1907-08
		159	178m		1/15	South Africa	Melbourne	1910-11
		214*	242m		-/26	South Africa	Adelaide	1910-11
		113	226m	206	-/12	England	Sydney	1911-12
Turner,A		136	279m	222	-/15	West Indies	Adelaide	1975-76
Walters,KD	(15)	155 §	322m		2/11	England	Brisbane[2]	1965-66
		115	263m		-/5	England	Melbourne	1965-66
		118	214m	185	-/12	West Indies	Sydney	1968-69
		110	194m		-/13	West Indies	Adelaide	1968-68
		242)	480m	412	-/24	West Indies	Sydney	1968-69
		103)	196m	181	-/7			
		102	208m		2/14	India	Chennai[1]	1969-70
		112	328m		-/9	England	Brisbane[2]	1970-71
		102*	200m		-/15	West Indies	Bridgetown	1972-73
		112	148m		1/19	West Indies	Port-of-Spain	1972-73
		104*	165m	138	-/15	New Zealand	Auckland	1973-74
		103	140m	119	1/11	England	Perth	1974-75
		107	247m		-/9	Pakistan	Adelaide	1976-77
		250	394m	342	2/30	New Zealand	Christchurch	1976-77
		107	276m	206	-/6	New Zealand	Melbourne	1980-81
Waugh,ME	(10)	138 §	237m	186	-/18	England	Adelaide	1990-91
		139*	307m	188	3/11	West Indies	St John's	1990-91
		112	327m	234	-/9	West Indies	Melbourne	1992-93
		137	239m	219	-/18	England	Birmingham	1993
		111	187m	139	-/15	New Zealand	Hobart	1993-94
		113*	283m	222	-/13	South Africa	Durban[2]	1993-94
		140	323m	215	1/14	England	Brisbane[2]	1994-95
		126	276m	192	-/12	West Indies	Kingston	1994-95
		116	262m	106	1/8	Pakistan	Sydney	1995-96
		111	261m	223	1/7	Sri Lanka	Perth	1995-96
Waugh,SR	(11)	177*	308m	242	-/24	England	Leeds	1989
		152*	329m	249	-/17	England	Lord's	1989
		134*	234m	234	-/14	Sri Lanka	Hobart	1989-90
		100	269m	207	-/5	West Indies	Sydney	1992-93
		157*	405m	305	-/19	England	Leeds	1993
		147*	380m	281	-/15	New Zealand	Brisbane[2]	1993-94
		164 §	380m	276	-/19	South Africa	Adelaide	1993-94
		200	555m	425	1/17	West Indies	Kingston	1994-95

		112*	366m	275	-/7	Pakistan	Brisbane[2]	1995-96
		131*	329m	252	-/12	Sri Lanka	Melbourne	1995-96
		170	421m	316	-/13	Sri Lanka	Adelaide	1995-96
Wellham,DM		103 §	266m	222	-/12	England	The Oval	1981
Wessels,KC	(4)	162 §	464m	343	-/17	England	Brisbane[2]	1982-83
		141 §	252m	188	-/21	Sri Lanka	Kandy	1982-83
		179	330m	233	1/24	Pakistan	Adelaide	1983-84
		173	482m	351	-/14	West Indies	Sydney	1984-85
Wood,GM	(9)	126	337m		1/8	West Indies	Georgetown	1977-78
		100	392m	283	-/6	England	Melbourne	1978-79
		112	363m	295	-/10	England	Lord's	1980
		111 §	318m	229	-/12	New Zealand	Brisbane[2]	1980-81
		125	286m	217	1/10	India	Adelaide	1980-81
		100	375m	305	-/3	Pakistan	Melbourne	1981-82
		100	261m	249	-/10	New Zealand	Auckland	1981-82
		172	601m	449	-/21	England	Nottingham	1985
		111	391m	287	-/14	West Indies	Perth	1988-89
Woodfull,WM	(7)	141	295m		-/12	England	Leeds	1926
		117	259m		-/6	England	Manchester	1926
		111	258m	286	-/6	England	Sydney	1928-29
		107	271m	309	-/7	England	Melbourne	1928-29
		102	325m	381	-/3	England	Melbourne	1928-29
		155	325m	391	-/9	England	Lord's	1930
		161	300m		-/5	South Africa	Melbourne	1931-32
Yallop,GN	(8)	121 §	228m		-/13	India	Adelaide	1977-78
		102 §	347m	307	-/8	England	Brisbane[2]	1978-79
		121	266m	212	-/13	England	Sydney	1978-79
		167	520m	392	-/14	India	Calcutta	1979-80
		172	504m		-/19	Pakistan	Faisalabad	1979-80
		114	177m	125	-/17	England	Manchester	1981
		141	402m	274	-/13	Pakistan	Perth	1983-84
		268	716m	517	-/29	Pakistan	Melbourne	1983-84

ENGLAND (592)			Time	Balls	6/4	Opponents		
Abel,R	(2)	120	n240h		-/11	South Africa	Cape Town	1888-89
		132*	325m		-/11	Australia	Sydney	1891-92
Allen,GOB		122 §	170m		1/14	New Zealand	Lord's	1931
Ames,LEG	(8)	105	220m		-/17	West Indies	Port-of-Spain	1929-30
		149	160m		-/17	West Indies	Kingston	1929-30
		137 §	205m		2/18	New Zealand	Lord's	1931
		103	144m		-/11	New Zealand	Christchurch	1932-33
		120	262m	333	-/14	Australia	Lord's	1934
		126	251m		-/16	West Indies	Kingston	1934-35
		148*	210m		1/14	South Africa	The Oval	1935
		115	145m	168	-/13	South Africa	Cape Town	1938-39
Amiss,DL	(11)	112	304m		-/15	Pakistan	Lahore[2]	1972-73
		158	326m		-/27	Pakistan	Hyderabad	1972-73
		138* §	365m		-/12	New Zealand	Nottingham	1973
		174	396m	429	-/19	West Indies	Port-of-Spain	1973-74
		262*	570m	563	1/40	West Indies	Kingston	1973-74
		118	340m	246	-/15	West Indies	Georgetown	1973-74
		188	>360h		-/29	India	Lord's	1974
		183	421m	370	-/19	Pakistan	The Oval	1974
		164*	406m	351	-/25	New Zealand	Christchurch	1974-75
		203	443m	320	-/28	West Indies	The Oval	1976
		179	496m	393	1/22	India	Delhi	1976-77

Atherton,MA	(10)	151	497m	382	-/16	New Zealand	Nottingham	1990
		131	338m	276	-/12	India	Manchester	1990
		105	451m	349	-/8	Australia	Sydney	1990-91
		144	412m	296	-/17	West Indies	Georgetown	1993-94
		135	539m	383	-/13	West Indies	St John's	1993-94
		101	325m	264	-/13	New Zealand	Nottingham	1994
		111	408m	307	-/14	New Zealand	Manchester	1994
		113	336m	247	-/17	West Indies	Nottingham	1995
		185*	645m	492	-/29	South Africa	Johannesburg[3]	1995-96
		160	469m	376	-/20	India	Nottingham	1996
Athey,CWJ		123	315m	203	-/14	Pakistan	Lord's	1987
Bailey,TE		134*	390m		-/13	New Zealand	Christchurch	1950-51
Bakewell,AH		107 §	230m		-/10	West Indies	The Oval	1933
Barber,RW		185	296m	272	-/19	Australia	Sydney	1965-66
Barnes,W		134	285h		-/7	Australia	Adelaide	1884-85
Barnett,CJ	(2)	129	341m		1/13	Australia	Adelaide	1936-37
		126	172m	183	-/18	Australia	Nottingham	1938
Barrington,KF	(20)	128 §	330h		-/20	West Indies	Bridgetown	1959-60
		121	350m		-/10	West Indies	Port-of-Spain	1959-60
		139 §	430m		-/19	Pakistan	Lahore[2]	1961-62
		151*	420m		-/15	India	Mumbai[2]	1961-62
		172	406m		-/26	India	Kanpur	1961-62
		113*	360h		-/13	India	Delhi	1961-62
		132*	227m		2/16	Australia	Adelaide	1962-63
		101	320m	344	-/4	Australia	Sydney	1962-63
		126 §	254m		1/15	New Zealand	Auckland	1962-63
		256	685m	621	-/26	Australia	Manchester	1964
		148*	432m		-/9	South Africa	Durban[2]	1964-65
		121	329m		1/16	South Africa	Johannesburg[3]	1964-65
		137	437m		1/11	New Zealand	Birmingham	1965
		163	339m	291	-/26	New Zealand	Leeds	1965
		102	329m		-/4	Australia	Adelaide	1965-66
		115	178m		2/8	Australia	Melbourne	1965-66
		148	310m		-/17	Pakistan	Lord's	1967
		109*	410m		-/5	Pakistan	Nottingham	1967
		142	347m		-/14	Pakistan	The Oval	1967
		143	390m		2/14	West Indies	Port-of-Spain	1967-68
Botham,IT	(14)	103	313m		1/12	New Zealand	Christchurch	1977-78
		100 §	190m		-/11	Pakistan	Birmingham	1978
		108	a180h			Pakistan	Lord's	1978
		137	201m	152	5/16	India	Leeds	1979
		119*	224m	212	-/15	Australia	Melbourne	1979-80
		114	206m	144	-/17	India	Mumbai[3]	1979-80
		149*	219m	148	1/27	Australia	Leeds	1981
		118	123m	102	6/13	Australia	Manchester	1981
		142	347m		2/12	India	Kanpur	1981-82
		128	199m	169	2/19	India	Manchester	1982
		208	276m	226	4/19	India	The Oval	1982
		103	156m	103	3/14	New Zealand	Nottingham	1983
		138	236m	167	2/22	New Zealand	Wellington	1983-84
		138	249m	174	4/13	Australia	Brisbane[2]	1986-87
Bowley,EH		109	128m		1/11	New Zealand	Auckland	1929-30
Boycott,G	(22)	113	297m	314	-/10	Australia	The Oval	1964
		117	423m	396	-/12	South Africa	Port Elizabeth	1964-65
		246* §	573m	555	1/29	India	Leeds	1967
		116	293m	254	-/20	West Indies	Georgetown	1967-68
		128	335m		-/18	West Indies	Manchester	1969

		106	269m	273	-/16	West Indies	Lord's	1969
		142*	412m		-/12	Australia	Sydney	1970-71
		119*	250m		-/12	Australia	Adelaide	1970-71
		121*	309m		-/12	Pakistan	Lord's	1971
		112	265m	206	1/14	Pakistan	Leeds	1971
		115	221m		-/20	New Zealand	Leeds	1973
		112	415m	385	-/12	West Indies	Port-of-Spain	1973-74
		107	419m	314	-/11	Australia	Nottingham	1977
		191	[illegible]	[illegible]	[illegible]	Australia	Leeds	1977
		(His 100th first-class century)						
		100*	325m		-/8	Pakistan	Hyderabad	1977-78
		131	417m		-/10	New Zealand	Nottingham	1978
		155	458m	341	-/12	India	Birmingham	1979
		125	418m	293	-/6	India	The Oval	1979
		128*	316m	252	-/12	Australia	Lord's	1980
		104*	345m		-/8	West Indies	St John's	1980-81
		137	441m	321	-/7	Australia	The Oval	1981
		105	441m	278	-/7	India	Delhi	1981-82
Braund,LC	(3)	103*	222m		16/12	Australia	Adelaide	1901-02
		102	171m		-/15	Australia	Sydney	1903-04
		104 §	240h		-/12	South Africa	Lord's	1907
Briggs,J		121	150h		-/15	Australia	Melbourne	1884-85
Broad,BC	(6)	162	435m	314	-/25	Australia	Perth	1986-87
		116	307m	263	1/12	Australia	Adelaide	1986-87
		112	329m	225	-/9	Australia	Melbourne	1986-87
		116	421m	339	-/13	Pakistan	Faisalabad	1987-88
		139	434m	361	-/13	Australia	Sydney	1987-88
		114 §	341m	244	-/11	New Zealand	Christchurch	1987-88
Brown,JT		140	148m		-/16	Australia	Melbourne	1894-95
Chapman,APF		121	152m	166	4/12	Australia	Lord's	1930
Compton,DCS	(17)	102 §	138m	172	-/15	Australia	Nottingham	1938
		120 §	140m		-/16	West Indies	Lord's	1939
		147 }	286m	350	-/14	Australia	Adelaide	1946-47
		103* }	284m	353	-/10			
		163 §	255h		-/19	South Africa	Nottingham	1947
		208	355m		-/20	South Africa	Lord's	1947
		115	190m		-/17	South Africa	Manchester	1947
		113	110m		-/15	South Africa	The Oval	1947
		184	410m	482	-/19	Australia	Nottingham	1948
		145*	327m	322	-/16	Australia	Manchester	1948
		114	156m	201	-/14	South Africa	Johannesburg[2]	1948-49
		114	240h		-/13	New Zealand	Leeds	1949
		116	220m		-/11	New Zealand	Lord's	1949
		112	320m		-/11	South Africa	Nottingham	1951
		133	349m		-/17	West Indies	Port-of-Spain	1953-54
		278	290m		1/33	Pakistan	Nottingham	1954
		158	339m		-/22	South Africa	Manchester	1955
Cowdrey,MC	(22)	102	239m		-/15	Australia	Melbourne	1954-55
		101	369m		1/9	South Africa	Cape Town	1956-57
		154 §	500m		-/16	West Indies	Birmingham	1957
		152	321m		-/14	West Indies	Lord's	1957
		100*	365m	302	-/7	Australia	Sydney	1958-59
		160	278m	279	4/14	India	Leeds	1959
		114	406m		-/11	West Indies	Kingston	1959-60
		119	270h		-/15	West Indies	Port-of-Spain	1959-60
		155	260m		-/22	South Africa	The Oval	1960
		159 §	263m		-/21	Pakistan	Birmingham	1962

		182	323m		1/23	Pakistan	The Oval	1962
		113	270m		-/7	Australia	Melbourne	1962-63
		128*	235m		-/10	New Zealand	Wellington	1962-63
		107	380m		-/17	India	Calcutta	1963-64
		151	374m		1/23	India	Delhi	1963-64
		119	298m		-/13	New Zealand	Lord's	1965
		105	188m	170	-/11	South Africa	Nottingham	1965
		104	197m			Australia	Melbourne	1965-66
		101	345m		-/12	West Indies	Kingston	1967-68
		148	271m		-/21	West Indies	Port-of-Spain	1967-68
		104	244m		-/15	Australia	Birmingham	1968
		(In his 100th Test match)						
		100	227m		-/12	Pakistan	Lahore[2]	1968-69
Crawley,JP		106	256m	217	-/12	Pakistan	The Oval	1996
Denness,MH	(4)	118	244m	228	-/12	India	Lord's	1974
		100	214m	193	-/10	India	Birmingham	1974
		188	492m	448	-/17	Australia	Melbourne	1974-75
		181	414m	392	-/25	New Zealand	Auckland	1974-75
Denton, D		104	100m		-/18	South Africa	Johannesburg[1]	1909-10
Dexter,ER	(9)	141	257m		-/24	New Zealand	Christchurch	1958-59
		136* §	285h		1/19	West Indies	Bridgetown	1959-60
		110	255h			West Indies	Georgetown	1959-60
		180	344m		-/31	Australia	Birmingham	1961
		126*	256m		-/15	India	Kanpur	1961-62
		205	495m		-/22	Pakistan	Karachi[1]	1961-62
		172	228m		5/18	Pakistan	The Oval	1962
		174	481m	382	-/22	Australia	Manchester	1964
		172	339m		-/27	South Africa	Johannesburg[3]	1964-65
D'Oliveira,BL	(5)	109 §	185m		-/13	India	Leeds	1967
		158	315m		-/21	Australia	The Oval	1968
		114*	285m		-/9	Pakistan	Dacca	1968-69
		117	346m		-/11	Australia	Melbourne	1970-71
		100	216m		2/13	New Zealand	Christchurch	1970-71
Douglas,JWHT		119 §	225m		-/14	South Africa	Durban[1]	1913-14
Duleepsinhji,KS	(3)	117	131m		1/10	New Zealand	Auckland	1929-30
		173 §	292m	321	-/21	Australia	Lord's	1930
		109	135h		-/13	New Zealand	The Oval	1931
Edrich,JH	(12)	120 §	318m	287	2/9	Australia	Lord's	1964
		310* §	532m	450	5/52	New Zealand	Leeds	1965
		109	310m		-/11	Australia	Melbourne	1965-66
		103	253m		-/12	Australia	Sydney	1965-66
		146	469m		1/10	West Indies	Bridgetown	1967-68
		164	462m		-/20	Australia	The Oval	1968
		115	296m	306	-/20	New Zealand	Lord's	1969
		111	347m		-/19	New Zealand	Nottingham	1969
		115*	346m		-/16	Australia	Perth	1970-71
		130	354m		-/14	Australia	Adelaide	1970-71
		100*	198m		1/9	India	Manchester	1974
		175	542m	420	-/21	Australia	Lord's	1975
Edrich,WJ	(6)	219	436m		-/25	South Africa	Durban[2]	1938-39
		119	314m	379	-/7	Australia	Sydney	1946-47
		189	362m		1/24	South Africa	Lord's	1947
		191	320m		3/22	South Africa	Manchester	1947
		111	314m	312	1/13	Australia	Leeds	1948
		100	185m		-/14	New Zealand	The Oval	1949
Evans,TG	(2)	104	140m		-/17	West Indies	Manchester	1950
		104	130m		-/16	India	Lord's	1952

Fane,FL		143	n240h		-/17	South Africa	Johannesburg[1]	1905-06
Fletcher,KWR	(7)	113	295m	259	-/13	India	Mumbai[2]	1972-73
		178	379m		2/21	New Zealand	Lord's	1973
		129*	365m	357	-/19	West Indies	Bridgetown	1973-74
		123*	334m		-/8	India	Manchester	1974
		122	513m	377	-/10	Pakistan	The Oval	1974
		146	446m	424	-/11	Australia	Melbourne	1974-75
		216	443m	413	-/30	New Zealand	Auckland	1974-75
Foster,RE		287 §	419m		-/37	Australia	Sydney	1903-04
Fowler,G	(3)	105 §	324m	303	-/8	New Zealand	The Oval	1983
		106	366m	259	-/13	West Indies	Lord's	1984
		201	565m	411	3/21	India	Chennai[1]	1984-85
Fry,CB	(2)	144	213m		-/23	Australia	The Oval	1905
		129	285h		-/7	South Africa	The Oval	1907
Gatting,MW	(10)	136	310m	255	-/21	India	Mumbai[3]	1984-85
		207	504m	308	3/20	India	Chennai[1]	1984-85
		160	356m	266	-/21	Australia	Manchester	1985
		100*	216m	127	-/13	Australia	Birmingham	1985
		183*	383m	294	2/20	India	Birmingham	1986
		121	259m	198	-/13	New Zealand	The Oval	1986
		100	180m	141	-/15	Australia	Adelaide	1986-87
		124	401m	281	-/16	Pakistan	Birmingham	1987
		150*	346m	302	-/21	Pakistan	The Oval	1987
		117	410m	286	-/14	Australia	Adelaide	1994-95
Gibb,PA	(2)	106 §	192m	192	-/7	South Africa	Johannesburg[1]	1938-39
		120	451m		-/2	South Africa	Durban[2]	1938-39
Gooch,GA	(20)	123	211m	162	1/17	West Indies	Lord's	1980
		116	310m		-/13	West Indies	Bridgetown	1980-81
		153	315m		2/21	West Indies	Kingston	1980-81
		127	227m		-/20	India	Chennai[1]	1981-82
		196	423m	310	-/27	Australia	The Oval	1985
		114	355m	280	1/12	India	Lord's	1986
		183	441m	368	-/22	New Zealand	Lord's	1986
		146	410m	303	-/15	West Indies	Nottingham	1988
		154	393m	281	1/19	New Zealand	Birmingham	1990
		333 }	627m	485	3/43	India	Lord's	1990
		123	147m	113	4/13			
		116	237m	163	-/16	India	Manchester	1990
		117	214m	188	-/12	Australia	Adelaide	1990-91
		154*	452m	331	-/18	West Indies	Leeds	1991
		174	329m	252	-/19	Sri Lanka	Lord's	1991
		114	294m	220	2/15	New Zealand	Auckland	1991-92
		135	415m	301	1/19	Pakistan	Leeds	1992
		133	309m	247	2/21	Australia	Manchester	1993
		120	324m	265	1/18	Australia	Nottingham	1993
		210	417m	317	-/29	New Zealand	Nottingham	1994
Gower,DI	(18)	111 §	251m	253	-/14	New Zealand	The Oval	1978
		102	254m	221	-/9	Australia	Perth	1978-79
		200* §	365m	279	1/24	India	Birmingham	1979
		154*	461m		1/16	West Indies	Kingston	1980-81
		114	370m	259	-/16	Australia	Adelaide	1982-83
		112*	281m	196	-/14	New Zealand	Leeds	1983
		108	228m	198	-/16	New Zealand	Lord's	1983
		152	426m	318	-/16	Pakistan	Faisalabad	1983-84
		173*	423m	284	-/16	Pakistan	Lahore[2]	1983-84
		166	379m	283	-/17	Australia	Nottingham	1985
		215	449m	314	1/25	Australia	Birmingham	1985

		157	337m	215	-/20	Australia	The Oval	1985
		131	281m	202	-/14	New Zealand	The Oval	1986
		136	277m	175	-/19	Australia	Perth	1986-87
		106	273m	198	-/16	Australia	Lord's	1989
		157*	365m	271	-/21	India	The Oval	1990
		100	254m	170	-/8	Australia	Melbourne	1990-91
		123	312m	236	-/15	Australia	Sydney	1990-91
Grace,WG	(2)	152 §	235m		-/12	Australia	The Oval	1880
		170	270m		-/22	Australia	The Oval	1886
Graveney,TW	(11)	175 §	503m		-/17	India	Mumbai[2]	1951-52
		111	166m	168	-/14	Australia	Sydney	1954-55
		258	471m		-/30	West Indies	Nottingham	1957
		164	324m		-/17	West Indies	The Oval	1957
		153	247m		-/22	Pakistan	Lord's	1962
		114	200m	214	-/15	Pakistan	Nottingham	1962
		109	230m		1/11	West Indies	Nottingham	1966
		165	361m		-/19	West Indies	The Oval	1966
		151	300h		2/12	India	Lord's	1967
		118	250m		-/20	West Indies	Port-of-Spain	1967-68
		105	275m		-/9	Pakistan	Karachi[1]	1968-69
Greig,AW	(8)	148	360m	291	-/24	India	Mumbai[2]	1972-73
		139 §	197m		-/16	New Zealand	Nottingham	1973
		148	404m	320	2/15	West Indies	Bridgetown	1973-74
		121	311m	254	1/14	West Indies	Georgetown	1973-74
		106	188m	180	1/8	India	Lord's	1974
		110	296m	229	-/17	Australia	Brisbane[2]	1974-75
		116	340m	264	-/15	West Indies	Leeds	1976
		103	426m	343	1/7	India	Calcutta	1976-77
Griffith,SC		140 §	354m		-/15	West Indies	Port-of-Spain	1947-48
Gunn,G	(2)	119 §	150m		-/20	Australia	Sydney	1907-08
		122*	287m		1!/7	Australia	Sydney	1907-08
Gunn,W		102*	250m		-/8	Australia	Manchester	1893
Hammond,WR	(22)	251	461m	605	-/30	Australia	Sydney	1928-29
		200	398m	472	-/17	Australia	Melbourne	1928-29
		119* }	263m	374	-/19	Australia	Adelaide	1928-29
		177 }	440m	603	-/17			
		138*	200m		-/13	South Africa	Birmingham	1929
		101*	>120h		1/5	South Africa	The Oval	1929
		113	325m	356	-/14	Australia	Leeds	1930
		136*	220m		-/6	South Africa	Durban[2]	1930-31
		100*	100m		-/13	New Zealand	The Oval	1931
		112	192m	242	-/16	Australia	Sydney	1932-33
		101	208m	205	-/12	Australia	Sydney	1932-33
		227	396m		-/22	New Zealand	Christchurch	1932-33
		336*	325m	398	10/34	New Zealand	Auckland	1932-33
		167	190m		-/21	India	Manchester	1936
		217	290m		-/30	India	The Oval	1936
		231*	458m		-/27	Australia	Sydney	1936-37
		140	219m		1/14	New Zealand	Lord's	1937
		240	369m	385	-/32	Australia	Lord's	1938
		181	337m	371	-/16	South Africa	Cape Town	1938-39
		120	178m	177	-/16	South Africa	Durban[2]	1938-39
		140	349m		-/7	South Africa	Durban[2]	1938-39
		138	180h		-/21	West Indies	The Oval	1939
Hampshire,JH		107 §	288m	258	-/15	West Indies	Lord's	1969
Hardstaff,J,jr	(4)	114 §	250m		-/9	New Zealand	Lord's	1937
		103	n180h		-/16	New Zealand	The Oval	1937

		169*	326m	395	-/20	Australia	The Oval	1938
		205*	315m		-/16	India	Lord's	1946
Hayes,FC		106* §	240m		-/12	West Indies	The Oval	1973
Hayward,TW	(3)	122	>180h		1!/15	South Africa	Johannesburg[1]	1895-96
		130	255h		-/18	Australia	Manchester	1899
		137	270h		-/20	Australia	The Oval	1899
Hearne,JW		114	225m	243	-/11	Australia	Melbourne	1911-12
Hendren,EH	(7)	132	140m		-/20	South Africa	Leeds	1924
		142	190m		2/14	South Africa	The Oval	1924
		127*	208m		-/18	Australia	Lord's	1926
		169	308m	314	-/16	Australia	Brisbane[1]	1928-29
		205*	398m		-/29	West Indies	Port-of-Spain	1929-30
		123			-/21	West Indies	Georgetown	1929-30
		132	243m	245	-/22	Australia	Manchester	1934
Hick,GA	(4)	178	390m	319	1/20	India	Mumbai[3]	1992-93
		110	272m	182	3/6	South Africa	Leeds	1994
		118*	302m	213	-/17	West Indies	Nottingham	1995
		141	393m	252	-/25	South Africa	Pretoria	1995-96
Hill,AJL		124				South Africa	Cape Town	1895-96
Hobbs,JB	(15)	187	225m		-/23	South Africa	Cape Town	1909-10
		126*	227m	206	-/8	Australia	Melbourne	1911-12
		187	334m	351	-/16	Australia	Adelaide	1911-12
		178	268m		-/22	Australia	Melbourne	1911-12
		107	167m	203	-/15	Australia	Lord's	1912
		122	210m		-/10	Australia	Melbourne	1920-21
		123	151m		-/13	Australia	Adelaide	1920-21
		211	280m		-/16	South Africa	Lord's	1924
		115	219m		-/7	Australia	Sydney	1924-25
		154	288m		-/11	Australia	Melbourne	1924-25
		119	294m		-/7	Australia	Adelaide	1924-25
		119	247m		-/10	Australia	Lord's	1926
		100	227m		-/10	Australia	The Oval	1926
		159	240h		-/20	West Indies	The Oval	1928
		142	278m	301	-/11	Australia	Melbourne	1928-29
Hussain,N	(2)	128 §	327m	227	1/18	India	Birmingham	1996
		107®	000m	180	-/12	India	Nottingham	1996
Hutchings,KL		126	163m		1!/21	Australia	Melbourne	1907-08
Hutton,L	(19)	100	202m		-/8	New Zealand	Manchester	1937
		100 §	199m	227	-/14	Australia	Nottingham	1938
		364	797m	844	-/35	Australia	The Oval	1938
		196 §	310m		-/21	West Indies	Lord's	1939
		165*	310m		-/17	West Indies	The Oval	1939
		122*	300m	356	-/5	Australia	Sydney	1946-47
		100	277m		-/8	South Africa	Leeds	1947
		158	290m	362	-/16	South Africa	Johannesburg[2]	1948-49
		123	249m		-/13	South Africa	Johannesburg[2]	1948-49
		101	>240h		-/14	New Zealand	Leeds	1949
		206	300h		-/25	New Zealand	The Oval	1949
		202*	470m		-/22	West Indies	The Oval	1950
		156*	370m		-/11	Australia	Adelaide	1950-51
		100	300h			South Africa	Leeds	1951
		150	317m		-/20	India	Lord's	1952
		104	315m		-/10	India	Manchester	1952
		145	325m	308	-/16	Australia	Lord's	1953
		169	457m		1/24	West Indies	Georgetown	1953-54
		205	534m		1/23	West Indies	Kingston	1953-54
Illingworth,R	(2)	113	195h		-/12	West Indies	Lord's	1969

		107	270m		1/8	India	Manchester	1971
Insole,DJ		110*	373m		-/7	South Africa	Durban[2]	1956-57
Jackson,Hon.FS	(5)	103	135h		-/13	Australia	The Oval	1893
		118	173m		-/18	Australia	The Oval	1899
		128	255m		-/16	Australia	Manchester	1902
		144*	268m		-/18	Australia	Leeds	1905
		113	223m		-/12	Australia	Manchester	1905
Jardine,DR		127	300h		-/5	West Indies	Manchester	1933
Jessop,GL		104	77m		-/17	Australia	The Oval	1902
Knight,B R	(2)	125 §	218m		-/14	New Zealand	Auckland	1962-63
		127	224m		-/16	India	Kanpur	1963-64
Knight,NV		113	259m	176	-/16	Pakistan	Leeds	1996
Knott,APE	(5)	101	181m		1/11	New Zealand	Auckland	1970-71
		116	188m	173	-/22	Pakistan	Birmingham	1971
		106*	227m	205	-/9	Australia	Adelaide	1974-75
		116	305m	212	-/14	West Indies	Leeds	1976
		135	292m	214	-/18	Australia	Nottingham	1977
Lamb,AJ	(14)	107	260m	202	1/8	India	The Oval	1982
		102* §	297m	293	-/10	New Zealand	The Oval	1983
		137*	262m	219	-/22	New Zealand	Nottingham	1983
		110	360m	259	-/13	West Indies	Lord's	1984
		100	228m	186	-/15	West Indies	Leeds	1984
		100*	251m	185	-/15	West Indies	Manchester	1984
		107 §	267m	195	1/10	Sri Lanka	Lord's	1984
		113	338m	212	-/15	West Indies	Lord's	1988
		125	281m	205	-/24	Australia	Leeds	1989
		132	364m	209	-/16	West Indies	Kingston	1989-90
		119	338m	225	-/14	West Indies	Bridgetown	1989-90
		139	276m	187	-/22	India	Lord's	1990
		109	205m	231	2/8	India	Manchester	1990
		142	303m	141	-/15	New Zealand	Wellington	1991-92
Legge,GB		196	281m		-/23	New Zealand	Auckland	1929-30
Lewis,AR		125	267m	228	1/16	India	Kanpur	1972-73
Lewis,CC		117	170m	140	2/15	India	Chennai[1]	1992-93
Leyland,M	(9)	137 §	301m	330	-/18	Australia	Melbourne	1928-29
		102			-/10	South Africa	Lord's	1929
		109	211m	258	1/14	Australia	Lord's	1934
		153	314m	314	-/19	Australia	Manchester	1934
		110	165m	174	1/15	Australia	The Oval	1934
		161	235m		1/17	South Africa	The Oval	1935
		126	251m		-/11	Australia	Brisbane[2]	1936-37
		111*	194m		-/11	Australia	Melbourne	1936-37
		187	381m	431	-/17	Australia	The Oval	1938
Lloyd,D		214*	448m	396	-/17	India	Birmingham	1974
Luckhurst,BW	(4)	131	340m		-/13	Australia	Perth	1970-71
		109	328m		-/11	Australia	Melbourne	1970-71
		108* §	327m	279	-/14	Pakistan	Birmingham	1971
		101	231m	170	1/10	India	Manchester	1971
MacLaren,AC	(5)	120	220m		-/12	Australia	Melbourne	1894-95
		109	189m		-/15	Australia	Sydney	1897-98
		124	317m		-/10	Australia	Adelaide	1897-98
		116	206m		-/20	Australia	Sydney	1901-02
		140	217m		-/22	Australia	Nottingham	1905
Makepeace,JWH		117	260m		-/4	Australia	Melbourne	1920-21
Mann,FG		136*	237m		1/12	South Africa	Port Elizabeth	1948-49
May,PBH	(13)	138 §	380m		-/19	South Africa	Leeds	1951
		135	249m		-/24	West Indies	Port-of-Spain	1953-54

		104	298m	281	-/10	Australia	Sydney	1954-55
		112	270m		-/18	South Africa	Lord's	1955
		117	270h		-/16	South Africa	Manchester	1955
		101	317m		-/12	Australia	Leeds	1956
		285*	595m		2/25	West Indies	Birmingham	1957
		104	183m		-/14	West Indies	Nottingham	1957
		113*	174m		2/12	New Zealand	Leeds	1958
		101	156m		4/7	New Zealand	Manchester	1958
		113	315m	298	-/11	Australia	Melbourne	1958-59
		124*	251m		-/14	New Zealand	Auckland	1958-59
		106	218m		-/18	India	Nottingham	1959
Mead,CP	(4)	102	>210h		-/12	South Africa	Johannesburg[1]	1913-14
		117	225h		-/8	South Africa	Port Elizabeth	1913-14
		182*	309m		-/21	Australia	The Oval	1921
		181	454m		-/13	South Africa	Durban[2]	1922-23
Milburn,C	(2)	126*	179m		3/17	West Indies	Lord's	1966
		139	301m		1/17	Pakistan	Karachi[1]	1968-69
Milton,CA		104* §	297m		-/12	New Zealand	Leeds	1958
Murray,JT		112 §	267m		-/13	West Indies	The Oval	1966
Parfitt,PH	(7)	111	312m		-/11	Pakistan	Karachi[1]	1961-62
		101*	197m		2/9	Pakistan	Birmingham	1962
		119	265m		-/18	Pakistan	Leeds	1962
		101*	225m	187	-/9	Pakistan	Nottingham	1962
		131* §	289m		-/14	New Zealand	Auckland	1962-63
		121	328m		-/18	India	Kanpur	1963-64
		122*	333m	289	-/18	South Africa	Johannesburg[3]	1964-65
Parks,JM	(2)	101* §†	210m			West Indies	Port-of-Spain	1959-60
		108*	247m		-/10	South Africa	Durban[2]	1964-65
Pataudi,Nawab of,sr		102 §	317m	380	-/6	Australia	Sydney	1932-33
Paynter,E	(4)	216*	319m	331	1/26	Australia	Nottingham	1938
		117 § }	176m	179	1/8	South Africa	Johannesburg[1]	1938-39
		100 § }	192m	162	-/10			
		243	334m	419	-/24	South Africa	Durban[2]	1938-39
Place,W		107	367m		-/6	West Indies	Kingston	1947-48
Pullar,G	(4)	131	320m		-/14	India	Manchester	1959
		175	360m	354	1/15	South Africa	The Oval	1960
		119	313m		-/14	India	Kanpur	1961-62
		165	414m		-/16	Pakistan	Dacca	1961-62
Radley,CT	(2)	158	648m	500	-/15	New Zealand	Auckland	1977-78
		106 §	310m		-/11	Pakistan	Birmingham	1978
Randall,DW	(7)	174 §	448m	353	-/21	Australia	Melbourne	1976-77
		150	582m	498	-/13	Australia	Sydney	1978-79
		126	353m	290	1/11	India	Lord's	1982
		105	249m	156	-/11	Pakistan	Birmingham	1982
		115	266m	215	-/13	Australia	Perth	1982-83
		164	365m	269	2/20	New Zealand	Wellington	1983-84
		104	347m	338	-/12	New Zealand	Auckland	1983-84
Ranjitsinhji,KS	(2)	154* §	185m		-/23	Australia	Manchester	1896
		175	223m		-/24	Australia	Sydney	1897-98
Read,WW		117	137m	155	-/20	Australia	The Oval	1884
Rhodes,W	(2)	179	397m		-/14	Australia	Melbourne	1911-12
		152	310m		-/21	South Africa	Johannesburg[1]	1913-14
Richards,CJ		133	240m	207	-/16	Australia	Perth	1986-87
Richardson,PE	(5)	104	222m		-/11	Australia	Manchester	1956
		117 §	528m		-/6	South Africa	Johannesburg[3]	1956-57
		126	278m		-/10	West Indies	Nottingham	1957
		107	295m		-/10	West Indies	The Oval	1957

		100 §	286m		-/7	New Zealand	Birmingham	1958
Robertson,JDB	(2)	133	345m		-/14	West Indies	Port-of-Spain	1947-48
		121 §	225h		1/11	New Zealand	Lord's	1949
Robins,RWV		108	130m		-/12	South Africa	Manchester	1935
Robinson,RT	(4)	160	508m	391	-/17	India	Delhi	1984-85
		175 §	408m	271	-/27	Australia	Leeds	1985
		148	392m	293	-/18	Australia	Birmingham	1985
		166 §	528m	366	-/16	Pakistan	Manchester	1987
Russell,CAG	(5)	135*	250m		1/10	Australia	Adelaide	1920-21
		101	244m		-/9	Australia	Manchester	1921
		102*	163m		-/11	Australia	The Oval	1921
		140 }	320m		-/11	South Africa	Durban[2]	1922-23
		111 }	265m		-/10			
Russell,RC	(2)	128*	350m	294	-/14	Australia	Manchester	1989
		124	383m	261	-/13	India	Lord's	1996
Sandham,A	(2)	152 §	360m		-/16	West Indies	Bridgetown	1929-30
		325	600m		-/28	West Indies	Kingston	1929-30
Sharp,J		105	176m	174	-/11	Australia	The Oval	1909
Sharpe,PJ		111	269m		-/14	New Zealand	Nottingham	1969
Sheppard,Rev.DS	(3)	119	350m		-/9	India	The Oval	1952
		113	296m		1/15	Australia	Manchester	1956
		113	301m		-/5	Australia	Melbourne	1962-63
Shrewsbury,A	(3)	105*	320m		-/10	Australia	Melbourne	1884-85
		164	411m		-/16	Australia	Lord's	1886
		106	250m		-/9	Australia	Lord's	1893
Simpson,RT	(4)	103 §	a145m		3/11	New Zealand	Manchester	1949
		156*	338m		-/12	Australia	Melbourne	1950-51
		137	255h		-/21	South Africa	Nottingham	1951
		101	203m		-/9	Pakistan	Nottingham	1954
Smith,MJK	(3)	100 §	214m		-/12	India	Manchester	1959
		108	a300h		2/?	West Indies	Port-of-Spain	1959-60
		121	320m		1/12	South Africa	Cape Town	1964-65
Smith,RA	(9)	143	355m	285	-/15	Australia	Manchester	1989
		101	206m	150	-/16	Australia	Nottingham	1989
		100* §	196m	155	-/14	India	Lord's	1990
		121*	243m	197	-/11	India	Manchester	1990
		148*	413m	271	-/20	West Indies	Lord's	1991
		109	353m	256	-/13	West Indies	The Oval	1991
		127 §	326m	231	-/18	Pakistan	Birmingham	1992
		128	448m	338	-/20	Sri Lanka	Colombo (SSC)	1992-93
		175	418m	315	3/25	West Indies	St John's	1993-94
Spooner,RH		119 §	<180h		1/13	South Africa	Lord's	1912
Steel,AG	(2)	135*	238m		-/16	Australia	Sydney	1882-83
		148	230m		-/13	Australia	Lord's	1884
Steele,DS		106 §	368m	296	-/9	West Indies	Nottingham	1976
Stewart,AJ	(8)	113* §	308m	240	-/14	Sri Lanka	Lord's	1991
		148	355m	265	-/17	New Zealand	Christchurch	1991-92
		107	320m	243	-/13	New Zealand	Wellington	1991-92
		190 §	351m	261	-/31	Pakistan	Birmingham	1992
		118 }	347m	221	-/18	West Indies	Bridgetown	1993-94
		143 }	475m	319	-/20			
		119	289m	229	-/20	New Zealand	Lord's	1994
		170	435m	315	-/24	Pakistan	Leeds	1996
Stoddart,AE	(2)	134	230m		-/15	Australia	Adelaide	1891-92
		173	320m		10/14	Australia	Melbourne	1894-95
Subba Row,R	(3)	100	270m			West Indies	Georgetown	1959-60
		112	244m		-/13	Australia	Birmingham	1961

		137	400m		1/15	Australia	The Oval	1961
Sutcliffe,H	(16)	122	200m		-/11	South Africa	Lord's	1924
		115 §	247m		-/11	Australia	Sydney	1924-25
		176)	431m		-/17	Australia	Melbourne	1924-25
		127)	379m		-/12			
		143	295m		-/14	Australia	Melbourne	1924-25
		161	439m		-/16	Australia	The Oval	1926
		102				South Africa	Johannesburg[1]	1927-28
		135	385m	462	-/9	Australia	Melbourne	1928-29
		114	225m		-/7	South Africa	Birmingham	1929
		100	176m		-/10	South Africa	Lord's	1929
		104 }	210m		-/9	South Africa	The Oval	1929
		109* }	200m		-/11			
		161	404m	387	-/10	Australia	The Oval	1930
		117 §	220m		-/10	New Zealand	The Oval	1931
		109*	195m		1/9	New Zealand	Manchester	1931
		194	436m	496	-/13	Australia	Sydney	1932-33
Tate,MW		100*	<120h		-/12	South Africa	Lord's	1929
Tavare,CJ	(2)	149	455m	303	-/18	India	Delhi	1981-82
		109 §	312m	255	-/11	New Zealand	The Oval	1983
Thorpe,GP	(2)	114* §	334m	280	-/11	Australia	Nottingham	1993
		123	301m	218	-/19	Australia	Perth	1994-95
Tyldesley,GE	(3)	122	253m		-/16	South Africa	Johannesburg[1]	1927-28
		100	165m		-/5	South Africa	Durban[2]	1927-28
		122 §	210h		1/13	West Indies	Birmingham	1928
Tyldesley,JT	(4)	112				South Africa	Cape Town	1898-99
		138	262m		-/20	Australia	Birmingham	1902
		100	168m		-/12	Australia	Leeds	1905
		112*	212m		-/15	Australia	The Oval	1905
Ulyett,G		149	240m		-/13	Australia	Melbourne	1881-82
Valentine,BH	(2)	136 §	177m		1/13	India	Mumbai[1]	1933-34
		112	160m	147	1/12	South Africa	Cape Town	1938-39
Walters,CF		102	151m		-/14	India	Chennai[1]	1933-34
Ward,Albert		117	224m		-/11	Australia	Sydney	1894-95
Warner,PF		132* §			-/19	South Africa	Johannesburg[1]	1898-99
Washbrook,C	(6)	112	247m	299	1/8	Australia	Melbourne	1946-47
		143	317m	312	-/22	Australia	Leeds	1948
		195	297m	308	-/18	South Africa	Johannesburg[2]	1948-49
		103*	180h		-/12	New Zealand	Leeds	1949
		114 §	320m		1/14	West Indies	Lord's	1950
		102	320m		-/9	West Indies	Nottingham	1950
Watkins,AJ	(2)	111	220m		-/15	South Africa	Johannesburg[2]	1948-49
		137 §	540h		-/15	India	Delhi	1951-52
Watson,W	(2)	109 §	346m	356	-/16	Australia	Lord's	1953
		116 §	259m		-/16	West Indies	Kingston	1953-54
Willey,P	(2)	100*	236m	203	-/16	West Indies	The Oval	1980
		102*	223m	203	1/15	West Indies	St John's	1980-81
Wood,H		134*				South Africa	Cape Town	1891-92
Woolley,FE	(5)	133*	215m		-/12	Australia	Sydney	1911-12
		115*	206m		1/11	South Africa	Johannesburg[1]	1922-23
		134*	145m		-/20	South Africa	Lord's	1924
		123	146m		1/15	Australia	Sydney	1924-25
		154	165m		-/20	South Africa	Manchester	1929
Woolmer,RA	(3)	149	499m	390	-/20	Australia	The Oval	1975
		120	306m	247	-/13	Australia	Lord's	1977
		137	386m	338	-/22	Australia	Manchester	1977
Worthington,TS		128	>210h		-/19	India	The Oval	1936

Wyatt,RES	(2)	113	245m		-/14	South Africa	Manchester	1929
		149	305m		-/17	South Africa	Nottingham	1935
SOUTH AFRICA (122)			Time	Balls	6/4	Opponents		
Balaskas,XC		122*	198m		-/15	New Zealand	Wellington	1931-32
Barlow,EJ	(6)	114 §	354m		-/13	Australia	Brisbane[2]	1963-64
		109	273m		-/11	Australia	Melbourne	1963-64
		201	392m		-/27	Australia	Adelaide	1963-64
		138	344m		-/16	England	Cape Town	1964-65
		127	362m		1/11	Australia	Cape Town	1969-70
		110	323m	247	1/13	Australia	Johannesburg[3]	1969-70
Bland,KC	(3)	126	324m	333	1/13	Australia	Sydney	1963-64
		144*	248m		2/17	England	Johannesburg[3]	1964-65
		127	‡270h		-/16	England	The Oval	1965
Catterall,RH	(3)	120	195m		2/15	England	Birmingham	1924
		120	200m		-/16	England	Lord's	1924
		119	135m		2/14	England	Durban[2]	1927-28
Christy,JAJ		103 §	126m		-/10	New Zealand	Christchurch	1931-32
Cronje,WJ	(5)	135	527m	411	-/12	India	Port Elizabeth	1992-93
		122	412m	297	-/11	Sri Lanka	Colombo (SSC)	1993-94
		122	250m	122	1/16	Australia	Johannesburg[3]	1993-94
		112	288m	235	1/10	New Zealand	Cape Town	1994-95
		101	227m	155	3/7	New Zealand	Auckland	1994-95
Cullinan,DJ		102	358m	232	-/17	Sri Lanka	Colombo (PSS)	1993-94
Dalton,EL	(2)	117	140m		-/18	England	The Oval	1935
		102	209m	237	-/9	England	Johannesburg[1]	1938-39
Endean,WR	(3)	162*	452m		-/9	Australia	Melbourne	1952-53
		116	275m		-/9	New Zealand	Auckland	1952-53
		116*	†240h		-/16	England	Leeds	1955
Faulkner,GA	(4)	123	170m		-/17	England	Johannesburg[1]	1909-10
		204	313m		-/26	Australia	Melbourne	1910-11
		115	239m		-/10	Australia	Adelaide	1910-11
		122*	257m	270	-/13	Australia	Manchester	1912
Frank,CN		152	512m		-/17	Australia	Johannesburg[1]	1921-22
Goddard,TL		112	251m		3/10	England	Johannesburg[3]	1964-65
Hathorn,CMH		102	135h		-/15	England	Johannesburg[1]	1905-06
Hudson,AC	(3)	163 §	521m	384	-/24	West Indies	Bridgetown	1991-92
		102	249m	175	-/13	Australia	Cape Town	1993-94
		135 §	311m	236	2/18	Zimbabwe	Harare	1994-95
Irvine,BL		102	178m	146	2/9	Australia	Port Elizabeth	1969-70
Kirsten,G		110	353m	241	-/16	England	Johannesburg[3]	1995-96
Kirsten,PN		104	295m	226	-/13	England	Leeds	1994
Lindsay,DT	(3)	182	274m		5/25	Australia	Johannesburg[3]	1966-67
		137	253m		-/14	Australia	Durban[2]	1966-67
		131	160m		4/14	Australia	Johannesburg[3]	1966-67
McGlew,DJ	(7)	255* §	534m		-/19	New Zealand	Wellington	1952-53
		104*	280m		-/19	England	Manchester	1955
		133	398m		-/13	England	Leeds	1955
		108	315m		1/12	Australia	Johannesburg[3]	1957-58
		105	572m		-/4	Australia	Durban[2]	1957-58
		127*	312m		-/10	New Zealand	Durban[2]	1961-62
		120	302m		1/10	New Zealand	Johannesburg[3]	1961-62
McLean,RA	(5)	101	144m		-/11	New Zealand	Durban[2]	1953-54
		142	205m		1/21	England	Lord's	1955
		100	260m		-/14	England	Durban[2]	1956-57
		109	157m	153	-/14	England	Manchester	1960
		113	174m		1/16	New Zealand	Cape Town	1961-62

McMillan,BM	(2)	113 §	226m	180	-/15	Pakistan	Johannesburg[3]	1994-95
		100*	299m	168	3/9	England	Johannesburg[3]	1995-96
Melville,A	(4)	103	210m		-/10	England	Durban[2]	1938-39
		189	360h		1/16	England	Nottingham	1947
		104*	138m		-/16			
		117	253m		-/13	England	Lord's	1947
Mitchell,B	(8)	123	340m		-/9	England	Cape Town	1930-31
		113 §	181m		-/6	New Zealand	Christchurch	1931-32
		164*	333m		-/17	England	Lord's	1935
		128	280m		-/11	England	The Oval	1935
		109	190m	234	-/14	England	Durban[2]	1938-39
		120	391m		-/14	England	The Oval	1947
		189*	410m					
		120	344m		-/11	England	Cape Town	1948-49
Murray,ARA		109 §	219m			New Zealand	Wellington	1952-53
Nourse,AD	(9)	231	298m	346	-/36	Australia	Johannesburg[1]	1935-36
		120	268m	295	1/12	England	Cape Town	1938-39
		103	364m	345	-/6	England	Durban[2]	1938-39
		149	240m		1/15	England	Nottingham	1947
		115	145m		2/13	England	Manchester	1947
		112	209m		-/11	England	Cape Town	1948-49
		129*	319m		-/11	England	Johannesburg[2]	1948-49
		114	274m	279	-/9	Australia	Cape Town	1949-50
		208	555m		-/25	England	Nottingham	1951
Nourse,AW		111	228m		-/13	Australia	Johannesburg[1]	1921-22
Owen-Smith,HG		129	160m		2/15	England	Leeds	1929
Pithey,AJ		154	440m		1/13	England	Cape Town	1964-65
Pollock,RG	(7)	122	221m	234	1/19	Australia	Sydney	1963-64
		175	283m		3/18	Australia	Adelaide	1963-64
		137	272m	236	-/18	England	Port Elizabeth	1964-65
		125	140m	145	-/21	England	Nottingham	1965
		209	361m		-/30	Australia	Cape Town	1966-67
		105	179m		1/13	Australia	Port Elizabeth	1966-67
		274	417m	401	-/43	Australia	Durban[2]	1969-70
Rhodes,JN		101* §	255m	202	1/14	Sri Lanka	Moratuwa	1993-94
Richards,BA	(2)	140	181m	164	1/20	Australia	Durban[2]	1969-70
		126	236m	212	3/16	Australia	Port Elizabeth	1969-70
Richardson,DJ		109	302m	206	-/7	New Zealand	Cape Town	1994-95
Rowan,EAB	(3)	156*	368m		-/18	England	Johannesburg[2]	1948-49
		143	388m	369	-/14	Australia	Durban[2]	1949-50
		236	550m		-/28	England	Leeds	1951
Sherwell,PW		115	105m		-/18	England	Lord's	1907
Siedle,IJ		141	297m		-/13	England	Cape Town	1930-31
Sinclair,JH	(3)	106	142m		1!/9	England	Cape Town	1898-99
		101	125m		2!/14	Australia	Johannesburg[1]	1902-03
		104	83m		6!/18	Australia	Cape Town	1902-03
Snooke,SJ		103	215m			Australia	Adelaide	1910-11
Taylor,HW	(7)	109	198m		1/11	England	Durban[1]	1913-14
		176	308m		-/25	England	Johannesburg[1]	1922-23
		101	225h		1/11	England	Johannesburg[1]	1922-23
		102	270m		1/6	England	Durban[2]	1922-23
		101	145m		-/9	England	Johannesburg[1]	1927-28
		121	220m		-/12	England	The Oval	1929
		117	167m		-/15	England	Cape Town	1930-31
Van der Bijl,PGV		125	438m	458	1/11	England	Durban[2]	1938-39
Viljoen,KG	(2)	111	210m		1/9	Australia	Melbourne	1931-32
		124	280m		-/10	England	Manchester	1935

Wade,WW		125	290m		-/12	England	Port Elizabeth	1948-49
Waite,JHB	(4)	113	340m		-/12	England	Manchester	1955
		115	305m		-/11	Australia	Johannesburg[3]	1957-58
		134	513m		-/6	Australia	Durban[2]	1957-58
		101	206m		-/13	New Zealand	Johannesburg[3]	1961-62
Wessels,KC	(2)	118 §	372m	264	-/18	India	Durban[2]	1992-93
		105 §	298m	217	-/15	England	Lord'	1994
White,GC	(2)	147	>240h		2!/19	England	Johannesburg[1]	1905-06
		118	240h		1/10	England	Durban[1]	1909-10
Winslow,PL		108	190m		3/13	England	Manchester	1955
Zulch,JW	(2)	105	184m		-/9	Australia	Adelaide	1910-11
		150	298m		-/15	Australia	Sydney	1910-11

WEST INDIES (318)			Time	Balls	6/4	Opponents		
Adams,JC	(5)	137	414m	262	-/21	England	Georgetown	1993-94
		125*	406m	312	-/14	India	Nagpur	1994-95
		174*	451m	371	-/19	India	Mohali	1994-95
		151	308m	226	-/24	New Zealand	Wellington	1994-95
		208*	433m	333	1/31	New Zealand	St John's	1995-96
Alexander,FCM		108	212m	186	1/9	Australia	Sydney	1960-61
Arthurton,KLT	(2)	157* §	447m	343	1/16	Australia	Brisbane[2]	1992-93
		126	323m	232	2/11	England	Kingston	1993-94
Atkinson,DS		219	411m		1/29	Australia	Bridgetown	1954-55
Bacchus,SFAF		250	512m	375	-/33	India	Kanpur	1978-79
Baichan,L		105* §	373m		-/5	Pakistan	Lahore[2]	1974-75
Barrow,I		105	235m		-/9	England	Manchester	1933
Best,CA		164	423m	245	-/19	England	Bridgetown	1989-90
Butcher,BF	(7)	103	†180h		-/15	India	Calcutta	1958-59
		142	335m		-/10	India	Chennai[2]	1958-59
		133	244m	261	2/17	England	Lord's	1963
		117	210m		1/10	Australia	Port-of-Spain	1964-65
		209*	461m		-/22	England	Nottingham	1966
		101	249m	134	-/14	Australia	Sydney	1968-69
		118	191m		-/18	Australia	Adelaide	1968-69
Campbell,SL		208	675m	496	-/29	New Zealand	Bridgetown	1995-96
Carew,GM		107	162m		-/16	England	Port-of-Spain	1947-48
Carew,MC		109 §	318m		-/12	New Zealand	Auckland	1968-69
Christiani,RJ		107 §	194m		-/9	India	Delhi	1948-49
Davis,CA	(4)	103	372m		-/6	England	Lord's	1969
		125*	n300h		-/15	India	Georgetown	1970-71
		105	330h			India	Port-of-Spain	1970-71
		183	602m		-/21	New Zealand	Bridgetown	1971-72
Depeiza,CC		122	330m		-/16	Australia	Bridgetown	1954-55
Dujon,PJL	(5)	110	239m		-/14	India	St John's	1982-83
		130	262m	187	2/15	Australia	Port-of-Spain	1983-84
		101	247m	228	-/12	England	Manchester	1984
		139	240m	158	-/21	Australia	Perth	1984-85
		106*	316m	175	-/13	Pakistan	Port-of-Spain	1987-88
Foster,MLC		125 §	232m		-/16	Australia	Kingston	1972-73
Fredericks,RC	(8)	163	408m		-/20	New Zealand	Kingston	1971-72
		150	510m		-/17	England	Birmingham	1973
		100	212m		-/13	India	Calcutta	1974-75
		104	215m		-/17	India	Mumbai[3]	1974-75
		169	212m	145	1/27	Australia	Perth	1975-76
		138	282m	253	1/14	England	Lord's	1976
		109	156m	124	-/18	England	Leeds	1976
		120	380m		-/12	Pakistan	Port-of-Spain	1976-77

Player	Tons	Score	Time	Balls	6/4	Opponent	Venue	Season
Ganteaume,AG		112 §	300m		-/13	England	Port-of-Spain	1947-48
Gomes,HA	(9)	101 §	205m		-/11	Australia	Georgetown	1977-78
		115	343m	269	-/11	Australia	Kingston	1977-78
		126*	344m	252	-/11	Australia	Sydney	1981-82
		124*	402m	273	-/9	Australia	Adelaide	1981-82
		123	446m	333	-/12	India	Port-of-Spain	1982-83
		143	380m	279	-/16	England	Birmingham	1984
		104*	314m	197	-/14	England	Leeds	1984
		127	472m	207	-/9	Australia	Perth	1984-85
		120*	304m	217	-/10	Australia	Adelaide	1984-85
Gomez,GE		101 §	255m		-/7	India	Delhi	1948-49
Greenidge,CG	(19)	107 §	260m	208	2/14	India	Bangalore	1974-75
		134	250m	198	-/18	England	Manchester	1976
		101	245m	155	-/13			
		115	214m	147	2/14	England	Leeds	1976
		100	†210h		3/15	Pakistan	Kingston	1976-77
		154*	248m		1/14	India	St John's	1982-83
		194	552m	368	-/23	India	Kanpur	1983-84
		120*	270m	189	3/10	Australia	Georgetown	1983-84
		127	286m	193	-/17	Australia	Kingston	1983-84
		214*	300m	241	-/29	England	Lord's	1984
		223	598m	425	-/30	England	Manchester	1984
		100	316m	235	-/12	New Zealand	Port-of-Spain	1984-85
		213	534m	381	7/20	New Zealand	Auckland	1986-87
		141	362m	265	4/14	India	Calcutta	1987-88
		103	246m	192	-/14	England	Lord's	1988
		104	294m	249	-/8	Australia	Adelaide	1988-89
		117	236m	182	1/11	India	Bridgetown	1988-89
		149	380m	207	3/18	England	St John's	1989-90
		(In his 100th Test match)						
		226	677m	480	3/11	Australia	Bridgetown	1990-91
Haynes,DL	(18)	105 §	435m	323	-/16	New Zealand	Dunedin	1979-80
		122	263m	199	3/17	New Zealand	Christchurch	1979-80
		184	490m	395	1/27	England	Lord's	1980
		136	372m		1/10	India	St John's	1982-83
		103*	270m	184	-/9	Australia	Georgetown	1983-84
		145	383m	222	1/19	Australia	Bridgetown	1983-84
		125	436m	269	-/17	England	The Oval	1984
		131	472m	283	-/14	England	St John's	1985-86
		121	311m	269	-/20	New Zealand	Wellington	1986-87
		100	243m	176	-/12	Australia	Perth	1988-89
		143	316m	272	-/16	Australia	Sydney	1988-89
		112*	177m	128	3/11	India	Bridgetown	1988-89
		109	303m	176	-/10	England	Bridgetown	1989-90
		167	533m	317	1/24	England	St John's	1989-90
		117	351m	204	-/8	Pakistan	Karachi[1]	1990-91
		111	318m	223	-/17	Australia	Georgetown	1990-91
		143*	406m	289	-/20	Pakistan	Port-of-Spain	1992-93
		125	351m	206	1/14	Pakistan	Bridgetown	1992-93
Headley,GA	(10)	176 §	390h		-/16	England	Bridgetown	1929-30
		114	200m		-/10	England	Georgetown	1929-30
		112	257m		1/12			
		223	390h		-/28	England	Kingston	1929-30
		102*	247m		-/10	Australia	Brisbane[1]	1930-31
		105	146m		-/13	Australia	Sydney	1930-31
		169*	375h		-/18	England	Manchester	1933
		270*	493m		-/30	England	Kingston	1934-35

		106 }	250m		-/13	England	Lord's	1939
		107 }	230m		-/8			
Holford,DAJ		105*	320m		-/6	England	Lord's	1966
Holt,JK	(2)	166	284m		1/26	England	Bridgetown	1953-54
		123	255m		-/17	India	Delhi	1958-59
Hooper,CL	(5)	100*	277m	171	3/7	India	Calcutta	1987-88
		134	315m	226	2/11	Pakistan	Lahore[2]	1990-91
		111	282m	202	1/14	England	Lord's	1991
		178*	297m	248	4/19	Pakistan	St John's	1992-93
		127	285m	180	2/14	England	The Oval	1995
Hunte,CC	(8)	142 §	300h		-/17	Pakistan	Bridgetown	1957-58
		260	506m		1/28	Pakistan	Kingston	1957-58
		114	253m		-/9	Pakistan	Georgetown	1957-58
		110	270m		-/9	Australia	Melbourne	1960-61
		182	500m		-/27	England	Manchester	1963
		108*	300h			England	The Oval	1963
		135	300h		-/19	England	Manchester	1966
		101	285m		-/16	India	Mumbai[2]	1966-67
Julien,BD	(2)	121	171m		2/18	England	Lord's	1973
		101	192m		-/12	Pakistan	Karachi[1]	1974-75
Kallicharran,AI	(12)	100* §	258m		1/7	New Zealand	Georgetown	1971-72
		101	179m		1/13	New Zealand	Port-of-Spain	1971-72
		158	369m	334	-/18	England	Port-of-Spain	1973-74
		119	251m	191	-/18	England	Bridgetown	1973-74
		124 §	281m	226	2/15	India	Bangalore	1974-75
		115			1/18	Pakistan	Karachi[1]	1974-75
		101	267m	207	-/13	Australia	Brisbane[2]	1975-76
		103*	257m		-/8	India	Port-of-Spain	1975-76
		127	256m		-/17	Australia	Port-of-Spain	1977-78
		126	263m	260	1/18	Australia	Kingston	1977-78
		187	396m		-/26	India	Mumbai[3]	1978-79
		106	221m	176	-/14	Australia	Adelaide	1979-80
Kanhai,RB	(15)	256	400m		-/42	India	Calcutta	1958-59
		217	420h		-/32	Pakistan	Lahore[1]	1958-59
		110	378m		1/19	England	Port-of-Spain	1959-60
		117 }	149m		2/14	Australia	Adelaide	1960-61
		115 }	222m		-/12			
		138	298m		-/19	India	Kingston	1961-62
		139			2/11	India	Port-of-Spain	1961-62
		129	372m		-/17	Australia	Bridgetown	1964-65
		121	182m		2/12	Australia	Port-of-Spain	1964-65
		104	215m		-/14	England	The Oval	1966
		153	300m		1/19	England	Port-of-Spain	1967-68
		150	412m	301	-/21	England	Georgetown	1967-68
		158*	390h		-/17	India	Kingston	1970-71
		105	305m		-/11	Australia	Bridgetown	1972-73
		157	340m		-/21	England	Lord's	1973
King,CL		100*	129m	109	4/10	New Zealand	Christchurch	1979-80
Lara,BC	(7)	277	474m	372	-/38	Australia	Sydney	1992-93
		167	256m	210	2/25	England	Georgetown	1993-94
		375	766m	538	-/45	England	St John's	1993-94
		147	247m	181	-/23	New Zealand	Wellington	1994-95
		145	281m	216	-/16	England	Manchester	1995
		152	253m	182	-/28	England	Nottingham	1995
		179	267m	206	1/26	England	The Oval	1995
Lloyd,CH	(19)	118 §	273m		1/17	England	Port-of-Spain	1967-68
		113*	178m		2/14	England	Bridgetown	1967-68

		129 §	208m		1/18	Australia	Brisbane[2]	1968-69
		178	358m		1/24	Australia	Georgetown	1972-73
		132	a240h		2/15	England	The Oval	1973
		163	205m	149	2/22	India	Bangalore	1974-75
		242*	429m		4/19	India	Mumbai[3]	1974-75
		149	218m	186	1/22	Australia	Perth	1975-76
		102	206m	121	-/14	Australia	Melbourne	1975-76
		102	175m		2/12	India	Bridgetown	1975-76
		157	200m		3/21	Pakistan	Bridgetown	1976-77
		121	187m	156	-/17	Australia	Adelaide	1979-80
		101	205m	159	-/11	England	Manchester	1980
		100	238m		-/17	England	Bridgetown	1980-81
		143	310mm		2/13	India	Port-of-Spain	1982-83
		106	218m		1/11	India	St John's	1982-83
		103	320m		-/7	India	Delhi	1983-84
		161*	496m		-/12	India	Calcutta	1983-84
		114	208m	154	3/14	Australia	Brisbane[2]	1984-85
Logie,AL	(2)	130	273m		2/12	India	Bridgetown	1982-83
		101	188m	136	-/15	India	Calcutta	1987-88
McMorris,EDAS		125 §	342m		-/11	India	Kingston	1961-62
Martin,FR		123*	347m		-/11	Australia	Sydney	1930-31
Murray,JR		101*	114m	88	2/11	New Zealand	Wellington	1994-95
Nurse,SM	(6)	201	382m		-/30	Australia	Bridgetown	1964-65
		137	345m		2/14	England	Leeds	1966
		136	331m		-/12	England	Port-of-Spain	1967-68
		137	200m		1/18	Australia	Sydney	1968-69
		168 §	215m		2/22	New Zealand	Auckland	1968-69
		258	476m		1/35	New Zealand	Christchurch	1968-69
Pairaudeau,BH		115 §	272m		-/16	India	Port-of-Spain	1952-53
Rae,AF	(4)	104	255m		-/11	India	Mumbai[2]	1948-49
		109	230m		3/5	India	Chennai[1]	1948-49
		106	280m		-/15	England	Lord's	1950
		109	300h			England	The Oval	1950
Richards,IVA	(24)	192*	319m	297	6/20	India	Delhi	1974-75
		101	182m	136	-/17	Australia	Adelaide	1975-76
		142	242m		1/10	India	Bridgetown	1975-76
		130	290m	203	-/21	India	Port-of-Spain	1975-76
		177	343m	296	2/23	India	Port-of-Spain	1975-76
		232 §	438m	313	4/31	England	Nottingham	1976
		135	288m	261	-/18	England	Manchester	1976
		291	472m	386	-/38	England	The Oval	1976
		140	329m	259	-/20	Australia	Brisbane[2]	1979-80
		145	196m	159	1/25	England	Lord's	1980
		120	417m	263	-/15	Pakistan	Multan	1980-81
		182*	383m		2/23	England	Bridgetown	1980-81
		114	305m		1/21	England	St John's	1980-81
		109	258m		2/9	India	Georgetown	1982-83
		120	267m		1/13	India	Mumbai[3]	1983-84
		178	377m	229	-/30	Australia	St John's	1983-84
		117	204m	154	1/17	England	Birmingham	1984
		208	376m	245	3/22	Australia	Melbourne	1984-85
		105	192m	147	3/13	New Zealand	Bridgetown	1984-85
		110*	87m	58	7/7	England	St John's	1985-86
		109*	179m	114	-/13	India	Delhi	1987-88
		123	302m	169	-/13	Pakistan	Port-of-Spain	1987-88
		146	195m	150	3/21	Australia	Perth	1988-89
		110	304m	178	1/13	India	Kingston	1988-89

Richardson,RB	(16)	131*	481m	313	-/17	Australia	Bridgetown	1983-84
		154	468m	326	1/21	Australia	St John's	1983-84
		138	331m	232	-/24	Australia	Brisbane²	1984-85
		185	455m	346	-/26	New Zealand	Georgetown	1984-85
		102	176m	140	1/19	England	Port-of-Spain	1985-86
		160	348m	278	-/18	England	Bridgetown	1985-86
		122	286m	194	-/12	Australia	Melbourne	1988-89
		106	194m	160	-/16	Australia	Adelaide	1988-89
		194	459m	367	-/20	India	Georgetown	1988-89
		156	482m	314	-/20	India	Kingston	1988-89
		104*	315m	240	-/15	Australia	Kingston	1990-91
		182	344m	259	2/26	Australia	Georgetown	1990-91
		104	273m	229	-/13	England	Birmingham	1991
		121	458m	312	1/11	England	The Oval	1991
		109	330m	253	-/11	Australia	Sydney	1992-93
		100	344m	223	1/12	Australia	Kingston	1994-95
Roach,CA	(2)	122	165m		-/20	England	Bridgetown	1929-30
		209	303m		3/22	England	Georgetown	1929-30
Rowe,LG	(7)	214 § }	427m		1/19	New Zealand	Kingston	1971-72
		100*§ }	153m		-/13			
		120	303m	258	1/17	England	Kingston	1973-74
		302	612m	430	1/36	England	Bridgetown	1973-74
		123	437m	340	1/10	England	Port-of-Spain	1973-74
		107	267m	235	-/14	Australia	Brisbane²	1975-76
		100	186m	165	1/10	New Zealand	Christchurch	1979-80
Samuels,RG		125	329m	219	3/15	New Zealand	St John's	1995-96
Shillingford,IT		120	345m		1/15	Pakistan	Georgetown	1976-77
Simmons,PV		110	253m	178	2/8	Australia	Melbourne	1992-93
Smith,OG	(4)	104 §	218m		-/14	Australia	Kingston	1954-55
		161 §	412m		1/18	England	Birmingham	1957
		168	416m		3/10	England	Nottingham	1957
		100	<180h		2/10	India	Delhi	1958-59
Sobers,GS	(26)	365*	614m		-/38	Pakistan	Kingston	1957-58
		125 }	260m		-/15	Pakistan	Georgetown	1957-58
		109* }			-/9			
		142* §	365m		1/8	India	Mumbai²	1958-59
		198	340m		-/28	India	Kanpur	1958-59
		106*	a195h		-/11	India	Calcutta	1958-59
		226	647m		-/24	England	Bridgetown	1959-60
		147	371m		-/17	England	Kingston	1959-60
		145	420h		1/18	England	Georgetown	1959-60
		132	174m		-/21	Australia	Brisbane²	1960-61
		168	270m	224	1/25	Australia	Sydney	1960-61
		153	280m		4/11	India	Kingston	1961-62
		104			2/13	India	Kingston	1961-62
		102	251m		-/14	England	Leeds	1963
		161	248m		1/26	England	Manchester	1966
		163*	330m		-/13	England	Lord's	1966
		174	243m		-/24	England	Leeds	1966
		113*	357m		1/14	England	Kingston	1967-68
		152	440m	362	-/18	England	Georgetown	1967-68
		110	134m		2/15	Australia	Adelaide	1968-69
		113	144m	126	-/20	Australia	Sydney	1968-69
		108*	150m		2/14	India	Georgetown	1970-71
		178	329m		1/19	India	Bridgetown	1970-71
		132				India	Port-of-Spain	1970-71
		142	363m		-/18	New Zealand	Bridgetown	1971-72

		150*	288m	227	-/19	England	Lord's	1973
Solomon,JS		100*	281m		-/9	India	Delhi	1958-59
Stollmeyer,JB	(4)	160	308m		-/12	India	Chennai[1]	1948-49
		104	242m		-/6	Australia	Sydney	1951-52
		152	326m		-/14	New Zealand	Auckland	1951-52
		104*	163m			India	Port-of-Spain	1952-53
Walcott,CL	(15)	152 §	259m		-/12	India	Delhi	1948-49
		108	164m		2/11	India	Calcutta	1948-49
		168*	285m		-/24	England	Lord's	1950
		115	168m		-/13	New Zealand	Auckland	1951-52
		125	255m		1/15	India	Georgetown	1952-53
		118	241m		-/11	India	Kingston	1952-53
		220	428m		1/28	England	Bridgetown	1953-54
		124	211m		1/18	England	Port-of-Spain	1953-54
		116	262m		-/20	England	Kingston	1953-54
		108	208m		-/14	Australia	Kingston	1954-55
		126 }	267m		-/14	Australia	Port-of-Spain	1954-55
		110 }	147m		-/17			
		155 }	294m		-/23	Australia	Kingston	1954-55
		110 }	196m		-/14			
		145	273m		-/19	Pakistan	Georgetown	1957-58
Weekes,ED	(15)	141	232m		-/15	England	Kingston	1947-48
		128 §	194m		-/16	India	Delhi	1948-49
		194	368m		-/18	India	Mumbai[2]	1948-49
		162 }	199m		-/24	India	Calcutta	1948-49
		101 }	187m		-/5			
		129	220m		-/17	England	Nottingham	1950
		207	431m		-/20	India	Port-of-Spain	1952-53
		161	338m		-/22	India	Port-of-Spain	1952-53
		109	173m		-/13	India	Kingston	1952-53
		206	354m		-/25	England	Port-of-Spain	1953-54
		139	210m		1/24	Australia	Port-of-Spain	1954-55
		123	148m		-/17	New Zealand	Dunedin	1955-56
		103	142m		-/16	New Zealand	Christchurch	1955-56
		156	211m		-/19	New Zealand	Wellington	1955-56
		197§	330m		-/18	Pakistan	Bridgetown	1957-58
Weekes,KH		137	135m		1/18	England	The Oval	1939
Williams,AB	(2)	100 §	169m	118	-/19	Australia	Georgetown	1977-78
		111	214m		-/11	India	Calcutta	1978-79
Worrell,FMM	(9)	131*	215m		-/14	England	Georgetown	1947-48
		261	335m		2/35	England	Nottingham	1950
		138	305m		-/17	England	The Oval	1950
		108	247m		-/7	Australia	Melbourne	1951-52
		100	151m		-/13	New Zealand	Auckland	1951-52
		237	569m		-/35	India	Kingston	1952-53
		167	438m		-/23	England	Port-of-Spain	1953-54
		191*	575m		-/26	England	Nottingham	1957
		197*	682m		2/17	England	Bridgetown	1959-60

NEW ZEALAND (140)			Time	Balls	6/4	Opponents		
Astle,NJ	(2)	125		154	2/22	West Indies	Bridgetown	1995-96
		103	217m	165	1/12	West Indies	St John's	1995-96
Barton,PT		109	276m		-/20	South Africa	Port Elizabeth	1961-62
Bracewell,JG		110	270m	200	-/10	England	Nottingham	1986
Burgess,MG	(5)	119*	255m		-/12	Pakistan	Dacca	1969-70
		104	237m	176	1/12	England	Auckland	1970-71
		101	185m		1/15	West Indies	Kingston	1971-72

		105	228m		-/12	England	Lord's	1973
		111	254m		-/9	Pakistan	Lahore[2]	1976-77
Cairns,CL		120	122m	96	9/10	Zimbabwe	Auckland	1995-96
Coney,JV	(3)	174*	488m	374	1/26	England	Wellington	1983-84
		111*	385m	243	-/12	Pakistan	Dunedin	1984-85
		101*	282m	192	-/14	Australia	Wellington	1985-86
Congdon,BE	(7)	104	320m		-/7	England	Christchurch	1965-66
		166*	527m		1/14	West Indies	Port-of-Spain	1971-72
		126	258m		-/11	West Indies	Bridgetown	1971-72
		176	409m		-/19	England	Nottingham	1973
		175	515m		-/12	England	Lord's	1973
		132	390m	360	-/14	Australia	Wellington	1973-74
		107*	297m	251	-/11	Australia	Christchurch	1976-77
Crowe,JJ	(3)	128	384m	285	-/20	England	Auckland	1983-84
		112	286m	207	1/10	West Indies	Kingston	1984-85
		120*	609m	397	-/13	Sri Lanka	Colombo (CCC)	1986-87
Crowe,MD	(17)	100	276m	247	-/19	England	Wellington	1983-84
		188	571m	462	1/26	West Indies	Georgetown	1984-85
		188	472m	328	-/26	Australia	Brisbane[2]	1985-86
		137	283m	226	-/21	Australia	Christchurch	1985-86
		106	339m	247	-/11	England	Lord's	1986
		119	381m	308	-/15	West Indies	Wellington	1986-87
		104	382m	264	1/8	West Indies	Auckland	1986-87
		137	234m	184	1/17	Australia	Adelaide	1987-88
		143	402m	333	-/14	England	Wellington	1987-88
		174	592m	410	-/16	Pakistan	Wellington	1988-89
		113	227m	174	-/17	India	Auckland	1989-90
		108*	552m	306	1/14	Pakistan	Lahore[2]	1990-91
		299	610m	523	3/29	Sri Lanka	Wellington	1990-91
		140	182m	163	3/17	Zimbabwe	Harare	1992-93
		107	159m	121	4/10	Sri Lanka	Colombo (SSC)	1992-93
		142	366m	255	3/20	England	Lord's	1994
		115	333m	237	-/15	England	Manchester	1994
Dempster,CS	(2)	136	274m		-/8	England	Wellington	1929-30
		120	235m		-/10	England	Lord's	1931
Donnelly,MP		206	355m		-/26	England	Lord's	1949
Dowling,GT	(3)	129	378m		-/17	India	Mumbai[2]	1964-65
		143	343m		2/16	India	Dunedin	1967-68
		239	556m	519	5/28	India	Christchurch	1967-68
Edgar,BA	(3)	129 §	414m		-/14	Pakistan	Christchurch	1978-79
		127	432m	317	-/7	West Indies	Auckland	1979-80
		161	516m	418	-/22	Australia	Auckland	1981-82
Franklin,TJ		101	432m	310	-/8	England	Lord's	1990
Greatbatch,MJ	(3)	107* §	407m	325	-/12	England	Auckland	1987-88
		146* §	656m	485	-/17	Australia	Perth	1989-90
		133	427m	317	-/16	Pakistan	Hamilton	1992-93
Guy,J W		102 §	473m		-/13	India	Hyderabad	1955-56
Hadlee,RJ	(2)	103	114m	92	2/11	West Indies	Christchurch	1979-80
		151*	407m	243	2/14	Sri Lanka	Colombo (CCC)	1986-87
Hadlee,WA		116	147m		-/11	England	Christchurch	1946-47
Harris,PGZ		101	266m		2/10	South Africa	Cape Town	1961-62
Hastings,BF	(4)	117*	278m		2/12	West Indies	Christchurch	1968-69
		105	273m		-/15	West Indies	Bridgetown	1971-72
		110	275m		-/10	Pakistan	Auckland	1972-73
		101	281m	274	-/8	Australia	Wellington	1973-74
Howarth,GP	(6)	122)	515m		-/12	England	Auckland	1977-78
		102)	320m		-/13			

		123	340m		-/14	England	Lord's	1978
		114	286m		1/11	Pakistan	Napier	1978-79
		147	358m	261	-/13	West Indies	Christchurch	1979-80
		137 §	353m		-/15	India	Wellington	1980-81
Jarvis,TW		182	540m	555	-/19	West Indies	Georgetown	1971-72
Jones,AH	(7)	150	444m	383	-/11	Australia	Adelaide	1987-88
		170	634m	448	2/15	India	Auckland	1989-90
		186	562m	454	-/15	Sri Lanka	Wellington	1990-91
		122 }	288m	217	-/8	Sri Lanka	Hamilton	1990-91
		100* }	255m	175	-/8			
		143	462m	398	-/15	England	Wellington	1991-92
		143	351m	283	-/11	Australia	Perth	1993-94
Latham,RT		119 §	282m	214	1/14	Zimbabwe	Bulawayo[1]	1992-93
Lees,WK		152	338m		2/21	Pakistan	Karachi[1]	1976-77
McGregor,SN		111	340m		-/12	Pakistan	Lahore[1]	1955-56
Mills,JE		117 §	258m		-/13	England	Wellington	1929-30
Morrison,JFM		117	261m	246	-/11	Australia	Sydney	1973-74
Page,ML		104	215m		-/15	England	Lord's	1931
Parore,AC		100* §	298m	249	-/9	New Zealand	Christchurch	1994-95
Parker,JM	(3)	108	258m	233	-/10	Australia	Sydney	1973-74
		121	408m	297	-/18	England	Auckland	1974-75
		104	289m		-/11	India	Mumbai[3]	1976-77
Pollard,V	(2)	116	437m		-/9	England	Nottingham	1973
		105*	235m		-/14	England	Lord's	1973
Rabone,GO		107	n360h		-/9	South Africa	Durban[2]	1953-54
Redmond,RE		107 §	145m		-/20	Pakistan	Auckland	1972-73
Reid,JF	(6)	123*	446m		-/11	India	Christchurch	1980-81
		180	685m	445	-/16	Sri Lanka	Colombo (CCC)	1983-84
		106	291m	325	-/8	Pakistan	Hyderabad	1984-85
		148	572m	427	-/15	Pakistan	Wellington	1984-85
		158*	486m	318	-/17	Pakistan	Auckland	1984-85
		108 §	365m	256	-/16	Australia	Brisbane[2]	1985-86
Reid,JR	(6)	135	196m		2/18	South Africa	Cape Town	1953-54
		119*	210h		1/10	India	Delhi	1955-56
		120	273m		-/15	India	Calcutta	1955-56
		142	259m		2/21	South Africa	Johannesburg[3]	1961-62
		100	252m		-/13	England	Christchurch	1962-63
		128	268m		3/15	Pakistan	Karachi[1]	1964-65
Rutherford,KR	(3)	107*	263m	181	-/12	England	Wellington	1987-88
		105	277m	227	2/13	Sri Lanka	Moratuwa	1992-93
		102	260m	215	1/9	Australia	Christchurch	1992-93
Sinclair,BW	(3)	138	346m		-/22	South Africa	Auckland	1963-64
		130	373m		-/12	Pakistan	Lahore[2]	1964-65
		114	229m		-/11	England	Auckland	1965-66
Smith,IDS	(2)	113*	239m	182	2/9	England	Auckland	1983-84
		173	237m	136	3/23	India	Auckland	1989-90
Spearman,CM		112	334m	219	1/9	Zimbabwe	Auckland	1995-96
Sutcliffe,B	(5)	101	170m		-/12	England	Manchester	1949
		116	267m		-/12	England	Christchurch	1950-51
		137* §	300h		-/15	India	Hyderabad	1955-56
		230*	>480h		-/30	India	Delhi	1955-56
		151*	357m		-/24	India	Calcutta	1964-65
Taylor,BR	(2)	105 §	158m		3/14	India	Calcutta	1964-65
		124 §	111m	102	5/14	West Indies	Auckland	1968-69
Thomson,SA		120*	233m	167	2/12	Pakistan	Christchurch	1993-94
Turner,GM	(7)	110 §	445m		-/7	Pakistan	Dacca	1969-70
		223*	572m		-/26	West Indies	Kingston	1971-72

		259	704m	759	-/22	West Indies	Georgetown	1971-72
		101 }	282m	260	-/9	Australia	Christchurch	1973-74
		110*	370m	355	-/11			
		117	411m		-/9	India	Christchurch	1975-76
		113	246m	236	-/14	India	Kanpur	1976-77
Vivian,HG		100 §	139m		-/14	South Africa	Wellington	1931-32
Wright,JG	(12)	110	460m	434	1/10	India	Auckland	1980-81
		141	352m	262	-/26	Australia	Christchurch	1981-82
		130	387m	297	-/24	England	Auckland	1983-84
		107	235m	200	1/17	Pakistan	Karachi[1]	1984-85
		119	427m	344	-/8	England	The Oval	1986
		138	575m	466	-/14	West Indies	Wellington	1986-87
		103	352m	276	-/16	England	Auckland	1987-88
		185	553m	443	-/23	India	Christchurch	1989-90
		113*	278m	208	1/12	India	Napier	1989-90
		117*	248m	197	1/17	Australia	Wellington	1989-90
		101	185m	140	-/14	Sri Lanka	Hamilton	1990-91
		116	406m	334	-/15	England	Wellington	1991-92
Young,BA		120	416m	314	-/7	Pakistan	Christchurch	1993-94

INDIA (232)			Time	Balls	6/4	Opponents		
Adhikari,HR		114* §	245m		-/10	West Indies	Delhi	1948-49
Amarnath,M	(11)	100	264m		-/4	Australia	Perth	1977-78
		101*	288m	223	-/5	West Indies	Kanpur	1978-79
		109*	391m	284	-/15	Pakistan	Lahore[2]	1982-83
		120	282m	200	1/15	Pakistan	Lahore[2]	1982-83
		103*	236m	188	-/12	Pakistan	Karachi[1]	1982-83
		117	375m		-/14	West Indies	Port-of-Spain	1982-83
		116	282m		-/10	West Indies	St John's	1982-83
		101*	408m		-/8	Pakistan	Lahore[2]	1984-85
		116*	395m	201	-/9	Sri Lanka	Kandy	1985-86
		138	382m	312	-/10	Australia	Sydney	1985-86
		131	454m	301	-/14	Sri Lanka	Nagpur	1986-87
Amarnath,NB		118 §	203m		-/21	England	Mumbai[1]	1933-34
Amarnath,S		124 §	259m		1/16	New Zealand	Auckland	1975-76
Amre,PK		103 §	374m	298	-/11	South Africa	Durban[2]	1992-93
Apte,ML		163*	584m			West Indies	Port-of-Spain	1952-53
Azharuddin,M	(14)	110 §	442m	324	-/10	England	Calcutta	1984-85
		105	279m	218	-/18	England	Chennai[1]	1984-85
		122	374m	270	-/16	England	Kanpur	1984-85
		199	500m		1/16	Sri Lanka	Kanpur	1986-87
		141	400m		-/11	Pakistan	Calcutta	1986-87
		110	308m	211	-/14	Pakistan	Jaipur	1986-87
		109	249m	175	-/10	Pakistan	Faisalabad	1989-90
		192	421m	259	-/26	New Zealand	Auckland	1989-90
		121	174m	112	-/22	England	Lord's	1990
		179	279m	243	1/21	England	Manchester	1990
		106	185m	162	-/17	Australia	Adelaide	1991-92
		182	326m	197	1/26	England	Calcutta	1992-93
		108	290m	217	1/11	Sri Lanka	Bangalore	1993-94
		152	361m	260	1/16	Sri Lanka	Ahmedabad	1993-94
Baig,AA		112 §	261m		-/12	England	Manchester	1959
Borde,CG	(5)	109	255m		-/16	West Indies	Delhi	1958-59
		177*	533		-/13	Pakistan	Chennai[2]	1960-61
		109	152m		-/17	New Zealand	Mumbai[2]	1964-65
		121			-/15	West Indies	Mumbai[2]	1966-67
		125	340m		-/14	West Indies	Chennai[1]	1966-67

Contractor,NJ		108	397m		-/10	Australia	Mumbai[2]	1959-60
Durani,SA		104	194m		-/14	West Indies	Port-of-Spain	1961-62
Engineer,FM	(2)	109	159m		-/18	West Indies	Chennai[1]	1966-67
		121	283m	182	-/14	England	Mumbai[2]	1972-73
Gaekwad,AD	(2)	102	357m		-/10	West Indies	Kanpur	1978-79
		201	671m	436	-/17	Pakistan	Jullundur	1983-84
Ganguly,S	(2)	131 §	434m	301	-/20	England	Lord's	1996
		136	359m	268	2/17	England	Nottingham	1996
Gavaskar,SM	(31)	116	265m		-/11	West Indies	Georgetown	1970-71
		117*	340m		-/10	West Indies	Bridgetown	1970-71
		124 }	392m		-/11	West Indies	Port-of-Spain	1970-71
		220	505m		-/22			
		101	290m		-/8	England	Manchester	1974
		116§	368m		1/15	New Zealand	Auckland	1975-76
		156	488m	352	-/13	West Indies	Port-of-Spain	1975-76
		102	245m		-/13	West Indies	Port-of-Spain	1975-76
		119	265m		-/20	New Zealand	Mumbai[3]	1976-77
		108	341m	220	-/13	England	Mumbai[3]	1976-77
		113 §	320m	264	-/12	Australia	Brisbane[2]	1977-78
		127	270m		-/20	Australia	Perth	1977-78
		118	354m		-12	Australia	Melbourne	1977-78
		111 }	357m		-/15	Pakistan	Karachi[1]	1978-79
		137	315m	240	-/20			
		205	398m		2/29	West Indies	Mumbai[3]	1978-79
		107 }	315h		-/18	West Indies	Calcutta	1978-79
		182*	399m	264	-/19			
		120	344m	218	-/18	West Indies	Delhi	1978-79
		221	489m	443	-/21	England	The Oval	1979
		115	329m	238	1/17	Australia	Delhi	1979-80
		123	303m	239	-/17	Australia	Mumbai[3]	1979-80
		166	593m	393	1/15	Pakistan	Chennai[1]	1979-80
		172	708m	476	-/21	England	Bangalore	1981-82
		155 §	399m	293	1/24	Sri Lanka	Chennai[1]	1982-83
		127*	433m	262	-/19	Pakistan	Faisalabad	1982-83
		147*	330m		1/17	West Indies	Georgetown	1982-83
		103*	236m	190	-/10	Pakistan	Bangalore	1983-84
		121	224m	128	2/15	West Indies	Delhi	1983-84
		236*	644m	425	-/23	West Indies	Chennai[1]	1983-84
		166*	551m	416	-/16	Australia	Adelaide	1985-86
		172	413m	400	-/19	Australia	Sydney	1985-86
		103	302m	203	-/11	Australia	Mumbai[3]	1986-87
		176	506m	302	-/22	Sri Lanka	Kanpur	1986-87
Hanumant Singh		105 §	149m		-/16	England	Delhi	1963-64
Hazare,VS	(7)	116 }	275m		-/14	Australia	Adelaide	1947-48
		145	313m		-/17			
		134*	371m		-/18	West Indies	Mumbai[2]	1948-49
		122	241m		-/14	West Indies	Mumbai[2]	1948-49
		164*	515m		-/15	England	Delhi	1951-52
		155	321m		-/19	England	Mumbai[2]	1951-52
		146*	285m		-/18	Pakistan	Mumbai[2]	1952-53
Jaisimha,ML	(3)	127	249m		2/14	England	Delhi	1961-62
		129	299m		1/18	England	Calcutta	1963-64
		101	291m		-/9	Australia	Brisbane[2]	1967-68
Kambli,VG	(4)	224	608m	411	-/23	England	Mumbai[3]	1992-93
		227	413m	301	-/28	Zimbabwe	Delhi	1992-93
		125	358m	220	1/16	Sri Lanka	Colombo (SSC)	1993-94
		120	315m	240	2/15	Sri Lanka	Colombo (PSS)	1993-94

Kapil Dev	(8)	126*	224m	124	1/11	West Indies	Delhi	1978-79
		116	173m	98	2/16	England	Kanpur	1981-82
		100*	142m	95	3/13	West Indies	Port-of-Spain	1982-83
		119	214m	138	-/21	Australia	Chennai[1]	1986-87
		163	240m	165	1/19	Sri Lanka	Kanpur	1986-87
		109	164m	124	-/18	West Indies	Chennai[1]	1987-88
		110	197m	142	-/19	England	The Oval	1990
		129	256m	180	1/14	South Africa	Port Elizabeth	1992-93
Kirmani,SMH	(2)	101*	306m	206	-/16	Australia	Mumbai[3]	1979-80
		102	319m	230	-/10	England	Mumbai[3]	1984-85
Kripal Singh,AG		100* §	246m		-/12	New Zealand	Hyderabad	1955-56
Kunderan,BK	(2)	192	410m		-/31	England	Chennai[2]	1963-64
		100	241m		-/15	England	Delhi	1963-64
Manjrekar,SV	(4)	108	343m	221	-/15	West Indies	Bridgetown	1988-89
		113*	351m	243	-/13	Pakistan	Karachi[1]	1989-90
		218	511m	401	-/28	Pakistan	Lahore[2]	1989-90
		100* §	529m	422	-/7	Zimbabwe	Harare	1992-93
Manjrekar,VL	(7)	133	266m		-/19	England	Leeds	1952
		118	249m		-/15	West Indies	Kingston	1952-53
		118 §	235m		-/20	New Zealand	Hyderabad	1955-56
		177	555h		-/20	New Zealand	Delhi	1955-56
		189*	444m		-/28	England	Delhi	1961-62
		108	294m		-/14	England	Chennai[2]	1963-64
		102*	200m		-/14	New Zealand	Chennai[2]	1964-65
Mankad,MH	(5)	116	180h		1/13	Australia	Melbourne	1947-48
		111	300m		-/6	Australia	Melbourne	1947-48
		184	270m		1/19	England	Lord's	1952
		223	472m		-/22	New Zealand	Mumbai[2]	1955-56
		231	525m		-/21	New Zealand	Chennai[2]	1955-56
Merchant,VM	(3)	114	255m		-/13	England	Manchester	1936
		128	315h		-/15	England	The Oval	1946
		154	440m		-/20	England	Delhi	1951-52
Modi,RS		112	284m		-/12	West Indies	Mumbai[2]	1948-49
Mushtaq Ali	(2)	112	160m		-/17	England	Manchester	1936
		106 §	203m		-/9	West Indies	Calcutta	1948-49
Nadkarni,RG		122*	418m		-/15	England	Kanpur	1963-64m
Pataudi,Nawab of,jr	(6)	103	168m		2/16	England	Chennai[2]	1961-62
		203*	430m		2/23	England	Delhi	1963-64
		128* §	343m	311	-/17	Australia	Chennai[2]	1964-65
		153	285m		-/29	New Zealand	Calcutta	1964-65
		113	233m		2/16	New Zealand	Delhi	1964-65
		148	350m		1/15	England	Leeds	1967
Patel,BP		115*	420m		-/10	West Indies	Port-of-Spain	1975-76
Patil,SM	(4)	174	301m	240	1/22	Australia	Adelaide	1980-81
		129*	212m	196	2/18	England	Manchester	1982
		114* §	216m		1/13	Sri Lanka	Chennai[1]	1982-83
		127	330h	231	-/18	Pakistan	Faisalabad	1984-85
Phadkar,DG	(2)	123	254m		-/15	Australia	Adelaide	1947-48
		115	389m		1/10	England	Calcutta	1951-52
Prabhakar,M		120	405m	274	-/16	West Indies	Mohali	1994-95
Ramchand,GS	(2)	106*	220m		-/14	New Zealand	Calcutta	1955-56
		109	248m		-/19	Australia	Mumbai[2]	1956-57
Roy,Pankaj	(5)	140	329m		-/20	England	Mumbai[2]	1951-52
		111	232m		-/15	England	Chennai[1]	1951-52
		150	376m		-/20	West Indies	Kingston	1952-53
		100	308m		-/15	New Zealand	Calcutta	1955-56
		173	472m		-/12	New Zealand	Chennai[2]	1955-56

Sardesai,DN	(5)	200*	550m		-/25	New Zealand	Mumbai[2]	1964-65
		106	140m		-/18	New Zealand	Delhi	1964-65
		212	487m		1/17	West Indies	Kingston	1970-71
		112	278m		-/11	West Indies	Port-of-Spain	1970-71
		150	288m		-/20	West Indies	Bridgetown	1970-71
Shastri,RJ	(11)	128	488m	327	-/15	Pakistan	Karachi[1]	1982-83
		102	370m		-/5	West Indies	St John's	1982-83
		139	405m	270	2/16	Pakistan	Faisalabad	1984-85
		142	389m	322	1/17	England	Mumbai[3]	1984-85
		111	455m	357	-/13	England	Calcutta	1984-85
		121*	388m	287	6/9	Australia	Mumbai[3]	1986-87
		125	>450h		1/8	Pakistan	Jaipur	1986-87
		107	441m	282	-/12	West Indies	Bridgetown	1988-89
		100	245m	185	1/12	England	Lord's	1990
		187	559m	435	-/23	England	The Oval	1990
		206	572m	472	2/17	Australia	Sydney	1991-92
Shodhan,RH		110 §	215m		-/15	Pakistan	Calcutta	1952-53
Sidhu,NS	(6)	116 §	295m	195	4/12	New Zealand	Bangalore	1988-89
		116	358m	237	-/13	West Indies	Kingston	1988-89
		106	403m	273	-/9	England	Chennai[1]	1992-93
		104	384m	273	-/7	Sri Lanka	Colombo (SSC)	1993-94
		124	280m	223	8/9	Sri Lanka	Lucknow[2]	1993-94
		107	296m	240	-/17	West Indies	Nagpur	1994-95
Solkar,ED		102	363m		-/8	West Indies	Mumbai[3]	1974-75
Srikkanth,K	(2)	116	190m	119	1/19	Australia	Sydney	1985-86
		123		149	2/18	Pakistan	Chennai[1]	1986-87
Tendulkar,SR	(10)	119*	225m	189	-/17	England	Manchester	1990
		148*	298m	215	-/14	Australia	Sydney	1991-92
		114	228m	161	-/16	Australia	Perth	1991-92
		111	370m	270	-/19	South Africa	Johannesburg[3]	1992-93
		165	361m	296	1/24	England	Chennai[1]	1992-93
		104*	217m	163	1/11	Sri Lanka	Colombo (SSC)	1993-94
		142	260m	224	-/22	Sri Lanka	Lucknow[2]	1993-94
		179	412m	319	1/24	West Indies	Nagpur	1994-95
		122	262m	176	1/19	England	Birmingham	1996
		177	460m	360	-/26	England	Nottingham	1996
Umrigar,PR	(12)	130*	262m		-/11	England	Chennai[1]	1951-52
		102	168m		1/15	Pakistan	Mumbai[2]	1952-53
		130	327m		2/12	West Indies	Port-of-Spain	1952-53
		117	232m		-/16	West Indies	Kingston	1952-53
		108	280m		-/13	Pakistan	Peshawar[1]	1954-55
		223 §	503m		-/26	New Zealand	Hyderabad	1955-56
		118	260m		-/13	England	Manchester	1959
		115	339m		-/11	Pakistan	Kanpur	1960-61
		117			-/14	Pakistan	Chennai[2]	1960-61
		112				Pakistan	Delhi	1960-61
		147*	400m		-/16	England	Kanpur	1961-62
		172*	248m			West Indies	Port-of-Spain	1961-62
Vengsarkar,DB	(17)	157*	379m	299	1/18	West Indies	Calcutta	1978-79
		109	336m	223	-/11	West Indies	Delhi	1978-79
		103	353m	295	-/13	England	Lord's	1979
		112	366m	283	2/12	Australia	Bangalore	1979-80
		146*	522m	370	1/11	Pakistan	Delhi	1979-80
		157	334m	264	-/21	England	Lord's	1982
		159	370m	238	1/20	West Indies	Delhi	1983-84
		100		142	-/13	West Indies	Mumbai[3]	1983-84
		137	360m	255	1/17	England	Kanpur	1984-85

		126*	327m	213	-/16	England	Lord's	1986
		102*	282m	216	-/10	England	Leeds	1986
		164*	432m	303	1/21	Australia	Mumbai[3]	1986-87
		153				Sri Lanka	Nagpur	1986-87
		166	429m	266	-/14	Sri Lanka	Cuttack	1986-87
		109		295	-/10	Pakistan	Ahmedabad	1986-87
		102	405m	257	-/8	West Indies	Delhi	1987-88
		102*	346m	266	-/11	West Indies	Calcutta	1987-88
Viswanath,GR	(14)	137 §	354m		-/25	Australia	Kanpur	1969-70
		113	267m	214	1/18	England	Mumbai[2]	1972-73
		139	376m	263	-/23	West Indies	Calcutta	1974-75
		112	220m		-/15	West Indies	Port-of-Spain	1975-76
		103*	147m		-/8	New Zealand	Kanpur	1976-77
		145 §	360m		-/16	Pakistan	Faisalabad	1978-79
		124	346m		-/17	West Indies	Chennai[1]	1978-79
		179	419m	261	-/21	West Indies	Kanpur	1978-79
		113	351m	337	-/14	England	Lord's	1979
		161*	405m	297	1/11	Australia	Bangalore	1979-80
		131	277m	207	-/18	Australia	Delhi	1979-80
		114	274m	222	-/11	Australia	Melbourne	1980-81
		107	268m	200	-/14	England	Delhi	1981-82
		222	638m	373	-/31	England	Chennai[1]	1981-82
Wadekar,AL		143	371m		-/12	New Zealand	Wellington	1967-68
Yashpal Sharma	(2)	100*	280m	239	3/10	Australia	Delhi	1979-80
		140	492m	301	2/18	England	Chennai[1]	1981-82

PAKISTAN (183)			Time	Balls	6/4	Opponents		
Aamer Malik	(2)	117	409m	300	-/15	India	Faisalabad	1989-90
		113	344m	276	-/11	India	Lahore[2]	1989-90
Aamer Sohail	(2)	205	343m	284	-/32	England	Manchester	1992
		105	280m	200	-/17	Australia	Lahore[2]	1994-95
Alimuddin	(2)	103*	325m		-/15	India	Karachi[1]	1954-55
		109	232m		-/17	England	Karachi[1]	1961-62
Asif Iqbal	(11)	146	190m	244	2/21	England	The Oval	1967
		104*	192m	170	-/16	England	Birmingham	1971
		175	274m		1/18	New Zealand	Dunedin	1972-73
		102	195m		-/16	England	Lahore[2]	1972-73
		166	334m		-/15	New Zealand	Lahore[2]	1976-77
		152*	268m		-/14	Australia	Adelaide	1976-77
		120	245m		-/15	Australia	Sydney	1976-77
		135	245m		1/20	West Indies	Kingston	1976-77
		104 §	178m		-/15	India	Faisalabad	1978-79
		104	237m		-/10	New Zealand	Napier	1978-79
		134*	306m		1/18	Australia	Perth	1978-79
Basit Ali		103	197m	139	3/9	New Zealand	Christchurch	1993-94
Hanif Mohammad	(12)	142	518m		1/17	India	Bahawalpur	1954-55
		103	270h		-/8	New Zealand	Dacca	1955-56
		337 §	973m		-/24	West Indies	Bridgetown	1957-58
		103	390h		-/7	West Indies	Karachi[1]	1958-59
		101*	365m		-/10	Australia	Karachi[1]	1959-60
		160	380m		-/17	India	Mumbai[2]	1960-61
		111 }	497m		-/14	England	Dacca	1961-62
		104 }	396m		-/8			
		104	193m		-/8	Australia	Melbourne	1964-65
		100*	203m		-/18	New Zealand	Christchurch	1964-65
		203*	445m		-/33	New Zealand	Lahore[2]	1964-65
		187*	540h		-/21	England	Lord's	1967

Haroon Rashid	(3)	122 §	298m		1/18	England	Lahore[2]	1977-78
		108	214m		6/10	England	Hyderabad	1977-78
		153 §	323m	242	3/16	Sri Lanka	Karachi[1]	1981-82
Ijaz Ahmed	(5)	122	297m	221	2/17	Australia	Faisalabad	1988-89
		121	450m	331	-/11	Australia	Melbourne	1989-90
		137	442m	332	2/17	Australia	Sydney	1995-96
		103	312m	213	2/13	New Zealand	Christchurch	1995-96
		141	279m	201	2/20	England	Leeds	1996
Ijaz Faqih		105 §		211	1/7	India	Ahmedabad	1986-87
Imran Khan	(6)	123	302m	199	-/13	West Indies	Lahore[2]	1980-81
		117	192m	121	5/10	India	Faisalabad	1982-83
		135*		230	5/14	India	Chennai[1]	1986-87
		118	256m	201	1/11	England	The Oval	1987
		109*	201m	145	1/17	India	Karachi[1]	1989-90
		136	485m	361	-/10	Australia	Adelaide	1989-90
Imtiaz Ahmed	(3)	209	380m		-/28	New Zealand	Lahore[2]	1955-56
		122	250m		-/14	West Indies	Kingston	1957-58
		135	320m		-/11	India	Chennai[2]	1960-61
Intikhab Alam		138	270m		4/15	England	Hyderabad	1972-73
Inzamamul Haq	(5)	123	314m	225	1/11	West Indies	St John's	1992-93
		135*	251m	195	1/19	New Zealand	Wellington	1993-94
		100*	197m	125	-/13	Sri Lanka	Kandy	1994-95
		101	205m	168	2/12	Zimbabwe	Harare	1994-95
		148	298m	218	1/19	England	Lord's	1996
Javed Burki	(3)	138 §	375h		1/17	England	Lahore[2]	1961-62
		140	356m		-/18	England	Dacca	1961-62
		101	225m		-/15	England	Lord's	1962
Javed Miandad	(23)	163 §	259m		-/22	New Zealand	Lahore[2]	1976-77
		206	410m		2/29	New Zealand	Karachi[1]	1976-77
		154* §	430m		3/13	India	Faisalabad	1978-79
		100	311m		1/8	India	Karachi[1]	1978-79
		160*	420m		1/17	New Zealand	Christchurch	1978-79
		129*	388m	284	-/15	Australia	Perth	1978-79
		106*	217m		1/11	Australia	Faisalabad	1979-80
		138	416m	264	2/13	Australia	Lahore[2]	1982-83
		126	276m	200	3/10	India	Faisalabad	1982-83
		280*	606m	460	1/19	India	Hyderabad	1982-83
		131	361m	271	-/13	Australia	Adelaide	1983-84
		104 }	269m	217	-/12	New Zealand	Hyderabad	1984-85
		103* }	245m	198	1/13			
		203*	465m		1/22	Sri Lanka	Faisalabad	1985-86
		260	617m	521	1/28	England	The Oval	1987
		114	405m	235	-/12	West Indies	Georgetown	1987-88
		102	436m	265	-/18	West Indies	Port-of-Spain	1987-88
		211	636m	441	1/29	Australia	Karachi[1]	1988-89
		107	254m	186	-/17	Australia	Faisalabad	1988-89
		118	360m	277	-/8	New Zealand	Wellington	1988-89
		271	558m	465	5/28	New Zealand	Auckland	1988-89
		145	369m	291	-/10	India	Lahore[2]	1989-90
		(In his 100th Test match)						
		153*	415m	337	-/19	England	Birmingham	1992
Khalid Ibadulla		166 §	330m	319	-/20	Australia	Karachi[1]	1964-65
Majid Khan	(8)	158	303m		-/18	Australia	Melbourne	1972-73
		110	269m		-/15	New Zealand	Auckland	1972-73
		100	247m		-/9	West Indies	Karachi[1]	1974-75
		112	128m		2/18	New Zealand	Karachi[1]	1976-77
		167	360h		-/25	West Indies	Georgetown	1976-77

		119*	411m		-/13	New Zealand	Napier	1978-79
		108	219m		-/16	Australia	Melbourne	1978-79
		110*	282m		-/14	Australia	Lahore[2]	1979-80
Mansoor Akhtar		111	289m	191	-/18	Australia	Faisalabad	1982-83
Mohammad Ilyas		126	205m		1/15	New Zealand	Karachi[1]	1964-65
Mohsin Khan	(7)	129	296m	173	-/17	Sri Lanka	Lahore[2]	1981-82
		200	496m	386	-/23	England	Lord's	1982
		135	349m	218	-/17	Australia	Lahore[2]	1982-83
		101* §	168m	161	1/10	India	Lahore[2]	1982-83
		149	393m	296	-/16	Australia	Adelaide	1983-84
		152	354m	239	1/19	Australia	Melbourne	1983-84
		104	258m	136	-/3	England	Lahore[2]	1983-84
Moin Khan	(3)	115*	233m	185	1/13	Australia	Lahore[2]	1994-95
		117*	283m	208	2/13	Sri Lanka	Sialkot	1994-95
		105	290m	191	1/10	England	Leeds	1996
Mudassar Nazar	(10)	114 §	591m		-/12	England	Lahore[2]	1977-78
		126	447m	337	-/13	India	Bangalore	1979-80
		119	294m	199	-/10	India	Karachi[1]	1982-83
		231	627m	444	1/21	India	Hyderabad	1982-83
		152*	495m	296	-/15	India	Lahore[2]	1982-83
		152	458m	308	-/14	India	Karachi[1]	1982-83
		199	552m	408	-/24	India	Faisalabad	1984-85
		106	255m	187	-/11	New Zealand	Hyderabad	1984-85
		124	416m	362	-/16	England	Birmingham	1987
		120	323m	257	-/18	England	Lahore[2]	1987-88
Mushtaq Mohammad	(10)	101	210m		-/19	India	Delhi	1960-61
		100*	324m		-/9	England	Nottingham	1962
		100	351m	283	-/13	England	Birmingham	1971
		121	292m	271	-/14	Australia	Sydney	1972-73
		201	383m		-/20	New Zealand	Dunedin	1972-73
		157	469m		-/17	England	Hyderabad	1972-73
		123	466m		-/12	West Indies	Lahore[2]	1974-75
		101			-/9	New Zealand	Hyderabad	1976-77
		107	298m		-/11	New Zealand	Karachi[1]	1976-77
		121	371m		-/14	West Indies	Port-of-Spain	1976-77
Nasim-ul-Ghani		101	180m		1/16	England	Lord's	1962
Nazir Mohammad		124*	517m			India	Lucknow[1]	1952-53
Qasim Omar	(3)	113	283m	224	-/12	Australia	Adelaide	1983-84
		210	685m	442	-/27	India	Faisalabad	1984-85
		206 §				Sri Lanka	Faisalabad	1985-86
Rameez Raja	(2)	122	388m	242	-/17	Sri Lanka	Colombo (PSS)	1985-86
		114	302m	279	1/12	India	Jaipur	1986-87
Sadiq Mohammad	(5)	137	313m		-/15	Australia	Melbourne	1972-73
		166	362m		-/19	New Zealand	Wellington	1972-73
		119	375m		-/12	England	Lahore[2]	1972-73
		103*			-/14	New Zealand	Hyderabad	1976-77
		105	296m		-/10	Australia	Melbourne	1976-77
Saeed Ahmed	(5)	150	349m		-/16	West Indies	Georgetown	1957-58
		166	461m		-/19	Australia	Lahore[2]	1959-60
		121 §	345m		-/11	India	Mumbai[2]	1960-61
		103	245m		-/10	India	Chennai[2]	1960-61
		172	341m		1/17	New Zealand	Karachi[1]	1964-65
Saeed Anwar	(3)	169	307m	248	-/26	New Zealand	Wellington	1993-94
		136	319m	218	-/12	Sri Lanka	Colombo (PPS)	1994-95
		176	377m	264	-/26	England	The Oval	1996
Saleem Malik	(14)	100* §	272m	191	-/10	Sri Lanka	Karachi[1]	1981-82
		107	251m	168	-/14	India	Faisalabad	1982-83

Mark Waugh (Australia) plays a shot against New Zealand in Hobart, November 1993. Waugh scored 111, his fifth Test century, and was one of three Australian batsmen to score a century in this match. (The others were Michael Slater and David Boon.)

Brian Lara (West Indies) pulls Chris Lewis (England) for four, to break compatriot Sir Garfield Sobers' record Test innings score of 365 in the fifth Test at St Johns in Antigua, 1994. Lara was eventually dismissed for 375.

		116	393m	270	-/17	England	Faisalabad	1983-84
		102*	205m	157	-/15	India	Faisalabad	1984-85
		119*	267m	169	1/21	New Zealand	Karachi[1]	1984-85
		102	267m	237	-/6	England	The Oval	1987
		102*	216m	144	-/13	India	Karachi[1]	1989-90
		102	268m	208	-/7	West Indies	Karachi[1]	1990-91
		101	287m	201	-/10	Sri Lanka	Sialkot	1991-92
		165	370m	297	1/19	England	Birmingham	1992
		140	285m	200	-/20	New Zealand	Christchurch	1993-94
		237	443m	328	-/34	Australia	Rawalpindi[2]	1994-95
		143	313m	242	-/19	Australia	Lahore[2]	1994-95
		100*	297m	223	-/10	England	The Oval	1996
Shoaib Mohammad	(7)	101			-/10	India	Chennai[1]	1986-87
		163	720m	516	1/17	New Zealand	Wellington	1988-89
		112	350m	254	-/17	New Zealand	Auckland	1988-89
		203*	486m	335	-/19	India	Lahore[2]	1989-90
		203*	656m	411	-/23	New Zealand	Karachi[1]	1990-91
		105	351m	223	1/15	New Zealand	Lahore[2]	1990-91
		142	527m	368	-/20	New Zealand	Faisalabad	1990-91
Taslim Arif		210*	435m		-/20	Australia	Faisalabad	1979-80
Waqar Hassan		189	430m		-/30	New Zealand	Lahore[1]	1955-56
Wasim Akram		123	244m	195	1/18	Australia	Adelaide	1989-90
Wasim Raja	(4)	107*	340m		1/10	West Indies	Karachi[1]	1974-75
		117*	260m		1/12	West Indies	Bridgetown	1976-77
		125	258m	207	2/17	India	Jullundur	1983-84
		112	300m	210	2/14	England	Faisalabad	1983-84
Wazir Mohammad	(2)	106	a180h		-/17	West Indies	Kingston	1957-58
		189	403m		-/22	West Indies	Port-of-Spain	1957-58
Zaheer Abbas	(12)	274§	550m		-/38	England	Birmingham	1971
		240	550m	410	-/22	England	The Oval	1974
		101	224m		1/13	Australia	Adelaide	1976-77
		176 §	315m		2/24	India	Faisalabad	1978-79
		235*	391m		2/29	India	Lahore[2]	1978-79
		135	388m	282	1/15	New Zealand	Auckland	1978-79
		134 §	269m	148	2/12	Sri Lanka	Lahore[2]	1981-82
		126	279m	205	3/12	Australia	Faisalabad	1982-83
		215	334m	254	2/23	India	Lahore[2]	1982-83
		(His 100th first-class century)						
		186	328m	246	-/23	India	Karachi[1]	1982-83
		168	264m	176	1/23	India	Faisalabad	1982-83
		168*	500m	341	1/6	India	Lahore[2]	1984-85
SRI LANKA (43)			Time	Balls	6/4	Opponents		
de Silva,PA	(8)	122 §	510m		3/17	Pakistan	Faisalabad	1985-86
		105	265m		-/16	Pakistan	Karachi[1]	1985-86
		167	491m	361	1/17	Australia	Brisbane[2]	1989-90
		267	509m	380	-/40	New Zealand	Wellington	1990-91
		123	261m	193	5/6	New Zealand	Auckland	1990-91
		148	388m	297	1/17	India	Colombo (PSS)	1993-94
		127	211m	156	1/19	Pakistan	Colombo (PSS)	1994-95
		105	402m	316	-/11	Pakistan	Faisalabad	1994-95
Dias,RL	(3)	109	260m	179	1/14	Pakistan	Lahore[2]	1981-82
		108 §	272m	215	-/18	New Zealand	Colombo (SSC)	1983-84
		106	312m	216	-/17	India	Kandy	1985-86
Gurusinha,AP	(7)	116*	495m	307	-/14	Pakistan	Colombo (PSS)	1985-86
		119 }	362m	261	1/17	New Zealand	Hamilton	1990-91
		102 }	331m	239	1/9			

			Time	Balls	6/4	Opponents		
		137	525m	399	-/18	Australia	Colombo (SSC)	1992-93
		128 §	607m	461	1/14	Zimbabwe	Harare	1994-95
		127	516m	429	1/11	New Zealand	Dunedin	1994-95
		143	353m	274	1/15	Australia	Melbourne	1995-96
Jayasuriya,ST		112	272m	188	2/14	Australia	Adelaide	1995-96
Kaluwitharana,RS §		132* §	203m	158	-/26	Australia	Colombo (SSC)	1992-93
Kuruppu,DSBP §		201* §	778m	562	-/24	New Zealand	Colombo (CCC)	1986-87
Madugalle,RS		103	403m	280	-/10	India	Colombo (SSC)	1985-86
Mahanama,RS	(3)	153	361m	297	-/18	New Zealand	Moratuwa	1992-93
		109	217m	154	-/14	New Zealand	Colombo (SSC)	1992-93
		151	520m	362	-/19	India	Colombo (PSS)	1993-94
Mendis,LRD	(4)	105 § }	179m	123	1/17	India	Chennai[1]	1982-83
		105 § }	236m		-/12			
		111	197m	143	3/11	England	Lord's	1984
		124	318m	228	2/12	India	Kandy	1985-86
Ranatunga,A	(4)	111	400m	290	1/4	India	Colombo (SSC)	1985-86
		135*	341m	208	4/14	Pakistan	Colombo (PSS)	1985-86
		127	266m	192	3/15	Australia	Colombo (SSC)	1992-93
		131 §	204m	140	1/18	South Africa	Moratuwa	1992-93
Ranatunga,S		118	467m	342	-/17	Zimbabwe	Harare	1994-95
		100*	421m	352	-/15	Zimbabwe	Bulawayo[2]	1994-95
Silva,SAR	(2)	102* §	316m	255	-/12	England	Lord's	1984
		111	492m	347	-/11	India	Colombo (PSS)	1985-86
Tillakaratne,HP	(4)	116	451m	287	-/14	Zimbabwe	Harare	1994-95
		108	332m	258	-/14	New Zealand	Dunedin	1994-95
		115	226m	176	-/20	Pakistan	Faisalabad	1994-95
		119	267m	206	-/12	Australia	Perth	1995-96
Wettimuny,S	(2)	157	372m	330	-/21	Pakistan	Faisalabad	1981-82
		190	636m	471	-/21	England	Lord's	1984

ZIMBABWE (9)			Time	Balls	6/4	Opponents		
Arnott,KJ		101* §	248m	200	-/12	New Zealand	Bulawayo[1]	1992-93
Flower,A	(2)	115	289m	236	-/15	India	Delhi	1992-93
		156	336m	245	1/18	Pakistan	Harare	1994-95
Flower,GW		201*	654m	523	1/10	Pakistan	Harare	1994-95
Houghton,DL	(4)	121 §	414m	322	-/15	India	Harare	1992-93
		266	675m	541	3/30	Sri Lanka	Bulawayo[2]	1994-95
		142	394m	268	2/17	Sri Lanka	Harare	1994-95
		104+	306m	204	-/12	New Zealand	Auckland	1995-96
Whittall,GJ		113*	243m	192	-/9	Pakistan	Harare	1994-95

BATSMAN RUN OUT IN EACH INNINGS OF A TEST

P.A.McAlister	Australia	v	England	Melbourne	1907-08
C.Kelleway	Australia	v	South Africa	Melbourne	1910-11
J.Ryder	Australia	v	England	Sydney	1920-21
J.Trim	West Indies	v	Australia	Melbourne	1951-52
J.B.Stollmeyer	West Indies	v	England	Bridgetown	1953-54
I.Meckiff	Australia	v	West Indies	Brisbane[2]	1960-61
J.S.Solomon	West Indies	v	Australia	Melbourne	1960-61
S.N.McGregor	New Zealand	v	South Africa	Dunedin	1963-64
R.M.Edwards	West Indies	v	New Zealand	Wellington	1968-69
C.H.Lloyd	West Indies	v	India	Kingston	1970-71
J.A.Jameson	England	v	India	The Oval	1971
Zaheer Abbas	Pakistan	v	Australia	Melbourne	1972-73
A.R.Border	Australia	v	Pakistan	Melbourne	1981-82
M.A.Taylor	Australia	v	West Indies	Adelaide	1988-89
Wasim Akram	Pakistan	v	West Indies	Faisalabad	1990-91

M.A.Taylor	Australia	v	England	Adelaide	1990-91
I.A.Healy	Australia	v	West Indies	Georgetown	1990-91
A.H.Jones	New Zealand	v	Pakistan	Christchurch	1993-94
J.Angel	Australia	v	England	Perth	1994-95

NOUGHT AND A CENTURY IN THE SAME MATCH *(§ in first Test)*

AUSTRALIA	Scores		Opponents		
W.L.Murdoch	0	153*	England	The Oval	1880
G.H.S.Trott	0	143	England	Lord's	1890
C.Hill	188	0	England	Melbourne	1897-98
D.G.Bradman	0	103*	England	Melbourne	1932-33
J.H.W.Fingleton	100	0	England	Brisbane[2]	1936-37
D.G.Bradman	138	0	England	Nottingham	1948
S.G.Barnes	0	141	England	Lord's	1948
R.N.Harvey	122	0	England	Manchester	1953
I.R.Redpath	0	132	West Indies	Sydney	1968-69
I.M.Chappell	138	0	India	Delhi	1969-70
I.C.Davis	105	0	Pakistan	Adelaide	1976-77
R.B.McCosker	0	105	Pakistan	Melbourne	1976-77
C.S.Serjeant	0	124	West Indies	Georgetown	1977-78
G.N.Yallop	0	114	England	Manchester	1981
G.R.Marsh	118	0	New Zealand	Auckland	1985-86
D.C.Boon	103	0	England	Adelaide	1986-87
M.E.Waugh	139*	0	West Indies	St John's	1990-91

ENGLAND	Scores		Opponents		
L.C.Braund	102	0	Australia	Sydney	1903-04
J.T.Tyldesley	0	100	Australia	Leeds	1905
G.Gunn	122*	0	Australia	Sydney	1907-08
F.E.Woolley	0	123	Australia	Sydney	1924-25
G.B.Legge	196	0	New Zealand	Auckland	1929-30
D.C.S.Compton	145*	0	Australia	Manchester	1948
L.Hutton	101	0	New Zealand	Leeds	1949
P.B.H.May	0	112	South Africa	Lord's	1955
M.C.Cowdrey	119	0	West Indies	Port-of-Spain	1959-60
Rev.D.S.Sheppard	0	113	Australia	Melbourne	1962-63
M.C.Cowdrey	101	0	West Indies	Kingston	1967-68
D.L.Amiss	158	0	Pakistan	Hyderabad	1972-73
D.W.Randall	0	150	Australia	Sydney	1978-79
I.T.Botham	0	118	Australia	Manchester	1981
G.Boycott	137	0	Australia	The Oval	1981
M.W.Gatting	100	0	Australia	Adelaide	1986-87
D.I.Gower	100	0	Australia	Melbourne	1990-91
C.C.Lewis	0	117	India	Chennai[1]	1992-93
M.A.Atherton	144	0	West Indies	Georgetown	1993-94
M.W.Gatting	117	0	Australia	Adelaide	1994-95
G.P.Thorpe	123	0	Australia	Perth	1994-95

SOUTH AFRICA	Scores		Opponents		
J.H.Sinclair	0	104	Australia	Cape Town	1902-03
G.A.Faulkner	122*	0	Australia	Manchester	1912
R.H.Catterall	0	120	England	Birmingham	1924
A.D.Nourse	0	231	Australia	Johannesburg[1]	1935-36
E.J.Barlow	114	0	Australia	Brisbane[2]	1963-64
A.C.Hudson §	163	0	West Indies	Bridgetown	1991-92

WEST INDIES	Scores		Opponents		
I.Barrow	105	0	England	Manchester	1933
F.C.M.Alexander	0	108	Australia	Sydney	1960-61
S.M.Nurse	201	0	Australia	Bridgetown	1964-65
G.S.Sobers	0	113*	England	Kingston	1967-68
C.A.Davis	103	0	England	Lord's	1969
G.S.Sobers	132	0	India	Port-of-Spain	1970-71
A.I.Kallicharran	0	103*	India	Port-of-Spain	1975-76
R.C.Fredericks	0	138	England	Lord's	1976
D.L.Haynes	0	122	New Zealand	Christchurch	1979-80
C.L.King	0	100*	New Zealand	Christchurch	1979-80
I.V.A.Richards	0	182*	England	Bridgetown	1980-81
I.V.A.Richards	208	0	Australia	Melbourne	1984-85
D.L.Haynes	0	109	England	Bridgetown	1989-90
R.B.Richardson	104	0	England	Birmingham	1991
K.L.T.Arthurton	157*	0	Australia	Brisbane[2]	1992-93

NEW ZEALAND	Scores		Opponents		
G.T.Dowling	129	0	India	Mumbai[2]	1964-65
B.F.Hastings	0	117*	West Indies	Christchurch	1968-69
M.D.Crowe	174	0	Pakistan	Wellington	1988-89
J.G.Wright	116	0	England	Wellington	1991-92
M.D.Crowe	0	107	Sri Lanka	Colombo (SSC)	1992-93

INDIA	Scores		Opponents		
M.H.Mankad	111	0	Australia	Melbourne	1947-48
Pankaj Roy	140	0	England	Mumbai[2]	1951-52
V.L.Manjrekar	133	0	England	Leeds	1952
M.L.Apte	0	163*	West Indies	Port-of-Spain	1952-53
V.L.Manjrekar	108	0	England	Chennai[2]	1963-64
G.R.Viswanath §	0	137	Australia	Kanpur	1969-70
S.M.Gavaskar	0	118	Australia	Melbourne	1977-78
D.B.Vengsarkar	0	103	England	Lord's	1979
N.S.Sidhu	116	0	West Indies	Kingston	1988-89
M.Azharuddin	0	109	Pakistan	Faisalabad	1989-90

PAKISTAN	Scores		Opponents		
Imtiaz Ahmed	209	0	New Zealand	Lahore[1]	1955-56
Imtiaz Ahmed	122	0	West Indies	Kingston	1957-58
Hanif Mohammad	160	0	India	Mumbai[2]	1960-61
Javed Burki	140	0	England	Dacca	1961-62
Asif Iqbal	0	152*	Australia	Adelaide	1976-77
Sadiq Mohammad	105	0	Australia	Melbourne	1976-77
Asif Iqbal	0	104	India	Faisalabad	1978-79
Ijaz Ahmed	122	0	Australia	Faisalabad	1988-89

SRI LANKA	Scores		Opponents		
A.Ranatunga	127	0	Australia	Colombo (SSC)	1992-93
P.A.de Silva	0	105	Pakistan	Faisalabad	1994-95
H.P.Tillakaratne	115	0	Pakistan	Faisalabad	1994-95

NINETY-NINES IN TEST MATCHES *(§ on debut)*

Over the years many batsmen have scored ninety-nine runs in a Test innings. M.J.K.Smith, G.Boycott (Boycott and S.R.Waugh are the only players to register a not out 99), R.B.Richardson, J.G.Wright, M.A.Atherton and Saleem Malik are the only batsmen to score 99 twice in their careers. In the Third Test* *between England and Pakistan at Karachi[1] in 1972-73 three batsmen, Majid Khan, Mushtaq Mohammad and D.L.Amiss were dismissed for 99.*

AUSTRALIA	How out	Opponent		
C.Hill	caught	England	Melbourne	1901-02
C.G.Macartney	caught	England	Lord's	1912
A.G.Chipperfield §	caught	England	Nottingham	1934
W.A.Brown	run out	India	Melbourne	1947-48
K.R.Miller	bowled	England	Adelaide	1950-51
A.R.Morris	run out	South Africa	Melbourne	1952-53
C.C.McDonald	caught	South Africa	Cape Town	1957-58
R.M.Cowper	caught	England	Melbourne	1965-66
I.M.Chappell	caught	India	Calcutta	1969-70
R.Edwards	lbw	England	Lord's	1975
K.J.Hughes	caught	England	Perth	1979-80
D.M.Jones	lbw	New Zealand	Perth	1989-90
M.E.Waugh	bowled	England	Lord's	1993
M.J.Slater	caught	New Zealand	Perth	1993-94
S.R.Waugh	not out	England	Perth	1994-95

ENGLAND	How out	Opponent		
H.Sutcliffe	bowled	South Africa	Cape Town	1927-28
E.Paynter	lbw	Australia	Lord's	1938
N.W.D.Yardley	caught	South Africa	Nottingham	1947
M.J.K.Smith	caught	South Africa	Lord's	1960
M.J.K.Smith	run out	Pakistan	Lahore[2]	1961-62
E.R.Dexter	bowled	Australia	Brisbane[2]	1962-63
D.L.Amiss	caught	Pakistan	Karachi[1]	1972-73
G.Boycott	caught	West Indies	Port-of-Spain	1973-74
G.Boycott*	not out	Australia	Perth	1979-80
G.A.Gooch	run out	Australia	Melbourne	1979-80
M.D.Moxon	caught	New Zealand	Auckland	1987-88
M.A.Atherton	run out	Australia	Lord's	1993
M.A.Atherton	c and b	South Africa	Leeds	1994

SOUTH AFRICA	How out	Opponent		
G.A.Faulkner	caught	England	Cape Town	1909-10
B.Mitchell	caught	England	Port Elizabeth	1948-49
T.L.Goddard	caught	England	The Oval	1960

WEST INDIES	How out	Opponent		
R.J.Christiani §	lbw	England	Bridgetown	1947-48
A.F.Rae	bowled	New Zealand	Auckland	1951-52
R.B.Kanhai	run out	India	Chennai[2]	1958-59
M.L.C.Foster	bowled	India	Port-of-Spain	1970-71
R.B.Richardson	bowled	India	Port-of-Spain	1988-89
R.B.Richardson	lbw	Australia	Bridgetown	1990-91

NEW ZEALAND	How out	Opponent		
J.E.F.Beck	run out	South Africa	Cape Town	1953-54
R.J.Hadlee	caught	England	Christchurch	1983-84
J.G.Wright	caught	Australia	Melbourne	1987-88
D.N.Patel	run out	England	Christchurch	1991-92
J.G.Wright	stumped	England	Christchurch	1991-92

INDIA	How out	Opponent		
Pankaj Roy	caught	Australia	Delhi	1959-60
M.L.Jaisimha	run out	Pakistan	Kanpur	1960-61

A.L.Wadekar	caught	Australia	Melbourne	1967-68
R.F.Surti	caught	New Zealand	Auckland	1967-68
N.S.Sidhu	lbw	Sri Lanka	Bangalore	1993-94

PAKISTAN	How out	Opponent		
Maqsood Ahmed	stumped	India	Lahore[1]	1954-55
Majid Khan	caught	England	Karachi[1]	1972-73
Mushtaq Mohammad	run out	England	Karachi[1]	1972-73
Javed Miandad	caught	India	Bangalore	1983-84
Saleem Malik	caught	England	Leeds	1987
Saleem Malik	caught	South Africa	Johannesburg[3]	1994-95
Aamer Sohail	bowled	Australia	Brisbane[2]	1995-96

ZIMBABWE	How out	Opponent		
A.D.R.Campbell	caught	Sri Lanka	Harare	1994-95

MOST FIFTIES *(All scores of 50 and over)*

Player	Country	50's	Inns	A	E	SA	WI	NZ	I	P	SL	Z
A.R.Border	Australia	**90**	265	0	29	1	17	11	13	14	5	0
S.M.Gavaskar	India	**79**	214	12	20	0	20	5	0	17	5	0
I.V.A.Richards	West Indies	**69**	182	19	23	0	0	3	16	8	0	0
Javed Miandad	Pakistan	**66**	189	13	11	0	6	13	19	0	3	1
G.A.Gooch	England	**66**	215	20	0	0	18	7	13	6	2	0
G.Boycott	England	**64**	193	21	0	3	20	8	6	6	0	0
M.C.Cowdrey	England	**60**	188	16	0	10	16	10	5	3	0	0
C.H.Lloyd	West Indies	**58**	175	18	18	0	0	0	19	3	0	0
D.L.Haynes	West Indies	**57**	202	19	18	1	0	8	6	5	0	0
D.I.Gower	England	**57**	204	21	0	0	7	8	8	11	2	0
G.S.Sobers	West Indies	**56**	160	10	23	0	0	1	15	7	0	0
K.F.Barrington	England	**55**	131	18	0	8	7	4	12	6	0	0
G.S.Chappell	Australia	**55**	151	0	21	0	12	6	3	12	0	0
C.G.Greenidge	West Indies	**53**	185	12	15	1	0	7	13	6	0	0
D.C.Boon	Australia	**53**	190	0	15	3	11	11	8	2	3	0
L.Hutton	England	**52**	138	19	0	11	11	7	4	0	0	0
D.B.Vengsarkar	India	**52**	185	9	11	0	13	3	0	10	6	0
G.R.Viswanath	India	**49**	155	13	16	0	11	5	0	4	0	0
K.D.Walters	Australia	**48**	123	0	17	3	11	7	8	2	0	0
M.A.Taylor	Australia	**47**	129	0	17	3	6	5	4	9	3	0
W.R.Hammond	England	**46**	140	16	0	20	2	5	3	0	0	0
D.C.S.Compton	England	**45**	131	14	0	18	4	4	2	3	0	0
R.N.Harvey	Australia	**45**	137	0	18	13	6	0	6	2	0	0
J.B.Hobbs	England	**43**	102	27	0	14	2	0	0	0	0	0
R.B.Kanhai	West Indies	**43**	137	15	14	0	0	0	11	3	0	0
R.B.Richardson	West Indies	**43**	146	16	10	0	0	3	7	6	1	0
D.G.Bradman	Australia	**42**	80	0	31	4	2	0	5	0	0	0
W.M.Lawry	Australia	**40**	123	0	20	5	7	0	8	0	0	0
I.M.Chappell	Australia	**40**	136	0	20	0	12	3	3	2	0	0

Most for the other countries:

Player	Country	50's	Inns	A	E	SA	WI	NZ	I	P	SL	Z
B.Mitchell	South Africa	**29**	80	4	23	0	0	2	0	0	0	0
M.D.Crowe	New Zealand	**35**	131	9	8	1	4	0	1	8	2	2
J.G.Wright	New Zealand	**35**	148	6	11	0	4	0	6	4	4	0
A.Ranatunga	Sri Lanka	**27**	104	4	4	2	0	6	4	6	0	1
A.Flower	Zimbabwe	**10**	26	0	0	1	0	2	3	3	1	0

MOST CONSECUTIVE FIFTIES

SEVEN									
E.D.Weekes	West Indies	141	128	194	162	101	90	56	1947-48 to 1948-49
SIX									
J.Ryder	Australia	78*	58	56	142	201*	88		1921-22 to 1924-25
E.H.Hendren	England	77	205*	56	123	61	55		1929-30
G.A.Headley	West Indies	93	53	270*	106	107	51		1934-35 to 1939
A.Melville	South Africa	67	78	103	189	104*	117		1938-39 to 1947
G.S.Sobers	West Indies	52	52	80	365*	125	109*		1957-58
E.R.Dexter	England	85	172	70	99	93	52		1962 to 1962-63
K.F.Barrington	England	63	132*	101	94	126	76		1962-63
K.D.Walters	Australia	76	118	110	50	242	103		1968-69
G.S.Chappell	Australia	68	54*	52	70	121	67		1975-76 to 1976-77
G.R.Viswanath	India	59	54	79	89	73	145		1977-78 to 1978-79
Zaheer Abbas	Pakistan	91	126	52	215	186	168		1982-83
A.R.Border	Australia	80	65*	76	51*	50	56		1989 to 1989-90
M.A.Taylor	Australia	108	52	101	77	59	101*		1989-90

G.Boycott (England) scored nine fifties in ten innings in 1970-71 and 1971: 70, 50, 77, 142,12, 76*, 58, 119*, 121*, 112.*

M.A.Noble (Australia) is the only player to score two separate fifties on the same day: 60 and 59* v England at Manchester in 1899 on the second day.*

OVER 60% OF A COMPLETED INNINGS TOTAL.

67.34	C.Bannerman	165*/245	Australia	v	England	Melbourne	1876-77
63.50	C.G.Greenidge	134/211	West Indies	v	England	Manchester	1976
63.41	A.P.Gurusinha	52*/82	Sri Lanka	v	India	Chandigarh	1990-91
62 89	J.R.Reid	100/159	New Zealand	v	England	Christchurch	1962-63
61 87	S.M.Nurse	258/417	West Indies	v	New Zealand	Christchurch	1968-69
61.85	M.Amarnath	60/97†	India	v	West Indies	Kingston	1975-76
61.11	G.N.Yallop	121/198	Australia	v	England	Sydney	1978-79
61.11	G.A.Gooch	154*/252	England	v	West Indies	Leeds	1991
60.65	V.T.Trumper	74/122	Australia	v	England	Melbourne	1903-04
60.26	H.A.Gomes	91/151	West Indies	v	India	Chennai[1]	1978-79
60.19	J.T.Tyldesley	62/103	England	v	Australia	Melbourne	1903-04
60.00	Kapil Dev	129/215	India	v	South Africa	Port Elizabeth	1992-93

† Five men were absent hurt.

D.L.Houghton (266) scored 62.29% of Zimbabwe's total 462 for 9 declared against Sri Lanka at Bulawayo[2] in 1994-95. D.L.Amiss (262) scored 60.64% of England 's total of 432 for 9 against West Indies at Kingston in 1973-74)*

THE NERVOUS NINETIES *(§ first Test, † last Test, ¶ only Test)*

AUSTRALIA		Opponents		
A.C.Bannerman	94	England	Sydney	1882-83
A.C.Bannerman	91	England	Sydney	1891-92
G.H.S.Trott	92	England	The Oval	1893
G.H.S.Trott	95	England	Melbourne	1894-95
C.Hill	96	England	Sydney	1897-98
C.Hill	99	England	Melbourne	1901-02
C.Hill	98 + 97	England	Adelaide	1901-02
C.Hill	91	South Africa	Cape Town	1902-03
V.S.Ransford	95	South Africa	Melbourne	1910-11
W.Bardsley	94	South Africa	Sydney	1910-11
R.B.Minnett §	90	England	Sydney	1911-12
W.W.Armstrong	90	England	Melbourne	1911-12
C.Hill	98	England	Adelaide	1911-12
C.G.Macartney	99	England	Lord's	1912
J.M.Gregory	93	England	Sydney	1920-21
T.J.E.Andrews	92	England	Leeds	1921

T.J.E.Andrews	94	England	The Oval	1921
A.J.Richardson §	98	England	Sydney	1924-25
J.M.Taylor	90	England	Melbourne	1924-25
S.J.McCabe	90	West Indies	Adelaide	1930-31
W.H.Ponsford	92*	West Indies	Adelaide	1930-31
A.G.Chipperfield §	99	England	Nottingham	1934
S.J.McCabe	93	England	Sydney	1936-37
C.L.McCool	95	England	Brisbane²	1946-47
D.Tallon	92	England	Melbourne	1946-47
W.A.Brown	99	India	Melbourne	1947-48
S.J.E.Loxton	93	England	Leeds	1948
K.R.Miller	99	England	Adelaide	1950-51
A.L.Hassett	92	England	Melbourne	1950-51
A.R.Morris	99	South Africa	Melbourne	1952-53
R.N.Harvey	92*	England	Sydney	1954-55
R.G.Archer	98	West Indies	Bridgetown	1954-55
R.Benaud	97	England	Lord's	1956
C.C.McDonald	99	South Africa	Cape Town	1957-58
R.N.Harvey	96	Pakistan	Dacca	1959-60
C.C.McDonald	91	West Indies	Melbourne	1960-61
R.B.Simpson	92	West Indies	Brisbane²	1960-61
R.B.Simpson	92	West Indies	Melbourne	1960-61
W.M.Lawry	98	England	Brisbane²	1962-63
R.B.Simpson	91	England	Sydney	1962-63
I.R.Redpath §	97	South Africa	Melbourne	1963-64
B.K.Shepherd	96	South Africa	Melbourne	1963-64
R.Benaud	90	South Africa	Sydney	1963-64
P.J.P.Burge	91	South Africa	Adelaide	1963-64
B.C.Booth	98	England	Manchester	1964
W.M.Lawry	94	England	The Oval	1964
R.M.Cowper	99	England	Melbourne	1965-66
W.M.Lawry	98	South Africa	Johannesburg³	1966-67
R.B.Simpson	94	South Africa	Durban²	1966-67
R.M.Cowper	92	India	Adelaide	1967-68
K.D.Walters	93	India	Brisbane²	1967-68
K.D.Walters	94*	India	Sydney	1967-68
I.R.Redpath	92	England	Leeds	1968
I.M.Chappell	96	West Indies	Adelaide	1968-69
I.M.Chappell	99	India	Calcutta	1969-70
R.W.Marsh	92*	England	Melbourne	1970-71
R.W.Marsh	91	England	Manchester	1972
R.W.Marsh	97	West Indies	Kingston	1972-73
I.M.Chappell	97	West Indies	Port-of-Spain	1972-73
K.D.Walters	94	New Zealand	Adelaide	1973-74
I.R.Redpath	93	New Zealand	Wellington	1973-74
I.M.Chappell	90	England	Brisbane²	1974-75
R.Edwards	99	England	Lord's	1975
R.B.McCosker	95*	England	Leeds	1975
G.J.Gilmour	95	West Indies	Adelaide	1975-76
G.M.Wood	90	West Indies	Kingston	1977-78
P.M.Toohey	97	West Indies	Kingston	1977-78
W.M.Darling	91	England	Sydney	1978-79
K.J.Hughes	92	India	Calcutta	1979-80
B.M.Laird §	93	West Indies	Brisbane²	1979-80
K.J.Hughes	99	England	Perth	1979-80
G.S.Chappell	98*	England	Sydney	1979-80
J.M.Wiener †	93	Pakistan	Lahore²	1979-80
R.W.Marsh	91	New Zealand	Perth	1980-81

G.N.Yallop	98	Sri Lanka	Kandy	1982-83
K.J.Hughes	94	Pakistan	Melbourne	1983-84
A.R.Border	98*	West Indies	Port-of-Spain	1983-84
A.R.Border	98	West Indies	St John's	1983-84
K.C.Wessels	98	West Indies	Adelaide	1984-85
K.C.Wessels	90	West Indies	Melbourne	1984-85
W.B.Phillips	91	England	Leeds	1985
G.M.Ritchie	94	England	Lord's	1985
G.R.Marsh	92	India	Sydney	1985-86
G.M.Ritchie	92	New Zealand	Wellington	1985-86
D.M.Jones	93	England	Adelaide	1986-87
P.R.Sleep	90	New Zealand	Melbourne	1987-88
S.R.Waugh	90	West Indies	Brisbane[2]	1988-89
S.R.Waugh	91	West Indies	Perth	1988-89
D.C.Boon	94	England	Lord's	1989
S.R.Waugh	92	England	Manchester	1989
D.M.Jones	99	New Zealand	Perth	1989-90
D.C.Boon	94*	England	Melbourne	1990-91
D.C.Boon	97	England	Sydney	1990-91
G.R.Marsh	94	West Indies	Georgetown	1990-91
M.A.Taylor	94	India	Brisbane[2]	1991-92
A.R.Border	91*	India	Adelaide	1991-92
G.R.J.Matthews	96	Sri Lanka	Moratuwa	1992-93
D.C.Boon	93	England	Manchester	1993
M.E.Waugh	99	England	Lord's	1993
M.J.Slater	99	New Zealand	Perth	1993-94
M.J.Slater	92	South Africa	Sydney	1993-94
D.C.Boon	96	South Africa	Cape Town	1993-94
M.J.Slater	95	South Africa	Durban[2]	1993-94
S.R.Waugh	98	Pakistan	Rawalpindi[2]	1994-95
M.G.Bevan	91	Pakistan	Lahore[2]	1994-95
S.R.Waugh	94*	England	Melbourne	1994-95
S.R.Waugh	99*	England	Perth	1994-94
M.A.Taylor	96	Sri Lanka	Perth	1995-96
R.T.Ponting §	96	Sri Lanka	Perth	1995-96
ENGLAND		Opponents		
W.H.Scotton	90	Australia	The Oval	1884
W.W.Read	94	Australia	The Oval	1886
F.S.Jackson §	91	Australia	Lord's	1893
A.Ward	93	Australia	Melbourne	1894-95
R.Abel	94	Australia	Lord's	1896
K.S.Ranjitsinhji	93*	Australia	Nottingham	1899
T.W.Hayward	90	Australia	Adelaide	1901-02
A.C.MacLaren	92	Australia	Sydney	1901-02
T.W.Hayward	91	Australia	Sydney	1903-04
J.T.Tyldesley	97	Australia	Melbourne	1903-04
G.L.Jessop	93	South Africa	Lord's	1907
J.B.Hobbs	93*	South Africa	Johannesburg[1]	1909-10
W.Rhodes	92	Australia	Manchester	1912
J.B.Hobbs	92	South Africa	Johannesburg[1]	1913-14
J.B.Hobbs	97	South Africa	Durban[2]	1913-14
F.E.Woolley	95 + 93	Australia	Lord's	1921
C.A.G.Russell	96	South Africa	Johannesburg[1]	1922-23
E.H.Hendren	92	Australia	Adelaide	1924-25
H.Sutcliffe	94	Australia	Leeds	1926
H.Sutcliffe	99	South Africa	Cape Town	1927-28
R.E.S.Wyatt	91	South Africa	Cape Town	1927-28

W.R.Hammond	90	South Africa	Durban[2]	1927-28
D.R.Jardine	98	Australia	Adelaide	1928-29
E.H.Hendren	95	Australia	Melbourne	1928-29
F.E.Woolley	95*	South Africa	Leeds	1929
E.H.Hendren	93	South Africa	Cape Town	1930-31
M.Leyland	91	South Africa	Johannesburg[1]	1930-31
H.Larwood	98	Australia	Sydney	1932-33
J.Hardstaff, jr	94	India	Manchester	1936
E.Paynter	99	Australia	Lord's	1938
P.A.Gibb §	93	South Africa	Johannesburg[1]	1938-39
B.H.Valentine	97	South Africa	Johannesburg[1]	1938-39
L.Hutton	92	South Africa	Johannesburg[1]	1938-39
J.Hardstaff, jr	94	West Indies	The Oval	1939
L.Hutton	94	Australia	Adelaide	1946-47
N.W.D.Yardley	99	South Africa	Nottingham	1947
J.Hardstaff, jr	98	West Indies	Bridgetown	1947-48
C.Washbrook	97	South Africa	Johannesburg[2]	1948-49
T.E.Bailey	93	New Zealand	Lord's	1949
R.T.Simpson	94	West Indies	Nottingham	1950
L.Hutton	98*	South Africa	Manchester	1951
T.E.Bailey	95	South Africa	Leeds	1951
R.T.Spooner	92	India	Calcutta	1951-52
D.C.S.Compton	93	West Indies	Bridgetown	1953-54
T.W.Graveney	92	West Indies	Port-of-Spain	1953-54
D.C.S.Compton	93	Pakistan	Manchester	1954
P.B.H.May	91	Australia	Melbourne	1954-55
P.B.H.May	97	South Africa	Leeds	1955
C.Washbrook	98	Australia	Leeds	1956
D.C.S.Compton	94	Australia	The Oval	1956
P.B.H.May	92	Australia	Sydney	1958-59
R.Subba Row	94	India	The Oval	1959
M.J.K.Smith	98	India	The Oval	1959
M.C.Cowdrey	97	West Indies	Kingston	1959-60
M.J.K.Smith	96	West Indies	Port-of-Spain	1959-60
R.Subba Row	90	South Africa	Lord's	1960
M.J.K.Smith	99	South Africa	Lord's	1960
M.C.Cowdrey	93	Australia	Leeds	1961
P.B.H.May	95	Australia	Manchester	1961
M.J.K.Smith	99	Pakistan	Lahore[2]	1961-62
T.W.Graveney	97	Pakistan	Birmingham	1962
E.R.Dexter	99	Australia	Brisbane[2]	1962-63
E.R.Dexter	93	Australia	Melbourne	1962-63
K.F.Barrington	94	Australia	Sydney	1962-63
M.C.Cowdrey	93*	Australia	The Oval	1964
R.W.Barber	97	South Africa	Johannesburg[3]	1964-65
K.F.Barrington	93	South Africa	Johannesburg[3]	1964-65
K.F.Barrington	91	South Africa	Lord's	1965
C.Milburn §	94	West Indies	Manchester	1966
T.W.Graveney	96	West Indies	Lord's	1966
J.M.Parks	91	West Indies	Lord's	1966
M.C.Cowdrey	96	West Indies	Nottingham	1966
K.F.Barrington	93	India	Leeds	1967
K.F.Barrington	97	India	Lord's	1967
J.H.Edrich	96	West Indies	Kingston	1967-68
G.Boycott	90	West Indies	Bridgetown	1967-68
T.W.Graveney	96	Australia	Birmingham	1968
A.P.E.Knott	96*	Pakistan	Karachi[1]	1968-69

A.P.E.Knott	96	New Zealand	Auckland	1970-71
A.P.E.Knott	90	India	The Oval	1971
B.W.Luckhurst	96	Australia	Nottingham	1972
A.P.E.Knott	92	Australia	The Oval	1972
B.Wood §	90	Australia	The Oval	1972
K.W.R.Fletcher	97*	India	Chennai[1]	1972-73
D.L.Amiss	99	Pakistan	Karachi[1]	1972-73
G.Boycott	92	New Zealand	Lord's	1973
G.Boycott	97	West Indies	The Oval	1073
G.Boycott	93	West Indies	Port-of-Spain	1973-74
G.Boycott	99	West Indies	Port-of-Spain	1973-74
J.H.Edrich	96	India	Lord's	1974
D.L.Amiss	90	Australia	Melbourne	1974-75
A.W.Greig	96	Australia	Lord's	1975
D.S.Steele	92	Australia	Leeds	1975
J.H.Edrich	96	Australia	The Oval	1975
J.M.Brearley	91	India	Mumbai[3]	1976-77
A.W.Greig	91	Australia	Lord's	1977
G.Miller	98*	Pakistan	Lahore[2]	1977-78
G.A.Gooch	91*	New Zealand	The Oval	1978
R.W.Taylor	97	Australia	Adelaide	1978-79
G.Boycott	99*	Australia	Perth	1979-80
D.I.Gower	98*	Australia	Sydney	1979-80
G.A.Gooch	99	Australia	Melbourne	1979-80
G.Miller	98	India	Manchester	1982
D.W.Randall	95	India	The Oval	1982
E.E.Hemmings	95	Australia	Sydney	1982-83
C.L.Smith	91	New Zealand	Auckland	1983-84
D.I.Gower	90	West Indies	St John's	1985-86
R.T.Robinson	96	India	Kanpur	1984-85
C.W.J.Athey	96	Australia	Perth	1986-87
M.W.Gatting	96	Australia	Sydney	1986-87
D.J.Capel	98	Pakistan	Karachi[1]	1987-88
G.A.Gooch	93	Pakistan	Karachi[1]	1987-88
M.D.Moxon	99	New Zealand	Auckland	1987-88
R.C.Russell §	94	Sri Lanka	Lord's	1988
R.A.Smith	96	Australia	Lord's	1989
A.J.Stewart	91	Australia	Sydney	1990-91
A.J.Lamb	91	Australia	Perth	1990-91
R.A.Smith	96	New Zealand	Christchurch	1991-92
A.J.Lamb	93	New Zealand	Christchurch	1991-92
M.A.Atherton	99	Australia	Lord's	1993
G.A.Hick	96	West Indies	Kingston	1993-94
M.A.Atherton	99	South Africa	Leeds	1994
G.A.Hick	98*	Australia	Sydney	1994-95
R.A.Smith	95	West Indies	Lord's	1995
G.P.Thorpe	94	West Indies	Manchester	1995
G.A.Hick	96	West Indies	The Oval	1995
R.C.Russell	91	West Indies	The Oval	1995
M.A.Atherton	95	West Indies	The Oval	1995

SOUTH AFRICA		Opponents		
L.J.Tancred	97	Australia	Johannesburg[1]	1902-03
C.B.Llewellyn	90	Australia	Johannesburg[1]	1902-03
A.W.Nourse	93*	England	Johannesburg[1]	1905-06
G.A.Faulkner	99	England	Cape Town	1909-10
A.W.Nourse	92*	Australia	Melbourne	1910-11

G.A.Faulkner	92	Australia	Sydney	1910-11
H.W.Taylor	93	Australia	Lord's	1912
H.W.Taylor	93	England	Durban[1]	1913-14
H.W.Taylor	91	England	Durban[2]	1922-23
R.H.Catterall	95	England	The Oval	1924
R.H.Catterall	98	England	Birmingham	1929
H.G.Deane	93	England	The Oval	1929
B.Mitchell	95	Australia	Adelaide	1931-32
H.B.Cameron	90	England	Lord's	1935
A.D.Nourse	91	Australia	Durban[2]	1935-36
P.G.V.van der Bijl †	97	England	Durban[2]	1938-39
K.G.Viljoen	93	England	Manchester	1947
A.D.Nourse	97	England	The Oval	1947
B.Mitchell	99	England	Port Elizabeth	1948-49
P.N.F.Mansell §	90	England	Leeds	1951
K.J.Funston	92	Australia	Adelaide	1952-53
J.C.Watkins	92	Australia	Melbourne	1952-53
W.R.Endean	93	New Zealand	Johannesburg[2]	1953-54
R.A.McLean	93	England	Johannesburg[3]	1956-57
T.L.Goddard	90	Australia	Johannesburg[3]	1957-58
S.O'Linn	98	England	Nottingham	1960
T.L.Goddard	99	England	The Oval	1960
T.L.Goddard	93	Australia	Sydney	1963-64
E.J.Barlow	92	New Zealand	Wellington	1963-64
E.J.Barlow	96	England	Johannesburg[3]	1964-65
A.J.Pithey	95	England	Johannesburg[3]	1964-65
R.G.Pollock	90	Australia	Johannesburg[3]	1966-67
J.N.Rhodes	91	India	Johannesburg[3]	1992-93
B.M.McMillan	98	India	Johannesburg[3]	1992-93
K.C.Wessels	95*	India	Port Elizabeth	1992-93
A.C.Hudson	90	Sri Lanka	Moratuwa	1993-94
K.C.Wessels	92	Sri Lanka	Colombo (SSC)	1993-94
A.C.Hudson	90	Australia	Adelaide	1993-94
B.M.McMillan	93	England	The Oval	1994
D.J.Cullinan	94	England	The Oval	1994
D.J.Richardson	93	New Zealand	Johannesburg[3]	1994-95
D.J.Cullinan	96	New Zealand	Auckland	1994-95
B.M.McMillan	98*	Zimbabwe	Harare	1995-96
D.J.Cullinan	91	England	Port Elizabeth	1995-96

WEST INDIES		Opponents		
R.K.Nunes	92	England	Kingston	1929-30
J.E.D.Sealy	92	England	Port-of-Spain	1934-35
L.N.Constantine	90	England	Port-of-Spain	1934-35
G.A.Headley	93	England	Port-of-Spain	1934-35
J.E.D.Sealy	91	England	Kingston	1934-35
V.H.Stollmeyer §	96	England	The Oval	1939
R.J.Christiani §	99	England	Bridgetown	1947-48
F.M.M.Worrell §	97	England	Port-of-Spain	1947-48
E.D.Weekes	90	India	Chennai[1]	1948-49
A.F.Rae	97	India	Mumbai[2]	1948-49
A.F.Rae	99	New Zealand	Auckland	1951-52
C.L.Walcott	98	India	Bridgetown	1952-53
J.K.Holt §	94	England	Kingston	1953-54
E.D.Weekes	90*	England	Kingston	1953-54
E.D.Weekes	94	England	Georgetown	1953-54
C.L.Walcott	90	England	Birmingham	1957

E.D.Weekes	90	England	Lord's	1957
R.B.Kanhai	96	Pakistan	Port-of-Spain	1957-58
R.B.Kanhai	99	India	Chennai[2]	1958-59
C.C.Hunte	92	India	Delhi	1958-59
G.S.Sobers	92	England	Port-of-Spain	1959-60
J.S.Solomon	96	India	Bridgetown	1961-62
F.M.M.Worrell	98*	India	Kingston	1961-62
R.B.Kanhai	90	England	Manchester	1963
R.B.Kanhai	[illegible]	England	Leeds	1963
S.M.Nurse	93	England	Nottingham	1966
G.S.Sobers	94	England	Nottingham	1966
R.B.Kanhai	90	India	Calcutta	1966-67
G.S.Sobers	95	India	Chennai[1]	1966-67
G.S.Sobers	95*	England	Georgetown	1967-68
R.B.Kanhai	94	Australia	Brisbane[2]	1968-69
M.C.Carew	90	Australia	Adelaide	1968-69
M.C.Carew	91	New Zealand	Auckland	1968-69
S.M.Nurse	95	New Zealand	Auckland	1968-69
B.F.Butcher	91	England	Leeds	1969
G.S.Sobers	93	India	Kingston	1970-71
M.L.C.Foster	99	India	Port-of-Spain	1970-71
C.A.Davis	90	New Zealand	Port-of-Spain	1971-72
R.C.Fredericks	98	Australia	Bridgetown	1972-73
D.L.Murray	90	Australia	Bridgetown	1972-73
A.I.Kallicharran	91	Australia	Port-of-Spain	1972-73
C.H.Lloyd	94	England	Birmingham	1973
R.C.Fredericks	94	England	Kingston	1973-74
A.I.Kallicharran	93	England	Kingston	1973-74
R.C.Fredericks	98	England	Georgetown	1973-74
C.G.Greenidge §	93	India	Bangalore	1974-75
A.I.Kallicharran	98	India	Mumbai[3]	1974-75
D.L.Murray	91	India	Mumbai[3]	1974-75
A.I.Kallicharran	92*	Pakistan	Lahore[2]	1974-75
K.D.Boyce	95*	Australia	Adelaide	1975-76
I.V.A.Richards	98	Australia	Melbourne	1975-76
C.H.Lloyd	91*	Australia	Melbourne	1975-76
A.I.Kallicharran	93	India	Bridgetown	1975-76
A.I.Kallicharran	97	England	Nottingham	1976
I.V.A.Richards	92	Pakistan	Bridgetown	1976-77
C.G.Greenidge	91 + 96	Pakistan	Georgetown	1976-77
A.I.Kallicharran	92	Australia	Port-of-Spain	1977-78
S.F.A.F.Bacchus	98	India	Bangalore	1978-79
A.I.Kallicharran	98	India	Chennai[1]	1978-79
H.A.Gomes	91	India	Chennai[1]	1978-79
I.V.A.Richards	96	Australia	Melbourne	1979-80
C.G.Greenidge	91 + 97	New Zealand	Christchurch	1979-80
D.L.Haynes	96	England	Port-of-Spain	1980-81
C.H.Lloyd	95	England	Kingston	1980-81
H.A.Gomes	90*	England	Kingston	1980-81
D.L.Haynes	92	India	Bridgetown	1982-83
M.D.Marshall	92	India	Kanpur	1983-84
P.J.L.Dujon	98	India	Ahmedabad	1983-84
A.L.Logie	97	Australia	Port-of-Spain	1983-84
H.A.Gomes	92*	England	Lord's	1984
C.G.Greenidge	95	Australia	Adelaide	1984-85
D.L.Haynes	90	New Zealand	Georgetown	1984-85
A.L.Logie	93	Australia	Perth	1988-89

R.B.Richardson	93	India	Bridgetown	1988-89
R.B.Richardson	99	India	Port-of-Spain	1988-89
A.L.Logie	98	England	Port-of-Spain	1989-90
R.B.Richardson	99	Australia	Bridgetown	1990-91
B.C.Lara	96	Pakistan	Port-of-Spain	1992-93
J.C.Adams	95*	England	Kingston	1993-94
B.C.Lara	91	India	Mohali	1994-95
S.L.Campbell	93	England	Lord's	1995
R.B.Richardson	93	England	The Oval	1995

NEW ZEALAND

R.C.Blunt	96	England	Lord's	1931
W.A.Hadlee	93	England	Manchester	1937
F.B.Smith	96	England	Leeds	1949
J.R.Reid	93	England	The Oval	1949
J.E.F.Beck	99	South Africa	Cape Town	1953-54
N.S.Harford §	93	Pakistan	Lahore[1]	1955-56
J.W.Guy	91	India	Calcutta	1955-56
J.R.Reid	92	South Africa	Cape Town	1961-62
J.R.Reid	97	Pakistan	Wellington	1964-65
R.W.Morgan	97	Pakistan	Christchurch	1964-65
B.A.G.Murray	90	Pakistan	Lahore[2]	1969-70
G.M.Turner	95	West Indies	Port-of-Spain	1971-72
G.M.Turner	98	England	Christchurch	1974-75
M.G.Burgess	95	India	Wellington	1975-76
R.W.Anderson §	92	Pakistan	Lahore[2]	1976-77
G.P.Howarth	94	England	The Oval	1978
J.G.Wright	93	England	Leeds	1983
R.J.Hadlee	92*	England	Nottingham	1983
R.J.Hadlee	99	England	Christchurch	1983-84
J.V.Coney	92	Sri Lanka	Colombo (CCC)	1983-84
J.F.Reid	97	Pakistan	Karachi[1]	1984-85
J.V.Coney	98	Australia	Christchurch	1985-86
J.V.Coney	93	Australia	Auckland	1985-86
J.G.Wright	99	Australia	Melbourne	1987-88
M.J.Greatbatch	90*	India	Hyderabad	1988-89
J.G.Wright	98	England	Lord's	1990
D.N.Patel	99	England	Christchurch	1991-92
J.G.Wright	99	England	Christchurch	1991-92
S.P.Fleming §	92	India	Hamilton	1993-94
B.A.Young	94	England	Lord's	1994
R.G.Twose	94	Zimbabwe	Auckland	1995-96

INDIA		Opponents		
M.H.Mankad	96	West Indies	Port-of-Spain	1952-53
V.L.Manjrekar	90	New Zealand	Calcutta	1955-56
Pankaj Roy	90	West Indies	Mumbai[2]	1958-59
N.J.Contractor	92	West Indies	Delhi	1958-59
C.G.Borde	96	West Indies	Delhi	1958-59
Pankaj Roy	99	Australia	Delhi	1959-60
M.L.Jaisimha	99	Pakistan	Kanpur	1960-61
N.J.Contractor	92	Pakistan	Delhi	1960-61
V.L.Manjrekar	96	England	Kanpur	1961-62
C.G.Borde	93	West Indies	Kingston	1961-62
S.A.Durani	90	England	Mumbai[2]	1963-64
Hanumant Singh	94	Australia	Chennai[2]	1964-65
F.M.Engineer	90	New Zealand	Chennai[2]	1964-65

A.L.Wadekar	91	England	Leeds	1967
A.L.Wadekar	99	Australia	Melbourne	1967-68
R.F.Surti	99	New Zealand	Auckland	1967-68
Nawab of Pataudi, jr	95	Australia	Mumbai[2]	1969-70
A.V.Mankad	97	Australia	Delhi	1969-70
A.L.Wadekar	91*	Australia	Delhi	1969-70
A.L.Wadekar	90	England	Kanpur	1972-73
G.R.Viswanath	97*	West Indies	Chennai[1]	1974-75
G.R.Viswanath	95	West Indies	Mumbai[3]	1974-75
M.Amarnath	90	Australia	Perth	1977-78
C.P.S.Chauhan	93	Pakistan	Lahore[2]	1978-79
S.M.Gavaskar	97	Pakistan	Lahore[2]	1978-79
G.R.Viswanath	96	Australia	Calcutta	1979-80
C.P.S.Chauhan	97	Australia	Adelaide	1980-81
R.J.Shastri	93	England	Delhi	1981-82
Kapil Dev	97	England	The Oval	1982
D.B.Vengsarkar	90	Sri Lanka	Chennai[1]	1982-83
M.Amarnath	91	West Indies	Bridgetown	1982-83
D.B.Vengsarkar	94	West Indies	St John's	1982-83
Kapil Dev	98	West Indies	St John's	1982-83
S.M.Gavaskar	90	West Indies	Ahmedabad	1983-84
M.Amarnath	95	England	Chennai[1]	1984-85
D.B.Vengsarkar	98*	Sri Lanka	Colombo (SSC)	1985-86
S.M.Gavaskar	90	Australia	Chennai[1]	1986-87
S.M.Gavaskar	91	Pakistan	Chennai[1]	1986-87
D.B.Vengsarkar	96	Pakistan	Chennai[1]	1986-87
S.M.Gavaskar	96	Pakistan	Bangalore	1986-87
Arun Lal	93	West Indies	Calcutta	1987-88
K.Srikkanth	94	New Zealand	Mumbai[3]	1988-89
N.S.Sidhu	97	Pakistan	Sialkot	1989-90
W.V.Raman	96	New Zealand	Christchurch	1989-90
M.Prabhakar	95	New Zealand	Napier	1989-90
S.V.Manjrekar	93	England	Manchester	1990
M.Prabhakar	95	Sri Lanka	Colombo (SSC)	1993-94
N.S.Sidhu	99	Sri Lanka	Bangalore	1993-94
S.R.Tendulkar	96	Sri Lanka	Bangalore	1993-94
N.S.Sidhu	98	New Zealand	Hamilton	1993-94
M.Azharuddin	97	West Indies	Nagpur	1994-95
R.S.Dravid §	95	England	Lord's	1996
PAKISTAN		Opponents		
Hanif Mohammad	96	India	Mumbai[2]	1952-53
Waqar Hassan	97	India	Calcutta	1952-53
Maqsood Ahmed	99	India	Lahore[1]	1954-55
A.H.Kardar	93	India	Karachi[1]	1954-55
Imtiaz Ahmed	91	West Indies	Bridgetown	1957-58
Wazir Mohammad	97*	West Indies	Georgetown	1957-58
Saeed Ahmed	97	West Indies	Port-of-Spain	1957-58
Saeed Ahmed	91	Australia	Karachi[1]	1959-60
Imtiaz Ahmed	98	England	The Oval	1962
Abdul Kadir §	95	Australia	Karachi[1]	1964-65
Hanif Mohammad	93	Australia	Melbourne	1964-65
Shafqat Rana	95	New Zealand	Lahore[2]	1969-70
Asif Iqbal	92	New Zealand	Dacca	1969-70
Sadiq Mohammad	91	England	Leeds	1971
Majid Khan	99	England	Karachi[1]	1972-73
Mushtaq Mohammad	99	England	Karachi[1]	1972-73

Majid Khan	98	England	The Oval	1974
Sadiq Mohammad	98*	Pakistan	Karachi[1]	1974-75
Majid Khan	98	New Zealand	Hyderabad	1976-77
Zaheer Abbas	90	Australia	Melbourne	1976-77
Majid Khan	92	West Indies	Port-of-Spain	1976-77
Sadiq Mohammad	97	England	Leeds	1978
Zaheer Abbas	96	India	Faisalabad	1978-79
Wasim Raja	97	India	Delhi	1979-80
Wasim Raja	94*	India	Kanpur	1979-80
Taslim Arif §	90	India	Calcutta	1979-80
Zaheer Abbas	90	Australia	Melbourne	1981-82
Mudassar Nazar	95	Australia	Melbourne	1981-82
Javed Miandad	92	Sri Lanka	Karachi[1]	1982-83
Zaheer Abbas	91	Australia	Faisalabad	1982-83
Mohsin Khan	94	India	Lahore[2]	1982-83
Mohsin Khan	91	India	Karachi[1]	1982-83
Javed Miandad	99	India	Bangalore	1983-84
Sarfraz Nawaz	90	England	Lahore[2]	1983-84
Qasim Omar	96	New Zealand	Dunedin	1984-85
Javed Miandad	94	India	Chennai[1]	1986-87
Saleem Malik	99	England	Leeds	1987
Saleem Yousuf	91	England	Birmingham	1987
Aamer Malik	98*	England	Karachi[1]	1987-88
Shoaib Mohammad	94	Australia	Karachi[1]	1988-89
Shoaib Mohammad	95	India	Karachi[1]	1989-90
Rameez Raja	98	Sri Lanka	Sialkot	1991-92
Imran Khan	93*	Sri Lanka	Sialkot	1991-92
Javed Miandad	92	New Zealand	Hamilton	1992-93
Basit Ali	92*	West Indies	Bridgetown	1992-93
Saeed Anwar	94	Sri Lanka	Colombo (PSS)	1993-94
Saleem Malik	99	South Africa	Johannesburg[3]	1994-95
Inzamamul Haq	95	South Africa	Johannesburg[3]	1994-95
Inzamamul Haq	95	Sri Lanka	Peshawar[2]	1994-95
Aamer Sohail	99	Australia	Brisbane[2]	1995-96

SRI LANKA		Opponents		
R.L.Dias	98	Pakistan	Faisalabad	1981-82
R.S.Madugalle	91*	Pakistan	Faisalabad	1981-82
R.L.Dias	97	India	Chennai[1]	1982-83
A.Ranatunga	90	Australia	Kandy	1982-83
S.Wettimuny	91	Australia	Kandy	1982-83
L.R.D.Mendis	94	England	Lord's	1984
R.L.Dias	95	India	Colombo (PSS)	1985-86
J.R.Ratnayeke	93	India	Kanpur	1986-87
P.A.de Silva	96	New Zealand	Auckland	1990-91
H.P.Tillakaratne	93	New Zealand	Colombo (SSC)	1992-93
H.P.Tillakaratne	93*	England	Colombo (SSC)	1992-93
P.A.de Silva	93	India	Colombo (SSC)	1993-94
H.P.Tillakaratne	92	South Africa	Moratuwa	1993-94
C.I.Dunusinghe §	91	New Zealand	Napier	1994-95
A.Ranatunga	90	New Zealand	Dunedin	1994-95

ZIMBABWE		Opponents		
G.W.Flower	96	India	Delhi	1992-93
A.D.R.Campbell	99	Sri Lanka	Harare	1994-95

There have been 503 scores in the nineties recorded in Test cricket (106 for Australia; 127 for England; 42 for South Africa; 82 for West Indies; 30 for New Zealand; 51 for India; 49 for Pakistan; 14 for Sri Lanka; and 2 for Zimbabwe). The following players scored these nineties:

8 A.I.Kallicharran(W)

6 G.Boycott(E), C.G.Greenidge(W), C.Hill(A), R.B.Kanhai(W), S.R.Waugh(A)

5 K.F.Barrington(E), D.C.Boon(A), S.M.Gavaskar(I), G.S.Sobers(W)

4 I.M.Chappell(A), M.C.Cowdrey(E), T.W.Graveney(E), Javed Miandad(P), A.P.E.Knott(E), A.L.Logie(W), Majid Khan(P), R.W.Marsh(A), P.B.H.May(E), R.B.Richardson(W), R.B.Simpson(A), M.J.K.Smith(E), D.B.Vengsarkar(I), A.L.Wadekar(I), E.D.Weekes(W), K.C.Wessels(A/SA), J.G.Wright(N), Zaheer Abbas(P)

3 M.Amarnath(I), M.A.Atherton (E), A.R.Border(A), D.C.S.Compton(E), J.V.Coney(N), D.J.Cullinan(SA), R.L.Dias(SL), J.H.Edrich(E), R.C.Fredericks(W), T.L.Goddard(SA), H.A.Gomes(W), G.A.Gooch(E), J.Hardstaff jr(E), D.L.Haynes(W), E.H.Hendren(E), G.A.Hick(E), J.B.Hobbs(E), K.J.Hughes(A), L.Hutton(E), W.M.Lawry(A), C.H.Lloyd(W), B.M.McMillan(SA), I.R.Redpath(A), J.R.Reid(N), I.V.A.Richards(W), Sadiq Mohammad(P), N.S.Sidhu(I), M.J.Slater(A), R.A.Smith(E), H.W.Taylor(SA), H.P.Tillakaratne(SL), G.R.Viswanath, K.D.Walters(A), F.E.Woolley(E)

2 D.L.Amiss(E), T.J.E.Andrews(A), T.E.Bailey(E), A.C.Bannerman(A), E.J.Barlow(SA), R.Benaud(A), C.G.Borde(I), M.C.Carew(W), R.H.Catterall(SA), C.P.S.Chauhan(I), N.J.Contractor(I), R.M.Cowper(A), P.A.de Silva(SL), E.R.Dexter(E), G.A.Faulkner(SA), D.I.Gower(E), A.W.Greig(E), R.J.Hadlee(N), Hanif Mohammad(P), R.N.Harvey(A), T.W.Hayward(E), A.C.Hudson(SA), Imtiaz Ahmed(P), Inzamamul Haq(P), D.M.Jones(A), Kapil Dev(I), A.J.Lamb(E), B.C.Lara(W), S.J.McCabe(A), C.C.McDonald(A), V.L.Manjrekar(I), G.R.Marsh(A), G.Miller(E), B.Mitchell(SA), Mohsin Khan(P), D.L.Murray(W), A.D.Nourse(SA), A.W.Nourse(SA), S.M.Nurse(W), A.F.Rae(W), A.Ranatunga(SL), G.M.Ritchie(A), Pankaj Roy(I), M.Prabhakar(I), R.C.Russell(E), Saeed Ahmed(P), Saleem Malik(P), J.E.D.Sealy(W), Shoaib Mohammad(P), R.Subba Row(E), H.Sutcliffe(E), G.H.S.Trott(A), G.M.Turner(N), C.L.Walcott(W), C.Washbrook(E), Wasim Raja(P), F.M.M.Worrell(W)

1 Aamer Malik(P), Abdul Kadir(P), R.Abel(E), J.C.Adams(W), R.W.Anderson(N), R.G.Archer(A), W.W.Armstrong(A), Arun Lal(I), Asif Iqbal(P), C.W.J.Athey(E), M.Azahruddin(I), S.F.A.F.Bacchus(A), R.W.Barber(E), W.Bardsley(A), Basit Ali(P), J.E.F.Beck(N), M.G.Bevan(A), R.C.Blunt(N), B.C.Booth(A), K.D.Boyce(W), J.M.Brearley(E), W.A.Brown(A), P.J.P.Burge(A), M.G.Burgess(N), B.F.Butcher(W), H.B.Cameron(SA), A.D.R.Campbell(Z), S.L.Campbell(W), D.J.Capel(E), G.S.Chappell(A), A.G.Chipperfield(A), R.J.Christiani(W), L.N.Constantine(W), W.M.Darling(A), C.A.Davis(W), H.G.Deane(SA), R.S.Dravid (I), P.J.L.Dujon(W), C.I.Dunusinghe(SL), S.A.Durani(I), R.Edwards(A), W.R.Endean(SA), F.M.Engineer(I), S.P.Fleming(N), K.W.R.Fletcher(E), G.W.Flower(Z), M.L.C.Foster(W), K.J.Funston(SA), M.W.Gatting(E), P.A.Gibb(E), G.J.Gilmour(A), M.J.Greatbatch(N), J.M.Gregory(A), J.W.Guy(N), W.A.Hadlee(N), W.R.Hammond(E), Hanumant Singh(I), N.S.Harford(N), A.L.Hassett(A), G.A.Headley(W), E.E.Hemmings(E), J.K.Holt(W), G.P.Howarth(N), C.C.Hunte(W), Imran Khan(P), F.S.Jackson(E), M.L.Jaisimha(I), D.R.Jardine(E), G.L.Jessop(E), A.H.Kardar(P), B.M.Laird(A), H.Larwood(E), M.Leyland(E), C.B.Llewellyn(SA), S.J.E.Loxton(A), B.W.Luckhurst(E), C.G.Macartney(A), C.L.McCool(A), R.B.McCosker(A), A.C.MacLaren(E), R.A.McLean(SA), R.S.Madugalle(SL), S.V.Manjrekar(I), A.V.Mankad(I), M.H.Mankad(I), P.N.F.Mansell(SA), Maqsood Ahmed(P), M.D.Marshall(W), G.R.J.Matthews (A), L.R.D.Mendis(SL), C.Milburn(E), K.R.Miller(A), R.B.Minnett(A), R.W.Morgan(N), A.R.Morris(A), M.D.Moxon(E), Mudassar Nazar(P), B.A.G.Murray(N), Mushtaq Mohammad(P), R.K.Nunes(W), S.O'Linn(SA), J.M.Parks(E), Nawab of Pataudi, jr(I), D.N.Patel(N), E.Paynter(E), W.B.Phillips(A), A.J.Pithey(SA), R.G.Pollock(SA), W.H.Ponsford(A), Qasim Omar(P), W.V.Raman(I), Rameez Raja(P), D.W.Randall(E), K.S.Ranjitsinhji(E), V.S.Ransford(A), J.R.Ratnayeke(SL), W.W.Read(E), J.F.Reid(N), J.N.Rhodes(SA), W.Rhodes(E), A.J.Richardson(A), D.J.Richardson(SA), R.T.Robinson(E), C.A.G.Russell(E), Saeed Anwar(P), Saleem Yousuf(P), Sarfraz Nawaz(P), W.H.Scotton(E), Shafqat Rana(P), R.J.Shastri(I), B.K.Shepherd(A), R.T.Simpson(E), P.R.Sleep(A), C.L.Smith(E), F.B.Smith(N), J.S.Solomon(W), R.T.Spooner(E), K.Srikkanth(I), D.S.Steele(E), A.J.Stewart(E), V.H.Stollmeyer(W), R.F.Surti(I), D.Tallon(A), L.J.Tancred(SA), Taslim Arif(P), J.M.Taylor(A), M.A.Taylor(A), R.W.Taylor(E), G.P.Thorpe(E), P.M.Toohey(A), J.T.Tyldesley(E), B.H.Valentine(E), P.G.V.van der Bijl(SA), K.G.Viljoen(SA), Waqar Hassan(P), A.Ward(E), J.C.Watkins(SA), M.E.Waugh (A), Wazir Mohammad(P), S.Wettimuny(SL), J.M.Wiener(A), B.Wood(E), G.M.Wood(A), R.E.S.Wyatt(E), G.N.Yallop(A), N.W.D.Yardley(E), B.A.Young(N)

BATTED ON EACH DAY OF A FIVE-DAY MATCH

	Scores						
M.L.Jaisimha	20*	74	India	v	Australia	Calcutta	1959-60
G.Boycott	107	80*	England	v	Australia	Nottingham	1977
K.J.Hughes	117	84	Australia	v	England	Lord's	1980
A.J.Lamb	23	110	England	v	West Indies	Lord's	1984
R.J.Shastri	111	7*	India	v	England	Calcutta	1984-85

LONGEST INNINGS FOR EACH COUNTRY

For	Min		Opponents		
Australia	762	R.B.Simpson (311)	England	Manchester	1964
England	797	L.Hutton (364)	Australia	The Oval	1938
South Africa	575	D.J.McGlew (105)	Australia	Durban[2]	1957-58
West Indies	682	F.M.M.Worrell (197*)	England	Bridgetown	1959-60
New Zealand	704	G.M.Turner (259)	West Indies	Georgetown	1971-72
India	708	S.M.Gavaskar (172)	England	Bangalore	1981-82
Pakistan	970	Hanif Mohammad(337)	West Indies	Bridgetown	1957-58
Sri Lanka	777	D.S.B.P.Kuruppu (201*)	New Zealand	Colombo (CCC)	1986-87
Zimbabwe	675	D.L.Houghton (266)	Sri Lanka	Bulawayo[2]	1994-95

MOST RUNS FROM STROKES WORTH FOUR OR MORE IN AN INNINGS

	6s	5s	4s							
238	5	-	52	J.H.Edrich	310*	England	v	New Zealand	Leeds	1965
196	10	-	34	W.R.Hammond	336*	England	v	New Zealand	Auckland	1932-33
190	3	-	43	G.A.Gooch	333	England	v	India	The Oval	1990
184	-	-	46	D.G.Bradman	334	Australia	v	England	Leeds	1930
184	2	-	43	D.G.Bradman	304	Australia	v	England	Leeds	1934
180	-	-	45	B.C.Lara	375	West Indies	v	England	St John's	1993-94
177	-	1	43	R.G.Pollock	274	South Africa	v	Australia	Durban[2]	1969-70
168	-	-	42	R.B.Kanhai	256	West Indies	v	India	Calcutta	1958-59
166	1	-	40	D.L.Amiss	262*	England	v	West Indies	Kingston	1973-74
160	-	-	40	P.A.de Silva	267	Sri Lanka	v	New Zealand	Wellington	1990-91
157	-	1	38	G.S.Sobers	365*	West Indies	v	Pakistan	Kingston	1957-58
152	2	-	35	F.M.M.Worrell	261	West Indies	v	England	Nottingham	1957
152	-	-	38	Zaheer Abbas	274	Pakistan	v	England	Birmingham	1971
152	-	-	38	I.V.A.Richards	291	West Indies	v	England	The Oval	1976
152	-	-	38	B.C.Lara	277	West Indies	v	Australia	Sydney	1992-93
150	1	-	36	L.G.Rowe	302	West Indies	v	England	Bridgetown	1973-74

REACHING CENTURY WITH A SIX

Batsman	Bowler					
J.Darling (178)	J.Briggs	Australia	v	England	Adelaide	1897-98
E.H.Bowley (109)	W.E.Merritt	England	v	New Zealand	Auckland	1929-30
P.R.Umrigar (130)	S.Ramadhin	India	v	West Indies	Port-of-Spain	1952-53
P.L.Winslow (108)	G.A.R.Lock	South Africa	v	England	Manchester	1955
K.F.Barrington (132*)	R.B.Simpson	England	v	Australia	Adelaide	1962-63
K.F.Barrington (121)	M.A.Seymour	England	v	South Africa	Johannesburg[3]	1964-65
J.H.Edrich (103)	P.I.Philpott	England	v	Australia	Sydney	1965-66
K.F.Barrington (115)	T.R.Veivers	England	v	Australia	Melbourne	1965-66
D.T.Lindsay (131)	D.A.Renneberg	South Africa	v	Australia	Johannesburg[3]	1966-67
K.F.Barrington (143)	L.R.Gibbs	England	v	West Indies	Port-of-Spain	1967-68
B.R.Taylor (124)	R.M.Edwards	New Zealand	v	West Indies	Auckland	1968-69
J.Benaud (142)	Intikhab Alam	Australia	v	Pakistan	Melbourne	1972-73
K.R.Stackpole (142)	M.L.C.Foster	Australia	v	West Indies	Kingston	1972-73
K.D.Walters (103)	R.G.D.Willis	Australia	v	England	Perth	1974-75
D.L.Amiss (179)	B.S.Chandrasekhar	England	v	India	Delhi	1976-77
I.C.Davis (105)	Salim Altaf	Australia	v	Pakistan	Adelaide	1976-77

R.B.McCosker (107)	R.G.D.Willis	Australia	v	England	Nottingham	1977
Haroon Rashid (108)	G.Miller	Pakistan	v	England	Hyderabad	1977-78
Kapil Dev (126*)	N.Phillip	India	v	West Indies	Delhi	1978-79
I.T.Botham (137)	Kapil Dev	England	v	India	Leeds	1979
C.L.King (100*)	G.P.Howarth	West Indies	v	New Zealand	Christchurch	1979-80
J.G.Wright (110)	D.R.Doshi	New Zealand	v	India	Auckland	1980-81
I.T.Botham (118)	M.R.Whitney	England	v	Australia	Manchester	1981
Imran Khan (117)	Kapil Dev	Pakistan	v	India	Faisalabad	1982-83
L.R.D.Mendis (105)	D.R.Doshi	Sri Lanka	v	India	Chennai[1]	1982-83
G.R.J.Matthews (115)	V.R.Brown	Australia	v	New Zealand	Brisbane[2]	1985-86
P.A.de Silva (122)	Imran Khan	Sri Lanka	v	Pakistan	Faisalabad	1985-86
Imran Khan (135*)	N.S.Yadav	Pakistan	v	India	Chennai[1]	1986-87
M.D.Crowe (104)	C.G.Butts	New Zealand	v	West Indies	Auckland	1986-87
Ijaz Ahmed (105)	Maninder Singh	Pakistan	v	India	Ahmedabad	1986-87
D.L.Haynes (112*)	N.D.Hirwani	West Indies	v	India	Bridgetown	1988-89
C.C.Lewis (117)	S.L.Venkatapathy Raju	England	v	India	Chennai[1]	1992-93
D.L.Haynes (125)	Asif Mujtaba	West Indies	v	Pakistan	Bridgetown	1992-93
C.L.Hooper (178*)	Nadeem Khan	West Indies	v	Pakistan	St John's	1992-93
P.A.de Silva (148)	A.R.Kumble	Sri Lanka	v	India	Colombo (PSS)	1993-94
P.A.de Silva (127)	Mushtaq Ahmed	Sri Lanka	v	Pakistan	Colombo (PSS)	1994-95
S.R.Tendulkar (179)	C.A.Walsh	India	v	West Indies	Nagpur	1994-95
R.G.Samuels (125)	D.N.Patel	West Indies	v	New Zealand	St John's	1995-96
S.R.Tendulkar (122)	M.M.Patel	India	v	England	Birmingham	1996
Inzamamul Haq (148)	G.A.Hick	Pakistan	v	England	Lord's	1996

MOST SIXES IN AN INNINGS

TEN	W.R.Hammond (336*)	England	v	New Zealand	Auckland	1932-33
NINE	C.L.Cairns (120)	New Zealand	v	Zimbabwe	Auckland	1995-96
EIGHT	N.S.Sidhu (124)	India	v	Sri Lanka	Lucknow[2]	1993-94
SEVEN	B.Sutcliffe (80*)	New Zealand	v	South Africa	Johannesburg[2]	1953-54
	I.V.A.Richards (110*)	West Indies	v	England	St John's	1985-86
	C G.Greenidge (213)	West Indies	v	New Zealand	Auckland	1986-87
SIX	J.H.Sinclair (104)	South Africa	v	Australia	Cape Town	1902-03
	I.V.A.Richards (192*)	West Indies	v	India	Delhi	1974-75
	Haroon Rashid (108)	Pakistan	v	England	Hyderabad	1977-78
	I.T.Botham (118)	England	v	Australia	Manchester	1981
	R.J.Shastri (121*)	India	v	Australia	Mumbai[3]	1986-87

MOST SIXES OFF CONSECUTIVE BALLS

FOUR	Kapil Dev (77*) off E.E.Hemmings	India	v	England	Lord's	1990
THREE	W.R.Hammond (336*) off J.Newman	England	v	New Zealand	Auckland	1932-33
	S.T.Clarke (35*) off Mohammad Nazir	West Indies	v	Pakistan	Faisalabad	1980-81

MOST FOURS OFF CONSECUTIVE BALLS

FIVE	D.T.Lindsay (60) off J.W.Gleeson	South Africa	v	Australia	Port Elizabeth	1969-70
	R.E.Redmond (107) off Majid Khan	New Zealand	v	Pakistan	Auckland	1972-73
	D.W.Hookes (56) off A.W.Greig	Australia	v	England	Melbourne	1976-77

MOST RUNS OFF ONE OVER

EIGHT-BALLS

25 (66061600)	B.Sutcliffe and R.W.Blair off H.J.Tayfield - New Zealand v South Africa (Johannesburg[2])	1953-54
24 (2x6, 3x4)	J.F.M.Morrison off Imran Khan - New Zealand v Pakistan (Karachi[1])	1976-77
22 (42444004)	P.G.van der Bijl off D.P.V.Wright - South Africa v England (Durban[2])	1938-39
22 (44422204)	R.C.Fredericks off G.J.Gilmour - West Indies v Australia (Perth)1975-76	
22 (?)	Javed Miandad and Wasim Raja off B.P.Bracewell - Pakistan v New Zealand (Christchurch)	1978-79

21 (44442300)	V.Y.Richardson off J.W.H.T.Douglas - Australia v England (Melbourne)	1924-25
21 (10206444)	K.R.Miller and R.R.Lindwall off S.Ramadhin - Australia v West Indies (Brisbane[2])	1951-52
21 (14466000)	E.J.Barlow and R.G.Pollock off R.B.Simpson - South Africa v Australia (Adelaide)	1963-64
21 (3x6?)	I.M.Chappell off Intikhab Alam - Australia v Pakistan (Adelaide)	1972-73
21 (34200444)	G.J.Cosier and G.S.Chappell off Saleem Altaf - Australia v Pakistan (Melbourne)	1976-77
21 (04614222)	J.R.Thomson and A.G.Hurst off S.Madan Lal - Australia v India (Brisbane[2])	1977-78
20 (66422000)	G.D.McKenzie off G.S.Sobers - Australia v West Indies (Sydney)	1968-69
20 (?)	I.M.Chappell and R.Edwards off Intikhab Alam - Australia v Pakistan (Adelaide)	1972-73
20 (?)	R.W.Marsh off Asif Iqbal - Australia v Pakistan (Adelaide)	1972-73
20 (44444?)	R.E.Redmond off Majid Khan - New Zealand v Pakistan (Auckland)	1972-73
20 (044440400)	A.I.Kallicharran off Asif Masood - West Indies v Pakistan (Karachi[1])	1974-75
20 (20**4**404402)	R.C.Fredericks off J.R.Thomson - West Indies v Australia (Perth)	1975-76
20 (64442000)	Zaheer Abbas off K.J.O'Keeffe - Pakistan v Australia (Adelaide)	1976-77
20 (00444440)	D.W.Hookes off A.W.Greig - Australia v England (Melbourne)	1976-77

SIX-BALLS (L 1 leg-bye (**bold** no-ball)

24 (462660L)	A.M.E.Roberts off I.T.Botham - West Indies v England (Port-Of-Spain)	1980-81
24 (44**4**0444)	S.M.Patil off R.G.D.Willis - India v England (Manchester)	1982
24 (464604)	I.T.Botham off D.A.Stirling - England v New Zealand (The Oval)	1986
24 (244266)	I.D.S.Smith off A.S.Wassan - New Zealand v India (Auckland)	1989-90
24 (006666)	Kapil Dev off E.E.Hemmings - India v England (Lord's)	1990
22 (116626)	M.W.Tate and W.Voce off A.E.Hall - England v South Africa (Johannesburg[1])	1930-31
22 (064066)	R.C.Motz off D.A.Allen - New Zealand v England (Dunedin)	1965-66
22 (664420)	R.C.Motz off E.A.S.Prasanna - New Zealand v India (Dunedin)	1967-68
22 (006664)	S.T.Clarke off Mohammad Nazir - West Indies v Pakistan (Faisalabad)	1979-80
22 (613642)	I.T.Botham and C.J.Tavare off D.K.Lillee - England v Australia (Manchester)	1981
22 (046444)	K.Srikkanth off R.G.Holland - India v Australia (Sydney)	1985-86
22 (224644)	I.T.Botham off M.G.Hughes - England v Australia (Brisbane[2])	1986-87
22 (440446)	P.A.J.DeFreitas off C.J.McDermott - England v Australia (Adelaide)	1994-95
21 (124464)	J.H.Sinclair and C.M.H.Hathorn off A.J.Y.Hopkins - South Africa v Australia (Cape Town)	1902-03
21 (122466)	D.G.Bradman and S.G.Barnes off J.C.Laker - Australia v England (Lord's)	1948
21 (660612)	B.S.Bedi and B.S.Chandrasekhar off P.J.Petherick - India v New Zealand (Kanpur)	1976-77
21 (**4**144044)	M.Amarnath and S.M.Gavaskar off Sikander Bakht - India v Pakistan (Karachi[1])	1978-79
21 (640461)	Imran Khan off Kapil Dev - Pakistan v India (Faisalabad)	1982-83
20 (664400)	E.A.V.Williams off J.C.Laker - West Indies v England (Bridgetown)	1947-48
20 (604046)	A.K.Davidson off D.A.Allen - Australia v England (Manchester)	1961
20 (44444?)	D.T.Lindsay off J.W.Gleeson - South Africa v Australia (Port Elizabeth)	1969-70
20 (444620)	D.L.Haynes off J.R.Thomson - West Indies v Australia (Port-of-Spain)	1977-78
20 (460406)	Yashpal Sharma off P.R.Sleep - India v Australia (New Delhi)	1979-80
20 (446420)	S.M.Patil off Jalaluddin - India v Pakistan (Lahore[2])	1982-83
20 (?)	N.S.Sidhu off E.J.Gray - India v New Zealand (Bangalore)	1988-89
20 (4444nn04)	Aamer Sohail off D.H.Brain - Pakistan v Zimbabwe (Bulawayo[2])	1994-95

CENTURY BEFORE LUNCH

FIRST DAY

	Lunch score					
V.T.Trumper (104)	103*	Australia	v	England	Manchester	1902
C.G.Macartney (151)	112*	Australia	v	England	Leeds	1926
D.G.Bradman (334)	105*	Australia	v	England	Leeds	1930
Majid Khan (112)	108*	Pakistan	v	New Zealand	Karachi[1]	1976-77

OTHER DAYS

	Overnight score	Lunch score						Day
K.S.Ranjitsinhji (154*)	41*	154*	England	v	Australia	Manchester	1896	3
C.Hill (142)	22*	138*	Australia	v	South Africa	Johannesburg[1]	1902-03	3
W.Bardsley (164)	32*	150*	Australia	v	South Africa	Lord's	1912	2

C.P.Mead (182*	19*	128*	England	v	Australia	The Oval	1921	2
J.B.Hobbs (211)	12*	114*	England	v	South Africa	Lord's	1924	2
H.G.Owen-Smith (129)	27*	129	South Africa	v	England	Leeds	1929	3
W.R.Hammond (336*)	41*	152*	England	v	New Zealand	Auckland	1932-33	2
L.E.G.Ames (148*)	25*	148*	England	v	South Africa	The Oval	1935	3
S.J.McCabe (189*)	59*	159*	Australia	v	South Africa	Johannesburg[1]	1935-36	4
G.S.Chappell (176)	76*	176	Australia	v	New Zealand	Christchurch	1981-82	2

FASTEST FIFTIES

Min						
22	V.T.Trumper (63)	Australia	v	South Africa	Johannesburg[1]	1902-03
28	J.T Brown (140)	England	v	Australia	Melbourne	1894-95
29	S.A.Durani (61*)	India	v	England	Kanpur	1963-64
30	E.A.V.Williams (72)	West Indies	v	England	Bridgetown	1947-48
30	B.R.Taylor (124)	New Zealand	v	West Indies	Auckland	1968-69
33	C.A.Roach (56)	West Indies	v	England	The Oval	1933
34	C.R.Browne (70*)	West Indies	v	England	Georgetown	1929-30
35	J.H.Sinclair (104)	South Africa	v	Australia	Cape Town	1902-03
35	C.G.Macartney (56)	Australia	v	South Africa	Sydney	1910-11
35	J.W.Hitch (51*)	England	v	Australia	The Oval	1921
38	R.Benaud (121)	Australia	v	West Indies	Kingston	1954-55
40	J.Darling (160)	Australia	v	England	Sydney	1897-98
40	S.J.McCabe (189*)	Australia	v	South Africa	Johannesburg[1]	1935-36
41	J.M.Gregory (119)	Australia	v	South Africa	Johannesburg[1]	1921-22
43	G.L.Jessop (104)	England	v	Australia	The Oval	1902
45	J.J.Lyons (55)	Australia	v	England	Lord's	1890
45	G.L.Jessop (93)	England	v	South Africa	Lord's	1907
45	P.W.Sherwell (115)	South Africa	v	England	Lord's	1907
45	F.B.Smith (54*)	New Zealand	v	England	Leeds	1949
45	R.R.Lindwall (50)	Australia	v	England	Lord's	1953

FASTEST FIFTIES (by balls)

Balls						
30	Kapil Dev (73)	India	v	Pakistan	Karachi[1]	1982-83
32	I.V.A.Richards (61)	West Indies	v	India	Kingston	1982-83
32	I.T.Botham (59)	England	v	New Zealand	The Oval	1986
33	R.C.Fredericks (169)	West Indies	v	Australia	Perth	1975-76
33	Kapil Dev (59)	India	v	Pakistan	Karachi	1978-79
33	Kapil Dev (65)	India	v	England	Manchester	1982
33	A.J.Lamb (60)	England	v	New Zealand	Auckland	1991-92
34	I.D.S.Smith (61)	New Zealand	v	Pakistan	Faisalabad	1990-91
35	I.V.A.Richards (110*)	West Indies	v	England	St John's	1985-86
35	R.B.Richardson (106)	West Indies	v	Australia	Adelaide	1988-89
36	B.R.Taylor (124)	New Zealand	v	West Indies	Auckland	1968-69
37	S.M.Gavaskar (121)	India	v	West Indies	Delhi	1983-84
39	M.J.Greatbatch (87)	New Zealand	v	Zimbabwe	Bulawayo[1]	1992-93
39	A.D.R.Campbell (63)	Zimbabwe	v	Pakistan	Rawalpindi[2]	1993-94
40	B.C.Lara (53)	West Indies	v	England	Leeds	1995
42	D.I.Gower (73)	England	v	Pakistan	Manchester	1992
43	J.M.Gregory (119)	Australia	v	South Africa	Johannesburg[1]	1921-22
43	A.Ranatunga (131)	Sri Lanka	v	South Africa	Moratuwa	1993-94
43	B.C.Lara (152)	West Indies	v	England	Nottingham	1995
45	C.L.Hooper (73*)	West Indies	v	England	Leeds	1995
47	P.V.Simmons (87)	West Indies	v	Pakistan	Bridgetown	1992-93
47	C.L.Cairns (120)	New Zealand	v	Zimbabwe	Auckland	1995-96
48	B.C.Lara (88)	West Indies	v	Australia	St John's	1994-95
50	R.S.Mahanama (109)	Sri Lanka	v	New Zealand	Colombo (SSC)	1992-93

50	M.E.Waugh (70)	Australia	v	England	Nottingham	1993
50	M.E.Waugh (126)	Australia	v	West Indies	Kingston	1994-95

FASTEST CENTURIES

Min						
70	J.M.Gregory (119)	Australia	v	South Africa	Johannesburg[1]	1921-22
75	G.L.Jessop (104)	England	v	Australia	The Oval	1902
78	R.Benaud (121)	Australia	v	West Indies	Kingston	1954-55
80	J.H.Sinclair (104)	South Africa	v	Australia	Cape Town	1902-03
81	I.V.A.Richards (110*)	West Indies	v	England	St John's	1985-86
86	B.R.Taylor (124)	New Zealand	v	West Indies	Auckland	1968-69
91	J.Darling (160)	Australia	v	England	Sydney	1897-98
91	S.J.McCabe (189*)	Australia	v	South Africa	Johannesburg[1]	1935-36
94	V.T.Trumper (185*)	Australia	v	England	Sydney	1903-04
95	J.T.Brown (140)	England	v	Australia	Melbourne	1894-95
95	P.W.Sherwell (115)	South Africa	v	England	Lord's	1907
98	D.Denton (104)	England	v	South Africa	Johannesburg[1]	1909-10
98	C.Hill (191)	Australia	v	South Africa	Sydney	1910-11
98	D.G.Bradman (167)	Australia	v	South Africa	Melbourne	1931-32
99	C.G.Macartney (116)	Australia	v	South Africa	Durban[1]	1921-22
99	D.G.Bradman (334)	Australia	v	England	Leeds	1948
100	G.J.Bonnor (128)	Australia	v	England	Sydney	1884-85
100	C.Hill (100)	Australia	v	South Africa	Mebourne	1910-11
100	L.E.G.Ames (149)	England	v	West Indies	Kingston	1929-30
100	W.R.Hammond (100*)	England	v	New Zealand	The Oval	1931
100	W.R.Hammond (167)	England	v	India	Manchester	1936

FASTEST CENTURIES (by balls)

Balls						
56	I.V.A.Richards (110*)	West Indies	v	England	St John's	1985-86
67	J.M.Gregory (119)	Australia	v	South Africa	Johannesburg[1]	1921-22
71	R.C.Fredericks (169)	West Indies	v	Australia	Perth	1975-76
74	Majid Khan (112)	Pakistan	v	New Zealand	Karachi[1]	1976-77
74	Kapil Dev (163)	India	v	Sri Lanka	Kanpur	1986-87
76	G.L.Jessop (104)	England	v	Australia	The Oval	1902
83	B.R.Taylor (124)	New Zealand	v	West Indies	Auckland	1968-69
85	C.H.Lloyd (163)	West Indies	v	India	Bangalore	1974-75
86	I.T.Botham (118)	England	v	Australia	Manchester	1981
86	Kapil Dev (116)	India	v	England	Kanpur	1981-82
86	C.L.Cairns (120)	New Zealand	v	Zimbabwe	Auckland	1995-96
87	I.T.Botham (147*)	England	v	Australia	Leeds	1981
87	M.Azharuddin (121)	India	v	England	Lord's	1990
88	R.R.Lindwall (100)	Australia	v	England	Melbourne	1946-47
88	R.J.Hadlee (103)	New Zealand	v	West Indies	Christchurch	1979-80
94	Zaheer Abbas (168)	Pakistan	v	India	Faisalabad	1982-83
94	S.M.Gavaskar (121)	India	v	West Indies	Delhi	1983-84
95	D.T.Lindsay (131)	South Africa	v	Australia	Johannesburg[3]	1966-67
95	Kapil Dev (100*)	India	v	West Indies	Port-of-Spain	1982-83
95	I.D.S.Smith (173)	New Zealand	v	India	Auckland	1989-90
95	G.A.Gooch (123)	England	v	India	Lord's	1990
97	K.Srikkanth (116)	India	v	Australia	Sydney	1985-86
98	G.S.Sobers (113)	West Indies	v	Australia	Sydney	1968-69
99	I.T.Botham (103)	England	v	New Zealand	Nottingham	1983
101	Kapil Dev (126*)	India	v	West Indies	Delhi	1978-79
102	I.V.A.Richards (109*)	West Indies	v	India	Delhi	1987-88
104	I.T.Botham (108)	England	v	Pakistan	Lord's	1978
105	I.V.A.Richards (145)	West Indies	v	England	Lord's	1980

105	Kapil Dev (109)	India	v	West Indies	Chennai[1]	1987-88
107	C.H.Lloyd (242*)	West Indies	v	India	Mumbai[3]	1974-75
108	M.D.Crowe (107)	New Zealand	v	Sri Lanka	Colombo (SSC)	1992-93
109	D.C.S.Compton (113)	England	v	South Africa	The Oval	1947
109	C.L.King (100*)	West Indies	v	New Zealand	Christchurch	1979-80
109	Kapil Dev (119)	India	v	Australia	Chennai[1]	1986-87
110	R.E.Redmond (107)	New Zealand	v	Pakistan	Auckland	1972-73
110	R.C.Fredericks (109)	West Indies	v	England	Leeds	1976
110	L.R.D.Mendis (105)	Sri Lanka	v	India	Chennai[1]	1982-83
110	S.R.Waugh (134*)	Australia	v	Sri Lanka	Hobart	1989-90
114	A.Rantunga (131)	Sri Lanka	v	South Africa	Moratuwa	1993-94

FASTEST DOUBLE CENTURIES

Min						
214	D.G.Bradman (334)	Australia	v	England	Leeds	1930
223	S.J.McCabe (232)	Australia	v	England	Nottingham	1938
226	V.T.Trumper (214*)	Australia	v	South Africa	Adelaide	1910-11
234	D.G.Bradman (254)	Australia	v	England	Lord's	1930
240	W.R.Hammond (336*)	England	v	New Zealand	Auckland	1932-33
241	S.E.Gregory (201)	Australia	v	England	Sydney	1894-95
245	D.C S.Compton (278)	England	v	Pakistan	Nottingham	1954
251	D.G Bradman (223)	Australia	v	West Indies	Brisbane[1]	1930-31
253	D.G.Bradman (226)	Australia	v	South Africa	Brisbane[2]	1931-32

FASTEST TRIPLE CENTURIES

Min						
288	W.R.Hammond (336*)	England	v	New Zealand	Auckland	1932-33
336	D.G.Bradman (334)	Australia	v	England	Leeds	1930

W.R.Hammond's third hundred was scored in 48 minutes.

D.G.Bradman scored his three hundreds in 99, 115 and 122 minutes respectively and reached 309 at the end of the first day.*

MOST RUNS IN A DAY

309(0-309*)	D.G.Bradman (334)	Australia	v	England	Leeds	1930
295(41*-336*)	W.R.Hammond (336*)	England	v	New Zealand	Auckland	1932-33
273(5*-278)	D.C.S.Compton (278)	England	v	Pakistan	Nottingham	1954
271(0-271*)	D.G.Bradman (304)	Australia	v	England	Leeds	1934
244(0-244)	D.G.Bradman (244)	Australia	v	England	The Oval	1934
239(0-239*)	F.M.M.Worrell (261)	West Indies	v	England	Nottingham	1950
223(0-223*)	W.R.Hammond (227)	England	v	New Zealand	Christchurch	1932-33
223(0-223*)	D.G.Bradman (223)	Australia	v	West Indies	Brisbane[1]	1930-31
217(0-217)	W.R.Hammond (217)	England	v	India	The Oval	1936
214(73*-287)	R.E.Foster (287)	England	v	Australia	Sydney	1903-04
213(19*-232)	S.J.McCabe (232)	Australia	v	England	Nottingham	1938
210(0-210*)	W.R.Hammond (240)	England	v	Australia	Lord's	1938
209(0-209)	C.A.Roach (209)	West Indies	v	England	Georgetown	1929-30
208(20*-228*)	G.S.Sobers (365*)	West Indies	v	Pakistan	Kingston	1957-58
208(0-208*)	V.T.Trumper (214*)	Australia	v	South Africa	Adelaide	1910-11
206(0-206)	L.Hutton (206)	England	v	New Zealand	The Oval	1949
205(0-205*)	W.H.Ponsford (266)	Australia	v	England	The Oval	1934
205(0-205)	Aamer Sohail (205)	Pakistan	v	England	Manchester	1992
203(0-203)	H.L.Collins (203)	Australia	v	South Africa	Johannesburg[1]	1921-22
203(0-203*)	R B Kanhai (256)	West Indies	v	India	Calcutta	1958-59
203(0*-203*)	P.A.de Silva (267)	Sri Lanka	v	New Zealand	Wellington	1990-91
201(0-201)	D.G.Bradman (201)	Australia	v	India	Adelaide	1947-48
200(0-200*)	D.G.Bradman (226)	Australia	v	South Africa	Brisbane[2]	1931-32
200(0-200*)	I.V.A.Richards (291)	West Indies	v	England	The Oval	1976

FEWEST BOUNDARIES IN AN INNINGS

Runs	Fours						
84	0	W.M.Lawry	Australia	v	England	Brisbane[2]	1970-71
77	0	G.Boycott	England	v	Australia	Perth	1978-79
67	0	E.A.B.Rowan	South Africa	v	England	Durban[2]	1938-39
120	2	P.A.Gibb	England	v	South Africa	Durban[2]	1938-39
94	2	K.F.Barrington	England	v	Australia	Sydney	1962-63
102	3	W.M.Woodfull	Australia	v	England	Melbourne	1928-29
161	5	W.M.Woodfull	Australia	v	South Africa	Melbourne	1931-32

G.Boycott's innings included one four but it was all-run and included two runs from an overthrow.

SLOWEST FIFTIES

Min						
357	T.E.Bailey (68)	England	v	Australia	Brisbane[2]	1958-59
350	C.J.Tavare (82)	England	v	Pakistan	Lord's	1982
333	B.A.Young (51)	New Zealand	v	South Africa	Durban[2]	1994-95
326	S.M.Gavaskar (51)	India	v	Sri Lanka	Colombo (SSC)	1985-86
318	Rameez Raja (62)	Pakistan	v	West Indies	Karachi[1]	1986-87
316	C.P.S.Chauhan (61)	India	v	Pakistan	Kanpur	1979-80
315	Shoaib Mohammad (53*)	Pakistan	v	Zimbabwe	Lahore[2]	1993-94
313	D.J.McGlew (70)	South Africa	v	Australia	Johannesburg[3]	1957-58
312	J.J.Crowe (120*)	New Zealand	v	Sri Lanka	Colombo (CCC)	1986-87
310	B.A.Edgar (55)	New Zealand	v	Australia	Wellington	1981-82
310	A.R.Border (75)	Australia	v	West Indies	Sydney	1988-89
306	C.J.Tavare (78)	England	v	Australia	Manchester	1981
304	P.L.Taylor (54*)	Australia	v	Pakistan	Karachi[1]	1988-89
302	D.N.Sardesai (60)	India	v	West Indies	Bridgetown	1961-62
300	G.S.Camacho (57)	West Indies	v	England	Bridgetown	1967-68
296	C.Z.Harris (56)	New Zealand	v	Sri Lanka	Moratuwa	1992-93
294	C.L.Smith (91)	England	v	New Zealand	Auckland	1983-84
290	G.Boycott (63)	England	v	Pakistan	Lahore[2]	1977-78
290	K.R.Rutherford (50*)	New Zealand	v	Australia	Auckland	1985-86
290	E.J.Gray (50)	New Zealand	v	England	Nottingham	1986
290	H.D.P.K.Dharmasena (54)	Sri Lanka	v	Zimbabwe	Bulawayo[2]	1994-95
289	C.J.Tavare (56)	England	v	India	Mumbai[3]	1981-82
289	B.A.Edgar (74)	New Zealand	v	Australia	Perth	1985-86
288	R.J.Shastri (109)	India	v	West Indies	Bridgetown	1988-89
285	P.R.Umrigar (78)	India	v	Australia	Mumbai[2]	1956-57
285	G.A.Gooch (84)	England	v	West Indies	The Oval	1988
284	K.S.More (55)	India	v	South Africa	Durban[2]	1992-93
284	J.G.Wright (72)	New Zealand	v	Australia	Wellington	1992-93
282	E.D.A.S.McMorris (73)	West Indies	v	England	Kingston	1959-60
280	P.E.Richardson (117)	England	v	South Africa	Johannesburg[3]	1956-57
279	Asif Mujtaba (54*)	Pakistan	v	Zimbabwe	Rawalpindi[2]	1993-94
278	G.Boycott (77)	England	v	Australia	Perth	1978-79
275	W.M.Lawry (57)	Australia	v	England	Melbourne	1962-63
275	S.Ranatunga (118)	Sri Lanka	v	Zimbabwe	Harare	1994-95
272	A.P.Gurusinha (128)	Sri Lanka	v	Zimbabwe	Harare	1994-95
271	B.A.Young (51)	New Zealand	v	South Africa	Cape Town	1994-95
270	Mudassar Nazar (111)	Pakistan	v	England	Lahore[2]	1977-78
270	M.D.Crowe (108*)	New Zealand	v	Pakistan	Lahore[2]	1990-91

SLOWEST CENTURIES

Min						
557	Mudassar Nazar (111)	Pakistan	v	England	Lahore[2]	1977-78

545	D.J.McGlew (105)	South Africa	v	Australia	Durban[2]	1957-58
535	A.P.Gurusinha (128)	Sri Lanka	v	Zimbabwe	Harare	1994-95
516	J.J.Crowe (120*)	New Zealand	v	Sri Lanka	Colombo (CCC)	1986-87
500	S.V.Manjrekar (104)	India	v	Zimbabwe	Harare	1992-93
488	P.E.Richardson (117)	England	v	South Africa	Johannesburg[3]	1956-57
487	C.T.Radley (158)	England	v	New Zealand	Auckland	1977-78
468	Hanif Mohammad (142)	Pakistan	v	India	Bahawalpur	1954-55
462	M.J.Greatbatch (146*)	New Zealand	v	Australia	Perth	1989-90
461	M.D.Crowe (108*)	New Zealand	v	Pakistan	Lahore[2]	1990-91
460	Hanif Mohammad (111)	Pakistan	v	England	Dacca	1961-62
458	K.W.R.Fletcher (122)	England	v	Pakistan	The Oval	1974
457	S.A.R.Silva (111)	Sri Lanka	v	India	Colombo (SSC)	1985-86
455	G.P.Howarth (122)	New Zealand	v	England	Auckland	1977-78
440	A.J.Watkins (137*)	England	v	India	Delhi	1951-52
438	G.Boycott (105)	England	v	India	Delhi	1981-82
437	D.B.Vengsarkar (146*)	India	v	Pakistan	Delhi	1979-80
437	A.P.Gurusinha (116*)	Sri Lanka	v	Pakistan	Colombo (PSS)	1985-86
435	J.W.Guy (102)	New Zealand	v	India	Hyderabad	1955-56
434	M.C.Cowdrey (154)	England	v	West Indies	Birmingham	1957
434	T.J.Franklin (101)	New Zealand	v	England	Lord's	1990
430	S.Ranatunga (118)	Sri Lanka	v	Zimbabwe	Harare	1994-95
428	S.M.Gavaskar (172)	India	v	England	Bangalore	1981-82
427	R.J.Shastri (109)	India	v	West Indies	Bridgetown	1988-89
425	H.A.Gomes (127)	West Indies	v	Australia	Perth	1984-85
424	R.J.Shastri (125)	India	v	Pakistan	Jaipur	1986-87
424	M.A.Atherton (105)	England	v	Australia	Sydney	1990-91
422	R.J.Shastri (111)	India	v	England	Calcutta	1984-85
421	S.Ranatunga (100*)	Sri Lanka	v	Zimbabwe	Bulawayo[2]	1994-95
420	M.D.Crowe (188)	New Zealand	v	West Indies	Georgetown	1984-85
416	W.J.Cronje (135)	South Africa	v	India	Port Elizabeth	1992-93
416	A.J.Stewart (143)	England	v	West Indies	Bridgetown	1993-94
414	J.H.B.Waite (134)	South Africa	v	Australia	Durban[2]	1957-58
414	A.W.Greig (103)	England	v	India	Calcutta	1976-77
414	J.G.Wright (110)	New Zealand	v	India	Auckland	1980-81
412	J.G.Wright (138)	New Zealand	v	West Indies	Wellington	1986-87
411	D.W.Randall (150)	England	v	Australia	Sydney	1978-79
409	M.L.Apte (163*)	India	v	West Indies	Port-of-Spain	1952-53
408	M.Amarnath (101)	India	v	Pakistan	Lahore[2]	1984-85
405	M.A.Atherton (151)	England	v	New Zealand	Nottingham	1990
404	J.F.Reid (148)	New Zealand	v	Pakistan	Wellington	1984-85
396	R.A.Woolmer (149)	England	v	Australia	The Oval	1975
395	A.P.Gurusinha (127)	Sri Lanka	v	New Zealand	Dunedin	1994-95
392	J.F.Reid (180)	New Zealand	v	Sri Lanka	Colombo (CCC)	1983-84
392	M.J.Greatbatch (107*)	New Zealand	v	England	Auckland	1987-88
390	R.A.Smith (128)	England	v	Sri Lanka	Colombo (SSC)	1992-93
388	H.A.Gomes (127*)	West Indies	v	Australia	Adelaide	1981-82
387	M.A.Atherton (111)	England	v	New Zealand	Manchester	1994
386	C.A.Davis (183)	West Indies	v	New Zealand	Bridgetown	1971-72
385	D.M.Jones (210)	Australia	v	India	Chennai	1986-87
385	Imran Khan (136)	Pakistan	v	Australia	Adelaide	1989-90
384	M.A.Taylor (100)	Australia	v	India	Adelaide	1991-92
382	D.L.Haynes (105)	West Indies	v	New Zealand	Dunedin	1979-80
376	B.A.Edgar (127)	New Zealand	v	West Indies	Auckland	1979-80
373	V.Pollard (116)	New Zealand	v	England	Nottingham	1973
370	H.P.Tillakaratne (116)	Sri Lanka	v	Zimbabwe	Harare	1994-95

SLOWEST DOUBLE CENTURIES

Min						
776	D.S.B.P.Kuruppu (201*)	Sri Lanka	v	New Zealand	Colombo (CCC)	1986-87
685	V.G.Kambli (224)	India	v	England	Chennai[1]	1992-93
666	G.W.Flower (201*)	Zimbabwe	v	Pakistan	Harare	1994-95
656	Shoaib Mohammad (203*)	Pakistan	v	New Zealand	Karachi[1]	1990-91
652	A.D.Gaekwad (201)	India	v	Pakistan	Jullundur	1983-84
608	R.B.Simpson (311)	Australia	v	England	Manchester	1964
596	A.R.Border (205)	Australia	v	New Zealand	Adelaide	1987-88
595	G.S.Sobers (226)	West Indies	v	England	Bridgetown	1959-60
591	Javed Miandad (211)	Pakistan	v	Australia	Karachi[1]	1988-89
584	Hanif Mohammad (337)	Pakistan	v	West Indies	Bridgetown	1957-58
570	S.G.Barnes (234)	Australia	v	England	Sydney	1946-47
568	G.R.Viswanath (222)	India	v	England	Chennai[1]	1981-82
566	A.R.Border (200*)	Australia	v	England	Leeds	1993
562	C.G.Greenidge (226)	West Indies	v	Australia	Bridgetown	1990-91
556	R.J.Shastri (206)	India	v	Australia	Sydney	1991-92
555	G.N.Yallop (268)	Australia	v	Pakistan	Melbourne	1983-84
550	S.R.Waugh (200)	Australia	v	West Indies	Kingston	1994-95
535	R.M.Cowper (307)	Australia	v	England	Melbourne	1965-66
531	W.M.Lawry (210)	Australia	v	West Indies	Bridgetown	1964-65
524	D.L.Houghton (266)	Zimbabwe	v	Sri Lanka	Bulawayo[2]	1994-95
523	G.M.Turner (223)	New Zealand	v	West Indies	Kingston	1971-72
522	G.M.Turner (259)	New Zealand	v	West Indies	Georgetown	1971-72
518	K.F.Barrington (256)	England	v	Australia	Manchester	1964
515	D.M.Jones (216)	Australia	v	West Indies	Adelaide	1988-89
513	V.G.Kambli (224)	India	v	England	Mumbai[3]	1992-93
512	M.A.Taylor (219)	Australia	v	England	Nottingham	1989

SLOWEST TRIPLE CENTURIES

Min						
858	Hanif Mohammad (337)	Pakistan	v	West Indies	Bridgetown	1957-58
753	R.B.Simpson (311)	Australia	v	England	Manchester	1964
693	R.M.Cowper (307)	Australia	v	England	Melbourne	1965-66
662	L.Hutton (364)	England	v	Australia	The Oval	1938
610	B.C.Lara (375)	West Indies	v	England	St John's	1993-94
605	L.G.Rowe (302)	West Indies	v	England	Bridgetown	1973-74

AN HOUR BEFORE SCORING FIRST RUN

Min						
97	T.G.Evans (10*)	England	v	Australia	Adelaide	1946-47
84	R.K.Chauhan (9)	India	v	Sri Lanka	Ahmedabad	1993-94
82	P.I.Pocock (13)	England	v	West Indies	Georgetown	1967-68
74	J.T.Murray (3*)	England	v	Australia	Sydney	1962-63
72	C.G.Rackemann (9)	Australia	v	England	Sydney	1990-91
72	H.H.Streak (19*)	Zimbabwe	v	Pakistan	Karachi[2]	1993-94
70	W.L.Murdoch (17)	Australia	v	England	Sydney	1882-83
69	R.M.Hogg (7*)	Australia	v	West Indies	Adelaide	1984-85
67	C.J.Tavare (82)	England	v	Pakistan	Lord's	1982
66	J.G.Wright (38)	New Zealand	v	Australia	Wellington	1981-82
65	Shujauddin (45)	Pakistan	v	Australia	Lahore[2]	1959-60
64	C.E.Eksteen (21)	South Africa	v	New Zealand	Auckland	1994-95
63	C.J.Tavare (9)	England	v	Australia	Perth	1982-83
63	P.C.R.Tufnell (2*)	England	v	India	Mumbai[3]	1992-93
62	M.A.Taylor (49)	Australia	v	England	Sydney	1994-95

AN HOUR WITHOUT ADDING TO SCORE

Min						
94	M.C.Snedden (23)	New Zealand	v	Australia	Wellington	1989-90
91	J.J.Crowe (21)	New Zealand	v	West Indies	Bridgetown	1984-85
90	B.Mitchell (58)	South Africa	v	Australia	Brisbane[2]	1931-32
90	C.J.Tavare (89)	England	v	Australia	Perth	1982-83
89	R.J.Shastri (23)	India	v	South Africa	Johannesburg[3]	1992-93
79	T.E.Bailey (8)	England	v	South Africa	Leeds	1955
77	D.B.Close (20)	England	v	West Indies	Manchester	1976
75	A.Ranatunga (37)	Sri Lanka	v	New Zealand	Colombo (CCC)	1983-84
70	D.L.Haynes (9)	West Indies	v	New Zealand	Auckland	1979-80
70	R.C.Russell (29*)	England	v	South Africa	Johannesburg[3]	1995-96
69	G.A.Gooch (84)	England	v	West Indies	The Oval	1988
67	W.H.Scotton (34)	England	v	Australia	The Oval	1886
66	S.M.Gavaskar (52)	India	v	Sri Lanka	Colombo (PSS)	1985-86
65	Nawab of Pataudi, jr (5)	India	v	England	Mumbai[2]	1972-73
64	Anil Dalpat (15)	Pakistan	v	New Zealand	Wellington	1984-85
64	M.A.Taylor (11)	Australia	v	England	Sydney	1990-91
64	S.Chanderpaul (80)	West Indies	v	England	The Oval	1995
63	D.R.Jardine (24)	England	v	Australia	Brisbane[2]	1932-33
63	W.R.Endean (18)	South Africa	v	England	Johannesburg[3]	1956-57
63	W.R.Playle (18)	New Zealand	v	England	Leeds	1958
63	J.M.Brearley (48)	England	v	Australia	Birmingham	1981
63	S.R.Waugh (47*)	Australia	v	England	Nottingham	1993
62	K.F.Barrington (137)	England	v	New Zealand	Birmingham	1965
61	J.F.Reid (148)	New Zealand	v	Pakistan	Wellington	1984-85
61	M.D.Marshall (6*)	West Indies	v	England	Birmingham	1991
60	B.Mitchell (73)	South Africa	v	England	Johannesburg[1]	1938-39
60	T.E.Bailey (80)	England	v	South Africa	Durban[2]	1956-57
60	C.J.Tavare (82)	England	v	Pakistan	Lord's	1982
60	A.R.Border (9)	Australia	v	Pakistan	Faisalabad	1982-83
60	S.M.Gavaskar (51)	India	v	Sri Lanka	Colombo (SSC)	1985-86
60	J.J.Crowe (120*)	New Zealand	v	Sri Lanka	Colombo (CCC)	1986-87

FEWEST RUNS IN A DAY

49	(5*-54*)	M.L.Jaisimha (99)	India	v	Pakistan	Kanpur	1960-61
52	(52*)	Mudassar Nazar(114)	Pakistan	v	England	Lahore[2]	1977-78
56	(1*-57*)	D.J.McGlew (70)	South Africa	v	Australia	Johannesburg[3]	1957-58
59	(0*-59*)	M.L.Jaisimha (74)	India	v	Australia	Calcutta	1959-60

PLAYER DISMISSED FROM THE FIRST BALL OF A TEST

Batsman	Bowler					
A.C.MacLaren	A.Coningham †	England	v	Australia	Melbourne	1894-95
T.W.Hayward	A.E.E.Vogler	England	v	South Africa	The Oval	1907
W.Bardsley	M.W.Tate	Australia	v	England	Leeds	1926
H.Sutcliffe	F.T.Badcock	England	v	New Zealand	Christchurch	1932-33
T.S.Worthington	E.L.McCormick	England	v	Australia	Brisbane[2]	1936-37
C.C.Hunte	Fazal Mahmood	West Indies	v	Pakistan	Port-of-Spain	1957-58
E.J.Barlow	G.D.McKenzie	South Africa	v	Australia	Durban[2]	1966-67
R.C.Fredericks	S.Abid Ali	West Indies	v	India	Port-of-Spain	1970-71
K.R.Stackpole §	R.J.Hadlee	Australia	v	New Zealand	Auckland	1973-74
S.M.Gavaskar	G.G.Arnold	India	v	England	Birmingham	1974
S.S.Naik §	A.M.E.Roberts	India	v	West Indies	Calcutta	1974-75
J.F.M.Morrison	G.G.Arnold	New Zealand	v	England	Christchurch	1974-75
Mohsin Khan	Kapil Dev	Pakistan	v	India	Jullundur	1983-84
S.M.Gavaskar	M.D.Marshall	India	v	West Indies	Calcutta	1983-84

S.M.Gavaskar	Imran Khan	India	v	Pakistan	Jaipur	1986-87
W.V.Raman	R.J.Hadlee	India	v	New Zealand	Napier	1989-90
S.J.Cook †	Kapil Dev	South Africa	v	India	Durban[2]	1992-93

† on debut. § in his last Test.

BATSMEN DISMISSED FOR A 'PAIR'

FOUR TIMES

B.S.Chandrasekhar (India): v NZ 1975-76; v E 1976-77; v A 1977-78 (twice).

THREE TIMES

R.Peel (England):v A 1894-95 (twice), 1896.
R.W.Blair (New Zealand): v WI 1955-56; v E 1962-63; v SA 1963-64.
D.L.Underwood (England):v WI 1966; v A 1974-75; v WI 1976.
B.S.Bedi (India):v E 1974; v WI 1974-75; v E 1976-77.
A.G.Hurst (Australia):v E 1978-79 (twice); v P 1978-79.
C.E.L.Ambrose (West Indies):v E 1988; v P 1990-91; v E 1991.
D.K.Morrison (New Zealand) v A 1987-88; v SL 1990-91; v A 1993-94.

TWICE

AUSTRALIA: K.D.Mackay v E 1956; v I 1959-60. G.D.McKenzie v SA 1963-64; v E 1968. J.W.Gleeson v SA 1969-70; v E 1970-71. W.M.Clark v WI 1977-78 (twice). R.M.Hogg v I 1979-80; v WI 1984-85. R.G.Holland v E 1985; v NZ 1985-86. M.E.Waugh v SL 1992-93 (twice).

ENGLAND: A.V.Bedser v A 1948; v WI 1950. D.L.Amiss v A 1968, 1974-75. P.I.Pocock v WI 1984 (twice). N.A.Foster v WI 1985-86; v P 1987-88. D.E.Malcolm v NZ 1990; v P 1992.

SOUTH AFRICA: L.J.Tancred v E 1907, 1912. Q.McMillan v A 1931-32 (twice). R.J.Crisp v A 1935-36 (twice).

WEST INDIES: C.A.Roach v E 1929-30, 1933. A.L.Valentine v E 1950, 1953-54. A.I.Kallicharran v E 1973-74; v NZ 1979-80.

INDIA: M.Amarnath v WI 1983-84 (twice). Maninder Singh v P 1982-83; v WI 1987-88.

PAKISTAN: Aaqib Javed v A 1989-90; v E 1992.

SRI LANKA: M.S.Ataputta v I 1990-91; v I 1993-94.

ONCE

AUSTRALIA: P.S.McDonnell v E 1882-83. T.W.Garrett v E 1882-83. E.Evans v E 1886. P.G.McShane v E 1887-88. A.C.Bannerman v E 1888. M.A.Noble v E 1899. S.E.Gregory v E 1899. C.E.McLeod v E 1901-02. J.Darling v E 1902. J.J.Kelly v E 1902. H.Trumble v E 1903-04. V.T.Trumper v E 1907-08. J.V.Saunders v E 1907-08. C.V.Grimmett v E 1930. W.A.S.Oldfield v SA 1931-32. J.H.W.Fingleton v E 1932-33. V.Y.Richardson v E 1932-33. C.L.Badcock v E 1938. I.W.Johnson v E 1946-47. J.Moroney v E 1950-51. J.B.Iverson v E 1950-51. L.V.Maddocks v E 1956. R.N.Harvey v E 1956. A.T.W.Grout v WI 1960-61. R.Benaud v E 1961. A.N.Connolly v WI 1968-69. R.Edwards v E 1972. K.R.Stackpole v NZ 1973-74. G.Dymock v E 1974-75. R.W.Marsh v E 1977. J.R.Thomson v E 1977. C.S.Serjeant v I 1977-78. A.L.Mann v I 1977-78. D.W.Hookes v P 1979-80. G.M.Wood v NZ 1980-81. M.R.Whitney v E 1981. B.Yardley v P 1982-83. R.J.Bright v P 1982-83. C.G.Rackemann v WI 1984-85. K.J.Hughes v WI 1984-85. M.G.Hughes v E 1986-87. D.M.Jones v P 1988-89. B.A.Reid v WI 1990-91. I.A.Healy v WI 1992-93. A.R.Border v WI 1992-93. J.L.Langer v NZ 1992-93. M.A.Taylor v P 1994-95. P.E.McIntyre v A 1994-95. B.P.Julian v W 1994-95. C.J.McDermott v P 1995-96. G.D.McGrath v P 1995-96.

ENGLAND: G.F.Grace v A 1880. W.Attewell v A 1891-92. G.A.Lohmann v SA 1895-96. E.G.Arnold v A 1903-04. A.E.Knight v A 1903-04. E.G.Hayes v SA 1905-06. M.C.Bird v SA 1909-10. H.Strudwick v A 1921. P.Holmes v SA 1927-28. C.I.J.Smith v WI 1934-35. J.T.Ikin v A 1946-47. J.J.Warr v A 1950-51. F.Ridgway v I 1951-52. R.T.Spooner v SA 1955. J.H.Wardle v A 1956. F.S.Trueman v A 1958-59. T.E.Bailey v A 1958-59. G.Pullar v P 1961-62. M.J.K.Smith v I 1961-62. J.T.Murray v P 1967. B.W.Luckhurst v P 1971. A.P.E.Knott v NZ 1973. G.G.Arnold v A 1974-75. G.A.Gooch v A 1975. A.Ward v WI 1976. J.C.Balderstone v WI 1976. M.Hendrick v NZ 1977-78. R.A.Woolmer v A 1981.

I.T.Botham v A 1981. E.E.Hemmings v A 1982-83. N.G.Cowans v I 1984-85. D.J.Capel v P 1987-88. W.Larkins v WI 1989-90. R.J.Bailey v WI 1989-90. C.C.Lewis v A 1993. P.C.R.Tufnell v A 1994-95. J.P.Crawley v A 1994-95. P.A.J.DeFreitas v A 1994-95. M.R.Ramprakash v W 1995. R.K.Illingworth v W 1995.

SOUTH AFRICA: C.S.Wimble v E 1891-92. J.T.Willoughby v E 1895-96. J.J.Kotze v A 1902-03. P.S.Twentyman-Jones v A 1902-03. A.E.E.Vogler v A 1910-11. T.A.Ward v A 1912. C.B.Llewellyn v E 1912. P.T.Lewis v E 1913-14. J.L.Cox v E 1913-14. C.D.Dixon v E 1913-14. G.A.L.Hearne v E 1922-23. A.E.Hall v E 1922-23. F.Nicholson v A 1935-36. X.C.Balaskas v A 1935-36. C.N.McCarthy v E 1948-49. D.J.McGlew v E 1955. W.R.Endean v E 1955. P.S.Heine v E 1956-57. C.Wesley v E 1960. M.A.Seymour v A 1969-70. A.A.Donald v WI 1991-92. C.R.Matthews v E 1994. D.J.Richardson v P 1994-95.

WEST INDIES: C.R.Browne v E 1929-30. H.C.Griffith v E 1933. E.E.Achong v E 1934-35. J.Trim v A 1951-52. A.P.Binns v A 1954-55. O.G.Smith v A 1954-55. S.Ramadhin v E 1957. E.D.Weekes v E 1957. F.C.M.Alexander v E 1957. L.R.Gibbs v P 1958-59. F.M.M.Worrell v A 1960-61. J.S.Solomon v I 1961-62. J.L.Hendriks v E 1966. W.W.Hall v E 1967-68. D.L.Murray v I 1974-75. C.G.Greenidge v A 1975-76. J.Garner v P 1976-77. D.A.Murray v P 1980-81. A.L.Logie v I 1983-84. M.A.Holding v A 1984-85. P.J.L.Dujon v P 1986-87. A.H.Gray v P 1986-87. D.Williams v A 1992-93. K.L.T.Arthurton v A 1992-93. J.R.Murray v P 1992-93.

NEW ZEALAND: K.C.James v E 1929-30. F.T.Badcock v E 1929-30. J.Cowie v E 1937. C.G.Rowe v A 1945-46. L.A.Butterfield v A 1945-46. L.S.M.Miller v SA 1953-54. M.B.Poore v E 1954-55. I.A.Colquhoun v E 1954-55. J.A.Hayes v E 1954-55. A.R.MacGibbon v I 1955-56. H.B.Cave v WI 1955-56. N.S.Harford v E 1958. R.C.Motz v SA 1961-62. M.J.F.Shrimpton v SA 1963-64. A.E.Dick v P 1964-65. G.A.Bartlett v E 1965-66. T.W.Jarvis v P 1972-73. W.K.Lees v E 1977-78. B.P.Bracewell v E 1978. B.L.Cairns v A 1980-81. B.A.Edgar v A 1980-81. G.B.Troup v I 1980-81. J.V.Coney v A 1981-82. I.D.S.Smith v A 1981-82. J.G.Bracewell v P 1984-85. K.R.Rutherford v WI 1984-85. J.G.Wright v E 1986. C.M.Kuggeleijn v I 1988-89. M.C.Snedden v I 1988-89. B.R.Hartland v E 1991-92. M.L.Su'a v P 1992-93. S.B.Doull v W 1994-95. D.J.Nash v SL 1994-95. C.Z.Harris N v W 1995-96.

INDIA: V.S.Hazare v E 1951-52. G.S.Ramchand v E 1952. Pankaj Roy v E 1952. P.G.Joshi v WI 1952-53. C.V.Gadkari v WI 1952-53. N.S.Tamhane v WI 1958-59. Surendranath v E 1959. R.B.Desai v A 1959-60. D.N.Sardesai v WI 1961-62. M.L.Jaisimha v NZ 1969-70. E.A.S.Prasanna v WI 1974-75. F.M.Engineer v WI 1974-75. D.B.Vengsarkar v WI 1978-79. Yashpal Sharma v A 1979-80. R.M.H.Binny v P 1979-80. D.R.Doshi v P 1982-83. S.Venkataraghavan v WI 1982-83. R.G.Patel v NZ 1988-89.

PAKISTAN: M.E.Z.Ghazali v E 1954. Nasim-ul-Ghani v WI 1957-58. Wazir Mohammad v WI 1957-58. Imtiaz Ahmed v E 1961-62. Javed Burki v NZ 1964-65. Salim Altaf v A 1976-77. Iqbal Qasim v E 1978. Majid Khan v A 1978-79. Wasim Bari v A 1978-79. Sikander Bakht v A 1978-79. Mudassar Nazar v E 1982. Wasim Akram v SL 1985-86. Waqar Younis v NZ 1990-91. Saeed Anwar v WI 1990-91. Aamer Sohail v NZ 1992-93. Mushtaq Ahmed v A 1994-95. Manzoor Elahi v Z 1994-95.

SRI LANKA: B.R.Jurangpathy v I 1986-87. R.G.de Alwis v I 1986-87. R.J.Ratnayake v I 1990-91. G.F.Labrooy v I 1990-91. A.Ranatunga v P 1991-92. S.D.Anurasiri v P 1991-92. C.I.Dunusinghe v N 1994-95.

ZIMBABWE: D.H.Brain v I 1992-93. S.G.Peall v P 1993-94. G.W.Flower v P 1993-94.

FASTEST 'PAIRS' *Timed from the start of first innings to dismissal in the second innings*

120 mins	M.E.Z.Ghazali	Pakistan	v	England	Manchester	1954
124 mins	R.N.Harvey	Australia	v	England	Manchester	1956
164 mins	Pankaj Roy	India	v	England	Manchester	1952

BATSMEN DISMISSED FOR A 'KING PAIR'

A.E.E.Vogler	South Africa	v	Australia	Sydney	1910-11
T.A.Ward	South Africa	v	Australia	Manchester	1912
R.J.Crisp	South Africa	v	Australia	Durban[2]	1935-36
C.Wesley	South Africa	v	England	Nottingham	1960
G.B.Troup	New Zealand	v	India	Wellington	1980-81
D.J.Richardson	South Africa	v	Pakistan	Johannesburg[3]	1994-95

DISMISSED FOR A 'PAIR' BY THE SAME FIELDING COMBINATION

R.Peel	st Jarvis b Turner	England	v	Australia	Sydney	1894-95
J.Darling	c Braund b Barnes	Australia	v	England	Sheffield	1902
P.T.Lewis	c Woolley b Barnes	South Africa	v	England	Durban[1]	1913-14
P.G.Joshi	c Worrell b Valentine	India	v	West Indies	Bridgetown	1952-53
K.D.Mackay	c Oakman b Laker	Australia	v	England	Manchester	1956
Maninder Singh	c Richardson b Walsh	India	v	West Indies	Mumbai[3]	1987-88

THREE 'PAIRS' IN A MATCH BY THE SAME TEAM

M.B.Poore, I.A.Colquhoun, J A.Hayes	New Zealand	v	England	Auckland	1954-55
D L.Amiss, D L.Underwood, G G.Arnold	England	v	Australia	Adelaide	1974-75
Majid Khan, Wasim Bari, Sikander Bakht	Pakistan	v	Australia	Perth	1978-79
M.S.Ataputta, R.J.Ratnayake, G.F.Labrooy	Sri Lanka	v	India	Chandigarh	1990-91

MOST CONSECUTIVE 'DUCKS'

FIVE					
R.G.Holland	(including two pairs	Australia	v	England	1985
	in consecutive Tests)	Australia	v	New Zealand	1985-86
FOUR					
R.Peel	(2 pairs in consecutive Tests)	England	v	Australia	1894-95
R.J.Crisp	(2 pairs in consecutive Tests)	South Africa	v	Australia	1935-36
Pankaj Roy	(including one pair)	India	v	England	1952
L.S.M.Miller	(including one pair)	New Zealand	v	South Africa	1953-54
R.B.Desai		India	v	England	1959
	(including one pair)	India	v	Australia	1959-60
W.M.Clark	(2 pairs in consecutive Tests)	Australia	v	West Indies	1977-78
P.I.Pocock	(2 pairs in consecutive Tests)	England	v	West Indies	1984
N.A.Foster	(including one pair)	England	v	Australia	1985
		England	v	West Indies	1985-86
R.G.de Alwis	(including one pair)	Sri Lanka	v	India	1986-87
		Sri Lanka	v	Australia	1987-88
M.E.Waugh	(2 pairs in consecutive Tests)	Australia	v	Sri Lanka	1992-93
M.L.Su'a	(including one pair)	New Zealand	v	Sri Lanka	1992-93
		New Zealand	v	Pakistan	1992-93
		New Zealand	v	Australia	1992-93
D.K.Morrison	(including one pair)	New Zealand	v	Australia	1993-94

R.J.Crisp was dismissed four times in five balls.

MOST 'DUCKS' IN A SERIES

					Innings	
SIX	A.G.Hurst	Australia	v	England	12	1978-79
FIVE	Pankaj Roy	India	v	England	7	1952
	R.C.Motz	New Zealand	v	South Africa	9	1961-62
	W.M.Clark	Australia	v	West Indies	7	1977-78
	M.Amarnath	India	v	West Indies	6	1983-84

MOST INNINGS BEFORE FIRST 'DUCK'

75	P.A.de Silva	Sri Lanka	1984	to	1994-95
58	C.H.Lloyd	West Indies	1966-67	to	1973-74
51	A.K.Davidson	Australia	1953	to	1961
46	B.F.Butcher	West Indies	1958-59	to	1966-67
44	M.J.Slater	Australia	1993	to	1994-95
41	R.N.Harvey	Australia	1947-48	to	1953
41	G.S.Sobers	West Indies	1953-54	to	1958-59
41	K.D.Ghavri	India	1974-75	to	1979-80
40	W.H.Ponsford	Australia	1924-25	to	1932-33
40	Sadiq Mohammad	Pakistan	1969-70	to	1976-77

MOST CONSECUTIVE INNINGS WITHOUT A 'DUCK'

119	D.I.Gower	England	1982	to	1990-91
96	R.B.Richardson	West Indies	1984-85	to	1991
89	A.R.Border	Australia	1982-83	to	1988-89
78	K.F.Barrington	England	1962	to	1967-68
75	P.A.de Silva	Sri Lanka	1984	to	1994-95
74	C.H.Lloyd	West Indies	1976	to	1984
72	H.W.Taylor	South Africa	1912	to	1931-32
72	G.M.Turner	New Zealand	1968-69	to	1982-83
68	K.D.Walters	Australia	1969-70	to	1976-77
67	W.R.Hammond	England	1929	to	1936
67	G.Boycott	England	1969	to	1978-79
66	H.A.Gomes	West Indies	1977-78	to	1984-85
62	A.P.E.Knott	England	1974	to	1981
62	G.R.Marsh	Australia	1986-87	to	1990-91

FEWEST 'DUCKS' IN A CAREER *(Qualification: 50 innings)*

Ducks	Innings					
0	44	J.W.Burke	Australia	1950-51	to	1958-59
0	40	R.A.Duff	Australia	1901-02	to	1907-08
0	37	R.J.Christiani	West Indies	1947-48	to	1953-54
0	37	J.C.Adams	West Indies	1991-92	to	1995-96
0	35	Waqar Hassan	Pakistan	1952-53	to	1959-60
0	34	B.D.Julien	West Indies	1973	to	1976-77
1	74	C.L.Walcott	West Indies	1947-48	to	1959-60
1	73	G.M.Turner	New Zealand	1968-69	to	1982-83
1	69	A.L.Hassett	Australia	1938	to	1953
1	61	A.K.Davidson	Australia	1953	to	1962-63
1	56	P.E.Richardson	England	1956	to	1963
1	55	C.G.Macartney	Australia	1907-08	to	1926
1	53	G.M.Ritchie	Australia	1982-83	to	1986-87
1	48	W.M.Ponsford	Australia	1924-25	to	1934
1	48	E.D.Solkar	India	1969-70	to	1976-77
1	48	W.B.Phillips	Australia	1983-84	to	1985-86
1	46	S.J.Snooke	South Africa	1905-06	to	1922-23
1	45	R.W.Barber	England	1960	to	1968
1	43	J.E.Cheetham	South Africa	1948-49	to	1955
1	42	U.C.Hathurusingha	Sri Lanka	1990-91	to	1995-96
1	41	R.G.Pollock	South Africa	1963-64	to	1969-70
1	40	A.Shrewsbury	England	1881-82	to	1893
2	84	H.Sutcliffe	England	1924	to	1935
2	83	C.C.McDonald	Australia	1951-52	to	1961
2	78	Saeed Ahmed	Pakistan	1957-58	to	1972-73
2	76	H.W.Taylor	South Africa	1912	to	1931-32
2	74	A.H.Jones	New Zealand	1986-87	to	1994-95
2	66	C.Washbrook	England	1937	to	1956
2	57	K.D.Ghavri	India	1974-75	to	1980-81
2	56	J.B.Stollmeyer	West Indies	1939	to	1954-55
2	53	G.R.J.Matthews	Australia	1983-84	to	1992-93
2	52	N.J.Contractor	India	1955-56	to	1961-62
2	50	P.Willey	England	1976	to	1986
3	129	M.A.Taylor	Australia	1988-89	to	1995-96
3	103	A.J.Stewart	England	1989-90	to	1996
3	93	G.R.Marsh	Australia	1985-86	to	1991-92
3	85	J.V.Coney	New Zealand	1973-74	to	1986-87
3	83	A.W.Nourse	South Africa	1902-03	to	1924
3	80	B.Mitchell	South Africa	1930-31	to	1948-49

3	80	G.A.Hick	England	1991	to	1996
3	79	Mohsin Khan	Pakistan	1977-78	to	1986-87
3	78	B.F.Butcher	West Indies	1958-59	to	1969
3	70	G.N.Yallop	Australia	1975-76	to	1984-85
4	175	C.H.Lloyd	West Indies	1966-67	to	1984-85
4	140	W.R.Hammond	England	1927-28	to	1946-47
4	125	K.D.Walters	Australia	1965-66	to	1980-81
4	102	J.B.Hobbs	England	1907-08	to	1930
4	101	M.Azharuddin	India	1984-85	to	1996
4	100	Mushtaq Mohammad	Pakistan	1958-59	to	1978-79
5	138	L.Hutton	England	1937	to	1954-55
5	131	K.F.Barrington	England	1955	to	1968
6	189	Javed Miandad	Pakistan	1976-77	to	1993-94
7	202	D.I.Gower	England	1978	to	1990-91

MOST 'DUCKS'

MOST 'DUCKS'	Country	0's	Tests	A	E	SA	WI	NZ	I	P	SL	Z
D.K.Morrison	New Zealand	**24**	47	7	4	1	1	-	2	6	3	-
B.S.Chandrasekhar	India	**23**	58	6	8	-	4	3	-	2	-	-
B.S.Bedi	India	**20**	67	11	1	-	7	1	-	-	-	-
C.A.Walsh	West Indies	**20**	82	7	5	-	-	-	2	5	1	-
Wasim Bari	Pakistan	**19**	81	11	4	-	2	-	2	-	-	-
D.L.Underwood	England	**19**	86	8	-	-	7	-	2	1	1	-
J.Garner	West Indies	**18**	59	5	5	-	-	4	-	4	-	-
K.R.Rutherford	New Zealand	**17**	56	3	3	2	3	-	1	2	3	-
T.G.Evans	England	**17**	91	5	-	6	1	3	1	1	-	-
J.A.Snow	England	**16**	49	6	-	1	7	-	1	1	-	-
J.E.Emburey	England	**16**	65	5	-	-	6	-	2	1	2	-
M.W.Gatting	England	**16**	79	6	-	-	2	2	3	3	-	-
D.C.Boon	Australia	**16**	107	-	5	-	3	3	-	2	3	-
Kapil Dev	India	**16**	131	3	4	-	4	2	-	2	1	-
E.A.S.Prasanna	India	**15**	49	7	4	-	2	2	-	-	-	-
M.A.Holding	West Indies	**15**	60	5	4	-	-	2	4	-	-	-
G.D.McKenzie	Australia	**15**	60	-	7	3	1	-	4	-	-	-
I.T.Botham	England	**15**	102	11	-	-	1	1	1	1	-	-
D.B.Vengsarkar	India	**15**	116	1	3	-	5	3	-	2	1	-
D.R.Doshi	India	**14**	33	4	4	-	-	1	-	5	-	-
R.M.Hogg	Australia	**14**	38	-	7	-	2	1	3	1	-	-
S.Ramadhin	West Indies	**14**	43	7	6	-	-	1	-	-	-	-
Pankaj Roy	India	**14**	43	8	1	-	2	1	-	2	-	-
J.R.Thomson	Australia	**14**	43	-	5	-	6	-	2	1	-	-
D.W.Randall	England	**14**	47	6	-	-	1	2	3	2	-	-
L.R.Gibbs	West Indies	**14**	79	5	5	-	-	-	1	3	-	-
M.D.Marshall	West Indies	**14**	81	3	6	-	-	1	1	3	-	-
D.E.Malcolm	England	**13**	36	3	-	-	3	2	2	-	-	-
T.M.Alderman	Australia	**13**	41	-	4	-	6	-	-	2	1	-
C.G.Borde	India	**13**	55	4	4	-	4	-	-	1	-	-
S.Venkataraghavan	India	**13**	57	5	2	-	5	1	-	-	-	-
C.E.L.Ambrose	West Indies	**13**	61	4	6	-	-	-	-	3	-	-
F.E.Woolley	England	**13**	64	7	-	6	-	-	-	-	-	-
J.B.Statham	England	**13**	70	5	-	5	2	-	-	1	-	-
C.J.McDermott	Australia	**13**	71	-	4	-	3	-	3	3	-	-
I.A.Healy	Australia	**13**	79	-	1	1	7	2	-	1	1	-
G.S.Chappell	Australia	**13**	87	-	5	-	3	3	1	1	-	-
R.W.Marsh	Australia	**13**	96	-	6	-	1	2	1	3	-	-

G.A.Gooch	England	**13**	118	5	-	-	3	4	1	-	-	-
R.W.Blair	New Zealand	**12**	19	-	6	4	2	-	-	-	-	-
R.C.Motz	New Zealand	**12**	32	-	2	6	-	-	1	3	-	-
A.L.Valentine	West Indies	**12**	36	5	4	-	-	1	2	-	-	-
R.A.McLean	South Africa	**12**	40	3	6	-	-	3	-	-	-	-
J.G.Bracewell	New Zealand	**12**	41	3	3	-	-	-	1	4	1	-
S.E.Gregory	Australia	**12**	58	-	11	1	-	-	-	-	-	-
M.A.Atherton	England	**12**	62	3	-	2	4	1	1	1	-	-
M.Amarnath	India	**12**	[illegible]	[illegible]	3	[illegible]	[illegible]	[illegible]	[illegible]	1	[illegible]	[illegible]
Wasim Akram	Pakistan	**12**	70	-	1	-	5	1	2	-	2	1
S.R.Waugh	Australia	**12**	81	-	5	1	1	2	1	2	-	-
R.J.Hadlee	New Zealand	**12**	86	3	5	-	1	-	3	2	-	-
R.G.D.Willis	England	**12**	90	5	-	-	3	1	2	-	1	-
G.S.Sobers	West Indies	**12**	93	6	1	-	-	2	2	1	-	-
S.M.Gavaskar	India	**12**	125	3	2	-	5	-	-	1	1	-
J.W.Gleeson	Australia	**11**	29	-	5	3	2	-	1	-	-	-
Maninder Singh	India	**11**	35	-	1	-	4	-	-	5	1	-
E.J.Chatfield	New Zealand	**11**	43	5	-	-	1	-	3	2	-	-
M.J.K.Smith	England	**11**	50	2	-	2	2	2	3	-	-	-
A.V.Bedser	England	**11**	51	5	-	2	3	1	-	-	-	-
A.T.W.Grout	Australia	**11**	51	-	4	2	3	-	1	1	-	-
F.M.M.Worrell	West Indies	**11**	51	8	2	-	-	-	1	-	-	-
D.M.Jones	Australia	**11**	52	-	3	-	1	2	2	3	-	-
V.L.Manjrekar	India	**11**	55	4	-	-	5	1	-	1	-	-
A.Ranatunga	Sri Lanka	**11**	61	1	1	-	-	1	2	6	-	-
F.S.Trueman	England	**11**	67	6	-	2	1	1	1	-	-	-
A.R.Border	Australia	**11**	156	-	3	-	4	2	2	-	-	-
A.G.Hurst	Australia	**10**	12	-	6	-	-	-	2	2	-	-
P.I.Pocock	England	**10**	25	-	-	-	7	-	3	-	-	-
S.L.Boock	New Zealand	**10**	28	2	-	-	3	-	-	5	-	-
J.Briggs	England	**10**	33	9	-	1	-	-	-	-	-	-
Fazal Mahmood	Pakistan	**10**	34	3	-	-	5	-	2	-	-	-
A.F.A.Lilley	England	**10**	35	9	-	1	-	-	-	-	-	-
A.A.Mallett	Australia	**10**	38	-	4	-	3	1	1	1	-	-
G.R.Dilley	England	**10**	39	2	-	-	5	1	1	1	-	-
P.A.J.DeFreitas	England	**10**	44	4	-	-	4	1	-	1	-	-
S.K.Warne	Australia	**10**	44	-	3	1	4	-	1	1	-	-
I.W.Johnson	Australia	**10**	45	-	6	1	1	-	1	1	-	-
Intikhab Alam	Pakistan	**10**	47	4	1	-	1	3	1	-	-	-
Iqbal Qasim	Pakistan	**10**	47	5	-	-	2	-	3	-	-	-
W.W.Hall	West Indies	**10**	48	2	4	-	-	-	2	2	-	-
D.L.Amiss	England	**10**	50	7	-	-	-	-	2	1	-	-
C.L.Hooper	West Indies	**10**	52	5	2	-	-	-	-	3	-	-
M.G.Hughes	Australia	**10**	53	-	3	1	5	-	1	-	-	-
R.W.Taylor	England	**10**	57	3	-	-	-	3	2	2	-	-
A.I.Kallicharran	West Indies	**10**	66	4	1	-	-	3	2	-	-	-
K.J.Hughes	Australia	**10**	70	-	3	-	4	1	1	1	-	-
I.M.Chappell	Australia	**10**	75	-	4	4	-	-	2	-	-	-
Zaheer Abbas	Pakistan	**10**	78	2	3	-	2	2	1	-	-	-
Saleem Malik	Pakistan	**10**	90	2	1	-	1	4	2	-	-	-
G.R.Viswanath	India	**10**	91	3	1	-	1	2	-	3	-	-
C.G.Greenidge	West Indies	**10**	96	3	5	-	-	-	2	-	-	-
G.Boycott	England	**10**	108	3	-	1	4	2	-	-	-	-
D.L.Haynes	West Indies	**10**	116	1	2	-	-	3	1	3	-	-
Most 'ducks' for Zimbabwe:												
H.H.Streak	Zimbabwe	**6**	12	-	-	1	-	-	-	4	1	-

Partnerships

HIGHEST PARTNERSHIP FOR EACH WICKET

Wkt	Runs	Partners	Team		Opponent	Venue	Season
1st	413	M.H.Mankad (231), Pankaj Roy (173)	IND	v	NZ	Chennai[2]	1955-56
2nd	451	W.H.Ponsford (266), D.G.Bradman (244)	AUST	v	ENG	The Oval	1934
3rd	467	A.H.Jones (186), M.D.Crowe (299)	NZ	v	SL	Wellington	1990-91
4th	411	P.B.H.May (285*), M.C.Cowdrey (154)	ENG	v	WI	Birmingham	1957
5th	405	S.G.Barnes (234), D.G.Bradman (234)	AUST	v	ENG	Sydney	1946-47
6th	346	J.H.W.Fingleton (136), D.G.Bradman (270)	AUST	v	ENG	Melbourne	1936-37
7th	347	D.S.Atkinson (219), C.C.Depeiza (122)	WI	v	AUST	Bridgetown	1954-55
8th	246	L.E.G.Ames (137), G.O.B.Allen (122)	ENG	v	NZ	Lord's	1931
9th	190	Asif Iqbal (146), Intikhab Alam (51)	PAK	v	ENG	The Oval	1967
10th	151	B.F.Hastings (110), R.O.Collinge (68*)	NZ	v	PAK	Auckland	1972-73

PARTNERSHIPS OF 300 AND OVER

Runs	Wkt	Partners	Match	Venue	Season
467	3rd	A.H.Jones (186), M.D.Crowe (299)	NZ v SL	Wellington	1990-91
451	2nd	W.H.Ponsford (266), D.G.Bradman (244)	AUST v ENG	The Oval	1938
451	3rd	Mudassar Nazar (231), Javed Miandad (280*)	PAK v IND	Hyderabad	1982-83
446	2nd	C.C.Hunte (260), G.S.Sobers (365*)	WI v PAK	Kingston	1957-58
413	1st	M.H.Mankad (231), Pankaj Roy (173)	IND v NZ	Chennai[2]	1955-56
411	4th	P.B.H.May (285*), M.C.Cowdrey (154)	ENG v WI	Birmingham	1957
405	5th	S.G.Barnes (234), D.G.Bradman (234)	AUST v ENG	Sydney	1946-47
399	4th	G.S.Sobers (226), F.M.M.Worrell (197*)	WI v E	Bridgetown	1959-60
397	3rd	Qasim Omar (206), Javed Miandad (203*)	PAK v SL	Faisalabad	1985-86
388	4th	W.H.Ponsford (181), D.G.Bradman (304)	AUST v ENG	Leeds	1934
387	1st	G.M.Turner (259), T.W.Jarvis (182)	NZ v WI	Georgetown	1971-72
382	2nd	L.Hutton (364), M.Leyland (187)	ENG v AUST	The Oval	1938
382	1st	W.M.Lawry (210), R.B.Simpson (201)	AUST v WI	Bridgetown	1964-65
370	3rd	W.J.Edrich (189), D.C.S.Compton (208)	ENG v SA	Lord's	1947
369	2nd	J.H.Edrich (310*), K.F.Barrington (163)	ENG v NZ	Leeds	1965
359	1st	L.Hutton (158), C.Washbrook (195)	ENG v SA	Johannesburg[2]	1948-49
351	2nd	G.A.Gooch (196), D.I.Gower (157)	ENG v AUST	The Oval	1985
350	4th	Mushtaq Mohammad (201), Asif Iqbal (175)	PAK v NZ	Dunedin	1972-73
347	7th	D.S.Atkinson (219), C.C.Depeiza (122)	WI v AUST	Bridgetown	1954-55
346	6th	J.H.W.Fingleton (136), D.G.Bradman (270)	AUST v ENG	Melbourne	1936-37
344*	2nd	S.M.Gavaskar (182*), D.B.Vengsarkar (157*)	IND v WI	Calcutta	1978-79
341	3rd	E.J.Barlow (201), R.G.Pollock (175)	SA v AUST	Adelaide	1963-64
338	3rd	E.D.Weekes (206), F.M.M.Worrell (167)	WI v ENG	Port-of-Spain	1953-54
336	4th	W.M.Lawry (151), K.D.Walters (242)	AUST v WI	Sydney	1968-69
332*	5th	A.R.Border (200*), S.R.Waugh (157*)	AUST v ENG	Leeds	1993
331	2nd	R.T.Robinson (148), D.I.Gower (215)	ENG v AUST	Birmingham	1985
329	1st	G.R.Marsh (138), M.A.Taylor (219)	AUST v ENG	Nottingham	1989
323	1st	J.B.Hobbs (178), W.Rhodes (179)	ENG v AUST	Melbourne	1911-12
322	4th	Javed Miandad (153*), Saleem Malik (165)	PAK v ENG	Birmingham	1992
319	3rd	A.Melville (189), A.D.Nourse (149)	SA v ENG	Nottingham	1947
316†	3rd	G.R.Viswanath (222), Yashpal Sharma (140)	IND v ENG	Chennai[1]	1981-82
308	7th	Waqar Hassan (189), Imtiaz Ahmed (209)	PAK v IND	Lahore[1]	1955-56
308	3rd	R.B.Richardson (154), I.V.A.Richards (178)	WI v AUST	St John's	1983-84
308	3rd	G.A.Gooch (333), A.J.Lamb (139)	ENG v IND	Lord's	1990
303	3rd	I.V.A.Richards (232), A.I.Kallicharran (97)	WI v ENG	Nottingham	1976
303	3rd	M.A.Atherton (135), R.A.Smith (175)	ENG v WI	St John's	1993-94
301	2nd	A.R.Morris (182), D.G.Bradman (173*)	AUST v ENG	Leeds	1948

† 415 runs were scored for this wicket in two separate partnerships, D.B.Vengsarkar retiring hurt and being succeeded by Yashpal Sharma after 99 runs had been added.

MOST CENTURY PARTNERSHIPS IN AN INNINGS

FOUR		Opponents		
England	382 (2nd), 135 (3rd), 215 (6th), 106 (7th)	Australia	The Oval	1938
West Indies	267 (4th), 101 (6th), 118 (7th), 106 (9th)	India	Delhi	1948-49
Pakistan	152 (1st), 112 (2nd), 154 (3rd), 121 (4th)	West Indies	Bridgetown	1957-58
India	144 (3rd), 172 (4th), 109 (5th), 102 (6th)	West Indies	Kanpur	1978-79

SUMMARY OF CENTURY PARTNERSHIPS

Country	1st	2nd	3rd	4th	5th	6th	7th	8th	9th	10th	Total
Australia	73	109	107	103	73	42	24	12	7	2	552
England	135	132	115	109	70	71	35	12	7	3	689
South Africa	33	22	31	24	12	14	13	5	1	1	156
West Indies	44	61	64	65	46	47	15	1	4	1	348
New Zealand	26	24	29	21	29	13	10	5	2	2	161
India	37	48	53	44	31	24	15	7	7	1	267
Pakistan	26	31	43	35	24	19	8	4	3	2	195
Sri Lanka	4	4	13	8	9	6	2	-	-	-	46
Zimbabwe	3	4	1	3	-	2	-	-	-	-	13
Total	381	435	456	412	294	238	122	46	31	12	2427

BATSMEN SHARING IN MOST CENTURY PARTNERSHIPS

		Total	1st	2nd	3rd	4th	5th	6th	7th	8th	9th	10th
A.R.Border	Australia	**62**	-	2	14	20	16	8	1	1	-	-
S.M.Gavaskar	India	**58**	22	18	8	6	2	1	-	-	1	-
Javed Miandad	Pakistan	**50**	-	2	22	15	8	3	-	-	-	-
G.Boycott	England	**47**	20	8	9	8	-	2	-	-	-	-
C.G.Greenidge	West Indies	**46**	22	9	5	4	2	3	1	-	-	-
G.S.Chappell	Australia	**44**	-	2	15	13	11	2	1	-	-	-
I.V.A.Richards	West Indies	**44**	-	11	12	12	5	2	1	1	-	-
G.S.Sobers	West Indies	**43**	-	3	4	12	12	10	2	-	-	-
D.C.Boon	Australia	**42**	6	13	16	5	1	1	-	-	-	-
M.C.Cowdrey	England	**42**	5	9	6	13	4	3	1	-	1	-
G.A.Gooch	England	**41**	18	11	7	2	2	1	-	-	-	-
L.Hutton	England	**41**	17	13	7	1	-	2	1	-	-	-
C.H.Lloyd	West Indies	**41**	-	-	6	14	9	10	1	-	1	-
D.L.Haynes	West Indies	**39**	18	14	5	1	-	1	-	-	-	-
D.I.Gower	England	**38**	-	7	10	11	5	3	2	-	-	-
K.F.Barrington	England	**35**	-	6	10	14	4	1	-	-	-	-
D.G.Bradman	Australia	**35**	-	14	11	3	6	1	-	-	-	-
R.B.Kanhai	West Indies	**34**	2	9	11	7	3	2	-	-	-	-
W.R.Hammond	England	**33**	1	6	12	11	2	1	-	-	-	-
H.Sutcliffe	England	**33**	21	10	1	-	-	1	-	-	-	-
J.H.Edrich	England	**32**	9	11	6	5	1	-	-	-	-	-
R.N.Harvey	Australia	**32**	-	6	13	9	3	1	-	-	-	-
J.B.Hobbs	England	**32**	24	6	1	-	-	-	1	-	-	-
I.M.Chappell	Australia	**30**	-	18	8	1	1	2	-	-	-	-
D.C.S.Compton	England	**30**	-	-	14	7	7	1	-	1	-	-
D.B.Vengsarkar	India	**30**	-	9	9	9	1	2	-	-	-	-
The most for the other countries is:												
B.Mitchell	South Africa	**24**	9	3	8	2	-	-	1	1	-	-
M.D.Crowe	New Zealand	**26**	-	1	12	3	7	2	1	-	-	-
P.A.de Silva	Sri Lanka	**15**	-	-	8	3	2	1	1	-	-	-
G.W.Flower	Zimbabwe	**6**	3	-	1	2	-	-	-	-	-	-

HIGHEST WICKET PARTNERSHIPS FOR EACH COUNTRY

AUSTRALIA

1st	382	W.M.Lawry (210), R.B.Simpson (201)	v	West Indies	Bridgetown	1964-65
2nd	451	W.H.Ponsford (266), D.G.Bradman (244)	v	England	The Oval	1934
3rd	295	C.C.McDonald (127), R.N.Harvey (204)	v	West Indies	Kingston	1954-55
4th	388	W.H.Ponsford (181), D.G.Bradman (304)	v	England	Leeds	1934
5th	405	S.G.Barnes (234), D.G.Bradman (234)	v	England	Sydney	1946-47
6th	346	J.H.W.Fingleton (136), D.G.Bradman (270)	v	England	Melbourne	1936-37
7th	217	K.D.Walters (250), G.J.Gilmour (101)	v	New Zealand	Christchurch	1976-77
8th	243	R.J.Hartigan (116), C.Hill (160)	v	England	Adelaide	1907-08
9th	154	S.E.Gregory (201), J.M.Blackham (74)	v	England	Sydney	1894-95
10th	127	J.M.Taylor (108), A.A.Mailey (46*)	v	England	Sydney	1924-25

ENGLAND

1st	359	L.Hutton (158), C.Washbrook (195)	v	South Africa	Johannesburg[2]	1948-49
2nd	382	L.Hutton (364), M.Leyland (187)	v	Australia	The Oval	1938
3rd	370	W.J.Edrich (189), D.C.S.Compton (208)	v	South Africa	Lord's	1947
4th	411	P.B.H.May (285*), M.C.Cowdrey (154)	v	West Indies	Birmingham	1957
5th	254	K.W.R.Fletcher (113), A.W.Greig (148)	v	India	Mumbai[2]	1972-73
6th	240	P.H.Parfitt (131*), B.R.Knight (125)	v	New Zealand	Auckland	1962-62
7th	197	M.K.J.Smith (96), J.M.Parks (101*)	v	West Indies	Port-of-Spain	1959-60
8th	246	L.E.G.Ames (137), G.O.B.Allen (122)	v	New Zealand	Lord's	1931
9th	163*	M.C.Cowdrey (128*), A.C.Smith (69*)	v	New Zealand	Wellington	1962-62
10th	130	R.E.Foster (287), W.Rhodes (40*)	v	Australia	Sydney	1903-04

SOUTH AFRICA

1st	260	B.Mitchell (123), I.J.Siedle (141)	v	England	Cape Town	1930-31
2nd	198	E.A.B.Rowan (236), C.B.van Ryneveld (83)	v	England	Leeds	1951
3rd	341	E.J.Barlow (201), R.G.Pollock (175)	v	Australia	Adelaide	1963-64
4th	214	H.W.Taylor (121), H.G.Deane (93)	v	England	The Oval	1929
5th	157	A.J.Pithey (95), J.H.B.Waite (64)	v	England	Johannesburg[2]	1964-65
6th	200	R.G.Pollock (274), H.R.Lance (61)	v	Australia	Durban[2]	1969-70
7th	246	D.J.McGlew (255*), A.R.A.Murray (109)	v	New Zealand	Wellington	1952-53
8th	124	A.W.Nourse (72), E.A.Halliwell (57)	v	Australia	Johannesburg[1]	1902-03
9th	137	E.L.Dalton (117), A.B.C.Langton (73*)	v	England	The Oval	1935
10th	103	H.G.Owen-Smith (129), A.J.Bell (26*)	v	England	Leeds	1929

WEST INDIES

1st	298	C.G.Greenidge (149), D.L.Haynes (167)	v	England	St John's	1989-90
2nd	446	C.C.Hunte (260), G.S.Sobers (365*)	v	Pakistan	Kingston	1957-58
3rd	338	E.D.Weekes (206), F.M.M.Worrell (167)	v	England	Port-of-Spain	1953-54
4th	399	G.S.Sobers (226), F.M.M.Worrell (197*)	v	England	Bridgetown	1959-60
5th	265	S.M.Nurse (137), G.S.Sobers (174)	v	England	Leeds	1966
6th	274*	G.S.Sobers (163*), D.A.J.Holford (105*)	v	England	Lord's	1966
7th	347	D.S.Atkinson (219), C.C.Depeiza (122)	v	Australia	Bridgetown	1954-55
8th	124	I.V.A.Richards (192*), K.D.Boyce (68)	v	India	Delhi	1974-75
9th	161	C.H.Lloyd (161*), A.M.E.Roberts (68)	v	India	Calcutta	1983-84
10th	106	C.L.Hooper (178*), C.A.Walsh (30)	v	Pakistan	St John's	1992-93

NEW ZEALAND

Wkt	Runs	Batsmen		Opponent	Venue	Season
1st	387	G.M.Turner (259), T.W.Jarvis (182)	v	West Indies	Georgetown	1971-72
2nd	241	J.G.Wright (116), A.H.Jones (143)	v	England	Wellington	1991-92
3rd	467	A.H.Jones (186), M.D.Crowe (299)	v	Sri Lanka	Wellington	1990-91
4th	229	B.E.Congdon (132), B.F.Hastings (101)	v	Australia	Wellington	1973-74
5th	183	M.G.Burgess (111), R.W.Anderson (92)	v	Pakistan	Lahore[2]	1976-77
6th	246*	J.J.Crowe (120*), R.J.Hadlee (151*)	v	Sri Lanka	Colombo (CCC)	1986-87
7th	186	W.K.Lees (152), R.J.Hadlee (87)	v	Pakistan	Karachi[1]	1976-77
8th	136	B.E.Congdon (166*), R.S.Cunis (51)	v	West Indies	Port-of-Spain	1971-72
9th	136	I.D.S.Smith (173), M.C.Snedden (22)	v	India	Auckland	1989-90
10th	151	B.F.Hastings (110), R.O.Collinge (68*)	v	Pakistan	Auckland	1972-73

INDIA

Wkt	Runs	Batsmen		Opponent	Venue	Season
1st	413	M.H.Mankad (231), Pankaj Roy (173)	v	New Zealand	Chennai[2]	1955-56
2nd	344*	S.M.Gavaskar (182*), D.B.Vengsarkar (157*)	v	West Indies	Calcutta	1978-79
3rd	316	G.R.Viswanath (222), Yashpal Sharma (140)	v	England	Chennai[1]	1981-82
4th	222	V.S.Hazare (89), V.L.Manjrekar (133)	v	England	Leeds	1952
5th	214	M.Azharuddin (110), R.J.Shastri (111)	v	England	Calcutta	1984-85
6th	298*	D.B.Vengsarkar (164*), R.J.Shastri (121*)	v	Australia	Mumbai[3]	1986-87
7th	235	R.J.Shastri (142), S.M.H.Kirmani (102)	v	England	Mumbai[2]	1984-85
8th	143	R.G.Nadkarni (75), F.M.Engineer (90)	v	New Zealand	Chennai[2]	1964-65
9th	149	P.G.Joshi (52*), R.B.Desai (85)	v	Pakistan	Mumbai[2]	1960-61
10th	109	H.R.Adhikari (81*), Ghulam Ahmed (50)	v	Pakistan	Delhi	1952-53

PAKISTAN

Wkt	Runs	Batsmen		Opponent	Venue	Season
1st	249	Khalid Ibadulla (116), Abdul Kadir (95)	v	Australia	Karachi[1]	1964-65
2nd	291	Zaheer Abbas (274), Mushtaq Mohammad (100)	v	England	Birmingham	1971
3rd	451	Mudassar Nazar (231), Javed Miandad (280*)	v	India	Hyderabad	1982-83
4th	350	Mushtaq Mohammad (201), Asif Iqbal (175)	v	New Zealand	Dunedin	1972-73
5th	281	Javed Miandad (163), Asif Iqbal (166)	v	New Zealand	Lahore[2]	1976-77
6th	217	Hanif Mohammad (203*), Majid Khan (80)	v	New Zealand	Lahore[2]	1964-65
7th	308	Waqar Hassan (189), Imtiaz Ahmed (209)	v	New Zealand	Lahore[1]	1955-56
8th	130	Hanif Mohammad (187*), Asif Iqbal (76)	v	England	Lord's	1967
9th	190	Asif Iqbal (146), Intikhab Alam (51)	v	England	The Oval	1967
10th	133	Wasim Raja (71), Wasim Bari (60*)	v	West Indies	Bridgetown	1976-77

SRI LANKA

Wkt	Runs	Batsmen		Opponent	Venue	Season
1st	159	S.Wettimuny (79), J.R.Ratnayeke (93)	v	India	Kanpur	1986-87
2nd	217	S.Wettimuny (157), R.L.Dias (98)	v	Pakistan	Faisalabad	1981-82
2nd	217	A.P.Gurusinha (128), S.Ranatunga (118)	v	Zimbabwe	Harare	1994-95
3rd	176	U.C.Hathurusingha (83), P.A.de Silva (105)	v	Pakistan	Faisalabad	1995-96
4th	240*	A.P.Gurusinha (116*), A.Ranatunga (135*)	v	Pakistan	Colombo (PSS)	1985-86
5th	150	S.Wettimuny (190), L.R.D.Mendis (111)	v	England	Lord's	1984
6th	138	S.A.R.Silva (102*), L.R.D.Mendis (94)	v	England	Lord's	1984
7th	144	P A de Silva (167), J R Ratnayeke (56)	v	Australia	Brisbane[2]	1989-90
8th	83	H.P.Tillakaratne (93*), M.Muralidharan (19)	v	England	Colombo (SSC)	1992-93
9th	52	P.A.de Silva (122), R.J.Ratnayake (56)	v	Pakistan	Faisalabad	1985-86
10th	64	J.R.Ratnayeke (59*), G.F.Labrooy (42)	v	England	Lord's	1988

ZIMBABWE

1st	120	G.W.Flower (71), S.V.Carlisle (58)	v	New Zealand	Auckland	1995-96
2nd	135	M.H.Dekker (68*), A.D.R.Campbell (75)	v	Pakistan	Rawalpindi[2]	1993-94
3rd	269	G.W.Flower (201*), A.Flower (156)	v	Pakistan	Harare	1994-95
4th	233*	G.W.Flower (201*), G.J.Whittall (113*)	v	Pakistan	Harare	1994-95
5th	97	A.Flower (63), G.J.Whittall (38)	v	South Africa	Harare	1995-96
6th	165	D.L.Houghton (121), A.Flower (59)	v	India	Harare	1992-93
7th	91	G.J.Whittall (54), P.A.Strang (49)	v	New Zealand	Hamilton	1995-96
8th	84	D.L.Houghton (266), J.A.Rennie (19*)	v	Sri Lanka	Bulawayo[2]	1994-95
9th	46	P.A.Strang (37), B.C.Strang (25*)	v	South Africa	Harare	1995-96
10th	42	H.H.Streak (53), A.C.I.Lock (8*)	v	South Africa	Harare	1995-96

Bowling

200 TEST WICKETS

Player (Country)	Tests	Wkts	Avge	A	E	SA	WI	NZ	I	P	SL	Z
				Opponents								
Kapil Dev (I)	131	**434**	29.64	79	85	8	89	25	-	99	45	4
R.J.Hadlee (N)	86	**431**	22.29	130	97	-	51	-	65	51	37	-
I.T.Botham (E)	102	**[illegible]**	[illegible]	[illegible]	-	-	61	64	59	40	11	-
M.D.Marshall (W)	81	**376**	20.94	87	127	-	-	36	76	50	-	-
Imran Khan (P)	88	**362**	22.81	64	47	-	80	31	94	-	46	-
D.K.Lillee (A)	70	**355**	23.92	-	167	-	55	38	21	71	3	-
R.G.D.Willis (E)	90	**325**	25.20	128	-	-	38	60	62	34	3	-
C.A.Walsh (W)	82	**309**	25.04	79	89	4	-	40	61	35	1	-
L.R.Gibbs (W)	79	**309**	29.09	103	100	-	-	11	63	32	-	-
F.S.Trueman (E)	67	**307**	21.57	79	-	27	86	40	53	22	-	-
Wasim Akram (P)	70	**300**	22.91	40	50	4	47	60	31	-	44	24
D.L.Underwood (E)	86	**297**	25.83	105	-	-	38	48	62	36	8	-
C.J.McDermott (A)	71	**291**	28.63	-	84	21	59	48	34	18	27	-
C.E.L.Ambrose (W)	61	**266**	21.26	90	117	8	-	13	5	30	3	-
B.S.Bedi (I)	67	**266**	28.71	56	85	-	62	57	-	6	-	-
J.Garner (W)	58	**259**	20.97	89	92	-	-	36	7	35	-	-
J.B.Statham (E)	70	**252**	24.84	69	-	69	42	20	25	27	-	-
M.A.Holding (W)	60	**249**	23.68	76	96	-	-	16	61	-	-	-
R.Benaud (A)	63	**248**	27.03	-	83	52	42	-	47	15	-	-
G.D.McKenzie (A)	60	**246**	29.78	-	96	41	47	-	47	15	-	-
B.S.Chandrasekhar (I)	58	**242**	29.74	38	95	-	65	36	-	8	-	-
A.V.Bedser (E)	51	**236**	24.89	104	-	54	11	13	44	10	-	-
Abdul Qadir (P)	67	**236**	32.80	45	82	-	42	26	27	-	14	-
G.S.Sobers (W)	93	**235**	34.03	51	102	-	-	19	59	4	-	-
R.R.Lindwall (A)	61	**228**	23.03	-	114	31	41	2	36	4	-	-
C.V.Grimmett (A)	37	**216**	24.21	-	106	77	33	-	-	-	-	-
Waqar Younis (P)	41	**216**	21.07	22	38	-	35	57	6	-	31	27
M.G.Hughes (A)	53	**212**	28.38	-	75	4	53	25	23	16	16	-
S.K.Warne (A)	44	**207**	23.52	-	61	33	25	35	1	37	9	-
A.M.E.Roberts (W)	47	**202**	25.61	51	50	-	-	3	67	31	-	-
J.A.Snow (E)	49	**202**	26.66	83	-	4	72	20	16	7	-	-
J.R.Thomson (A)	51	**200**	28.00	-	100	-	62	6	22	10	-	-

100 OR MORE TEST WICKETS

AUSTRALIA	Tests	Balls	Runs	Wkts	Avge	5wi	10wm	Best
D.K.Lillee	70	18467	8493	355	23.92	23	7	7/83
C.J.McDermott	71	16586	8332	291	28.63	14	2	8/97
R.Benaud	63	19108	6704	248	27.03	16	1	7/72
G.D.McKenzie	60	17681	7328	246	29.78	16	3	8/71
R.R.Lindwall	61	13650	5251	228	23.03	12	0	7/38
C.V.Grimmett	37	14513	5231	216	24.21	21	7	7/40
M.G.Hughes	53	12285	6017	212	28.38	7	1	8/87
S.K.Warne	44	13118	4870	207	23.52	10	3	8/71
J.R.Thomson	51	10535	5601	200	28.00	8	0	6/46
A.K.Davidson	44	11587	3819	186	20.53	14	2	7/93
G.F.Lawson	46	11118	5501	180	30.56	11	2	8/112
K.R.Miller	55	10461	3906	170	22.97	7	1	7/60
T.M.Alderman	41	10181	4616	170	27.15	14	1	6/47
W.A.Johnston	40	11048	3826	160	23.91	7	0	6/44
W.J.O'Reilly	27	10024	3254	144	22.59	11	3	7/54

H.Trumble	32	8099	3072	141	21.78	9	3	8/65
M.H.N.Walker	34	10094	3792	138	27.47	6	0	8/143
A.A.Mallett	38	9990	3940	132	29.84	6	1	8/59
B.Yardley	33	8909	3986	126	31.63	6	1	7/98
R.M.Hogg	38	7633	3503	123	28.47	6	2	6/74
M.A.Noble	42	7159	3025	121	25.00	9	2	7/17
B.A.Reid	27	6244	2784	113	24.63	5	2	7/51
I.W.Johnson	45	8780	3182	109	29.19	3	0	7/44
G.Giffen	31	6391	2791	103	27.09	7	1	7/117
A.N.Connolly	29	7818	2981	102	29.22	4	0	6/47
C.T.B.Turner	17	5179	1670	101	16.53	11	2	7/43
ENGLAND	Tests	Balls	Runs	Wkts	Avge	5wi	10wm	Best
I.T.Botham	102	21815	10878	383	28.40	27	4	8/34
R.G.D.Willis	90	17357	8190	325	25.20	16	0	8/43
F.S.Trueman	67	15178	6625	307	21.57	17	3	8/31
D.L.Underwood	86	21862	7674	297	25.83	17	6	8/51
J.B.Statham	70	16056	6261	252	24.84	9	1	7/39
A.V.Bedser	51	15918	5876	236	24.89	15	5	7/44
J.A.Snow	49	12021	5387	202	26.66	8	1	7/40
J.C.Laker	46	12027	4101	193	21.24	9	3	10/53
S.F.Barnes	27	7873	3106	189	16.43	24	7	9/103
G.A.R.Lock	49	13147	4451	174	25.58	9	3	7/35
M.W.Tate	39	12523	4055	155	26.16	7	1	6/42
F.J.Titmus	53	15118	4931	153	32.22	7	0	7/79
J.E.Emburey	65	15571	5728	147	38.96	6	0	7/78
H.Verity	40	11173	3510	144	24.37	5	2	8/43
C.M.Old	46	8858	4020	143	28.11	4	0	7/50
A.W.Greig	58	9802	4541	141	32.20	6	2	8/86
P.A.J.DeFreitas	44	9838	4700	140	33.57	4	0	7/70
G.R.Dilley	41	8192	4107	138	29.76	6	0	6/38
T.E.Bailey	61	9712	3856	132	29.21	5	1	7/34
W.Rhodes	58	8231	3425	127	26.96	6	1	8/68
P.H.Edmonds	51	12028	4273	125	34.18	2	0	7/66
D.A.Allen	39	11297	3779	122	30.97	4	0	5/30
R.Illingworth	61	11934	3807	122	31.20	3	0	6/29
D.E.Malcolm	36	7922	4441	122	36.40	5	2	9/57
A.R.C.Fraser	32	7967	3509	119	29.48	8	0	8/75
J.Briggs	33	5332	2094	118	17.74	9	4	8/11
G.G.Arnold	34	7650	3254	115	28.29	6	0	6/45
G.A.Lohmann	18	3821	1205	112	10.75	9	5	9/28
D.V.P.Wright	34	8135	4224	108	39.11	6	1	7/105
R.Peel	20	5216	1715	101	16.98	5	1	7/31
J.H.Wardle	28	6597	2080	102	20.39	5	1	7/36
C.Blythe	19	4546	1863	100	18.63	9	4	8/59
SOUTH AFRICA	Tests	Balls	Runs	Wkts	Avge	5wi	10wm	Best
H.J.Tayfield	37	13568	4405	170	25.91	14	2	9/113
T.L.Goddard	41	11736	3226	123	26.22	5	0	6/53
P.M.Pollock	28	6522	2806	116	24.18	9	1	6/38
A.A.Donald	25	5781	2835	114	24.86	6	2	8/71
N.A.T.Adcock	26	6391	2195	104	21.10	5	0	6/43
WEST INDIES	Tests	Balls	Runs	Wkts	Avge	5wi	10wm	Best
M.D.Marshall	81	17585	7876	376	20.94	22	4	7/22
C.A.Walsh	82	17578	7739	309	25.04	11	2	7/37
L.R.Gibbs	79	27115	8989	309	29.09	18	2	8/38

J.Garner	58	13175	5433	259	20.97	7	0	6/56
C.E.L.Ambrose	61	14319	5657	266	21.26	14	3	8/45
M.A.Holding	60	12680	5898	249	23.68	13	2	8/92
G.S.Sobers	93	21599	7999	235	34.03	6	0	6/73
A.M.E.Roberts	47	11136	5174	202	25.61	11	2	7/54
W.W.Hall	48	10421	5066	192	26.38	9	1	7/69
S.Ramadhin	43	13939	4579	158	28.98	10	1	7/49
A.L.Valentine	36	12953	4215	139	30.32	8	2	8/104
C.E.H.Croft	27	6165	2913	125	23.30	3	0	8/29
I.R.Bishop	26	5742	2565	117	21.92	6	0	6/40
V.A.Holder	40	9095	3627	109	33.27	3	0	6/28

NEW ZEALAND	Tests	Balls	Runs	Wkts	Avge	5wi	10wm	Best
R.J.Hadlee	86	21918	9611	431	22.29	36	9	9/52
D.K.Morrison	47	10016	5445	157	34.68	10	0	7/89
B.L.Cairns	43	10628	4279	130	32.91	6	1	7/74
E.J.Chatfield	43	10360	3958	123	32.17	3	1	6/73
R.O.Collinge	35	7689	3393	116	29.25	3	0	6/63
B.R.Taylor	30	6334	2953	111	26.60	4	0	7/74
J.G.Bracewell	41	8403	3653	102	35.81	4	1	6/32
R.C.Motz	32	7034	3148	100	31.48	5	0	6/63

INDIA	Tests	Balls	Runs	Wkts	Avge	5wi	10wm	Best
Kapil Dev	131	28741	12867	434	29.64	23	2	9/83
B.S.Bedi	67	21367	7637	266	28.71	14	1	7/98
B.S.Chandrasekhar	58	15963	7199	242	29.74	16	2	8/79
E.A.S.Prasanna	49	14353	5742	189	30.38	10	2	8/76
M.H.Mankad	44	14686	5236	162	32.32	8	2	8/52
S.Venkataraghavan	57	14877	5634	156	36.11	3	1	8/72
R.J.Shastri	80	15751	6187	151	40.97	2	0	5/75
S.P.Gupte	36	11284	4403	149	29.55	12	1	9/102
A.R.Kumble	26	7583	2996	114	26.28	6	1	7/59
D.R.Doshi	33	9322	3502	114	30.71	6	0	6/102
K.D.Ghavri	39	7042	3656	109	33.54	4	0	5/33
N.S.Yadav	35	8349	3580	102	35.09	3	0	5/76

PAKISTAN	Tests	Balls	Runs	Wkts	Avge	5wi	10wm	Best
Imran Khan	88	19458	8258	362	22.81	23	6	8/58
Wasim Akram	70	16016	6875	300	22.91	20	3	7/119
Abdul Qadir	67	17126	7742	236	32.80	15	5	9/56
Waqar Younis	41	8484	4553	216	21.07	19	4	7/76
Sarfraz Nawaz	55	13931	5798	177	32.75	4	1	9/86
Iqbal Qasim	50	13019	4807	171	28.11	8	2	7/49
Fazal Mahmood	34	9834	3434	139	24.70	13	4	7/42
Intikhab Alam	47	10474	4494	125	35.92	5	2	7/52

Most Test wickets for the other countries:

SRI LANKA	Tests	Balls	Runs	Wkts	Avge	5wi	10wm	Best
M.Muralidaran	23	6099	2745	81	33.88	5	0	5/64
R.J.Ratnayake	23	4955	2563	73	35.11	5	0	6/66

ZIMBABWE	Tests	Balls	Runs	Wkts	Avge	5wi	10wm	Best
H.H.Streak	12	2986	1257	58	21.67	3	0	6/90
D.H.Brain	9	1810	915	30	30.50	1	0	5/42

BEST BOWLING AVERAGES *(Qualification: 25 wickets)*

Player	Country	Tests	Balls	Runs	Wkts	Avge	5w	10w
G.A.Lohmann	England	18	3821	1205	112	**10.75**	9	5
J.J.Ferris	Australia/England	9	2302	775	61	**12.70**	6	1
A.E.Trott	Australia/England	5	948	390	26	**15.00**	2	0
M.J.Proctor	South Africa	7	1514	616	41	**15.02**	1	0
W.Barnes	England	21	2289	793	51	**14.54**	3	0
W.Bates	England	15	2364	821	50	**16.42**	4	1
S.F.Barnes	England	27	7873	3106	189	**16.43**	24	7
C.T.B.Turner	Australia	17	5179	1670	101	**16.53**	11	2
R.Peel	England	20	5216	1715	101	**16.98**	5	1
J.Briggs	England	33	5332	2094	118	**17.74**	9	4
R.Appleyard	England	9	1596	534	31	**17.87**	1	0
W.S.Lees	England	5	1256	467	26	**17.96**	2	0
H.Ironmonger	Australia	14	4695	1330	74	**17.97**	4	2
G.B.Lawrence	South Africa	5	1334	512	28	**18.28**	2	0
F.R.Spofforth	Australia	18	4185	1731	94	**18.41**	7	4
F.H.Tyson	England	17	3452	1413	76	**18.56**	4	1
C.Blythe	England	19	4446	1863	100	**18.63**	9	4
G.F.Bissett	South Africa	4	989	469	25	**18.76**	2	0
A.S.Kennedy	England	5	1683	599	31	**19.32**	2	0

BEST STRIKE RATES *(Qualification: 25 wickets)*

Player	Country	Balls/wkt	Tests	Balls	Runs	Wkts	Avge
G.A.Lohmann	England	**34.11**	18	3821	1205	112	10.75
A.E.Trott	Australia/England	**36.46**	5	948	390	26	15.00
M.J.Proctor	South Africa	**36.92**	7	1514	616	41	15.02
J.J.Ferris	Australia/England	**37.73**	9	2302	775	61	12.70
B.J.T.Bosanquet	England	**38.80**	7	970	604	25	24.16
Waqar Younis	Pakistan	**39.27**	41	8484	4553	216	21.07
G.F.Bissett	South Africa	**39.56**	4	989	469	25	18.76
S.F.Barnes	England	**41.65**	27	7873	3106	189	16.43

MOST ECONOMICAL CAREER BOWLING *(Qualification: 2000 balls)*

Player	Country	Runs/100 balls	Tests	Balls	Runs	Wkts	Avge
W.Attewell	England	**21.96**	10	2850	626	28	22.35
C.Gladwin	England	**26.82**	8	2129	571	15	38.06
T.L.Goddard	South Africa	**27.48**	41	11736	3226	123	26.22
R.G.Nadkarni	India	**27.92**	41	9165	2559	88	29.07
H.Ironmonger	Australia	**28.32**	14	4695	1330	74	17.97
J.C.Watkins	South Africa	**29.09**	15	2805	816	29	28.13
K.D.Mackay	Australia	**29.71**	37	5792	1721	50	34.42
A.R.A.Murray	South Africa	**29.90**	10	2374	710	18	39.44

25 OR MORE WICKETS IN A TEST SERIES *(§ in first series. # in last series. † in only series.)*

AUSTRALIA	Opp	Season	Tests	Balls	Mdns	Runs	Wkts	Avge	5w	10w	Best
C.V.Grimmett #	SA	1935-36	5	2077	140	642	44	14.59	5	3	7/40
T.M.Alderman §	ENG	1981	6	1950	76	893	42	21.26	4	0	6/135
R.M.Hogg §	ENG	1978-79	6	1740	60	527	41	12.85	5	2	6/74
T.M.Alderman	ENG	1989	6	1622	68	712	41	17.36	6	1	6/128
D.K.Lillee	ENG	1981	6	1870	81	870	39	22.30	2	1	7/89
W.J.Whitty	SA	1910-11	5	1395	55	632	37	17.08	2	0	6/17
A.A.Mailey §	ENG	1920-21	5	1465	27	946	36	26.27	4	2	9/121
G.Giffen	ENG	1894-95	5	2060	111	820	34	24.11	3	0	6/155
G.F.Lawson	ENG	1982-83	5	1384	51	687	34	20.20	4	1	6/47

S.K.Warne	ENG	1993	6	2639	178	877	34	25.79	1	0	5/82
C.V.Grimmett	WI	1930-31	5	1433	60	593	33	17.96	2	1	7/87
C.V.Grimmett	SA	1931-32	5	1836	108	557	33	16.87	3	1	7/83
A.K.Davidson	WI	1960-61	4	1391	25	612	33	18.54	5	1	6/53
J.R.Thomson	ENG	1974-75	5	1401	34	592	33	17.93	2	0	6/46
M.A.Noble	ENG	1901-02	5	1380	68	608	32	19.00	4	1	7/17
H.V.Hordern #	ENG	1911-12	5	1665	43	780	32	24.37	4	2	7/90
C.J.McDermott	ENG	1994-95	5	1397	56	675	32	21.09	4	0	6/38
J.V.Saunders #	ENG	1907-08	5	1603	52	716	31	23.09	3	0	5/28
H.Ironmonger	SA	1931-32	4	1331	112	296	31	9.54	3	1	6/18
R.Benaud	ENG	1958-59	5	1866	65	584	31	18.83	2	0	5/83
D.K.Lillee	ENG	1972	5	1499	83	548	31	17.67	3	1	6/66
C.J.McDermott	IND	1991-92	5	1586	75	670	31	21.61	3	1	5/54
M.G.Hughes	ENG	1993	6	1778	79	845	31	27.25	1	0	5/92
R.Benaud	SA	1957-58	5	1937	56	658	30	21.93	4	0	5/49
G.D.McKenzie	WI	1968-69	5	1649	27	758	30	25.26	1	1	8/71
C.J.McDermott	ENG	1985	6	1406	21	901	30	30.03	2	0	8/141
C.V.Grimmett	ENG	1930	5	2098	78	925	29	31.89	4	1	6/167
A.K.Davidson	IND	1959-60	5	1469	85	431	29	14.86	2	1	7/93
R.Benaud	IND	1959-60	5	1934	146	568	29	19.58	2	0	5/43
G.D.McKenzie	ENG	1964	5	1536	61	654	29	22.55	2	0	7/153
J.R.Thomson	WI	1975-76	6	1205	15	831	29	28.65	2	0	6/50
G.F.Lawson	ENG	1989	6	1663	68	791	29	27.27	1	0	6/72
H.Trumble	ENG	1901-02	5	1604	93	561	28	20.03	2	0	6/74
W.J.O'Reilly	ENG	1934	5	2002	128	698	28	24.92	2	1	7/54
A.A.Mallett	IND	1969-70	5	1792	129	535	28	19.10	3	1	6/64
W.M.Clark §	IND	1977-78	5	1585	27	701	28	25.03	0	0	4/46
E.A.McDonald	ENG	1921	5	1235	32	668	27	24.74	2	0	5/32
W.J.O'Reilly	ENG	1932-33	5	2302	144	724	27	26.81	2	1	5/63
W.J.O'Reilly	SA	1935-36	5	1502	112	460	27	17.03	2	0	5/20
R.R.Lindwall	ENG	1948	5	1337	57	530	27	19.62	2	0	6/20
W.A.Johnston	ENG	1948	5	1856	91	630	27	23.33	1	0	5/36
D.K.Lillee	WI	1975-76	5	1035	7	712	27	26.37	1	0	5/63
B.A.Reid	ENG	1990-91	4	1039	47	432	27	16.00	2	1	7/51
S.K.Warne	ENG	1994-95	5	1537	84	549	27	20.33	2	1	8/71
E.Jones	ENG	1899	5	1276	73	657	26	25.26	2	1	7/88
H.Trumble	ENG	1902	3	1036	55	371	26	14.26	2	2	8/65
R.R.Lindwall	ENG	1953	5	1444	62	490	26	18.84	3	0	5/54
J.W.Gleeson	WI	1968-69	5	2006	57	844	26	32.46	2	0	5/61
M.H.N.Walker	WI	1972-73	5	1627	83	539	26	20.73	3	0	6/114
C.V.Grimmett	ENG	1934	5	2379	148	668	25	26.72	2	0	7/83
W.J.O'Reilly	ENG	1936-37	5	1982	89	555	25	22.20	2	0	5/51
A.K.Davidson	SA	1957-58	5	1613	47	425	25	17.00	2	0	6/34
D.K.Lillee	ENG	1974-75	6	1462	36	596	25	23.84	0	-	4/49
A.G.Hurst	ENG	1978-79	6	1634	44	577	25	23.08	1	0	5/28

ENGLAND	Opp	Season	Tests	Balls	Mdns	Runs	Wkts	Avge	5w	10w	Best
S.F.Barnes #	SA	1913-14	4	1356	56	536	49	10.93	7	3	9/103
J.C.Laker	AUST	1956	5	1703	127	442	46	9.60	4	2	10/53
A.V.Bedser	AUST	1953	5	1591	58	682	39	17.48	5	1	7/44
M.W.Tate	AUST	1924-25	5	2528	62	881	38	23.18	5	1	6/99
G.A.Lohmann	SA	1895-96	3	520	38	203	35	5.80	4	2	9/28
S.F.Barnes	AUST	1911-12	5	1782	64	778	34	22.88	3	0	5/44
S.F.Barnes	SA	1912	3	768	38	282	34	8.29	5	3	8/29
G.A.R.Lock	NZ	1958	5	1056	93	254	34	7.47	3	1	7/35
F.S.Trueman	WI	1963	5	1420	53	594	34	17.47	4	2	7/44
I.T.Botham	AUST	1981	6	1635	81	700	34	20.58	3	1	6/95

H.Larwood #	AUST	1932-33	5	1322	42	644	33	19.51	2	1	5/28
T.Richardson	AUST	1894-95	5	1747	63	849	32	26.53	4	0	6/104
F.R.Foster §	AUST	1911-12	5	1660	58	692	32	21.62	3	0	6/91
W.Rhodes	AUST	1903-04	5	1032	36	488	31	15.74	3	1	8/68
A.S.Kennedy †	SA	1922-23	5	1683	91	599	31	19.32	2	0	5/76
J.A.Snow	AUST	1970-71	6	1805	47	708	31	22.83	2	0	7/40
I.T.Botham	AUST	1985	6	1510	36	855	31	27.58	1	0	5/109
J.N.Crawford #	AUST	1907-08	5	1426	36	742	30	24.73	3	0	5/48
A.V.Bedser	AUST	1950-51	5	1560	34	482	30	16.06	2	1	5/46
A.V.Bedser	SA	1951	5	1655	84	517	30	17.23	3	1	7/58
F.S.Trueman §	IND	1952	4	718	25	386	29	13.31	2	0	8/31
D.L.Underwood	IND	1976-77	5	1517	95	509	29	17.55	1	0	5/84
R.G.D.Willis	AUST	1981	6	1516	56	666	29	22.96	1	0	8/43
F.H.Tyson	AUST	1954-55	5	1208	16	583	28	20.82	2	1	7/27
R.Peel	AUST	1894-95	5	1831	77	721	27	26.70	1	0	6/67
M.W.Tate §	SA	1924	5	1304	68	424	27	15.70	1	0	6/42
J.B.Statham	SA	1960	5	1218	54	491	27	18.18	2	1	6/63
F.J.Titmus	IND	1963-64	5	2393	156	747	27	27.66	2	0	6/73
J.A.Snow	WI	1967-68	4	990	29	504	27	18.66	3	1	7/49
R.G.D.Willis	AUST	1977	5	1000	36	534	27	19.77	3	0	7/78
W.S.Lees †	SA	1905-06	5	1256	69	467	26	17.96	2	0	6/78
C.Blythe	SA	1907	3	603	26	270	26	10.38	3	1	8/59
W.Voce	AUST	1936-37	5	1297	20	560	26	21.53	1	1	6/41
J.H.Wardle	SA	1956-57	4	1118	37	359	26	13.80	3	1	7/36
J.K.Lever §	IND	1976-77	5	898	29	380	26	14.61	2	1	7/46
D.G.Cork §	WI	1995	5	1106	30	661	26	25.42	1	0	7/43
A.Fielder #	AUST	1907-08	4	1299	31	627	25	25.08	1	0	6/82
J.C.White	AUST	1928-29	5	2440	134	760	25	30.40	3	1	8/126
F.S.Trueman	SA	1960	5	1083	31	508	25	20.32	1	0	5/27

SOUTH AFRICA	Opp	Season	Tests	Balls	Mdns	Runs	Wkts	Avge	5w	10w	Best
H.J.Tayfield	ENG	1956-57	5	2280	105	636	37	17.18	4	1	9/113
A.E.E.Vogler	ENG	1909-10	5	1349	33	783	36	21.75	4	1	7/94
H.J.Tayfield	AUST	1952-53	5	2228	58	843	30	28.10	2	1	7/81
G.A.Faulkner	ENG	1909-10	5	1255	45	635	29	21.89	2	0	6/87
G.B.Lawrence †	NZ	1961-62	5	1334	62	512	28	18.28	2	0	8/53
A.E.Hall §	ENG	1922-23	4	1505	82	501	27	18.55	2	1	7/63
H.J.Tayfield	ENG	1955	5	1881	124	568	26	21.84	3	0	5/60
N.A.T.Adcock	ENG	1960	5	1578	69	587	26	22.57	2	0	6/65
T.L.Goddard	AUST	1966-67	5	1533	101	422	26	16.23	1	0	6/53
M.J.Procter #	AUST	1969-70	4	858	50	353	26	13.57	1	0	6/73
C.B.Llewellyn	AUST	1902-03	3	796	23	448	25	17.92	4	1	6/92
R.O.Schwarz	AUST	1910-11	5	1006	19	651	25	26.04	2	0	6/47
J.M.Blanckenberg	ENG	1922-23	5	1510	60	613	25	24.52	2	0	6/76
G.F.Bissett †	ENG	1927-28	4	989	28	469	25	18.76	2	0	7/29
T.L.Goddard §	ENG	1955	5	1894	148	528	25	21.12	2	0	5/31
J.T.Partridge §	AUST	1963-64	5	1980	33	833	25	33.32	2	0	7/91
P.M.Pollock	AUST	1963-64	5	1275	11	710	25	28.40	2	0	6/95

WEST INDIES	Opp	Season	Tests	Balls	Mdns	Runs	Wkts	Avge	5w	10w	Best
M.D.Marshall	ENG	1988	5	1219	49	443	35	12.66	3	1	7/22
A.L.Valentine §	ENG	1950	4	2535	197	674	33	20.42	2	2	8/104
C.E.H.Croft §	PAK	1976-77	5	1307	45	676	33	20.48	1	0	8/29
M.D.Marshall	IND	1983-84	6	1326	59	621	33	18.81	2	0	6/37
C.E.L.Ambrose	AUST	1992-93	5	1563	77	542	33	16.42	3	1	7/25
C.C.Griffith	ENG	1963	5	1343	54	519	32	16.21	3	0	6/36
A.M.E.Roberts	IND	1974-75	5	1251	51	585	32	18.28	3	1	7/64

	Opp	Season	Tests	Balls	Mdns	Runs	Wkts	Avge	5w	10w	Best
J.Garner	AUST	1983-84	5	1253	55	523	31	16.87	3	0	6/60
W.W.Hall	IND	1958-59	5	1330	65	530	30	17.66	2	1	6/50
M.A.Holding	IND	1983-84	6	1342	43	663	30	22.10	1	0	5/102
J.Garner	ENG	1984	5	1307	60	540	29	18.62	1	0	5/55
A.L.Valentine	IND	1952-53	5	2580	178	828	28	29.57	2	0	5/64
M.A.Holding	ENG	1976	4	957	54	356	28	12.71	3	1	8/92
A.M.E.Roberts	ENG	1976	5	1330	69	537	28	19.17	3	1	6/37
M.D.Marshall	AUST	1984-85	5	1277	47	554	28	19.78	4	1	5/38
C.E.L.Ambrose	ENG	1991	5	1494	60	560	28	20.00	2	0	6/52
W.W.Hall	IND	1961-62	5	1006	37	475	27	15.74	2	0	6/49
M.D.Marshall	NZ	1984-85	4	1021	30	486	27	18.00	1	1	7/80
J.Garner	ENG	1985-86	5	937	30	436	27	16.14	0	-	4/43
M.D.Marshall	ENG	1985-86	5	1017	36	482	27	17.85	0	-	4/38
I.R.Bishop	ENG	1995	6	1455	49	649	27	24.03	1	0	5/32
S.Ramadhin §	ENG	1950	4	2267	170	604	26	23.23	3	1	6/86
R.Gilchrist #	IND	1958-59	4	1189	73	419	26	16.11	1	0	6/55
L.R.Gibbs	ENG	1963	5	1497	74	554	26	21.30	2	1	5/98
L.R.Gibbs	AUST	1972-73	5	1950	108	696	26	26.76	1	0	5/102
J.Garner	ENG	1980	5	1276	73	371	26	14.26	0	-	4/30
C.A.Walsh	IND	1987-88	4	823	24	437	26	16.80	2	0	5/54
C.E.L.Ambrose	AUST	1988-89	5	1227	38	558	26	21.46	1	0	5/72
C.E.L.Ambrose	ENG	1993-94	5	1346	62	519	26	19.96	2	1	6/24
C.A.Walsh	ENG	1995	6	1740	57	786	26	30.23	1	0	5/45
J.Garner §	PAK	1976-77	5	1317	41	688	25	27.52	0	-	4/48

NEW ZEALAND	Opp	Season	Tests	Balls	Mdns	Runs	Wkts	Avge	5w	10w	Best
R.J.Hadlee	AUST	1985-86	3	1017	42	401	33	12.15	5	2	9/52
B.R.Taylor	WI	1971-72	4	1034	39	478	27	17.70	2	0	7/74

INDIA	Opp	Season	Tests	Balls	Mdns	Runs	Wkts	Avge	5w	10w	Best
B.S.Chandrasekhar	ENG	1972-73	5	1747	83	662	35	18.91	4	0	8/79
M.H.Mankad	ENG	1951-52	5	2224	151	571	34	16.79	1	1	8/55
S.P.Gupte	NZ	1955-56	5	2140	152	669	34	19.67	4	0	7/128
Kapil Dev	PAK	1979-80	6	1271	53	566	32	17.68	3	1	7/56
B.S.Bedi	AUST	1977-78	5	1759	39	740	31	23.87	3	1	5/55
Kapil Dev	WI	1983-84	6	1223	39	537	29	18.51	2	1	9/83
B.S.Chandrasekhar	AUST	1977-78	5	1579	24	704	28	25.14	3	1	6/52
Kapil Dev	AUST	1979-80	6	1339	53	625	28	22.32	2	0	5/74
S.P.Gupte	WI	1952-53	5	1977	87	789	27	29.22	3	0	7/162
K.D.Ghavri	WI	1978-79	6	1230	42	634	27	23.48	1	0	5/51
D.R.Doshi §	AUST	1979-80	6	1838	87	630	27	23.33	2	0	6/103
E.A.S.Prasanna	AUST	1969-70	5	1770	107	672	26	25.84	3	1	6/74
M.H.Mankad	PAK	1952-53	4	1592	100	514	25	20.56	3	1	8/52
E.A.S.Prasanna	AUST	1967-68	4	1581	34	686	25	27.44	2	0	6/104
B.S.Bedi	ENG	1972-73	5	2237	134	632	25	25.28	1	0	5/63
B.S.Bedi	ENG	1976-77	5	1788	106	574	25	22.96	2	0	6/71
Kapil Dev	AUST	1991-92	5	1704	76	645	25	25.80	2	0	5/97

PAKISTAN	Opp	Season	Tests	Balls	Mdns	Runs	Wkts	Avge	5w	10w	Best
Imran Khan	IND	1982-83	6	1339	69	558	40	13.95	4	2	8/60
Abdul Qadir	ENG	1987-88	3	1408	69	437	30	14.56	3	2	9/56
Waqar Younis	NZ	1990-91	3	869	50	315	29	10.86	3	2	7/76
Waqar Younis	ZIM	1993-94	3	784	31	373	27	13.81	4	1	7/91
Imran Khan	WI	1976-77	5	1417	54	790	25	31.60	1	0	6/90
Wasim Akram	NZ	1993-94	3	958	41	431	25	17.24	2	0	7/119

Most wickets in a series for the other countries:

SRI LANKA	Opp	Season	Tests	Balls	Mdns	Runs	Wkts	Avge	5w	10w	Best
R.J.Ratnayake	IND	1985-86	3	977	35	459	20	22.95	2	0	6/85

ZIMBABWE	Opp	Season	Tests	Balls	Mdns	Runs	Wkts	Avge	5w	10w	Best
H.H.Streak	P	1995	3	708	31	298	22	13.54	2	0	6/90

TEN WICKETS IN A MATCH *(§ In first Test. # In last Test. † In only Test)*

AUSTRALIA (73)		Opponents		
R.A.L.Massie §	16-137	England	Lord's	1972
F.R.Spofforth	14-90	England	The Oval	1882
C.V.Grimmett	14-199	South Africa	Adelaide	1931-32
M.A.Noble	13-77	England	Melbourne	1901-02
F.R.Spofforth	13-110	England	Melbourne	1878-79
B.A.Reid	13-148	England	Melbourne	1990-91
C.V.Grimmett #	13-173	South Africa	Durban[2]	1935-36
M.G.Hughes	13-217	West Indies	Perth	1988-89
A.A.Mailey	13-236	England	Melbourne	1920-21
C.T.B.Turner	12-87	England	Sydney	1887-88
H.Trumble	12-89	England	The Oval	1896
A.K.Davidson	12-124	India	Kanpur	1959-60
B.A.Reid	12-126	India	Melbourne	1991-92
S.K.Warne	12-128	South Africa	Sydney	1993-94
G.Dymock	12-166	India	Kanpur	1979-80
H.Trumble	12-173	England	The Oval	1902
H.V.Hordern	12-175	England	Sydney	1911-12
H.Ironmonger	11-24	South Africa	Melbourne	1931-32
E.R.H.Toshack	11-31	India	Brisbane[2]	1947-48
S.K.Warne	11-77	Pakistan	Brisbane[2]	1995-96
H.Ironmonger	11-79	West Indies	Melbourne	1930-31
C.V.Grimmett §	11-82	England	Sydney	1924-25
C.G.Macartney	11-85	England	Leeds	1909
M.R.Whitney	11-95	India	Perth	1991-92
A.R.Border	11-96	West Indies	Sydney	1988-89
M.A.Noble	11-103	England	Sheffield	1902
R.Benaud	11-105	India	Calcutta	1956-57
S.K.Warne	11-110	England	Brisbane[2]	1994-95
F.R.Spofforth	11-117	England	Sydney	1882-83
C.G.Rackemann	11-118	Pakistan	Perth	1983-84
D.K.Lillee	11-123	New Zealand	Auckland	1976-77
W.J.O'Reilly	11-129	England	Nottingham	1934
G.F.Lawson	11-134	England	Brisbane[2]	1982-83
D.K.Lillee	11-138	England	Melbourne	1979-80
C.J.McDermott	11-157	England	Perth	1990-91
D.K.Lillee	11-159	England	The Oval	1981
G.E.Palmer	11-165	England	Sydney	1881-82
D.K.Lillee	11-165	England	Melbourne	1976-77
G.F.Lawson	11-181	West Indies	Adelaide	1984-85
C.V.Grimmett	11-183	West Indies	Adelaide	1930-31
A.K.Davidson	11-222	West Indies	Brisbane[2]	1960-61
C.T.B.Turner	10-63	England	Lord's	1888
R.M.Hogg	10-66	England	Melbourne	1978-79
C.V.Grimmett	10-88	South Africa	Cape Town	1935-36
G.D.McKenzie	10-91	India	Chennai[2]	1964-65
C.V.Grimmett	10-110	South Africa	Johannesburg[1]	1935-36
R.J.Bright	10-111	Pakistan	Karachi[1]	1979-80
N.J.N.Hawke	10-115	West Indies	Georgetown	1964-65

W.J.O'Reilly	10-122	England	Leeds	1938
R.M.Hogg	10-122	England	Perth	1978-79
G.E.Palmer	10-126	England	Melbourne	1882-83
D.K.Lillee	10-127	West Indies	Melbourne	1981-82
H.Trumble	10-128	England	Manchester	1902
W.J.O'Reilly	10-129	England	Melbourne	1932-33
D.K.Lillee	10-135	Pakistan	Melbourne	1976-77
F R.Spofforth	10-144	England	Sydney	1884-85
A.A.Mallett	10-144	India	Chennai[1]	1969-70
R.G.Holland	10-144	West Indies	Sydney	1984-85
G.D.McKenzie	10-151	India	Melbourne	1967-68
T.M.Alderman	10-151	England	Leeds	1989
K.R.Miller	10-152	England	Lord's	1956
G.D.McKenzie	10-159	West Indies	Melbourne	1968-69
G.Giffen	10-160	England	Sydney	1891-92
H.V.Hordern #	10-161	England	Sydney	1911-12
E.Jones	10-164	England	Lord's	1899
C.J.McDermott	10-168	India	Adelaide	1991-92
R.G.Holland	10-174	New Zealand	Sydney	1985-86
D.K.Lillee	10-181	England	The Oval	1972
B.Yardley	10-185	West Indies	Sydney	1981-82
C.V.Grimmett	10-201	England	Nottingham	1930
L.O.Fleetwood-Smith	10-239	England	Adelaide	1936-37
G.R.J.Matthews	10-249	India	Chennai[1]	1986-87
A.A.Mailey	10-302	England	Adelaide	1920-21

ENGLAND (89)		Opponents		
J.C.Laker	19-90	Australia	Manchester	1956
S.F.Barnes	17-159	South Africa	Johannesburg[1]	1913-14
J.Briggs	15-28	South Africa	Cape Town	1888-89
G.A Lohmann	15-45	South Africa	Port Elizabeth	1895-96
C.Blythe	15-99	South Africa	Leeds	1907
H.Verity	15-104	Australia	Lord's	1934
W.Rhodes	15-124	Australia	Melbourne	1903-04
A.V.Bedser	14-99	Australia	Nottingham	1953
W.Bates	14-102	Australia	Melbourne	1882-83
S.F.Barnes #	14-144	South Africa	Durban[1]	1913-14
S.F.Barnes	13-57	South Africa	The Oval	1912
D.L.Underwood	13-71	Pakistan	Lord's	1974
J.J.Ferris ¶	13-91	South Africa	Cape Town	1891-92
I.T.Botham	13-106	India	Mumbai[3]	1979-80
A.W.Greig	13-156	West Indies	Port-of-Spain	1973-74
S.F.Barnes	13-162	Australia	Melbourne	1901-02
T.Richardson	13-244	Australia	Manchester	1896
J.C.White	13-256	Australia	Adelaide	1928-29
G.A.Lohmann	12-71	South Africa	Johannesburg[1]	1895-96
J.H.Wardle	12-89	South Africa	Cape Town	1956-57
D.L.Underwood	12-97	New Zealand	Christchurch	1970-71
R.Tattersall	12-101	South Africa	Lord's	1951
D.L.Underwood	12-101	New Zealand	The Oval	1969
F.Martin §	12-102	Australia	The Oval	1890
G.A.Lohmann	12-104	Australia	The Oval	1886
A.V.Bedser	12-112	South Africa	Manchester	1951
F.S.Trueman	12-119	West Indies	Birmingham	1963
G.Geary	12-130	South Africa	Johannesburg[1]	1927-28
J.Briggs	12-136	Australia	Adelaide	1891-92
A.P.Freeman	12-171	South Africa	Manchester	1929

G.A.R.Lock	11-48	West Indies	The Oval	1957
G.A.R.Lock	11-65	New Zealand	Leeds	1958
R.Peel	11-68	Australia	Manchester	1888
D.L.Underwood	11-70	New Zealand	Lord's	1969
J.Briggs	11-74	Australia	Lord's	1886
W.H.Lockwood	11-76	Australia	Manchester	1902
N.G.B.Cook	11-83	Pakistan	Karachi[1]	1983-84
G.A.R.Lock	11-84	New Zealand	Christchurch	1958-59
F.S.Trueman	11-88	Australia	Leeds	1961
A.E.R.Gilligan	11-90	South Africa	Birmingham	1924
A.V.Bedser	11-93	India	Manchester	1946
C.S.Marriott †	11-96	West Indies	The Oval	1933
J.B.Statham	11-97	South Africa	Lord's	1960
T.E.Bailey	11-98	West Indies	Lord's	1957
C.Blythe	11-102	Australia	Birmingham	1909
S.F.Barnes	11-110	South Africa	Lord's	1912
J.C.Laker	11-113	Australia	Leeds	1956
C.Blythe	11-118	South Africa	Cape Town	1905-06
I.T.Botham	11-140	New Zealand	Lord's	1978
A.V.Bedser §	11-145	India	Lord's	1946
P.C.R.Tufnell	11-147	New Zealand	Christchurch	1991-92
W.Voce	11-149	West Indies	Port-of-Spain	1929-30
F.S.Trueman	11-152	West Indies	Lord's	1963
H.Verity	11-153	India	Chennai[1]	1933-34
N.A.Foster	11-163	India	Chennai[1]	1984-85
T.Richardson	11-173	Australia	Lord's	1896
I.T.Botham	11-176	Australia	Perth	1979-80
D.L.Underwood	11-215	Australia	Adelaide	1974-75
M.W.Tate	11-228	Australia	Sydney	1924-25
F.E.Woolley	10-49	Australia	The Oval	1912
W.Voce	10-57	Australia	Brisbane[2]	1936-37
R.Reel	10-58	Australia	Sydney	1887-88
J.T.Hearne	10-60	Australia	The Oval	1896
J.K.Lever §	10-70	India	Delhi	1976-77
G.O.B.Allen	10-78	India	Lord's	1936
D.L.Underwood	10-82	Australia	Leeds	1972
G.A.Lohmann	10-87	Australia	Sydney	1886-87
A.P.Freeman	10-93	West Indies	Manchester	1928
C.Blythe #	10-104	South Africa	Cape Town	1909-10
R.M.Ellison	10-104	Australia	Birmingham	1985
A.V.Bedser	10-105	Australia	Melbourne	1950-51
S.F.Barnes	10-105	South Africa	Durban[1]	1913-14
S.F.Barnes	10-115	South Africa	Leeds	1912
J.C.Laker	10-119	South Africa	The Oval	1951
H.Larwood	10-124	Australia	Sydney	1932-33
F.H.Tyson	10-130	Australia	Sydney	1954-55
D.E.Malcolm	10-137	West Indies	Port-of-Spain	1989-90
D.E.Malcolm	10-138	South Africa	The Oval	1994
G.A Lohmann	10-142	Australia	Sydney	1891-92
J.A.Snow	10-142	West Indies	Georgetown	1967-68
J.Briggs	10-148	Australia	The Oval	1893
A.W.Greig	10-149	New Zealand	Auckland	1977
T.Richardson §	10-156	Australia	Manchester	1893
D.V.P.Wright	10-175	South Africa	Lord's	1947
K.Farnes §	10-179	Australia	Nottingham	1934
G.T.S.Stevens	10-195	West Indies	Bridgetown	1929-30
T.Richardson #	10-204	Australia	Sydney	1897-98

Above: Philip de Freitas (England) falls lbw for 0 as Australian spinner Shane Warne takes the first wicket of a hat-trick in the second Test against England at Melbourne's MCG in 1994.

Below: Shane Warne has Darren Gough (England) caught behind by keeper Ian Healy for 0 — the second wicket in Warne's hat-trick.

Above: Shane Warne takes his third and final successive wicket as Devon Malcolm (England) is caught by David Boon for 0.

Below: The whole Australian team celebrates Shane Warne's historic hat-trick.

A.P.Freeman	10-207	South Africa	Leeds	1929
I.T.Botham	10-253	Australia	The Oval	1981

¶ *Ferris's only Test for England.*

SOUTH AFRICA (13)		Opponents		
H.J.Tayfield	13-165	Australia	Melbourne	1952-53
H.J.Tayfield	13-192	England	Johannesburg[3]	1956-57
S.J.Snooke	12-127	England	Johannesburg[1]	1905-06
A.A.Donald	12-139	India	Port Elizabeth	1992-93
A.E.E.Vogler	12-181	England	Johannesburg[1]	1909-10
A.E.Hall §	11-112	England	Cape Town	1922-23
A.A.Donald	11-113	Zimbabwe	Harare	1995-96
E.P.Nupen	11-150	England	Johannesburg[1]	1930-31
S.F.Burke §	11-196	New Zealand	Cape Town	1961-62
P.M.Pollock	10-87	England	Nottingham	1965
P.S.de Villiers	10-108	Pakistan	Johannesburg[3]	1994-95
C.B.Llewellyn	10-116	Australia	Johannesburg[1]	1902-03
P.S.de Villiers	10-123	Australia	Sydney	1993-94

WEST INDIES (24)		Opponents		
M.A.Holding	14-149	England	The Oval	1976
C.A.Walsh	13-55	New Zealand	Wellington	1994-95
A.M.E.Roberts	12-121	India	Chennai[1]	1974-75
C.E.L.Ambrose	11-84	England	Port-of-Spain	1993-94
M.D.Marshall	11-89	India	Port-of-Spain	1988-89
M.A.Holding	11-107	Australia	Melbourne	1981-82
M.D.Marshall	11-120	New Zealand	Bridgetown	1984-85
W.W.Hall	11-126	India	Kanpur	1958-59
K.D.Boyce	11-147	England	The Oval	1973
S.Ramadhin	11-152	England	Lord's	1950
L.R.Gibbs	11-157	England	Manchester	1963
A.L.Valentine §	11-204	England	Manchester	1950
W.Ferguson	11-229	England	Port-of-Spain	1947-48
M.D.Marshall	10-92	England	Lord's	1988
H.H.H.Johnson §	10-96	England	Kingston	1947-48
C A Walsh	10-101	India	Kingston	1988-89
L R Gibbs	10-106	England	Manchester	1966
M.D.Marshall	10-107	Australia	Adelaide	1984-85
G.E.Gomez	10-113	Australia	Sydney	1951-52
C.E.L.Ambrose	10-120	Australia	Adelaide	1992-93
A.M.E.Roberts	10-123	England	Lord's	1976
C.E.L.Ambrose	10-127	England	Bridgetown	1989-90
A.L.Valentine	10-160	England	The Oval	1950
K.C.G.Benjamin	10-174	England	Nottingham	1995

NEW ZEALAND (16)		Opponents		
R.J.Hadlee	15-123	Australia	Brisbane[2]	1985-86
R.J.Hadlee	11-58	India	Wellington	1975-76
R.J.Hadlee	11-102	West Indies	Dunedin	1979-80
C.Pringle	11-152	Pakistan	Faisalabad	1990-91
R.J.Hadlee	11-155	Australia	Perth	1985-86
D.J.Nash	11-169	England	Lord's	1994
R.J.Hadlee	10-88	India	Mumbai[3]	1988-89
R.J.Hadlee	10-100	England	Wellington	1977-78
R.J.Hadlee	10-102	Sri Lanka	Colombo (CCC)	1983-84
J.G.Bracewell	10-106	Australia	Auckland	1985-86
E.J.Chatfield	10-124	West Indies	Port-of-Spain	1984-85

J.Cowie	10-140	England	Manchester	1937
R.J.Hadlee	10-140	England	Nottingham	1986
B.L.Cairns	10-144	England	Leeds	1983
G.B.Troup	10-166	West Indies	Auckland	1979-80
R.J.Hadlee	10-176	Australia	Melbourne	1987-88

INDIA (22)		Opponents		
N.D.Hirwani §	16-136	West Indies	Chennai[1]	1987-88
J.M.Patel	14-124	Australia	Kanpur	1959-60
M.H.Mankad	13-131	Pakistan	Delhi	1952-53
B.S.Chandrasekhar	12-104	Australia	Melbourne	1977-78
M.H.Mankad	12-108	England	Chennai[1]	1951-52
S.Venkataraghavan	12-152	New Zealand	Delhi	1964-65
L.Sivaramakrishnan	12-181	England	Mumbai[3]	1984-85
R.G.Nadkarni	11-122	Australia	Chennai[2]	1964-65
S.L.Venkatapathy Raju	11-125	Sri Lanka	Ahmedabad	1993-94
A.R.Kumble	11-128	Sri Lanka	Lucknow[2]	1993-94
E.A.S.Prasanna	11-140	New Zealand	Auckland	1975-76
Kapil Dev	11-146	Pakistan	Chennai[1]	1979-80
B.S.Chandrasekhar	11-235	West Indies	Mumbai[2]	1966-67
Maninder Singh	10-107	Sri Lanka	Nagpur	1986-87
Maninder Singh	10-126	Pakistan	Bangalore	1986-87
Ghulam Ahmed	10-130	Australia	Calcutta	1956-57
Kapil Dev	10-135	West Indies	Ahmedabad	1983-84
E.A.S.Prasanna	10-174	Australia	Chennai[1]	1969-70
S.A.Durani	10-177	England	Chennai[2]	1961-62
C.Sharma	10-188	England	Birmingham	1986
B.S.Bedi	10-194	Australia	Perth	1977-78
S.P.Gupte	10-223		Kanpur	1958-59

PAKISTAN (30)		Opponents		
Imran Khan	14-116	Sri Lanka	Lahore[2]	1981-82
Abdul Qadir	13-101	England	Lahore[2]	1987-88
Fazal Mahmood	13-114	Australia	Karachi[1]	1956-57
Waqar Younis	13-135	Zimbabwe	Karachi[2]	1993-94
Fazal Mahmood	12-94	India	Lucknow[1]	1952-53
Fazal Mahmood	12-99	England	The Oval	1954
Fazal Mahmood	12-100	West Indies	Dacca	1958-59
Waqar Younis	12-130	New Zealand	Faisalabad	1990-91
Imran Khan	12-165	Australia	Sydney	1976-77
Zulfiqar Ahmed	11-79	New Zealand	Karachi[1]	1955-56
Imran Khan	11-79	India	Karachi[1]	1982-83
Iqbal Qasim	11-118	Australia	Karachi[1]	1979-80
Waqar Younis	11-119	Sri Lanka	Kandy	1994-95
Imran Khan	11-121	West Indies	Georgetown	1987-88
Sarfraz Nawaz	11-125	Australia	Melbourne	1978-79
Intikhab Alam	11-130	New Zealand	Dunedin	1972-73
Wasim Akram	11-160	Australia	Melbourne	1989-90
Wasim Akram	11-179	New Zealand	Wellington	1993-94
Imran Khan	11-180	India	Faisalabad	1982-83
Sikander Bakht	11-190	India	Delhi	1979-80
Abdul Qadir	11-218	Australia	Faisalabad	1982-83
Imran Khan	10-77	England	Leeds	1987
Waqar Younis	10-106	New Zealand	Lahore[1]	1990-91
Wasim Akram	10-128	New Zealand	Dunedin	1984-85
Mushtaq Ahmed	10-171	New Zealand	Christchurch	1995-96
Iqbal Qasim	10-175	India	Mumbai[3]	1979-80

Intikhab Alam	10-182	New Zealand	Dacca	1969-70
Abdul Qadir	10-186	England	Karachi[1]	1987-88
Abdul Qadir	10-194	England	Lahore[2]	1983-84
Abdul Qadir	10-211	England	The Oval	1987

SRI LANKA (1)

		Opponents		
W.P.U.J.C.Vaas	10-90	New Zealand	Napier	1994-95

Best for Zimbabwe:

ZIMBABWE

H.H.Streak	9-105	Pakistan	Harare	1994-95

SIX WICKETS IN AN INNINGS ON DEBUT

IN BOTH INNINGS

F.Martin	6/50, 6/52	England	v	Australia	The Oval	1890
R.A.L.Massie	8/84, 8/52	Australia	v	England	Lord's	1972
N.D.Hirwani	8/61, 8/75	India	v	West Indies	Chennai[1]	1987-88

IN FIRST INNINGS

W.H.Ashley	7/95	South Africa	v	England	Port Elizabeth	1888-89
W.H.Lockwood	6/101	England	v	Australia	Lord's	1893
G.H.T.Simpson-Hayward	6/43	England	v	South Africa	Johannesburg[1]	1909-10
G.M.Parker	6/152	South Africa	v	England	Birmingham	1924
A.J.Bell	6/99	South Africa	v	England	Lord's	1929
A.V.Bedser	7/49	England	v	India	Lord's	1946
J.C.Laker	7/103	England	v	West Indies	Bridgetown	1947-48
T.E.Bailey	6/118	England	v	New Zealand	Leeds	1949
G.F.Cresswell	6/168	New Zealand	v	England	The Oval	1949
A.L.Valentine	8/104	West Indies	v	England	Manchester	1950
A.M.Moir	6/155	New Zealand	v	England	Christchurch	1950-51
S.F.Burke	6/128	South Africa	v	New Zealand	Cape Town	1961-62
Arif Butt	6/89	Pakistan	v	Australia	Melbourne	1964-65
S.Abid Ali	6/55	India	v	Australia	Adelaide	1967-68
Mohammad Nazir	7/99	Pakistan	v	New Zealand	Karachi[1]	1969-70
J.K.Lever	7/46	England	v	India	Delhi	1976-77
R.M.Hogg	6/74	Australia	v	England	Brisbane[2]	1978-79
D.R.Doshi	6/103	India	v	Australia	Chennai[1]	1979-80
P.L.Taylor	6/78	Australia	v	England	Sydney	1986-87
P.M.Such	6/67	England	v	Australia	Manchester	1993

IN SECOND INNINGS

T.K.Kendall	7/55	Australia	v	England	Melbourne	1876-77
W.H.Cooper	6/120	Australia	v	England	Melbourne	1881-82
A.E.Trott	8/43	Australia	v	England	Adelaide	1894-95
M.A.Noble	6/49	Australia	v	England	Melbourne	1897-98
A.E.Hall	7/63	South Africa	v	England	Cape Town	1922-23
C.V.Grimmett	6/37	Australia	v	England	Sydney	1924-25
J.Langridge	7/56	England	v	West Indies	Manchester	1933
C.S.Marriott	6/59	England	v	West Indies	The Oval	1933
F.A.Ward	6/102	Australia	v	England	Brisbane[2]	1936-37
C.N.McCarthy	6/43	South Africa	v	England	Durban[2]	1948-49
P.S.Pollock	6/38	South Africa	v	New Zealand	Durban[2]	1961-62
L.J.Coldwell	6/85	England	v	Pakistan	Lord's	1962

A.I.C.Dodemaide	6/58	Australia	v	New Zealand	Melbourne	1987-88
D.G.Cork	7/43	England	v	West Indies	Lord's	1995

TEN WICKETS IN A MATCH ON DEBUT

F.Martin	10/104	England	v	Australia	The Oval	1890
T.Richardson	10/156	England	v	Australia	Manchester	1893
A.E.Hall	11/112	South Africa	v	England	Cape Town	1922-23
C.V.Grimmett	11/82	Australia	v	England	Sydney	1924-25
C.S.Marriott	11/96	England	v	West Indies	The Oval	1933
K.Farnes	10/179	England	v	Australia	Nottingham	1934
A.V.Bedser	11/145	England	v	India	Lord's	1946
H.H.H.Johnson	10/96	West Indies	v	England	Kingston	1947-48
A.L.Valentine	11/204	West Indies	v	England	Manchester	1950
S.F.Burke	11/196	South Africa	v	New Zealand	Cape Town	1961-62
R.A.L.Massie	16/137	Australia	v	England	Lord's	1972
J.K.Lever	10/70	England	v	India	Delhi	1976-77
N.D.Hirwani	16/136	India	v	West Indies	Chennai[1]	1987-88

EIGHT WICKETS IN AN INNINGS *(§ In first Test. # In last Test)*

AUSTRALIA (14)		Opponents		
A.A.Mailey	9-121	England	Melbourne	1920-21
F.Laver	8-31	England	Manchester	1909
A.E.Trott §	8-43	England	Adelaide	1894-95
R.A.L.Massie §	8-53	England	Lord's	1972
A.A.Mallett	8-59	Pakistan	Adelaide	1972-73
H.Trumble	8-65	England	The Oval	1902
G.D.McKenzie	8-71	West Indies	Melbourne	1968-69
S.K.Warne	8-71	England	Brisbane[2]	1994-95
R.A.L.Massie §	8-84	England	Lord's	1972
M.G.Hughes	8-87	West Indies	Perth	1988-89
C.J.McDermott	8-97	England	Perth	1990-91
G.F.Lawson	8-112	West Indies	Adelaide	1984-85
C.J.McDermott	8-141	England	Manchester	1985
M.H.N.Walker	8-143	England	Melbourne	1974-75

ENGLAND (26)		Opponents		
J.C.Laker	10-53	Australia	Manchester	1956
G.A.Lohmann	9-28	South Africa	Johannesburg[1]	1895-96
J.C.Laker	9-37	Australia	Manchester	1956
D.E.Malcolm	9-57	South Africa	The Oval	1994
S.F.Barnes	9-103	South Africa	Johannesburg[1]	1913-14
G.A.Lohmann	8-7	South Africa	Port Elizabeth	1895-96
J.Briggs	8-11	South Africa	Cape Town	1888-89
S.F.Barnes	8-29	South Africa	The Oval	1912
F.S.Trueman	8-31	India	Manchester	1952
I.T.Botham	8-34	Pakistan	Lord's	1978
G.A.Lohmann	8-35	Australia	Sydney	1886-87
H.Verity	8-43	Australia	Lord's	1934
R.G.D.Willis	8-43	Australia	Leeds	1981
D.L.Underwood	8-51	Pakistan	Lord's	1974
S.F.Barnes	8-56	South Africa	Johannesburg[1]	1913-14
G.A.Lohmann	8-58	Australia	Sydney	1891-92
C.Blythe	8-59	South Africa	Leeds	1907
W.Rhodes	8-68	Australia	Melbourne	1903-04
A.R.C.Fraser	8-75	West Indies	Bridgetown	1993-94
L.C.Braund	8-81	Australia	Melbourne	1903-04
A.W.Greig	8-86	West Indies	Port-of-Spain	1973-74

T.Richardson #	8-94	Australia	Sydney	1897-98
I.T.Botham	8-103	West Indies	Lord's	1984
B.J.T.Bosanquet	8-107	Australia	Nottingham	1905
N.A.Foster	8-107	Pakistan	Leeds	1987
J.C.White	8-126	Australia	Adelaide	1928-29
SOUTH AFRICA (5)		Opponents		
H.J.Tayfield	9-113	England	Johannesburg[3]	1956-57
G.B.Lawrence	8-53	New Zealand	Johannesburg[3]	1961-62
H.J.Tayfield	8-69	England	Durban[2]	1956-57
S.J.Snooke	8-70	England	Johannesburg[1]	1905-06
A.A.Donald	8-71	Zimbabwe	Harare	1995-96
WEST INDIES (6)		Opponents		
J.M.Noreiga	9-95	India	Port-of-Spain	1970-71
C.E.H.Croft	8-29	Pakistan	Port-of-Spain	1976-77
L.R.Gibbs	8-38	India	Bridgetown	1961-62
C.E.L.Ambrose	8-45	England	Bridgetown	1989-90
M.A.Holding	8-92	England	The Oval	1976
A.L.Valentine §	8-104	England	Manchester	1950
NEW ZEALAND (1)		Opponents		
R.J.Hadlee	9-52	Australia	Brisbane[2]	1985-86
INDIA (12)		Opponents		
J.M.Patel	9-69	Australia	Kanpur	1959-60
Kapil Dev	9-83	West Indies	Ahmedabad	1983-84
S.P.Gupte	9-102	West Indies	Kanpur	1958-59
M.H.Mankad	8-52	Pakistan	Delhi	1952-53
M.H.Mankad	8-55	England	Chennai[1]	1951-52
N.D.Hirwani §	8-61	West Indies	Chennai[1]	1987-88
S.Venkataraghavan	8-72	New Zealand	Delhi	1964-65
N.D.Hirwani §	8-75	West Indies	Chennai[1]	1987-88
E.A.S.Prasanna	8-76	New Zealand	Auckland	1975-76
B.S.Chandrasekhar	8-79	England	Delhi	1972-73
Kapil Dev	8-85	Pakistan	Lahore[2]	1982-83
Kapil Dev	8-106	Australia	Adelaide	1985-86
PAKISTAN (5)		Opponents		
Abdul Qadir	9-56	England	Lahore[2]	1887-88
Sarfraz Nawaz	9-86	Australia	Melbourne	1978-79
Imran Khan	8-58	Sri Lanka	Lahore[2]	1981-82
Imran Khan	8-60	India	Karachi[1]	1982-83
Sikander Bakht	8-69	India	Delhi	1979-80
SRI LANKA (1)		Opponents		
J.R.Ratnayeke	8-83	Pakistan	Sialkot	1985-86

Best for Zimbabwe:

ZIMBABWE

H.H.Streak	6-90	Pakistan	Harare	1994-95

DISTRIBUTION OF FIVE WICKETS IN AN INNINGS

Taken Against	Taken For: A	E	SA	WI	NZ	I	P	SL	Z	Total Against
Australia	0	214	34	49	23	35	22	3	0	380
England	247	0	76	79	28	50	30	1	0	511
South Africa	53	86	0	1	6	1	0	2	1	150
West Indies	58	70	0	0	15	29	21	0	0	193
New Zealand	13	53	19	17	0	23	33	8	0	166
India	32	47	2	44	19	0	29	8	1	182
Pakistan	28	31	1	12	13	27	0	9	4	125
Sri Lanka	6	5	3	0	6	10	12	0	0	42
Zimbabwe	0	0	1	0	3	1	7	1	0	13
Total For	437	506	136	202	113	176	154	32	6	1762

HAT-TRICKS IN TEST MATCHES *(§ In first Test. # On final Test appearance. ¶ Over both innings.)*

F.R.Spofforth	Australia	v	England	Melbourne	1878-79
W.Bates	England	v	Australia	Melbourne	1882-83
J.Briggs	England	v	Australia	Sydney	1891-92
G.A.Lohmann	England	v	South Africa	Port Elizabeth	1895-96
J.T.Hearne	England	v	Australia	Leeds	1899
H.Trumble	Australia	v	England	Melbourne	1901-02
H.Trumble #	Australia	v	England	Melbourne	1903-04
T.J.Matthews (2)	Australia	v	South Africa	Manchester	1912
M.J.C.Allom §	England	v	New Zealand	Christchurch	1929-30
T.W.J.Goddard	England	v	South Africa	Johannesburg[1]	1938-39
P.J.Loader	England	v	West Indies	Leeds	1957
L.F.Kline	Australia	v	South Africa	Cape Town	1957-58
W.W.Hall	West Indies	v	Pakistan	Lahore[1]	1958-59
G.M.Griffin #	South Africa	v	England	Lord's	1960
L.R.Gibbs	West Indies	v	Australia	Adelaide	1960-61
P.J.Petherick §	New Zealand	v	Pakistan	Lahore[2]	1976-77
C.A.Walsh ¶	West Indies	v	Australia	Brisbane[2]	1988-89
M.G.Hughes ¶	Australia	v	West Indies	Perth	1988-89
D.W.Fleming §	Australia	v	Pakistan	Rawalpindi[2]	1994-95
S.K.Warne	Australia	v	England	Melbourne	1994-95
D.G.Cork	England	v	West Indies	Lord's	1995

Matthews did the hat-trick in each innings on the second afternoon of the match.

FOUR WICKETS IN FIVE BALLS

M.J.C.Allom | England | v | New Zealand | Christchurch | 1929-30

In his first Test - in his eighth over (W0WWW).

C.M.Old | England | v | Pakistan | Birmingham | 1978

In the same over (WW0WW) his third ball was a no ball.

Wasim Akram | Pakistan | v | West Indies | Lahore[2] | 1990-91

In the same over (WW1WW) - a catch was dropped from the third ball.

THREE WICKETS IN FOUR BALLS

F.R.Spofforth	Australia	v	England	The Oval	1882
F.R.Spofforth	Australia	v	England	Sydney	1884-85
J.Briggs	England	v	South Africa	Cape Town	1888-89
W.P.Howell	Australia	v	South Africa	Cape Town	1902-03
E.P.Nupen	South Africa	v	England	Johannesburg[1]	1930-31
W J.O'Reilly	Australia	v	England	Manchester	1934

B.Mitchell	South Africa	v	Australia	Johannesburg[1]	1935-36
W.Voce	England	v	Australia	Sydney	1936-37
R.R.Lindwall	Australia	v	England	Adelaide	1946-47
K.Cranston	England	v	South Africa	Leeds	1947
C.N.McCarthy	South Africa	v	England	Durban[2]	1948-49
R.Appleyard	England	v	New Zealand	Auckland	1954-55
R.Benaud	Australia	v	West Indies	Georgetown	1954-55
Fazal Mahmood	Pakistan	v	Australia	Karachi[1]	1956-57
J.W.Martin	Australia	v	West Indies	Melbourne	1960-61
L.R.Gibbs	West Indies	v	Australia	Sydney	1960-61
K.D.Mackay	Australia	v	England	Birmingham	1961
W.W.Hall	West Indies	v	India	Port-of-Spain	1961-62
D.Shackleton	England	v	West Indies	Lord's	1963
G.D.McKenzie	Australia	v	West Indies	Port-of-Spain	1964-65
F.J.Titmus	England	v	New Zealand	Leeds	1965
P.Lever	England	v	Pakistan	Leeds	1971
D.K.Lillee	Australia	v	England	Manchester	1972
D.K.Lillee	Australia	v	England	The Oval	1972
C.M.Old	England	v	Pakistan	Birmingham	1978
S.T.Clarke	West Indies	v	Pakistan	Karachi[1]	1980-81
R..Hadlee	New Zealand	v	Australia	Melbourne	1980-81
R..Shastri	India	v	New Zealand	Wellington	1980-81
I.T.Botham	England	v	Australia	Leeds	1985
Kapil Dev	India	v	Australia	Adelaide	1985-86
C.G.Rackemann	Australia	v	Pakistan	Adelaide	1989-90
D.E.Malcolm	England	v	West Indies	Port-of-Spain	1989-90
Wasim Akram	Pakistan	v	West Indies	Lahore[2]	1990-91
A.R.Border	Australia	v	West Indies	Georgetown	1990-91
Wasim Akram	Pakistan	v	England	Lord's	1992
S.K.Warne	Australia	v	England	Brisbane[2]	1994-95

K.Cranston, F.J.Titmus, C.M.Old and Wasim Akram each took four wickets in an over.

WICKET WITH FIRST BALL IN TEST CRICKET

Bowler	Batsman dismissed					
A.Coningham	A.C.MacLaren	Australia	v	England	Melbourne	1894-95
W.M.Bradley	F.J.Laver	England	v	Australia	Manchester	1899
E.G.Arnold	V.T.Trumper	England	v	Australia	Sydney	1903-04
G.G.Macaulay	G.A.L.Hearne	England	v	South Africa	Cape Town	1922-23
M.W.Tate	M.J.Susskind	England	v	South Africa	Birmingham	1924
M.Henderson	E.W.Dawson	New Zealand	v	England	Christchurch	1929-30
H.D.Smith	E.Paynter	New Zealand	v	England	Christchurch	1932-33
T.F.Johnson	W.W.Keeton	West Indies	v	England	The Oval	1939
R.Howorth	D.V.Dyer	England	v	South Africa	The Oval	1947
Intikhab Alam	C.C.McDonald	Pakistan	v	Australia	Karachi[1]	1959-60
R.K.Illingworth	P.V.Simmons	England	v	West Indies	Nottingham	1991

WICKET IN FIRST OVER IN TEST CRICKET

Ball	Bowler	Batsman dismissed				
1st	A.Coningham	A.C.MacLaren	Australia	v England	Melbourne	1894-95
1st	W.M.Bradley	F.J.Laver	England	v Australia	Manchester	1899
1st	E.G.Arnold	V.T.Trumper	England	v Australia	Sydney	1903-04
1st	G.G.Macaulay	G.A.L.Hearne	England	v South Africa	Cape Town	1922-23
1st	M.W.Tate	M.J.Susskind	England	v South Africa	Birmingham	1924
1st	M.Henderson	E.W.Dawson	New Zealand	v England	Christchurch	1929-30
1st	H.D.Smith	E.Paynter	New Zealand	v England	Christchurch	1932-33
1st	T.F.Johnson	W.W.Keeton	West Indies	v England	The Oval	1939
1st	R.Howorth	D.V.Dyer	England	v South Africa	The Oval	1947
1st	Intikhab Alam	C.C.McDonald	Pakistan	v Australia	Karachi[1]	1959-60

1st	R.K.Illingworth	P.V.Simmons	England	v West Indies	Nottingham	1991
2nd	G.A.Rowe	T.C.O'Brien	South Africa	v England	Johannesburg[1]	1895-96
2nd	W.Barber	H.B.Cameron	England	v South Africa	Leeds	1935
2nd	J.H.Cameron	H.Gimblett	West Indies	v England	Lord's	1939
2nd	C.L.McCool	D.A.N.McRae	Australia	v New Zealand	Wellington	1945-46
2nd	G.W.A.Chubb	J.T.Ikin	South Africa	v England	Nottingham	1951
2nd	R.Appleyard	Hanif Mohammad	England	v Pakistan	Nottingham	1954
2nd	F.M.Misson	C.C.Hunte	Australia	v West Indies	Melbourne	1960-61
2nd	P.I.Philpott	C.C.Hunte	Australia	v West Indies	Kingston	1964-65
2nd	B.A.G.Murray	S.Abid Ali	New Zealand	v India	Wellington	1967-68
2nd	G.Dymock	J.M.Parker	Australia	v New Zealand	Adelaide	1973-74
3rd	I.W.Johnson	L.Hutton	Australia	v England	Sydney	1946-47
3rd	R.O.Jenkins	E.A.B.Rowan	England	v South Africa	Durban[2]	1948-49
3rd	M.S.Hardikar	R.B.Kanhai	India	v West Indies	Mumbai[2]	1958-59
3rd	P.D.Lashley	G.Boycott	West Indies	v England	Leeds	1966
3rd	E.W.Freeman	S.Abid Ali	Australia	v India	Brisbane[2]	1967-68
3rd	K.Thompson	F.M.Engineer	New Zealand	v India	Wellington	1967-68
3rd	M.Hendrick	E.D.Solkar	England	v India	Manchester	1974
3rd	B.P.Bracewell	G.A.Gooch	New Zealand	v England	The Oval	1978
3rd	A.K.Kuruppuarachchi	Mudassar Nazar	Sri Lanka	v Pakistan	Colombo (CCC)	1985-86
3rd	G.A.Hick	P.V.Simmons	England	v West Indies	Lord's	1991
3rd	C.A.Lambert	M.R.Ramprakash	West Indies	v England	The Oval	1991
3rd	D.K.Liyanage	T.M.Moody	Sri Lanka	v Australia	Colombo (PIS)	1992-93
3rd	H.K.Olonga	Saeed Anwar	Zimbabwe	v Pakistan	Harare	1994-95
4th	G.L.Weir	G.B.Legge	New Zealand	v England	Wellington	1929-30
4th	D.V.P.Wright	J.H.W.Fingleton	England	v Australia	Nottingham	1938
4th	F.W.Freer	C.Washbrook	Australia	v England	Sydney	1946-47
4th	A.M.B.Rowan	L.Hutton	South Africa	v England	Nottingham	1947
4th	J.C.Laker	C.L.Walcott	England	v West Indies	Bridgetown	1947-48
4th	H.J.Rhodes	Pankaj Roy	England	v India	Leeds	1959
4th	D.A.J.Holford	F.J.Titmus	West Indies	v England	Manchester	1966
4th	D.S.Steele	A.A.Mallett	England	v Australia	Lord's	1975
4th	J.E.Emburey	B.A.Edgar	England	v New Zealand	Lord's	1978
4th	E.E.Hemmings	Javed Miandad	England	v Pakistan	Birmingham	1982
4th	C.S.Cowdrey	Kapil Dev	England	v India	Mumbai[3]	1984-85
4th	F.S.Ahangama	M.Azharuddin	Sri Lanka	v India	Colombo (SSC)	1985-86
4th	W.V.Raman	C.A.Walsh	India	v West Indies	Chennai[1]	1987-88
4th	J.C.Adams	W.J.Cronje	West Indies	v South Africa	Bridgetown	1991-92
4th	S.G.Peall	Aamer Sohail	Zimbabwe	v Pakistan	Karachi[2]	1993-94
5th	G.H.T.Simpson-Hayward	J.W.Zulch	England	v South Africa	Johannesburg[1]	1909-10
5th	S.A.Banerjee	D.S.Atkinson	India	v West Indies	Calcutta	1948-49
5th	L.J.Coldwell	Imtiaz Ahmed	England	v Pakistan	Lord's	1962
5th	B.W.Yuile	E.R.Dexter	New Zealand	v England	Auckland	1962-63
5th	A.A.Mallett	M.C.Cowdrey	Australia	v England	The Oval	1968
5th	G.A.Chevalier	A.P.Sheahan	South Africa	v Australia	Cape Town	1969-70
5th	R.D.Jackman	C.G.Greenidge	England	v West Indies	Bridgetown	1980-81
5th	C.Sharma	Mohsin Khan	India	v Pakistan	Lahore[2]	1984-85
5th	D.Gough	M.J.Greatbatch	England	v New Zealand	Manchester	1994
5th	R.C.Irani	M.Azharuddin	England	v India	Birmingham	1996
6th	D.P.B.Morkel	P.Holmes	South Africa	v England	Johannesburg[1]	1927-28
6th	E.W.Clark	R.H.Catterall	England	v South Africa	The Oval	1929
6th	V.V.Kumar	Imtiaz Ahmed	India	v Pakistan	Delhi	1960-61
6th	M.W.W.Selvey	R.C.Fredericks	England	v West Indies	Manchester	1976
6th	D.R.Pringle	Yashpal Sharma	England	v India	Lord's	1982
7th	R.A.Gaunt	R.J.Westcott	Australia	v South Africa	Durban[2]	1957-58
7th	A.L.Mann	G.R.Viswanath	Australia	v India	Brisbane[2]	1977-78
	M.Leyland	G.Challenor	England	v West Indies	The Oval	1928

B.Sutcliffe	A.Wharton	New Zealand	v England	Leeds	1949
E.W.Dempster	D.J.McGlew	New Zealand	v South Africa	Auckland	1952-53
A.F.Lissette	A.P.Binns	New Zealand	v West Indies	Dunedin	1955-56
L.A.King	M.L.Jaisimha	West Indies	v India	Kingston	1961-62

500 BALLS IN AN INNINGS

		O	M	R	W					
588	S.Ramadhin	98	35	179	2	West Indies	v	England	Birmingham	1957
571	T.R.Veivers	95.1	36	155	3	Australia	v	England	Manchester	1964
552	A.L.Valentine	92	49	140	3	West Indies	v	England	Nottingham	1950
522	L.O.Fleetwood-Smith	87	11	298	1	Australia	v	England	The Oval	1938
512	Fazal Mahmood	85.2	20	247	2	Pakistan	v	West Indies	Kingston	1957-58
510	W.J.O'Reilly	85	26	178	3	Australia	v	England	The Oval	1938
504	Haseeb Ahsan	84	19	202	6	Pakistan	v	India	Chennai[2]	1960-61

700 BALLS IN A MATCH

		O	M	R	W					
774	S.Ramadhin	129	51	228	9	West Indies	v	England	Birmingham	1957
766	H.Verity	95.6	23	184	4	England	v	South Africa	Durban[2]	1938-39
749	J.C.White	124.5	37	256	13	England	v	Australia	Adelaide	1928-29
738	N.Gordon	92.2	17	256	1	South Africa	v	England	Durban[2]	1938-39
728	A.B.C.Langton	91	24	203	4	South Africa	v	England	Durban[2]	1938-39
712	M.W.Tate	89	19	228	11	England	v	Australia	Sydney	1924-25
708	G.Giffen	118	42	239	8	Australia	v	England	Sydney	1894-95

OUTSTANDING ANALYSES IN A TEST INNINGS

O	M	R	W						
51.2	23	53	10	J.C.Laker	England	v	Australia	Manchester	1956
14.2	6	28	9	G.A.Lohmann	England	v	South Africa	Johannesburg[1]	1895-96
16.4	4	37	9	J.C.Laker	England	v	Australia	Manchester	1956
9.4	5	7	8	G.A.Lohmann	England	v	South Africa	Port Elizabeth	1895-96
14.2	5	11	8	J.Briggs	England	v	South Africa	Cape Town	1888-89
19.1	11	17	7	J.Briggs	England	v	South Africa	Cape Town	1888-89
7.4	2	17	7	M.A.Noble	Australia	v	England	Melbourne	1901-02
11	3	17	7	W.Rhodes	England	v	Australia	Birmingham	1902
6.3	4	7	6	A.E.R.Gilligan	England	v	South Africa	Birmingham	1924
11.4	6	11	6	S.Haigh	England	v	South Africa	Cape Town	1898-99
11.6	7	12	6	D.L.Underwood	England	v	New Zealand	Christchurch	1970-71
17.5	13	12	6	S.L.Venkatapathy Raju	India	v	Sri Lanka	Chandigarh	1990-91
14	7	13	6	H.J.Tayfield	South Africa	v	New Zealand	Johannesburg[2]	1953-54
18	11	15	6	C.T.B.Turner	Australia	v	England	Sydney	1886-87
16	8	15	6	M.H.N.Walker	Australia	v	Pakistan	Sydney	1972-73
2.3	1	2	5	E.R.H.Toshack	Australia	v	India	Brisbane[2]	1947-48
7.2	5	6	5	H.Ironmonger	Australia	v	South Africa	Melbourne	1931-32
12	8	5	4	Pervez Sajjad	Pakistan	v	New Zealand	Rawalpindi[1]	1964-65
9	7	5	4	K.Higgs	England	v	New Zealand	Christchurch	1965-66
8	6	6	4	P.H.Edmonds	England	v	Pakistan	Lord's	1978
6.3	2	7	4	J.C.White	England	v	Australia	Brisbane[1]	1928-29
5	2	7	4	J.H.Wardle	England	v	Australia	Manchester	1953
6	3	7	4	R.Appleyard	England	v	New Zealand	Auckland	1954-55
3.4	3	0	3	R.Benaud	Australia	v	India	Delhi	1959-60

MOST WICKETS BY A BOWLER IN ONE DAY

15	J.Briggs	15-28	England	v	South Africa	Cape Town	1888-89
14	H.Verity	14-80	England	v	Australia	Lord's	1934

DISMISSING ALL ELEVEN BATSMEN IN A MATCH

J.C.Laker	19-90	England	v	Australia	Manchester	1956
S.Venkataraghavan	12-152	India	v	New Zealand	Delhi	1964-65
G.Dymock	12-166	Australia	v	India	Kanpur	1979-80
Abdul Qadir	13-101	Pakistan	v	England	Lahore[2]	1987-88
Waqar Younis	12-130	Pakistan	v	New Zealand	Faisalabad	1990-91

OVER 200 RUNS CONCEDED IN AN INNINGS

O	M	R	W						
87	11	298	1	L.O.Fleetwood-Smith	Australia	v	England	The Oval	1938
80.2	13	266	5	O.C.Scott	West Indies	v	England	Kingston	1929-30
54	5	259	0	Khan Mohammad	Pakistan	v	West Indies	Kingston	1957-58
85.2	20	247	2	Fazal Mahmood	Pakistan	v	West Indies	Kingston	1957-58
70	10	229	1	S.L.Boock	New Zealand	v	Pakistan	Auckland	1988-89
82	17	228	5	M.H.Mankad	India	v	West Indies	Kingston	1952-53
64.2	8	226	6	B.S.Bedi	India	v	England	Lord's	1974
54	3	224	2	M.Muralidaran	Sri Lanka	v	Australia	Perth	1995-96
38.4	3	220	7	Kapil Dev	India	v	Pakistan	Faisalabad	1982-83
52	7	217	3	I.T.Botham	England	v	Pakistan	The Oval	1987
71	8	204	6	I.A.R.Peebles	England	v	Australia	The Oval	1930
75	16	202	3	M.H.Mankad	India	v	West Indies	Mumbai[2]	1948-49
84	19	202	6	Haseeb Ahsan	Pakistan	v	India	Chennai[2]	1960-61

OVER 300 RUNS CONCEDED IN A MATCH

O	M	R	W						
105.2	13	374	9	O.C.Scott	West Indies	v	England	Kingston	1929-30
63	3	308	7	A.A.Mailey	Australia	v	England	Sydney	1924-25
61.3	6	302	10	A.A.Mailey	Australia	v	England	Adelaide	1920-21

BOWLERS UNCHANGED IN A COMPLETED INNINGS

AUSTRALIA

		Opponents		
G.E.Palmer (7-68)	E.Evans (3-64)	England (133)	Sydney	1881-82
F.R.Spofforth (5-30)	G.E.Palmer (4-32)	England (77)	Sydney	1884-85
C.T.B.Turner (6-15)	J.J.Ferris (4-27)	England (45)	Sydney	1886-87
C.T.B.Turner (5-36)	J.J.Ferris (5-26)	England (62)	Lord's	1888
G.Giffen (5-26)	C.T.B.Turner (4-33)	England (72)	Sydney	1894-95
H.Trumble (3-38)	M.A.Noble (7-17)	England (61)	Melbourne	1901-02
M.A.Noble (5-54)	J.V.Saunders (5-43)	England (99)	Sydney	1901-02

ENGLAND

		Opponents		
F.Morley (2-34)	R.G.Barlow (7-40)	Australia (83)	Sydney	1882-83
G.A.Lohmann (7-36)	J.Briggs(3-28)	Australia (68)	The Oval	1886
G.A.Lohmann (5-17)	R.Peel (5-18)	Australia (42)	Sydney	1887-88
J.Briggs (8-11)	A.J.Fothergill (1-30)	South Africa (43)	Cape Town	1888-89
J.J.Ferris (7-37)	F.Martin (2-39)	South Africa (83)	Cape Town	1891-92
J.Briggs (6-49)	G.A.Lohmann (3-46)	Australia (100)	Adelaide	1891-92
T.Richardson (6-39)	G.A.Lohmann (3-13)	Australia (53)	Lord's	1896
S.Haigh (6-11)	A.E.Trott (4-19)	South Africa (35)	Cape Town	1898-99
S.F.Barnes (6-42)	C.Blythe (4-64)	Australia (112)	Melbourne	1901-02
G.H.Hirst (4-28)	C.Blythe (6-44)	Australia (74)	Birmingham	1909
F.R.Foster (5-16)	S.F.Barnes (5-25)	South Africa (58)	Lord's	1912
A.E.R.Gilligan (6-7)	M.W.Tate (4-12)	South Africa (30)	Birmingham	1924
G.O.B.Allen (5-36)	W.Voce (4-16)	Australia (58)	Brisbane[2]	1936-37

PAKISTAN

		Opponents		
Fazal Mahmood (6-34)	Khan Mohammad (4-43)	Australia (80)	Karachi[1]	1956-57
Wasim Akram (4-32)	Waqar Younis (6-34)	Sri Lanka (71)	Kandy	1994-95

WEST INDIES		Opponents		
C.E.L.Ambrose (6-24)	C.A.Walsh (3-16)	England (46)	Port-of-Spain	1993-94

MOST LBW'S IN AN INNINGS BY ONE BOWLER

FIVE					
T.M.Alderman	Australia	v	Pakistan	Melbourne	1989-90
C.E.L.Ambrose	West Indies	v	England	Bridgetown	1989-90
FOUR					
P.S.Heine	South Africa	v	England	Leeds	1955
G.A.R.Lock	England	v	New Zealand	Leeds	1958
Abdul Qadir	Pakistan	v	England	Karachi[1]	1977-78
Kapil Dev	India	v	Australia	Kanpur	1979-80
R.J.Hadlee	New Zealand	v	West Indies	Dunedin	1979-80
L.S.Pascoe	Australia	v	England	Lord's	1980
R.M.Ellison	England	v	West Indies	Kingston	1985-86
Abdul Qadir	Pakistan	v	England	Faisalabad	1987-88
N.D.Hirwani	India	v	New Zealand	Bangalore	1988-89
T.M.Alderman	Australia	v	England	Leeds	1989
T.M.Alderman	Australia	v	England	Lord's	1989
G.P.Wickramasinghe	Sri Lanka	v	Pakistan	Faisalabad	1991-92
Waqar Younis	Pakistan	v	Zimbabwe	Karachi[2]	1993-94

MOST LBW'S IN A MATCH BY ONE BOWLER

SEVEN					
R.J.Hadlee	New Zealand	v	West Indies	Dunedin	1979-80
Abdul Qadir	Pakistan	v	England	Faisalabad	1987-88
Waqar Younis	Pakistan	v	Zimbabwe	Karachi[2]	1993-94
SIX					
Imran Khan	Pakistan	v	India	Faisalabad	1982-83
T.M.Alderman	Australia	v	Pakistan	Melbourne	1989-90
C.E.L.Ambrose	West Indies	v	England	Bridgetown	1989-90
Waqar Younis	Pakistan	v	West Indies	St John's	1992-93
FIVE					
Fazal Mahmood	Pakistan	v	India	Lucknow[1]	1952-53
Kapil Dev	India	v	Australia	Kanpur	1979-80
N.D.Hirwani	India	v	New Zealand	Bangalore	1988-89
T.M.Alderman	Australia	v	England	Leeds	1989
T.M.Alderman	Australia	v	England	Lord's	1989
Wasim Akram	Pakistan	v	West Indies	Lahore[2]	1990-91
G.P.Wickramasinghe	Sri Lanka	v	Pakistan	Faisalabad	1991-92
C.C.Lewis	England	v	New Zealand	Auckland	1991-92

FIFTY WICKETS AT A TEST GROUND

Player	Country	Ground	M	Balls	Mdns	Runs	Wkts	Avge	5w	10w	Best
Lillee,DK	Aust	Melbourne	14	3833	105	1798	82	21.92	7	4	7/83
Hadlee,RJ	NZ	Christchurch	14	3679	112	1635	76	21.51	6	0	7/116
Botham,IT	Eng	Lord's	15	3194	125	1693	69	24.53	8	1	8/34
Trueman,FS	Eng	Lord's	12	3087	113	1394	63	22.12	5	1	6/31
Abdul Qadir	Pak	Karachi[1]	13	3655	128	1571	59	26.62	5	1	5/44
Imran Khan	Pak	Lahore[2]	11	2443	93	937	56	16.73	3	1	8/58
Hadlee,RJ	NZ	Wellington	12	2623	90	1075	53	20.28	3	2	7/23
Botham,IT	Eng	The Oval	11	2615	90	1379	52	26.51	2	1	6/125
Gibbs,LR	WI	Port-of-Spain	13	4754	239	1646	52	31.65	2	0	6/108
Bedser,AV	Eng	Manchester	7	1816	88	686	51	13.45	5	2	7/52
Imran Khan	Pak	Karachi[1]	11	2406	100	938	51	18.39	2	1	8/60
Abdul Qadir	Pak	Lahore[2]	12	3099	105	1348	51	26.43	3	2	9/56

50 WICKETS IN THE CALENDAR YEAR *# includes one match in which player did not bowl.*

Player (Country)	Year	Tests	Balls	Mdns	Runs	Wkts	Avge	5w	10w	Best
D.K.Lillee (A)	1981	13	3710	162	1781	85	20.95	5	2	7/83
J.Garner (W)	1984	15	3620	149	1603	77	20.81	4	0	6/60
Kapil Dev (I)	1983	18	3469	112	1738	75	23.17	5	1	9/83
Kapil Dev (I)	1979	18	3651	147	1720	74	23.24	5	0	6/63
M.D.Marshall (W)	1984	13	3251	121	1471	73	20.15	9	1	7/53
S.K.Warne (A)	1993	16	5054	316	1697	72	23.56	2	0	6/31
G.D.McKenzie (A)	1964	14	4106	119	1737	71	24.46	4	1	7/153
S.F.Barnes (E)	1912	10	2394	106	959	64	14.98	8	3	8/29 #
R.J.Hadlee (N)	1985	10	2588	102	1116	64	17.43	6	2	9/52
I.T.Botham (E)	1978	12	2757	91	1160	63	18.41	6	1	8/34
F.S.Trueman (E)	1963	11	2563	90	1061	62	17.11	6	2	7/44
I.T.Botham (E)	1981	12	3338	136	1590	62	25.64	4	1	6/95
Imran Khan (P)	1982	9	2359	112	824	62	13.29	5	2	8/58
C.A.Walsh (W)	1995	12	3051	111	1347	62	21.72	4	1	7/37
M.D.Marshall (W)	1988	10	2477	83	1072	60	17.86	4	1	7/22
R.G.D.Willis (E)	1978	14	2921	94	1056	57	18.52	4	0	5/32
M.G.Hughes (A)	1993	12	3033	127	1448	57	25.40	2	0	5/64
C.J.McDermott (A)	1991	9	2416	84	1188	56	21.21	4	1	8/97
A.A.Mailey (A)	1921	10	2849	63	1567	55	28.49	4	2	9/121 #
R.Benaud (A)	1959	9	3248	177	1031	55	18.74	4	0	5/76
Waqar Younis (P)	1993	7	1626	59	838	55	15.23	6	1	7/91
T.M.Alderman (A)	1981	9	2672	105	1222	54	22.62	4	0	6/135
M.D.Marshall (W)	1983	11	2371	99	1119	54	20.72	2	0	6/37
H.Trumble (A)	1902	8	2520	140	994	53	18.75	4	2	8/65
M.H.Mankad (I)	1952	10	3512	218	1170	53	22.07	5	2	8/52
M.A.Holding (W)	1976	11	2305	88	1080	53	20.37	4	1	8/92
B.S.Chandrasekhar (I)	1976	11	3139	108	1458	52	28.03	3	0	6/94
J.Garner (W)	1980	13	2758	139	897	52	17.25	1	0	6/56
R.G.D.Willis (E)	1982	13	2428	72	1236	52	23.76	2	0	6/101
G.D.McGrath (A)	1995	10	2319	92	1138	52	21.88	4	0	6/47
S.K.Warne (A)	1995	12	3051	156	1254	52	24.11	1	1	7/23
M.A.Noble (A)	1902	12	2208	100	989	51	19.39	6	2	7/17
J.M.Gregory (A)	1921	12	2702	84	1292	51	25.33	3	0	7/69
R.G.D.Willis (E)	1977	11	2146	58	1108	50	22.16	5	0	7/78
T.M.Alderman (A)	1989	10	2414	106	1019	50	20.38	6	1	6/128
S.K.Warne (A)	1994	8	3099	174	1084	50	21.68	4	1	7/56

FOUR OR MORE BOWLERS CONCEDING 100 RUNS IN AN INNINGS

FIVE BOWLERS

Australia (8d-758) v West Indies Kingston 1954-55
(D.T.Dewdney 1/115; F.M.King 2/126; D.S.Atkinson 1/132; O.G.Smith 2/145; F.M.M.Worrell 1/116 - nb G.S.Sobers 1/99 in the same innings)

West Indies (8d-652) v England Lord's 1973
(G.G.Arnold 0/111; R.G.D.Willis 4/118; A.W.Greig 3/180; D.L.Underwood 0/105; R.Illingworth 1/114)

Australia (6d-607) v New Zealand Brisbane[2] 1993-94
(D.K.Morrison 0/104; C.L.Cairns 1/128; S.B.Doull 2/105; R.P.de Groen 1/120; D.N.Patel 1/125)

FOUR BOWLERS

England (849) v West Indies Kingston 1929-30
(H.C.Griffith 2/555; G.Gladstone 1/139; O.C.Scott 5/266; F.R.Martin 1/128)

Australia (6d-729) v England Lord's 1930
(G.O.B.Allen 0/115; M.W.Tate 1/148; J.C.White 1/172; R.W.V.Robins 1/172)

Australia (554) v South Africa Melbourne 1931-32
(A.J.Bell 1/101; N.A.Quinn 1/113; C.L.Vincent 4/154; Q.McMillan 4/150)

England (524) v Australia Sydney 1932-33

(T.W.Wall 3/104; L.E.Nagel 2/110; W.J.O'Reilly 3/117; C.V.Grimmett 1/118)

Australia (701) v England The Oval 1934

(W.E.Bowes 4/164; G.O.B.Allen 4/170; E.W.Clark 2/110; H.Verity 0/123)

England (8d-658) v Australia Nottingham 1938

(E.L.McCormick 1/108; W.J.O'Reilly 3/164; L.O.Flrrtwood-Smith 4/153; F.A.Ward 0/142)

England (5-654) v South Africa Durban[2] 1938-39

(A.B.C.Langton 1/132; N.Gordon 1/174; B.Mitchell 1/133; E.L.Dalton 2/100)

Australia (674) v India Adelaide 1947-48

(C.R.Rangachari 4/141; M.H.Mankad 2/170; C.T.Sarwate 0/121; V.S.Hazare 0/110)

Australia (7d-549) v South Africa Port Elizabeth 1949-50

(C.N.McCarthy 0/121; M.G.Melle 2/132; H.J.Tayfield 2/103; N.B.F.Mann 2/154)

Australia (530) v South Africa Adelaide 1952-53

(M.G.Melle 1/105; E.R.H.Fuller 2/119; H.J.Tayfield 4/142; P.N.F.Mansell 2/113)

West Indies (8d-681) v England Port-of-Spain 1953-54

(F.S.Trueman 1/131; T.E.Bailey 0/104; J.C.Laker 2/154; G.A.R.Lock 2/178)

England (6d-558) v Pakistan Nottingham 1954

(Fazal Mahmood 0/148; Khan Mohammad 3/155; A.H.Kardar 1/110; Khalid Wazir 2/116)

Australia (8d-601) v England Brisbane[2] 1954-55

(A.V.Bedser 1/131; J.B.Statham 2/123; F.H.Tyson 1/160; T.E.Bailey 3/140)

England (5d-544) v Pakistan Birmingham 1962

(Mahmood Hussain 2/130; A.D'Souza 1/161; Intikhab Alam 2/117; Nasim-ul-Ghani 0/109)

South Africa (595) v Australia Adelaide 1963-64

(R.A.Gaunt 2/115; G.D.McKenzie 1/135; N.J.N.Hawke 3/139; R.Benaud 0/101)

Australia (8d-656) v England Manchester 1964

(J.S.E.Price 3/183; T.W.Cartwright 2/118; F.J.Titmus 0/100; J.B.Mortimore 0/122)

Australia (6d-650) v West Indies Bridgetown 1964-65

(W.W.Hall 2/117; C.C.Griffith 0/131; G.S.Sobers 1/143; L.R.Gibbs 2/168)

Australia (516) v England Adelaide 1965-66

(I.J.Jones 6/118; D.J.Brown 1/109; F.J.Titmus 3/116; D.A.Allen 0/103)

Australia (547) v West Indies Sydney 1968-69

(W.W.Hall 3/113; R.M.Edwards 2/139; G.S.Sobers 0/109; L.R.Gibbs 2/124)

New Zealand (9d-551) v England Lord's 1973

(J.A.Snow 3/109; G.G.Arnold 1/108; C.M.Old 5/113; N.Gifford 0/107)

Australia (6d-511) v New Zealand Wellington 1973-74

(M.G.Webb 2/114; R.O.Collinge 1/103; D.R.Hadlee 2/107; H.J.Howarth 0/113)

Pakistan (7d-600) v England The Oval 1974

(G.G.Arnold 1/106; R.G.D.Willis 2/102; C.M.Old 0/143; D.L.Underwood 2/106)

West Indies (585) v Australia Perth 1975-76

(D.K.Lillee 2/123; J.R.Thomson 3/128; G.J.Gilmour 2/103; A.A.Mallett 0/103)

Pakistan (9d-565) v New Zealand Karachi[1] 1976-77

(R.O.Collinge 2/141; R.J.Hadlee 4/138; B.L.Cairns 1/142; D.R.O'Sullivan 2/131)

India (7d-644) v West Indies Kanpur 1978-79

(M.D.Marshall 1/123; V.A.Holder 0/118; R.R.Jumadeen 3/137; D.R.Parry 2/127)

England (5d-633) v India Birmingham 1979

(Kapil Dev 5/146; K.D.Ghavri 0/129; B.S.Chandrasekhar 0/113; S.Venkataraghavan 0/107)

Australia (528) v India Adelaide 1980-81

(Kapil Dev 2/112; K.D.Ghavri 0/106; D.R.Doshi 3/146; N.S.Yadav 4/143)

Pakistan (7d-500) v Sri Lanka Lahore[2] 1981-82

(A.L.F.de Mel 3/120; J.R.Ratnayeke 3/121; D.S.de Silva 1/129; R.G.C.E.Wijesuriya 0/105)

Pakistan (652) v India Faisalabad 1982-83

(Kapil Dev 7/220; S.Madan Lal 2/109; D.R.Doshi 0/130; Maninder Singh 1/103)

Pakistan (3d-581) v India Hyderabad 1982-83

(Kapil Dev 0/111; B.S.Sandhu 2/107; Maninder Singh 0/135; D.R.Doshi 1/143)

Pakistan (624) v Australia Adelaide 1983-84

(G.F.Lawson 2/127; R.M.Hogg 1/123; D.K.Lillee 6/171; T.G.Hogan 1/107)

West Indies (606) v England Birmingham 1984
(R.G.D.Willis 2/108; I.T.Botham 1/127; D.R.Pringle 5/108; N.G.B.Cook 1/127)

India (8d-553) v England Kanpur 1984-85
(N.G.Cowans 2/115; N.A.Foster 3/123; P.H.Edmonds 1/112; C.S.Cowdrey 1/103)

New Zealand (7d-533) v Australia Brisbane[2] 1985-86
(C.J.McDermott 1/119; D.R.Gilbert 2/102; G.R.J.Matthews 3/110; R.G.Holland 0/106)

England (8d-592) v Australia Perth 1986-87
(G.F.Lawson 0/126; C.D.Matthews 3/112; B.A.Reid 4/115; G.R.J.Matthews 1/124)

Australia (5d-514) v England Adelaide 1986-87
(G.R.Dilley 1/111; P.A.J.DeFreitas 1/128; J.E.Emburey 1/117; P.H.Edmonds 2/134)

India (7d-676) v Sri Lanka Kanpur 1986-87
(A.L.F.de Mel 1/119; G.F.Labrooy 1/164; J.R.Ratnayeke 4/132; E.A.R.de Silva 0/133)

Australia (7d-601) v England Leeds 1989
(P.A.J.DeFreitas 2/140; N.A.Foster 3/109; P.J.Newport 2/153; D.R.Pringle 0/123)

Pakistan (5-699) v India Lahore[2] 1989-90
(M.Prabhakar 1/107; Maninder Singh 2/191; Arshad Ayub 0/182; R.J.Shastri 105)

England (4d-653) v India Lord's 1990
(Kapil Dev 1/120; M.Prabhakar 1/187; S.K.Sharma 1/122; N.D.Hirwani 1/102)

India (454) v England Lord's 1990
D.E.Malcolm 1/106; A.R.C.Fraser 5/104; C.C.Lewis 1/108; E.E.Hemmings 2/109)

India (9d-606) v England The Oval 1990
(D.E.Malcolm 2/110; A.R.C.Fraser 2/112; N.F.Williams 2/148; E.E.Hemmings 2/117)

England (9d-580) v New Zealand Christchurch 1991-92
(D.K.Morrison 2/133; C.L.Cairns 1/118; C.Pringle 3/127; D.N.Patel 2/132)

Australia (4d-653) v England Leeds 1993
(M.J.McCague 0/110; M.C.Ilott 3/161; A.R.Caddick 0/138; M.P.Bicknell 1/155)

Pakistan (5d-548) v New Zealand Wellington 1993-94
(D.K.Morrison 2/139; R.P.de Groen 0/104; S.B.Doull 0/112; M.N.Hart 1/102)

West Indies (5d-593) v England St John's 1993-94
(A.R.C.Fraser 2/121; A.R.Caddick 3/158; P.C.R.Tufnell 0/110; C.C.Lewis 0/140)

West Indies (8d-592) v England The Oval 1995
(D.E.Malcolm 3/160; A.R.C.Fraser 1/155; M.Watkinson 0/113; D.G.Cork 3/145)

Wicketkeeping

MOST DISMISSALS IN TEST CAREER

Player	Country	Tests	Dis	C	S	A	E	SA	WI	NZ	I	P	SL	Z
						Opponents								
R.W.Marsh	A	96	**355**	343	12	-	148	-	65	58	16	68	-	-
I.A.Healy	A	79	**275**	255	20	-	89	12	55	34	19	36	30	-
P.J.L.Dujon	WI	81	**272**	267 ¶	5	86	84	-	-	20	60	22	-	-
A.P.E.Knott	E	95	**269**	250	19	105	-	-	43	26	54	41	-	-
Wasim Bari	P	81	**228**	201	27	66	54	-	21	32	55	-	-	-
T.G.Evans	E	91	**219**	173	46	76	-	59	37	28	12	7	-	-
S.M.H.Kirmani	I	88	**198**	160	38	41	42	-	36	28	-	50	1	-
D.L.Murray	WI	62	**189**	181	8	40	94	-	-	7	27	21	-	-
A.T.W.Grout	A	51	**187**	163	24	-	76	33	41	-	20	17	-	-
I.D.S.Smith	NZ	63	**176**	168	8	39	42	-	16	-	29	23	27	-
R.W.Taylor	E	57	**174**	167	7	57				45	40	29	3	-
R.C.Russell	E	49	**152**	141	11	28	-	27	39	16	20	16	6	-
J.H.B.Waite	SA	50	**141**	124	17	28	56	-	-	57	-	-	-	-
W.A.S.Oldfield	A	54	**130**	78	52	-	90	27	13	-	-	-	-	-
K.S.More	I	49	**130**	110	20	13	37	11	21	13		21	11	3
J.M.Parks	E	46	**114**	103 §	11	21		30	31	22	9	1	-	-
D.J.Richardson	SA	28	**107**	107	0	17	15	-	6	23	16	7	17	6
Saleem Yousuf	P	32	**104**	91	13	15	15	-	22	22	11	-	19	-

Best for the other countries are:

Player	Country	Tests	Dis	C	S	A	E	SA	WI	NZ	I	P	SL	Z
S.A.R.Silva	SL	9	**34**	33	1	-	6	-	-	2	22	4	-	-
A.Flower	Z	16	**41**	39 †	2	-	-	2	-	14	3	17	5	-

§ Including 2 catches in 3 Tests when not keeping wicket. ¶ Including 2 catches in 2 Tests when not keeping wicket.
† includes 5 catches in 4 Tests when not keeping wicket.

MOST DISMISSALS IN A MATCH *(§ In first Test)*

AUSTRALIA

9 (8c, 1s)	G.R.A.Langley	England	Lord's	1956
9 (9c)	R.W.Marsh	England	Brisbane[2]	1982-83
9 (9c)	I.A.Healy	England	Brisbane[2]	1994-95
8 (8c)	J.J.Kelly	England	Sydney	1901-02
8 (8c)	G.R.A.Langley	West Indies	Kingston	1954-55
8 (6c, 2s)	A.T.W.Grout	Pakistan	Lahore[2]	1959-60
8 (8c)	A.T.W.Grout	England	Lord's	1961
8 (7c, 1s) §	H.B.Taber	South Africa	Johannesburg[3]	1966-67
8 (8c)	R.W.Marsh	West Indies	Melbourne	1975-76
8 (8c)	R.W.Marsh	New Zealand	Christchurch	1976-77
8 (7c, 1s)	R.W.Marsh	India	Sydney	1980-81
8 (8c)	R.W.Marsh	England	Adelaide	1982-83
8 (8c)	I.A.Healy	West Indies	Adelaide	1992-93
8 (8c)	I.A.Healy	England	Melbourne	1994-95
8 (8c)	I.A.Healy	Sri Lanka	Adelaide	1995-96

ENGLAND

11 (11c)	R.C.Russell	South Africa	Johannesburg[3]	1995-96
10 (10c)	R.W.Taylor	India	Mumbai[3]	1979-80
9 (7c, 2s)	R.C.Russell	South Africa	Port Elizabeth	1995-96
8 (6c, 2s)	L.E.G.Ames	West Indies	The Oval	1933
8 (8c)	J.M.Parks	New Zealand	Christchurch	1965-66

SOUTH AFRICA

9 (9c)	D.J.Richardson	India	Port Elizabeth	1992-93
8 (8c)	D.T.Lindsay	Australia	Johannesburg[3]	1966-67
8 (8c)	D.J.Richardson	Sri Lanka	Colombo (SSC)	1993-94

WEST INDIES

9 (9c)	D.A.Murray	Australia	Melbourne	1981-82
9 (9c)	C.O.Browne	England	Lord's	1995
8 (8c)	J.R.Murray	Australia	Perth	1992-93

NEW ZEALAND

8 (8c)	W.K.Lees	Sri Lanka	Wellington	1982-83
8 (8c)	I.D.S.Smith	Sri Lanka	Hamilton	1990-91

INDIA

7 (1c, 6s)	K.S.More	West Indies	Chennai[1]	1987-88
7 (5c, 2s)	K.S.More	England	Mumbai[3]	1992-93

PAKISTAN

9 (9c)	Rashid Latif	New Zealand	Auckland	1993-94
8 (8c)	Wasim Bari	England	Leeds	1971
8 (7c, 1s)	Rashid Latif	Australia	Sydney	1995-96

SRI LANKA

9 (9c)	S.A.R.Silva	India	Colombo (SSC)	1985-86
9 (8c, 1s)	S.A.R.Silva	India	Colombo (PSS)	1985-86

ZIMBABWE

7 (7c)	W.R.James	Sri Lanka	Bulawayo[2]	1994-95

MOST DISMISSALS IN A SERIES *(§ In first series. # In last series)*

AUSTRALIA

Total	C	S	Tests	Player	Opponents	Season
28	28	-	5	R.W.Marsh	England	1982-83
26	26	-	6	R.W.Marsh	West Indies	1975-76
26	21	5	6	I.A.Healy	England	1993
25	23	2	5	I.A.Healy	England	1994-95
24	24	-	5	I.A.Healy	England	1990-91
23	20	3	5	A.T.W.Grout	West Indies	1960-61
23	21	2	5	R.W.Marsh	England	1972
23	23	-	6	R.W.Marsh	England	1981
23	19	4	5	I.A.Healy	West Indies	1992-93
22 §	22	-	5	S.J.Rixon	India	1977-78
21 #	13	8	5	R.A.Saggers	South Africa	1949-50
21 §	16	5	5	G.R.A.Langley	West Indies	1951-52
21	20	1	5	A.T.W.Grout	England	1961
21 #	21	-	5	R.W.Marsh	Pakistan	1983-84
20	16	4	5	D.Tallon	England	1946-47
20	16	4	4	G.R.A.Langley	West Indies	1954-55
20	17	3	5	A.T.W.Grout	England	1958-59
20 §	19	1	5	H.B.Taber	South Africa	1966-67

ENGLAND

Total	C	S	Tests	Player	Opponents	Season
27	25	2	5	R.C.Russell	South Africa	1995-96
24	21	3	6	A.P.E.Knott	Australia	1970-71

23	22	1	6	A.P.E.Knott	Australia	1974-75
21	21	-	5	H.Strudwick	South Africa	1913-14
21	20	1	5	S.J.Rhodes	Australia	1994-95
20	20	-	-	T.G.Evans	South Africa	1956-57
20	18	2	6	R.W.Taylor	Australia	1978-79
20	19	1	6	P.R.Downton	Australia	1985

SOUTH AFRICA

Total	C	S	Tests	Player	Opponents	Season
26	23	3	5	J.H.B.Waite	New Zealand	1961-62
24	24	-	5	D.T.Lindsay	Australia	1966-67
23	16	7	5	J.H.B.Waite	New Zealand	1953-54

WEST INDIES

Total	C	S	Tests	Player	Opponents	Season
24 §	22	2	5	D.L.Murray	England	1963
23	22	1	5	F.C.M.Alexander	England	1959-60
23	23	-	5	P.J.L.Dujon	Australia	1990-91
20	19	1	5	P.J.L.Dujon	Australia	1983-84
20	20	-	5	P.J.L.Dujon	England	1988

NEW ZEALAND

Total	C	S	Tests	Player	Opponents	Season
23 §	21	2	5	A.E.Dick	South Africa	1961-62

INDIA

Total	C	S	Tests	Player	Opponents	Season
19 §	12	7	5	N.S.Tamhane	Pakistan	1954-55
19	17	2	6	S.M.H.Kirmani	Pakistan	1979-80

PAKISTAN

Total	C	S	Tests	Player	Opponents	Season
17	15	2	6	Wasim Bari	India	1982-83

SRI LANKA

Total	C	S	Tests	Player	Opponents	Season
22	21	1	3	S.A.R.Silva	India	1985-86

ZIMBABWE

Total	C	S	Tests	Player	Opponents	Season
13	13	0	2	W.R.James	Sri Lanka	1994-95

MOST DISMISSALS IN AN INNINGS *(§ In first Test. # in last Test)*

AUSTRALIA

6 (6c) §	A.T.W.Grout	South Africa	Johannesburg[3]	1957-58
6 (6c)	R.W.Marsh	England	Brisbane[2]	1982-83
5 (1c, 4s)	W.A.S.Oldfield	England	Melbourne	1924-25
5 (2c, 3s)	G.R.A.Langley	West Indies	Georgetown	1954-55
5 (5c)	G.R.A.Langley	West Indies	Kingston	1954-55
5 (5c)	G.R.A.Langley	England	Lord's	1956
5 (4c, 1s)	A.T.W.Grout	South Africa	Durban[2]	1957-58
5 (5c)	A.T.W.Grout	Pakistan	Lahore[2]	1959-60
5 (4c, 1s)	A.T.W.Grout	West Indies	Brisbane[2]	1960-61
5 (5c)	A.T.W.Grout	England	Lord's	1961
5 (5c)	A.T.W.Grout	England	Sydney	1965-66

5 (5c) §	H.B.Taber	South Africa	Johannesburg[3]	1966-67
5 (5c)	H.B.Taber	West Indies	Sydney	1968-69
5 (5c) #	H.B.Taber	South Africa	Port Elizabeth	1969-70
5 (5c)	R.W.Marsh	England	Manchester	1972
5 (5c)	R.W.Marsh	England	Nottingham	1972
5 (5c)	R.W.Marsh	New Zealand	Sydney	1973-74
5 (5c)	R.W.Marsh	New Zealand	Christchurch	1973-74
5 (5c)	R.W.Marsh	West Indies	Melbourne	1975-76
5 (5c)	R.W.Marsh	New Zealand	Christchurch	1976-77
5 (5c) §	J.A.Maclean	England	Brisbane[2]	1978-79
5 (5c)	K.J.Wright	Pakistan	Melbourne	1978-79
5 (5c)	R.W.Marsh	West Indies	Brisbane[2]	1979-80
5 (5c)	R.W.Marsh	India	Sydney	1980-81
5 (5c)	R.W.Marsh	Pakistan	Perth	1981-82
5 (5c)	R.W.Marsh	Pakistan	Perth	1983-84
5 (5c) #	R.W.Marsh	Pakistan	Sydney	1983-84
5 (5c)	W.B.Phillips	West Indies	Kingston	1983-84
5 (5c)	I.A.Healy	Pakistan	Adelaide	1989-90
5 (5c)	I.A.Healy	England	Melbourne	1990-91
5 (5c)	I.A.Healy	England	Adelaide	1990-91
5 (5c)	I.A.Healy	New Zealand	Brisbane[2]	1993-94
5 (5c)	I.A.Healy	Pakistan	Rawalpindi[2]	1994-95
5 (4c, 1s) §	P.A.Emery	Pakistan	Lahore[2]	1994-95
5 (5c)	I.A.Healy	England	Brisbane[2]	1994-95
5 (5c)	I.A.Healy	England	Melbourne	1994-95
5 (5c)	I.A.Healy	Sri Lanka	Adelaide	1995-96

ENGLAND

7 (7c)	R.W.Taylor	India	Mumbai[3]	1979-80
6 (6c)	J.T.Murray	India	Lord's	1967
6 (6c)	R.C.Russell	Australia	Melbourne	1990-91
6 (6c)	R.C.Russell	South Africa (1st Innings)	Johannesburg[3]	1995-96
5 (5c)	J.G.Binks	India	Calcutta	1963-64
5 (3c, 2s)	J.M.Parks	Australia	Sydney	1965-66
5 (5c)	J.M.Parks	New Zealand	Christchurch	1965-66
5 (4c, 1s)	A.P.E.Knott	India	Manchester	1974
5 (5c)	R.W.Taylor	New Zealand	Nottingham	1978
5 (5c)	R.W.Taylor	Australia	Brisbane[2]	1978-79
5 (5c)	C.J.Richards	Australia	Melbourne	1986-87
5 (5c)	R.C.Russell	West Indies	Bridgetown	1989-90
5 (5c)	R.C.Russell	South Africa (2nd Innings)	Johannesburg[3]	1995-96
5 (4c, 1s)	R.C.Russell	South Africa	Port Elizabeth	1995-96

SOUTH AFRICA

6 (6c)	D.T.Lindsay	Australia	Johannesburg[3]	1966-67
5 (5c)	D.J.Richardson	India	Port Elizabeth	1992-93

WEST INDIES

5 (5c)	F.C.M.Alexander	England	Bridgetown	1959-60
5 (5c)	D.L.Murray	England	Leeds	1976
5 (5c)	D.L.Murray	Pakistan	Georgetown	1976-77
5 (5c)	D.A.Murray	India	Delhi	1978-79
5 (5c)	D.A.Murray	Australia	Melbourne	1981-82
5 (5c)	P.J.L.Dujon	India	Kingston	1982-83
5 (5c)	P.J.L.Dujon	England	Bridgetown	1985-86
5 (5c)	P.J.L.Dujon	Australia	St John's	1990-91
5 (5c)	D.Williams	Australia	Brisbane[2]	1992-93

5 (5c)	J.R.Murray	Australia	Perth	1992-93
5 (5c)	C.O.Browne	England	Nottingham	1005

NEW ZEALAND

7 (7c)	I.D.S.Smith	Sri Lanka	Hamilton	1990-91
5 (5c)	R.I.Harford	India	Wellington	1967-68
5 (5c)	K.J.Wadsworth	Pakistan	Auckland	1972-73
5 (5c)	W.K.Lees	Sri Lanka	Wellington	1982-83
5 (4c, 1s)	I.D.S.Smith	England	Auckland	1983-84
5 (5c)	I.D.S.Smith	Sri Lanka	Auckland	1990-91
5 (5c)	A.C.Parore	England	Auckland	1991-92
5 (4c, 1s)	A.C.Parore	Sri Lanka	Colombo (SSC)	1992-93

INDIA

6 (5c, 1s)	S.M.H.Kirmani	New Zealand	Christchurch	1975-76
5 (3c, 2s)	B.K.Kunderan	England	Mumbai[1]	1961-62
5 (5c)	S.M.H.Kirmani	Pakistan	Faisalabad	1982-83
5 (0c, 5s)	K.S.More	West Indies	Chennai[1]	1987-88

PAKISTAN

7 (7c)	Wasim Bari	New Zealand	Auckland	1978-79
5 (4c, 1s)	Imtiaz Ahmed	Australia	Lahore[2]	1959-60
5 (5c)	Wasim Bari	England	Leeds	1971
5 (5c)	Saleem Yousuf	Sri Lanka	Karachi[1]	1985-86
5 (5c)	Saleem Yousuf	New Zealand	Faisalabad	1990-91
5 (4c, 1s)	Moin Khan	West Indies	Bridgetown	1992-93
5 (5c)	Rashid Latif	Zimbabwe	Lahore[2]	1993-94
5 (5c)	Rashid Latif	New Zealand	Auckland	1993-94
5 (4c, s1)	Rashid Latif	Australia	Sydney	1995-96
5 (5c)	Rashid Latif	New Zealand	Christchurch	1995-96

SRI LANKA

6 (6c)	S.A.R.Silva	India	Colombo (SSC)	1985-86
5 (5c)	S.A.R.Silva	India	Colombo (PSS)	1985-86
5 (5c)	H.P.Tillakaratne	New Zealand	Hamilton	1990-91
5 (5c)	P.B.Dasanayake	Zimbabwe	Harare	1994-95

ZIMBABWE

5 (5c)	W.R.James	Sri Lanka	Bulawayo[2]	1994-95
4 (4c)	A.Flower	New Zealand	Harare	1992-93
4 (4c)	A.Flower	Pakistan	Karachi[2]	1993-94
4 (4c)	W.R.James	Sri Lanka	Harare	1994-95
4 (4c)	A.Flower	Pakistan	Harare	1994-95

MOST STUMPINGS IN A SERIES

9	P.W.Sherwell	South Africa	v	Australia	in Australia	1910-11

MOST STUMPINGS IN A MATCH

6	K.S.More	India	v	West Indies	Chennai[1]	1987-88

MOST STUMPINGS IN AN INNINGS

5	K.S.More	India	v	West Indies	Chennai[1]	1987-88

WICKETKEEPERS WITH 30 DISMISSALS IN THE CALENDAR YEAR

Player	Country	Year	Tests	C	S	Dismissals
I.A.Healy	Australia	1993	15	57	9	66
P.J.L.Dujon	West Indies	1984	15	54	1	55
R.W.Marsh	Australia	1981	13	52	1	53
R.W.Taylor	England	1978	14	43	1	44
R.W.Marsh	Australia	1982	12	42	1	43
R.W.Marsh	Australia	1975	10	38	2	40
R.C.Russell	England	1990	12	39	1	40
P.J.L.Dujon	West Indies	1991	10	40	0	40
A.P.E.Knott	England	1974	14	37	2	39
D.L.Murray	West Indies	1976	12	37	2	39
A.P.E.Knott	England	1971	11	34	4	38
S.M.H.Kirmani	India	1983	18	35	3	38
P.J.L.Dujon	West Indies	1988	12	37	1	38
R.W.Marsh	Australia	1974	9	36	1	37
A.T.W.Grout	Australia	1961	9	33	3	36
I.A.Healy	Australia	1995	12	32	4	36
K.J.Wright	Australia	1979	10	31	4	35
R.W.Taylor	England	1982	14	35	0	35
P.J.L.Dujon	West Indies	1983	11	34	1	35
Wasim Bari	Pakistan	1983	11	32	3	35
A.T.W.Grout	Australia	1964	10	33	1	34
I.A.Healy	Australia	1991	10	34	0	34
R.W.Marsh	Australia	1977	10	33	0	33
Wasim Bari	Pakistan	1979	9	31	2	33
J.R.Murray	West Indies	1995	9	33	0	33
R.C.Russell	England	1995	7	30	3	33
J.R.Murray	West Indies	1995	9	33	0	33
P.R.Downton	England	1985	9	31	1	32
T.G.Evans	England	1957	9	29	2	31
J.M.Parks	England	1966	10	28	3	31
S.M.H.Kirmani	India	1979	14	27	4	31
A.T.W.Grout	Australia	1959	8	24	6	30
A.P.E.Knott	England	1973	13	30	0	30
I.A.Healy	Australia	1995	11	28	2	30
D.J.Richardson	South Africa	1995	8	30	0	30

NO BYES CONCEDED IN TOTAL OF 500 RUNS

4-671	H.P.Tillakaratne	Sri Lanka	v	New Zealand	Wellington	1990-91
5d-660	A.C.Parore	New Zealand	v	West Indies	Wellington	1994-95
8d-659	T.G.Evans	England	v	Australia	Sydney	1946-47
652	S.M.H.Kirmani	India	v	Pakistan	Faisalabad	1982-83
4d-632	A.J.Stewart	England	v	Australia	Lord's	1993
619	J.L.Hendriks	West Indies	v	Australia	Sydney	1968-69
5d-616	I.D.S.Smith	New Zealand	v	Pakistan	Auckland	1988-89
7d-601	R C Russell	England	v	Australia	Leeds	1989
5d-593	R.C.Russell	England	v	West Indies	St John's	1993-94
8d-567	A.C.Parore	New Zealand	v	England	Nottingham	1994
9d-559	W.W.Wade	South Africa	v	England	Cape Town	1938-39
551	J.J.Kelly	Australia	v	England	Sydney	1897-98
9d-551	A.P.E.Knott	England	v	New Zealand	Lord's	1973
7d-548	L.K.Germon	New Zealand	v	West Indies	St John's	1995-96
5d-544	Imtiaz Ahmed	Pakistan	v	England	Birmingham	1962
3d-543	T.M.Findlay	West Indies	v	New Zealand	Georgetown	1971-72
9d-536	I.A.Healy	Australia	v	West Indies	Bridgetown	1990-91
9d-532	A.P.E.Knott	England	v	Australia	The Oval	1975

531	D.T.Lindsay	South Africa	v	England	Johannesburg[3]	1964-65
528	S.M.H.Kirmani	India	v	Australia	Adelaide	1980-81
528	R.C.Russell	England	v	Australia	Lord's	1989
7d-526	A.P.E.Knott	England	v	West Indies	Port-of-Spain	1967-68
521	W.A.S.Oldfield	Australia	v	England	Brisbane[1]	1928-29
520	J.H.B.Waite	South Africa	v	Australia	Melbourne	1952-53
515	P.J.L.Dujon	West Indies	v	Australia	Adelaide	1988-89
4d-514	R.G.de Alwis	Sri Lanka	v	Australia	Kandy	1982-83
5d-514	C.J.Richards	England	v	Australia	Adelaide	1986-87
6d-512	B.N.French	England	v	New Zealand	Wellington	1987-88
510	J.L.Hendriks	West Indies	v	Australia	Melbourne	1968-69
509	W.B.Phillips	Australia	v	West Indies	Bridgetown	1983-84
6d-507	K.J.Wadsworth	New Zealand	v	Pakistan	Dunedin	1972-73
8d-503	S.M.H.Kirmani	India	v	Pakistan	Faisalabad	1978-79
6d-500	R.S.Kaluwitharana	Sri Lanka	v	Australia	Melbourne	1995-96

MOST BYES CONCEDED IN AN INNINGS

37	F.E.Woolley	England	v	Australia	The Oval	1934

(At the age of 47, standing-in for the injured L.E.G.Ames).

33	J.T.Murray	England	v	India	Mumbai[2]	1961-62
33	J.M.Parks	England	v	West Indies	Kingston	1967-68

Fielding

MOST CATCHES IN TESTS

				Opponents								
Player	Country	Tests	C	A	E	SA	WI	NZ	I	P	SL	Z
A.R.Border	A	156	**156**	-	57	5	19	31	14	22	8	-
G.S.Chappell	A	87	**122**	-	61	-	16	18	5	22	-	-
I.V.A.Richards	WI	121	**122**	24	29	-	-	7	39	23	-	-
I.T.Botham	E	102	**120**	61	-	-	15	14	14	14	2	-
M.C.Cowdrey	E	114	**120**	40	-	22	21	15	11	11	-	-
R.B.Simpson	A	62	**110**	-	30	27	29	-	21	3	-	-
W.R.Hammond	E	85	**110**	43	-	30	22	9	6	-	-	-
G.S.Sobers	WI	93	**109**	27	40	-		11	27	4	-	-
S.M.Gavaskar	I	125	**108**	19	35	-	17	11	-	19	7	-
M.A.Taylor	A	72	**105**	-	31	6	19	15	7	16	11	-
I.M.Chappell	A	75	**105**	-	31	11	24	16	17	6	-	-
G.A.Gooch	E	118	**103**	29	-	1	28	13	21	7	4	-

The most successful catchers for the other countries are:

Player	Country	Tests	C	A	E	SA	WI	NZ	I	P	SL	Z
B.Mitchell	SA	42	**56**	10	43	-	-	3	-	-	-	-
M.D.Crowe	NZ	77	**70**	10	19	7	12	-	2	15	4	1
Javed Miandad	P	124	**93**	10	22	-	12	20	18	-	11	-
† H.P.Tillakaratne	SL	25	**37**	1	4	6	-	12	6	6	-	2
D.L.Houghton	Z	16	**11**	-	-	2	-	4	-	5	-	-

† Tillakaratne also played 11 Tests as a wicket-keeper, taking 32 catches.

MOST CATCHES IN A SERIES *(§ In first Test series)*

AUSTRALIA

C	Tests	Player	Against	Season
15 §	5	J.M.Gregory	England	1920-21
14	6	G.S.Chappell	England	1974-75
13 §	5	R.B.Simpson	South Africa	1957-58
13	5	R.B.Simpson	West Indies	1960-61
12	5	D.F.Whatmore	India	1979-80
12	6	A.R.Border	England	1981

ENGLAND

C	Tests	Player	Against	Season
12 §	5	L.C.Braund	Australia	1901-02
12	5	W.R.Hammond	Australia	1934
12	3	J.T.Ikin	South Africa	1951
12	6	A.W.Greig	Australia	1974-75
12	6	I.T.Botham	Australia	1981

SOUTH AFRICA

C	Tests	Player	Against	Season
12	5	A.E.E.Vogler	England	1909-10
12	5	B.Mitchell	England	1930-31
12	5	T.L.Goddard	England	1956-57

WEST INDIES

C	Tests	Player	Against	Season
12	5	G.S.Sobers	Australia	1960-61

NEW ZEALAND

C	Tests	Player	Against	Season
9	3	B.A.Young	Pakistan	1993-94
8	5	B.Sutcliffe	South Africa	1953-54
8	4	B.A.G.Murray	India	1967-68
8	4	J.J.Crowe	West Indies	1984-85

INDIA

12	5	E.D.Solkar	England	1972-73
11	3	M.Azharuddin	Sri Lanka	1993-94
10	4	A.L.Wadekar	New Zealand	1967-68
10	4	E.D.Solkar	Australia	1969-70

PAKISTAN

9	5	W.Mathias	West Indies	1957-58

SRI LANKA

8	2	H.P.Tillakaratne	New Zealand	1992-93

ZIMBABWE

7	3	M.H.Dekker	Sri Lanka	1994-95

MOST CATCHES IN A MATCH *(§ In first Test. # In last Test)*

AUSTRALIA

7	G.S.Chappell	v	England	Perth	1974-75
6	J.M.Gregory	v	England	Sydney	1920-21
6 #	V.Y.Richardson	v	South Africa	Durban2	1935-36
6 #	R.N.Harvey	v	England	Sydney	1962-63
6	I.M.Chappell	v	New Zealand	Adelaide	1973-74
6	D.F.Whatmore	v	India	Kanpur	1979-80

ENGLAND

6	A.Shrewsbury	v	Australia	Sydney	1887-88
6	F.E.Woolley	v	Australia	Sydney	1911-12
6	M.C.Cowdrey	v	West Indies	Lord's	1963
6	A.W.Greig	v	Pakistan	Leeds	1974
6	A.J.Lamb	v	New Zealand	Lord's	1983
6	G.A.Hick	v	Pakistan	Leeds	1992

SOUTH AFRICA

6	A.E.E.Vogler	v	England	Durban[1]	1909-10
6	B.Mitchell	v	Australia	Melbourne	1931-32

WEST INDIES

6	G.S.Sobers	v	England	Lord's	1973
6	J.C.Adams	v	England	Bridgetown	1993-94

NEW ZEALAND

6	B.A.Young	v	Pakistan	Auckland	1993-94

INDIA

7 §	Yajurvindra Singh	v	England	Bangalore	1976-77
6	E.D.Solkar	v	West Indies	Port-of-Spain	1970-71

PAKISTAN

5	Majid Khan	v	Australia	Karachi[1]	1979-80
5	Inzamamul Haq	v	Zimbabwe	Rawalpindi[2]	1993-94

SRI LANKA

7	H.P.Tillakaratne	v	New Zealand	Colombo (SSC)	1992-93

ZIMBABWE

4	M.H.Dekker	v	Sri Lanka	Harare	1994-95

MOST CATCHES IN AN INNINGS *(§ In first Test. # In last Test)*

AUSTRALIA

5	V.Y.Richardson #	v	South Africa	Durban²	1935-36
4	H.Trumble	v	England	Lord's	1899
4	S.J.E.Loxton	v	England	Brisbane²	1950-51
4	G.B.Hole	v	South Africa	Sydney	1952-53
4	R.G.Archer	v	West Indies	Georgetown	1954-55
4	A.K.Davidson	v	India	Delhi	1959-60
4	R.B.Simpson	v	West Indies	Sydney	1960-61
4	R.N.Harvey #	v	England	Sydney	1962-63
4	R.B.Simpson	v	West Indies	Bridgetown	1964-65
4	I.M.Chappell	v	New Zealand	Adelaide	1973-74
4	G.S.Chappell	v	England	Perth	1974-75
4	A.Turner	v	Pakistan	Sydney	1976-77
4	D.F.Whatmore	v	India	Kanpur	1979-80
4	A.R.Border	v	Pakistan	Karachi¹	1979-80
4	K.J.Hughes	v	New Zealand	Perth	1980-81
4	D.C.Boon	v	Pakistan	Karachi¹	1988-89
4	M.A.Taylor	v	West Indies	Bridgetown	1994-95

ENGLAND

4	L.C.Braund	v	Australia	Sheffield	1902
4	W.Rhodes	v	Australia	Manchester	1905
4	L.C.Braund	v	Australia	Sydney	1907-08
4	F.E.Woolley	v	Australia	Sydney	1911-12
4	H.Larwood	v	Australia	Brisbane¹	1928-29
4	J.E.McConnon	v	Pakistan	Manchester	1954
4	P.B.H.May	v	Australia	Adelaide	1954-55
4	P.H.Parfitt	v	Australia	Nottingham	1972
4	A.W.Greig	v	Pakistan	Leeds	1974
4	P.H.Edmonds	v	New Zealand	Christchurch	1977-78
4	A.J.Lamb	v	New Zealand	Lord's	1983
4	G.A.Hick	v	Pakistan	Leeds	1992
4	G.A.Hick	v	India	Calcutta	1992-93
4	G.A.Hick	v	New Zealand	Nottingham	1994

SOUTH AFRICA

4	A.E.E.Vogler	v	England	Durban¹	1909-10
4	A.W.Nourse	v	England	Durban²	1922-23
4	B.Mitchell	v	Australia	Melbourne	1931-32
4	T.L.Goddard	v	Australia	Sydney	1963-64
4	A.J.Traicos §	v	Australia	Durban²	1969-70
4	A.C.Hudson	v	India	Cape Town	1992-93

WEST INDIES

4	E.D.Weekes	v	India	Kingston	1952-53
4	G.S.Sobers	v	England	Port-of-Spain	1959-60
4	G.S.Sobers	v	England	Nottingham	1966
4	R.C.Fredericks	v	Australia	Port-of-Spain	1972-73
4	G.S.Sobers	v	England	Lord's	1973
4	I.V.A.Richards	v	India	Kingston	1988-89
4	A.L.Logie	v	Pakistan	Lahore²	1990-91
4	J.C.Adams	v	England	Bridgetown	1993-94
4	B.C.Lara	v	Australia	Kingston	1994-95

NEW ZEALAND

4	J.J.Crowe	v	West Indies	Bridgetown	1984-85
4	M.D.Crowe	v	West Indies	Kingston	1984-85

INDIA

5	Yajurvindra Singh §	v	England	Bangalore	197-77
5	M Azharuddin	v	Pakistan	Karachi[1]	1989-90
5	K.Srikkanth	v	Australia	Perth	1991-92
4	A.L.Wadekar	v	England	Birmingham	1967
4	A.L.Wadekar	v	New Zealand	Christchurch	1967-68

PAKISTAN

4	W.Mathias	v	West Indies	Bridgetown	1957-58
4	Hanif Mohammad	v	England	Dacca	1968-69
4	Aamer Malik §	v	England	Faisalabad	1987-88
4	Inzamamul Haq	v	Zimbabwe	Rawalpindi[2]	1993-94

SRI LANKA

4	Y.Goonasekera	v	New Zealand	Wellington	1982-83
4	H.P.Tillakaratne	v	New Zealand	Colombo (SSC)	1992-93

ZIMBABWE

4	M.H.Dekker	v	Sri Lanka	Harare	1994-95

PLAYERS WITH 15 CATCHES IN THE CALENDAR YEAR

Player	Country	Year	Tests	C
J.M.Gregory	Australia	1921	12	27
R.B.Simpson	Australia	1964	14	26
M.A.Taylor	Australia	1993	15	25
M.A.Taylor	Australia	1995	12	24
A.W.Greig	England	1974	13	23
I.M.Chappell	Australia	1974	9	21
M.A.Taylor	Australia	1995	11	21
I.T.Botham	England	1979	9	20
G.S.Chappell	Australia	1974	9	19
G.R.J.Roope	England	1978	9	19
M.D.Crowe	New Zealand	1985	10	19
A.L.Logie	West Indies	1988	12	19
L.C.Braund	England	1902	9	18
W.R.Endean	South Africa	1953	7	18
R.N.Harvey	Australia	1959	9	18
R.B.Simpson	Australia	1961	9	18
G.R.J.Roope	England	1973	8	18
A.R.Border	Australia	1980	10	18
A.R.Border	Australia	1981	10	18
I.M.Chappell	Australia	1969	8	17
J.M.Brearley	England	1977	10	17
A.W.Greig	England	1977	10	17
J.M.Brearley	England	1978	10	17
I.T.Botham	England	1981	13	17
C.H.Lloyd	West Indies	1984	14	17
G.A.Gooch	England	1986	11	17
D.C.Boon	Australia	1989	11	17
G.B.Hole	Australia	1953	7	16
G.S.Chappell	Australia	1975	10	16
I.V.A.Richards	West Indies	1980	11	16
D.B.Vengsarkar	India	1979	18	16
G.S.Chappell	Australia	1980	10	16
I.V.A.Richards	West Indies	1981	11	16
M.E.Waugh	Australia	1991	9	16 #
A.R.Border	Australia	1985	12	16

M.E.Waugh	Australia	1993	15	16
W.R.Hammond	England	1928	10	15
M.C.Cowdrey	England	1957	9	15
A.L.Wadekar	India	1968	7	15
K.R.Stackpole	Australia	1969	8	15
M.H.Denness	England	1974	14	15
J.J.Crowe	New Zealand	1985	10	15
C.L.Hooper	West Indies	1991	10	15
A.R.Border	Australia	1993	16	15

 # Waugh achieved the feat in his debut calendar year.

MOST SUBSTITUTE CATCHES BY ONE FIELDER IN A MATCH

FOUR

Gursharan Singh	India	v	West Indies	Ahmedabad	1983-84

THREE

H.Strudwick	England	v	Australia	Melbourne	1903-04
J.E.D.Sealy	West Indies	v	England	Port-of-Spain	1929-30
W.V.Rodriguez	West Indies	v	India	Port-of-Spain	1961-62
Yajurvindra Singh	India	v	West Indies	Chennai[1]	1978-79
Haroon Rashid	Pakistan	v	England	Leeds	1982
M.J.Greatbatch	New Zealand	v	England	Christchurch	1987-88
W.V.Raman	India	v	England	Chennai[1]	1992-93

MOST SUBSTITUTE CATCHES BY ONE FIELDER IN AN INNINGS

THREE

H.Strudwick	England	v	Australia	Melbourne	1903-04
Haroon Rashid	Pakistan	v	England	Leeds	1982
Gursharan Singh	India	v	West Indies	Ahmedabad	1983-84

All Round

1000 RUNS AND 100 WICKETS

	Tests	Runs	Wkts	Tests for Double
AUSTRALIA				
R.Benaud	63	2201	248	32
A K.Davidson	44	1328	186	34
G.Giffen	31	1238	103	30
M.G.Hughes	53	1032	212	52
I.W.Johnson	45	1000	109	45
R.R.Lindwall	61	1502	228	38
K.R.Miller	55	2958	170	33
M.A.Noble	42	1997	121	27
ENGLAND				
T.E.Bailey	61	2290	132	47
I.T.Botham	102	5200	383	21
J.E.Emburey	64	1721	147	46
A.W.Greig	58	3599	141	37
R.Illingworth	61	1836	122	47
W.Rhodes	58	2325	127	44
M W.Tate	39	1198	155	33
F.J.Titmus	53	1449	153	40
SOUTH AFRICA				
T.L.Goddard	41	2516	123	36
WEST INDIES				
M.D.Marshall	81	1810	376	49
G.S.Sobers	93	8032	235	48
NEW ZEALAND				
J.G.Bracewell	41	1001	102	41
R.J.Hadlee	86	3124	431	28
INDIA				
Kapil Dev	131	5248	434	25
M.H.Mankad	44	2109	162	23
R.J.Shastri	80	3830	151	44
PAKISTAN				
Abdul Qadir	67	1029	236	62
Imran Khan	88	3807	362	30
Intikhab Alam	47	1493	125	41
Sarfraz Nawaz	55	1045	177	55
Wasim Akram	70	1652	300	45

1000 RUNS, 50 WICKETS AND 50 CATCHES

AUSTRALIA	Tests	Runs	Wkts	Catches
R.Benaud	63	2201	248	65
R.B.Simpson	62	4869	71	110
S.R.Waugh	81	5002	77	61

ENGLAND				
I.T.Botham	102	5200	383	120
A.W.Greig	58	3599	141	87
W.R.Hammond	85	7249	83	110
W.Rhodes	58	2325	127	60
F.E.Woolley	64	3283	83	64
WEST INDIES				
C.L.Hooper	52	2548	51	57
G.S.Sobers	93	8032	235	109
INDIA				
Kapil Dev	131	5248	434	64

1000 RUNS AND 100 WICKETKEEPING DISMISSALS

	Tests	Runs	Dismissals	Tests for Double
AUSTRALIA				
I.A.Healy	79	2803	275	36
R.W.Marsh	96	3633	355	25
W.A.S.Oldfield	54	1427	130	41
ENGLAND				
T.G.Evans	91	2439	219	42
A.P.E.Knott	95	4389	269	30
J.M.Parks	46	1962	114	41
R.C.Russell	49	1807	152	37
R.W.Taylor	57	1156	174	47
SOUTH AFRICA				
J.H.B.Waite	50	2405	141	36
D.J.Richardson	28	1006	107	28
WEST INDIES				
P.J.L.Dujon	81	3322	272	30
D.L.Murray	62	1993	189	33
NEW ZEALAND				
I.D.S.Smith	63	1815	177	42
INDIA				
S.M.H.Kirmani	88	2759	198	42
K.S.More	46	1277	125	39
PAKISTAN				
Saleem Yousuf	32	1055	104	32
Wasim Bari	81	1366	228	53

250 RUNS AND 20 WICKETS IN A SERIES *(§ In first Test series)*

	Tests	Runs	Wkts				
G.Giffen	5	475	34	Australia	v	England	1894-95
L.C.Braund §	5	256	21	England	v	Australia	1901-02
G.A.Faulkner	5	545	29	South Africa	v	England	1909-10
G.J.Thompson	5	267	23	England	v	South Africa	1909-10
J.M.Gregory §	5	442	23	Australia	v	England	1920-21
K.R.Miller	5	362	20	Australia	v	West Indies	1951-52
K.R.Miller	5	439	20	Australia	v	West Indies	1954-55
R.Benaud	5	329	30	Australia	v	South Africa	1957-58

G.S.Sobers	5	424	23	West Indies	v	India	1961-62
G.S.Sobers	5	322	20	West Indies	v	England	1963
G.S.Sobers	5	722	20	West Indies	v	England	1966
T.L.Goddard	5	294	26	South Africa	v	Australia	1966-67
A.W.Greig	5	430	24	England	v	West Indies	1973-74
I.T.Botham	6	291	23	England	v	Australia	1978-79
Kapil Dev	6	278	32	India	v	Pakistan	1979-80
I T.Botham	6	399	34	England	v	Australia	1981
Kapil Dev	6	318	22	India	v	England	1981-82
R.J.Hadlee	4	301	21	New Zealand	v	England	1983
I.T.Botham	6	250	31	England	v	Australia	1985

250 RUNS AND 20 WICKET-KEEPING DISMISSALS IN A SERIES

	Tests	Runs	Dismissals				
J H.B Waite	5	263	26	South Africa	v	New Zealand	1961-62
D T.Lindsay	5	606	24	South Africa	v	Australia	1966-67
A P.E.Knott	6	364	23	England	v	Australia	1974-75
P.J.L.Dujon	5	305	20	West Indies	v	England	1988
I.A.Healy	6	296	26	Australia	v	England	1993

500 RUNS IN A SERIES BY A WICKET-KEEPER

	Tests	Runs	Avge				
B.K.Kunderan	5	525	52.50	India	v	England	1963-64
D.T.Lindsay	5	606	86.57	South Africa	v	Australia	1966-67

MATCH DOUBLE - 100 RUNS AND 10 WICKETS

A.K.Davidson	44 80	5-135 6-87	Australia	v	West Indies	Brisbane[2]	1960-61
I.T.Botham	114	6-58 7-48	England	v	India	Mumbai[3]	1979-80
Imran Khan	117	6-98 5-82	Pakistan	v	India	Faisalabad	1982-83

A CENTURY AND 5 WICKETS IN AN INNINGS OF THE SAME MATCH *(§ In first Test)*

			Opponents		
AUSTRALIA					
C.Kelleway	114	5-33	South Africa	Manchester	1912
J.M.Gregory	100	7-69	England	Melbourne	1920-21
K.R.Miller	109	6-107	West Indies	Kingston	1954-55
R.Benaud	100	5-84	South Africa	Johannesburg[3]	1957-58
ENGLAND					
A.W.Greig	148	6-164	West Indies	Bridgetown	1973-74
I.T.Botham	103	5-73	New Zealand	Christchurch	1977-78
I.T.Botham	108	8-34	Pakistan	Lord's	1978
I.T.Botham	114	6-58 + 7-48	India	Mumbai[3]	1979-80
I.T.Botham	149*	6-95	Australia	Leeds	1981
I.T.Botham	138	5-59	New Zealand	Wellington	1983-84
SOUTH AFRICA					
J.H.Sinclair	106	6-26	England	Cape Town	1898-99
G.A.Faulkner	123	5-120	England	Johannesburg[1]	1909-10
WEST INDIES					
D.S.Atkinson	219	5-56	Australia	Bridgetown	1954-55
O.G.Smith	100	5-90	India	Delhi	1958-59

G.S.Sobers	104	5-63	India	Kingston	1961-62
G.S.Sobers	174	5-41	England	Leeds	1966
NEW ZEALAND					
B.R.Taylor §	105	5-86	India	Calcutta	1964-65
INDIA					
M.H.Mankad	184	5-196	England	Lord's	1952
P.R.Umrigar	172*	5-107	West Indies	Port-of-Spain	1961-62
PAKISTAN					
Mushtaq Mohammad	201	5-49	New Zealand	Dunedin	1972-73
Mushtaq Mohammad	121	5-28	West Indies	Port-of-Spain	1976-77
Imran Khan	117	6-88 + 5-82	India	Faisalabad	1982-83
Wasim Akram	123	5-100	Australia	Adelaide	1989-90

A FIFTY AND TEN WICKETS IN THE SAME MATCH *(§ In first Test)*

AUSTRALIA			Opponents		
H.Trumble	64* + 7*	8-65 + 4-108	England	The Oval	1902
A.K.Davidson	44 + 80	5-132 + 6-87	West Indies	Brisbane[2]	1960-61
A.R.Border	75 + 16*	7-46 + 4-50	West Indies	Sydney	1988-89
ENGLAND			Opponents		
W.Bates	55	7-28 + 7-74	Australia	Melbourne	1882-83
F.E.Woolley	62 + 4	5-29 + 5-20	Australia	The Oval	1912
A.W.Greig	51	5-98 + 5-51	New Zealand	Auckland	1974-75
J.K.Lever §	53	7-46 + 3-24	India	Delhi	1976-77
I.T.Botham	114	6-58 + 7-48	India	Mumbai[3]	1979-80
SOUTH AFRICA			Opponents		
P.S.de Villiers	66*	6-81 + 4-27	Pakistan	Johannesburg[3]	1994-95
WEST INDIES			Opponents		
K.D.Boyce	72 + 9	5-70 + 6-77	England	The Oval	1973
M.D.Marshall	63	4-40 + 7-80	New Zealand	Bridgetown	1984-85
NEW ZEALAND			Opponents		
R.J.Hadlee	51 + 17	5-34 + 6-68	West Indies	Dunedin	1979-80
R.J.Hadlee	54	9-52 + 6-71	Australia	Brisbane[2]	1985-86
R.J.Hadlee	68	6-80 + 4-60	England	Nottingham	1986
D.J.Nash	56	6-76 + 5-93	England	Lord's	1994
INDIA			Opponents		
Kapil Dev	84	4-90 + 7-56	Pakistan	Chennai[1]	1979-80
PAKISTAN			Opponents		
Imran Khan	117	6-98 + 5-82	India	Faisalabad	1982-83
Abdul Qadir	61	5-88 + 5-98	England	Karachi[1]	1987-88

A CENTURY AND FIVE DISMISSALS IN AN INNINGS BY A WICKET-KEEPER

D.T.Lindsay	182	6c	South Africa	v	Australia	Johannesburg[3]	1966-67
I.D.S.Smith	113*	4c, 1s	New Zealand	v	England	Auckland	1983-84
S.A.R.Silva	111	5c	Sri Lanka	v	India	Colombo (PSS)	1985-86

The Captains

RESULT SUMMARY

AUSTRALIA (39)	Tests as Captain	Opponents E	SA	WI	NZ	I	P	SL	Z	Results W	L	D	Tie	Toss Won
D.W.Gregory	**3**	3	-	-	-	-	-	-	-	2	1	-	-	2
W.L.Murdoch	**16**	16	-	-	-	-	-	-	-	5	7	4	-	7
T.P.Horan	**2**	2	-	-	-	-	-	-	-	-	2	-	-	1
H.H.Massie	**1**	1	-	-	-	-	-	-	-	1	-	-	-	1
J.M.Blackham	**8**	8	-	-	-	-	-	-	-	3	3	2	-	4
H.J.H.Scott	**3**	3	-	-	-	-	-	-	-	-	3	-	-	1
P.S.McDonnell	**6**	6	-	-	-	-	-	-	-	1	5	-	-	4
G.Giffen	**4**	4	-	-	-	-	-	-	-	2	2	-	-	3
G.H.S.Trott	**8**	8	-	-	-	-	-	-	-	5	3	-	-	5
J.Darling	**21**	18	3	-	-	-	-	-	-	7	4	10	-	7
H.Trumble	**2**	2	-	-	-	-	-	-	-	2	-	-	-	1
M.A.Noble	**15**	15	-	-	-	-	-	-	-	8	5	2	-	11
C.Hill	**10**	5	5	-	-	-	-	-	-	5	5	-	-	5
S.E.Gregory	**6**	3	3	-	-	-	-	-	-	2	1	3	-	1
W.W.Armstrong	**10**	10	-	-	-	-	-	-	-	8	-	2	-	4
H.L.Collins	**11**	8	3	-	-	-	-	-	-	5	2	4	-	7
W.Bardsley	**2**	2	-	-	-	-	-	-	-	-	-	2	-	1
J.Ryder	**5**	5	-	-	-	-	-	-	-	1	4	-	-	2
W.M.Woodfull	**25**	15	5	5	-	-	-	-	-	14	7	4	-	12
V.Y.Richardson	**5**	-	5	-	-	-	-	-	-	4	-	1	-	1
D.G.Bradman	**24**	19	-	-	-	5	-	-	-	15	3	6	-	10
W.A.Brown	**1**	-	-	-	1	-	-	-	-	1	-	-	-	0
A.L.Hassett	**24**	10	10	4	-	-	-	-	-	14	4	6	-	18
A.R.Morris	**2**	1	-	-	-	-	-	-	-	-	2	-	-	2
I.W.Johnson	**17**	9	-	5	-	2	1	-	-	7	5	5	-	6
R.R.Lindwall	**1**	-	-	-	-	1	-	-	-	-	-	1	-	0
I.D.Craig	**5**	-	5	-	-	-	-	-	-	3	-	2	-	3
R.Benaud	**28**	14	1	5	-	5	3	-	-	12	4	11	1	11
R.N.Harvey	**1**	1	-	-	-	-	-	-	-	1	-	-	-	0
R.B.Simpson	**39**	8	9	10	-	10	2	-	-	12	12	15	-	19
B.C.Booth	**2**	2	-	-	-	-	-	-	-	-	1	1	-	1
W.M.Lawry	**25**	9	4	5	-	7	-	-	-	9	8	8	-	8
B.N.Jarman	**1**	1	-	-	-	-	-	-	-	-	-	1	-	1
I.M.Chappell	**30**	16	-	5	6	-	3	-	-	15	5	10	-	17
G.S.Chappell	**48**	15	-	12	8	3	9	1	-	21	13	14	-	29
G.N.Yallop	**7**	6	-	-	-	-	1	-	-	1	6	-	-	6
K.J.Hughes	**28**	6	-	7	-	6	9	-	-	4	13	11	-	13
A.R.Border	**93**	29	6	18	17	11	6	6	-	32	22	38	1	46
M.A.Taylor	**18**	5	-	4	-	-	6	3	-	10	4	4	-	6
	557	285	59	81	32	50	40	10	-	232	156	167	2	276

ENGLAND (71)	Tests as Captain	Opponents A	SA	WI	NZ	I	P	SL	Z	Results W	L	D	Tie	Toss Won
James Lillywhite	**2**	2	-	-	-	-	-	-	-	1	1	-	-	0
Lord Harris	**4**	4	-	-	-	-	-	-	-	2	1	1	-	2
A.Shaw	**4**	4	-	-	-	-	-	-	-	-	2	2	-	4
A.N.Hornby	**2**	2	-	-	-	-	-	-	-	-	1	1	-	1
Hon.I.F.W.Bligh	**4**	4	-	-	-	-	-	-	-	2	2	-	-	3
A.Shrewsbury	**7**	7	-	-	-	-	-	-	-	5	2	-	-	3

A.G.Steel	**4**	4	-	-	-	-	-	-	-	3	1	-	-	2
W.W.Read	**2**	1	1	-	-	-	-	-	-	2	-	-	-	0
W.G.Grace	**13**	13	-	-	-	-	-	-	-	8	3	2	-	4
C.A.Smith	**1**	-	1	-	-	-	-	-	-	1	-	-	-	0
M.P.Bowden	**1**	-	1	-	-	-	-	-	-	1	-	-	-	1
A.E.Stoddart	**8**	8	-	-	-	-	-	-	-	3	4	1	-	2
T.C.O'Brien	**1**	-	1	-	-	-	-	-	-	1	-	-	-	0
Lord Hawke	**4**	-	4	-	-	-	-	-	-	4	-	-	-	4
A.C.MacLaren	**22**	22	-	-	-	-	-	-	-	4	11	7	-	11
P.F.Warner	**10**	5	5	-	-	-	-	-	-	4	6	-	-	5
Hon F.S.Jackson	**5**	5	-	-	-	-	-	-	-	2	-	3	-	5
R.E.Foster	**3**	-	3	-	-	-	-	-	-	1	-	2	-	3
F.L.Fane	**5**	3	2	-	-	-	-	-	-	2	3	-	-	3
A.O.Jones	**2**	2	-	-	-	-	-	-	-	-	2	-	-	1
H.D.G.Leveson Gower	**3**	-	3	-	-	-	-	-	-	1	2	-	-	0
J.W.H.T.Douglas	**18**	12	6	-	-	-	-	-	-	8	8	2	-	7
C.B Fry	**6**	3	3	-	-	-	-	-	-	4	-	2	-	4
Hon.L.H.Tennyson	**3**	3	-	-	-	-	-	-	-	-	1	2	-	2
F.T.Mann	**5**	-	5	-	-	-	-	-	-	2	1	2	-	3
A.E.R.Gilligan	**9**	5	4	-	-	-	-	-	-	4	4	1	-	2
A.W Carr	**6**	4	2	-	-	-	-	-	-	1	-	5	-	3
A.P.F.Chapman	**17**	9	5	3	-	-	-	-	-	9	2	6	-	9
R.T.Stanyforth	**4**	-	4	-	-	-	-	-	-	2	1	1	-	0
G.T.S.Stevens	**1**	-	1	-	-	-	-	-	-	-	1	-	-	0
J.C.White	**4**	1	3	-	-	-	-	-	-	1	1	2	-	3
A.H.H.Gilligan	**4**	-	-	-	4	-	-	-	-	1	-	3	-	1
Hon.F.S.G.Calthorpe	**4**	-	-	4	-	-	-	-	-	1	1	2	-	2
R.E.S.Wyatt	**16**	5	5	5	1	-	-	-	-	3	5	8	-	12
D.R.Jardine	**15**	5	-	2	4	4	-	-	-	9	1	5	-	7
C.F.Walters	**1**	1	-	-	-	-	-	-	-	-	1	-	-	0
G.O.B.Allen	**11**	5	-	3	-	3	-	-	-	4	5	2	-	6
R.W.V.Robins	**3**	-	-	-	3	-	-	-	-	1	-	2	-	2
W.R.Hammond	**20**	8	5	3	1	3	-	-	-	4	3	13	-	12
N.W.D.Yardley	**14**	6	5	3	-	-	-	-	-	4	7	3	-	9
K.Cranston	**1**	-	-	-	1	-	-	-	-	-	-	1	-	0
F.G.Mann	**7**	-	5	-	2	-	-	-	-	2	-	5	-	5
F.R.Brown	**15**	5	5	1	4	-	-	-	-	5	6	4	-	3
N.D.Howard	**4**	-	-	-	-	4	-	-	-	1	-	3	-	2
D.B.Carr	**1**	-	-	-	-	1	-	-	-	-	1	-	-	1
L.Hutton	**23**	10	-	5	2	4	2	-	-	11	4	8	-	7
Rev.D.S.Sheppard	**2**	-	-	-	-	-	2	-	-	1	-	1	-	1
P.B.H.May	**41**	13	10	8	7	3	-	-	-	20	10	11	-	26
M.C.Cowdrey	**27**	6	5	10	-	2	4	-	-	8	4	15	-	17
E.R.Dexter	**30**	10	-	5	3	5	7	-	-	9	7	14	-	13
M.J.K.Smith	**25**	5	8	1	6	5	-	-	-	5	3	17	-	10
D.B.Close	**7**	-	-	1	-	3	3	-	-	6	-	1	-	4
T.W.Graveney	**1**	1	-	-	-	-	-	-	-	-	-	1	-	0
R.Illingworth	**31**	11	-	6	8	3	3	-	-	12	5	14	-	15
A R.Lewis	**8**	-	-	-	-	5	3	-	-	1	2	5	-	3
M.H.Denness	**19**	6	-	5	2	3	3	-	-	6	5	8	-	9
J.H.Edrich	**1**	1	-	-	-	-	-	-	-	-	1	-	-	0
A.W.Greig	**14**	4	-	5	-	5	-	-	-	3	5	6	-	6
J.M.Brearley	**31**	18	-	-	3	5	5	-	-	18	4	9	-	13
G.Boycott	**4**	-	-	-	3	-	1	-	-	1	1	2	-	3
I.T.Botham	**12**	3	-	9	-	-	-	-	-	-	4	8	-	6
K.W.R.Fletcher	**7**	-	-	-	-	6	-	1	-	1	1	5	-	5
R.G.D.Willis	**18**	5	-	-	7	3	3	-	-	7	5	6	-	8

D.I.Gower	**32**	12	-	10	-	6	3	1	-	5	18	9	-	14
M.W.Gatting	**23**	6	-	1	6	2	8	-	-	2	5	16	-	14
J.E.Emburey	**2**	-	-	2	-	-	-	-	-	-	2	-	-	1
C.S.Cowdrey	**1**	-	-	1	-	-	-	-	-	-	1	-	-	0
G.A.Gooch	**34**	8	-	8	6	5	5	2	-	10	12	12	-	16
A.J.Lamb	**3**	1	-	2	-	-	-	-	-	-	3	-	-	2
A.J.Stewart	**2**	-	-	-	-	1	-	1	-	-	2	-	-	1
M.A.Atherton	**35**	7	8	11	3	3	3	-	-	8	13	14	-	16
	729	285	110	115	75	84	55	5	-	248	207	275	-	359

SOUTH AFRICA (26)	Tests as Captain	Opponents								Results				Toss Won
		A	E	WI	NZ	I	P	SL	Z	W	L	D	Tie	
O.R.Dunell	**1**	-	1	-	-	-	-	-	-	-	-	-	-	1
W.H.Milton	**2**	-	2	-	-	-	-	-	-	-	2	-	-	1
E.A.Halliwell	**3**	1	2	-	-	-	-	-	-	-	3	-	-	1
A.R.Richards	**1**	-	1	-	-	-	-	-	-	-	1	-	-	0
M.Bisset	**2**	-	2	-	-	-	-	-	-	-	2	-	-	0
H.M.Taberer	**1**	1	-	-	-	-	-	-	-	-	-	1	-	1
J.H.Anderson	**1**	1	-	-	-	-	-	-	-	-	1	-	-	0
P.W.Sherwell	**13**	5	8	-	-	-	-	-	-	5	6	2	-	5
S.J.Snooke	**5**	-	5	-	-	-	-	-	-	3	2	-	-	3
F.Mitchell	**3**	2	1	-	-	-	-	-	-	-	3	-	-	2
L.J.Tancred	**3**	1	2	-	-	-	-	-	-	-	2	1	-	2
H.W.Taylor	**18**	3	15	-	-	-	-	-	-	1	10	7	-	11
H.G.Deane	**12**	-	12	-	-	-	-	-	-	2	4	6	-	9
E.P.Nupen	**1**	-	1	-	-	-	-	-	-	1	-	-	-	0
H.B.Cameron	**9**	5	2	-	2	-	-	-	-	2	5	2	-	3
H.F.Wade	**10**	5	5	-	-	-	-	-	-	1	4	5	-	5
A.Melville	**10**	-	10	-	-	-	-	-	-	-	4	6	-	4
A.D.Nourse	**15**	5	10	-	-	-	-	-	-	1	9	5	-	7
J.E.Cheetham	**15**	5	3	-	7	-	-	-	-	7	5	3	-	6
D.J.McGlew	**14**	1	8	-	5	-	-	-	-	4	6	4	-	4
C.B.van Ryneveld	**8**	4	4	-	-	-	-	-	-	2	4	2	-	3
T.L.Goddard	**13**	5	5	-	3	-	-	-	-	1	2	10	-	4
P.L.van der Merwe	**8**	5	3	-	-	-	-	-	-	4	1	3	-	4
A Bacher	**4**	4	-	-	-	-	-	-	-	4	-	-	-	4
K.C.Wessels	**16**	5	3	1	-	4	-	3	-	5	3	8	-	11
W.J.Cronje	**10**	1	5	-	4	-	1	-	1	6	2	4	-	5
	200	59	110	1	21	4	1	3	1	49	82	69	-	96

WEST INDIES (22)	Tests as Captain	Opponents								Results				Toss Won
		A	E	SA	NZ	I	P	SL	Z	W	L	D	Tie	
R.K.Nunes	**4**	-	4	-	-	-	-	-	-	-	3	1	-	2
E.L.G.Hoad	**1**	-	1	-	-	-	-	-	-	-	-	1	-	1
N.Betancourt	**1**	-	1	-	-	-	-	-	-	-	-	1	-	0
M.P.Fernandes	**1**	-	1	-	-	-	-	-	-	1	-	-	-	1
G.C.Grant	**12**	5	7	-	-	-	-	-	-	3	7	2	-	5
R.C.Grant	**3**	-	3	-	-	-	-	-	-	-	1	2	-	2
G.A.Headley	**1**	-	1	-	-	-	-	-	-	-	-	1	-	1
J.D.C.Goddard	**22**	4	11	-	2	5	-	-	-	8	7	7	-	12
J.B.Stollmeyer	**13**	3	5	-	-	5	-	-	-	3	4	6	-	7
D.S.Atkinson	**7**	3	-	-	4	-	-	-	-	3	3	1	-	3
F.C.M.Alexander	**18**	-	5	-	-	5	8	-	-	7	4	7	-	9
F.M.M.Worrell	**15**	5	5	-	-	5	-	-	-	9	3	2	1	9
G.S.Sobers	**39**	10	13	-	8	8	-	-	-	9	10	20	-	27
R.B.Kanhai	**13**	5	8	-	-	-	-	-	-	3	3	7	-	6

C.H.Lloyd	**74**	22	18	-	3	20	1	-	-	36	12	26	-	35
A.I.Kallicharran	**9**	3	-	-	-	6	-	-	-	1	2	6	-	4
D.L.Murray	**1**	1	-	-	-	-	-	-	-	-	-	1	-	1
I.V.A.Richards	**50**	11	19	-	7	8	5	-	-	27	8	15	-	24
C.G.Greenidge	**1**	-	-	-	-	-	1	-	-	-	1	-	-	1
D.L.Haynes	**4**	-	1	-	-	-	3	-	-	1	1	2	-	2
R.B.Richardson	**24**	9	10	1	-	-	3	1	-	11	6	7	-	12
C.A.Walsh	**8**	-	1	-	4	3	-	-	-	3	1	4	-	5
	322	81	115	1	28	65	31	1	-	125	77	119	1	169

NEW ZEALAND (23)	Tests as				Opponents						Results			Toss
	Captain	A	E	SA	WI	I	P	SL	Z	W	L	D	Tie	Won
T.C.Lowry	**7**	7	1	-	-	-	-	-	-	-	2	5	-	5
M.L.Page	**7**	-	5	2	-	-	-	-	-	-	3	4	-	4
W.A.Hadlee	**8**	1	7	-	-	-	-	-	-	-	2	6	-	4
B.Sutcliffe	**4**	-	-	2	2	-	-	-	-	-	3	1	-	4
W.M.Wallace	**2**	-	-	2	-	-	-	-	-	-	1	1	-	0
G.O.Rabone	**5**	-	2	3	-	-	-	-	-	-	4	1	-	2
H.B.Cave	**9**	-	-	-	1	5	3	-	-	-	5	4	-	5
J.R.Reid	**34**	-	13	8	3	4	6	-	-	3	18	13	-	17
M.E.Chapple	**1**	-	1	-	-	-	-	-	-	-	-	1	-	0
B.W.Sinclair	**3**	-	2	-	-	1	-	-	-	-	1	2	-	3
G.T.Dowling	**19**	-	5	-	5	6	3	-	-	4	7	8	-	10
B.E.Congdon	**17**	6	5	-	3	-	3	-	-	1	7	9	-	4
G.M.Turner	**10**	2	-	-	-	6	2	-	-	1	6	3	-	2
J.M.Parker	**1**	-	-	-	-	-	1	-	-	-	-	1	-	0
M.G.Burgess	**10**	1	6	-	-	-	3	-	-	1	6	3	-	4
G.P.Howarth	**30**	5	7	-	7	3	3	5	-	11	7	12	-	17
J.V.Coney	**15**	6	3	-	3	-	3	-	-	5	4	6	-	8
J.J.Crowe	**6**	3	2	-	-	-	-	1	-	-	1	5	-	3
J.G.Wright	**14**	2	4	-	-	6	2	-	-	3	3	8	-	8
M.D.Crowe	**16**	4	3	-	-	-	3	4	2	2	7	7	-	8
I.D.S.Smith	**1**	-	-	-	-	-	-	1	-	-	-	1	-	1
K.R.Rutherford	**18**	2	3	4	2	1	4	2	-	2	11	5	-	12
L.K.Germon	**8**	-	-	-	2	3	1	-	2	-	3	5	-	4
	245	32	75	21	28	35	37	13	4	33	101	110	-	125

INDIA (25)	Tests as				Opponents						Results			Toss
	Captain	A	E	SA	WI	NZ	P	SL	Z	W	L	D	Tie	Won
C.K.Nayudu	**4**	-	4	-	-	-	-	-	-	-	3	1	-	1
Maharajkumar of Vizianagram	**3**	-	3	-	-	-	-	-	-	-	2	1	-	1
Nawab of Pataudi, sr	**3**	-	3	-	-	-	-	-	-	-	1	2	-	3
N.B.Amarnath	**15**	5	-	-	5	-	5	-	-	2	6	7	-	4
V.S.Hazare	**14**	-	9	-	5	-	-	-	-	1	5	8	-	8
M.H.Mankad	**6**	-	-	-	1	-	5	-	-	-	1	5	-	1
Ghulam Ahmed	**3**	-	-	-	2	1	-	-	-	-	2	1	-	1
P.R.Umrigar	**8**	3	-	-	1	4	-	-	-	2	2	4	-	6
H.R.Adhikari	**1**	-	-	1	-	-	-	-	-	-	-	1	-	1
D.K.Gaekwad	**4**	-	4	-	-	-	-	-	-	-	4	-	-	2
Pankaj Roy	**1**	-	1	-	-	-	-	-	-	-	1	-	-	1
G.S.Ramchand	**5**	5	-	-	-	-	-	-	-	1	2	2	-	4
N.J.Contractor	**12**	-	5	-	2	-	5	-	-	2	2	8	-	7
Nawab of Pataudi, jr	**40**	11	8	-	10	1	-	-	-	9	19	12	-	20
C.G.Borde	**1**	1	-	-	-	-	-	-	-	-	1	-	-	0

A.L.Wadekar	**16**	-	11	-	5	-	-	-	-	4	4	8	-	7
S.Venkataraghavan	**5**	-	4	-	1	-	-	-	-	-	2	3	-	2
S.M.Gavaskar	**47**	9	14	-	6	4	13	1	-	9	8	30	-	22
B.S.Bedi	**22**	5	5	-	4	5	3	-	-	6	11	5	-	13
G.R.Viswanath	**2**	-	1	-	-	-	1	-	-	-	1	1	-	2
Kapil Dev	**34**	6	3	-	11	-	8	6	-	4	7	22	1	15
D.B.Vengsarkar	**10**	-	-	-	7	3	-	-	-	2	5	3	-	4
R.J.Shastri	**1**	-	-	-	1	-	-	-	-	1	-	-	-	1
K.Srikkanth	**1**						1					1		L
M.Azharuddin	**37**	5	9	4	3	7	-	7	2	11	9	17	-	22
	298	50	84	4	65	35	44	14	2	54	98	145	1	150

PAKISTAN (18)	Tests as Captain	Opponents A	E	SA	WI	NZ	I	SL	Z	Results W	L	D	Tie	Toss Won
A.H.Kardar	**23**	1	4	-	5	3	10	-	-	6	6	11	-	10
Fazal Mahmood	**10**	2	-	-	3	-	5	-	-	2	2	6	-	6
Imtiaz Ahmed	**4**	1	3	-	-	-	-	-	-	-	2	2	-	4
Javed Burki	**5**	-	5	-	-	-	-	-	-	-	4	1	-	3
Hanif Mohammad	**11**	2	3	-	-	6	-	-	-	2	2	7	-	6
Saeed Ahmed	**3**	-	3	-	-	-	-	-	-	-	-	3	-	1
Intikhab Alam	**17**	3	6	-	2	6	-	-	-	1	5	11	-	12
Majid Khan	**3**	-	3	-	-	-	-	-	-	-	-	3	-	1
Mushtaq Mohammad	**19**	5	-	-	5	6	3	-	-	8	4	7	-	10
Wasim Bari	**6**	-	6	-	-	-	-	-	-	-	2	4	-	4
Asif Iqbal	**6**	-	-	-	-	-	6	-	-	-	2	4	-	3
Javed Miandad	**34**	9	8	-	4	7	-	6	-	14	6	14	-	12
Imran Khan	**48**	8	8	-	9	2	15	6	-	14	8	26	-	25
Zaheer Abbas	**14**	3	3	-	-	3	5	-	-	3	1	10	-	6
Wasim Akram	**12**	3	3	-	3	1	-	-	2	5	4	3	-	3
Waqar Younis	**1**	-	-	-	-	-	-	-	1	1	-	-	-	1
Saleem Malik	**12**	3	-	1	-	3	-	2	3	7	3	2	-	6
Rameez Raja	**3**	-	-	-	-	-	-	3	-	1	2	-	-	2
	231	40	55	1	31	37	44	17	6	64	53	114	-	115

SRI LANKA (6)	Tests as Captain	Opponents A	E	SA	WI	NZ	I	P	Z	Results W	L	D	Tie	Toss Won
B.Warnapura	**4**	1	1	-	-	-	1	2	-	-	3	1	-	2
L.R.D.Mendis	**19**	1	1	-	-	4	6	7	-	2	8	9	-	10
D.S.De Silva	**2**	-	-	-	-	2	-	-	-	-	2	-	-	1
R.S.Madugalle	**2**	1	1	-	-	-	-	-	-	-	2	-	-	0
A.Ranatunga	**34**	7	1	3	1	7	7	5	3	5	13	16	-	19
P.A.de Silva	**5**	1	1	-	-	-	-	3	-	-	3	2	-	2
	66	10	5	3	1	13	14	17	3	7	31	28	-	34

ZIMBABWE (2)	Tests as Captain	Opponents A	E	SA	WI	NZ	I	P	SL	Results W	L	D	Tie	Toss Won
D.L.Houghton	**4**	-	-	-	-	2	2	-	-	-	2	2	-	1
A.Flower	**12**	-	-	1	-	2	-	6	3	1	5	6	-	7
	16	-	-	1	-	4	2	6	3	1	7	8	-	8

MOST CONSECUTIVE MATCHES AS CAPTAIN

			From	To
Australia	93	A.R.Border	1984-85	1993-94
England	35	P.B.H.May	1955	1959
South Africa	18	H.W.Taylor	1913-14	1924
West Indies	39	G.S.Sobers	1964-65	1971-72
New Zealand	34	J.R.Reid	1955-56	1965
India	37	M.Azharuddin	1989-90	# 1996
Pakistan	23	A.H.Kardar	1952-53	1957-58
Sri Lanka	28	A.Ranatunga	1992-93	1995-96
Zimbabwe	12	A.Flower	1993-94	# 1995-96

 # to date.

In addition to those listed above, the following had unbroken captaincy runs of 20 or more matches

30	I.M.Chappell (A)
29	C.H.Lloyd (WI)
27	M.A.Atherton (E)
25	W.M.Woodfull (A), R.Illingworth (E), D.I.Gower (E)
23	C.H.Lloyd (WI), M.W.Gatting (E)
22	B.S.Bedi(I), S.M.Gavaskar(I)
21	Nawab of Pataudi, jr (I)
20	M.J.K.Smith (E), W.M.Lawry (A), J.M.Brearley (E), Kapil Dev (I)

WINNING ALL FIVE TOSSES IN A SERIES

Captains				Venue	
Hon F.S.Jackson	England	v	Australia	England	1905
M.A.Noble	Australia	v	England	England	1909
H.G.Deane	South Africa	v	England	South Africa	1927-28
J.D.C.Goddard	West Indies	v	India	India	1948-49
A.L.Hassett	Australia	v	England	England	1953
P.B.H.May (3) } M.C.Cowdrey (2) }	England	v	West Indies	West Indies	1959-60
M.C.Cowdrey	England	v	South Africa	England	1960
Nawab of Pataudi , jr	India	v	England	India	1963-64
G.S.Sobers	West Indies	v	England	England	1966
G.S.Sobers	West Indies	v	New Zealand	West Indies	1971-72
C.H.Lloyd	West Indies	v	India	West Indies	1982-83

The following Australian captains won five tosses during six-match series in Australia: I.M.Chappell v England 1974-75; G.S.Chappell v West Indies 1975-76; G.N.Yallop v England 1978-79.

K.W.R.Fletcher (England) won five successive tosses during the six-match series in India in 1981-82.

M.C.Cowdrey won the toss for England in nine consecutive Tests from 1959-60 to 1961.

R.B.Richardson (West Indies) won the toss in all 4 Tests in the series against Australia in the West Indies in 1994-95 and 8 consecutive tosses from 1993-94 to 1995.

CAPTAINS WHO SENT THE OPPOSITION IN

(§ In first match as captain. # In last Test as captain. ¶ In only Test as captain.)

AUSTRALIA	Opponents	Result		
P.S.McDonnell §	England	Lost by 13 runs	Sydney	1886-87
P.S.McDonnell	England	Lost by 126 runs	Sydney	1887-88
G.Giffen §	England	Lost by 94 runs	Melbourne	1894-95
M.A.Noble	England	Won by 9 wkts	Lord's	1909
A.L.Hassett	West Indies	Won by 7 wkts	Sydney	1951-52
A.L.Hassett	England	Drawn	Leeds	1953
A.R.Morris #	England	Lost by 38 runs	Sydney	1954-55
I.W.Johnson	England	Drawn	Sydney	1954-55
R.Benaud	England	Won by 9 wkts	Melbourne	1958-59
R.Benaud	Pakistan	Won by 8 wkts	Dacca	1959-60

R.Benaud	West Indies	Won by 2 wkts	Melbourne	1960-61
R.B.Simpson §	South Africa	Won by 8 wkts	Melbourne	1963-64
R.B.Simpson	Pakistan	Drawn	Melbourne	1964-65
R.B.Simpson	West Indies	Drawn	Port-of-Spain	1964-65
R.B.Simpson	South Africa	Lost by 8 wkts	Durban[2]	1966-67
W.M.Lawry	West Indies	Won by Innings + 30 runs	Melbourne	1968-69
W.M.Lawry	India	Won by 10 wkts	Calcutta	1969-70
W.M.Lawry	England	Drawn	Perth	1970-71
I.M.Chappell §	England	Lost by 62 runs	Sydney	1970-71
I.M.Chappell	New Zealand	Drawn	Sydney	1973-74
I.M.Chappell	England	Won by 9 wkts	Perth	1974-75
I.M.Chappell	England	Drawn	Melbourne	1974-75
G.S.Chappell	West Indies	Won by 8 wkts	Melbourne	1975-76
G.S.Chappell	West Indies	Won by 7 wkts	Sydney	1975-76
G.S.Chappell	New Zealand	Won by 10 wkts	Auckland	1976-77
G.S.Chappell	England	Drawn	The Oval	1977
R.B.Simpson	West Indies	Lost by 198 runs	Port-of-Spain	1977-78
G.N.Yallop	England	Lost by 166 runs	Perth	1978-79
G.N.Yallop	England	Lost by 205 runs	Adelaide	1978-79
G.N.Yallop #	Pakistan	Lost by 71 runs	Melbourne	1978-79
K.J.Hughes §	Pakistan	Won by 7 wkts	Perth	1978-79
G.S.Chappell	England	Won by 6 wkts	Sydney	1979-80
G.S.Chappell	West Indies	Lost by 408 runs	Adelaide	1979-80
G.S.Chappell	New Zealand	Won by 10 wkts	Brisbane[2]	1980-81
G.S.Chappell	New Zealand	Won by 8 wkts	Perth	1980-81
G.S.Chappell	India	Lost by 59 runs	Melbourne	1980-81
K.J.Hughes	England	Won by 4 wkts	Nottingham	1981
K.J.Hughes	England	Drawn	Lord's	1981
G.S.Chappell	Pakistan	Won by 10 wkts	Brisbane[2]	1981-82
G.S.Chappell	New Zealand	Drawn	Wellington	1981-82
G.S.Chappell	England	Drawn	Perth	1982-83
G.S.Chappell	England	Won by 7 wkts	Brisbane[2]	1982-83
G.S.Chappell	England	Lost by 3 runs	Melbourne	1982-83
K.J.Hughes	Pakistan	Won by 10 wkts	Sydney	1983-84
K.J.Hughes	West Indies	Lost by Innings + 112 runs	Perth	1984-85
A.R.Border	West Indies	Drawn	Melbourne	1984-85
A.R.Border	England	Won by 4 wkts	Lord's	1985
A.R.Border	New Zealand	Won by 4 wkts	Sydney	1985-86
A.R.Border	England	Lost by 7 wkts	Brisbane[2]	1986-87
A.R.Border	New Zealand	Won by 9 wkts	Brisbane[2]	1987-88
A.R.Border	New Zealand	Drawn	Melbourne	1987-88
A.R.Border	West Indies	Lost by 169 runs	Perth	1988-89
A.R.Border	West Indies	Lost by 285 runs	Melbourne	1988-89
A.R.Border	Pakistan	Drawn	Sydney	1989-90
A.R.Border	England	Won by 10 wkts	Brisbane[2]	1990-91
A.R.Border	West Indies	Lost by 343 runs	Bridgetown	1990-91
A.R.Border	India	Won by 10 wkts	Brisbane[2]	1991-92
A.R.Border	New Zealand	Drawn	Wellington	1992-93

ENGLAND	Opponents	Result		
A.E.Stoddart	Australia	Lost by Innings + 147 runs	Sydney	1894-95
Lord Hawke	South Africa	Won by Innings + 33 runs	Cape Town	1895-96
A.C.MacLaren	Australia	Lost by 229 runs	Melbourne	1901-02
A.O.Jones #	Australia	Lost by 49 runs	Sydney	1907-08
J.W.H.T.Douglas	Australia	Won by Innings + 225 runs	Melbourne	1911-12
A.W.Carr	Australia	Drawn	Leeds	1926
A.P.F.Chapman	South Africa	Lost by 28 runs	Johannesburg[1]	1930-31

A.P.F.Chapman #	South Africa	Drawn	Durban[2]	1930-31
R.E.S.Wyatt	West Indies	Won by 4 wkts	Bridgetown	1934-35
R.E.S.Wyatt	West Indies	Lost by 217 runs	Port-of-Spain	1934-35
R.E.S.Wyatt #	South Africa	Drawn	The Oval	1935
G.O.B.Allen §	India	Won by 9 wkts	Lord's	1936
W.R.Hammond #	New Zealand	Drawn	Christchurch	1946-47
F.R.Brown §	New Zealand	Drawn	Manchester	1949
L.Hutton	Pakistan	Drawn	Lord's	1954
L.Hutton	Australia	Lost by Innings + 154 runs	Brisbane[2]	1954-55
L.Hutton #	New Zealand	Won by 8 wkts	Dunedin	1954-55
P.B.H.May	Australia	Lost by 10 wkts	Adelaide	1958-59
E.R.Dexter	New Zealand	Won by Innings + 47 runs	Wellington	1962-63
E.R.Dexter	Australia	Drawn	Lord's	1964
M.J.K.Smith	South Africa	Drawn	Johannesburg[3]	1964-65
M.J.K.Smith	South Africa	Drawn	The Oval	1965
D.B.Close #	Pakistan	Won by 8 wkts	The Oval	1967
R.Illingworth	Australia	Drawn	Nottingham	1972
M.H.Denness	Australia	Lost by 163 runs	Adelaide	1974-75
M.H.Denness	New Zealand	Drawn	Christchurch	1974-75
M.H.Denness #	Australia	Lost by Innings + 85 runs	Birmingham	1975
A.W.Greig #	Australia	Lost by 45 runs	Melbourne	1976-77
G.Boycott	New Zealand	Lost by 72 runs	Wellington	1977-78
J.M.Brearley	Australia	Lost by 138 runs	Perth	1979-80
I.T.Botham	West Indies	Lost by Innings + 79 runs	Port-of-Spain	1980-81
I.T.Botham	West Indies	Lost by 298 runs	Bridgetown	1980-81
J.M.Brearley #	Australia	Drawn	The Oval	1981
K.W.R.Fletcher	India	Drawn	Chennai[1]	1981-82
R.G.D.Willis	Australia	Lost by 8 wkts	Adelaide	1982-83
D.I.Gower	Sri Lanka	Drawn	Lord's	1984
D.I.Gower	Australia	Drawn	Manchester	1985
D.I.Gower	Australia	Won by Innings + 118 runs	Birmingham	1985
D.I.Gower	West Indies	Lost by Innings + 30 runs	Bridgetown	1985-86
D.I.Gower	West Indies	Lost by 240 runs	St John's	1985-86
M.W.Gatting	New Zealand	Drawn	The Oval	1986
M.W.Gatting	Australia	Won by Innings + 14 runs	Melbourne	1986-87
M.W.Gatting	Pakistan	Drawn	Birmingham	1987
M.W.Gatting	New Zealand	Drawn	Auckland	1987-88
G.A.Gooch	Sri Lanka	Won by 7 wkts	Lord's	1988
D.I.Gower	Australia	Lost by 210 runs	Leeds	1989
G.A.Gooch	West Indies	Drawn	Port-of-Spain	1989-90
A.J.Lamb §	West Indies	Lost by 164 runs	Bridgetown	1989-90
G.A.Gooch	Pakistan	Drawn	Birmingham	1992
G.A.Gooch	Australia	Lost by 179 runs	Manchester	1993
M.A.Atherton	Australia	Lost by 295 runs	Melbourne	1994-95
M.A.Atherton	South Africa	Drawn	Johannesburg[3]	1995-96
M.A.Atherton	Pakistan	Drawn	Leeds	1996

SOUTH AFRICA	Opponents	Result		
E.A.Halliwell §	England	Lost by 288 runs	Port Elizabeth	1895-96
P.W.Sherwell	Australia	Lost by 530 runs	Melbourne	1910-11
P.W.Sherwell #	Australia	Lost by 7 wkts	Sydney	1910-11
H.W.Taylor	England	Lost by Innings + 18 runs	Birmingham	1924
H.G.Deane	England	Lost by 87 runs	Cape Town	1927-28
H.G.Deane	England	Won by 4 wkts	1927-28	
H.G.Deane	England	Won by 8 wkts	Durban[2]	1927-28
H.G Deane	England	Drawn	The Oval	1929
T.L.Goddard	Australia	Drawn	Sydney	1963-64

P.L.van der Merwe #	Australia	Won by 7 wkts	Port Elizabeth	1966-67
K.C.Wessels §	West Indies	Lost by 52 runs	Bridgetown	1991-92
K.C.Wessels	India	Won by 9 wickets	Port Elizabeth	1992-93
K.C.Wessels	Australia	Drawn	Durban[2]	1993-94
W.J.Cronje	England	Drawn	Pretoria	1995-96

WEST INDIES	Opponents	Result		
R.S.Grant	England	Drawn	Manchester	1939
F.C.M.Alexander	Pakistan	Lost by 41 runs	Dacca	1958-59
F.M.M.Worrell	India	Won by Innings + 30 runs	Bridgetown	1961-62
G.S.Sobers	Australia	Lost by 382 runs	Sydney	1968-69
G.S.Sobers	New Zealand	Won by 5 wkts	Auckland	1968-69
G.S.Sobers	India	Drawn	Kingston	1970-71
G.S.Sobers	New Zealand	Drawn	Port-of-Spain	1971-72
R.B.Kanhai	England	Won by 7 wkts	Port-of-Spain	1973-74
R.B.Kanhai	England	Drawn	Bridgetown	1973-74
C.H.Lloyd	Pakistan	Drawn	Lahore[2]	1974-75
C.H.Lloyd	India	Won by 10 wkts	Kingston	1975-76
C.H.Lloyd	Pakistan	Drawn	Georgetown	1976-77
C.H.Lloyd	Pakistan	Lost by 266 runs	Port-of-Spain	1976-77
C H Lloyd	Australia	Won by Innings + 106 runs	Port-of-Spain	1977-78
C H Lloyd	Australia	Won by 9 wkts	Bridgetown	1977-78
A.I.Kallicharran	India	Drawn	Mumbai[3]	1978-79
D.L.Murray ¶	Australia	Drawn	Brisbane[2]	1979-80
C.H.Lloyd	England	Drawn	Manchester	1980
I V A.Richards §	England	Drawn	Kingston	1980
C H Lloyd	Australia	Won by 5 wkts	Adelaide	1981-82
C.H.Lloyd	India	Won by 4 wkts	Kingston	1982-83
C.H.Lloyd	India	Drawn	Port-of-Spain	1982-83
C H Lloyd	India	Won by 10 wkts	Bridgetown	1982-83
C H Lloyd	India	Drawn	St John's	1982-83
I.V.A.Richards	Australia	Drawn	Port-of-Spain	1983-84
C.H.Lloyd	Australia	Won by 10 wkts	Bridgetown	1983-84
C.H.Lloyd	Australia	Won by 10 wkts	Kingston	1983-84
C.H.Lloyd	England	Won by 9 wkts	Lord's	1984
C.H.Lloyd	Australia	Won by 8 wkts	Brisbane[2]	1984-85
I.V.A.Richards	New Zealand	Won by 10 wkts	Bridgetown	1984-85
I.V.A.Richards	England	Won by 7 wkts	Port-of-Spain	1985-86
I.V.A.Richards	England	Won by 10 wkts	Port-of-Spain	1985-86
I.V.A.Richards	New Zealand	Drawn	Wellington	1986-87
I.V.A.Richards	India	Drawn	Mumbai[3]	1987-88
I.V.A.Richards	Pakistan	Won by 2 wkts	Bridgetown	1987-88
I.V.A.Richards	England	Won by 10 wkts	Leeds	1988
I.V.A.Richards	India	Won by 8 wkts	Bridgetown	1988-89
I.V.A.Richards	India	Won by 7 wkts	Kingston	1988-89
I.V.A.Richards	Australia	Drawn	Port-of-Spain	1990-91
I.V.A.Richards	England	Lost by 115 runs	Leeds	1991
I.V.A.Richards	England	Won by 7 wkts	Birmingham	1991
R.B.Richardson	England	Lost by 208 runs	Bridgetown	1993-94
C.A.Walsh	New Zealand	Drawn	Christchurch	1994-95
R.B.Richardson	Australia	Drawn	St John's	1994-95
R.B.Richardson	Australia	Won by 9 wickets	Port-of-Spain	1994-95
R.B.Richardson	England	Won by 9 wickets	Leeds	1995
C.A.Walsh	New Zealand	Won by 10 wickets	Bridgetown	1995-96

NEW ZEALAND	Opponents	Result		
T.C.Lowry	England	Drawn	Auckland	1929-30
T.C.Lowry #	England	Drawn	Manchester	1931

B.Sutcliffe	West Indies	Drawn	Auckland	1951-52
B.Sutcliffe	South Africa	Lost by 9 wkts	Johannesburg[2]	1953-54
J.R.Reid	South Africa	Drawn	Auckland	1963-64
J.R.Reid	Pakistan	Drawn	Lahore[2]	1964-65
G.T.Dowling	India	Lost by 272 runs	Auckland	1967-68
G.T.Dowling	West Indies	Won by 6 wkts	Wellington	1968-69
G.T.Dowling	England	Drawn	Auckland	1970-71
B.E.Congdon	England	Drawn	Lord's	1973
B.E.Congdon	Australia	Won by 5 wkts	Christchurch	1973-74
B.E.Congdon	Australia	Lost by 297 runs	Auckland	1973-74
G.M.Turner	Australia	Drawn	Christchurch	1976-77
M.G.Burgess	Pakistan	Lost by 128 runs	Christchurch	1978-79
G.P.Howarth	West Indies	Drawn	Christchurch	1979-80
G.P.Howarth	West Indies	Drawn	Auckland	1979-80
G.P.Howarth	Australia	Drawn	Melbourne	1980-81
G.P.Howarth	Australia	Won by 5 wkts	Auckland	1981-82
G.P.Howarth	Australia	Lost by 8 wkts	Christchurch	1981-82
G.P.Howarth	Sri Lanka	Won by 6 wkts	Wellington	1982-83
G.P.Howarth	England	Won by 5 wkts	Leeds	1983
G.P Howarth	England	Lost by 127 runs	Lord s	1983
G.P.Howarth	Sri Lanka	Drawn	Colombo (SSC)	1983-84
G.P.Howarth	Pakistan	Won by Innings + 99 runs	Auckland	1984-85
G.P.Howarth	Pakistan	Won by 2 wkts	Dunedin	1984-85
G.P.Howarth #	West Indies	Lost by 10 wkts	Kingston	1984-85
J.V.Coney §	Australia	Won by Innings + 41 runs	Brisbane[2]	1985-86
J.V.Coney	Australia	Won by 6 wkts	Perth	1985-86
J.V.Coney	Australia	Drawn	Wellington	1985-86
J.V.Coney	Australia	Drawn	Christchurch	1985-86
J.V.Coney	England	Won by 8 wkts	Nottingham	1986
J.V.Coney #	West Indies	Won by 5 wkts	Christchurch	1986-87
J.J.Crowe §	Sri Lanka	Drawn	Colombo (CCC)	1986-87
J.J.Crowe	England	Drawn	Christchurch	1987-88
J.G.Wright	Australia	Drawn	Perth	1989-90
J.G.Wright	England	Drawn	Lord's	1990
J.G.Wright #	England	Lost by 114 runs	Birmingham	1990
M.D.Crowe	Pakistan	Lost by 65 runs	Faisalabad	1990-91
I.D.S.Smith ¶	Sri Lanka	Drawn	Auckland	1990-91
M.D.Crowe	England	Lost by Innings + 4 runs	Christchurch	1991-92
M.D.Crowe	England	Lost by 168 runs	Auckland	1991-92
K.R.Rutherford §	Pakistan	Lost by 33 runs	Hamilton	1992-93
M.D.Crowe	Australia	Lost by Innings + 60 runs	Christchurch	1992-93
M.D.Crowe	Australia	Drawn	Perth	1993-94
K.R.Rutherford	Pakistan	Won 5 wkts	Christchurch	1993-94
K.R.Rutherford	Sri Lanka	Lost by 241 runs	Napier	1994-95
K.R.Rutherford	Sri Lanka	Drawn	Dunedin	1994-95
L.K.Germon	Pakistan	Lost by 161 runs	Christchurch	1995-96
L.K.Germon	West indies	Drawn	St John's	1995-96

INDIA	Opponents	Result		
Nawab of Pataudi, sr	England	Drawn	Manchester	1946
N.B.Amarnath	Pakistan	Drawn	Calcutta	1952-53
P.R.Umrigar	Australia	Lost by 94 runs	Calcutta	1956-57
Nawab of Pataudi, jr	England	Drawn	Kanpur	1963-64
Nawab of Pataudi, jr	Australia	Drawn	Calcutta	1964-65
Nawab of Pataudi, jr	Australia	Lost by 39 runs	Brisbane[2]	1967-68
Nawab of Pataudi, jr	Australia	Lost by 144 runs	Sydney	1967-68
Nawab of Pataudi, jr	New Zealand	Lost by 6 wkts	Christchurch	1967-68

A.L.Wadekar	West Indies	Drawn	Bridgetown	1970-71
Nawab of Pataudi, jr	West Indies	Lost by 267 runs	Bangalore	1974-75
B.S.Bedi	West Indies	Drawn	Port-of-Spain	1975-76
S.M.Gavaskar	Australia	Drawn	Adelaide	1980-81
S.M.Gavaskar	New Zealand	Lost by 62 runs	Wellington	1980-81
S.M.Gavaskar	Pakistan	Drawn	Lahore[2] (1st)	1982-83
S.M Gavaskar	Pakistan	Drawn	Lahore[2] (5th)	1982-83
Kapil Dev	Pakistan	Drawn	Jullundur	1983-84
Kapil Dev	West Indies	Lost by 1[illegible] runs	Ahmedabad	1983-84
Kapil Dev	Australia	Drawn	Melbourne	1985-86
Kapil Dev	England	Won by 5 wkts	Lord's	1986
D.B.Vengsarkar	West Indies	Drawn	Georgetown	1988-89
D.B.Vengsarkar	West Indies	Lost by 217 runs	Port-of-Spain	1988-89
K.Srikkanth §	Pakistan	Drawn	Karachi[1]	1989-90
M.Azharuddin	New Zealand	Drawn	Auckland	1990-91
M.Azharuddin	England	Lost by 247 runs	Lord's	1990
M.Azharuddin	Australia	Drawn	Sydney	1991-92
M.Azharuddin	Australia	Lost by 38 runs	Adelaide	1991-92
M.Azharuddin	South Africa	Drawn	Durban[2]	1992-93
M.Azharuddin	Sri Lanka	Drawn	Kandy	1993-94
M.Azharuddin	England	Drawn	Lord's	1996
PAKISTAN	Opponents	Result		
Fazal Mahmood §	West Indies	Won by 10 wkts	Karachi[1]	1958-59
Javed Burki	England	Lost by Innings + 117 runs	Leeds	1962
Javed Burki	England	Drawn	Nottingham	1962
Hanif Mohammad	New Zealand	Drawn	Wellington	1964-65
Hanif Mohammad	New Zealand	Won by Innings + 64 runs	Rawalpindi[1]	1964-65
Intikhab Alam	Australia	Lost by 52 runs	Sydney	1972-73
Mushtaq Mohammad	India	Won by 8 wkts	Lahore[2]	1978-79
Mushtaq Mohammad	New Zealand	Drawn	Auckland	1978-79
Javed Miandad	Australia	Lost by 286 runs	Perth	1981-82
Javed Miandad	Sri Lanka	Won by Innings + 102 runs	Lahore[2]	1981-82
Imran Khan	Australia	Won by 9 wkts	Lahore[2]	1982-83
Imran Khan	India	Won by Innings + 86 runs	Karachi[1]	1982-83
Imran Khan	India	Won by 10 wkts	Faisalabad	1982-83
Zaheer Abbas	Australia	Lost by Innings + 9 runs	Perth	1983-84
Zaheer Abbas	England	Drawn	Lahore[2]	1983-84
Javed Miandad	Sri Lanka	Won by 8 wkts	Sialkot	1985-86
Imran Khan	India	Drawn	Calcutta	1986-87
Imran Khan	England	Drawn	Manchester	1987
Imran Khan	West Indies	Drawn	Port-of-Spain	1987-88
Imran Khan	New Zealand	Drawn	Wellington	1988-89
Imran Khan	India	Drawn	Faisalabad	1989-90
Imran Khan	India	Drawn	Lahore[2]	1989-90
Imran Khan	India	Drawn	Sialkot	1989-90
Imran Khan	Australia	Lost by 92 runs	Melbourne	1989-90
Javed Miandad	New Zealand	Won by Innings + 43 runs	Faisalabad	1990-91
Imran Khan	Sri Lanka	Won by 3 wkts	Faisalabad	1991-92
Wasim Akram	West Indies	Lost by 10 wickets	Bridgetown	1992-93
Saleem Malik §	New Zealand	Won 5 wkts	Auckland	1993-94
Saleem Malik	Sri Lanka	Won by Innings + 52 runs	Kandy	1994-95
Saleem Malik	Australia	Drawn	Rawalpindi[2]	1994-95
Rameez Raja	Sri Lanka	Lost by 42 runs	Faisalabad	1995-96
SRI LANKA	Opponents	Result		
D.S.de Silva §	New Zealand	Lost by Innings + 25 runs	Christchurch	1982-83
L.R.D.Mendis	Pakistan	Won by 8 wkts	Colombo (CCC)	1985-86

A.Ranatunga §	Australia	Drawn	Brisbane[2]	1989-90
A.Ranatunga	Australia	Lost by 173 runs	Hobart	1989-90
A.Ranatunga	New Zealand	Drawn	Wellington	1990-91
A.Ranatunga	New Zealand	Drawn	Hamilton	1990-91
P.A.de Silva	Pakistan	Drawn	Gujranwala	1991-92
A.Ranatunga	Australia	Lost by 16 runs	Colombo (SSC)	1992-93
A.Ranatunga	Australia	Drawn	Colombo (PIS)	1992-93
A.Ranatunga	New Zealand	Drawn	Moratuwa	1992-93
A.Ranatunga	Australia	Lost by 10 wickets	Melbourne	1995-96

ZIMBABWE	Opponents	Result		
A.Flower	Pakistan	Lost by 52 runs	Rawalpindi[2]	1993-94
A.Flower	Pakistan	Drawn	Lahore[2]	1993-94

SUMMARY	Captains	Instances	W	L	D
Australia	14	58	25	18	15
England	29	53	10	21	22
South Africa	8	14	4	6	4
West Indies	11	48	24	5	19
New Zealand	14	49	12	15	22
India	11	29	1	11	17
Pakistan	11	32	12	7	13
Sri Lanka	4	11	1	4	6
Zimbabwe	1	2	0	1	1
TOTAL	103	296	89	88	119

CENTURY ON DEBUT AS CAPTAIN

0	143	G.H.S.Trott	Australia	v	England	Lord's	1896
109	50*	A.C.MacLaren	England	v	Australia	Sydney	1897-98
133	22	M.A.Noble	Australia	v	England	Sydney	1903-04
191		C.Hill	Australia	v	South Africa	Sydney	1910-11
109	8	H.W.Taylor	South Africa	v	England	Durban[1]	1913-14
12	158	W.W.Armstrong	Australia	v	England	Sydney	1920-21
112		A.L.Hassett	Australia	v	South Africa	Johannesburg[2]	1949-50
164*		V.J.Hazare	India	v	England	Delhi	1951-52
10	104	J.B.Stollmeyer	West Indies	v	Australia	Sydney	1951-52
107	68	G.O.Rabone	New Zealand	v	South Africa	Durban[2]	1953-54
104*	48	D.J.McGlew	South Africa	v	England	Manchester	1955
239	5	G.T.Dowling	New Zealand	v	India	Christchurch	1967-68
126		B.E.Congdon	New Zealand	v	West Indies	Bridgetown	1971-72
30	163	C.H.Lloyd	West Indies	v	India	Bangalore	1974-75
123	109*	G.S.Chappell	Australia	v	West Indies	Brisbane[2]	1975-76
116	35*	S.M.Gavaskar	India	v	New Zealand	Auckland	1975-76
7	102	G.N.Yallop	Australia	v	England	Brisbane[2]	1978-79
120*		J.J.Crowe	New Zealand	v	Sri Lanka	Colombo (CCC)	1986-87
10	102	D.B.Vengsarkar	India	v	West Indies	Delhi	1987-88
119	10	A.J.Lamb	England	v	West Indies	Bridgetown	1989-90
121		D.L.Houghton	Zimbabwe	v	India	Harare	1992-93

HIGHEST INDIVIDUAL INNINGS BY CAPTAINS

333	G.A.Gooch	England	v	India	Lord's	1990
311	R.B.Simpson	Australia	v	England	Manchester	1964
299	M.D.Crowe	New Zealand	v	Sri Lanka	Wellington	1990-91
285*	P.B.H.May	England	v	West Indies	Birmingham	1957
270	D.G.Bradman	Australia	v	England	Melbourne	1936-37
242*	C.H.Lloyd	West Indies	v	India	Mumbai[3]	1974-75
240	W.R.Hammond	England	v	Australia	Lord's	1938

239	G.T.Dowling	New Zealand	v	India	Christchurch	1967-68
237	Saleem Malik	Pakistan	v	Australia	Rawalpindi[2]	1994-95
235	G.S.Chappell	Australia	v	Pakistan	Faisalabad	1979-80
234	D.G.Bradman	Australia	v	England	Sydney	1946-47
225	R.B.Simpson	Australia	v	England	Adelaide	1965-66
219	D.S.Atkinson	West Indies	v	Australia	Bridgetown	1954-55
215	D.I.Gower	England	v	Australia	Birmingham	1985
212	D.G.Bradman	Australia	v	England	Adelaide	1936-37
211	W.L.Murdoch	Australia	v	England	The Oval	1884
211	Javed Miandad	Pakistan	v	Australia	Karachi[1]	1988-89
208	A.D.Nourse	South Africa	v	England	Nottingham	1951
205	E.R.Dexter	England	v	Pakistan	Karachi[1]	1961-62
205	L.Hutton	England	v	West Indies	Kingston	1953-54
205	W.M.Lawry	Australia	v	West Indies	Melbourne	1968-69
205	S.M.Gavaskar	India	v	West Indies	Mumbai[3]	1978-79
205	A.R.Border	Australia	v	New Zealand	Adelaide	1987-88
204	G.S.Chappell	Australia	v	India	Sydney	1980-81
203*	Nawab of Pataudi jr	India	v	England	Delhi	1963-64
203*	Hanif Mohammad	Pakistan	v	New Zealand	Lahore[2]	1964-65
203*	Javed Miandad	Pakistan	v	Sri Lanka	Faisalabad	1985-86
203	H.L.Collins	Australia	v	South Africa	Johannesburg[1]	1921-22
201*	J.Ryder	Australia	v	England	Adelaide	1924-25
201	D.G.Bradman	Australia	v	India	Adelaide	1947-48
201	R.B.Simpson	Australia	v	West Indies	Bridgetown	1964-65
201	G.S.Chappell	Australia	v	Pakistan	Brisbane[2]	1981-82
200*	A.R.Border	Australia	v	England	Leeds	1993

CENTURY IN EACH INNINGS BY A CAPTAIN

189	104*	A.Melville	South Africa	v	England	Nottingham	1947
132	127*	D.G.Bradman	Australia	v	India	Melbourne	1947-48
153	115	R.B.Simpson	Australia	v	Pakistan	Karachi[1]	1964-65
145	121	I.M.Chappell	Australia	v	New Zealand	Wellington	1973-74
123	109*	G.S.Chappell	Australia	v	West Indies	Brisbane[2]	1975-76
107	182*	S.M.Gavaskar	India	v	West Indies	Calcutta	1978-79
140	114*	A.R.Border	Australia	v	New Zealand	Christchurch	1985-86
333	123	G.A.Gooch	England	v	India	Lord's	1990

CENTURY AND A NINETY IN SAME MATCH BY A CAPTAIN

104	93	Hanif Mohammad	Pakistan	v	Australia	Melbourne	1964-65
152	95*	G.S.Sobers	West Indies	v	England	Georgetown	1967-68
119	94	L.R.D.Mendis	Sri Lanka	v	England	Lord's	1984

CENTURIES BY RIVAL CAPTAINS IN THE SAME TEST

H.W.Taylor	South Africa	109	J.W.H.T.Douglas	England	119	Durban[2]	1913-14
A.P.F.Chapman	England	121	W.M.Woodfull	Australia	155	Lord's	1930
W.R.Hammond	England	240	D.G.Bradman	Australia	102*	Lord's	1938
A.Melville	South Africa	103	W.R.Hammond	England	140	Durban[2]	1938-39
L.Hutton	England	145	A.L.Hassett	Australia	104	Lord's	1953
P.B.H.May	England	117	D.J.McGlew	South Africa	104*	Manchester	1955
D.J.McGlew	South Africa	120	J.R.Reid	New Zealand	142	Johannesburg[1]	1961-62
E.R.Dexter	England	174	R.B.Simpson	Australia	311	Manchester	1964
G.S.Sobers	West Indies	113*	M.C.Cowdrey	England	101	Kingston	1967-68
W.M.Lawry	Australia	151	G.S.Sobers	West Indies	113	Sydney	1968-69
G.S.Sobers	West Indies	142	B.E.Congdon	New Zealand	126	Bridgetown	1971-72
R.B.Kanhai	West Indies	105	I.M.Chappell	Australia	106*	Bridgetown	1972-73
B.E.Congdon	New Zealand	132	I.M.Chappell	Australia	145 + 121	Wellington	1973-74
S.M.Gavaskar	India	205	A.I.Kallicharran	West Indies	187	Mumbai[3]	1978-79

Javed Miandad	Pakistan	106*	G.S.Chappell	Australia	235	Faisalabad	1979-80
Imran Khan	Pakistan	117	S.M.Gavaskar	India	127*	Faisalabad	1982-83
C.H.Lloyd	West Indies	143	Kapil Dev	India	100*	Port-of-Spain	1982-83
Kapil Dev	India	119	A.R.Border	Australia	106	Chennai[1]	1986-87
M.W.Gatting	England	150*	Imran Khan	Pakistan	118	The Oval	1987
D.B.Vengsarkar	India	102	I.V.A.Richards	West Indies	146	Delhi	1987-88
Javed Miandad	Pakistan	107	A.R.Border	Australia	113*	Faisalabad	1988-89
G.A.Gooch	England	333 + 123	M.Azharuddin	India	121	Lord's	1990
G.A.Gooch	England	116	M.Azharuddin	India	179	Manchester	1990

SEVEN WICKETS IN AN INNINGS BY A CAPTAIN

9-83	Kapil Dev	India	v	West Indies	Ahmedabad	1983-84
8-60	Imran Khan	Pakistan	v	India	Karachi[1]	1982-83
8-106	Kapil Dev	India	v	Australia	Adelaide	1985-86
7-37	C.A.Walsh	West Indies	v	New Zealand	Wellington	1994-95
7-40	Imran Khan	Pakistan	v	England	Leeds	1987
7-44	I.W.Johnson	Australia	v	West Indies	Georgetown	1954-55
7-46	A.R.Border	Australia	v	West Indies	Sydney	1988-89
7-52	Intikhab Alam	Pakistan	v	New Zealand	Dunedin	1972-73
7-52	Imran Khan	Pakistan	v	England	Birmingham	1982
7-53	D.S.Atkinson	West Indies	v	New Zealand	Auckland	1955-56
7-80	G.O.B.Allen	England	v	India	The Oval	1936
7-80	Imran Khan	Pakistan	v	West Indies	Georgetown	1987-88
7-91	Waqar Younis	Pakistan	v	Zimbabwe	Karachi[2]	1993-94
7-100	M.A.Noble	Australia	v	England	Sydney	1903-04

TEN WICKETS IN A MATCH BY A CAPTAIN

13-55	C.A.Walsh	West Indies	v	New Zealand	Wellington	1994-95
13-135	Waqar Younis	Pakistan	v	Zimbabwe	Karachi[2]	1993-94
12-100	Fazal Mahmood	Pakistan	v	West Indies	Dacca	1958-59
11-79	Imran Khan	Pakistan	v	India	Karachi[1]	1982-83
11-90	A.E.R.Gilligan	England	v	South Africa	Birmingham	1924
11-96	A.R.Border	Australia	v	West Indies	Sydney	1988-89
11-121	Imran Khan	Pakistan	v	West Indies	Georgetown	1987-88
11-130	Intikhab Alam	Pakistan	v	New Zealand	Dunedin	1972-73
11-150	E.P.Nupen	South Africa	v	England	Johannesburg[1]	1930-31
11-180	Imran Khan	Pakistan	v	India	Faisalabad	1982-83
10-77	Imran Khan	Pakistan	v	England	Leeds	1987
10-78	G.O.B.Allen	England	v	India	Lord's	1936
10-135	Kapil Dev	India	v	West Indies	Ahmedabad	1983-84
10-182	Intikhab Alam	Pakistan	v	New Zealand	Dacca	1969-70
10-194	B.S.Bedi	India	v	Australia	Perth	1977-78

A CENTURY AND FIVE WICKETS IN AN INNINGS BY A CAPTAIN

219	5-56	D.S.Atkinson	West Indies	v	Australia	Bridgetown	1954-55
174	5-41	G.S.Sobers	West Indies	v	England	Leeds	1966
121	5-28	Mushtaq Mohammad	Pakistan	v	West Indies	Port-of-Spain	1976-77
117	6-98 } 5-82 }	Imran Khan	Pakistan	v	India	Faisalabad	1982-83

HUNDRED RUNS AND EIGHT WICKETS IN A MATCH BY A CAPTAIN.

121	565-28	3-69	Mushtaq Mohammad	Pakistan	v	West Indies	Port-of-Spain	1976-77
174	5-41	3-39	G.S.Sobers	West Indies	v	England	Leeds	1966
117	6-98	5-82	Imran Khan	Pakistan	v	India	Faisalabad	1982-83
67*	465-49	3-66	Imran Khan	Pakistan	v	England	Leeds	1982
35	683-71	5-36	G.O.B.Allen	England	v	Australia	Brisbane[2]	1936-37

YOUNGEST CAPTAINS

Years	Days						
21	77	Nawab of Pataudi, jr	India	v	West Indies	Bridgetown	1961-62
22	15	Waqar Younis	Pakistan	v	Zimbabwe	Karachi[2]	1993-94
22	194	I.D.Craig	Australia	v	South Africa	Johannesburg[3]	1957-58
22	260	Javed Miandad	Pakistan	v	Australia	Karachi[1]	1979-80
22	306	M.Bisset	South Africa	v	England	Johannesburg[1]	1898-99
23	144	M.P.Bowden	England	v	South Africa	Cape Town	1888-89
23	217	G.C.Grant	West Indies	v	Australia	Adelaide	1930-31
23	292	Hon I.F.W.Bligh	England	v	Australia	Melbourne	1882-83
24	23	Javed Burki	Pakistan	v	England	Birmingham	1962
24	48	Kapil Dev	India	v	West Indies	Kingston	1982-83
24	125	W.J.Cronje	South Africa	v	Australia	Adelaide	1993-94
24	194	I.T.Botham	England	v	West Indies	Nottingham	1980
24	222	H.W.Taylor	South Africa	v	England	Durban[1]	1913-14
25	40	D.B.Carr	England	v	India	Chennai[1]	1951-52
25	57	K.J.Hughes	Australia	v	Pakistan	Perth	1978-79
25	117	D.S.Sheppard	England	v	Pakistan	Nottingham	1954
25	133	D.I.Gower	England	v	Pakistan	Lord's	1982
25	135	M.A.Atherton	England	v	Australia	Birmingham	1993
25	217	A.Flower	Zimbabwe	v	Pakistan	Karachi[2]	1993-94

OLDEST CAPTAINS

Years	Days						
50	320	W.G.Grace	England	v	Australia	Nottingham	1899
45	245	G.O.B.Allen	England	v	West Indies	Kingston	1947-48
43	276	W.R.Hammond	England	v	New Zealand	Christchurch	1946-47
43	232	W.Bardsley	Australia	v	England	Manchester	1926
42	247	N.Betancourt	West Indies	v	England	Port-of-Spain	1929-30
42	130	S.E.Gregory	Australia	v	England	The Oval	1912
42	86	W.W.Armstrong	Australia	v	England	The Oval	1921
41	330	J.W.H.T.Douglas	England	v	South Africa	Manchester	1924
41	178	V.Y.Richardson	Australia	v	South Africa	Durban[2]	1935-36
41	95	N.B.Amarnath	India	v	Pakistan	Calcutta	1952-53
41	80	R.Illingworth	England	v	West Indies	Lord's	1973
41	44	T.W.Graveney	England	v	Australia	Leeds	1968
40	279	A.D.Nourse	South Africa	v	England	The Oval	1951
40	277	D.S.de Silva	Sri Lanka	v	New Zealand	Wellington	1982-83
40	245	F.R.Brown	England	v	South Africa	The Oval	1951
40	223	J.M.Blackham	Australia	v	England	Sydney	1894-95
40	125	C.H.Lloyd	West Indies	v	Australia	Sydney	1984-85
40	109	C.B.Fry	England	v	Australia	The Oval	1912
40	3	G.A.Gooch	England	v	Australia	Leeds	1993

General

MOST TEST MATCH APPEARANCES

For	Total		Opponents A	E	SA	WI	NZ	I	P	SL	Z
Australia	**156**	A.R.Border	-	47	6	31	23	20	22	7	-
England	**118**	G.A.Gooch	42	-	3	26	15	19	10	3	-
South Africa	**50**	J.H.B.Waite	14	21	-	-	15	-	-	-	-
West Indies	**121**	I.V.A.Richards	34	36	-	-	7	28	16	-	-
New Zealand	**86**	R.J.Hadlee	23	21	-	10	-	14	12	6	-
India	**131**	Kapil Dev	20	27	4	25	10	-	29	14	2
Pakistan	**124**	Javed Miandad	24	22	-	17	18	28	-	12	3
Sri Lanka	**61**	A.Ranatunga	9	4	3	1	11	14	16	-	3
Zimbabwe	**16**	A.D.R.Campbell	-	-	-	-	4	2	6	3	-
		A.Flower	-	-	-	-	4	2	6	3	-
		G.W.Flower	-	-	-	-	4	2	6	3	-
		D.L.Houghton	-	-	-	-	4	2	6	3	-

MOST CONSECUTIVE APPEARANCES

		From		To	
153	A.R.Border (Australia)	Melbourne	1978-79	Durban[2]	1993-94
106	S.M.Gavaskar (India)	Mumbai[3]	1974-75	Chennai[1]	1986-87
87	G.R.Viswanath (India)	Georgetown	1970-71	Karachi[1]	1982-83
85	G.S.Sobers (West Indies)	Port-of-Spain	1954-55	Port-of-Spain	1971-72
72	D.L.Haynes (West Indies)	Brisbane[2]	1979-80	Lord's	1988
71	I.M.Chappell (Australia)	Adelaide	1965-66	Melbourne	1975-76
66	Kapil Dev (India)	Faisalabad	1978-79	Delhi	1984-85
65	A.P.E.Knott (England)	Auckland	1970-71	The Oval	1977
65	I.T.Botham (England)	Wellington	1977-78	Karachi[1]	1983-84
65	Kapil Dev (India)	Chennai[1]	1984-85	Hamilton	1993-94
64	I.A.Healy (Australia)	Karachi[1]	1988-89	Rawalpindi[2]	1994-95
61	R.B.Kanhai (West Indies)	Birmingham	1957	Sydney	1968-69
61	I.V.A.Richards (West Indies)	Nottingham	1980	Chennai[1]	1987-88
58 §	J R.Reid (New Zealand)	Manchester	1949	Leeds	1965
58 §	A.W.Greig (England)	Manchester	1972	The Oval	1977
56	S.M.H.Kirmani (India)	Chennai[1]	1979-80	Kanpur	1984-85
53	K.J.Hughes (Australia)	Brisbane[2]	1978-79	Sydney	1982-83
53	Javed Miandad (Pakistan)	Lahore[2]	1977-78	Sydney	1983-84
52	F.E.Woolley (England)	The Oval	1909	The Oval	1926
52	P.B.H.May (England)	The Oval	1953	Leeds	1959
52	R.W.Marsh (Australia)	Brisbane[2]	1970-71	The Oval	1977
51	G.S.Chappell (Australia)	Perth	1970-71	The Oval	1977
51	D.I.Gower (England)	Mumbai[3]	1981-82	Lord's	1986
50	M.Azharuddin (India)	Mumbai[3]	1987-88	Nottingham	# 1996

The most for South Africa is 45 § by A.W.Nourse; for Sri Lanka 35 # by P.A.de Silva; and for Zimbabwe 16 by 4 players as above.

§ Entire Test career. # To date. Note: Kapil Dev played 66 consecutive Tests before being dropped for one Test because of disciplinary reasons. He then played a further 65 consecutive Tests before retiring.

LONGEST CAREERS *(From debut to final day of last match)*

Years	Days		Team (s)	From		To	
30	315	W.Rhodes	England	Nottingham	1899	Kingston	1929-30
26	355	D.B.Close	England	Manchester	1949	Manchester	1976
25	13	F.E.Woolley	England	The Oval	1909	The Oval	1934
24	10	G.A.Headley	West Indies	Bridgetown	1929-30	Kingston	1953-54
23	41	A.J.Traicos	South Africa/Zimbabwe	Durban[2]	1969-70	Delhi	1992-93
22	233	J.B.Hobbs	England	Melbourne	1907-08	The Oval	1930

22	120	G.Gunn	England	Sydney	1907-08	Kingston	1929-30
22	18	S.E.Gregory	Australia	Lord's	1890	The Oval	1912
21	336	F.R.Brown	England	The Oval	1931	Lord's	1953
21	313	A.W.Nourse	South Africa	Johannesburg[1]	1902-03	The Oval	1924
20	218	Imran Khan	Pakistan	Birmingham	1971	Faisalabad	1991-92
20	132	R.B.Simpson	Australia	Johannesburg[1]	1957-58	Kingston	1977-78
20	79	M.C.Cowdrey	England	Brisbane[2]	1954-55	Melbourne	1974-75
20	6	G.S.Sobers	West Indies	Kingston	1953-54	Port-of-Spain	1973-74
20	1	Mushtaq Mohammad	Pakistan	Lahore[1]	1958-59	Perth	1978-79

Longest for the other countries:

19	0	N.B.Amarnath	India	Mumbai[1]	1933-34	Calcutta	1952-53
18	72	B.Sutcliffe	New Zealand	Christchurch	1946-47	Birmingham	1965
13	316	A.Ranatunga	Sri Lanka	Colombo (PSS)	1981-82	Melbourne #	1995-96

 # To date.

LONGEST INTERVALS BETWEEN APPEARANCES

Years	Days		Team (s)	From		To	
22	222	A.J.Traicos	Sth.Africa/Zimbabwe	Pt.Elizabeth	1969-70	Harare	1992-93
17	316	G.Gunn	England	Sydney	1911-12	Bridgetown	1929-30
17	111	Younis Ahmed	Pakistan	Lahore[2]	1969-70	Jaipur	1986-87
14	92	J.M.M.Commaille	South Africa	Cape Town	1909-10	Birmingham	1924
14	28	D.C.Cleverley	New Zealand	Christchurch	1931-32	Wellington	1945-46
13	53	F.Mitchell	England/South Africa	Cape Town	1898-99	Manchester	1912
13	32	G.M.Carew	West Indies	Bridgetown	1934-35	Port-of-Spain	1947-48
12	160	N.B.Amarnath	India	Chennai[1]	1933-34	Lord's	1946
12	81	W.E.Hollies	England	Kingston	1934-35	Nottingham	1947
12	10	Nawab of Pataudi, sr	England/India	Nottingham	1934	Lord's	1946
11	361	F.R.Brown	England	Manchester	1937	The Oval	1949
11	345	H.L.Jackson	England	Manchester	1949	Leeds	1961
11	320	G.A.Faulkner	South Africa	The Oval	1912	Lord's	1924
11	306	S.J.Pegler	South Africa	The Oval	1912	Birmingham	1924
11	298	M.P.Donnelly	New Zealand	The Oval	1937	The Oval	1949
11	225	D.Shackleton	England	Delhi	1951-52	Lord's	1963
10	158	S.J.Snooke	South Africa	The Oval	1912	Durban[2]	1922-23
10	48	J.Langridge	England	Lord's	1936	The Oval	1946

Longest for Australia:

9	305	R.B.Simpson	Australia	Sydney	1967-68	Brisbane[2]	1977-78

The most matches between appearances is 104 by Younis Ahmed (as above).

PLAYERS WHO REPRESENTED TWO COUNTRIES

Player	Country (Tests)	Seasons	Country (Tests)	Seasons	Total Tests
Amir Elahi	India (1)	1947-48	Pakistan (5)	1952-53	6
J.J.Ferris	Australia (8)	1886-87 to 1890	England (1)	1891-92	9
S.C.Guillen	West Indies (5)	1951-52	New Zealand (3)	1955-56	8
Gul Mahomed	India (8)	1946 to 1952-53	Pakistan (1)	1956-57	9
F.Hearne	England (2)	1888-89	South Africa (4)	1891-92 to 1895-96	6
A.H.Kardar	India (3)	1946 §	Pakistan (23)	1952-53 to 1957-58	26
W.E.Midwinter	Australia (8)	1876-77 to 1886-87	England (4)	1881-82	12
F.Mitchell	England (2)	1898-99	South Africa (3)	1912	5
W.L.Murdoch	Australia (18)	1876-77 to 1890	England (1)	1891-92	19
Nawab of Pataudi, sr	England (3)	1932-33 to 1934	India (3)	1946	6
A.J.Traicos	South Africa (3)	1969-70	Zimbabwe (4)	1992-93	7
A.E.Trott	Australia (3)	1894-95	England (2)	1898-99	5
K.C.Wessels	Australia (24)	1982-83 to 1985-86	South Africa (16)	1991-92 to 1994	40
S.M.J.Woods	Australia (3)	1888	England (3)	1895-96	6

§ As "Abdul Hafeez".

ON THE FIELD THROUGHOUT A MATCH

						Days
Nazar Mohammad	Pakistan	v	India	Lucknow[1]	1952-53	4
D.J.McGlew	South Africa	v	New Zealand	Wellington	1952-53	4
C.A.Milton	England	v	New Zealand	Leeds	1958	5#†
J.H.Edrich	England	v	New Zealand	Leeds	1965	5
D.Lloyd	England	v	India	Birmingham	1974	3
G.Boycott	England	v	Australia	Leeds	1977	4
Taslim Arif	Pakistan	v	Australia	Faisalabad	1979-80	4
S.M.Gavaskar	India	v	West Indies	Georgetown	1982-83	5#
D.S.B.P.Kuruppu	Sri Lanka	v	New Zealand	Colombo (CCC)	1986-87	5†
M.A.Taylor	Australia	v	Pakistan	Sydney	1989-90	6§
M.A.Taylor	Australia	v	South Africa	Melbourne	1993-94	5

† In first Test. # Rain prevented play on two days. § Rain prevented play on three days. Rain prevented play on one day.

OLDEST PLAYERS ON TEST DEBUT

Years	Days						
49	119	J.Southerton	England	v	Australia	Melbourne	1876-77
47	284	Miran Bux	Pakistan	v	India	Lahore[1]	1954-55
46	253	D.D.Blackie	Australia	v	England	Sydney	1928-29
46	237	H.Ironmonger	Australia	v	England	Brisbane[2]	1928-29
45	154	A.J.Traicos #	Zimbabwe	v	India	Harare	1992-93
42	242	N.Betancourt	West Indies	v	England	Port-of-Spain	1929-30
41	337	E.R.Wilson	England	v	Australia	Sydney	1920-21
41	27	R.J.D.Jamshedji	India	v	England	Mumbai[1]	1933-34
40	345	C.A.Wiles	West Indies	v	England	Manchester	1933
40	295	O.Henry	South Africa	v	India	Durban[2]	1992-93
40	216	S.Kinneir	England	v	Australia	Sydney	1911-12
40	110	H.W.Lee	England	v	South Africa	Johannesburg[1]	1930-31
40	56	G.W.A.Chubb	South Africa	v	England	Nottingham	1951
40	37	C.Ramaswami	India	v	England	Manchester	1936

 # Traicos had previously played three Tests for South Africa in 1969-70.
The oldest player to make his debut for New Zealand was H.M.McGirr who was 38 years 101 days old when he appeared against England at Auckland in 1929-30; and for Sri Lanka D.S.De Silva who was 39 years 251 days old when he made his debut in his country's inaugural Test against England at Colombo (PSS) in 1981-82.

YOUNGEST TEST PLAYERS

Years	Days						
15	124	Mushtaq Mohammad	Pakistan	v	West Indies	Lahore[1]	1958-59
16	189	Aaqib Javed	Pakistan	v	New Zealand	Wellington	1988-89
16	205	S.R.Tendulkar	India	v	Pakistan	Karachi[1]	1989-90
16	221	Aftab Baloch	Pakistan	v	New Zealand	Dacca	1969-70
16	248	Nasim-ul-Ghani	Pakistan	v	West Indies	Bridgetown	1957-58
16	352	Khalid Hassan	Pakistan	v	England	Nottingham	1954
17	5	Zahid Fazal	Pakistan	v	West Indies	Karachi[1]	1990-91
17	69	Ataur Rehmann	Pakistan	v	England	Leeds	1992
17	118	L.Sivaramakrishnan	India	v	West Indies	St John's	1982-83
17	122	J.E.D.Sealy	West Indies	v	England	Bridgetown	1929-30
17	189	C.D.U.S.Weerasinghe	Sri Lanka	v	India	Colombo (PSS)	1985-86
17	193	Maninder Singh	India	v	Pakistan	Karachi[1]	1932-83
17	239	I.D.Craig	Australia	v	South Africa	Melbourne	1952-53
17	245	G.S.Sobers	West Indies	v	England	Kingston	1953-54
17	265	V.L.Mehra	India	v	New Zealand	Mumbai[2]	1955-56
17	300	Hanif Mohammad	Pakistan	v	India	Delhi	1952-53
17	341	Intikhab Alam	Pakistan	v	Australia	Karachi[1]	1959-60
17	364	Waqar Younis	Pakistan	v	India	Karachi[1]	1989-90

18	1	M.S.Atapattu	Sri Lanka	v	India	Chandigarh	1990-91
18	13	A.G.Milkha Singh	India	v	Australia	Chennai[2]	1959-60
18	26	Majid Khan	Pakistan	v	Australia	Karachi[1]	1964-65
18	31	M.R.Bynoe	West Indies	v	Pakistan	Lahore[1]	1958-59
18	41	Salahuddin	Pakistan	v	New Zealand	Rawalpindi[1]	1964-65
18	44	Khalid Wazir	Pakistan	v	England	Lord's	1954
18	78	A.Ranatunga	Sri Lanka	v	England	Colombo (PSS)	1981-82
18	81	B.R.Jurangpathy	Sri Lanka	v	India	Kandy	1985-86
18	105	J.B.Stollmeyer	West Indies	v	England	Lord's	1939
18	136	Ijaz Ahmed	Pakistan	v	India	Chennai[1]	1986-87
18	149	D.B.Close	England	v	New Zealand	Manchester	1949
18	173	A.T.Roberts	West Indies	v	New Zealand	Auckland	1955-56
18	186	Haseeb Ahsan	Pakistan	v	West Indies	Bridgetown	1957-58
18	190	Imran Khan	Pakistan	v	England	Birmingham	1971
18	197	D.L.Freeman	New Zealand	v	England	Christchurch	1932-33
18	212	H.K.Olonga	Zimbabwe	v	Pakistan	Harare	1994-95
18	232	T.W.Garrett	Australia	v	England	Melbourne	1876-77
18	236	Wasim Akram	Pakistan	v	New Zealand	Auckland	1984-85
18	242	A.P.H.Scott	West Indies	v	India	Kingston	1952-53
18	249	B.S.Chandrasekhar	India	v	England	Mumbai[2]	1963-64
18	255	Shadab Kabir	Pakistan	v	England	Lord's	1996
18	260	Mohammad Ilyas	Pakistan	v	Australia	Melbourne	1964-65
18	267	H.G.Vivian	New Zealand	v	England	The Oval	1931
18	270	R.J.Shastri	India	v	New Zealand	Wellington	1980-81
18	288	C.Sharma	India	v	Pakistan	Lahore[2]	1984-85
18	295	R.O.Collinge	New Zealand	v	Pakistan	Wellington	1964-65
18	311	P.A.De Silva	Sri Lanka	v	England	Lord's	1984
18	312	S.Venkataraghavan	India	v	New Zealand	Chennai[2]	1964-65
18	316	B.P.Bracewell	New Zealand	v	England	The Oval	1978
18	323	Saleem Malik	Pakistan	v	Sri Lanka	Karachi[1]	1981-82
18	340	P.R.Adams	South Africa	v	England	Port Elizabeth	1995-96

OLDEST TEST PLAYERS *(Age on final day of their last Test match)*

Years	Days						
52	165	W.Rhodes	England	v	West Indies	Kingston	1929-30
50	327	H.Ironmonger	Australia	v	England	Sydney	1932-33
50	320	W.G.Grace	England	v	Australia	Nottingham	1899
50	303	G.Gunn	England	v	West Indies	Kingston	1929-30
49	139	J.Southerton	England	v	Australia	Melbourne	1876-77
47	302	Miran Bux	Pakistan	v	India	Peshawar[1]	1954-55
47	249	J.B.Hobbs	England	v	Australia	The Oval	1930
47	87	F.E.Woolley	England	v	Australia	The Oval	1934
46	309	D.D.Blackie	Australia	v	England	Adelaide	1928-29
46	206	A.W.Nourse	South Africa	v	England	The Oval	1924
46	202	H.Strudwick	England	v	Australia	The Oval	1926
46	41	E.H.Hendren	England	v	West Indies	Kingston	1934-35
45	305	A.J.Traicos	Zimbabwe	v	India	Delhi	1992-93
45	245	G.O.B.Allen	England	v	West Indies	Kingston	1947-48
45	215	P.Holmes	England	v	India	Lord's	1932
45	140	D.B.Close	England	v	West Indies	Manchester	1976
44	341	E.G.Wynyard	England	v	South Africa	Johannesburg[1]	1905-06
44	317	J.M.M.Commaille	South Africa	v	England	Cape Town	1927-28
44	238	R.Abel	England	v	Australia	Manchester	1902
44	236	G.A.Headley	West Indies	v	England	Kingston	1953-54
44	105	Amir Elahi	Pakistan	v	India	Calcutta	1952-53

RELATED TEST PLAYERS

FATHER AND TWO SONS

N.B.Amarnath and his sons M. and S.(India)
W.A.Hadlee and his sons D.R. and R.J.(New Zealand)

FATHERS AND SONS

N.B. and M., S.Amarnath (India)
W.M. and R.W.Anderson (New Zealand)
W.P. and G.E.Bradburn (New Zealand)
B.L. and C.L.Cairns (New Zealand)
M.C. and C.S.Cowdrey (England)
D.K. and A.D.Gaekwad (India)
E.J. and S.E.Gregory (Australia)
W.A. and D.R., R.J.Hadlee (New Zealand)
J.Hardstaff, sr and J.Hardstaff, jr (England)
P.G.Z. and C.Z.Harris (New Zealand)
G.A. and R.G.A.Headley (West Indies)
F.Hearne (England and South Africa) and G.A.L.Hearne (South Africa)
L. and R.A.Hutton (England)
M.Jahangir Khan (India) and Majid Khan (Pakistan)
J.D. and D.T.Lindsay (South Africa)
V.L. and S.V.Manjrekar (India)
M.H. and A.V.Mankad (India)
F.T. and F.G.Mann (England)
Hanif Mohammad and Shoaib Mohammad (Pakistan)
Nazar Mohammad and Mudassar Nazar (Pakistan)
A.W. and A.D.Nourse (South Africa)
J.H. and J.M.Parks (England)
Nawab of Pataudi, sr (England and India) and Nawab of Pataudi, jr (India)
P.M. and S.M.Pollock (South Africa)
Pankaj and Pranab Roy (India)
O.C. and A.P.H.Scott (West Indies)
M.J. and A.J.Stewart (England)
F.W. and M.W.Tate (England)
C.L. and D.C.H.Townsend (England)
L.R. and L.Tuckett (South Africa)
H.G. and G.E.Vivian (New Zealand)
S.Wazir Ali (India) and Khalid Wazir (Pakistan)

FOUR BROTHERS

Hanif, Mushtaq, Sadiq and Wazir Mohammad (Pakistan)
Hanif, Mushtaq and Sadiq all played against New Zealand at Karachi[1] in 1969-70

THREE BROTHERS

G.S., I.M. and T.M.Chappell (Australia)
E.M., G.F. and W.G.Grace (England)
A., F. and G.G.Hearne (England) - F.Hearne also played for South Africa
A., D. and S.Ranatunga (Sri Lanka)
A.B., L.J. and V.M.Tancred (South Africa)
All three Grace brothers played against Australia at The Oval in 1880.
A. and G.G.Hearne (E) and F.Hearne (SA) all played in the match between South Africa and England at Cape Town in 1891-92.

TWO BROTHERS

AUSTRALIA

K.A. and R.G.Archer
A.C. and C.Bannerman
J. and R.Benaud
G. and W.F.Giffen
D.W. and E. Gregory
M.R. and R.N.Harvey
C.E. and R.W.McLeod
A.E, and G.H.S.Trott
H. and J.W.Trumble
M.E. and S.R.Waugh

WEST INDIES

D.S. and E.S.Atkinson
F.J. and J.H.Cameron
C.M. and R.J.Christiani
B.A. and C.A.Davis
G.C. and R.S.Grant
N.E. and R.E.Marshall
E.L. and W.H.St Hill
J.B. and V.H.Stollmeyer

SRI LANKA

M.S. and S.Wettimuny

ENGLAND

A.E.R. and A.H.H.Gilligan
A.W. and I.A.Greig
G. and J.R.Gunn
D.W. and P.E.Richardson
C.L. and R.A.Smith
C.T. and G.B.Studd
G.E. and J.T.Tyldesley
C.E.M. and E.R.Wilson

NEW ZEALAND

B.P. and J.G.Bracewell
J.J. and M.D.Crowe
D.R. and R.J.Hadlee
G.P. and H.J.Howarth
J.M. and N. M.Parker

PAKISTAN

Rameez Raja and Wasim Raja
Azmat Rana and Shafqat Rana
Pervez Sajjad and Waqar Hassan
Saeed Ahmed and Younis Ahmed
Moin Khan and Nadeem Khan
Manzoor Elahi and Saleem Elahi

SOUTH AFRICA

P.A.M. and R.H.M.Hands
G. and P.N.Kirsten
A.J. and D.B.Pithey
P.M. and R.G.Pollock
A.R. and W.H.M.Richards
A.M.B. and E.A.B.Rowan
S.D. and S.J.Snooke
G.L. and L.E.Tapscott
D. and H.W.Taylor
H.F. and W.W.Wade

INDIA

M. and S.Amarnath
L.Amar Singh and L.Ramji
A L. and M.L.Apte
B P. and S.P.Gupte
A G Kripal Singh and
A G Milkha Singh
C.K. and C.S.Nayudu
S Nazir Ali and S.Wazir Ali

ZIMBABWE

A. and G.W.Flower
B.C. and P.A.Strang

Umpires

MOST TEST MATCHES

Tests		Venue	From	To
66	H.D. Bird	England (54)	1973	1996
		Zimbabwe (3)	1992-93	
		West Indies (3)	1992-93	
		New Zealand (2)	1993-94	
		Pakistan (1)	1994-95	
		India (1)	1994-95	
		Australia (2)	1995-96	
48	F.Chester	England	1924	1955
42	C.S. Elliot	England (41)	1957	1974
		New Zealand (1)	1970-71	
36	D.J.Constant	England	1971	1988
33	J.S.Buller	England	1956	1969
33	A.R.Crafter	Australia	1978-79	1991-92
33	Khizer Hayat	Pakistan (30)	1979-80	
		New Zealand (1)	1993-94	
		South Africa (1)	1994-95	
		Australia (1)	1995-96	
32	R.W. Crockett	Australia	1901-02	1924-25
31	D.Sang Hue	West Indies	1961-62	1980-81
30	D.R. Shepherd	England (23)	1985	1996
		South Africa (4)	1992-93	1993-94
		West Indies (2)	1994-95	
		Zimbabwe (1)	1995-96	
29	J.Phillips	England (11)	1893	1905
		Australia (13)	1884-85	1897-98
		South Africa (5)	1905-06	
29	F.S.Lee	England	1949	1962
29	C.J.Egar	Australia	1960-61	1968-69
28	D.M.Archer	West Indies	1980=81	1991-92
27	R.C.Bailhache	Australia	1974-75	1988-89
26	Mahboob Shah	Pakistan (23)	1974-75	1995-96
		South Africa (1)	1993-94	
		Zimbabwe (1)	1994-95	
		Pakistan (2)	1995-96	
25	B.J.Meyer	England	1978	1993
26	B.L.Aldridge	New Zealand (20)	1985-86	1994-95
		Sri Lanka (3)	1993-94	
		Zimbabwe (1)	1994-95	
		Pakistan (2)	1995-96	
25	L.P.Rowan	Australia	1962-63	1970-71
25	R.Gosein	West Indies	1964-65	1977-78
25	S.G.Randell	Australi a(21)	1984-85	1995-96
		England (1)	1994	
		Zimbabwe (1)	1994-95	
		New Zealand (1)	1994-95	
		South Africa (1)		

Most for other countries:

19	V.K.Ramaswamy	India (14)	1981-85	1995-96
		Pakistan (2)	1986-87	
		New Zealand (2)	1994-95	
		England (1)	1995	
16	K.T.Francis	Sri Lanka (12)	1981-82	1994-95
		New Zealand (1)	1993-94	
		South Africa (1)	1994-95	
		India (1)	1995-96	
		England (1)	1996	
14	R.G.A.Ashman	South Africa	1935-36	1949-50
13	I.D.Robinson	Zimbabwe (7)	1992-93	1994-95
		West Indies (1)	1993-94	
		Sri Lanka (2)	1994-95	
		South Africa (1)	1994-95	
		England (1)	1995	
		India (1)	1995-96	

C.J.Egar & L.P.Rowan stood together in 19 Tests, four more than the partnership of R.Gosein & D.Sang Hue.

Individual Career Records

These career records for all players appearing in official Test matches are complete to 27 August 1996.
(* not out)

AUSTRALIA	BATTING AND FIELDING										BOWLING						
	Tests	I	N	Runs	HS	Avge	100	50	0's	C/S	Balls	Runs	Wks	Avge	5w	10w	BB
a'Beckett,EL	4	7	0	143	41	20.42	0	0	0	4	1062	317	3	105.66	0	0	1/41
Alderman,TM	41	53	22	203	26*	6.54	0	0	13	27	10181	4616	170	27.15	14	1	6/47
Alexander,G	2	4	0	52	33	13.00	0	0	0	2	168	93	2	46.50	0	0	2/69
Alexander,HH	1	2	1	17	17*	17.00	0	0	1	0	276	154	1	154.00	0	0	1/129
Allan,FE	1	1	0	5	5	5.00	0	0	0	0	180	80	4	20.00	0	0	2/30
Allan,PJ	1						0	0	0	0	192	83	2	41.50	0	0	2/58
Allen,RC	1	2	0	44	30	22.00	0	0	0	2							
Andrews,TJE	16	23	1	592	94	26.90	0	4	0	12	156	116	1	116.00	0	0	1/23
Angel,J	4	7	1	35	11	5.83	0	0	2	1	748	463	10	46.30	0	0	3/54
Archer,KA	5	9	0	234	48	26.00	0	0	1	0							
Archer,RG	19	30	1	713	128	24.58	1	2	4	20	3576	1318	48	27.45	1	0	5/53
Armstrong,WW	50	84	10	2863	159*	38.68	6	8	6	44	8022	2923	87	33.59	3	0	6/35
Badcock,CL	7	12	1	160	118	14.54	1	0	4	3							
Bannerman,AC	28	50	2	1108	94	23.08	0	8	3	21	292	163	4	40.75	0	0	3/111
Bannerman,C	3	6	2	239	165*	59.75	1	0	0	0							
Bardsley,W	41	66	5	2469	193*	40.47	6	14	6	12							
Barnes,SG	13	19	2	1072	234	63.05	3	5	1	14	594	218	4	54.50	0	0	2/25
Barnett,BA	4	8	1	195	57	27.85	0	1	0	3/2							
Barrett,JE	2	4	1	80	67*	26.66	0	1	1	1							
Beard,GR	3	5	0	114	49	22.80	0	0	0	0	259	109	1	109.00	0	0	1/26
Benaud,J	3	5	0	223	142	44.60	1	0	0	0	24	12	2	6.00	0	0	2/12
Benaud,R	63	97	7	2201	122	24.45	3	9	8	65	19108	6704	248	27.03	16	1	7/72
Bennett,MJ	3	5	2	71	23	23.66	0	0	0	5	665	325	6	54.16	0	0	3/79
Bevan,MG	6	10	0	324	91	32.40	0	3	1	5	90	67	1	67.00	0	0	1/21
Blackham,JM	35	62	11	800	74*	15.68	0	4	6	37/24							
Blackie,DD	3	6	3	24	11*	8.00	0	0	2	2	1260	444	14	31.71	1	0	6/94
Blewett,GS	9	15	1	468	115	33.42	2	2	1	11	240	122	2	61.00	0	0	2/25
Bonnor,GJ	17	30	0	512	128	17.06	1	2	5	16	164	84	2	42.00	0	0	1/5
Boon,DC	107	190	20	7422	200	43.65	21	32	16	99	36	14	0	-	0	0	0/0
Booth,BC	29	48	6	1773	169	42.21	5	10	5	17	436	146	3	48.66	0	0	2/33
Border,AR	156	265	44	11174	205	50.56	27	63	11	156	4009	1525	39	39.10	2	1	7/46
Boyle,HF	12	16	4	153	36*	12.75	0	0	2	10	1744	641	32	20.03	1	0	6/42
Bradman,DG	52	80	10	6996	334	99.94	29	13	7	32	160	72	2	36.00	0	0	1/8
Bright,RJ	25	39	8	445	33	14.35	0	0	6	13	5541	2180	53	41.13	4	1	7/87
Bromley,EH	2	4	0	38	26	9.50	0	0	0	2	60	19	0	-	0	0	0/19
Brown,WA	22	35	1	1592	206*	46.82	4	9	1	14							
Bruce,W	14	26	2	702	80	29.25	0	5	1	12	988	440	12	36.66	0	0	3/88
Burge,PJP	42	68	8	2290	181	38.16	4	12	5	23							
Burke,JW	24	44	7	1280	189	34.59	3	5	0	18	814	230	8	28.75	0	0	4/37
Burn,EJK	2	4	0	41	19	10.25	0	0	1	0							
Burton,FJ	2	4	2	4	2*	2.00	0	0	0	1/1							
Callaway,ST	3	6	1	87	41	17.40	0	0	1	0	471	142	6	23.66	1	0	5/37
Callen,IW	1	2	2	26	22*	0	0	0	0	1	440	191	6	31.83	0	0	3/83
Campbell,GD	4	4	0	10	6	2.50	0	0	2	1	951	503	13	38.69	0	0	3/79
Carkeek,W	6	5	2	16	6*	5.33	0	0	0	6/0							
Carlson,PH	2	4	0	23	21	5.75	0	0	2	2	368	99	2	49.50	0	0	2/41
Carter,H	28	47	9	873	72	22.97	0	4	4	44/21							
Chappell,GS	87	151	19	7110	247*	53.86	24	31	12	122	5327	1913	47	40.70	1	0	5/61
Chappell,IM	75	136	10	5345	196	42.42	14	26	11	105	2873	1316	20	65.80	0	0	2/21
Chappell,TM	3	6	1	79	27	15.80	0	0	0	2							

AUSTRALIA (cont.)				**BATTING AND FIELDING**									**BOWLING**				
	Tests	I	N	Runs	HS	Avge	100	50	0's	C/S	Balls	Runs	Wks	Avge	5w	10w	BB
Charlton,PC	2	4	0	29	11	7.25	0	0	0	0	45	24	3	8.00	0	0	3/18
Chipperfield,AG	14	20	3	552	109	32.47	1	2	1	15	924	437	5	87.40	0	0	3/91
Clark,WM	10	19	2	98	33	5.76	0	0	8	6	2793	1265	44	28.75	0	0	4/46
Colley,DJ	3	4	0	84	54	21.00	0	1	0	1	729	312	6	52.00	0	0	3/83
Collins,HL	19	31	1	1352	203	45.06	4	6	0	13	654	252	4	63.00	0	0	2/47
Coningham,A	1	2	0	13	10	6.50	0	0	0	0	186	76	2	38.00	0	0	2/17
Connolly,AN	29	45	20	260	37	10.40	0	0	10	17	7818	2981	102	29.22	4	0	6/47
Cooper,BB	1	2	0	18	15	9.00	0	0	0	2							
Cooper,WH	2	3	1	13	7	6.50	0	0	0	1	466	226	9	25.11	1	0	6/120
Corling,GE	5	4	1	5	3	1.66	0	0	2	0	1159	447	12	37.25	0	0	4/60
Cosier,GJ	18	32	1	897	168	28.93	2	3	3	14	899	341	5	68.20	0	0	2/26
Cottam,JT	1	2	0	4	3	2.00	0	0	0	1							
Cotter,A	21	37	2	457	45	13.05	0	0	6	8	4633	2549	89	28.64	7	0	7/148
Coulthard,G	1	1	1	6	6*	-	0	0	0	0							
Cowper,RM	27	46	2	2061	307	46.84	5	10	3	21	3005	1139	36	31.63	0	0	4/48
Craig,ID	11	18	0	358	53	19.88	0	2	3	2							
Crawford,WPA	4	5	2	53	34	17.66	0	0	1	1	437	107	7	15.28	0	0	3/28
Darling,J	34	60	2	1657	178	28.56	3	8	8	27							
Darling,LS	12	18	1	474	85	27.88	0	3	2	8	162	65	0	-	0	0	0/3
Darling,WM	14	27	1	697	91	26.80	0	6	1	5							
Davidson,AK	44	61	7	1328	80	24.59	0	5	1	42	11587	3819	186	20.53	14	2	7/93
Davis,IC	15	27	1	692	105	26.61	1	4	9	3							
Davis,SP	1	1	0	0	0	0.00	0	0	0	1	150	70	0	-	0	0	0/70
De Courcy,JH	3	6	1	81	41	16.20	0	0	3	0							
Dell,AR	2	2	2	6	3*	-	0	0	0	0	559	160	6	26.66	0	0	3/65
Dodemaide,AIC	10	15	6	202	50	22.44	0	1	6	0	2184	963	34	28.32	1	0	6/58
Donnan,H	5	10	1	75	15	8.33	0		10	1	54	22	0	-	0	0	0/22
Dooland,B	3	5	1	76	29	19.00	0		00	3	880	419	9	46.55	0	0	4/69
Duff,RA	22	40	3	1317	146	35.59	2		06	14	180	85	4	21.25	0	0	2/43
Duncan,JRF	1	1	0	3	3	3.00	0		00	0	112	30	0	-	0	0	0/30
Dyer,GC	6	6	0	131	60	21.83	0	1	1	22/2							
Dymock,G	21	32	7	236	31*	9.44	0	0	7	1	5545	2116	78	27.12	5	1	7/67
Dyson,J	30	58	7	1359	127*	26.64	2	5	4	10							
Eady,CJ	2	4	1	20	10*	6.66	0	0	0	2	223	112	7	16.00	0	0	3/30
Eastwood,KH	1	2	0	5	5	2.50	0	0	1	0	40	21	1	21.00	0	0	1/21
Ebeling,HI	1	2	0	43	41	21.50	0	0	0	0	186	89	3	29.66	0	0	3/74
Edwards,JD	3	6	1	48	26	9.60	0	0	3	1							
Edwards,R	20	32	3	1171	170*	40.37	2	9	4	7	12	20	0	-	0	0	0/20
Edwards,WJ	3	6	0	68	30	11.33	0	0	2	0							
Emery,PA	1	1	1	8	8*	-	0	0	0	5/1							
Emery,SH	4	2	0	6	5	3.00	0	0	0	2	462	249	5	49.80	0	0	2/46
Evans,E	6	10	2	82	33	10.25	0	0	3	5	1247	332	7	47.42	0	0	3/64
Fairfax,AG	10	12	4	410	65	51.25	0	4	0	15	1520	645	21	30.71	0	0	4/31
Favell,LE	19	31	3	757	101	27.03	1	5	2	9							
Ferris,JJ	8	16	4	98	20*	8.16	0	0	1	4	2030	684	48	14.25	4	0	5/26
Fingleton,JHW	18	29	1	1189	136	42.46	5	3	3	13							
Fleetwood-Smith,LO	10	11	5	54	16*	9.00	0	0	2	0	3093	1570	42	37.38	2	1	6/110
Fleming,DW	4	4	0	40	24	10.00	0	0	2	2	902	435	17	25.58	0	0	4/75
Francis,BC	3	5	0	52	27	10.40	0	0	1	1							
Freeman,EW	11	18	0	345	76	19.16	0	2	0	5	2183	1128	34	33.17	0	0	4/52
Freer,FW	1	1	1	28	28*	-	0	0	0	0	160	74	3	24.66	0	0	2/49
Gannon,JB	3	5	4	3	3*	3.00	0	0	1	3	726	361	11	32.81	0	0	4/77
Garrett,TW	19	33	6	339	51*	12.55	0	1	5	7	2708	970	36	26.94	2	0	6/78
Gaunt,RA	3	4	2	6	3	3.00	0	0	0	1	716	310	7	44.28	0	0	3/53

AUSTRALIA (cont.)				**BATTING AND FIELDING**								**BOWLING**					
	Tests	I	N	Runs	HS	Avge	100	50	0's	C/S	Balls	Runs	Wks	Avge	5w	10w	BB
Gehrs,DRA	6	11	0	221	67	20.09	0	2	1	6	6	4	0	-	0	0	0/4
Giffen,G	31	53	0	1238	161	23.35	1	6	5	24	6391	2791	103	27.09	7	1	7/117
Giffen,WF	3	6	0	11	3	1.83	0	0	1	1							
Gilbert,DR	9	12	4	57	15	7.12	0	0	1	0	1647	843	16	52.68	0	0	3/48
Gilmour,GJ	15	22	1	483	101	23.00	1	3	3	8	2661	1406	54	26.03	3	0	6/85
Gleeson,JW	29	46	8	395	45	10.39	0	0	11	17	8857	3367	93	36.20	3	0	5/61
Graham,H	6	10	0	301	107	30.10	2	0	2	3							
Gregory,DW	3	5	2	60	43	20.00	0	0	0	0	20	9	0	-	0	0	0/9
Gregory,EJ	1	2	0	11	11	5.50	0	0	1	1							
Gregory,JM	24	34	3	1146	119	36.96	2	7	3	37	5582	2648	85	31.15	4	0	7/69
Gregory,RG	2	3	0	153	80	51.00	0	2	0	1	24	14	0	-	0	0	0/14
Gregory,SE	58	100	7	2282	201	24.53	4	8	12	25	30	33	0	-	0	0	0/4
Grimmett,CV	37	50	10	557	50	13.92	0	1	7	17	14513	5231	216	24.21	21	7	7/40
Groube,TU	1	2	0	11	11	5.50	0	0	1	0							
Grout,ATW	51	67	8	890	74	15.08	0	3	11	163/24							
Guest,CEJ	1	1	0	11	11	11.00	0	0	0	0	144	59	0	-	0	0	0/8
Hamence,RA	3	4	1	81	30*	27.00	0	0	0	1							
Hammond,JR	5	5	2	28	19	9.33	0	0	1	2	1031	488	15	32.53	0	0	4/38
Harry,J	1	2	0	8	6	4.00	0	0	0	1							
Hartigan,RJ	2	4	0	170	116	42.50	1	0	0	1	12	7	0	-	0	0	0/7
Hartkopf,AEV	1	2	0	80	80	40.00	0	1	1	0	240	134	1	134.00	0	0	1/120
Harvey,MR	1	2	0	43	31	21.50	0	0	0	0							
Harvey,RN	79	137	10	6149	205	48.41	21	24	7	64	414	120	3	40.00	0	0	1/8
Hassett,AL	43	69	3	3073	198*	46.56	10	11	1	30	111	78	0	-	0	0	0/1
Hawke,NJN	27	37	15	365	45*	16.59	0	0	6	9	6974	2677	91	29.41	6	1	7/105
Hayden,ML	1	2	0	20	15	10.00	0	0	0	1							
Hazlitt,GR	9	12	4	89	34*	11.12	0	0	2	4	1563	623	23	27.08	1	0	7/25
Healy,IA	79	117	14	2803	113*	27.21	2	17	13	255/20							
Hendry,HSTL	11	18	2	335	112	20.93	1	0	1	10	1706	640	16	40.00	0	0	3/36
Hibbert,PA	1	2	0	15	13	7.50	0	0	0	1							
Higgs,JD	22	36	16	111	16	5.55	0	0	5	3	4752	2057	66	31.16	2	0	7/143
Hilditch,AMJ	18	34	0	1073	119	31.55	2	6	3	13							
Hill,C	49	89	2	3412	191	39.21	7	19	9	33							
Hill,JC	3	6	3	21	8*	7.00	0	0	1	2	606	273	8	34.12	0	0	3/35
Hoare,DE	1	2	0	35	35	17.50	0	0	1	2	232	156	2	78.00	0	0	2/68
Hodges,JR	2	4	1	10	8	3.33	0	0	1	0	136	84	6	14.00	0	0	2/7
Hogan,TG	7	12	1	205	42*	18.63	0	0	1	2	1436	706	15	47.06	1	0	5/66
Hogg,RM	38	58	13	439	52	9.75	0	1	14	7	7633	3503	123	28.47	6	2	6/74
Hohns,TV	7	7	1	136	40	22.66	0	0	1	3	1528	581	17	34.11	0	0	3/59
Hole,GB	18	33	2	789	66	25.45	0	6	2	21	398	126	3	42.00	0	0	1/9
Holland,RG	11	15	4	35	10	3.18	0	0	7	5	2889	1352	34	39.76	3	2	6/54
Hookes,DW	23	41	3	1306	143*	34.36	1	8	4	12	96	41	1	41.00	0	0	1/4
Hopkins,AJY	20	33	2	509	43	25.45	0	0	4	11	1327	696	26	26.76	0	0	4/81
Horan,TP	15	27	2	471	124	18.84	1	1	3	6	373	143	11	13.00	1	0	6/40
Hordern,HV	7	13	2	254	50	23.09	0	1	1	6	2148	1075	46	23.36	5	2	7/90
Hornibrook,PM	6	7	1	60	26	10.00	0	0	1	7	1579	664	17	39.05	1	0	7/92
Howell,WP	18	27	6	158	35	7.52	0	0	8	12	3892	1407	49	28.71	1	0	5/81
Hughes,KJ	70	124	6	4415	213	37.41	9	22	10	50	85	28	0	-	0	0	0/0
Hughes,MG	53	70	8	1032	72*	16.64	0	2	10	23	12285	6017	212	28.38	7	1	8/87
Hunt,WA	1	1	0	0	0	0.00	0	0	1	1	96	39	0	-	0	0	0/4
Hurst,AG	12	20	3	102	26	6.00	0	0	10	3	3054	1200	43	27.90	2	0	5/28
Hurwood,A	2	2	0	5	5	2.50	0	0	1	2	517	170	11	15.45	0	0	4/22
Inverarity,RJ	6	11	1	174	56	17.40	0	1	1	4	372	93	4	23.25	0	0	3/26
Iredale,FA	14	23	1	807	140	36.68	2	4	2	16	12	3	0	-	0	0	0/3

AUSTRALIA (cont.)				**BATTING AND FIELDING**								**BOWLING**						
	Tests	I	N	Runs	HS	Avge	100	50	0's	C/S	Balls	Runs	Wks	Avge	5w	10w	BB
Ironmonger,H	14	21	5	42	12	2.62	0	0	6	3	4695	1330	74	17.97	4	2	7/23
Iverson,JB	5	7	3	3	1*	0.75	0	0	2	2	1108	320	21	15.23	1	0	6/27
Jackson,A	8	11	1	474	164	47.40	1	2	1	7							
Jarman,BN	19	30	3	400	78	14.81	0	2	5	50/4							
Jarvis,AH	11	21	3	303	82	16.83	0	1	1	9/9							
Jenner,TJ	9	14	5	208	74	23.11	0	1	1	5	1881	749	24	31.20	1	0	5/90
Jennings,CB	6	8	2	107	32	17.83	0	0	2	5							
Johnson,IW	45	66	12	1000	77	18.51	0	6	10	30	8780	3182	109	29.19	3	0	7/44
Johnson,LJ	1	1	1	25	25*	0	0	0	0	2	282	74	6	12.33	0	0	3/8
Johnston,WA	40	49	25	273	29	11.37	0	0	7	16	11048	3826	160	23.91	7	0	6/44
Jones,DM	52	89	11	3631	216	46.55	11	14	11	34	198	64	1	64.00	0	0	1/5
Jones,E	19	26	1	126	20	5.04	0	0	5	21	3748	1857	64	29.01	3	1	7/88
Jones,SP	12	24	4	432	87	21.60	0	1	3	12	262	112	6	18.66	0	0	4/47
Joslin,LR	1	2	0	9	7	4.50	0	0	0	0							
Julian,BP	7	9	1	128	56*	16.00	0	1	3	4	1098	599	15	39.93	0	0	4/36
Kelleway,C	26	42	4	1422	147	37.42	3	6	1	24	4363	1683	52	32.36	1	0	5/33
Kelly,JJ	36	56	17	664	46*	17.02	0	0	7	43/20							
Kelly,TJD	2	3	0	64	35	21.33	0	0	0	1							
Kendall,TK	2	4	1	39	17*	13.00	0	0	0	2	563	215	14	15.35	1	0	7/55
Kent,MF	3	6	0	171	54	28.50	0	2	0	6							
Kerr,RB	2	4	0	31	17	7.75	0	0	1	1							
Kippax,AF	22	34	1	1192	146	36.12	2	8	1	13	72	19	0	-	0	0	0/2
Kline,LF	13	16	9	58	15*	8.28	0	0	3	9	2373	776	34	22.82	1	0	7/75
Laird,BM	21	40	2	1341	92	35.28	0	11	2	16	18	12	0	-	0	0	0/3
Langer,JL	6	9	0	241	69	26.77	0	3	2	2							
Langley,GRA	26	37	12	374	53	14.96	0	1	3	83/15							
Laughlin,TJ	3	5	0	87	35	17.40	0	0	0	3	516	262	6	43.66	1	0	5/101
Laver,FJ	15	23	6	196	45	11.52	0	0	4	8	2361	964	37	26.05	2	0	8/31
Law,SG	1	1	1	54	54*	-	0	1	0	1	18	9	0	-	0	0	0/9
Lawry,WM	67	123	12	5234	210	47.15	13	27	6	30	14	6	0	-	0	0	0/0
Lawson,GF	46	68	12	894	74	15.96	0	4	6	10	11118	5501	180	30.56	11	2	8/112
Lee,PK	2	3	0	57	42	19.00	0	0	1	1	436	212	5	42.40	0	0	4/111
Lillee,DK	70	90	24	905	73*	13.71	0	1	10	23	18467	8493	355	23.92	23	7	7/83
Lindwall,RR	61	84	13	1502	118	21.15	2	5	9	26	13650	5251	228	23.03	12	0	7/38
Love,HSB	1	2	0	8	5	4.00	0	0	0	3							
Loxton,SJE	12	15	0	554	101	36.93	1	3	1	7	906	349	8	43.62	0	0	3/55
Lyons,JJ	14	27	0	731	134	27.07	1	3	1	3	316	149	6	24.83	1	0	5/30
McAlister,PA	8	16	1	252	41	16.80	0	0	0	10							
Macartney,CG	35	55	4	2131	170	41.78	7	9	1	17	3561	1240	45	27.55	2	1	7/58
McCabe,SJ	39	62	5	2748	232	48.21	6	13	4	41	3746	1543	36	42.86	0	0	4/13
McCool,CL	14	17	4	459	104*	35.30	1	1	0	14	2504	958	36	26.61	3	0	5/41
McCormick,EL	12	14	5	54	17*	6.00	0	0	3	8	2107	1079	36	29.97	0	0	4/101
McCosker,RB	25	46	5	1622	127	39.56	4	9	5	21							
McDermott,CJ	71	90	13	940	42*	12.20	0	0	13	19	16586	8332	291	28.63	14	2	8/97
McDonald,CC	47	83	4	3107	170	39.32	5	17	2	14	8	3	0	-	0	0	0/3
McDonald,EA	11	12	5	116	36	16.57	0	0	1	3	2885	1431	43	33.27	2	0	5/32
McDonnell,PS	19	34	1	950	147	28.78	3	2	6	6	52	53	0	-	0	0	0/11
McGrath,GD	19	20	5	32	9	2.13	0	0	8	2	4543	2107	78	27.01	4	0	6/47
McIlwraith,J	1	2	0	9	7	4.50	0	0	0	1							
McIntyre,PE	1	2	0	0	0	0.00	0	0	2	0	165	87	2	43.50	0	0	2/51
Mackay,KD	37	52	7	1507	89	33.48	0	13	6	16	5792	1721	50	34.42	2	0	6/42
McKenzie,GD	60	89	12	945	76	12.27	0	2	15	34	17681	7328	246	29.78	16	3	8/71
McKibbin,TR	5	8	2	88	28*	14.66	0	0	2	4	1032	496	17	29.17	0	0	3/35
McLaren,JW	1	2	2	0	0*	-	0	0	0	0	144	70	1	70.00	0	0	1/23

AUSTRALIA (cont.) — **BATTING AND FIELDING** — **BOWLING**

	Tests	I	N	Runs	HS	Avge	100	50	0's	C/S	Balls	Runs	Wks	Avge	5w	10w	BB
Maclean,JA	4	8	1	79	33*	11.28	0	0	2	18/0							
McLeod,CE	17	29	5	573	112	23.87	1	4	5	9	3374	1325	33	40.15	2	0	5/65
McLeod,RW	6	11	0	146	31	13.27	0	0	0	3	1089	384	12	32.00	1	0	5/55
McShane,PG	3	6	1	26	12*	5.20	0	0	3	2	108	48	1	48.00	0	0	1/39
Maddocks,LV	7	12	2	177	69	17.70	0	1	3	18/1							
Maguire,JN	3	5	1	28	15*	7.00	0	0	2	2	616	323	10	32.30	0	0	4/57
Mailey,AA	21	29	9	222	46*	11.10	0	0	3	14	6119	3358	99	33.91	6	2	9/121
Mallett,AA	38	50	13	430	43*	11.62	0	0	10	30	9990	3940	132	29.84	6	1	8/59
Malone,MF	1	1	0	46	46	46.00	0	0	0	0	342	77	6	12.83	1	0	5/63
Mann,AL	4	8	0	189	105	23.62	1	0	2	2	552	316	4	79.00	0	0	3/12
Marr,AP	1	2	0	5	5	2.50	0	0	1	0	48	14	0	-	0	0	0/3
Marsh,GR	50	93	7	2854	138	33.18	4	15	3	38							
Marsh,RW	96	150	13	3633	132	26.51	3	16	12	343/12	72	54	0	-	0	0	0/3
Martin,JW	8	13	1	214	55	17.83	0	1	3	5	1846	832	17	48.94	0	0	3/56
Martyn,DR	7	12	1	317	74	28.81	0	3	1	1	6	0	0	-	0	0	0/0
Massie,HH	9	16	0	249	55	15.56	0	1	2	5							
Massie,RAL	6	8	1	78	42	11.14	0	0	3	1	1739	647	31	20.87	2	1	8/53
Matthews,CD	3	5	0	54	32	10.80	0	0	1	1	570	313	6	52.16	0	0	3/95
Matthews,GRJ	33	53	8	1849	130	41.08	4	12	2	17	6271	2942	61	48.22	2	1	5/103
Matthews,TJ	8	10	1	153	53	17.00	0	1	1	7	1081	419	16	26.18	0	0	4/29
May,TBA	24	28	12	225	42*	14.06	0	0	3	6	6577	2606	75	34.74	3	0	5/9
Mayne,LC	6	11	3	76	13	9.50	0	0	0	3	1251	628	19	33.05	0	0	4/33
Mayne,RE	4	4	1	64	25*	21.33	0	0	1	2	6	1	0	-	0	0	0/1
Meckiff,I	18	20	7	154	45*	11.84	0	0	2	9	3734	1423	45	31.62	2	0	6/38
Meuleman,KD	1	1	0	0	0	0.00	0	0	1	1							
Midwinter,WE	8	14	1	174	37	13.38	0	0	1	5	949	333	14	23.78	1	0	5/78
Miller,KR	55	87	7	2958	147	36.97	7	13	5	38	10461	3906	170	22.97	7	1	7/60
Minnett,RB	9	15	0	391	90	26.06	0	3	3	0	589	290	11	26.36	0	0	4/34
Misson,FM	5	5	3	38	25*	19.00	0	0	1	6	1197	616	16	38.50	0	0	4/58
Moody,TM	8	14	0	456	106	32.57	2	3	1	9	432	147	2	73.50	0	0	1/17
Moroney,J	7	12	1	383	118	34.81	2	1	3	0							
Morris,AR	46	79	3	3533	206	46.48	12	12	4	15	111	50	2	25.00	0	0	1/5
Morris,S	1	2	1	14	10*	14.00	0	0	0	0	136	73	2	36.50	0	0	2/73
Moses,H	6	10	0	198	33	19.80	0	0	0	1							
Moss,JK	1	2	1	60	38*	60.00	0	0	0	0							
Moule,WH	1	2	0	40	34	20.00	0	0	0	1	51	23	3	7.66	0	0	3/23
Murdoch,WL	18	33	5	896	211	32.00	2	1	3	13/1							
Musgrove,H	1	2	0	13	9	6.50	0	0	0	0							
Nagel,LE	1	2	1	21	21*	21.00	0	0	1	0	262	110	2	55.00	0	0	2/110
Nash,LJ	2	2	0	30	17	15.00	0	0	0	6	311	126	10	12.60	0	0	4/18
Nitschke,HC	2	2	0	53	47	26.50	0	0	0	3							
Noble,MA	42	73	7	1997	133	30.25	1	16	4	26	7159	3025	121	25.00	9	2	7/17
Noblet,G	3	4	1	22	13*	7.33	0	0	1	1	774	183	7	26.14	0	0	3/21
Nothling,OE	1	2	0	52	44	26.00	0	0	0	0	276	72	0	-	0	0	0/12
O'Brien,LPJ	5	8	0	211	61	26.37	0	2	1	3							
O'Connor,JDA	4	8	1	86	20	12.28	0	0	0	3	692	340	13	26.15	1	0	5/40
O'Donnell,SP	6	10	3	206	48	29.42	0	0	1	4	940	504	6	84.00	0	0	3/37
Ogilvie,AD	5	10	0	178	47	17.80	0	0	3	5							
O'Keeffe,KJ	24	34	9	644	85	25.76	0	1	3	15	5384	2018	53	38.07	1	0	5/101
Oldfield,WAS	54	80	17	1427	65*	22.65	0	4	9	78/52							
O'Neill,NC	42	69	8	2779	181	45.55	6	15	6	21	1392	667	17	39.23	0	0	4/41
O'Reilly,WJ	27	39	7	410	56*	12.81	0	1	6	7	10024	3254	144	22.59	11	3	7/54
Oxenham,RK	7	10	0	151	48	15.10	0	0	2	4	1802	522	14	37.28	0	0	4/39
Palmer,GE	17	25	4	296	48	14.09	0	0	3	13	4517	1678	78	21.51	6	2	7/65

AUSTRALIA (cont.)	BATTING AND FIELDING										BOWLING						
	Tests	I	N	Runs	HS	Avge	100	50	0's	C/S	Balls	Runs	Wks	Avge	5w	10w	BB
Park,RL	1	1	0	0	0	0.00	0	0	1	0	6	9	0	-	0	0	0/9
Pascoe,LS	14	19	9	106	30*	10.60	0	0	3	2	3403	1668	64	26.06	1	0	5/59
Pellew,CE	10	14	1	484	116	37.23	2	1	0	4	78	34	0	-	0	0	0/3
Phillips,WB	27	48	2	1485	159	32.28	2	7	1	52/0							
Phillips,WN	1	2	0	22	14	11.00	0	0	0	0							
Philpott,PI	8	10	1	93	22	10.33	0	0	0	5	2262	1000	26	38.46	1	0	5/90
Ponsford,WH	29	48	4	2122	266	48.22	7	6	1	21							
Ponting,RT	3	4	0	193	96	48.25	0	2	0	4	24	8	1	8.00	0	0	1/8
Pope,RJ	1	2	0	3	3	1.50	0	0	1	0							
Rackemann,CG	11	12	4	43	15*	5.37	0	0	5	2	2546	1028	39	26.35	3	1	6/86
Ransford,VS	20	38	6	1211	143*	37.84	1	7	2	10	43	28	1	28.00	0	0	1/9
Redpath,IR	66	120	11	4737	171	43.45	8	31	9	83	64	41	0	-	0	0	0/0
Reedman,JC	1	2	0	21	17	10.50	0	0	0	1	57	24	1	24.00	0	0	1/12
Reid,BA	27	34	14	93	13	4.65	0	0	6	5	6244	2784	113	24.63	5	2	7/51
Reiffel,PR	21	27	9	412	56	22.88	0	2	1	11	3869	1744	63	27.68	3	0	6/71
Renneberg,DA	8	13	7	22	9	3.66	0	0	3	2	1598	830	23	36.08	2	0	5/39
Richardson,AJ	9	13	0	403	100	31.00	1	2	1	1	1812	521	12	43.41	0	0	2/20
Richardson,VY	19	30	0	706	138	23.53	1	1	5	24							
Rigg,KE	8	12	0	401	127	33.41	1	1	0	5							
Ring,DT	13	21	2	426	67	22.42	0	4	2	5	3024	1305	35	37.28	2	0	6/72
Ritchie,GM	30	53	5	1690	146	35.20	3	7	1	14	6	10	0	-	0	0	0/10
Rixon,SJ	13	24	3	394	54	18.76	0	2	4	42/5							
Robertson,WR	1	2	0	2	2	1.00	0	0	1	0	44	24	0	-	0	0	0/24
Robinson,RD	3	6	0	100	34	16.66	0	0	0	4							
Robinson,RH	1	2	0	5	3	2.50	0	0	0	1							
Rorke,GF	4	4	2	9	7	4.50	0	0	1	1	703	203	10	20.30	0	0	3/23
Rutherford,JW	1	1	0	30	30	30.00	0	0	0	0	36	15	1	15.00	0	0	1/11
Ryder,J	20	32	5	1394	201*	51.62	3	9	1	17	1897	743	17	43.70	0	0	2/20
Saggers,RA	6	5	2	30	14	10.00	0	0	0	16/8							
Saunders,JV	14	23	6	39	11*	2.29	0	0	8	5	3565	1796	79	22.73	6	0	7/34
Scott,HJH	8	14	1	359	102	27.61	1	1	0	8	28	26	0	-	0	0	0/9
Sellers,RHD	1	1	0	0	0	0.00	0	0	1	1	30	17	0	-	0	0	0/17
Serjeant,CS	12	23	1	522	124	23.72	1	2	4	13							
Sheahan,AP	31	53	6	1594	127	33.91	2	7	3	17							
Shepherd,BK	9	14	2	502	96	41.93	0	5	1	2	26	9	0	-	0	0	0/3
Sievers,MW	3	6	1	67	25*	13.40	0	0	0	4	602	161	9	17.88	1	0	5/21
Simpson,RB	62	111	7	4869	311	46.81	10	27	8	110	6881	3001	71	42.26	2	0	5/57
Sincock,DJ	3	4	1	80	29	26.66	0	0	0	2	724	410	8	51.25	0	0	3/67
Slater,KN	1	1	1	1	1*	-	0	0	0	0	256	101	2	50.50	0	0	2/40
Slater,MJ	33	57	3	2611	219	48.35	7	10	3	11	7	4	1	4.00	0	0	1/4
Sleep,PR	14	21	1	483	90	24.15	0	3	4	4	2982	1397	31	45.06	1	0	5/72
Slight,J	1	2	0	11	11	5.50	0	0	1	0							
Smith,DBM	2	3	1	30	24*	15.00	0	0	1	0							
Smith,SB	3	5	0	41	12	8.20	0	0	0	1							
Spofforth,FR	18	29	6	217	50	9.43	0	1	6	11	4185	1731	94	18.41	7	4	7/44
Stackpole,KR	43	80	5	2807	207	37.42	7	14	5	47	2321	1001	15	66.73	0	0	2/33
Stevens,GB	4	7	0	112	28	16.00	0	0	0	2							
Taber,HB	16	27	5	353	48	16.04	0	0	3	56/4							
Tallon,D	21	26	3	394	92	17.13	0	2	3	50/8							
Taylor,JM	20	28	0	997	108	35.60	1	8	1	11	114	45	1	45.00	0	0	1/25
Taylor,MA	72	129	9	5502	219	45.85	14	33	3	105	42	26	1	26.00	0	0	1/11
Taylor,PL	13	19	3	431	87	26.93	0	2	1	10	2227	1068	27	39.55	1	0	6/78
Thomas,G	8	12	1	325	61	29.54	0	3	0	3							
Thoms,GR	1	2	0	44	28	22.00	0	0	0	0							

AUSTRALIA (cont.)

	BATTING AND FIELDING										BOWLING						
	Tests	I	N	Runs	HS	Avge	100	50	0's	C/S	Balls	Runs	Wks	Avge	5w	10w	BB
Thomson,AL	4	5	4	22	12*	22.00	0	0	1	0	1519	654	12	54.50	0	0	3/79
Thomson,JR	51	73	20	679	49	12.81	0	0	14	20	10535	5601	200	28.00	8	0	6/46
Thomson,NFD	2	4	0	67	41	16.75	0	0	0	3	112	31	1	31.00	0	0	1/14
Thurlow,HM	1	1	0	0	0	0.00	0	0	1	0	234	86	0	-	0	0	0/33
Toohey,PM	15	29	1	893	122	31.89	1	7	3	9	2	4	0	-	0	0	0/4
Toshack,ERH	12	11	6	73	20*	14.60	0	0	1	4	3140	989	47	21.04	4	1	6/29
Travers,JPF	1	2	0	10	9	5.00	0	0	0	1	48	14	1	14.00	0	0	1/14
Tribe,GE	3	3	1	35	25*	17.50	0	0	0	0	760	330	2	165.00	0	0	2/48
Trott,AE	3	5	3	205	85*	102.50	0	2	1	4	474	192	9	21.33	1	0	8/43
Trott,GHS	24	42	0	921	143	21.92	1	4	7	21	1890	1019	29	35.13	0	0	4/71
Trumble,H	32	57	14	851	70	19.79	0	4	7	45	8099	3072	141	21.78	9	3	8/65
Trumble,JW	7	13	1	243	59	20.25	0	1	1	3	600	222	10	22.20	0	0	3/29
Trumper,VT	48	48	8	3163	214*	39.04	8	13	7	31	546	317	8	39.62	0	0	3/60
Turner,A	14	27	1	768	136	29.53	1	3	2	15							
Turner,CTB	17	32	4	323	29	11.53	0	0	6	8	5179	1670	101	16.53	11	2	7/43
Veivers,TR	21	30	4	813	88	31.26	0	7	3	7	4191	1375	33	41.66	0	0	4/68
Veletta,MRJ	8	11	0	207	39	18.81	0	0	0	12							
Waite,MG	2	3	0	11	8	3.66	0	0	1	1	552	190	1	190.00	0	0	1/150
Walker,MHN	34	43	13	586	78*	19.53	0	1	5	12	10094	3792	138	27.47	6	0	8/143
Wall,TW	18	24	5	121	20	6.36	0	0	5	11	4812	2010	56	35.89	3	0	5/14
Walters,FH	1	2	0	12	7	6.00	0	0	0	2							
Walters,KD	74	125	14	5357	250	48.26	15	33	4	43	3295	1425	49	29.08	1	0	5/66
Ward,FA	4	8	5	36	18	6.00	0	0	2	1	1268	574	11	52.18	1	0	6/102
Warne,SK	44	58	9	669	74*	13.65	0	1	10	30	13118	4870	207	23.52	10	3	8/71
Watkins,JR	1	2	1	39	36	39.00	0	0	0	1	48	21	0	-	0	0	0/21
Watson,GD	5	9	0	97	50	10.77	0	1	3	1	552	254	6	42.33	0	0	2/67
Watson,WJ	4	7	1	106	30	17.66	0	0	1	2	6	5	0	-	0	0	0/5
Waugh,ME	54	86	4	3627	140	44.23	10	22	7	68	2928	1342	38	35.31	1	0	5/40
Waugh,SR	81	125	26	5002	200	50.52	11	28	12	61	6115	2713	77	35.23	3	0	5/28
Wellham,DM	6	11	0	257	103	23.36	1	0	0	5							
Wessels,KC	24	42	1	1761	179	42.95	4	9	3	19	90	42	0	-	0	0	0/2
Whatmore,DF	7	13	0	293	77	22.53	0	2	1	13	30	11	0	-	0	0	0/11
Whitney,MR	12	19	8	68	13	6.18	0	0	4	2	2672	1325	39	33.95	2	1	7/27
Whitty,WJ	14	19	7	161	39*	13.41	0	0	3	4	3357	1373	65	21.12	3	0	6/17
Wiener,JM	6	11	0	281	93	25.54	0	2	0	4	78	41	0	-	0	0	0/19
Wilson,JW	1						0	0	0	0	216	64	1	64.00	0	0	1/25
Wood,GM	59	112	6	3374	172	31.83	9	13	9	41							
Woodcock,AJ	1	1	0	27	27	27.00	0	0	0	1							
Woodfull,WM	35	54	4	2300	161	46.00	7	13	6	7							
Woods,SMJ	3	6	0	32	18	5.33	0	0	2	1	217	121	5	24.20	0	0	2/35
Woolley,RD	2	2	0	21	13	10.50	0	0	0	7/0							
Worrall,J	11	22	3	478	76	25.15	0	5	2	13	255	127	1	127.00	0	0	1/97
Wright,KJ	10	18	5	219	55*	16.84	0	4	2	31/4							
Yallop,GN	39	70	3	2756	268	41.13	8	9	3	23	192	116	1	116.00	0	0	1/21
Yardley,B	33	54	4	978	74	19.56	0	4	8	31	8909	3986	126	31.63	6	1	7/98
Zoehrer,TJ	10	14	2	246	52*	20.50	0	1	0	18/1							

ENGLAND

	BATTING AND FIELDING										BOWLING						
	Tests	I	N	Runs	HS	Avge	100	50	0's	C/S	Balls	Runs	Wks	Avge	5w	10w	BB
Abel,R	13	22	2	744	132*	37.20	2	2	1	13							
Absolom,CA	1	2	0	58	52	29.00	0	1	0	0							
Agnew,JP	3	4	3	10	5	10.00	0	0	0	0	552	373	4	93.25	0	0	2/51
Allen,DA	39	51	15	918	88	25.50	0	5	4	10	11297	3779	122	30.97	4	0	5/30

ENGLAND (cont.)				BATTING AND FIELDING								BOWLING					
	Tests	I	N	Runs	HS	Avge	100	50	0's	C/S	Balls	Runs	Wks	Avge	5w	10w	BB
Allen,GOB	25	33	2	750	122	24.19	1	3	1	20	4386	2379	81	29.37	5	1	7/80
Allom,MJC	5	3	2	14	8*	14.00	0	0	0	0	817	265	14	18.92	1	0	5/38
Allott,PJW	13	18	3	213	52*	14.20	0	1	2	4	2225	1084	26	41.69	1	0	6/61
Ames,LEG	47	72	12	2434	149	40.56	8	7	5	74/23							
Amiss,DL	50	88	10	3612	262*	46.30	11	11	10	24							
Andrew,KV	2	4	1	29	15	9.66	0	0	0	1/0							
Appleyard,R	9	9	6	51	19*	17.00	0	0	0	4	1596	554	31	17.87	1	0	5/51
Archer,AG	1	2	1	31	24*	31.00	0	0	0	0							
Armitage,T	2	3	0	33	21	11.00	0	0	0	0	12	15	0	-	0	0	0/15
Arnold,EG	10	15	3	160	40	13.33	0	0	5	8	1683	788	31	25.41	1	0	5/37
Arnold,GG	34	46	11	421	59	12.02	0	1	5	9	7650	3254	115	28.29	6	0	6/45
Arnold,J	1	2	0	34	34	17.00	0	0	1	0							
Astill,WE	9	15	0	190	40	12.66	0	0	2	7	2182	856	25	34.24	0	0	4/58
Atherton,MA	62	114	3	4627	185*	41.68	10	29	12	43	408	302	2	151.00	0	0	1/20
Athey,CWJ	23	41	1	919	123	22.97	1	4	2	13							
Attewell,W	10	15	6	150	43*	16.66	0	0	4	9	2850	626	28	22.35	0	0	4/42
Bailey,RJ	4	8	0	119	43	14.87	0	0	2	0							
Bailey,TE	61	91	14	2290	134*	29.74	1	10	7	32	9712	3856	132	29.21	5	1	7/34
Bairstow,DL	4	7	1	125	59	20.83	0	1	1	12/1							
Bakewell,AH	6	9	0	409	107	45.44	1	3	0	3	18	8	0	-	0	0	0/8
Balderstone,JC	2	4	0	39	35	9.75	0	0	2	1	96	80	1	80.00	0	0	1/80
Barber,RW	28	45	3	1495	185	35.59	1	9	1	21	3426	1806	42	43.00	0	0	4/132
Barber,W	2	4	0	83	44	20.75	0	0	0	1	2	0	1	0.00	0	0	1/0
Barlow,GD	3	5	1	17	7*	4.25	0	0	1	0							
Barlow,RG	17	30	4	591	62	22.73	0	2	3	14	2456	767	34	22.55	3	0	7/40
Barnes,SF	27	39	9	242	38*	8.06	0	0	8	12	7873	3106	189	16.43	24	7	9/103
Barnes,W	21	33	2	725	134	23.38	1	5	3	19	2289	793	51	15.54	3	0	6/28
Barnett,CJ	20	35	4	1098	129	35.41	2	5	1	14	256	93	0	-	0	0	0/1
Barnett,KJ	4	7	0	207	80	29.57	0	2	1	1	36	32	0	-	0	0	0/32
Barratt,F	5	4	1	28	17	9.33	0	0	0	2	750	235	5	47.00	0	0	1/8
Barrington,KF	82	131	15	6806	256	58.67	20	35	5	58	2715	1300	29	44.85	0	0	3/4
Barton,VA	1	1	0	23	23	23.00	0	0	0	0							
Bates,W	15	26	2	656	64	27.33	0	5	0	9	2364	821	50	16.42	4	1	7/28
Bean,G	3	5	0	92	50	18.40	0	1	0	4							
Bedser,AV	51	71	15	714	79	12.75	0	1	11	26	15918	5876	236	24.89	15	5	7/44
Benjamin,JE	1	1	0	0	0	0.00	0	0	1	0	168	80	4	20.00	0	0	4/42
Benson,MR	1	2	0	51	30	25.50	0	0	0	0							
Berry,R	2	4	2	6	4*	3.00	0	0	1	2	653	228	9	25.33	1	0	5/63
Bicknell,MP	2	4	0	26	14	6.25	0	0	2	0	522	263	4	65.75	0	0	3/99
Binks,JG	2	4	0	91	55	22.75	0	1	0	8							
Bird,MC	10	16	1	280	61	18.66	0	2	2	5	264	120	8	15.00	0	0	3/11
Birkenshaw,J	5	7	0	148	64	21.14	0	1	1	3	1017	469	13	36.07	1	0	5/57
Blakey,RJ	2	4	0	7	6	1.75	0	0	2	2							
Bligh,Hon.IFW	4	7	1	62	19	10.33	0	0	2	7							
Blythe,C	19	31	12	183	27	9.63	0	0	4	6	4546	1863	100	18.63	9	4	8/59
Board,JH	6	12	2	108	29	10.80	0	0	3	8/3							
Bolus,JB	7	12	0	496	88	41.33	0	4	0	2	18	16	0	-	0	0	0/16
Booth,MW	2	2	0	46	32	23.00	0	0	0	0	312	130	7	18.57	0	0	4/49
Bosanquet,BJT	7	14	3	147	27	13.36	0	0	0	9	970	604	25	24.16	2	0	8/107
Botham,IT	102	161	6	5200	208	33.54	14	22	14	120	21815	10878	383	28.40	27	4	8/34
Bowden,MP	2	2	0	25	25	12.50	0	0	1	1							
Bowes,WE	15	11	5	28	10*	4.66	0	0	2	2	3655	1519	68	22.33	6	0	6/33
Bowley,EH	5	7	0	252	109	36.00	1	0	0	2	252	116	0	-	0	0	0/7
Boycott,G	108	193	23	8114	246*	47.72	22	42	10	33	944	382	7	54.57	0	0	3/47

ENGLAND (cont.) — **BATTING AND FIELDING** / **BOWLING**

	Tests	I	N	Runs	HS	Avge	100	50	0's	C/S	Balls	Runs	Wks	Avge	5w	10w	BB
Bradley,WM	2	2	1	23	23*	23.00	0	0	1	0	625	233	6	38.83	1	0	5/67
Braund,LC	23	41	3	987	104	25.97	3	2	7	39	3803	1810	47	38.51	3	0	8/81
Brearley,JM	39	66	3	1442	91	22.88	0	9	6	52							
Brearley,W	4	5	2	21	11*	7.00	0	0	2	0	705	359	17	21.11	1	0	5/110
Brennan,DV	2	2	0	16	16	8.00	0	0	1	0							
Briggs,J	33	50	5	815	121	18.11	1	2	10	12	5332	2094	118	17.74	9	4	8/11
Broad,BC	25	44	2	1661	162	39.54	6	6	3	10	6	4	0	-	0	0	0/4
Brockwell,W	7	12	0	202	49	16.83	0	0	1	6	582	309	5	61.80	0	0	3/33
Bromley-Davenport,HR	4	6	0	128	84	21.33	0	1	1	1	155	98	4	24.50	0	0	2/46
Brookes,D	1	2	0	17	10	8.50	0	0	0	1							
Brown,A	2	1	1	3	3*	0	0	0	0	1	323	150	3	50.00	0	0	3/27
Brown,DJ	26	34	5	342	44*	11.79	0	0	6	7	5098	2237	79	28.31	2	0	5/42
Brown,FR	22	30	1	734	79	25.31	0	5	1	22	3260	1398	45	31.06	1	0	5/49
Brown,G	7	12	2	229	84	29.90	0	2	2	9/3							
Brown,JT	8	16	3	470	140	36.15	1	1	2	7	35	22	0	-	0	0	0/22
Brown,SJE	1	2	1	11	10*	11.00	0	0	0	1	198	138	2	69.00	0	0	1/60
Buckenham,CP	4	7	0	43	17	6.14	0	0	1	2	1182	593	21	28.23	1	0	5/115
Butcher,AR	1	2	0	34	20	17.00	0	0	0	0	12	9	0	-	0	0	0/9
Butcher,RO	3	5	0	71	32	14.20	0	0	1	3							
Butler,HJ	2	2	1	15	15*	15.00	0	0	1	1	552	215	12	17.91	0	0	4/34
Butt,HR	3	4	1	22	13	7.33	0	0	1	1/1							
Caddick,AR	9	15	2	174	29*	13.38	0	0	0	3	2284	1198	29	41.31	2	0	6/65
Calthorpe,Hon.FSG	4	7	0	129	49	18.42	0	0	1	3	204	91	1	91.00	0	0	1/38
Capel,DJ	15	25	1	374	98	15.58	0	2	4	6	2000	1064	21	50.66	0	0	3/88
Carr,AW	11	13	1	237	62	19.75	0	1	0	3							
Carr,DB	2	4	0	135	76	33.75	0	1	0	0	210	140	2	70.00	0	0	2/84
Carr,DW	1	1	0	0	0	0.00	0	0	1	0	414	282	7	40.28	1	0	5/146
Cartwright,TW	5	7	2	26	9	5.20	0	0	2	2	1611	544	15	36.26	1	0	6/94
Chapman,APF	26	36	4	925	121	28.90	1	5	2	32	40	20	0	-	0	0	0/10
Charlwood,HRJ	2	4	0	63	36	15.75	0	0	1	0							
Chatterton,W	1	1	0	48	48	48.00	0	0	0	0							
Childs,JH	2	4	4	2	2*	0	0	0	0	1	516	183	3	61.00	0	0	1/13
Christopherson,S	1	1	0	17	17	17.00	0	0	0	0	136	69	1	69.00	0	0	1/52
Clark,EW	8	9	5	36	10	9.00	0	0	1	0	1931	899	32	28.09	1	0	5/98
Clay,JC	1						0	0	0	1	192	75	0	-	0	0	0/30
Close,DB	22	37	2	887	70	25.34	0	4	3	24	1212	532	18	29.55	0	0	4/35
Coldwell,LJ	7	7	5	9	6*	4.50	0	0	1	1	1668	610	22	27.72	1	0	6/85
Compton,DCS	78	131	15	5807	278	50.06	17	28	10	49	2716	1410	25	56.40	1	0	5/70
Cook,C	1	2	0	4	4	2.00	0	0	1	0	180	127	0	-	0	0	0/40
Cook,G	7	13	0	203	66	15.61	0	2	1	9	42	27	0	-	0	0	0/2
Cook,NGB	15	25	4	179	31	8.52	0	0	2	5	4174	1689	52	32.48	4	1	6/65
Cope,GA	3	3	0	40	22	13.33	0	0	1	1	864	277	8	34.62	0	0	3/102
Copson,WH	3	1	0	6	6	6.00	0	0	0	1	762	297	15	19.80	1	0	5/85
Cork,DG	16	23	3	361	56*	18.05	0	1	2	7	3752	1949	67	29.09	3	0	7/43
Cornford,WL	4	4	0	36	18	9.00	0	0	0	5/3							
Cottam,RMH	4	5	1	27	13	6.75	0	0	0	2	903	327	14	23.35	0	0	4/50
Coventry,Hon.CJ	2	2	1	13	12	13.00	0	0	0	0							
Cowans,NG	19	29	7	175	36	7.95	0	0	5	9	3452	2003	51	39.27	2	0	6/77
Cowdrey,CS	6	8	1	101	38	14.42	0	0	1	5	399	309	4	77.25	0	0	2/65
Cowdrey,MC	114	188	15	7624	182	44.06	22	38	9	120	119	104	0	-	0	0	0/1
Coxon,A	1	2	0	19	19	9.50	0	0	1	0	378	172	3	57.33	0	0	2/90
Cranston,J	1	2	0	31	16	15.50	0	0	0	1							
Cranston,K	8	14	0	209	45	14.92	0	0	2	3	1010	461	18	25.61	0	0	4/12
Crapp,JF	7	13	2	319	56	29.00	0	3	1	7							

ENGLAND (cont.)				**BATTING AND FIELDING**										**BOWLING**			
	Tests	I	N	Runs	HS	Avge	100	50	0's	C/S	Balls	Runs	Wks	Avge	5w	10w	BB
Crawford,JN	12	23	2	469	74	22.33	0	2	1	13	2203	1150	39	29.48	3	0	5/48
Crawley,JP	12	19	1	508	106	28.22	1	4	3	11							
Croft,RDB	1	2	1	11	6	11.00	0	0	0	1	286	125	2	52.50	0	0	2/116
Curtis,TS	5	9	0	140	41	15.55	0	0	1	3	18	7	0	-	0	0	0/7
Cuttell,WR	2	4	0	65	21	16.25	0	0	0	2	285	73	6	12.16	0	0	3/17
Dawson,EW	5	9	0	175	55	19.44	0	1	0	0							
Dean,H	3	4	2	10	8	5.00	0	0	1	2	447	153	11	13.90	0	0	4/19
DeFreitas,PAJ	44	68	5	934	88	14.82	0	4	10	14	9838	4700	140	33.57	4	0	7/70
Denness,MH	28	45	3	1667	188	39.69	4	7	2	28							
Denton,D	11	22	1	424	104	20.19	1	1	4	8							
Dewes,JG	5	10	0	121	67	12.10	0	1	1	0							
Dexter,ER	62	102	8	4502	205	47.89	9	27	6	29	5317	2306	66	34.93	0	0	4/10
Dilley,GR	41	58	19	521	56	13.35	0	2	10	10	8192	4107	138	29.76	6	0	6/38
Dipper,AE	1	2	0	51	40	25.50	0	0	0	0/0							
Doggart,GHG	2	4	0	76	29	19.00	0	0	1	3							
D'Oliveira,BL	44	70	8	2484	158	40.06	5	15	4	29	5706	1859	47	39.55	0	0	3/46
Dollery,HE	4	7	0	72	37	10.28	0	0	2	1							
Dolphin,A	1	2	0	1	1	0.50	0	0	1	1/0							
Douglas,JWHT	23	35	2	962	119	29.15	1	6	3	9	2812	1496	45	33.02	1	0	5/46
Downton,PR	30	48	8	785	74	19.62	0	4	4	70/5							
Druce,NF	5	9	0	252	64	28.00	0	1	0	5							
Ducat,A	1	2	0	5	3	2.50	0	0	0	1							
Duckworth,G	24	28	12	234	39*	14.62	0	0	2	45/15							
Duleepsinhji,KS	12	19	2	995	173	58.52	3	5	0	10	6	7	0	-	0	0	0/7
Durston,FJ	1	2	1	8	6*	8.00	0	0	0	0	202	136	5	27.20	0	0	4/102
Ealham,MA	2	3	0	81	51	27.00	0	1	0	1	480	192	7	27.42	0	0	4/21
Edmonds,PH	51	65	15	875	64	17.50	0	2	5	42	12028	4273	125	34.18	2	0	7/66
Edrich,JH	77	127	9	5138	310*	43.54	12	24	6	43	30	23	0	-	0	0	0/6
Edrich,WJ	39	63	2	2440	219	40.00	6	13	3	39	3234	1693	41	41.29	0	0	4/68
Elliott,H	4	5	1	61	37*	15.25	0	0	0	8/3							
Ellison,RM	11	16	1	202	41	13.46	0	0	1	2	2264	1048	35	29.94	3	1	6/77
Emburey,JE	65	97	20	1721	75	22.35	0	10	16	35	15571	5728	147	38.96	6	0	7/78
Emmett,GM	1	2	0	10	10	5.00	0	0	1	0							
Emmett,T	7	13	1	160	48	13.33	0	0	1	9	728	284	9	31.55	1	0	7/68
Evans,AJ	1	2	0	18	14	9.00	0	0	0	0							
Evans,TG	91	133	14	2439	104	20.49	2	8	17	173/46							
Fagg,AE	5	8	0	150	39	18.75	0	0	0	5							
Fairbrother,NH	10	15	1	219	83	15.64	0	1	1	4	12	9	0	-	0	0	0/9
Fane,FL	14	27	1	682	143	26.23	1	3	3	6							
Farnes,K	15	17	5	58	20	4.83	0	0	4	1	3932	1719	60	28.65	3	1	6/96
Farrimond,W	4	7	0	116	35	16.57	0	0	0	5/2							
Fender,PGH	13	21	1	380	60	19.00	0	2	3	14	2178	1185	29	40.86	2	0	5/90
Ferris,JJ	1	1	0	16	16	16.00	0	0	0	0	272	91	13	7.00	2	1	7/37
Fielder,A	6	12	5	78	20	11.14	0	0	0	4	1491	711	26	27.34	1	0	6/82
Fishlock,LB	4	5	1	47	19*	11.75	0	0	1	1							
Flavell,JA	4	6	2	31	14	7.75	0	0	0	0	792	367	7	52.42	0	0	2/65
Fletcher,KWR	59	96	14	3272	216	39.90	7	19	6	54	285	193	2	96.50	0	0	1/6
Flowers,W	8	14	0	254	56	18.14	0	1	0	2	858	296	14	21.14	1	0	5/46
Ford,FGJ	5	9	0	168	48	18.66	0	0	1	5	210	129	1	129.00	0	0	1/47
Foster,FR	11	15	1	330	71	23.57	0	3	1	11	2447	926	45	20.57	4	0	6/91
Foster,NA	29	45	7	446	39	11.73	0	0	9	7	6261	2891	88	32.85	5	1	8/107
Foster,RE	8	14	1	602	287	46.30	1	1	1	13							
Fothergill,AJ	2	2	0	33	32	16.50	0	0	0	0	321	90	8	11.25	0	0	4/19
Fowler,G	21	37	0	1307	201	35.32	3	8	3	10	18	11	0	-	0	0	0/0

ENGLAND (cont.)				BATTING AND FIELDING										BOWLING			
	Tests	I	N	Runs	HS	Avge	100	50	0's	C/S	Balls	Runs	Wks	Avge	5w	10w	BB
Fraser,ARC	32	46	10	265	29	7.36	0	0	7	7	7967	3509	119	29.48	8	0	8/75
Freeman,AP	12	16	5	154	50*	14.00	0	1	2	4	3732	1707	66	25.86	5	3	7/71
French,BN	16	21	4	308	59	18.11	0	1	2	38/1							
Fry,CB	26	41	3	1223	144	32.18	2	7	3	17	10	3	0	-	0	0	0/3
Gallian,JER	3	6	0	74	28	12.33	0	0	2	1	84	62	0	-	0	0	0/6
Gatting,MW	79	138	14	4409	207	35.55	10	21	16	59	752	317	4	79.25	0	0	1/14
Gay,LH	1	2	0	37	33	18.50	0	0	0	3/1							
Geary,G	14	20	4	249	66	15.56	0	2	3	13	3810	1353	46	29.41	4	1	7/70
Gibb,PA	8	13	0	581	120	44.69	2	3	1	3/1							
Gifford,N	15	20	9	179	25*	16.27	0	0	1	8	3084	1026	33	31.09	1	0	5/55
Gilligan,AER	11	16	3	209	39*	16.07	0	0	2	3	2404	1046	36	29.05	2	1	6/7
Gilligan,AHH	4	4	0	71	32	17.75	0	0	0	0							
Gimblett,H	3	5	1	129	67*	32.25	0	1	0	1							
Gladwin,C	8	11	5	170	51*	28.33	0	1	0	2	2129	571	15	38.06	0	0	3/21
Goddard,TWJ	8	5	3	13	8	6.50	0	0	1	3	1563	588	22	26.72	1	0	6/29
Gooch,GA	118	215	6	8900	333	42.58	20	46	13	103	2655	1069	23	46.47	0	0	3/39
Gough,D	12	18	3	319	65	21.26	0	2	3	7	2521	1376	43	32.00	1	0	6/49
Gover,AR	4	1	1	2	2*	0	0	0	0	1	816	359	8	44.87	0	0	3/85
Gower,DI	117	204	18	8231	215	44.25	18	39	7	74	36	20	1	20.00	0	0	1/1
Grace,EM	1	2	0	36	36	18.00	0	0	1	1							
Grace,GF	1	2	0	0	0	0.00	0	0	2	2							
Grace,WG	22	36	2	1098	170	32.29	2	5	2	39	666	236	9	26.22	0	0	2/12
Graveney,TW	79	123	13	4882	258	44.38	11	20	8	80	260	167	1	167.00	0	0	1/34
Greenhough,T	4	4	1	4	2	1.33	0	0	1	1	1129	357	16	22.31	1	0	5/35
Greenwood,A	2	4	0	77	49	19.25	0	0	0	2							
Greig,AW	58	93	4	3599	148	40.43	8	20	5	87	9802	4541	141	32.20	6	2	8/86
Greig,IA	2	4	0	26	14	6.50	0	0	0	0	188	114	4	28.50	0	0	4/53
Grieve,BAF	2	3	2	40	14*	40.00	0	0	0	0							
Griffith,SC	3	5	0	157	140	31.40	1	0	1	5/0							
Gunn,G	15	29	1	1120	122*	40.00	2	7	3	15	12	8	0	-	0	0	0/8
Gunn,JR	6	10	2	85	24	10.62	0	0	1	3	999	387	18	21.50	1	0	5/76
Gunn,W	11	20	2	392	102*	21.77	1	1	1	5							
Haig,NE	5	9	0	126	47	14.00	0	0	2	4	1026	448	13	34.46	0	0	3/73
Haigh,S	11	18	3	113	25	7.53	0	0	4	8	1294	622	24	25.91	1	0	6/11
Hallows,C	2	2	1	42	26	42.00	0	0	0	0							
Hammond,WR	85	140	16	7249	336*	58.45	22	24	4	110	7969	3138	83	37.80	2	0	5/36
Hampshire,JH	8	16	1	403	107	26.86	1	2	2	9							
Hardinge,HTW	1	2	0	30	25	15.00	0	0	0	0							
Hardstaff,J jr	23	38	3	1636	205*	46.74	4	10	4	9							
Hardstaff,J sr	5	10	0	311	72	31.10	0	3	0	1							
Harris,Lord	4	6	1	145	52	29.00	0	1	0	2	32	29	0	-	0	0	0/14
Hartley,JC	2	4	0	15	9	3.75	0	0	2	2	192	115	1	115.00	0	0	1/62
Hawke,Lord	5	8	1	55	30	7.85	0	0	2	3							
Hayes,EG	5	9	1	86	35	10.75	0	0	2	2	90	52	1	52.00	0	0	1/28
Hayes,FC	9	17	1	244	106*	15.25	1	0	6	7							
Hayward,TW	35	60	2	1999	137	34.46	3	12	7	19	887	514	14	36.71	0	0	4/22
Hearne,A	1	1	0	9	9	9.00	0	0	0	1							
Hearne,F	2	2	0	47	27	23.50	0	0	0	1							
Hearne,GG	1	1	0	0	0	0.00	0	0	1	0							
Hearne,JT	12	18	4	126	40	9.00	0	0	3	4	2976	1082	49	22.08	4	1	6/41
Hearne,JW	24	36	5	806	114	26.00	1	2	3	13	2926	1462	30	48.73	1	0	5/49
Hemmings,EE	16	21	4	383	95	22.52	0	2	5	5	4437	1825	43	42.44	1	0	6/58
Hendren,EH	51	83	9	3525	205*	47.63	7	21	4	33	47	31	1	31.00	0	0	1/27
Hendrick,M	30	35	15	128	15	6.40	0	0	8	25	6208	2248	87	25.83	0	0	4/28

ENGLAND (cont.)	Tests	I	N	Runs	HS	Avge	100	50	0's	C/S	Balls	Runs	Wks	Avge	5w	10w	BB
				BATTING AND FIELDING							BOWLING						
Heseltine,C	2	2	0	18	18	9.00	0	0	1	3	157	84	5	16.80	1	0	5/38
Hick,GA	46	80	6	2672	178	36.10	4	15	3	62	2925	1236	22	56.18	0	0	4/126
Higgs,K	15	19	3	185	63	11.56	0	1	2	4	4112	1473	71	20.74	2	0	6/91
Hill,A	2	4	2	101	49	50.50	0	0	1	1	340	130	7	18.57	0	0	4/27
Hill,AJL	3	4	0	251	124	62.75	1	1	0	1	40	8	4	2.00	0	0	4/8
Hilton,MJ	4	6	1	37	15	7.40	0	0	2	1	1244	477	14	34.07	1	0	5/61
Hirst,GH	24	38	3	790	85	22.57	0	5	5	18	3967	1770	59	30.00	3	0	5/48
Hitch,JW	7	10	3	103	51*	14.71	0	1	1	4	462	325	7	46.42	0	0	2/31
Hobbs,JB	61	102	7	5410	211	56.94	15	28	4	17	376	165	1	165.00	0	0	1/19
Hobbs,RNS	7	8	3	34	15*	6.80	0	0	1	8	1291	481	12	40.08	0	0	3/25
Hollies,WE	13	15	8	37	18*	5.28	0	0	4	2	3554	1332	44	30.27	5	0	7/50
Holmes,ERT	5	9	2	114	85*	16.28	0	1	2	4	108	76	2	38.00	0	0	1/10
Holmes,P	7	14	1	357	88	27.46	0	4	3	3							
Hone,L	1	2	0	13	7	6.50	0	0	0	2/0							
Hopwood,JL	2	3	1	12	8	6.00	0	0	0	0	462	155	0	-	0	0	0/16
Hornby,AN	3	6	0	21	9	3.50	0	0	1	0	28	0	1	0.00	0	0	1/0
Horton,MJ	2	2	0	60	58	30.00	0	1	0	2	238	59	2	29.50	0	0	2/24
Howard,ND	4	6	1	86	23	17.20	0	0	0	4							
Howell,H	5	8	6	15	5	7.50	0	0	0	0	918	559	7	79.85	0	0	4/115
Howorth,R	5	10	2	145	45*	18.12	0	0	0	2	1536	635	19	33.42	1	0	6/124
Humphries,J	3	6	1	44	16	8.80	0	0	0	7							
Hunter,J	5	7	2	93	39*	18.60	0	0	0	8/3							
Hussain,N	12	21	3	713	128	39.61	2	2	3	7							
Hutchings,KL	7	12	0	341	126	28.41	1	1	1	9	90	81	1	81.00	0	0	1/5
Hutton,L	79	138	15	6971	364	56.67	19	33	5	57	260	232	3	77.33	0	0	1/2
Hutton,RA	5	8	2	219	81	36.50	0	2	1	9	738	257	9	28.55	0	0	3/72
Iddon,J	5	7	1	170	73	28.33	0	2	3	0	66	27	0	-	0	0	0/3
Igglesden,AP	3	5	3	6	3*	3.00	0	0	2	1	555	329	6	54.83	0	0	2/91
Ikin,JT	18	31	2	606	60	20.89	0	3	4	31	572	354	3	118.00	0	0	1/38
Illingworth,R	61	90	11	1836	113	23.24	2	5	7	45	11934	3807	122	31.20	3	0	6/29
Illingworth,RK	9	14	7	128	28	18.28	0	0	3	5	1485	613	19	32.26	0	0	4/94
Ilott,MC	5	6	2	28	15	7.00	0	0	0	0	1042	542	12	45.16	0	0	3/48
Insole,DJ	9	17	2	408	110*	27.20	1	1	2	8							
Irani,RC	2	3	0	76	41	25.33	0	0	0	0	126	74	2	3700	0	0	1/22
Jackman,RD	4	6	0	42	17	7.00	0	0	2	0	1070	445	14	31.78	0	0	4/110
Jackson,Hon.FS	20	33	4	1415	144*	48.79	5	6	3	10	1587	799	24	33.29	1	0	5/52
Jackson,HL	2	2	1	15	8	15.00	0	0	0	1	498	155	7	22.14	0	0	2/26
Jameson,JA	4	8	0	214	82	26.75	0	1	0	0	42	17	1	17.00	0	0	1/17
Jardine,DR	22	33	6	1296	127	48.00	1	10	2	26	6	10	0	-	0	0	0/10
Jarvis,PW	9	15	2	132	29*	10.15	0	0	1	2	1912	965	21	45.95	0	0	4/107
Jenkins,RO	9	12	1	198	39	18.00	0	0	0	4	2118	1098	32	34.31	1	0	5/116
Jessop,GL	18	26	0	569	104	21.88	1	3	3	11	742	354	10	35.40	0	0	4/68
Jones,AO	12	21	0	291	34	13.85	0	0	2	15	228	133	3	44.33	0	0	3/73
Jones,IJ	15	17	9	38	16	4.75	0	0	2	4	3546	1769	44	40.20	1	0	6/118
Jupp,H	2	4	0	68	63	17.00	0	1	1	2/0							
Jupp,VWC	8	13	1	208	38	17.33	0	0	0	5	1301	616	28	22.00	0	0	4/37
Keeton,WW	2	4	0	57	25	14.25	0	0	1	0							
Kennedy,AS	5	8	2	93	41*	15.50	0	0	1	5	1683	599	31	19.32	2	0	5/76
Kenyon,D	8	15	0	192	87	12.80	0	1	1	5							
Killick,ET	2	4	0	81	31	20.25	0	0	0	2							
Kilner,R	9	8	1	233	74	33.28	0	2	0	6	2368	734	24	30.58	0	0	4/51
King,JH	1	2	0	64	60	32.00	0	1	0	0	162	99	1	99.00	0	0	1/99
Kinneir,S	1	2	0	52	30	26.00	0	0	0	0							
Knight,AE	3	6	1	81	70*	16.20	0	1	3	1							

ENGLAND (cont.)	**BATTING AND FIELDING**										**BOWLING**						
	Tests	I	N	Runs	HS	Avge	100	50	0's	C/S	Balls	Runs	Wks	Avge	5w	10w	BB
Knight,BR	29	38	7	812	127	26.19	2	0	2	14	5377	2223	70	31.75	0	0	4/38
Knight,DJ	2	4	0	54	38	13.50	0	0	0	1							
Knight,NV	6	11	0	320	113	29.09	1	2	0	10							
Knott,APE	95	149	15	4389	135	32.75	5	30	8	250/19							
Knox,NA	2	4	1	24	8*	8.00	0	0	0	0	126	105	3	35.00	0	0	2/39
Laker,JC	46	63	15	676	63	14.08	0	2	6	12	12027	4101	193	21.24	9	3	10/53
Lamb,AJ	79	139	10	4656	142	36.09	14	18	9	75	30	23	1	23.00	0	0	1/6
Langridge,J	8	9	0	242	70	26.88	0	1	0	6	1074	413	19	21.73	2	0	7/56
Larkins,W	13	25	1	493	64	20.54	0	3	6	8							
Larter,JDF	10	7	2	16	10	3.20	0	0	2	5	2172	941	37	25.43	2	0	5/57
Larwood,H	21	28	3	485	98	19.40	0	2	4	15	4969	2212	78	28.35	4	1	6/32
Lathwell,MN	2	4	0	78	33	19.50	0	0	1	0							
Lawrence,DV	5	6	0	60	34	10.00	0	0	0	0	1089	676	18	37.55	1	0	5/106
Leadbeater,E	2	2	0	40	38	20.00	0	0	0	3	289	218	2	109.00	0	0	1/38
Lee,HW	1	2	0	19	18	9.50	0	0	0	0							
Lees,WS	5	9	3	66	25*	11.00	0	0	0	2	1256	467	26	17.96	2	0	6/78
Legge,GB	5	7	1	299	196	49.83	1	0	2	1	30	34	0	-	0	0	0/34
Leslie,CFH	4	7	0	106	54	15.14	0	1	1	1	96	44	4	11.00	0	0	3/31
Lever,JK	21	31	5	306	53	11.76	0	1	2	11	4433	1951	73	26.72	3	1	7/46
Lever,P	17	18	2	350	88*	21.87	0	2	1	11	3571	1509	41	36.80	2	0	6/38
Leveson Gower,HDG	3	6	2	95	31	23.75	0	0	0	1							
Levett,WHV	1	2	1	7	5	7.00	0	0	0	3/0							
Lewis,AR	9	16	2	457	125	32.64	1	3	2	0							
Lewis,CC	32	51	3	1105	117	23.02	1	4	6	25	5852	3490	93	37.52	3	0	6/111
Leyland,M	41	65	5	2764	187	46.06	9	10	6	13	1103	585	6	97.50	0	0	3/91
Lilley,AFA	35	52	8	903	84	20.52	0	4	10	70/22	25	23	1	23.00	0	0	1/23
Lillywhite,J	2	3	1	16	10	8.00	0	0	0	1	340	126	8	15.75	0	0	4/70
Lloyd,D	9	15	2	552	214*	42.46	1	0	0	11	24	17	0	-	0	0	0/4
Lloyd,TA	1	1	1	10	10*	-	0	0	0	0							
Loader,PJ	13	19	6	76	17	5.84	0	0	3	2	2662	878	39	22.51	1	0	6/36
Lock,GAR	49	63	9	742	89	13.74	0	3	8	59	13147	4451	174	25.58	9	3	7/35
Lockwood,WH	12	16	3	231	52*	17.76	0	1	3	4	1970	884	43	20.55	5	1	7/71
Lohmann,GA	18	26	2	213	62*	8.87	0	1	7	28	3821	1205	112	10.75	9	5	9/28
Lowson,FA	7	13	0	245	68	18.84	0	2	2	5							
Lucas,AP	5	9	1	157	55	19.62	0	1	0	1	120	54	0	-	0	0	0/23
Luckhurst,BW	21	41	5	1298	131	36.05	4	5	4	14	57	32	1	32.00	0	0	1/9
Lyttelton,Hon.A	4	7	1	94	31	15.66	0	0	0	2/0	48	19	4	4.75	0	0	4/19
Macaulay,GG	8	10	4	112	76	18.66	0	1	1	5	1701	662	24	27.58	1	0	5/64
MacBryan,JCW	1						0	0	0	0							
McCague,MJ	3	5	0	21	11	4.20	0	0	2	1	593	390	6	65.00	0	0	4/121
McConnon,JE	2	3	1	18	11	9.00	0	0	0	4	216	74	4	18.50	0	0	3/19
McGahey,CP	2	4	0	38	18	9.50	0	0	1	1							
MacGregor,G	8	11	3	96	31	12.00	0	0	1	14/3							
McIntyre,AJW	3	6	0	19	7	3.16	0	0	1	8/0							
MacKinnon,FA	1	2	0	5	5	2.50	0	0	1	0							
MacLaren,AC	35	61	4	1931	140	33.87	5	8	4	29							
McMaster,JEP	1	1	0	0	0	0.00	0	0	1	0							
Makepeace,JWH	4	8	0	279	117	34.87	1	2	0	0							
Malcolm,DE	36	53	18	224	29	6.40	0	0	13	5	7922	4441	122	36.40	5	2	9/57
Mallender,NA	2	3	0	8	4	2.66	0	0	0	0	449	215	10	21.50	1	0	5/50
Mann,FG	7	12	2	376	136*	37.60	1	0	0	3							
Mann,FT	5	9	1	281	84	35.12	0	2	0	4							
Marks,VJ	6	10	1	249	83	27.66	0	3	0	0	1082	484	11	44.00	0	0	3/78
Marriott,CS	1	1	0	0	0	0.00	0	0	1	1	247	96	11	8.72	2	1	6/59

ENGLAND (cont.)	BATTING AND FIELDING										BOWLING						
	Tests	I	N	Runs	HS	Avge	100	50	0's	C/S	Balls	Runs	Wks	Avge	5w	10w	BB
Martin,F	2	2	0	14	13	7.00	0	0	0	2	410	141	14	10.07	2	1	6/50
Martin,JW	1	2	0	26	26	13.00	0	0	1	0	270	129	1	129.00	0	0	1/111
Martin,PJ	7	11	0	92	29	8.36	0	0	2	5	1338	529	17	31.11	0	0	4/60
Mason,JR	5	10	0	129	32	12.90	0	0	1	3	324	149	2	74.50	0	0	1/8
Matthews,ADG	1	1	1	2	2*	[illegible]	0	0	0	1	180	65	2	32.50	0	0	1/13
May,PBH	66	106	9	4537	285*	46.77	13	22	8	42							
Maynard,MP	4	8	0	87	35	10.87	0	0	2	3							
Mead,CP	17	26	2	1185	182*	49.37	4	3	3	4							
Mead,W	1	2	0	7	7	3.50	0	0	1	1	265	91	1	91.00	0	0	1/91
Midwinter,WE	4	7	0	95	36	13.57	0	0	1	5/0	776	272	10	27.20	0	0	4/81
Milburn,C	9	16	2	654	139	46.71	2	2	0	7							
Miller,AM	1	2	2	24	20*	-	0	0	0	0							
Miller,G	34	51	4	1213	98*	25.80	0	7	5	17	5149	1859	60	30.98	1	0	5/44
Milligan,FW	2	4	0	58	38	14.50	0	0	0	1	45	29	0	-	0	0	0/0
Millman,G	6	7	2	60	32*	12.00	0	0	2	13/2							
Milton,CA	6	9	1	204	104*	25.50	1	0	0	5	24	12	0	-	0	0	0/12
Mitchell,A	6	10	0	298	72	29.80	0	2	1	9	6	4	0	-	0	0	0/4
Mitchell,F	2	4	0	88	41	22.00	0	0	0	2							
Mitchell,TB	5	6	2	20	9	5.00	0	0	1	1	894	498	8	62.25	0	0	2/49
Mitchell-Innes,NS	1	1	0	5	5	5.00	0	0	0	0							
Mold,AW	3	3	1	0	0*	0.00	0	0	2	1	491	234	7	33.42	0	0	3/44
Moon,LJ	4	8	0	182	36	22.75	0	0	1	4							
Morley,F	4	6	2	6	2*	1.50	0	0	2	4	972	296	16	18.50	1	0	5/56
Morris,H	3	6	0	115	44	19.16	0	0	0	3							
Morris,JE	3	5	2	71	32	23.66	0	0	0	3							
Mortimore,JB	9	12	2	243	73*	24.30	0	1	1	3	2162	733	13	56.38	0	0	3/36
Moss,AE	9	7	1	61	26	10.16	0	0	1	1	1657	626	21	29.80	0	0	4/35
Moxon,MD	10	17	1	455	99	28.43	0	3	2	10	48	30	0	-	0	0	0/3
Mullally,AD	6	9	4	54	24	10.80	0	0	2	0	1677	675	22	30.68	0	0	3/44
Munton,TA	2	2	1	25	25*	25.00	0	0	1	0	405	200	4	50.00	0	0	2/22
Murdoch,WL	1	1	0	12	12	12.00	0	0	0	0/1							
Murray,JT	21	28	5	506	112	22.00	1	2	3	52/3							
Newham,W	1	2	0	26	17	13.00	0	0	0	0							
Newport,PJ	3	5	1	110	40*	27.50	0	0	1	1	669	417	10	41.70	0	0	4/87
Nichols,MS	14	19	7	355	78*	29.58	0	2	0	11	2565	1152	41	28.09	2	0	6/35
Oakman,ASM	2	2	0	14	10	7.00	0	0	0	7	48	21	0	-	0	0	0/21
O'Brien,TC	5	8	0	59	20	7.37	0	0	3	4							
O'Connor,J	4	7	0	153	51	21.85	0	1	1	2	162	72	1	72.00	0	0	1/31
Old,CM	46	66	9	845	65	14.82	0	2	10	22	8858	4020	143	28.11	4	0	7/50
Oldfield,N	1	2	0	99	80	49.50	0	1	0	0							
Padgett,DEV	2	4	0	51	31	12.75	0	0	0	0	12	8	0	-	0	0	0/8
Paine,GAE	4	7	1	97	49	16.16	0	0	1	5	1044	467	17	27.47	1	0	5/168
Palairet,LCH	2	4	0	49	20	12.25	0	0	0	2							
Palmer,CH	1	2	0	22	22	11.00	0	0	1	0	30	15	0	-	0	0	0/15
Palmer,KE	1	1	0	10	10	10.00	0	0	0	0	378	189	1	189.00	0	0	1/113
Parfitt,PH	37	52	6	1882	131*	40.91	7	6	5	42	1326	574	12	47.83	0	0	2/5
Parker,CWL	1	1	1	3	3*	-	0	0	0	0	168	32	2	16.00	0	0	2/32
Parker,PWG	1	2	0	13	13	6.50	0	0	1	0							
Parkhouse,WGA	7	13	0	373	78	28.69	0	2	1	3							
Parkin,CH	10	16	3	160	36	12.30	0	0	1	3	2095	1128	32	35.25	2	0	5/38
Parks,JH	1	2	0	29	22	14.50	0	0	0	0	126	36	3	12.00	0	0	2/26
Parks,JM	46	68	7	1962	108*	32.16	2	9	5	103/11	54	51	1	51.00	0	0	1/43
Pataudi,Nawab of, sr	3	5	0	144	102	28.80	1	0	0	0							
Patel,MM	2	2	0	45	27	22.50	0	0	0	2	276	180	1	180.00	0	0	1/101

ENGLAND (cont.) **BATTING AND FIELDING** **BOWLING**

	Tests	I	N	Runs	HS	Avge	100	50	0's	C/S	Balls	Runs	Wks	Avge	5w	10w	BB
Paynter,E	20	31	5	1540	243	59.23	4	7	3	7							
Peate,E	9	14	8	70	13	11.66	0	0	1	2	2096	682	31	22.00	2	0	6/85
Peebles,IAR	13	17	8	98	26	10.88	0	0	3	5	2882	1391	45	30.91	3	0	6/63
Peel,R	20	33	4	427	83	14.72	0	3	8	17	5216	1715	101	16.98	5	1	7/31
Penn,F	1	2	1	50	27*	50.00	0	0	0	0	12	2	0	-	0	0	0/2
Perks,RTD	2	2	2	3	2*	0	0	0	0	1	829	355	11	32.27	2	0	5/100
Philipson,H	5	8	1	63	30	9.00	0	0	0	8/3							
Pigott,ACS	1	2	1	12	8*	12.00	0	0	0	0	102	75	2	37.50	0	0	2/75
Pilling,R	8	13	1	91	23	7.58	0	0	1	10/4							
Place,W	3	6	1	144	107	28.80	1	0	0	0							
Pocock,PI	25	37	4	206	33	6.24	0	0	10	15	6650	2976	67	44.41	3	0	6/79
Pollard,R	4	3	2	13	10*	13.00	0	0	0	3	1102	378	15	25.20	1	0	5/24
Poole,CJ	3	5	1	161	69*	40.25	0	2	0	1	30	9	0	-	0	0	0/9
Pope,GH	1	1	1	8	8*	-	0	0	0	0	218	85	1	85.00	0	0	1/49
Pougher,AD	1	1	0	17	17	17.00	0	0	0	2	105	26	3	8.66	0	0	3/26
Price,JSE	15	15	6	66	32	7.33	0	0	5	7	2724	1401	40	35.02	1	0	5/73
Price,WFF	1	2	0	6	6	3.00	0	0	1	2/0							
Prideaux,RM	3	6	1	102	64	20.40	0	1	0	0	12	0	0	-			0/0
Pringle,DR	30	50	4	695	53	15.10	0	1	6	10	5287	2518	70	35.97	3	0	5/95
Pullar,G	28	49	4	1974	175	43.86	4	12	3	2	66	37	1	37.00	0	0	1/1
Quaife,WG	7	13	1	228	68	19.00	0	1	1	4	15	6	0	-	0	0	0/6
Radford,NV	3	4	1	21	12*	7.00	0	0	1	0	678	351	4	87.75	0	0	2/131
Radley,CT	8	10	0	481	158	48.10	2	2	1	4							
Ramprakash,MR	19	33	1	533	72	16.65	0	2	6	13	265	149	0	-	0	0	0/3
Randall,DW	47	79	5	2470	174	33.37	7	12	14	31	16	3	0	-	0	0	0/1
Ranjitsinhji,KS	15	26	4	989	175	44.95	2	6	2	13	97	39	1	39.00	0	0	1/23
Read,HD	1						0	0	0	0	270	200	6	33.33	0	0	4/136
Read,JM	17	29	2	463	57	17.14	0	2	3	8							
Read,WW	18	27	1	720	117	27.69	1	5	0	16	60	63	0	-	0	0	0/27
Reeve,DA	3	5	0	124	59	24.80	0	1	1	1	149	60	2	30.00	0	0	1/4
Relf,AE	13	21	3	416	63	23.11	0	1	1	14	1764	624	25	24.96	1	0	5/85
Rhodes,HJ	2	1	1	0	0*	-	0	0	0	0	449	244	9	27.11	0	0	4/50
Rhodes,SJ	11	17	5	294	65*	24.50	0	1	1	46/2							
Rhodes,W	58	98	21	2325	179	30.19	2	11	6	60	8231	3425	127	26.96	6	1	8/68
Richards,CJ	8	13	0	285	133	21.92	1	0	2	20/1							
Richardson,DW	1	1	0	33	33	33.00	0	0	0	1							
Richardson,PE	34	56	1	2061	126	37.47	5	9	1	6	120	48	3	16.00	0	0	2/10
Richardson,T	14	24	8	177	25*	11.06	0	0	3	5	4497	2220	88	25.22	11	4	8/94
Richmond,TL	1	2	0	6	4	3.00	0	0	0	0	114	86	2	43.00	0	0	2/69
Ridgway,F	5	6	0	49	24	8.16	0	0	2	3	793	379	7	54.14	0	0	4/83
Robertson,JDB	11	21	2	881	133	46.36	2	6	0	6	138	58	2	29.00	0	0	2/17
Robins,RWV	19	27	4	612	108	26.60	1	4	4	12	3318	1758	64	27.46	1	0	6/32
Robinson,RT	29	49	5	1601	175	36.38	4	6	5	8	6	0	0	-	0	0	0/0
Roope,GRJ	21	32	4	860	77	30.71	0	7	3	35	172	76	0	-	0	0	0/2
Root,CF	3						0	0	0	0	642	194	8	24.25	0	0	4/84
Rose,BC	9	16	2	358	70	25.57	0	2	0	4							
Royle,VPFA	1	2	0	21	18	10.50	0	0	0	2	16	6	0	-	0	0	0/6
Rumsey,FE	5	5	3	30	21*	15.00	0	0	0	0	1145	461	17	27.11	0	0	4/25
Russell,CAG	10	18	2	910	140	56.87	5	2	2	8							
Russell,RC	49	77	15	1807	128	29.14	2	6	5	141/11							
Russell,WE	10	18	1	362	70	23.27	0	2	2	4	144	44	0	-	0	0	0/19
Salisbury,IDK	9	17	2	255	50	17.00	0	1	2	3	1773	1154	18	64.11	0	0	4/163
Sandham,A	14	23	0	879	325	38.21	2	3	3	4							
Schultz,SS	1	2	1	20	20	20.00	0	0	0	0	35	26	1	26.00	0	0	1/16

ENGLAND (cont.)

	BATTING AND FIELDING										BOWLING						
	Tests	I	N	Runs	HS	Avge	100	50	0's	C/S	Balls	Runs	Wks	Avge	5w	10w	BB
Scotton,WH	15	25	2	510	90	22.17	0	3	2	4	20	20	0	-	0	0	0/20
Selby,J	6	12	1	256	70	23.27	0	2	0	1/0							
Selvey,MWW	3	5	3	15	5*	7.50	0	0	1	1	492	343	6	57.16	0	0	4/41
Shackleton,D	7	13	7	113	42	18.83	0	0	0	1	2078	768	18	42.66	0	0	4/72
Sharp,J	3	6	2	188	105	47.00	1	1	0	1	183	111	3	37.00	0	0	3/67
Sharpe,JW	3	6	4	44	26	22.00	0	0	0	0	975	305	11	27.72	1	0	6/84
Sharpe,PJ	12	21	4	786	111	46.23	1	4	1	17							
Shaw,A	7	12	1	111	40	10.09	0	0	1	4	1099	285	12	23.75	1	0	5/38
Sheppard,Rev.DS	22	33	2	1172	119	37.80	3	6	2	12							
Sherwin,M	3	6	4	30	21*	15.00	0	0	1	5/2							
Shrewsbury,A	23	40	4	1277	164	35.47	3	4	1	29	12	2	0	-	0	0	0/2
Shuter,J	1	1	0	28	28	28.00	0	0	0	0							
Shuttleworth,K	5	6	0	46	21	7.66	0	0	1	1	1071	427	12	35.58	1	0	5/47
Sidebottom,A	1	1	0	2	2	2.00	0	0	0	0	112	65	1	65.00	0	0	1/65
Simpson,RT	27	45	3	1401	156*	33.35	4	6	6	5	45	22	2	11.00	0	0	2/4
Simpson-Hayward,GHT	5	8	1	105	29*	15.00	0	0	1	1	898	420	23	18.26	2	0	6/43
Sims,JM	4	4	0	16	12	4.00	0	0	1	6	887	480	11	43.63	1	0	5/73
Sinfield,RA	1	1	0	6	6	6.00	0	0	0	0	378	123	2	61.50	0	0	1/51
Slack,WN	3	6	0	81	52	13.50	0	1	2	3							
Smailes,TF	1	1	0	25	25	25.00	0	0	0	0	120	62	3	20.66	0	0	3/44
Small,GC	17	24	7	263	59	15.47	0	1	4	9	3921	1871	55	34.01	2	0	5/48
Smith,AC	6	7	3	118	69*	29.50	0	1	0	20/0							
Smith,CA	1	1	0	3	3	3.00	0	0	0	0	154	61	7	8.71	1	0	5/19
Smith,CIJ	5	10	0	102	27	10.20	0	0	2	1	930	393	15	26.20	1	0	5/16
Smith,CL	8	14	1	392	91	30.15	0	2	1	5	102	39	3	13.00	0	0	2/31
Smith,D	2	4	0	128	57	32.00	0	1	1	1							
Smith,DM	2	4	0	80	47	20.00	0	0	1	0							
Smith,DR	5	5	1	38	34	9.50	0	0	2	2	972	359	6	59.83	0	0	2/60
Smith,DV	3	4	1	25	16*	8.33	0	0	1	0	270	97	1	97.00	0	0	1/12
Smith,EJ	11	14	1	113	22	8.69	0	0	2	17/3							
Smith,H	1	1	0	7	7	7.00	0	0	0	1							
Smith,MJK	50	78	6	2278	121	31.63	3	11	11	53	214	128	1	128.00	0	0	1/10
Smith,RA	62	112	15	4240	175	43.71	9	28	8	39	72	17	0	-	0		0/6
Smith,TPB	4	5	0	33	24	6.60	0	0	0	1	538	319	3	106.33	0	0	2/172
Smithson,GA	2	3	0	70	35	23.33	0	0	1	0							
Snow,JA	49	71	14	772	73	13.54	0	2	17	16	12021	5387	202	26.66	8	1	7/40
Southerton,J	2	3	1	7	6	3.50	0	0	1	2	263	107	7	15.28	0	0	4/46
Spooner,RH	10	15	0	481	119	32.06	1	4	2	4							
Spooner,RT	7	14	1	354	92	27.23	0	3	3	10/2							
Stanyforth,RT	4	6	1	13	6*	2.60	0	0	1	7/2							
Staples,SJ	3	5	0	65	39	13.00	0	0	0	0	1149	435	15	29.00	0	0	3/50
Statham,JB	70	87	28	675	38	11.44	0	0	13	28	16056	6261	252	24.84	9	1	7/39
Steel,AG	13	20	3	600	148	35.29	2	0	1	5	1364	605	29	20.86	0	0	3/27
Steele,DS	8	16	0	673	106	42.06	1	5	1	7	88	39	2	19.50	0	0	1/1
Stephenson,JP	1	2	0	36	25	18.00	0	0	0	0							
Stevens,GTS	10	17	0	263	69	15.47	0	1	2	9	1186	648	20	32.40	2	1	5/90
Stevenson,GB	2	2	1	28	27*	28.00	0	0	0	0	312	183	5	36.60	0	0	3/111
Stewart,AJ	58	103	6	3935	190	40.56	8	20	3	70/5	20	13	0	-	0	0	0/5
Stewart,MJ	8	12	1	385	87	35.00	0	2	1	6							
Stoddart,AE	16	30	2	996	173	35.57	2	3	3	6	162	94	2	47.00	0	0	1/10
Storer,W	6	11	0	215	51	19.54	0	1	0	11/0	168	108	2	54.00	0	0	1/24
Street,GB	1	2	1	11	7*	11.00	0	0	0	0/1							
Strudwick,H	28	42	13	230	24	7.93	0	0	5	60/12							
Studd,CT	5	9	1	160	48	20.00	0	0	2	5	384	98	3	32.66	0	0	2/35

ENGLAND (cont.)	BATTING AND FIELDING										BOWLING						
	Tests	I	N	Runs	HS	Avge	100	50	0's	C/S	Balls	Runs	Wks	Avge	5w	10w	BB
Studd,GB	4	7	0	31	9	4.42	0	0	1	8							
Subba Row,R	13	22	1	984	137	46.85	3	4	0	6	6	2	0	-	0	0	0/2
Such,PM	8	11	4	65	14*	9.28	0	0	0	2	1697	805	22	36.59	1	0	6/67
Sugg,FH	2	2	0	55	31	27.50	0	0	0	0							
Sutcliffe,H	54	84	9	4555	194	60.73	16	23	2	23							
Swetman,R	11	17	2	254	65	16.93	0	1	2	24/2							
Tate,FW	1	2	1	9	5*	9.00	0	0	0	2	96	51	2	25.50	0	0	2/7
Tate,MW	39	52	5	1198	100*	25.48	1	5	5	11	12523	4055	155	26.16	7	1	6/42
Tattersall,R	16	17	7	50	10*	5.00	0	0	1	8	4228	1513	58	26.08	4	1	7/52
Tavare,CJ	31	56	2	1755	149	32.50	2	12	5	20	30	11	0	-	0	0	0/0
Taylor,JP	2	4	2	34	17*	17.00	0	0	1	0	288	156	3	52.00	0	0	1/18
Taylor,K	3	5	0	57	24	11.40	0	0	0	1	12	6	0	-	0	0	0/6
Taylor,LB	2	1	1	1	1*	0	0	0	0	1	381	178	4	44.50	0	0	2/34
Taylor,RW	57	83	12	1156	97	16.28	0	3	10	167/7	12	6	0	-	0	0	0/6
Tennyson,Hon.LH	9	12	1	345	74*	31.36	0	4	1	6	6	1	0	-	0	0	0/1
Terry,VP	2	3	0	16	8	5.33	0	0	0	2							
Thomas,JG	5	10	4	83	31*	13.83	0	0	3	0	774	504	10	50.40	0	0	4/70
Thompson,GJ	6	10	1	273	63	30.33	0	2	0	5	1367	638	23	27.73	0	0	4/50
Thomson,NI	5	4	1	69	39	23.00	0	0	1	3	1488	568	9	63.11	0	0	2/55
Thorpe,GP	32	59	5	2174	123	40.25	2	18	5	29	132	37	0	-	0	0	0/1
Titmus,FJ	53	76	11	1449	84*	22.29	0	10	4	35	15118	4931	153	32.22	7	0	7/79
Tolchard,RW	4	7	2	129	67	25.80	0	1	1	5							
Townsend,CL	2	3	0	51	38	17.00	0	0	0	0	140	75	3	25.00	0	0	3/50
Townsend,DCH	3	6	0	77	36	12.83	0	0	0	1	6	9	0	-	0	0	0/9
Townsend,LF	4	6	0	97	40	16.16	0	0	0	2	399	205	6	34.16	0	0	2/22
Tremlett,MF	3	5	2	20	18*	6.66	0	0	2	0	492	226	4	56.50	0	0	2/98
Trott,AE	2	4	0	23	16	5.75	0	0	1	0	474	198	17	11.64	1	0	5/49
Trueman,FS	67	85	14	981	39*	13.81	0	0	11	64	15178	6625	307	21.57	17	3	8/31
Tufnell,NC	1	1	0	14	14	14.00	0	0	0	0/1							
Tufnell,PCR	22	32	17	62	22*	4.13	0	0	9	10	6378	2671	68	39.27	4	1	7/47
Turnbull,MJL	9	13	2	224	61	20.36	0	1	1	1							
Tyldesley,GE	14	20	2	990	122	55.00	3	6	2	2	3	2	0	-	0	0	0/2
Tyldesley,JT	31	55	1	1661	138	30.75	4	9	4	16							
Tyldesley,RK	7	7	1	47	29	7.83	0	0	1	1	1615	619	19	32.57	0	0	3/50
Tylecote,EFS	6	9	1	152	66	19.00	0	1	4	5/5							
Tyler,EJ	1	1	0	0	0	0.00	0	0	1	0	145	65	4	16.25	0	0	3/49
Tyson,FH	17	24	3	230	37*	10.95	0	0	3	4	3452	1411	76	18.56	4	1	7/27
Ulyett,G	25	39	0	949	149	24.33	1	7	6	19	2627	1020	50	20.40	1	0	7/36
Underwood,DL	86	116	35	937	45*	11.56	0	0	19	44	21862	7674	297	25.83	17	6	8/51
Valentine,BH	7	9	2	454	136	64.85	2	1	0	2							
Verity,H	40	44	12	669	66*	20.90	0	3	4	30	11173	3510	144	24.37	5	2	8/43
Vernon,GF	1	2	1	14	11*	14.00	0	0	0	0							
Vine,J	2	3	2	46	36	46.00	0	0	0	0							
Voce,W	27	38	15	308	66	13.39	0	1	6	15	6360	2733	98	27.88	3	2	7/70
Waddington,A	2	4	0	16	7	4.00	0	0	1	1	276	119	1	119.00	0	0	1/35
Wainwright,E	5	9	0	132	49	14.66	0	0	0	2	127	73	0	-	0	0	0/11
Walker,PM	3	4	0	128	52	32.00	0	1	0	5	78	34	0	-	0	0	0/8
Walters,CF	11	18	3	784	102	52.26	1	7	0	6							
Ward,Alan	5	6	1	40	21	8.00	0	0	4	3	761	453	14	32.35	0	0	4/61
Ward,Albert	7	13	0	487	117	37.46	1	3	1	1							
Wardle,JH	28	41	8	653	66	19.78	0	2	5	12	6597	2080	102	20.39	5	1	7/36
Warner,PF	15	28	2	622	132*	23.92	1	3	4	3							
Warr,JJ	2	4	0	4	4	1.00	0	0	3	0	584	281	1	281.00	0	0	1/76
Warren,A	1	1	0	7	7	7.00	0	0	0	1	236	113	6	18.83	1	0	5/57

ENGLAND (cont.)	**BATTING AND FIELDING**										**BOWLING**						
	Tests	I	N	Runs	HS	Avge	100	50	0's	C/S	Balls	Runs	Wks	Avge	5w	10w	BB
Washbrook,C	37	66	6	2569	195	42.81	6	12	2	12	36	33	1	33.00	0	0	1/25
Watkin,SL	3	5	0	25	13	5.00	0	0	1	1	534	305	11	27.72	0	0	4/65
Watkins,AJ	15	24	4	810	137*	40.50	2	4	2	17	1364	554	11	50.36	0	0	3/20
Watkinson,M	4	6	1	167	82*	33.40	0	1	1	1	672	348	10	34.80	0	0	3/64
Watson,W	23	37	3	879	116	25.85	2	3	3	8							
Webbe,AJ	1	2	0	4	4	2.00	0	0	1	2							
Wellard,AW	2	4	0	47	38	11.75	0	0	1	2	456	237	7	33.85	0	0	4/81
Wells,AP	1	2	1	3	3*	3.00	0	0	0	0							
Wharton,A	1	2	0	20	13	10.00	0	0	0	0							
Whitaker,JJ	1	1	0	11	11	11.00	0	0	0	1							
White,C	6	10	0	157	51	15.70	0	1	1	3	565	334	8	41.75	0	0	3/18
White,DW	2	2	0	0	0	0.00	0	0	2	0	220	119	4	29.75	0	0	3/65
White,JC	15	22	9	239	29	18.38	0	0	1	6	4801	1581	49	32.26	3	1	8/126
Whysall,WW	4	7	0	209	76	29.85	0	2	0	7	16	9	0	-	0	0	0/9
Wilkinson,LL	3	2	1	3	2	3.00	0	0	0	0	573	271	7	38.71	0	0	2/12
Willey,P	26	50	6	1184	102*	26.90	2	5	2	3	1091	456	7	65.14	0	0	2/73
Williams,NF	1	1	0	38	38	38.00	0	0	0	0	246	148	2	74.00	0	0	2/148
Willis,RGD	90	128	55	840	28*	11.50	0	0	12	39	17357	8190	325	25.20	16	0	8/43
Wilson,CEM	2	4	1	42	18	14.00	0	0	0	0							
Wilson,D	6	7	1	75	42	12.50	0	0	0	1	1472	466	11	42.36	0	0	2/17
Wilson,ER	1	2	0	10	5	5.00	0	0	0	0	123	36	3	12.00	0	0	2/28
Wood,A	4	5	1	80	53	20.00	0	1	1	10/1							
Wood,B	12	21	0	454	90	21.61	0	2	1	6	98	50	0	-	0	0	0/2
Wood,GEC	3	2	0	7	6	3.50	0	0	0	5/1							
Wood,H	4	4	1	204	134*	68.00	1	1	0	2/1							
Wood,R	1	2	0	6	6	3.00	0	0	1	0							
Woods,SMJ	3	4	0	122	53	30.50	0	1	0	4	195	129	5	25.80	0	0	3/28
Woolley,FE	64	98	7	3283	154	36.07	5	23	13	64	6495	2815	83	33.91	4	1	7/76
Woolmer,RA	19	34	2	1059	149	33.09	3	2	4	10	546	299	4	74.75	0	0	1/8
Worthington,TS	9	11	0	321	128	29.18	1	1	4	8	633	316	8	39.50	0	0	2/19
Wright,CW	3	4	0	125	71	31.25	0	1	0	0							
Wright,DVP	34	39	13	289	45	11.11	0	0	7	10	8135	4224	108	39.11	6	1	7/105
Wyatt,RES	40	64	6	1839	149	31.70	2	12	6	16	1395	642	18	35.66	0	0	3/4
Wynward,EG	3	6	0	72	30	12.00	0	0	2	0	24	17	0	-	0	0	0/2
Yardley,NWD	20	34	2	812	99	25.37	0	4	2	14	1662	707	21	33.66	0	0	3/67
Young,HI	2	2	0	43	43	21.50	0	0	1	1	556	262	12	21.83	0	0	4/30
Young,JA	8	10	5	28	10*	5.60	0	0	3	5	2368	757	17	44.52	0	0	3/65
Young,RA	2	4	0	27	13	6.75	0	0	1	6/0							

SOUTH AFRICA	**BATTING AND FIELDING**										**BOWLING**						
	Tests	I	N	Runs	HS	Avge	100	50	0's	C/S	Balls	Runs	Wks	Avge	5w	10w	BB
Adams,PR	2	3	1	29	29	14.50	0	0	1	2	643	231	8	28.87	0	0	3/75
Adcock,NAT	26	39	12	146	24	5.40	0	0	9	4	6391	2195	104	21.10	5	0	6/43
Anderson,JH	1	2	0	43	32	21.50	0	0	0	1							
Ashley,WH	1	2	0	1	1	0.50	0	0	1	0	173	95	7	13.57	1	0	7/95
Bacher,A	12	22	1	679	73	32.33	0	6	1	10							
Balaskas,XC	9	13	1	174	122*	14.50	1	0	5	5	1572	806	22	36.63	1	0	5/49
Barlow,EJ	30	57	2	2516	201	45.74	6	15	3	35	3021	1362	40	34.05	1	0	5/85
Baumgartner,HV	1	2	0	19	16	9.50	0	0	0	1	166	99	2	49.50	0	0	2/99
Beaumont,R	5	9	0	70	31	7.77	0	0	2	2	6	0	0	-	0	0	0/0
Begbie,DW	5	7	0	138	48	19.71	0	0	0	2	160	130	1	130.00	0	0	1/38
Bell,AJ	16	23	12	69	26*	6.27	0	0	6	6	3342	1567	48	32.64	4	0	6/99
Bissett,GF	4	4	2	38	23	19.00	0	0	0	0	989	469	25	18.76	2	0	7/29

SOUTH AFRICA (cont.)

	BATTING AND FIELDING										BOWLING						
	Tests	I	N	Runs	HS	Avge	100	50	0's	C/S	Balls	Runs	Wks	Avge	5w	10w	BB
Bisset,M	3	6	2	103	35	25.75	0	0	0	2/1							
Blanckenberg,JM	18	30	7	455	59	19.78	0	2	2	9	3888	1817	60	30.28	4	0	6/76
Bland,KC	21	39	5	1669	144*	49.08	3	9	2	10	394	125	2	62.50	0	0	2/16
Bock,EG	1	2	2	11	9*	-	0	0	0	0	138	91	0	-	0	0	0/42
Bond,GE	1	1	0	0	0	0.00	0	0	1	0	16	16	0	-	0	0	0/16
Bosch,T	1	2	2	5	5*	-	0	0	0	0	297	104	3	34.66	0	0	2/61
Botten,JT	3	6	0	65	33	10.83	0	0	2	1	828	337	8	42.12	0	0	2/56
Brann,WH	3	5	0	71	50	14.20	0	1	1	2							
Briscoe,AW	2	3	0	33	16	11.00	0	0	0	1							
Bromfield,HD	9	12	7	59	21	11.80	0	0	3	13	1810	599	17	35.23	1	0	5/88
Brown,LS	2	3	0	17	8	5.66	0	0	0	0	318	189	3	63.00	0	0	1/30
Burger,CGD	2	4	1	62	37*	20.66	0	0	0	1							
Burke,SF	2	4	1	42	20	14.00	0	0	1	0	660	257	11	23.36	2	1	6/128
Buys,ID	1	2	1	4	4*	4.00	0	0	1	0	144	52	0	-	0	0	0/20
Cameron,HB	26	45	4	1239	90	30.21	0	10	3	39/12							
Campbell,T	5	9	3	90	48	15.00	0	0	1	7/1							
Carlstein,PR	8	14	1	190	42	14.61	0	0	1	3							
Carter,CP	10	15	5	181	45	18.10	0	0	3	2	1475	694	28	24.78	2	0	6/50
Catterall,RH	24	43	2	1555	120	37.92	3	11	3	12	342	162	7	23.14	0	0	3/15
Chapman,HW	2	4	1	39	17	13.00	0	0	0	1	126	104	1	104.00	0	0	1/51
Cheetham,JE	24	43	6	883	89	23.86	0	5	1	13	6	2	0	-	0	0	0/2
Chevalier,GA	1	2	1	0	0*	0.00	0	0	1	1	253	100	5	20.00	0	0	3/68
Christy,JAJ	10	18	0	618	103	34.33	1	5	1	3	138	92	2	46.00	0	0	1/15
Chubb,GWA	5	9	3	63	15*	10.50	0	0	0	0	1425	577	21	27.47	2	0	6/51
Cochran,JAK	1	1	0	4	4	4.00	0	0	0	0	138	47	0	-	0	0	0/47
Coen,SK	2	4	2	101	41*	50.50	0	0	0	1	12	7	0	-	0	0	0/7
Commaille,JMM	12	22	1	355	47	16.90	0	0	1	1							
Commins,JB	3	6	1	125	45	25.00	0	0	1	2							
Conyngham,DP	1	2	2	6	3*	0	0	0	0	1	366	103	2	51.50	0	0	1/40
Cook,FJ	1	2	0	7	7	3.50	0	0	1	0							
Cook,SJ	3	6	0	107	43	17.83	0	0	1	0							
Cooper,AHC	1	2	0	6	6	3.00	0	0	1	1							
Cox,JL	3	6	1	17	12*	3.40	0	0	3	1	576	245	4	61.25	0	0	2/74
Cripps,G	1	2	0	21	18	10.50	0	0	0	0	15	23	0	-	0	0	0/23
Crisp,RJ	9	13	1	123	35	10.25	0	0	5	3	1428	747	20	37.35	1	0	5/99
Cronje,WJ	27	46	5	1516	135	36.97	5	4	4	10	1639	512	8	64.00	0	0	2/17
Cullinan,DJ	19	31	2	1095	102	37.75	1	9	2	13							
Curnow,SH	7	14	0	168	47	12.00	0	0	0	5							
Dalton,EL	15	24	2	698	117	31.72	2	3	1	5	864	490	12	40.83	0	0	4/59
Davies,EQ	5	8	3	9	3	1.80	0	0	2	0	768	481	7	68.71	0	0	4/75
Dawson,OC	9	15	1	293	55	20.92	0	1	1	10	1294	578	10	57.80	0	0	2/57
Deane,HG	17	27	2	628	93	25.12	0	3	1	8							
de Villiers,PS	14	19	5	230	66*	16.42	0	1	2	8	4009	1733	70	24.75	4	2	6/43
Dixon,CD	1	2	0	0	0	0.00	0	0	2	1	240	118	3	39.33	0	0	2/62
Donald,AA	25	32	17	233	33	15.53	0	0	5	6	5781	2835	114	24.86	6	2	8/71
Dower,RR	1	2	0	9	9	4.50	0	0	1	2							
Draper,RG	2	3	0	25	15	8.33	0	0	0	0							
Duckworth,CAR	2	4	0	28	13	7.00	0	0	0	3							
Dumbrill,R	5	10	0	153	36	15.30	0	0	0	3	816	336	9	37.33	0	0	4/30
Duminy,JP	3	6	0	30	12	5.00	0	0	1	2	60	39	1	39.00	0	0	1/17
Dunell,OR	2	4	1	42	26*	14.00	0	0	1	1							
Du Preez,JH	2	2	0	0	0	0.00	0	0	2	2	144	51	3	17.00	0	0	2/22
Du Toit,JF	1	2	2	2	2*	0	0	0	0	1	85	47	1	47.00	0	0	1/47
Dyer,DV	3	6	0	96	62	16.00	0	1	0	0							

SOUTH AFRICA (cont.)				**BATTING AND FIELDING**								**BOWLING**						
	Tests	I	N	Runs	HS	Avge	100	50	0's	C/S	Balls	Runs	Wks	Avge	5w	10w	BB
Eksteen,CE	6	10	2	87	22	10.87	0	0	1	4	1458	447	8	55.87	0	0	3/12
Elgie,MK	3	6	0	75	56	12.50	0	1	2	4	66	46	0	-	0	0	0/18
Endean,WR	28	52	4	1630	162*	33.95	3	8	3	41							
Farrer,WS	6	10	2	221	40	27.62	0	0	0	2	0						
Faulkner,GA	25	47	4	1754	204	40.79	4	8	2	20	4227	2180	82	26.58	4	0	7/84
Fellows-Smith,JP	4	8	2	166	35	27.66	0	0	0	2	114	61	0	-	0	0	0/13
Fichardt,CG	2	4	0	15	10	3.75	0	0	1	2							
Finlason,CE	1	2	0	6	6	3.00	0	0	1	0	12	7	0	-	0	0	0/7
Floquet,CE	1	2	1	12	11*	12.00	0	0	0	0	48	24	0	-	0	0	0/24
Francis,HH	2	4	0	39	29	9.75	0	0	0	1							
Francois,CM	5	9	1	252	72	31.50	0	1	0	5	684	225	6	37.50	0	0	3/23
Frank,CN	3	6	0	236	152	39.33	1	0	0	0							
Frank,WHB	1	2	0	7	5	3.50	0	0	0	0	58	52	1	52.00	0	0	1/52
Fuller,ERH	7	9	1	64	17	8.00	0	0	2	3	1898	668	22	30.36	1	0	5/66
Fullerton,GM	7	13	0	325	88	25.00	0	3	1	10/2							
Funston,KJ	18	33	1	824	92	25.75	0	5	2	7							
Gamsy,D	2	3	1	39	30*	19.50	0	0	0	5/0							
Gleeson,RA	1	2	1	4	3	4.00	0	0	0	2							
Glover,GK	1	2	1	21	18*	21.00	0	0	0	0	65	28	1	28.00	0	0	1/28
Goddard,TL	41	78	5	2516	112	34.46	1	18	4	48	11736	3226	123	26.22	5	0	6/53
Gordon,N	5	6	2	8	7*	2.00	0	0	3	1	1966	807	20	40.35	2	0	5/103
Graham,R	2	4	0	6	4	1.50	0	0	2	2	240	127	3	42.33	0	0	2/22
Grieveson,RE	2	2	0	114	75	57.00	0	1	0	7/3							
Griffin,GM	2	4	0	25	14	6.25	0	0	1	0	432	192	8	24.00	0	0	4/87
Hall,AE	7	8	2	11	5	1.83	0	0	4	4	2361	886	40	22.15	3	1	7/63
Hall,GG	1	1	0	0	0	0.00	0	0	1	0	186	94	1	94.00	0	0	1/94
Halliwell,EA	8	15	0	188	57	12.53	0	1	3	9/2							
Halse,CG	3	3	3	30	19*	0	0	0	0	1	587	260	6	43.33	0	0	3/50
Hands,PAM	7	12	0	300	83	25.00	0	2	2	3	37	18	0	-	0	0	0/1
Hands,RHM	1	2	0	7	7	3.50	0	0	1	0							
Hanley,MA	1	1	0	0	0	0.00	0	0	1	0	232	88	1	88.00	0	0	1/57
Harris,TA	3	5	1	100	60	25.00	0	1	0	1							
Hartigan,GPD	5	10	0	114	51	11.40	0	1	3	0	252	141	1	141.00	0	0	1/72
Harvey,RL	2	4	0	51	28	12.75	0	0	0	0							
Hathorn,CMH	12	20	1	325	102	17.10	1	0	1	5							
Hearne,F	4	8	0	121	30	15.12	0	0	2	2	62	40	2	20.00	0	0	2/40
Hearne,GAL	3	5	0	59	28	11.80	0	0	2	3							
Heine,PS	14	24	3	209	31	9.95	0	0	3	8	3890	1455	58	25.08	4	0	6/58
Henry,O	3	3	0	53	34	17.66	0	0	0	2	427	189	3	63.00	0	0	2/56
Hime,CFW	1	2	0	8	8	4.00	0	0	1	0	55	31	1	31.00	0	0	1/20
Hudson,AC	25	44	2	1444	163	34.38	3	10	4	24							
Hutchinson,P	2	4	0	14	11	3.50	0	0	2	3							
Ironside,DEJ	3	4	2	37	13	18.50	0	0	0	1	985	275	15	18.33	1	0	5/51
Irvine,BL	4	7	0	353	102	50.42	1	2	0	2							
Jack,SD	2	2	0	7	7	3.50	0	0	1	1	462	196	8	24.50	0	0	4/69
Johnson,CL	1	2	0	10	7	5.00	0	0	0	1	140	57	0	-	0	0	0/57
Kallis,JH	2	2	0	8	7	4.00	0	0	0	1	24	2	0	-	0	0	0/2
Keith,HJ	8	16	1	318	73	21.20	0	2	3	9	108	63	0	-	0	0	0/19
Kempis,GA	1	2	1	0	0*	0.00	0	0	1	0	168	76	4	19.00	0	0	3/53
Kirsten,G	20	35	2	1265	110	38.33	1	9	1	18	125	135	2	67.50	0	0	1/0
Kirsten,PN	12	22	2	626	104	31.30	1	4	2	8	54	30	0	-	0	0	0/5
Kotze,JJ	3	5	0	2	2	0.40	0	0	4	3	413	243	6	40.50	0	0	3/64
Kuiper,AP	1	2	0	34	34	17.00	0	0	1	1							
Kuys,F	1	2	0	26	26	13.00	0	0	1	0	60	31	2	15.50	0	0	2/31

SOUTH AFRICA (cont.)				BATTING AND FIELDING										BOWLING			
	Tests	I	N	Runs	HS	Avge	100	50	0's	C/S	Balls	Runs	Wks	Avge	5w	10w	BB
Lance,HR	13	22	1	591	70	28.14	0	5	1	7	948	479	12	39.91	0	0	3/30
Langton,ABC	15	23	4	298	73*	15.68	0	2	5	8	4199	1827	40	45.67	1	0	5/58
Lawrence,GB	5	8	0	141	43	17.62	0	0	2	2	1334	512	28	18.28	2	0	8/53
Le Roux,FL	1	2	0	1	1	0.50	0	0	1	0	54	24	0	-	0	0	0/5
Lewis,PT	1	2	0	0	0	0.00	0	0	2	0							
Lindsay,DT	19	31	1	1130	182	37.66	3	5	2	57/2							
Lindsay,JD	3	5	2	21	9*	7.00	0	0	2	4/1							
Lindsay,NV	1	2	0	35	29	17.50	0	0	0	1							
Ling,WVS	6	10	0	168	38	16.80	0	0	3	1	18	20	0	-	0	0	0/20
Llewellyn,CB	15	28	1	544	90	20.14	0	4	6	7	2292	1421	48	29.60	4	1	6/92
Lundie,EB	1	2	1	1	1	1.00	0	0	0	0	286	107	4	26.75	0	0	4/101
Macaulay,MJ	1	2	0	33	21	16.50	0	0	0	0	276	73	2	36.50	0	0	1/10
McCarthy,CN	15	24	15	28	5	3.11	0	0	6	6	3499	1510	36	41.94	2	0	6/43
McGlew,DJ	34	64	6	2440	255*	42.06	7	10	4	18	32	23	0	-	0	0	0/7
McKinnon,AH	8	13	7	107	27	17.83	0	0	0	1	2546	925	26	35.57	0	0	4/128
McLean,RA	40	73	3	2120	142	30.28	5	10	11	23	4	1	0	-	0	0	0/1
McMillan,BM	23	35	6	1236	113	42.62	2	7	1	28	4241	1789	60	29.81	0	0	4/65
McMillan,Q	13	21	4	306	50*	18.00	0	1	4	8	2021	1243	36	34.52	2	0	5/66
Mann,NBF	19	31	1	400	52	13.33	0	1	4	3	5796	1920	58	33.10	1	0	6/59
Mansell,PNF	13	22	2	355	90	17.75	0	2	3	15	1506	736	11	66.90	0	0	3/58
Markham,LA	1	1	0	20	20	20.00	0	0	0	0	104	72	1	72.00	0	0	1/34
Marx,WFE	3	6	0	125	36	20.83	0	0	1	0	228	144	4	36.00	0	0	3/85
Matthews,CR	18	25	6	348	62*	18.31	0	1	4	4	3932	1502	52	28.88	2	0	5/42
Meintjes,DJ	2	3	0	43	21	14.33	0	0	0	3	246	115	6	19.16	0	0	3/38
Melle,MG	7	12	4	68	17	8.50	0	0	1	4	1667	851	26	32.73	2	0	6/71
Melville,A	11	19	2	894	189	52.58	4	3	2	8							
Middleton,J	6	12	5	52	22	7.42	0	0	2	1	1064	442	24	18.41	2	0	5/51
Mills,C	1	2	0	25	21	12.50	0	0	0	2	140	83	2	41.50	0	0	2/83
Milton,WH	3	6	0	68	21	11.33	0	0	0	1	79	48	2	24.00	0	0	1/5
Mitchell,B	42	80	9	3471	189*	48.88	8	21	3	56	2519	1380	27	51.11	1	0	5/87
Mitchell,F	3	6	0	28	12	4.66	0	0	1	0							
Morkel,DPB	16	28	1	663	88	24.55	0	4	3	13	1704	821	18	45.61	0	0	4/93
Murray,ARA	10	14	1	289	109	22.23	1	1	1	3	2374	710	18	39.44	0	0	4/169
Nel,JD	6	11	0	150	38	13.63	0	0	1	1							
Newberry,C	4	8	0	62	16	7.75	0	0	1	3	558	268	11	24.36	0	0	4/72
Newson,ES	3	5	1	30	16	7.50	0	0	0	3	874	265	4	66.25	0	0	2/58
Nicholson,F	4	8	1	76	29	10.85	0	0	4	3/0							
Nicolson,JFW	3	5	0	179	78	35.80	0	1	0	0	24	17	0	-	0	0	0/5
Norton,NO	1	2	0	9	7	4.50	0	0	0	0	90	47	4	11.75	0	0	4/47
Nourse,AD	34	62	7	2960	231	53.81	9	14	3	12	20	9	0	-	0	0	0/0
Nourse,AW	45	83	8	2234	111	29.78	1	15	3	43	3234	1553	41	37.87	0	0	4/25
Nupen,EP	17	31	7	348	69	14.50	0	2	5	9	4159	1788	50	35.76	5	1	6/46
Osche,AE	2	4	0	16	8	4.00	0	0	0	0							
Osche,AL	3	4	1	11	4*	3.66	0	0	0	1	649	362	10	36.20	0	0	4/79
O'Linn,S	7	12	1	297	98	27.00	0	2	0	4							
Owen-Smith,HG	5	8	2	252	129	42.00	1	1	0	4	156	113	0	-	0	0	0/3
Palm,AW	1	2	0	15	13	7.50	0	0	0	1							
Parker,GM	2	4	2	3	2*	1.50	0	0	2	0	366	273	8	34.12	1	0	6/152
Parkin,DC	1	2	0	6	6	3.00	0	0	1	1	130	82	3	270.33	0	0	3/82
Partridge,JT	11	12	5	73	13*	10.42	0	0	0	6	3684	1373	44	31.20	3	0	7/91
Pearse,COC	3	6	0	55	31	9.16	0	0	2	1	144	106	3	35.33	0	0	3/56
Pegler,SJ	16	28	5	356	35*	15.47	0	0	6	5	2989	1572	47	33.44	2	0	7/65
Pithey,AJ	17	27	1	819	154	31.50	1	4	2	3	12	5	0	-	0	0	0/5
Pithey,DB	8	12	1	138	55	12.54	0	1	1	6	1424	577	12	48.08	1	0	6/58

SOUTH AFRICA (cont.)				**BATTING AND FIELDING**							**BOWLING**						
	Tests	I	N	Runs	HS	Avge	100	50	0's	C/S	Balls	Runs	Wks	Avge	5w	10w	BB
Plimsoll,JB	1	2	1	16	8*	16.00	0	0	0	0	237	143	3	47.66	0	0	3/128
Pollock,PM	28	41	13	607	75*	21.67	0	2	3	9	6522	2806	116	24.18	9	1	6/38
Pollock,RG	23	41	4	2256	274	60.97	7	11	1	17	414	204	4	51.00	0	0	2/50
Pollock,SM	5	6	1	133	36*	26.60	0	0	0	2	899	377	16	23.56	1	0	5/32
Poore,RM	3	6	0	76	20	12.66	0	0	0	3	9	4	1	4.00	0	0	1/4
Pothecary,JE	3	4	0	26	12	6.50	0	0	0	2	828	354	9	39.33	0	0	4/58
Powell,AW	1	2	0	16	11	8.00	0	0	0	2	20	10	1	10.00	0	0	1/10
Prince,CFH	1	2	0	6	5	3.00	0	0	0	0							
Pringle,MW	4	6	2	67	33	16.75	0	0	1	0	652	270	5	54.00	0	0	2/62
Procter,MJ	7	10	1	226	48	25.11	0	0	1	4	1514	616	41	15.02	1	0	6/73
Promnitz,HLE	2	4	0	14	5	3.50	0	0	0	2	528	161	8	20.12	1	0	5/58
Quinn,NA	12	18	3	90	28	6.00	0	0	1	1	2922	1145	35	32.71	1	0	6/92
Reid,N	1	2	0	17	11	8.50	0	0	0	0	126	63	2	31.50	0	0	2/63
Rhodes,JN	27	43	2	1223	101*	29.82	1	7	3	14	12	5	0	-	0	0	0/0
Richards,AR	1	2	0	6	6	3.00	0	0	1	0							
Richards,BA	4	7	0	508	140	72.57	2	2	0	3	72	26	1	26.00	0	0	1/12
Richards,WHM	1	2	0	4	4	2.00	0	0	1	0							
Richardson,DJ	28	41	3	1006	109	26.47	1	7	4	107/0							
Robertson,JB	3	6	1	51	17	10.20	0	0	0	2	738	321	6	53.50	0	0	3/143
Rose-Innes,A	2	4	0	14	13	3.50	0	0	2	2	128	89	5	17.80	1	0	5/43
Routledge,TW	4	8	0	72	24	9.00	0	0	1	2							
Rowan,AMB	15	23	6	290	41	17.05	0	0	3	7	5193	2084	54	38.59	4	0	5/68
Rowan,EAB	26	50	5	1965	236	43.66	3	12	4	14	19	7	0	-	0	0	0/0
Rowe,GA	5	9	3	26	13*	4.33	0	0	3	4	998	456	15	30.40	1	0	5/115
Rushmere,MW	1	2	0	6	3	3.00	0	0	0	0							
Samuelson,SV	1	2	0	22	15	11.00	0	0	0	1	108	64	0	-	0	0	0/64
Schultz,BN	7	6	2	6	6	1.50	0	0	3	1	1421	600	30	20.00	2	0	5/48
Schwarz,RO	20	35	8	374	61	13.85	0	1	6	18	2639	1417	55	25.76	2	0	6/47
Seccull,AW	1	2	1	23	17*	23.00	0	0	0	1	60	37	2	18.50	0	0	2/37
Seymour,MA	7	10	3	84	36	12.00	0	0	3	2	1458	588	9	65.33	0	0	3/80
Shalders,WA	12	23	1	355	42	16.13	0	0	4	3	48	6	1	6.00	0	0	1/6
Shepstone,GH	2	4	0	38	21	9.50	0	0	1	2	115	47	0	-	0	0	0/8
Sherwell,PW	13	22	4	427	115	23.72	1	1	1	20/16							
Siedle,IJ	18	34	0	977	141	28.73	1	5	3	7	19	7	1	7.00	0	0	1/7
Sinclair,JH	25	47	1	1069	106	23.23	3	3	7	9	3598	1996	63	31.68	1	0	6/26
Smith,CJE	3	6	1	106	45	21.20	0	0	0	2							
Smith,FW	3	6	1	45	12	9.00	0	0	1	2							
Smith,VI	9	16	6	39	11*	3.90	0	0	4	3	1655	769	12	64.08	0	0	4/143
Snell,RP	5	8	1	95	48	13.57	0	0	1	1	1025	538	19	28.31	0	0	4/74
Snooke,SD	1	1	0	0	0	0.00	0	0	1	2							
Snooke,SJ	26	46	1	1008	103	22.40	1	5	1	24	1620	702	35	20.05	1	1	8/70
Solomon,WRT	1	2	0	4	2	2.00	0	0	0	1							
Stewart,RB	1	2	0	13	9	6.50	0	0	0	2							
Steyn,PJR	3	6	0	127	46	21.16	0	0	0	0							
Stricker,LA	13	24	0	342	48	14.25	0	0	5	3	174	105	1	105.00	0	0	1/36
Susskind,MJ	5	8	0	268	65	33.50	0	4	0	1							
Symcox,PL	6	7	0	164	50	23.42	0	1	0	0	989	426	9	47.33	0	0	3/75
Taberer,HM	1	1	0	2	2	2.00	0	0	0	0	60	47	1	48.00	0	0	1/25
Tancred,AB	2	4	1	87	29	29.00	0	0	0	2							
Tancred,LJ	14	26	1	530	97	21.20	0	2	5	3							
Tancred,VM	1	2	0	25	18	12.50	0	0	0	0							
Tapscott,GL	1	2	0	5	4	2.50	0	0	0	1							
Tapscott,LE	2	3	1	58	50*	29.00	0	1	0	0	12	2	0	-	0	0	0/2
Tayfield,HJ	37	60	9	862	75	16.90	0	2	5	26	13568	4405	170	25.91	14	2	9/113

SOUTH AFRICA (cont.) — **BATTING AND FIELDING** / **BOWLING**

	Tests	I	N	Runs	HS	Avge	100	50	0's	C/S	Balls	Runs	Wks	Avge	5w	10w	BB
Taylor,AI	1	2	0	18	12	9.00	0	0	0	0							
Taylor,D	2	4	0	85	36	21.25	0	0	0	0							
Taylor,HW	42	76	4	2936	176	40.77	7	17	2	19	342	156	5	31.20	0	0	3/15
Theunissen,NH	1	2	1	2	2*	2.00	0	0	1	0	80	51	0	-	0	0	0/51
Thornton,PG	1	1	1	1	1*	0	0	0	0	1	24	20	1	20.00	0	0	1/20
Tomlinson,DS	1	1	0	9	9	9.00	0	0	0	0	60	38	0	-	0	0	0/38
Traicos,AJ	3	4	2	8	5*	4.00	0	0	1	4	470	207	4	51.75	0	0	2/70
Trimborn,PHJ	4	4	2	13	11*	6.50	0	0	1	7	747	257	11	23.36	0	0	3/12
Tuckett,L	9	14	3	131	40*	11.90	0	0	3	9	2104	980	19	51.57	2	0	5/68
Tuckett,LR	1	2	1	0	0*	0.00	0	0	1	2	120	69	0	-	0	0	0/24
Twentyman Jones,PS	1	2	0	0	0	0.00	0	0	2	0							
Van der Bijl,PGV	5	9	0	460	125	41.11	1	2	0	1							
Van der Merwe,EA	2	4	1	27	19	9.00	0	0	1	3/0							
Van der Merwe,PL	15	23	2	533	76	25.38	0	3	3	11	79	22	1	22.00	0	0	1/6
Van Ryneveld,CB	19	33	6	724	83	26.81	0	3	2	14	1554	671	17	39.47	0	0	4/67
Varnals,GD	3	6	0	97	23	16.16	0	0	0	0	12	2	0	-	0	0	0/2
Viljoen,KG	27	50	2	1365	124	28.43	2	9	5	5	48	23	0	-	0	0	0/10
Vincent,CL	25	38	12	526	60	20.23	0	2	4	27	5851	2631	84	31.32	3	0	6/51
Vintcent,CH	3	6	0	26	9	4.33	0	0	1	1	369	193	4	48.25	0	0	3/8
Vogler,AEE	15	26	6	340	65	17.00	0	2	4	20	2764	1455	64	22.73	5	1	7/94
Wade,HF	10	18	2	327	40*	20.43	0	0	4	4							
Wade,WW	11	19	1	511	125	28.38	1	3	3	15/2							
Waite,JHB	50	86	7	2405	134	30.44	4	16	9	124/17							
Walker,KA	2	3	0	11	10	3.66	0	0	1	3	495	197	6	32.83	0	0	4/63
Ward,TA	23	42	9	459	64	13.90	0	2	5	19/13							
Watkins,JC	15	27	1	612	92	23.53	0	3	2	12	2805	816	29	28.13	0	0	4/22
Wesley,C	3	5	0	49	35	9.80	0	0	2	1							
Wessels,KC	16	29	2	1027	118	38.03	2	6	2	12							
Westcott,RJ	5	9	0	166	62	18.44	0	1	2	0	32	22	0	-	0	0	0/22
White,GC	17	31	2	872	147	30.06	2	4	3	10	498	301	9	33.44	0	0	4/47
Willoughby,JT	2	4	0	8	5	2.00	0	0	2	0	275	159	6	26.50	0	0	2/37
Wimble,CS	1	2	0	0	0	0.00	0	0	2	0							
Winslow,PL	5	9	0	186	108	20.66	1	0	1	1							
Wynne,OE	6	12	0	219	50	18.25	0	1	0	3							
Zulch,JW	16	32	2	985	150	32.83	2	4	0	4	24	28	0	-	0	0	0/2

WEST INDIES — **BATTING AND FIELDING** / **BOWLING**

	Tests	I	N	Runs	HS	Avge	100	50	0's	C/S	Balls	Runs	Wks	Avge	5w	10w	BB
Achong,EE	6	11	1	81	22	8.10	0	0	2	6	918	378	8	47.25	0	0	2/64
Adams,JC	24	37	9	1851	208*	66.10	5	8	0	27	1120	594	14	42.42	1	0	5/17
Alexander,FCM	25	38	6	961	108	30.03	1	7	5	85/5							
Ali,Imtiaz	1	1	1	1	1*	-	0	0	0	0	204	89	2	44.50	0	0	2/37
Ali,Inshan	12	18	2	172	25	10.75	0	0	3	7	3718	1621	34	47.67	1	0	5/59
Allan,DW	5	7	1	75	40*	12.50	0	0	0	15/3							
Allen,IBA	2	2	2	5	4*	0	0	0	0	1	282	180	5	36.00	0	0	2/69
Ambrose,CEL	61	87	19	850	53	12.50	0	1	13	13	14319	5657	266	21.26	14	3	8/45
Arthurton,KLT	33	50	5	1382	157*	30.71	2	8	8	22	473	183	1	183.00	0	0	1/17
Asgarali,NR	2	4	0	62	29	15.50	0	0	1	0							
Atkinson,DS	22	35	6	922	219	31.79	1	5	4	11	5201	1647	47	35.04	3	0	7/53
Atkinson,ES	8	9	1	126	37	15.75	0	0	3	2	1634	589	25	23.56	1	0	5/42
Austin,RA	2	2	0	22	20	11.00	0	0	0	2	6	5	0	-	0	0	0/5
Bacchus,SFAF	19	30	0	782	250	26.06	1	3	7	17	6	3	0	-	0	0	0/3
Baichan,L	3	6	2	184	105*	46.00	1	0	0	2							

WEST INDIES (cont.)				**BATTING AND FIELDING**									**BOWLING**				
	Tests	I	N	Runs	HS	Avge	100	50	0's	C/S	Balls	Runs	Wks	Avge	5w	10w	BB
Baptiste,EAE	10	11	1	233	87*	23.30	0	1	1	2	1362	562	16	35.12	0	0	3/31
Barrett,AG	6	7	1	40	19	6.66	0	0	1	0	1612	603	13	46.38	0	0	3/43
Barrow,I	11	19	2	276	105	16.23	1	0	3	17/5							
Bartlett,EL	5	8	1	131	84	18.71	0	1	1	2							
Benjamin,KCG	21	27	7	184	40*	9.20	0	0	6	1	4000	2257	80	28.21	4	1	6/66
Benjamin,WKM	21	26	1	433	85	17.32	0	2	5	12	3711	1648	61	27.01	0	0	4/46
Best,CA	8	13	1	342	164	28.50	1	1	1	8	30	21	0	-	0	0	0/2
Betancourt,N	1	2	0	52	39	26.00	0	0	0	0							
Binns,AP	5	8	1	64	27	9.14	0	0	3	14/3							
Birkett,LS	4	8	0	136	64	17.00	0	1	1	4	126	71	1	71.00	0	0	1/16
Bishop,IR	26	39	9	356	31	11.86	0	0	5	3	5742	2565	117	21.92	6	0	6/40
Boyce,KD	21	30	3	657	95*	24.33	0	4	4	5	3501	1801	60	30.01	2	1	6/77
Browne,CO	5	8	3	137	34	27.40	0	0	0	23/1							
Browne,CR	4	8	1	176	70*	25.14	0	1	2	1	840	288	6	48.00	0	0	2/72
Butcher,BF	44	78	6	3104	209*	43.11	7	16	3	15	256	90	5	18.00	1	0	5/34
Butler,LS	1	1	0	16	16	16.00	0	0	0	0	240	151	2	75.50	0	0	2/151
Butts,CG	7	8	1	108	38	15.42	0	0	1	2	1554	595	10	59.50	0	0	4/73
Bynoe,MR	4	6	0	111	48	18.50	0	0	0	4	30	5	1	5.00	0	0	1/5
Camacho,GS	11	22	0	640	87	29.09	0	4	1	4	18	12	0	-	0	0	0/12
Cameron,FJ	5	7	1	151	75*	25.16	0	1	1	0	786	278	3	92.66	0	0	2/74
Cameron,JH	2	3	0	6	5	2.00	0	0	1	0	232	88	3	29.33	0	0	3/66
Campbell,SL	11	18	1	885	208	52.05	1	6	1	14							
Carew,GM	4	7	1	170	107	28.33	1	0	1	1	18	2	0	-	0	0	0/2
Carew,MC	19	36	3	1127	109	34.15	1	5	1	13	1174	437	8	54.62	0	0	1/11
Challenor,G	3	6	0	101	46	16.83	0	0	2	0							
Chanderpaul,S	11	16	4	667	82	55.58	0	8	0	6	618	332	2	166.00	0	0	1/63
Chang,HS	1	2	0	8	6	4.00	0	0	0	0							
Christiani,CM	4	7	2	98	32*	19.60	0	0	1	6/1							
Christiani,RJ	22	37	3	896	107	26.35	1	4	0	19/2	234	108	3	36.00	0	0	3/52
Clarke,CB	3	4	1	3	2	1.00	0	0	1	0	456	261	6	43.50	0	0	3/59
Clarke,ST	11	16	5	172	35*	15.63	0	0	2	2	2477	1170	42	27.85	1	0	5/126
Constantine,LN	18	33	0	635	90	19.24	0	4	4	28	3583	1746	58	30.10	2	0	5/75
Croft,CEH	27	37	22	158	33	10.53	0	0	6	8	6165	2913	125	23.30	3	0	8/29
Cuffy,CE	2	3	1	1	1	0.50	0	0	1	0	314	190	5	38.00	0	0	4/80
Cummins,AC	5	6	1	98	50	19.60	0	1	1	1	618	342	8	42.75	0	0	4/54
Da Costa,OC	5	9	1	153	39	19.12	0	0	1	5	372	175	3	58.33	0	0	1/14
Daniel,WW	10	11	4	46	11	6.57	0	0	2	4	1754	910	36	25.27	1	0	5/39
Davis,BA	4	8	0	245	68	30.62	0	3	0	1							
Davis,CA	15	29	5	1301	183	54.20	4	4	1	4	894	330	2	165.00	0	0	1/27
Davis,WW	15	17	4	202	77	15.53	0	1	2	10	2773	1472	45	32.71	0	0	4/19
De Caires,FI	3	6	0	232	80	38.66	0	2	1	1	12	9	0	-	0	0	0/9
Depeiza,CC	5	8	2	187	122	31.16	1	0	1	7/4	30	15	0	-	0	0	0/3
Dewdney,DT	9	12	5	17	5*	2.42	0	0	3	0	1641	807	21	38.42	1	0	5/21
Dhanraj,R	4	4	0	17	9	4.25	0	0	0	1	1087	595	8	74.37	0	0	2/49
Dowe,UG	4	3	2	8	5*	8.00	0	0	0	3	1014	534	12	44.50	0	0	4/69
Dujon,PJL	81	115	11	3322	139	31.94	5	16	8	267/5							
Edwards,RM	5	8	1	65	22	9.28	0	0	2	0	1311	626	18	34.77	1	0	5/84
Ferguson,W	8	10	3	200	75	28.57	0	2	1	11	2568	1165	34	34.26	3	1	6/92
Fernandes,MP	2	4	0	49	22	12.25	0	0	1	0							
Findlay,TM	10	16	3	212	44*	16.30	0	0	1	19/2							
Foster,MLC	14	24	5	580	125	30.52	1	1	0	3	1776	600	9	66.66	0	0	2/41
Francis,GN	10	18	4	81	19*	5.78	0	0	4	7	1619	763	23	33.17	0	0	4/40
Frederick,MC	1	2	0	30	30	15.00	0	0	1	0							
Fredericks,RC	59	109	7	4334	169	42.49	8	26	7	62	1187	548	7	78.28	0	0	1/12

WEST INDIES (cont.)				**BATTING AND FIELDING**										**BOWLING**			
	Tests	I	N	Runs	HS	Avge	100	50	0's	C/S	Balls	Runs	Wks	Avge	5w	10w	BB
Fuller,RL	1	1	0	1	1	1.00	0	0	0	0	48	12	0	-	0	0	0/2
Furlonge,HA	3	5	0	99	64	19.80	0	1	1	0							
Ganteaume,AG	1	1	0	112	112	112.00	1	0	0	0							
Garner,J	58	68	14	672	60	12.44	0	1	17	42	13169	5433	259	20.97	7	0	6/56
Gaskin,BBM	2	3	0	17	10	5.66	0	0	1	1	474	158	2	79.00	0	0	1/15
Gibbs,GL	1	2	0	12	12	6.00	0	0	1	1	24	7	0	-	0	0	0/2
Gibbs,LR	79	109	39	488	25	6.97	0	0	15	52	27115	8989	309	29.09	18	2	8/38
Gibson,OD	1	2	0	43	29	21.50	0	0	0	0	204	132	2	66.00	0	0	2/81
Gilchrist,R	13	14	3	60	12	5.45	0	0	4	4	3227	1521	57	26.68	1	0	6/55
Gladstone,G	1	1	1	12	12*	-	0	0	0	0	300	189	1	189.00	0	0	1/139
Goddard,JDC	27	39	11	859	83*	30.67	0	4	5	22	2931	1050	33	31.81	1	0	5/31
Gomes,HA	60	91	11	3171	143	39.63	9	13	5	18	2401	930	15	62.00	0	0	2/20
Gomez,GE	29	46	5	1243	101	30.31	1	8	5	18	5236	1590	58	27.41	1	1	7/55
Grant,GC	12	21	5	413	71*	25.81	0	3	1	10	24	18	0	-	0	0	0/1
Grant,RS	7	11	1	220	77	22.00	0	1	3	13	986	353	11	32.06	0	0	3/68
Gray,AH	5	8	2	48	12*	8.00	0	0	2	6	888	377	22	17.13	0	0	4/39
Greenidge,AE	6	10	0	222	69	22.20	0	2	2	5							
Greenidge,CG	108	185	16	7558	226	44.72	19	34	11	96	26	4	0	-	0	0	0/0
Greenidge,GA	5	9	2	209	50	29.85	0	1	1	3	156	75	0	-	0	0	0/2
Grell,MG	1	2	0	34	21	17.00	0	0	0	1	30	17	0	-	0	0	0/7
Griffith,CC	28	42	10	530	54	16.56	0	1	5	16	5631	2683	94	28.54	5	0	6/36
Griffith,HC	13	23	5	91	18	5.05	0	0	6	4	2663	1243	44	28.25	2	0	6/103
Guillen,SC	5	6	2	104	54	26.00	0	1	1	9/2							
Hall,WW	48	66	14	818	50*	15.73	0	2	7	11	10421	5066	192	26.38	9	1	7/69
Harper,RA	25	32	3	535	74	18.44	0	3	5	36	3615	1291	46	28.06	1	0	6/57
Haynes,DL	116	202	25	7487	184	42.29	18	39	10	65	18	8	1	8.00	0	0	1/2
Headley,GA	22	40	4	2190	270*	60.83	10	5	2	14	398	230	0	-	0	0	0/0
Headley,RGA	2	4	0	62	42	15.50	0	0	0	2							
Hendriks,JL	20	32	8	447	64	18.62	0	2	4	42/5							
Hoad,ELG	4	8	0	98	36	12.25	0	0	1	1							
Holder,VA	40	59	11	682	42	14.20	0	0	7	16	9095	3627	109	33.27	3	0	6/28
Holding,MA	60	76	10	910	73	13.78	0	6	15	22	12680	5898	249	23.68	13	2	8/92
Holford,DAJ	24	39	5	768	105*	22.58	1	3	3	18	4816	2009	51	39.39	1	0	5/23
Holt,JK	17	31	2	1066	166	36.75	2	5	2	8	30	20	1	20.00	0	0	1/20
Hooper,CL	52	87	7	2548	178*	31.85	5	12	10	57	6066	2672	51	52.39	2	0	5/40
Howard,AB	1						0	0	0	0	372	140	2	70.00	0	0	2/140
Hunte,CC	44	78	6	3245	260	45.06	8	13	5	16	270	110	2	55.00	0	0	1/17
Hunte,EAC	3	6	1	166	58	33.20	0	2	0	5/0							
Hylton,LG	6	8	2	70	19	11.66	0	0	0	1	965	418	16	26.12	0	0	4/27
Johnson,HHH	3	4	0	38	22	9.50	0	0	1	0	789	238	13	18.30	2	1	5/41
Johnson,TF	1	1	1	9	9*	0	0	0	0	1	240	129	3	43.00	0	0	2/53
Jones,CEL	4	7	0	63	19	9.00	0	0	0	3	102	11	0	-	0	0	0/2
Jones,PE	9	11	2	47	10*	5.22	0	0	1	4	1842	751	25	30.04	1	0	5/85
Julien,BD	24	34	6	866	121	30.92	2	3	0	14	4542	1868	50	37.36	1	0	5/57
Jumadeen,RR	12	14	10	84	56	21.00	0	1	2	4	3140	1141	29	39.34	0	0	4/72
Kallicharran,AI	66	109	10	4399	187	44.43	12	21	10	51	406	158	4	39.50	0	0	2/16
Kanhai,RB	79	137	6	6227	256	47.53	15	28	7	50/0	183	85	0	-	0	0	0/1
Kentish,ESM	2	2	1	1	1*	0	0	0	1	1	540	178	8	22.25	1	0	5/49
King,CL	9	16	3	418	100*	32.15	1	2	3	5	582	282	3	94.00	0	0	1/30
King,FM	14	17	3	116	21	8.28	0	0	4	5	2869	1159	29	39.96	1	0	5/74
King,LA	2	4	0	41	20	10.25	0	0	1	2	476	154	9	17.11	1	0	5/46
Lambert,CB	1	2	0	53	39	26.50	0	0	0	2	4	4	1	4.00	0	0	1/4
Lara,BC	33	55	2	3197	375	60.32	7	17	3	45	42	12	0	-	0	0	0/0
Lashley,PD	4	7	0	159	49	22.71	0	0	1	4	18	1	1	1.00	0	0	1/1

WEST INDIES (cont.)				**BATTING AND FIELDING**									**BOWLING**				
	Tests	I	N	Runs	HS	Avge	100	50	0's	C/S	Balls	Runs	Wks	Avge	5w	10w	BB
Legall,RA	4	5	0	50	23	10.00	0	0	0	8/1							
Lewis,DM	3	5	2	259	88	86.33	0	3	0	8/0							
Lloyd,CH	110	175	14	7515	242*	46.67	19	39	4	90	1716	622	10	62.20	0	0	2/13
Logie,AL	52	78	9	2470	130	35.79	2	16	8	57	7	4	0	-	0	0	0/0
McMorris,EDAS	13	21	0	564	125	26.85	1	3	1	5							
McWatt,CA	6	9	2	202	54	28.85	0	2	0	9/1	24	16	1	16.00	0	0	1/16
Madray,IS	2	3	0	3	2	1.00	0	0	1	2	210	108	0	-	0	0	0/12
Marshall,MD	81	107	11	1810	92	18.85	0	10	15	25	17585	7876	376	20.94	22	4	7/22
Marshall,NE	1	2	0	8	8	4.00	0	0	1	0	279	62	2	31.00	0	0	1/22
Marshall,RE	4	7	0	143	30	20.42	0	0	1	1	52	15	0	-	0	0	0/3
Martin,FR	9	18	1	486	123*	28.58	1	0	1	2	1346	619	8	77.37	0	0	3/91
Martindale,EA	10	14	3	58	22	5.27	0	0	3	5	1605	804	37	21.72	3	0	5/22
Mattis,EH	4	5	0	145	71	29.00	0	1	1	3	36	14	0	-	0	0	0/4
Mendonça,IL	2	2	0	81	78	40.50	0	1	0	8/2							
Merry,CA	2	4	0	34	13	8.50	0	0	0	1							
Miller,R	1	1	0	23	23	23.00	0	0	0	0	96	28	0	-	0	0	0/28
Moseley,EA	2	4	0	36	26	9.00	0	0	1	1	522	261	6	43.50	0	0	2/70
Mudie,GH	1	1	0	5	5	5.00	0	0	0	0	174	40	3	13.33	0	0	3/23
Murray,DA	19	31	3	601	84	21.46	0	3	3	57/5							
Murray,DL	62	96	9	1993	91	22.90	0	11	7	181/8							
Murray,JR	24	31	3	712	101*	25.42	1	2	6	86/2							
Nanan,R	1	2	0	16	8	8.00	0	0	0	2	216	91	4	22.75	0	0	2/37
Neblett,JM	1	2	1	16	11*	16.00	0	0	0	0	216	75	1	75.00	0	0	1/44
Noreiga,JM	4	5	2	11	9	30.62	0	0	1	2	1322	493	17	29.00	2	0	9/95
Nunes,RK	4	8	0	245	92	30.62	0	2	1	2/0							
Nurse,SM	29	54	1	2523	258	47.60	6	10	3	21	42	7	0	-	0	0	0/0
Padmore,AL	2	2	1	8	8*	8.00	0	0	1	0	474	135	1	135.00	0	0	1/36
Pairaudeau,BH	13	21	0	454	115	21.61	1	3	3	6	6	3	0	-	0	0	0/3
Parry,DR	12	20	3	381	65	22.41	0	3	3	4	1909	936	23	40.69	1	0	5/15
Passailaigue,CC	1	2	1	46	44	46.00	0	0	0	3	12	15	0	-	0	0	0/15
Patterson,BP	28	38	16	145	21*	6.59	0	0	8	5	4829	2875	93	30.91	5	0	5/24
Payne,TRO	1	1	0	5	5	5.00	0	0	0	5/0							
Philip,N	9	15	5	297	47	29.70	0	0	1	5	1820	1041	28	37.17	0	0	4/48
Pierre,LR	1						0	0	0	0	42	28	0	-	0	0	0/9
Rae,AF	15	24	2	1016	109	46.18	4	4	1	10							
Ramadhin,S	43	58	14	361	44	8.20	0	0	14	9	13939	4579	158	28.98	10	1	7/49
Richards,IVA	121	182	12	8540	291	50.23	24	45	10	122	5170	1964	32	61.37	0	0	2/17
Richardson,RB	86	146	12	5949	194	44.39	16	27	8	90	66	18	0	-	0	0	0/0
Rickards,KR	2	3	0	104	67	34.66	0	1	0	0							
Roach,CA	16	32	1	952	209	30.70	2	6	6	5	222	103	2	51.50	0	0	1/18
Roberts,AME	47	62	11	762	68	14.94	0	3	6	9	11355	5174	202	25.61	11	2	7/54
Roberts,AT	1	2	0	28	28	14.00	0	0	1	0							
Rodriguez,WV	5	7	0	96	50	13.71	0	1	1	3	573	374	7	53.42	0	0	3/51
Rowe,LG	30	49	2	2047	302	43.55	7	7	2	17	86	44	0	-	0	0	0/1
St Hill,EL	2	4	0	18	12	4.50	0	0	1	0	558	221	3	73.66	0	0	2/110
St Hill,WH	3	6	0	117	38	19.50	0	0	0	1	12	9	0	-	0	0	0/9
Samuels,RG	2	4	1	141	125	47.00	1	0	0	4							
Scarlett,RO	3	4	1	54	29*	18.00	0	0	0	2	804	209	2	104.50	0	0	1/46
Scott,APH	1	1	0	5	5	5.00	0	0	0	0	264	140	0	-	0	0	0/52
Scott,OC	8	13	3	171	35	17.10	0	0	1	0	1405	925	22	42.04	1	0	5/266
Sealey,BJ	1	2	0	41	29	20.50	0	0	0	0	30	10	1	10.00	0	0	1/10
Sealy,JED	11	19	2	478	92	28.11	0	3	2	6/1	156	94	3	31.33	0	0	2/7
Shepherd,JN	5	8	0	77	32	9.62	0	0	2	4	1445	479	19	25.21	1	0	5/104
Shillingford,GC	7	8	1	57	25	8.14	0	0	1	2	1181	537	15	35.80	0	0	3/63

WEST INDIES (cont.)				BATTING AND FIELDING										BOWLING			
	Tests	I	N	Runs	HS	Avge	100	50	0's	C/S	Balls	Runs	Wks	Avge	5w	10w	BB
Shillingford,IT	4	7	0	218	120	31.14	1	0	0	1							
Shivnarine,S	8	14	1	379	63	29.15	0	4	2	6	336	167	1	167.00	0	0	1/13
Simmons,PV	24	44	2	1000	110	23.81	1	4	3	23	474	181	3	60.33	0	0	2/34
Singh,CK	2	3	0	11	11	3.66	0	0	2	2	506	166	5	33.20	0	0	2/28
Small,JA	3	6	0	79	52	13.16	0	1	2	3	366	184	3	61.33	0	0	2/67
Small,MA	2	1	1	3	3*	-	0	0	0	0	270	153	4	38.25	0	0	3/40
Smith,CW	5	10	1	222	55	24.66	0	1	0	4/1							
Smith,OG	26	42	0	1331	168	31.69	4	6	8	9	4431	1625	48	33.85	1	0	5/90
Sobers,GS	93	160	21	8032	365*	57.78	26	30	12	109	21599	7999	235	34.03	6	0	6/73
Solomon,JS	27	46	7	1326	100*	34.00	1	9	7	13	702	268	4	67.00	0	0	1/20
Stayers,SC	4	4	1	58	35*	19.33	0	0	1	0	636	364	9	40.44	0	0	3/65
Stollmeyer,JB	32	56	5	2159	160	42.33	4	12	2	20	990	507	13	39.00	0	0	3/32
Stollmeyer,VH	1	1	0	96	96	96.00	0	1	0	0							
Taylor,J	3	5	3	4	4*	2.00	0	0	2	0	672	273	10	27.30	1	0	5/109
Thompson,PIC	1	1	0	1	1	1.00	0	0	0	0	132	135	4	33.75	0	0	2/58
Trim,J	4	5	1	21	12	5.25	0	0	2	2	794	291	18	16.16	1	0	5/34
Valentine,AL	36	51	21	141	14	4.70	0	0	12	13	12953	4215	139	30.32	8	2	8/104
Valentine,VA	2	4	1	35	19*	11.66	0	0	1	0	288	104	1	104.00	0	0	1/55
Walcott,CL	44	74	7	3798	220	56.68	15	14	1	53/11	1194	408	11	37.09	0	0	3/50
Walcott,LA	1	2	1	40	24	40.00	0	0	0	0	48	32	1	32.00	0	0	1/17
Walsh,CA	82	108	33	716	30*	9.54	0	0	20	12	17578	7739	309	25.04	11	2	7/37
Watson,CD	7	6	1	12	5	2.40	0	0	2	1	1458	724	19	38.10	0	0	4/62
Weekes,ED	48	81	5	4455	207	58.61	15	19	6	49	122	77	1	77.00	0	0	1/8
Weekes,KH	2	3	0	173	137	57.66	1	0	0	0							
White,AW	2	4	1	71	57*	23.66	0	1	0	1	491	152	3	50.66	0	0	2/34
Wight,CV	2	4	1	67	23	22.33	0	0	0	0	30	6	0	-	0	0	0/6
Wight,GL	1	1	0	21	21	21.00	0	0	0	0							
Wiles,CA	1	2	0	2	2	1.00	0	0	1	0							
Willett,ET	5	8	3	74	26	14.80	0	0	2	0	1326	482	11	43.81	0	0	3/33
Williams,AB	7	12	0	469	111	39.08	2	1	1	5							
Williams,D	3	6	0	21	15	3.50	0	0	3	15/1							
Williams,EAV	4	6	0	113	72	18.83	0	1	1	2	796	241	9	26.77	0	0	3/51
Williams,SC	12	19	2	386	62	22.70	0	1	2	14							
Wishart,KL	1	2	0	52	52	26.00	0	1	1	0							
Worrell,FMM	51	87	9	3860	261	49.48	9	22	11	43	7141	2672	69	38.72	2	0	7/70

NEW ZEALAND				BATTING AND FIELDING										BOWLING			
	Tests	I	N	Runs	HS	Avge	100	50	0's	C/S	Balls	Runs	Wks	Avge	5w	10w	BB
Alabaster,JC	21	34	6	272	34	9.71	0	0	2	7	3992	1863	49	38.02	0	0	4/46
Alcott,CFW	6	7	2	113	33	22.60	0	0	0	3	1206	541	6	90.16	0	0	2/102
Allott,GI	2	2	1	0	0*	0.00	0	0	1	0	396	209	4	52.25	0	0	3/56
Anderson,RW	9	18	0	423	92	23.50	0	3	1	1							
Anderson,WM	1	2	0	5	4	2.50	0	0	0	1							
Andrews,B	2	3	2	22	17	22.00	0	0	0	1	256	154	2	77.00	0	0	2/40
Astle,NJ	4	8	0	367	125	45.87	2	1	0	6	30	10	0	-	0	0	0/3
Badcock,FT	7	9	2	137	64	19.57	0	2	3	1	1608	610	16	38.12	0	0	4/80
Barber,RT	1	2	0	17	12	8.50	0	0	0	1							
Bartlett,GA	10	18	1	263	40	15.47	0	0	4	8	1768	792	24	33.00	1	0	6/38
Barton,PT	7	14	0	285	109	20.35	1	1	1	4							
Beard,DD	4	7	2	101	31	20.20	0	0	0	2	806	302	9	33.55	0	0	3/22
Beck,JEF	8	15	0	394	99	26.26	0	3	1	0							
Bell,W	2	3	3	21	21*	0	0	0	0	1	491	235	2	117.50	0	0	1/54
Bilby,GP	2	4	0	55	28	13.75	0	0	0	3							

NEW ZEALAND (cont.)	**BATTING AND FIELDING**										**BOWLING**						
	Tests	I	N	Runs	HS	Avge	100	50	0's	C/S	Balls	Runs	Wks	Avge	5w	10w	BB
Blain,TE	11	20	3	456	78	26.82	0	1	2	19/2							
Blair,RW	19	34	6	189	64*	6.75	0	1	12	5	3525	1515	43	35.23	0	0	4/85
Blunt,RC	9	13	1	330	96	27.50	0	1	1	5	936	472	12	39.33	0	0	3/17
Bolton,BA	2	3	0	59	33	19.66	0	0	1	1							
Boock,SL	30	41	8	207	37	6.27	0	0	10	14	6598	2564	74	34.64	4	0	7/87
Bracewell,BP	6	12	2	24	8	2.40	0	0	5	1	1036	585	14	41.78	0	0	3/110
Bracewell,JG	41	60	11	1001	110	20.42	1	4	13	31	8403	3653	102	35.81	4	1	6/32
Bradburn,GE	5	9	2	105	30*	15.00	0	0	0	4	616	336	5	67.20	0	0	3/134
Bradburn,WP	2	4	0	62	32	15.50	0	0	0	2							
Brown,VR	2	3	1	51	36*	25.50	0	0	1	3	342	176	1	176.00	0	0	1/17
Burgess,MG	50	92	6	2684	119*	31.20	5	14	5	34	498	212	6	35.33	0	0	3/23
Burke,C	1	2	0	4	3	2.00	0	0	0	0	66	30	2	15.00	0	0	2/30
Burtt,TB	10	15	3	252	42	21.00	0	0	1	2	2593	1170	33	35.45	3	0	6/162
Butterfield,LA	1	2	0	0	0	0.00	0	0	2	0	78	24	0	-	0	0	0/24
Cairns,BL	43	65	8	928	64	16.28	0	2	7	30	10628	4279	130	32.91	6	1	7/74
Cairns,CL	16	26	0	675	120	25.96	1	4	2	7	3226	1782	51	34.94	2	0	6/52
Cameron,FJ	19	30	20	116	27*	11.60	0	0	4	2	4570	1849	62	29.82	3	0	5/34
Cave,HB	19	31	5	229	22*	8.80	0	0	5	8	4074	1467	34	43.14	0	0	4/21
Chapple,ME	14	27	1	497	76	19.11	0	3	2	10	248	84	1	84.00	0	0	1/24
Chatfield,EJ	43	54	33	180	21*	8.57	0	0	11	7	10360	3958	123	32.17	3	1	6/73
Cleverley,DC	2	4	3	19	10*	19.00	0	0	0	0	222	130	0	-	0	0	0/51
Collinge,RO	35	50	13	533	68*	14.40	0	2	9	10	7689	3393	116	29.25	3	0	6/63
Colquhoun,IA	2	4	2	1	1*	0.50	0	0	2	4/0							
Coney,JV	52	85	14	2668	174*	37.57	3	16	3	64	2835	966	27	35.77	0	0	3/28
Congdon,BE	61	114	7	3448	176	32.22	7	19	9	44	5620	2154	59	36.50	1	0	5/65
Cowie,J	9	13	4	90	45	10.00	0	0	3	3	2028	969	45	21.53	4	1	6/40
Cresswell,GF	3	5	3	14	12*	7.00	0	0	1	0	650	292	13	22.46	1	0	6/168
Cromb,IB	5	8	2	123	51*	20.50	0	1	1	1	960	442	8	55.25	0	0	3/113
Crowe,JJ	39	65	4	1601	128	26.24	3	6	6	41	18	9	0	-	0	0	0/0
Crowe,MD	77	131	11	5444	299	45.36	17	18	9	70	1377	676	14	48.28	0	0	2/25
Cunis,RS	20	31	8	295	51	12.82	0	1	6	1	4250	1887	51	37.00	1	0	6/76
D'Arcy,JW	5	10	0	136	33	13.60	0	0	0	0							
Davis,HT	1	2	2	0	0*	-	0	0	0	0	126	93	1	93.00	0	0	1/93
de Groen,RP	5	10	4	45	22	7.50	0	0	1	0	1060	505	11	45.90	0	0	3/40
Dempster,CS	10	15	4	723	136	65.72	2	5	0	2	5	10	0	-	0	0	0/10
Dempster,EW	5	8	2	106	47	17.66	0	0	2	1	544	219	2	109.50	0	0	1/24
Dick,AE	17	30	4	370	50*	14.23	0	1	4	47/4							
Dickinson,GR	3	5	0	31	11	6.20	0	0	0	3	451	245	8	30.62	0	0	3/66
Donnelly,MP	7	12	1	582	206	52.90	1	4	2	7	30	20	0	-	0	0	0/20
Doull,SB	11	18	2	210	31*	13.12	0	0	5	8	2013	1077	33	32.63	2	0	5/66
Dowling,GT	39	77	3	2306	239	31.16	3	11	6	23	36	19	1	19.00	0	0	1/19
Dunning,JA	4	6	1	38	19	7.60	0	0	2	2	830	493	5	98.60	0	0	2/35
Edgar,BA	39	68	4	1958	161	30.59	3	12	7	14	18	3	0	-	0	0	0/3
Edwards,GN	8	15	0	377	55	25.13	0	3	2	7							
Emery,RWG	2	4	0	46	28	11.50	0	0	0	0	46	52	2	26.00	0	0	2/52
Fisher,FE	1	2	0	23	14	11.50	0	0	0	0	204	78	1	78.00	0	0	1/78
Fleming,SP	20	34	1	1143	92	34.63	0	8	2	19							
Foley,H	1	2	0	4	2	2.00	0	0	0	0							
Franklin,TJ	21	37	1	828	101	23.00	1	4	2	8							
Freeman,DL	2	2	0	2	1	1.00	0	0	0	0	240	169	1	169.00	0	0	1/91
Gallichan,N	1	2	0	32	30	16.00	0	0	0	0	264	113	3	37.66	0	0	3/99
Gedye,SG	4	8	0	193	55	24.12	0	2	0	0							
Germon,LK	8	13	3	268	49	26.80	0	0	1	21/1							
Gillespie,SR	1	1	0	28	28	28.00	0	0	0	0	162	79	1	79.00	0	0	1/79

NEW ZEALAND (cont.)	BATTING AND FIELDING										BOWLING						
	Tests	I	N	Runs	HS	Avge	100	50	0's	C/S	Balls	Runs	Wks	Avge	5w	10w	BB
Gray,EJ	10	16	0	248	50	15.50	0	1	0	6	2076	886	17	52.11	0	0	3/73
Greatbatch,MJ	39	67	5	1981	146*	31.95	3	10	9	27	6	0	0	-	0	0	0/0
Guillen,SC	3	6	0	98	41	16.33	0	0	2	4/1							
Guy,JW	12	23	2	440	102	20.95	1	3	3	2							
Hadlee,DR	26	42	5	530	56	14.32	0	1	9	8	4883	2389	71	33.64	0	0	4/30
Hadlee,RJ	86	134	19	3124	151*	27.16	2	15	12	39	21918	9611	431	22.29	36	9	9/52
Hadlee,WA	11	19	1	543	116	30.16	1	2	1	6							
Harford,NS	8	15	0	229	93	15.26	0	2	4	0							
Harford,RI	3	5	2	7	6	2.33	0	0	1	11/0							
Harris,CZ	7	14	1	160	56	12.30	0	1	4	3	570	295	5	59.00	0	0	2/75
Harris,PGZ	9	18	1	378	101	22.23	1	1	3	6	42	14	0	-	0	0	0/14
Harris,RM	2	3	0	31	13	10.33	0	0	0	0							
Hart,MN	14	24	4	353	45	17.65	0	0	3	8	3086	1438	29	49.58	1	0	5/77
Hartland,BR	9	18	0	303	52	16.83	0	1	3	5							
Haslam,MJ	4	2	1	4	3	4.00	0	0	0	22	493	245	2	122.50	0	0	1/33
Hastings,BF	31	56	6	1510	117*	30.20	4	7	6	23	22	9	0	-	0	0	0/3
Hayes,JA	15	22	7	73	19	4.86	0	0	4	3	2675	1217	30	40.56	0	0	4/36
Henderson,M	1	2	1	8	6	8.00	0	0	0	1	90	64	2	32.00	0	0	2/38
Horne,PA	4	7	0	71	27	10.14	0	0	2	3							
Hough,KW	2	3	2	62	31*	62.00	0	0	0	1	462	175	6	29.16	0	0	3/79
Howarth,GP	47	83	5	2531	147	32.44	6	11	7	29	614	271	3	90.33	0	0	1/13
Howarth,HJ	30	42	18	291	61	12.12	0	1	7	33	8833	3178	86	36.95	2	0	5/34
James,KC	11	13	2	52	14	4.72	0	0	4	11/5							
Jarvis,TW	13	22	1	625	182	29.76	1	2	6	3	12	3	0	-	0	0	0/0
Jones,AH	39	74	8	2922	186	44.27	7	11	2	25	328	194	1	194.00	0	0	1/40
Kennedy,RJ	4	5	1	28	22	7.00	0	0	2	0	636	380	6	63.33	0	0	3/28
Kerr,JL	7	12	1	212	59	19.27	0	1	2	4							
Kuggeleijn,CM	2	4	0	7	7	1.75	0	0	3	1	97	67	1	67.00	0	0	1/50
Larsen,GR	8	13	4	127	26*	14.11	0	0	2	5	1961	689	24	28.70	0	0	3/57
Latham,RT	4	7	0	219	119	31.28	1	0	1	6	18	6	0	-	0		0/6
Lees,WK	21	37	4	778	152	23.57	1	1	4	52/7	5	4	0	-	0	0	0/4
Leggatt,IB	1	1	0	0	0	0.00	0	0	1	2	24	6	0	-	0	0	0/6
Leggatt,JG	9	18	2	351	61	21.93	0	2	1	0							
Lissette,AF	2	4	2	2	1*	1.00	0	0	2	1	288	124	3	41.33	0	0	2/73
Loveridge,GR	1	1	1	4	4*	-	0	0	0	0							
Lowry,TC	7	8	0	223	80	27.87	0	2	2	8	12	5	0	-	0	0	0/5
McEwan,PE	4	7	1	96	40*	16.00	0	0	1	5	36	13	0	-	0	0	0/6
MacGibbon,AR	26	46	5	814	66	19.85	0	3	7	13	5659	2160	70	30.85	1	0	5/64
McGirr,HM	2	1	0	51	51	51.00	0	1	0	0	180	115	1	115.00	0	0	1/65
McGregor,SN	25	47	2	892	111	19.82	1	3	5	9							
McLeod,EG	1	2	1	18	16	18.00	0	0	0	0	12	5	0	-	0	0	0/5
McMahon,TG	5	7	4	7	4*	2.33	0	0	2	7/1							
McRae,DAN	1	2	0	8	8	4.00	0	0	1	0	84	44	0	-	0	0	0/44
Matheson,AM	2	1	0	7	7	7.00	0	0	0	2	282	136	2	68.00	0	0	2/7
Meale,T	2	4	0	21	10	5.25	0	0	0	0							
Merritt,WE	6	8	1	73	19	10.42	0	0	1	2	936	617	12	51.41	0	0	4/104
Meuli,EM	1	2	0	38	23	19.00	0	0	0	0							
Milburn,BD	3	3	2	8	4*	8.00	0	0	1	6/2							
Miller,LSM	13	25	0	346	47	13.84	0	0	5	1	2	1	0	-	0	0	0/1
Mills,JE	7	10	1	241	117	26.77	1	0	2	1							
Moir,AM	17	30	8	327	41*	14.86	0	0	5	2	2650	1418	28	50.64	2	0	6/155
Moloney,DAR	3	6	0	156	64	26.00	0	1	1	3	12	9	0	-	0	0	0/9
Mooney,FLH	14	22	2	343	46	17.15	0	0	1	22/8	8	0	0	-	0	0	0/0
Morgan,RW	20	34	1	734	97	22.24	0	5	5	12	1114	609	5	121.80	0	0	1/16

NEW ZEALAND (cont.)	Tests	I	N	Runs	HS	Avge	100	50	0's	C/S	Balls	Runs	Wks	Avge	5w	10w	BB
				BATTING AND FIELDING							**BOWLING**						
Morrison,BD	1	2	0	10	10	5.00	0	0	1	1	186	129	2	64.50	0	0	2/129
Morrison,DK	47	69	24	359	42	7.97	0	0	24	14	10016	5445	157	34.68	10	0	7/89
Morrison,JFM	17	29	0	656	117	22.62	1	3	4	9	264	71	2	35.50	0	0	2/52
Motz,RC	32	56	3	612	60	11.54	0	3	12	9	7034	3148	100	31.48	5	0	6/63
Murray,BAG	13	26	1	598	90	23.92	0	5	1	21	6	0	1	0.00	0	0	1/0
Murray,DJ	8	16	1	303	52	20.20	0	1	3	6							
Nash,DJ	14	21	6	236	56	15.73	0	1	3	7	2772	1308	44	29.72	2	1	6/76
Newman,JA	3	4	0	33	19	8.25	0	0	0	0	425	254	2	127.00	0	0	2/76
O'Sullivan,DR	11	21	4	158	23*	9.29	0	0	2	2	2744	1221	18	67.83	1	0	5/148
Overton,GWF	3	6	1	8	3*	1.60	0	0	2	1	729	258	9	28.66	0	0	3/65
Owens,MB	8	12	6	16	8*	2.66	0	0	5	3	1074	585	17	34.41	0	0	4/99
Page,ML	14	20	0	492	104	24.60	1	2	1	6	379	231	5	46.20	0	0	2/21
Parker,JM	36	63	2	1498	121	24.55	3	5	4	30	40	24	1	24.00	0	0	1/24
Parker,NM	3	6	0	89	40	14.83	0	0	0	2							
Parore,AC	27	46	6	1072	100*	26.80	1	6	2	60/2							
Patel,DN	31	54	6	1061	99	22.10	0	5	5	11	5651	2748	65	42.27	3	0	6/50
Petherick,PJ	6	11	4	34	13	4.85	0	0	1	4	1305	685	16	42.81	0	0	3/90
Petrie,EC	14	25	5	258	55	12.90	0	1	2	25							
Playle,WR	8	15	0	151	65	10.06	0	1	3	4							
Pocock,BA	6	12	0	135	34	11.25	0	0	3	1	12	10	0	-	0	0	0/10
Pollard,V	32	59	7	1266	116	24.34	2	7	4	19	4421	1853	40	46.32	0	0	3/3
Poore,MB	14	24	1	355	45	15.43	0	0	6	1	788	367	9	40.77	0	0	2/28
Priest,MW	1	1	0	26	26	26.00	0	0	0	0	72	26	1	26.00	0	0	1/26
Pringle,C	14	21	4	175	30	10.29	0	0	6	3	2985	1389	30	46.30	1	1	7/52
Puna,N	3	5	3	31	18*	15.50	0	0	0	1	480	240	4	60.00	0	0	2/40
Rabone,GO	12	20	2	562	107	31.22	1	2	0	5	1385	635	16	39.68	1	0	6/68
Redmond,RE	1	2	0	163	107	81.50	1	1	0	0							
Reid,JF	19	31	3	1296	180	46.28	6	2	4	9	18	7	0	-	0	0	0/0
Reid,JR	58	108	5	3428	142	33.28	6	22	5	43/1	7725	2835	85	33.35	1	0	6/60
Roberts,ADG	7	12	1	254	84*	23.09	0	1	2	4	440	182	4	45.50	0	0	1/12
Roberts,AW	5	10	1	248	66*	27.55	0	3	0	4	459	209	7	29.85	0	0	4/101
Robertson,GK	1	1	0	12	12	12.00	0	0	0	0	144	91	1	91.00	0	0	1/91
Rowe,CG	1	2	0	0	0	0.00	0	0	2	1							
Rutherford,KR	56	99	8	2463	107*	27.06	3	18	17	31	256	161	1	161.00	0	0	1/38
Scott,RH	1	1	0	18	18	18.00	0	0	0	0	138	74	1	74.00	0	0	1/74
Scott,VJ	10	17	1	458	84	28.62	0	3	1	7	18	14	0	-	0	0	0/5
Shrimpton,MJF	10	19	0	265	46	13.94	0	0	6	2	257	158	5	31.60	0	0	3/35
Sinclair,BW	21	40	1	1148	138	29.43	3	3	5	8	60	32	2	16.00	0	0	2/32
Sinclair,IM	2	4	1	25	18*	8.33	0	0	2	1	233	120	1	120.00	0	0	1/79
Smith,FB	4	6	1	237	96	47.40	0	2	0	1							
Smith,HD	1	1	0	4	4	4.00	0	0	0	0	120	113	1	113.00	0	0	1/113
Smith,IDS	63	88	17	1815	173	25.56	2	6	7	168/8	18	5	0	-	0	0	0/5
Snedden,CA	1						0	0	0	0	96	46	0	-	0	0	0/46
Snedden,MC	25	30	8	327	33*	14.86	0	0	6	7	4775	2199	58	37.91	1	0	5/68
Sparling,JT	11	20	2	229	50	12.72	0	1	2	3	708	327	5	65.40	0	0	1/9
Spearman,CM	5	10	0	352	112	35.20	1	1	2	4							
Stirling,DA	6	9	2	108	26	15.42	0	0	0	1	902	601	13	46.23	0	0	4/88
Su'a,ML	13	18	5	165	44	12.69	0	0	5	8	2843	1377	36	38.25	2	0	5/73
Sutcliffe,B	42	76	8	2727	230*	40.10	5	15	5	20	538	344	4	86.00	0	0	2/38
Taylor,BR	30	50	6	898	124	20.40	2	2	8	10	6334	2953	111	26.60	4	0	7/74
Taylor,DD	3	5	0	159	77	31.80	0	1	0	2							
Thomson,K	2	4	1	94	69	31.33	0	1	1	0	21	9	1	9.00	0	0	1/9
Thomson,SA	19	35	4	958	120*	30.90	1	5	3	7	1990	953	19	50.15	0	0	3/63
Tindill,EWT	5	9	1	73	37*	9.12	0	0	1	6/1							

NEW ZEALAND (cont.) **BATTING AND FIELDING** **BOWLING**

	Tests	I	N	Runs	HS	Avge	100	50	0's	C/S	Balls	Runs	Wks	Avge	5w	10w	BB
Troup,GB	15	18	6	55	13*	4.58	0	0	7	2	3183	1454	39	37.28	1	1	6/95
Truscott,PB	1	2	0	29	26	14.50	0	0	0	1							
Turner,GM	41	73	6	2991	259	44.64	7	14	1	42	12	5	0	-	0	0	0/5
Twose,RG	7	11	1	314	94	31.40	0	3	1	2	156	80	3	26.66	0	0	2/36
Vance,RH	4	7	0	207	68	29.57	0	1	0	0							
Vaughan,JTC	3	6	1	143	44	28.60	0	0	0	3	561	246	5	49.20	0	0	3/30
Vivian,GE	5	6	0	110	43	18.33	0	0	1	3	198	107	1	107.00	0	0	1/14
Vivian,HG	7	10	0	421	100	42.10	1	5	0	4	1311	633	17	37.23	0	0	4/85
Wadsworth,KJ	33	51	4	1010	80	21.48	0	5	5	92/4							
Wallace,WM	13	21	0	439	66	20.90	0	5	0	5	6	5	0	-	0	0	0/5
Walmsley,KP	2	3	0	8	4	2.66	0	0	1	0	666	344	7	49.14	0	0	3/70
Ward,JT	8	12	6	75	35*	12.50	0	0	2	16/1							
Watson,W	15	18	6	60	11	5.00	0	0	3	4	3486	1387	40	34.67	1	0	6/78
Watt,L	1	2	0	2	2	1.00	0	0	1	0							
Webb,MG	3	2	0	12	12	6.00	0	0	1	0	732	471	4	117.75	0	0	2/114
Webb,PN	2	3	0	11	5	3.66	0	0	0	2							
Weir,GL	11	16	2	416	74*	29.71	0	3	1	3	342	209	7	29.85	0	0	3/38
White,DJ	2	4	0	31	18	7.75	0	0	0	0	3	5	0	-	0	0	0/5
Whitelaw,PE	2	4	2	64	30	32.00	0	0	0	0							
Wright,JG	82	148	7	5334	185	37.82	12	23	7	38	30	5	0	-	0	0	0/1
Young,BA	18	36	1	1052	120	30.05	1	8	4	29							
Yuile,BW	17	33	6	481	64	17.81	0	1	3	12	2897	1213	34	35.67	0	0	4/43

INDIA **BATTING AND FIELDING** **BOWLING**

	Tests	I	N	Runs	HS	Avge	100	50	0's	C/S	Balls	Runs	Wks	Avge	5w	10w	BB
Abid Ali,S	29	53	3	1018	81	20.36	0	6	3	32	4164	1980	47	42.12	1	0	6/55
Adhikari,HR	21	36	8	872	114*	31.14	1	4	5	8	170	82	3	27.33	0	0	3/68
Amarnath,M	69	113	10	4378	138	42.50	11	24	12	47	3676	1782	32	55.68	0	0	4/63
Amarnath,NB	24	40	4	878	118	24.38	1	4	5	13	4241	1481	45	32.91	2	0	5/96
Amarnath,S	10	18	0	550	124	30.55	1	3	1	4	11	5	1	5.00	0	0	1/5
Amar Singh,L	7	14	1	292	51	22.46	0	1	1	3	2182	858	28	30.64	2	0	7/86
Amir Elahi	1	2	0	17	13	8.50	0	0	0	0							
Amre,PK	11	13	3	425	103	42.50	1	3	0	9							
Ankola,SA	1	1	0	6	6	6.00	0	0	0	0	180	128	2	64.00	0	0	1/35
Apte,AL	1	2	0	15	8	7.50	0	0	0	0							
Apte,ML	7	13	2	542	163*	49.27	1	3	1	2	6	3	0	-	0	0	0/3
Arshad Ayub	13	19	4	257	57	17.13	0	1	1	2	3662	1438	41	35.07	3	0	5/50
Arun,B	2	2	1	4	2*	4.00	0	0	0	2	252	116	4	29.00	0	0	3/76
Arun Lal	16	29	1	729	93	26.03	0	6	1	13	16	7	0	-	0	0	0/1
Azad,K	7	12	0	135	24	11.25	0	0	2	3	750	373	3	124.33	0	0	2/84
Azharuddin,M	71	101	4	4362	199	44.96	14	15	4	71	7	12	0	-	0	0	0/4
Baig,AA	10	18	0	428	112	23.77	1	2	1	6	18	15	0	-	0	0	0/2
Banerjee,S	1	1	0	3	3	3.00	0	0	0	0	108	47	3	15.66	0	0	3/47
Banerjee,SA	1	1	0	0	0	0.00	0	0	1	3	306	181	5	36.20	0	0	4/120
Banerjee,SN	1	2	0	13	8	6.50	0	0	0	0	273	127	5	25.40	0	0	4/54
Baqa Jilani,M	1	2	1	16	12	16.00	0	0	0	0	90	55	0	-	0	0	0/55
Bedi,BS	67	101	28	656	50*	8.98	0	1	20	26	21367	7637	266	28.71	14	1	7/98
Bhandari,P	3	4	0	77	39	19.25	0	0	0	1	78	39	0	-	0	0	0/12
Bhat,AR	2	3	1	6	6	3.00	0	0	1	0	438	151	4	37.75	0	0	2/65
Binny,RMH	27	41	5	830	83*	23.05	0	5	7	11	2870	1534	47	32.63	2	0	6/65
Borde,CG	55	97	11	3061	177*	35.59	5	18	13	37	5695	2417	52	46.48	1	0	5/88
Chandrasekhar,BS	58	80	39	167	22	4.07	0	0	23	25	15963	7199	242	29.74	16	2	8/79
Chauhan,CPS	40	68	2	2084	97	31.57	0	16	6	38	174	106	2	53.00	0	0	1/4

INDIA (cont.)				**BATTING AND FIELDING**							**BOWLING**						
	Tests	I	N	Runs	HS	Avge	100	50	0's	C/S	Balls	Runs	Wks	Avge	5w	10w	BB
Chauhan,RK	15	11	3	65	15*	8.12	0	0	0	8	3365	1189	34	34.97	0	0	3/8
Chowdhury,NR	2	2	1	3	3*	3.00	0	0	1	0	516	205	1	205.00	0	0	1/130
Colah,SHM	2	4	0	69	31	17.25	0	0	0	2							
Contractor,NJ	31	52	1	1611	108	31.58	1	11	2	18	186	80	1	80.00	0	0	1/9
Dani,HT	1						0	0	0	1	60	19	1	19.00	0	0	1/9
Desai,RB	28	44	13	418	85	13.48	0	1	8	9	5597	2761	74	37.31	2	0	6/56
Dilawar Hussain	3	6	0	254	59	42.33	0	3	0	6/1							
Divecha,RV	5	5	0	60	26	12.00	0	0	0	5	1044	361	11	32.81	0	0	3/102
Doshi,DR	33	38	10	129	20	4.60	0	0	14	10	9322	3502	114	30.71	6	0	6/102
Dravid,RS	2	3	0	187	95	62.33	0	2	0	1							
Durani,SA	29	50	2	1202	104	25.04	1	7	4	14	6446	2657	75	35.42	3	1	6/73
Engineer,FM	46	87	3	2611	121	31.08	2	16	7	66/16							
Gadkari,CV	6	10	4	129	50*	21.50	0	1	2	6	102	45	0	-	0	0	0/8
Gaekwad,AD	40	70	4	1985	201	30.07	2	10	4	15	334	187	2	93.50	0	0	1/4
Gaekwad,DK	11	20	1	350	52	18.42	0	1	3	5	12	12	0	-	0	0	0/4
Gaekwad,HG	1	2	0	22	14	11.00	0	0	0	0	222	47	0	-	0	0	0/47
Gandotra,A	2	4	0	54	18	13.50	0	0	0	1	6	5	0	-	0	0	0/5
Ganguly,S	2	3	0	315	136	105.00	2	0	0	0	227	125	6	20.83	0	0	3/71
Gavaskar,SM	125	214	16	10122	236*	51.12	34	45	12	108	380	206	1	206.00	0	0	1/34
Ghavri,KD	39	57	14	913	86	21.23	0	2	2	16	7042	3656	109	33.54	4	0	5/33
Ghorpade,JM	8	15	0	229	41	15.26	0	0	3	4	150	131	0	-	0	0	0/17
Ghulam Ahmed	22	31	9	192	50	8.72	0	1	9	11	5650	2052	68	30.17	4	1	7/49
Gopalan,MJ	1	2	1	18	11*	18.00	0	0	0	3	114	39	1	39.00	0	0	1/39
Gopinath,CD	8	12	1	242	50*	22.00	0	1	4	2	48	11	1	11.00	0	0	1/11
Guard,GM	2	2	0	11	7	5.50	0	0	0	2	396	182	3	60.66	0	0	2/69
Guha,S	4	7	2	17	6	3.40	0	0	1	2	674	311	3	103.66	0	0	2/66
Gul Mahomed	8	15	0	166	34	11.06	0	0	2	3	77	24	2	12.00	0	0	2/21
Gupte,BP	3	3	2	28	17*	28.00	0	0	0	0	678	349	3	116.33	0	0	1/54
Gupte,SP	36	42	13	183	21	6.31	0	0	6	14	11284	4403	149	29.55	12	1	9/102
Gursharan Singh	1	1	0	18	18	18.00	0	0	0	2							
Hanumant Singh	14	24	2	686	105	31.18	1	5	3	11	66	51	0	-	0	0	0/5
Hardikar,MS	2	4	1	56	32*	18.66	0	0	1	3	108	55	1	55.00	0	0	1/9
Hazare,VS	30	52	6	2192	164*	47.65	7	9	4	11	2840	1220	20	61.00	0	0	4/29
Hindelkar,DD	4	7	2	71	26	14.20	0	0	0	3/0							
Hirwani,ND	15	18	10	45	17	5.62	0	0	4	5	4058	1858	64	29.03	4	1	8/61
Ibrahim,KC	4	8	0	169	85	21.12	0	1	1	0							
Indrajitsinhji,KS	4	7	1	51	23	8.50	0	0	1	6/3							
Irani,JK	2	3	2	3	2*	3.00	0	0	1	2/1							
Jadeja,AD	8	12	1	295	73	26.81	0	2	1	3							
Jahingir Khan,M	4	7	0	39	13	5.57	0	0	1	4	606	255	4	63.75	0	0	4/60
Jai,LP	1	2	0	19	19	9.50	0	0	1	0							
Jaisimha,ML	39	71	4	2056	129	30.68	3	12	9	17	2097	829	9	92.11	0	0	2/54
Jamshedji,RJD	1	2	2	5	4*	0	0	0	0	2	210	137	3	45.66	0	0	3/137
Jayantilal,K	1	1	0	5	5	5.00	0	0	0	0							
Joshi,PG	12	20	1	207	52*	10.89	0	1	3	18/9							
Joshi,S	1	2	0	24	12	12.00	0	0	0	0							
Kambli,VG	17	21	1	1084	227	54.20	4	3	3	6							
Kanitkar,HS	2	4	0	111	65	27.75	0	1	0	0							
Kapil Dev	131	184	15	5248	163	31.05	8	27	16	64	28741	12867	434	29.64	23	2	9/83
Kapoor,AR	2	3	0	58	42	19.33	0	0	0	1	324	154	1	154.00	0	0	1/90
Kardar,AH	3	5	0	80	43	16.00	0	0	1	1							
Kenny,RB	5	10	1	245	62	27.72	0	3	2	1							
Kirmani,SMH	88	124	22	2759	102	27.04	2	12	7	160/38	18	13	1	13.00	0	0	1/9
Kishenchand,G	5	10	0	89	44	8.90	0	0	5	1							

INDIA (cont.)				BATTING AND FIELDING										BOWLING			
	Tests	I	N	Runs	HS	Avge	100	50	0's	C/S	Balls	Runs	Wks	Avge	5w	10w	BB
Kripal Singh,AG	14	20	5	422	100*	28.13	1	2	4	4	1518	584	10	58.40	0	0	3/43
Krishnamurthy,P	5	6	0	33	20	5.50	0	0	2	7/1							
Kulkarni,RR	3	2	0	2	2	1.00	0	0	1	1	366	227	5	45.40	0	0	3/85
Kulkarni,UN	4	8	5	13	7	4.33	0	0	1	0	448	238	5	47.60	0	0	2/37
Kumar,VV	2	2	0	6	6	3.00	0	0	1	2	605	202	7	28.85	1	0	5/64
Kumble,AR	26	28	5	293	52*	12.73	0	1	5	10	7583	2996	114	26.28	6	1	7/59
Kunderan,BK	18	34	4	981	192	32.70	2	3	1	23/7	24	13	0	-	0	0	0/13
Lall Singh	1	2	0	44	29	22.00	0	0	0	1							
Lamba,R	4	5	0	102	53	20.40	0	1	1	5							
Madan Lal,S	39	62	16	1042	74	22.65	0	5	7	15	5997	2846	71	40.08	4	0	5/23
Mahomed Nissar	6	11	3	55	14	6.87	0	0	2	2	1211	707	25	28.28	3	0	5/90
Maka,ES	2	1	1	2	2*	0	0	0	0	2/1							
Malhotra,A	7	10	1	226	72*	25.11	0	1	2	2	18	3	0	-	0	0	0/0
Maninder Singh	35	38	12	99	15	3.80	0	0	11	9	8218	3288	88	37.36	3	2	7/27
Manjrekar,SV	35	59	6	2004	218	37.81	4	9	3	24/1	17	15	0	-	0		0/4
Manjrekar,VL	55	92	10	3208	189*	39.12	7	15	11	19/2	204	44	1	44.00	0	0	1/16
Mankad,AV	22	42	3	991	97	25.41	0	6	3	12	41	43	0	-	0	0	0/0
Mankad,MH	44	72	5	2109	231	31.47	5	6	7	33	14686	5236	162	32.32	8	2	8/52
Mantri,MK	4	8	1	67	39	9.57	0	0	2	8/1							
Meherhomji,KR	1	1	1	0	0*	0	0	0	0	1/0							
Mehra,VL	8	14	1	329	62	25.30	0	2	1	1	36	6	0	-	0	0	0/1
Merchant,VM	10	18	0	859	154	47.72	3	3	2	7	54	40	0	-	0	0	0/17
Mhambrey,PL	2	3	1	58	28	29.00	0	0	0	1	258	148	2	74.00	0	0	1/43
Milka Singh,AG	4	6	0	92	35	15.33	0	0	0	2	6	2	0	-	0	0	0/2
Modi,RS	10	17	1	736	112	46.00	1	6	0	3	30	14	0	-	0	0	0/14
Mongia,NR	13	18	2	495	80	30.93	0	1	1	28/2							
More,KS	49	64	14	1285	73	25.70	0	7	7	110/20	12	12	0	-	0		0/12
Muddiah,VM	2	3	1	11	11	5.50	0	0	1	0	318	134	3	44.66	0	0	2/40
Mushtaq Ali,S	11	20	1	612	112	32.21	2	3	1	7	378	202	3	67.33	0	0	1/45
Nadkarni,RG	41	67	12	1414	122*	25.70	1	7	6	22	9165	2559	88	29.07	4	1	6/43
Naik,SS	3	6	0	141	77	23.50	0	1	1	0							
Naoomal Jeoomal	3	5	1	108	43	27.00	0	0	0	0	108	68	2	34.00	0	0	1/4
Narasimha Rao,MV	4	6	1	46	20*	9.20	0	0	0	8	463	227	3	75.66	0	0	2/46
Navle,JG	2	4	0	42	13	10.50	0	0	0	1							
Nayak,SV	2	3	1	19	11	9.50	0	0	0	1	231	132	1	132.00	0	0	1/16
Nayudu,CK	7	14	0	350	81	25.00	0	2	0	4	858	386	9	42.88	0	0	3/40
Nayudu,CS	11	19	3	147	36	9.18	0	0	3	3	522	359	2	179.50	0	0	1/19
Nazir Ali,S	2	4	0	30	13	7.50	0	0	0	0	138	83	4	20.75	0	0	4/83
Nyalchand,S	1	2	1	7	6*	7.00	0	0	0	0	384	97	3	32.33	0	0	3/97
Pai,AM	1	2	0	10	9	5.00	0	0	0	0	114	31	2	15.50	0	0	2/29
Palia,PE	2	4	1	29	16	9.66	0	0	0	0	42	13	0	-	0	0	0/2
Pandit,CS	5	8	1	171	39	24.42	0	0	0	14/2							
Parkar,GA	1	2	0	7	6	3.50	0	0	0	1							
Parkar,RD	2	4	0	80	35	20.00	0	0	0	0							
Parsana,DD	2	2	0	1	1	0.50	0	0	1	0	120	50	1	50.00	0	0	1/32
Patankar,CT	1	2	1	14	13	14.00	0	0	0	3/0							
Pataudi,Nawab of, jr	46	83	3	2793	203*	34.91	6	16	7	27	132	88	1	88.00	0	0	1/10
Pataudi,Nawab of, sr	3	5	0	55	22	11.00	0	0	0	0							
Patel,BP	21	38	5	972	115*	29.45	1	5	0	17							
Patel,JM	7	10	1	25	12	2.77	0	0	5	2	1725	637	29	21.96	2	1	9/69
Patel,RG	1	2	0	0	0	0.00	0	0	2	1	84	51	0	-	0	0	0/14
Patiala,Yuvaraj of	1	2	0	84	60	42.00	0	1	0	0							
Patil,SM	29	47	4	1588	174	36.93	4	7	4	12	645	240	9	26.66	0	0	2/28
Patil,SR	1	1	1	14	14*	0	0	0	0	1	138	51	2	25.50	0	0	1/15

INDIA (cont.)				BATTING AND FIELDING								BOWLING					
	Tests	I	N	Runs	HS	Avge	100	50	0's	C/S	Balls	Runs	Wks	Avge	5w	10w	BB
Phadkar,DG	31	45	7	1229	123	32.34	2	8	3	21	5994	2285	62	36.85	3	0	7/159
Prabhakar,M	39	58	9	1598	120	32.61	1	9	3	20	7481	3581	96	37.30	3	0	6/132
Prasanna,EAS	49	84	20	735	37	11.48	0	0	15	18	14353	5742	189	30.38	10	2	8/76
Punjabi,PH	5	10	0	164	33	16.40	0	0	0	5							
Rai Singh,K	1	2	0	26	24	13.00	0	0	0	0							
Rajinder Pal	1	2	1	6	3*	6.00	0	0	0	0	78	22	0	-	0	0	0/3
Rajindernath,V	1						0	0	0	0/4							
Rajput,LS	2	4	0	105	61	26.25	0	1	1	1							
Raman,WV	8	13	1	367	96	30.58	0	3	3	5	258	66	2	33.00	0	0	1/7
Ramaswami,C	2	4	1	170	60	56.66	0	1	0	0							
Ramchand,GS	33	53	5	1180	109	24.58	2	5	6	20	4976	1899	41	46.31	1	0	6/49
Ramji,L	1	2	0	1	1	0.50	0	0	1	1	138	64	0	-	0	0	0/64
Rangachari,CR	4	6	3	8	8*	2.66	0	0	3	0	846	493	9	54.77	1	0	5/107
Rangnekar,KM	3	6	0	33	18	5.50	0	0	2	1							
Ranjane,VB	7	9	3	40	16	6.66	0	0	1	1	1265	649	19	34.15	0	0	4/72
Rathore,V	3	4	0	46	20	11.50	0	0	0	5							
Razdan,V	2	2	1	6	6*	6.00	0	0	1	0	240	141	5	28.20	1	0	5/79
Reddy,B	4	5	1	38	21	9.50	0	0	7	9/2							
Rege,MR	1	2	0	15	15	7.50	0	0	1	1							
Roy,A	4	7	0	91	48	13.00	0	0	2	0							
Roy,Pankaj	43	79	4	2442	173	32.56	5	9	14	13	104	66	1	66.00	0	0	1/6
Roy,Pranab	2	3	1	71	60*	35.50	0	1	0	1							
Sandhu,BS	8	11	4	214	71	30.57	0	2	1	1	1020	557	10	55.70	0	0	3/87
Sardesai,DN	30	55	4	2001	212	39.23	5	9	4	4	59	45	0	-	0	0	0/3
Sarwate,CT	9	17	1	208	37	13.00	0	0	4	0	658	374	3	124.66	0	0	1/16
Saxena,RC	1	2	0	25	16	12.50	0	0	0	0	12	11	0	-	0	0	0/11
Sekhar,TA	2	1	1	0	0*	-	0	0	0	0	216	129	0	-	0	0	0/43
Sen,P	14	18	4	165	25	11.78	0	0	12	0/11							
Sengupta,AK	1	2	0	9	8	4.50	0	0	0	0							
Sharma,AK	1	2	0	53	30	26.50	0	0	0	1	24	9	0	-	0	0	0/9
Sharma,C	23	27	9	396	54	22.00	0	1	2	7	3470	2163	61	35.45	4	1	6/58
Sharma,G	5	4	1	11	10*	3.66	0	0	2	2	1307	418	10	41.80	0	0	4/88
Sharma,PH	5	10	0	187	54	18.70	0	1	0	1	24	8	0	-	0	0	0/2
Sharma,SK	2	3	1	56	38	28.00	0	0	1	1	414	247	6	41.16	0	0	3/37
Shastri,RJ	80	121	14	3830	206	35.79	11	12	9	36	15751	6187	151	40.97	2	0	5/75
Shinde,SG	7	11	5	85	14	14.16	0	0	0	0	1515	717	12	59.75	1	0	6/91
Shodhan,RH	3	4	1	181	110	60.33	1	0	0	1	60	26	0	-	0	0	0/1
Shukla,RC	1						0	0	0	0	294	152	2	76.00	0	0	2/82
Sidhu,NS	36	54	2	2087	107	40.13	6	10	6	8	6	9	0	-	0		0/9
Sivaramakrishnan,L	9	9	1	130	25	16.25	0	0	1	9	2367	1145	26	44.03	3	1	6/64
Sohoni,SW	4	7	2	83	29*	16.60	0	0	0	2	532	202	2	101.00	0	0	1/16
Solkar,ED	27	48	6	1068	102	25.42	1	6	1	53	2265	1070	18	59.44	0	0	3/28
Sood,MM	1	2	0	3	3	1.50	0	0	1	0							
Srikkanth,K	43	72	3	2062	123	29.88	2	12	7	40	216	113	0	-	0	0	0/1
Srinath,J	21	28	12	324	60	20.25	0	3	1	11	4657	2063	57	36.19	0	0	4/33
Srinivasan,TE	1	2	0	48	29	24.00	0	0	0	0							
Subramanya,V	9	15	1	263	75	18.78	0	2	1	9	444	201	3	67.00	0	0	2/32
Sunderam,G	2	1	1	3	3*	-	0	0	0	0	396	166	3	55.33	0	0	2/46
Surendranath,R	11	20	7	136	27	10.46	0	0	4	4	2602	1053	26	40.50	2	0	5/75
Surti,RF	26	48	4	1263	99	28.70	0	9	5	26	3870	1962	42	46.71	1	0	5/74
Swamy,VN	1						0	0	0	0	108	45	0	-	0	0	0/15
Tamhane,NS	21	27	5	225	54*	10.22	0	1	8	35/16							
Tarapore,KK	1	1	0	2	2	2.00	0	0	0	0	114	72	0	-	0	0	0/72
Tendulkar,SR	41	60	7	2911	179	54.92	10	14	3	32	486	220	4	55.00	0	0	2/10

INDIA (cont.) — BATTING AND FIELDING / BOWLING

	Tests	I	N	Runs	HS	Avge	100	50	0's	C/S	Balls	Runs	Wks	Avge	5w	10w	BB
Umrigar,PR	59	94	8	3631	223	42.22	12	14	5	33	4725	1473	35	42.08	2	0	6/74
Vengsarkar,DB	116	185	22	6868	166	42.13	17	35	15	78	47	36	0	-	0	0	0/3
Venkatapathy Raju,SL	24	28	10	229	31	12.72	0	0	2	5	6600	2439	85	28.69	5	1	6/12
Venkataraghavan,S	57	76	12	748	64	11.68	0	2	13	44	14877	5634	156	36.11	3	1	8/72
Venkatesh Prasad,BK	3	5	3	17	13	8.50	0	0	0	0	855	375	15	25.00	1	0	5/76
Venkataramana,M	1	2	2	0	0*	0	0	0	0	1	70	58	1	58.00	0	0	1/10
Viswanath,GR	91	155	10	6080	222	41.93	14	35	10	63	70	46	1	46.00	0	0	1/11
Viswanath,S	3	5	0	31	20	6.20	0	0	2	11							
Vizianagaram, Maharaj of	3	6	2	33	19*	8.25	0	0	0	1							
Wadekar,AL	37	71	3	2113	143	31.07	1	14	7	46	61	55	0	-	0	0	0/4
Wassan,AS	4	5	1	94	53	23.50	0	1	1	1	712	504	10	50.40	0	0	4/108
Wazir Ali,S	7	14	0	237	42	12.92	0	0	1	1	30	25	0	-	0	0	0/0
Yadav,NS	35	40	12	404	43	14.42	0	0	4	10	8349	3580	102	35.09	3	0	5/76
Yadav,V	1	1	0	30	30	30.00	0	0	0	1/2							
Yajurvindra Singh	4	7	1	109	43*	7.16	0	0	0	11	120	50	0	-	0	0	0/2
Yashpal Sharma	37	59	11	1606	140	33.45	2	9	4	16	30	17	1	17.00	0	0	1/6
Yograj Singh	1	2	0	10	6	5.00	0	0	0	0	90	63	1	63.00	0	0	1/63

PAKISTAN — BATTING AND FIELDING / BOWLING

	Tests	I	N	Runs	HS	Avge	100	50	0's	C/S	Balls	Runs	Wks	Avge	5w	10w	BB
Aamer Malik	14	19	3	565	117	35.31	2	3	3	15/1	156	89	1	89.00	0	0	1/0
Aamer Nazir	6	11	6	31	11	6.20	0	0	2	2	1057	597	20	29.85	1	0	5/46
Aamer Sohail	32	59	2	2037	205	35.73	2	13	4	30	1511	677	17	39.82	0	0	4/54
Aaqib Javed	21	25	6	100	28*	5.26	0	0	7	2	3754	1786	54	33.07	1	0	5/84
Abdul Kadir	4	8	0	272	95	34.00	0	2	2	0/1							
Abdul Qadir	67	77	10	1029	61	15.35	0	3	7	15	17126	7742	236	32.80	15	5	9/56
Afaq Hussain	2	4	4	66	35*	0	0	0	0	2	240	106	1	106.00	0	0	1/40
Aftab Baloch	2	3	1	97	69*	48.50	0	1	0	0	44	17	0	-	0	0	0/2
Aftab Gul	6	8	0	182	33	22.75	0	0	0	3	6	4	0	-	0	0	0/4
Agha Saadat Ali	1	1	1	8	8*	0	0	0	0	3							
Agha Zahid	1	2	0	15	14	7.50	0	0	0	0							
Akram Raza	9	12	2	153	32	15.30	0	0	3	8	1520	732	13	56.30	0	0	3/46
Alimuddin	25	45	2	1091	109	25.37	2	7	6	8	84	75	1	75.00	0	0	1/17
Amir Elahi	5	7	1	65	47	10.83	0	0	1	0	400	248	7	35.42	0	0	4/134
Anil Dalpat	9	12	1	167	52	15.18	0	1	0	23/3							
Anwar Hussain	4	6	0	42	17	7.00	0	0	0	0	36	29	1	29.00	0	0	1/25
Anwar Khan	1	2	1	15	12	15.00	0	0	0	0	32	12	0	-	0	0	0/12
Arif Butt	3	5	0	59	20	11.80	0	0	1	0	666	288	14	20.57	1	0	6/89
Ashfaq Ahmed	1	2	1	1	1*	1.00	0	0	1	0	138	53	2	26.50	0	0	2/31
Ashraf Ali	8	8	3	229	65	45.80	0	2	0	17/5							
Asif Iqbal	58	99	7	3575	175	38.85	11	12	9	36	3864	1502	53	28.33	2	0	5/48
Asif Masood	16	19	10	93	30*	10.33	0	0	5	5	3038	1568	38	41.26	1	0	5/111
Asif Mujtaba	23	38	3	852	65*	24.34	0	8	5	18	306	158	2	79.00	0	0	1/0
Ataur Rehman	13	15	6	76	19	8.44	0	0	3	2	1973	1071	31	34.54	0	0	4/50
Atif Rauf	1	2	0	25	16	12.50	0	0	0	0							
Azeem Hafeez	18	21	5	134	24	8.37	0	0	2	1	4291	2202	63	34.95	4	0	6/46
Azhar Khan	1	1	0	14	14	14.00	0	0	0	0	18	2	1	2.00	0	0	1/2
Azmat Rana	1	1	0	49	49	49.00	0	0	0	0							
Basit Ali	19	33	1	858	103	26.81	1	5	5	6	6	6	0	-	0	0	0/6
D'Souza,A	6	10	8	76	23*	38.00	0	0	0	3	1587	745	17	43.82	1	0	5/112
Ehteshamuddin	5	3	1	2	2	1.00	0	0	1	2	940	375	16	23.43	1	0	5/47
Farooq Hamid	1	2	0	3	3	1.50	0	0	1	0	184	107	1	107.00	0	0	1/82
Farrukh Zaman	1						0	0	0	0	80	15	0	-	0	0	0/7

PAKISTAN (cont.)				**BATTING AND FIELDING**										**BOWLING**			
	Tests	I	N	Runs	HS	Avge	100	50	0's	C/S	Balls	Runs	Wkts	Avge	5w	10w	BB
Fazal Mahmood	34	50	6	620	60	14.09	0	1	10	11	9834	3434	139	24.70	13	4	7/42
Ghazali,MEZ	2	4	0	32	18	8.00	0	0	2	0	48	18	0	-	0	0	0/18
Ghulam Abbas	1	2	0	12	12	6.00	0	0	1	0							
Gul Mahomed	1	2	1	39	27*	39.00	0	0	0	0							
Hanif Mohammad	55	97	8	3915	337	43.98	12	15	5	40/0	206	95	1	95.00	0	0	1/1
Haroon Rashid	23	36	1	1217	153	34.77	3	5	2	16	8	3	0	-	0	0	0/3
Haseeb Ahsan	12	16	7	61	14	6.77	0	0	3	1	2835	1330	27	49.25	2	0	6/202
Ijaz Ahmed	30	46	2	1723	141	39.15	5	9	2	21	54	18	1	18.00	0	0	1/9
Ijaz Ahmed jr	2	3	0	29	16	9.66	0	0	0	3	24	6	0	-	0	0	0/1
Ijaz Butt	8	16	2	279	58	19.92	0	1	1	5/0							
Ijaz Faqih	5	8	1	183	105	26.14	1	0	2	0	534	299	4	74.75	0	0	1/38
Imran Khan	88	126	25	3807	136	37.69	6	18	8	28	19458	8258	362	22.81	23	6	8/58
Imtiaz Ahmed	41	72	1	2079	209	29.28	3	11	9	77/16	6	0	0	-	0	0	0/0
Intikhab Alam	47	77	10	1493	138	22.28	1	8	10	20	10474	4494	125	35.92	5	2	7/52
Inzamamul Haq	33	57	7	2367	148	47.34	5	16	4	34							
Iqbal Qasim	50	57	15	549	56	13.07	0	1	10	42	13019	4807	171	28.11	8	2	7/49
Israr Ali	4	8	1	33	10	4.71	0	0	1	1	318	165	6	27.50	0	0	2/29
Jalaluddin	6	3	2	3	2	3.00	0	0	0	0	1200	538	11	48.90	0	0	3/77
Javed Akhtar	1	2	1	4	2*	4.00	0	0	0	0	96	52	0	-	0	0	0/52
Javed Burki	25	48	4	1341	140	30.47	3	4	3	7	42	23	0	-	0	0	0/3
Javed Miandad	124	189	21	8832	280*	52.57	23	43	6	93/1	1470	682	17	40.11	0	0	3/74
Kabir Khan	4	5	2	24	10	8.00	0	0	1	1	655	370	9	41.11	0	0	3/26
Kardar,AH	23	37	3	847	93	24.91	0	5	1	15	2712	954	21	45.42	0	0	3/35
Khalid Hassan	1	2	1	17	10	17.00	0	0	0	0	126	116	2	58.00	0	0	2/116
Khalid Ibadulla	4	8	0	253	166	31.62	1	0	0	3	336	99	1	99.00	0	0	1/42
Khalid Wazir	2	3	1	14	9*	7.00	0	0	0	0							
Khan Mohammad	13	17	7	100	26*	10.00	0	0	3	4	3157	1292	54	23.92	4	0	6/21
Liaquat Ali	5	7	3	28	12	7.00	0	0	1	1	808	359	6	59.83	0	0	3/80
Mahmood Hussain	27	39	6	336	35	10.18	0	0	8	5	5910	2628	68	38.64	2	0	6/67
Majid Khan	63	106	5	3930	167	38.91	8	19	9	70	3584	1456	27	53.92	0	0	4/45
Mansoor Akhtar	19	29	3	655	111	25.19	1	3	4	9							
Manzoor Elahi	6	10	2	123	52	15.37	0	1	3	7	444	194	7	27.71	0	0	2/38
Maqsood Ahmed	16	27	1	507	99	19.50	0	2	2	13	462	191	3	63.66	0	0	2/12
Masood Anwar	1	2	0	39	37	19.50	0	0	0	0	161	102	3	34.00	0	0	2/59
Mathias,W	21	36	3	783	77	23.72	0	3	3	22	24	20	0	-	0	0	0/20
Miran Bux	2	3	2	1	1*	1.00	0	0	1	0	348	115	2	57.50	0	0	2/82
Mohammad Akram	5	8	2	8	5	1.33	0	0	3	4	919	463	10	46.30	0	0	3/39
Mohammad Aslam	1	2	0	34	18	17.00	0	0	0	0							
Mohammad Farooq	7	9	4	85	47	17.00	0	0	1	1	1427	682	21	32.47	0	0	4/70
Mohammad Ilyas	10	19	0	441	126	23.21	1	1	1	6	84	63	0	-	0	0	0/1
Mohammad Munaf	4	7	2	63	19	12.60	0	0	0	0	769	341	11	31.00	0	0	4/42
Mohammad Nazir	14	18	10	144	29*	18.00	0	0	3	4	3262	1124	34	33.05	3	0	7/99
Mohsin Kamal	9	11	7	37	13*	9.25	0	0	1	4	1348	822	24	34.25	0	0	4/116
Mohsin Khan	48	79	6	2709	200	37.10	7	9	3	34	86	30	0	-	0	0	0/0
Moin Khan	20	31	5	782	117*	30.07	3	2	2	46/4							
Mudassar Nazar	76	116	8	4114	231	38.09	10	17	7	48	5967	2532	66	38.36	1	0	6/32
Mufasir-ul-Haq	1	1	1	8	8*	0	0	0	0	1	222	84	3	28.00	0	0	2/50
Munir Malik	3	4	1	7	4	2.33	0	0	1	1	684	358	9	39.77	1	0	5/128
Mushtaq Ahmed	24	37	7	246	27	8.20	0	0	8	9	5706	2607	89	29.29	5	1	7/56
Mushtaq Mohammad	57	100	7	3643	201	39.17	10	19	4	42	5260	2309	79	29.22	3	-	5/28
Nadeem Abbasi	3	2	0	46	36	23.00	0	0	0	6							
Nadeem Ghauri	1	1	0	0	0	0.00	0	0	1	0	48	20	0	-	0	0	0/20
Nadeem Khan	1	1	0	25	25	25.00	0	0	0	0	312	195	2	97.50	0	0	2/147
Nasim-ul-Ghani	29	50	5	747	101	16.60	1	2	8	11	4406	1959	52	37.67	2	0	6/76

PAKISTAN (cont.)	BATTING AND FIELDING										BOWLING						
	Tests	I	N	Runs	HS	Avge	100	50	0's	C/S	Balls	Runs	Wks	Avge	5w	10w	BB
Naushad Ali	6	11	0	156	39	14.18	0	0	0	9/0							
Naved Anjum	2	3	0	44	22	14.66	0	0	0	0	342	162	4	40.50	0	0	2/57
Nazar Mohammad	5	8	1	277	124*	39.57	1	1	1	7	12	4	0	-	0	0	0/4
Niaz Ahmed	2	3	3	17	16*	0	0	0	0	1	294	94	3	31.33	0	0	2/72
Pervez Sajjad	19	20	11	123	24	13.66	0	0	2	9	4145	1410	59	23.89	3	0	7/74
Qasim Omar	26	43	2	1502	210	36.63	3	5	2	15	6	0	0	-	0	0	0/0
Rameez Raja	55	91	5	2747	122	31.94	2	21	6	31							
Rashid Khan	4	6	3	155	59	51.66	0	1	1	2	738	360	8	45.00	0	0	3/129
Rashid Latif	19	29	4	623	68*	24.92	0	3	1	59/8	12	10	0	-	0	0	0/10
Rehman,SF	1	2	0	10	8	5.00	0	0	0	1	204	99	1	99.00	0	0	1/43
Rizwan-uz-Zaman	11	19	1	345	60	19.16	0	3	2	4	132	46	4	11.50	0	0	3/26
Sadiq Mohammad	41	74	2	2579	166	35.81	5	10	6	28	200	98	0	-	0	0	0/0
Saeed Ahmed	41	78	4	2991	172	40.41	5	16	2	13	1980	802	22	36.45	0	0	4/64
Saeed Anwar	17	31	0	1400	176	45.16	3	10	3	9	18	4	0	-	0	0	0/0
Salahuddin	5	8	2	117	34*	19.50	0	0	0	3	546	187	7	26.71	0	0	2/36
Saleem Elahi	2	4	0	43	17	10.75	0	0	0	1							
Saleem Jaffer	14	14	6	42	10*	5.25	0	0	4	2	2471	1139	36	31.63	1	0	5/40
Saleem Malik	90	134	21	5101	237	45.14	14	25	10	56	428	247	5	49.40	0	0	1/3
Saleem Yousuf	32	44	5	1055	91*	27.05	0	5	2	91/13							
Salim Altaf	21	31	12	276	53*	14.52	0	1	4	3	4001	1710	46	37.17	0	0	4/11
Saqlain Mushtaq	4	7	2	53	34	10.60	0	0	2	3	1074	492	13	37.84	0	0	3/74
Sarfraz Nawaz	55	72	13	1045	90	17.71	0	4	6	26	13926	5798	177	32.75	4	1	9/86
Shadab Kabir	2	4	0	87	35	21.75	0	0	0	2	6	9	0	-	0	0	0/9
Shafiq Ahmed	6	10	1	99	27*	11.00	0	0	3	0	8	1	0	-	0	0	0/1
Shafqat Rana	5	7	0	221	95	31.57	0	2	1	5	36	9	1	9.00	0	0	1/2
Shahid Israr	1	1	1	7	7*	0	0	0	0	2/0							
Shahid Mahboob	1						0	0	0	0	294	131	2	65.50	0	0	2/131
Shahid Mahmood	1	2	0	25	16	12.50	0	0	0	0	36	23	0	-	0	0	0/23
Shahid Saeed	1	1	0	12	12	12.00	0	0	0	0	90	43	0	-	0	0	0/7
Shakeel Ahmed	3	5	0	74	33	14.80	0	0	1	4							
Sharpe,D	3	6	0	134	56	22.33	0	1	0	2							
Shoaib Mohammad	45	68	7	2705	203*	44.34	7	13	6	22	396	170	5	34.00	0	0	2/8
Shujauddin	19	32	6	395	47	15.19	0	0	3	8	2313	801	20	40.05	0	0	3/18
Sikander Bakht	26	35	12	146	22*	6.34	0	0	4	7	4873	2412	67	36.00	3	1	8/69
Tahir Naqqash	15	19	5	300	57	21.42	0	1	1	3	2800	1398	34	41.11	2	0	5/40
Talat Ali	10	18	2	370	61	23.12	0	2	2	4	20	7	0	-	0	0	0/1
Taslim Arif	6	10	2	501	201*	62.62	1	2	1	7/2	30	28	1	28.00	0	0	1/28
Tauseef Ahmed	34	38	20	318	35*	17.66	0	0	6	9	7778	2950	93	31.72	3	0	6/45
Waqar Hassan	21	35	1	1071	189	31.50	1	6	0	10	6	10	0	-	0	0	0/10
Waqar Younis	41	53	11	403	34	9.59	0	0	7	6	8484	4553	216	21.07	19	4	7/76
Wasim Akram	70	98	12	1652	123	19.20	1	4	12	26	16016	6875	300	22.91	20	3	7/119
Wasim Bari	81	112	26	1366	85	15.88	0	6	19	201/27	8	2	0	-	0	0	0/2
Wasim Raja	57	92	14	2821	125	36.16	4	18	8	20	4092	1826	51	35.80	0	0	4/50
Wazir Mohammad	20	33	4	801	189	27.62	2	3	8	5	24	15	0	-	0	0	0/5
Younis Ahmed	4	7	1	177	62	29.50	0	1	1	0	6	6	0	-	0	0	0/6
Zaheer Abbas	78	124	11	5062	274	44.79	12	20	10	34	370	132	3	44.00	0	0	2/21
Zahid Fazal	9	16	0	288	78	18.00	0	1	0	5							
Zakir Khan	2	2	2	9	9*	0	0	0	0	1	444	259	5	51.80	0	0	3/80
Zulfiqar Ahmed	9	10	4	200	63*	33.33	0	1	1	5	1285	366	20	18.30	2	1	6/42
Zulqarnain	3	4	0	24	13	6.00	0	0	0	8/2							

SRI LANKA				BATTING AND FIELDING								BOWLING					
	Tests	I	N	Runs	HS	Avge	100	50	0's	C/S	Balls	Runs	Wks	Avge	5w	10w	BB
Ahangama,FS	3	3	1	11	11	5.50	0	0	1	1	804	348	18	19.33	1	0	5/52
Amalean,KN	2	3	2	9	7*	9.00	0	0	0	1	244	156	7	22.28	0	0	4/97
Amerasinghe,MJG	2	4	1	54	34	18.00	0	0	0	3	300	150	3	50.00	0	0	2/73
Anurasiri,SD	18	23	4	88	24	4.63	0	0	3	4	3697	1442	37	38.97	0	0	4/71
Atapattu,MS	3	6	0	1	1	0.16	0	0	5	0							
Dasanayake,PB	11	17	2	196	36	13.06	0	0	3	20/5							
de Alwis,RG	11	19	0	152	28	8.00	0	0	5	21/2							
de Mel,ALF	17	28	5	326	34	14.17	0	0	5	9	3518	2180	59	36.94	3	0	6/109
de Silva,AM	3	3	0	10	9	3.33	0	0	1	4/1							
de Silva,DS	12	22	3	406	61	21.36	0	2	3	5	3031	1424	38	37.47	1	0	5/59
de Silva,EAR	10	16	4	185	50	15.41	0	1	3	4	2388	1032	8	129.00	0	0	2/67
de Silva,GRA	4	7	2	41	14	8.20	0	0	2	0	956	385	7	55.00	0	0	2/38
de Silva,PA	53	93	4	3176	267	35.68	8	13	4	22	1149	605	17	35.58	0	0	3/39
Dharmasena,HDPK	10	18	1	307	62*	18.05	0	2	3	4	2595	1046	23	45.47	1	0	6/99
Dias,RL	20	36	1	1285	109	36.71	3	8	2	9	24	16	0	-	0	0	0/16
Dunusinghe,CI	5	10	0	160	91	16.00	0	1	3	13/2							
Fernando,ERNS	5	10	0	112	46	11.20	0	0	3	0							
Goonasekera,Y	2	4	0	48	23	12.00	0	0	0	6							
Goonatillake,HM	5	10	2	191	56	23.87	0	1	1	10/3							
Guneratne,RPW	1	2	2	0	0*	-	0	0	0	0	102	84	0	-	0	0	0/84
Gurusinha,AP	39	68	7	2312	143	37.90	7	6	3	30	1378	674	20	33.70	0	0	2/7
Hathurusingha,UC	24	42	1	1260	83	30.73	0	8	1	6	1704	668	16	41.75	0	0	4/66
Jayasekera,RSA	1	2	0	2	2	1.00	0	0	1	0							
Jayasuriya,ST	17	27	5	771	112	35.04	1	4	2	17	648	386	4	96.50	0	0	2/46
Jeganathan,S	2	4	0	19	8	4.75	0	0	1	0	32	12	0	-	0	0	0/12
John,VB	6	10	5	53	27*	10.60	0	0	4	2	1281	614	28	21.92	2	0	5/60
Jurangpathy,BR	2	4	0	1	1	0.25	0	0	3	2	150	93	1	93.00	0	0	1/69
Kalpage,RS	8	14	1	265	63	20.38	0	2	0	6	917	405	6	67.50	0	0	2/27
Kaluperuma,LW	2	4	1	12	11*	4.00	0	0	2	2	162	93	0	-	0	0	0/24
Kaluperuma,SMS	4	8	0	88	23	11.00	0	0	1	6	240	124	3	41.33	0	0	2/17
Kaluwitharana,RS	6	10	1	350	132	38.88	1	2	2	12/0							
Kuruppu,DSBP	4	7	2	320	201*	64.00	1	0	0	1/0							
Kuruppuarachchi,AK	2	2	2	0	0*	-	0	0	0	0	272	152	8	19.00	1	0	5/44
Labrooy,GF	9	14	3	158	70*	14.36	0	1	3	3	2158	1194	27	44.22	1	0	5/133
Liyanage,DK	8	8	0	66	23	8.25	0	0	1	0	1271	622	17	36.58	0	0	4/56
Madugalle,RS	21	39	4	1029	103	29.40	1	7	4	9	84	38	0	-	0	0	0/0
Madurasinghe,MAWR	3	6	1	24	11	4.80	0	0	1	0	396	172	3	57.33	0	0	3/60
Mahanama,RS	37	63	0	1838	153	29.17	3	9	5	26	36	30	0	-	0	0	0/3
Mendis,LRD	24	43	1	1329	124	31.64	4	8	2	9							
Muralidaran,M	23	32	17	205	24*	13.66	0	0	6	13	6099	2745	81	33.88	5	0	5/64
Pushpakumara,KR	7	12	6	45	17*	7.50	0	0	1	4	1078	691	18	38.38	1	0	7/116
Ramanayake,CPH	18	24	9	143	34*	9.53	0	0	7	6	3654	1880	44	42.72	1	0	5/82
Ranasinghe,AN	2	4	0	88	77	22.00	0	1	1	0	114	69	1	69.00	0	0	1/23
Ranatunga,A	61	104	6	3471	135*	35.41	4	23	11	25	2168	942	14	67.28	0	0	2/17
Ranatunga,D	2	3	0	87	44	29.00	0	0	0	0							
Ranatunga,S	8	15	1	522	118	37.28	2	2	0	2							
Ratnayake,RJ	23	36	6	433	56	14.43	0	2	5	9	4955	2563	73	35.11	5	0	6/66
Ratnayeke,JR	22	38	6	807	93	25.21	0	5	5	1	3833	1972	56	35.21	4	0	8/83
Samarasekera,MAR	4	7	0	118	57	16.85	0	1	1	3	192	104	3	34.66	0	0	2/38
Samaraweera,DP	7	14	0	211	42	15.07	0	0	1	5							
Senanayake,CP	3	5	0	97	64	19.40	0	1	1	2							
Silva,KJ	1	2	1	6	6*	6.00	0	0	1	0	210	120	1	120.00	0	0	1/120
Silva,SAR	9	16	2	353	111	25.21	2	0	1	33/1							
Tillakaratne,HP	36	61	8	2166	119	40.86	4	12	5	69/0	22	11	0	-	0	0	0/1

SRI LANKA (cont.)	BATTING AND FIELDING										BOWLING						
	Tests	I	N	Runs	HS	Avge	100	50	0's	C/S	Balls	Runs	Wks	Avge	5w	10w	BB
Vaas,WPJUC	12	21	2	320	51	16.84	0	1	2	1	2615	1117	48	23.27	4	1	6/87
Warnapura,B	4	8	0	96	38	12.00	0	0	1	2	90	46	0	-	0	0	0/1
Warnaweera,KPJ	10	12	3	39	20	4.33	0	0	3	0	2359	1021	32	31.90	0	0	4/25
Weerasinghe,CDUS	1	1	0	3	3	3.00	0	0	0	0	114	36	0	-	0	0	0/8
Wettimuny,MD	2	4	0	28	17	7.00	0	0	1	2							
Wettimuny,S	23	43	1	1221	190	29.07	2	6	5	10	24	37	0	-	0	0	0/16
Wickramasinghe,GP	23	37	4	280	28	8.48	0	0	7	8	4355	2219	46	48.23	1	0	5/73
Wickremasinghe,AGD	3	3	1	17	13*	8.50	0	0	0	9/1							
Wijegunawardene,KIW	2	4	1	14	6*	4.66	0	0	0	0	364	148	7	21.14	0	0	4/52
Wijesuriya,RGCE	4	7	2	22	8	4.40	0	0	2	1	586	294	1	294.00	0	0	1/68
Wijetunge,PK	1	2	0	10	10	5.00	0	0	1	0	312	118	2	59.00	0	0	1/58

ZIMBABWE	BATTING AND FIELDING										BOWLING						
	Tests	I	N	Runs	HS	Avge	100	50	0's	C/S	Balls	Runs	Wks	Avge	5w	10w	BB
Arnott,KJ	4	8	1	302	101*	43.14	1	1	1	3							
Brain,DH	9	12	1	109	28	9.90	0	0	4	1	1810	915	30	30.50	1	0	5/42
Brandes,EA	8	12	2	102	39	10.20	0	0	2	3	1648	806	22	36.63	0	0	3/45
Briant,GA	1	2	0	17	16	8.50	0	0	0	0							
Bruk-Jackson,GK	2	4	0	39	31	9.75	0	0	1	0							
Burmester,MG	3	4	2	54	30*	27.00	0	0	1	1	436	227	3	75.66	0	0	3/78
Butchart,IP	1	2	0	23	15	11.50	0	0	0	1	18	11	0	-	0	0	0/11
Campbell,ADR	16	27	1	815	99	31.34	0	7	4	10	30	7	0	-	0	0	0/1
Carlisle,SV	5	8	1	171	58	24.42	0	1	1	8							
Crocker,GJ	3	4	1	69	33	23.00	0	0	0	0	456	217	3	72.33	0	0	2/65
Dekker,MH	9	13	1	233	68*	19.41	0	2	3	10	60	15	0	-	0	0	0/4
Flower,A	16	26	5	1049	156	49.95	2	8	1	39/2	1	0	0	-	0	0	0/0
Flower,GW	16	27	1	794	201*	30.53	1	4	3	8	432	214	2	107.00	0	0	1/8
Houghton,DL	16	25	2	1113	266	48.39	4	2	0	11	5	0	0	-	0	0	0/0
James,WR	4	4	0	61	33	15.25	0	0	0	16/0							
Jarvis,MP	5	4	2	10	6*	5.00	0	0	1	1	1273	393	11	35.72	0	0	3/30
Lock,ACI	1	2	1	8	8*	8.00	0	0	1	0	180	105	5	21.00	0	0	3/68
Olonga,HK	2	1	0	0	0	0.00	0	0	1	3	162	112	2	56.00	0	0	1/27
Peall,SG	4	6	1	59	30	11.80	0	0	2	1	888	303	4	75.75	0	0	2/89
Pycroft,AJ	3	5	0	152	60	30.40	0	1	0	2							
Ranchod,U	1	2	0	8	7	4.00	0	0	0	0	72	45	1	45.00	0	0	1/45
Rennie,JA	3	4	1	24	19*	8.00	0	0	1	0	658	256	3	85.33	0	0	2/22
Shah,AH	2	3	0	59	28	19.66	0	0	0	0	186	125	1	125.00	0	0	1/46
Strang,BC	5	8	3	49	25*	9.80	0	0	3	4	1297	437	18	24.27	1	0	5/101
Strang,PA	7	10	1	204	49	22.66	0	0	1	4	1200	548	7	78.28	0	0	3/65
Streak,HH	12	17	3	216	53	15.42	0	1	6	4	2986	1257	58	21.67	3	0	6/90
Traicos,AJ	4	6	2	11	5	2.75	0	0	1	4	1141	562	14	40.14	1	0	5/86
Whittall,GJ	12	19	2	455	113*	26.76	1	2	1	6	1596	675	19	35.52	0	0	4/70
Wishart,CB	2	4	1	56	24	18.66	0	0	0	1							

COMPLETE TEST RECORD FOR PLAYERS REPRESENTING TWO COUNTRIES

	BATTING AND FIELDING										BOWLING						
	Tests	I	N	Runs	HS	Avge	100	50	0's	C/S	Balls	Runs	Wks	Avge	5w	10w	BB
Amir Elahi (I/P)	6	9	1	82	47	10.25	0	0	1	0	400	248	7	35.42	0	0	4/134
Ferris,JJ (A/E)	9	17	4	114	20*	8.76	0	0	1	4	2002	775	61	12.70	6	1	7/37
Guillen,SC (W/N)	8	12	2	202	54	20.20	0	1	3	13/3							
Gul Mahomed (I/P)	9	17	1	205	34	12.81	0	0	2	3	77	24	2	12.00	0	0	2/21
Hearne,F (E/SA)	6	10	0	168	30	16.80	0	0	2	3	62	40	2	20.00	0	0	2/40
Kardar,AH (I/P)	26	42	3	927	93	23.76	0	5	2	16	2712	954	21	45.42	0	0	3/35
Midwinter,WE (A/E)	12	21	1	269	37	13.45	0	0	1	10	1725	605	24	25.20	1	0	5/78
Mitchell,F (E/SA)	5	10	0	116	41	11.60	0	0	1	2							
Murdoch,WL (A/E)	19	34	5	908	211	31.31	2	1	3	13/2							
Pataudi, Nawab of, sr (E/I)	6	10	0	199	102	19.90	1	0	0	0							
Traicos,AJ (SA/Z)	7	10	4	19	5*	3.16	0	0	2	8	1611	769	18	42.72	0	0	3/186
Trott,AE (A/E)	5	9	3	228	85*	38.00	0	2	2	4	948	390	26	15.00	2	0	8/43
Wessels,KC (A/SA)	40	71	3	2788	179	41.00	6	15	5	30	90	42	0	-	0	0	0/2
Woods,SMJ (A/E)	6	10	0	154	53	15.40	0	1	2	5	412	250	10	25.00	0	0	3/28

NOTES

NOTES

NOTES